Other Mood Disorders

Mood Disorder Due to a General Medical Condition

Substance-Induced Mood Disorder

Mood Disorder Not Otherwise Specified

ANXIETY DISORDERS

Panic Disorder
Without Agoraphobia
With Agoraphobia

Agoraphobia Without History of Panic Disorder

Specific Phobia

Social Phobia

Obsessive-Compulsive Disorder

Posttraumatic Stress Disorder

Acute Stress Disorder

Generalized Anxiety Disorder

Anxiety Disorder Due to a General Medical Condition

Substance-Induced Anxiety Disorder

Anxiety Disorder Not Otherwise Specified

SOMATOFORM DISORDERS

Somatization Disorder

Undifferentiated Somatoform Disorder

Conversion Disorder

Hypochondriasis

Body Dysmorphic Disorder

Pain Disorder

Somatoform Disorder Not Otherwise Specified

FACTITIOUS DISORDERS

Factitious Disorder

Factitious Disorder Not Otherwise Specified

DISSOCIATIVE DISORDERS

Dissociative Amnesia

Dissociative Fugue

Dissociative Identity Disorder

Depersonalization Disorder

Dissociative Disorder Not Otherwise Specified

SEXUAL AND GENDER IDENTITY DISORDERS

Sexual Dysfunctions
Sexual Desire Disorders
Hypoactive Sexual Desire Disorder
Sexual Aversion Disorder
Sexual Arousal Disorders
Female Sexual Arousal Disorder
Male Erectile Disorder

Orgasmic Disorders
Female Orgasmic Disorder
Male Orgasmic Disorder
Premature Ejaculation
Sexual Pain Disorders
Dyspareunia
Vaginismus
Sexual Dysfunction Due to a General Medical Condition
Substance-Induced Sexual Dysfunction
Sexual Dysfunction Not Otherwise Specified

Paraphilias
Exhibitionism
Fetishism
Frotteurism
Pedophilia
Sexual Masochism
Sexual Sadism
Transvestic Fetishism
Voyeurism
Paraphilia Not Otherwise Specified

Gender Identity Disorders
Gender Identity Disorder
Gender Identity Disorder Not Otherwise Specified
Sexual Disorder Not Otherwise Specified

EATING DISORDERS

Anorexia Nervosa

Bulimia Nervosa

Eating Disorder Not Otherwise Specified

SLEEP DISORDERS

Primary Sleep Disorders
Dyssomnias
Primary Insomnia
Primary Hypersomnia
Narcolepsy
Breathing-Related Sleep Disorder
Circadian Rhythm Sleep Disorder
Dyssomnia Not Otherwise Specified
Parasomnias
Nightmare Disorder
Sleep Terror Disorder
Sleepwalking Disorder
Parasomnia Not Otherwise Specified

Sleep Disorders Related to Another Mental Disorder

Other Sleep Disorders
Sleep Disorder Due to a General Medical Condition
Substance-Induced Sleep Disorder

IMPULSE CONTROL DISORDERS NOT ELSEWHERE CLASSIFIED

Intermittent Explosive Disorder

Kleptomania

Pyromania

Pathological Gambling

Trichotillomania

Impulse-Control Disorder Not Otherwise Specified

Adj
Adj
M
Adju___ _____ Disorder With Disturbance of Conduct

Adjustment Disorder With Mixed Disturbance of Emotions and Conduct

Adjustment Disorder With Mixed Anxiety and Depressed Mood

Adjustment Disorder Unspecified

OTHER CONDITIONS THAT MAY BE A FOCUS OF CLINICAL ATTENTION
Psychological Factors Affecting Medical Condition
Medication-Induced Movement Disorders
Other Medication-Induced Disorder
Relational Problems
Problems Related to Abuse or Neglect
Additional Conditions That May Be a Focus of Clinical Attention

AXIS II:
PERSONALITY DISORDERS

Paranoid Personality Disorder

Schizoid Personality Disorder

Schizotypal Personality Disorder

Antisocial Personality Disorder

Borderline Personality Disorder

Histrionic Personality Disorder

Narcissistic Personality Disorder

Avoidant Personality Disorder

Dependent Personality Disorder

Obsessive-Compulsive Personality Disorder

Personality Disorder Not Otherwise Specified

Mental Retardation
Mild Mental Retardation
Moderate Mental Retardation
Severe Mental Retardation
Profound Mental Retardation
Mental Retardation, Severity Unspecified

AXIS III: GENERAL MEDICAL CONDITIONS

AXIS IV: PSYCHOSOCIAL AND ENVIRONMENTAL PROBLEMS

AXIS V: GLOBAL ASSESSMENT OF FUNCTIONING

essentials of **abnormal psychology** in a changing world

essentials of **abnormal** **psychology** in a changing world

Jeffrey S. Nevid
St. John's University

Beverly Greene
St. John's University

Paul A. Johnson
Confederation College

Steven Taylor
University of British Columbia

second canadian edition

PEARSON
Prentice
Hall

Toronto

Library and Archives Canada Cataloguing in Publication

Essentials of abnormal psychology in a changing world / Jeffrey S. Nevid ... [et al.]. — 2nd
Canadian ed.
Includes bibliographical references and index.
ISBN 978-0-13-205373-0

1. Psychology, Pathological—Textbooks. I. Nevid, Jeffrey S.

RC454.E88 2009   616.89   C2007-903860-3

ISBN-13: 978-0-13-205373-0
ISBN-10: 0-13-205373-X

Vice President, Editorial Director: Gary Bennett
Executive Acquisitions Editor: Ky Pruesse
Executive Marketing Manager: Judith Allen
Developmental Editor: Emily Jardeleza
Production Editor: Amanda Wesson
Copy Editor: Joe Zingrone
Proofreader: Sally Glover
Production Coordinator: Janis Raisen
Composition: Susan MacGregor
Photo Research: Sandy Cooke
Art Director: Julia Hall
Cover and Interior Design: Alex Li
Cover Image: Picture Press/First Light

1 2 3 4 5   11 10 09 08

Printed and bound in the United States of America.

Brief Contents

CONTENTS

Abnormal psychology is among the most popular areas of study in psychology for good reason. The problems it addresses are of immense personal and social importance—problems that touch the lives of us all in one way or another. They include problems that are all too pervasive, such as depression, sexual dysfunctions, obesity, and alcohol and substance abuse. They include problems that are less common but have a profound impact on all of us, such as schizophrenia.

The problems addressed in this book are thus not of the few. The majority of us will experience one or more of them at some time or another. Or a friend or loved one will. Even those who are not personally affected by these problems will be touched by society's response—or lack of response—to them. We hope that this text will serve both as an educational tool and as a vehicle to raise awareness among students and general readers alike.

Essentials of Abnormal Psychology in a Changing World, Second Canadian Edition, maintains the style and substance that has distinguished the U.S. editions of the text, including the use of many case examples and self-scoring questionnaires; a clear and engaging writing style that is accessible but does not compromise rigour; research-based and comprehensive coverage; superior pedagogy; and integration of sociocultural material throughout, including coverage of issues relating to Canadian cultural diversity, gender, and lifestyle.

Essentials of Abnormal Psychology provides students with the basic concepts in the field in a convenient 14-chapter format. The first 13 chapters cover historical and theoretical perspectives, approaches to psychological assessment and treatment, and the major types of psychological disorders—including adjustment disorders, anxiety disorders, mood disorders, substance-related disorders, personality disorders, gender identity and sexual disorders, schizophrenia, and disorders of childhood and adolescence. The concluding Chapter 14 covers topics that lie at the interface of abnormal psychology and society: psychiatric commitment, patients' rights, and the insanity defence. Throughout the text, we highlight important Canadian research, case examples, and societal and legal perspectives on abnormal psychology. We also present the best international research from a Canadian perspective. In this sense, the book has both a Canadian and global focus.

This new second Canadian edition updates and integrates sociocultural material relating to ethnicity, gender, culture, and lifestyle throughout the text and in highlighted boxed features ("Focus on Diversity"). Attention to issues of diversity is clearly consistent with the importance given to cultural factors in the DSM-IV-TR and the need to bring these important issues to the attention of the beginning student in abnormal psychology.

We approached the writing of this text with the belief that a textbook should do more than offer a portrait of a field of knowledge. It should be a teaching device—a means of presenting information in ways that arouse interest and encourage understanding and critical thinking. To these ends, we speak to the reader in a clear expository style. We attempt to render complex material accessible. We put a human face on the subjects we address by including many case examples drawn from our own clinical files and those of other mental health professionals. We stimulate and involve students through carefully chosen pedagogical features, questionnaires, highlights, and applications. We also include a built-in study guide designed to help students master difficult material. And yes, we keep abreast of our ever-changing subject by bringing to our readers a wealth of new scientific information drawn from leading scientific journals and organizations. To summarize the material covered in each chapter in an easy-to-remember format, we also include Concept Maps at the end of each chapter.

Essentials exposes students to the multiple perspectives that inform our present understandings of abnormal behaviour—the psychological, sociocultural, and biological domains. We adopt an interactionist approach, which recognizes that abnormal behaviour typically involves a complex interplay of multiple factors representing different domains. Because the concept of integrating diverse perspectives is often difficult for beginning students to grasp, the unique "Tying It Together" features interspersed throughout the text help students explore how multiple factors interact in the development of psychological disorders.

FEATURES OF THE TEXT

Textbooks walk balance beams, as it were, and they can fall off in three directions, not just two. That is, they must do justice to their subject matter while also meeting the needs of instructors and students.

In subject matter, *Essentials* is comprehensive, providing depth and breadth as well as showcasing the most important new research discoveries. It covers the history of societal response to abnormal behaviours, historic and contemporary models of abnormal behaviours, methods of assessment, psychological and biological models of treatment, contemporary issues, the comprehensive range of problem behaviours set forth in the DSM, and a number of other behavioural problems that entail psychological factors—most notably in the interfaces between psychology and health.

Canadian Content

Unlike most textbooks on abnormal psychology, this second Canadian edition of *Essentials of Abnormal Psychology in a Changing World* showcases a wealth of Canadian content. We chose to do this for several reasons. First and foremost, there is a great deal of important, internationally acclaimed Canadian work being done on the research and treatment of abnormal behaviour. We highlight this important work while placing it in an international context. In other words, we have tried to present the best research on abnormal psychology, while at the same time alerting our readers to the fact that much of this work comes from Canada. Why would we do this? The answer is to help our readers understand that there is important, relevant research being conducted right where they live, and quite probably on their own campus. Our Canadian focus helps readers understand that key research does not originate just in other countries—it's happening in students' own backyards, perhaps from the professor who is teaching their course.

The second reason for highlighting Canadian content is to refute the myth that mental disorders are things that happen to people who live someplace else, such as in other regions or countries. Mental disorder touches all of us; there are people in our country, communities, and campuses who are afflicted with psychological problems. By citing Canadian examples of people who have battled psychological problems, we hope to bring home the fact that mental illness can reach any of us. Fortunately, effective treatments are available for many of these disorders.

Our third reason for a Canadian focus is pragmatic. The prevalence of mental disorders differs from country to country, as do the treatments and laws regarding mental disorders and patient rights. Some disorders, such as dependence on crack cocaine, are much more common in the U.S. than in Canada. Substance-use disorders in Canada more commonly involve other substances. The health-care system in Canada is also different from those in other countries. Accordingly, it is important to have a Canadian focus so that readers can understand how people with mental health problems are treated in Canada. Finally, the issues regarding mental disorders and the law are different in Canada compared to many other countries. For example, in the U.S., a person might be deemed to be *not guilty by reason of insanity*. In Canada, such a judgment would be *not criminally responsible on account of a mental disorder*. In other words, the Canadian courts often recognize that an accused is guilty of a given crime, but not responsible because he or she is under the influence of a mental disorder.

This text illustrates the important fact that abnormal psychology does not occur in a cultural vacuum; the expression and treatment of psychological problems are strongly influenced by cultural factors. Our task of updating and Canadianizing this text was made much easier by the fact that so much of the key research on abnormal behaviour has been conducted in Canada.

"Focus on Diversity" Features

The second Canadian edition of *Essentials* helps broaden students' perspectives so they understand the importance of issues relating to gender, culture, ethnicity, and lifestyle in the diagnosis and treatment of psychological disorders. Students will see how behaviour deemed normal in one culture could be labelled abnormal in another; how states of psychological distress might be experienced differently in other cultures; how some abnormal behaviour patterns are culture-bound; and how therapists can cultivate a sensitivity to cultural factors in their approach to treating people from diverse backgrounds. Multicultural material is incorporated throughout the text and is highlighted in boxed "Focus on Diversity" features that cover the following specific topics:

- Healing the Whole Person: The Canadian Aboriginal Perspective (Chapter 1)
- Canadian Multicultural Issues in Psychotherapy (Chapter 2)
- Culture-Bound Syndromes (Chapter 3)
- Koro and Dhat Syndromes: Far Eastern Somatoform Disorders? (Chapter 6)
- Ethnicity and Alcohol Abuse (Chapter 9)

"Did You Know That?" Chapter Openers

Each chapter begins with a set of "Did You Know That?" questions designed to whet students' appetites for specific information contained in the chapter and to encourage them to read further. These chapter-opening questions (e.g., "Did You Know That... despite beliefs that it is a wonder drug, the antidepressant Prozac has not been shown to be any more effective than the earlier generation of antidepressants?") also encourage students to think critically and evaluate common conceptions in light of scientific evidence. The sections of running text in which the pertinent material is discussed are underlined in the chapter for easy reference.

"A Closer Look" Features

The "A Closer Look" features highlight cutting-edge developments in the field (e.g., virtual reality therapy) and in practice (e.g., "Suicide Prevention") that enable students to apply information from the text to their own lives. Examples include the following:

- Antipsychotic Medications: A Major Psychiatric Breakthrough (Chapter 1)
- The Homeless in Canada: Still Waiting for True Community Mental Health Care (Chapter 1)
- Thinking Critically About Abnormal Psychology (Chapter 1)
- Canadian Mental Health Promotion (Chapter 2)
- Emerging Trends in Biological Treatments (Chapter 2)
- Would You Tell Your Problems to a Computer? (Chapter 3)
- Stress and the Wellness Continuum Model (Chapter 4)
- Emotions and the Heart (Chapter 4)
- Psychological Methods for Lowering Arousal (Chapter 4)
- Cancer Risk Reduction (Chapter 4)
- Virtual Therapy (Chapter 5)
- Coping with a Panic Attack (Chapter 5)
- The Recovered Memory Controversy (Chapter 6)
- St. John's Wort—A Natural "Prozac"? (Chapter 7)
- Suicide Prevention (Chapter 7)
- The Controlled Social Drinking Controversy (Chapter 9)
- Other Eating Problems and Related Conditions (Chapter 10)
- To Sleep, Perchance to Dream (Chapter 10)
- Rape Prevention (Chapter 11)

- The Cost of Autism Treatment in Canada (Chapter 13)
- Savant Syndrome (Chapter 13)
- A Canadian Definition of Learning Disabilities (Chapter 13)
- The Duty to Warn (Chapter 14)

Concept Maps

These are diagram spreads at the end of each chapter that summarize key concepts and findings in bubble form. Concept maps provide readers with a "big picture" and are a useful way of understanding and remembering the material covered in each chapter.

Self-Scoring Questionnaires

Self-scoring questionnaires (for example, "Are you Type A?"; the "Fear of Fat Scale"; and the "Life Orientation Test") involve students in the discussion at hand and permit them to evaluate their own behaviour. In some cases, students may become more aware of troubling concerns, such as states of depression or problems with drug or alcohol use, which they may wish to bring to the attention of a professional. We have screened the questionnaires to ensure they will provide students with useful information both to reflect on and to serve as a springboard for class discussion.

Built-In Study Guide

Essentials of Abnormal Psychology contains a built-in study guide consisting of "Study Break" sections that follow each of the major sections in the chapters. These components provide students with the opportunity to review the material they have just read, test their knowledge by completing a set of multiple-choice questions, and think critically about the issues that were raised in the preceding passages of the text. "Study Break" sections are organized into four subsections:

- **Review It** (question and answer review)
- **Define It** (listing of key terms)
- **Recall It** (multiple-choice quiz—answers can be found on *Essential*'s Companion Website)
- **Think About It** (questions that encourage critical thinking and invite students to relate the material to their own experiences)

Glossary

Key terms are boldfaced in the text and defined both in the margins and in the glossary at the back of the text. The origins of key terms are often discussed. By learning to attend to commonly found Greek and Latin word origins, students can acquire skills that will help them decipher the meanings of new words. These decoding skills are a valuable objective for general education as well as a specific asset for the study of abnormal psychology.

SUPPLEMENTS

No matter how comprehensive a textbook is, today's instructors and students require a complete educational package to advance teaching and comprehension. *Essentials of Abnormal Psychology* is accompanied by the following supplements.

Supplements for Instructors

Instructors can download these supplements from our online catalogue. Simply visit **vig.pearsoned.ca** and look up this textbook using the catalogue's search function.

Instructor's Resource Manual. The Instructor's Resource Manual is a true "course organizer," integrating a variety of resources for teaching abnormal psychology. It includes lecture suggestions, discussion questions, and student activities.

Test Item File. This test bank contains over 3000 multiple-choice, true/false, and short-answer/essay questions. The Test Item File is available in both Word and MyTest formats. MyTest is compatible with both Windows and Macintosh software. Please visit **www.pearsonmytest.com** to access MyTest.

Supplements for Students

Companion Website. An interactive website at **www.pearsoned.ca/nevid** is available for instructors and students who use *Essentials of Abnormal Psychology in a Changing World*, Second Canadian Edition. In addition to chapter outlines, learning objectives, flashcards, and weblinks, the Companion Website also contains answers to the Recall It questions found in the numerous "Study Break" boxes in the text.

The Companion Website also includes the Grade Tracker functionality. With Grade Tracker, the results from the self-test quizzes you take are preserved in a gradebook. Each time you return to the Companion Website, you can refer back to these results, track your progress, and measure your improvement. Use the access code found on the card bound into this book to sign on to the Grade Tracker website. Your instructor might also take advantage of the Class Manager function to assign marks for participation or for quiz scores. Ask your instructor if he or she will be distributing a Course ID that will allow you to enroll in the class.

ACKNOWLEDGMENTS

The field of abnormal psychology is a moving target, because the literature base that informs our understanding is continually expanding. We are deeply indebted to a number of talented individuals who helped us hold our camera steady in taking a portrait of the field, focus in on the salient features of our subject matter, and develop our snapshots through prose.

First, our professional colleagues, who reviewed chapters from the first and second Canadian edition: Carolyn Szostak, University of British Columbia-Okanagan; Kathy Foxall, Wilfrid Laurier University; Thomas Keenan, Niagara College; Linda Knight, John Abbott College; Joanna Sargent, Georgian College; Rajesh Malik, Dawson College; Kristen Buscaglia, Niagara College; Jillian Esmonde Moore, Georgian College; Beverley Bouffard, York University; Jocelyn Lymburner, Kwantlen University College. Second, the publishing professionals at or collaborating with Pearson Education Canada—they helped guide the development, editing, proofreading, and marketing of this edition, especially Ky Pruesse, executive acquisitions editor; Emily Jardeleza, developmental editor; Judith Allen, executive marketing manager; Amanda Wesson, production editor; Joe Zingrone, copy editor; Sally Glover, proofreader; and Lisa Brant, photo researcher.

Jeffrey S. Nevid is professor of psychology at St. John's University in New York, where he directs the doctoral program in clinical psychology, teaches graduate courses in research methods and behaviour therapy, and supervises doctoral trainees in psychotherapy. He earned his Ph.D. in clinical psychology from the State University of New York at Albany and was awarded a National Institute of Mental Health post-doctoral fellowship in mental health evaluation research at Northwestern University. He has published numerous articles in such areas as clinical and community psychology, health psychology, training models in clinical psychology, and methodological issues in clinical research. He formerly taught at Hofstra University before joining the faculty at St. John's. He holds a diploma in clinical psychology from the American Board of Professional Psychology, is a fellow of the Academy of Clinical Psychology, has served on the editorial board of the *Journal of Consulting and Clinical Psychology*, and has authored or co-authored several textbooks in psychology and related fields.

Beverly A. Greene is professor of psychology at St. John's University and a licensed psychologist in private practice in New York City. She is a fellow of the American Psychological Association, the Academy of Clinical Psychology, and the American Orthopsychiatric Association. She received her doctorate in clinical psychology from Adelphi University and holds a diploma in clinical psychology (ABPP). She has served on the editorial boards of the journals *Violence Against Women, Journal of Cultural Diversity and Ethnic Minority Psychology, Women & Therapy*, and *Journal of Feminist Family Therapy*. She was also the founding co-editor of *Psychological Perspectives on Lesbian, Gay and Bisexual Issues*. She also co-edited (with Leslie Jackson), *Psychotherapy with African American Women: Psychodynamic Perspectives* (Guilford Press, 2000). Dr. Greene is the recipient of numerous national awards for her contributions to issues relating to diversity in professional psychology. She was the recipient of the Women of Color Psychologies Publication Award (1991), the Distinguished Humanitarian Award from the American Association of Applied and Preventive Psychology (1994), and the Psychotherapy With Women Research Award from the APA Division of Psychology of Women (1995, 1996). Her co-edited book, *Women of Color: Integrating Ethnic and Gender Identities in Psychotherapy*, was honoured with the 1995 Distinguished Publication Award and the 1995 Women of Color Psychologies Publication Award, sponsored by the Association for Women in Psychology. She was also the recipient of a 1996 Outstanding Achievement Award from the APA Committee on Lesbian, Gay and Bisexual Concerns for pioneering scholarship and training efforts relating to the interaction of gender, ethnicity, and sexual orientation in contemporary psychology.

Paul Johnson has 25 years' experience in post-secondary education as a professor, program co-ordinator, and curriculum and program validation advisor at Confederation College. Paul recently served on the Ministry of Training, Colleges and Universities (MTCU) committee that developed the new provincial college curriculum standards for general education and essential employability skills. He has received international recognition for academic leadership from The Chair Academy and the National Institute for Staff and Organizational Development (NISOD). Paul has also practised psychology in the Psychotherapy and Psychiatric Departments of St. Joseph's Hospital in Thunder Bay. As well, he has been a health-promotion consultant in his community for many years. Along with Helen Bee and Denise Boyd, Paul co-authored *Lifespan Development* (Pearson Education Canada), now in its third Canadian edition.

Steven Taylor, PhD, ABPP, is a professor and clinical psychologist in the Department of Psychiatry at the University of British Columbia, and is editor-in-chief of the *Journal of Cognitive Psychotherapy*. He serves on the editorial board of several journals, including the *Journal of Consulting and Clinical Psychology*. He has published over 200 journal articles and book chapters, and over a dozen books on anxiety disorders and related topics. Dr. Taylor has received career awards from the Canadian Psychological Association, the British Columbia Psychological Association, the Association for Advancement of Behaviour Therapy, and the Anxiety Disorders Association of America. He is a fellow of several scholarly organizations including the Canadian Psychological Association, the American Psychological Association, the Association for Psychological Science, and the Academy of Cognitive Therapy. His clinical and research interests include cognitive-behavioural treatments and mechanisms of anxiety disorders and related conditions, as well as the behavioural-genetics of these disorders.

What Is Abnormal Psychology?

Did You Know That...

See the underlined text on the pages indicated below for more information on these interesting and often misunderstood facts.

- About one in five adults in Canada will be diagnosed with a psychological disorder at some point in their lives? (p. 2)

- Behaviour we consider abnormal may be perceived as perfectly normal in another culture? (p. 4)

- The modern medical model of abnormal behaviour can be traced to the work of a Greek physician some 2500 years ago? (p. 10)

- Innocent people were drowned in medieval times as a way of certifying they were not possessed by the devil? (p. 11)

- A night on the town in London a few hundred years ago may have included peering at the residents of a local asylum? (p. 12)

- Although we may find that depression and negative thinking are highly correlated, it does not follow that negative thinking necessarily causes depression? (p. 25)

- A survey of 1500 Canadians may provide a more accurate reflection of voting preferences and attitudes of the Canadian public than one based on millions of participants? (p. 28)

- Case studies have been conducted on people who have been dead for hundreds of years? (p. 30)

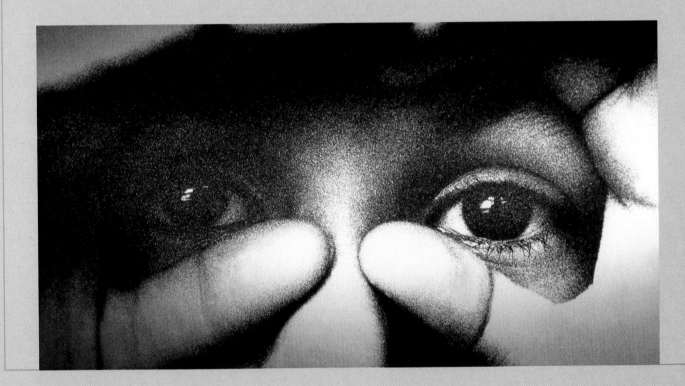

clinical psychologist Person with graduate training in psychology who specializes in abnormal behaviour. They must be registered and licensed with a provincial psychological regulatory body in order to provide psychological services in that province.

psychiatrist Physician who specializes in the diagnosis and treatment of mental disorders.

psychological disorders Disturbances of psychological functioning or behaviour associated with states of personal distress or impaired social, occupational, or interpersonal functioning. Also called *mental disorders*.

abnormal psychology Branch of psychology that deals with the description, causes, and treatment of abnormal behaviour patterns.

ABNORMAL BEHAVIOUR MIGHT appear to be the concern of only a few. After all, only a minority of the population will ever be admitted to a psychiatric hospital. Most people never seek the help of a **clinical psychologist** or **psychiatrist**. Only a few people plead not criminally responsible on account of a mental disorder. Many of us have what we call an "eccentric" relative, but few of us have relatives we would consider truly bizarre.

The truth of the matter is that abnormal behaviour affects virtually everyone in one way or another. Abnormal behaviour patterns that involve a disturbance of psychological functioning or behaviour are classified as **psychological disorders** (also called mental disorders). Health Canada's (2002a) Report on Mental Illness in Canada suggests about 20% of Canadians will experience a psychological disorder at some time in their lives. Table 1.1 shows the percentage of people who have one of several major classes of psychological disorders during any one-year period. The report also found that psychological disorders requiring hospitalization were most common among people in the 25- to 44-year age range and declined with increasing age. Women, essentially at all ages, had higher rates and more days of hospitalization for the seven most common psychological disorders leading to hospital admission (Health Canada, 2002a). If we also include the mental health problems of our family members, friends, and co-workers, then perhaps none of us remain unaffected.

Abnormal psychology is the branch of the science of psychology that addresses the description, causes, and treatment of abnormal behaviour patterns. Let us pause for a moment to consider our use of terms. We prefer to use the term psychological disorder when referring to abnormal behaviour patterns associated with disturbances of psychological functioning, rather than mental disorder. There are a number of reasons why we have adopted this approach. First, psychological disorder puts the study of abnormal behaviour squarely within the

TABLE 1.1

Estimated Percentage of the Adult Population Who Have a Mental Disorder During Any One-Year Period in Canada

Psychological Disorder	Estimated Percentage of the Population Who Have a Disorder During Any One-Year Period
Mood Disorders	
Major (unipolar) depression	4.8%
Bipolar disorder	1.0%
Dysthymia	0.8–3.1%
Schizophrenia	0.3%
Anxiety Disorders	
Panic disorder	1.5%
Agoraphobia	0.7%
Social Phobia	3.0%
Eating Disorders	
Anorexia	0.7% women
	0.2% men
Bulimia	1.5% women
	0.1% men

Source: Based on Bland, R.C., Newman, S.C., & Orn, H. (1988a); Health Canada (2002a); Offord, D.R. et al. (1996); Gravel, R., Connolly, D., & Bédard, M. (2004); Woodside, D. B. et al. (2001). Adapted and reproduced with the permission of the Minister of Public Works and Government Services Canada, 2007.

purview of the field of psychology. Second, the term mental disorder is generally associated with the **medical model** perspective that considers abnormal behaviour patterns to be symptoms of underlying mental illnesses or disorders. Although the medical model remains a prominent perspective for understanding abnormal behaviour patterns, we shall see that other perspectives, including psychological and sociocultural perspectives, also inform our understanding of abnormal behaviour. Third, mental disorder as a phrase reinforces the traditional distinction between mental and physical phenomena. As we'll see, there is increasing awareness of the interrelationships between the body and the mind that calls into question this distinction.

In this chapter, we first address the task of defining abnormal behaviour. We see that throughout history, and even in the preceding prehistory, abnormal behaviour has been viewed from different perspectives or models. We chronicle the development of concepts of abnormal behaviour and its treatment. We see that, historically speaking, treatment usually referred to what was done to, rather than for, people with abnormal behaviour. Finally, we describe the ways in which psychologists and other scholars study abnormal behaviour today.

medical model Biological perspective in which abnormal behaviour is viewed as symptomatic of underlying illness.

HOW DO WE DEFINE ABNORMAL BEHAVIOUR?

Most of us become anxious or depressed from time to time, but our behaviour is not deemed abnormal. It is normal to become anxious in anticipation of an important job interview or a final examination. It is appropriate to feel depressed when you have lost someone close to you or when you have failed at a test or on the job. But when do we cross the line between normal and abnormal behaviour?

One answer is that emotional states like anxiety and depression may be considered abnormal when they are not appropriate to the situation. It is normal to feel down because of failure on a test, but not when one's grades are good or excellent. It is normal to feel anxious during a job interview, but not whenever entering a department store or boarding a crowded elevator.

Abnormal behaviour may also be suggested by the magnitude of the problem. Although some anxiety is normal enough before a job interview, feeling your heart hammering away so relentlessly that it might leap from your chest—and consequently cancelling the interview—are not. Nor is it normal to feel so anxious in this situation that your clothing becomes soaked with perspiration.

Criteria for Determining Abnormality

Psychologists generally apply some combination of the following criteria in making a determination that behaviour is abnormal:

1. *Behaviour is unusual.* Behaviour that is unusual is often considered abnormal. Only a few of us report seeing or hearing things that are not really there; "seeing things" and "hearing things" are almost always considered abnormal in our culture, except, perhaps, in cases of religious experience. Yet, **hallucinations** are not deemed unusual in some non-Western cultures. Being overcome with feelings of panic when entering a department store or when standing in a crowded elevator is also uncommon and considered abnormal. But uncommon behaviour is not in itself abnormal. Only one person can hold the record for swimming or running the fastest 100 metres. The record-holding athlete differs from the rest of us but, again, is not considered abnormal. Thus, rarity or statistical deviance is not a sufficient basis for labelling behaviour abnormal; nevertheless, it is one yardstick often used to judge abnormality.

hallucinations Perceptions that occur in the absence of an external stimulus that are confused with reality.

2. *Behaviour is socially unacceptable or violates social norms.* All societies have norms (standards) that define the kinds of behaviours acceptable in given contexts. <u>Behaviour deemed normal in one culture may be viewed as abnormal in another.</u> In our society, standing on a soapbox in a park and repeatedly shouting "Kill!" to passersby would be labelled abnormal; shouting "Kill!" in the arena at a professional wrestling match is usually within normal bounds, however tasteless it may seem.

Although the use of norms remains one of the important standards for defining abnormal behaviour, we should be aware of some limitations of this definition.

One implication of basing the definition of abnormal behaviour on social norms is that norms reflect relative standards, not universal truths. What is normal in one culture may be abnormal in another. For example, Canadians who assume strangers are devious and try to take advantage are usually regarded as distrustful, perhaps even **paranoid**. But such suspicions were justified among the Mundugumor, a tribe of cannibals in Papua New Guinea studied by anthropologist Margaret Mead (1935). Within that culture, male strangers, even the male members of one's own family, *were* typically malevolent toward others.

Clinicians such as psychologists or psychiatrists need to weigh cultural differences in determining what is normal and abnormal. In the case of the Mundugumor, this need is more or less obvious. Sometimes, however, differences are subtler. For example, what is seen as normal, outspoken behaviour by most Canadian women might be interpreted as brazen behaviour when viewed in the context of another, more traditional culture. Moreover, what strikes one generation as abnormal may be considered by others to fall within the normal spectrum. For example, until the mid-1970s, homosexuality was classified as a mental disorder by the psychiatric profession (see Chapter 11, "Gender Identity Disorder, Paraphilias, and Sexual Dysfunctions"). Today, however, the psychiatric profession no longer considers homosexuality a mental disorder. Indeed, roughly two-thirds of Canadians now express approval of same-sex relationships (Bibby, 2006).

Another implication of basing normality on compliance with social norms is the tendency to brand nonconformists as mentally disturbed. We may come to brand behaviour we do not like or understand as "sick," rather than accept that behaviour may be normal even if it offends or puzzles us.

3. *Perception or interpretation of reality is faulty.* Normally speaking, our sensory systems and cognitive processes permit us to form accurate mental representations of the environment. But seeing things and hearing voices that are not present are considered hallucinations, which in our culture are often taken as signs of an

paranoid Having irrational suspicions.

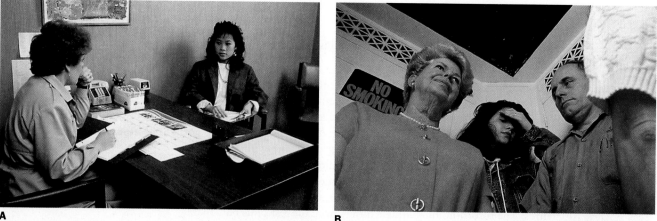

A   **B**

When is anxiety abnormal? Negative emotions such as anxiety are considered abnormal when they are judged to be excessive or inappropriate to the situation. Anxiety is generally regarded as normal when it is experienced during a job interview (photo A), so long as it is not so severe that it prevents the interviewee from performing adequately. Anxiety is deemed to be abnormal if it is experienced whenever one boards an elevator (photo B).

underlying disorder. Similarly, holding unfounded ideas or **delusions**, such as **ideas of persecution** that the Mounties or the Mafia are out to get you, may be regarded as signs of mental disturbance—unless, of course, they *are*. (There's a quip about a politician who acknowledged that he might, indeed, be paranoid. His paranoia, however, did not mean he was without enemies.)

It is normal in Canada to say that one "talks" to God through prayer. If, however, a person claims to have literally seen God or heard the voice of God—as opposed to, say, being divinely inspired—we may come to regard her or him as mentally disturbed.

4. *The person is in significant personal distress.* States of personal distress caused by troublesome emotions, such as anxiety, fear, or depression, may be considered abnormal. As noted earlier, however, anxiety and depression are sometimes appropriate responses to a situation. Real threats and losses occur from time to time, and the *lack* of an emotional response to them would be regarded as abnormal. Appropriate feelings of distress are not considered abnormal unless they become prolonged or persist long after the source of anguish has been removed (after most people would have adjusted) or if they are so intense that they impair the individual's ability to function.

5. *Behaviour is maladaptive or self-defeating.* Behaviour that leads to unhappiness rather than self-fulfillment can be regarded as abnormal. Behaviour that limits our ability to function in expected roles, or to adapt to our environments, may also be considered abnormal. According to these criteria, heavy alcohol consumption that impairs health or social and occupational functioning may be viewed as abnormal. **Agoraphobia**, behaviour characterized by an intense fear of venturing into public places, may be considered abnormal in that it is both uncommon and also maladaptive because it impairs the individual's ability to fulfill work and family responsibilities.

6. *Behaviour is dangerous.* Behaviour that is dangerous to oneself or other people may be considered abnormal. Here, too, social context is crucial. In wartime, people who sacrifice themselves or charge the enemy with little apparent concern for their own safety may be characterized as courageous, heroic, and patriotic. But people who threaten or attempt suicide because of the pressures of civilian life are usually considered abnormal.

Football and hockey players, even adolescents who occasionally get into altercations, may be normal enough. Given the cultural demands of these sports, nonaggressive football and hockey players would not last long in varsity or professional ranks. But individuals involved in frequent unsanctioned fights may be regarded as abnormal. Physically aggressive behaviour is most often maladaptive in modern life. Moreover, outside the contexts of sports and warfare, physical aggression is discouraged as a way of resolving interpersonal conflicts—although it is by no means uncommon.

Abnormal behaviour thus has multiple definitions. Depending on the case, some criteria may be weighted more heavily than others. But in most cases, a combination of these criteria is used to define abnormality. Precisely how mental health professionals assess and classify abnormal behaviour is described in Chapter 3, "Classification and Assessment of Abnormal Behaviour."

It is one thing to recognize and label behaviour as abnormal; it is another to understand

delusions Firmly held but inaccurate beliefs that persist despite evidence that they have no basis in reality.

ideas of persecution Form of delusional thinking characterized by false beliefs that one is being persecuted or victimized by others.

agoraphobia Excessive, irrational fear of open places.

Is this abnormal? One of the criteria used to determine whether behaviour is abnormal is whether it deviates from acceptable standards of conduct or social norms. The behaviour and attire of these spectators might be considered abnormal in the context of a classroom or workplace, but perhaps not at a sporting event.

and explain it. Philosophers, physicians, natural scientists, and psychologists have used various approaches, or *models*, in the effort to explain abnormal behaviour. Some approaches have been based on superstition; others have invoked religious explanations. Some current views are predominantly biological; others, psychological. We consider various historical and contemporary approaches to understanding abnormal behaviour. First, let us look further at the importance of cultural beliefs and expectations in determining which behaviour patterns are deemed abnormal.

Cultural Bases of Normal Behaviour

Behaviour considered normal in one culture may be deemed abnormal in another. Hallucinations (hearing voices or seeing things that are not in fact present) are a common experience among Australian Aborigines but are generally taken as a sign of abnormality in our culture. Aborigines also believe they can communicate with the spirits of their ancestors and that dreams are shared among people, especially close relatives. Such beliefs may be regarded in Western culture as delusions (fixed false beliefs). Hallucinations and delu-

FOCUS ON DIVERSITY

Healing the Whole Person: The Canadian Aboriginal Perspective

Canadian census data shows that our Aboriginal population continues to be the fastest-growing segment of the population. The highest concentrations of Canada's more than 1.3 million Aboriginal peoples are in the North and West, and just over one-half are now living in urban centres throughout Canada (Statistics Canada, 2003a). Along with rapid population growth, there is evidence of the resurgence of Canadian Aboriginal cultures especially in the arts, media, education, commerce, and health (Aboriginal Planet, 2002; Arthur & Stewart, 2001; Fraser, 1994; Letendre, 2002).

Despite this optimistic outlook, Aboriginal peoples in Canada are still dealing with the effects of generations of physical, mental, emotional, and spiritual distress caused by the decimation of their communities, lands, and cultural identities. Consequently, both on- and off-reserve Aboriginal peoples have to contend with extensive mental health, addiction, and medical issues in their communities as compared to the rest of Canadians. In particular, Canadian Aboriginals suffer from disproportionately higher rates of major depression, anxiety, posttraumatic stress disorder, alcoholism and substance abuse, sexual abuse, family violence, chronic disease such as heart disease and diabetes, lower life expectancy, and suicide (Health Reports, 2002; Kirby & Keon, 2004, 2006; Kirmayer, MacDonald, & Brass, 2001; MacMillan et al., 1996).

Centuries of extreme social, cultural, and geographic disruption have contributed to the distress suffered by Aboriginal people. Firstly, the arrival of

European settlers resulted in an estimated 90% decline in Aboriginal populations (Trigger & Swagerty, 1996). The remaining Aboriginals were exposed to widespread, inescapable, social, and cultural disruption caused by government-sanctioned separation of children from their parents and communities, plus systematic efforts to force Aboriginals to take on non-Aboriginal cultural values at the cost of becoming disconnected from their own. This process of cultural assimilation was enforced by relocation and social regrouping of Aboriginal peoples onto remote reserves, placing Aboriginal children into residential boarding schools, and by unwittingly creating a forced dependence on government support. Poverty and powerlessness further marginalized Aboriginal peoples and their cultural traditions from mainstream society (Hogan & Barlow, 2000; Kirby & Keon, 2006; Poonwassie & Charter, 2001). Surviving and recovering from this long-standing personal and social devastation is a testament to Aboriginal peoples' strength and long-suffering determination. Moreover, it gives credence to the significance and legitimacy of their perception of life and, despite great odds, a distinctive Aboriginal perspective has survived to challenge the established Canadian ideas of treatments and cures.

Mainstream Treatment of Aboriginal Illnesses Has Proved Lacking

Mainstream health-care approaches have not been readily accessible or reasonably successful at treating and preventing Aboriginal peoples' physical and mental health problems (McCormick, 2000; Wieman, 2001). There were well-intentioned attempts to change the way

sions are taken to be common features of schizophrenia in Western culture. Should we thus conclude that Aborigines are seriously disturbed or have schizophrenia? What standards should be applied in judging abnormal behaviour in other cultures? Even Aborigines perceive "madness" in some members of their community, although the criteria they use to label someone as mentally disturbed may differ from those used by health professionals in Western society.

The very words that Western cultures use to describe psychological disorders—words such as *depression* or even *mental health*—may have very different meanings in other cultures or no equivalent meaning at all. In many non-Western societies, depression may be closer in meaning to the concept of "soul loss" than to Western concepts involving a sense of loss of purpose and meaning in life (Shweder, 1985). Abnormal behaviour patterns may also take different forms in different cultures. Westerners may experience anxiety, for example, in the form of excessive worrying about paying the mortgage, losing a job, and so on. Yet, "[i]n a number of African cultures, anxiety is expressed as fears of failure in procreation, in dreams and complaints about witchcraft" (Kleinman, 1987). Some Australian Aborigines develop intense fears of sorcery, which may be accompanied by the

that "experts" dealt with Aboriginal health problems during the last decades of the 20th century, but at best, medical and counselling professionals adopted as truth a range of overgeneralized, simplified, and underresearched beliefs about Aboriginal cultural values and behaviours. This overreliance on Aboriginal cultural stereotypes led to a "cookie-cutter," "one-size-fits-all," condescending approach to treatment and counselling that has netted few overall gains in health and well-being for Aboriginal peoples (Brass, 2001; Kirmayer, Brass, & Tait, 2000; Waldram, 2001, 2004) This lack of success creates a formidable challenge and opportunity, especially for the non-Aboriginal health-care practitioner, to become an effective partner in a meaningful healing process.

Aboriginal Healing

Aboriginal healing and wellness promotion place a high value on the balance between the interconnected physical, mental, emotional, and spiritual aspects of life. As such, healing and wellness promotion are multi-levelled, targeting the individual as well as the family and the community, while respecting both individual and the group languages, customs, history, and environment (Ellerby et al., 2000; McCormick, 2000; Smith & Morrissette, 2001). This may ultimately evolve into a healing paradigm in which not only will Canadian health practitioners change the way they approach Aboriginal peoples, but the Aboriginal healing perspective will influence how practitioners approach members of any and all cultural minority groups. Ultimately, a holistic healing perspective may come to permeate and trans-

A Canadian Aboriginal smudging ceremony. Sacred medicinal plants such as sweetgrass, tobacco, sage, and cedar are ignited in a bowl or seashell and allowed to smoulder. Following ancient, traditional rituals, the smoke is used to purify, cleanse, and heal the mind, body, soul, and spirit. Although there is no one thing that on its own leads to healing, a smudging ceremony is an important aspect of the larger Aboriginal healing perspective. It serves to strengthen cultural identity, which builds self-respect. As the Aboriginal people become aware of who they are, then a sense of connectedness with nature and the Creator, healthier ways of living, and improved physical and mental well-being will follow (A. Magiskan, personal communication, February 10, 2004).

Source: Ann Magiskan is of Ojibwa heritage and is responsible for the Native Heritage programs at Fort William Historical Park.

form mainstream health, mental health, social services, and care practices in Canada (Chaimowitz, 2000; Kirby & Keon, 2006; McDougall & Arthur, 2001; Poonwassie & Charter, 2001).

belief that one is in mortal danger from evil spirits (Spencer, 1983). Trancelike states in which young Aboriginal women become mute, immobile, and unresponsive are also quite common. If women do not recover from a trance within hours or at most a few days, they may be brought to a sacred site for healing.

Depression may also be expressed differently in different cultures (Bebbington, 1993; Thakker & Ward, 1998). This doesn't mean that depression doesn't exist in all cultures. Rather, it suggests we need to consider how people in different cultures experience states of emotional distress, including depression and anxiety, rather than imposing our perspectives on their experiences. In some Asian cultures, for example, depression is experienced largely in terms of physical symptoms such as headaches, fatigue, or weakness, rather than by feelings of guilt or sadness that are common in Western cultures (American Psychiatric Association [APA], 2000a).

Cultural differences in how abnormal behaviour patterns are expressed lead us to realize that we must determine that our concepts of abnormal behaviour are recognizable and valid before they are applied to other cultures (Bebbington, 1993; Kleinman, 1987). The reverse is equally true. The concept of "soul loss" may characterize psychological distress in some non-Western societies but has little or no relevance to middle-class North Americans. Evidence from multinational studies conducted by the World Health Organization (WHO) in the 1960s and 1970s shows that the behaviour pattern we characterize as schizophrenia exists in countries as wide-ranging as Colombia, India, China, Denmark, Nigeria, and the former Soviet Union, among others (Jablensky et al., 1992). Rates of schizophrenia and its general features were actually quite similar among all countries studied. However, some differences have been observed in the specific features of schizophrenia across cultures (Thakker & Ward, 1998).

Societal views of abnormal behaviour also vary across cultures. In our society, models based on medical disease and psychological factors have achieved prominence in explaining abnormal behaviour. But in traditional cultures, concepts of abnormal behaviour often invoke supernatural causes, such as possession by demons or the devil (Lefley, 1990). The notion of supernatural causation or demonology held prominence in Western society until the Age of Enlightenment.

STUDY BREAK

How Do We Define Abnormal Behaviour?

Review It

- **What are the criteria used by mental health professionals to define abnormal behaviour?** Psychologists generally consider behaviour abnormal when it meets some combination of the following criteria: (1) unusual or statistically infrequent; (2) socially unacceptable or in violation of social norms; (3) fraught with misperceptions or misinterpretations of reality; (4) associated with states of severe personal distress; (5) maladaptive or self-defeating; or (6) dangerous.

- **What are psychological disorders?** Psychological disorders (also called *mental disorders*) involve abnormal behaviour patterns associated with disturbances in mental health or psychological functioning.

- **How are cultural beliefs and norms related to the classification and understandings of abnormal behaviour?** Behaviours deemed normal in one cul-

ture may be considered abnormal in another. Concepts of health and illness may also have different meanings in different cultures. Abnormal behaviour patterns may also take different forms in different cultures, and societal views or models explaining abnormal behaviour also vary across cultures.

Define It

clinical psychologist
psychiatrist
psychological disorders
abnormal psychology
medical model

hallucinations
paranoid
delusions
ideas of persecution
agoraphobia

Recall It*

1. When clinicians make judgments about whether a person's behaviour is socially unacceptable or violates social norms, they must account for _____.

   a. ideas of persecution
   b. universal truths

c. cultural differences

d. subject's expectations

2. Joanie has persistent delusions that she is the queen of England. She also hallucinates that the woman sitting next to her is talking to the members of parliament through secret microphones in her head. Which criterion of abnormal behaviour most closely matches her behaviour?

a. severe mental distress

b. self-defeating behaviour

c. unusual behaviour

d. faulty perception of reality

3. Claire experiences persistent symptoms of anxiety and depression. Which criterion of abnormal behaviour most closely matches her symptoms?

a. severe mental distress

b. self-defeating behaviour

c. unusual behaviour

d. faulty perception of reality

4. When Australian Aborigines report hearing the voices of recently deceased loved ones, they are considered from our cultural perspective to be experiencing _____.

a. delusions

b. hallucinations

c. compulsions

d. obsessions

5. Which of the following statements is NOT true?

a. Abnormal behaviour patterns are identical in most all respects in every culture researchers have studied.

b. Behaviour considered normal in one culture may be deemed abnormal in another.

c. Beliefs about the nature of health and illness often vary across cultures.

d. The words we use to describe abnormal behaviour patterns may have different meanings in other cultures.

* Recall It answers can be found on the Companion Website for this text.

Think About It

• On what basis can we claim that problems of abnormal psychology affect virtually every one of us in one way or another?

• How would you recognize abnormal behaviour?

• What criteria would you use to distinguish abnormal behaviour from normal behaviour?

• What behaviours have you observed in members of other cultural groups that might be considered abnormal in your own?

• What behaviours in your own cultural group might be considered abnormal by members of other groups?

HISTORICAL PERSPECTIVES ON ABNORMAL BEHAVIOUR

Throughout the history of Western culture, concepts of abnormal behaviour have been shaped, to some degree, by the prevailing **world view** of the time. Throughout much of history, beliefs in supernatural forces, demons, and evil spirits held sway. Abnormal behaviour was often taken as a sign of **possession**. In more modern times, the predominant—but by no means universal—world view has shifted toward beliefs in science and reason. Abnormal behaviour has come to be viewed in our culture as the product of physical and psychosocial factors, not demonic possession.

The Demonological Model

Let us begin our journey with an example from prehistory. Archaeologists have unearthed human skeletons from the Stone Age with egg-sized cavities in the skulls. One interpretation of these holes is that our prehistoric ancestors believed abnormal behaviour reflected the invasion of evil spirits. Perhaps they used this harsh method—called **trephining**—to create a pathway through the skull to provide an outlet for those irascible spirits. Fresh bone growth indicates that some people managed to survive the ordeal.

Threat of trephining may have persuaded people to comply with group or tribal norms to the best of their abilities. Because no written records or accounts of the purposes

world view Prevailing view of the times. (English translation of the German *Weltanschauung*.)

possession In demonology, a type of superstitious belief in which abnormal behaviour is taken as a sign that the individual has become possessed by demons or the devil, usually as a form of retribution or the result of making a pact with the devil.

trephining Harsh, prehistoric practice of cutting a hole in a person's skull, possibly as an ancient form of surgery for brain trauma, or possibly as a means of releasing the demons that prehistoric people may have believed caused abnormal behaviaour in the afflicted persons.

of trephination exist, other explanations are possible. Perhaps trephination was used as a primitive form of surgery to remove shattered pieces of bone or blood clots that resulted from head injuries (Maher & Maher, 1985).

Explanation of abnormal behaviour in terms of supernatural or divine causes is termed the **demonological model**. Ancients peoples explained natural forces in terms of divine will and spirits. The ancient Babylonians believed the movements of the stars and planets were fashioned by the adventures and conflicts of the gods. The ancient Greeks believed their gods toyed with humans; when aroused to wrath, they could unleash forces of nature to wreak havoc on disrespectful or arrogant humans, even clouding their minds with madness.

In ancient Greece, people who behaved abnormally were often sent to temples dedicated to Aesculapius, the god of healing. Priests believed Aesculapius would visit the afflicted persons while they slept in the temple and offer them restorative advice through dreams. Rest, a nutritious diet, and exercise were also believed to contribute to treatment. Incurables might be driven from the temple by stoning.

demonological model The model that explains abnormal behaviour in terms of supernatural forces.

Origins of the Medical Model: An "Ill Humour"

Not all ancient Greeks believed in the demonological model. The seeds of naturalistic explanations of abnormal behaviour were sown by Hippocrates and developed by other physicians in the ancient world, especially Galen.

Hippocrates (ca. 460–377 BC), the celebrated physician of the Golden Age of Greece, challenged the prevailing beliefs of his time by arguing that illnesses of the body and mind were the result of natural causes, not possession by supernatural spirits. He believed the health of the body and mind depended on the balance of **humours** or vital fluids: phlegm, black bile, blood, and yellow bile. An imbalance of humours, he thought, accounted for abnormal behaviour. A lethargic or sluggish person was believed to have an excess of phlegm, from which we derive the word **phlegmatic**. An overabundance of black bile was believed to cause depression, or **melancholia**. An excess of blood created a **sanguine** disposition: cheerful, confident, and optimistic. An excess of yellow bile made people "bilious" and **choleric**—quick-tempered, that is.

Although we no longer subscribe to Hippocrates's theory of bodily humours, his theory is of historical importance because of its break from demonology. It also foreshadowed the development of the modern medical model, the view that abnormal behaviour results from underlying biological processes. Hippocrates made many contributions to modern thought and, indeed, to modern medical practice. He had even begun to classify abnormal behaviour patterns, using three main categories that find some equivalents today: *melancholia* to characterize excessive depression, *mania* to refer to exceptional excitement, and *phrenitis* (from the Greek "inflammation of the brain") to characterize the bizarre kinds of behaviour that might typify schizophrenia. Medical schools continue to pay homage to Hippocrates by having new physicians swear the Hippocratic oath in his honour.

Galen (ca. AD 130–200), a Greek physician who attended Roman emperor-philosopher Marcus Aurelius, adopted and expanded on the teachings of Hippocrates. Among Galen's contributions was the discovery that arteries carry blood, not air, as had been formerly believed.

humours Historic: the vital bodily fluids considered responsible for one's disposition and health, as in Hippocrates's belief that the health of the body and mind depended on the balance of four humours in the body: phlegm, black bile, blood, and yellow bile.

phlegmatic Slow and stolid.

melancholia State of severe depression.

sanguine Having a cheerful disposition.

choleric Having or showing bad temper.

Medieval Times

The Middle Ages, or medieval times, cover the millennium of European history from about AD 476 through AD 1450. After the passing of Galen, belief in supernatural causes, especially the doctrine of possession, increased in influence and eventually dominated medieval thought. The doctrine of possession held that abnormal behaviours were a sign of possession by evil spirits or the devil. This belief was embodied within the teachings of the Roman Catholic Church, which became the unifying force in Western Europe following the decline of the Roman Empire. Although belief in possession antedated the Church and is found in ancient Egyptian and Greek writings, the Church revitalized it. The treatment of choice for abnormal behaviour was **exorcism**. Exorcists were employed to persuade evil spirits that the bodies of their intended victims were basically uninhabitable. Methods included prayer, waving a cross at the victim, beating and flogging, even starving the victim. If the victim still displayed unseemly behaviour, there were yet more powerful remedies, such as the rack, a device of torture. It seems clear that recipients of these "remedies" would be motivated to conform their behaviour to social expectations as best they could.

The Renaissance—the great European revival in learning, art, and literature—began in Italy in the 1400s and spread gradually throughout Europe. The Renaissance is considered the transition from the medieval world to the modern. Therefore, it is ironic that fear of witches also reached its height during the Renaissance.

Witchcraft

The late 15th through the late 17th centuries were especially dangerous times to be unpopular with your neighbours. These were times of massive persecutions of people, particularly women, who were accused of witchcraft. Officials of the Roman Catholic Church believed witches made pacts with the devil, practised satanic rituals, and committed heinous acts such as eating babies and poisoning crops. In 1484, Pope Innocent VIII decreed that witches be executed. Two Dominican priests compiled a manual for witch-hunting, called the *Malleus Maleficarum* ("The Witches' Hammer"), to help inquisitors identify suspected witches. Over 100 000 accused witches were killed in the next two centuries.

There were also creative "diagnostic" tests for detecting possession and witchcraft. <u>In the case of the water-float test, innocent people were drowned in medieval times as a way of certifying they were not possessed by the devil.</u> The water-float test was based on the principle that pure metals settle to the bottom during smelting, whereas impurities bob up to the surface. Suspects who sank and were drowned were ruled pure. Suspects who were able to keep their heads above water were regarded as being in league with the devil—and in real trouble. This trial is the source of the phrase, "Damned if you do and damned if you don't."

Modern scholars once believed the so-called witches of the Middle Ages and the Renaissance were actually people who were mentally disturbed. They were believed to have been persecuted because their abnormal behaviour was taken as evidence that they were in league with the devil. It is true that many suspected witches confessed to impossible behaviours, such as flying or engaging in sexual intercourse with the devil. At face value, such confessions might suggest disturbances in thinking and perception that are consistent with a modern diagnosis of a psychological disorder, such as schizophrenia. Most of these confessions can be discounted, however, because they were extracted under torture by inquisitors who were bent on finding evidence to support accusations of witchcraft (Spanos, 1978). In other cases, the threat of torture and alternate forms of intimidation were sufficient to extract false confessions. Although some of those who were persecuted as witches probably did show abnormal behaviour patterns, most did not (Schoenman, 1984). Rather, accusations of witchcraft appeared to be a convenient means of disposing of social nuisances and political rivals, of seizing property, and of suppressing heresy (Spanos, 1978). In English villages, many of the accused were poor, unmarried elderly women, who were forced to beg their neighbours for food. If misfortune befell people who declined to help, the beggar might be accused of causing misery by having cast a curse on the uncharitable family (Spanos, 1978). If the woman was generally unpopular, accusations of witchcraft were more likely to be followed up.

Although demons were believed to play roles both in abnormal behaviour and witchcraft, there was a

Exorcism. This medieval woodcut illustrates the practice of exorcism, which was used to expel evil spirits who were believed to have possessed people.

difference between the two. Victims of possession may have been perceived to be afflicted as retribution for wrongdoing, but it was allowed that some people who showed abnormal behaviour might be totally innocent victims of demonic possession. Witches, however, were believed to have voluntarily entered into a pact with the devil and renounced God. Witches were generally seen as more deserving of torture and execution (Spanos, 1978).

Historical trends do not follow straight lines. Although the demonological model held sway during the Middle Ages and much of the Renaissance, it did not universally supplant belief in naturalistic causes (Schoenman, 1984). In medieval England, for example, demonic possession was only rarely invoked as the cause of abnormal behaviour in cases in which a person was held to be insane by legal authorities (Neugebauer, 1979). Most explanations involved natural causes for unusual behaviour, such as illness or trauma to the brain. In England, in fact, some disturbed people were kept in hospitals until they were restored to sanity (Allderidge, 1979). The Renaissance Belgian physician Johann Weyer (1515–1588) also took up the cause of Hippocrates and Galen by arguing that abnormal behaviour and thought patterns were caused by physical problems.

Asylums in Europe and the New World

By the late 15th and early 16th centuries, asylums, or madhouses, began to crop up throughout Europe. Many were former leprosariums, which were no longer needed as a result of the decline in leprosy that occurred in the late Middle Ages. Asylums often gave refuge to beggars as well as the disturbed, and conditions were generally appalling. Residents were often chained to their beds and left to lie in their own waste or wander about unassisted. Some asylums became public spectacles. In one asylum in London, Bethlehem Hospital—from which the word bedlam is derived—the public could buy tickets to observe the bizarre antics of inmates, much as we would view a sideshow in a circus or animals at a zoo.

The first asylum in what is now North America was the Hôtel Dieu of Quebec. It was founded in 1639 by the Duchess d'Aiguillon to care for people with psychological disorders and intellectual disabilities, as well as the poor and destitute and the physically disabled. The Catholic community took responsibility for the treatment of patients and oversaw the development of other asylums throughout Quebec (Hurd et al., 1916). Outside Quebec, however, people with psychological disorders received little treatment and were commonly shut away in jails, poorhouses, charity shelters, or other convenient strongholds. No means of addressing their needs came until well into the 19th century, when mental hospitals began to appear in other parts of Canada (Sussman, 1998).

The Reform Movement and Moral Therapy in Europe and North America

The modern era of treatment can be traced to the efforts of individuals such as the Frenchmen Jean-Baptiste Pussin and Philippe Pinel in the late 18th and early 19th centuries. They argued that people who behave abnormally suffer from diseases and should be treated humanely. This view was not popular at the time. Deranged people were generally regarded by the public as threats to society, not as sick people in need of treatment.

From 1784 to 1802, Pussin, a layman, was placed in charge of a ward for people considered "incurably insane" at La Bicêtre, a large mental hospital in Paris. Although Pinel is often credited with freeing the inmates of La Bicêtre from their chains, Pussin was actually the first official to unchain a group of the "incurably insane." These unfortu-

"Bedlam." The bizarre antics of the patients at Bethlehem Hospital in London in the 18th century were a source of entertainment for the well-heeled gentry of the town (note the two well-dressed women in the middle of the painting). The word bedlam derives from the name of this hospital.

The unchaining of inmates at La Bicêtre by 18th-century French reformer Philippe Pinel. Continuing the work of Jean-Baptiste Pussin, Pinel stopped harsh practices such as bleeding and purging and moved inmates from darkened dungeons to sunny, airy rooms. Pinel also took the time to converse with inmates in the belief that understanding and concern would help restore them to normal functioning.

nates had been considered too dangerous and unpredictable to be left unchained. But Pussin believed that if they were treated with kindness, there would be no need for chains. As he predicted, most of the shut-ins became manageable and calm when their chains were removed. They could walk the hospital grounds and take in fresh air. Pussin also forbade the staff from treating the residents harshly, and he discharged employees who ignored his directives.

Pinel (1745–1826) became medical director for the incurables' ward at La Bicêtre in 1793 and continued the humane treatment Pussin had begun. He stopped harsh practices, such as bleeding and purging, and moved patients from darkened dungeons to well-ventilated, sunny rooms. Pinel also spent hours talking to inmates, in the belief that showing understanding and concern would help restore them to normal functioning.

The philosophy of treatment that emerged from these efforts was labelled **moral therapy** (a mistranslation of "well-being" or "morale") (Lightner, 1999). It was based on the belief that providing humane treatment in a relaxed, decent, and encouraging environment could restore functioning. Similar reforms were instituted at about this time in England by William Tuke and later in the United States and Canada by Dorothea Dix.

Dorothea Dix (1802–1887), a Boston schoolteacher, travelled throughout the United States, Europe, and Canada decrying the deplorable conditions in jails and almshouses where deranged people were often placed. As a direct result of her social activism, mental hospitals were established in Canada, initially in the Maritimes during the 1840s, and later in the century throughout the other provinces.

moral therapy A 19th-century treatment philosophy that emphasized that hospitalized mental patients should be treated with care and understanding in a pleasant environment, not shackled in chains.

Treatment Takes a Step Backward in Canada

In the latter half of the 19th century, however, the belief that abnormal behaviours could be successfully treated or cured by moral therapy fell into disfavour. Mental institutions in Canada grew in size and number and came to provide little more than custodial care. Resources became scarce and conditions deteriorated. Mental hospitals became unclean and frightening places. Hurd et al. (1916) cited reports from that era that contained descriptors like "horrors," "revolting scenes," "misery, starvation, and suffering," "naked for... months," "the stench... scarcely bearable," and "beds... full of vermin" (pp. 134–135). Straitjackets, handcuffs, cribs, straps, and other devices were used to restrain excitable or violent patients.

Deplorable hospital conditions remained commonplace through the middle of the 20th century. By the 1950s, the population in Canadian psychiatric hospitals had risen to 66 000 patients. At this time, there were more patients occupying psychiatric hospital beds than there were patients in hospital beds due to all other causes (Greenland, Griffin, &

Hoffman, 2001). With few effective psychiatric treatments available, the provincial psychiatric hospital system continued to expand across Canada until the 1960s (Hector, 2001).

The Community Mental Health Movement in Canada: The Exodus from Provincial Psychiatric Hospitals

phenothiazines Group of antipsychotic drugs or "major tranquillizers" used in the treatment of schizophrenia.

An important factor that spurred the exodus from psychiatric hospitals was the advent of a new class of drugs— *phenothiazines*. The **phenothiazines**, a group of antipsychotic drugs that helped quell the most flagrant behaviour patterns associated with schizophrenia, were introduced in Canada in the early 1950s. Two psychiatrists, unbeknownst to each other, had begun experimenting with chlorpromazine, a drug that was being used in conjunction with anaesthetics for surgery. They were curious about its soothing qualities and potential worth as a treatment for psychotic symptoms and it wasn't long before their pioneering research produced far-reaching outcomes. In 1954, Dr. Ruth Kajander (see "A Closer Look: Antipsychotic Medications" on page 15) was the first in North America to publicly report on the drug's therapeutic value (Gold, Lalinec-Michaud, & Bernazzani, 1995; Sussman, 1999). A month later, McGill University psychiatrist Dr. Heinz Lehmann published the first research paper for the North American audience describing his success in using chlorpromazine to treat schizophrenia (Griffin, 1993; Sussman, 1999). As a result of Kajander's and Lehmann's research, the widespread use of chlorpromazine as an antipsychotic drug in Canada and the United States quickly followed. It reduced the need for indefinite hospital stays and permitted many people with schizophrenia to be discharged to less restrictive living arrangements in their community, such as halfway houses, group homes, and independent living arrangements.

In response to the growing call for reform in the mental health system, the Canadian Mental Health Association (CMHA) published a report, *More for the Mind: A Study of Psychiatric Services in Canada* (Tyhurst et al., 1963), which recommended that mental illness be treated as a medical condition in a medical facility. This report paved the way for long-term custodial care patients, the so-called back-ward patients in bleak institutions, to be integrated into community general hospitals. This policy of **deinstitutionalization** was predicated on the belief—the hope, perhaps—that psychiatric patients would benefit from the opportunity to lead more independent and fulfilling lives in the community, while relying on general hospitals for short-term care during episodes of illness. Indeed, the psychiatric hospital population across Canada plummeted from more than 50 000 in 1960 to 15 000 by 1975 (Wasylenki, 2001).

deinstitutionalization Practice of discharging large numbers of hospitalized mental patients to the community and of reducing the need for new admissions through the development of alternative treatment approaches such as halfway houses and crisis intervention services.

In the initial stages, during the 1960s and 1970s, there was a shift from long stays in provincial psychiatric hospitals to shorter but more frequent stays in general hospital psychiatric units. However, although the number of general hospital beds used for this purpose rose, it failed to match the shrinking number of psychiatric hospitals beds. At the same time, the availability of more community mental health supports and services lagged far behind the rapid exodus of mental health patients from psychiatric hospitals (Sealy & Whitehead, 2004). The general hospital psychiatric units treated patients with less severe forms of mental disorders, while patients with severe and persistent mental disorders had to rely on the much-scaled-down provincial psychiatric hospital system. In effect, this created a two-tier mental health-care system, whereby middle- and upper-class patients had easier access to psychiatrists and general hospital psychiatric care than less fortunate Canadians who were relegated to shrinking psychiatric hospital services or worse, were left to lead a subsistence existence in the community (Kirby & Keon, 2004).

The number of general hospital beds allocated for psychiatric patients peaked during the mid-1980s to mid-1990s and has been declining ever since (Sealy & Whitehead, 2004). Funding started becoming available for programs outside of the hospital setting to meet the needs of patients with severe and persistent mental disorders. But services continued to be narrow in focus and not well co-ordinated, thus making it difficult for patients to receive adequate and consistent care. The community programs and services that were supposed to replace institutional care have thus far been inadequate (Kirby & Keon, 2004; Wasylenki, 2001). Deinstitutionalization in Canada has left mental patients to rely on dramatically fewer hospital beds and a fragmented system of community services and supports. In "A Closer Look: The Homeless in Canada" on page 18, we consider the plight of the homeless Canadians with mental health issues who got lost in the shuffle between the movement toward the closure of psychiatric institutions and the promised, but thus far inadequate, community mental health-care system.

Until recently, Canada lacked a comprehensive mental health-care policy; mental health legislation falls under the jurisdiction of the provinces and territories. A mental health act serves a variety of purposes including the regulation of psychiatric assessment, admission and treatment, patients' rights, and the confidentiality of patient records. The federal government's role in mental health care falls under the authority of the Canada Health Act. Under this arrangement, the provinces and territories administer and deliver mental health-care services while the government of Canada determines national principles, monitors the implementation of the Canada Health Act, and provides funding assistance. Unfortunately, the Act does not directly address mental health care. In fact, mental health was deemed the "orphan child" of medicare in the final report of the Romanow Commission on the Future of Health Care in Canada (2002). Following this, senators Michael Kirby and Wilbert Keon (2006) conducted the most comprehensive study of its kind in Canada on mental health, mental illness, and addiction. Their report, *Out of the Shadows at Last: Transforming Mental Health, Mental Illness and Addiction Services in Canada*, focused squarely on mental health promotion, prevention of mental illness, and the creation of a continuum of care for those who suffer from mental illness and addiction. The report recommended that a Canadian Mental Health Commission be established to implement a national mental health-care strategy. In March 2007, the federal government announced funding for the Commission, to be led by Senator Kirby.

A CLOSER LOOK

Antipsychotic Medications: A Major Psychiatric Breakthrough

Until the use of phenothiazines to treat schizophrenia, psychotic symptoms were typically controlled with powerful sedatives that basically "knocked patients out" to the point that they could barely talk or eat (Kajander, 2004). Chlorpromazine, a phenothiazine synthesized by a French chemist in 1950, was originally used in conjunction with anaesthesia to stabilize a patient's shock reaction to surgery. Within a year of discovering the calming and stabilizing effects of chlorpromazine on surgical patients, Parisian psychiatrists, inspired by its psychiatric treatment possibilities, began using it successfully to treat agitated psychotic patients. Despite these encouraging findings, chlorpromazine was initially marketed in North America as a treatment for postsurgical nausea and vomiting (Healy, 2002), while its potential as an antipsychotic medication was yet unknown in North America. It was within this context that in 1953, two Canadian psychiatrists, each unaware of the other's research activities, began experimenting with chlorpromazine to assess its calming effect in the treatment of psychotic patients.

Dr. Ruth Kajander. Ruth Kajander, a long-time practising psychiatrist in Thunder Bay, Ontario, is recognized as a pioneer at a time when, half a century ago in Canada, women and immigrants (especially post-WWII Germans) were not readily acknowledged for their accomplishments. (Photo: Courtesy of Dr. Ruth Kajander – photo by Karsh)

(continued)

(continued)

On speculation, pharmaceutical sales representatives provided McGill University psychiatrist Dr. Heinz Lehmann with articles recently published by the French psychiatrists who first described the calming effect of chlorpromazine on agitated psychiatric patients. Lehmann immediately began conducting chlorpromazine **clinical drug trials**. About the same time, a newly arrived German immigrant medical intern, Dr. Ruth Kajander (née Koeppe), happened to be working with a surgeon at Oshawa General Hospital who was using chlorpromazine as an adjunct to anaesthesia. Kajander, armed with psychiatric training, was intrigued by the tranquillizing effect that chlorpromazine had on surgical patients and suddenly realized its potential for treating agitated psychotic patients (Kajander, 2004). Soon after, Kajander

began conducting her own research into the clinical effects of chlorpromazine at the London (Ontario) Psychiatric Hospital. In February 1954, at the Ontario Neuropsychiatric Association conference, Kajander became the first person on this side of the Atlantic to publicly report on the drug's antipsychotic therapeutic properties (Sussman, 1999; Gold, Lalinec-Michaud, & Bernazzani, 1995). A month later, Dr. Lehmann published the first North American research paper on chlorpromazine. His paper described his eyewitness accounts of the successful use of chlorpromazine as a treatment for schizophrenia (Griffin, 1993; Sussman, 1999). As in France two years earlier, chlorpromazine was quickly and widely adopted as the treatment of choice for schizophrenia and other psychotic conditions in Canada, the United States, and the rest of the industrialized world.

clinical drug trials The controlled investigation of a new drug to determine how well it works, dosage limits, side effects, and safety.

Pathways to the Present: From Demonology to Science

Beliefs in possession or demonology persisted until the rise of the natural sciences in the late 17th and early 18th centuries. Society at large began to turn toward reason and science as ways of explaining natural phenomena and human behaviour. The nascent sciences of biology, chemistry, physics, and astronomy offered promise that knowledge could be derived from scientific methods of observation and experimentation. The 18th and 19th centuries witnessed rapid developments in medical science. Scientific discoveries uncovered the microbial causes of some kinds of diseases and gave rise to preventive measures. Emerging models of abnormal behaviour also began to surface, including the medical model, psychological models, and sociocultural models.

Medical Model Against the backdrop of advances in medical science, German physician Wilhelm Griesinger (1817–1868) argued that abnormal behaviour was rooted in diseases of the brain. Griesinger's views influenced another German physician, Emil Kraepelin (1856–1926), who wrote an influential textbook on psychiatry in 1883 in which he likened mental disorders to physical diseases. Griesinger and Kraepelin paved the way for the development of the modern medical model, which attempts to explain abnormal behaviour on the basis of underlying biological defects or abnormalities, not evil spirits. According to the medical model, people behaving abnormally suffer from mental illnesses or disorders that can be classified, like physical illnesses, according to their distinctive causes and symptoms. Not all adopters of the medical model believe every pattern of abnormal behaviour is a product of defective biology, but they maintain that patterns of abnormal behaviour can be likened to physical illnesses in that their features can be conceptualized as symptoms of underlying disorders, whatever their cause.

dementia praecox Term given by Emil Kraepelin to the disorder we now call schizophrenia.

Kraepelin specified two main groups of mental disorders or diseases: **dementia praecox** (from roots meaning "precocious [premature] insanity"), which we now call *schizophrenia*, and *manic-depressive psychosis*, which is now labelled *bipolar disorder*. Kraepelin believed dementia praecox was caused by a biochemical imbalance and manic-depressive psychosis by an abnormality in body metabolism. But his major contribution was the development of a classification system that forms the cornerstone for current diagnostic systems.

general paresis Degenerative brain disorder that occurs during the final stage of syphilis.

The medical model was supported by evidence that a form of derangement called **general paresis** represented an advanced stage of syphilis in which the syphilis bacterium directly invades brain tissue. Scientists grew optimistic that other biological causes, as well as treatments, would soon be discovered for other so-called mental disorders. This early optimism has remained largely unfulfilled because the causes of most patterns of abnormal behaviour remain obscure.

Much of the terminology in current use reflects the influence of the medical model. Because of the medical model, many professionals and laypeople speak of people whose behaviour is deemed abnormal as being mentally *ill*. It is because of the medical model that so many speak of the *symptoms* of abnormal behaviour, rather than its features or characteristics. Other terms spawned by the medical model include *mental health, syndrome, diagnosis, patient, mental patient, mental hospital, prognosis, treatment, therapy, cure, relapse,* and *remission.*[1]

The medical model is a major advance over demonology. It inspired the idea that abnormal behaviour should be treated by learned professionals and not be punished. Compassion supplanted hatred, fear, and persecution.

Psychological Models

Although the medical model was gaining influence in the 19th century, there were those who believed organic factors alone could not explain the many forms of abnormal behaviour. In Paris, a highly respected neurologist, Jean-Martin Charcot (1825–1893), experimented with the use of **hypnosis** in treating **hysteria** (which is now called *conversion disorder*), a condition in which people present with physical symptoms like paralysis or numbness that cannot be explained by any underlying physical cause. The thinking at the time was that they must have an affliction of the nervous system that caused their symptoms. Yet Charcot and his associates demonstrated that these symptoms could be removed in hysterical patients or actually induced in normal patients by means of hypnotic suggestion.

Among those who attended Charcot's demonstrations was a young Austrian physician named Sigmund Freud (1856–1939). Freud reasoned that if hysterical symptoms could be made to disappear or appear through hypnosis—the mere "suggestion of ideas"—they must be psychological in origin (Jones, 1953). He concluded that whatever psychological factors give rise to hysteria, they must lie outside the range of conscious awareness. This was the kernel of the idea that underlies his model of abnormal behaviour, the **psychodynamic model**, which holds that the causes of abnormal behaviours lie in the interplay of forces within the unconscious mind. "I received the proudest impression," Freud wrote of his experience with Charcot, "of the possibility that there could be powerful mental processes which nevertheless remained hidden from the consciousness of men" (cited in Sulloway, 1983, p. 32).

Freud was also influenced by the Viennese physician Joseph Breuer (1842–1925), 14 years his senior. Breuer too had used hypnosis to treat a 21-year-old woman, Anna O., with hysterical complaints for which there was no apparent medical basis, such as paralysis in her limbs, numbness, and disturbances of vision and hearing (Jones, 1953). A "paralysed" muscle in her neck prevented her from turning her head. Immobilization of the fingers of her left hand made it all but impossible for her to feed herself. Breuer believed there was a strong psychological component to the symptoms. He treated her by encouraging her to talk about them, sometimes under hypnosis. Recalling and talking about events connected with the appearance of the symptoms—especially events that evoked feelings of fear, anxiety, or guilt—appeared to provide symptom relief, at least for a time. Anna referred to the treatment as the "talking cure" or, when joking, as "chimney sweeping."

Hysterical symptoms were taken to represent the transformation of these blocked-up emotions, forgotten but not lost, into physical complaints. In Anna's case, the symptoms

hypnosis Trancelike state induced by suggestion in which one is generally passive and responsive to the commands of the hypnotist.

hysteria Former term for *conversion disorder*.

psychodynamic model Theoretical model of Freud and his followers in which behaviour is viewed as the product of clashing forces within the personality.

---

[1]Because the medical model is not the only way of viewing abnormal behaviour patterns, we adopt a more neutral language in this text in describing abnormal behaviour patterns. For example, we often refer to "features" or "characteristics" of abnormal behaviour patterns or psychological disorders rather than "symptoms." But our adoption of nonmedical jargon is not an absolute rule. In some cases, there may be no handy substitutes for terms that derive from the medical model, such as the term *remission* or the reference to patients in mental hospitals as "mental patients." In other cases we may use terms such as *disorder, therapy,* and *treatment* because they are commonly used by psychologists who "treat" "mental disorders" with psychological "therapies."

The Homeless in Canada: Still Waiting for True Community Mental Health Care

The number of homeless people across Canada has more than doubled in the last decade. Projections state that nightly, tens of thousands of Canadians are homeless (Hwang, 2001). Although difficult to measure, it is estimated that between 20% and 35% of homeless people need treatment for their mental health problems (Golden et al., 1999; Milstone, 1995). A year-long study of Toronto homeless shelter users found about one-third (31%) of homeless people were experiencing both psychological and substance-use disorders, while roughly equal numbers were experiencing either a psychological disorder (19%) or a substance-use disorder (21%) (Tolomiczenko & Goering, 1998). In 5% of the cases, a prevalence of severe psychological disorder, primarily schizophrenia, was found.

Facing the Challenge of Mental Health Promotion for Homeless People

While it's true that many provincial psychiatric hospitals closed their doors and general hospitals reduced the number of psychiatric beds beginning in the 1990s, problems arose when provinces failed to adequately fund or integrate community support services intended to replace the need for long-term hospitalization (Muckle & Turnbull, 2006). Far too often, homeless people with a range of psychological problems fell through the cracks of the mental health and social service systems and were left largely to fend for themselves. In particular, there has been an ongoing lack of available housing, transitional care facilities, and effective case management for homeless Canadians who have psychological disorders and addictions (Kirby & Keon, 2006). To compound the problem, not only is there limited access to adequate housing and community support services that magnifies the length and severity of a homeless person's mental health problems (Golden et al., 1999; Social Services Ottawa, 1999; Stuart & Arboleda-Florez, 2000), but also large numbers of those who suffer from medical ailments are typically forced to endure increased hospital stays and treatment costs (Podymow, Turnbull, Tadic, & Muckle, 2006).

Deinstitutionalization: The Final Phase

At long last, we may be on the verge of a new era in Canadian mental health care. In their comprehensive

Psychiatric homeless. A multifaceted effort is needed to meet the needs of the psychiatric homeless population, including access to affordable housing and to medical, drug and alcohol, and mental health treatment, as well as other social services. Far too often, homeless people with a range of psychological problems fall through the cracks of the mental health and social service systems, and are left largely to fend for themselves.

report, *Out of the Shadows at Last*, senators Kirby and Keon (2006) described how a continuum of mental health care could be made available to every Canadian, including some of our most vulnerable members of society—homeless Canadians with psychological disorders. Based on the recommendations of Kirby and Keon's report, the newly formed Canadian Mental Health Care Commission will develop a national strategy to oversee the delivery of mental health services, such as integrated, seamless access to personalized and culturally sensitive care through community mental health-care services and supports (Kirby & Keon, 2006). Such a system may include, but would not be limited to, the following: access to non-health services including safe and adequate housing, employment assistance and adequate income, opportunities to rely on peer support and develop meaningful social relationships, opportunities to foster self-respect and a sense of being an accepted member of society (Kirby & Keon, 2006; Russell, Hubley & Palepu, 2005), and harm reduction programs that target alcohol and drug abuse (Everett, 2002; Turnbull, Muckle & Tadic, 2004; Wasylenki, 2001).

seemed to disappear once the emotions were brought to the surface and "discharged." Breuer labelled the therapeutic effect **catharsis**, a Greek term meaning "purgation or purification of feelings." Cases of hysteria, such as that of Anna O., seemed to have been a common occurrence in the later Victorian period but are relatively rare today (Spitzer et al., 1989).

Freud's theoretical model was the first major psychological model of abnormal behaviour. As we'll see in Chapter 2, "Theoretical Perspectives and Methods of Treatment," other psychological perspectives on abnormal behaviour soon followed based on behavioural, humanistic, and cognitive approaches. We'll also see that each of these psychological perspectives, as well as the physiological perspective, spawned particular forms of therapy to treat psychological disorders.

Sociocultural Models: Viewing Abnormal Behaviour From a Broader Context

Sociocultural theorists believe we must consider the broader social contexts in which behaviour occurs to better understand the roots of abnormal behaviour. They believe the causes of abnormal behaviour may be found in the failures of society rather than the person. Psychological problems may be rooted in the social ills of society, such as poverty, lack of economic opportunity, rapidly changing social values and morals, and racial and gender discrimination.

According to the more radical sociocultural theorists, such as the psychiatrist Thomas Szasz, mental illness is no more than a myth—a label used to stigmatize and subjugate people whose behaviour is socially deviant (Szasz, 1961). Szasz argues that so-called mental illnesses are really "problems in living," not diseases in the sense that influenza, hypertension, and cancer are. Nearly half a century later, Canadian psychiatrist Gordon Warme (2006) has rekindled these sentiments by claiming that biological explanations of abnormal behaviour are still unconvincing and that "most, if not all, of the effects of psychiatry are magical" (p. 2).

Sociocultural theorists also maintain that once the label of "mental illness" is applied, it is very difficult to remove. The label also affects other people's responses to the "patient." Mental patients are stigmatized and socially degraded. Job opportunities may be denied, friendships may dissolve, and the "patient" may become increasingly alienated from society. Szasz argues that treating people as mentally ill strips them of their dignity because it denies them responsibility for their own behaviour and choices. He claims that troubled people should be encouraged to take more responsibility for managing their lives and solving their problems.

Although not all sociocultural theorists subscribe to the more radical views of Szasz, they alert us to consider the importance of taking sociocultural factors relating to gender, race, ethnicity, lifestyle, and social ills such as poverty and discrimination into account in understanding people whose behaviour leads them to be perceived as mentally ill or abnormal. It should come as no surprise that the effects of stigma and discrimination remain a daily experience for many Canadians diagnosed with psychological or addictive disorders—a topic we'll come back to in Chapter 3, "Classification and Assessment of Abnormal Behaviour."

We next consider the ways in which psychologists and other mental health professionals study abnormal behaviour.

catharsis (1) Discharge of states of tension associated with repression of threatening impulses or material. (2) the free expression or purging of feelings. Also called *abreaction* by later psychoanalysts.

Historical Perspectives on Abnormal Behaviour

Review It

- **How have views about abnormal behaviour changed over time?** Ancient societies attributed abnormal behaviour to divine or supernatural forces. There were some authorities in ancient times, such as the Greek physicians Hippocrates and Galen, who believed that abnormal behaviour reflected natural causes. In medieval times, belief in possession held sway, and exorcists were used to rid people who behaved abnormally of the evil spirits that were believed to possess them. The 19th-century German physician Wilhelm Griesinger argued that abnormal behaviour was caused by diseases of the brain. He, along with another German physician who followed him, Emil Kraepelin, were influential in the development of the modern medical model, which likens abnormal behaviour patterns to physical illnesses.

- **How has the treatment of people with psychological disorders changed over time?** Asylums, or madhouses, began to crop up throughout Europe in the late 15th and early 16th centuries. Conditions in these asylums were dreadful and in some, such as Bethlehem Hospital in England, a circus atmosphere prevailed. With the rise of moral therapy in the 19th century, largely spearheaded by the Frenchmen Jean-Baptiste Pussin and Philippe Pinel, conditions in mental hospitals improved. Proponents of moral therapy believed that mental patients could be restored to functioning if they were treated with dignity and understanding. The decline of moral therapy in the latter part of the 19th century led to a period of apathy and to the belief that the "insane" could not be successfully treated. Conditions in mental hospitals deteriorated, and they offered little more than custodial care.

  Not until the middle of the 20th century did public outrage and concern about the plight of mental patients mobilize a change in government policy. As a consequence, psychiatric services were commonly relocated to general hospital psychiatric units as an alternative to long-term hospitalization. This movement toward deinstitutionalization was spurred by the introduction of psychoactive drugs, called phenothiazines, which curbed the more flagrant features of schizophrenia.

- **What are the roles of psychiatric hospitals and general hospital psychiatric units today?** The hospitals provide a structured treatment environment for people in acute crisis and for those who are unable to adapt to community living. Mental health care in a hospital today aims to restore patients to community functioning. Community mental health care services are meant to provide continuing care to people with psychological disorders outside of the hospital.

- **What is deinstitutionalization and how successful has it been?** Deinstitutionalization is the policy of reducing the need for long-term hospitalization of mental patients by shifting care to community-based settings. Although deinstitutionalization has greatly reduced the population of provincial psychiatric hospitals, it has not yet fulfilled its promise of restoring people with psychological disorders to a reasonable quality of life in the community. One example of the challenges yet to be met is the number of homeless people with psychological and substance abuse problems who are not receiving adequate care in the community.

Define It

world view	moral therapy
possession	deinstitutionalization
trephining	phenothiazines
demonological model	clinical drug trials
humours	dementia praecox
phlegmatic	general paresis
melancholia	hypnosis
sanguine	hysteria
choleric	psychodynamic model
exorcism	catharsis

Recall It*

1. The physician of ancient Greece who first identified the belief that illnesses of the body and mind resulted from natural causes rather than supernatural causes was _____.

   a. Galen
   b. Plato
   c. Hippocrates
   d. Aristotle

2. Which form of treatment was used widely in the Middle Ages to treat people who were deemed to be mentally disturbed?

   a. trephining
   b. bleeding

c. meditation

d. exorcism

3. If someone subjected to the water-float test was found to be spiritually pure, the suspect _____.

   a. was released and returned to the community

   b. was required to provide service to the Church to assure the purity of his or her soul

   c. drowned

   d. was given an exorcism to prevent future demonic possession

4. The first asylums in Europe were _____.

   a. former military forts

   b. former leprosariums

   c. built in rural areas to provide a tranquil setting to help restore normal functioning

   d. established as special "wards" in existing hospitals

5. Which is NOT true of the policy of deinstitutionalization?

   a. It has led to a major reduction in the patient population of psychiatric hospitals.

b. It was instituted to help correct past abuses of patients confined to mental hospitals.

c. It has mostly eliminated the problem of homeless people with mental health issues.

d. It has caused people with serious psychological disorders to rely increasingly on community support services.

* Recall It answers can be found on the Companion Website for this text.

Think About It

- How did the thinking of Hippocrates and Galen anticipate the development of the modern medical model?

- What role did hypnotism play in the development of psychological models of abnormal behaviour?

- What do you believe should be done about the problem of homelessness for people with psychological disorders?

RESEARCH METHODS IN ABNORMAL PSYCHOLOGY

Abnormal psychology is a branch of the scientific discipline of psychology, which means the pursuit of knowledge in the field is based on the application of the scientific method. Here, we examine how researchers apply the scientific method in investigating abnormal behaviour.

Let us begin by asking you to imagine you are in your first psychology class and the professor enters the room carrying a small wire-mesh cage with a white rat. She smiles and sets the cage on her desk. The professor removes the rat from the cage and places it on the desk. She asks the class to observe its behaviour. As a serious student, you attend closely. The animal moves to the edge of the desk, pauses, peers over, and seems to jiggle its whiskers at the floor below. It manoeuvres along the edge, tracking the perimeter. Now and then it pauses and vibrates its whiskers downward in the direction of the floor.

The professor picks up the rat and returns it to the cage. She asks the class to describe the animal's *behaviour*.

A student responds, "The rat seems to be looking for a way to escape."

The professor writes each response on the blackboard. Another student raises her hand. "The rat is making a visual search of the environment," she says. "Maybe it's looking for food."

The professor prompts other students for their descriptions.

"It's looking around," says one.

"Trying to escape," says another.

Your turn arrives. Trying to be scientific, you say, "We can't say what its motivation might be. All we know is that it's scanning its environment."

"How so?" the professor asks.

"Visually," you reply, confidently.

The professor writes the response and then turns to the class, shaking her head. "Each of you observed the rat," she said, "but none of you described its *behaviour*. Each of you made certain *inferences*, that the rat was 'looking for a way down' or 'scanning its environment' or 'looking for food,' and the like. These are not unreasonable inferences, but they are inferences, not descriptions. They also happen to be wrong. You see, the rat is blind. It's been blind since birth. It couldn't possibly be looking around, at least not in a visual sense."

Description, Explanation, Prediction, and Control: The Objectives of Science

description In science, the representation of observations without interpretation or inferences as to their nature or meaning. Contrast with *inference*, which is the process of drawing conclusions based on observations.

inference Conclusion that is drawn from data.

theory (1) Plausible or scientifically defensible explanation of events. (2) Formulation of the relationships underlying observed events. Theories are helpful to scientists because they provide a means of organizing observations and lead to predictions about future events.

Description is one of the primary objectives of science. To understand abnormal behaviour, we must first learn to describe it. Description allows us to recognize abnormal behaviour and provides the basis for explaining it.

Descriptions should be clear, unbiased, and based on careful observation. Our anecdote about the blind rat illustrates the point that our observations and our attempts to describe them can be influenced or biased by our expectations. Our expectations reflect our models of behaviour, and they may incline us to perceive events—such as the rat's movements and other people's behaviour—in certain ways. Describing the rat in the classroom as "scanning" and "looking" for something is an **inference** or conclusion we draw from our observations based on our model of how animals explore their environments. Description would involve a precise accounting of the animal's movements around the desk, measuring how far in each direction it moves, how long it pauses, how it bobs its head from side to side, and so on.

Inference is also important in science, however. Inference allows us to jump from the particular to the general—to suggest laws and principles of behaviour that can be woven into models and **theories** of behaviour. In Chapter 2, we consider the major theoretical perspectives or models of abnormal behaviour. Let us note here that without a way of organizing our descriptions of phenomena in terms of models and theories, we would be left with a buzzing confusion of unconnected observations. The crucial issue is to distinguish between description and inference—to recognize when we jump from a description of events to an inference based on an interpretation of events. For example, we do not *describe* a person's behaviour as "schizophrenic," but rather we *interpret* behaviour as schizophrenic on the basis of our model of schizophrenia. To do otherwise, we would affix ourselves to a given label or model and lose the intellectual flexibility needed to revise our inferences in the light of new evidence or ways of conceptualizing information.

Theories help scientists explain puzzling behaviour and predict future behaviour. Prediction entails the discovery of factors that anticipate the occurrence of events. Geology, for example, seeks clues in the forces affecting the earth that can forecast natural events such as earthquakes and volcanic eruptions. Scientists who study abnormal behaviour seek clues in overt behaviour, biological processes, family interactions, and so forth, to predict the development of abnormal behaviours as well as factors that might predict response to various treatments. It is not sufficient for theoretical models to help us explain or make sense of events or behaviours that have already occurred. Useful theories must allow us to predict the occurrence of particular behaviours.

The idea of controlling human behaviour—especially the behaviour of people with serious problems—is controversial. The history of societal response to abnormal behaviours, including abuses such as exorcism and cruel forms of physical restraint, render the idea particularly distressing. Within science, however, the word *control* need not imply that people are coerced into doing the bidding of others like puppets dangling on strings. Psychologists, for example, are committed to the dignity of the individual, and the concept of human dignity requires that people be free to make decisions and exercise choices. Within this context, *controlling behaviour* means using scientific knowledge to help people shape their own goals and more efficiently use their resources to accomplish them. Today, in Canada, even when helping professionals restrain people who are violently disturbed, their goal is to assist them to overcome their agitation and regain the ability to exercise meaningful choices in their lives[2]. Ethical standards prohibit the use of injurious techniques in research or practice.

Psychologists and other scientists use the *scientific method* to advance the description, explanation, prediction, and control of abnormal behaviour.

The Scientific Method

The scientific method involves systematic attempts to test our assumptions and theories about the world through gathering objective evidence. Various means are used in applying the scientific method, including observational and experimental methods. Here, let us focus on the basic steps involved in using the scientific method in experimentation:

1. *Formulating a research question.* Scientists derive research questions from their observations and theories of events and behaviour. For instance, based on their clinical observations and understandings of the underlying mechanisms in depression, they may formulate questions about whether certain experimental drugs or particular types of psychotherapy can help people overcome depression.

2. *Framing the research question in the form of a hypothesis.* A **hypothesis** is a precise prediction about behaviour examined through research. For example, scientists might hypothesize that people who are clinically depressed will show greater improvement on measures of depression if they are given an experimental drug than if they receive an inert placebo ("sugar pill").

   hypothesis Assumption that is tested through experimentation.

3. *Testing the hypothesis.* Scientists test hypotheses through carefully controlled observation and experimentation. They might test the hypothesis about the experimental drug by setting up an experiment in which one group of people with depression is given the experimental drug and another group is given the placebo. They would then administer tests to see if the people who received the active drug showed greater improvement over a period of time than those who received the placebo.

4. *Drawing conclusions about the hypothesis.* In the final step, scientists draw conclusions from their findings about the correctness of their hypotheses. Psychologists use statistical methods to determine the likelihood that differences between groups are **significant** as opposed to chance fluctuations. Psychologists are reasonably confident that group differences are significant—that is, not due to chance—when the probability that chance alone can explain the difference is less than 5%. When well-designed research findings fail to bear out hypotheses, scientists can modify the theories from which the hypotheses are derived. Research findings often lead to modifications in theory, new hypotheses, and, in turn, subsequent research.

   significant In statistics, a magnitude of difference that is taken as indicating meaningful differences between groups because of the low probability that it occurred by chance.

We will consider the major research methods used by psychologists and others in studying abnormal behaviour: the naturalistic-observation, correlational, experimental, epidemiological, kinship, and case-study methods. Before we do so, however, let us consider some of the principles that guide ethical conduct in research.

Ethics in Research

Ethical principles are designed to protect the rights of people, respect the dignity and integrity of the individual, impart responsible caring, protect human welfare, and preserve scientific integrity. Psychological practitioners, researchers, and scientists follow ethical standards that address the following major concerns: psychologists are prohibited from using methods that cause psychological or physical harm to subjects or clients; psychologists must inform participants and obtain a signed consent form stating they are aware of

---

[2]Here we are talking about violently confused and disordered behaviour, not criminal behaviour. Both criminals and disturbed people may be dangerous to others, but with criminals the intention of restraint is usually limited to protecting society.

risks of participation; psychologists must ensure confidentiality; and they must aim to maximize what is of benefit to subjects or clients (Canadian Psychological Association, 2000). Psychologists also must follow ethical guidelines that protect animal subjects in research.

Institutions such as universities and hospitals have review committees, often called *research ethics boards* (REBs), that review proposed research studies in light of ethical guidelines (National Council on Ethics in Human Research, 2002). Investigators must receive approval before they are permitted to begin their studies. Two of the major principles on which ethical research guidelines are based are (1) informed consent, and (2) confidentiality.

The principle of **informed consent** requires that people be free to choose whether they wish to participate in research studies. They must be given sufficient information in advance about the study's purposes and methods, and its risks and benefits, to allow them to make an informed decision about their participation. Subjects must also be free to withdraw from a study at any time without penalty. In some cases, researchers may withhold certain information until all the data are collected. For instance, subjects in placebo control studies of experimental drugs are told that they may receive an inert placebo rather than the active drug. After the study is concluded, participants who received the placebo would be given the option of receiving the active treatment. In studies in which information was withheld or deception was used, subjects must be **debriefed** afterward. That is, they must receive an explanation of the true methods and purposes of the study and why it was necessary to keep them in the dark.

Subjects also have a right to expect that their identities will not be revealed. Investigators are required to protect their **confidentiality** by keeping the records of their participation secure and by not disclosing their identities to others.

The Naturalistic-Observation Method

The **naturalistic-observation method** is used to observe behaviour in the field, where it happens. Anthropologists have lived in preliterate societies in order to study human diversity. Sociologists have followed the activities of adolescent gangs in inner cities. Psychologists have spent weeks observing the behaviour of homeless people in train stations and bus terminals. They have even observed the eating habits of slender and overweight people in fast-food restaurants, searching for clues to obesity.

Scientists take every precaution to ensure their naturalistic observations are **unobtrusive** so as to prevent any interference with the behaviour they observe. Otherwise, the presence of the observer may distort the observed behaviour. Over the years, naturalistic observers have sometimes found themselves in controversial situations. For example, they have allowed sick or injured apes to die when medicine could have saved them. Observers of substance abuse and other criminal behaviour have allowed illicit behaviour to go unreported to authorities. In such cases, the ethical trade-off is that unobtrusive observation can yield information of benefit to all.

Naturalistic observation provides a good deal of information on how subjects behave, but it does not necessarily reveal why they do so. Men who frequent bars and drink, for example, are more likely to get into fights than men who do not. But such observations do not show that alcohol *causes* aggression. As we see in the following pages, questions of cause and effect are best approached by means of controlled experiments.

Correlation

Correlation is a statistical measure of the relationships between two factors or **variables**. In the naturalistic-observation study that occurred in the fast-food restaurant, eating behaviours were related—or correlated—to patrons' weights. They were not directly manipulated. In other words, the investigators did not manipulate the weights or eating rates of their subjects, but merely measured the two variables in some fashion and examined whether they were statistically related to each other. When one variable (weight level) increases as the second variable (rate of eating) increases, there is a **positive correlation** between them. If one variable decreases as the other increases, there is a **negative correlation** between the variables.

---

informed consent Agreement by individuals to participate in research based upon a prior disclosure of information about the study's purposes, methods, risks, and benefits, sufficient to allow subjects to make informed decisions about their participation.

debriefed Providing research participants with a fuller accounting of a study's aims and purposes after their participation, including information about any deception that may have been used or other information that may have been withheld.

confidentiality The principle of safeguarding information so that it remains secret and is not disclosed to other parties.

naturalistic-observation method Method of scientific research in which the behaviour of subjects is carefully and unobtrusively observed and measured in their natural environments.

unobtrusive Not interfering.

correlation Relationship or association between two or more variables. A correlation between variables may suggest, but does not prove, that a causal relationship exists between them.

variables Conditions that are measured (dependent variables) or manipulated (independent variables) in scientific studies.

positive correlation Statistical relationship between two variables such that increases in one variable are associated with increases in the other.

negative correlation Statistical relationship between two variables such that increases in one variable are associated with decreases in the other.

Although correlational research reveals whether or not there is a statistical relationship between variables, it does not prove the variables are causally related. <u>Causal connections sometimes work in unexpected directions, and sometimes there is no causal connection between variables that are merely correlated.</u> There are correlations between depression and negative thoughts, and it may seem logical that depression is caused by such thoughts. However, it is also possible that feelings of depression give rise to negative thoughts. Perhaps the direction of causality works both ways, with negative thinking contributing to depression and depression in turn influencing negative thinking. Moreover, depression and negative thinking may both reflect a common causative factor, such as stress, and not be causally related to each other at all.

Although correlational research does not reveal cause and effect, it can be used to serve the scientific objective of prediction. When two variables are correlated, we can use one to predict the other. Knowledge of correlations among alcoholism, family history, and attitudes toward drinking helps us predict which adolescents are at great risk of developing problems with alcohol, although causal connections are complex and somewhat nebulous. But knowing which factors predict future problems may help us direct preventive efforts toward these high-risk groups to help prevent problems from developing.

Naturalistic observation. Anthropologists learn about other cultures by observing how members of these other societies live from day to day, in some cases actually living for a time in the societies they study. Here, a North American anthropologist is shown sitting among members of an African pygmy tribe.

The Longitudinal Study One type of correlational study is the **longitudinal study**, in which subjects are studied at periodic intervals over lengthy periods, perhaps for decades. By studying people over time, researchers can investigate the events associated with the onset of abnormal behaviour and, perhaps, learn to identify factors that predict the development of such behaviour. However, such research is time-consuming and costly. It requires a commitment that may literally outlive the original investigators. Therefore, long-term longitudinal studies are relatively uncommon. In Chapter 12, "Schizophrenia," we examine one of the best-known longitudinal studies, the Danish high-risk study that has tracked since 1962 the development of a group of children whose mothers had schizophrenia and so were at increased risk of developing the disorder (Mednick, 1970).

Prediction is based on the *correlation* between events or factors that are separated in time. As in other forms of correlational research, we must be careful not to infer *causation* from *correlation*. A **causal relationship** between two events involves a time-ordered relationship in which the second event is the direct result of the first. We need to meet two strict conditions to posit a causal relationship between two factors:

1. The effect must follow the cause in a time-ordered sequence of events.
2. Other plausible causes of the observed effects (rival hypotheses) must be eliminated.

Through the experimental method, scientists seek to demonstrate causal relationships by first manipulating the causal factor and then measuring its effects under controlled conditions that minimize the risk of possible rival hypotheses.

The Experimental Method

The term *experiment* can cause some confusion. Broadly speaking, an experiment is a trial or test of a hypothesis. From this vantage point, any method that actually seeks to test a hypothesis could be considered experimental—including naturalistic observation and correlational studies. But investigators usually limit the use of the term **experimental method**

longitudinal study Research study in which subjects are followed over time. Longitudinal studies have helped researchers identify factors in early life that may predict the later development of disorders such as schizophrenia.

causal relationship Relationship between two factors or events in which one is necessary and sufficient to bring about the other. Also called a *cause-and-effect relationship*.

experimental method Scientific method that aims to discover cause-and-effect relationships by means of manipulating the independent variable(s) and observing their effects on the dependent variable(s).

TABLE 1.2

Examples of Independent and Dependent Variables in Experimental Research

Independent Variables	Dependent Variables
Type of treatment: for example, different types of drug treatments or psychological treatments	*Behavioural variables:* for example, measures of adjustment, activity levels, eating behaviour, smoking behaviour
Treatment factors: for example, brief vs. long-term treatment, inpatient vs. outpatient treatment	*Physiological variables:* for example, measures of physiological responses such as heart rate, blood pressure, and brain wave activity
Experimental manipulations: for example, types of beverage consumed (alcoholic vs. nonalcoholic)	*Self-report variables:* for example, measures of anxiety, mood, or marital or life satisfaction

independent variable Factor in an experiment that is manipulated so its effects can be measured or observed.

dependent variable Measure of outcome in a scientific study that is assumed to be dependent on the effects of the independent variable.

to refer to studies in which researchers seek to uncover cause-and-effect relationships by manipulating possible causal factors directly.

The factors or variables hypothesized to play a causal role are manipulated or controlled by the investigator in experimental research. These are called the **independent variables**. The observed effects are labelled **dependent variables**, because changes in them are believed to depend on the independent or manipulated variable. Dependent variables are observed and measured, not manipulated, by the experimenter. Examples of independent and dependent variables of interest to investigators of abnormal behaviour are shown in the accompanying Table 1.2 above.

In an experiment, subjects are exposed to an *independent variable*, for example, the type of beverage (alcoholic vs. nonalcoholic) they consume in a laboratory setting. They are then observed or examined to determine whether the independent variable makes a difference in their behaviour, or, more precisely, whether the independent variable affects the dependent variable—in this case, whether they behave more aggressively if they consume alcohol.

experimental subject (1) In an experiment, a subject receiving a treatment or intervention, in contrast to a *control subject*. (2) More generally, one who participates in an experiment.

control subject Subject who does not receive the experimental treatment or manipulation but for whom all other conditions are held constant.

Experimental and Control Subjects Well-controlled experiments assign subjects to experimental and control groups at random. **Experimental subjects** are given the experimental treatment. **Control subjects** are not. Care is taken to hold other conditions constant for each group. By using random assignment and holding other conditions constant, experimenters can be reasonably confident that the experimental treatment, and not uncontrolled factors such as room temperature or differences between the types of subjects in the experimental and control groups, brought about the differences in outcome between the experimental and control groups.

When experimenters use random assignment to ensure that subject characteristics are randomly distributed across groups, it is reasonable to assume that differences between groups involve the treatments they receive, rather than differences in the types of subjects making up the groups. Still, it is possible that apparent treatment effects stem from subjects' expectancies about the treatments they receive rather than from the active components in the treatments themselves. For example, knowing you are being given an alcoholic beverage to drink might affect your behaviour, quite apart from the alcoholic content of the beverage itself.

blind In the context of research design, a state of being unaware of whether or not one has received a treatment.

Controlling for Subject Expectancies In order to control for subject expectancies, experimenters rely on procedures that render subjects **blind**, or uniformed, as to what treatments they are receiving. For example, the taste of an alcoholic beverage such as vodka may be masked by mixing it with tonic water in certain amounts to keep subjects blind as to whether the drinks they receive contain alcohol or tonic water only. In this way, subjects who truly receive alcohol should have no different expectations than those receiving the nonalcoholic control beverage. Similarly, drug-treatment studies are often designed to control for subjects' expectations by keeping subjects in the dark as to whether they are receiving the experimental drug or an *inert* placebo control.

The term **placebo** derives from the Latin meaning "I shall please," referring to the fact that belief in the effectiveness of a treatment (its pleasing qualities) may inspire hopeful expectations that help people mobilize themselves to overcome their problems, regardless of whether the substance they receive is chemically active or inert. In medical research on chemotherapy, a placebo—also referred to as a "sugar pill"—is an inert substance that physically resembles an active drug. By comparing the effects of the active drug with those of the placebo, the experimenter can determine whether or not the drug has specific effects beyond those accounted for by expectations.

In a *single-blind placebo-control study*, subjects are randomly assigned to treatment conditions in which they receive an active drug (experimental condition) or a placebo (placebo-control condition), but are kept blind, or uninformed, about which drug they are receiving. It is also helpful to keep the dispensing researchers blind as to which substances the subjects are receiving, lest the researchers' expectations come to affect the results. So in the case of a *double-blind placebo design*, neither the researcher nor the subject is told whether an active drug or a placebo is being administered. Of course, this approach assumes the subjects and the experimenters cannot "see through" the blind. In some cases, however, telltale side effects or obvious drug effects may break the blind (Basoglu et al., 1997). Still, the double-blind placebo control is among the strongest and most popular experimental designs, especially in drug-treatment research.

Placebo-control groups have also been used in psychotherapy research in order to control for subject expectancies. Assume you were to study the effects of therapy method A on mood. It would be inadequate to assign the experimental group to therapy method A randomly and the control group to a no-treatment waiting list. The experimental group might show improvement because of group participation, not because of therapy method A. Participation might raise expectations of success, and these expectations might be sufficient to engender improvement. Changes in control subjects placed on the "waiting list" would help to account for effects due to the passage of time, but they would not account for placebo effects, such as the benefits of therapy that result from instilling a sense of hope.

An *attention-placebo* control group design can be used to separate the effects of a particular form of psychotherapy from placebo effects. In an attention-placebo group, subjects are exposed to a believable or credible treatment that contains the nonspecific factors that therapies share—such as the attention and emotional support of a therapist—but not the specific ingredients of therapy represented in the active treatment. Attention-placebo treatments commonly substitute general discussions of participants' problems for the specific ingredients of therapy contained in the experimental treatment. Unfortunately, although attention-placebo subjects may be kept blind as to whether or not they are receiving the experimental treatment, the therapists themselves are generally aware of which treatment is being administered. Therefore, the attention-placebo method may not control for therapists' expectations.

Epidemiological Method

The **epidemiological method** studies the rates of occurrence of abnormal behaviour in various settings or population groups. One type of epidemiological study is the **survey method**, which relies on interviews or questionnaires. Surveys are used to ascertain the rates of occurrence of various disorders in the population as a whole and in various subgroups classified according to such factors as race, ethnicity, gender, or social class. Rates of occurrence of a given disorder are expressed in terms of **incidence** (recall Table 1.1 on page 2), or the number of new cases of a disorder occurring during a specific period of time, and **prevalence**, which refers to the overall number of cases of a disorder existing in a population during a given period of time. Prevalence rates, then, include both new and continuing cases.

Epidemiological studies may point to potential causal factors in illnesses and disorders, even though they lack the power of experiments. By finding that illnesses or disorders cluster in certain groups or locations, researchers may be able to identify certain distinguishing characteristics that place these groups or regions at higher risk. Yet, such epidemiological studies cannot control for selection factors—that is, they cannot rule out

placebo (pluh-SEE-bo) Inert medication or form of bogus treatment intended to control for the effects of expectancies. Sometimes referred to as a "sugar pill."

epidemiological method Method of research involved in tracking the rates of occurrence of particular disorders among different groups.

survey method Method of scientific research in which large samples of people are questioned by the use of a survey instrument.

incidence Number of new cases of a disorder occurring within a specific period of time.

prevalence Overall number of cases of a disorder existing in a population during a given period of time.

rival hypotheses that other unrecognized factors might play a causal role in putting a certain group at greater risk. Therefore, they must be considered suggestive of possible causal influences that must be tested further in experimental studies.

population Total group of people, other organisms, or events.

Samples and Populations In the best of possible worlds, we would conduct surveys in which every member of the **population** of interest would participate. In that way, we could be sure the survey results accurately represent the population we wish to study. In reality, unless the population of interest is rather narrowly defined (say, for example, designating the population of interest as the students living on your dormitory floor), chances are it is extremely difficult, if not impossible, to survey every member of a given population. Even census takers can't count every head in the general population. Consequently, most surveys are based on a **sample** or subset of a population. Researchers take steps when constructing a sample to ensure that it *represents* the target population. A researcher who sets out to study smoking rates in a local community by interviewing people drinking coffee in late-night cafés will probably overestimate its true prevalence.

sample Part of a population.

One method of obtaining a representative sample is **random sampling**. A random sample is drawn in such a way that each member of the population of interest has an equal probability of selection. Epidemiologists sometimes construct random samples by surveying at random a given number of households within a target community. By repeating this process in a random sample of Canadian communities, the overall sample can approximate the general Canadian population, based on even a tiny percentage of the overall population. In fact, a representative nationwide sample of about 1500 eligible voters may be more accurate in predicting an election result than a haphazard sample of millions.

random sample Sample drawn in such a way that every member of a population has an equal probability of being selected.

Random sampling is often confused with random assignment. Random sampling refers to the process of randomly choosing individuals within a target population to participate in a survey or research study. By contrast, random assignment refers to a process by which members of a research sample are assigned at random to different experimental conditions or treatments.

Kinship Studies

Kinship studies attempt to disentangle the roles of heredity and environment in determining behaviour. Heredity plays a critical role in determining a wide range of traits. The structures we inherit make our behaviour possible (humans can walk and run) and at the same time place limits on us (humans cannot fly without artificial equipment). Heredity plays a role in determining not only our physical characteristics (hair colour, eye colour, height, and the like) but also many of our psychological characteristics. The science of heredity is called **genetics**. Human behavioural genetics is the study of the interactive effect of genetic and environmental factors on behaviour, especially personality patterns and psychological disorders.

genetics Science of heredity.

genes Units found on chromosomes that carry heredity.

Genes are the basic building blocks of heredity. They are the structures that regulate the development of traits. Some traits, such as blood type, are transmitted by a single pair of genes, one of which is derived from each parent. Other traits, referred to as **polygenic**, are determined by complex combinations of genes. **Chromosomes**, the rod-shaped structures that house our genes, are found in the nuclei of the body's cells. Each consists of more than a thousand genes. A normal human cell contains 46 chromosomes, organized into 23 pairs. Chromosomes consist of large complex molecules of deoxyribonucleic acid (DNA). Genes occupy various segments along the length of chromosomes. There are about 20 000–25 000 genes in every cell in our bodies.

polygenic Traits or characteristics that are determined by more than one gene.

chromosomes Structures found in the nuclei of cells that carry the units of heredity, or *genes*.

The set of traits specified by our genetic code is referred to as our **genotype**. Our appearance and behaviour are not determined by our genotype alone. We are also influenced by environmental factors such as nutrition, exercise, accident and illness, learning, and culture. The constellation of our actual or expressed traits is called our **phenotype**. Our phenotype represents the interaction of genetic and environmental influences. People who possess genotypes for particular psychological disorders are said to have a *genetic predisposition* that makes them more likely to develop the disorder in response to stress or other factors, such as physical or psychological trauma.

genotype (1) Genetic constitution of an individual or a group. (2) Sum total of traits that one inherits from one's parents.

phenotype Representation of the total array of traits of an organism, as influenced by the interaction of nature (genetic factors) and nurture (environmental factors).

The more closely people are related, the more genes they have in common. Children receive half their genes from each parent. There is thus a 50% overlap in genetic heritage between each parent and his or her offspring. Siblings (brothers and sisters) similarly share half their genetic heritage. Aunts and uncles related by blood to their nephews and nieces have a 25% overlap; first cousins, a 12.5% overlap (see Figure 1.1).

In order to determine whether a pattern of abnormal behaviour has a genetic basis, researchers locate one case of a person with the disorder and then study how the disorder is distributed among that person's family members. The case first diagnosed is referred to as the index case or **proband**. If the distribution of the disorder among family members of the proband approximates their degree of kinship, there may be a genetic involvement in the disorder. However, the closer their kinship, the more likely people also are to share environmental backgrounds. For this reason, twin and adoptee studies are of particular value.

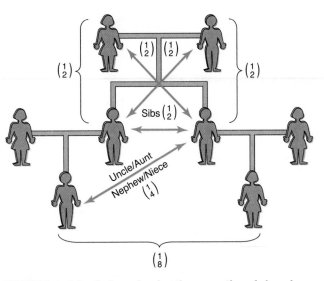

FIGURE 1.1 A family tree showing the proportion of shared inheritance among relatives.
The more closely people are related, the more genes they have in common. Kinship studies, including twin studies and adoptee studies, afford researchers insight into the heritability of various patterns of abnormal behaviour.

Twin Studies Sometimes a fertilized egg cell (or zygote) divides into two cells that separate, so each develops into a separate person. In such cases, there is a 100% overlap in genetic makeup, and the offspring are known as identical or **monozygotic (MZ) twins**. Sometimes a woman releases two egg cells, or ova, in the same month, and they are both fertilized. In such cases, the *zygotes* (fertilized egg cells) develop into fraternal or **dizygotic (DZ) twins**. DZ twins overlap 50% in their genetic heritage, just as other siblings do.

Identical or MZ twins are important in the study of the relative influences of heredity and environment because differences between MZ twins are the result of environmental rather than genetic influences. MZ twins look more alike and are closer in height than DZ twins. In twin studies, researchers identify probands for a given disorder who are members of MZ or DZ twin pairs and then study the other twins in the pairs. A role for genetic factors is suggested when MZ twins are more likely than DZ twins to share a disorder. Differences in the rates of **concordance** (agreement for the given trait or disorder) for MZ versus DZ twins are found for some forms of abnormal behaviour, such as schizophrenia and bipolar disorder. Even among MZ twins, though, environmental influences cannot be ruled out. Parents and teachers, for example, often encourage MZ twins to behave in similar ways. Put it another way: if one twin does X, everyone expects the other to do X also. Expectations have a way of influencing behaviour and making for self-fulfilling prophecies. We should also note that twins might not be typical of the general population, so we need to be cautious when generalizing the results of twin studies to the larger population. Twins tend to have had shorter gestational periods, lower birth weights, and a greater frequency of congenital malformations than nontwins (Kendler & Prescott, 2006). Perhaps differences in prenatal experiences influence their later development in ways that set them apart from nontwins.

proband Initial diagnosed case of a given disorder.

monozygotic (MZ) twins Twins who develop from the same fertilized egg and therefore share identical genes. Also called identical twins. Abbreviated *MZ twins*. Contrast with fraternal or *dizygotic (DZ) twins*.

dizygotic (DZ) twins Twins who develop from separate fertilized eggs. Also called fraternal twins. Abbreviated *DZ twins*. Often contrasted with *monozygotic (MZ) twins* in studies of heritability of particular traits or disorders.

concordance Agreement.

Adoptee Studies **Adoptee studies** can provide powerful arguments for or against genetic factors in the appearance of psychological traits and disorders. Assume that children are reared by adoptive parents from a very early age—perhaps from birth. The children share environmental backgrounds with their adoptive parents but not their genetic heritages. Then assume we compare the traits and behaviour patterns of these children to those of their biological parents and their adoptive parents. If the children show a greater similarity to their biological parents than their adoptive parents on certain traits or disorders, we have strong evidence indeed for genetic factors in these traits and disorders.

Although adoptee studies may represent the strongest source of evidence for genetic factors in explaining abnormal behaviour patterns, we should recognize that adoptees, like twins, may not be typical of the general population. In later chapters we explore how

adoptee studies Studies of adopted-away children that examine whether their behaviour patterns and psychological functioning more closely resemble those of their biological parents or adoptive parents.

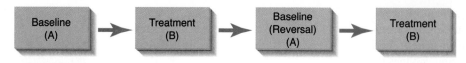

FIGURE 1.2 **Diagram of an A-B-A-B reversal design.**

adoptee and other kinship studies add to our understanding of genetic and environmental influences in many psychological disorders.

The Case-Study Method

case study Carefully drawn biography that is typically constructed on the basis of clinical interviews, observations, psychological tests, and, in some cases, historical records.

single-case experimental designs Type of case study in which the subject (case) is used as his or her own control by varying the conditions to which the subject is exposed (by use of a *reversal* phase) or by means of a *multiple-baseline* design.

reversal design An A-B-A-B type of experimental single-subject design in which treatment is instituted following a baseline phase and then withdrawn (reversal phase) so as to examine effects on behaviour.

baseline Period of time preceding the implementation of a treatment. Used to gather data regarding the rate of occurrence of the target behaviour before treatment is introduced.

Case studies have been important influences in the development of theories and treatment of abnormal behaviour. Freud developed his theoretical model primarily on the basis of case studies, such as that of Anna O. Therapists representing other theoretical viewpoints have also reported cases studies.

Types of Case Studies Case studies involve intensive studies of individuals. Some case studies are based on historical material, involving subjects who have been dead for hundreds of years. Freud, for example, conducted a case study of the Renaissance artist and inventor Leonardo da Vinci. More commonly, case studies reflect an in-depth analysis of an individual's course of treatment. They typically include detailed histories of the subject's background and response to treatment. The therapist attempts to glean information from a particular client's experience in therapy that may be of help to other therapists treating similar clients.

Despite the richness of clinical material that case studies can provide, they are much less rigorous as research designs than experiments. There are bound to be distortions or gaps in memory when people discuss historical events, especially those of their childhoods. Some people may intentionally colour events to make a favourable impression on the interviewer; others aim to shock the interviewer with exaggerated or fabricated recollections. Interviewers themselves may unintentionally guide subjects into slanting the histories they report in ways that are compatible with their own theoretical perspectives.

Single-Case Experimental Designs The lack of control available in the traditional case-study method led researchers to develop more sophisticated methods, called **single-case experimental designs**, in which subjects are used as their own controls. One of the most common forms of the single-case experimental design is the A-B-A-B or **reversal design** (see Figure 1.2). The reversal design consists of the repeated measurement of clients' behaviour across four successive phases:

1. A baseline phase (A). The baseline phase, which occurs prior to the inception of treatment, is characterized by repeated measurement of the target problem behaviours at periodic intervals. This measurement allows the experimenter to establish a **baseline** rate for the behaviour before treatment begins.

2. A treatment phase (B). Now the target behaviours are measured as the client undergoes treatment.

3. A second baseline phase (A, again). Treatment is now temporarily withdrawn or suspended. This is the reversal in the reversal design, and it is expected that the positive effects of treatment should now be reversed because the treatment has been withdrawn.

4. A second treatment phase (B, again). Treatment is reinstated and the target behaviours are reassessed.

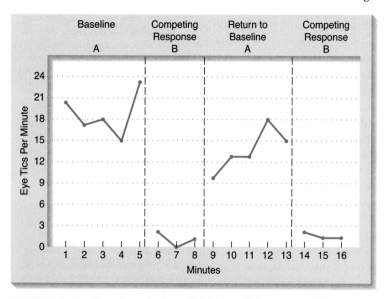

FIGURE 1.3 **Treatment results from the Azrin and Peterson study.**
Notice how the target response, eye tics per minute, decreased when the competing response was introduced in the first "B" phase. It then increased to near baseline levels when the competing response was withdrawn during the second "A" phase. It decreased again when the competing response was reinstated in the second "B" phase.

Source: Azrin, N. H., & Peterson, A. L. (1989). Reduction of an eye tic controlled by blinking. *Behavior Therapy, 20,* 467–473. Copyright 1989 by the Association for Advancement of Behavior Therapy. Reprinted by permission of the publisher.

Clients' target behaviours or response patterns are compared from one phase to the next in order to determine the effects of treatment. The experimenter looks for evidence of a correspondence between the subject's behaviour and the particular phase of the design to determine whether or not the independent variable (that is, the treatment) has produced the intended effects. If the behaviour improves whenever treatment is introduced (during the first and second treatment phases) but returns (or is reversed) to baseline levels during the reversal phase, the experimenter can be reasonably confident the treatment had the intended effect.

The method is illustrated by a case in which Azrin and Peterson (1989) used a controlled blinking treatment to eliminate a severe eye tic—a form of squinting in which the subject's eyes shut tightly for a fraction of a second—in a nine-year-old girl. The tic occurred about 20 times a minute when the girl was at home. In the clinic, the rate of eye tics or squinting was measured for five minutes during a baseline period (A). Then the girl was prompted to blink her eyes softly every five seconds (B). The experimenters reasoned that voluntary "soft" blinking would activate motor (muscle) responses incompatible with those producing the tic, thereby suppressing it. As seen in Figure 1.3, the tic was virtually eliminated in just a few minutes of practising the incompatible or competing response, ("soft" blinking) but returned to near baseline levels during the reversal phase (A) when the competing response was withdrawn. The positive effects were quickly reinstated during the second treatment period (B). The child was also taught to practise the blinking response at home during scheduled three-minute practice periods and whenever the tic occurred or she felt an urge to squint. The tic was completely eliminated during the first six weeks of the treatment program and remained absent at a follow-up evaluation two years later.

Although reversal designs offer better controls than traditional treatment case studies, it is not always possible or ethical to reverse certain behaviours or treatment effects. Participants in a stop-smoking program who reduce or quit smoking during treatment may not revert to their baseline smoking rates when treatment is temporarily withdrawn during a reversal phase.

The *multiple-baseline design* is a type of single-case experimental design that does not require a reversal phase. In a multiple-baseline design *across behaviours*, treatment is applied, in turn, to two or more behaviours following a baseline period. A treatment effect is inferred if changes in each of these behaviours corresponded to the time at which each was subjected to treatment. Because no reversal phase is required, many of the ethical and practical problems associated with reversal designs are avoided.

A multiple-baseline design was used to evaluate the effects of a social skills training program in the treatment of a shy, unassertive seven-year-old girl named Jane (Bornstein, Bellack, & Hersen, 1977). The program taught Jane to maintain eye contact, speak more loudly, and make requests of other people through **modelling** (therapist demonstration of the target behaviour), **rehearsal** (practice), and therapist **feedback** regarding the effectiveness of practice. However, the behaviours were taught sequentially, not simultaneously. Measurement of each behaviour and an overall rating of assertiveness were obtained during a baseline period from observations of Jane's role playing of social situations with other children, such as playing social games at school and conversing in class. As shown in Figure 1.4, Jane's performance of each behaviour improved following treatment. The rating of overall assertiveness showed more gradual improvement as the number of behaviours included in the program increased. Treatment gains were generally maintained at a follow-up evaluation.

To show a clear-cut treatment effect, changes in target behaviours should occur only when they are subjected to treatment. In some cases, however, changes in the treated behaviours may lead to

modelling In behaviour therapy, a technique for helping a client acquire new behaviour by means of having the therapist or members of a therapy group demonstrate a target behaviour that is then imitated by a client.

rehearsal In behaviour therapy, a practice opportunity in which a person enacts a desired response and receives feedback from others.

feedback Information about one's behaviour.

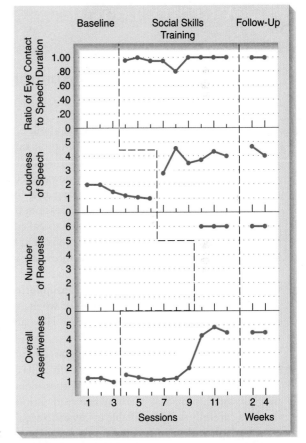

FIGURE 1.4 Treatment results from the study by Bornstein, Bellack, and Hersen.
The blue dotted line shows the point at which social skills training was applied to each of the targeted behaviours. Here we see that the targeted behaviours (eye contact, loudness of speech, and number of requests) improved only when they were subject to the treatment approach (social skills training). We thus have evidence that the treatment—and not another, unidentified factor—accounted for the results. The section on the bottom shows ratings of Jane's overall level of assertiveness during the baseline assessment period, the social skills training program, and the follow-up period.

changes in the yet untreated behaviours, apparently because of generalization of the effect. Fortunately, though, generalization effects have tended to be the exception, rather than the rule, in experimental research (Kazdin, 1992).

No matter how tightly controlled the design or how impressive the results, single-case designs suffer from weak external validity because it does not show whether a treatment effective for one person is effective for others. Replication with other individuals can help strengthen external validity. If these results prove encouraging, they may lead to controlled experiments to provide even more convincing evidence of treatment effectiveness.

Scientists may use different methods to study phenomena of interest to them, but they share in common a skeptical, hard-nosed way of thinking called critical thinking. **Critical thinking** involves a willingness to challenge the conventional wisdom and common knowledge that many of us take for granted. It also means finding *reasons* to support beliefs, rather than relying on feelings or gut impressions. When people think critically, they maintain open minds. They suspend their beliefs until they have obtained and evaluated evidence that either supports or refutes them. In "A Closer Look: Thinking Critically About Abnormal Psychology," we examine the features of critical thinking and how they can be applied in our study of abnormal psychology.

critical thinking A style of thinking characterized by the adoption of a questioning attitude and careful weighing of available evidence to determine if claims made by others stand up to scrutiny.

A CLOSER LOOK

Thinking Critically About Abnormal Psychology

We are exposed to a flood of information about our mental health that comes streaming down to us through a variety of media—television, radio, internet, and print media including books, magazines, and newspapers. We may hear a news report touting a new drug as a "breakthrough" in the treatment of anxiety, depression, or obesity, only to learn some time later that the so-called breakthrough doesn't live up to expectations or carries serious side effects. Some reports in the media are accurate and reliable; others are misleading, biased, or contain half-truths, exaggerated claims, or unsupported conclusions. The situation is compounded when even reputed experts disagree with one another. How are we to know what to believe?

To sort through the welter of sometimes confusing information, we need to arm ourselves with skills of critical thinking, which involves adopting a questioning attitude toward information you hear and read. Critical thinkers carefully weigh available evidence to see if claims people make can stand up to scrutiny. Becoming a critical thinker means never taking claims at face value. It means looking carefully at both sides of an argument. Sad to say, most of us take certain "truths" for granted. Critical thinkers, however, never say, "This is true because so-and-so says it is true." They seek to evaluate assertions and claims for themselves.

We encourage you to apply critical thinking skills to questions posed in the "Think About It" sections contained within the "Study Break" boxes in each chapter. We will now review some general principles of critical thinking.

Features of Critical Thinking

Critical thinkers adopt a skeptical attitude toward information they receive. They carefully examine the definitions of terms, evaluate the logical bases of arguments, and evaluate claims in light of available evidence. Here are some key features of critical thinking:

1. *Maintain a skeptical attitude.* Don't take anything at face value, not even claims made by respected scientists or textbook authors. Consider evidence yourself and seek additional information to help you evaluate claims made by others.
2. *Consider the definitions of terms.* Statements may be true or false depending on how the terms that are used are defined. Consider the statement "Stress is bad for you." If we define stress in terms of hassles and work or family pressures that stretch our ability to cope to the max, then there is perhaps substance to the statement. However, if we define stress (see Chapter 4, "Stress, Psychological Factors, and Health,") more broadly to include any factors that impose a demand on us to adjust, including events such as a new marriage or the birth of a child, then perhaps certain types of stress can be positive, even if they are stressful. Perhaps, as we'll see, we all need some amount of stress to be active and alert.
3. *Weigh the assumptions or premises on which arguments are based.* Consider a case in which we are comparing differences in the rates of psychological disorders across racial or ethnic groups in our society. Assuming we find differences, should we conclude that ethnicity or racial identity accounts for these differences? This conclusion might be valid if

(continued)

we can assume all other factors that distinguish one racial or ethnic group from another are held constant. However, ethnic or racial minorities in Canada and the United States are disproportionately represented among the poor, and the poor are more apt to develop more severe psychological disorders. Differences among racial or ethnic groups may thus be a function of poverty, not race or ethnicity per se. These differences may also be due to negative stereotyping of racial minorities by clinicians in making diagnostic judgments, rather than to differences in underlying rates of the disorder.

4. *Bear in mind that correlation is not causation.* Critical thinkers recognize that correlation is not causation. Consider the relationship between depression and stress. Evidence shows a positive correlation between these variables, which means depressed people tend to have higher levels of stress in their lives (Hammen, 2005; Pianta & Egeland, 1994). But does stress cause depression? Perhaps it does. Or perhaps depression leads to greater stress. After all, depressive symptoms may be stressful in themselves and may lead to additional stress as the person finds it increasingly difficult to meet life responsibilities, such as keeping up with work at school or on the job. It is also possible that the two variables are not causally linked at all but are linked through a third variable, perhaps an underlying genetic factor. It is conceivable that people inherit clusters of genes that make them more prone to encounter both depression and stress.

5. *Consider the kinds of evidence on which conclusions are based.* Some conclusions, even seemingly "scientific" conclusions, are based on anecdotes and personal endorsements. They are not founded on sound research. There is much controversy today about so-called recovered memories that may suddenly arise in adulthood, usually during the course of psychotherapy or hypnosis, and usually involving incidents of sexual abuse committed during childhood by the person's parents or family members. Are such memories accurate? Or might they be tales spun of imaginary thread? (See Chapter 6, "Dissociative and Somatoform Disorders.")

6. *Do not oversimplify.* Consider the statement "Alcoholism is inherited." In Chapter 9, "Substance Abuse and Dependence," we review evidence suggesting that genetic factors may create a predisposition to alcoholism, at least in males. But the origins of alcoholism, as well as of schizophrenia, depression, and physical health problems such as cancer and heart disease, are more complex, reflecting a complicated interplay of biological and environmental factors. In only a few cases are diseases the direct result of a single defective gene or genes. People may even inherit a predisposition to develop a particular psychological or physical disorder but avoid developing it if they are raised in a supportive family environment and learn to manage stress esffectively.

7. *Do not overgeneralize.* In Chapter 6, we consider evidence showing that a history of severe abuse in childhood figures prominently in the great majority of cases of people who later develop multiple personalities. Does this mean that all (or even most) abused children go on to develop multiple personalities? Actually, very few do.

Thinking Critically About Online Information

With today's online services, a world of information is literally at your fingertips. If you have access to the internet, you can obtain information relating to the following:

- Listings and abstracts (brief descriptions) of scientific studies published in leading psychology journals. Much of this information is provided free of charge.

- Do-it-yourself psychology quizzes and questionnaires.

- Access to online encyclopedias containing hundreds if not thousands of entries relating to psychological issues.

- Access to homepages of leading psychology organizations, like the Canadian Psychological Association (CPA), the Canadian Mental Health Association (CMHA), and the Canadian Alliance on Mental Illness and Mental Health (CAMIMH), that provide information about professional psychology and topics in psychology of general interest to the lay public.

- Forums and chat lines that bring together people who share similar concerns, such as people who have suffered loss of loved ones and people with family members who have psychological disorders.

- Information on topics relating to psychology provided by federal health agencies, including Health Canada's Mental Health Site and the Canadian Health Network (CHN).

The internet holds a vast repository of health-related information. Anyone can post information online, so the casual browser may not know how to distinguish accurate, scientifically based information from misinformation. The beauty—and the risk—of the internet is that it

(continued)

is freely available to anyone to post just about anything, from credible scientific information to advertising hype to complete malarkey. Don't believe everything you read online: Think critically!

1. *Check out the credentials of the source.* Who is it that is posting the material? Is it a well-respected medical or scientific institution or an individual or group of individuals with no scientific credentials or perhaps even with a grudge against the scientific establishment? The most reliable sources are scientific journals that are subject to peer review, a process by which other scientists carefully scrutinize each potential contributor's work before publication. In addition to scientific journals, the more reliable sources of health and medical information are those that are frequently updated, like websites maintained by government agencies such as Health Canada and its many divisions, as well as those sponsored by leading psychology organizations, including the Canadian Psychological Association and the Canadian Psychiatric Association.

2. *Look for citations.* Scientists back up what they say with citations to original scientific sources. The references listed at the end of this book, for example, represent the sources your authors used in preparing these chapters. If online authors cite findings from scientific literature, you should expect them to supply some of the references they use, such as noting the journals or other periodicals in which the studies were published (including the year, volume, and page numbers). Having this information allows the reader to check the original sources to see if the statements made are accurate. In some cases, however, scientific organizations like the Canadian Mental Health Association (CMHA) and scholarly organizations like the CPA prepare information for the general public that is no less reliable, although it may not be annotated with source notes or references.

3. *Beware of any product claims.* Many commercial organizations use the internet to tout or sell services and products. Don't assume that product claims are scientifically valid. Think of them as electronic advertising, basically an internet version of a television commercial. Be skeptical (and keep a tight grip on your wallet). Don't be misled by the offer of a money-back guarantee. These are not guarantees that the product will work as advertised. Rather, they guarantee you'll get your money back if they don't succeed (although often there are strings attached).

STUDY BREAK

Research Methods in Abnormal Psychology

Review It

- **What are the basic objectives of the scientific method and the steps involved in applying it?** The scientific approach focuses on four general objectives: description, explanation, prediction, and control. There are four steps to the scientific method: formulating a research question, framing the research question in the form of a hypothesis, testing the hypothesis, and drawing conclusions about the correctness of the hypotheses.

- **How are ethical standards applied in conducting research?** Psychologists follow the ethical principles of the profession that governs research with human and nonhuman subjects. Two of the key ethical provisions in research with humans are informed consent and confidentiality. Psychologists conducting research in institutional settings are required to obtain approval from institutional review boards to ensure that their methods meet ethical standards.

- **What are the methods used by psychologists to study abnormal behaviour?** The naturalistic-observation method allows scientists to measure behaviour under naturally occurring conditions. Correlational research explores the relationship between variables, which may help predict future behaviour and suggest possible underlying causes. But correlational research does not directly test cause-and-effect relationships. Longitudinal research is a type of correlational design that involves the study of selected subjects at periodic intervals over long periods of times, sometimes spanning decades. Research samples need to be representative of a target population.

    In the experimental method, the investigator directly controls or manipulates the independent variable under controlled conditions in order to demonstrate cause-and-effect relationships. Experiments use random assignment as the basis for determining which subjects (called experimental subjects) receive an experimental treatment and which others (called control subjects) do not. Researchers use various methods to attempt to control for subjects' and researchers' expectations, including single-blind, placebo-control, double-blind placebo-control, and attention-placebo control group designs.

The epidemiological method examines the rates of occurrence of abnormal behaviour in various population groups or settings. Evidence of how disorders cluster in certain groups or geographic areas may reveal underlying causes. Kinship studies attempt to disentangle the contributions of environment and heredity.

Case-study methods can provide a richness of clinical material, but they are limited by the difficulties of obtaining accurate and unbiased client histories, by possible therapist biases, and by a lack of control groups. Single-case experimental designs are intended to help researchers overcome some of the limitations of the case-study method.

Define It

description	incidence
inference	prevalence
theory	population
hypothesis	sample
significant	random sample
informed consent	genetics
debriefed	genes
confidentiality	polygenic
naturalistic-observation	chromosomes
method	genotype
unobtrusive	phenotype
correlation	proband
variables	twins monozygotic
positive correlation	(MZ) twins
negative correlation	dizygotic (DZ) twins
longitudinal studies	concordance
causal relationship	adoptee studies
experimental method	case study
independent variable	single-case
dependent variable	experimental
experimental subject	designs
control subject	reversal design
blind	baseline
placebo	modelling
epidemiological method	rehearsal
survey	feedback
	critical thinking
	method

Recall It*

1. Pete observes a rat in a laboratory cage box and says, "It must be looking for food!" His inference primarily serves which objective of science?

   a. description
   b. explanation
   c. obfuscation
   d. control

2. Pamela is interested in learning more about the problem of obesity. She designs a correlational study that compares weight level and risk of heart disease. She finds that as weight increases so does the risk of heart disease. Pamela's study has found a _____ correlation.

   a. random
   b. complementary
   c. positive
   d. negative

3. We call the suspected causal variables that investigators manipulate in experimental studies _____.

   a. dependent variables
   b. codependent variables
   c. independent variables
   d. reciprocal variables

4. Experimenters use attention-placebo groups in order to control for _____.

   a. subjects' but not experimenters' expectations
   b. neither subjects' nor experimenters' expectations
   c. experimenters' but not subjects' expectations
   d. both subjects' and experimenters' expectations

5. Which is not an example of an experimental single-subject design?

   a. reversal design
   b. multiple-baseline design
   c. A-B-A-B design
   d. case studies

* Recall It answers can be found on the Companion Website for this text.

Think About It

- Why should we not assume that because two variables are correlated they are causally linked?

- Why should experimenters assign subjects to experimental and control groups at random?

- How do investigators attempt to separate out the effects of heredity and environment?

- What are the limitations of the case study in drawing cause-and-effect relationships?

WEBLINKS

Canadian Psychological Association (CPA)
www.cpa.ca
This is the homepage for Canada's national psychological association. It is the central source for information about the profession of psychology in Canada.

Canadian Psychiatric Association (CPA)
www.cpa-apc.org
This is the homepage for Canada's national professional association for psychiatrists. It contains psychiatric e-journals and information on a variety of professional matters.

Canadian Mental Health Association (CMHA)
www.cmha.ca
The CMHA is a voluntary organization that is dedicated to promotion of mental health for all Canadians. Its website contains a diverse selection of mental health resources.

Mental Health Page at Health Canada
www.hc-sc.gc.ca/hl-vs/mental/index_e.html
This website provides convenient access to a range of online materials related to the promotion of mental health, mental health programs and services in Canada, and the mental health issues, problems, and disorders encountered by Canadians.

Centre for Addiction and Mental Health (CAMH)
www.camh.net
CAMH is Canada's largest teaching and research centre for mental health and addiction problems. The site contains resources on a wide range of mental health and addiction concerns.

What Is Abnormal Psychology?

How Do We Define Abnormal Behaviour?

Criteria for Determining Abnormality
Psychologists generally apply some combination of the following criteria in making a determination that behaviour is abnormal:

Unusualness
- Unusual or statistically infrequent behaviour

Social Deviance
- Behaviour that is social unacceptable or in violation of social norms

Faulty perceptions or interpretations of reality
- Misperceptions or misinterpretations of reality

Significant personal distress
- States of severe, prolonged and inappropriate emotional distress

Maladaptive or self-defeating behaviours
- Leading to unhappiness, or limiting one's ability to function in expected roles or adapt to environments

Dangerousness
- Dangerous to oneself or to other people

Cultural Bases of Normal Behaviour
Behaviours deemed normal in one culture may be considered abnormal in another.

Idiomatic concepts
- Concepts of health and illness may have different meanings in different cultures

Idiosyncratic customs
- Abnormal behaviour patterns may take different forms in different cultures

Localized belief systems
- Societal views or models explaining abnormal behaviour vary across cultures

Historical Perspectives on Abnormal Behaviour

Views About Abnormal Behaviour and Treatment Change Over Time
Prevailing worldviews shape concepts of abnormal behaviour and treatment.

The Demonological Model
- Ancient societies attributed abnormal behaviour to divine or supernatural forces.

Origins of Naturalistic Explanations
- Hippocrates (460-377 BC) believed an imbalance of vital bodily fluids caused abnormal behaviour.

Medieval Times (AD 476-1450)
- Belief in demonic possession held sway, and exorcists were used to rid people who behaved abnormally of the evil spirits that were believed to possess them.

Witchcraft (1400s–1600s)
- During the Renaissance, ideas about demonic possession coexisted with naturalistic explanations of abnormal behaviour.

Asylums in Europe and the New World
- As a refuge to both beggars and the disturbed, asylums in Europe were generally dreadful or, in some cases, circus-like. In North America, treatment-based asylums first appeared in Quebec (1639).

The Reform Movement and Moral Therapy (1700s–1800s)
- Proponents of moral therapy believed that mental patients could be restored to functioning if they were treated with dignity and understanding.

Transition in the Modern Era
Institutionalization dominated from the late 1800s until the 1950s as new treatments and community supports became available.

Decline of Moral Therapy
- The erroneous belief that the "insane" could not be successfully treated lead to deteriorating conditions in mental hospitals with little more than custodial care until the 1950s.

Deinstitutionalization
- The policy of reducing the need for long-term hospitalization of mental patients by shifting care to community-based settings.

Community Mental Health
- A work still in progress today in Canada, mental patients rely on dramatically fewer hospital beds and a fragmented system of community services and supports.

Scientific Models of Abnormal Behaviour
Core explanations of abnormal behaviour are based on the medical model, psychological models, and sociocultural models.

Medical Model
- Abnormal behaviour is based on underlying biological defects or abnormalities. Disorders can be classified, like physical illnesses, according to their distinctive causes and symptoms.

Psychological Models
- The first psychological explanation of abnormal behaviour originated with Freud. His psychodynamic model holds that the causes of abnormal behaviours lie in the interplay of forces within the unconscious mind. A diversity of psychological models soon followed.

Sociocultural Models
- Psychological problems may be rooted in the failures of society, such as poverty, social decay, racial and gender discrimination, and lack of economic opportunity. The stigma of "mental Illness" can also strip people of their dignity and give rise to discrimination.

Research Methods in Abnormal Psychology

The Scientific Method and Research Ethics

- The assumptions and theories of abnormal psychology undergo systematic and principled testing.

Abnormal Psychology as a Scientific Discipline
The study of abnormal behaviour is grounded in the four objectives of the scientific method.

Description (what)
- Clear, unbiased details of observations without interpretation or inferences as to their nature or meaning.

Explanation (why)
- Inferences based on an interpretation of events in accordance with models and theories of behaviour.

Prediction (when)
- Theories provide a means of organizing observations and lead to predictions about future behaviour.

Control (how)
- The use of scientific knowledge to help people shape their own goals and more efficiently use their resources to accomplish them.

Scientific Method
Four steps of the scientific method are

1) formulate a research question,
2) frame the research question in the form of a hypothesis,
3) test the hypothesis, and
4) draw conclusions about the correctness of the hypothesis.

Ethics

- Psychologists rigorously follow the ethical principles of the profession that govern research with human and nonhuman subjects.

Research Methods
The study of abnormal psychology abides rigorous scientific methods.

Naturalistic Observation
- Research in which the behaviour of subjects is carefully and unobtrusively observed and measured in their natural environments.

Correlational Study
- Research to determine the relationship or association between two or more variables. A correlation between variables may suggest, but does not prove, that a causal relationship exists between them.

Experimental Method
- A way to discover cause-and-effect relationships by means of manipulating the independent variable(s) and observing their effects on the dependent variable(s).

Epidemiological Method
- A way to examine the rates of occurrence of abnormal behaviour in various population groups or settings.

Kinship Studies
- Given that the more closely people are related, the more genes they have in common, twin studies and adoptee studies provide researchers insight into the heritability of various patterns of abnormal behaviour.

Case-study Method
- A way to construct a biography that is typically on the basis of clinical interviews, observations, psychological tests, and, in some cases, historical records.

CHAPTER 2

Theoretical Perspectives and Methods of Treatment

Did You Know That...

See the underlined text on the pages indicated below for more information on these interesting and often misunderstood facts.

- Freud likened the mind to a giant iceberg, with only the tip rising into conscious awareness? (p. 51)

- People can make themselves miserable by the ways in which they interpret events? (p. 66)

- Despite beliefs that it is a wonder drug, the antidepressant Prozac has not been shown to be any more effective than the earlier generation of antidepressants? (p. 79)

- Severely depressed people who have failed to respond to other treatments may show rapid improvement if they undergo a form of treatment in which they have jolts of electricity passed through their heads? (p. 79)

- In classical psychoanalysis, you are asked to express whatever thought happens to come to mind, no matter how trivial or silly? (p. 83)

- The average client receiving psychotherapy is better off than 80% of people with similar problems who go untreated? (p. 94)

SINCE EARLIEST TIMES humans have sought explanations for strange or deviant behaviour. In ancient times and through the Middle Ages, beliefs about abnormal behaviour centred on the role of demons and other supernatural forces. But even in ancient times, there were some scholars, such as Hippocrates and Galen, who sought natural explanations of abnormal behaviour. In contemporary times, superstition and demonology have given way to theoretical models engendered by the natural and social sciences. These approaches pave the way not only for a scientifically based understanding of abnormal behaviour, but also for ways of treating people with psychological disorders.

In this chapter, we examine the major contemporary perspectives on abnormal behaviour—the biological, psychological, and sociocultural perspectives. Each of these major perspectives provides a window for examining abnormal behaviour. They each contribute to our understanding of abnormal behaviour, but none captures a complete view of our subject matter. Many theorists today believe abnormal behaviour patterns are complex phenomena that are best understood by adopting an interactionist perspective, which takes into account the interaction of multiple factors representing biological, psychological, and sociocultural domains.

Contemporary approaches to understanding abnormal behaviour have also given rise to methods of therapy or treatment for psychological disorders. Biological perspectives, for example, have led to the development of drug therapies and other medical interventions, such as electroconvulsive therapy (ECT) and repetitive transcranial magnetic stimulation (rTMS). Each of the psychological perspectives—the psychodynamic, learning, humanistic-existential, and cognitive-behavioural perspectives—has spawned corresponding psychological approaches to treatment or models of psychotherapy. Sociocultural perspectives have focused attention on the need to remediate underlying social ills that may contribute to the development of abnormal behaviour—ills such as poverty, overcrowding, and prolonged unemployment.

BIOLOGICAL PERSPECTIVES

The medical model, inspired by physicians from Hippocrates through Kraepelin, remains a powerful force in contemporary understanding of abnormal behaviour, representing a biological perspective. We prefer to use the term *biological perspectives* rather than *medical model* to refer to approaches that emphasize the role of biological factors in explaining abnormal behaviour and the use of biologically based components in treating psychological disorders. We can speak of biological perspectives without adopting the tenets of the medical model, which treats abnormal behaviour patterns as *disorders* and their features as *symptoms*. For example, certain behaviour patterns (shyness or a lack of musical ability) may have a strong genetic component but are not considered "symptoms" of underlying "disorders."

Knowledge of the biological underpinnings of abnormal behaviour has grown rapidly in recent years. In Chapter 1 (see the section on kinship studies), we focused on the methods of studying the role of heredity or genetics. Many exciting advances are being made in genetics, epigenetics, and stem cell research that are taking us to an entirely new level of understanding of abnormal behaviour. We know that other biological factors, especially the functioning of the nervous system, are also involved in many forms of abnormal behaviour. To better understand the role of biological systems in abnormal behaviour patterns, we first need to learn how molecular structures alter and regulate cellular function. Then we move on to learn how the nervous system is organized and how nerve cells communicate with each other.

Genetics

As you'll recall from Chapter 1, heredity plays an important role in human behaviour. From a biological perspective, heredity is described in terms of *genetics*—the study of how traits are passed down from one generation to the next and how these traits affect the way we look, function, and behave. We'll begin this section by looking at the latest ground-breaking research about the role genetics plays in the origin of abnormalities.

DNA Deoxyribonucleic acid is a double-strand complex molecule of helical structure that contains the genetic instructions for building and maintaining living organisms.

The Human Genome A *genome* comprises all the genetic material encoded in the **DNA** (deoxyribonucleic acid) located in the nucleus of cells in living organisms. DNA—the long, complex molecular structures that make up the genome—is characterized by four letters that represent its essential organic compounds: A—adenine; T—thymine; C—cytosine; and G—guanine. It is the sequential order of the *base pairs*, A–T and G–C, that determines our unique genetic code.

In each of our cells, there are an estimated 2.8 billion of these base-pair compounds that form the familiar DNA double helix structures of the human genome. (Amazingly, if you stretched out and aligned all the DNA strands coiled up in the nucleus of just one of your body cells, they would total about two metres in length.) The DNA in each cell is bundled into 23 pairs of chromosomes of various sizes, each pair consisting of anywhere from 23 million to 237 million base pairs. Each chromosome is further organized into gene segments containing the inherited set of instructions that determine the traits particular to each individual, such as eye colour, body shape, and the like (see Figure 2.1). From smallest to largest, our chromosomes contain in the range of 231 to 3141 genes. In total, the human genome is comprised of 20 000 to 25 000 genes.

FIGURE 2.1 The genome and the epigenome.
The *genome* consists of all the DNA found in the nucleus of body cells. Chromosomes contain genes that are wrapped around histones (a protein material). The gene-coiled histones are called nucleosomes and the clusters of nucleosomes resemble beads on a string. Among the nucleosomes are epigenetic markers, which collectively make up the *epigenome*. Epigenetic markers regulate gene expression by opening or condensing the space between nucleosomes. When the nucleosome space is open, gene expression is possible, but when the nucleosome space is condensed, the gene is silenced (e.g., unable to produce proteins). Researchers are investigating ways to correct epigenetic errors that interfere with normal gene regulation.

Source: Artwork copyright © Alexandra Johnson. Printed with permission.

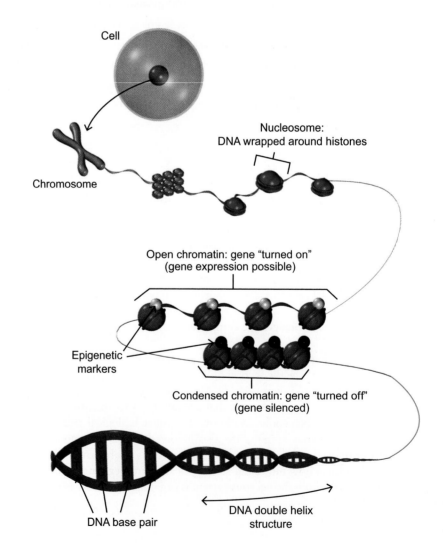

Cell

Nucleosome:
DNA wrapped around histones

Chromosome

Open chromatin: gene "turned on"
(gene expression possible)

Epigenetic markers

Condensed chromatin: gene "turned off"
(gene silenced)

DNA base pair

DNA double helix structure

Most of our genes contain the cellular instructions for combining 20 standard *amino acids* to build a wide array of **proteins** (35 000 or so). Each protein is a unique combination of amino acids and every cell in our body is constructed and maintained by proteins. For example, different proteins are used to build everything from bones, muscles, and organs to brain cells. In addition, all biological processes—metabolism, immune function, muscle contraction, and neurotransmission—rely on proteins.

Genetic errors occur when the number or order of the DNA base pairs is wrong. When the DNA sequence is interrupted, the result can be an alteration or breakdown of a cell's normal protein production, maintenance, and repair processes. If these errors are serious enough, bodily structures and functions can become abnormal or fail.

proteins Organic compounds consisting of amino acids that perform most life functions and make up the majority of cellular structures.

Genetic and Chromosomal Disorders

Sometimes, genetic errors are transmitted from parent to child and result in serious health conditions. *Cystic fibrosis* and *Huntington's disease* are just two of the hundreds of known inherited genetic disorders. Genetic errors can also develop prenatally from exposure to **teratogens** or **mutagens**. For example, maternal alcohol consumption during pregnancy contributes to *fetal alcohol effects* (Mattson & Riley, 2000) and a maternal diet lacking in folic acid (a source of vitamin B) can result in *spina bifida* (Daly, Kirke, Molloy, Wier, & Scott, 1995). Chromosomal diseases, another type of genetic disorder, result from too many, too few, or incomplete chromosomes. For example, trisomy 21 is a condition where a person has three copies of the number 21 chromosome, which results in *Down syndrome* (see Chapter 13, "Abnormal Behaviour in Childhood and Adolescence"). *Turner syndrome*, characterized by underdeveloped sexual features in females, results from missing one X-chromosome. In other instances, people can have a genetic vulnerability to developing certain disorders, but may never display any symptoms of the disorder unless they are exposed to specific environmental risk factors later in life. This may be the case in some forms of schizophrenia or depression, which generally don't appear before adolescence (McClellan, Susser, & King, 2006; Petronis, Popendikyte, Kan, & Sasaki, 2002).

teratogens Any substances or conditions, such as drugs, X-rays, and infectious diseases, that interfere with normal prenatal development.

mutagens Any substances or conditions, such as pesticides, heavy metals, or ionizing radiation, that produce heritable changes in cellular DNA.

Epigenetics

Recent genetics research has revealed that DNA errors tell only one part of the story when it comes to explaining the causes of human diseases and disorders. Each of your body's cells contains an identical DNA code. But if each cell carries the same genetic code (your genotype), how is it that they come to differentiate into specialized cell types (your phenotype) such as muscle, skin, or brain cells? The answer seems to be found in a molecular structure that overlays the *genome*, called the **epigenome** (Callinan & Feinberg, 2006). (See Figure 2.1 on page 42.)

Epigenetics research, particularly in the past few years (Weinhold, 2006), has shown that the epigenome plays a vital role in gene regulation through two key means: **gene expression** and **gene silencing**. Under normal circumstances some genes are *expressed* (turned on) while others are *silenced* (turned off). So, for example, although a person's muscle cells and brain cells both have the same genome (DNA sequence), it is each cell's unique epigenome that dictates which pattern of genes within that cell will be activated. Simply put, we could say that it is the epigenome that causes "brain" genes to be active in brain cells but silenced in muscle cells and vice versa.

The epigenome also regulates hundreds of other critically precise tasks in our cells. It controls all of the ongoing functional and maintenance cellular processes by signalling a gene or polygene when to turn on or off. When a cell needs to make more proteins, the epigenome triggers the genes to comply until a sufficient amount of protein has been produced; then, the epigenome signals the genes to stop the process until more protein is needed. In this way, the epigenome is responsible for "telling" the genes when to go to work, whether it be, for example, producing more saliva, balancing blood sugar levels, or controlling brain cell activity.

On the flip side, faulty gene regulation can result when epigenomic mechanisms fail to regulate or signal genes to turn on or off. This is the case in many forms of cancer, for example, where genes that should normally be suppressed are activated, resulting in cellular proliferation (cancer tumours) (Esteller, 2006; Weinhold, 2006; Rodenhiser & Mann, 2006). Conversely, cancer can also develop when genes that are normally activated to keep cancer

epigenome The sum total of inherited and acquired molecular variations to the genome that lead to changes in gene regulation without changing the DNA sequence of the genome itself.

epigenetics The study of the heritable and acquired changes in gene regulation (phenotype) that occur without affecting DNA sequence (genotype).

gene expression The process by which a gene sequence becomes activated ("turned on") and is translated into the proteins that determine the structure and functions of body cells.

gene silencing The process of preventing or suppressing ("switching off") a gene sequence from being translated into proteins.

cell growth in check are silenced (Egger, Laing, Aparicio, & Jones, 2004). Thus, merely possessing the necessary gene for a certain trait does not guarantee that it will be expressed because we now know that genes remain silent unless activated by an epigenome.

As is true with the genome, the epigenome also transfers species-specific information from one generation to the next. For the most part, any epigenetic modifications that are acquired during the lifetime of an organism are typically expunged during the initial stages of prenatal development (Kimmins & Sassone-Corsi, 2005). In some cases however, acquired epigenetic modifications of the epigenome can be passed on from one generation to the next. For example, cloned embryos are likely to possess many non-normal epigenetic modifications, and so stem cells derived from such embryos may be susceptible to serious problems, including a propensity toward cancer (Balch et al., 2005; Egger et al., 2004; Laird, 2005; Maitra et al., 2005). Moreover, some animal studies indicate that epigenetic changes acquired during the lifetime of the animal can be transmitted to their offspring (Anway, Cupp, Uzumca, & Skinner, 2005; Jirtle & Skinner, 2007; Roemer, Reik, Dean, & Klose, 1997). Examples include inheritance of epigenetic changes to liver, heart, and brain proteins in mice and endocrine and reproductive changes in rats. There are also some preliminary studies showing tentative evidence that acquired epigenetic traits may be inherited in humans, as seen in changes to chromosome *centromeres,* which are key to normal cell division (Amor et al., 2004; Peaston & Whitelaw, 2006; Whitelaw & Whitelaw, 2006).

Epigenetic mechanisms have been implicated in a host of major human maladies ranging from cancer and neurological disorders to autoimmune disorders (Rodenhiser & Mann, 2006). In the area of mental health, Canadian researchers are at the forefront of investigating the role epigenetics plays in the origin and course of psychological disorders such as schizophrenia, bipolar disorders, and Alzheimer's disease (Petronis, 2003, 2004; Petronis et al., 2000, Rodenhiser & Mann, 2006; Schumacher & Petronis, 2006; Szyf, 2006). Epigenetics has suddenly provided scientists with a significant reinterpretation of the interplay between genes and the environment. We are just now beginning to understand what may well be the next revolution in the theory and treatment of human disease and disorders.

Stem Cells

stem cells Undifferentiated cells that are capable of indefinite self-replication and differentiation into specialized cells.

differentiate When unspecialized cells divide into any of the many cells that make up the body, such as heart, liver, or brain.

Our knowledge of **stem cells** has increased dramatically since the 1960s, when a team of Canadian researchers first demonstrated the existence of stem cells and identified their self-renewing capacity to **differentiate** into any type of mature cell (McCulloch & Till, 1960; Till & McCulloch, 1961; Becker, McCulloch, & Till, 1963; Siminovitch, McCulloch, & Till, 1963). Today, we classify stem cells into two broad categories (see Figure 2.2 on page 45). One category includes *embryonic stem cells* that are *totipotent,* meaning they have the capacity to become any type of body cell or develop into another complete individual as in the case of monozygotic twins. In humans, the fertilized egg is totipotent until the eight-cell stage following conception. At this point, embryonic stem cells become *pluripotent*—they lose their ability to be totipotent, but they retain the potential to become one of the more than 200 cells in the body. Some common sources of pluripotent stems cells include umbilical cords, amniotic fluid, and the placenta. The second category of stem cells, called *somaticstem cells,* includes *multipotent* cells that have a more limited capacity than embryonic stem cells to differentiate into specialized cells. For example, *neural stem cells* can further differentiate into different types of brain cells, but cannot develop into other cells types such as skin, muscle, blood, and so on. Multipotent cells are found in most adult tissues, but it should be noted that they can also be found in embryo and fetus tissues. The least flexible somatic stems cells are *unipotent.* These stem cells can only produce one type of mature cell—for example, liver stem cells give rise only to liver cells. The primary functions of adult stem cells are to replace dying and repair damaged body cells.

Advances in stem cell research hold tremendous promise for treating diseases and healing defects, as we'll see when we discuss biological therapies later in the chapter.

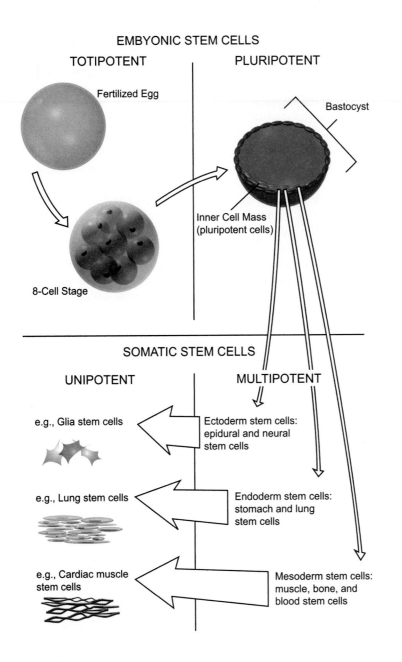

EMBYONIC STEM CELLS

TOTIPOTENT

Fertilized Egg

8-Cell Stage

PLURIPOTENT

Bastocyst

Inner Cell Mass
(pluripotent cells)

SOMATIC STEM CELLS

UNIPOTENT

e.g., Glia stem cells

e.g., Lung stem cells

e.g., Cardiac muscle
stem cells

MULTIPOTENT

Ectoderm stem cells:
epidural and neural
stem cells

Endoderm stem cells:
stomach and lung
stem cells

Mesoderm stem cells:
muscle, bone, and
blood stem cells

FIGURE 2.2 Categories of human stem cells.
Totipotent stem cells will develop into any human cell. *Pluripotent* stem cells will grow into three very broad categories of cells: endoderm (e.g., gastrointestinal and respiratory), ectoderm (e.g., nerves and skin), and mesoderm (e.g., bones, muscle, and blood). *Multipotent* stem cells descend from pluripotent stem cells, but have a more limited range of development. For example, multipotent nerve stem cells can form only into neural and glial cells. *Unipotent* stem cells can produce only one type of cell. Embryonic stems cells are of particular interest to researchers because of their potential to treat a wide range of human diseases and disorders.

Source: Artwork copyright © Alexandra Johnson. Printed with permission.

The Nervous System

Perhaps you would not be nervous if you did not have a nervous system, but even calm people have nervous systems. The nervous system is made up of nerve cells called **neurons**. Neurons communicate with one another or transmit "messages." These messages somehow account for events as diverse as sensing an itch from a bug bite; coordinating a figure skater's vision and muscles; composing a symphony; solving an architectural equation; and, in the case of hallucinations, hearing or seeing things that are not really there.

Every neuron has a cell body or **soma**, dendrites, and an axon (see Figure 2.3 on page 46). The cell body contains the nucleus of the cell and metabolizes oxygen to carry out its work. Short fibres called **dendrites** project from the cell body to receive messages from adjoining neurons. Each neuron has a single **axon** that projects trunk-like from the cell body. Axons can extend as long as several feet if they are conveying messages between the toes and the spinal cord. They may branch and project in various directions. Axons terminate in small branching structures that are aptly termed **terminals**. Swellings called **knobs** occupy the tips of axon terminals. Neurons convey messages in one direction, from the dendrites or cell body along the axon to the axon terminals. The messages are then conveyed from terminal knobs to other neurons, muscles, or glands.

neurons Nerve cells.

soma Cell body.

dendrites Root-like structures at the end of a neuron that receive nerve impulses from other neurons.

axon Long, thin part of a neuron along which nervous impulses travel.

terminals In neuropsychology, the small branching structures found at the tips of axons.

knob Swollen ending of an axon terminal.

neurotransmitter Chemical substance that serves as a type of messenger by transmitting neural impulses from one neuron to another.

synapse Junction between the terminal knob of one neuron and the dendrite or soma of another through which nerve impulses pass.

receptor site Part of a dendrite on the receiving neuron that is structured to receive a neurotransmitter.

norepinephrine Type of neurotransmitter of the catecholamine class.

Alzheimer's disease Progressive brain disease characterized by gradual loss of memory and intellectual functioning, personality changes, and eventual loss of ability to care for oneself.

acetylcholine Type of neurotransmitter involved in the control of muscle contractions. Abbreviated *ACh*.

dopamine Neurotransmitter of the catecholamine class that is believed to play a role in schizophrenia.

serotonin Type of neurotransmitter, imbalances of which have been linked to mood disorders and anxiety.

Neurons transmit messages to other neurons by means of chemical substances called **neurotransmitters**. Neurotransmitters induce chemical changes in receiving neurons. These changes cause axons to conduct the messages in electrical form.

The junction between a transmitting neuron and a receiving neuron is termed a **synapse**. A transmitting neuron is termed *presynaptic*. A receiving neuron is said to be *postsynaptic*. A synapse consists of an axon terminal from a transmitting neuron, a dendrite of a receiving neuron, and a small fluid-filled gap between the two called the *synaptic cleft*. The message does not jump the synaptic cleft like a spark. Instead, axon terminals release neurotransmitters into the cleft like myriad ships casting off into the seas (see Figure 2.4 on page 47).

Each kind of neurotransmitter has a distinctive chemical structure. It will fit only into one kind of harbour or **receptor site** on the receiving neuron. Consider the analogy of a lock and key. Only the right key (neurotransmitter) operates the lock, causing the postsynaptic neuron to forward the message.

Once released, some molecules of a neurotransmitter reach port at receptor sites of other neurons. "Loose" neurotransmitters may be broken down in the synaptic clefts by enzymes or be reabsorbed by the axon terminal (a process termed *reuptake*), so as to prevent the receiving cell from continuing to fire.

Malfunctions in neurotransmitter systems in the brain are linked to various kinds of mental health problems. For example, excesses and deficiencies of the neurotransmitter **norepinephrine** have been connected with mood disorders (see Chapter 7, "Mood Disorders and Suicide") and eating disorders (see Chapter 10, "Eating Disorders and Sleep Disorders"). **Alzheimer's disease,** which involves the progressive loss of memory and cognitive functioning, is associated with reductions in the levels in the brain of the neurotransmitter **acetylcholine.** Irregularities involving excessive availability of the neurotransmitter **dopamine** appear to be involved in schizophrenia (see Chapter 12, "Schizophrenia"). **Serotonin,** another neurotransmitter, is linked to various psychological disorders, including anxiety disorders (see Chapter 5, "Anxiety Disorders"), mood disorders (see Chapter 7), sleep disorders, and eating disorders (see Chapter 10). Although neurotransmitters are believed to play a role in various psychological disorders, precise causal relationships have not yet been determined.

FIGURE 2.3 Anatomy of a neuron.
Neurons typically consist of cell bodies (or somas), dendrites, and one or more axons. The axon of this neuron is wrapped in a myelin sheath, which insulates it from the bodily fluids surrounding the neuron and facilitates transmission of neural impulses (messages that travel within the neuron).

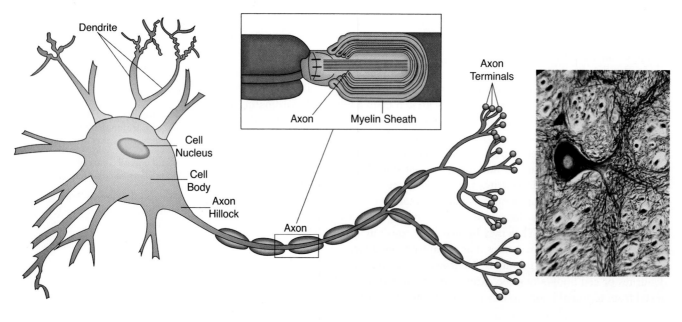

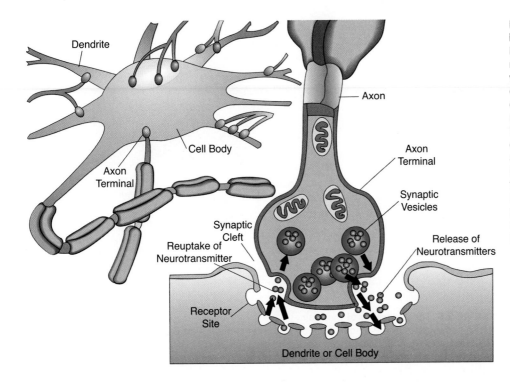

Dendrite

Cell Body

Axon Terminal

Axon

Axon Terminal

Synaptic Vesicles

Synaptic Cleft

Reuptake of Neurotransmitter

Release of Neurotransmitters

Receptor Site

Dendrite or Cell Body

FIGURE 2.4 Transmission of neural impulses across the synapse. Neurons transmit messages or neural impulses across synapses, which consist of the axon terminal of the transmitting neuron, the gap or synaptic cleft between the neurons, and the dendrite of the receiving neuron. The "message" consists of neurotransmitters that are released by synaptic vesicles (sacs) into the synaptic cleft and taken up by receptor sites on the receiving neuron. Finally, neurotransmitters are broken down and reabsorbed by the axon terminal (reuptake) to be recycled.

Parts of the Nervous System

The nervous system consists of two major parts, the **central nervous system** and the **peripheral nervous system**. These parts are further divided. The central nervous system consists of the brain and spinal cord. The peripheral nervous system is made up of nerves that (1) receive and transmit sensory messages (messages from sense organs such as the eyes and ears) to the brain and spinal cord, and (2) transmit messages from the brain or spinal cord to the muscles, causing them to contract; and to glands, causing them to secrete hormones.

We begin our overview of the parts of the central nervous system with the back of the head, where the spinal cord meets the brain, and work forward (see Figure 2.5 on page 48). The lower part of the brain or *hindbrain* consists of the medulla, pons, and cerebellum. Many nerves that link the spinal cord to higher brain levels pass through the **medulla**. The medulla plays roles in such vital functions as heart rate, respiration, and blood pressure, and also in sleep, sneezing, and coughing. The **pons** transmits information about body movement and is involved in functions related to attention, sleep, and respiration.

Behind the pons is the **cerebellum** (Latin for "little brain"). The cerebellum is involved in balance and motor (muscle) behaviour. Injury to the cerebellum may impair motor coordination and cause stumbling and loss of muscle tone.

The **reticular activating system** (RAS) starts in the hindbrain and rises through the midbrain into the lower forebrain. The RAS plays vital roles in sleep, attention, and arousal. RAS injury may leave an animal **comatose**. RAS stimulation triggers messages that heighten alertness. Depressant drugs such as alcohol—which dampen nervous system activity—lower RAS activity.

Important areas in the frontal part of the brain or *forebrain* are the thalamus, hypothalamus, limbic system, basal ganglia, and cerebrum. The **thalamus** relays sensory information (such as touch and vision) to higher brain regions. The thalamus is also involved in sleep and attention, and co-ordination with other structures such as the RAS.

The **hypothalamus** is a tiny structure located between the thalamus and the pituitary gland. The hypothalamus is vital in regulating body temperature, concentration of fluids, storage of nutrients, and motivation and emotion. By implanting electrodes in parts of the hypothalamus of animals and observing the effects when a current is switched on, researchers have found that the hypothalamus is involved in a range of motivational drives and behaviours, including hunger, thirst, sex, parenting behaviours, and aggression.

central nervous system The brain and spinal cord.

peripheral nervous system Part of the nervous system that consists of the somatic nervous system and the autonomic nervous system.

medulla Area of the hindbrain involved in the regulation of heartbeat and respiration.

pons Brain structure, located in the hindbrain, which is involved in respiration.

cerebellum Part of the hindbrain involved in co-ordination and balance.

reticular activating system Part of the brain involved in processes of attention, sleep, and arousal. Abbreviated *RAS*.

comatose In a coma, a state of deep, prolonged unconsciousness.

thalamus Structure in the brain involved in relaying sensory information to the cortex and in processes relating to sleep and attention.

hypothalamus Structure in the lower middle part of the brain involved in regulating body temperature, emotion, and motivation.

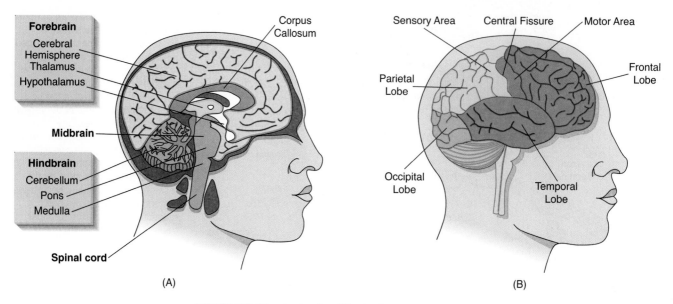

Forebrain
Cerebral Hemisphere
Thalamus
Hypothalamus

Corpus Callosum

Midbrain

Hindbrain
Cerebellum
Pons
Medulla

Spinal cord

(A)

Sensory Area   Central Fissure   Motor Area

Parietal Lobe

Frontal Lobe

Occipital Lobe

Temporal Lobe

(B)

FIGURE 2.5 The geography of the brain.
Part A shows parts of the hindbrain, midbrain, and forebrain. Part B shows the four lobes of the cerebral cortex: frontal, parietal, temporal, and occipital. In part B, the sensory (tactile) and motor areas lie across the central fissure from one another. Researchers are investigating the potential relationships between various patterns of abnormal behaviour and irregularities in the formation or functioning of the structures of the brain.

limbic system Group of forebrain structures, consisting of the amygdala, hippocampus, thalamus, and hypothalamus that are involved in processes of learning and memory as well as basic drives involving hunger, thirst, sex, and aggression.

hippocampus Named for its sea horse shape, it plays a key role in the formation of memories.

amygdala Named for its almond shape, it is involved in the regulation of defensive emotions like fear and anger.

basal ganglia Ganglia located between the thalamus and the cerebrum in the brain that are involved in the coordination of motor activity.

cerebrum Large mass of the forebrain, consisting of two hemispheres.

cerebral cortex Wrinkled surface area of the cerebrum, often referred to as grey matter because of the appearance produced by the high density of cell bodies. Higher mental functions, such as thinking and planning, are assumed to occur in the cerebral cortex.

corpus callosum Thick bundle of fibres that connects the two hemispheres of the brain.

The hypothalamus, together with parts of the thalamus, the hippocampus, the amygdala, and other structures, make up the **limbic system**. The limbic system plays a role in memory and learning, the expression of emotion, and in regulating the more basic drives involving hunger, thirst, sex, and aggression. The **hippocampus** is primarily involved in the formation of long-term memories. Damage to the hippocampus is associated with Alzheimer's disease and epilepsy. The **amygdala** processes sensory information reciprocally with the cerebral cortex to regulate emotion and emotion-related actions. It is involved in the arousal of innate and learned defensive, negative emotions such as fear, avoidance, and aggression. The amygdala is also involved in the formation of emotional memories. The **basal ganglia** lie in front of the thalamus and help regulate postural movements and co-ordination.

The **cerebrum** is the "crowning glory," responsible for the round shape of the human head. The surface of the cerebrum is convoluted with ridges and valleys. This surface is the **cerebral cortex**, the thinking, planning, and executive centre of the brain. The hemispheres of the cerebral cortex are connected by the **corpus callosum**, a thick fibre bundle. Although the two hemispheres function together through the corpus callosum, each hemisphere performs somewhat specialized functions. The left hemisphere controls the right side of the body and is mostly responsible for language, interpreting events literally, and dealing with details, and it excels at logical, objective, and sequential thinking. The right hemisphere controls the left side of the body and is superior at spatial perceptual tasks, interpreting emotional and facial expressions, and interpreting events metaphorically, and it excels at intuitive, subjective, and holistic thinking.

The human activities of thought and language involve the two hemispheres of the cerebrum. Each hemisphere is divided into four parts or lobes, as shown in Figure 2.5 above. The *occipital lobe* is primarily involved in vision; the *temporal lobe* is involved in processing sounds or auditory stimuli. The *parietal lobe* is involved in determining our sense of body position. The *sensory area* of the parietal lobe receives messages from skin and muscle sensors all over the body. Neurons in the motor area (or *motor cortex*) of the *frontal lobe* are involved in controlling muscular responses, enabling us to move our limbs. The *prefrontal cortex* (the part of the frontal lobe that lies in front of the motor cortex) is involved in attention, working memory, decision making, problem solving, and speech.

The peripheral nervous system connects the brain to the outer world. Without the peripheral nervous system, people could not perceive the world or act on it. The two main divisions of the peripheral nervous system are the *somatic nervous system* and the *autonomic nervous system*.

The **somatic nervous system** transmits messages about sights, sounds, smells, temperature, body position, and so on, to the brain. Messages from the brain and spinal cord to the somatic nervous system regulate intentional body movements such as raising an arm, winking, or walking, breathing, and subtle movements that maintain posture and balance.

Psychologists are particularly interested in the **autonomic nervous system** (ANS) because its activities are linked to emotional response. *Autonomic* means "automatic." The ANS regulates the glands and **involuntary** activities such as heart rate, breathing, digestion, and dilation of the pupils of the eyes, even when we are sleep.

The ANS has two branches or subdivisions, the **sympathetic** and the **parasympathetic**. These branches have mostly opposing effects. Many organs and glands are served by both branches of the ANS. The sympathetic division is most involved in processes that mobilize the body's resources in times of stress, such as drawing energy from stored reserves to prepare a person to deal with imposing threats or dangers (see Chapter 4, "Stress, Psychological Factors, and Health"). When we face a threat or dangerous situation, the sympathetic branch of the ANS accelerates the heart rate and breathing rate, which helps prepare our bodies to either fight or flee. Sympathetic activation in the face of a threatening stimulus is associated with emotional responses such as fear or anxiety. When we relax, the parasympathetic branch decelerates the heart rate. The parasympathetic division is most active during processes that replenish energy reserves, such as digestion.

Evaluating Biological Perspectives on Abnormal Behaviour

There is no question that biological structures and processes are involved in many patterns of abnormal behaviour, as we see in later chapters. Factors such as genetic errors, abnormal gene expression caused by faulty epigenetic structures, disturbances in neurotransmitter functioning and underlying brain abnormalities or defects are implicated in many types of psychological disorders. For some disorders, such as Alzheimer's disease, biological processes play the direct causative role. Even then, however, the onset and course of the disease can be mediated by changes in the epigenome. In other cases, such as with schizophrenia, biological factors, especially epigenetics, appear to interact with stressful environmental factors in the development of the disorder.

Genetic influences are implicated in a wide range of psychological disorders, including schizophrenia, bipolar (manic-depressive) disorder, major depression, alcoholism, autism, Alzheimer's disease, anxiety disorders, learning disabilities, and antisocial personality disorder (Merikangas & Risch, 2003; NIMH, 2003; Plomin & Kovas, 2005; Plomin & McGuffin, 2003; Santos-Rebouças & Pimentel, 2007). Yet genetic factors cannot account entirely for any of these disorders. Environmental factors and epigenetic changes also play an important role.

While we continue to learn more about the biological foundations of abnormal behaviour patterns, the interface between biology and behaviour can be construed as a two-way street. For example, in the field of human **behavioural genetics**, researchers study the interactive effect of genetic and environmental factors on behaviour—especially how they affect the development of personality patterns and psychological disorders (see the section "Interactionist Perspectives" later in this chapter). Moreover, researchers have uncovered links between psychological factors and many physical disorders and conditions (see Chapter 4).

Researchers are also investigating whether the combination of psychological and drug treatments for such problems as depression, anxiety disorders, and substance abuse disorders, among others, may increase the therapeutic benefits of either of the two approaches alone. Although Canadian psychiatry has become increasingly medicalized in recent years, some within the psychiatric community have warned their colleagues not to overlook the role of psychological factors in explaining and treating mental health problems (Leszcz et al., 2002).

somatic nervous system Division of the peripheral nervous system that relays information from the sense organs to the brain and transmits messages from the brain to the skeletal muscles, resulting in body movements.

autonomic nervous system Division of the peripheral nervous system that regulates the activities of glands and involuntary functions, such as respiration, heartbeat, and digestion. Abbreviated *ANS*. Also see *sympathetic* and *parasympathetic* branches of the ANS.

involuntary Automatic or without conscious direction, as in bodily processes like heartbeat and respiration.

sympathetic Pertaining to the division of the autonomic nervous system that becomes active to meet the demands of stress, as in adjusting to cold temperatures or in expending bodily reserves of energy through physical exertion or through emotional reactions such as anxiety or fear. See *parasympathetic*.

parasympathetic Relating to the activity of the parasympathetic branch of the autonomic nervous system. See *sympathetic*.

behavioural genetics The study of how hereditary and environmental factors interact to produce behaviour.

Biological Perspectives

Review It

- **What is the distinguishing feature of the biological perspectives on abnormal behaviour?** Biological perspectives focus on the biological underpinnings of abnormal behaviour, including the roles of genetics, neurotransmitter functioning, and brain abnormalities and defects.

Define It

DNA	serotonin
proteins	central nervous system
teratogens	peripheral nervous system
mutagens	medulla
epigenome	pons
epigenetics	cerebellum
gene expression	reticular activating system
gene silencing	comatose
stem cells	thalamus
differentiate	hypothalamus
neurons	limbic system
soma	hippocampus
dendrites	amygdala
axon	basal ganglia
terminals	cerebrum
knob	cerebral cortex
neurotransmitter	corpus callosum
synapse	somatic nervous system
receptor site	autonomic nervous system
norepinephrine	involuntary
Alzheimer's disease	sympathetic
acetylcholine	parasympathetic
dopamine	behavioural genetics

Recall It*

1. The chemical substances that enable neurons to transmit messages to each other are called _____.

   a. epigenomic promoters
   b. hormones
   c. neurotransmitters
   d. neuropeptides

2. Alzheimer's disease is linked to deficiencies of _____.

   a. dopamine
   b. acetylcholine
   c. norepinephrine
   d. serotonin

3. The _____ nervous system consists of the brain and spinal cord.

   a. cerebro-spinal
   b. parasympathetic
   c. somatic
   d. central

4. Henry has problems maintaining balance and coordinating his muscle movements. Assuming his problems are the result of a brain injury, the part of the brain most likely to be affected is the _____.

   a. thalamus
   b. pons
   c. medulla
   d. cerebellum

5. The _____ connects the two hemispheres of the brain.

   a. pons
   b. thalamus
   c. corpus callosum
   d. medulla

* Recall It answers can be found on the Companion Website for this text.

Think About It

- Do you believe abnormal behaviour is more a function of nature (biology) or nurture (environment)? Explain.
- Do you believe biology is destiny? Why or why not?

PSYCHOLOGICAL PERSPECTIVES

At about the time that biological models of abnormal behaviour were beginning to achieve prominence with the contributions of Kraepelin, Griesinger, and others, another approach to understanding the bases of abnormal behaviour began to emerge. This approach emphasized the psychological roots of abnormal behaviour and was most closely identified with the work of the Austrian physician Sigmund Freud. Over time other psychological models would emerge from the behaviourist, humanistic-existential, and cognitivist traditions. Let's begin our study of psychological perspectives with Freud's contribution and the development of psychodynamic models.

Psychodynamic Models

Psychodynamic theory is based on the contributions of Sigmund Freud and his followers. The psychodynamic model espoused by Freud, called **psychoanalytic theory**, is based on the belief that psychological problems are derived from unconscious psychological conflicts, which can be traced to childhood. Freud held that much of our behaviour is driven by unconscious motives and conflicts of which we are unaware. These underlying conflicts revolve around primitive sexual and aggressive instincts or drives and the need to keep these primitive impulses out of direct awareness. Why? Because awareness of these primitive impulses, including murderous urges and incestuous impulses, would flood the conscious self with crippling anxiety. Within the Freudian view, abnormal behaviour patterns such as hysteria represent "symptoms" of the dynamic struggles taking place within the mind. In the case of hysteria, the "symptom" represents the *conversion* of an unconscious psychological conflict into a physical problem.

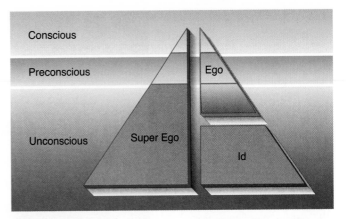

FIGURE 2.6 The parts of the mind, according to Sigmund Freud. According to psychodynamic theory, the mind is akin to an iceberg in that only a small part of it rises to conscious awareness at any moment in time. Although material in the preconscious mind may be brought into consciousness by focusing our attention on it, the impulses and ideas in the unconscious tend to remain veiled in mystery.

The Structure of the Mind Freud's clinical experiences led him to conclude that the mind is like an iceberg (see Figure 2.6 above). Only the tip of an iceberg is visible above the surface of the water. The great mass of the iceberg lies below the surface, darkening the deep. Freud came to believe that people, similarly, perceive but a few of the ideas, wishes, and impulses that dwell within them and determine their behaviour. Freud held that the larger part of the mind, which includes our deepest wishes, fears, and instinctual urges, remains below the surface of consciousness. Freud labelled the region that corresponds to our present awareness the **conscious** part of the mind. The regions that lie beneath the surface of awareness were labelled the *preconscious* and the *unconscious*.

In the **preconscious** mind, memories of experience can be found that are not in awareness but can be brought into awareness with focus. Your telephone number, for example, remains in the preconscious until you focus on it. The **unconscious** mind, the largest part of the mind, remains shrouded in mystery. Its contents can only be brought to awareness with great difficulty, if at all. Freud believed the unconscious is the repository of biological drives or instincts such as sex and aggression.

The Structure of Personality According to Freud's **structural hypothesis**, the personality is divided into three mental entities or **psychic** structures: the *id*, *ego*, and *superego*. Psychic structures cannot be seen or measured directly, but their presence is suggested by observable behaviour and expressed in thoughts and emotions.

The **id** is the only psychic structure present at birth. It is the repository of our baser drives and instinctual impulses, including hunger, thirst, sex, and aggression. The id, which operates completely in the unconscious, was described by Freud as "a chaos, a cauldron of seething excitations" (1933/1964, p. 73). The id follows the **pleasure principle**. It demands instant gratification of instincts without consideration of social rules or customs or the needs of others. It operates by **primary process thinking**, which is a mode of relating to the world through imagination and fantasy. This enables the id to achieve gratification by conjuring up a mental image of the object of desire.

During the first year of life, the child discovers its every demand is not instantly gratified. It must learn to cope with delay of gratification. The **ego** develops during this first year to organize reasonable ways of coping with frustration. Standing for "reason and good sense" (Freud, 1933/1964, p. 76), the ego seeks to curb the demands of the id and to direct behaviour in keeping with social customs and expectations. Gratification can thus be achieved, but not at the expense of social disapproval. The id floods your consciousness with hunger pangs. Were it to have its way, the id might also prompt you to wolf down any food at hand or even to swipe someone else's plate. But the ego creates the ideas

psychoanalytic theory Theoretical model of personality developed by Freud. Also called *psychoanalysis*.

conscious Aware.

preconscious In psychodynamic theory, descriptive of material that lies outside of present awareness but which can be brought into awareness by focusing attention. See also *unconscious*.

unconscious (1) In psychodynamic theory, pertaining to impulses or ideas that are not readily available to awareness, in many instances because they are kept from awareness by means of *repression*. (2) Also in psychodynamic theory, the part of the mind that contains repressed material and primitive urges of the id. (3) More generally, a state of unawareness or loss of consciousness.

structural hypothesis In Freud's theory, the belief that the clashing forces within the personality could be divided into three psychic structures: the id, the ego, and the superego.

psychic (1) Relating to mental phenomena. (2) A person who claims to be sensitive to supernatural forces.

id In psychodynamic theory, the unconscious psychic structure that is present at birth. The id contains instinctual drives and is governed by the pleasure principle.

pleasure principle In psychodynamic theory, the governing principle of the id, involving the demands for immediate gratification of instinctual needs.

primary process thinking In psychodynamic theory, the mental process in infancy by which the id seeks gratification of primitive impulses by means of imagining it possesses what it desires. Thinking that is illogical, magical, and fails to discriminate between reality and fantasy.

ego In psychodynamic theory, the psychic structure corresponding to the concept of the self. The ego is governed by the reality principle and is responsible for finding socially acceptable outlets for the urgings of the id. The ego is characterized by the capacity to tolerate frustration and delay gratification.

reality principle In psychodynamic theory, the governing principle of the ego that involves consideration of what is socially acceptable and practical in gratifying needs.

secondary process thinking In psychodynamic theory, the reality-based thinking processes and problem-solving activities of the ego.

self Centre of consciousness that organizes sensory impressions and governs one's perceptions of the world. The sum total of a person's thoughts, sensory impressions, and feelings.

superego In psychodynamic theory, the psychic structure that represents the incorporation of the moral values of the parents and important others and floods the ego with guilt and shame when it falls short of meeting those standards. The superego is governed by the moral principle and consists of two parts: the conscience and the ego ideal.

identification (1) In psychodynamic theory, the process of incorporating the personality or behaviour of others. (2) In social learning theory, a process of imitation by which children acquire behaviours similar to those of role models.

moral principle In psychodynamic theory, the principle that governs the superego to set moral standards and enforce adherence to them.

ego ideal In Freud's view, the configuration of higher social values and moral ideals embodied in the superego.

defence mechanisms In psychodynamic theory, the reality-distorting strategies used by the ego to shield itself from conscious awareness of anxiety-evoking or troubling material.

repression In psychodynamic theory, a type of defence mechanism involving the ejection from awareness of anxiety-provoking ideas, images, or impulses, without the conscious awareness that one has done so.

psychoanalysis (1) Theoretical model of personality developed by Sigmund Freud. (2) Method of psychotherapy developed by Sigmund Freud.

Sigmund Freud at about the age of 30.

of walking to the refrigerator, making yourself a sandwich, and pouring a glass of milk.

The ego is governed by the **reality principle**. It considers what is practical and possible, as well as the urgings of the id. The ego engages in **secondary process thinking**—the remembering, planning, and weighing of circumstances that permit a compromise between the fantasies of the id and the realities of the world outside. The ego lays the groundwork for the development of the conscious sense of the **self**.

During middle childhood, the **superego** develops. The moral standards and values of parents and other key people become internalized through a process of **identification**. The superego operates according to the **moral principle**; it demands strict adherence to moral standards. The superego represents the moral values of an ideal self, called the **ego ideal**. It also serves as a conscience or internal moral guardian that monitors the ego and passes judgment on right and wrong. It metes out punishment in the form of guilt and shame when it finds that the ego has failed to adhere to the superego's moral standards. Ego stands between the id and the superego. It endeavours to satisfy the cravings of the id without offending the moral standards of the superego.

Defence Mechanisms Although part of the ego rises to consciousness, some of its activity is carried out unconsciously. In the unconscious, the ego serves as a kind of gatekeeper or censor that screens impulses from the id. It uses **defence mechanisms** (psychological defences) to prevent socially unacceptable impulses from rising into consciousness. If it were not for these defence mechanisms, the darkest sins of our childhoods, the primitive demands of our ids, and the censures of our superegos might disable us psychologically. **Repression**, or motivated forgetting (banishment of unacceptable ideas or motives to the unconscious), is considered the most basic of the defence mechanisms. A number of these defence mechanisms are described in Table 2.1 on page 53.

A dynamic unconscious struggle thus takes place between the id and the ego. It pits biological drives that strive for expression (the id) against the ego, which seeks to restrain them or channel them into socially acceptable outlets. When these conflicts are not resolved smoothly, they can lead to the development of symptoms or features associated with psychological disorders, such as hysterical symptoms, phobias, and behavioural problems. Because we cannot view the unconscious mind directly, Freud developed a method of mental detective work called **psychoanalysis**, which is described later in this chapter.

The use of defence mechanisms to cope with feelings like anxiety, guilt, and shame is considered normal. These mechanisms enable us to constrain impulses from the id as we go about our daily business. In his *Psychopathology of Everyday Life*, Freud noted that slips of the tongue and ordinary forgetfulness could represent hidden motives that are kept out of consciousness by repression. If a friend means to say, "I hear what you're saying," but it comes out, "I hate what you're saying," perhaps the friend is expressing a repressed emotion. If a lover storms out in anger but forgets his umbrella, perhaps he is unconsciously creating an excuse for returning. Defence mechanisms may also give rise to abnormal behaviour, however. The person who regresses to an infantile state under pressures of enormous stress is clearly not acting adaptively to the situation.

TABLE 2.1

Major Defence Mechanisms in Psychodynamic Theory

Type of Defence Mechanism	Description	Example
Repression	Expulsion from awareness of unacceptable ideas or motives.	A person remains unaware of harbouring hateful or destructive impulses toward others.
Regression	The return of behaviour that is typical of earlier stages of development.	Under stress, a college student starts biting his nails or becomes totally dependent on others.
Displacement	The transfer of unacceptable impulses away from threatening persons toward safer or less threatening objects.	A worker slams a door after his boss chews him out.
Denial	Refusal to recognize a threatening impulse or desire.	A person harshly rebukes his or her spouse but denies feeling angry.
Reaction formation	Behaving in a way that is the opposite of one's true wishes or desires in order to keep these repressed.	A sexually frustrated person goes on a personal crusade to stamp out indecency.
Rationalization	The use of self-justifications to explain unacceptable behaviour.	A woman says, when asked why she continues to smoke, "Cancer doesn't run in my family."
Projection	Imposing one's own impulses or wishes onto another person.	A sexually inhibited person misinterprets other people's friendly approaches as sexual advances.
Sublimation	The channelling of unacceptable impulses into socially constructive pursuits.	A person channels aggressive impulses into competitive sports.

Stages of Psychosexual Development Freud proposed that sexual drives are the dominant factors in the development of personality, even in childhood. In Freud's view, all activities that are physically pleasurable, such as eating or moving one's bowels, are in essence "sexual." The instinctual drive for "sexual" pleasure, present from birth, was deemed to be the motivating force behind most human behaviour.

The internal drive for "sexual" pleasure represents what Freud termed the **libido**, or sexual energy. Freud believed libidinal energy is expressed through sexual pleasure in different body parts, called **erogenous zones**, as a child matures. In Freud's view, the stages of human development are **psychosexual** in nature, because they correspond to the transfer of libidinal energy from one erogenous zone to another. Freud proposed the existence of five psychosexual stages of development: oral, anal, phallic, latency, and genital.

In the first year of life, the **oral stage**, infants achieve sexual pleasure by sucking their mothers' breasts and by mouthing anything that happens to be nearby. Oral stimulation, in the form of sucking and biting, is a source of both sexual gratification and nourishment. One of Freud's central beliefs is that the child may encounter conflict during each of the psychosexual stages of development. Conflict during the oral stage centres around the issue of whether or not the infant receives adequate oral gratification. Too much gratification could lead the infant to expect that everything in life is given with little or no effort on its part. In contrast, early **weaning** might lead to frustration. Too little or too much gratification at any stage could lead to **fixation** in that stage, which leads to the development of personality traits characteristic of that stage. Oral

libido In psychodynamic theory, sexual drive or energy.

erogenous zone Part of the body that is sensitive to sexual stimulation.

psychosexual Descriptive of the stages of human development in Freud's theory in which sexual energy (libido) becomes expressed through different erogenous zones of the body during different developmental stages.

oral stage In psychodynamic theory, the first of Freud's stages of psychosexual development, during which pleasure is primarily sought through such oral activities as sucking and biting.

weaning Process of accustoming a child to eat solid food rather than seek nourishment through breastfeeding or sucking a baby bottle.

fixation In psychodynamic theory, arrested development in the form of attachment to objects of an earlier stage that occurs as the result of excessive or inadequate gratification at that stage.

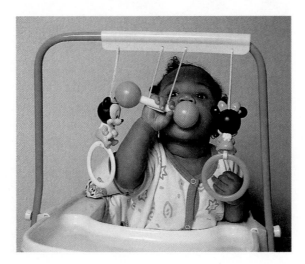

The oral stage of psychosexual development? According to Freud, a child's early encounters with the world are largely experienced through the mouth.

anal stage The second stage of psychosexual development in Freud's theory, in which gratification is achieved through anal activities, such as by the elimination of bodily wastes.

anal fixation In psychodynamic theory, attachment to objects and behaviours that characterize the anal stage.

anal retentive In psychodynamic theory, a personality type characterized by excessive needs for self-control, such as extreme neatness and punctuality.

anal expulsive In psychodynamic theory, a personality type characterized by excessive self-expression, such as extreme sloppiness or messiness.

phallic stage In psychodynamic theory, Freud's third stage of psychosexual development, characterized by sexual interest focused on the phallic region and the development of incestuous desires for the parent of the opposite gender and rivalry with the parent of the same gender (the Oedipus complex).

Oedipus complex In psychodynamic theory, the conflict that occurs during the phallic stage of development in which a boy incestuously desires his mother and perceives his father as a rival for his mother's love and attention.

Electra complex In psychodynamic theory, the term used to describe the conflict in a young girl during the phallic stage of development involving her incestuous desires to possess her father and her resentment of her mother, whom she blames for lacking a penis.

gender roles Characteristic ways in which males and females are expected to behave within a given culture.

castration anxiety In psychodynamic theory, the boy's unconscious fear that he will be castrated as a form of punishment for having incestuous wishes for his mother.

fixations could include an exaggerated desire for "oral activities," which could become expressed in later life in smoking, alcohol abuse, overeating, and nail-biting. Like the infant who depends on the mother's breast for survival and gratification of oral pleasure, orally fixated adults may also become clinging and dependent in their interpersonal relationships.

During the **anal stage** of psychosexual development, gratification is achieved through anal activities, such as by the elimination of bodily wastes. The child begins to learn she or he can delay gratification of the need to eliminate when the urge is felt. During toilet training, the issue of self-control may become a source of conflict between a parent and child. **Anal fixations** that derive from this conflict are associated with two sets of traits. Harsh toilet training may lead to the development of **anal-retentive** traits, which involve excessive needs for self-control. These include perfectionism and extreme fastidiousness—a penchant for orderliness, cleanliness, and neatness. By contrast, excessive gratification during the anal period might lead to **anal expulsive** traits, which include carelessness and messiness.

The next stage of psychosexual development, the **phallic stage**, generally begins during the third year of life. The major erogenous zone during this stage is the phallic region (the penis in boys, the clitoris in girls). Conflict between parent and child may occur over masturbation—the rubbing of phallic areas for sexual pleasure—to which parents may react with threats and punishments. Perhaps the most controversial of Freud's beliefs was his suggestion that phallic-stage children develop unconscious incestuous wishes for the parent of the opposite gender and begin to view the parent of the same sex as a rival. Freud dubbed this conflict the **Oedipus complex**. The female version of the Oedipus complex has been named by some followers (although not by Freud himself) the **Electra complex**.

Freud believed the Oedipus conflict represents a central psychological conflict of early childhood, the resolution of which has far-reaching consequences in later development and in determining the acquisition of **gender roles**. He also believed that **castration anxiety** plays an important role in resolving the complex for boys. Freud hypothesized that boys develop castration anxiety, based on the fantasy that their rivals for their mother's affections, namely their fathers, would seek to punish them for their incestuous wishes by removing the organ that has become connected with sexual pleasure. To prevent castration, Freud argued, boys repress their incestuous wishes for their mothers and identify with their fathers. Keep in mind that Freudian theory posits that these developments (incestuous

Are young children interested in sex? According to Freud, even young children have sexual impulses. Freud's view of childhood sexuality shocked the scientific establishment of his day, and many of Freud's own followers believe that Freud placed too much emphasis on sexual motivation.

wishes and castration anxiety) are largely unconscious and are part and parcel of normal development. Successful resolution of the Oedipus complex involves the boy repressing his incestuous wishes for his mother and identifying with and modelling his father.

The Electra complex in girls is somewhat of a mirror image of the Oedipal one in boys. Freud believed little girls naturally become envious of boys' penises. Girls come to desire to possess their fathers, in a way substituting their fathers' penises for their own missing ones. But the rivalry with their mothers for their fathers' affection places them in peril of losing their mothers' love and protection. Successful resolution of the complex for the girl involves repression of the incestuous wishes for her father and identification with and emulation of her mother.

The Oedipus complex comes to a point of resolution, whether fully resolved or not, when a child reaches the age of five or six. From the identification with the parent of the same gender comes the internalization of parental values in the form of the superego. Children then enter the **latency stage** of psychosexual development, a period of late childhood during which sexual impulses remain in a latent state. Interests are directed toward school and play activities. But sexual drives are once again aroused with the **genital stage**, beginning with puberty, which reaches fruition in mature sexuality, marriage, and the bearing of children. The sexual feelings toward the parent of the opposite gender that had remained repressed during the latency period emerge during adolescence but are displaced or transferred onto socially appropriate members of the opposite gender. Boys might still look for girls "just like the girl that married dear old Dad." And girls might still be attracted to boys who resemble their fathers.

In Freud's view, successful adjustment during the genital stage involves attaining sexual gratification through sexual intercourse with someone of the opposite gender, presumably within the context of marriage. Other forms of sexual expression, such as oral or anal stimulation, masturbation, and homosexual activity, are considered **pregenital** fixations, or immature forms of sexual conduct.

Other Psychodynamic Theorists Freud left a rich intellectual legacy that has stimulated the thinking of many theorists. Psychodynamic theory has been shaped over the years by the contributions of other theorists who are sometimes referred to collectively as **neo-Freudians**. They shared certain central tenets in common with Freud, such as the belief that behaviour reflects unconscious motivation, inner conflict, and the operation of defensive responses to anxiety. They tended to de-emphasize the roles of basic instincts such as sex and aggression, however, and placed greater emphasis on roles for conscious choice, self-direction, and creativity (see Table 2.2 on pages 56 and 57). These theorists also differed from each other in various ways.

Psychodynamic Perspectives on Normality and Abnormality Freud believed there is a thin line between normal and abnormal. Both normal and abnormal behaviour are motivated or driven by irrational drives of the id. The difference may be largely a matter of degree. Normality is a matter of the balance of energy among the psychic structures of id, ego, and superego. In normal people, the ego has the strength to control the instincts of the id and to withstand the condemnation of the superego. The presence of acceptable outlets for the expression of some primitive impulses, such as the expression of mature sexuality in marriage, decreases the pressures within the id and at the same time lessens the burdens of the ego in repressing the remaining impulses. Being reared by reasonably tolerant parents might prevent the superego from becoming overly harsh and condemnatory.

In psychological disorders, the balance of energy is lopsided. Some unconscious impulses may "erupt," producing anxiety or leading to the development of **neuroses** such as hysteria and phobias. The neurotic symptom—a fear of knives, for example—serves a purpose of shielding the self from awareness of these threatening unconscious impulses (using a knife to murder someone or attack the self). So long as the symptom is maintained (the person avoids knives), the murderous or suicidal impulses are kept at bay. If the superego becomes overly powerful, it may create excessive feelings of guilt and lead to depression. An underdeveloped superego is believed to play a role in explaining the antisocial tendencies of people who intentionally hurt others without feelings of guilt.

latency stage According to psychoanalytic theory, the fourth stage of psychosexual development, which is characterized by repression of sexual impulses.

genital stage In psychodynamic theory, the fifth stage of psychosexual development that corresponds to mature sexuality and is characterized by the expression of libido through sexual intercourse with an adult member of the opposite gender.

pregenital In psychodynamic theory, referring to characteristics which are typical of stages of psychosexual development that precede the genital stage.

neo-Freudians Term used to describe the "second generation" of theorists who followed in the Freudian tradition. On the whole, neo-Freudians (such as Jung, Adler, Horney, Sullivan) placed greater emphasis on the importance of cultural and social influences on behaviour and lesser importance on sexual impulses and the functioning of the id.

neurosis Type of nonpsychotic behavioural disturbance, characterized chiefly by the use of defensive behaviours to control anxiety, in which a person is generally able to function but is impaired in some aspect(s) of functioning. Plural: *neuroses*.

TABLE 2.2

Neo-Freudian Psychodynamic Theorists

Theorist	Ideology
Carl Jung (1875–1961) **analytical psychology** Jung's psychodynamic theory, which emphasizes such concepts as the collective unconscious, the existence of archetypes, and the notion of the self as a unifying force of personality. **collective unconscious** In Carl Jung's theory, the hypothesized storehouse of archetypes and racial memories. **archetypes** Jung's concept of primitive images or concepts that reside in the collective unconscious.	**Analytical Psychology** Jung developed his own psychodynamic theory, **analytical psychology**, which states that an understanding of human behaviour must incorporate the facts of self-awareness and self-direction as well as the impulses of the id and the mechanisms of defence. He believed that not only do we have a personal unconscious, a repository of repressed memories and impulses, but we also inherit a **collective unconscious**. To Jung, the collective unconscious represents the accumulated experience of humankind, which he believed is passed down genetically through the generations. The collective unconscious is believed to contain primitive images or **archetypes**, which reflect on the history of our species, including vague, mysterious mythical images like the all-powerful God, the fertile and nurturing mother, the young hero, the wise old man, and themes of rebirth or resurrection. Although archetypes remain unconscious, in Jung's view, they influence our thoughts, dreams, and emotions and render us responsive to cultural themes in stories and films.
Alfred Adler (1870–1937) **inferiority complex** In Adler's view, the feelings of inferiority believed to be a central source of motivation. **drive to superiority** In Adler's theory, a term describing the desire to compensate for feelings of inferiority. **creative self** In Alfred Adler's theory, the self-aware part of the personality that strives to achieve its potential. **individual psychology** Psychodynamic theory developed by Alfred Adler.	**Individual Psychology** Adler believed that people are basically driven by an **inferiority complex**, not by sexual instinct as Freud had maintained. All of us, because of our small size during childhood, encounter feelings of inferiority to some degree. These feelings lead to a **drive to superiority**, which motivates us to achieve prominence and social dominance. In the healthy personality, however, strivings for dominance are tempered by devotion to helping other people. Adler, like Jung, believed self-awareness plays a major role in the formation of personality. The **creative self** is a self-aware aspect of personality that strives to overcome obstacles and develop an individual's potential. With the hypothesis of the creative self, Adler shifted the emphasis of psychodynamic theory from the id to the ego. Because our potentials are uniquely individual, Adler's views have been termed **individual psychology**.
Karen Horney (1885–1952)	**Self-Theory** For Horney, the hallmark of a healthy personality is having an accurate view of oneself that increases the freedom to realize one's potential in life. In contrast, the neurotic adult's sense of self is split between an idealized self that strives to achieve unobtainable ideals and a despised self that loathes the way one actually is. Neurosis is rooted in a childhood perception that one's parents were indifferent toward them—lacked warmth and affection. Based on her clinical observations, Horney established a feminine psychology that opened up new ways of thinking about women's issues.
Harry Stack Sullivan (1892–1949)	**Self-System** Sullivan emphasized the importance of the social context of psychological problems and child–parent relationships in particular in determining the nature of later interpersonal relationships. For example, children of rejecting parents tend to become self-doubting and anxious. These personality features persist and impede the development of close relationships in adult life.
Heinz Hartmann (1894–1970) **ego psychology** Approach of modern psychodynamic theorists which posits that the ego has energy and strivings of its own apart from the id. Ego psychologists focus more on the conscious strivings of the ego than on the hypothesized unconscious functioning of the id. **ego analysts** Psychodynamically oriented therapists who are influenced by ego psychology.	**Ego-Psychology** Hartmann was one of the originators of **ego psychology**, which posits that the ego has energy and motives of its own. Freud believed ego functions are largely defensive, fuelled by the id, and perpetually threatened by the irrational. Hartmann and other **ego analysts** found Freud's views of the ego—and of people in general—too pessimistic and ignoble. Hartmann argued that the cognitive functions of the ego could be free of conflict. The choices to seek an education, dedicate oneself to art and poetry, and further humanity are not merely defensive forms of sublimation, as Freud had seen them.

TABLE 2.2

Neo-Freudian Psychodynamic Theorists (continued)

Theorist	Ideology
Erik Erikson (1902–1994)	**Ego-Psychology (Psychosocial)** Another ego analyst, Erikson, emphasized the importance of children's social relationships that result from the interaction between internal drives and sociocultural demands. Whereas Freud's developmental theory ends with the genital stage, beginning in early adolescence, Erikson focused on developmental processes that he believed continue throughout adulthood. In Erikson's view, a person must successfully resolve the psychosocial crises at each of the eight stages of human development, as summarized in Table 2.3 on page 58. Failure to find satisfactory solutions to the tasks associated with each psychosocial stage can lead to maladaptive behaviour.
Margaret Mahler (1897–1985) **object-relations theory** In psychodynamic theory, the viewpoint that focuses on the influences of internalized representations (called "objects") within a person's ego structure of the personalities of parents and other figures of strong attachment. **introjection** In psychodynamic theory, the process of unconsciously incorporating features of the personality of another person within one's own ego structure.	**Object-Relations Theory** One popular contemporary psychodynamic approach is termed **object-relations theory**, which focuses on how children come to develop symbolic representations of important others in their lives, especially their parents. Mahler was one of the major contributors to object-relations theory; she saw the process of separating from the mother during the first three years of life as crucial to personality development (discussed further in Chapter 8, "Personality Disorders"). According to psychodynamic theory, we introject or incorporate into our own personalities elements of major figures in our lives. **Introjection** is more powerful when we fear rejection by others or losing others to death. Thus, we might be particularly apt to incorporate elements of people who disapprove of us or who see things differently. In Mahler's view, these symbolic representations, which are formed from images and memories of others, come to influence our perceptions and behaviour. We experience internal conflict as the attitudes of introjected people battle with our own. Some of our perceptions may be distorted or seem unreal to us. Some of our impulses and behaviour may seem unlike us, as if they come out of the blue. With such conflict, we may not be able to tell where the influences of other people end and our "real selves" begin. The aim of Mahler's therapeutic approach was to help clients separate their own ideas and feelings from those of the introjected objects so they could develop as wholly unique individuals.

Freud believed the underlying conflicts in neuroses have childhood origins, which are buried in the depths of the unconscious. Through psychoanalysis, he sought to help people uncover and learn to deal with these underlying conflicts to free themselves of the need to maintain the overt symptom.

Perpetual vigilance and defence take their toll. The ego can weaken and, in extreme cases, lose the ability to keep a lid on the id. **Psychosis** results when the urges of the id spill forth into consciousness, untempered by an ego that either has been weakened or is underdeveloped. The fortress of the ego is overrun, and the person loses the ability to distinguish between fantasy and reality. Behaviour becomes detached from reality. Primary process thinking and bizarre behaviour rule the day. Psychoses are characterized, in general, by more severe disturbances of functioning than neuroses, by the appearance of bizarre behaviour and thoughts, and by faulty perceptions of reality, such as hallucinations ("hearing voices" or seeing things that are not present). Speech may become incoherent and there may be bizarre posturing and gestures. The most prominent form of psychosis is schizophrenia, which is discussed in Chapter 12, "Schizophrenia."

psychosis Type of major psychological disorder in which people show impaired ability to interpret reality and difficulties in meeting the demands of daily life. Schizophrenia is a prominent example of a psychotic disorder. Plural: *psychoses.*

Freud equated psychological health with the *abilities to love and to work*. The normal person can care deeply for other people, find sexual gratification in an intimate relationship, and engage in productive work. To accomplish these ends, there must be an opportunity for sexual impulses to be expressed in a relationship with a partner of the opposite gender. Other impulses must be channelled (sublimated) into socially productive pursuits, such as work, enjoyment of art or music, or creative expression. When some impulses are expressed directly and others are sublimated, the ego has a relatively easy time of it repressing those that remain in the boiling cauldron.

TABLE 2.3

Erikson's Psychosocial Stages

Psychosocial Stage	Period of Development	Description
Trust versus mistrust	Birth–1 year	With responsive care and love, infants learn to trust that the world is good. Mistrust occurs when infants experience inconsistent or harsh care.
Autonomy versus shame and doubt	1–3 years	Children develop autonomy when they are given opportunities to make appropriate choices. Otherwise, children become unsure about their ability to do things by themselves.
Initiative versus guilt	3–6 years	Children develop autonomy when they are ambitious and want to pursue their own tasks. If they are criticized, or not allowed to initiate activities, they feel stupid or as if they are wrong for trying.
Industry versus inferiority	6–11 years	Children want to do tasks well and develop a sense of competence. If their efforts are not encouraged by caregivers or teachers, they can feel inadequate.
Identity versus role confusion	Adolescence	Adolescents want to develop a sense of who they are and what their place is in society. Failure to develop self-determined values and social and vocational identities will leave them confused about the future roles they should play as adults.
Intimacy versus isolation	Young adulthood	The formation of strong friendships and commitment to loving and caring relationships is possible once people can comfortably share their identities with others. Avoiding close relationships can lead to loneliness and isolation.
Generativity versus stagnation	Middle adulthood	Contributing to the next generation or the common good becomes important. The alternative is turning inward and becoming self-centred or uninvolved.
Ego integrity versus despair	Late adulthood	Older adults reflect on the kind of life they have lived. If they can accept and feel satisfied that their lives were lives worth living, ego integrity results. If they are disappointed over lost opportunities and regrets, they may fear death and experience despair.

Other psychodynamic theorists, such as Jung and Adler, emphasized the need to develop a differentiated self—the unifying force that provides direction to behaviour and helps develop a person's potential. Adler also believed that psychological health involves efforts to compensate for feelings of inferiority by striving to excel in one or more of the arenas of human endeavour. For Mahler, similarly, abnormal behaviour derives from failure to separate ourselves from those we have psychologically brought within us. The notion of a guiding self provides bridges between psychodynamic theories and other theories, such as humanistic theories (which also speak of a self and the fulfillment of inner potential) and social-cognitive theory (which speaks in terms of self-regulatory processes).

Evaluating Psychodynamic Perspectives Psychodynamic theory has had a pervasive influence, not only on concepts of abnormal behaviour but more broadly on art, literature, philosophy, and the general culture. It has focused attention on our inner lives—our dreams, fantasies, and hidden motives. People unschooled in Freud habitually look for the symbolic meanings of each other's slips of the tongue and assume that abnormalities can be traced to early childhood. Terms like *ego* and *repression* have become commonplace, although their everyday meanings do not fully overlap with those intended by Freud.

One of the major contributions of the psychodynamic model was the increased awareness that people may be motivated by hidden drives and impulses of a sexual or aggressive nature. Freud's beliefs about childhood sexuality were both illuminating and controversial. Before Freud, children were perceived as *pure innocents*, free of sexual desire. Freud recognized, however, that young children, even infants, seek pleasure through stimulation of the oral and anal cavities and the phallic region. Yet his beliefs that primitive drives give rise to incestuous desires, intrafamily rivalries and conflicts, and castration anxiety and penis envy remain sources of controversy, even within psychodynamic circles. For one thing, these processes are deemed to occur largely if not entirely at an unconscious level and so are difficult if not impossible to study, let alone validate, by scientific means. For another, little evidence supports even the existence of the Oedipus and Electra complexes, let alone their universality (Kupfersmid, 1995).

Freud's views of female psychosexual development have been roundly attacked by women and modern-day psychoanalysts. One of the most prominent critics, the psychoanalyst Karen Horney, for example, argued that evidence of penis envy is not confirmed by observations of children and that Freud's view reflects the cultural prejudice in Western society against women. To Horney, cultural expectations played a greater role in shaping women's self-images in his day and time. In Freud's day, motherhood and family life were, by and large, the only socially proper avenues of fulfillment for women. Today, the choices available to women are more varied, and normality is not conceptualized in terms of rigidly defined gender roles.

Many critics, including some of Freud's followers, believe he placed too much emphasis on sexual and aggressive impulses and underemphasized social relationships. Critics have also argued that the psychic structures—the id, ego, and superego—may be little more than useful fictions, poetic ways to represent inner conflict. Sir Karl Popper (as cited in Goleman, 1985) argued that Freud's hypothetical mental processes are not scientific concepts because they cannot be directly observed or tested. Therapists can speculate, for example, that a client "forgot" about an appointment because "unconsciously" she or he did not want to attend the session. Such unconscious motivation is not subject to scientific verification, however.

Yet for all the criticism and skepticism directed at psychoanalytic theory, new research shows support for some of Freud's specific predictions and claims. For example, modern cognitive psychology has confirmed that through repetition, our behaviour can become automatic and as a consequence we perform many everyday tasks with minimal conscious awareness (Power, 2000). *Neuropsychological* studies are also helping us to better understand conscious and unconscious mental processes and how early life experiences can influence one's susceptibility to abnormal behaviour (Etkin, Egner, Peraza, Kandel, & Hirsch, 2006; Muris, 2006; Snodgrass, Bernat, & Shevrin, 2004; Stein, Solms, & van Honk, 2006). Cognitive science provides a contemporary description of Freud's notion of *repression*. For instance, Brewin and Andrews (2000) describe how forgetting is both an active and a selective process and it follows that normal memory processes involve both the filtering and exclusion of material from conscious awareness. Research by Andersen and Miranda (2000) has shown another example of how early childhood experiences have effects lasting into adulthood. In particular, *transference* (see the section on psychodynamic therapies later in this chapter) not only has clinical implications, it is a common social experience whereby inferences we make about a new person we meet are biased by emotionally laden mental representations of a significant other person from our lives. In effect, when we meet a new person that reminds us of a significant other we may relate to the new person as we would to the significant other. James Reason (2000) suggests that although a majority of slips of the tongue are related to force of habit and sound or language errors, Freud's explanation was at least partially right. In some cases, slips of the tongue are indeed associated with repressed fears or desires. To the extent that a slip of the tongue reflects unconscious intentions, it would be considered a *Freudian slip*. Aspects of Freud's theory about dreams have support from recent neuropsychological research that shows a close link between brain structures associated with dreaming and those that are organized around primitive biological emotions and motivations (Peterson, Henke, & Hayes, 2002; Solms, 2000).

Today, many of Freud's insights about human behaviour are being subsumed into the nomenclature and research protocols of other branches of psychology, especially cognitive psychology and neuropsychology. As Canadian neuropsychoanalyst Norman Doidge (2006) remarked on the occasion of Freud's 150th birthday in 2006, Freud began his medical career as a neurologist and originally penned a manuscript called the "project" in which his goal was to unite the science of the mind with the biology of the brain. Freud, realizing the limitations of the knowledge of the brain in his day, instead went on to develop his grand theory of the mind: psychoanalysis. With the availability of today's neuroimaging techniques, we are at the point where we can finish off what Freud started a century earlier (Doidge, 2006; Kandel, 1999; Solms, 2004).

Learning Perspectives

Psychodynamic models of Freud and his followers were the first major psychological theories of abnormal behaviour, but other relevant psychologies were also taking shape early in the 20th century. Among the most important was the behavioural perspective or **behaviourism**, which is identified with contributions by the Russian physiologist Ivan Pavlov (1849–1936), the discoverer of the conditioned reflex, and the American psychologists John B. Watson (1878–1958) and B. F. Skinner (1904–1990). The behavioural perspective focuses on the role of learning in explaining both normal and abnormal behaviour. From a learning perspective, abnormal behaviour represents the acquisition or learning of inappropriate, maladaptive behaviours. Abnormal behaviour can also be described in terms of not learning or underlearning appropriate, adaptive behaviours.

From the medical and psychodynamic perspectives, abnormal behaviour is *symptomatic*, respectively, of underlying biological or psychological problems. From the learning perspective, however, abnormal behaviour need not be symptomatic of anything. The abnormal behaviour itself is the problem. Abnormal behaviour is regarded as learned in much the same way as normal behaviour. Why, then, do some people behave abnormally? One reason is found in situational factors: Their learning histories, that is, might differ from most people's. For example, harsh punishment for early exploratory behaviour, such as childhood sexual exploration in the form of masturbation, might give rise to adult anxieties over autonomy or sexuality. Poor child-rearing practices, as shown by a lack of praise or rewards for good behaviour and harsh and capricious punishment of misconduct, might give rise to antisocial behaviour. Then, too, children with abusive or neglectful parents might learn to pay more attention to inner fantasies than to the world outside, giving rise, at worst, to difficulty in separating reality from fantasy.

Watson and other behaviourists, such as B. F. Skinner, believed that human behaviour is basically the product of genetic endowment and environmental or situational influences. Like Freud, Watson and Skinner discarded concepts of personal freedom, choice, and self-direction. But whereas Freud saw us as driven by irrational unconscious forces, behaviourists see us as products of environmental influences that shape and manipulate our behaviour. To Watson and Skinner, even the belief that we have free will is determined by the environment, just as surely as is learning to raise our hands in class before speaking. Behaviourists focus on the roles of two major forms of learning in shaping normal and abnormal behaviour: classical conditioning and operant conditioning.

Role of Classical Conditioning

Pavlov discovered the conditioned reflex (now called a *conditioned response*) quite by accident. In his laboratory, he harnessed dogs to an apparatus like that in Figure 2.7 on page 61 to study their salivary response to food. Yet he observed that the animals would start salivating and secreting gastric juices even before they started eating. These responses appeared to be elicited by the sounds made by his laboratory assistants when they wheeled in the food cart. So Pavlov undertook a clever experimental program that showed that animals could learn to salivate to other stimuli, such as the sound of a bell, if these stimuli were *associated* with feeding.

Because dogs don't normally salivate to the sound of bells, Pavlov reasoned that they had acquired this response, called a **conditioned response** (CR) or conditioned reflex, because it had been paired with a stimulus, called an **unconditioned stimulus** (US)—in this case, food—which naturally elicits salivation (see Figure 2.8). The salivation to food, an unlearned response, is called the **unconditioned response** (UR), and the bell, a previously neutral stimulus, is called the **conditioned stimulus** (CS). Can you recognize classical conditioning in your everyday life? Do you flinch in the waiting room at the sound of the dentist's drill? The drill sounds may be conditioned stimuli for conditioned responses of fear and muscle tension.

Phobias or excessive fears may be acquired by classical conditioning. For instance, a person may develop a phobia for riding on elevators following a traumatic experience while riding on an elevator. In this example, a previously neutral stimulus (elevator) becomes paired or associated with an aversive stimulus (trauma), which leads to the conditioned response (phobia). From the learning perspective, normal behaviour involves responding adaptively to

behaviourism School of psychology that defines psychology as the study of observable or overt behaviour and focuses on investigating the relationships between stimuli and responses.

conditioned response (1) In classical conditioning, a learned or acquired response to a previously neutral stimulus. (2) A response to a conditioned stimulus. Abbreviated *CR.*

unconditioned stimulus Stimulus that elicits an instinctive or unlearned response from an organism. Abbreviated *US* or *UCS.*

unconditioned response Unlearned response or a response to an unconditioned stimulus. Abbreviated *UR* or *UCR.*

conditioned stimulus Previously neutral stimulus that comes to evoke a conditioned response following repeated pairings with a stimulus (unconditioned stimulus) that had already evoked that response. Abbreviated *CS.*

FIGURE 2.7 The apparatus used in Ivan Pavlov's experiments on conditioning.
Pavlov used an apparatus such as this to demonstrate the process of conditioning. To the left is a two-way mirror, behind which a researcher rings a bell. After ringing the bell, meat is placed on the dog's tongue. Following several pairings of the bell and the meat, the dog learns to salivate in response to the bell. The animal's saliva passes through the tube to a vial, where its quantity may be taken as a measure of the strength of the conditioned response.

stimuli—including conditioned stimuli. After all, if we do not learn to be afraid of drawing our hand too close to a hot stove after one or two experiences of being burned or nearly burned, we might suffer unnecessary burns. On the other hand, acquiring inappropriate and maladaptive fears on the basis of conditioning may cripple our efforts to function in the world. Chapter 5, "Anxiety Disorders," explains how conditioning may help explain anxiety disorders such as phobias and **posttraumatic stress disorder**.

In later years, Pavlov's interest turned to the study of the psychophysiology of personality. Pavlov conceptualized personality in terms of excitatory and inhibitory responses that influenced later personality theorists Hans Eysenck and Jeffrey Gray (Corr, 2004). We will discuss Reinforcement Sensitivity Theory (RST) in Chapter 8, "Personality Disorders."

Role of Operant Conditioning Operant conditioning involves the acquisition of behaviours, called *operant behaviours*, that are emitted by an organism and that operate upon or manipulate the environment to produce certain effects. The psychologist B. F. Skinner (1938) showed that food-deprived pigeons would learn to peck buttons when food pellets drop into their cages as a result. It takes a while for the birds to happen on the first peck, but after a few repetitions of the button pecking to food association, pecking behaviour, an operant response, becomes fast and furious until the pigeons have had their fill.

In operant conditioning, organisms acquire responses or skills that lead to **reinforcement**. Reinforcers are changes in the environment (stimuli) that increase the frequency of the preceding behaviour.

Positive reinforcers boost the frequency of behaviour when they are presented. Food, money, social approval, and the opportunity to mate are examples of positive reinforcers. **Negative reinforcers** increase the frequency of behaviour when they are removed. Fear, pain, discomfort, and social disapproval are examples of negative reinforcers. We learn responses that lead to their removal (like learning to turn on the air conditioner to remove unpleasant heat and humidity from a room).

Adaptive, normal behaviour involves learning responses or skills that permit us to obtain positive reinforcers and escape or avoid negative reinforcers. Thus, we learn adaptive behaviours that permit us to obtain such positive reinforcers as money, food, and social approval, and to escape or avoid such negative reinforcers as fear, pain, and social condemnation. But if our early learning environments do not provide opportunities for learning new skills, we might be hampered in our efforts to develop the skills needed to obtain reinforcers. A lack of social skills, for example, may reduce opportunities for social reinforcement (approval or praise from others), especially when a person withdraws from social situations. This may lead to depression and social isolation. In Chapter 7, "Mood Disorders and Suicide," we examine links between changes in reinforcement levels and the development of depression.

We can also differentiate *primary* and *secondary* or conditioned reinforcers. **Primary reinforcers** influence behaviour because they satisfy basic physical needs. We do not learn to respond to these basic reinforcers; we are born with that capacity. Food, water, sexual

posttraumatic stress disorder Type of anxiety disorder involving impaired functioning following exposure to a traumatic experience, such as combat, physical assault or rape, or natural or technological disasters, in which a person experiences such problems as reliving or re-experiencing the trauma, intense fear, avoidance of event-related stimuli, generalized numbing of emotional responsiveness, and heightened autonomic arousal.

reinforcement Stimulus that increases the frequency of the response it follows. See *positive* and *negative* and *primary* and *secondary* reinforcers.

positive reinforcers Types of reinforcers that increase the frequency of a behaviour when they are presented. Food and social approval are generally, but not always, positive reinforcers. Contrast with *negative reinforcer*.

negative reinforcers Reinforcers whose removal increases the frequency of an operant behaviour. Anxiety, pain, and social disapproval often function as negative reinforcers; that is, their removal tends to increase the rate of the immediately preceding behaviour. Contrast with *positive reinforcer*.

primary reinforcers Natural reinforcers or stimuli that have reinforcement value without learning. Water, food, warmth, and relief from pain are examples of primary reinforcers. Contrast with *secondary reinforcers*.

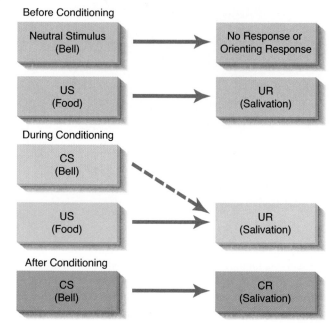

Before Conditioning

| Neutral Stimulus (Bell) | → | No Response or Orienting Response |
| US (Food) | → | UR (Salivation) |

During Conditioning

| CS (Bell) | ⤏ | |
| US (Food) | → | UR (Salivation) |

After Conditioning

| CS (Bell) | → | CR (Salivation) |

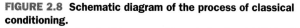

FIGURE 2.8 Schematic diagram of the process of classical conditioning.

Before conditioning, food (an unconditioned stimulus or US) that is placed on a dog's tongue will naturally elicit salivation (an unconditioned response or UR). The bell, however, is a neutral stimulus that may elicit an orienting response but not salivation. During conditioning, the bell (the conditioned stimulus, CS) is rung while food (the US) is placed on the dog's tongue. After several conditioning trials have occurred, the bell (the CS) will elicit salivation (the conditioned response or CR) when it is rung, even though it is not accompanied by food (the US). The dog is said to have been conditioned or to have learned to display the conditioned response (CR) in response to the conditioned stimulus (CS). Learning theorists have suggested that irrational excessive fears of harmless stimuli may be acquired through principles of classical conditioning.

secondary reinforcers Stimuli that gain reinforcement value through their association with established reinforcers. Money and social approval are typically secondary reinforcers. Contrast with *primary reinforcer*.

punishments Unpleasant stimuli that suppress the frequency of the behaviours they follow.

positive punishers Types of punishers that decrease the frequency of behaviour when they are presented. Physical aggression and social disapproval are generally, but not always, positive punishers. Contrast with *negative punishers*.

negative punishers Types of punishers that decrease the frequency of behaviour when they are taken away. Removal of negative punishers, such as treats, opportunity to play, and social approval, tends to decrease the rate of the immediately preceding behaviour. Contrast with *positive punishers*.

stimulation, and escape from pain are examples of primary reinforcers. **Secondary reinforcers** influence behaviour through their association with established reinforcers. Thus, we learn to respond to secondary reinforcers. People learn to seek money—a secondary reinforcer—because it can be exchanged for primary reinforcers like food and heat (or air conditioning).

Punishments are aversive stimuli that decrease or suppress the frequency of the preceding behaviour when they are applied. Negative reinforcers, by contrast, increase the frequency of the preceding behaviour when they are removed. A loud noise, for example, can be either a punishment (if by its introduction the probability of the preceding behaviour decreases) or a negative reinforcer (if by its removal the probability of the preceding behaviour increases).

Positive punishers reduce the frequency of behaviour when they are presented. Hitting, yelling, scolding, and social disapproval are examples of positive punishers. **Negative punishers**

Ivan Pavlov. Here, Russian physiologist Ivan Pavlov (the bearded man in the centre) demonstrates his apparatus for classical conditioning to students. How might the principles of classical conditioning explain the acquisition of excessive irrational fears that we refer to as phobias?

decrease the frequency of behaviour when they are removed. The removal of enjoyable activities or the use of **time-out** are examples of negative punishers. Negative punishment can be considered a form of **extinction**.

Punishment, especially physical aggression, may suppress but not eliminate undesirable behaviour. The behaviour may return when the punishment is withdrawn. One limitation of punishment is that it does not lead to the development of more desirable alternative behaviours. Another is that it may also encourage people to withdraw from such learning situations. Punished children may cut classes, drop out of school, or run away. Punishment may generate anger and hostility rather than constructive learning. Finally, because people also learn by observation, punishment may become imitated as a means for solving interpersonal problems.

Reinforcing desirable behaviour is thus generally preferable to punishing misbehaviour. But reinforcing appropriate behaviour requires paying attention to it, and not just to misbehaviour. Some children who develop conduct problems can gain the attention of other people only by misbehaving. They learn that by acting out, others will pay attention to them. For them, getting scolded may actually serve as a positive reinforcer, increasing the rate of response of the behaviour it follows. Learning theorists point out that it is not sufficient to expect good conduct from children. Instead, adults need to teach children proper behaviour and regularly reinforce them for performing it.

B. F. Skinner.

Evaluating Learning Perspectives   One of the principal values of learning models, in contrast to psychodynamic approaches, is their emphasis on observable behaviour and environmental factors, such as reinforcers and punishments, which can be systematically manipulated to observe their effects on behaviour. Learning perspectives have spawned a major model of therapy called **behaviour therapy** (also called *behaviour modification*), which involves the systematic application of learning principles to help people make adaptive behavioural changes. Behaviour therapy techniques have been applied to helping people overcome a wide range of psychological problems including phobias and other anxiety disorders, sexual dysfunctions, and depression. Moreover, reinforcement-based programs are now widely used in helping parents learn better parenting skills and helping children learn in the classroom.

Critics contend that behaviourism cannot explain the richness of human behaviour and that human experience cannot be reduced to observable responses. Many learning theorists, too—especially social-cognitive theorists—have been dissatisfied with the strict behaviouristic view that environmental influences—reinforcements and punishments—mechanically control our behaviour. Humans experience thoughts and dreams and formulate goals and aspirations; behaviourism seems not to address much of what it means to be human.

time-out Procedures that deny the opportunity to receive reinforcement for a specific period of time.

extinction The gradual reduction of a behaviour through repeated non-reinforcement.

behaviour therapy A learning-based model of therapy.

Humanistic-Existential Perspectives

A "third force" in modern psychology emerged during the mid-20th century—humanistic-existential psychology. Humanistic theorists such as psychologists Carl Rogers (1902–1987) and Abraham Maslow (1908–1970) believed that human behaviour cannot be explained as the product of either unconscious conflicts or simple conditioning. Rejecting the determinism implicit in these theories, they saw people as *actors* in the drama of life, not *reactors* to instinctual or environmental pressures. They focused on the importance of subjective conscious experience and self-direction. Humanistic psychology is closely linked with the school of European philosophy called *existentialism*. The existentialists, notably the philosophers Martin Heidegger (1889–1976) and Jean-Paul Sartre (1905–1980), focused on the search for meaning and the importance of choice in human existence. Along with our freedom to choose, existentialists believe our humanness makes us responsible for the directions our lives will take.

Carl Rogers. One of the principal forces in humanistic psychology.

Each of us possesses a singular cluster of traits and talents that gives rise to an individual set of feelings and needs and grants us a unique perspective on life. The humanists maintain that people have an inborn tendency toward *self-actualization*—to strive to become all they are capable of being. The existentialists contend that despite the finality of death, we can each fill our lives with meaning and purpose if we recognize and accept our genuine needs and feelings. By being true to ourselves, we live *authentically*. We may not decide to act out every wish and fancy, but self-awareness of authentic feelings and subjective experiences can help us make more meaningful choices.

To understand abnormal behaviour, in the humanist-existentialist's view, we need to understand the roadblocks that people encounter in striving for self-actualization and authenticity. To accomplish this, psychologists must learn to view the world from clients' own perspectives because their subjective views of their world lead them to interpret and evaluate their experiences in either self-enhancing or self-defeating ways. The humanistic-existential viewpoint is sometimes called the *phenomenological* perspective because it involves the attempt to understand the subjective or phenomenological experience of others—the stream of conscious experiences people have of "being in the world."

Humanistic Concepts of Abnormal Behaviour Rogers developed the most influential humanistic account of abnormal behaviour (Rogers, 1951). His central belief was that abnormal behaviour results from the development of a distorted concept of the self. When parents show children **conditional positive regard**—accept them only when they behave in an approved manner—children may learn to disown the thoughts, feelings, and behaviours their parents have rejected. With conditional positive regard, children may learn to develop **conditions of worth**, to think of themselves as worthwhile only if they behave in certain approved ways. For example, children who are valued by their parents only when they are compliant may deny to themselves ever having feelings of anger. Children in some families learn it is unacceptable to hold their own ideas, lest they depart from their parents' views. Parental disapproval causes them to see themselves as rebels and their feelings as wrong, selfish, or evil. If they wish to retain self-esteem, they may have to deny many or most of their genuine feelings or disown parts of themselves. They may thus develop a distorted self-concept or view of themselves and become strangers to their true selves.

Rogers believed anxiety might arise from the partial perception of feelings and ideas that are inconsistent or discrepant with one's distorted self-concept. Because anxiety is unpleasant, we may deny to ourselves that these feelings and ideas even exist. And so the actualization of our authentic self is stifled by the denial of important ideas and emotions. Psychological energy is channelled toward continued denial and self-defence, not growth. Under such conditions, we cannot hope to perceive our genuine values or personal talents, leading to frustration and setting the stage for abnormal behaviour.

So, we cannot fulfill all of the wishes of others and remain true to ourselves. This does not mean that self-actualization invariably leads to conflict. Rogers was more optimistic about human nature than Freud. Rogers believed that people hurt one another or become antisocial in their behaviour only when they are frustrated in their endeavours to reach their unique potentials. But when parents and others treat children with love and tolerance for their differences, children, too, grow to be loving—even if some of their values and preferences differ from their parents' choices. In Rogers's view, the pathway to self-actualization involves a process of self-discovery and self-acceptance, of getting in touch with our true feelings, accepting them as our own, and acting in ways that genuinely reflect them. These are the goals of Rogers's method of psychotherapy, called *person-centred therapy*.

A Neo-Humanistic Perspective Psychologist Leslie Greenberg of York University has been at the forefront of advancing the *humanistic approach*, which has been influenced by contemporary developments in the areas of neuroscience and cognitive theory. A key feature of his neo-humanistic approach is that it attempts to reconcile the theoretical differences between the major psychological theories we have discussed so far in this chapter. For example, Greenberg (2002a, 2002b) views humans as being comprised of multiple facets—emotions, motivations, cognitions, and actions—and each is of value for survival. In comparison, the different psychological theories have traditionally emphasized that one domain of human functioning is superior to the others (Greenberg & Safran, 1987; Elliot et al., 2004; Greenberg, 2002a, 2002b). This theoretical competition has created major theoretical dilemmas by pitting emotions against reason, conscious against unconscious processes, conformity against self-determination, and mind against both behaviour and biology, to name a few. Accordingly, each theory has given rise to divergent therapeutic approaches but, despite their serious differences, they all have a common therapeutic goal: they all attempt to regulate and minimize undesirable emotions (Greenberg, 2002a, 2002b). Instead of merely reducing unpleasant emotions, Greenberg's theory embraces the notion that emotions—both pleasant and unpleasant—serve essential adaptive purposes and should therefore be heeded. For example, emotions have survival value when they warn us of potentially dangerous situations, aid us in interpersonal communications (especially nonverbal), and enhance learning by arousing attention and motivation. To suppress or radically modify our emotions is to deny ourselves this important survival function.

The cornerstone of this approach is our **emotional intelligence**. Emotional intelligence dictates how well we experience and express our emotions in a purposeful way to cope with life. Strengthening our emotional intelligence leads to well-being, and this is the premise for a neo-humanistic therapy referred to as emotion-focused therapy (EFT).

Evaluating Humanistic-Existential Perspectives The strengths of humanistic-existential perspectives in understanding abnormal behaviour lie largely in their focus on conscious experience and their innovation of therapy methods that assist people along pathways of self-discovery, self-acceptance, and self-determination. The humanistic-existential movement put concepts of purpose, free choice, inherent goodness, responsibility, and authenticity back on centre stage and brought them into modern psychology. Ironically, the primary strength of the humanistic-existential approach—its focus on conscious experience—may also be its primary weakness. Conscious experience is private and subjective. Therefore, the validity of formulating theories in terms of consciousness has been questioned. How can psychologists be certain they accurately perceive the world through the eyes of their clients?

Nor can the concept of self-actualization—which is so basic to Maslow and Rogers—be proved or disproved. Like a psychic structure, a self-actualizing force is not directly measurable or observable. It is inferred from its supposed effects. Self-actualization also yields circular explanations for behaviour. When someone is observed engaging in striving, what do we learn by attributing striving to a self-actualizing tendency? The source of the tendency remains a mystery. And when someone is observed not to be striving, what do we gain by attributing the lack of endeavour to a blocked or frustrated self-actualizing tendency? We must still determine the source of frustration or blockage.

There is now a Canadian initiative to study these types of issues. Founded in Langley, British Columbia, in 1998, the International Network on Personal Meaning (INPM) is an organization of 300 members in 30 countries dedicated to the scientific research and advancement of the role of meaning in our daily lives (Wong, 2002). This multidisciplinary society addresses our needs for health, spirituality, and community through scholarly and educational activities. The INPM has also spawned a professional branch of its organization to advance the role of existential psychology and therapy within psychology, the International Society for Existential Psychology and Psychotherapy (ISEPP, 2006), and it launched a peer-reviewed journal in 2004, *The International Journal for Existential Psychology and Psychotherapy*.

The neo-humanistic perspective already shows promise as a treatment approach that integrates elements of neuroscience with developmental, cognitive, psychodynamic, humanistic-existential, and learning theory. Critics suggest that neo-humanistic intervention is best suited for personal growth and development and, indeed, Greenberg (2002a) agrees that it is inappropriate for acute conditions such as panic disorder or disorders of

emotional intelligence "The ability to perceive emotions, to access and generate emotions so as to assist thought, to understand emotions and emotional knowledge, and to reflectively regulate emotions so as to promote emotional and intellectual growth" (Mayer & Salovey, 1997).

impulse control. Nonetheless, it has been shown to be effective in the treatment of moderate depression, couples therapy, disorders related to childhood maltreatment and trauma, and interpersonal problems.

Cognitive-Behavioural Perspectives

In their attempt to turn psychology into a scientific discipline, the early behaviourists focused on outward measurable behaviour and denied the legitimacy of internal mental processes in human behaviour. But the pioneering Canadian psychologist Donald Hebb thought differently. He believed that "psychology without thought was unthinkable," notes Hebb's fellow McGill University psychologist, Peter Milner (Milner, 2006, p. 36). In *The Organization of Behavior*, Hebb (1949) outlined his pivotal theory describing how mental process could be explained by neural functioning, and this opened the way for cognition to become a worthy scientific field of study (Milner, 2006).

The word *cognitive* derives from the Latin *cognitio*, meaning "knowledge." Cognitive-behaviour theorists study the cognitions—the thoughts, beliefs, expectations, and attitudes—that accompany and may underlie abnormal behaviour. They focus on how reality is coloured by our expectations, attitudes, and so forth, and how inaccurate or biased processing of information about the world—and our place within it—can give rise to emotional difficulties and dysfunctional behaviours. Cognitive-behaviour theorists believe that our interpretations of the events in our lives, and not the events themselves, determine our emotional states and actions.

Albert Ellis Psychologist Albert Ellis (1913–2007) (1977, 1993, 2003) was a prominent cognitive-behaviour theorist who believed that troubling events in themselves do not lead to anxiety, depression, or disturbed behaviour. Rather, it is the irrational beliefs about unfortunate experiences that foster negative emotions and maladaptive behaviour. Consider someone who loses a job, becomes anxious and despondent about it, and spends the day just moping around the house. It may seem that being fired is the direct cause of the person's misery, but the misery actually stems from the person's beliefs about the loss and not directly from the loss itself.

Ellis used an "ABC approach" to explain the causes of the misery. Being fired is an *activating event* (A). The ultimate outcome or *consequence* (C) is a dysfunctional emotional, physiological, and behavioural response (Ellis, 2003; Harris, Davies, & Dryden, 2006). But the activating event (A) and the consequences (C) are mediated by various *beliefs* (B). Some of these beliefs might include, "That job was the major thing in my life"; "What a useless washout I am"; "My family will go hungry"; "I'll never be able to find another job as good"; or "I can't do a thing about it." These exaggerated and irrational beliefs compound depression, nurture helplessness, and distract us from evaluating what to do. For instance, the beliefs, "I can't do a thing about it" and "What a useless washout I am" promote helplessness.

The situation can be diagrammed like this:

Activating events → Beliefs → Consequences

catastrophize To exaggerate or magnify the negative consequences of events; to "blow things out of proportion."

Ellis emphasized that apprehension about the future and feelings of disappointment are perfectly normal when people face losses. However, the adoption of irrational beliefs leads people to **catastrophize** the magnitude of losses, leading to profound distress and states of depression. By intensifying emotional responses and nurturing feelings of helplessness, such beliefs impair coping ability.

Ellis asserted there are three core irrational beliefs held by many people worldwide:

1. "I must be thoroughly competent, adequate, achieving, and lovable at all times, or else I am an incompetent worthless person. . . ."
2. "Other significant people in my life must treat me kindly and fairly at all times, or else I can't stand it, and they are bad, rotten, and evil persons who should be severely blamed, damned, and vindictively punished for their horrible treatment of me. . . ."

3. "Things and conditions absolutely must be the way I want them to be and must never be too difficult or frustrating. Otherwise life is awful, terrible, horrible, catastrophic, and unbearable. . . ." (Ellis, 2003, pp. 236–237)

Ellis noted that the desire for others' approval is understandable, but it is irrational to assume you cannot survive without it. It would be marvellous to excel in everything we do, but it's absurd to demand it of ourselves. Sure, in tennis it would be great to serve and volley like a pro, but most people haven't the leisure time or aptitude to perfect the game. Insisting on perfection deters people from playing simply for fun.

Ellis developed a model of therapy called *rational-emotive behaviour therapy* (REBT) to help people dispute these conditioned habitual irrational beliefs and substitute more rational ones. Ellis admitted that childhood experiences are involved in the origins of irrational beliefs, but cognitive appraisal—the here and now—causes people misery. For most people who are anxious and depressed, the ticket to greater happiness does not lie in discovering and liberating deep-seated conflicts, but in recognizing and modifying irrational self-demands.

Aaron Beck   Another prominent cognitive theorist, psychiatrist Aaron Beck, proposes that depression may result from "cognitive errors" such as judging oneself entirely on the basis of one's flaws or failures and interpreting events in a negative light (as though wearing blue-coloured glasses) (A. T. Beck et al., 1979). Beck stresses the pervasive roles of four basic types of cognitive errors that contribute to emotional distress:

1. *Selective abstraction.* People may selectively abstract (focus exclusively on) the parts of their experiences that reflect on their flaws and ignore evidence of their competencies.
2. *Overgeneralization.* People may overgeneralize from a few isolated experiences. For example, they may see their futures as hopeless because they were laid off or believe they will never marry because they were rejected by a dating partner.
3. *Magnification.* People may blow out of proportion or magnify the importance of unfortunate events. Students may catastrophize a bad test grade by jumping to the conclusion that they will flunk out of college and their lives will be ruined.
4. *Absolutist thinking.* Absolutist thinking is seeing the world in black and white terms rather than in shades of grey. Absolutist thinkers may assume any grade less than a perfect "A," or a work evaluation less than a rave, is a total failure.

Like Ellis, Beck has developed a major model of therapy called *cognitive therapy* (now commonly referred to as cognitive behaviour therapy) that focuses on helping individuals with psychological disorders identify and correct faulty ways of thinking.

Social-cognitive theorists, who share much in common with the cognitive-behaviour theorists, focus on the ways in which social information is encoded. Let's now consider *social-cognitive theory*, which broadens the focus of both traditional behaviourist and cognitive theory by considering the role of social factors in learning and behaviour.

Albert Bandura   **Social-cognitive theory** represents the contributions of theorists such as Alberta-born Albert Bandura (Zimmerman, & Schunk, 2002). Social-cognitive theorists emphasize the roles of thinking or cognition and of learning by observation or modelling in human behaviour. For example, social-cognitive theorists suggest that phobias may be learned *vicariously*, by observing the fearful reactions of others in real life or shown on television or in movies.

Social-cognitive theorists also view people as impacting on their environment, just as the environment impacts on them. They see people as self-aware and purposeful learners who seek information about their environment, who do not just respond automatically to the stimuli that impinge on them. For example, Bandura (1986, 1989, 2001) uses the term **reciprocal determinism** to describe how a person's behaviour both acts upon

social-cognitive theory A broader view of learning theory that emphasizes both situational determinants of behaviour (reinforcements and punishments) and cognitive factors (expectancies, values, attitudes, beliefs, etc.).

reciprocal determinism The ongoing process of two-way interactions among personal factors (cognitive abilities—expectancies, values, attitudes, and beliefs, as well as affective and biological characteristics), behaviours (skills, talents, habits, and interpersonal relations), and environmental factors (physical surroundings and other people).

Aaron Beck. One of the leading cognitive theorists.

and is influenced by one's personal and environmental factors. For example, if you were lost and approached someone for help, you may elicit a different reaction from the stranger depending on whether you came across as friendly versus fearful or threatening. In turn, the stranger's reaction to your request for help might, in part, be influenced by his or her interpretation of your intentions based on your behaviour. As well, the circumstances play a role, too—the intentions of a smiling stranger may be viewed quite differently on a dimly lit street corner than in a shopping mall.

Social-cognitive theorists concur with traditional behaviourists that theories of human nature should be tied to observable behaviour. They assert, however, that factors *within* a person should also be considered in explaining human behaviour. For example, behaviour cannot be predicted from situational factors alone (Rotter, 1972). Whether or not people behave in certain ways also depends on certain cognitive factors, such as the person's **expectancies** about the outcomes of behaviour. For example, we see in Chapter 9 that people who hold more positive expectancies about the outcomes of using drugs are more likely to use them and to use them in larger quantities.

expectancies In social-cognitive theory, a personal variable describing people's predictions of future outcomes.

Donald Meichenbaum
University of Waterloo professor emeritus Donald Meichenbaum is a cofounder of cognitive-behavioural modification (CBM). Like the other cognitive behaviourists, Meichenbaum's (1976, 1977) perspective considers the interdependence of thoughts, emotions, and actions (interpersonal in particular). Aggressive boys and adolescents, for example, are likely to incorrectly encode other people's behaviour as threatening (see Chapter 13, "Abnormal Behaviour in Childhood and Adolescence"). They assume other people intend them ill when they do not. Aggressive children and adults may behave in ways that elicit coercive or hostile behaviour from others, which serves to confirm their aggressive expectations (Meichenbaum, 1993). Information may also be distorted by what cognitive-behaviour therapists call *cognitive distortions* or errors in thinking. For example, people who are depressed tend to develop an unduly negative view of their personal situation by exaggerating the importance of unfortunate events they experience (Meichenbaum, 1993). From Meichenbaum's perspective, behavioural interventions can be used to initiate change anywhere along the chain of cognitive, affective, and behavioural events.

Evaluating Cognitive-Behavioural Perspectives
As we'll see in later chapters, cognitive-behavioural theorists have had an enormous impact on our understanding of abnormal behaviour patterns and development of therapeutic approaches. The overlap between the learning-based and cognitive approaches is best represented by the emergence of cognitive-behavioural therapy (CBT), a form of therapy that focuses on modifying self-defeating beliefs in addition to overt behaviours.

A major issue concerning cognitive-behavioural perspectives is their range of applicability. Cognitive-behavioural therapists have largely focused on emotional disorders relating to anxiety and depression but have had less impact on the development of treatment approaches or conceptual models of more severe forms of disturbed behaviour, such as schizophrenia. Moreover, in the case of depression, it remains unclear, as we see in Chapter 7, to what extent distorted thinking patterns are causes of depression or merely effects of depression.

STUDY BREAK

Psychological Perspectives

Review It

• **What are the major psychological perspectives on abnormal behaviour?** Psychodynamic perspectives reflect the views of Freud and his followers, who believed that abnormal behaviour stems from psychological causes involving underlying psychic forces within the personality. Learning theorists posit that the principles of learning can be used to explain both abnormal and normal behaviour.

Humanistic-existential theorists believe it is important to understand the obstacles that people encounter as they strive toward self-actualization and authenticity. Cognitive-behavioural theorists focus on the role of distorted and self-defeating thinking in explaining abnormal behaviour.

Define It

psychoanalytic theory	analytical psychology
conscious	collective unconscious
preconscious	archetypes
unconscious	inferiority complex
structural hypothesis	drive to superiority
psychic	creative self
id	individual psychology
pleasure principle	neo-Freudians
primary process thinking	ego psychology
ego	ego analysts
reality principle	object-relations theory
secondary process	introjection
thinking	psychosis
superego	behaviourism
identification	conditioned response
moral principle	unconditioned stimulus
ego ideal	unconditioned response
defence mechanisms	conditioned stimulus
repression	posttraumatic stress
psychoanalysis	disorder
libido	reinforcement
erogenous zone	positive reinforcers
psychosexual	negative reinforcers
oral stage	primary reinforcers
weaning	secondary reinforcers
fixation	punishments
anal stage	positive punishers
anal fixation	negative punishers
anal retentive	time-out
anal expulsive	extinction
phallic stage	behaviour therapy
Oedipus complex	conditional positive
Electra complex	regard
gender roles	conditions of worth
castration anxiety	emotional intelligence
latency stage	catastrophize
genital stage	social-cognitive theory
pregenital	reciprocal determinism
	expectancies

Recall It*

1. In Freud's theory, the _____ is the part of the mind that holds wishes and impulses that remain hidden from awareness.

    a. conscious
    b. superconscious
    c. preconscious
    d. unconscious

2. According to Freud, the part of the mind that plans ways of satisfying basic impulses in socially acceptable ways is called the _____.

    a. id
    b. ego
    c. superego
    d. conscious self

3. To Jung, the _____ represents the accumulated experiences of humankind that are passed down through our genes.

    a. personal unconscious
    b. collective unconscious
    c. anima
    d. animus

4. A leader of the humanistic movement in psychology was _____.

    a. Albert Ellis
    b. Albert Bandura
    c. Walter Mischel
    d. Carl Rogers

5. Cognitive-behaviourist theorists emphasize the role of _____ in shaping personality.

    a. biological influences
    b. thinking patterns
    c. classical conditioning
    d. self-actualization

* Recall It answers can be found on the Companion Website for this text.

Think About It

- Underlying the psychodynamic approach is the belief that we are not usually aware of the deeper motives and impulses that drive our behaviour. Do you agree? Why or why not? Can you think of examples of behaviours in others (or yourself) in which defence mechanisms may have played a role?
- How is your present behaviour influenced by your learning history? What learning principles (classical conditioning and operant conditioning) can you use to account for your behaviour—normal or abnormal?
- Whom would you consider to be a self-actualizer? What about yourself? Are you a self-actualizer? Why or why not?
- Can you think of examples from your personal life in which your thinking style reflected one or more of

the cognitive distortions identified by Beck—selective abstraction, overgeneralization, magnification, or absolutist thinking? What effects did these thought patterns have on your moods? On your level of motivation? Do you think you can change how you think about your experiences? Why or why not?

SOCIOCULTURAL PERSPECTIVES

To what extent does abnormal behaviour arise from forces within a person as the psychodynamic theorists propose, or from the learning of maladaptive behaviours, as the learning theorists suggest? The sociocultural perspective informs us that a fuller accounting of abnormal behaviour requires that we also consider the impact of social and cultural factors, including factors relating to ethnicity, gender and social roles, and poverty. Sociocultural theorists seek causes of abnormal behaviour that may reside in the failures of society rather than in the person. Some of the more radical psychosocial theorists we discussed in Chapter 1, like Thomas Szasz and Gordon Warme, even deny the existence of psychological disorders or mental illness, believing abnormal behaviour is merely a label that society attaches to people who act differently in order to stigmatize and subjugate them.

Still others, such as Acadia University community psychologist Patrick O'Neil (2004), say it is important to keep the focus on dysfunctional social systems rather than on an individual's dysfunction when dealing with social problems. O'Neil cautions that it is easy for social researchers to inadvertently divert their attention toward an individual's "problem" rather than on the social causes of that problem, and doing so contributes to a "blame the victim" mentality. For example, if we were to consider the problem of drug abuse from a sociocultural perspective, we should focus on the social structures that underlie substance abuse problems instead of the personal characteristics or "failings" of the drug addict. The former requires sweeping social changes that, for example, would reduce poverty and improve living conditions. The latter perpetuates interventions that deal with the problem of drug dependence one drug user or one drug dealer at a time.

Evaluating Sociocultural Perspectives

As you recall from the discussion of homelessness in Chapter 1, low-income Canadians experience higher rates of mental health problems than the rest of society. The reasons why are not easy to determine. One line of thinking suggests that poverty gives rise to mental illness. Psychosocial stress resulting from chronic unemployment, financial difficulties, or inadequate housing can create a sense of futility or emotional upset that may lead to the development of mental illness (Health Canada, 2002a). Additionally, low-income Canadians have less access to mental health counselling opportunities than higher-income individuals, and this creates a further barrier to getting well (Health Canada, 1999a).

downward drift hypothesis The belief that people with psychological problems may drift downward in socioeconomic status.

An alternative view is the **downward drift hypothesis**, which suggests that mental illness leads to poverty. According to this perspective, having a mental illness makes it difficult to hold down a well-paying job. The lack of gainful employment may lead people to drift downward in social status, thereby explaining the linkage between low socioeconomic status and severe behaviour problems (Canadian Health Network, 1999a).

Yet another view posits that the connections are not so simple. There may be one or more other variables that influence both poverty and mental illness, such as discrimination, dysfunctional family relationships, interpersonal conflict, or a lack of social-support networks.

Certainly it is desirable for social critics such as Szasz to rivet our attention on the political implications of our responses to deviance. The views of Szasz and other critics of the mental health establishment have been influential in bringing about much needed changes to better protect the rights of mental patients in psychiatric institutions. Many professionals, however, believe the more radical sociocultural theorists like Szasz go too far in arguing that mental illness is merely a fabrication invented by society to stigmatize social deviants.

All in all, the sociocultural theorists have focused much needed attention on the social stressors that may lead to abnormal behaviour. Throughout the text we consider how sociocultural factors relating to gender, race, ethnicity, and lifestyle better inform our understanding of abnormal behaviour and our response to people deemed mentally ill. Later in this chapter we consider how issues relating to race, culture, and ethnicity impact the therapeutic process.

A CLOSER LOOK

Canadian Mental Health Promotion

Mental health is the expressed means to think, feel, act, and relate in ways that allow us to carry out everyday tasks plus have extra resources to cope with opportunities and challenges. Mental health is one of the quality-of-life measures that lie on a continuum ranging from nominal to optimal (Alberta Mental Health Board [AMHB], 2001; Canadian Mental Health Association [CMHA], n.d.; Kahan & Goodstadt, 2002; Stephens, Dulberg, & Joubert, 1999; World Health Organization [WHO], 2001).

Personal and Social Costs of Poor Mental Health

While most Canadians would agree that mental health care is a priority, the true extent and cost of poor mental health has been underestimated (Stephens & Joubert, 2001; Canadian Alliance on Mental Illness and Mental Health [CAMIMH], 2000; Prevention-Dividend Project, 2003). Measures of nonmedical services and of short-term disability are excluded because large numbers of Canadians seek treatment outside of the medical system. Specifically, direct costs related to visits to nonmedical mental health professionals are not fully accounted for. Indirect costs, including lost days of work, lowered productivity, and the drain on other resources (such as family and co-workers) are even harder to track. When morbidity and mortality issues are factored into the equation, poor mental health is one of the costliest health conditions in Canada (CAMIMH, 2000), with the conservative estimated cost of treatment to be over $14 billion annually (Stephens & Joubert, 2001).

Risk Factors

In a recent major Canadian study of mental health, Stephens, Dulberg, and Joubert (1999) determined that key risk factors include age, education, childhood traumas, current stress, life events, social supports, gender, and physical health. To confound matters, exposure to multiple risk factors can have an exponential effect that dramatically increases the likelihood of adverse outcomes

(Masten, 2001). Exposure to just two risk factors can engender a four-fold increase in adverse outcomes, and four or more risk factors can increase adversity ten-fold (Rutter, 1999; Luthar & Cicchetti, 2000). In addition to acting synergistically, risk factors can also generate a negative chain reaction whereby exposure to new risks perpetuates and intensifies existing problems.

This can set into motion a self-reinforcing negative spiral (Stephens, Dulberg, & Joubert, 1999; Baylis, 2002). Individually, risk factors do not present a high probability of psychopathology, but have a strong effect in combination. Multiple risk factors greatly increase the likelihood of adverse outcomes (Masten, 2001).

Prevention and Resilience

Prevention efforts focus on risk factors with the expectation that when these are reduced or eliminated, the incidence of mental health problems will drop. Strategies that promote resilience and enhance an individual's psychological resources can also contribute to problem reduction and even prevention (Stephens, Dulberg, & Joubert, 1999). In light of this, viable mental health promotion strategies are needed to establish conditions that foster resilience and support. For instance, the more protective factors there are available to a child, the more likely the child is to experience resilience in the face of adversity and to cope effectively with challenges to both mental and physical functioning (Baylis, 2002; Stephens, Dulberg, & Joubert, 1999).

Resilience is the display of positive adaptation in face of adversity (Baylis, 2002). It's the capacity to bounce back from our lows and learn from them in a positive way. It's the vital sense of flexibility and the capacity to re-establish one's own balance. It's the essential feeling of being in control with regard to oneself and the outside world (Mental Health Promotion [MHP], 2003). Resilience does not come solely from within an individual, but is engendered by family and community. We need to foster resilience within families and communities rather than merely trying to make an individual resilient. Neither children nor adults should be viewed in isolation—as the

(continued)

(continued)

sole focus of change, treatment, or enhancement (Baylis, 2002). Studies have shown that integrated health promotion strategies work best (Kahan & Goodstadt, 2002).

Promoting Mental Health

Preventing mental health problems and mental health promotion are two sides of the same coin and, as such, are mutually compatible and reinforcing processes.

Mental health promotion is a proactive, holistic, multilevelled, synergistic process that fosters resilience as one progresses toward an optimal sense of well-being (see Figure 2.9 in this box) (Johnson, 1989). It is *proactive* to the extent that it builds up knowledge, resources, and strengths for overall wellness and it enhances the capacity of individuals to take control of their lives (MHP, 2003). (Find out more about wellness in Chapter 4, "Stress, Psychological Factors, and Health.") Through education, community efforts, and government policy, mental health promotion champions optimal mental health, reduces the stigma of mental illness, and engenders a mental wellness style of life (Baylis, 2002). Mental health promotion also moves beyond the commonly held notion that mental health is the mere absence of mental illness (Kahan & Goodstadt, 2002). Moreover, it applies equally to all people, sick or well, disabled or not, problematic or not (MHP, 2003). Mental health promotion is also *holistic* in nature and places high importance on mental, emotional, social, physical, and spiritual functioning (WHO, 2003). It considers the reciprocal interactions of these personal domains on *multiple levels* including the physical environment, family, community, and population culture, politics, and economics (MHP, 2003; Kahan & Goodstadt, 2002). As is true with risk factors, there is a *synergistic* effect among health promoting factors. Exposure to a combination of mental health promotion factors can be greater than the sum total effect of the individual factors (Dryden et al., 1998).

Mental Health Promotion Initiatives

There is a demonstrated need for a different kind of investment in

the mental health of Canadians of all ages (Stephens & Joubert, 2001). Canada is sitting on the cusp of change when it comes to mental health promotion and prevention (CAMIMH, 2000), and psychology's role will likely expand across all health-related areas (Arnett, 2006). Below are just some of the initiatives that cover the full spectrum of mental health promotion services and supports:

- Health Canada (2001a) sponsors five Centres of Excellence for Children's Well-Being across Canada that focus on child welfare, communities, early childhood development, special needs, and youth engagement.

- Health Canada's Mental Health Promotion Branch (MHP, 2003) was formed in 1995 "to maintain positive mental health and well-being for the Canadian population [and to] reduce the burden of mental health problems and disorders."

- The federal government introduced the Public Health Agency of Canada (2004) to focus on illness prevention and health promotion.

- In their report, *Out of the Shadows at Last: Transforming Mental Health, Mental Illness and Addiction Services in Canada*, Canadian senators Kirby and Keon (2006) recommend that a Canadian Mental Health Commission be established for mental health promotion and prevention of mental illness.

FIGURE 2.9 The mental wellness continuum.

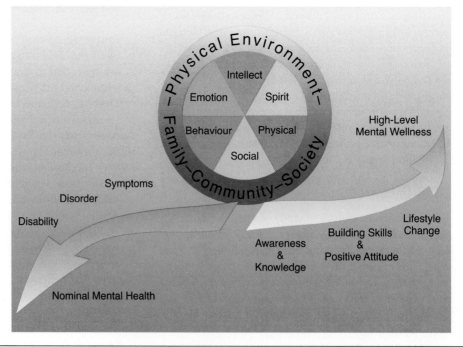

STUDY BREAK

Sociocultural Perspectives

Review It

- **What is the basic idea that underlies sociocultural perspectives?** Sociocultural theorists believe we need to broaden our outlook on abnormal behaviour by taking into account the role of social ills in society, including poverty, racism, and lack of opportunity, in the development of abnormal behaviour patterns.

Define It

downward drift hypothesis

Recall It*

1. The theorist associated with the belief that mental illness is merely a label given to people who act differently in order to stigmatize and subjugate them is _____.

   a. Aaron Beck
   b. Thomas Szasz
   c. Fritz Perls
   d. Abraham Maslow

2. Which of the following is NOT a type of sociocultural variable?

   a. social class
   b. ethnicity
   c. ego defences
   d. gender

3. Each of the following is a contribution of sociocultural theory EXCEPT _____.

   a. It has helped bring about much needed changes to protect the rights of mental patients in psychiatric institutions.
   b. It has focused our attention on the political implications of our responses to deviance.
   c. It has focused our attention on the factors within the individual that give rise to abnormal behaviour patterns.
   d. It has focused much needed attention on the social stressors underlying abnormal behaviour patterns.

* Recall It answers can be found on the Companion Website for this text.

Think About It

- Do you believe the root causes of abnormal behaviour lie in the environment? The person? A combination of the two? Why or why not?

INTERACTIONIST PERSPECTIVES

We have seen several models or perspectives for understanding and treating psychological disorders. The fact that there are different ways of looking at the same phenomenon does not mean one model must be right and the others wrong.

No one theoretical perspective can account for the complex forms of abnormal behaviour we encounter in this text. Each of the perspectives we have discussed—the biological, psychological, and sociocultural frameworks—contributes something to our understanding, but none offers a complete view. We are only beginning to uncover the subtle and often complex interactions involving the multitude of factors that give rise to abnormal behaviour patterns.

Many theorists today adopt an *interactionist* perspective. They believe we need to take into account the interaction of multiple factors representing biological, psychological, sociocultural, and environmental domains in order to explain abnormal behaviour. We'll describe two prominent interactionist models—the diathesis-stress and the biopsychosocial models.

The Diathesis-Stress Model

The **diathesis-stress model** holds that psychological disorders result from the combination or interaction of a diathesis (vulnerability or predisposition) with stress (see Figure 2.10 below). The model proposes that some people possess a vulnerability or **diathesis**, possibly genetic in nature, which increases their risk of developing a particular disorder. Yet whether they develop the disorder depends on the kinds and level of stress they experience.

diathesis-stress model Model of abnormal behaviour that posits that abnormal behaviour patterns, such as schizophrenia, involve the interaction of genetic and environmental influences. In this model, a genetic or acquired predisposition or diathesis increases an individual's vulnerability to develop the disorder in response to stressful life circumstances. If, however, the level of stress is kept under the person's particular threshold, the disorder may never develop, even among people with the predisposition.

diathesis A predisposition or vulnerability.

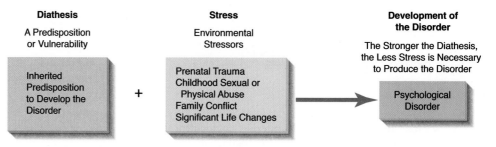

FIGURE 2.10 The diathesis-stress model.

Diathesis
A Predisposition or Vulnerability

Inherited Predisposition to Develop the Disorder

+

Stress
Environmental Stressors

Prenatal Trauma
Childhood Sexual or Physical Abuse
Family Conflict
Significant Life Changes

Development of the Disorder
The Stronger the Diathesis, the Less Stress is Necessary to Produce the Disorder

Psychological Disorder

Stress may take the form of biological events such as prenatal trauma, birth complications, and physical illness; psychosocial factors such as childhood sexual or physical abuse and family conflict; and negative life events such as prolonged unemployment and loss of loved ones.

In some cases, people with a diathesis for a particular disorder may remain free of the disorder or develop a milder form of the disorder if the level of stress in their lives remains low or they develop effective coping responses for handling the stress they encounter. However, the stronger the diathesis, the less stress is generally needed to produce the disorder. In some cases the diathesis may be so strong that the disorder develops even under the most benign life circumstances.

The diathesis-stress hypothesis was originally developed as an explanatory framework for understanding the development of schizophrenia (see Chapter 12). It has since been applied to other psychological disorders, such as depression. Although the term *diathesis* generally refers to an inherited predisposition, a diathesis may involve psychological factors such as dysfunctional thinking patterns or personality traits. For example, a dysfunctional pattern of thinking may put individuals at greater risk of developing depression in the face of upsetting or stressful life events such as prolonged unemployment or divorce (see Chapter 7).

The Biopsychosocial (Systems) Model

biopsychosocial model A conceptual model that emphasizes that human behaviour is linked to complex interactions among biological, psychological, and sociocultural factors.

The diathesis-stress model is not the only interactionist account of how abnormal behaviour patterns develop. Another prominent interdisciplinary approach is the **biopsychosocial model,** which, compared to the diathesis-stress model, expands and more clearly delineates the number of factors and dynamic interactions between a person and his or her environment. For example, the biopsychosocial model encompasses the dynamic interplay of three major *systems* or domains. Two systems can be thought of as being *internal*: the biological, which includes genetic, epigenetic, and neurophysiologic factors; and the psychological, which includes psychoanalytic, behavioural, humanistic-existential, and cognitive-behavioural factors. The third system includes what is considered to be *external* or outside of us: the sociocultural and environmental factors. Together, these biopsychosocial systems determine the range of known variables involved in the development of abnormal behaviour (Jaerisch & Bird, 2003: Martin, 2005; Petronis, 2000, 2003, 2004; Schumacher & Petronis, 2006; Szyf, 2006).

The Epigenome: Where Nature Meets Nurture In a landmark international study of 80 pairs of monozygotic (MZ) twins, researchers discovered that young pairs of MZ twins had indistinguishable epigenetic patterns and physical traits compared to each other, whereas pairs of MZ twins in their 50s showed substantial differences in their epigenetic patterns and phenotypic characteristics (Fraga et al., 2005). The disparity was even more pronounced in older pairs of MZ twins who shared distinctive lifestyles and spent less time in their lives together. Considering that MZ twins are genetically identical, we must look for reasons other than genetics to explain the changes that appear with age. The authors of this study suggest that over the course of a lifetime, environmental factors (e.g., differences in diet, smoking, fitness levels) contribute to changes in epigenetic markers and, by extension, phenotypic changes. They conclude that both internal and external factors (e.g., biopsychosocial factors) work to change the epigenome and, thus, the expression of genetic information, which may explain differences in phenotypic characteristics, including frequency and onset of disease.

Although the study of the relationship between the epigenome and human dysfunction is still in its infancy, early indications point toward the critical influence that external and internal factors have on epigenetic changes (Esteller, 2006; Fraga et al., 2005; Hiltunen, Turunen, Hakkinen et al., 2002; Luch, 2005; Mathers & Hesketh, 2007; Rossman, 2003; Weinhold, 2006). In turn, epigenetic changes affect gene expression, which can lead to an increased risk of developing both physical and psychological disorders (Petronis, 2000, 2003, 2004; Schumacher & Petronis, 2006; Szyf, 2006). Furthermore, it has been found that epigenetic markings on DNA are altered throughout life by interactions with external and internal factors (Bennett-Baker, Wilkowski, & Burke, 2003; Martin, 2005; Richardson, 2003).

Evaluating Interactionist Perspectives

Research shows how biopsychosocial factors play a major role in the aging process, diseases, and abnormal behaviour. Indeed, the discovery of epigenetic factors and the pivotal role they play on our overall well-being may prove to be the proverbial "missing link" that helps us explain how psychological, sociocultural, and environmental factors interface with our genetic code. We'll explore the interactionist perspective more fully in Chapter 4. Throughout the rest of the book, you will also find that many forms of abnormal behaviour involve a complex interplay of multiple influences that include psychological, biological, and/or sociocultural factors.

STUDY BREAK

Interactionist Perspectives

Review It

- **What is the distinguishing feature of the interactionist perspectives?** The diathesis-stress model posits that some people have predispositions (diatheses) for particular disorders, but whether these disorders actually develop depends on the type and severity of the stressors they experience. The biopsychosocial approach examines the interplay of biological, psychological, and sociocultural factors in abnormal behaviour. External and internal factors can alter epigenetic patterns, which can affect gene expression. This can lead to an increased risk of both physical and psychological disorders.

Define It

diathesis-stress model   biopsychosocial model
diathesis

Recall It*

1. The psychological model that holds that abnormal behaviour patterns involve a combination of a genetic predisposition and exposure to stress is the _____ model.

   a. perceived self-efficacy
   b. diathesis-stress

   c. neural sensitivity
   d. genetic-stress model

2. The diathesis-stress model was originally developed as an explanatory framework for understanding the development of _____.

   a. personality disorders
   b. posttraumatic stress disorder
   c. schizophrenia
   d. depression

3. Over the course of a lifetime, environmental factors such as diet, smoking, fitness levels _____.

   a. can trigger a schizophrenic diathesis reaction.
   b. have no affect on the epigenome.
   c. cause permanent transgenerational genetic mutations.
   d. can contribute to changes in the frequency and onset of disease.

* Recall It answers can be found on the Companion Website for this text.

Think About It

- Think of an example of how your own behaviour reflects interactions of biological, psychological, and sociocultural influences. Give an example.

METHODS OF TREATMENT

Carla, a 19-year-old undergraduate student, had been crying more or less continuously for several days. She felt her life was falling apart, that her academic aspirations were in shambles, and she was a disappointment to her parents. The thought of suicide had crossed her mind. She could not seem to drag herself out of bed in the morning and had withdrawn from her friends. Her misery seemed to descend on her from nowhere, although she could pinpoint some pressures in her life: a couple of poor grades at school, a recent break-up with a boyfriend, and some adjustment problems with roommates.

The psychologist who examined her arrived at a diagnosis of major depressive disorder. Had she broken her leg, her treatment from a qualified professional would have followed a fairly standard course. Yet the treatment that Carla or someone else with a psychological disorder receives is likely to vary not only with the type of disorder involved but also with the therapeutic orientation and professional background of the helping professional. A psychiatrist might recommend a course of antidepressant medication, perhaps in combination with some form of psychotherapy. A cognitively oriented psychologist might suggest a program of cognitive therapy to help Carla identify dysfunctional thoughts that may underlie her depression, whereas a psychodynamic therapist might recommend she begin psychodynamically oriented therapy to uncover inner conflicts originating in childhood that may lie at the root of her depression.

In these next sections, we focus on ways of treating psychological disorders. In later chapters, we see how these treatment approaches are applied to particular disorders. Here, we focus on the treatments themselves. We will see that the biological and psychological perspectives have spawned corresponding approaches to treatment. First, however, we consider the major types of mental health professionals who treat psychological or mental disorders and the different roles they play.

Types of Mental Health Professionals in Canada

Clinical psychologists, psychiatrists, and social workers comprise the majority of licensed mental health professionals in Canada. These three groups are regulated under provincial and territorial jurisdictions. But for the fourth broad cluster, psychotherapists and counsellors, there remains a lack of common pan-Canadian titles and clearly defined scopes of practice. To date, only Quebec, Alberta, British Columbia, and Ontario have passed, or are in the process of passing, legislation that regulates the practices of psychotherapy and or counselling. Distinguishing among the various helping professionals can be confusing to the public (Farberman, 1997), and thus, people seeking treatment are advised to inquire about the training and licensure of helping professionals.

Another reason for confusion is that all different types of mental health providers, such as clinical psychologists, psychiatrists, clinical social workers, and a wide range of other mental health professionals, practise **psychotherapy** or "talk therapy"—a psychologically based method of treatment involving a series of verbal interchanges between clients and therapists taking place over a period of time, usually on a one-session-per-week basis. The particular approach used by individual psychotherapists reflects their theoretical orientation, such as psychodynamic, behavioural, humanistic, cognitive, and so on. Some therapists adopt an **eclectic orientation**, which means they draw on the theories and techniques espoused by two or more theoretical orientations. We'll return to consider these different approaches to psychotherapy. But first, let's consider the different roles that the major types of mental health professionals play.

Clinical Psychologists A clinical psychologist is a psychologist trained in the assessment, diagnosis, and treatment of psychological problems. All psychologists, including clinical psychologists, must have at least a master's degree. In most provinces, they must have a doctoral degree (Ph.D. or Psy.D.) to be licensed to practise psychology independently (Edwards, 2000). Psychologists use various techniques to diagnose psychological problems, including clinical interviews, psychological tests, and behavioural observations

psychotherapy Method of helping involving a systematic interaction between a therapist and a client that brings psychological principles to bear on influencing the client's thoughts, feelings, or behaviours in order to help that client overcome abnormal behaviour or adjust to problems in living.

eclectic orientation Adoption of principles or techniques from various systems or theories.

(CPA, 2002). They also use psychotherapy as a means of treating these problems. Psychologists often receive extensive training in research, which helps them conduct studies in clinical settings and critically evaluate the clinical literature.

Psychiatrists Psychiatrists are licensed physicians who have earned medical degrees such as the Doctor of Medicine (MD). They have also completed a postdoctoral residency program in psychiatry that provides specialized training in diagnosing and treating psychological problems. Like psychologists, psychiatrists conduct psychotherapy and diagnostic interviews. Unlike psychologists, they can prescribe drugs and administer other biological treatments, such as electroconvulsive therapy (ECT). Psychiatrists often rely on psychologists for psychological testing to help determine a diagnosis or course of treatment.

Social Workers Social workers earn a graduate degree in social work at the master's level (Master of Social Work: M.S.W.) or doctoral level (Doctor of Social Work: D.S.W.). They receive supervised training in helping people adjust and utilize social-support services and community agencies. Many social workers conduct psychotherapy or specialize in marital or family therapy.

Biological Therapies

There is a growing emphasis in Canadian psychiatry on the biologically based treatment of abnormal behaviour, especially drug therapies (Bibeau et al., 1999; Garfinkel & Dorian, 2000; Gauthier, 1999). Biologically based approaches are generally administered by medical doctors, many of whom have specialized training in psychiatry or **psychopharmacology**. Many family physicians or general practitioners also prescribe psychotherapeutic or psychotropic drugs for their patients, however.

Although the biological or medical approaches have had dramatic success in treating some forms of abnormal behaviour, they also have their limitations. For one, biological therapies may have unwelcome or dangerous side effects. There is also the potential for abuse. One of the most commonly prescribed minor tranquillizers, Valium, has become a major drug of abuse among people who become psychologically and physiologically dependent on it. Psychosurgery has been all but eliminated as a form of treatment because of serious harmful effects of earlier procedures. There are, however, some new experimental biologically based techniques that show promise, such as transcranial magnetic stimulation (TMS), gene splicing, epigenetic therapy, and stem cell interventions.

Different classes of psychotropic drugs are used in the treatment of various types of mental health problems.

Anti-anxiety Drugs Anti-anxiety drugs (also called *anxiolytics*, from the Greek *anxietas*, meaning "anxiety," and *lysis*, meaning "bringing to an end") are drugs that combat anxiety and reduce states of muscle tension. They include mild tranquillizers, such as *diazepam* (Valium); barbiturates, such as *meprobamate* (Miltown); and hypnotic-sedatives, such as *triazolam* (Halcion) and *flurazepam* (Dalmane).

Anti-anxiety drugs depress the level of activity in certain parts of the central nervous system (CNS). In turn, the CNS decreases the level of sympathetic nervous system activity, reducing the respiration rate and heart rate, and lessening states of anxiety and tension. Minor tranquillizers such as Valium grew in popularity when physicians became concerned about the use of more potent sedatives, such as barbiturates, which are highly addictive and extremely dangerous when taken in overdoses or mixed with alcohol. Unfortunately, it has become clear that the minor tranquillizers also can, and often do, lead to physiological dependence (addiction). People who are dependent on Valium may go into convulsions when they abruptly stop taking it. Deaths have been reported among people who mix mild tranquillizers with alcohol or who are unusually sensitive to them. There are other less severe side effects, such as fatigue, drowsiness, and impaired motor co-ordination, which might nonetheless reduce one's ability to function or to operate an automobile. Regular usage of benzodiazepines can also produce **tolerance**, a physiological sign of dependence, which refers to the need over time for increasing dosages of a drug to achieve the same effect. Quite commonly,

psychopharmacology Field of study that examines the effects of drugs on behaviour and psychological functioning and explores the use of psychoactive drugs in the treatment of emotional disorders.

tolerance Physical habituation to a drug so that with frequent usage, higher doses are needed to attain similar effects.

patients become involved in tugs of war with their physicians as they demand increased dosages despite their physicians' concerns about the potential for abuse and dependence.

When used on a short-term basis, anti-anxiety drugs can be safe and effective in treating anxiety and insomnia. Yet drugs by themselves do not teach people more adaptive ways of solving their problems and may encourage them to rely on a chemical agent to cope with stress rather than develop active means of coping. Drug therapy is thus often combined with psychotherapy to help people with anxiety complaints deal with the psychological and situational bases of their problems (Talbot & McMurray, 2004). However, combining drug therapy and psychotherapy may present special problems and challenges. For one, drug-induced relief from anxiety may reduce clients' motivation to try to solve their problems. For another, medicated clients who develop skills for coping with stress in psychotherapy may fail to retain what they have learned once the tranquillizers are discontinued, or find themselves too tense to employ their newly acquired skills.

Rebound anxiety is another problem associated with regular use of minor tranquillizers. Many people who regularly use anti-anxiety drugs report that anxiety or insomnia returns in a more severe form once they discontinue them. For some, this may represent a fear of not having the drugs to depend on. For others, rebound anxiety might reflect changes in biochemical processes that are not well understood at present.

Antipsychotic Drugs

Antipsychotic drugs, also called **neuroleptics**, are commonly used to treat the more flagrant features of schizophrenia or other psychotic disorders, such as hallucinations, delusions, and states of confusion. Many of these drugs, including *chlorpromazine* (Thorazine), belong to the phenothiazine class of chemicals. Phenothiazines appear to control psychotic features by blocking the action of the neurotransmitter dopamine at receptor sites in the brain. Although the underlying causes of schizophrenia remain unknown, researchers suspect a dysregulation of the dopamine system in the brain may be involved (see Chapter 12). *Clozapine* (brand name Clozaril), a neuroleptic of a different chemical class than the phenothiazines, has been shown to be effective in treating many people with schizophrenia whose symptoms were unresponsive to other neuroleptics (see Chapter 12). The use of clozapine must be carefully monitored, however, because of potentially dangerous side effects.

The use of neuroleptics has greatly reduced the need for more restrictive forms of treatment for severely disturbed patients, such as physical restraints and confinement in padded cells, and has lessened the need for long-term hospitalization. The introduction of major tranquillizers in the mid-1950s was one of the major factors that led to a massive exodus of chronic mental patients from institutions. Many ex-hospitalized patients have been able to resume family life and hold jobs while continuing to take their medications.

Neuroleptics are not without their problems, including potential side effects such as muscular rigidity and tremors. Although these side effects are generally controllable by use of other drugs, long-term use of antipsychotic drugs (possibly except clozapine) can produce a potentially irreversible and disabling motor disorder called *tardive dyskinesia* (see Chapter 12), characterized by uncontrollable eye blinking, facial grimaces, lip smacking, and other involuntary movements of the mouth, eyes, and limbs. Researchers are experimenting with lowered dosages, intermittent drug regimens, and use of new medications to reduce the risk of such complications.

Antidepressants

Three major classes of **antidepressants** are used in treating depression: **tricyclics**, **monoamine oxidase (MAO) inhibitors**, and **selective serotonin-reuptake inhibitors (SSRIs)**. The first two kinds of antidepressants, tricyclics and monoamine oxidase (MAO) inhibitors, increase the availability of the neurotransmitters norepinephrine and serotonin in the brain. Some of the more common tricyclics are *imipramine* (Tofranil) and *amitriptyline* (Elavil). The MAO inhibitors include such drugs as *phenelzine* (Nardil) and *tranylcypromine* (Parnate). Tricyclic antidepressants (TCAs) are more commonly favoured over MAO inhibitors because of potentially serious side effects associated with MAO inhibitors.

The third class of antidepressants, selective serotonin-reuptake inhibitors or SSRIs, have more specific effects on serotonin function in the brain. Drugs in this class, which

rebound anxiety Occurrence of strong anxiety following withdrawal from a tranquillizer.

neuroleptics Group of antipsychotic drugs used in the treatment of schizophrenia, such as the phenothiazines (e.g., Thorazine).

antidepressants Types of drugs that act to relieve depression. Tricyclics, MAO inhibitors, and selective serotonin-reuptake inhibitors are the major classes of antidepressants.

tricyclics Group of antidepressant drugs that increase the activity of norepinephrine and serotonin in the brain by interfering with the reuptake of these neurotransmitters by transmitting neurons. Also called *TCAs* (tricyclic antidepressants).

monoamine oxidase (MAO) inhibitors Antidepressants that act to increase the availability of neurotransmitters in the brain by inhibiting the actions of an enzyme, monoamine oxidase, that normally breaks down or degrades neurotransmitters (norepinephrine and serotonin) in the synaptic cleft.

selective serotonin-reuptake inhibitors (SSRIs) Type of antidepressant medication that prevents serotonin from being taken back up by the transmitting neuron, thus increasing its action.

include *fluoxetine* (Prozac), are now the most widely prescribed antidepressant on the market. They increase the availability of serotonin in the brain by interfering with its reuptake by the transmitting neuron.

Slightly more than half of the people with clinically significant depression who are treated with antidepressants of the tricyclic class will respond favourably (Depression Guideline Panel, 1993b). A favourable response to treatment does not mean depression is eliminated, however. Overall, the effects of tricyclic antidepressants (TCAs) appear to be modest (Greenberg et al., 1992). Nor does a particular antidepressant appear to be clearly more effective than any other (Kennedy, Lam, Cohen, Ravindran, & CANMAT Depression Working Group, 2001). Even Prozac, which was hailed by some as a "wonder drug," appears, on the basis of present evidence, to be no more effective than the TCAs (Greenberg et al., 1994). The preferred antidepressant depends on individual patient characteristics including the subtype and severity of depression, tolerance of side effects and safety, and interaction with other approaches such as psychotherapy (Kennedy et al., 2001).

We shall see that antidepressants also have beneficial effects in treating a wide range of psychological disorders including an array of anxiety disorders (see Chapter 5) and eating disorders (see Chapter 10). As research into the underlying causes of these disorders continues, we may find that dysregulation of neurotransmitters plays a key role in their development.

Lithium Lithium carbonate, a salt of the metal lithium in tablet form, has demonstrated remarkable effectiveness in stabilizing the dramatic mood swings associated with bipolar disorder (formerly manic depression) (see Chapter 7). Because of its potential toxicity, the blood levels of patients maintained on lithium must be carefully monitored (Yatham et al, 2005). Like people with diabetes who must take insulin throughout their lifetimes to control their disease, people with bipolar disorder may have to continue using lithium indefinitely to control the disorder.

Electroconvulsive Therapy In 1939, the Italian psychiatrist Ugo Cerletti introduced the technique of **electroconvulsive therapy** (ECT) in psychiatric treatment. Cerletti had observed the practice in some slaughterhouses of using electric shock to render animals unconscious. He observed that the shocks also produced convulsions. Cerletti incorrectly believed, as did other researchers in Europe at the time, that convulsions of the type found in epilepsy were incompatible with schizophrenia and a method of inducing convulsions might be used to cure schizophrenia.

electroconvulsive therapy Induction of a convulsive seizure by means of passing an electric current through the head; used primarily in the treatment of severe depression. Abbreviated *ECT*.

After the introduction of the phenothiazines in the 1950s, the use of ECT became generally limited to the treatment of severe depression. The introduction of antidepressants has further limited the use of ECT. Even though rates of ECT use are down from the 1960s, one Ontario study found that rates (roughly 12.5 per 100 000) have remained constant since the 1990s and are three times higher for elderly than younger patients (Rapoport, Mamdani, & Herrmann, 2006).

Electroconvulsive therapy remains a source of controversy. For instance, many people, including many professionals, are uncomfortable about the idea of passing an electric shock through a person's head, even if the level of shock is closely regulated and the convulsions are controlled by drugs. Then there are the potential side effects. ECT often produces dramatic relief from severe depression, but concerns remain about its potential for inducing cognitive deficits, such as memory loss. A review of the evidence, however, finds memory losses following ECT to be temporary, except perhaps for some persistent loss of memory for events transpiring immediately around the time of the procedure itself (Devanand et al., 1994).

A recent Canadian review found that up to 15% of depressive patients experience *treatment-resistant depression* (TRD) (Berlim & Turecki, 2007). Although controversies concerning the use of ECT persist, the facts support its effectiveness in helping people overcome severe depression that fails to respond to psychotherapy or antidepressant medication (Rabheru, 2001; Rapoport, Mamdani, & Herrmann, 2006). Moreover, ECT may help reduce the risk of suicide among severely depressed people (Martin et al., 1985). However, ECT is usually considered a treatment of last resort, after less intrusive methods of treating TRD have been tried and failed.

Emerging Trends in Biological Treatments

Gene therapy, epigenetic drugs, and stem cell interventions for medical and psychological disorders are still in the early stages of development, but there have been some encouraging results thus far.

Gene Therapy

Gene therapy holds great promise for the development of treatments and potential cures for the 3000 or so known human genetic disorders. For example, gene therapy makes it possible to provide individuals who have a missing or defective gene with a corrected copy of that gene. Gene therapy often involves gene splicing or *recombinant* (as in recombining) DNA techniques in which genetically altered bacterium or virus cells carrying healthy gene segments are first cultivated and then injected into the body, where they replace defective DNA

with healthy DNA segments (see Figure 2.11). The replacement genes then begin to produce proteins, hormones, or other substances that may be needed in treating a person's illness. And, with respect to the human nervous system, gene-splicing techniques carry the potential to cure a variety of nerve-tissue disorders such as spinal-cord injuries, stroke (cerebrovascular accidents), and multiple sclerosis (MS).

Epigenetic Therapy

Unlike genetic mutations, epigenetic defects are reversible and thus, directly treatable. This bodes well for the future of epigenetic treatments according to pioneering epigenesist Moshe Szyf (2004), a pharmacologist researcher at McGill University, who coined the term *pharmacoepigenomics* to describe the emerging field of epigenetics and pharmacology. Most of the epigenetic research thus far has focused on physical diseases which has lead to an explosion of epigenetic preclinical and

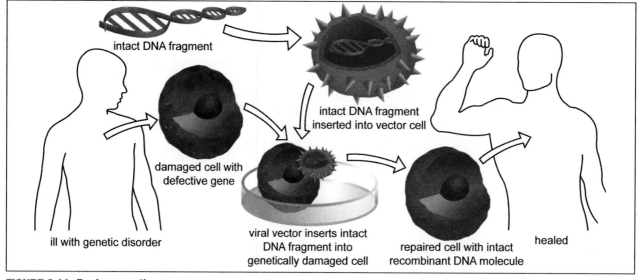

FIGURE 2.11 *Ex vivo* **gene therapy.**
Delivering recombinant DNA into a group of cells in a patient's body can be done through the *ex vivo* (outside the body) process. This process begins with the removal of genetically damaged cells from the patient. Meanwhile, the healthy gene segments from a different source are spliced into viral or bacterial *vectors* (the vehicles used to transport the recombinant DNA). Once the vector containing the healthy gene segment joins with the DNA of the patient's cells, the treated cells are then cultured in a petri dish and returned to the patient's body where normal cellular functioning can begin.

Source: Artwork copyright © Alexandra Johnson. Printed with permission.

repetitive transcranial magnetic stimulation (rTMS) A procedure that uses strong magnetic pulses to stimulate the brain.

An alternative form of brain stimulation treatment for depression—**repetitive transcranial magnetic stimulation (rTMS)**—is now used in Canada. In rTMS, a strong magnetic field is directed through a coil held against the head for several daily hour-long sessions. Some early indications have shown rTMS to be an effective, painless, noninvasive procedure with zero to low side effects (Fitzgerald et al., 2006a, 2006b). In some cases, it can be a practical alternative to ECT, as it is a less costly treatment and is not associated with anaesthetic and other ECT risks (Rosa et al., 2006; Schulze-Rauschen-

(continued)

clinical drug trials for diseases, such as cancer and neurological disorders (Eckhardt, Beck, Gut, & Berlin, 2004; Egger, Laing, Aparicio, & Jones, 2004; Flanagan et al., 2006; Peedicayil, 2006; Santos-Rebouças & Pimentel, 2007). However, just as Canadians led the way in the development of antipsychotic drugs half a century ago (refer back to Chapter 1), Canadian scientists are again on the forefront, this time tracking down the epigenetic features associated with the psychotic symptoms of schizophrenia and major mood disorders (Centre for Addiction and Mental Health, 2006; Petronis, 2003, 2004; Szyf, 2004; Wang, 2006). The hope is that the discovery of a new class of epigenetic drugs will work by precisely targeting molecular epigenome structures that underlie a range of neurological and psychological disorders ranging from addictions, autism, and Alzheimer's to psychotic disorders such as schizophrenia. The expectation is that these new epigenetic drugs will reduce or prevent symptoms by either activating or silencing disease-related genes and their proteins. Epigenetic drugs could also have a distinct advantage over conventional psychotropic drugs by both minimizing unwanted side effects and increasing drug safety.

Stem Cell Therapy

Stem cell therapy is of most value in medical conditions where there are damaged or diseased body tissues. Different kinds of stem cells, you will recall, are naturally present in organs and body systems to repair damaged tissue. In one type of stem cell procedure, the nuclei of stem cells are removed and replaced with nuclei from the patient. The genetically modified stem cells are then cloned to produce more cells that can be used to repair the patient's damaged or missing cells. This procedure avoids the body's *immune rejection* of the transplanted stem cells because they are genetically compatible with the patient. These procedures are now commonly used in bone marrow transplants to treat leukemia and other types of cancer, as well as various blood disorders.

Researchers are also looking into other experimental treatments, such as the use of stem cells to treat spinal cord injuries. For example, recent animal research

studies using embryonic stem cells have demonstrated that both mice and rats can recover from paralysis and regain movement (Bernreuther et al., 2006; Cao et al., 2005; Deshpande et al., 2006; Kerr et al., 2001). And, closer to the field of abnormal psychology, an international team of scientists, Cunningham, Kwang-soo, and Dong-wook, have reported that when they injected dopamine- and serotonin-producing stem cells into the brains of mice with symptoms of anxiety and depression, the rodents acted as if they had been administered antidepressant medications (as cited in Tae-gyu, 2006, October 22). This research shows potential for treating human psychological disorders with embryonic stem cells, as these neurotransmitters are associated with depression, anxiety disorders, and possibly schizophrenia.

Stem cell therapy, like genetic modification and epigenetic treatments, has the potential to revolutionize medicine and we may soon see dramatic cures for medical conditions such as Alzheimer's and Parkinson's diseases, spinal cord injuries, and a host of other neurological and psychiatric disorders (Goldman & Windrem, 2006; Lindvall, 2003; Taupin 2006).

Biotechnology Lab. Modern biotechnology labs are designed to perform biotechnology research, studies, experiments, analysis, or testing.

bach et al., 2005). The antidepressant "action," "reaction," "response" also appears to be clinically effective and safe in some studies with adolescent patients (Fregni et al., 2006; Loo, McFarquhar, & Walter, 2006). Find out more about the use of rTMS in the treatment of depression in Chapter 7.

Psychosurgery Psychosurgery is even more controversial than ECT and rarely practised today. Although no longer performed, the most widely used form of psychosurgery was

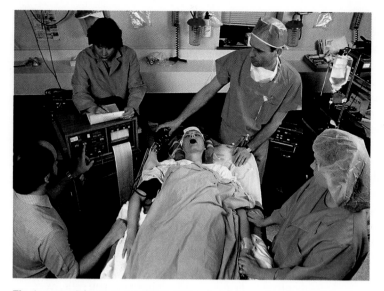

Electroconvulsive therapy (ECT). ECT is helpful in many cases of severe or prolonged depression that do not respond to other forms of treatment. Still, its use remains controversial.

prefrontal lobotomy Form of psychosurgery in which certain neural pathways in the brain are severed in the attempt to control disturbed behaviour.

the **prefrontal lobotomy**, in which the nerve pathways linking the thalamus to the prefrontal lobes of the brain are surgically severed. It was believed that by severing the connections between the thalamus and the higher brain centres in the frontal lobe of the cerebral cortex, the patient's violent or aggressive tendencies could be controlled. The prefrontal lobotomy was developed by the Portuguese neurologist António Egas Moniz, who in 1949 won a Nobel Prize for the procedure. By the 1960s, more than 10 000 mental patients in Canada had undergone the operation (Simmons, 1987). Although the operation did reduce violent and agitated behaviour in many cases, it was not always successful. In a cruel, ironic twist, one of Moniz's treatment failures later shot him, leaving him paralyzed from a bullet that lodged in his spine.

Many distressing side effects are associated with the prefrontal lobotomy, including hyperactivity, impaired learning ability and reduced creativity, distractibility, apathy, overeating, withdrawal, epileptic-type seizures, and even death. The occurrence of these side effects, combined with the introduction of the phenothiazines, led to the elimination of the operation. Several more sophisticated psychosurgery techniques have been introduced in more recent years for various purposes. Generally speaking, they are limited to smaller parts of the brain and produce less damage than the prefrontal lobotomy. These operations have been performed to treat such problems as intractable aggression, depression, and psychotic behaviour; chronic pain; some forms of epilepsy; and persistent obsessive-compulsive disorder (Baer et al., 1995; Irle et al., 1998; Sachdev & Hay, 1996). Follow-up studies of such procedures have shown marked improvement in about a quarter to half of cases. Concerns about possible complications of these procedures, including decrements in intellectual functioning (Irle et al., 1998), have greatly limited their use.

We now consider the major types of psychotherapy and their relationships to the theoretical models from which they derive.

Psychodynamic Therapies

Psychoanalysis is the form of psychodynamic therapy originated by Sigmund Freud. Practitioners of psychoanalysis, called *psychoanalysts*, view psychological problems as rooted in early childhood experiences and unconscious conflicts. Freud used psychoanalysis to help clients gain insight into and resolve unconscious conflicts. Working through these conflicts, the ego would be freed of the need to maintain defensive behaviours—such as phobias, obsessive-compulsive behaviours, hysterical complaints, and the like—that shield it from recognition of inner turmoil.

Freud summed up the goal of psychoanalysis by saying, "Where id was, there shall ego be." This meant, in part, that psychoanalysis could help shed the light of awareness, represented by the conscious ego, on the inner workings of the id. But Freud did not expect or intend that clients should seek to become conscious of all repressed material—of all their impulses, wishes, fears, and memories. The aim, rather, was to replace defensive behaviour with more adaptive behaviour. By so doing, clients could find gratification without incurring social or self-condemnation.

Through this process a man with a phobia of knives might become aware he had been repressing impulses to vent a murderous rage against his father. His phobia keeps him from having contact with knives, thereby serving a hidden purpose of keeping his homicidal impulses in check. A woman with a loss of sensation in her hand that could not be explained medically might come to see she harboured guilt over urges to masturbate. The loss of sensation may have prevented her from acting on these urges. Through confronting hidden impulses and the conflicts they produce, clients learn to sort out their feelings and find more constructive and socially acceptable ways of handling their impulses and wishes. The ego is then freed to focus on more constructive interests.

The major methods that Freud used to accomplish these goals were free association, dream analysis, and analysis of the transference relationship.

Free Association You are asked to lie down on a couch and to say anything that enters your mind. The psychoanalyst (or *analyst* for short) sits in a chair behind you, out of direct view. For the next 45 or 50 minutes, you let your mind wander, saying whatever pops in, or saying nothing at all. The analyst remains silent most of the time, prompting you occasionally to utter whatever crosses your mind, no matter how seemingly trivial, no matter how personal. This process continues, typically for three or four sessions a week, for a period of several years. At certain points in the process, the analyst offers an *interpretation*, drawing your attention to connections between your disclosures and unconscious conflicts.

<u>Free association is the process of uttering uncensored thoughts as they come to mind.</u> Free association is believed to gradually break down the defences that block awareness of unconscious processes. Clients are told not to censor or screen out thoughts, but to let their minds wander "freely" from thought to thought. Psychoanalysts do not believe that the process of free association is truly free. Repressed impulses press for expression or release, leading to a **compulsion to utter**. Although free association may begin with small talk, the compulsion to utter eventually leads the client to disclose more meaningful material.

The ego, however, continues to try to avert the disclosure of threatening impulses and conflicts. Consequently, clients may show **resistance**—an unwillingness or inability to recall or discuss disturbing or threatening material. Clients might report that their minds suddenly go blank when they venture into sensitive areas. They might switch topics abruptly, or accuse the analyst of trying to pry into material that is too personal or embarrassing to talk about. Or they might conveniently "forget" the next appointment after a session in which sensitive material is touched on. The analyst monitors the dynamic conflict between the "compulsion to utter" and resistance. Signs of resistance are often suggestive of meaningful material. Now and then, the analyst brings interpretations of this material to the attention of the client to help the client gain better **insight** into deep-seated feelings and conflicts.

free association In psychoanalysis, the method of verbalizing thoughts as they occur without any conscious attempt to edit or censor them.

compulsion to utter In psychodynamic theory, the urge to express repressed material verbally.

resistance During psychoanalysis, the blocking of thoughts or feelings that would evoke anxiety if they were consciously experienced. Resistance may also take the form of missed sessions by a client or a client's verbal confrontation with the analyst as threatening material is about to be uncovered.

insight In psychotherapy, the attainment of awareness and understanding of one's true motives and feelings.

Dream Analysis To Freud, dreams represented the "royal road to the unconscious." During sleep, the ego's defences are lowered and unacceptable impulses find some form of expression in dreams. Because the defences are not completely eliminated, the impulses take a disguised or symbolized form in dreams. In psychoanalytic theory, dreams have two levels of content:

1. **Manifest content**: the material of the dream the dreamer experiences and reports, and
2. **Latent content**: the unconscious material the dream symbolizes or represents.

A man might dream of flying in an airplane. Flying is the apparent or manifest content of the dream. Freud believed that flying may symbolize erection, so perhaps the latent content of the dream reflects unconscious issues related to fears of impotence. Such symbols may vary from person to person. Analysts therefore ask clients to free-associate to the manifest content of the dream to provide clues to the latent content.

manifest content In psychodynamic theory, the reported content or apparent meaning of dreams.

latent content In psychodynamic theory, the underlying or symbolic content of dreams.

Transference Freud found that clients not only responded to him as an individual but also in ways that reflected their feelings and attitudes toward other important people in their lives. A young female client might respond to him as a father figure, **displacing** or transferring onto Freud her feelings toward her own father. A man might also view him as a father figure, responding to him as a rival in a manner Freud believed might reflect the man's unresolved Oedipal complex.

displacement In psychodynamic theory, a type of defence mechanism that involves the transferring of impulses toward threatening or unacceptable objects onto more acceptable or safer objects.

transference relationship In psycho-analysis, a client's transfer or generalization to the analyst of feelings and attitudes the client holds toward important figures in his or her life.

The process of analyzing and working through the **transference relationship** is considered an essential component of psychoanalysis. Freud believed the transference relationship provides a vehicle for the re-enactment of childhood conflicts with parents. Clients may react to the analyst with the same feelings of anger, love, or jealousy they felt toward their own parents. Freud termed the enactment of these childhood conflicts the *transference neurosis*. This "neurosis" had to be successfully analyzed and worked through for clients to succeed in psychoanalysis.

Childhood conflicts usually involve unresolved feelings of anger or rejection or needs for love. For example, a client may interpret any slight criticism by the therapist as a devastating blow, transferring feelings of self-loathing that the client had repressed from childhood experiences of parental rejection. Transferences may also distort or colour the client's relationships with others, such as a spouse or employer. Clients might relate to their spouses as they had to their parents, perhaps demanding too much from them or unjustly accusing them of being insensitive or uncaring. Or they might not give new friends or lovers the benefit of a fair chance if they had been mistreated by others who played similar roles in their past. The analyst helps the client recognize transference relationships, especially the therapy transference, and to work through the residues of childhood feelings and conflicts that lead to self-defeating behaviour in the present.

According to Freud, transference is a two-way street. Freud felt he transferred his underlying feelings onto his clients, perhaps viewing a young man as a competitor or a woman as a rejecting love interest. Freud referred to the feelings that he projected onto clients as **countertransference**. Psychoanalysts in training are expected to undergo psychoanalysis themselves to help them uncover motives that might lead to countertransferences in their therapeutic relationships. In their therapeutic training, psychoanalysts learn to monitor their own reactions in therapy so as to become better aware of when and how countertransferences intrude on the therapy process.

countertransference In psychoanalysis, the transfer of feelings that the analyst holds toward other persons in her or his life onto the client.

Although the analysis of the therapy transference is a crucial element of psychoanalytic therapy, it generally takes months or years for a transference relationship to develop and be resolved. This is one reason why psychoanalysis is typically a lengthy and expensive process.

Modern Psychodynamic Approaches Although some psychoanalysts continue to practise traditional psychoanalysis in much the same manner as Freud, briefer and less intensive forms of psychodynamic treatment have emerged (Strupp, 1992). These newer approaches are often referred to as "brief psychodynamic therapies." They are able to reach clients who are seeking more focused and less costly forms of treatment, perhaps once or twice a week.

Like Freudian psychoanalysis, the newer psychodynamic approaches aim to uncover unconscious motives and break down resistances and psychological defences, yet focus more on the client's present relationships and encourage the client to make adaptive behaviour changes. As a result of the briefer format, therapy may entail a more open and direct exploration of the client's defences and transference relationships than was traditionally the case. Unlike the traditional approach, the client and therapist generally sit facing each other. Rather than offer an occasional interpretation, the therapist engages in more frequent verbal give-and-take with the client, as in the following vignette. Note how the therapist uses interpretation to help the client, Mr. Arianes, achieve insight into how his relationship with his wife involves a transference of his childhood relationship with his mother:

Mr. Arianes: I think you've got it there, Doc. We weren't communicating. I wouldn't tell her [his wife] what was wrong or what I wanted from her. Maybe I expected her to understand me without saying anything.

Therapist: Like the expectations a child has of its mother.

Mr. Arianes: Not my mother!

Therapist: Oh?

Mr. Arianes:	No, I always thought she had too many troubles of her own to pay attention to mine. I remember once I got hurt on my bike and came to her all bloodied up. When she saw me she got mad and yelled at me for making more trouble for her when she already had her hands full with my father.
Therapist:	Do you remember how you felt then?
Mr. Arianes:	I can't remember, but I know that after that I never brought my troubles to her again.
Therapist:	How old were you?
Mr. Arianes:	Nine. I know that because I got that bike for my ninth birthday. It was a little too big for me still, that's why I got hurt on it.
Therapist:	Perhaps you carried this attitude into your marriage.
Mr. Arianes:	What attitude?
Therapist:	The feeling that your wife, like your mother, would be unsympathetic to your difficulties. That there was no point in telling her about your experiences because she was too preoccupied or too busy to care.
Mr. Arianes:	But she's so different from my mother. I come first with her.
Therapist:	On one level you know that. On another, deeper level there may well be the fear that people—or maybe only women, or maybe only women you're close to—are all the same, and you can't take a chance at being rejected again in your need.
Mr. Arianes:	Maybe you're right, Doc, but all that was so long ago, and I should be over that by now.
Therapist:	That's not the way the mind works. If a shock or a disappointment is strong enough it can permanently freeze our picture of ourselves and our expectations of the world. The rest of us grows up—that is, we let ourselves learn about life from experience and from what we see, hear, or read of the experiences of others, but that one area where we really got hurt stays unchanged. So what I mean when I say you might be carrying that attitude into your relationship with your wife is that when it comes to your hopes of being understood and catered to when you feel hurt or abused by life, you still feel very much like that nine-year-old boy who was rebuffed in his need and gave up hope that anyone would or could respond to him.

SOURCE: BASCH, 1980, PP. 29–30. REPRINTED WITH PERMISSION.

Some modern psychodynamic therapies focus more on the role of the ego and less on the role of the id. Therapists adopting this view believe Freud placed too much emphasis on sexual and aggressive impulses and underplayed the importance of the ego. These therapists, such as Heinz Hartmann, are generally described as *ego analysts*. Other modern psychoanalysts, such as Melanie Klein and Margaret Mahler, are identified with object-relations approaches to psychodynamic therapy. **Object-relations** therapists focus on helping people separate their own ideas and feelings from the elements of others they have incorporated or introjected within themselves. They can then develop more as individuals—as their own persons.

Newer psychoanalytical therapies are more time limited in nature. One form in particular, cognitive analytic therapy (CAT), established by Anthony Ryle (1982), has gathered international following and shows promise particularly in the treatment of both borderline personality disorder and eating disorders (Garfinkel, 2002; Ryle & Kerr, 2001; Winston, 2000). CAT integrates elements of psychoanalysis and cognitive therapy and is limited to about 16 sessions. Typically, the first four sessions address developmental issues

object-relations Person's relationships to the internalized representations or "objects" of others' personalities that have been introjected within the person's ego structure. See *object-relations theory*.

and the remaining sessions focus on current behaviour (Association for Cognitive Analytic Therapy, 2003). Another variant, interpersonal psychotherapy (IPT), has proven to be an effective short-term treatment for depression (Ravitz, 2004). It focuses on helping the client overcome interpersonal problems, in part by developing conflict-resolution strategies, changing one's role in interpersonal relationships, and developing new supportive social networks.

Behaviour Therapy

Behaviour therapists apply the principles of learning to help clients make adaptive changes in their behaviour. Because the focus is on changing behaviour—not on personality change or deep probing into the past—behaviour therapy is relatively brief, lasting typically from a few weeks to a few months. Behaviour therapists, like other therapists, seek to develop warm therapeutic relationships with clients, but they believe the special efficacy of behaviour therapy derives from learning-based techniques rather than from the nature of the therapeutic relationship.

Behaviour therapy first gained widespread attention as a means of helping people overcome fears and phobias, problems that had proved resistant to insight-oriented therapies. Among these methods are systematic desensitization, gradual exposure, and modelling. **Systematic desensitization** involves a therapeutic program of exposure (in imagination or by means of pictures or slides) to progressively more fearful stimuli while one remains deeply relaxed. First the person uses a relaxation technique, such as progressive muscle relaxation (discussed in Chapter 4), to become deeply relaxed. The client is then instructed to imagine (or perhaps view, as through a series of slides) progressively more anxiety-arousing scenes. If fear is evoked, the client focuses on restoring relaxation. The process is repeated until the scene can be tolerated without anxiety. The client then progresses to the next scene in the *fear-stimulus hierarchy*. The procedure is continued until the person can remain relaxed while imagining the most distressing scene in the hierarchy.

In **gradual exposure** (also called *in vivo*, meaning "in life," exposure), people troubled by phobias purposely expose themselves to the stimuli that evoke their fear. Like systematic desensitization, the person progresses at his or her own pace through a hierarchy of progressively more anxiety-evoking stimuli. A person with a fear of snakes, for example, might first look at a harmless, caged snake from across the room and then gradually approach and interact with the snake in a step-by-step process, progressing to each new step only when feeling completely calm at the prior step. Gradual exposure is often combined with cognitive techniques that focus on replacing anxiety-arousing irrational thoughts with calming rational thoughts.

In modelling, clients first observe and then imitate others who approach or interact with fear-evoking situations or objects. After observing the model, the client may be assisted or guided by the therapist or the model in performing the target behaviour. The client receives ample reinforcement from the therapist for each attempt. Modelling approaches were pioneered by Albert Bandura and his colleagues, who had remarkable success using modelling techniques to treat various phobias, especially fears of animals, such as snakes and dogs (Bandura, Blanchard, & Ritter, 1969; Bandura, Jeffery, & Wright, 1974).

Behaviour therapists also use techniques based on operant conditioning, or systematic use of rewards and punishments, to shape desired behaviour. For example, parents and teachers may be trained to reinforce children systematically for appropriate behaviour by showing appreciation and to extinguish inappropriate behaviour by ignoring it. In institutional settings, **token economies** seek to increase adaptive behaviour by allowing patients to earn tokens for performing appropriate behaviours, such as self-grooming and making their beds. The tokens can eventually be exchanged for desired rewards. Token systems have also been used to treat children with conduct-disorder problems.

Other techniques of behaviour therapy discussed in later chapters include aversive conditioning (used in the treatment of substance-abuse problems like smoking and alcoholism), social-skills training (used in the treatment of social anxieties and skills deficits associated with schizophrenia), and self-control techniques (used in helping people reduce excess weight and quit smoking).

---

systematic desensitization Behaviour therapy technique for overcoming phobias by means of exposure (in imagination or by means of slides) to progressively more fearful stimuli while one remains deeply relaxed.

gradual exposure In behaviour therapy, a method of overcoming fears through a stepwise process of direct exposure to increasingly fearful stimuli.

token economies Behavioural treatment programs in institutional settings in which a controlled environment is constructed such that people are reinforced for desired behaviours by receiving tokens (such as poker chips) that may be exchanged for desired rewards or privileges.

Humanistic-Existential Therapies

Psychodynamic therapists tend to focus on unconscious processes such as internal conflicts. By contrast, humanistic therapists focus on clients' subjective, conscious experiences. Like behaviour therapists, humanistic-existential therapists also focus more on what clients are experiencing in the present—the here and now—rather than on the past. But there are also similarities between the psychodynamic and humanistic-existential therapies. Both assume the past affects present behaviour and feelings and both seek to expand clients' self-insight. The major form of humanistic therapy is **person-centred therapy** (formerly called **client-centred therapy**), which was developed by the psychologist Carl Rogers.

Person-Centred Therapy Rogers (1951) believed that people have natural motivational tendencies toward growth, fulfillment, and health. In Rogers's view, psychological disorders develop largely from the roadblocks that others place in the journey toward self-actualization. When others are selective in their approval of our childhood feelings and behaviour, we may come to disown the criticized parts of ourselves. To earn social approval, we may don social masks or façades. We learn "to be seen and not heard" and may become deaf even to our own inner voices. Over time, we may develop distorted self-concepts that are consistent with others' views of us but are not of our own making and design. As a result, we may become poorly adjusted, unhappy, and confused as to who and what we are.

Well-adjusted people make choices and take actions consistent with their personal values and needs. *Person-centred therapy* creates conditions of warmth and acceptance in the therapeutic relationship—these conditions help clients become more aware and accepting of their true selves. Rogers was a major shaper of contemporary psychotherapy and was rated the single most influential psychotherapist in a survey of therapists (D. Smith, 1982). Rogers did not believe therapists should impose their own goals or values on their clients. His focus of therapy, as the name implies, is centred on the person.

Person-centred therapy is *nondirective*. The client, not the therapist, takes the lead and directs the course of therapy. The therapist uses *reflection*—the restating or paraphrasing of the client's expressed feelings without interpreting them or passing judgment on them. This encourages the client to further explore his or her feelings and get in touch with deeper feelings and parts of the self that had become disowned because of social condemnation.

Rogers stressed the importance of creating a warm therapeutic relationship that would encourage the client to engage in self-exploration and self-expression. The effective person-centred therapist should possess four basic qualities or attributes: *unconditional positive regard*, *empathy*, *genuineness*, and *congruence*. First, the therapist must be able to express **unconditional positive regard** for clients. In contrast to the conditional approval the client may have received from parents and others in the past, the therapist must be unconditionally accepting of the client as a person, even if the therapist sometimes objects to the client's choices or behaviours. Unconditional positive regard provides clients with a sense of security that encourages them to explore their feelings without fear of disapproval. As clients feel accepted or prized for themselves, they are encouraged to accept themselves in turn. To Rogers, every human being has intrinsic worth and value. Traditional psychodynamic theory holds that people are basically motivated by primitive forces, such as sexual and aggressive impulses. Rogers believed, however, that people are basically good and are motivated to pursue prosocial goals.

Therapists who display **empathy** are able to reflect or mirror accurately their clients' experiences and feelings. Therapists try to see the world through their clients' eyes or frames of reference.

person-centred therapy Carl Rogers's method of psychotherapy, emphasizing the establishment of a warm, accepting therapeutic relationship that frees clients to engage in a process of self-exploration and self-acceptance.

client-centred therapy Another name for Carl Rogers's *person-centred therapy*.

unconditional positive regard In Carl Rogers's view, the expression of unconditional acceptance of another person's basic worth as a person, regardless of whether one approves of all of the behaviour of the other person. The ability to express unconditional positive regard is considered a quality of an effective person-centred therapist.

empathy In Carl Rogers's theory, the ability to understand a client's experiences and feelings from the client's frame of reference. It is considered one of the principal characteristics of effective person-centred therapists.

Modelling. Modelling techniques are often used to help people overcome phobic behaviours. Here, a woman models approaching and petting a dog to a phobic child. As the phobic child observes the woman harmlessly engage in the desired behaviour, he is more likely to imitate that behaviour.

genuineness In Carl Rogers's view, the ability to recognize and express one's true feelings. Genuineness is considered to be a characteristic of the effective person-centred therapist.

congruence In Carl Rogers's theory, the fit between one's self-concept and one's thoughts, behaviours, and feelings. One of the principal characteristics of effective person-centred therapists.

They listen carefully to clients and set aside their own judgments and interpretations of events. Showing empathy encourages clients to get in touch with feelings of which they may be only dimly aware.

Genuineness is the ability to be open about one's feelings. Rogers admitted he had negative feelings at times during therapy sessions, typically boredom, but he attempted to express these feelings openly rather than hide them (Bennett, 1985).

Congruence refers to the fit between one's thoughts, feelings, and behaviour. The congruent person is one whose behaviour, thoughts, and feelings are integrated and consistent. Congruent therapists serve as models of psychological integrity to their clients. Here, Rogers (C.R.) uses reflection to help a client, Jill, focus more deeply on her inner feelings:

Jill: I'm having a lot of problems dealing with my daughter. She's 20 years old; she's in college; I'm having a lot of trouble letting her go . . . . And I have a lot of guilt feelings about her; I have a real need to hang on to her.

C.R.:   A need to hang on so you can kind of make up for the things you feel guilty about. Is that part of it?

Jill: There's a lot of that . . . . Also, she's been a real friend to me, and filled my life . . . . And it's very hard . . . a lot of empty places now that she's not with me.

C.R.:   The old vacuum, sort of, when she's not there.

Jill: Yes. Yes. I also would like to be the kind of mother that could be strong and say, you know, "Go and have a good life," and this is really hard for me, to do that.

C.R.:   It's very hard to give up something that's been so precious in your life, but also something that I guess has caused you pain when you mentioned guilt.

Jill: Yeah. And I'm aware that I have some anger toward her that I don't always get what I want. I have needs that are not met. And, uh, I don't feel I have a right to those needs. You know . . . she's a daughter; she's not my mother. Though sometimes I feel as if I'd like her to mother me . . . it's very difficult for me to ask for that and have a right to it.

C.R.:   So, it may be unreasonable, but still, when she doesn't meet your needs, it makes you mad.

Jill: Yeah I get very angry, very angry with her.

C.R.:   (*Pause*) You're also feeling a little tension at this point, I guess.

Jill: Yeah. Yeah. A lot of conflict . . . (C.R.: M-hm.). A lot of pain.

C.R.:   A lot of pain. Can you say anything more about what that's about?

SOURCE: FARBER, BRINK, & RASKIN, 1996, PP. 74–75. REPRINTED WITH PERMISSION.

Emotion-Focused Psychotherapy Emotion-focused therapy (EFT) is based on the premise that "emotion, motivation, cognition, and action occur as an integrated response package" (Greenberg, 2002a, p. 26). From this perspective, there are multiple factors that contribute to maladaptive emotions, including our genetic makeup and temperament. Early in our development, reciprocal interpersonal relationships are formed with "significant others" and gradually we develop well-ingrained patterns of emotional responses. If our early emotional responses were intense, we may fall prey to "reliving" past hurts, fears, and rages in current situations. For example, "inattentiveness from a spouse can activate intense feelings of neglect from a loveless childhood. These feelings then become maladaptive responses to the present situation" (Greenberg, 2002a, p. 32).

An essential tenet of EFT is not to eliminate intense or uncomfortable feelings, but view them as a signal to take action—"emotion moves us and reason guides us" (Greenberg,

2002a, p. x). The challenge is to know "when to change emotion and when to be changed by it" (Greenberg, 2002a, p. xi). During a counselling session, for instance, an emotion-focused therapist acts as a coach who begins by helping people become more aware and accepting of their emotions. This is followed by helping them transform their negative emotions into more adaptive ones—for example, turning unproductive anger into adaptive sadness and then acceptance though the use of emotion-shifting techniques such as role play or guided imagery. This strategy is based on the premise that even though "thinking usually changes thoughts, only feeling can change emotions" (Greenberg, 2006, p. 91). Lastly, the emotional experiences are reflected upon and assimilated to allow a new meaning of self to emerge (Greenberg, 2006). This type of therapeutic collaboration between therapist and client promotes the development of the client's *emotional intelligence* (Elliot et al., 2004).

Cognitive-Behavioural Therapies

There is nothing either good or bad, but thinking makes it so.

SHAKESPEARE, HAMLET

In these words, Shakespeare did not mean to imply that misfortunes or ailments are painless or easy to manage. His point, rather, is that the ways in which we evaluate upsetting events can heighten our discomfort and impair our ability to cope. Several hundred years later, cognitive therapists adopted this simple but elegant expression as a kind of motto for their approach to therapy.

Cognitive-behaviour therapists focus on helping clients identify and correct maladaptive beliefs, automatic types of thinking, and self-defeating attitudes that create or compound emotional problems and dysfunctional ways of behaving. They believe negative emotions such as anxiety and depression are caused by the interpretations we place on troubling events, not on the events themselves. Canadian psychologists Keith Dobson (University of Calgary) and David Dozois (University of Western Ontario) suggest that "all cognitive-behavioural therapies share three fundamental propositions:

1. cognitive activity affects behaviour
2. cognitive activity may be monitored and altered
3. desired behaviour change may be affected through cognitive change" (Dobson & Dozois, 2001, p. 4).

Here, we focus on the contributions of three prominent types of cognitive-behavioural therapy: Albert Ellis's rational-emotive behaviour therapy, Aaron Beck's cognitive therapy, and the cognitive-behavioural therapy of Donald Meichenbaum.

Rational-Emotive Behaviour Therapy Albert Ellis (1977, 1993, 2003) believed the adoption of irrational, self-defeating beliefs gives rise to psychological problems and negative feelings. Consider the irrational belief that one must have the approval almost all of the time of the people who are important to you. Ellis found it understandable to want other people's approval and love, but he argued that it is irrational to believe we cannot survive without it. Another irrational belief is that we must be thoroughly competent and achieving in everything we seek to accomplish. We are doomed to eventually fall short of these irrational expectations. When we do fall short, we may experience negative emotional consequences, such as depression and lowered self-esteem. Emotional difficulties such as anxiety and depression are not directly caused by negative events, but rather by how we distort their meaning by viewing them through the dark-coloured glasses of irrational beliefs. Thinking irrationally transforms challenging events, such as forthcoming examinations, into looming disasters ("It would be so awful if I did poorly I wouldn't be able to stand it."). Ellis's rational-emotive behaviour therapy (REBT) seeks to free people from such irrational beliefs and their consequences. In REBT, therapists actively *dispute* irrational beliefs and their premises and assist clients to develop more rational, adaptive beliefs.

Ellis and Dryden (1987) described the case of a 27-year-old woman, Jane, who was socially inhibited and shy, particularly with attractive men. Through REBT, Jane identified some of her underlying irrational beliefs, such as "I must speak well to people I find attractive" and "When

I don't speak well and impress people as I should, I'm a stupid, inadequate person!" (p. 68). REBT helped Jane discriminate between these irrational beliefs and rational alternatives, such as, "If people do reject me for showing them how anxious I am, that will be most unfortunate, but I can stand it" (p. 68). REBT encouraged Jane to debate or dispute irrational beliefs by posing challenging questions to herself: (1) "*Why* must I speak well to people I find attractive?" and (2) "When I don't speak well and impress people, how does that make me a *stupid and inadequate person*?" (p. 69). Jane learned to form rational responses to her self-questioning: for example, (1) "There is no reason I must speak well to people I find attractive, but it would be desirable if I do so, so I shall make an effort—but not kill myself—to do so," and (2) "When I speak poorly and fail to impress people, that only makes me a *person who spoke unimpressively this time*—not a *totally stupid or inadequate person*" (p. 69).

Jane also rehearsed more rational ideas several times a day. Examples included, "I would like to speak well, but I never *have to*," and "When people I favour reject me, it often reveals more about them and their tastes than about me" (pp. 69–70). After nine months of REBT, Jane was able to talk comfortably to men she found attractive and was preparing to take a job as a teacher, a position she had previously avoided due to fear of facing a class.

Ellis recognized that irrational beliefs may be formed on the basis of early childhood experiences. Changing them requires finding rational alternatives in the here and now, however. Rational-emotive behaviour therapists also help clients substitute more effective interpersonal behaviour for self-defeating or maladaptive behaviour. Ellis often gave clients specific tasks or homework assignments, like disagreeing with an overbearing relative or asking someone for a date. He assisted them in practising or rehearsing adaptive behaviours.

Beck's Cognitive Therapy As formulated by psychiatrist Aaron Beck and his colleagues (Beck, 1976; Beck et al., 1979; Beck, Freeman, & Associates, 2003), cognitive therapy, like REBT, focuses on clients' maladaptive cognitions. Cognitive therapists encourage clients to recognize and change errors in their thinking, called *cognitive distortions*, that affect their moods and impair their behaviour, such as tendencies to magnify negative events and minimize personal accomplishments.

Cognitive therapists have clients record the thoughts that are prompted by upsetting events they experience and note the connections between their thoughts and their emotional responses. They then help them dispute distorted thoughts and replace them with rational alternatives. Therapists also use behavioural homework assignments, such as encouraging depressed clients to fill their free time with structured activities such as gardening or completing work around the house. Carrying out such tasks serves to counteract the apathy and loss of motivation that tend to characterize depression and may also provide concrete evidence of competence, which helps combat self-perceptions of helplessness and inadequacy.

Another type of homework assignment involves reality testing. Clients are asked to test out their negative beliefs in the light of reality. For example, a depressed client who feels unwanted by everyone might be asked to call two or three friends on the phone to gather data about the friends' reactions to the calls. The therapist might then ask the client to report on the assignment: "Did they immediately hang up the phone? Or did they seem pleased you called? Did they express any interest at all in talking to you again or getting together sometime? Does the evidence support the conclusion that *no one* has any interest in you?" Such exercises help clients replace distorted beliefs with rational alternatives.

Consider this case in which a depressed man was encouraged to test his belief he was about to be fired from his job. The case also illustrates several cognitive distortions or errors in thinking, such as selectively perceiving only one's flaws (in this case, self-perceptions of laziness) and expecting the worst (expectations of being fired):

A 35-year-old man, a frozen-foods distributor, had suffered from chronic depression since his divorce six years earlier. During the past year, the depression had worsened and he found it increasingly difficult to call upon customers or go to the office. Each day that he avoided working made it more difficult for him to go the office and face his boss. He was convinced that he was in imminent danger of being fired since he had not made any sales calls for more than a month. Since he had not earned any commissions in a while, he felt he was not adequately supporting his two daughters and was concerned that he wouldn't have the money to send them to college. He was convinced that his basic problem was laziness, not depression. His therapist pointed out the illogic in his thinking. First of all, there was no real evidence that his boss was about to fire him. His boss had actually encouraged him to get help and was paying for part of the treatment. His therapist also pointed out that judging himself as lazy was unfair because it overlooked the fact that he had been an industrious, successful salesman before he became depressed. While not fully persuaded, the client agreed to a homework assignment in which he was to call his boss and also make a sales call to one of his former customers. His boss expressed support and reassured him that his job was secure. The customer ribbed him about "being on vacation" during the preceding six weeks but placed a small order. The client discovered that the small unpleasantness he experienced in facing the customer and being teased paled in comparison to the intense depression he felt at home while he was avoiding work. Within the next several weeks he gradually worked himself back to a normal routine, calling upon customers and making future plans. This process of viewing himself and the world from a fresh perspective led to a general improvement in his mood and behaviour.

ADAPTED FROM BURNS AND BECK, 1978, PP. 124–126

Rational-emotive behaviour therapy and Beck's cognitive therapy have much in common, especially the focus on helping clients replace self-defeating thoughts and beliefs with more rational ones. Perhaps the major difference between the two approaches is one of therapeutic style. REBT therapists tend to be more confrontational and forceful in their approach to disputing clients' irrational beliefs (Dryden, 1984; Ellis, Young, & Lockwood, 1989). Cognitive therapists tend to adopt a more gentle, collaborative approach in helping clients discover and correct the distortions in their thinking.

Meichenbaum's Cognitive-Behavioural Therapy Today many, if not most, behaviour therapists identify with the broader cognitive-behavioural therapy (CBT). Donald Meichenbaum's cognitive-behavioural therapy developed from the attempt to integrate therapeutic techniques that focus not only on making overt behavioural changes but also on changing dysfunctional thoughts and cognitions (Meichenbaum, 1977). Cognitive-behavioural therapy draws on the assumptions that cognitions and information processing play important roles in the genesis and maintenance of maladaptive behaviour and that the impact of external events is filtered through thinking processes (Beidel & Turner, 1986).

Cognitive-behavioural therapists use an assortment of behavioural and cognitive techniques in therapy. The following case illustration shows how behavioural techniques (exposure to fearful situations) and cognitive techniques (changing maladaptive thoughts) were used in the treatment of *agoraphobia*, a type of anxiety disorder characterized by excessive fears of venturing out in public:

Ms. X was a 41-year-old woman with a 12-year history of agoraphobia. She feared venturing into public places alone and required her husband or children to accompany her from place to place. *In vivo* (actual) exposure sessions were arranged in a series of progressively more fearful encounters—a fear-stimulus hierarchy. The first step in the hierarchy, for example, involved taking a shopping trip while accompanied by the therapist. After accomplishing this task, she gradually moved upwards in the hierarchy. By the third week of treatment, she was able to complete the last step in her hierarchy—shopping by herself in a crowded supermarket. Cognitive restructuring was conducted along with the exposure training. Ms. X was asked to imagine herself in various fearful situations and to report the self-statements (self-talk) she experienced. The therapist helped her

Donald Meichenbaum.

identify disruptive self-statements, such as "I am going to make a fool of myself." This particular self-statement was challenged by questioning whether it was realistic to believe that she would actually lose control, and, secondly, by disputing the belief that the consequences of losing control, were it to happen, would truly be disastrous. She progressed rapidly with treatment and became capable of functioning more independently. But she still harboured concerns about relapsing in the future. The therapist focused at this point on deeper cognitive structures involving her fears of abandonment by the people she loved if she were to relapse and be unable to attend to their needs. In challenging these beliefs, the therapist helped her realize that she was not as helpless as she perceived herself to be and that she was loved for other reasons than her ability to serve others. She also explored the question, "Who am I improving for?" She realized that she needed to find reasons to overcome her phobia that were related to meeting her own personal needs, not simply the needs of her loved ones. At a follow-up interview nine months after treatment, she was functioning independently, which allowed her to pursue her own interests, such as taking night courses and seeking a job.

ADAPTED FROM BIRAN, 1988, PP. 173–176

It could be argued that any behavioural method involving imagination or mental imagery, such as systematic desensitization, bridges behavioural and cognitive domains. Cognitive therapies such as Ellis's rational-emotive behaviour therapy and Beck's cognitive therapy might also be regarded as forms of cognitive-behavioural therapy because they incorporate cognitive and behavioural treatment methods. The dividing lines between the psychotherapies may not be as clearly drawn as authors of textbooks—who are given the task of classifying them—might desire. Not only are traditional boundaries between the cognitive and behavioural therapies blurred, but many therapists endorse an *eclectic* orientation in which they incorporate principles and techniques derived from different schools of therapy.

Eclectic Therapy

Each of the major psychological models of abnormal behaviour—the psychodynamic, learning theory, humanistic-existentialist, and cognitive-behavioural approaches—has spawned its own approaches to psychotherapy. Although many therapists identify with one or another of these schools of therapy, an increasing number of therapists identify with an eclectic approach that draws on techniques and teachings of different therapeutic approaches. Eclectic therapists look beyond the theoretical barriers that divide one school of psychotherapy from another in an effort to define what is common among the schools of therapy and what is useful in each of them. They seek to enhance their therapeutic effectiveness by incorporating principles and techniques from different therapeutic orientations (Wolfe & Goldfried, 1988). An eclectic therapist might use behaviour therapy techniques to help a client change specific maladaptive behaviours, for example, along with psychodynamic techniques to help the client gain insight into the childhood roots of the problem. The eclectic approach embodies the contemporary idea of a "best practices" model in which therapists make use of the best available treatment for a specific condition.

Surveys of therapists have consistently shown that the largest single group of psychologists and other psychotherapists (ranging from around one-third to more than half of those sampled) identified with an eclectic therapeutic orientation (Garfield, 1994). Researchers find that therapists who adopt an eclectic approach tend to be older and more experienced

(Beitman, Goldfried, & Norcross, 1989). Perhaps they have learned through experience the value of drawing on diverse contributions to the practice of therapy.

Group, Family, and Marital Therapy

In group therapy, a group of clients meet together with a therapist or pair of therapists. Group therapy has several advantages over individual treatment. For one, group therapy is less costly because several clients are treated at the same time. Many clinicians also believe group therapy may be more effective in treating groups of clients who have similar problems, such as complaints relating to anxiety, depression, lack of social skills, or adjustment to divorce or other life stresses. The group format provides clients with the opportunity to learn how people with similar problems cope with them and provides the social support of the group as well as the therapist. Group therapy also provides members with opportunities to work through their problems in relating to others. For example, the therapist or other members may point out to a particular member when he or she acts in a bossy manner or tends to withdraw when criticized, patterns of behaviour that may mirror the behaviour the client shows in relationships with others outside the group. Group members may also rehearse social skills with one another in a supportive atmosphere.

Despite these advantages, clients may prefer individual therapy for various reasons. For one, clients might not wish to disclose their problems to others in a group. Some clients prefer the individual attention of the therapist. Others are too socially inhibited to feel comfortable in a group setting, even though they might be the ones who could most profit from a group experience. Because of such concerns, group therapists require that group disclosures be kept confidential, that group members relate to each other supportively and nondestructively, and that group members receive the attention they need.

In family therapy, the family, not the individual, is the unit of treatment. Family therapy aims to help troubled families resolve their conflicts and problems so they functions better as a unit and individual members are subjected to less stress from family conflicts.

Faulty patterns of communications within the family often contribute to family problems. In family therapy, members of the family unit learn to communicate more effectively and air their disagreements constructively. Family conflicts often emerge at transitional points in the life cycle when patterns are altered by changes in one or more members. Conflicts between parents and children, for example, often emerge when adolescent children seek greater independence or autonomy. Family members with low self-esteem may be unable to tolerate different attitudes or behaviours from other members of the family and may resist their efforts to change or become more independent.

Family therapists work with families to resolve these conflicts and help them adjust to life changes among members. Family therapists are sensitive to tendencies of families to scapegoat one member as the source of the problem, or the "identified client." Disturbed families seem to adopt a sort of myth: change the identified client, the "bad apple," and the "barrel" or family will once again become functional. Family therapists encourage families to work together to resolve their disputes and conflicts, instead of resorting to scapegoating.

One widely adopted approach to family therapy, called *conjoint family therapy*, was developed by Virginia Satir (1967). Satir conceptualized the family in terms of a pattern or system of communications and interactions that needs to be studied and changed to enhance family functioning as well as the growth of individual family members.

Another prominent approach to family therapy is *structural family therapy* (Minuchin, 1974). This approach also adopts a family system model of abnormal behaviour. It conceptualizes problem behaviours of individual members of the family as arising from dysfunctional relationship patterns within the family system, rather than as problems involving only the individuals themselves. Family members may develop psychological or physical problems in response to stressful role relationships in the family. The family system usually resists efforts of individual members to change these role relationships, no matter how distorted or dysfunctional they become. Structural family therapists analyze the family roles played by individual members and help families restructure themselves in ways that are more supportive of the members. For example, a child may feel in competition with other siblings for a parent's attention and develop enuresis, or bed-wetting, as a means of securing attention. The structural family therapist would help the family understand the hidden messages in the child's behaviour and assist the family to make changes in their relationships to meet the child's needs more adequately. In so doing, the therapist shows the family how the member with the identified problem (enuresis) is responding to wider problems in the family.

Marital therapy may be considered a subtype of family therapy, in which the family unit is the marital couple. Like other forms of family therapy, marital therapy focuses on improving communication and analyzing role relationships in order to improve the marital relationship. For example, one partner may play a dominant role and resist any request to share power with the other. The marital therapist would help bring these role relationships into the open, so alternative ways of relating to one another could be explored that would lead to a more satisfying relationship.

Evaluating Methods of Treatment

The use of psychotropic drugs clearly has helped many people with severe psychological problems. Many thousands of people with schizophrenia who were formerly hospitalized are able to function more effectively in the community because of antipsychotic drugs. For example, drugs have been developed that quell the more flagrant features of schizophrenia, although they do not bring about a cure. Nor can drugs alone prepare psychiatric inmates for re-entry into society. Acquiring social and vocational skills that will permit them to assume more independent communal roles requires psychosocial or psychoeducational training.

Antidepressant drugs have helped relieve depression in many cases and have shown therapeutic benefits in treating other disorders, such as panic disorder, obsessive-compulsive disorder (OCD), and eating disorders. Electroconvulsive therapy and repetitive transcranial magnetic stimulation are helpful in relieving depression in many people who have been unresponsive to other treatments.

In the case of depression, it may be that some forms of psychotherapy are as effective as drug therapy (see Chapter 7). Moreover, problems persist with respect to the side effects of various psychotropic drugs. Minor tranquillizers have often been turned into drugs of abuse among people who become dependent on them for relieving the effects of stress rather than seeking more adaptive ways of solving their problems. Medical practitioners have too often been happy to use their prescription pads to "quick-fix" people with anxiety complaints, rather than to help them examine their lives or refer them for psychological treatment. Physicians often feel pressured, of course, by patients who seek a chemical solution to their life problems.

What, then, of the effectiveness of psychotherapy? Does psychotherapy work? Are some forms of therapy more effective than others? Are some forms of therapy more effective for some types of clients or for some types of problems than for others? The effectiveness of psychotherapy receives strong support from the research literature. Reviews of the scientific literature often utilize a statistical technique called **meta-analysis**, which averages the results of a large number of studies in order to determine an overall level of effectiveness.

In the most frequently cited meta-analysis of psychotherapy research, M. L. Smith and G. V. Glass (1977) analyzed the results of some 375 controlled studies comparing various types of therapies (psychodynamic, behavioural, humanistic, etc.) against control groups. The results of their analyses showed the average psychotherapy client in these studies was better off than 75% of the clients who remained untreated. In 1980, Smith and Glass and their colleague T. I. Miller reported the results of a larger analysis based on 475 controlled outcome studies, which showed the average person who received therapy was better off at the end of treatment than 80% of those who did not (Smith, Glass, & Miller, 1980).

Other meta-analyses also show positive outcomes for psychotherapy, including analyses of both behavioural approaches (Bowers & Clum, 1988; Lipsey & Wilson, 1993, 1995)

meta-analysis Statistical technique for combining the results of different studies into an overall average. In psychotherapy research, meta-analysis is used to compute the average benefit or size of effect associated with psychotherapy overall, or with different forms of therapy, in relation to control groups.

and brief psychodynamic approaches (Anderson & Lambert, 1995; Crits-Christoph, 1992). Evidence indicates that psychotherapy is effective not only in the confines of clinical-research centres, but also in settings that are more typical of ordinary clinical practice (Shadish et al., 1997). Although not all researchers endorse the use of meta-analysis as a methodological tool, the technique has achieved widespread acceptance within psychology and has provided some of the strongest evidence to date supporting the effectiveness of psychotherapy.

Evidence also shows that the greatest gains in psychotherapy are typically achieved in the first several months of treatment (Barkham et al., 1996; Howard et al., 1986). By the end of eight treatment sessions, roughly 50% of patients show measurable improvement (Goode, 1998). By six months of treatment, this figure rises to about 75%; by one year, about 75% of patients experience a remission of the complaints that brought them to therapy, at least to a point that the complaints no longer interfere with their ability to function normally (Howard et al., 1986; Kopta et al., 1994).

Comparing Different Therapeutic Approaches There are major methodological problems in comparing different therapies in any head-to-head test. Among the problems are differences that may exist in the types of therapists who practise one form of therapy or another, differences in the types of problems treated, and difficulties obtaining consent from clients and clinic administrators to permit random assignment to different therapies. Not surprisingly, few direct comparisons between different approaches to therapy have been reported. As an alternative to direct comparisons, investigators have turned to the use of meta-analysis to compare the relative level of effectiveness of different therapies when each is compared against control groups.

Meta-analyses show only negligible differences, overall, in outcomes among the various therapies when such therapies are compared to control groups (Crits-Christoph, 1992; M. L. Smith, Glass, & Miller, 1980; Wampold et al., 1997a, 1997b). Such minor differences suggest that the effectiveness of psychotherapy may have more to do with the features they share in common than with the specific techniques that set them apart (Lambert & Bergin, 1994).

These common features are called **nonspecific treatment factors**. Nonspecific or common factors in psychotherapy stem largely from the therapist–client relationship. These factors include the following: (1) empathy, support, and attention shown by the therapist; (2) *therapeutic alliance*, or the attachment the client develops toward the therapist and the therapy process; and (3) the *working alliance*, which refers to the development of an effective working relationship in which the therapist and client work together to identify and confront the important issues and problems the client faces (Binder & Strupp, 1997; Connors et al., 1997; Lambert & Okiishi, 1997; Weinberger, 1995).

Should we conclude that different therapies are about equally effective? One possibility is that different therapies are about equal in their effects overall but may not be equal in their effects with every patient (Wampold et al., 1997a). That is, a given therapy may be more effective for a particular patient or for a particular type of problem. It is thus insufficient to ask which therapy works best. We must ask which therapy works best for which type of problem. Which clients are best suited for which type of therapy? What are the advantages and limitations of particular therapies? Behaviour therapy, for example, has shown impressive results in treating various types of anxiety disorders, sleep disorders, and sexual dysfunctions, and in improving the adaptive functioning of people with schizophrenia and mental retardation. Psychodynamic and humanistic approaches may be more effective in fostering self-insight and personality growth. Cognitive-behavioural therapy has demonstrated impressive results in treating depression and anxiety disorders. By and large, however, the process of determining which treatment, which type of practitioner, and under what conditions is most effective for a given client remains a challenge.

nonspecific treatment factors Characteristics that are not specific to any one form of psychotherapy, but tend to be shared by psychotherapies, such as the attention a client receives from a therapist and the therapist's encouragement of the client's sense of hope and positive expectancies.

Nonspecific factors. Are the benefits of psychotherapy due to nonspecific factors that various psychotherapists share in common, such as the mobilization of hope, the attention and support provided by the therapist, and the development of a good working alliance between the client and therapist? It appears that both specific and nonspecific factors are involved in accounting for therapeutic change.

Canadian Multicultural Issues in Psychotherapy

We live in a nation that has become increasingly multiethnic and multicultural. The 2001 census listed more than 200 ethnic groups, and Canada now has its largest proportion of foreign-born citizens in 70 years. Almost one in five people is foreign-born and the same proportion has a mother tongue other than English or French (Statistics Canada, 2003a).

In the past, the diagnosis and treatment of psychological disorders was heavily influenced by European and North American thought. But this Western cultural perspective is not universally appropriate for people who hold different cultural beliefs (see Table 2.4). Cultural learning and values make a difference in what people bring to therapy (Beiser, 2003a). Canada's substantial cultural diversity creates serious mental health issues that cannot be ignored, especially at a time when biomedical models of mental health care dominate (Agbayewa, 2000; Beiser, 2003b; Bibeau et al., 1999; Macnaughton, 2000).

Mental health-care practitioners in Canada have become increasingly responsive to the cultural factors that influence the delivery of mental health services. People from different cultural backgrounds often experience and express mental distress in ways that may be open to misinterpretation by someone from another culture. For example, expressions like "I am feeling blue," "I blew my top," "I feel out of sorts," "He's forever changing his mind," and "She is getting on my nerves" are common English idioms that can carry disparate meanings vis-à-vis a person's mental state in a different culture and/or language (Hamid, 2000). In addition, misunderstanding of nonverbal communication can lead to serious mistakes by therapists when a client and therapist have differing cultural traditions and customs (Singh, McKay, & Singh, 1998). This highlights the need to understand culture-specific idioms and nonverbal cues of distress when supporting a person's mental health needs, although the assumptions must be verified in each case to avoid erroneous stereotyping.

There are two broad approaches to the delivery of mental health-care services to Canada's culturally diverse groups. One model calls for the training of culturally skilled practitioners adept at working with clients from various cultural backgrounds (Arthur & Januszkowski, 2001; Lo & Fung, 2003; Macnaughton, 2000). To be culturally skilled, a counsellor must be able to demonstrate competency in self-awareness of how his or her personal world view influences the counselling relationship, knowledge of the history and development of various Canadian cultural groups, intervention skills that address the need to vary the counselling relationship depending on the client's cultural expectations, and advocacy skills that promote cultural sensitivity of mental health problems in organizations and institutions (Arthur & Stewart, 2001).

In many Canadian settings, there are too few culturally skilled practitioners available to meet the high demand for culturally diverse mental health services. Additional methods to respond to the challenge presented by diverse populations are also needed within existing mental health-care settings. The cultural consultation services (CCS) model was designed by Lawrence Kirmayer and others at McGill University to work within existing systems. Their model made use of a culturally and professionally diverse team including interpreters/culture brokers, community organizations, clinicians with generic cultural competency, and clinicians with expertise in a specific culture or ethnic group. Although the consultants were accessed as needed, there was a core cultural team consisting of psychiatrists,

TABLE 2.4	
World Views	
Traditional Western View	**Alternative World View**
The mind and the brain are separate.	The mind and the brain are inextricably connected.
"Mental illness" is discretely separate from "mental health" and mental health is associated with "control" over symptoms.	There is a continuum of mental health that values balance or harmony among all aspects of the whole person in context of his or her sociocultural and physical environment.
Belief in and foremost value placed on an independent "self" whereby mental health is perceived as a personal problem.	Belief in the interdependence of the person and their family and community whereby mental health is perceived in terms of a person's "collective identity."

Sources: Macnaughton (2000); Pettifor (2001).

(continued)

social workers, psychiatric nurses, medical anthropologists, a physician, and a full-time clinical psychologist. A database was used to track the specific skills of each cultural consultant. Benefits of the CCS model included being able to avoid the pitfall of sweeping generalizations or cultural stereotypes while targeting mental health issues in the context of a person's particular cultural view of the problem. Moreover, there was a greatly reduced language barrier for assessment, diagnosis, and treatment, much improved short- and long-term client functioning, decreased use of mental health services, and increased clinician satisfaction (Kirmayer et al., 2003).

STUDY BREAK

Methods of Treatment

Review It

- **What are the major biological approaches to treating abnormal behaviour patterns?** Biological approaches include drug therapy, electroconvulsive therapy (ECT), repetitive transcranial magnetic stimulation (rTMS), and (rarely) psychosurgery.

- **What is psychotherapy?** Psychotherapy involves a systematic interaction between a therapist and client that incorporates psychological principles to help the client overcome abnormal behaviour, solve problems in living, or develop as an individual.

- **What is psychodynamic therapy?** Psychodynamic therapy originated with psychoanalysis, the approach to treatment developed by Freud. Psychoanalysts use techniques such as free association and dream analysis to help people gain insight into their unconscious conflicts and work them through in the light of their adult personalities. More recent psychodynamic therapies are generally briefer and less intensive.

- **What is behaviour therapy?** Behaviour therapy applies the principles of learning to help people make adaptive behavioural changes. Behaviour therapy techniques include systematic desensitization, gradual exposure, modelling, operant conditioning approaches, and social-skills training.

- **What is humanistic-existential therapy?** Humanistic approaches focus on the client's subjective, conscious experience in the here and now. Rogers's person-centred therapy helps people increase their awareness and acceptance of inner feelings that had met with social condemnation and been disowned. The effective person-centred therapist possesses the qualities of unconditional positive regard, empathy, genuineness, and congruence. Greenberg's approach, emotion-focused therapy (EFT), does not aim to eliminate intense or uncomfortable feelings, but to transform them into more adaptive feelings.

- **What are three major approaches to cognitive-behavioural therapy?** Cognitive-behavioural therapies focus on modifying the maladaptive cognitions that are believed to underlie emotional problems and self-defeating behaviour. Ellis's rational-emotive behaviour therapy focuses on disputing the irrational beliefs that occasion emotional distress and substituting adaptive behaviour for maladaptive behaviour. Beck's cognitive-behaviour therapy focuses on helping clients identify, challenge, and replace distorted cognitions, such as tendencies to magnify negative events and minimize personal accomplishments. Meichenbaum's cognitive-behavioural therapy integrates behavioural and cognitive approaches in treatment.

- **What are the general aims of group therapy, family therapy, and marital therapy?** Group therapy provides opportunities for mutual support and shared learning experiences within a group setting to help individuals overcome psychological difficulties and develop more adaptive behaviours. Family therapists work with conflicted families to help them resolve their differences. Family therapists focus on clarifying family communications, resolving role conflicts, guarding against scapegoating individual members, and helping members develop greater autonomy. Marital therapists focus on helping couples improve their communications and resolve their differences.

- **Does psychotherapy work?** Evidence from meta-analyses of psychotherapy outcome studies that compare psychotherapy with control groups supports the value of various approaches to psychotherapy.

- **How are multicultural issues involved in psychotherapy?** Therapists need to take cultural factors into account and become more aware of how their own biases may affect the therapeutic process. Western forms of psychotherapy may be inappropriate in treating members of cultural groups when conflicts in underlying cultural values emerge.

Define It

psychotherapy	transference
eclectic orientation	relationship
psychopharmacology	countertransference
tolerance	neuroleptics
rebound anxiety	antidepressants
selective serotonin-	tricyclics
reuptake inhibitors	monoamine oxidase
(SSRIs)	(MAO) inhibitors
electroconvulsive	object-relations
therapy	systematic
repetitive transcranial	desensitization
magnetic	gradual exposure
stimulation (rTMS)	person-centred therapy
token economies	client-centred therapy
prefrontal lobotomy	unconditional positive
free association	regard
compulsion to utter	empathy
resistance	genuineness
insight	congruence
manifest content	meta-analysis
latent content	nonspecific treatment
displacement	factors

Recall It*

1. Which form of biological treatment is used most widely?

   a. electroconvulsive therapy
   b. repetitive transcranial magnetic stimulation
   c. drug therapy
   d. psychosurgery

2. Traditional psychoanalysts believe that psychological problems are _____.

   a. related to underlying conflicts in identity
   b. rooted in early childhood experiences and unconscious conflicts
   c. rooted in dysfunctional relationships in the present
   d. misperceptions of oneself and one's current relationships

3. Jennifer is receiving treatment for depression. During therapy she comes to view her therapist as failing to pay enough attention to her, in much the same way that she felt her father had ignored her. Freudian therapists might say Jennifer is experiencing _____.

   a. abreaction
   b. catharsis
   c. transference
   d. countertransference

4. Jonathan consults a therapist to help overcome his fear of spiders. The therapist uses a combination of systematic desensitization and gradual exposure. His therapist most likely practises _____.

   a. behaviour therapy
   b. cognitive therapy
   c. humanistic therapy
   d. object-relations therapy

5. Cognitive therapists primarily focus on helping clients _____.

   a. actualize their unique potentials as individuals
   b. uncover deep-seated conflicts from childhood
   c. change maladaptive thinking patterns
   d. free themselves from unwanted impulses

* Recall It answers can be found on the Companion Website for this text.

Think About It

- What type of therapy would you prefer if you were seeking treatment for a psychological disorder? Why? What problems do you see in taking pills to cope with anxiety or depression that may stem from academic or social difficulties?

WEBLINKS

Centre for Addiction and Mental Health (CAMH): About Therapy
www.camh.net/Care_Treatment/Resources_clients_families_friends/
Challenges_and_Choices/challenges_choices_abouttherapy.html
A question-and-answer format is used to assist mental healthcare consumers find the
right type of therapy and therapist.

British Psychological Society Centre for Outcomes, Research and Effectiveness
www.nelmh.org/downloads/other_info/treatment_choice_psychological_therapies.pdf
Clinical best practice guidelines to aid decisions about which forms of psychological
therapy are most appropriate for which mental health consumer.

International Network on Personal Meaning (INPM)
www.meaning.ca
The INPM website provides a humanistic-existential context for the promotion of
personal meaning and spirituality. It provides a good source of articles on the topic and
an opportunity to exchange ideas through an e-forum.

Internet Mental Health
www.mentalhealth.com
Canadian psychiatrist Dr. Phillip Long created this online encyclopedia of mental health
information, which is one of the best "one-stop shopping" websites. It covers a vast
array of topics from medications to self-diagnosis.

Theoretical Perspectives and Methods of Treatment

Biological Perspectives

Genetics

Genome
- All the genetic material encoded in the DNA located in the nucleus of cells in living organisms.

DNA
- Long, complex molecular structures that determine our unique genetic code.

Genetic and Chromosomal Disorders
- Genetic errors occur when the number or order of the DNA base pairs is wrong. Chromosomal diseases result from too many, too few, or incomplete chromosomes.

Epigenetics

Epigenome
- Inherited and acquired molecular variations to the genome.

Epigenetic Mechanisms
- Regulates gene expression (turned on) and gene silencing (turned off).

Epigenetic Errors
- Epigenetic mechanisms that fail to properly regulate or signal the genes to turn on or off.

Stem Cells

Defined
- Undifferentiated cells that are capable of indefinite self-replication and differentiation into specialized cells.

Types
1. Totipotent
2. Pluripotent
3. Multipotent
4. Unipotent

The Nervous System

Neurons
- Cells of the nervous system use neurotransmission to communicate with each other and with the body.

Neurotransmitters
- Chemical substances that foster neural impulses.

Parts of the Nervous System
- Central Nervous System (CNS): the brain and spinal cord send and receive messages in the body.
- Peripheral Nervous System (PNS): the somatic and autonomic nervous systems carry messages between the CNS and the body.

Psychological Perspectives

Psychodynamic Models
Theories based on the belief that psychological problems are derived from unconscious psychological conflicts that can be traced to childhood.

Sigmund Freud—Psychoanalysis
- Key Concepts: levels of consciousness, personality structures (id, ego, super ego), ego defences, stages of psychosexual development.

Neo-Freudians place less emphasis on basic instincts and focus more on conscious choice.

Learning Models
The view that abnormal behaviour can be described in terms of not learning or underlearning appropriate, adaptive behaviours.

Ivan Pavlov—Classical Conditioning
- Key concepts: the conditioned response, unconditioned stimulus, unconditioned response, and conditioned stimulus.

B. F. Skinner—Operant Conditioning
- Key concepts: the effect of reinforcers and punishments on behaviour.

Humanistic-Existential Models
Theories that focus on self-actualization and living authentically.

Carl Rogers
- Key concepts: conditional positive regard and conditions of worth.

Neo-Humanism
- Key concept: emotional intelligence.

Cognitive-Behavioural Models
Focus on the cognitions—the thoughts, beliefs, expectations, and attitudes—that accompany and may underlie abnormal behaviour.

Albert Ellis—Rational Emotive Behavioural Therapy
- An "ABC approach" to explain the causes of negative emotions and abnormal behaviour.

Aaron Beck
- Cognitive errors in thinking include selective abstraction, overgeneralization, magnification, and absolutist thinking.

Albert Bandura
- Social-cognitive theorists focus on the roles of thinking or cognition, learning by observation, and modelling in human behaviour.

Donald Meichenbaum—Cognitive-Behaviour Modification
- Integrative technique that focuses on making overt behavioural changes and changing dysfunctional thoughts and cognitions.

Sociocultural Perspectives

The Sociocultural Perspective
The view that the causes of abnormal behaviour may reside in the failures of society rather than in the person.

Thomas Szasz
- Key concept: abnormal behaviour is a label that society attaches to people who act differently in order to stigmatize and subjugate them.

- Theorists emphasize the impact of social and cultural factors, including factors relating to ethnicity, gender and social roles, and poverty on abnormal behaviour.

- The *downward drift hypothesis* suggests that mental illness leads to poverty.

Interactionist Perspectives

Diathesis-Stress Model
The theory that a genetic or acquired predisposition, or diathesis, increases the individual's vulnerability to develop a disorder in response to stressful life circumstances.

- Diathesis: a vulnerability caused by genetic or acquired predispositions involving psychological factors and personality traits.
- Stress: biological events, psychosocial factors, and negative life events.

Biopsychosocial Models
The theory that human behaviour is linked to complex interactions among biological, psychological, and sociocultural factors.

- Internal Systems: biological—genetic, epigenetic, and neurophysiologic factors; psychological—psychodynamic, behavioural, humanistic-existential, and cognitive-behavioural factors.
- External Systems: sociocultural and environmental factors.
- Epigenetic markings on DNA are altered throughout life by interactions with internal and external factors.

Methods of Treatment

Mental Health Professionals
- Three main types in Canada: clinical psychologist, psychiatrists, and social workers.

Biological Therapies
- Psychopharmacology: anti-anxiety drugs, antipsychotic drugs, antidepressants, and lithium.
- Brain Stimulation Techniques: electroconvulsive therapy (ECT) and repetitive transcranial magnetic stimulation (rTMS).
- Psychosurgery: Early methods, e.g., the prefrontal lobotomy, have given way to more sophisticated psychosurgery techniques.
- Emerging Trends: Gene therapy, epigenetic therapy, and stem cell therapy.

Psychodynamic Therapies
- Traditional focus: to gain insight into, and resolve, unconscious conflicts.
- Methods: free association, dream analysis, and analysis of the transference relationship.
- Modern focus: briefer and target ego and cognitive functions.
- Methods: cognitive analytic therapy (CAT) and interpersonal psychotherapy (IPT).

Behaviour Therapy
- Focus: changing behaviour.
- Methods: systematic desensitization, gradual exposure, modelling, token economies, aversive conditioning, social skills training, and self-control techniques.

Humanistic-Existential Therapies
- Focus: the client's subjective, conscious experiences in the "here and now."
- Methods: person-centred therapy and emotion-focused therapy (EFT).

Cognitive-Behavioural Therapies
- Focus: correcting maladaptive beliefs, automatic types of thinking, and self-defeating attitudes.
- Methods: rational-emotive behaviour therapy (REBT), Beck's cognitive therapy, and Meichenbaum's cognitive-behaviour therapy.

Eclectic Therapy
- Focus: draws upon techniques and teachings of different therapeutic approaches. It's based on the "best practices" concept.

Group, Family, and Marital Therapy
- Group therapy: provides mutual support and shared learning experiences.
- Family and marital therapy: focus on improving communication and analyzing roles in order to improve relationships.

Evaluating Methods of Treatment
- Psychotherapy outcome studies support the value of various approaches to psychotherapy.
- Nonspecific treatment factors: empathy, support, and attention shown by the therapist; therapeutic alliance; and the working alliance.

CHAPTER 3

Classification and Assessment of Abnormal Behaviour

CHAPTER OUTLINE

Classification of Abnormal Behaviour
Reliability and Validity Issues in
Assessment
Methods of Assessment

Did You Know That...

See the underlined text on the pages indicated below for more information on these interesting and often misunderstood facts.

- Some men in India develop a psychological disorder involving excessive concerns or anxiety over losing semen? (p. 111)

- A psychological test can be highly reliable yet also invalid? (p. 115)

- Researchers find that people report more personal problems when they are interviewed by computers than by humans? (p. 120)

- The most widely used personality inventory includes a number of questions that bear no obvious relationship to the traits the instrument purports to measure? (p. 124)

- Some clinicians form diagnostic impressions on the basis of how people interpret inkblots? (p. 126)

- Researchers today can probe the workings of the brain without surgery? (p. 135)

SYSTEMS OF CLASSIFICATION of abnormal behaviour date to ancient times. Hippocrates classified abnormal behaviours on the basis of his theory of humours. Although his theory proved to be flawed, he arrived at some diagnostic categories that generally correspond to those in modern diagnostic systems. His description of melancholia, for example, is similar to present conceptions of depression. During the Middle Ages, some so-called authorities classified abnormal behaviours according to those that represented possession and those that represented natural causes. The 19th-century German psychiatrist Emil Kraepelin is generally considered the first modern theorist to develop a comprehensive model of classification based on the distinctive features or "symptoms" associated with abnormal behaviour patterns. The most commonly used classification systems today are largely an outgrowth and extension of Kraepelin's work: the Diagnostic and Statistical Manual of Mental Disorders (DSM) and the International Classification of Diseases (ICD). These two systems classify abnormal behaviour patterns as mental disorders on the basis of specified diagnostic criteria.

Why is it important to classify abnormal behaviour? For one thing, classification is the core of science. Without labelling and organizing patterns of abnormal behaviour, researchers could not communicate with one another, and progress toward understanding these disorders would come to a halt. Moreover, important decisions are made on the basis of classification. Certain psychological disorders respond better to one therapy or drug than others. Classification also helps clinicians predict behaviour. Some patterns of abnormal behaviour, such as schizophrenia, follow more or less predictable courses of development. Classification also helps researchers identify populations with similar patterns of abnormal behaviour. By classifying groups of people as depressed, for example, researchers might be able to identify common factors that help explain the origins of depression.

This chapter reviews the classification and assessment of abnormal behaviour, beginning with the major systems clinicians use in Canada to classify and report abnormal behaviour patterns: the Diagnostic and Statistical Manual of Mental Disorders (DSM) and the International Classification of Diseases (ICD).

CLASSIFICATION OF ABNORMAL BEHAVIOUR

First introduced in 1952, the DSM is now in its fourth edition, called the DSM-IV. Recently, a text revision—the Diagnostic And Statistical Manual Of Mental Disorders, 4th Edition, Text Revision, better known as the DSM-IV-TR—was published, in which the descriptive and background information on each disorder was updated (American Psychiatric Association (APA), 2000a). The definitions, diagnostic categories, and diagnostic criteria in DSM-IV-TR remain the same as those in DSM-IV.

The WHO first published an international mortality and morbidity diagnostic classification standards manual in 1893 (WHO, 2001a). The latest in the series, the International Statistical Classification of Diseases and Related Health Problems, is now in its tenth edition and for brevity, is known as ICD-10. Subsequently, the Canadian Institute for Health Information (CIHI, 2001) petitioned the WHO for permission to make Canadian enhancements to the ICD-10 and the result was the ICD-10-CA, the Canadian modification.

Throughout Canada, DSM-IV-TR is generally preferred for determining a clinical diagnosis. At the same time, the ICD-10 has been adopted as the Canadian standard for coding, reporting, and tracking health information (Alberta Mental Health Board, 2002; CIHI, 2001). Although there is a co-ordinated effort to ensure the two manuals are mutually compatible, these two diagnostic systems still require a diagnostic code conversion mechanism. For instance, the Alberta Mental Health Board (AMHB) (2002) has developed a cross-reference that effectively links the DSM-IV-TR with the codes found in Chapter 5, "Mental and Behavioural Disorders," of the ICD-10-CA.

We focus on the DSM as a method of classification because of its widespread adoption by mental health professionals. However, many psychologists and other professionals criticize the DSM on several grounds, such as relying too strongly on the medical model. Our focus on the DSM reflects recognition of its widespread use and should not be interpreted as a wholesale endorsement.

In the DSM, abnormal behaviour patterns are classified as *mental disorders*. Mental disorders involve either emotional distress (typically depression or anxiety) and/or significant impairment in psychological functioning. Impaired functioning involves difficulties in meeting responsibilities at work, within the family, or within society at large. It also includes behaviour that places people at risk for personal suffering, pain, or death.

Diagnosis of mental disorders in the DSM system requires that the behaviour pattern not represent an expected or culturally appropriate response to a stressful event, such as the loss of a loved one. People who show signs of bereavement or grief following the death of loved ones are not considered disordered, even if their behaviour is significantly impaired. If their behaviour remains significantly impaired over an extended period of time, however, a diagnosis of a mental disorder might become appropriate.

The DSM and Models of Abnormal Behaviour

The DSM system, like the medical model, treats abnormal behaviours as signs or symptoms of underlying pathologies. However, the DSM does not assume abnormal behaviours necessarily reflect biological causes or defects. It recognizes that the causes of most mental disorders remain uncertain: Some disorders may have purely biological causes, and some psychological. Still others are likely to reflect a multifactorial model that comprises the interaction of biological, psychological, social (socioeconomic, sociocultural, and ethnic), and physical environmental factors.

The authors of the DSM recognize that their use of the term *mental disorder* is problematic because it perpetuates a long-standing but dubious distinction between mental and physical disorders (APA, 2000a). They point out there is much that is "physical" in mental disorders and much that is "mental" in physical disorders. The diagnostic manual continues to use the term *mental disorder* because its developers have not been able to agree on an appropriate substitute. In this text, we use the term *psychological disorder* instead of *mental disorder* because we feel it is more appropriate to place the study of abnormal behaviour more squarely within a psychological context. Moreover, the term *psychological* has the advantage of encompassing behavioural patterns as well as strictly "mental" experiences such as emotions, thoughts, beliefs, and attitudes.

J.C. Wakefield (1992a, 1992b, 1997, 2001) proposed that the term *disorder* be conceptualized as "harmful dysfunction." A harmful dysfunction represents a failure of a mental or physical system to perform its natural function, resulting in negative consequences or harm to an individual. By this definition, dysfunction alone is not enough to constitute a disorder. For example, even though the body was naturally designed to have two kidneys, and it would be dysfunctional to have only one, the failure of one kidney to function properly (or even the loss of a kidney altogether) may not be harmful to an individual's well-being. By contrast, a dysfunction involving a breakdown in the brain's ability to store or retrieve information would constitute a disorder if it leads to harmful consequences such as memory deficits that make it difficult for the person to function effectively. We find Wakefield's conceptualization of disorders as harmful dysfunctions to be instructive to our approach to this text, although we recognize that not all psychologists share his point of view (see Lilienfeld & Marino, 1995). One problem is that we may lack agreement on what constitutes the "natural function" of mental systems (Bergner, 1997).

Finally, we should recognize that the DSM is used to classify disorders, not people. Rather than classify someone as a *schizophrenic* or a *depressive*, we refer to them as *an individual with schizophrenia* or *a person with major depression*. This difference in terminology is not simply a matter of semantics. To label someone a schizophrenic carries an unfortunate and stigmatizing implication that a person's identity is defined in terms of the disorder that he or she may have or exhibit.

Features of the DSM The DSM is descriptive, not explanatory. It describes the diagnostic features—or, in medical terms, symptoms—of abnormal behaviours, and does not attempt to explain their origins. A clinician, using the DSM classification system, arrives at a diagnosis by matching clients' behaviours with the criteria that define particular patterns of abnormal behaviour (mental disorders). An example of diagnostic criteria for pathological gambling, an impulse-control disorder, is shown in Table 3.1.

Abnormal behaviour patterns are categorized according to the clinical features they share. For example, abnormal behaviour patterns chiefly characterized by anxiety are classified as anxiety disorders (see Chapter 5, "Anxiety Disorders"). Behaviours chiefly characterized by disruptions in mood are categorized as mood disorders (see Chapter 7, "Mood Disorders and Suicide"). The DSM employs a multiaxial or multidimensional system of assessment that provides a broad range of information about an individual's functioning, not just a diagnosis (see Table 3.2 on page 106). The system contains the following axes:

1. *Axis I: Clinical* **Syndromes** and *Other Conditions That May Be a Focus of Clinical Attention.* Axis I incorporates a wide range of diagnostic classes such as anxiety disorders, mood disorders, schizophrenia and other psychotic disorders, adjustment disorders, and disorders usually first diagnosed during infancy, childhood, or adolescence (except for mental retardation, which is coded on Axis II). This axis also includes relationship problems, academic or occupational problems, or bereavement, which do not in themselves constitute definable psychological disorders. Psychological factors that affect medical conditions, such as anxiety that exacerbates an asthmatic condition or depressive symptoms that delay recovery from surgery, are also coded on Axis I.

syndrome Cluster of symptoms that is characteristic of a particular disorder.

TABLE 3.1

Sample Diagnostic Criteria for Pathological Gambling

A. A persistent and repeated pattern of maladaptive gambling behaviour that is characterized by at least five of the following ten behaviours:

1. Continually preoccupied with gambling by reliving past and anticipating future gambling experiences

2. Gambles with increasingly larger bets in order to reach a desired level of excitement

3. Repeatedly tries, but fails, to control, reduce, or stop gambling

4. Feels restless or irritable when attempting to control or stop gambling

5. Uses gambling to escape from problems or to get relief from uncomfortable feelings, such as helplessness, guilt, uneasiness, sadness, or boredom

6. Will often try to recoup gambling losses by gambling again another day

7. Tells lies to significant other to conceal the extent of gambling

8. Commits crimes, such as forgery, fraud, theft, or embezzlement, to cover gambling debts

9. Has risked or lost an important relationship or the opportunity for educational or career advancement because of gambling

10. Will rely on others for money to escape financial ruin caused by gambling

B. The gambling behaviour is not attributable to a manic episode.

Source: Adapted from the DSM-IV-TR (APA, 2000a).

TABLE 3.2

The Multiaxial Classification System of the DSM-IV-TR

Axis	Type of Information	Brief Description
Axis	Clinical Syndromes	The patterns of abnormal behaviour ("mental disorders") that impair functioning and are stressful to the individual
	Other Conditions That May Be a Focus of Clinical Attention	Other problems that may be the focus of diagnosis of treatment but do not constitute mental disorders, such as academic, vocational, or social problems, and psychological factors that affect medical conditions (such as delayed recovery from surgery due to depressive symptoms)
Axis II	Personality Disorders	Personality disorders involve excessively rigid, enduring, and maladaptive ways of relating to others and adjusting to external demands. Mental retardation involves a delay in the development of intellectual and adaptive abilities.
	Mental Retardation	
Axis III	General Medical Conditions	Chronic and acute illnesses and medical conditions that are important to the understanding or treatment of the psychological disorder or that may play a direct role in causing the psychological disorder
Axis IV	Psychosocial and Environmental Problems	Problems in the social or physical environment that affect the diagnosis, treatment, and outcome of psychological disorders
Axis V	Global Assessment of Functioning	Overall judgment of current functioning with respect to the psychological, social, and occupational functioning; the clinician may also rate the highest level of functioning occurring for at least a few months during the past year

Source: Adapted from the DSM-IV-TR (APA, 2000).

2. *Axis II: Personality Disorders and Mental Retardation.* Personality disorders are enduring and rigid patterns of maladaptive behaviour that generally impair interpersonal relationships and social adaptation. These include antisocial, paranoid, narcissistic, and borderline personality disorders (see Chapter 8, "Personality Disorders"). Mental retardation involves pervasive intellectual impairment and is also coded on Axis II.

   People may be given either Axis I or Axis II diagnoses or a combination of the two when both apply. For example, a person may receive a diagnosis of an anxiety disorder (Axis I) and a second diagnosis of a personality disorder (Axis II).

3. *Axis III: General Medical Conditions.* All medical conditions and diseases that may be important to the understanding or treatment of an individual's mental disorder are coded under Axis III. Such would be the case if **hypothyroidism** is a direct cause of an individual's mood disorder (such as major depression). Medical conditions that affect the understanding or treatment of a mental disorder but are not direct causes of the disorder are also listed on Axis III. For instance, the presence of a heart condition may determine whether a particular course of pharmacotherapy should be presecribed to a depressed person.

4. *Axis IV: Psychosocial and Environmental Problems.* Axis IV identifies any psychosocial and environmental problems believed to affect a diagnosis, treatment, or outcome of a mental disorder. Psychosocial and environmental problems include negative life events (such as a job termination or a marital separation or divorce), homelessness or inadequate housing, lack of social support, the death or loss of a friend, or exposure to war or disasters. Some positive life events may also be listed, such as a job promotion, but only when they create problems for an individual, such as difficulties adapting to a new job. A listing of these types of problems is found in Table 3.3 on page 107.

5. *Axis V: Global Assessment of Functioning (GAF).* The clinician uses a scale similar to that shown in Table 3.4 on page 108 to judge a client's current level of overall psychological, social, and occupational functioning. The clinician may also indicate the highest level of functioning achieved for at least a few months during the preceding year. The level of current functioning is taken to indicate the current need

hypothyroidism Physical condition caused by deficiencies of the hormone thyroxin that is characterized by sluggishness and lowered metabolism.

TABLE 3.3

Psychosocial and Environmental Problems

Problem Categories	Examples
Problems with Primary Support Group	Death of family members; health problems of family members; marital disruption in the form of separation, divorce, or estrangement; sexual or physical abuse within the family; child neglect; birth of a sibling
Problems Related to the Environment	Death or loss of a friend; social isolation or living alone; difficulties adjusting to a new culture (acculturation); discrimination; adjustment to transitions occurring during the life cycle, such as retirement
Educational Problems	Illiteracy; academic difficulties; problems with teachers or classmates; inadequate or impoverished school environment
Occupational Problems	Work-related problems including stressful workloads and problems with bosses or co-workers; changes in employment; job dissatisfaction; threat of loss of job; unemployment
Housing Problems	Inadequate housing or homelessness; living in an unsafe neighbourhood; problems with neighbours or landlord
Economic Problems	Financial hardships or extreme poverty; inadequate social services support
Problems with Access to Health Care Services	Inadequate health-care services or disability insurance support; difficulties with transportation to health-care facilities
Problems Related to Interaction With the Legal System/Crime	Arrest or imprisonment; becoming involved in a lawsuit or trial; being a victim of crime
Other Psychosocial Problems	Natural or human-made disasters; war or other hostilities; problems with caregivers outside the family, such as counsellors, social workers, and physicians; lack of availability of social service agencies

Source: Adapted from the DSM-IV-TR (APA, 2000).

for treatment or intensity of care. The level of highest functioning is suggestive of the level of functioning that might be restored.

An example of a diagnosis in the DSM-IV-TR multiaxial system is shown in Table 3.5 on page 108.

Evaluation of the DSM System The two basic criteria used in assessing the value of a diagnostic system such as the DSM are its reliability and validity. A diagnostic system may be considered **reliable** or consistent if various diagnosticians using the system arrive at the same diagnoses when they evaluate the same cases.

The most appropriate test of the **validity** of the DSM is its correspondence with observed behaviour. Certain DSM classes, such as anxiety disorders, appear to have generally good validity in terms of grouping people who display similar behaviours (T. A. Brown et al., 2001; Turner et al., 1986). Both the validity and reliability of some other diagnostic classes, such as personality disorders, remain areas of active study and debate (Kendell & Jablensky, 2003).

Another measure of validity, called predictive validity, is based on the ability of the diagnostic system to predict the course the disorder is likely to follow or its response to treatment. Evidence is accumulating that persons classified in certain categories respond better to certain types of medication. Persons with bipolar disorder, for example, respond reasonably well to lithium (see Chapter 7). Specific forms of psychological treatment may also be more effective with certain diagnostic groupings. For example, persons who have *specific phobias* (such as fear of heights) are generally highly responsive to behavioural techniques for reducing fears (see Chapter 5).

McGill University transcultural psychiatrists (e.g., Engelsmann, 2000; Kirmayer & Minas, 2000; Kirmayer, 2001; Prince, 2000) have argued that psychiatry in general and the DSM in particular should become more sensitive to diversity in culture and ethnicity.

reliable In psychological assessment, the consistency of a measuring instrument, such as a psychological test or rating scale. There are various ways of measuring reliability, such as test-retest reliability, internal consistency, and interrater reliability. Also see *validity*.

validity (1) With respect to tests, the degree to which a test measures the traits or constructs that it purports to measure. (2) With respect to experiments, the degree to which an experiment yields scientifically accurate and defensible results.

TABLE 3.4

Global Assessment of Functioning (GAF) Scale

Code	Severity of Symptoms	Examples
91–100	Superior functioning across a wide variety of activities of daily life	Lacks symptoms Handles life problems without them "getting out of hand"
81–90	Absent or minimal symptoms, no more than everyday problems or concerns	Mild anxiety before exams Occasional argument with family members
71–80	Transient and predictable reactions to stressful events, OR no more than slight impairment in functioning	Difficulty concentrating after argument with family Temporarily falls behind in schoolwork
61–70	Some mild symptoms, OR some difficulty in social, occupational, or school functioning, but functioning pretty well	Feels down, mild insomnia Occasional truancy or theft within household
51–60	Moderate symptoms, OR any serious impairment in social, occupational, or school functioning	Occasional panic attacks Few friends, conflicts with co-workers
41–50	Serious symptoms, OR any serious impairment in social, occupational, or school functioning	Suicidal thoughts, frequent shoplifting Unable to hold job, has no friends
31–40	Some impairment in reality testing or communication, OR major impairment in several areas	Speech illogical Depressed and unable to work, neglects family, and avoids friends
21–30	Strong influence or behaviour of delusions or hallucinations, OR serious impairment in communication or judgment, OR inability to function in almost all areas	Grossly innappropriate behaviour, speech sometimes incoherent Stays in bed all day, no job, home, or friends
11–20	Some danger of hurting self or others, OR occasionally fails to maintain personal hygiene, OR gross impairment in communication	Suicidal gestures, frequently violent Smears feces
1–10	Persistent danger of severely hurting self or others, OR persistent inability to maintain minimal personal hygiene, OR seriously suicidal act	Largely incoherent or mute Serious suicidal attempt, recurrent violence

Source: Adapted from the DSM-IV-TR (APA, 2000).

The behaviours included as diagnostic criteria in the DSM are determined by a consensus of mostly U.S.- and Canadian-trained psychiatrists, psychologists, and social workers. Had the American Psychiatric Association asked Asian-trained or Latin American-trained professionals to develop the diagnostic manual, for example, there might have been some different or revised diagnostic categories.

In fairness to the DSM, however, the latest edition—the DSM-IV-TR—does place greater emphasis than did earlier editions on weighing cultural factors when assessing abnormal behaviour (APA, 2000a). It recognizes that clinicians unfamiliar with an individual's cultural background may incorrectly classify an individual's behaviour as abnormal when it in fact falls within the normal spectrum in the individual's culture. In Chapter 1, we noted the same behaviour may be deemed normal in one culture but abnormal in

TABLE 3.5

Example of a Diagnosis in the Multiaxial DSM-IV-TR System

Axis I	Generalized Anxiety Disorder
Axis II	Dependent Personality Disorder
Axis III	Hypertension
Axis IV	Problem With Primary Support Group (marital separation); Occupational Problem (unemployment)
Axis V	GAF = 62

another. The DSM specifies that for a diagnosis of a mental disorder to be made, the behaviour in question must not merely represent a culturally expectable and sanctioned response to a particular event, even though it may seem odd in light of the examiner's own cultural standards. The DSM-IV-TR also recognizes that abnormal behaviours may take different forms in different cultures and that some abnormal behaviour patterns are culturally specific (see the feature, "Culture-Bound Syndromes" on page 110). All told, the DSM-IV (and DSM-IV-TR) is widely recognized as an improvement over previous editions, but questions still remain about the reliability and validity of certain diagnostic categories (Langenbucher et al., 2000; Thakker & Ward, 1998; Widiger & Clark, 2000).

Advantages and Disadvantages of the DSM System

Many consider the major advantage of the DSM to be its designation of specific diagnostic criteria. The DSM permits a clinician to readily match a client's complaints and associated features with specific standards to see which diagnosis best fits their case. The multiaxial system paints a comprehensive picture of clients by integrating information concerning abnormal behaviours, medical conditions that affect abnormal behaviours, psychosocial and environmental problems that may be stressful to an individual, and level of functioning. The possibility of multiple diagnoses prompts clinicians to consider presenting problems (Axis I) along with the relatively long-standing personality problems (Axis II) that may contribute to them.

Criticisms have also been levelled against the DSM system. As noted, questions remain about the system's reliability and validity. Some critics challenge specific diagnostic criteria, such as the requirement that major depression be present for two weeks before diagnosis (Kendler & Gardner, 1998). Others challenge its reliance on the medical model—a *categorical* approach to diagnosis in which a disorder is either present or absent. In the DSM system, problem behaviours are viewed as symptoms of underlying mental disorders in much the same way that physical symptoms are signs of underlying physical disorders. The very use of the term *diagnosis* presumes the medical model is an appropriate basis for classifying abnormal behaviours. An alternative approach, the *dimensional* model, quantifies multiple aspects of behaviour on the basis of degree of severity—a person may rate low on depression, but high on psychosis. The dimensional model is under consideration for the upcoming revision of the DSM (DSM-V) (Rounsaville et al., 2002; Trull, Tragesser, Solhan, & Schwartz-Mette, 2007).

Some clinicians feel that behaviour, abnormal or otherwise, is too complex and meaningful to be treated merely as symptomatic. They assert that the medical model focuses too much on what might be happening within an individual and not enough on external influences on behaviour such as social factors (socioeconomic, sociocultural, and ethnic) and physical environmental factors. Culture, for example, dictates how we define abnormality. Culture can also influence the expression and interpretation of symptoms, and therefore affects how a person will cope and how others in their culture will respond to that person's behaviour (Alarcón et al., 2002).

An additional problem is that the medical model focuses on categorizing psychological (or mental) disorders rather than describing people's behavioural strengths and weaknesses. Nor does the DSM attempt to place behaviour within a contextual framework that examines the settings, situations, and cultural contexts in which behaviour occurs. To behaviourally oriented psychologists, the understanding of behaviour, abnormal or otherwise, is best approached by examining the interaction between a person and their environment. The DSM aims to determine what "disorders" people "have"—not what they can "do" in particular situations. An alternative model of assessment, the behavioural model, focuses more on behaviours than on underlying processes—more on what people "do" than on what they "are" or "have." Behaviourists and behaviour therapists also use the DSM, of course, in part because mental health centres and health insurance carriers require the use of a diagnostic code, and in part because they want to communicate in a common language with practitioners of other theoretical persuasions. Many behaviour therapists view the DSM diagnostic code as a convenient means of labelling patterns of abnormal behaviour; a shorthand for a more extensive behavioural analysis of a problem.

Another concern about the DSM system is the potential for stigmatization of people labelled with psychiatric diagnoses. Our society is strongly biased against people who are

Culture-Bound Syndromes

Some patterns of psychological distress are limited to just one or a few cultures (Osborne, 2001). These **culture-bound disorders** are believed to be a manifestation, however exaggerated, of common folklore and belief patterns within the particular culture. For example, the psychiatric syndrome **taijin-kyofu-sho** (TKS) is common in Japan but rare elsewhere. TKS is characterized by excessive fear that one may behave in ways that will embarrass or offend other people (McNally, Cassiday, & Calamari, 1990). People with TKS may dread blushing in front of others for fear of causing them embarrassment, not for fear of embarrassing themselves. In Western culture, an excessive fear of social embarrassment is called a *social phobia* (see Chapter 5). Unlike people with TKS, however, people with social phobias have excessive concerns that they will be rejected by or embarrassed in front of others, not that they will embarrass other people. The syndrome primarily affects young Japanese men and is believed to be related to an emphasis in Japanese culture on not embarrassing others as well as deep concerns about issues of shame (McNally et al., 1990; Spitzer et al., 1994). Chang (1984) reports that TKS is diagnosed in 7% to 36% of the people treated by psychiatrists in Japan. Table 3.6 lists some other culture-bound syndromes identified in the DSM-IV-TR.

Culture-bound syndromes are portrayed in the same way as other psychological disorders in the DSM. However, in the case of some culture-bound disorders, there is scant evidence that these syndromes exist today (Trimble, Manson, Dinges, & Medicine, 1984). Such may be the case with two exotic conditions attributed to Aboriginal peoples on this continent referred to as *pibloktoq*, a dissociative episode of excitement, seizures, and short-term coma allegedly found in Inuit communities; and *ghost sickness*, a psychotic-like preoccupation with death seemingly found among Aboriginal peoples in America. These conditions are either extremely rare or they may have never existed at all—at least not in the same way that depression, schizophrenia, or alcoholism exist in Aboriginal cultures (Waldram, 2004).

We generally think of culture-bound syndromes as abnormal behaviour patterns associated with folk cultures in non-Western societies. Yet some disorders, such as anorexia nervosa (discussed in Chapter 10, "Eating Disorders and Sleep Disorders") and dissociative identity disorder (formerly called multiple personality disorder; discussed in Chapter 6, "Dissociative and Somatoform Disorders"), are recognized as culture-bound syndromes specific to industrialized or technological societies such as Canada (Hall, 2001; Ross, Norton, & Wozney, 1989). They occur rarely, if at all, in other societies.

TABLE 3.6

Examples of Culture-Bound Syndromes

Culture-Bound Syndrome	Description
amok	A disorder principally occurring in men in southeastern Asian and Pacific island cultures as well as in traditional Puerto Rican and Navajo cultures in the West, it describes a type of dissociative episode (a sudden change in consciousness or self-identity) marked by a violent or aggressive outburst following a period of brooding. These episodes are usually precipitated by a perceived slight or insult. During the episode, the person may experience amnesia or have a sense of acting automatically, as if robotic. Violence may be directed at people or objects and is often accompanied by perceptions of persecution. A return to the person's usual state of functioning follows the episode. In the West, we use the expression *running amok* to refer to an episode of losing oneself and running around in a violent frenzy. The word *amok* is derived from the Malaysian *amoq*, meaning "engaging furiously in battle."
	(continued)

culture-bound disorders Referring to patterns of behaviour that are found within only one or a few cultural contexts.

taijin-kyofu-sho Psychiatric syndrome found in Japan that involves excessive fear of offending or causing embarrassment to others. Abbreviated *TKS*.

labelled as mentally ill (Everett, 2006). They are often shunned by others and treated unfairly when it comes to many aspects of daily living, such as finding safe and adequate housing, employment, or obtaining insurance benefits. This, in turn, impedes their prospects for social integration and can contribute to a cycle of social disadvantages including unemployment, family discord, divorce, substance abuse, and so on (Kirby &

TABLE 3.6

Examples of Culture-Bound Syndromes (*Continued*)

Culture-Bound Syndrome	Description
ataque de nervios ("attack of nerves")	A way of describing states of emotional distress among Latin American and Latin Mediterranean groups, it most commonly involves features such as shouting uncontrollably, fits of crying, trembling, feelings of warmth or heat rising from the chest to the head, and aggressive verbal or physical behaviour. These episodes are usually precipitated by a stressful event affecting the family (e.g., receiving news of the death of a family member) and are accompanied by feelings of being out of control. After the attack, the person returns quickly to his or her usual level of functioning, although there may be amnesia for events that occurred during the episode.
bouffée délirante	A French term used to describe a syndrome occurring in West Africa and Haiti that is characterized by a sudden change in behaviour in which a person becomes highly agitated, aggressive, or confused, and experiences a speeding up of body movements. Auditory or visual hallucinations and paranoid thinking may be present.
dhat syndrome	A disorder (described further in Chapter 6) affecting males found principally in India that involves intense fear or anxiety over the loss of semen through nocturnal emissions, ejaculations, or through excretion with urine (despite the folk belief, semen doesn't actually mix with urine). In Indian culture, there is a popular belief that loss of semen depletes a man of his vital natural energy.
falling out or *blacking out*	Occurring principally among southern U.S. and Caribbean groups, this disorder involves an episode of sudden collapsing or fainting. The attack may occur without warning or be preceded by dizziness or feelings of "swimming" in the head. Although the eyes remain open, the individual reports an inability to see. The person can hear what others are saying and understand what is occurring but feels powerless to move.
ghost sickness	A disorder occurring among American Indian groups. It involves a preoccupation with death and with the "spirits" of the deceased. Symptoms associated with the condition include bad dreams, feelings of weakness, loss of appetite, fear, anxiety, and a sense of foreboding. Hallucinations, loss of consciousness, and states of confusion may also be present, as well as other symptoms.
koro	Found primarily in China and some other South and East Asian countries, this syndrome (also discussed further in Chapter 6) refers to an episode of acute anxiety involving the fear that one's genitals (the penis in men and the vulva and nipples in women) are shrinking and retracting into the body and that death may result.
zar	A term used in a number of countries in North Africa and the Middle East to describe the experience of spirit possession. Possession by spirits is often used in these cultures to explain dissociative episodes (sudden changes in consciousness or identity) that may be characterized by periods of shouting, banging of the head against the wall, laughing, singing, or crying. Affected people may seem apathetic or withdrawn or refuse to eat or carry out their usual responsibilities.

Source: Adapted from the DSM-IV-TR (APA, 2000) and other sources.

Keon, 2006; Stuart, 2005). Stigma also affects individuals directly when they internalize negative stereotypes, which can contribute to feelings of guilt, shame, inferiority, and the wish to conceal their condition (Everett, 2006; Stuart, 2005). Indeed, the burden of stigmatization has been portrayed as causing greater and longer-lasting suffering than the mental disorder itself (Shulze & Angermeyer, 2003). Even family members, by association, may adopt attitudes of self-loathing and self-blame when they share in the negative stereotyping of people identified as mentally ill.

Some critics argue that recent editions of the DSM have been overzealous in removing theoretical concepts that explain the causes of abnormal behaviours. Description alone, such critics claim, is too superficial and many clinicians are recommending a return to a more etiologically based diagnostic system for the next edition of the DSM. For instance, given the advances being made in the areas of genetics and brain-imaging research, some say an effort should be made to include neurobiological explanations of abnormal behaviour in the DSM-V (Charney et al., 2002).

Many critics also claim the DSM focuses too much on current behaviours and not enough on a person's history or childhood experiences. To address this, there are plans to incorporate developmental factors into the next edition. For example, the interactions between an individual and his or her social and physical environments play an important role in that person's development over the course their life. By including in the DSM the salient risks and vulnerabilities at each stage of life for each mental disorder, clinicians will be in a better position to intervene or even prevent the onset of abnormal behaviours at earlier stages of development (Pine et al., 2002).

The DSM system, despite its critics, has become part and parcel of the everyday practice of most Canadian mental health professionals. It may be the one reference manual found on the bookshelves of nearly all such professionals, dog-eared from repeated use. Perhaps the DSM is best considered a work in progress, not a final product.

Now let us consider various ways of assessing abnormal behaviour. We begin by considering the basic requirements for methods of assessment so that they'll be reliable and valid.

STUDY BREAK

Classification of Abnormal Behaviour

Review It

- **What is the DSM and what are its major features?** The *Diagnostic and Statistical Manual of Mental Disorders* (DSM) is the most widely accepted system for classifying mental disorders. The DSM uses specific diagnostic criteria to group patterns of abnormal behaviours that share common clinical features and a multiaxial system of evaluation.

- **Why is the DSM considered a multiaxial system?** The DSM system consists of five axes of classification: Axis I (Clinical Syndromes), Axis II (Personality Disorders), Axis III (General Medical Conditions), Axis IV (Psychosocial and Environmental Problems), and Axis V (Global Assessment of Functioning, or GAF).

- **What are the major strengths and weaknesses of the DSM?** Strengths of the DSM include its use of specified diagnostic criteria and a multiaxial system to provide a comprehensive picture of a individual's functioning. Weaknesses include questions about the reliability and validity of certain diagnostic categories, and for some, the adoption of a medical model framework for classifying abnormal behaviour patterns.

Define It

syndrome	validity
hypothyroidism	culture-bound disorders
reliable	taijin-kyofu-sho

Recall It*

1. Which of the following is NOT considered a feature of a mental disorder in the DSM system?

    a. emotional distress
    b. difficulties meeting usual responsibilities
    c. significant change in an underlying physical condition
    d. impaired functioning

2. Critics of the DSM system have often claimed that it relies too heavily on the _____ model of abnormal behaviour.

    a. medical
    b. psychodynamic

c. sociocultural

d. social deviance

3. According to Wakefield, the term *disorder* might be conceptualized as _____.

a. socially impaired behaviour

b. physiologically based problems

c. harmful dysfunction

d. a way of stigmatizing people who act differently

4. The current version of the DSM places more emphasis than previous versions on _____.

a. descriptive criteria for defining disorders

b. underlying dynamics involved in psychological disorders

c. cultural factors

d. theoretical bases of abnormal behaviour

5. Each of the following is a criticism of the DSM *except* _____.

a. its reliance on the medical model of classification

b. its use of specific diagnostic criteria

c. its emphasis on classification of disorders rather than describing behavioural strengths and weaknesses

d. concerns about the validity and reliability of particular diagnostic groupings

* Recall It answers can be found on the Companion Website for this text.

Think About It

• How do you see the advantages and disadvantages of using a system like the DSM to classify abnormal behaviour patterns? Can you think of other ways we might classify abnormal behaviour patterns?

RELIABILITY AND VALIDITY ISSUES IN ASSESSMENT

Important decisions are made on the basis of classification and assessment. For example, recommendations for specific treatment techniques vary according to our assessment of the problems that a client might exhibit. Therefore, methods of assessment, like diagnostic categories, must be *reliable* and *valid*.

Reliability

The reliability of a method of assessment, like that of a diagnostic system, refers to its consistency. A gauge of height would be unreliable if people looked taller or shorter at every measurement. A reliable measure of abnormal behaviour must also yield comparable results on different occasions. Different people should be able to check the yardstick and agree on the measured height of a subject. A yardstick that shrinks and expands markedly with the slightest change in temperature would be unreliable. So would one that is difficult to read.

There are three main approaches for demonstrating the reliability of assessment techniques.

Internal Consistency Correlational techniques are used to show whether the different parts or items of an assessment instrument, such as a personality scale or test, yield results that are consistent with one another and with the instrument as a whole. **Internal consistency** is crucial for tests intended to measure single traits or construct dimensions. When the individual items or parts of a test are highly correlated with one another, we can assume they are measuring a common trait or construct. For example, if responses to a set of items on a depression scale are not highly correlated with one another, there is no basis for assuming the items measure a single common dimension or construct—in this case, depression.

One commonly used method of assessing internal consistency, **coefficient alpha**, is based on a statistical computation of the average intercorrelations (interrelationships) of all the items making up a particular test. The higher coefficient alpha is, the greater the internal consistency of the test.

internal consistency Reliability as measured by the cohesiveness or interrelationships of the items on a test or scale.

coefficient alpha Measure of internal consistency or reliability: the average intercorrelation among the items comprising a particular scale or test.

Some tests are multidimensional in content. They contain subscales or factors that measure different construct dimensions. One such test is the Minnesota Multiphasic Personality Inventory (MMPI), which assesses various dimensions of abnormal behaviour. In such cases, subscales within the test intended to measure individual traits, such as the hypochondriasis and depression subscales, are expected to show internal consistency. Subscales need not correlate with each other, however, unless the traits they are presumed to measure are interrelated.

Temporal Stability

Reliable methods of assessment also have **temporal stability** (stability over time). They yield similar results on separate occasions. We would not trust a bathroom scale that yielded different results each time we weighed ourselves—unless we had stuffed or starved ourselves between weighings. The same principle applies to methods of psychological assessment. Temporal stability is measured by means of **test-retest reliability**, which represents the correlation between two administrations of the test separated by a period of time. The higher the correlation, the greater the temporal stability or test-retest reliability of the test.

Assessment of test-retest reliability is most important in the measurement of traits assumed to remain stable over time, such as intelligence and aptitude. Yet measures of test-retest reliability on intelligence and aptitude tests can be compromised because of a *warm-up effect*; that is, scores can improve due to familiarity with the test.

Interrater Reliability

Interrater reliability—also referred to as *interjudge reliability*—is usually of great importance in making diagnostic decisions and for measures requiring ratings of behaviour. A diagnostic system is not reliable unless expert raters agree as to their diagnoses on the basis of the system. Two teachers may be asked to use a behavioural rating scale to evaluate a child's aggressiveness, hyperactivity, and sociability. The level of agreement between the raters would be an index of the reliability of the scale.

Validity

The validity of assessment techniques or measures refers to the degree to which the instruments in question measure what they are intended to measure. There are various kinds of validity, such as *content*, *construct*, and *criterion validity*.

Content Validity

The **content validity** of an assessment technique is the degree to which its content covers a representative sample of the behaviours associated with the construct dimension or trait in question. For example, depression includes features such as sadness and lack of participation in previously enjoyed activities. To have content validity, techniques assessing depression should thus have features or items that address these areas. One type of content validity, called **face validity**, is the degree to which questions or test items bear an apparent relationship to the constructs or traits they purport to measure. A face-valid item on a test of assertiveness could be, "I have little difficulty standing up for my rights." An item that lacks face validity as a measure of assertiveness could read, "I usually subscribe to magazines that contain features about world events."

The limitation of face validity is its reliance on subjective judgment in determining whether or not the test measures what it is supposed to measure. The apparent or face validity of an assessment technique is not sufficient to establish its scientific value. A scientific test may also be valid if its results relate to some standard or criterion, even though the items themselves do not have high face validity. This brings us to criterion validity.

Criterion Validity

Criterion validity represents the degree to which the assessment technique correlates with an independent, external criterion (standard) of what the technique is intended to assess. There are two general types of criterion validity: concurrent validity and predictive validity.

Concurrent validity is the degree to which test responses predict scores on criterion measures taken at about the same time. Most psychologists presume intelligence is in part responsible for academic success. The concurrent validity of intelligence test scores is thus frequently studied by correlating test scores with criteria such as school grades and teacher ratings of academic abilities.

A test of depression might be validated in terms of its ability to identify people who meet diagnostic criteria for depression. Two related concepts are important here: sensitivity and specificity. **Sensitivity** refers to the degree to which a test correctly identifies people who have the disorder the test is intended to detect. Tests that lack sensitivity produce a high number of *false negatives*—individuals identified as not having the disorder who truly have the disorder. **Specificity** refers to the degree to which the test avoids classifying people as having a particular disorder who truly do not have the disorder. Tests that lack specificity produce a high number of *false positives*—people identified as having the disorder who truly do not have the disorder. By taking into account the sensitivity and specificity of a given test, we can determine the ability of the test to correctly classify individuals.

Predictive validity refers to the ability of a test to predict future behaviour. A test of academic aptitude may be validated in terms of its ability to predict school performance in a particular area.

Construct Validity

Construct validity is the degree to which a test corresponds to the theoretical model of the underlying construct or trait it purports to measure. Consider a test that purports to measure anxiety. Anxiety is not a concrete object or phenomenon. It can't be measured directly, counted, weighed, or touched. Anxiety is a theoretical construct that helps explain phenomena like a pounding heart or the sudden inability to speak when you ask an attractive person out on a date. Anxiety may be indirectly measured by such means as self-report (rating one's own level of anxiety) and physiological techniques (measuring the level of sweat on the palms of one's hands).

The construct validity of a test of anxiety requires the results of the test to predict other behaviours that would be expected given your theoretical model of anxiety. Assume that your theoretical model predicts that anxious college students would experience greater difficulties than calmer students in speaking coherently when asking someone for a date, but not when they are merely rehearsing the invitation in private. If the speech behaviour of high and low scorers on a test purported to measure test anxiety fits these predicted patterns, we can say the evidence supports the construct validity of the test. Construct validity involves a continuing process of testing relationships among variables that are predicted from a theoretical framework. We can never claim to have proven the construct validity of a test because it is always possible to come up with an alternative theoretical account of these relationships.

A test may be reliable (gives you consistent responses) but still not measure what it purports to measure (and is therefore invalid). A test of musical aptitude might have excellent reliability but be invalid as a measure of general intelligence. 19th-century **phrenologists** believed they could gauge people's personalities by measuring the bumps on their heads. Their callipers provided reliable measures of their subjects' bumps and protrusions; the measurements, however, did not provide valid estimates of subjects' psychological traits. The phrenologists were bumping in the dark, so to speak.

Sociocultural and Ethnic Factors in the Assessment of Abnormal Behaviour

Researchers and clinicians also need to be aware of sociocultural and ethnic factors when they assess personality traits and psychological disorders. Assessment techniques may be reliable and valid in one culture but not in another, even when they are translated accurately (Kleinman, 1987). In one study, Chan (1991) administered a Chinese-language version of the

sensitivity Ability of a test or diagnostic instrument to identify people as having a given characteristic or disorder who truly have the characteristic or disorder.

specificity Ability of a test or diagnostic instrument to avoid classifying people as having a characteristic or disorder who truly do not have the characteristic or disorder.

predictive validity Degree to which a test response or score is predictive of some criterion behaviour (such as school performance) in the future.

construct validity Degree to which a test or instrument measures the hypothetical construct that it purports to measure.

phrenologist Practitioner of the study of bumps on a person's head as indications of the individual's underlying traits or characteristics.

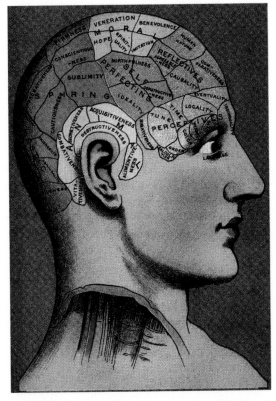

Phrenology. In the 19th century, some people believed that mental faculties and abilities were based in certain parts of the brain and that people's acumen in such faculties could be assessed by gauging the protrusions and indentations of the skull.

Beck Depression Inventory (BDI), a widely used inventory of depression in Canada, to a sample of Chinese students and psychiatric patients in Hong Kong. The Chinese BDI met tests of reliability, as judged by internal consistency, and of validity, as judged by its ability to distinguish people with depression from nondepressives among a small sample of Chinese psychiatric patients. Yet other investigators found that Chinese people in both Hong Kong and the People's Republic of China tended to achieve higher scores on a subscale of the Chinese MMPI that is suggestive of deviant responses (Cheung, Song, & Butcher, 1991). These higher scores appeared to reflect cultural differences, however, rather than greater psychopathology (Cheung et al., 1991; Cheung & Ho, 1997).

Most diagnostic schedules consider culture to some degree, but researchers believe they fail to provide adequate norms for different cultural and ethnic groups. Translations of instruments should not only translate words, they should also provide instructions that encourage examiners to address the importance of cultural beliefs, norms, and values, so that diagnosticians and interviewers will be prompted to seriously consider an individual's background when making assessments of abnormal behaviour patterns.

Interviewers need also be sensitized to problems that can arise when interviews are conducted in a language other than the client's mother tongue (Kirmayer, Groleau, Guzder, Blake, & Jarvis, 2003). Problems can arise when interviewers who use a second language fail to appreciate its idioms and subtleties (Hamid, 2000). J. S. Nevid recalls a case in a U.S. mental hospital in which the interviewer, a foreign-born psychiatrist, reported that a patient exhibited the delusional belief that he was outside his body. This assessment was based on the patient's response to a question posed by the psychiatrist. The psychiatrist had asked the patient if he was feeling anxious and the patient replied, "Yes, Doc, I feel like I'm jumping out of my skin at times."

STUDY BREAK

Reliability and Validity Issues in Assessment

Review It

• **What are the major characteristics by which methods of assessment are judged?** Methods of assessment must be reliable and valid. Reliability of assessment techniques is shown in various ways, including internal consistency, temporal stability, and interrater reliability. Validity is measured by means of content validity, criterion validity, and construct validity.

Define It

internal consistency
coefficient alpha
temporal stability
test-retest reliability
interrater reliability
content validity
face validity

criterion validity
concurrent validity
sensitivity
specificity
predictive validity
construct validity
phrenologist

Recall It*

1. Which of the following is NOT a method used to establish reliability of assessment techniques?

   a. internal consistency
   b. construct reliability
   c. interrater reliability
   d. temporal stability

2. Coefficient alpha is a statistical method used to assess _____.

   a. internal consistency
   b. interrater reliability
   c. predictive reliability
   d. temporal stability

3. Sal uses his bathroom scale to weigh himself every morning. If his weight remains steady and the scale gives him consistent measures, we can say the scale shows _____.

   a. internal consistency
   b. intertest consistency
   c. construct validity
   d. temporal stability

4. The degree to which a test measures what it purports to measure reflects its _____.

a. reliability
b. stability
c. validity
d. rigour

5. A test developer claims a new test intended to measure anxiety is highly correlated with behaviours theoretically associated with anxiety. This test can be said to have _____.

a. construct validity
b. concurrent validity
c. pattern validity
d. content validity

* Recall It answers can be found on the Companion Website for this text.

Think About It

- Suppose you wanted to develop a new psychological test or measure. How would you go about demonstrating it was reliable and valid?

METHODS OF ASSESSMENT

Here, we explore methods of assessment that clinicians use to arrive at diagnostic impressions, including interviews, psychological testing, self-report questionnaires, behavioural measures, and physiological measures. The role of assessment, however, goes further than classification. A careful assessment provides a wealth of information about clients' personalities and cognitive functioning. This information helps clinicians acquire a broader understanding of their clients' problems and recommend appropriate forms of treatment.

The Clinical Interview

The clinical interview is the most widely used means of assessment. It is employed by all helping professionals and paraprofessionals. The interview is usually a client's first face-to-face contact with a clinician. Clinicians often begin by asking clients to describe the presenting complaint in their own words. They may say something like, "Can you describe to me the problems you've been having lately?" (Therapists learn not to ask, "What brings you here?" to avoid receiving such answers as "A car," "A bus," or "My social worker.") The clinician will then usually probe aspects of the presenting complaint, such as behavioural abnormalities and feelings of discomfort, the circumstances regarding the onset of the problem, history of past episodes, and how the problem affects the client's daily functioning. The clinician may explore possible precipitating events, such as changes in life circumstances, social relationships, employment, or schooling. The interviewer encourages the client to describe the problem in her or his own words in order to understand it from the client's point of view.

Although the format of an intake process may vary from clinician to clinician, most interviews cover topics such as:

1. *Identifying data*. Information regarding the client's sociodemographic characteristics: address and telephone number, marital status, age, gender, racial/ethnic characteristics, religion, employment, family composition, and so on.

2. *Description of the presenting problem(s)*. How does the client perceive the problem? What troubling behaviours, thoughts, or feelings are reported? How do they affect the client's functioning? When did they begin?

3. *Psychosocial history*. Information describing the client's developmental history: educational, social, and occupational history; early family relationships.

4. *Medical/psychiatric history*. History of medical and psychiatric treatment and hospitalizations. Is the present problem a recurrent episode of a previous problem?

How was the problem handled in the past? Was treatment successful? Why or why not?

5. *Medical problems/medication.* Description of present medical problems and present treatment, including medication. The clinician is alert to ways in which medical problems may affect the presenting psychological problem. For example, drugs for certain medical conditions can affect mood and general levels of arousal.

Differences in Theoretical Approaches Each interviewer is guided by his or her own theoretical approach. A behaviourally oriented interviewer might seek detailed information about the events that precede and follow the occurrence of the problem behaviour—searching for stimuli that trigger the problem behaviour and for reinforcements that maintain it.

Consider the case of Pamela:

> A young woman of 19, Pamela, is seen for an initial evaluation. She complains of fear of driving her car across a bridge on a route that she must take to attend college. She reports that she fears "freezing up" at the wheel and causing an accident if she were to drive across the bridge. Upon interview, she reports that the problem began six months earlier, shortly after she experienced intense anxiety driving across a different bridge. It nearly caused her to lose control of her car. Now she takes three buses to make the trip, increasing her commutes by more than an hour each way. But she has heard that the bus company may terminate her route, so she would have to take another local bus to make connections, adding another half hour or more to the trip. She wonders whether she should transfer to a community college nearer home, even though it doesn't offer the program of study that most interests her.
>
> THE AUTHORS' FILES

A behavioural interviewer might try to determine the stimulus cues that evoke Pamela's fear. For example, is the fear greater or lesser depending on the height of the bridge? The depth of the ground or water below? The steepness of the incline? The narrowing of the road? Can Pamela quantify the fear she encounters at the inclines, overpasses, and bridges in the roadways she uses? Such information might help the therapist map out a strategy of gradual exposure to these stimuli (see Chapter 5).

A psychodynamically oriented interviewer might focus on Pamela's early childhood experiences, seeking clues as to how her fear of driving over bridges may symbolize unconscious conflicts. Might the crossing of a bridge symbolically represent separation from her parents and signify conflict concerning issues of independence and separation? Did Pamela experience separation anxiety as a child that might be reactivated in her current travel? Does her travel phobia protect her from facing adult challenges that require more independence and self-confidence than she can muster—such as attending a college outside her immediate community and pursuing the more demanding career opportunities the college offers?

Whatever the theoretical orientation of the interviewer, interviewing skills and techniques have a few features in common. Psychologists and other professionals are trained to establish **rapport** and feelings of trust with a client. These feelings help put the client at ease and encourage candid communication. Effective interviewers do not pressure clients to disclose sensitive information. Clients are generally more willing to disclose their personal feelings and experiences to someone who shows concern and understanding, someone they feel they can trust. When an interviewer is skilful, clients are less likely to fear they will be criticized or judged for revealing sensitive information.

Interview Formats There are three general types of clinical interviews: **unstructured interviews, semi-structured interviews,** and **structured interviews.** In an unstructured

rapport In psychotherapy, the interpersonal relationship between a therapist and a client that is characterized by harmony, trust, and co-operation.

unstructured interviews Type of clinical interview in which interviewers determine which questions to ask rather than following a standard interview format.

semi-structured interviews Type of clinical interview in which interviewers are guided by a general outline but are free to modify the order in which questions are asked and to branch off in other directions.

structured interviews Means by which an interviewer obtains clinical information from a client by asking a fairly standard series of questions concerning such issues as the client's presenting complaints or problems, mental state, life circumstances, and psychosocial or developmental history.

interview, the clinician adopts his or her own style of questioning rather than following any standard format. In a semi-structured interview, the clinician follows a general outline of questions designed to gather essential information, but is free to ask the questions in any particular order and to branch off in other directions in order to follow up on clinically important information. In a structured interview, the interview follows a preset series of questions in a particular order.

The major advantage of the unstructured interview is its spontaneity and conversational style. There is an active give-and-take between the interviewer and the client because the interviewer is not bound to follow any specific set of questions. The major disadvantage is the lack of standardization. Different interviewers may ask questions in different ways. For example, one interviewer might ask, "How have your moods been lately?" and another might pose the question, "Have you had any periods of crying or tearfulness during the past week or two?" Client response may depend to a certain extent on how the questions were asked. Another drawback is that the conversational flow of the interview may fail to touch on important clinical information needed to form a diagnostic impression. A semi-structured interview provides more structure and uniformity, but at the possible expense of spontaneity. Clinicians may seek to strike a balance by conducting a semi-structured interview in which they follow a general outline of questions but allow themselves the flexibility to depart from the interview protocol to pursue issues that seem important.

Structured interviews (also called *standardized interviews*) provide the highest level of reliability and consistency in reaching diagnostic judgments, which is why they are used frequently in research settings. Yet many clinicians prefer using a semi-structured approach because of its greater flexibility. A leading example of structured interview protocol is the Structured Clinical Interview for the DSM (SCID). The SCID includes **closed-ended questions** to determine the presence of behaviour patterns that suggest specific diagnostic categories and **open-ended questions** that allow clients to elaborate their problems and feelings. The SCID guides the clinician in testing diagnostic hypotheses as the interview progresses. Recent research supports the reliability of the SCID across various clinical settings (J. B. Williams et al., 1992).

In the course of an interview, a clinician may also conduct a more formal assessment of their client's cognitive functioning by administering a **mental status examination**. This involves a formal assessment of the client's appearance (appropriateness of attire and grooming), mood, attention, perceptual and thinking processes, memory, orientation (knowing who they are, where they are, and the present date), level of awareness or insight into their problems, and judgment in making life decisions. The interviewer compiles all the information available from the interview and review of the client's background and presenting problems to arrive at a diagnostic impression.

closed-ended questions Questionnaire or test items that have a limited range of response options.

open-ended questions Type of questions that provide an unlimited range of response options.

mental status examination Structured clinical evaluation to determine various aspects of a client's mental functioning.

Psychological Tests of Intelligence and Personality

Psychological tests are structured methods of assessment used to evaluate reasonably stable traits such as intelligence and personality. Tests are usually standardized on large numbers of subjects and provide norms that compare clients' scores with an average. By comparing test results from samples of people who are free of psychological disorders with those of people who have diagnosable psychological disorders, we may gain some insight into the types of response patterns that are indicative of abnormal behaviour.

Intelligence Tests
The assessment of abnormal behaviour often includes an evaluation of intelligence. Formal tests of intelligence are used to help diagnose mental retardation. They evaluate the intellectual impairment that may be the result of other disorders, such as organic mental disorders caused by damage to the brain. They also provide a profile of a client's intellectual strengths and weaknesses, which helps in the development of a treatment plan suited to the client's competencies.

Intelligence is a controversial concept in psychology, however. Even attempts at definition stir debate. David Wechsler, the originator of a widely used series of intelligence tests, defined intelligence as "capacity . . . to understand the world . . . and . . . resourcefulness

intelligence (1) Global capacity to understand the world and cope with its challenges. (2) Trait or traits associated with successful performance on intelligence tests.

Would You Tell Your Problems to a Computer?

Picture yourself seated before a computer screen. A message on the screen asks you to type in your name and press *Enter*. Not wanting to offend, you comply. This message then appears: "Hello, my name is Sigmund. I'm programmed to ask you a set of questions to learn more about you. May I begin?" You nod your head yes, momentarily forgetting the computer can only "perceive" keystrokes. You type "yes" and the interview begins.

Computerized clinical interviews have been used for more than 25 years. Consider a computerized interview system named CASPER. Interview questions and response options, such as the following, are presented on the screen:

"About how many days in the past month did you have difficulty falling asleep, staying asleep, or waking too early (include sleep disturbed by bad dreams)?"

"During the past month, how have you been getting along with your spouse/partner? (1) Very satisfactory; (2) Mostly satisfactory; (3) Sometimes satisfactory, sometimes unsatisfactory; (4) Mostly unsatisfactory; (5) Very unsatisfactory."

FARRELL ET AL., 1987, P. 692

The client presses a numeric key to respond to each item. CASPER is a branching program that follows up on problems suggested by the client's responses. For example, if the client indicates difficulty in falling or remaining asleep, CASPER asks whether or not sleep has become a major problem—"something causing you great personal distress or interfering with your daily functioning" (Farrell et al., 1987, 693). If the client indicates yes, the computer will return to the problem after other items have been presented and ask the client to rate the duration and intensity of the problem. Clients may also add or drop complaints—change their minds, that is.

A study found that a brief diagnostic interview conducted over the phone by a computer equipped with voice-response technology achieved similar results to a human interviewer using a more intensive interview protocol, the SCID (Kobak et al., 1997). Moreover, people generally reveal more personal problems to CASPER than they do when interviewed by a human. Perhaps people are less concerned about being "judged" by computers. Perhaps the computer interview is especially helpful in identifying problems the client is embarrassed or unwilling to report to a human. Perhaps the computer seems more willing to take the time to note all complaints.

Reviews of research suggest that computer programs are as capable as skilled clinicians at obtaining information from clients and reaching an accurate diagnosis, and are less expensive and more time-efficient (Bloom, 1992; Kobak et al., 1996). It seems that most of the resistance to using computer interviews for this purpose comes from clinicians rather than clients.

Computer-assisted treatments for mental health problems are also available. The most basic form of e-therapy is through email correspondence and generally addresses less serious problems—it more often entails giving advice or is psycho-educational in nature (Rochlen, Zack, & Speyer, 2004). Text messaging and chat rooms have also been gaining in popularity because of their "real-time" quality, which allows for immediacy and clarification (Castelnuovo, Gaggioli, Mantovani, & Riva, 2003). Self-help groups, such as Alcoholics Anonymous, have been using a chat-room format as a form of group therapy since the 1990s (Griffiths, 2005). Today, computer video-conferencing between therapists and clients offers a promising alternative mode of mental health treatment (Bouchard et al., 2004; Ruskin et al., 2004). It may prove to be especially useful in circumstances where face-to-face therapy is impractical, such as in many remote and northern regions of Canada.

---

to cope with its challenges" (1975). From his perspective, intelligence has to do with the ways in which we (1) mentally represent the world, and (2) adapt to its demands. There are various intelligence tests, including group tests and those that are administered individually, such as the Stanford-Binet Intelligence Scale (SBIS) and the Wechsler scales. Individual tests allow examiners to observe the behaviour of a respondent while recording answers. Examiners can thus gain insight as to whether factors such as testing conditions, language problems, illness, or level of motivation contribute to a given test performance.

The SBIS was originated by Frenchmen Alfred Binet and Theodore Simon in 1905 in response to the French public school system's quest for a test that could identify children who might profit from special education. The initial Binet-Simon scale yielded a score called a **mental age** (MA) that represented a child's overall level of intellectual functioning.

mental age Age equivalent that corresponds to the person's level of intelligence, as measured by performance on the Stanford-Binet Intelligence Scale. Abbreviated *MA*.

A child who received an MA of eight was said to be functioning as a typical eight-year-old. Children received "months" of credit for correct answers, and their MAs were determined by adding them up.

Louis Terman of Stanford University adapted the Binet-Simon test for American children in 1916, and it became known by its full current name: the Stanford-Binet Intelligence Scale (SBIS). The SBIS also yielded an **intelligence quotient** (IQ), which reflected the relationship between a child's MA and chronological age (CA), according to this formula:

$$IQ = MA/CA \times 100$$

intelligence quotient Measure of intelligence derived on the basis of scores on an intelligence test. Called a quotient because it was originally derived by dividing a respondent's *mental age* by her or his actual age. Abbreviated *IQ*.

Examination of this formula shows that children who received identical mental age scores might differ markedly in IQ, with a younger child attaining a higher IQ.

Binet assumed that intelligence grew as children developed, so older children would answer more correct answers. He thus age-graded his questions and arranged them according to difficulty level, a practice carried over into the Stanford-Binet, as shown in Table 3.7 below.

Today, the SBIS is used for children and adults, and test takers' IQ scores are based on their deviation from the norms of their age group. A score of 100 is defined as the mean. People who answer more items correctly than the average obtain IQ scores above 100; those who answer fewer items correctly obtain scores of less than 100.

This method of deriving an IQ score, called the **deviation IQ**, was used by psychologist David Wechsler in developing various intelligence tests for children and adults, known as the Wechsler scales. The Wechsler scales group questions into subtests like those shown in Table 3.8 on page 122, each of which measures a different intellectual task. The Wechsler scales are thus designed to offer insight into a person's relative strengths and weaknesses, and not simply yield an overall score.

deviation IQ Intelligence quotient derived by determining the deviation between the individual's score and the norm (mean).

Wechsler's scales include both *verbal* and *performance* subtests. Verbal subtests generally require knowledge of verbal concepts; performance subtests rely more on spatial-relations skills. (Figure 3.1 on page 123 shows items similar to those on performance subtests of the Wechsler scales.) Wechsler's scales allow for computation of verbal and performance IQs.

Students from various backgrounds yield different profiles. Post-secondary students, generally speaking, perform better on verbal subtests than on performance subtests. Australian Aboriginal children outperform white Australian children on performance-type tasks that involve visual-spatial skills (Kearins, 1981). Such skills are likely to foster survival in the harsh Australian outback. Intellectual attainments, like psychological adjustment, are connected with the demands of particular sociocultural and physical environmental settings.

Wechsler IQ scores are based on how respondents' answers deviate from those attained by their age-mates. The mean whole test score at any age is defined as 100. Wechsler distributed IQ scores so that 50% of the scores of a population would lie within a "broad average" range of 90 to 110.

TABLE 3.7	
Items Similar to Those on the Stanford-Binet	
Age	**Sample Item**
2	"Point to your toes."
6	"Tell me what's next: A minute is short; an hour is _____."
10	"Try to repeat these numbers: 8-9-4-2-6-1."
11	"How are 'beginning' and 'end' alike?"
Adult	"What does this mean? 'The watched pot never boils'?"

Source: Fernald, D. (1997). *Psychology*. Upper Saddle River, NJ: Prentice Hall, p. 242.

TABLE 3.8

Examples of Subtests from the Wechsler Adult Intelligence Scale

Verbal Subtests	Performance Subtests
Information Who wrote the *Iliad*?	**Digit Symbol** Fill in as many boxes as you can with symbols corresponding to particular numbers within the time allowed.
Comprehension Why do people need to obey traffic laws? What does the saying, "The early bird catches the worm" mean?	**Picture Completion** Determine the missing parts of a picture.
Arithmetic John wanted to buy a shirt that cost $31.50, but only had $17.00. How much more money would he need to buy the shirt?	**Block design** Use blocks like those in Figure 3.1 to match particular designs.
Similiarities How are a stapler and a paper clip alike?	**Picture arrangement** Arrange story-book pictures in the correct order to tell a coherent story.
Digit Spam (Forward order) Listen to this series of numbers and repeat them back to me in the same order: 4 7 5 6 (Backward order) Listen to this series of numbers and then repeat them backward: 3 9 7 1	**Symbol search** Determine whether either of two target shapes match those presented in a row of shapes.
Vocabulary What does capricious mean?	**Object assembly** Arrange the pieces of a puzzle so that they form a meaningful object.
Letter-Number Sequencing Listen to this series of numbers and letters and repeat them back, first saying the numbers from least to most, and then saying the numbers in alphabetical order.	

Simulated items similar to those in the Wechsler Intelligence Scales for Adults and Children. Copyright 1949, 1974, 1981, 1991 by The Psychological Corporation. Reproduced by permission. All rights reserved.

Most IQ scores cluster around the mean (see Figure 3.2 on page 124). Just 5% are above 130 or below 70. Wechsler labelled people who attained scores of 130 or above as "very superior," those with scores below 70 as "intellectually deficient." IQ scores below 70 are one of the criteria used in diagnosing mental retardation.

Personality Tests Clinicians use various formal tests to assess personality. We consider two types of personality tests: *self-report tests* and *projective tests*. Some self-report tests are intended to measure a particular trait or construct, such as anxiety or depression. The Beck Depression Inventory (BDI) (Beck et al., 1961), for instance, is a widely used measure of depression. In many clinic sites, such as the training clinic where the first author supervises clinical psychology students, the BDI is used routinely to screen new clients for depression. Here, our focus is on multidimensional self-report personality tests or inventories, as represented by the most widely used of these instruments, the Minnesota Multiphasic Personality Inventory (MMPI).

Do you like automobile magazines? Are you easily startled by noises in the night? Are you bothered by periods of anxiety or shakiness? Self-report inventories use structured items similar to these to measure personality traits such as anxiety, depression, emotionality, hypomania, masculinity–femininity, and introversion. Comparison of clients' responses on scales measuring these traits to those of a normative sample reveals their relative standing.

Self-report personality inventories are also called **objective tests**. They are objective in that the range of possible responses to items is limited. Empirical objective standards—rather than psychological theory—are also used to derive test items. Tests might ask respondents to check adjectives that apply to them, to mark statements as true or false, to select preferred activities from lists, or to indicate whether items apply to them "always," "sometimes," or "never." Tests with **forced-choice formats** require respondents to mark

objective tests Tests that allow a limited, specified range of response options or answers so they can be scored objectively.

forced-choice formats Method of structuring test questions that requires respondents to select among a set number of possible answers.

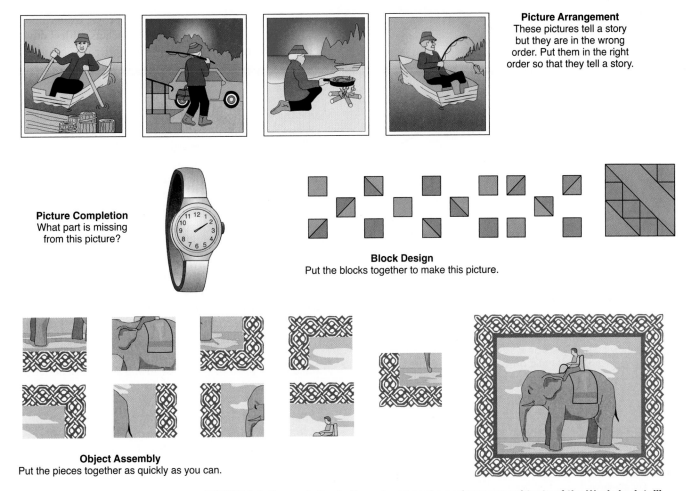

Picture Arrangement
These pictures tell a story but they are in the wrong order. Put them in the right order so that they tell a story.

Picture Completion
What part is missing from this picture?

Block Design
Put the blocks together to make this picture.

Object Assembly
Put the pieces together as quickly as you can.

FIGURE 3.1 Items similar to those found on the performance subtests of the Wechsler Intelligence Scales.
The Wechsler scales yield verbal and performance IQs that are based on the extent to which an individual's test scores deviate from the norm for her or his age group.

which of a group of statements is truest for them, or to select their most preferred activity from a list. They cannot answer "none of the above." Forced-choice formats are commonly used in interest inventories, as in this item:

I would rather
   a. be a forester.
   b. work in an office setting.
   c. play in a band.

With objective personality tests, items are selected according to some empirical standard. With the Minnesota Multiphasic Personality Inventory (MMPI-2), the standard was whether or not items differentiated clinical diagnostic groups from normal comparison groups. The MMPI-2 contains more than 500 true–false statements that assess interest patterns, habits, family relationships, somatic complaints, attitudes, beliefs, and behaviours characteristic of psychological disorders. It is widely used as a test of personality as well as assisting in the diagnosis of abnormal behaviour patterns. The MMPI-2 consists of a number of individual scales comprised of items that tended to be answered differently by members of carefully selected diagnostic groups, such as patients diagnosed with schizophrenia or depression, than by members of normal comparison groups.

Consider a hypothetical item: "I often read detective novels." If groups of depressed people tended to answer the item in a direction different from normal groups, the item would be placed on the depression scale—regardless of whether or not it had face validity.

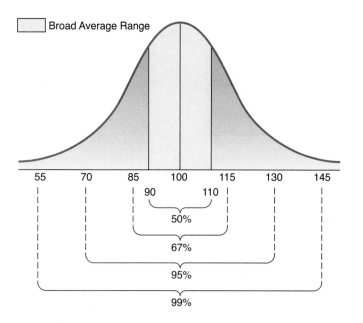

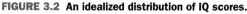

FIGURE 3.2 An idealized distribution of IQ scores.
The distribution of IQ scores is based on a bell-shaped curve, which is referred to by psychologists as a normal curve. Wechsler defined the deviation IQ in such a way that 50% of the scores fall within the broad average range of 90 to 110.

contrasted groups approach Method of concurrent validity in which group membership is used as the criterion by which the validity of a test is measured. The ability of the test to differentiate among two or more comparison groups (e.g., people with schizophrenia vs. normals) is taken as evidence of concurrent validity.

validity scales Groups of test items that serve to detect whether the results of a particular test are valid or whether a person responded in a random manner or in a way intended to create a favourable or unfavourable impression.

standard scores Scores that indicate the relative standing of raw scores in relation to the distribution of normative scores. For example, raw scores on the MMPI-2 scales are converted into standard scores that indicate the degree to which each of the individual raw scores deviates from the mean.

Many items that discriminate normal people from clinical groups are transparent in meaning, such as, "I feel down much of the time." Some items are subtler in meaning or bear no obvious relationship to the measured trait.

Derivation of scales on the basis of their ability to distinguish the response patterns of comparison groups such as clinical and normal groups is called the **contrasted groups approach.** The contrasted groups technique establishes concurrent validity; group membership is the criterion by which the validity of the test is measured.

Eight clinical scales were derived through the contrasted-groups approach. Two additional clinical scales were developed by using nonclinical comparison groups: a scale measuring masculine–feminine interest patterns and one measuring social introversion. The clinical scales are described in Table 3.9 on page 125. The MMPI-2 also has **validity scales** that assess tendencies to distort test responses in a favourable ("faking good") or unfavourable ("faking bad") direction.

The respondent's raw score for each of the clinical scales on the MMPI-2 scale is simply the number of items scored in a clinical direction. Raw scores are converted into **standard scores** with a mean of 50 and a standard deviation of 10. A standard score of 65 or higher on a particular scale places an individual at approximately the 92nd percentile or higher of the revised normative sample and is considered clinically significant.

The MMPI-2 is interpreted according to individual scale elevations and interrelationships among scales. For example, a "2-7 profile," commonly found among people seeking therapy, refers to a test pattern in which scores for scales 2 (Depression) and 7 (Psychasthenia) are clinically significant. Clinicians may refer to *atlases* or descriptions of people who usually attain various profiles.

MMPI-2 scales are regarded as reflecting continua of personality traits associated with the diagnostic categories represented by the test. For example, a high score on *psychopathic deviation* suggests the respondent holds a higher-than-average number of nonconformist beliefs and may be rebellious, which are characteristics often found in people with antisocial personality disorder. However, because it is not tied specifically to DSM criteria, it cannot be used to establish a diagnosis of antisocial personality disorder or any other psychological disorder. Perhaps it is unfair to expect that the MMPI, which was originally developed in the 1930s and 1940s under a largely outmoded diagnostic system, should provide diagnostic judgments consistent with the current version of the DSM system. Even so, MMPI profiles may suggest possible diagnoses that can be considered in light of other evidence. Moreover, instead of making a full diagnosis, many clinicians use the MMPI to gain general information about respondents' personality traits and attributes that may underlie their psychological problems.

The validity of the original and revised MMPI is supported by a large body of research demonstrating its ability to discriminate between control and psychiatric samples and between groups composed of people with different types of psychological disorders, such as anxiety vs. depressive disorders (Garb, 2003; Graham, 1993, 2000; Keiller & Graham, 1993). Moreover, the MMPI-2 introduced *content scales* that have enabled clinicians to gain greater understanding of their clients' specific problems (Graham, 2000; McGrath, Pogge, & Stokes, 2002). These content scales measure an individual's specific complaints and concerns, such as anxiety, anger, family troubles, and problems of low self-esteem.

Another widely used assessment tool, the Millon Clinical Multiaxial Inventory (MCMI), was originally designed to provide a description of a person's personality characteristics and an assessment of clinical syndromes within the DSM system (Millon, 1982, 2003). In previous editions of the MCMI, there was a concern that it underestimated the severity of depression (Patrick, 1988) while over-diagnosing personality disorders

TABLE 3.9

Clinical Scales of the MMPI-2

Scale Number	Scale Label	Items Similar to Those Found on MMPI Scale	Sample Traits of High Scorers
1	Hypochondriasis	My stomach frequently bothers me. At times, my body seems to ache all over.	Many physical complaints, cynical defeatist attitudes, often perceived as whiny, demanding
2	Depression	Nothing seems to interest me anymore. My sleep is often disturbed by worrisome thoughts.	Depressed mood; pessimistic, worrisome, despondent, lethargic
3	Hysteria	I sometimes become flushed for no apparent reason. I tend to take people at their word when they're trying to be nice to me.	Naïve, egocentric, little insight into problems, immature; develops physical complaints in response to stress
4	Psychopathic Deviate	My parents often disliked my friends. My behaviour sometimes got me into trouble at school.	Difficulties incorporating values of society, rebellious, impulsive, antisocial tendencies; strained family relationships; poor work and school history
5	Masculinity–Femininity	I like reading about electronics. (M) I would like to work in the theatre. (F)	Males endorsing feminine attributes: have cultural and artistic interests, effeminate, sensitive, passive Females endorsing male interests: Aggressive, masculine, self-confident, active, assertive, vigorous
6	Paranoia	I would have been more successful in life but people didn't give me a fair break. It's not safe to trust anyone these days.	Suspicious, guarded, blames others, resentful, aloof, may have paranoid delusions
7	Psychasthenia	I'm one of those people who have to have something to worry about. I seem to have more fears than most people I know.	Anxious, fearful, tense, worried, insecure, difficulties concentrating, obsessional, self-doubting
8	Schizophrenia	Things seem unreal to me at times. I sometimes hear things that other people can't hear.	Confused and illogical thinking, feels alienated and misunderstood, socially isolated or withdrawn, may have blatant psychotic symptoms such as hallucinations or delusional beliefs, or may lead detached, schizoid lifestyle
9	Hypomania	I sometimes take on more tasks than I can possibly get done. People have noticed that my speech is sometimes pressured or rushed.	Energetic, possibly manic, impulsive, optimistic, sociable, active, flighty, irritable, may have overly inflated or grandiose self-image or unrealistic plans
10	Social Introversion	I don't like loud parties. I was not very active in school activities.	Shy, inhibited, withdrawn, introverted, lacks self-confidence, reserved, anxious in social situations

(Guthrie & Mobley, 1994; Piersma, 1987). However, its diagnostic capability seems to have improved with the third edition (Millon et al., 2004). Because of its simplicity of administration, scoring, and interpretation, the MCMI-III and other related Millon clinical inventories can be used on a routine basis in both clinical locales (hospitals, outpatient clinics) and nonclinical settings (college and university counselling centres, private practices, the courts).

Like the MCMI, the Personality Assessment Inventory (PAI) is another commonly used objective personality test that is closely tied to the DSM Axis I and II categories (Piotrowski,

2000). The PAI has several subscales, including ones that have treatment implications (e.g., they measure potential for harm to self or others, level of stress, and motivation for treatment). The validity of the PAI is about equal to that of the MMPI (Braxton et al., 2007; Kurtz & Blais, 2007), but the PAI can be completed in almost half the time—an important feature for clients who may have difficulty staying on a task for extended periods of time, such as those who are cognitively impaired, impulsive, or depressed.

Self-report tests have the benefits of relative ease and economy of administration. Once the examiner has read the instructions to clients and ascertained they can read and comprehend the items, clients can complete the tests on their own. Because the tests permit limited response options, such as marking items either true or false, they can be scored with high interrater reliability. Moreover, the accumulation of research findings on respondents provides a quantified basis for interpreting test responses. Such tests often uncover information that might not be revealed during a clinical interview or by observing a person's behaviour.

A disadvantage of self-rating tests is that they rely on clients themselves as the source of data. Test responses may therefore reflect underlying response biases, such as tendencies to answer items in a socially desirable direction, rather than accurate self-perceptions. For this reason, self-report inventories like the MMPI contain validity scales to help uncover response biases. Yet even validity scales may not detect all sources of bias (Bagby, Nicholson, & Buis, 1998; Nicholson et al., 1997). Examiners may also look for corroborating information, for example by interviewing others who are familiar with a client's behaviour.

Psychodynamically oriented critics suggest that self-report instruments tell us little about possible unconscious processes. The use of such tests may also be limited to relatively high-functioning individuals who can read well, respond to verbal material, and focus on a potentially tedious task. Clients who are disorganized, unstable, or confused may not be able to complete tests.

Projective Personality Tests   Projective tests, unlike objective tests, offer no clear, specified answers. Clients are presented with ambiguous stimuli, such as vague drawings or inkblots, and are usually asked to describe what the stimuli look like or to relate stories about them. The tests are called projective because they were derived from the psychodynamic projective hypothesis, the belief that people impose or "project" their psychological needs, drives, and motives, much of which may lie in the unconscious, onto their interpretations of unstructured or ambiguous stimuli.

The psychodynamic model holds that potentially disturbing impulses and wishes, often of a sexual or aggressive nature, are often hidden from consciousness by defence mechanisms. Defence mechanisms may thwart direct probing of threatening material. Indirect methods of assessment, however, such as projective tests, may offer clues to unconscious processes. More behaviourally oriented critics contend, however, that the results of projective tests are based more on clinicians' subjective interpretations of test responses than on empirical evidence.

The two most prominent projective techniques are the Rorschach inkblot test and the Thematic Apperception Test (TAT). The Rorschach test, in which a person's responses to inkblots are used to reveal aspects of his or her personality, was developed by Swiss psychiatrist Hermann Rorschach (1884–1922). As a child, Rorschach was intrigued by the game of dripping ink on paper and folding the paper to make symmetrical figures. He noted that people saw different things in the same blot, and believed their *percepts* reflected their personalities as well as the stimulus cues provided by the blot. In high school, his friends gave him the nickname *Klecks*, which means "inkblot" in German. As a psychiatrist, Rorschach experimented with hundreds of blots to identify those that could help in the diagnosis of psychological problems. He finally found a group of 15 blots that seemed to do the job and could be administered in a single session. Ten blots are used today because Rorschach's publisher did not have the funds to reproduce all 15 blots in the first edition of the text on the subject. Rorschach never had the opportunity to learn how popular and influential his inkblot test would become. He died at the age of 38 of complications from a ruptured appendix the year following its publication.

Five of the inkblots are black and white and the other five have colour (see Figure 3.3). Each inkblot is printed on a separate card, which is handed to subjects in sequence. Subjects are asked to tell the examiner what the blot might be or what it reminds them of. A follow-up inquiry explores what features of the blot (its colour, form, or texture) the person used in forming an impression of what it resembled.

Clinicians who use the Rorschach tend to interpret responses in the following ways. Clients who use the entire blot in their responses show ability to perceive part–whole relationships and integrate events in meaningful ways. People whose responses are based solely on minor details of the blots may have obsessive-compulsive tendencies that, in psychodynamic theory, protect them from having to cope with the larger issues in their lives. Clients who respond to the negative (white) spaces tend to see things in their own way, suggestive of negativism or stubbornness.

Relationships between form and colour are suggestive of clients' capacity to control impulses. When clients use the colour of the blot but are primarily guided by its form, they are believed capable of feeling deeply but also of holding their feelings in check. When colour dominates—as in perceiving any reddened area as "blood"—clients may not be able to exercise control over impulses. A response consistent with the form or contours of the blot is suggestive of adequate **reality testing**. People who see movement in the blots may be revealing intelligence and creativity. Content analysis may shed light on underlying conflicts. For example, adult clients who see animals but not people may have problems relating to people. Clients who appear confused about whether or not percepts of people are male or female may, according to psychodynamic theory, be in conflict over their own gender.

The validity of the Rorschach has been the subject of extensive debate. One problem is the lack of a standard scoring procedure. Interpretation of a person's responses is not objective; it depends to some degree on the subjective judgment of the examiner. Two examiners may interpret the same Rorschach response differently. Recent attempts to develop a comprehensive scoring approach, such as the Exner system (Exner, 1991, 1993), have advanced the effort to standardize scoring of responses. But the debate over the reliability of the Rorschach, including the Exner system, continues (see Meyer, 1997; Wood, Nezworski, & Stejskal, 1996, 1997). Yet even if a Rorschach response can be scored reliably, the interpretation of the response—what it means—remains an open question.

Critics and even some proponents of the Rorschach technique such as Hertz (1986) recognize that evidence is lacking to support the interpretation of some particular responses. However, evidence has accumulated pointing to the validity of certain Rorschach responses (e.g., Leavitt & Labott, 1997; Parker, Hanson, & Hinsley, 1988; Viglione, 1999; M. F. Weiner, 1997), such as responses meant to assess dependency-related behaviours (Bornstein, 1999a). Still, some reviewers do not believe the Rorschach has yet met the test of scientific utility or validity (Hunsley & Bailey, 1999). Perhaps the Rorschach should be thought of more as a method for gathering information about the ways in which individuals construct meaning from unstructured or ambiguous situations than as a formal diagnostic tool per se (Weiner, 2000). The Rorschach is most valuable when making predictions in a clinical setting about mental functions such as stress thresholds and impulse control that are not readily accessible from self-report methods (Bornstein, 2001).

The Thematic Apperception Test (TAT) was developed by psychologist Henry Murray (1943) at Harvard University in the 1930s. *Apperception* is a French word that can be translated as "interpreting (new ideas or impressions) on the basis of existing ideas (cognitive structures) and past experience." The TAT consists of a series of cards, like that shown in Figure 3.4 on page 128, each of which depicts an ambiguous scene. Respondents are asked to construct stories about the cards. It is assumed their tales reflect their experiences and outlooks on life—and, perhaps, also shed light on deep-seated needs and conflicts.

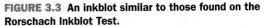

FIGURE 3.3 An inkblot similar to those found on the Rorschach Inkblot Test.
What does the blot look like to you? What could it be? Rorschach assumed that people project their personalities into their responses to ambiguous inkblots as well as responding to the stimulus characteristics of the blot.

reality testing Ability to perceive the world accurately and to distinguish reality from fantasy.

FIGURE 3.4 The Thematic Apperception Test (TAT). Psychologists ask test takers to provide their impressions of what is happening in the scene depicted in the drawing. They ask test takers what led up to the scene and how it will turn out. How might your responses reveal aspects of your own personality?

neuropsychological assessment Methods of psychological assessment used to detect signs of underlying neurological damage or brain defects.

Respondents are asked to describe what is happening in each scene, what led up to it, what the characters are thinking and feeling, and what will happen next. Psychodynamically oriented clinicians assume that respondents identify with the protagonists in their stories and project their psychological needs and conflicts into the events they *apperceive*. On a more superficial level, the stories also suggest how respondents might interpret or behave in similar situations in their own lives. TAT results are also suggestive of clients' attitudes toward others, particularly family members and lovers.

The TAT has been used extensively in research on motivation as well as in clinical practice. For example, psychologist David McClelland helped pioneer the TAT assessment of social motives such as the needs for achievement and power (McClelland, Alexander, & Marks, 1982). The rationales for this research are that we are likely to be somewhat preoccupied with our needs, and our needs are projected into our reactions to ambiguous stimuli and situations.

One criticism of the TAT is that the stimulus properties of some of the cards, such as cues depicting sadness or anger, may exert too strong a "stimulus pull" on the subject. The pictures themselves may pull for certain types of stories. If so, clients' responses may represent reactions to the stimulus cues rather than projections of their personalities (Murstein & Mathes, 1996). The TAT, like the Rorschach, is open to criticism that the scoring and interpretation of responses largely depends on clinicians' subjective impressions. The validity of the TAT in eliciting deep-seated material or tapping underlying psychopathology also remains to be demonstrated.

One general problem with projective instruments such as the TAT and Rorschach is that the more healthily test takers talk or see in response to projective instruments, the more likely they will be judged as having psychological problems (Murstein & Mathes, 1996). Proponents of projective testing argue that in skilled hands, tests like the TAT and the Rorschach can yield meaningful material that might not be revealed in interviews or by self-rating inventories (Stricker & Gold, 1999). Moreover, allowing subjects freedom of expression through projective testing reduces the tendency of individuals to offer socially desirable responses. Despite the lack of direct evidence for the projective hypothesis, the appeal of projective tests among clinicians remains high (Camara, Nathan, & Puente, 2000).

Neuropsychological Assessment

Neuropsychological assessment is used to evaluate whether or not psychological problems reflect underlying neurological damage or brain defects. When neurological impairment is suspected, a neurological evaluation may be requested from a *neurologist*—a medical doctor who specializes in disorders of the nervous system. A clinical *neuropsychologist* may also be consulted to administer neuropsychological assessment techniques, such as behavioural observation and psychological testing, to reveal signs of possible brain damage. Neuropsychological inventories may be used in conjunction with brain-imaging techniques, such as MRI and CT scans, not only to suggest whether or not clients are suffering from brain damage but also to determine which parts of the brain might be involved (Fiez, 2001).

One of the most widely used neuropsychological inventories is the Halstead-Reitan Neuropsychological Battery.

The Halstead-Reitan Neuropsychological Battery
Psychologist Ralph Reitan developed the battery by adapting tests used by his mentor, Ward Halstead, an experimental psychologist, to study brain-behaviour relationships among organically impaired individuals. The battery contains tests that measure perceptual, intellectual, and motor skills and performance. A battery of tests permits the psychologist to observe patterns of results, and

various patterns of performance deficits are suggestive of certain kinds of organic defects. The tests in the battery include the following:

1. *The Category Test.* This test measures abstract thinking ability, as indicated by an individual's proficiency at forming principles or categories that relate different stimuli to one another. A series of groups of stimuli that vary in shape, size, location, colour, and other characteristics are flashed on a screen. The subject's task is to discern the principle that links them, such as shape or size, and to indicate which stimuli in each grouping represent the correct category by pressing a key. By analyzing the patterns of correct and incorrect choices, the subject normally learns to identify the principles that determine the correct choice. Performance on the test is believed to reflect functioning in the frontal lobe of the cerebral cortex.
2. *The Rhythm Test.* This is a test of concentration and attention. The subject listens to 30 pairs of tape-recorded rhythmic beats and indicates whether the beats in each pair are the same or different. Performance deficits are associated with damage to the right temporal lobe of the cerebral cortex.
3. *The Tactual Performance Test.* This test requires the blindfolded subject to fit wooden blocks of different shapes into corresponding depressions on a form board. Afterward, the subject draws the board from memory as a measure of visual memory.

The Luria Nebraska Test Battery The Luria Nebraska Test Battery is based on the work of the Russian neuropsychologist A. R. Luria and was developed by psychologists at the University of Nebraska (Golden, Hammeke, & Purisch, 1980). Like the Halstead-Reitan, the Luria Nebraska reveals patterns of skill deficits that are suggestive of particular sites of brain damage. The Luria Nebraska is more efficiently administered than the Halstead-Reitan, requiring about a third of the time to complete.

A wide range of skills is assessed. Tests measure tactile, kinesthetic, and spatial skills; complex motor skills; auditory skills; receptive and expressive speech skills; reading, writing, and arithmetic skills; and general intelligence and memory functioning. Although the Luria Nebraska is promising, more research is needed to substantiate its reliability and validity.

Neuropsychological tests attempt to reveal brain dysfunctions without surgical procedures. We will later consider other contemporary techniques that allow us to probe the workings of the brain without surgery.

Behavioural Assessment

The traditional model of assessment, or **psychometric approach,** holds that psychological tests reveal *signs* of reasonably stable traits or dispositions that largely determine behaviour. The psychometric approach aims to classify people in terms of personality types according to traits such as anxiety, introversion–extraversion, obsessiveness, hostility, impulsivity, and aggressiveness. This model inspired development of trait-based tests such as the Rorschach, TAT, and the MMPI.

The alternative model of **behavioural assessment** treats test results as samples of behaviour that occur in specific situations rather than signs of underlying personality types or traits. According to the behavioural approach, behaviour is primarily determined by environmental or situational factors, such as stimulus cues and reinforcements.

The behavioural model has inspired the development of techniques that aim to sample an individual's behaviour in settings as similar as possible to the real-life situation, thus maximizing the relationship between the testing situation and the criterion. Behaviour may be observed and measured in such settings as the home, school, or work environment. The examiner may also try to simulate situations in the clinic or laboratory that serve as **analogues** of the problems the individual confronts in daily life.

The examiner may conduct a **functional analysis** of the problem behaviour—relating it to the *antecedents* or stimulus cues that trigger it and the *consequences* or reinforcements that maintain it. Knowledge of the environmental conditions in which a problem behaviour occurs may help the therapist work with a client and family to change the conditions

psychometric approach Method of psychological assessment which seeks to use psychological tests to identify and measure the reasonably stable traits in an individual's personality that are believed to largely determine their behaviour.

behavioural assessment Approach to clinical assessment that focuses on the objective recording or description of problem behaviour rather than inferences about personality traits.

analogue Something that resembles something else in many respects.

functional analysis Analysis of behaviour in terms of antecedent stimuli and consequent stimuli (potential reinforcers).

The examiner may conduct a **behavioural interview** by posing questions to learn more about the history and situational aspects of problem behaviour. If a client seeks help because of panic attacks, the behavioural interviewer might ask how the client experiences these attacks—when, where, how often, under what circumstances. The interviewer looks for precipitating cues, such as thought patterns (e.g., thoughts of dying or losing control) or situational factors (e.g., entering a department store) that may provoke an attack. The interviewer also seeks information about reinforcers that may maintain the panic. Does the client flee the situation when an attack occurs? Is escape reinforced by relief from anxiety? Has the client learned to lessen anticipatory anxiety by avoiding exposure to situations in which attacks have occurred?

The examiner may also use observational methods to connect the problem behaviour to the stimuli and reinforcements that help maintain it. Consider the case of Kerry:

> A seven-year-old boy, Kerry, is brought by his parents for evaluation. His mother describes him as a "royal terror." His father complains he won't listen to anyone. Kerry throws temper tantrums in the supermarket, screaming and stomping his feet if his parents refuse to buy him what he wants. At home, he breaks his toys by throwing them against the wall and demands new ones. Sometimes, though, he appears sullen and won't talk to anyone for hours. At school, he appears inhibited and has difficulty concentrating. His progress at school is slow and he has difficulty reading. His teachers complain he has a limited attention span and doesn't seem motivated.
>
> THE AUTHORS' FILES

The psychologist may use direct home observation to assess the interactions between Kerry and his parents. Alternatively, the psychologist may observe Kerry and his parents through a one-way mirror in the clinic. Such observations may suggest interactions that explain the child's noncompliance. For example, Kerry's noncompliance may follow parental requests that are vague (e.g., a parent says, "Play nicely now," and Kerry responds by throwing toys) or inconsistent (e.g., a parent says, "Go play with your toys but don't make a mess," to which Kerry responds by scattering the toys). Observation may suggest ways in which Kerry's parents can improve communication and cue and reinforce desirable behaviours.

Direct or behavioural observation is the hallmark of behavioural assessment. Through behavioural observation, clinicians can observe and quantify problem behaviour. Observations may be videotaped to permit subsequent analysis of behavioural patterns. Observers are trained to identify and record targeted patterns of behaviour. Behaviour coding systems have been developed that enhance the reliability of recording.

There are advantages and disadvantages to direct observation. One advantage is that direct observation does not rely on a client's self-reports, which may be distorted by efforts to make a favourable or unfavourable impression. In addition to providing accurate measurements of problem behaviour, behavioural observation can suggest strategies for intervention. A mother might report that her son is so hyperactive he cannot sit still long enough to complete homework assignments. By using a one-way mirror, the clinician may discover the boy becomes restless only when he encounters a problem he cannot solve right away. The child may thus be helped by being taught ways of coping with frustration and of solving certain kinds of academic problems.

Direct observation also has its drawbacks. One issue is the possible lack of consensus in defining problems in behavioural terms. In coding a child's behaviour for hyperactivity, clinicians must agree on which aspects of the behaviour represent hyperactivity. Another potential problem is a lack of reliability or inconsistency of measurement across time or between observers. Reliability is reduced when an observer is inconsistent in the coding of specific behaviours or when two or more observers code behaviour inconsistently.

Observers may also show response biases. An observer who has been sensitized to expect that a child is hyperactive may perceive normal variations in behaviour as subtle

behavioural interview Approach to clinical interviewing that focuses on relating problem behaviour to antecedent stimuli and reinforcement consequences.

cues of hyperactivity and erroneously record them as instances of hyperactive behaviour. Such expectations are less likely to affect behavioural ratings when the target behaviours are defined concretely (Foster & Cone, 1986).

Reactivity is another potential problem. Reactivity refers to the tendency for the behaviour being observed to be influenced by the way in which it is measured. With respect to behavioural observation, people may put their best feet forward when they know they are being observed. Using covert observation techniques, such as hidden cameras or one-way mirrors, may reduce reactivity. Covert observation may not be feasible, however, because of ethical concerns or practical constraints. Another approach is to accustom subjects to observation by watching them a number of times before collecting data (Foster & Cone, 1986).

Another potential problem is *observer drift*—the tendency of observers or groups of raters to deviate from the coding system in which they were trained as time elapses. One suggestion to help control this problem is to regularly retrain observers to ensure continued compliance with the coding system (Kazdin, 1992). As time elapses, observers may also become fatigued or distracted. It may be helpful to limit the duration of observations and to provide frequent breaks.

Behavioural observation is limited to measuring overt behaviours. Many clinicians also wish to assess subjective or private experiences—for example, feelings of depression and anxiety or distorted thought patterns. Such clinicians may combine direct observation with forms of assessment that permit clients to reveal internal experiences. Staunch behavioural clinicians tend to consider self-reports unreliable and to limit their data to direct observation.

Behavioural clinicians may supplement behavioural observations with traditional forms of assessment, such as the MMPI, or perhaps even with projective tests, such as the Rorschach or TAT. However, they are likely to interpret test data as samples of clients' behaviour at a particular point in time, and not as signs of stable traits. Trait-oriented clinicians may similarly employ behavioural assessment to learn how personality "traits" are "revealed" in different settings and to see how particular traits affect clients' daily functioning.

In addition to behavioural interviews and direct observation, behavioural assessment may involve the use of other techniques, such as self-monitoring, contrived or analogue measures, and behavioural rating scales.

Self-Monitoring Training clients to record or monitor the problem behaviour in their daily lives is another method of relating problem behaviour to the settings in which it occurs. In **self-monitoring**, clients assume the primary responsibility for assessing the problem behaviour.

Self-monitoring permits direct measurement of the problem behaviour when and where it occurs. Behaviours that can be easily counted, such as food intake, cigarette smoking, nail-biting, hair pulling, study periods, or social activities are well suited for self-monitoring. Clients are usually best aware of the frequency of these behaviours and their situational contexts. Self-monitoring can also produce highly accurate measurement because the behaviour is recorded as it occurs, not reconstructed from memory.

There are various devices for keeping track of a targeted behaviour. A behavioural diary or log is a handy way to record calories ingested or cigarettes smoked. Such logs are organized in columns and rows to track the frequency of occurrence of the problem behaviour and the situations in which it occurs (time, setting, feeling state, etc.). A record of eating may include entries for the type of food eaten, the number of calories, the location in which the eating occurred, the feeling states associated with eating, and the consequences of eating (e.g., how the client felt afterward). In reviewing an eating diary with the clinician, a client can identify problematic eating patterns, such as eating when feeling bored or in response to television food commercials, and devise better ways of handling these cues.

Behavioural diaries can also help clients increase desirable but low-frequency behaviours, such as assertive behaviour and dating behaviour. Unassertive clients might track occasions

reactivity Tendency for behaviour to be influenced by the process by which it is measured.

self-monitoring In behavioural assessment, the process of recording or observing one's own behaviour, thoughts, or emotions.

that seem to warrant an assertive response and jot down their actual responses to each occasion. Clients and clinicians then review the log to highlight problematic situations and rehearse assertive responses. A client who is anxious about dating might record social contacts with the opposite gender. To measure the effects of treatment, clinicians may encourage clients to engage in a **baseline** period of self-monitoring before treatment is begun.

Self-monitoring, though, is not without its disadvantages. Some clients are unreliable and do not keep accurate records. They become forgetful or sloppy, or they under-report undesirable behaviours, such as overeating or smoking, because of embarrassment or fear of criticism. To offset these biases, clinicians may, with clients' consent, corroborate the accuracy of self-monitoring by gathering information from other parties, such as clients' spouses. Private behaviours such as eating or smoking alone cannot be corroborated in this way, however. Sometimes, other means of corroboration, such as physiological measures, are available. For example, biochemical analysis of the carbon monoxide in clients' breath samples or of nicotine metabolites in their saliva or blood can be used to corroborate reports of abstinence from smoking.

Another issue in self-monitoring is *reactivity*, or changes in measured behaviour that stem from the act of measurement. Some clients may change undesirable behaviours merely as a consequence of focusing on them or recording them. When reactivity leads to more adaptive behaviour, it renders the measurement process an effective therapeutic tool, although it can make it difficult to tease out the effects due to measurement from those due to treatment.

Self-monitoring may actually be an important, perhaps even necessary feature of some behaviour change programs, such as weight management programs. A study showed that the more consistently participants monitored what they ate, the more weight they lost (Baker & Kirschenbaum, 1993). This is not to imply that self-monitoring alone is sufficient to produce a desired behaviour change. Motivation to change and skills needed to make behaviour changes are also important.

Analogue or Contrived Measures Analogue or contrived measures are intended to simulate the setting in which a behaviour naturally takes place but are carried out in laboratory or controlled settings. Role-playing exercises are common analogue measures. Clinicians cannot follow clients who have difficulty expressing dissatisfaction to authority figures throughout the day. Instead, they may rely on role-playing exercises, such as having the clients enact challenging an unfair grade. A scene might be described to the client as follows: "You've worked very hard on a term paper and received a very poor grade, say a D or an F. You approach the professor, who asks, 'Is there some problem?' What do you do now?" The client's enactment of the scene may reveal deficits in self-expression that can be addressed in therapy or assertiveness training.

The Behavioural Approach Task or BAT (Lang & Lazovik, 1963) is a popular analogue measure of a phobic person's approach to a feared object such as a snake. Approach behaviour is broken down into levels of response, such as looking in the direction of a snake from about six metres, touching a box holding a snake, and touching a snake. The BAT provides direct measurement of a response to a stimulus in a controlled situation. The subject's approach behaviour can be quantified by assigning a score to each level of approach.

Behavioural Rating Scales A **behavioural rating scale** is a checklist that provides information about the frequency, intensity, and range of problem behaviours. Behavioural rating scales differ from self-report personality inventories in that items assess specific behaviours rather than personality characteristics, interests, or attitudes.

Behavioural rating scales are often used by parents to assess children's problem behaviours. The Child Behaviour Problem Checklist (CBCL) (Achenbach, 1978; Achenbach & Edelbrock, 1979), for example, asks parents to rate their children on more than 100 specific problem behaviours, including the following:

refuses to eat
is disobedient

baseline Period of time preceding the implementation of a treatment. Used to gather data regarding the rate of occurrence of the target behaviour before treatment is introduced.

behavioural rating scale Method of behavioural assessment that involves the use of a scale to record the frequency of occurrence of target behaviours.

hits
is unco-operative
destroys own things

The scale yields an overall problem behaviour score and subscale scores on dimensions such as delinquency, aggressiveness, and physical problems. A clinician can compare a child's score on these dimensions with norms based on samples of age-mates.

Cognitive Assessment

Cognitive assessment involves the measurement of cognitions—thoughts, beliefs, and attitudes. Cognitive therapists believe that people who hold self-defeating or dysfunctional cognitions are at greater risk of developing emotional problems, such as depression, in the face of stressful or disappointing life experiences. They help clients replace dysfunctional thinking patterns with self-enhancing, rational thought patterns.

Several methods of cognitive assessment have been developed. One of the most straightforward is the thought record or diary. Depressed clients may carry such diaries to record dysfunctional thoughts as they arise. Aaron Beck (Beck et al., 1979) designed a thought diary or "Daily Record of Dysfunctional Thoughts" to help clients identify thought patterns connected with troubling emotional states. Each time a client experiences a negative emotion such as anger or sadness, entries are made to identify:

1. The situation in which the emotional state occurred
2. The automatic or disruptive thoughts that passed through the client's mind
3. The type or category of disordered thinking that the automatic thought(s) represented (e.g., selective abstraction, overgeneralization, magnification, or absolutist thinking—see Chapter 2)
4. A rational response to the troublesome thought
5. The emotional outcome or final emotional response

A thought diary can become part of a treatment program in which a client learns to replace dysfunctional thoughts with rational alternative thoughts.

Cognitive assessment of Pamela's travel phobia (see page 118) might involve asking her to describe the thoughts that pass through her mind when she imagines herself approaching the fearful situation. Pamela might also be asked to keep a diary of the thoughts she experiences while preparing for a drive or while driving toward a phobic stimulus such as a bridge or an overpass. By examining thoughts, a therapist can help Pamela identify styles of thinking that are linked to phobic episodes, such as catastrophizing ("I'm going to lose control of the car") and self-deprecation ("I'm just a jerk. I can't handle anything"). Several more formal methods of assessing cognitions assessment have been developed, including those described next.

Methods of Cognitive Assessment The Automatic Thoughts Questionnaire (ATQ-30; Hollon & Kendall, 1980) has clients rate the weekly frequency and degree of conviction associated with 30 automatic negative thoughts. (Automatic thoughts are thoughts that seem to just pop into our minds.) Sample items include the following:

I don't think I can go on.
I hate myself.
I've let people down.

A total score is obtained by summing the frequencies of occurrence of each item. Higher scores are considered typical of depressive thought patterns. The scale discriminates between subjects who attain high or low scores with higher scores being more indicative of depressive symptoms (Blankstein & Segal, 2001). The 30-item ATQ has been statistically sorted into four categories or factors of related thoughts (see Table 3.10).

A similar measure, the 26-item Cognition Checklist (CCL), contains a listing of 26 anxious or depressing thoughts of a type similar to such items as "I'm a failure," and "I

TABLE 3.10

Items Defining Factors on the Automatic Thoughts Questionnaire	
Factor 1: Personal Maladjustment and Desire for Change	Something has to change. What's the matter with me? I wish I were a better person. What's wrong with me? I'm so disappointed in myself.
Factor 2: Negative Self-Concept and Negative Expectations	My future is bleak. I'm a failure. I'll never make it. My life's not going the way I wanted it to. I'm a loser. Why can't I ever succeed? I'm no good.
Factor 3: Low Self-Esteem	I'm worthless. I hate myself.
Factor 4: Giving Up/Helplessness	I can't finish anything. It's just not worth it.

Source: Adapted from Hollon & Kendall (1980).

feel like something terrible is going to happen to me" (Beck et al., 1987). Clients rate the frequency of occurrence of these thoughts to give clinicians a sense of whether they are troubled by the kinds of disruptive thoughts that people with anxiety and depressive disorders frequently encounter (Steer et al., 1994).

Another cognitive measure, the Dysfunctional Attitudes Scale (DAS; Beck et al., 1991; Weissman & Beck, 1978), consists of an inventory of beliefs or attitudes believed to measure vulnerability to depression (Blankstein & Segal, 2001). For example, "I feel like I'm nothing if someone I love doesn't love me back." Subjects use a seven-point scale to rate the degree to which they endorse each belief. Recent evidence suggests that the DAS may actually be measuring depression itself rather than vulnerability to depression (Calhoon, 1996). Whatever the case, it clearly taps into a style of thinking associated with depression.

Cognitive assessment has opened a new domain to the psychologist in understanding how disruptive thoughts are related to abnormal behaviour. Over the past three decades or so, cognitive and cognitive-behavioural therapists have been exploring what B. F. Skinner labelled the "black box"—people's internal states—to learn how thoughts and attitudes influence emotional states and behaviour.

The behavioural objection to cognitive techniques is that clinicians have no direct means of verifying clients' subjective experiences—their thoughts and beliefs. These are private experiences that can be reported but not observed and measured directly. Even though thoughts remain private experiences, reports of cognitions in the form of rating scales or checklists can be quantified and validated by reference to external criteria.

Physiological Measurement

electrodermal response Changes in the electrical conductivity of the skin following exposure to a stimulus.

galvanic skin response Measure of the change in electrical activity of the skin caused by increased activity of the sweat glands that accompanies states of sympathetic nervous system arousal, such as when a person is anxious. Abbreviated *GSR*.

We can also learn about abnormal behaviour by studying people's physiological responses. Anxiety, for example, is associated with arousal of the sympathetic division of the autonomic nervous system (see Chapter 2). Anxious people, therefore, show elevated heart rates and blood pressure, which can be measured directly by means of the pulse and a blood pressure cuff. People also sweat more heavily when they are anxious. When we sweat, our skin becomes wet, increasing its ability to conduct electricity. Sweating can be measured by means of the **electrodermal response** or **galvanic skin response** (GSR). (*Electrodermal* contains the Greek word *derma*, meaning "skin." *Galvanic* is named after the Italian physicist and physician Luigi Galvani, who was a pioneer in research in electricity.) Measures of the GSR assess the amount of electricity that passes through two points on the skin, usually on the hand. We assume the person's anxiety level correlates with the amount of electricity conducted across the skin.

The GSR is just one example of a physiological response measured through probes or sensors connected to the body. Another example is the **electroencephalograph** (EEG), which measures brainwaves by attaching electrodes to the scalp.

Changes in muscle tension are also often associated with states of anxiety or tension. They can be detected through the **electromyograph** (EMG), which monitors muscle tension through sensors attached to targeted muscle groups. (*Myo-* derives from the Greek *mys*, meaning "mouse" or "muscle." The Greeks observed that muscles moved mouselike beneath the skin.) Placement of EMG probes on the forehead can indicate muscle tension associated with tension headaches. Other probes are used to assess sexual arousal (see Chapter 11, "Gender Identity Disorder, Paraphilias, and Sexual Dysfunctions").

Ambulatory blood pressure devices allow clinicians to monitor clients' blood pressure at intervals throughout the day. Clients may log their concurrent activities or feeling states to reveal how changes in blood pressure are connected with stress.

electroencephalograph Instrument for measuring the electrical activity of the brain (brainwaves). Abbreviated *EEG*.

electromyograph Instrument often used in biofeedback training for measuring muscle tension. Abbreviated *EMG*.

ambulatory Able to walk about on one's own.

Concept of Response Systems

P.J. Lang (1968) suggested that fear or anxiety consists of three different response systems: behavioural, physiological, and verbal. The behavioural response is avoidance of fear-inducing objects or situations. The physiological response can be measured in terms of changes in heart rate, GSR, or other bodily responses. The verbal system involves measurement of the subjective experience of anxiety. These response systems may act independently, however, so changes in one may not generalize to another. For example, people may report that they feel progressively less anxious when they confront a fearful situation, but their hearts may continue to pound. Or people may be able to approach a phobic situation although they report lingering feelings of anxiety or fear. Because response systems can be independent, most researchers recommend that investigations include multiple measures of anxiety or fear across response domains, such as self-reports of subjective feelings, behavioural approach measures, and physiological measurement.

computerized tomography Generation of a computer-enhanced image of the internal structures of the brain by means of passing a narrow X-ray beam through the head at different angles. Abbreviated *CT scan*.

positron emission tomography Brain-imaging technique in which a computer-generated image of the neural activity of regions of the brain is formed by tracing the amounts of glucose used in the various regions. Abbreviated *PET scan*.

Probing the Workings of the Brain

Advances in medical technology have made it possible to study the workings of the brain without the need for surgery.

One of the most common is the electroencephalograph (EEG), which is a record of the electrical activity of the brain (see Figure 3.5). The EEG detects minute amounts of electrical activity in the brain, or brainwaves, that are conducted between electrodes. Certain brainwave patterns are associated with mental states such as relaxation and with the different stages of sleep. The EEG is used to examine brainwave patterns associated with psychological disorders, such as schizophrenia, and with brain damage. It is also used to study various abnormal behaviour patterns. The EEG is also used by medical personnel to reveal brain abnormalities such as tumours.

Brain-imaging techniques generate images that reflect the structure and functioning of the brain. In **computerized tomography** (CT scan), a narrow X-ray beam is aimed at the head (Figure 3.6 on page 136). The radiation that passes through is measured from multiple angles. The CT scan reveals abnormalities in shape and structure that may be suggestive of lesions, blood clots, or tumours. A computer enables scientists to integrate the measurements into a three-dimensional picture of the brain. Evidence of brain damage that was once detectable only by surgery may now be displayed on a monitor.

Another imaging method, **positron emission tomography** (the PET scan), is used to study the functioning of various parts of the brain (see Figure 3.7 on page 136). In this method, a small amount of a radioactive compound or tracer is mixed with glucose and injected into the bloodstream. When it

FIGURE 3.5 The Electroencephalogram.
The EEG is a record of brainwave activity as recorded by an electroencephalograph. It can be used to study differences in brainwaves between groups of normal people and people with problems such as schizophrenia or organic brain damage.

reaches the brain, patterns of neural activity are revealed by measurement of the positrons—positively charged particles—emitted by the tracer. The glucose metabolized by parts of the brain generates a computer image of neural activity. Areas of greater activity metabolize more glucose. The PET scan has been used to learn which parts of the brain are most active (metabolize more glucose) when we are listening to music, solving a math problem, or using language. It can also be used to reveal differences in brain activity in people with schizophrenia (see Chapter 12, "Schizophrenia").

A third imaging technique is **magnetic resonance imaging** (**MRI**) (see Figure 3.8 on page 137). In MRI, a person is placed in a doughnut-shaped tunnel that generates a strong magnetic field. Radio waves of certain frequencies are directed at the head. As a result, parts of the brain emit signals that can be measured from several angles. As with the CT scan, the signals are integrated into a computer-generated image of the brain, which can be used to investigate brain abnormalities associated with schizophrenia (see Chapter 12) and other disorders such as obsessive-compulsive disorder (OCD).

Functional magnetic resonance imaging (fMRI) is a form of resonance imaging that yields far more information than a basic MRI and produces static pictures of brain structure. In MRI, computer-generated images show which regions of the brain are active during a specific mental activity, whether it is solving verbal riddles or visual puzzles, experiencing feelings, or initiating actions. The fMRI procedure has recently brought forth many intriguing discoveries in the neurobiology of stress (see Chapter 4, "Stress, Psychological Factors, and Health").

Brain electrical activity mapping (BEAM), a sophisticated type of EEG, uses a computer to analyze brainwave patterns and reveal areas of relative activity and inactivity from moment to moment (see Figure 3.9 on page 137) (Duffy, 1994; Silberstein et al., 1998). Twenty or more electrodes are attached to the scalp and simultaneously feed information

magnetic resonance imaging Formation of a computer-generated image of the anatomical details of the brain by measuring the signals that these structures emit when a subject's head is placed in a strong magnetic field. Abbreviated *MRI*.

functional magnetic resonance imaging A form of magnetic resonance imaging of the brain that records which regions of the brain are active during specific mental activities. Abbreviated *fMRI*.

brain electrical activity mapping Method of brain imaging that involves computer analysis of data from multiple electrodes that are placed on a subject's scalp in order to reveal areas of the brain with relatively higher or lower levels of electrical activity. Abbreviated *BEAM*.

FIGURE 3.6 The computerized tomography (CT) scan.
The CT scan aims a narrow X-ray beam at the head, and the resultant radiation is measured from multiple angles as it passes through. The computer enables researchers to consolidate the measurements into a three-dimensional image of the brain. The CT scan reveals structural abnormalities in the brain that may be implicated in various patterns of abnormal behaviour.

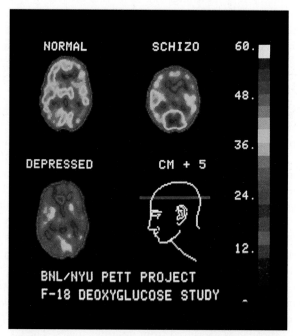

FIGURE 3.7 The positron emission tomography (PET) scan.
In the PET scan, a small amount of a radioactive tracer is mixed with glucose and injected into the bloodstream. When it reaches the brain, patterns of neural activity are revealed by measurement of the positively charged particles that are emitted by the tracer. The glucose metabolized by parts of the brain generates a computer image of neural activity. Areas of greater activity metabolize more glucose. These PET-scan images suggest differences in the metabolic processes of the brains of people with depression, schizophrenia, and controls who are free of psychological disorders.

about brain activity to a computer. The computer analyzes the signals and displays the pattern of brain activity on a colour monitor, providing a vivid image of the electrical activity of the brain at work. BEAM and other similar techniques have been helpful in studying the brain activity of people with schizophrenia and children with attention-deficit hyperactivity disorder, among other physical and psychological disorders. In later chapters, we see how modern imaging techniques are furthering our understanding of various patterns of abnormal behaviour.

In conclusion, people's psychological problems, which are no less complex than people themselves, are thus assessed in many ways. In hospital settings, for instance, clients are commonly reviewed by a multidisciplinary team that may include psychologists, psychiatrists, social workers, neuropsychologists, neuroimaging specialists, and other mental health experts as needed. Clients are generally asked to explain their problems as best they can, and sometimes a computer does the asking. Psychologists can also draw on batteries of tests that assess anything from intelligence and personality to neuropsychological integrity. Many psychologists prefer to observe people's behaviour directly when possible and sometimes devices that measure and record physiological markers of emotional states (e.g., changes in blood pressure, muscle tension, perspiration) are also used. Modern technology has provided several means of studying the structure and function of the brain. The methods of assessment selected by clinicians reflect the problems of their clients, the clinicians' theoretical orientations, and the clinicians' mastery of specialized technologies.

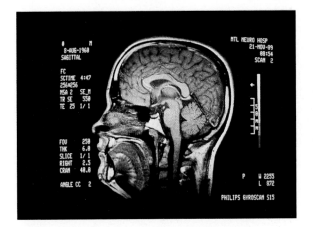

FIGURE 3.8 Magnetic resonance imaging (MRI).
In MRI, a person is placed in a donut-shaped tunnel that generates a strong magnetic field. Radio waves are directed at the brain, which emit signals that are measured from several angles and integrated into a computer-generated image of the brain.

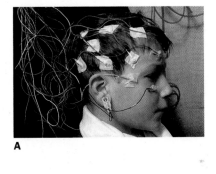

A

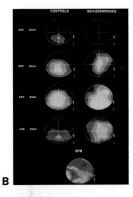

B

FIGURE 3.9 Brain electrical activity mapping (BEAM).
Beam is a type of EEG in which electrodes are attached to the scalp (photo A) to measure electrical activity in various regions of the brain. The left column of photo B shows the average level of electrical activity in the brains of ten normal people (controls) at four time intervals. The column to the right shows the average level of activity of subjects with schizophrenia during the same intervals. Higher activity levels are represented in increasing order by yellows, reds, and whites. The computer-generated image in the bottom centre summarizes differences in activity levels between the brains of normal subjects and those with schizophrenia. Areas of the brain depicted in blue show small differences between the groups. White areas represent larger differences.

STUDY BREAK

Methods of Assessment

Review It

- **What is a clinical interview?** A clinical interview involves the use of a set of questions designed to elicit relevant information from people seeking treatment. Interview formats include structured, semistructured, and unstructured approaches.

- **What are psychological tests?** Psychological tests are structured methods of assessment used to evaluate reasonably stable traits such as intelligence and personality.

- **What are the major types of psychological tests used by clinicians?** Tests of intelligence, such as the Stanford-Binet Intelligence Scale and the Wechsler scales, are used for various purposes in clinical assessment, including determining evidence of mental retardation or cognitive impairment, and assessing strengths and weaknesses. Self-report personality inventories, such as the MMPI, use structured items to measure various personality traits, such as anxiety, depression, and masculinity–femininity. These tests are considered objective in the sense that they make use of a limited range of possible responses to items and an empirical or objective method of test construction. Projective personality tests, such as the Rorschach and TAT, ask subjects to interpret ambiguous stimuli in the belief their answers may shed light on their unconscious processes. Concerns persist about the validity of these tests, however.

- **What is neuropsychological assessment?** Neuropsychological assessment involves the use of psychological tests to indicate possible neurological impairment or brain defects. The Halstead-Reitan Neuropsychological Battery and Luria Nebraska Test Battery measure perceptual skills, cognitive skills, and motor skills and performance that relate to specific areas of brain function.

- **What are some of the methods used in behavioural assessment?** In behavioural assessment, test responses are taken as samples of behaviour rather than as signs of underlying traits or dispositions. The behavioural examiner may conduct a functional assessment, which relates a problem behaviour to its antecedents and consequents. Methods of behavioural assessment include behavioural interviewing, self-monitoring, use of analogue or contrived measures, direct observation, and behavioural rating scales.

- **What is cognitive assessment?** Cognitive assessment focuses on the measurement of thoughts, beliefs, and attitudes in order to help identify distorted thinking patterns. Specific methods of assessment include the use of a thought record or diary and the use of rating scales such as the Automatic Thoughts Questionnaire (ATQ), the Cognition Checklist (CCL), and the Dysfunctional Attitudes Scale (DAS).

- **How do clinicians and researchers study physiological functioning?** Measures of physiological functioning include heart rate, blood pressure, galvanic skin response (GSR), muscle tension, and brainwave activity. Brain-imaging techniques such as EEG, CT scans, PET scans, MRI, fMRI, and BEAM probe the inner workings and structures of the brain.

Define It

rapport	behavioural assessment
unstructured interviews	analogue
semi-structured	functional analysis
interviews	behavioural interview
structured interviews	reactivity
closed-ended questions	self-monitoring
open-ended questions	baseline
intelligence	behavioural rating scale
mental status	electrodermal response
examination	galvanic skin response
mental age	electroencephalograph
intelligence quotient	electromyograph
deviation IQ	ambulatory
objective tests	computerized
forced-choice formats	tomography
contrasted groups	emission tomography
approach	magnetic resonance
validity scales positron	imaging
standard scores	functional magnetic
reality testing	resonance imaging
psychometric approach	neuropsychological
brain electrical activity	assessment
mapping	

Recall It*

1. A(n) _____ interview is an interview format in which a clinician follows a general outline of questions but is free to ask questions in any particular order and to branch off in other directions to gather more clinically important information.

   a. unstructured
   b. superstructured
   c. semi-structured
   d. structured

2. In using the Stanford-Binet Intelligence Scale (SBIS) today, we derive an IQ score based on _____.

   a. the sum of correct answers on a test
   b. the proportion of correct answers on a test
   c. the relationship between a child's performance and norms reflecting the child's age group
   d. the relationship between a child's mental age and chronological age

3. Stacy takes a personality test in which each item requires that she indicate which of two statements is more true for her. This test is a(n) _____ test.

   a. projective
   b. subjective
   c. objective
   d. comparison-based

4. The _____ is an example of a projective test.

   a. MMPI
   b. Stanford-Binet
   c. Rorschach
   d. Halstead-Reitan

5. The brain-imaging technique that relies on the use of radio waves is the _____.

   a. PET scan
   b. MRI
   c. CT scan
   d. EEG

* Recall It answers can be found on the Companion Website for this text.

Think About It

- Which methods of assessment do you feel are most helpful in evaluating people with mental health problems? Explain.
- Consider the debate over the use of projective tests. Do you believe that a person's response to inkblots or other unstructured stimuli might reveal aspects of his or her underlying personality? Why or why not?

WEBLINKS

Mental Health Info Source
www.cmellc.com/topics
This is a mental health education website. It contains access to e-journals and information on a wide range of mental disorders.

Mental Help Net
www.mentalhelp.net
This site has articles and descriptions of psychological disorders. It also provides links to assessment tools and other mental health resources and services.

Psychiatry Online
www.priory.com/psych.htm
This site provides an international forum for psychiatry and has links to the latest articles, papers, and journals.

The Section on Clinical Psychology of the Canadian Psychological Association
www.cpa.ca/clinical
The Canadian Psychological Association site is home to the Section on Clinical Psychology. It is a central source for information about the clinical psychology profession in Canada.

Classification and Assessment of Abnormal Behaviour

Classification of Abnormal Behaviour

Internationally Recognized Diagnostic Systems

1. Diagnostic and Statistical Manual of Mental Disorders (DSM-IV-TR)
2. International Statistical Classification of Diseases and Related Health Problems (ICD-10)

The DSM and Models of Abnormal Behaviour

1. Axis I (Clinical Syndromes)
2. Axis II (Personality Disorders)
3. Axis III (General Medical Conditions)
4. Axis IV (Psychosocial and Environmental Problems)
5. Axis V (Global Assessment of Functioning)

Evaluation of the DSM System

- Certain DSM classes have generally good reliability and validity, but other diagnostic classes, such as personality disorders, are under review.

Advantages and Disadvantages of the DSM System

- Strengths: use of specified diagnostic criteria and a multiaxial system to provide a comprehensive picture of the person's functioning.
- Weaknesses: questions about reliability and validity of certain diagnostic categories, and the adoption of a medical model framework for classifying abnormal behaviour patterns.

Reliability and Validity Issues in Assessment

Reliability

- Types: internal consistency, temporal stability, and interrater reliability

Validity

- Types: content validity, criterion validity, and construct validity

Sociocultural and Ethnic Factors in the Assessment of Abnormal Behaviour

- Researchers, clinicians, and interviewers need to be aware of sociocultural and ethnic factors when they assess personality traits and psychological disorders.

Methods of Assessment

The Clinical Interview

- The interview involves the use of a set of questions designed to elicit relevant information from people seeking treatment.
- Formats: structured, semi-structured, and unstructured approaches.

Psychological Tests of Intelligence and Personality

- Intelligence tests:
  Stanford-Binet
  Intelligence Scale
  Wechsler scales
- Self-report personality inventories:
  Beck Depression Inventory, MMPI-2 and the MCMI
- Projective personality tests: Rorschach Inkblot Test and the Thematic Apperception Test (TAT)

Neuropsychological Assessment

- These psychological tests are used to indicate possible neurological impairment or brain defects.
- Types: Halstead-Reitan Neuropsychological Battery and Luria Nebraska Test Battery.

Behavioural Assessment

- Responses are taken as samples of behaviour rather than as signs of underlying traits or dispositions.
- Types: self-monitoring, analogue or contrived measures, and behavioural rating scales.

Cognitive Assessment

- Focus on measurement of thoughts, beliefs, and attitudes in order to help identify distorted thinking patterns.
- Types: Automatic Thoughts Questionnaire (ATQ), the Cognition Checklist (CCL), and the Dysfunctional Attitudes Scale (DAS).

Physiological Measurement

- Types: heart rate, blood pressure, galvanic skin response (GSR), muscle tension (EMG), and brainwave activity

Concept of Response Systems

- The behavioural, physiological, and verbal response systems should be assessed separately.

Probing the Workings of the Brain

- Methods: EEG, CT scan, PET scan, MRI, fMRI, and BEAM

Stress, Psychological Factors, and Health

Did You Know That...

See the underlined text on the pages indicated below for more information on these interesting and often misunderstood facts.

- Stress can be good for you? (p. 143)
- If you have been having trouble concentrating on your schoolwork because of the break-up of a recent romance, you could be experiencing a mental disorder? (p. 144)
- As you read this page, millions of microscopic warriors in your body are engaged in search-and-destroy missions against invading hordes? (p. 147)
- Stress can increase your susceptibility to a common cold? (p. 148)
- Optimistic people recover more rapidly than pessimistic people from coronary artery bypass surgery? (p. 153)
- A sense of humour may buffer the impact of stress? (p. 154)
- People can relieve the pain of migraine headaches by raising the temperature in a finger? (p. 160)
- Cancer patients who maintain a "fighting spirit" experience better outcomes than those who resign themselves to their illness? (p. 168)

AN AGE-OLD DEBATE concerns relationships between the mind and body. Mental functioning certainly depends on the brain, but because the workings of the mind are of a different quality than biological processes, there is continuing temptation to regard them separately. The 17th-century French philosopher René Descartes (1596–1650) influenced modern thinking with his belief in dualism, or separateness, between the mind and body. Today, scientists and clinicians have come to recognize that the mind and body are more closely intertwined than would be suggested by a dualistic model—that psychological factors influence and are influenced by physical functioning (Lehtinen, Ozamiz, Underwood, Weiss, 2005). Psychologists who study the interrelationships between psychology and physical health are called **health psychologists**.

We begin focusing on relationships between the mind and body by examining the role of stress in both mental and physical functioning. The term **stress** refers to the disequilibrium that accompanies pressure or force placed on a body. Take, for example, an under-ocean earthquake that causes a shift in the ocean floor that generates a sudden release of energy. The resulting stress displaces the water above, forming a huge seismic wave—a tsunami—which can radiate outward for thousands of kilometres and cause mass destruction on distant shorelines and low-lying coastal areas. In psychology, we use the term *stress* to refer to the mental, emotional, or physical adaptation or adjustment an organism makes in the face of any tangible or perceived pressure or demand. Some reactions are healthy—sometimes called **eustress** (good stress). Some are relatively benign— **neustress** (neutral stress), and some are destructive— **distress** (bad stress). A **stressor** is a source of stress. Stressors (or stresses) include psychological factors such as examinations in school and problems in social relationships; life changes such as the death of a loved one, divorce, job termination; daily hassles such as traffic jams; and physical environmental factors such as exposure to extreme temperatures or noise levels. Some degree of stress is beneficial to us; it helps keep us active and alert. But stress that is prolonged or intense can over-tax our coping ability and turn into emotional distress, such as a state of anxiety or depression, and physical complaints such as fatigue and headaches.

Stress is implicated in a wide range of physical and psychological problems. We begin our study of the effects of stress by discussing a category of psychological disorders called *adjustment disorders*, which involve maladaptive stress reactions. We then consider the role of stressors and other psychological and sociocultural factors in physical disorders.

health psychologists Psychologists involved in the study of the interrelationships between psychological factors and physical illness.

stress The mental, emotional, or physical adaptation or adjustment an organism makes in the face of any tangible or perceived pressure or demand.

eustress The enjoyable and curative experience that accompanies pressures or demands.

neustress Neither a taxing nor an enhancing experience that accompanies pressures or demands.

distress The psychologically harmful and disease-producing experience that accompanies pressures or demands.

stressor Source of stress.

ADJUSTMENT DISORDERS

Adjustment disorders are the first psychological disorders we discuss in this book, and they are among the mildest. An adjustment disorder is a maladaptive reaction to an identified stressor that develops within a few months of the onset of the stressor. The maladaptive reaction is characterized by significant impairment in social, occupational, or academic functioning, or by states of emotional distress that exceed those normally induced by the stressor. For the diagnosis to apply, the stress-related reaction must not be sufficient to meet the diagnostic criteria for other clinical syndromes, such as anxiety disorders or mood disorders. The maladaptive reaction may be resolved if the stressor is removed or the individual learns to cope with it. If the maladaptive reaction lasts for more than six months after the stressor (or its consequences) have been removed, the diagnosis may be changed.

adjustment disorder Maladaptive reaction to an identified stressor or stressors that occurs shortly following exposure to the stressor(s) and results in impaired functioning or signs of emotional distress that exceed what would normally be expected in the situation. The reaction may be resolved if the stressor is removed or the individual learns to adapt to it successfully.

Hassles. One of the major sources of stress in everyday life is common hassles like traffic jams.

Difficulty in concentrating or adjustment disorder? An adjustment disorder is a maladaptive reaction to a stressful event that may take the form of impaired functioning at school or work, such as having difficulties keeping one's mind on one's studies.

If your relationship with someone comes to an end (an identified stressor) and your grades are falling because you are unable to keep your mind on schoolwork, you may fit the bill for an adjustment disorder. If Uncle Harry has been feeling down and pessimistic since his divorce from Aunt Jane, he too may be diagnosed with an adjustment disorder. So, too, might Cousin Billy if he has been cutting classes and spraying obscene words on school walls or showing other signs of disturbed conduct. There are several subtypes of adjustment disorders that vary in terms of the type of maladaptive reaction (see Table 4.1).

The concept of an adjustment disorder as a *mental disorder* highlights some of the difficulties in attempting to define what is normal and what is not. When something important goes wrong in life, we should feel bad about it. If there is a crisis in business, if we are victimized by a crime, if there is a flood or a devastating ice storm, it is understandable that we might become anxious or depressed. There might, in fact, be something more seriously wrong with us if we did not react in a "maladaptive" way, at least temporarily. However, if our emotional reaction exceeds an expectable response, or our ability to function is impaired (e.g., avoidance of social interactions, difficulty getting out of bed, or falling behind in our schoolwork), then a diagnosis of adjustment disorder may be indi-

TABLE 4.1

Subtypes of Adjustment Disorders

Disorder	Chief Features
Adjustment Disorder with Depressed Mood	The chief features are sadness, crying, and feelings of hopelessness.
Adjustment Disorder with Anxiety	The chief features are worrying, nervousness, and jitters (or in children, separation fears from primary attachment figures).
Adjustment Disorder with Mixed Anxiety and Depressed Mood	The chief feature involves a combination of anxiety and depression.
Adjustment Disorder with Disturbance of Conduct	The chief feature is violation of the rights of others or violation of social norms appropriate for one's age. Sample behaviours include vandalism, truancy, fighting, reckless driving, and defaulting on legal obligations (e.g., stopping alimony payments).
Adjustment Disorder with Mixed Disturbance of Emotions and Conduct	The predominant feature involves both emotional disturbance, such as depression or anxiety, and conduct disturbance (as described above).
Adjustment Disorder Unspecified	A residual category that applies to cases not classifiable in one of the other subtypes.

Sources: Adapted from the DSM-IV-TR (APA, 2000a).

cated. Thus, if you are having trouble concentrating on your schoolwork following the break-up of a romantic relationship, you may have a mild type of psychological disorder—an adjustment disorder.

STUDY BREAK

Adjustment Disorders

Review It

- **What are adjustment disorders?** Adjustment disorders are maladaptive reactions to identified stressors.

- **How are adjustment disorders recognized?** They are recognized on the basis of emotional reactions that are greater than normally expected given the circumstances or by evidence of significant impairment in functioning. Impairment usually takes the form of problems at work or school or in social relationships or activities.

Define It

health psychologists	distress
stress	stressor
eustress	adjustment disorder
neustress	

Recall It*

1. In psychology, stress can best be defined as _____.

   a. unpleasant demands placed on an organism to adjust
   b. the adaptation or adjustment made in response to pressure or demands
   c. any physical or psychological pressure exerted on a body
   d. a painful stimulus resulting in undesired consequences

2. Psychologists use the term *stressors* to refer to _____.

   a. people who possess keen sensitivity to stress and stimulation
   b. sources of stress

   c. sources of distress
   d. a person's physical reactions to a stressful event

3. A(n) _____ is a maladaptive reaction to a stressful event that develops within a few months of the onset of the event.

   a. affective disorder
   b. adjustment disorder
   c. diathesis
   d. personality disorder

4. Adjustment disorders _____ psychological disorders.

   a. are among the mildest
   b. vary between mild and severe
   c. are among the most severe
   d. are the most severe

5. When an adjustment disorder lasts more than _____ months after the removal of the stressor or its consequences, the diagnosis may be changed.

   a. 3
   b. 6
   c. 9
   d. 12

* Recall It answers can be found on the Companion Website for this text.

Think About It

- The lines between normal reactions to stressful events and abnormal reactions in the form of adjustment disorders may sometimes become blurry. Think of two people experiencing the same stressful event, such as the break-up of a relationship, the loss of a loved one, or adjusting to college. What would you expect would be a normal reaction to these events? What would constitute an abnormal reaction or adjustment disorder? Explain the differences.

STRESS AND ILLNESS

Psychological sources of stress not only diminish our capacity for adjustment, but may also be detrimental to our health. For instance, Vancouver-based physician and author Gabor Maté (2003) cites recent research that describes the important role that emotions and psychological stress have in the development of chronic illness. Maté maintains that a breakdown in the interplay of the body's emotional, nervous, hormonal, and immune systems

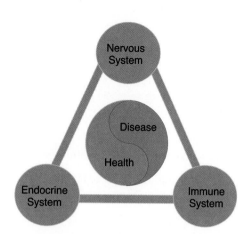

FIGURE 4.1 Neuroimmune biology.
A new multidisciplinary field of study that focuses on the mechanisms of hormones and neurotransmitters and the immune system that regulate all aspects of bodily functioning in health and disease.

Source: Berczi, I. (2001). Neuroimmune biology — An introduction. I. Berczi & R. M. Gorczynski (Eds.), *New Foundation of Biology* (pp. 3–45). New York: Elsevier Science.

psychoneuroimmunology Field of scientific investigation that studies relationships between psychological factors, such as coping styles, attitudes, and behaviour patterns, and immunological functioning.

can have major impacts on our health. This mind–body approach to medicine is grounded in the field of **psychoneuroimmunology**—the study of the relationships between psychological factors, especially stress, and the workings of the endocrine system, the immune system, and the nervous system (Kiecolt-Glaser & Glaser, 1992; Maier, Watkins, & Fleshner, 1994). A parallel discipline is known as neuroimmune biology. Istvan Berczi (2001) of the University of Manitoba's Faculty of Medicine is the co-editor of the new journal/book series *Neuroimmune Biology*. Neuroimmune biology is a multidisciplinary field of study that looks at how the nervous, endocrine, and immune systems affect health and disease (see Figure 4.1). Here, we examine what we've learned about these relationships.

Stress and Neurobiology

Bruce Perry, senior consultant to the Alberta Ministry of Children's Services, describes how stress and traumatic experiences can produce qualitatively different neurobiological effects at different stages of development—especially during early childhood (Perry, 2002; Perry, Pollard, Blakely, Baker, & Vigilante, 1995; Perry & Szalavitz, 2007). In addition, it has been shown that the more intense and prolonged the stress, the greater the negative impact on long-term behaviour. This coincides with recent neurological studies that have found that severe stress during early childhood is associated with relatively permanent changes in the shape, function, and molecular organization of neurons in regions of the brain that help regulate emotion and memory (Teicher, 2002). In particular, severe maltreatment during childhood (physical, sexual, and/or emotional abuse) is related to molecular and neurobiological damage in the emotional and memory parts of the brain that are still growing. As a result, brain-imaging studies of adults who were traumatized as children have revealed atypical left/right cerebral hemisphere functioning and reductions in the size of both the hippocampus, where memory processing takes place, and the amygdala, which regulates negative emotions (recall the nervous system in Chapter 2). These neurological changes are associated with a range of childhood and adult psychiatric disorders.

Recent fMRI studies of posttraumatic stress disorder (PTSD; see Chapter 5, "Anxiety Disorders") by Ruth Lanius of the University of Western Ontario have shown that people who have experienced traumatic life events, such as horrific car accidents or severe sexual assault, use atypical regions of their brain when they recall the events (Lanius et al., 2003, 2004). Lanius compared people who experienced traumatic events and developed PTSD to those who did not develop PTSD. When prompted to recall the traumatic event, PTSD patients displayed activation of several right-brain regions whereas non-PTSD people showed heightened activity in left-brain areas (Lanius et al., 2004). In other studies, it was shown that even within PTSD patients, there were brain-function differences. When prompted to recall traumatic events, about 70% of PTSD patients experienced heightened physiological arousal and 30% experienced dissociative states with no related physiological arousal. These nondissociative and dissociative PTSD reactions were linked to different neural pathways involving the prefrontal cortex and limbic structures of the brain (Lanius, Williamson, & Menon, 2002; Lanius et al., 2002).

Stress and the Endocrine System

endocrine system System of ductless glands in the body that directly secrete hormones into the bloodstream.

hormones Substances secreted by endocrine glands that regulate bodily functions and promote the development or growth of body structures.

Stress has a domino effect on the **endocrine system**, the body's system of glands that release secretions, called **hormones**, directly into the bloodstream. (Other glands, such as the salivary glands that produce saliva, release secretions into a system of ducts.) The endocrine system consists of glands distributed throughout the body. Figure 4.2 on page 147 shows the major endocrine glands and the hormones they produce.

Several endocrine glands are involved in the body's stress response. First, the hypothalamus, a small structure in the midbrain, releases a hormone that stimulates the nearby pituitary gland to secrete *adrenocorticotrophic hormone* (ACTH). ACTH, in turn, stimulates the adrenal glands, which are located above the kidneys. Under the influence of

ACTH, the outer layer of the adrenal glands, called the *adrenal cortex*, releases a group of **steroids** (cortisol and cortisone are examples). These cortical steroids (also called *corticosteroids*) are hormones that have a number of different functions in the body. They boost resistance to stressors; foster muscle development; and induce the liver to release sugar, which provides needed bursts of energy for responding to a threatening stressor (e.g., a lurking predator or assailant) or emergency situation. They also assist the body in defending against allergic reactions and inflammation.

The sympathetic branch of the autonomic nervous system, or ANS, stimulates the inner layer of the adrenal glands, called the *adrenal medulla*, to release a mixture of chemicals called **catecholamines**—epinephrine (adrenaline) and norepinephrine (noradrenaline). These chemicals function as hormones when released into the bloodstream. Norepinephrine is also produced in the nervous system and functions as a neurotransmitter. The mixture of epinephrine and norepinephrine mobilizes the body to deal with a threatening stressor by accelerating the heart rate and by also stimulating the liver to release stored glucose (sugar), making more energy available where it can be of use in protecting ourselves in a threatening situation.

The stress hormones produced by the adrenal glands help the body prepare to cope with an impending threat or stressor. Once the stressor has passed, the body returns to a normal state. During states of chronic stress, however, the body may continue to pump out stress hormones, which can have damaging effects throughout the body, including suppressing the ability of the immune system to protect against various infections and disease (Kemeny, 2003).

Stress and the Immune System

Given the intricacies of the human body and the rapid advance of scientific knowledge, we might consider ourselves dependent on highly trained medical specialists to contend with illness. Actually, our bodies cope with most diseases on their own through the functioning of the immune system.

The **immune system** is the body's wall of defence against disease. It combats disease in a number of ways. Your body is constantly engaged in search-and-destroy missions against invading microbes, even as you're reading this page. Millions of white blood cells, or leukocytes, are the immune system's foot soldiers in this microscopic warfare. Leukocytes systematically envelop and kill **pathogens** like bacteria, viruses, and fungi; worn-out body cells; and cells that have become cancerous.

Leukocytes recognize invading pathogens by their surface fragments, called **antigens**—literally *anti*body *gen*erators. Some leukocytes produce **antibodies**, kinds of specialized proteins, which attach to these foreign bodies, inactivate them, and mark them for destruction.

Special "memory lymphocytes" (lymphocytes are a type of leukocyte) are held in reserve rather than marking foreign bodies for destruction or going to war against them. They can remain in the bloodstream for years and form the basis for a quick immune response to an invader the second time around.

Researchers are particularly interested in how stress may affect the immune system. A weakened immune system can make us more vulnerable to common illnesses, such as colds and the flu, and may increase our risks of developing chronic diseases, including cancer.

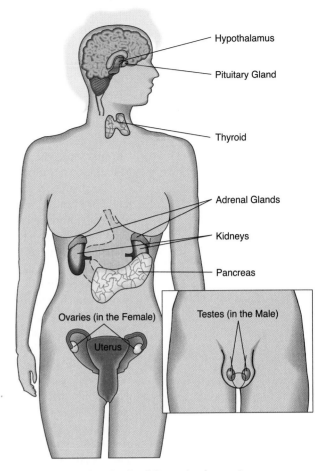

FIGURE 4.2 Major glands of the endocrine system.
The glands of the endocrine system pour secretions—called hormones—directly into the bloodstream. Although hormones may travel throughout the body, they act only on specific receptor sites. Many hormones are implicated in stress reactions and various patterns of abnormal behaviour.

steroids Group of hormones including testosterone, estrogen, progesterone, and corticosteroids.

catecholamines A group of chemically related substances that function as neurotransmitters in the brain (dopamine and norepinephrine) and as hormones (epinephrine and norepinephrine).

immune system The body's apparatus for recognizing and destroying antigens (foreign bodies) that invade the body, mutated cells, and worn-out cells.

leukocytes White blood cells. Leukocytes comprise part of the body's immune system.

pathogen Organism such as a bacterium or virus that can cause disease.

antigen Substance that triggers an immune system response (the contraction for *anti*body *gen*erator).

antibodies Substances produced by white blood cells that identify and target antigens for destruction.

Exposure to physical sources of stress such as cold or loud noise, especially when intense or prolonged, can dampen immunological functioning. So, too, can various psychological stressors ranging from sleep deprivation to final examinations (Maier, Watkins, & Fleshner, 1994). Medical students, for example, show poorer immune functioning during exam time than they do a month before exams, when their lives are relatively less stressful (Glaser et al., 1987). Traumatic stressors, such as exposure to earthquakes or other natural or technological disasters or to violence, can also dampen immunological functioning (Ironson et al., 1997; Solomon et al., 1997). Life stressors such as divorce and chronic unemployment can take a toll on the immune system as well (O'Leary, 1990). Chronic stress may make it take longer for wounds to heal (Kiecolt-Glaser, Marucha, Malarkey, Mercado, & Glaser, 1995).

Social support appears to moderate the harmful effects of stress on the immune system. For example, investigators find that medical and dental students with larger numbers of friends show better immune functioning than students with fewer friends (Jemmott et al., 1983; Kiecolt-Glaser, Speicher, Holliday, & Glaser, 1984). Consider, too, that lonely students show a greater suppression of the immune response than do students with greater social support (Glaser, Kiecolt-Glaser, Speicher, & Holiday, 1985). Newly separated and divorced people also show evidence of suppressed immune response, especially those who remain attached to their ex-partners (Kiecolt-Glaser et al., 1987, 1988).

Exposure to stressors is linked to an increased risk of developing a common cold. In one study, people who reported higher levels of daily stressors, such as pressures at work, showed lower levels in their bloodstreams of antibodies that fend off cold viruses (Stone et al., 1994). In another study, exposure to severe chronic stressors lasting a month or longer of the type associated with underemployment, unemployment, or interpersonal problems with family members or friends was associated with a greater risk of developing a common cold after exposure to cold viruses (Cohen et al., 1998). Yet social support may boost resistance to the common cold. Researchers found that people who have more varied types of social relationships—with spouses, children, other relatives, friends, colleagues, members of organizations and religious groups, and so on—were less likely than others to come down with a cold after exposure to cold viruses (Cohen, Doyle, Skoner, Rabin, & Gwaltney, 1997; Gilbert, 1997). And when they did get sick, they tended to develop milder symptoms.

We should caution that much of the research in the field of psychoneuroimmunology is correlational in nature. Researchers examine immunological functioning in relation to different indices of stress, but do not (nor would they want to) directly manipulate stress to observe its effect on subjects' immune systems or general health. Correlational research helps us better understand relationships between variables and may point to possible underlying causal factors, but does not in itself demonstrate causal connections.

The General Adaptation Syndrome

general adaptation syndrome In Hans Selye's view, the body's three-stage response to states of prolonged or intense stress. Abbreviated *GAS*.

alarm reaction First stage of the general adaptation syndrome following response to a stressor, it is characterized by heightened sympathetic activity.

fight-or-flight reaction Hypothesized inborn tendency to respond to a threat by means of fighting the threat or fleeing.

Canadian pioneering stress researcher Hans Selye (1976) coined the term **general adaptation syndrome** (GAS) to describe a common biological response pattern to prolonged or excessive stress. Selye pointed out that our bodies respond similarly to many kinds of unpleasant stressors, whether the source of stress is an invasion of microscopic disease organisms, a divorce, or the aftermath of a flood. The GAS model suggests that our bodies under stress are like clocks with alarm systems that do not shut off until their energy is perilously depleted.

The GAS consists of three stages: (1) the alarm reaction, (2) the resistance stage, and (3) the exhaustion stage (see Figure 4.3 on page 149). Perception of an immediate stressor (e.g., a car that swerves in front of your own on the highway) triggers the **alarm reaction**. The alarm reaction mobilizes the body for defence. It is initiated by the brain and regulated by the endocrine system and the sympathetic branch of the autonomic nervous system (ANS) (see Figure 4.4 on page 150). In 1929, Harvard University physiologist Walter Cannon termed this response pattern the **fight-or-flight reaction**. We noted earlier how the endocrine system responds to stressors. During the alarm reaction, the adrenal glands, under control of the pituitary gland in the brain, pump out cortical steroids and catecholamines that help mobilize the body's defences (see Table 4.2 on page 150).

The fight-or-flight reaction likely helped our early ancestors cope with the many perils they faced. This reaction may have been provoked by the sight of a predator or by a rustling sound in the undergrowth. But our ancestors usually did not experience prolonged activation of the alarm reaction. Once a threat was eliminated, the body reinstates a lower level of arousal. Our ancestors fought off predators or fled quickly; if not, they failed to contribute their genes to the genetic pools of their groups. In short, they died. Sensitive alarm reactions bestowed survival. Yet our ancestors did not invest years in the academic grind, struggle to balance the budget each month, or face any of the many daily stresses that repeatedly or persistently tax our body's ability to cope—everything from battling traffic in the morning to balancing school and work or rushing from job to job. Consequently, much of the time, our alarm system is turned on, which may eventually increase the likelihood of developing stress-related disorders.

When a stressor is persistent, we progress to the **resistance stage**, or adaptation stage, of the GAS. Endocrine and sympathetic system responses (release of stress hormones, for example) remain at high levels, but not quite as high as during the alarm reaction. During this stage, the body tries to renew spent energy and repair damage. But when stressors continue to persist or new ones enter the picture, we may advance to the final or **exhaustion stage** of the GAS. Although there are individual differences in capacity to resist stress, all of us will eventually exhaust or deplete our bodily resources. The exhaustion stage is characterized by dominance of the parasympathetic branch of the ANS. Consequently, our heart and respiration rates decelerate. Do we benefit from the respite? Not necessarily. If the source of stress persists, we may develop what Selye termed *diseases of adaptation*. These range from allergic reactions to heart disease—and, at times, even death. The lesson is clear: chronic stress can damage our health, leaving us more vulnerable to a range of diseases and other physical health problems.

Cortical steroids are perhaps one reason that persistent stress may eventually lead to health problems. Although cortical steroids in some ways help the body cope with stress, persistent secretion of these steroids suppresses the activity of the immune system. Cortical steroids have negligible effects when they are released only periodically. Continuous secretion, however, weakens the immune system by disrupting the production of antibodies. As a result, we grow more vulnerable to various diseases, even the common cold (Cohen, Tyrell, & Smith, 1991).

Hans Selye (1907–1982). Selye spent the formative years of his career at McGill University (1932–1945) and the remainder at the Université de Montréal (1945–1977). After that, he established the International Institute of Stress and the Canadian Institute of Stress. The internationally renowned scientist whose name is synonymous with "stress" spent a lifetime in ongoing research on general adaptation syndrome and wrote nearly 40 books and more than 1700 papers on stress and related problems. Selye was appointed a companion of the Order of Canada in 1968.

resistance stage In Selye's view, the second stage of the general adaptation syndrome, involving the attempt to withstand prolonged stress and preserve bodily resources. Also called the *adaptation stage*.

exhaustion stage Third stage of the general adaptation syndrome (GAS), which is characterized by a lowering of resistance, increased parasympathetic activity, and possible physical deterioration.

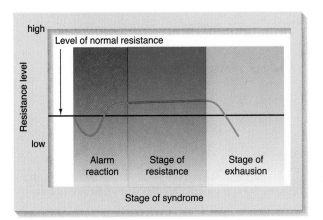

FIGURE 4.3 The general adaptation syndrome.
There are three stages of the general adaptation syndrome: (1) The fight-or-flight activation of the ANS indicates the *alarm stage*; (2) the *stage of resistance* follows, during which adaptation to the stressor is sustained, but at considerable mental and physical cost; and (3) as coping resources are depleted, the body's resistance drops and symptoms of illness appear during the stage of *exhaustion*.

Source: Based on Selye, 1956. Wood, Wood, Wood, Desmarais, 2008, p. 382, Pearson Education Canada. Reprinted with permission by Pearson Education Canada Inc.

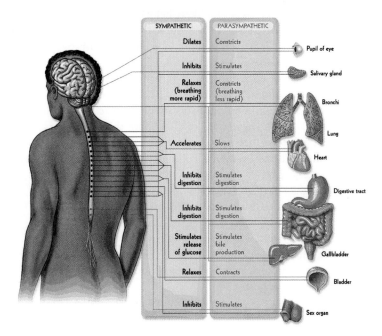

FIGURE 4.4 The Automatic Nervous System.
The ANS consists of two subdivisions: (1) the sympathetic nervous system, which chiefly activates the body during stress, and (2) the parasympathetic nervous system, which signals the body to return to its normal level of homeostasis after an emergency.

Source: From Lefton, Lester A., Linda Brannon Psychology, 8/e. Published by Allyn and Bacon, Boston, MA. Copyright © 2003 Pearson Education. Reprinted by permission of the publisher.

Although Selye's model speaks to the general response pattern of the body under stress, different biological processes may be involved in response to particular kinds of stressors. For example, persistent exposure to excessive noise may invoke different bodily processes than other sources of stress, such as overcrowding, or psychological sources of stress, such as divorce or separation.

Stress and Life Changes

Another way in which researchers have looked at the stress–illness connection is by quantifying life stress in terms of *life changes*. Both positive life events, like marriage, and negative events, like a job termination, can be stressful because the changes they involve impose demands on us to adjust.

Although positive and negative life changes can be stressful, positive life changes seem to be less disruptive than negative ones (Thoits, 1983). In other words, marriage tends to

TABLE 4.2
Stress-Related Changes in the Body Associated with the Alarm Reaction
Pupils dilate
Respiration rate, heart rate, blood pressure, and sweating increase
Blood shifts from the internal organs to the skeletal muscles
Muscles tense
Salivation, digestion, and bladder contraction is inhibited
Sugar is released by the liver
Blood clotting ability is increased
Corticosteroids are released
Epinephrine and norepinephrine are released
Stressors trigger the alarm reaction. The reaction is defined by activation of the sympathetic branch of the ANS and by secretion of corticosteroids, catecholamines. The alarm reaction mobilizes the body for combat or flight.

be less stressful than ending a steady dating relationship. Or to put it another way, a change for the better may be a change, but it is less of a hassle. Let us also note that "eventlessness" (i.e., the absence of life changes) may be just as stressful and indicative of the risk of illness as negative life events (Theorell, 1992).

Other researchers have found that, in addition to major life events, daily hassles such as arguing with a friend, losing or misplacing important items, delays due to bad weather, noisy neighbours, and so on can also have a negative impact on health. For example, University of British Columbia psychologist Anita DeLongis (1985) developed the Revised Hassles Scale (HS-R), an instrument that measures the cumulative effect of both undesirable (hassles) and desirable (uplifts) everyday stressors. The HS-R has been shown to predict changes in physical and mental health (Delongis, Folkman, & Lazarus, 1988; Johnson & Bornstein, 1991), especially in the short term (Johnson & Sherman, 1997).

Psychological Factors That Moderate Stress

Stress may be a fact of life, but the ways in which we handle stress help determine our ability to cope with it. Individuals react differently to stress depending on psychological factors such as the meaning they ascribe to stressful events. For example, whether a major life event, such as pregnancy, is a positive or negative stressor depends on a couple's desire for a child and their readiness to care for one. We can say the stress of pregnancy is moderated by the perceived value of children in a couple's eyes and their self-efficacy—their confidence in their ability to raise a child. As we see next, psychological factors such as coping styles, self-efficacy expectancies, hardiness, optimism, social support, and a sense of humour may moderate or buffer the effects of stress.

Styles of Coping
What do you do when faced with a serious problem? Do you pretend it doesn't exist? Like Scarlett O'Hara in *Gone With the Wind*, do you say to yourself, "I'll think about it tomorrow" and then banish it from your mind? Or do you take charge and confront it squarely?

Pretending that problems don't exist is a form of denial. Denial is an example of **emotion-focused coping** (Lazarus & Folkman, 1984). In emotion-focused coping, people take measures that immediately reduce the impact of the stressor, such as denying its existence or withdrawing from the situation. Emotion-focused coping, however, does not eliminate the stressor (a serious illness, for example) or help the individual develop better ways of managing. In **problem-focused coping**, by contrast, people examine the stressors they face and do what they can to change them or modify their own reactions to render stressors less harmful. These basic styles of coping—emotion focused and problem focused—have been applied to ways in which people respond to illness.

Denial of illness can take various forms, including the following:

1. Failure to recognize the seriousness of the illness;
2. Minimization of the emotional distress the illness causes;
3. Misattribution of symptoms to other causes (for example, assuming the appearance of blood in the stool represents nothing more than a local abrasion); and
4. Ignoring threatening information about the illness (Levine et al., 1987)

Denial can be dangerous to your health, especially if it leads to avoidance of or noncompliance with needed medical treatment. Avoidance is another form of emotion-based coping. In one study, people who had a more avoidant style of coping with cancer (e.g., by trying not to think or talk about it) showed greater disease progression when evaluated a year later than did people who more directly confronted the illness (Epping-Jordan, Compas, & Howell, 1994). Like denial, avoidance may deter people from complying with medical treatments, which can lead to a worsening of their medical conditions. It's also possible that avoidance may contribute to heightened emotional distress and arousal, which may impair immunological functioning.

Another form of emotion-focused coping, the use of wish-fulfillment fantasies, is also linked to poorer adjustment in coping with serious illness. Examples of wish-fulfillment

emotion-focused coping Style of coping with stress that attempts to minimize emotional responsiveness rather than deal with the source of stress directly (e.g., the use of denial to avoid thinking about the stress, or the use of tranquillizers to quell feelings of anxiety).

problem-focused coping Form of coping with stress characterized by directly confronting its source.

fantasies include ruminating about what might have been had the illness not occurred and longing for better times. Wish-fulfillment fantasy offers the patient no means of coping with life's difficulties other than an imaginary escape.

Does this mean that people are invariably better off when they know all the facts concerning their illnesses? Not necessarily. Whether or not you will be better off knowing all the facts may depend on your preferred style of coping. A mismatch between an individual's style of coping and the amount of information provided may hamper recovery. In one study, cardiac patients with a repressive style of coping (relying on denial) who received information about their conditions showed a higher incidence of medical complications than repressors who were largely kept in the dark (Shaw, Cohen, Doyle, & Palesky, 1985). Sometimes ignorance helps people manage stress—at least temporarily.

Problem-focused coping involves strategies that deal directly with the source of stress, like seeking information about the illness through self-study and medical consultation. Information seeking may help an individual maintain a more optimistic frame of mind by creating an expectancy that the information will prove to be useful.

Self-Efficacy Expectancies Self-efficacy expectancies refer to our expectations regarding our abilities to cope with the challenges we face, to perform certain behaviours skilfully, and to produce positive changes in our lives (Bandura, 1982, 1986). We may be better able to manage stress, including the stress of coping with illness, if we feel confident (have higher self-efficacy expectancies) in our ability to cope effectively. A forthcoming exam may be more or less stressful depending on your confidence in your ability to achieve a good grade. Researchers find that spider-phobic women show high levels of the stress hormones epinephrine and norepinephrine when they interact with a phobic object, such as by allowing a spider to crawl on their laps (Bandura et al., 1985). As their confidence or self-efficacy expectancies for coping with these tasks increased, their levels of these stress hormones declined. Epinephrine and norepinephrine arouse the body by way of the sympathetic branch of the ANS. As a consequence, we are likely to feel shaky, to have "butterflies in the stomach" and general feelings of nervousness. Because high self-efficacy expectancies appear to be associated with lower secretion of catecholamines, people who believe they can cope with their problems may be less likely to feel nervous.

Psychological Hardiness Psychological hardiness refers to a cluster of traits that may help people manage stress. Research on the subject is largely indebted to Suzanne Kobasa (1979) and her colleagues. They investigated business executives who resisted illness despite heavy burdens of stress—three key traits distinguished the psychologically hardy executives (Kobasa, Maddi, & Kahn, 1982, pp. 169–170):

1. The hardy executives were high in *commitment*. Rather than feeling alienated from their tasks and situations, they involved themselves fully. That is, they believed in what they were doing.
2. The hardy executives were high in *challenge*. They believed change was the normal state of things, not sterile sameness or stability for the sake of stability.
3. The hardy executives were also high in perceived *control* over their lives (Maddi & Kobasa, 1984). They believed and acted as though they were effectual rather than powerless in controlling the rewards and punishments of life. In terms suggested by social-cognitive theorist Julian Rotter (1966), psychologically hardy individuals have an internal **locus of control**.

People who are psychologically hardy appear to cope more adaptively with stress, such as by using more active, problem-solving approaches (Williams, Wiebe, & Smith, 1992). Psychological hardiness also appears to be positively related to other indices of mental health and recovery from traumatic stress disorders such as posttraumatic stress disorder (PTSD) (King, King, Fairbank, Keane, & Adams, 1998; Maddi & Khoshaba, 1994). Other evidence shows a relationship between proneness to illness and psychological hardiness in people with behaviour patterns that may place them at risk of cardiovascular illness, such as the **Type A behaviour pattern** (TABP). Type A people are highly driven, impatient, com-

psychological hardiness Cluster of stress-buffering traits characterized by commitment, challenge, and control.

locus of control One's perception of the site (internal or external) of the capacity to generate reinforcement. People who believe they have the capacity to generate or attain reinforcements are said to have an internal locus of control. People who rely on others or luck for reinforcement are said to have an external locus of control.

Type A behaviour pattern Pattern of behaviour characterized by a sense of time urgency, competitiveness, and general hostility. Abbreviated *TABP*.

petitive, and generally hostile and quick to anger. Psychologically hardy Type A people have been shown to be more resistant to coronary heart disease than nonhardy Type A people (e.g., Booth-Kewley & Friedman, 1987; Kobasa, Maddi, & Zola, 1983). Kobasa suggests that hardy people are better able to handle stress because they perceive themselves as *choosing* their stress-creating situations. They perceive the stressors they face as making life more interesting and challenging, not as simply burdening them with additional pressures. A sense of control is a key factor in psychological hardiness.

Psychological hardiness. Psychological hardiness is a psychological factor that moderates the effects of stress. Psychologically hardy business executives resist illness despite heavy stress loads. Psychologically hardy executives are committed to their work (they believe in what they are doing), seek challenges, and perceive themselves to be in control of their lives.

Optimism Research suggests that seeing a glass as half full is healthier than seeing it as half empty. That is, people who are more optimistic generally cope with stress better than those who are pessimistic, which may then lower their risk of illness (Scheier & Carver, 1992; Seligman, 1990). In one study on the relationships between optimism and health, Scheier and Carver (1985) administered a measure of optimism, the Life Orientation Test (LOT), to college students. The students tracked their physical symptoms for one month. It turned out those students who received higher optimism scores reported fewer symptoms such as fatigue, dizziness, muscle soreness, and blurry vision. (Subjects' symptoms at the beginning of the study were statistically taken into account, so it could not be argued that the study simply shows healthier people are more optimistic.)

Other research also reveals links between optimism and better health outcomes. For example, pain patients who expressed more pessimistic thoughts during flare-ups of pain reported more severe pain and distress (Gil, Williams, Keefe, & Beckham, 1990). The pessimistic thoughts included, "I can no longer do anything," "No one cares about my pain," and "It isn't fair I have to live this way." In a study of first-year law school students, optimism was associated with better mood and better immune-system responses (Segerstrom, Taylor, Kemeny, & Fahey, 1998). In another study, optimistic women were less likely than pessimistic women to experience postpartum depression (depression following childbirth) (Carver & Gaines, 1987). More optimistic women also suffered less depression and anxiety in the months following a diagnosis of breast cancer (Epping-Jordan et al., 1999). Coronary artery bypass patients who expressed more optimism about the procedure they were about to undergo also showed better outcomes (fewer complications requiring additional hospitalization or surgery) than did more pessimistic patients (Scheier et al., 1999).

Research to date shows only correlational links between optimism and health. Perhaps we shall soon learn whether learning to alter attitudes—to learn to see a glass as half full—plays a causal role in maintaining or restoring health. You can evaluate your own level of optimism by completing the accompanying Life Orientation Test in the "Questionnaire" box.

Humour: Does "A Merry Heart Doeth Good Like a Medicine?" The notion that humour eases the burdens of the day has been with humankind for millennia (Lefcourt & Martin, 1986). Consider the biblical adage, "A merry heart doeth good like a medicine" (Proverbs 17:22).

Research evidence buttresses the biblical maxim by suggesting that humour may indeed play a stress-buffering role and perhaps more. Rod Martin (1996) at the University of Western Ontario and others have been investigating the interrelationship of humour, well-being, and stress coping. In one study, negative life events had less of a depressing effect on students who had a better sense of humour and those who were better able to produce humour under conditions of stress (Martin & Lefcourt, 1983). Moreover, higher levels of humour were associated with a more positive self-concept, higher self-esteem, and more positive emotions during both good times and bad (Kuiper, Grimshaw, Leite, &

Kirsh, 2004; Kuiper & Martin, 1993, 1998; Martin, 2007). <u>This line of research suggests that humour may not only serve as a buffer against stress but actually enhance enjoyment of positive life events and good times</u> (Martin et al., 1993). A recent review of the literature found that the relationship between the effects of humour and laughter on the immune system, blood pressure, longevity, and illness symptoms is not strong because of methodological problems and inconsistencies in the research studies (Kuiper, et al., 2004; Martin, 2001, 2007). In addition, we should be careful about drawing causal inferences from correlational relationships. Persons with a better-developed sense of humour may also possess other qualities that buffer the impact of stress.

Social Support The role of social support as a buffer against stress is well documented (Wills & Filer Fegan, 2001). In one study of people with heart disease, higher levels of social support were associated with fewer depressive symptoms when measured a year later (Holahan, Moos, Holahan, & Brennan, 1995). People with more social support may actually live longer, as suggested by studies in Alameda County, California (Berkman & Breslow, 1983; Berkman & Syme, 1979) and Tecumseh, Michigan (House, Robbins, & Metzner 1982), and in another study conducted in Sweden (Goleman, 1993). In the Swedish study, researchers followed middle-aged men who had experienced high levels of emotional stress due to such factors as financial trouble or serious problems with family members. Men who were highly stressed but lacked social support were three times more likely to die within a period of seven years than were those whose lives were low in stress (Goleman, 1993). Yet men with highly stressed lives who had ample amounts of emotional support showed no higher death rates. Having other people available may help people find alternative ways of coping with stressors or simply provide them with the emotional support they need during difficult times.

QUESTIONNAIRE

The Life Orientation Test

Do you see a glass as half full or half empty? Do you expect bad things to happen or do you find the silver lining in every cloud? The Life Orientation Test can afford you insight as to how optimistic or pessimistic you are.

Directions: Indicate whether or not each of the items represents your feelings by writing a number in the blank space according to the following code. Then turn to the scoring key at the next Study Break on page 159.

4 = strongly agree
3 = agree
2 = neutral
1 = *dis*agree
0 = strongly *dis*agree

_____ 1. In uncertain times, I usually expect the best.
_____ 2. It's easy for me to relax.
_____ 3. If something can go wrong for me, it will.
_____ 4. I always look on the bright side of things.
_____ 5. I'm always optimistic about my future.
_____ 6. I enjoy my friends a lot.
_____ 7. It's important for me to keep busy.
_____ 8. I hardly ever expect things to go my way.

_____ 9. Things never work out the way I want them to.
_____ 10. I don't get upset too easily.
_____ 11. I'm a believer in the idea that "every cloud has a silver lining."
_____ 12. I rarely count on good things happening to me.

Source: Scheier & Carver (1985). The Life Orientation Test (pp. 219–247). In *Health Psychology*, 4th ed. Mahwah, NJ: Erlbaum. Reprinted with permission.

Stress and the Wellness Continuum Model

Specific stressors affect some domains of human functioning more than others. Some stressors are more closely tied to specific *internal domains*, while others are related to *external domains* (see Table 4.3). Additionally, stressors may range from acute to chronic, mild to severe, predictable to unforeseen, controllable to insurmountable, and from merely annoying to a major life-changing event. Although some stressors would be considered distressing to almost anyone, keep in mind that perception plays an important role in defining and governing your response to a stressor: one person's distressor may be another's eustressor.

The wellness continuum (see Table 4.4) represents a **dimensional model** of health, which embodies, but goes beyond, the *biopsychosocial model* (described in Chapter 2). The wellness continuum model serves two important purposes: It offers a quality of life measure ranging from nominal to optimal functioning and, over time, it provides you with a sense of direction—to let you know whether you are moving toward wellness or toward illness. Wellness can also be measured within either just one or more than one of the domains collectively. Generally, the more *distress indicators* you experience across domains, the more ill you are likely to be or become. Conversely, the more *eustress indicators* you exhibit across domains, the more well you are likely to be or become.

When you experience severe or prolonged distress, you are prone to developing harmful *distress outcomes* in one

TABLE 4.3

Examples of Distressors and Eustressors Within Each Stressor Domain

Distressors	Stressor Domains	Eustressors
	Internal Domains	
Excessive guilt, moral conflicts, lack of meaning, grieving, no time to reflect, church politics, religious doubts	**Spiritual**	Making a moral decision, meaningful life purpose, reflective solitude, religious affirmation, helping someone in need, a peak experience
Mental fatigue, mental overload, mental stagnation, boring work, too little change, return to school, creative block	**Intellectual**	Active learning, interesting work, a creative insight, making a plan, solving problems, reading for fun
Intense anger, unexpressed anger, lack of love, failure, loneliness, low self-esteem, bad news	**Emotional**	Appropriate emotional control, freedom to love and be loved, success, good self-esteem, having a good laugh, experiencing empathy
Drug dependence, smoking, Type A behaviour, unsafe habits, no time to play, underskilled, poor stress management	**Behavioural**	Self-control, absence of Type A behaviour, hardiness traits, safe habits, playfulness, effective stress management, a skillful performance
Embarrassment, being teased, being ridiculed, arguments, rejection, drop in status, over-conformity	**Social**	Effective communication, desirable status, socially active, sharing with loved ones, give and receive compliments, achieving agreements
Poor diet, sedentary lifestyle, lack of exercise, insufficient sleep, unhealthy weight, diseases, injuries, not enough relaxation	**Physical**	Balanced diet, active lifestyle, regular exercise, sufficient sleep, healthy weight, deep relaxation, immunization
	External Domains	
Pollution, natural disasters, ugly surroundings, noise, overcrowding, high crime rate, dangerous workplace, poverty, discrimination	**Environmental & Sociocultural**	Fresh air, water and soil, pleasant climate, beautiful surroundings, sufficient financial resources, secure home and workplace, appreciating cultural diversity, discovering your cultural roots, a just political decision

dimensional model An approach to diagnosis that quantifies indicators on a continuous scale (e.g., from low to average to high).

(continued)

(continued)

TABLE 4.4

Examples of Distress and Eustress Outcomes Along the Wellness Continuum

Illness ←——————————→ Wellness Continuum ←——————————→ Wellness

Distress Outcomes	Distress Indicators		Eustress Indicators	Eustress Outcomes
Loss of life meaning, lack of conscience, angst, despair, futility, suicide, martyrdom	Little joy, daily struggle, prolonged grief, inappropriate guilt, emptiness, sense of helplessness, doubt, cynicism, unforgiving attitude, expecting magical solutions	**Spiritual**	Joyfulness, hopefulness, sense of commitment, trusting nature, peacefulness, reflective, generosity, compassion, faithfulness, loving attitude	Joy, transcendence
Short-term memory deficit, impaired judgment, irrational thinking	Forgetfulness, speeded-up thinking, confusion, lethargy, no new ideas, boredom, poor concentration, fuzzy thinking, mental dullness	**Intellectual**	Alert, creative, logical, poetic, open-minded, capable, thoughtful, solving problems, focused	Compos mentis
Major psychological disorder, emotional instability, intense inappropriate emotions	Irritability, impulsiveness, mood swings, urge to cry, urge to flee, urge to hurt, impatience, nightmares, feeling helpless, lacking confidence, experiencing dread, bad tempered	**Emotional**	Expressive, stable, self-confident, independent, content, enthusiastic, sensitive, secure, patient	Contentment
Accidents, compulsions, addictions, self-damaging acts, low productivity	Accident prone, increased substance use, procrastination, excessive work, talking fast, teeth grinding, fidgety, low sex interest, change in eating, finger-tapping, restlessness, rushing	**Behavioural**	Self-disciplined, not injury prone, self-starting, productive, calmed pace	Aplomb
Alienated from society, friendless, ostracized, dysfunctional relationships, violence	Isolation, clamming up, withdrawing from others, phoniness, nagging others, mistrust, poor communication, intolerance, lashing out, acting out	**Social**	Outgoing, honest, tolerant, assertive, helpful, forgiving, affectionate, caring, respectful	Intimacy, harmony
Coronary artery disease, cancer, migraines, ulcers, rheumatoid arthritis, weak immunity, sudden death	Change in appetite, headaches, tension, insomnia, weight change, frequent colds, muscle aches, digestive upset, pounding heart, dry mouth, fatigue, chest pain, diarrhea, trembling, sweating	**Physical**	Strength, zest, tip-top shape, free of pain, sexy, vital, rested, relaxed	Longevity, fitness
		External Domains		
Pollution, toxic land, air and water, sterile land, air and water, dramatic climate change, lawlessness, anarchy	Don't reduce, reuse or recycle, wasteful attitude, negligent, irresponsible, disregard warnings, destroy nature, deface property, "not in my back yard" attitude, "not my problem" attitude, apathetic toward plight of others, intolerant of cultural differences	**Environmental & Socio-cultural**	Frugal attitude, conscientious	Ecological balance, civil society, peace and social order

(continued)

or more domains (Lehtinen, Ozamiz, Underwood, & Weiss, 2005). But when you experience eustress in one or more domains, you become more resilient to distressors and thus more likely to develop health-promoting *eustress outcomes*. When you practise wellness behaviours, you may also discover that there is a compounding effect of eustressors across several domains that can result in a sud-

den leap to a much higher level of wellness. As you approach optimal functioning, though, you cannot give up and neglect to maintain wellness behaviours. Once you begin to coast, you will initiate the inevitable slide back down the wellness continuum toward ill health. Optimum wellness requires an ongoing effort and, with persistence, wellness behaviours can become a lifestyle.

STUDY BREAK

Stress and Illness

Review It

- **How is stress implicated in physical illness?** Evidence links exposure to various forms of stress to weakened immune-system functioning, which in turn may increase vulnerability to physical disorders.

- **What is the general adaptation syndrome?** This is the name given by Hans Selye to the generalized pattern of response of the body to persistent or enduring stress, as characterized by three stages: (1) the alarm reaction, (2) the resistance stage, and (3) the exhaustion stage.

- **How are psychological factors related to our capacity to endure stress?** Many psychological factors, including coping styles, self-efficacy expectancies, psychological hardiness, optimism, social support, and a sense of humour, can have positive effects on our health by buffering the effects of stress.

Define It

psychoneuroimmunology	alarm reaction
endocrine system	fight-or-flight reaction
hormones	resistance stage
steroids	exhaustion stage
catecholamines	emotion-focused coping
immune system	problem-focused coping
leukocytes	psychological hardiness
pathogen	locus of control
antigen	Type A behaviour
antibodies	pattern
general adaptation	dimensional model
syndrome	

Recall It*

1. _____ are also called white blood cells.

   a. Antigens
   b. Leukocytes
   c. Antibodies
   d. Immunoglobulins

2. The immune system helps protect us against repeat infections by producing "memory _____" that form the basis for a quick response to an invader the second time it attacks.

   a. antigens
   b. lymphocytes
   c. antibodies
   d. corpuscles

3. Recent evidence on relationships between stress and immune system functioning suggest that _____.

   a. stress has no significant effect on immunological functioning
   b. stress dampens immunological functioning
   c. stress enhances immunological functioning
   d. stress initially dampens immunological functioning, but when prolonged, it begins stimulating an immune response

4. The term _____ was used by Hans Selye to describe the common biological response pattern to persistent stress.

   a. *general adaptation syndrome*
   b. *the hypothalamic-adreno syndrome*
   c. *the stress reaction cycle*
   d. *Kleinfelter's syndrome*

5. Psychological hardiness includes all of the following traits EXCEPT _____.

   a. control
   b. commitment

c. challenge
d. competitiveness

* Recall It answers can be found on the Companion Website for this text.

Think About It

• The authors suggest that the relationship between stress and illness may work both ways. What does this mean? In what ways might physical health problems lead to increased stress? In what ways might stress increase our vulnerability to physical health problems?

Scoring Key for the Life Orientation Test

In order to arrive at your total score for the test, first *reverse* your score on items 3, 8, 9, and 12. That is,

4 is changed to 0
3 is changed to 1
2 remains the same
1 is changed to 3
0 is changed to 4

Now add the numbers of items 1, 3, 4, 5, 8, 9, 11, and 12. (Items 2, 6, 7, and 10 are "fillers"; that is, your responses are not scored as part of the test.) Your total score can vary from 0 to 32.

Scheier and Carver (1985) provide the following norms for the LOT, based on the testing of 357 undergraduate men and 267 undergraduate women. The average (mean) score for men was 21.03 (standard deviation = 4.56) and the mean score for women was 21.41 (standard deviation = 5.22). All in all, approximately two out of three undergraduates obtained scores between 16 and 26. Scores above 26 may be considered quite optimistic, and scores below 16 quite pessimistic. Scores between 16 and 26 are within a broad average range, and higher scores within this range are relatively more optimistic.

PSYCHOLOGICAL FACTORS AND PHYSICAL DISORDERS

We noted at the start of the chapter that psychological factors can influence physical functioning; physical factors can also influence mental functioning. In these next sections, we examine the role of psychological factors in various physical disorders. Physical disorders in which psychological factors are believed to play a causal or contributing role have traditionally been termed **psychosomatic** or **psychophysiological**. The term *psychosomatic* is derived from the Greek roots *psyche*, meaning "soul" or "intellect," and *soma*, meaning "body." Disorders that involve psychological components range from asthma and headaches to heart disease.

psychosomatic Relating to physical disorders in which psychological factors are believed to play a causal or contributing role.

psychophysiological Referring to physiological correlates or underpinnings of psychological events.

Ulcers are another of the traditionally identified psychosomatic disorders. Ulcers affect about 2.5% of Canadian adults aged 18 and older (Shields, 2004). However, their status as a psychosomatic disorder has been re-evaluated in light of landmark research that showed that a bacterium, *H. pylori*, and not stress or diet, is the cause of the great majority of ulcers (Boren, Faulk, Roth, Larson, & Normark, 1993; Mason, 1994). Researchers suspect that ulcers arise when the bacterium damages the protective lining of the stomach or intestines. Treatment with a regimen of antibiotics can help cure ulcers by attacking the bacterium directly (Altman, 1994). We don't yet know why some people with the bacterium develop ulcers and others don't. It is conceivable that psychological stress may be involved (Levenstein, Ackerman, Kiecolt-Glaser, & Dubois, 1999).

The field of psychosomatic medicine was developed to explore the possible health-related connections between the mind and body. Today, evidence points to the importance of psychological factors in a much wider range of physical disorders than those traditionally identified as psychosomatic. In this section, we discuss several of the traditionally identified psychosomatic disorders as well as two other diseases in which psychological factors may play a role in the course or treatment of the disease—cancer and AIDS.

Headaches

Headaches are symptomatic of many medical disorders. When they occur in the absence of other symptoms, however, they may be classified as stress related. By far the most frequent kind of headache is the tension headache (Mark, 1998). Stress can lead to persistent contractions of the muscles of the scalp, face, neck, and shoulders, giving rise to periodic or chronic tension headaches. Such headaches develop gradually and are generally characterized by dull, steady pain on both sides of the head and feelings of pressure or tightness. Tension-type headache is found in 30% of adult Canadians—of these, 17% said their last attack necessitated bed rest (Medical Society of Nova Scotia [MSNS], 1997).

Most other headaches, including the severe migraine headache, are believed to involve changes in the blood flow to the brain. Migraine headaches are found in 8% of Canadians aged 12 and older, and females of all ages are three times as likely as males to have them (Martin, 2001; Statistics Canada, 1999). Of the adult migraine sufferers (17% of Canadian adults), 77% said that their last attack limited their regular activities and 39% required bed rest. In addition, 79% report that their migraine attacks have a negative impact on their family and social relationships (MSNS, 1997). Typical migraines last for hours or days. They may occur as often as daily or as seldom as every other month. Piercing or throbbing sensations may become so intense that they seem intolerable. Sleep, mood, and thinking processes may be affected as the individual's mental state becomes dominated by the misery of a brutal migraine. Migraine attacks usually last from 4 to 72 hours. There are two major types of migraines: migraine without aura (formerly called *common migraine*) and migraine with aura (formerly called *classic migraine*) (Transport Canada, 2003). An aura is a cluster of warning sensations that precedes an attack. Auras are typified by perceptual distortions, such as flashing lights, bizarre images, or blind spots. Roughly one in five migraine sufferers experiences auras. Other than the presence or absence of the aura, the two types of migraine are the same.

Theoretical Perspectives Why, under stress, do some people develop tension headaches? The underlying cause remains uncertain, but recent studies suggest tension headaches are linked to an increased sensitivity of the pain transmission circuits where neural signals from face and head muscles are intercepted (Holroyd, 2002). As for migraine headaches, investigators suspect that migraine pain results from the dilation of blood vessels that surround the brain, which, in turn, shoot pain signals through highly sensitized pain-transmission circuits in the brain (Olesen & Goadsby, 2000). The levels of the brain chemical serotonin also seem to play a role (Edelson, 1998). As serotonin levels fall, blood vessels in the brain contract (narrow) and then dilate (expand). This stretching stimulates nerve endings that give rise to the throbbing, piercing sensations associated with migraine. For those with a genetic predisposition to migraines, many factors may trigger migraine attacks. These include stress; stimuli like bright lights; barometric pressure; pollen; certain drugs; the chemical monosodium glutamate (MSG), which is often used to enhance the flavour of food; red wine; and even hunger (Martin & Seneviratne, 1997). Hormonal changes of the sort that affect women prior to and during menstruation can also trigger an attack.

Treatment Commonly available pain relievers, such as aspirin, ibuprofen, and acetaminophen, may reduce or eliminate pain associated with tension headaches. A recent study reported that a combination of acetaminophen, Aspirin, and caffeine (the ingredients in the over-the-counter pain reliever Excedrin) produced greater relief from the pain of migraine headaches than a placebo control (Lipton et al., 1998). Drugs that help regulate levels of serotonin in the brain can also help relieve migraine headache pain (Lipton, Stewart, Stone, Lainez, & Sawyer, 2000; Lohman, 2001).

Psychological treatment can also help relieve tension or migraine headache pain in many cases. These treatments include cognitive-behaviour therapy, biofeedback, relaxation training, coping-skills training, and some forms of cognitive therapy (Blanchard & Diamond, 1996; Gatchel, 2001; Turk, Meichenbaum, & Genest, 1983). **Biofeedback training** (BFT) helps people gain control over various bodily functions, such as muscle tension and brainwaves, by giving them information (feedback) about these functions in the form of auditory signals (e.g., "bleeps") or visual displays. People learn to make the signal change in the desired direction. Training people to use relaxation skills combined with biofeedback has also been shown to be effective. *Electromyographic* (EMG)

biofeedback training Method of feeding back to an individual information about bodily functions so the person is able to gain better control over them. Abbreviated *BFT*.

Risk. What's wrong with this picture? How many risk factors for cardiovascular disorders can you identify in this photograph?

biofeedback is a form of BFT that involves relaying information about muscle tension in the forehead. EMG biofeedback thus heightens awareness of muscle tension in this region and provides cues that people can use to learn to reduce it.

Some people have relieved the pain of migraine headaches by raising the temperature in a finger. This biofeedback technique, called thermal BFT, modifies patterns of blood flow throughout the body, including to the brain, which helps control migraine headaches (Blanchard et al., 1990; Gauthier, Ivers, & Carrier, 1996). One way of providing thermal feedback is by attaching a **thermistor** to a finger. A console "bleeps" more slowly[3] as the temperature rises. The temperature rises because more blood is flowing into the limb—away from the head. The client can imagine the finger growing warmer to bring about changes in the body's distribution of blood.

Transcranial magnetic stimulation (TMS and rTMS) treatments have been shown to provide relief to migraine headache sufferers that is usually immediate, with no side effects. In one recent study, pain relief was found to be more pronounced for some migraine sufferers than others, lasting from several hours to a few days in some patients, and up to several weeks in about half of those who were treated with rTMS (Fumal et al., 2006). TMS can be a worthwhile adjunct treatment for sustained pain relief and prevention of migraine headaches (Clarke, Upton, Kamath, Al-Harbi, & Castellanos, 2006).

Cardiovascular Disease

thermistor Small device that is strapped to the skin for registering body temperature, as used in biofeedback training.

cardiovascular disease Disease or disorder of the cardiovascular system, such as coronary heart disease and hypertension..

arteriosclerosis Disease involving the thickening and hardening of the arteries.

atherosclerosis Disease process consisting of arteriosclerosis with the deposition of fatty substances along the walls of the arteries.

myocardial infarction Breakdown of the tissue of the heart due to an obstruction of the blood vessels that supply blood to the affected area—a heart attack.

stroke Destruction of brain tissues resulting from the blockage of a blood vessel that serves the brain, or from bleeding in the brain. Also called a cerebrovascular accident (CVA).

Cardiovascular disease (CVD, heart and artery disease) is the leading cause of death in Canada, claiming about 79 000 lives annually and accounting for close to four in ten deaths (37%), most often as the result of ischemic heart disease (also known as coronary heart disease, including angina pectoris—21%), myocardial infarction (also known as a heart attack—10%), or cerebrovascular disease (commonly called a stroke—7%) (Heart and Stroke Foundation of Canada [HSFC], 2003a; Statistics Canada, 1999).

The exact number of Canadians who have cardiovascular disease is not known, but it is estimated that about one-quarter of the population, some eight million Canadians, have CVD (HSFC, 2003a; Statistics Canada, 1999). In coronary heart disease (CHD), the flow of blood to the heart is insufficient to meet its needs. The underlying disease process in CHD is **arteriosclerosis** or "hardening of the arteries," a condition in which artery walls become thicker, harder, and less elastic, which makes it more difficult for blood to flow freely. The major underlying cause of arteriosclerosis is **atherosclerosis**, a process involving the build-up of fatty deposits along artery walls that leads to the formation of artery-clogging plaque. If a blood clot should form in an artery narrowed by plaque, it may nearly or completely block the flow of blood to the heart. The result is a heart attack (also called **myocardial infarction**), a life-threatening event in which heart tissue dies due to a lack of oxygen-rich blood. If a blood clot chokes off the supply of blood in an artery serving the brain, a **stroke** may occur, leading to the destruction of brain tissue that can result in loss of certain functions or movements (controlled by the part of the brain affected), coma, or even death.

Psychological and behavioural factors play a large part in determining an individual's risk profile for CVD. Canadian research shows that certain behavioural patterns of consumption, such as heavy drinking, smoking, overeating, and consumption of a high-fat diet, as well as leading a sedentary lifestyle, are all linked to increased risk of CVD and premature death (Bouchard, Shephard, & Stephens, 1993; Health Canada, 2003a; HSFC, 2003b).

[3]Or more rapidly. The choice of direction is decided by the therapist or therapist and client.

Smoking alone is believed to be responsible for 25% of male deaths and 20% of female deaths from CHD in Canada, and the smoking-related death rate has been rising much faster for females (Health Canada, 2003b). Negative emotional states, especially anger and anxiety, have also been implicated in the development of cardiovascular disorders (see the "A Closer Look" feature on pages 161–162). Investigators have also implicated a personality pattern, the aforementioned Type A behaviour pattern (TAPB), as another psychological risk factor in CHD.

Type A Behaviour Pattern The Type A behaviour pattern, a style of behaviour that characterizes people who are hard-driving, ambitious, impatient, and highly competitive, has been associated with a modestly higher risk of CHD (T. Q. Miller, Turner, Tindale, Posavac, & Dugoni, 1991). Evidence indicates that psychological interventions focused on helping people rein in their Type A behaviour can significantly reduce the risk of subsequent heart attacks in people who have already suffered one (Brody, 1996b; Friedman et al., 1986). Perhaps there is a lesson in this for us all.

Hostility—quickness to anger—is the element of the Type A behaviour pattern most closely linked to cardiovascular risk (Donker, 2000; Niaura et al., 2002) (see the "A Closer Look" section below). People with TABP tend to have "short fuses" and are prone to get angry easily. "Questionnaire: Are You Type A?" on page 164 helps you assess whether or not you fit the Type A profile. If you would like to begin modifying Type A behaviour, a good place to start is with lessening your sense of time urgency. Here are some suggestions (Friedman & Ulmer, 1984):

Reducing Type A behaviour. Slowing down the pace of your daily life and making time for loved ones are among the ways of reducing Type A behaviour. Can you think of other ways that can help you decrease Type A behaviour?

1. Increase social activity with family and friends.
2. Each day, spend a few minutes recalling distant events. Peruse photos of family and old friends.
3. Read books—biographies, literature, drama, politics, nature, science, science fiction. (Books on business and on climbing the corporate ladder are not recommended!)

A CLOSER LOOK

Emotions and the Heart

Might your emotions be putting you at risk of developing coronary heart disease? It appears so. Evidence has accumulated that points to emotional stress in the form of persistent negative emotions, especially anxiety and anger, as a major risk factor for CHD and other heart problems.

The Anxious Heart

Investigators have linked phobic anxiety, the type of anxiety characterized by unfounded fears and panicky feelings, to a greater risk of death in men as the result of irregular heart rhythms. A study of some 34 000 men, none of whom were diagnosed at the outset of the study with CHD, showed those scoring at the high end of an index of phobic anxiety were six times more likely to suffer sudden coronary death over a two-year period than were less anxious men (Hilchey, 1994; Kawachi et al., 1994). Researchers suspect that persistent, high levels of anxiety may produce "electrical storms" in the heart, resulting in irregular heart rhythms that may lead to sudden coronary death. Fortunately, the number of cardiac-related deaths during the two-year study period was relatively small (only 16 among 34 000).

Other investigators have linked states of anxiety and tension with an increased risk of coronary symptoms and death in people with established coronary heart disease (Denollet et al., 1996; Gullette et al., 1997). In other recent research, people exposed to mental stress, like the kind experienced when we are required to work under pressure, can induce episodes of restricted blood flow to

(continued)

(continued)

the heart (called *ischemic events*) in people with CHD. People who experienced ischemic events in response to mental stress were more likely to later experience a heart attack or other cardiac event than were nonresponders (Jian et al., 1996). Researchers also find a connection between anxiety in middle-aged men and the later risk of developing hypertension, a major risk factor for CHD (Markovitz et al., 1993). Highly anxious men were about twice as likely as their more relaxed counterparts to develop hypertension. We don't yet know whether this relationship also applies to women.

Anger and Hostility

Occasional feelings of anger may not damage the heart in healthy people, but chronic anger—the type of anger you see in people who seem angry all the time—may be as dangerous a risk factor for CHD as smoking, obesity, family history, or consuming a high-fat diet (e.g., Brody, 1996b; "Coronary Disease: Taking Emotions to Heart," 1996). Anger is closely associated with hostility, which involves an attitude of blaming others and perceiving the world in negative terms (Eckhardt, Barbour, & Stuart, 1997; Eckhardt & Deffenbacher, 1995). Hostile people are quick to anger and become angry more often and more intensely than do other people when they feel they have been mistreated. Although anger may not directly cause heart disease, it may aggravate the underlying disease process and precipitate heart attacks in vulnerable people (Kiecolt-Glaser, McGuire, Robles, & Glaser, 2002; Suinn, 2001). Researchers find that among people with heart disease, the risk of suffering a heart attack doubles in the few hours following an anger episode as compared to other times (Talan, 1994).

Linking Emotions and the Heart

Although more research is needed to better understand the underlying mechanism linking negative emotions to heart disease (Januzzi & DeSantis, 1999), it is believed that the stress hormones epinephrine and norepinephrine play a significant role. Emotional arousal in the form of anxiety or anger is accompanied by the release of these stress hormones by the adrenal glands. These hormones mobilize the body's resources to deal with threatening situations. They increase the heart rate, breathing rate, and blood pressure, which increases the flow of oxygen-rich blood to the muscles to prepare for defensive action—to fight or to flee—in the face of a threatening stressor. When people are persistently or repeatedly anxious or angry, the body may remain over-aroused for long periods of time, continuing

to pump out these stress hormones, which eventually may have damaging effects on the heart and blood vessels. Stress hormones also appear to increase the stickiness of the clotting factors in blood, which might increase the chances that potentially dangerous blood clots may form (Januzzi & DeSantis, 1999). People with higher levels of hostility also tend to have higher blood pressures than their less hostile counterparts (Räikkönen, Matthews, Flory, & Owens, 1999). High blood pressure is a major risk factor for heart attacks and strokes.

Investigators continue to explore relationships between heart disease and emotional states. At the same time, cognitive-behavioural therapists are focusing on ways of helping chronically anxious and angry people learn to control their emotional responses in anxiety-provoking or angering situations (e.g., Deffenbacher, Dahlen, Lynch, Morris, & Gowensmith, 2000). By helping people to remain calm in these situations, psychological treatment may prove to have beneficial effects on the heart as well as the mind (Gidron & Davidson, 1996). Along these lines, a study reported that men with coronary heart disease who attended a hostility-reduction program showed less anger and lower blood pressures after treatment than did controls (Gidron, Davidson, & Bata, 1999).

Emotions and the heart. Emotional stress in the form of persistent negative emotions, such as anxiety and anger, has emerged as a major risk factor in heart-related disorders.

4. Visit art galleries and museums. Consider works for their aesthetic value, not their prices.
5. Go to the movies, theatre, concerts, or ballet.
6. Write letters to family and old friends.
7. Take an art course; start violin or piano lessons.
8. Keep in mind that life is by nature unfinished. You needn't have all your projects finished by a certain date.
9. Ask family members what they did during the day. *Listen* to the answer.

Here are some additional suggestions for reducing anger and hostility, the elements believed to be the most toxic components of the Type A profile (Brody, 1996b; Friedman & Ulmer, 1984):

1. Don't get involved in discussions that you know lead to pointless arguments.
2. When others do things that disappoint you, consider situational factors that might explain their behaviour. Don't jump to the conclusion that others intend to get you upset.
3. Focus on the beauty and pleasure in things.
4. Don't curse.
5. Express appreciation to people for their support and assistance.
6. Play for the fun of it, not to beat your opponent.
7. Check out your face in the mirror from time to time. Look for signs of anger and aggravation; ask yourself if you really need to look like that.
8. Don't sweat the small stuff. Let it go. Avoid grudges and let bygones be bygones.

Social Environmental Stress Social environmental stress also appears to heighten the risk of CHD (Krantz, Contrada, Hills, & Friedler, 1988). Such factors as overtime work, assembly-line labour, and exposure to conflicting demands are linked to increased risk of CHD (Jenkins, 1988).

The stress–CHD connection is not straightforward, however. For example, the effects of demanding occupations are apparently moderated by factors such as psychological hardiness and whether or not people find their work meaningful (Krantz et al., 1988). One model relates the demands of an occupation to the degree of control afforded an individual worker. Waiters and waitresses, store managers, and firefighters are examples of workers who hold highly demanding jobs. Architects, scientists, physicians, and some others have occupations in which they exert a good deal of control over their job-related activity. **High-strain jobs** are high in demand and low in the amount of personal control they afford. High-strain jobs apparently place workers at highest risk for CHD (Krantz et al., 1988; Williams et al., 1997). Workers in high-strain occupations have been found to have about one-and-a-half times the risk of suffering CHD as workers in low-strain occupations (LaCroix & Haynes, 1987). Working women in general do not have higher risks of CHD than homemakers or men. Yet women who are working in high-strain jobs—those involving repetitive jobs with nonsupportive bosses in which they're not allowed to make decisions on their own and are given too much work and too little time to complete it—are at greater risk for CHD or for CHD-associated risk factors such as hostility and anxiety (Krantz et al., 1988; Williams et al., 1997).

high-strain jobs Jobs that impose great stress on workers.

We finish this section with encouraging news. North Americans are taking better care of their health. The incidence of CHD and deaths from heart disease have been declining steadily during the past 50 years, thanks largely to reductions in smoking, to improved treatment of heart patients, and perhaps also to other changes in lifestyle such as reduced intake of dietary fat (Brody, 1994a; McGovern et al., 1996; Traven, Kuller, Ives, Rutan, & Perper, 1995). Better-educated people are also more likely to modify unhealthy behaviour patterns and reap the benefits of change. Is there a message in there for you?

Asthma

Asthma is a respiratory disorder in which the main tubes of the windpipe—the bronchi—constrict and become inflamed, and large amounts of mucus are secreted. During asthma

Are You Type A?

People with the Type A behaviour pattern (TABP) are impatient, competitive, and aggressive. They feel rushed, under pressure; they keep one eye glued to the clock. They are prompt and often arrive early for appointments. They walk, talk, and eat rapidly. They grow restless when others work slowly.

Type A people don't just stroll out on the tennis court to bat the ball around. They scrutinize their form, polish their strokes, and demand consistent self-improvement.

Are you Type A? The following questionnaire may afford you insight.

Directions: Write a check mark under the Yes if the behaviour pattern described is typical of you. Place one under the No if it is not. Work rapidly and answer all items. Then check the scoring key on page 171.

DO YOU   Yes   No

1. Strongly emphasize important words in your ordinary speech?   ____   ____

2. Walk briskly from place to place or meeting to meeting?   ____   ____

3. Think that life is by nature dog eat dog?   ____   ____

4. Get fidgety when you see someone complete a job slowly?   ____   ____

5. Urge others to complete what they're trying to express?   ____   ____

6. Find it exceptionally annoying to get stuck in line?   ____   ____

7. Envision all the things you have to get to even when someone is talking to you?   ____   ____

8. Eat while you're getting dressed, or jot notes down while you're driving?   ____   ____

9. Catch up on work during vacations?   ____   ____

10. Direct the conversation to things that interest you?   ____   ____

11. Feel as if things are going to pot because you're relaxing for a few minutes?   ____   ____

12. Get so wrapped up in your work that you fail to notice beautiful scenery passing by?   ____   ____

13. Get so wrapped up in money, promotions, and awards that you neglect expressing your creativity?   ____   ____

14. Schedule appointments and meetings back to back?   ____   ____

15. Arrive early for appointments and meetings?   ____   ____

16. Make fists or clench your jaws to drill home your views?   ____   ____

17. Think that you have achieved what you have because of your ability to work fast?   ____   ____

18. Have the feeling that uncompleted work must be done now and fast?   ____   ____

19. Try to find more efficient ways to get things done?   ____   ____

20. Struggle always to win games instead of having fun?   ____   ____

21. Interrupt people who are talking?   ____   ____

22. Lose patience with people who are late for appointments and meetings?   ____   ____

23. Get back to work right after lunch?   ____   ____

24. Find that there's never enough time?   ____   ____

25. Believe that you're getting too little done, even when other people tell you that you're doing fine?   ____   ____

attacks, people wheeze, cough, and struggle to breathe in enough air. They may feel as though they are suffocating.

Asthma affects nearly 2.3 million people aged 12 and older in Canada (Chen, Johansen, Thillaiampalam, & Sambell, 2005). Of Canadian children who have asthma or symptoms of asthma, between one-half and two-thirds are diagnosed by age five (National Asthma Control Task Force [NACTF], 2000). Rates of asthma are on the rise,

Psychological Methods for Lowering Arousal

Stress induces bodily responses such as excessive levels of sympathetic nervous system arousal, which if persistent may impair our ability to function optimally and possibly increase the risk of stress-related illnesses. Psychological treatments have been shown to lower states of bodily arousal that may be prompted by stress. In this feature, we consider two widely used psychological methods of lowering arousal: meditation and progressive relaxation.

Meditation

Meditation comprises several ways of narrowing consciousness to moderate the stressors of the outer world. Yogis study the design on a vase or a mandala. The ancient Egyptians riveted their attention on an oil-burning lamp, which is the inspiration for the tale of Aladdin's lamp. Islamic mystics in Turkey, so-called whirling dervishes, fix on their movements and the cadences of their breathing.

There are many meditation methods, but they share the common thread of narrowing one's attention by focusing on repetitive stimuli. Through passive observation, the regular person–environment connection is transformed. Problem solving, worry, planning, and routine concerns are suspended, and consequently, levels of sympathetic arousal are reduced.

Thousands of North Americans regularly practise **transcendental meditation** (TM), a simplified kind of Indian meditation brought to North America in 1959 by Maharishi Mahesh Yogi. Practitioners of TM repeat **mantras**—relaxing sounds like *ieng* and *om*. Benson (1975) studied TM practitioners aged 17 to 41—students, business people, artists. His subjects included relative novices and veterans of nine years of practice.

Benson found that TM yields a so-called relaxation response in many people. The relaxation response is characterized by reductions in the body's metabolic rate and by a reduction in blood pressure in people who have hypertension (high blood pressure) (Benson, Manzetta, & Rosner, 1973; Brody, 1996a). Meditators also produced more alpha waves—brainwaves connected with relaxation.

Although there are differences among meditative techniques, the following suggestions illustrate some general guidelines:

1. Try meditation once or twice a day for 10 to 20 minutes at a time.
2. Keep in mind that when you're meditating, what you *don't* do is more important than what you do. So embrace a passive attitude. Tell yourself, "What happens, happens." In meditation, you take what you get. You don't *strive* for more. Striving of any kind hinders meditation.
3. Place yourself in a hushed, calming environment. For example, don't face a light directly.
4. Avoid eating for an hour before you meditate. Avoid caffeine (found in coffee, tea, many soft drinks, and chocolate) for at least two hours.
5. Get into a relaxed position. Modify it as needed. You can scratch or yawn if you feel the urge.
6. For a focusing device, you can concentrate on your breathing or sit in front of a serene object like a plant or incense. Benson suggests "perceiving" (not "mentally saying") the word *one* each time you breathe out. That is, think the word, but "less actively" than you normally would. Other researchers suggest thinking the word *in* as you breathe in and *out* or *ah-h-h* as you breathe out. They also suggest mantras like *ah-nam*, *rah-mah*, and *shi-rim*.
7. When preparing for meditation, repeat your mantra aloud many times—if you're using a mantra. Enjoy it. Then say it progressively more softly. Close your eyes. Focus on the mantra. Allow your thinking of the mantra to become more and more "passive" so you "perceive" rather than think it. Again, embrace your "what happens, happens" attitude. Keep on focusing on the mantra. It may become softer or louder, or fade and then reappear.
8. If unsettling thoughts drift while you're meditating, allow them to sort of "pass through." Don't worry about squelching them, or you may become tense.
9. Remember to take what comes. Meditation and relaxation cannot be forced. You cannot force the relaxing effects of meditation. Like sleep, you can only set the stage for it and then permit it to happen.
10. Let yourself drift. (You won't get lost.) What happens, happens.

(continued)

---

transcendental meditation Popular form of meditation introduced to North America by the Maharishi Mahesh Yogi that focuses on the repeating of a mantra to induce a meditative state. Abbreviated *TM*.

mantra In meditation, a resonant-sounding word or sound that is repeated to induce a state of relaxation and a narrowing of consciousness.

(continued)

Progressive Relaxation

Progressive relaxation was originated by University of Chicago physician Edmund Jacobson in 1938. Jacobson noticed that people tense their muscles under stress, intensifying their uneasiness. They tend to be unaware of these contractions, however. Jacobson reasoned that if muscle contractions contribute to tension, muscle relaxation might reduce it. But clients who were asked to focus on relaxing muscles often had no idea what to do. Jacobson's method of progressive relaxation teaches people how to monitor muscle tension and relaxation. With this method, people first tense then relax selected muscle groups in the arms; facial area; the chest, stomach, and lower back muscles; the hips, thighs, and calves; and so on. The sequence heightens awareness of muscle tension and helps people differentiate feelings of tension from relaxation. The method is progressive in that people progress from one group of muscles to another in practising the technique. Since the 1930s, progressive relaxation has been used by a number of behaviour therapists, including Joseph Wolpe and Arnold Lazarus (1966). The following instructions from Wolpe and Lazarus (1966, pp. 177–178) illustrate how the technique is applied to relaxing the arms. Relaxation should be practised in a favourable setting. Settle back on a recliner, couch, or a bed with a pillow. Select a place and time when you're unlikely to be disturbed. Make the room warm and comfortable. Dim sources of light. Loosen tight clothing. Tighten muscles about two-thirds as hard as you could if you were trying your hardest. If you sense that a muscle could have a spasm, you are tightening too much. After tensing, let go of tensions completely.

> **Relaxation of Arms (time: four–five minutes)** Settle back as comfortably as you can. Let yourself relax to the best of your ability... Now, as you relax like that, clench your right fist. Just clench your fist tighter and tighter, and study the tension as you do so. Keep it clenched and feel the tension in your right fist, hand, forearm... and now relax. Let the fingers of your right hand become loose, and observe the contrast in your feelings...

Now, let yourself go and try to become more relaxed all over... Once more, clench your right fist really tight... hold it, and notice the tension again... Now let go, relax; your fingers straighten out, and you notice the difference once more... Now repeat that with your left fist. Clench your left fist while the rest of your body relaxes; clench that fist tighter and feel the tension... and now relax. Again enjoy the contrast... Repeat that once more, clench the left fist, tight and tense.... Now do the opposite of tension—relax and feel the difference. Continue relaxing like that for a while... Clench both fists tighter and together, both fists tense, forearms tense, study the sensations... and relax; straighten out your fingers and feel that relaxation. Continue relaxing your hands and forearms more and more... Now bend your elbows and tense your biceps, tense them harder and study the tension feelings... all right, straighten out your arms, let them relax and feel that difference again. Let the relaxation develop... Once more, tense your biceps; hold the tension and observe it carefully... Straighten the arms and relax; relax to the best of your ability... Each time, pay close attention to your feelings when you tense up and when you relax. Now straighten your arms, straighten them so that you feel most tension in the tricep muscles along the back of your arms; stretch your arms and feel that tension... And now relax. Get your arms back into a comfortable position. Let the relaxation proceed on its own. The arms should feel comfortably heavy as you allow them to relax... Straighten the arms once more so that you feel the tension in the triceps muscles; straighten them. Feel that tension... and relax. Now let's concentrate on pure relaxation in the arms without any tension. Get your arms comfortable and let them relax further and further. Continue relaxing your arms even further. Even when your arms seem fully relaxed, try to go that extra bit further; try to achieve deeper and deeper levels of relaxation.

having almost quintupled among Canadian children under the age of 14 between the late 1970s and 1995 (Millar & Hill, 1998). Attacks can last from a few minutes to several hours and vary greatly in intensity. Series of attacks can harm the bronchial system, causing mucus to collect and muscles to lose their elasticity. Sometimes the bronchial system is weakened to the point where a subsequent attack is lethal. Fortunately, few sufferers die from asthma, and the mortality rate has dropped by half from a peak in the 1980s to just over 1 in 100 000 (Chen et al., 2005)

Theoretical Perspectives The National Asthma Control Task Force (2000) has described the risk factors for asthma as a complex interaction of causal factors. Many predisposing factors are implicated in asthma, including atopy (a greater than usual reaction to foreign substances), gender (boys develop asthma more often than girls), and genetics (more common in families where at least one parent has asthma). Asthmatic reactions in susceptible people can be triggered by exposure to allergens such as pollen, mould spores, and animal dander; by cold, dry air; by emotional responses such as anger; by stress; and even by exercise or participation in sports. Factors that exacerbate the development of asthma in people when they are exposed to causal factors include respiratory infections, air pollution, smoking, and the grind of low-income jobs. Psychological factors, such as emotional stress, loss of loved ones, and intense disappointment, appear to increase susceptibility to asthmatic attacks (Moran, 1991). Asthma, moreover, has psychological consequences. Some sufferers avoid strenuous activity, including exercise, for fear of increasing their demand for oxygen and triggering attacks.

Treatment Although asthma cannot be cured, it can be controlled and quality of life can be improved for the individual and his or her family. Recent reports point to a role for psychological treatment by showing that asthma sufferers can improve their breathing during an attack by muscle relaxation training (Lehrer, Sargunaraj, & Hochron, 1992; Lehrer et al., 1994), education about asthma along with guided self-management planning (NACTF, 2000), and, for asthmatic children, family therapy that helps reduce family conflict (Lehrer et al., 1992). Symptom reduction can be achieved by reducing exposure to allergens, by desensitization therapy ("allergy shots") to help the body acquire more resistance to allergens, by use of inhalers, and by drugs that open bronchial passages during asthma attacks (called *bronchodilators*) and others (called *anti-inflammatories*) that reduce future attacks by helping keep bronchial tubes open.

Cancer

The word *cancer* is arguably the most feared word in the English language, and rightly so. The lifetime probability of dying from cancer was 29% for men and 24% for women in Canada in 2006 (Canadian Cancer Society, 2006). Cancer claimed over 70 000 lives in Canada in 2006. Canadian men have a 38% chance of developing cancer at some point in their lives; for Canadian women, the odds are 44%. The number of new cancer cases and deaths are rising steadily due largely to Canada's increasing and aging population. Cancer risk can be halved by following the Seven Steps to Health described in "A Closer Look: Cancer Risk Reduction."

Personality, Stress, and Cancer A weakened or compromised immune system may increase susceptibility to cancer. We've seen that psychological factors, such as exposure to stress, may affect the immune system. Research with animals has shown that exposure to stress can hasten the onset of a virus-induced cancer (Riley, 1981). Might exposure to stress in humans increase the risk of cancer? Several studies show an increased incidence of stressful life events, such as the loss of loved ones, preceding the development of some forms of cancer (Levenson & Bemis, 1991). However, because other studies show no linkage between stress and cancer onset, the question remains open to further inquiry.

Psychological Factors in Treatment and Recovery Cancer is a physical disease treated medically by means of surgery, radiation, and chemotherapy. Yet psychologists and mental health professionals can play key roles in helping cancer patients deal with the emotional consequences of coping with the disease (Andersen, 2002). Feelings of hopelessness and helplessness are common reactions to receiving a cancer diagnosis, but such feelings may hinder recovery (Andersen, 1992), perhaps by depressing the patient's immune system.

Evidence shows that breast cancer patients who maintain a "fighting spirit" experience better outcomes than those who resign themselves to their illness (Pettingale, 1985). A ten-year follow-up of breast cancer patients found that those who met their diagnosis with anger and a fighting spirit rather than stoic acceptance showed significantly higher survival rates. The will to fight the illness may help increase survival.

Social support may also help. Women with metastatic breast cancer who participated in a group support program survived a year and a half longer on average than did women assigned to a no-treatment control group (Spiegel et al., 1989). How psychological approaches affect the course of cancer is unclear, however. One possible mode of action is enhancement of the immune system (Andersen, 1992).

Investigators have examined the value of training cancer patients to use coping skills, such as relaxation, stress management, and coping thoughts, to relieve the stress and pain of coping with cancer. These interventions may also help cancer patients cope with the anticipatory side effects of chemotherapy. Cues associated with chemotherapy, such as the hospital environment itself, may become conditioned stimuli that elicit nausea and vomiting even before the drugs are administered (Redd, 1995). By pairing relaxation, pleasant imagery, and attentional distraction with these cues, investigators find that nausea and vomiting can be lessened (Redd, 1995). Playing video games as a form of distraction has also helped lessen the discomfort of chemotherapy in children with cancer (Kolko & Rickard-Figueroa, 1985).

Psychosocial interventions have had positive effects on emotional and behavioural adjustment in adult cancer patients, as well as reducing symptomatic distress arising from the disease and from chemotherapy treatment (Compas, Haaga, Keefe, Leitenberg, & Williams, 1998; Meyer & Mark, 1995). Although it is too early to tell whether psychosocial techniques actually prolong life in cancer patients, preliminary evidence indicates that they may (Fawzy & Fawzy, 1994; Kogon, Biswas, Pearl, Carlson, & Spiegel, 1997). Other investigators find relaxation training to have a beneficial effect on reducing states of tension, depression, and anger in cancer patients undergoing radiation therapy (Decker, Cline-Elsen, & Gallagher, 1992). Psychological treatment also leads to improved quality of life of cancer patients and reduces emotional distress; it helps patients develop more effective coping skills (Andersen, 1997).

A CLOSER LOOK

Cancer Risk Reduction

Canadians may reduce their risk of developing cancer by making some key lifestyle choices and living environment changes. The Canadian Cancer Society (2003) asserts that at least 50% of cancers can be prevented by taking the following measures:

1. Reduce your exposure to tobacco.

2. Make healthy food choices—follow *Canada's Food Guide to Healthy Living* (Health Canada, 2002b).

3. Get physically active—follow Canada's Physical Activity Guide to Healthy Active Living (Health Canada, 2002b).

4. Protect yourself from the sun.

5. Practise early detection through self-examination and screening by health-care professionals.

6. Be aware of and report any bodily changes to your doctor or dentist.

7. Be informed about environmental risks and reduce your exposure to carcinogens.

You can also find out if you have an increased risk for developing cancer through genetic testing.

Cancer involves the development of aberrant or mutant cells that form growths (tumours) that spread to healthy tissue. Cancerous cells can take root anywhere— the blood, the bones, lungs, digestive tract, and genital organs. When they are not contained early, cancer may metastasize or establish colonies throughout the body, leading to death.

Learning to modify expectations is also important. Cancer patients who are able to maintain or restore their psychological well-being appear to be able to do so by readjusting their expectations of themselves in line with their present capabilities (Heidrich, Forsthoff, & Ward, 1994).

Acquired Immunodeficiency Syndrome (AIDS)

Acquired immunodeficiency syndrome—AIDS—is a lethal viral disease caused by the **human immunodeficiency virus** (HIV). HIV attacks a person's immune system, leaving it helpless to fend off diseases that it normally would hold in check.

HIV is transmitted mainly through sexual contact (vaginal and anal intercourse; oral–genital contact) and needle sharing among injecting drug users. Almost 56 000 Canadians were living with HIV in 2006, and about 2500 new infections are added every year (Public Health Agency of Canada, 2006). Unfortunately, some 15 000 Canadian men and women are unaware that they are infected (Health Canada, 2003c). HIV is not contracted by donating blood, airborne germs, insects, or by casual contact such as using public toilets, holding or hugging infected people, sharing eating utensils with them, or living or going to school with them. Routine screening of the blood supplies for HIV have reduced the risk of infection from blood transfusions to virtually nil.

At present, there is no cure or vaccine for HIV infection, but recent advances in treatment that use a combination of antiviral drugs has brought hope that the disease may one day be controlled (Yeni et al, 2002). The lack of a cure or effective vaccine means that prevention programs focusing on reducing or eliminating risky sexual and injection practices represent our best hope for controlling the epidemic. Psychologists have become involved in the fight against HIV and AIDS because behaviour is the major determinant of the risk of contracting the deadly virus and because HIV and AIDS, like cancer, have devastating psychological effects on infected persons, their families and friends, and society at large.

Adjustment of People with HIV and AIDS   Given the nature of the disease and the stigma suffered by people with HIV and AIDS, it is not surprising that many people with HIV, although certainly not all, develop psychological problems, most commonly anxiety and depression (e.g., Catz & Kelly, 2001; Heckman et al., 2004). Psychological factors also affect AIDS progression. These include negative expectancies about one's future health, a psychological response to coping with the disease based on denial and avoidance, and sensitivity to rejection (Cole, Kemeny, & Taylor, 1997; Solano et al., 1993).

Psychological and Psychopharmacological Interventions   Behaviour-change programs focus on altering and reducing risky sexual and injection practices (e.g., Carey et al., 2004; Kelly & Kalichman, 2002). Psychological treatment, typically in the form of support groups, self-help groups, and organized therapy groups, has also been used to provide psychological assistance to people with HIV and AIDS, their families, and friends. Treatment may incorporate training in active coping skills, such as stress management techniques like self-relaxation and positive mental imagery, and cognitive strategies to control intrusive negative thoughts and preoccupations. Coping skills training and cognitive-behavioural therapy have been shown to help improve psychological functioning and ability to handle stress in people living with HIV or AIDS, and to reduce their feelings of depression and anxiety (Lutgendorf et al., 1997). Antidepressant medication has also been found to be helpful in treating depression in people with HIV (Elliott et al., 1998; Markowitz et al., 1998). Whether treatment of depression or coping skills training for handling stress can improve immunological functioning or prolong life in people with HIV and AIDS remains an open question.

Preventing AIDS   We end this section on a sobering note. The new reality is that young people will come of age when the threat of AIDS hangs over every sexual encounter. AIDS presents the public health community with an as yet unparalleled challenge: to help prevent the spread of AIDS and to treat people who have been infected with HIV and who have developed AIDS.

acquired immunodeficiency syndrome A condition caused by the human immunodeficiency virus (HIV) that is characterized by debilitation of the immune system, leaving the body vulnerable to opportunistic diseases. Abbreviated *AIDS*.

human immunodeficiency virus The virus that causes AIDS. Abbreviated *HIV*.

As frightening as AIDS may be, it is preventable. However, researchers find that information about risk reduction alone is not sufficient to induce widespread changes in sexual behaviour (Geringer, Marks, Allen, & Armstrong, 1993; Kelly et al., 1995; Klepinger, Billy, Tanfer, & Grady, 1993; Fisher, Fisher, Williams, & Malloy, 1994). People not only need to know about the dangers of unsafe sexual practices, they also need to know how to change their behaviour (e.g., learning how to refuse invitations to engage in unsafe sex and how to communicate effectively with one's partner about safer sex), and they must be motivated to change their high-risk behaviour (Fisher et al., 1994). Other factors not to be overlooked in prevention efforts are drug and alcohol use and peer group norms. The likelihood of people engaging in safer-sex practices is linked to the avoidance of alcohol and drugs before sex and to the perception that safer-sex practices are the social norm within one's peer group.

In this chapter, we focused on relationships between stress and health, and also on the psychological factors involved in health. Psychology has much to offer to the study and treatment of physical disorders. Psychological approaches may help in the treatment of such physical disorders as headaches and coronary heart disease. Psychologists also help people reduce the risks of contracting health problems such as cardiovascular disorders, cancer, and AIDS. Emerging fields like psychoneuroimmunology promise to further enhance our knowledge of the intricate relationships between the mind and body.

STUDY BREAK

Psychological Factors and Physical Disorders

Review It

- **How are psychological factors involved in physical illness?** Psychological factors are involved in the origins, course, and treatment of many physical health problems. The most common headache is the muscle-tension headache, which is often stress related. Behavioural methods of relaxation training and biofeedback are of help in treating headaches. Psychological factors that increase the risk of coronary heart disease include patterns of consumption, leading a sedentary lifestyle, Type A behaviour pattern, and persistent negative emotions.

  Psychological factors such as emotional stress, loss of loved ones, and intense disappointment may trigger asthma attacks in susceptible individuals. Although relationships between personality and risk of cancer remain under study, behavioural risk factors for cancer include dietary practices (especially high fat intake), heavy alcohol use, smoking, and suntanning. Research shows that a fighting spirit may help people recover from cancer. Psychological interventions help cancer patients cope better with the symptoms of the disease and its treatment.

  Our behaviour patterns influence our risk for contracting AIDS. Psychologists have become involved in the prevention and treatment of AIDS because this disease, like cancer, has devastating psychological effects on victims, their families and

friends, and society at large, and because AIDS can be prevented through reducing risky behaviour.

Define It

psychosomatic
psychophysiological
biofeedback training
thermistor
cardiovascular disease
arteriosclerosis
atherosclerosis
stroke

transcendental
  meditation
mantra
high-strain jobs
acquired immuno-
  deficiency syndrome
human immuno-
  deficiency virus
myocardial infarction

Recall It*

1. Christine complains of a headache that began this afternoon and was slow to develop. She feels a dull but steady pain on both sides of her head and feelings of pressure or tightness through her shoulders, neck, and head. Her headache is most likely a _____ headache.

   a. migraine
   b. hypoglycemic
   c. muscle-tension
   d. cluster

2. Harold has a "winning is everything" attitude in all that he does. He is often angry, especially when things don't turn out the way he expects. He constantly feels

pressured by not having enough time and cannot stand waiting in line, not even for five minutes. Harold may be described as having a _____ personality pattern.

a. Type A
b. Type B
c. Type C
d. reactive Type B

3. The underlying disease process in coronary heart disease is _____.

a. myocardial infarction
b. coronary thrombosis
c. arteriosclerosis
d. hypertension

4. _____ involves the growth of masses of aberrant cells in the body.

a. Muscular dystrophy
b. AIDS
c. Cancer
d. Cirrhosis

5. The risk of HIV infection from blood transfusions today is _____.

a. lower than it was in the 1980s but still a significant problem
b. common in some parts of the country
c. uncommon except in public hospitals that rely on community blood supplies
d. extremely low

* Recall It answers can be found on the Companion Website for this text.

Think About It

• Examine your own personality and behaviour patterns. How might they be helping to promote your health? In what ways might they damage your health or increase your risk of developing health-related problems? What changes can you make in your lifestyle to adopt healthier behaviours?

ANSWER KEY FOR "ARE YOU TYPE A?"

Yes answers are suggestive of the Type A behaviour pattern (TABP). In appraising whether or not you show the TABP, you need not be concerned with the precise number of yes answers. We have no normative data for you. As Friedman and Rosenman (1974, p. 85) note, however, you should have little trouble spotting yourself as "hard core" or "moderately afflicted"—that is, if you are honest with yourself.

WEBLINKS

The Canadian Cancer Society
www.cancer.ca/ccs/internet/frontdoor/0,,3172___langId-en,00.html
This is Canada's primary source for research, health promotion, advocacy, and information about cancer.

Canadian Health Network
www.canadian-health-network.ca
This website is jointly hosted by Health Canada and other major health organizations across the country. In addition to mental health, it also features a comprehensive human health resource base.

The Canadian Institute of Stress
http://stresscanada.org
Founded in 1979 by Dr. Hans Selye and other visionaries, the Canadian Institute of Stress is an international leader in preparing workplaces, communities, and individuals to plan and deal with successful, not stressful, future change.

The Heart and Stroke Foundation of Canada
www.heartandstroke.ca
This is a reliable Canadian source for research, health promotion, advocacy, and information about heart disease and stroke.

Stress, Psychological Factors, and Health

Adjustment Disorders

Characteristics

- Maladaptive reaction to an identified stressor or stressors
- Occurs shortly following exposure to stressor(s)
- Results in impaired functioning or signs of emotional distress that exceed what would normally be expected in the situation

Subtypes

- Adjustment Disorder with Depressed Mood
- Adjustment Disorder with Anxiety
- Adjustment Disorder with Mixed Anxiety and Depressed Mood
- Adjustment Disorder with Disturbance of Conduct
- Adjustment Disorder with Mixed Disturbance of Emotions and Conduct
- Adjustment Disorder Unspecified

Stress and Illness

Stress and Neurobiology

- Psychoneuroimmunology: the study of the relationships among psychological factors, especially stress, and the workings of the endocrine system, the immune system, and the nervous system.
- Neurological changes associated with severe stress during early childhood are related to childhood and adult psychiatric disorders.

Stress and the Endocrine System

- Endocrine glands are involved in the body's stress response.
- During states of chronic stress, the body may continue to pump out stress hormones, which can have damaging effects throughout the body.

Stress and the Immune System

- The immune system is the body's system of defence against disease. Exposure to physical and psychological sources of stress can dampen immunological functioning.

The General Adaptation Syndrome

- Selye's three-stage response to states of prolonged or intense stress:
  1. Alarm reaction (fight or flight reaction)
  2. Stage of resistance
  3. Stage of exhaustion

Stress and Life Changes

- Positive and negative life changes can be stressful. Positive life changes seem to be less disruptive than negative life changes.

Psychological Factors That Moderate Stress

- Coping styles: emotion-focused and problem-focused coping
- Self-efficacy expectations
- Psychological hardiness
  - Optimism
  - Humour
  - Social Support

Stress and the Wellness Continuum Model

- The wellness continuum model: a quality of life measure ranging from nominal to optimal functioning. Distressors are associated with illness; eustressors are associated with wellness.

Psychological Factors and Physical Disorders

Headaches

- Tension headache: stress can lead to persistent contractions of the muscles of the scalp, face, neck, and shoulders.
- Migraine headache: involves changes in the blood flow to the brain.
- Treatment: Biofeedback training, transcranial magnetic stimulation (TMS).

Cardiovascular Disease

- Psychological factors that increase the risk of coronary heart disease include patterns of consumption, leading a sedentary lifestyle, Type A behaviour pattern, and persistent negative emotions.

Emotions and the Heart

- Emotional stress in the form of persistent negative emotions, especially anxiety, anger, and hostility, are major risk factors for CHD and other heart problems.

Social Environmental Stress

- Social environmental stress heightens the risk of CHD. High-strain jobs that are high in demand and low in the amount of personal control they afford will place workers at highest risk for CHD.

Asthma

- Emotional stress, loss of loved ones, and intense disappointment may trigger asthma attacks in susceptible individuals.

Cancer

- Behavioural risk factors for cancer include dietary practices (especially high fat intake), heavy alcohol use, smoking, and sunbathing.

Acquired Immunodeficiency Syndrome (AIDS)

- AIDS can be prevented through reducing risky behaviour.

Psychological Methods for Lowering Arousal

- Meditation: Benson "relaxation response" is characterized by reductions in the body's metabolic rate and by a reduction in blood pressure.
- Progressive relaxation: teaches people how to monitor muscle tension and relaxation by training them to first tense, then relax, selected muscle groups.

CHAPTER 5

Anxiety Disorders

CHAPTER OUTLINE

Types of Anxiety Disorders
Theoretical Perspectives
Treatment of Anxiety Disorders

Did You Know That...

See the underlined text on the pages indicated below for more information on these interesting and often misunderstood facts.

- As many as 17% of people will suffer from an anxiety disorder at some point in their lives? (p. 177)

- People experiencing panic attacks are likely to believe they are having heart attacks, even though there is nothing wrong with their hearts? (p. 178)

- Although women are less likely to experience traumatic incidents than men, they are more likely to develop posttraumatic stress disorder (PTSD) at some point in their lives? (p. 186)

- According to one theory, humans may be genetically programmed to more readily acquire fears of snakes than of cuddly animals? (p. 192)

- The same drugs used to treat depression can also help treat anxiety disorders? (p. 201)

ANXIETY IS A STATE OF apprehension or foreboding. There is much in our world to be anxious about—our health, social relationships, examinations, careers, international relations, and the condition of the environment are but a few sources of possible concern. It is normal, even adaptive, to be somewhat anxious about these aspects of life. **Anxiety** serves us when it prompts us to seek regular medical checkups or motivates us to study for tests. Anxiety is an appropriate response to threats, but anxiety can be abnormal when its level is out of proportion to a threat or when it seems to come out of the blue—that is, when it is not in response to environmental changes. In extreme forms, anxiety can impair our daily functioning. Consider the case of Dick:

anxiety Emotional state characterized by physiological arousal, unpleasant feelings of tension, and a sense of apprehension, foreboding, and dread about the future.

> Slowly, trains snake their way through the city each morning. Most commuters pass the time reading the morning newspapers, sipping coffee, or catching a few last winks. For Dick, the morning commute was an exercise in terror. He noticed perspiration clinging to his shirt, but the air conditioning seemed to be working fine, for a change. So how then was he to account for the sweat? As the train entered the tunnel and darkness shrouded the windows, Dick was gripped by sheer terror. He sensed his heart beating faster, the muscles in his neck tightening. Queasiness soured his stomach. He felt as though he might pass out. Other commuters, engrossed in their morning papers or their private thoughts, paid no heed to Dick, nor did they seem concerned about the darkness that enveloped the train.
>
> Dick had known these feelings all too well before. But now the terror was worse. Other days he could bear it. This time it seemed to start earlier than usual, before the train had entered the tunnel. "Just don't think about it," he told himself, hoping it would pass. "I must think of something to distract myself." He tried humming a song, but the panic grew worse. He tried telling himself that it would be all right, that at any moment the train would enter the station and the doors would open. Not this day, however. On this day, the train came to a screeching halt. The conductor announced a "signalling problem." Dick tried to calm himself: "It's only a short delay. We'll be moving soon." But the train did not start moving soon. More apologies from the conductor. A train had broken down further ahead in the tunnel. Dick realized it could be a long delay, perhaps hours. Suddenly, he felt the urgent desire to escape. "But how?" he wondered.
>
> Dick felt like he was losing control. Wild imaginings flooded his mind. He saw himself bolting down the aisles in a futile attempt to escape, bowling people over, trying vainly to pry open the doors. He was filled with a sense of doom. Something terrible was about to happen to him. "Is this the first sign of a heart attack?" he wondered anxiously. By now, perspiration had soaked his clothes. His once-neat tie hung awry. His breathing became heavy and laboured, drawing attention from other passengers. "What do they think of me?" he thought. "Will they help me if I need them?"
>
> The train jerked into motion. He realized he would soon be free. "I'm going to be okay," he told himself. "The feelings will pass. I'm going to be myself again." The train pulled slowly into the station, 20 minutes late. The doors opened and the passengers hurried off. Stepping out himself, Dick adjusted his tie and readied himself to start the day. He felt as though he'd been in combat. Nothing that his boss could dish out could hold a candle to what he'd experienced on the 7:30 train.
>
> THE AUTHORS' FILES

Dick suffered a panic attack, one of many he had experienced before seeking treatment. The attacks varied in frequency. Sometimes they occurred daily, sometimes once a week or so. He never knew whether an attack would occur on a particular day. He knew, however, that he couldn't go on living that way. He feared that one day he would suffer a heart attack on the train. He pictured some passengers trying vainly to revive him while others stared blankly in the detached distant way that people stare at traffic accidents. He pictured emergency workers rushing onto the train, bearing him on a stretcher to an ambulance. For a while, he considered changing jobs, accepting a less remunerative job closer to home, one that would free him of the need to take the train. He also considered driving to work, but the roads were too thick with traffic. No choice, he figured; either commute by train or switch jobs. His wife, Jill, was unaware of his panic attacks. She wondered why his shirts were heavily stained with perspiration and why Dick was talking about changing jobs. She worried about making ends meet on a lower income. She had no idea it was the train ride, and not his job, that Dick was desperate to avoid.

Panic attacks, like the ones suffered by Dick, are a feature of **panic disorder**, a type of **anxiety disorder**. During a panic attack, one's level of anxiety can rise to a level of sheer terror.

Panic attacks are an extreme form of anxiety. Anxiety encompasses many physical features, cognitions, and behaviours, as shown in Table 5.1. Although anxious people need not experience all of them, it is easy to see why anxiety is distressing.

panic disorder Type of anxiety disorder characterized by recurrent episodes of panic.

anxiety disorder Type of psychological disorder in which anxiety is the prominent feature.

TABLE 5.1

Some Features of Anxiety

Physical Features of Anxiety	Behavioural Features of Anxiety	Cognitive Features of Anxiety
Jumpiness, jitteriness	Avoidance and escape behaviours	Worrying about something
Trembling or shaking of the hands or limbs	Clinging, dependent behaviours	A nagging sense of dread or apprehension about the future
Sensations of a tight band around the forehead	Agitated behaviours	Belief that something dreadful is going to happen, with no clear cause
Tightness in the pit of the stomach or chest	Seeking reassurance	Preoccupation with bodily sensations
Heavy perspiration	Repeatedly checking that something bad hasn't happened	Keen awareness of bodily sensations
Sweaty palms		Feeling threatened by people or events that are normally of little or no concern
Light-headedness or faintness		Fear of losing control
Dryness in the mouth or throat		Fear of inability to cope with one's problems
Difficulty talking		Thinking the world is caving in
Shortness of breath or shallow breathing		Thinking things are getting out of hand
Heart pounding or racing		Thinking things are swimming by too rapidly to take charge of them
Tremulousness in one's voice		Worrying about every little thing
Cold fingers or limbs		Thinking the same distrubing thought over and over
Dizziness		Thinking that one must flee crowded places or else pass out
Weakness or numbness		Finding one's thoughts jumbled or confused
Difficulty swallowing		Not being able to shake off nagging thoughts

TABLE 5.1

Some Features of Anxiety (continued)		
Physical Features of Anxiety	**Behavioural Features of Anxiety**	**Cognitive Features of Anxiety**
A "lump in the throat"		Thinking that one is going to die, even when one's doctor finds nothing medically wrong
Stiffness of the neck or back		Difficulty concentrating or focusing one's thoughts
Choking or smothering sensations		
Cold, clammy hands		
Upset stomach or nausea		
Hot or cold spells		
Frequent urination		
Feeling flushed		
Diarrhea		
Feeling irritable or "on edge"		

TYPES OF ANXIETY DISORDERS

According to a Simon Fraser University review of worldwide research on the prevalence of anxiety disorders, as many as 17% of adults will develop an anxiety disorder at some point in their lives (Somers et al., 2006). These disorders may persist for years or decades, especially if the person does not receive treatment.

The anxiety disorders, along with dissociative disorders and somatoform disorders (see Chapter 6, "Dissociative and Somatoform Disorders"), were classified as neuroses throughout most of the 19th century. The term *neurosis* derives from the root meaning "an abnormal or diseased condition of the nervous system." The Scottish physician William Cullen coined it in the 18th century. As the derivation implies, it was assumed neuroses had biological origins. They was seen as an affliction of the nervous system.

At the beginning of the 20th century, Cullen's organic assumptions were largely replaced by Sigmund Freud's psychodynamic views. Freud maintained that neuroses stem from the threatened emergence of unacceptable anxiety-evoking ideas into conscious awareness. Various neuroses—anxiety disorders, somatoform disorders, and dissociative disorders—might look different enough on the surface. According to Freud, however, they all represent ways in which the ego attempts to defend itself against anxiety. Freud's assumption of common **etiology**, in other words, united the disorders as neuroses. Freud's concepts were so widely accepted in the early 1900s that they formed the basis for the classification systems found in the first two editions of the *Diagnostic and Statistical Manual of Mental Disorders* (DSM).

etiology Cause or origin; the study of causality.

Since 1980, the DSM has not contained a category termed *neuroses*. The present DSM is based on similarities in observable behaviour and distinctive features rather than on causal assumptions. Many clinicians continue to use the terms *neurosis* and *neurotic* in the manner in which Freud described them, however. Some clinicians use "neuroses" as a convenient means of grouping milder behavioural problems in which people maintain relatively good contact with reality. *Psychoses*, such as schizophrenia, are typified by loss of touch with reality and by the appearance of bizarre behaviour, beliefs, and hallucinations. Anxiety is not limited to the diagnostic categories traditionally termed *neuroses*, moreover. People with adjustment problems, depression, and psychotic disorders may also encounter problems with anxiety.

TABLE 5.2

Diagnostic Features of Anxiety Disorders

Panic Disorder without Agoraphobia	Occurrence of recurrent, unexpected panic attacks about which there is persistent concern but without accompanying agoraphobia.
Panic Disorder with Agoraphobia	Occurrence of recurrent, unexpected panic attacks about which there is persistent concern, along with agoraphobia. Agoraphobia is the fear and avoidance of places or situations in which it would be difficult or embarrassing to escape, or in which help might be unavailable in the event of a panic attack or panic-type symptoms.
Generalized Anxiety Disorder	Persistent and excessive levels of anxiety and worry that are not tied to any particular object, situation, or activity.
Specific Phobia	Clinically significant anxiety relating to exposure to specific objects or situations; often accompanied by avoidance of these stimuli.
Social Phobia	Clinically significant anxiety relating to exposure to social situations or performance situations; often accompanied by avoidance of these situations.
Obsessive-Compulsive Disorder	Recurrent obsessions, compulsions, or both.
Posttraumatic Stress Disorder	Re-experiencing of a traumatic event accompanied by heightened arousal, numbing of general responsiveness, and avoidance of stimuli associated with the event.
Acute Stress Disorder	Similar to posttraumatic stress disorder but limited to the days and weeks following exposure to the trauma.

Source: Adapted from DSM-IV (APA, 2000a). Note: All of these disorders are coded on Axis I in the DSM-IV.

The DSM-IV recognizes the following specific types of anxiety disorders: panic disorder (with or without agoraphobia), specific phobia, social phobia, generalized anxiety disorder, obsessive-compulsive disorder, and acute and posttraumatic stress disorders. Table 5.2 lists the diagnostic features of anxiety disorders. These are not mutually exclusive—people frequently meet diagnostic criteria for more than one disorder.

Panic Disorder

Panic disorder involves the occurrence of repeated, unexpected panic attacks. Panic attacks are intense anxiety reactions accompanied by physical symptoms such as a pounding heart; rapid respiration, shortness of breath, or difficulty breathing; heavy perspiration; and weakness or dizziness. The attacks are accompanied by feelings of terror and a sense of imminent danger or impending doom and by an urge to escape the situation. They are usually accompanied by thoughts of losing control, going crazy, or dying. People who experience panic attacks tend to be keenly aware of changes in their heart rates (Taylor, 2000). They often believe they are having a heart attack even though there is nothing wrong with their hearts.

National surveys in Canada and the U.S. reveal that 1% to 5% of people develop panic disorders at some point in their lives (Barlow, 2002; Bland et al., 1988a, 1988b; Grant et al., 2006). Panic attacks occur suddenly and quickly reach a peak of intensity, usually in ten minutes or less. They typically last for about 20 minutes and are associated with a strong sense of uncontrollability. For a diagnosis of panic disorder to be made, there must be recurrent unexpected panic attacks—attacks that are not triggered by specific objects or situations. They seem to come out of the blue. Although the first attacks occur unexpectedly, over time, they may become associated with certain situations or cues, such as entering a crowded department store, or, like Dick, riding on a subway train.

Panic sufferers are sometimes unaware of subtle changes in their bodily sensations that may precipitate an attack, and so the panic may be perceived as spontaneous because these underlying changes are not detected. If panic sufferers are unable to identify the actual *triggers*, they may attribute their sensations to more serious causes, such as an impending heart attack or break with reality ("going crazy").

Panic. Panic attacks are associated with strong physical reactions, especially cardiovascular symptoms.

After a panic attack, the person may feel exhausted, as if he or she has survived a truly traumatic experience, as in the following case:

> I was inside a very busy shopping precinct and all of a sudden it happened; in a matter of seconds I was like a madwoman. It was like a nightmare, only I was awake: everything went black and sweat poured out of me—my body, my hands, and even my hair got wet through. All of the blood seemed to drain out of me; I went white as a ghost. I felt as if I was going to collapse; it was as if I had no control over my limbs—my back and legs were very weak and I felt as though it was impossible to move. It was as if I had been taken over by some stronger force. I saw all the people looking at me—just faces, no bodies, all merged into one. My heart started pounding in my head and my ears. I thought that my heart was going to stop. I could see black and yellow lights. I could hear the voices of people but from a long way off. I could not think of anything except the way that I was feeling and how I had to get out and run quickly or I would die. I had to escape and get into fresh air. Outside it subsided a little but I felt limp and weak; my legs were like jelly, as though I had run a race and lost. I had a lump in my throat like a golf ball. The incident seemed to me to have lasted hours. I was absolutely drained when I got home and I just broke down and cried. It took until the next day to feel normal again.
>
> ADAPTED FROM HAWKRIGG, 1975, PP. 1280–1282

People often describe panic attacks as the worst experiences of their lives. Their coping abilities are overwhelmed. They may feel they must flee. If flight seems useless, they may freeze. There is a tendency to cling to others for help or support. Some people with panic attacks fear going out alone. Recurrent panic attacks may become so difficult to cope with that sufferers become suicidal. Table 5.3 on page 181 lists the diagnostic features of panic attacks, although not all of these features need to be present. A diagnosis of panic disorder is based on the following criteria: (1) encountering repeated (at least two) unexpected panic attacks; and (2) at least one of the attacks is followed by at least a month of persistent fear of subsequent attacks, or worry about the implications or consequences of the attack (e.g., fear of losing one's mind or "going crazy" or having a heart attack), or significant change in behaviour (e.g., refusing to leave the house or venture into public for fear of having another attack) (APA, 2000a).

Panic disorder usually begins in late adolescence or the early 20s. Women are two to three times more likely than men to develop panic disorder (APA, 2000a). What little we know about the long course of panic disorder suggests it tends to follow a chronic course that waxes and wanes in severity over time (Taylor, 2000).

G. Ron Norton and colleagues at the University of Winnipeg were the first to discover that panic attacks are common among college students and other nonclinical samples. Norton's research and later studies by others showed that these panics are quite common but tend to be milder than those experienced by people with diagnosable panic disorder (Norton et al., 1992).

Agoraphobia

Panic disorder is often associated with *agoraphobia*. About a third to half of people with panic disorder also have agoraphobia, and the majority of people with agoraphobia have a history of panic attacks (APA, 2000a). **Agoraphobia** involves fear of places and situations from which it might be difficult or embarrassing to escape in the event of panicky symptoms or a full-fledged panic attack; or of situations in which help may be unavailable if such problems should occur. People with agoraphobia may fear shopping in crowded stores; walking through crowded streets; crossing bridges; travelling by bus, train, or car; eating in restaurants; or even just leaving the house. They may structure their lives around avoiding exposure to fearful situations and in some cases become housebound for months or even years.

agoraphobia A fear of places and situations from which it might be difficult or embarrassing to escape in the event of panicky symptoms or a full-fledged panic attack; or of situations in which help may be unavailable if such problems should occur.

Agoraphobia is more common in women than men (APA, 2000a). It frequently begins in late adolescence or early adulthood. Approximately 2% of adults have experienced agoraphobia at some point in their lives (Grant et al., 2006; Kessler et al., 2006). Agoraphobia may occur with or without an accompanying panic disorder. In panic disorder with agoraphobia, the person may live in fear of recurrent attacks and avoid public places where attacks have occurred or might occur. Because panic attacks can occur unexpectedly, some people restrict their activities for fear of making public spectacles of themselves or finding themselves without help (Taylor, 2000). Others venture outside only with a companion. Still others forge ahead despite intense anxiety.

People with panic disorder who must leave the house to work are less likely than those who do not work or who work from home to develop agoraphobia (Mineka & Zinbarg, 2006). This is because the necessity of leaving the house forces the person to confront his or her feared situations and thereby overcome their fears. In North American culture, it is more acceptable for women than men to stay home and adopt a traditionally feminine role. This might explain why agoraphobia is more common in women than men.

People with agoraphobia who have no history of panic disorder may experience mild panicky symptoms, such as dizziness, which lead them to avoid venturing away from places where they feel safe or secure. They, too, tend to become dependent on others for support. The following case of agoraphobia without a history of panic disorder illustrates the dependencies often associated with agoraphobia:

Helen, a 59-year-old widow, became increasingly agoraphobic after the death of her husband three years earlier. By the time she came for treatment, she was essentially housebound, refusing to leave her home except under the strongest urging of her daughter, Mary, age 32, and only if Mary accompanied her. Her daughter and 36-year-old son, Pete, did her shopping for her and took care of her other needs as best they could. Yet the burden of caring for their mother, on top of their other responsibilities, was becoming too great for them to bear. They insisted that Helen begin treatment and she begrudgingly acceded to their demands.

Helen was accompanied to her evaluation session by Mary. The 59-year-old woman appeared frail when she entered the office clutching Mary's arm, and insisted that Mary stay throughout the interview. Helen recounted that she had lost her husband and mother within three months of one another; her father had died 20 years earlier. Although she had never experienced a panic attack, she always considered herself an insecure, fearful person. Even so, she had been able to function in meeting the needs of her family until the deaths of her husband and mother left her feeling abandoned and alone. She had now become afraid of "just about everything" and was terrified of being out on her own, lest something bad would happen and she wouldn't be able to cope. Even at home, she was fearful that she might lose Mary and Pete. She needed constant reassurance that they wouldn't abandon her.

THE AUTHORS' FILES

Generalized Anxiety Disorder

generalized anxiety disorder Type of anxiety disorder characterized by general feelings of dread and foreboding and heightened states of sympathetic arousal. Formerly referred to as *free-floating anxiety*. Abbreviated *GAD*.

Generalized anxiety disorder (GAD) is characterized by persistent feelings of anxiety that are not triggered by any specific object, situation, or activity, but rather seems to be what Freud labelled "free floating." People with GAD are chronic worriers, and excessive, uncontrollable worrying is considered the key feature of the disorder (Behar & Borkovec, 2006). They may be excessively worried about life circumstances such as finances, the well-being of their children, social relationships, or even very minor things. Children with generalized anxiety are likely to be worried about academics, athletics, and other social aspects of school life. Other related features include restlessness; feeling tense, "keyed up," or "on edge"; becoming easily fatigued; having difficulty concentrating or finding

TABLE 5.3

Diagnostic Features of Panic Attacks

A panic attack involves an episode of intense fear or discomfort in which at least four of the following features develop suddenly and reach a peak within ten minutes:

1. Heart palpitations, pounding heart, tachycardia (rapid heart rate)
2. Sweating
3. Trembling or shaking
4. Shortness of breath or smothering sensations
5. Choking sensations
6. Chest pains or discomfort
7. Feelings of nausea or other signs of abdominal distress
8. Feelings of dizziness, unsteadiness, light-headedness, or faintness
9. Feelings of strangeness or unreality about one's surroundings (derealization) or detachment from oneself (depersonalization)
10. Fear of losing control or going crazy
11. Fear of dying
12. Numbness or tingling sensations
13. Chills or hot flushes

Source: Adapted from DSM-IV (APA, 2000a).

one's mind going blank; irritability; muscle tension; and disturbances of sleep such as difficulty falling asleep, staying asleep, or having restless and unsatisfying sleep (APA, 2000a). Not surprisingly, the features of GAD—anxiety, worry, and physical symptoms—cause a significant level of emotional distress or impaired functioning (Craske & Waters, 2005).

Generalized anxiety disorder tends to initially arise in the mid-teens to mid-20s and typically follows a lifelong course. The lifetime prevalence of GAD in the general population is estimated to be about 5% (Block et al., 2006). The disorder is believed to be twice as common in women as men. GAD frequently occurs together (comorbidly) with other disorders such as mood or anxiety disorders like panic disorder and obsessive-compulsive disorder. The following case illustrates a number of features of GAD.

Earl was a 52-year-old supervisor at an automobile plant. His hands trembled as he spoke. His cheeks were pale. His face was somewhat boyish, making his hair seem greyed with worry.

He was reasonably successful in his work, although he noted that he was not a "star." His marriage of nearly three decades was in "reasonably good shape," although sexual relations were "less than exciting—I shake so much that it isn't easy to get involved." The mortgage on his house was not a burden and would be paid off within five years, but Earl said, "I don't know what it is; I think about money all the time." His three children were doing well. One was employed, one was in college, and one was in high school. But "with everything going on these days, how can you help worrying about them? I'm up for hours worrying about them," Earl said.

"But it's the strangest thing." Earl shook his head. "I swear I'll find myself worrying when there's nothing in my head. I don't know how to describe it. It's like I'm worrying first and then there's something in my head to worry about. It's not like I start thinking about this or that and I see it's bad and then I worry. And then the shakes come, and then, of course, I'm worrying about worrying, if you know what I mean. I want to run away; I don't want anyone to see me. You can't direct workers when you're shaking."

Going to work had become a major chore. "I can't stand the noises of the assembly lines. I just feel jumpy all the time. It's like I expect something awful to happen. When it gets bad like that I'll be out of work for a day or two with shakes."

Earl had been worked up "for everything; my doctor took blood, saliva, urine, you name it. He listened to everything; he put things inside me. He had other people look at me. He told me to stay away from coffee and alcohol. Then from tea. Then from chocolate and Coca-Cola, because there's a little bit of caffeine [in them]. He gave me Valium [a minor tranquillizer] and I thought I was in heaven for a while. Then it stopped working, and he switched me to something else. Then that stopped working, and he switched me back. Then he said he was 'out of chemical miracles' and I better see a shrink or something. Maybe it was something from my childhood."

THE AUTHORS' FILES

Phobic Disorders

fear Unpleasant, negative emotion characterized by the perception of a specific threat, sympathetic nervous system activity, and tendencies to avoid the feared object.

The word *phobia* derives from the Greek *phobos*, meaning "fear." The concepts of fear and anxiety are closely related. **Fear** is the feeling of anxiety and agitation in response to a threat. Phobic disorders are persistent fears of objects or situations that are disproportionate to the threats they pose. To experience a sense of gripping fear when your car is about to go out of control is normal because there is an objective basis to the fear. In phobic disorders, however, the fear exceeds any reasonable appraisal of danger. People with a driving phobia, for example, might become fearful even when they are driving well below the speed limit on a sunny, uncrowded highway. Or they might be so afraid they will not drive or even ride in a car. People with phobias are not out of touch with reality; they generally recognize their fears are excessive or unreasonable.

A curious thing about phobias is that they usually involve fears of the ordinary things in life, not the extraordinary. People with phobias become frightened of ordinary experiences that most people take for granted, such as taking an elevator or driving on a highway. Phobias can become disabling when they interfere with daily tasks like taking buses, planes, or trains, driving, shopping, or leaving the house. Different types of phobias usually appear at different ages, as noted in Table 5.4 on page 183. The ages of onset appear to reflect levels of physical and cognitive development and life experiences. Fear of heights, for example, typically emerges when a child learns to crawl or walk and therefore is at risk for falling (Cox & Taylor, 1999). Let us consider the two types of phobic disorders classified within the DSM system: *specific phobia* and *social phobia* (also known as social anxiety disorder).

specific phobia Persistent but excessive fear of a specific object or situation, such as a fear of heights or of small animals.

acrophobia Excessive fear of heights.

claustrophobia Excessive fear of small, enclosed places.

Specific Phobias **Specific phobias** are persistent, excessive fears of specific objects or situations, such as fear of heights (**acrophobia**), fear of enclosed spaces (**claustrophobia**), or fear of small animals such as mice or snakes and various other "creepy-crawlies." A person experiences high levels of fear and physiological arousal when encountering the phobic object, which prompts strong urges to escape the situation or avoid the feared stimulus. To rise to the level of a psychological disorder, the phobia must make a significant impact on a person's lifestyle or functioning or cause significant distress. You may have a fear of snakes, but unless your fear interferes with your daily life or causes you significant emotional distress it would not warrant a diagnosis of phobic disorder.

According to the DSM-IV-TR, there are five diagnostic subtypes of specific phobia: (a) animal type (e.g., phobias of dogs or bugs); (b) natural environment type (e.g., phobias of storms, heights, or water); (c) blood-injection-injury type (e.g., phobias of seeing blood or receiving an injection); (d) situational type (e.g., phobias of specific situations such as enclosed spaces or public transportation); and (e) other types (e.g., a phobia of choking or contracting an illness). (Note that the close association between panic disorder and agoraphobia—i.e., most people with agoraphobia have a history of panic or panic-like episodes—is why agoraphobia is grouped with panic disorder rather than being classified as a subtype of specific phobias.)

Specific phobias often begin in childhood. Many children develop passing fears of specific objects or situations. Some, however, go on to develop chronic clinically significant phobias (Antony & Barlow, 2002). Claustrophobia seems to develop later than most other specific phobias, with a mean age of onset of 20 years (see Table 5.4).

Specific phobias are among the most common psychological disorders, affecting close to one in ten people at some point in their lives (APA, 2000a). They occur more frequently in women than men, perhaps because of cultural factors that socialize women to be dependent on men for protection from threatening objects in the environment (Antony & Barlow, 2002). Clinicians need to be aware of cultural factors when making diagnostic judgments. Fears of magic or spirits are common in some cultures and should not be considered a sign of a phobic disorder unless the fear is excessive in light of the cultural context in which it occurs and leads to significant emotional distress or impaired functioning.

Social Phobia It is not abnormal to experience some fear of social situations such as dating, attending parties or social gatherings, or giving a talk or presentation to a class or group. Yet people with **social phobia** have such an intense fear of social situations that they may avoid them altogether or endure them only with great distress. Underlying social phobia is an excessive fear of negative evaluations from others. As noted by Lynn Alden and colleagues at the University of British Columbia, people with social phobia often worry about their social presentation ("Do I look foolish?") and are frightened of doing or saying something humiliating or embarrassing (Crozier & Alden, 2001; Mellings & Alden, 2000). Research by Martin Antony, currently at Ryerson University, shows that people with social phobia tend to see themselves as not being as good as others (Antony, Rowa, Liss, Swallow, & Swinson, 2005). They tend to be severely critical of their social skills (Taylor & Alden, 2005) and become absorbed in evaluating their own performance when interacting with others (Woody, 1996). Some even experience full-fledged panic attacks in social situations.

> **social phobia** Excessive fear of engaging in behaviours that involve public scrutiny.

Surveys conducted in Canada and the United States suggest that between 3% and 13% of people develop social phobia at some point in their lives (APA, 2000a; Shields, 2004). Results from a survey of nearly 2000 people from Winnipeg and regions of Alberta indicated that the following were common social fears (M. B. Stein et al., 2000):

- Giving a speech in front of others (fear reported by 15% of those surveyed)
- Walking into a room when people are already seated (13%)
- Dealing with authority figures (10%)
- Making eye contact (10%)
- Using a public washroom when others are present (9%)
- Going to a party or other social gathering (9%)
- Writing in public (7%)

TABLE 5.4

Typical Age of Onset for Various Phobias

	No. Of Cases	Mean Age of Onset
Animal phobia	50	7
Blood phobia	40	9
Injection phobia	59	8
Dental phobia	60	12
Social phobia	80	16
Claustrophobia	40	20
Agoraphobia	100	28

Source: Adapted from Öst (1987, p. 199).

According to McMaster University psychiatrist and anxiety expert Richard Swinson (2005), there is controversy about whether social phobia is over-diagnosed; that is, controversy about whether psychologists and psychiatrists are confusing ordinary shyness with a psychiatric disorder. Like all psychological disorders, social phobia is diagnosed only when it causes significant suffering or significantly impairs a person's level of functioning in important spheres of life, such as social relationships or performance at work or school.

According to a survey conducted by Statistics Canada, people with social phobia (as diagnosed by rigorous assessment methods), compared to people without the disorder, have lower levels of educational attainment, more employment difficulties, lower income, greater dependence on welfare and social assistance, lower likelihood of marriage, and greater social isolation (Shields, 2004). To illustrate some of these problems, one of our patients, Megan, was on the verge of dropping out of university because she was so anxious about giving presentations in class. Megan did not simply experience the pre-presentation jitters that we all commonly experience; she felt full-blown terror about giving class presentations, even though she was always well-prepared to give her papers.

Social phobia is apparently more common among women than men (APA, 2000a; Shields, 2004), perhaps because of the greater social or cultural pressures placed on young women to please others and earn their approval. People with social phobia may find excuses for declining social invitations. They may eat lunch at their desks to avoid socializing with co-workers. Or they may find themselves in social situations and attempt a quick escape at the first sign of anxiety. Relief from anxiety negatively reinforces escape behaviour, but escape prevents people with phobias from learning to cope with fear-evoking situations more adaptively. Leaving the scene before anxiety dissipates only strengthens the association between the social situation and anxiety. Some people with social phobia are unable to order food in a restaurant for fear the server or their companions might make fun of the foods they order or how they pronounce them. Others fear meeting new people and dating. People with social phobia often turn to tranquillizers or try to "medicate" themselves with alcohol when preparing for social interactions (see Figure 5.1).

The roots of social phobia may begin in childhood. People with social phobia typically report they were shy as children (Crozier & Alden, 2001; Stein & Walker, 2002). Consistent with the *diathesis-stress model*, shyness may represent a diathesis or predisposition that makes one more vulnerable to develop social phobia in the face of stressful experiences, such as traumatic social encounters (e.g., being embarrassed in front of others). Social phobia tends to begin in adolescence and typically follows a chronic and persistent course in life (Antony & Swinson, 2000).

FIGURE 5.1 Percentage of people with social phobia reporting specific difficulties associated with their fears of social situations.
More than 90% of people with social phobia feel handicapped by anxiety in their jobs.
Source: Adapted from Statistics Canada, "How Healthy Are Canadians? Annual Report 2004" *Health Reports – Supplement*, Catalogue 82-003, December 24, 2004.

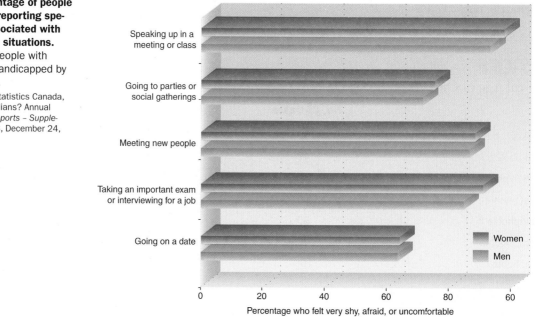

Obsessive-Compulsive Disorder (OCD) An **obsession** is an intrusive, unwanted, and recurrent thought, image, or urge that seems beyond a person's ability to control. Obsessions can be potent and persistent enough to interfere with daily life and can cause significant distress or anxiety. Obsessions may involve persistent, unwanted doubts; the person may wonder endlessly whether he or she has locked the doors and shut the windows, for example. Some sufferers are plagued by personally repugnant images, such as the recurrent fantasy of a young mother that her children had been run over by traffic on the way home from school.

A **compulsion** is a repetitive behaviour (such as hand-washing or checking door locks) or mental acts (such as praying, repeating certain words, or counting) that a person feels compelled or driven to perform (APA, 2000a). Compulsions often occur in response to obsessional thoughts and are frequent and forceful enough to interfere with daily life or cause significant distress. A compulsive hand-washer, Corinne, engaged in elaborate hand-washing rituals. She spent three to four hours daily at the sink and complained, "My hands look like lobster claws." Some people literally take hours checking and rechecking that all the appliances are off before they leave home, and then doubts still remain.

Most compulsions fall into two categories: checking rituals and cleaning rituals. Rituals can become the focal point of life. Checking rituals, like repeatedly checking that the gas jets are turned off or that doors are securely locked, cause delays and annoy companions; cleaning can occupy several hours a day. Table 5.5 shows some relatively common obsessions and compulsions.

Compulsions often appear to at least partially relieve the anxiety created by obsessional thinking (Clark, 2004). By washing one's hands 40 or 50 times in a row each time a public doorknob is touched, the compulsive hand-washer may experience some relief from the anxiety engendered by the obsessive thought that germs or dirt still linger in the folds of skin. The person may believe the compulsive act will help prevent some dreaded event from occurring, even though there is no realistic basis to the belief or the behaviour far exceeds what is reasonable under the circumstances.

Obsessive-compulsive disorder (OCD) affects between 2% and 3% of adults during their lifetimes, and is typically chronic, waxing and waning in response to life stressors (APA, 2000a). The disorder seems to affect women and men in about equal numbers (APA, 2000a). The DSM diagnoses obsessive-compulsive disorder when people are troubled by recurrent obsessions, compulsions, or both such that they cause marked distress, occupy more than an hour a day, or significantly interfere with normal routines or occupational or social functioning.

Phobic disorder. Some people, such as the person shown here, have a fear of germs and becoming infected by them.

obsession Intrusive, unwanted, and recurrent thought, image, or urge that seems beyond an individual's ability to control.

compulsion Repetitive or ritualistic behaviour that a person feels compelled to perform, such as compulsive hand-washing.

TABLE 5.5	
Examples of Obsessive Thoughts and Compulsive Behaviours	
Obsessive Thought Patterns	**Compulsive Behaviour Patterns**
Thinking that one's hands remain dirty despite repeated washing.	Rechecking one's work time and time again.
Difficulty shaking the thought that a loved one has been hurt or killed.	Rechecking the doors are locked or electrical appliances are switched off before leaving home.
Repeatedly thinking that one has left the door to the house unlocked.	Constantly washing one's hands to keep them clean and germ free.
Worrying constantly that the gas jets in the house were not turned off.	
Repeatedly thinking that one has done terrible things to loved ones.	

The line between obsessions and the firmly held but patently false beliefs that are labelled *delusions*, which are found in schizophrenia, is sometimes less than clear. Obsessions, such as the belief that one is contaminating other people, can, like delusions, become almost unshakable. As noted by internationally recognized OCD expert David Clark at the University of New Brunswick, although adults with OCD may be uncertain at a given time about whether their obsessions or compulsions are unreasonable or excessive, they will eventually concede their concerns are groundless or excessive (Clark, 2004). True delusions fail to be shaken. Children with OCD may not come to recognize their concerns are groundless, however.

The case of Jack illustrates a checking compulsion:

Jack, a successful chemical engineer, was urged by his wife Mary, a pharmacist, to seek help for "his little behavioural quirks," which she had found increasingly annoying. Jack was a compulsive checker. When they left the apartment, he would insist on returning to check that the lights or gas jets were off, or that the refrigerator doors were shut. Sometimes he would apologize at the elevator and return to the apartment to carry out his rituals. Sometimes the compulsion to check struck him in the garage. He would return to the apartment, leaving Mary fuming. Going on vacation was especially difficult for Jack. The rituals occupied the better part of the morning of their departure. Even then, he remained plagued by doubts.

Mary had also tried to adjust to Jack's nightly routine of bolting out of bed to recheck the doors and windows. Her patience was running thin. Jack realized his behaviour was impairing their relationship as well as causing himself distress, yet he was reluctant to enter treatment. He gave lip service to wanting to be rid of his compulsive habits. However, he also feared that surrendering his compulsions would leave him defenceless against the anxieties they helped ease.

THE AUTHORS' FILES

Acute and Posttraumatic Stress Disorders

In adjustment disorders (discussed in Chapter 4), people have difficulty adjusting to life stressors—business or marital problems, chronic illness, or bereavement over a loss. Here, we focus on stress-related disorders that arise from exposure to *traumatic* events. Exposure to traumatic events can produce acute or prolonged stress-related disorders that are labelled, respectively, **acute stress disorder** (ASD) and **posttraumatic stress disorder** (PTSD). Both types of stress disorders have occurred among soldiers exposed to combat, rape survivors, victims of motor vehicle and other accidents, and people who have witnessed the destruction of their homes and communities by natural disasters like floods, earthquakes, or tornadoes, or technological disasters like railroad or airplane crashes.

In these disorders, the traumatic event involves either actual or threatened death or serious physical injury, or threat to one's own or another's physical safety (APA, 2000a). The person's response to the threat involves feelings of intense fear, helplessness, or a sense of horror. Children with PTSD may have experienced the threat differently, such as by showing confused or agitated behaviour. Exposure to trauma is quite common in the general population, even in countries that are not experiencing civil wars, like Canada and the U.S. In the latter countries, more than two-thirds of people experience some traumatic event in their lives (Galea, Nandi, & Vlahov, 2005). The life prevalence of traumatic stressors is illustrated in Table 5.6, which presents the results from a survey of over a thousand people from Winnipeg (Stein et al., 1997). As in previous studies, the investigators found that men were generally more likely to experience traumatic stressors, although women were more likely to experience particular stressors such as sexual assault. Although men generally encounter more traumatic experiences, women are more likely to develop PTSD in response to trauma (Tolin & Foa, 2006). Little is known about the reasons for this difference.

acute stress disorder Traumatic stress reaction occurring in the days and weeks following exposure to a traumatic event. Abbreviated *ASD*.

posttraumatic stress disorder Type of anxiety disorder involving impaired functioning following exposure to a traumatic experience, such as combat, physical assault or rape, or natural or technological disasters, in which the person experiences, for at least a month, such problems as reliving or re-experiencing the trauma, intense fear, avoidance of event-related stimuli, generalized numbing of emotional responsiveness, and heightened autonomic arousal. Abbreviated *PTSD*.

TABLE 5.6

Lifetime Prevalence of Traumatic Events in a Community Sample of 1000 Winnipeg Residents

Type of Traumatic Event	Women (%)	Men (%)
More common in women		
Rape (at or after age 18)	16	2
Sexual molestation before age 18	19	5
More common in men		
Combat	1	7
Witnessing severe injury or death	19	39
Being threatened with a weapon	12	20
Serious motor vehicle accident	20	29
Equally common in women and men		
Robbery or hold-up	11	13
Physical attack	21	25
Violent death of a friend or family member	35	34
Fire	9	8
Natural disaster	13	14
Other	17	19
Any trauma	74	81

Sample consisted of 524 women and 478 men

Source: Reprinted from: Stein, M. B., Walker, J. R., Hazen, A. L., & Forde, D. R. (1997). Full and partial posttraumatic stress disorder: Findings from a community survey. *American Journal of Psychiatry, 154*, 1114–1119. Copyright (1997). Reprinted with permission from the American Journal of Psychiatry, (Copyright 1999). American Psychiatric Association.

There are, unfortunately, many different examples of traumatic stressors leading to PTSD. Many Canadian First Nations women were abused and developed PTSD after being removed from their communities and placed in residential schools (Söchting, 2004). An estimated 19% of U.S. Vietnam War veterans developed PTSD (Dohrenwend et al., 2006). A Canadian government report acknowledged that PTSD is an important problem for the Canadian military, and that more resources are needed to identify and treat people afflicted with this disorder (Marin, 2001). According to some estimates, as many as 10% to 20% of Canadian armed forces, especially among those stationed in hot spots like Afghanistan, have developed PTSD (Wente, 2006). Some of the survivors of school shootings such as the Columbine High School massacre (1999) and some survivors of the Montreal shootings at École Polytechnique (1989), Concordia University (1992), and Dawson College (2006) also may have developed PTSD, although the precise figures are unknown. After the September 11, 2001, terrorist attacks on New York's World Trade Center, about 8% of Manhattan residents developed PTSD (Galea et al., 2002). Most were traumatized because they were in the vicinity of the towers. The effect of this experience was apparently worsened when these residents saw television images of people falling or jumping from the towers (Ahern et al., 2002). To put a face to these tragedies, consider the following case:

Jennifer Charron, a Canadian-born graphic artist, had studios in World Trade Center's north tower, on the 91st and 92nd floors. Jennifer slept late on the morning of September 11, 2001, planning to go to her studios later in the afternoon. She heard about the first jet on the radio, and rushed to her apartment window just in time to see the unthinkable happen again. "I watched this big plane come across the sky and slam into the south tower," the 30-year-old recalls. "I close my eyes [today] and I can still see it." Jennifer spent the rest of September 11 on the phone trying to account for co-workers, numbed by the thought of how things might have been for her if the terrorists had struck in mid-afternoon. "You

Not everyone who experiences trauma develops traumatic stress reactions. There are many important factors influencing a person's resiliency or vulnerability (Bonnano, 2005; Taylor, 2005). Vulnerability factors include a person's degree of neurobiological responsivity to traumatic experiences; the severity of the trauma and degree of exposure; the use of coping responses to stress; the availability of post-trauma social support; and perhaps perceptions of helplessness and leftover emotional effects, such as guilt and depression (Taylor, 2005).

The risk of being traumatized and developing PTSD is higher for people living in war-torn countries and for those engaging in hazardous activities or occupations. The latter was dramatically illustrated by a recent study of 100 women working as prostitutes in Vancouver (Farley, Lynne, & Cotton, 2005). Ninety percent of these women had been physically assaulted in prostitution. Many reported stabbings and beatings; concussions and broken bones (e.g., broken jaws, ribs, collarbones, fingers); as well as cuts, black eyes, and other injuries—often when they refused to perform specific sexual acts. Most of the women (72%) were classified as having PTSD and 95% said they wanted to leave prostitution but felt unable to do so.

Surveys suggest that about 7% to 9% of Canadian or U.S. adults are affected by PTSD at some point in their lives (Keane, Marshall, & Taft, 2006; van Ameringen, Mancini, Pipe, & Boyle, 2004). The diagnostic category of acute stress disorder was introduced with the publication of the DSM-IV and we know little about its prevalence.

Features of Traumatic Stress Reactions Some of the basic features of traumatic stress reactions are re-experiencing the traumatic event; avoidance of cues or stimuli associated with the event; a numbing of general or emotional responsiveness; heightened states of bodily arousal; and significant emotional distress or impairment of functioning. In the

Civilian Trauma. ASD and PTSD are not limited to combat veterans. Survivors of disasters and catastrophes, like severe motor vehicle accidents, may also develop traumatic stress disorders.

case of an acute stress reaction, there may be an inability to perform necessary tasks such as obtaining needed medical or legal assistance, or a failure to mobilize one's resources to obtain support from family as the result of not informing family members about the traumatic experience (APA, 2000a).

Acute stress disorder is further characterized by extreme anxiety and by *dissociation*— feelings of detachment from oneself or one's environment. People with an acute stress disorder may feel they are "in a daze" or that the world seems unreal. The diagnosis of acute stress disorder is applied to a traumatic stress reaction that occurs during the days and weeks immediately following the traumatic experience. Many people with acute stress disorder go on to develop more persistent stress-related problems, leading to a diagnosis of PTSD (Harvey & Bryant, 2002). By contrast to ASD, PTSD may persist for months, years, or even decades.

ASD frequently occurs in the context of combat or exposure to natural or technological disasters. A soldier may come through a horrific battle not remembering important features of the battle, and feeling numb and detached from the environment. People who are injured or who nearly lose their lives in a hurricane, tsunami, or ice storm may walk around "in a fog" for days or weeks afterward; be bothered by intrusive images, flashbacks, and dreams of the disaster; or relive the experience as though it were happening again.

In acute and posttraumatic stress disorders, the traumatic event may be re-experienced in various ways. There can be intrusive memories, recurrent disturbing dreams, or the feeling that the event is indeed recurring (as in "flashbacks" to the event). Exposure to events that resemble the traumatic experience can cause intense psychological distress. People with traumatic stress reactions tend to avoid stimuli that evoke recollections of the trauma. For example, they may not be able to handle a television account or a friend's wish to talk about it. They may have feelings of detachment or estrangement from other people. They may show less responsiveness to the external world after the traumatic event, losing the ability to enjoy previously preferred activities or to have loving feelings.

Have you ever been awakened by a nightmare and been reluctant to return to sleep for fear of re-entering the orb of the dream? Nightmares in traumatic stress reactions often involve the re-experiencing of the traumatic event, which can lead to abrupt awakenings and difficulty falling back to sleep—because of fear associated with the nightmare and elevated levels of arousal. Other features of heightened arousal include difficulty falling or staying asleep, irritability or anger outbursts, hypervigilance (being continuously on guard), difficulty concentrating, and an exaggerated startle response (jumping in response to sudden noises or other stimuli) (APA, 2000a).

Although PTSD may wax and wane over time, it can last for years, even decades. Yet there is some good news: People who obtain treatment for PTSD typically recover sooner from its symptoms than those who do not seek help (Taylor, 2005).

STUDY BREAK

Types of Anxiety Disorders

Review It

- **What is an anxiety disorder?** Anxiety, a generalized sense of apprehension or fear, is normal and desirable under some conditions, but can become abnormal when it is excessive or inappropriate. Abnormal behaviour patterns in which anxiety is the most prominent feature are labelled anxiety disorders.

- **What is panic disorder?** Panic disorder is characterized by repeated panic attacks, which involve intense physical features, notably cardiovascular symptoms, and which may be accompanied by sheer terror and fears of losing control, losing one's mind, or dying. Panic disorder is often associated with agoraphobia.

- **What is generalized anxiety disorder?** Generalized anxiety disorder is a type of anxiety disorder involving persistent anxiety and worry that seems to be "free floating" or not tied to specific situations.

- **What are phobic disorders?** Phobias are excessive fears of specific objects or situations. Phobias involve a behavioural component—avoidance of the phobic stimulus—in addition to physical and cognitive features. Specific phobias are excessive fears of particular objects or situations, such as mice, spiders, tight places, or heights. Social phobia involves an intense fear of being judged negatively by others.

- **What is obsessive-compulsive disorder?** Obsessive-compulsive disorder or OCD involves recurrent patterns of obsessions, compulsions, or a combination of the two. Obsessions are nagging, persistent thoughts that create anxiety and seem beyond a person's ability to control. Compulsions are apparently irresistible repetitious urges to perform certain behaviours, such as repeated elaborate washing after using a bathroom.

- **What are acute and posttraumatic stress disorders?** Both acute stress disorder and posttraumatic stress disorder involve maladaptive stress reactions that follow exposure to traumatic events. Acute stress disorder occurs in the days and weeks following exposure to a traumatic event. Posttraumatic stress disorder persists for months or even years or decades after the traumatic experience and may not begin until months or years after the event.

Define It

anxiety
panic disorder
anxiety disorder
etiology
agoraphobia
generalized anxiety disorder
fear
specific phobia

acrophobia
claustrophobia
social phobia
obsession
compulsion
acute stress disorder
posttraumatic stress
  disorder

Recall It*

1. In panic disorder, the initial panic attacks occur _____.

   a. away from home
   b. in crowded situations
   c. unexpectedly
   d. when cued by particular stimuli

2. Noel has an excessive, unrealistic fear of heights. His phobia is _____.

   a. agoraphobia
   b. acrophobia
   c. claustrophobia
   d. hydrophobia

3. Specific phobias affect about 1 in _____ people at some point in their lives.

   a. 2
   b. 5
   c. 10
   d. 20

4. Tricia performs elaborate rituals involved in washing her hands repeatedly throughout the day but still feels her hands are contaminated with germs. Her hand-washing rituals are best described as _____.

   a. delusions
   b. abreactions
   c. obsessions
   d. compulsions

5. Which is NOT a feature of posttraumatic stress disorder?

   a. an exaggerated startle response
   b. difficulty falling or remaining asleep
   c. hypervigilance
   d. delusions centring on the traumatic event

* Recall It answers can be found on the Companion Website for this text.

Think About It

- Anxiety may be a normal emotional reaction in some situations, but not in others. Think of a situation in which you would consider anxiety to be a normal reaction and one in which you would consider it to be a maladaptive reaction. What are the differences? What criteria do you use to draw a line between normal and abnormal?

THEORETICAL PERSPECTIVES

The anxiety disorders offer something of a theoretical laboratory. Many theories of abnormal behaviour were developed with these disorders in mind. Here we consider the contributions of these theoretical perspectives to our understanding of anxiety disorders.

Psychodynamic Perspectives

From the psychodynamic perspective, anxiety is a danger signal that threatening impulses of a sexual or aggressive (murderous) nature are nearing the level of awareness. To fend off these threatening impulses, the ego tries to stem or divert the tide by mobilizing its defence mechanisms. For example, with phobias, the defence mechanisms of **projection** and displacement come into play. A phobic reaction is believed to involve the projection of a person's own threatening impulses onto a phobic object. For instance, a fear of knives or other sharp instruments may represent the projection of one's own destructive impulses onto the phobic object. The phobia serves a useful function. Avoiding contact with sharp instruments prevents these destructive wishes from becoming consciously realized or acted on. The threatening impulses remain safely repressed. Similarly, people with acrophobia may harbour unconscious wishes to jump that are controlled by avoiding heights. The phobic object or situation symbolizes or represents these unconscious wishes or desires. The person is aware of the phobia, but not of the unconscious impulses that it symbolizes.

Freud's (1909/1959) historic case of "Little Hans," a five-year-old boy who feared he would be bitten by a horse if he left his house, illustrates his principle of displacement. Freud hypothesized that Hans's fear of horses represented the displacement of an unconscious fear of his father. According to Freud's conception of the Oedipus complex, boys have unconscious incestuous desires to possess their mothers and fears of retribution from their fathers, whom they see as rivals in love. Hans's fear of being bitten by horses thus symbolized an underlying fear of castration.

A learning theorist view of Hans's childhood fear would suggest that he "learned" it from being frightened by an accident involving a horse and a transport vehicle, which generalized to fears of horses. The story of Little Hans has sparked a spirited debate in the psychological annals.

Applying the psychodynamic model to other anxiety disorders, we might hypothesize that in generalized anxiety disorder, unconscious conflicts remain hidden, but anxiety leaks through to the level of awareness. The person is unable to account for the anxiety because its source remains shrouded in unconsciousness, however. In panic disorder, unacceptable sexual or aggressive impulses approach the boundaries of consciousness and the ego strives desperately to repress them, generating high levels of conflict that bring on a full-fledged panic attack. Panic dissipates when the impulse has been safely repressed.

Obsessions are believed to represent the leakage of unconscious impulses into consciousness, and compulsions are acts that help keep these impulses repressed. Obsessive thoughts about contamination by dirt or germs may represent the threatened emergence of unconscious infantile wishes to soil oneself and play with feces. The compulsion (in this case, cleanliness rituals) helps keep such wishes at bay or partly repressed.

The psychodynamic model remains largely speculative, in large part because of the difficulty (some would say impossibility) of arranging scientific tests to determine the existence of the unconscious impulses and conflicts believed to lie at the root of these disorders.

Learning Perspectives

From the behavioural perspective, anxiety disorders are acquired through the process of conditioning. According to O. Hobart Mowrer's (1948) **two-factor model**, both classical and operant conditioning are involved in the development of phobias. The fear component of phobia is assumed to be acquired by means of classical conditioning. It is assumed that previously neutral objects and situations gain the capacity to evoke fear by being

projection In psychodynamic theory, a defence mechanism in which one's own impulses are attributed to another person.

two-factor model O. Hobart Mowrer's theory that both operant and classical conditioning are involved in the acquisition of phobic responses. The fear component of phobia is acquired by means of classical conditioning (pairing of a previously neutral stimulus with an aversive stimulus), and the avoidance component is acquired by means of operant conditioning (relief from anxiety negatively reinforces avoidance behaviour).

paired with noxious or aversive stimuli. A child who is frightened by a barking dog may acquire a phobia for dogs. A child who receives a painful injection may develop a phobia for hypodermic syringes. Consistent with this model, evidence shows that many cases of acrophobia, claustrophobia, and blood and injection phobias involve earlier pairings of the phobic object with aversive experiences (Cox & Taylor, 1999).

As Mowrer pointed out, the avoidance component of phobias is acquired and maintained by operant conditioning. That is, relief from anxiety negatively reinforces avoiding fear-inducing stimuli. A person with an elevator phobia learns to avoid anxiety over taking the elevator by opting for the stairs instead. Avoiding the phobic stimulus thus lessens anxiety, which negatively reinforces the avoidance behaviour. Yet there is a significant cost to avoiding the phobic stimulus. The person is not able to "unlearn" (extinguish) the fear via exposure to the phobic stimulus in the absence of any aversive consequences.

Learning theorists have also noted the role of observational learning in acquiring fears. Modelling (observing parents or others reacting fearfully to a stimulus) and receiving negative information (hearing from others or reading that a particular stimulus—spiders, for example—are fearful or disgusting) may also lead to phobias (Cox & Taylor, 1999).

Some investigators suggest that people may be genetically prepared to more readily acquire phobic responses to certain classes of stimuli than others (Mineka & Zinbarg, 2006). We're more likely to learn to fear spiders than rabbits, for example. This model, called **prepared conditioning**, suggests that evolutionary forces would have favoured the survival of human ancestors who were genetically predisposed to acquire fears of threatening objects, such as large animals, snakes and other creepy-crawlies, and of heights, enclosed spaces, and strangers.

Posttraumatic stress disorder may also be explained from a conditioning framework. From a classical conditioning perspective, traumatic experiences function as unconditioned stimuli that become paired with neutral (conditioned) stimuli such as the sights, sounds, and smells associated with the trauma scene—for example, the battlefield or the neighbourhood in which a person has been raped or assaulted (Taylor, 2005). Subsequent exposure to similar stimuli evokes the anxiety (a conditioned emotional response) associated with PTSD. The conditioned stimuli that reactivate the conditioned response include memories or dream images of the trauma or visits to the scene. Consequently, the person avoids these stimuli. Avoidance is an operant response, which is reinforced by relief from anxiety. However, avoidance prolongs PTSD because sufferers do not have the opportunity to learn to manage their conditioned reactions. Extinction (gradual weakening or elimination) of conditioned anxiety may only occur when conditioned stimuli (e.g., cues associated with the trauma) are presented in a supportive therapeutic setting in the absence of the troubling unconditioned stimuli.

From a learning perspective, generalized anxiety is precisely that: a product of stimulus generalization. People concerned about broad life themes, such as finances, health, and family matters, are likely to experience their apprehensions in a variety of settings. Anxiety would thus become connected with almost any environment or situation. Similarly, agoraphobia would represent a kind of generalized fear triggered by cues associated with various situations in which it might be hazardous or embarrassing to have a panic attack (such as travelling far from home or being in a shopping mall). Some learning theorists assume that panic attacks, which appear to descend out of nowhere, are triggered by cues that are subtle and not readily identified.

There are challenges to the learning theory account of phobias. For example, many people with phobias insist they cannot recall painful exposures to the dreaded stimuli. Learning theorists may assume such memory failures are understandable because many phobias are acquired in early childhood. Yet many phobias, such as social phobia, develop at later ages and appear to involve cognitive processes relating to an exaggerated appraisal of threat in social situations (excessive fears of embarrassment or criticism) rather than pairing of these situations with aversive experiences.

From the learning perspective, compulsive behaviours are operant responses that are negatively reinforced by relief of the anxiety engendered by obsessional thoughts. If a person obsesses that dirt or foreign bodies contaminate other people's hands, shaking hands or turning a doorknob may evoke powerful anxiety. Compulsive hand-washing following

prepared conditioning Belief that people are genetically prepared to acquire fear responses to certain classes of stimuli, such as fears of large animals, snakes, heights, or strangers. Although the development of such phobias may have had survival value for prehistoric ancestors, such behaviour patterns may be less functional today.

exposure to a possible contaminant provides some relief from anxiety. They thus become more likely to repeat the obsessive-compulsive cycle the next time they are exposed to anxiety-evoking cues such as shaking hands or touching doorknobs.

Cognitive Perspectives

Cognitive theorists and researchers focus on how dysfunctional patterns of thinking may set the stage for anxiety disorders. Here, we examine some of the most common thinking patterns associated with anxiety disorders.

Self-Defeating or Irrational Beliefs

Self-defeating thoughts can heighten and perpetuate anxiety disorders. When faced with fear-evoking stimuli, a person may think, "I've got to get out of here" or "My heart is going to burst out of my chest" (Antony & Swinson, 2000). Thoughts like these intensify autonomic arousal, disrupt planning, magnify the aversiveness of stimuli, prompt avoidance behaviour, and decrease one's confidence about controlling a situation.

Irrational beliefs may involve exaggerated needs to be approved of by everyone one meets and to avoid any situation in which negative appraisal from others might arise (Antony & Swinson, 1998). The following is one such example: "What if I have an anxiety attack in front of other people? They might think I'm crazy!"

Cognitive theorists relate obsessive-compulsive disorder with tendencies to exaggerate the risk of unfortunate events (Clark, 2004). Because they expect terrible things to happen, people with OCD engage in rituals to prevent them. An accountant who imagines awful consequences for slight mistakes on a client's tax forms may feel compelled to repeatedly check her or his work. Other irrational beliefs, such as perfectionism, also enter the picture (Antony & Swinson, 1998). The perfectionist exaggerates the consequences of turning in less-than-perfect work, and may feel compelled to redo his or her efforts until every detail is flawless.

Cognitive theorists further argue that obsessions arise as a result of trying too hard to control one's thinking (Clark, 2004). All of us, from time to time, have unwanted, intrusive thoughts. These are the mental flotsam that drifts along the stream of consciousness, which some theorists have called "normal obsessions." Compared to obsessions in OCD, normal obsessions are easier to dismiss, less frequent, cause less discomfort, and are less likely to lead to compulsions (Taylor, Abramowitz, & McKay, 2006). Normal obsessions are extremely common. To illustrate, Table 5.7 shows the frequency of students from the

TABLE 5.7		
Prevalence of Unwanted Intrusive Thoughts ("Normal Obsessions") among Students Sampled from the University of New Brunswick		
Unwanted Intrusive Thought	**Women (%)**	**Men (%)**
Harm-related thoughts		
Leaving the heat or stove on, resulting in an accident	79	66
Leaving the house unlocked, resulting in a break-in	77	69
Running the car off the road	64	56
Insulting a family member	59	55
Swerving into traffic	55	52
Becoming contaminated by touching a door knob	35	24
Sexual thoughts		
Seeing strangers naked	51	80
Having sex in public	49	78
Performing a personally repugnant sexual act	43	52
Having sex with an authority figure (e.g., teacher, boss)	38	63

Source: This article was published in *Behaviour Research and Therapy*, 31, Purdon, C., & Clark, D. A., Obsessive intrusive thoughts in nonclinical subjects. Part I. Content and relation with depressive, anxious and obsessional symptoms, 713–720. Copyright Elsevier (1993). Reprinted with permission from Elsevier.

University of New Brunswick who had ever experienced normal obsessions (Purdon & Clark, 1993). Notice that the frequencies are extremely high. Women were more likely to have unwanted harm-related thoughts, whereas men were more likely to have unwanted sexual thoughts. Researchers at the University of Toronto and Northwestern University also reported evidence of normal compulsions; normal individuals are more likely to wash their hands if they believe that they might have behaved immorally (Zhong & Liljenquist, 2006). This suggests that people tend to associate moral impurity with physical dirtiness. This association may be particularly strong in people with OCD.

If nearly everyone experiences normal obsessions, then why do only some people develop more severe and frequent obsessions, such as those characterizing OCD? Part of the answer seems to lie in the way a person appraises his or her unwanted intrusive thoughts (Janeck, Calamari, Riemann & Heffelfinger, 2003; Taylor, 2002). Irrational beliefs about intrusive thoughts are likely to increase one's odds of developing clinical obsessions. Research by University of Waterloo psychologist Christine Purdon suggests that people with OCD may become particularly upset about their failure to control (suppress) their obsessions, which may make the person anxious and depressed and thereby worsen their OCD (Purdon, 2004; Purdon, Rowa, & Antony, 2005). Similarly, research by Amy Janeck (University of British Columbia) and colleagues reveals that OCD people are excessively preoccupied with their thoughts; they are highly aware of them and monitor them while engaging in "too much thinking about thinking" (Janeck et al., 2003). This may be because people with OCD regard their obsessions as unacceptable and repugnant. To add to the cognitive difficulties experienced by people with OCD, research by investigators including Adam Radomsky at Concordia University has shown that repeated checking undermines memory confidence (Radomsky, Gilchrist, & Dussault, 2006). For example, the more you check and recheck that a stove has been properly switched off by repeatedly turning it on and off, the more uncertain you will be later on about whether you finally did switch off the stove. This is apparently because repeated checking makes it more difficult to visually recall the last check as opposed to previous checks (Radomsky et al., 2006). It is not known whether the same applies to other compulsions such as repeated handwashing.

The distinction between normal and abnormal obsessions is illustrated by two examples from our case files:

Mindy was carving a Halloween pumpkin for her young daughter. As she wielded the knife, she had the unwanted intrusive image of stabbing her daughter. This greatly frightened Mindy—she believed "the unwanted image means that, subconsciously, I must want to kill my daughter." Mindy desperately tried to push the image out of her mind, and became greatly alarmed when it returned. Because she placed so much significance on it, the image became highly important to her, and therefore kept popping into her mind.

In comparison, one of our colleagues, Joan, had a similar unwanted image of stabbing her daughter while carving a Halloween pumpkin. Joan believed the image was "mental garbage." She ignored the image and continued carving. Thus, the image held no significance for Joan and therefore did not return.

THE AUTHORS' FILES

Oversensitivity to Threat An oversensitivity to threatening cues is a cardinal feature of anxiety disorders (Beck & Clark, 1997). People with phobias perceive danger in situations that most people consider safe, such as riding on elevators or driving over bridges. We all possess an internal alarm system that is sensitive to cues of threat. This system may have had evolutionary advantages to ancestral humans by increasing the chances of survival in a hostile environment (Beck & Clark, 1997). Ancestral humans who responded quickly to any sign of threat, like a rustling sound in a bush that may have indicated a lurking predator about to pounce, may have been better prepared to take defensive action (to fight or flee) than those with less sensitive alarm systems. The emotion of fear is a key element in this alarm system and may have motivated our ancestors to take defensive action, which in turn may have helped them survive. People today who have anxiety disorders may have inherited an acutely sensitive internal alarm that leads them to be overly responsive to cues of threat. Rather than helping them cope effectively with threats, it may lead to inappropriate anxiety reactions in response to a wide range of cues that actually pose no danger to them.

Research led by Michel Dugas at Concordia University suggests that the intolerance of uncertainty plays an important role in GAD (Buhr & Dugas, 2006; Dugas et al., 2005; Dugas, Marchand, & Ladouceur, 2005). This intolerance is a special sort of sensitivity to threat, which arises from the belief that it is unacceptable that threatening things occur. People who are intolerant of uncertainty become upset by the possibility of threatening events even when the probability of these events is very small. Considering that daily life is fraught with uncertainties, people who are intolerant of uncertainty are unlikely to frequently worry and become anxious about threats.

Anxiety Sensitivity **Anxiety sensitivity** is a fear of fear. It refers to beliefs that internal emotions or bodily arousal will get out of control, leading to harmful consequences (Taylor, 1999). People with a high degree of anxiety sensitivity may be prone to panic when they experience bodily signs of anxiety, such as a racing heart or shortness of breath, because they take these symptoms to be signs of an impending catastrophe, like a heart attack. Evidence collected at the University of British Columbia and elsewhere suggests that anxiety sensitivity is influenced by a combination of genetic factors and learning experiences. The latter teach people to be afraid of anxiety-related sensations—for example, observing one's parents becoming frightened of sensations such as rapid heartbeat or shortness of breath (Jang, Stein, Taylor, & Lively, 1999; Stewart et al., 2001).

Anxiety sensitivity is an important risk factor for panic attacks, as indicated by longitudinal research (Schmidt, Zvolensky, & Maner, 2006). As we will see next, panic-prone individuals also tend to misattribute changes in their bodily sensations to dire consequences.

Misattributions for Panic Sensations Cognitive models of panic disorder posit that panic attacks involve catastrophic misinterpretations of such bodily sensations as heart palpitations, dizziness, or light-headedness (Clark, 1986). Rather than attribute changes in physical sensations to more benign causes, panic-prone people believe they represent the first signs of an impending heart attack or other threatening event such as a loss of control or "going crazy." Changes in bodily sensations in otherwise healthy individuals may be induced by various factors such as unrecognized hyperventilation, temperature changes, or reactions to certain drugs or medications. Or they may be fleeting, normally-occurring changes in bodily states that typically go unnoticed by most people.

A cognitive model of panic disorder involving an interaction of cognitive and physiological factors is depicted in Figure 5.2 above. The model suggests that people with a proneness to panic disorder perceive certain internal bodily cues or external stimuli as unduly threatening or dangerous, perhaps because they are overly sensitive to these cues or have associated them with earlier panic attacks. The sense of threat induces anxiety or feelings of apprehension, which intensify physical sensations by producing an accelerated heart rate, rapid breathing, and sweating, among other bodily symptoms. These changes

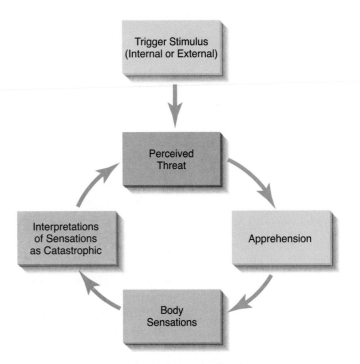

FIGURE 5.2 A cognitive model of panic disorder.
This model involves the interaction of cognitive and physiological factors. In panic-prone people, perceptions of threat from internal or external cues lead to feelings of apprehension or anxiety, which lead to changes in body sensations (e.g., cardiovascular symptoms). These changes lead, in turn, to catastrophic interpretations, thereby intensifying the perception of threat, which further heightens anxiety, and so on in a vicious cycle that may culminate in a full-blown panic attack.

Source: Adapted from Clark (1986).

anxiety sensitivity A "fear of fear," or fear that one's emotions or states of bodily arousal will get out of control and lead to harmful consequences.

in bodily sensations, in turn, are misinterpreted as signs of an impending panic attack or, worse, an imminent catastrophe ("I'm having a heart attack!"), which in either case reinforces perceptions of threat, which further heightens anxiety, leading to yet more anxiety-related bodily symptoms, and so on in a vicious cycle that can quickly spiral to a full-fledged panic attack. Thus, catastrophic misinterpretations of bodily cues may set into motion a vicious cycle that brings on panic attacks in panic-prone individuals.

Mounting evidence points to the important role of cognitive factors in anxiety disorders. As the cognitive model would predict, for instance, people with panic disorder do have a greater tendency to misinterpret bodily sensations as signs of impending catastrophe than do people without anxiety disorders or those with other types of anxiety disorders (Mathews & MacLeod, 2005). Studies also show, as the cognitive model would predict, that panic-prone people have greater awareness of and sensitivity to their internal physiological cues, such as heart palpitations (Taylor, 1999, 2000). More research is needed, however, to determine the extent to which cognitive factors play a direct causal role in panic disorder or other anxiety disorders.

In addition to irrational beliefs and misinterpretations, other sorts of cognitive factors appear to play an important role in anxiety disorders. Research shows that people with anxiety disorders, compared to people without them, are more likely to selectively attend to threatening information, and there is some evidence that people with anxiety disorders are more likely to selectively remember threatening information (Mathews & MacLeod, 2005). These biases in attention and memory make intuitive sense; if you're anxious or frightened of something—say, spiders—then you're more likely to search for sources of potential threat (e.g., scanning a room for spiders) and you're more likely to recall where you've seen spiders in the past. The biases in attention and memory could be either vulnerability factors or a consequence of anxiety disorders, and could worsen the disorders by increasing the chances that a person would notice or remember anxiety-provoking things.

Biological Perspectives

We also have a growing body of evidence that biological factors play a role in anxiety disorders. Many questions remain concerning the interactions of biological and other factors, however.

Genetic Factors Increasing evidence points to the role of genetic factors in anxiety disorders. Consistent with a genetic contribution, studies of twin pairs reveal higher concordance (agreement) rates between MZ (monozygotic or identical twins) than DZ (dizygotic or fraternal) twins for many anxiety disorders (Kendler & Prescott, 2006). Research conducted at the University of British Columbia, for example, suggests that social anxiety and PTSD symptoms are influenced, at least to some extent, by genes (Stein et al., 2002). Table 5.8 on page 197, for example, shows the heritability coefficients for trauma exposure and PTSD symptoms. Findings from the Canadian civilian sample (Stein, Jang, Taylor, Vernon, & Livesley, 2002) are compared with results from a U.S. Vietnam-era twin registry (Lyons et al., 1993; True et al., 1993). Heritability coefficients range from zero to one, with larger numbers indicating that genes make a greater contribution to the variability of the variable in question. The results in Table 5.8 show two important things: first, genes make a significant but modest contribution to PTSD symptoms in both civilian and Vietnam-era populations; and second, the risk of experiencing a traumatic event is also influenced by genes. For example, the chances of being mugged, beaten up in a bar fight, or being sexually assaulted (i.e., examples of assaultive trauma) are all moderately heritable. Recent research from UBC suggests the genes that contribute to assaultive trauma are also the same ones that contribute to antisocial personality traits (Jang et al., 2003). In other words, if you have antisocial tendencies (as illustrated, for example, by a tendency to engage in criminal behaviour or to hang around with criminals in dangerous parts of town), then your risk increases for being exposed to certain types of traumatic events.

Many different genes are probably involved in the etiology of anxiety disorders, with each gene making a small, additive contribution to a person's risk of developing these disorders (Jang, 2005; Leonardo & Hen, 2006). There is no single gene for any of them. The

TABLE 5.8

Heritability Coefficients for Trauma Exposure and PTSD Symptoms

Variable	Canadian Civilian Twin Sample (UBC Twin Study)	U.S. Vietnam-Era Twin Sample
Trauma Exposure		
Assaultive trauma	0.20	—
Volunteered for SEA* service	—	0.36
SEA* service	—	0.35
Combat exposure	—	0.47
Received combat decoration	—	0.54
PTSD Symptoms		
Re-experiencing	0.36	0.25
Avoidance	0.28	0.00
Numbing	0.36	0.28
Hyperarousal	0.29	0.26

*SEA = Southeast Asia. Heritability coefficients range from 0 to 1. The larger the number, the greater the influence of genetic factors on the variability of the variable in question.

Source: Data synthesized from Lyons et al. (1993), Stein et al. (2002), and True et al. (1993).

process of "gene hunting" is a slow, laborious process, and many initial discoveries are not replicated in later research. So, when you read a newspaper announcing that researchers have discovered "the" gene for, say, panic disorder, you need to ask the all-important question of whether the findings have been replicated.

Research replicated in several studies suggests that some genes have narrow effects, influencing a person's risk for developing a particular anxiety disorder. For example, genetic factors for phobias may specifically influence fear conditioning. Other genes have broader effects, influencing the risk for many different types of anxiety disorders as well as the risk for other disorders (Kendler & Prescott, 2006). The genes with broad effects may be the ones linked to **neuroticism**. Neuroticism is not an anxiety disorder, but a personality trait characterized by an enduring tendency to experience negative emotional states. People with high levels of neuroticism (also called *negative emotionality* or *internalizing*) tend to cope poorly with stress and frequently experience feelings of anxiety, anger, guilt, and depression. People high on this trait are at increased risk of developing anxiety disorders and other emotional problems (Craske & Waters, 2005; Krueger & Markon, 2006).

A growing body of research suggests that genes exert their influence by interacting with particular environmental events (Moffitt, Caspi, & Rutter, 2006). For example, people possessing a particular form of a gene involved in the serotonin neurotransmitter system (i.e., the "short" version of the serotonin-transporter gene) are more likely than people without this genetic variant to react to stressful life events by developing anxiety or depressive symptoms (Fox et al., 2005; Leonardo & Hen, 2006). In other words, both genes and the environment are important; people with genetic vulnerability for developing anxiety disorders appear to be at risk primarily when they experience particular sorts of environmental events.

Neurotransmitters The neurotransmitter **gamma-aminobutyric acid (GABA)** is implicated in anxiety. GABA is an *inhibitory* neurotransmitter, which means it helps tone down excess activity in the nervous system by preventing neurons from overly exciting their neighbours. When the action of GABA is inadequate, neurons can fire excessively, possibly bringing about seizures. In less dramatic cases, inadequate action of GABA may contribute to states of anxiety. This view of the role of GABA is supported by the action of the family of anti-anxiety drugs referred to as **benzodiazepines**, which include the well-known Valium and Ativan. Benzodiazepines regulate GABA receptors, thus enhancing GABA's calming (inhibitory) effects (Lydiard, 2003).

Dysfunctions involving serotonin or norepinephrine receptors in the brain have also been implicated in anxiety disorders (Baldwin, 2006). This may explain why so-called

Neuroticism Trait describing a general neurotic quality involving such characteristics as anxious, worrisome behaviour, apprehension about the future, and avoidance behaviour.

gamma-aminobutyric acid An inhibitory neurotransmitter believed to play a role in regulating anxiety. Abbreviated *GABA*.

benzodiazepines Class of minor tranquillizers that includes Valium and Ativan.

antidepressant drugs that affect these neurotransmitter systems in the brain often have beneficial effects in treating some types of anxiety disorder. Investigators also suspect that genes involved in the regulation of serotonin may play a role in determining symptoms of anxiety and depression (Hariri, Brown, & Tamminga, 2006; Pezawas et al., 2005).

Biological Aspects of Panic Disorder

The strong physical components of panic disorder have led some theorists to speculate that panic attacks have biological underpinnings, perhaps involving an underlying brain dysfunction (Gorman, Kent, Sullivan, & Coplan, 2000). Support for a biological basis of panic disorder is found in studies showing that people with panic disorder are more likely than people without to experience panicky symptoms in response to certain biological challenges, such as infusion of the chemical sodium lactate or manipulation of carbon dioxide (CO_2) levels in the blood either by intentional **hyperventilation** (which reduces levels of CO_2 in the blood) or inhalation of carbon dioxide (which increases CO_2 levels) (Barlow, 2002).

Cognitive theorists propose that cognitive factors may be involved in explaining these biological sensitivities. Theorists point out that biological challenges produce intense physical sensations that may be catastrophically misinterpreted by panic-prone people as signs of an impending heart attack or loss of control (Antony, Ledley, Liss, & Swinson, 2006; Barlow, 2002). Perhaps these misinterpretations—not underlying biological sensitivities—may in turn induce panic.

Supportive evidence for the cognitive perspective comes from research showing that cognitive-behavioural therapy, which focuses on changing faulty interpretations of bodily sensations, eliminates CO_2-induced panic in panic disorder patients (Barlow, 2002).

The fact that panic attacks often seem to come out of the blue also seems to support the belief that the attacks are biologically triggered. However, it is possible the cues that set off many panic attacks may be internal, involving changes in bodily sensations, rather than external. Changes in physical cues combined with catastrophic thinking may lead to a spiralling of anxiety that culminates in a full-blown panic attack.

Biological Aspects of Obsessive-Compulsive Disorder

Another biological model that receives attention suggests obsessive-compulsive disorder may involve heightened arousal of a particular *anxiety circuit*, a neural network in the brain involved in signalling danger. In OCD, the brain may be constantly sending messages that something is wrong and requires immediate attention, leading to obsessional thoughts and repetitive compulsive behaviours. The compulsive aspects of OCD may also involve disturbances in other brain circuits that usually suppress repetitive behaviours, leading people to feel like they are "stuck in gear" and cannot seek the sense that a particular action (e.g., checking a door lock) has been performed correctly (Szechtman & Woody, 2004). The frontal cortex regulates brain centres in the lower brain that control bodily movement. Perhaps a disruption in these neural pathways is involved in the failure to inhibit the repetitive handwashing and compulsive checking behaviours seen in people with OCD. Evidence also points to differences in brain functioning of people with OCD compared to nonpatient controls (Friedlander & Desrocher, 2006). The significance of these differences in explaining OCD remains unclear, however, and the ability of such models to account for OCD has been called in question (Taylor et al., 2005).

TYING IT TOGETHER

Unravelling the complex interactions of environmental, physiological, and psychological factors in explaining how anxiety disorders develop remains a challenge (see Figure 5.3). There may be different causal pathways at work. To illustrate, let us offer some possible causal pathways involved in phobic disorders and panic disorder.

Some people may develop phobias by way of classical conditioning—the pairing of a previously neutral stimulus with an unpleasant or traumatic experience. A person may develop a fear of small animals because of experiences in which he or she was bitten or

hyperventilation Pattern of overly rapid breathing, sometimes associated with anxiety, in which the amount of oxygen inhaled is in excess of metabolic requirements, leading to harmless but sometimes unpleasant sensations such as feeling faint or light-headed.

Social-Environmental Factors
Threatening or Traumatic Events
Observing Fear Responses in Others
Challenging Demands in New Situations
Cultural Factors Leading to Socialization
   in Passive or Dependent Roles
Lack of Social Support

Biological Factors
Genetic Predisposition
Disturbances in Neurotransmitter Activity
   or Suffocation Alarm System
Abnormalities in Brain Circuits Involved
   in Signalling Danger or Inhibiting
   Repetitive Behaviours

Behavioural Factors
Conditioning Experiences
Lack of Extinction Opportunities

Emotional and Cognitive Factors
Unresolved Psychological Conflicts
   (Freudian or Psychodynamic)
Cognitive Factors (anxiety sensitivity,
   self-defeating or irrational thinking,
   catastrophic misinterpretations of
   bodily cues, over-sensitivity to threats,
   low self-efficacy)

FIGURE 5.3 Multiple factors in anxiety disorders.

nearly bitten. A fear of riding on elevators may arise from experiences of being trapped in elevators or other enclosed spaces.

Bear in mind that not all people who have traumatic experiences develop related phobias. Perhaps some people have a genetic predisposition that sensitizes them to more readily acquire conditioned responses to stimuli associated with aversive situations. Or perhaps people are more sensitized to these experiences because of an inherited predisposition to respond with greater negative arousal to aversive situations. Whatever factors may be involved in the acquisition of a phobia, people with persistent phobias may have learned to avoid any further contact with the phobic stimulus and so do not avail themselves of opportunities to unlearn the phobia through repeated uneventful contacts with the feared object or situation. Then there are people who acquire phobias without any prior aversive experiences with the phobic stimulus, or at least none they can recall. We can conjecture that cognitive factors, such as observing other people's aversive responses, may play a contributing role in these cases.

Possible causal pathways in panic disorder highlight roles for biological, cognitive, and environmental factors. Some people may inherit a genetic predisposition or diathesis that makes them more likely to panic in response to changes in bodily sensations. This genetic predisposition may involve dysregulations in neurotransmitter systems that control emotional responding. Cognitive factors may also be involved. Bodily sensations, such as dizziness, tingling, or numbness, may be misconstrued as signs of impending death, insanity, or loss of control. This in turn may lead, like dominoes falling in line, to an anxiety reaction that quickly spirals into a full-fledged panic attack. Whether the anxiety reaction spirals into a state of panic may depend on another vulnerability factor: the individual's level of anxiety sensitivity. People with a high level of anxiety sensitivity (extreme fear of their own bodily sensations) may be more likely to panic in response to changes in their physical sensations. In some cases, anxiety sensitivity may be so high that panic ensues even in individuals without a genetic predisposition. Environmental factors may come into play as panic attacks come to be triggered by specific environmental cues, such as stimuli associated with situations (boarding a subway train or elevator) in which attacks have occurred in the past.

Theoretical Perspectives

Review It

- **How are anxiety disorders conceptualized within the psychodynamic perspective?** Psychodynamic theorists view anxiety disorders as attempts by the ego to control the conscious emergence of threatening impulses. Feelings of anxiety are warning signals that threatening impulses are nearing awareness. The ego mobilizes defence mechanisms to divert these impulses, thus leading to different anxiety disorders.

- **How do learning theorists view anxiety disorders?** Learning theorists explain anxiety disorders through conditioning and observational learning. Mowrer's two-factor model incorporates classical and operant conditioning in the explanation of phobias. Phobias, however, appear to be moderated by cognitive factors, such as irrational beliefs. The principles of reinforcement may help explain patterns of obsessive-compulsive behaviour. People may be genetically predisposed to acquire certain types of phobias that may have had survival value for our prehistoric ancestors. Cognitive factors, such as irrational beliefs and misattributions for panic attacks, may also play a role in anxiety disorders.

- **How does the biological perspective seek to inform our understanding of anxiety disorders?** The biological perspective seeks to uncover the biological underpinnings of anxiety disorders through studying the roles of genetic factors, neurotransmitters, and induction of panic by means of biological challenges.

Define It

projection	neuroticism
two-factor model	benzodiazepines
prepared conditioning	hyperventilation
anxiety sensitivity	gamma-aminobutyric acid

Recall It*

1. Within the psychodynamic perspective, phobias are conceptualized as involving processes of _____.

   a. denial and repression
   b. denial and displacement
   c. displacement and projection
   d. regression and rationalization

2. Within the classic psychodynamic model, compulsions are believed to represent _____.

   a. leakage of repressed conflicts into consciousness
   b. overcontrol of unconscious desires by the superego
   c. efforts to keep repressed impulses from emerging into consciousness
   d. wish fulfillment from unresolved dream material

3. Within the behavioural perspective, we can conceptualize the development of generalized anxiety in terms of _____.

   a. stimulus generalization
   b. response generalization
   c. response discrimination
   d. discrimination learning

4. From a learning perspective, we can conceptualize compulsive behaviours as operant responses that are reinforced by _____.

   a. anxiety associated with obsessive thoughts
   b. relief from anxiety
   c. avoidance of anxiety-inducing cues
   d. social reinforcement

5. Anxiety sensitivity refers to _____.

   a. fear of future events
   b. fear of ambiguous situations
   c. fear of fear
   d. unusual sensitivity to external threats

* Recall It answers can be found on the Companion Website for this text.

Think About It

- Compare and contrast the psychodynamic and learning-based explanations of the classic case of Little Hans. How does this case illustrate the differences between the two models?
- Have you developed any specific phobias, such as fears of small animals, insects, heights, or enclosed spaces? What factors do you think contributed to the development of this phobia (or phobias)? How has the phobia made an impact on your life? How have you coped with it?

TREATMENT OF ANXIETY DISORDERS

Each of the major theoretical perspectives has spawned approaches for treating anxiety disorders. Psychological approaches may differ from one another in their techniques and expressed aims, but they seem to have one thing in common: In one way or another, they encourage clients to face rather than avoid the sources of their anxieties. The biological perspective, by contrast, has focused largely on the use of drugs that quell anxiety.

Psychodynamic Approaches

From the psychodynamic perspective, anxieties reflect the energies attached to unconscious conflicts and the ego's efforts to keep them repressed. Traditional psychoanalysis fosters awareness of how clients' anxiety disorders symbolize their inner conflicts, so the ego can be freed from expending its energy on repression. The ego can thus attend to more creative and enhancing tasks.

More modern psychodynamic therapies also foster clients' awareness of inner sources of conflict. They focus more than traditional approaches on exploring sources of anxiety that arise from current rather than past relationships, however, and they encourage clients to develop more adaptive behaviours. Such therapies are briefer and more directive than traditional psychoanalysis.

Humanistic Approaches

Humanistic theorists believe that many of our anxieties stem from social repression of our genuine selves. Anxiety occurs when the incongruity between one's true inner self and one's social façade draws closer to the level of awareness. A person senses something bad will happen, but is unable to say what it is because the disowned parts of oneself are not directly expressed in consciousness. Because of the disapproval of others, people may fail to develop their individual talents and recognize their authentic feelings. Humanistic therapies thus aim at helping people get in touch with and express their genuine talents and feelings. As a result, clients become free to discover and accept their true selves, rather than reacting with anxiety whenever their true feelings and needs begin to surface.

Biological Approaches

A variety of drugs are used to treat anxiety disorders. Benzodiazepines such as *clonazepam* (brand name Rivotril) and *alprazolam* (brand name Xanax) are often used. Although they tend to have a calming effect, physical dependence (addiction) can develop with chronic use of benzodiazepines, leading to withdrawal symptoms when use of the drugs is stopped abruptly. Withdrawal symptoms include rebound anxiety, insomnia, and restlessness (Joffe & Gardner, 2000). These symptoms prompt many patients to return to using the drugs.

Antidepressant drugs are not only effective in treating depression, they have also proven helpful in treating panic disorder, PTSD, social phobia, and obsessive-compulsive disorder (Cloos, 2005; Fedoroff & Taylor, 2001; Taylor, 2005). Antidepressants may help counter anxiety by normalizing the activity of neurotransmitters in the brain. Some antidepressants in common use for treating panic disorder include the tricyclics *imipramine* (brand name Tofranil) and *clomipramine* (brand name Anafranil) and the selective serotonin reuptake inhibitors (SSRIs) *paroxetine* (brand name Paxil) and *sertraline* (brand name Zoloft). However, troublesome side effects may occur, such as heavy sweating and heart palpitations, which lead many patients to prematurely stop using the drugs. *Alprazolam* also can be helpful in treating panic disorder, social phobia, and generalized anxiety disorder (Antony & Swinson, 2000; Cloos, 2005; Fedoroff & Taylor, 2001).

Obsessive-compulsive disorder often responds to SSRI-type antidepressants—drugs such as *fluoxetine* (Prozac) and *clomipramine* (brand name Anafranil) that work specifically on increasing the availability of the neurotransmitter serotonin in the brain (Dell'Osso, Nestadt, Allen, & Hollander, 2006). The effectiveness of these drugs leads researchers to suspect that a problem with serotonin transmission in the brain may be involved in the development of OCD in at least some people with the disorder (Denys, van Nieuwerburgh, Deforce, & Westenberg, 2006). But as noted by University of Ottawa researchers, some patients fail to respond to these drugs, and among those who do respond, a complete remission of symptoms is uncommon (Blier, Habib, & Flament, 2006). In such cases, neurosurgery is sometimes performed, in which connections between brain regions are severed. For example, a cingulotomy might be performed, in which the cingulate gyrus—a small section of brain connecting the limbic system and frontal lobes—is severed. Although some neurosurgical studies have found positive results, it is still too early to say whether neurosurgery is safe and effective for people with OCD who have failed to benefit from other treatments (Schruers, Koning, Luermans, Haack, & Griez, 2005).

A potential problem with drug therapy is that patients may attribute clinical improvement to the drugs and not their own resources. Nor do such drugs produce cures. Relapses are common after patients discontinue medication (Antony & Swinson, 2000). Re-emergence of panic is likely unless cognitive-behavioural treatment is provided to help panic patients modify their cognitive overreactions to bodily sensations (Taylor, 2000). Drug therapy is sometimes combined with cognitive-behavioural therapy, although it is currently unclear whether combined treatment is more effective than either treatment alone (Pull, 2007).

Learning-Based Approaches

Behavioural treatments based on learning approaches include a variety of techniques aimed at helping individuals confront the objects or situations that elicit their fears and anxieties.

Systematic Desensitization

Adam has a phobia for receiving injections. His behaviour therapist treats him as he reclines in a comfortable padded chair. In a state of deep muscle relaxation, Adam observes slides projected on a screen. A slide of a nurse holding a needle has just been shown three times, 30 seconds at a time. Each time, Adam has shown no anxiety. So now a slightly more discomforting slide is shown: one of the nurse aiming the needle toward someone's bare arm. After 15 seconds, our armchair adventurer notices twinges of discomfort and raises a finger as a signal (speaking might disturb his relaxation). The projector operator turns off the light, and Adam spends a couple of minutes imagining his "safe scene"—lying on a beach beneath the tropical sun. Then the slide is shown again. This time Adam views it for 30 seconds before feeling anxiety.

RATHUS, 1996

fear-stimulus hierarchy Ordered series of increasingly fearful stimuli. Used in the behavioural techniques of *systematic desensitization* and *gradual exposure*.

Adam is undergoing systematic desensitization, a fear-reduction procedure originated by psychiatrist Joseph Wolpe (1958). Systematic desensitization is a gradual process. Clients learn to handle progressively more disturbing stimuli while they remain relaxed. About 10 to 20 stimuli are arranged in a sequence or hierarchy—called a **fear-stimulus hierarchy**—according to their capacity to evoke anxiety. By using their imagination or by viewing photos, clients are exposed to the items in the hierarchy, gradually imagining themselves approaching the target behaviour—be it the ability to receive an injection or remain in an enclosed room or elevator—without undue anxiety.

Joseph Wolpe developed systematic desensitization on the assumption that maladaptive anxiety responses, like other behaviours, are learned or conditioned. He assumed they can be unlearned by counterconditioning. In counterconditioning, a response incompatible with anxiety is made to appear under conditions that usually elicit anxiety. Muscle relaxation is generally used as the incompatible response, and followers of Wolpe usually use the method of progressive relaxation (described in Chapter 4) to help clients acquire relaxation skills. For this reason, Adam's therapist is teaching Adam to experience relaxation in the presence of (otherwise) anxiety-evoking slides of needles.

Behaviourally oriented therapists, like Wolpe, explain the benefits of systematic desensitization and similar therapies in terms of principles of counterconditioning. Cognitively oriented therapists note, however, that remaining in the presence of phobic imagery, rather than running from it, is also likely to enhance one's confidence about being able to manage the phobic stimuli without anxiety.

Gradual Exposure This method helps people overcome phobias through a stepwise approach of actual exposure to the phobic stimuli. The effectiveness of exposure therapy is well established, making it the treatment of choice for specific phobias (Antony & McCabe, 2005; Antony & Swinson, 2000). Here exposure therapy was used in treating a case of claustrophobia:

Gradual exposure. In gradual exposure, a client is exposed to a fear-stimulus hierarchy in real life situations, often with a therapist or companion serving in a supportive role. The therapist or companion gradually withdraws direct support, so as to encourage the person to accomplish the exposure tasks increasingly on his or her own. Gradual exposure is often combined with cognitive techniques that focus on helping the client replace anxiety-producing thoughts and beliefs with calming, rational alternatives.

Claustrophobia (fear of enclosed spaces) is quite common. Kevin's claustrophobia took the form of a fear of riding on elevators. Interestingly, Kevin worked as an elevator mechanic! Kevin spent his workdays repairing elevators. Unless it was absolutely necessary, however, Kevin managed to complete the repairs without riding in the elevator. He would climb the stairs to the floor where an elevator was stuck, make repairs, and hit the down button. He would then race downstairs to see that the elevator had operated correctly. When his work required an elevator ride, panic would seize him as the doors closed. Kevin tried to cope by praying for divine intervention to prevent him from passing out before the doors opened.

Kevin related the origin of his phobia to an accident three years earlier in which he had been pinned in his overturned car for nearly an hour. He remembered feelings of helplessness and suffocation. Kevin developed claustrophobia—a fear of situations from which he could not escape, such as flying on an airplane, driving through a tunnel, taking public transportation, and, of course, riding in an elevator. Kevin's fear had become so incapacitating that he was seriously considering switching jobs, although the change would require considerable financial sacrifice. Each night, he lay awake wondering whether he would be able to cope the next day if he were required to test-ride an elevator.

Kevin's therapy involved gradual exposure. Gradual exposure, like systematic desensitization, is a step-by-step procedure that involves a fear-stimulus hierarchy. In gradual exposure, however, the target behaviour is approached in actuality rather than symbolically. Moreover, the individual is active rather than relaxed in a recliner.

A typical hierarchy for overcoming a fear of riding on an elevator might include the following steps:

1. Standing outside the elevator
2. Standing in the elevator with the door open
3. Standing in the elevator with the door closed
4. Taking the elevator down one floor
5. Taking the elevator up one floor
6. Taking the elevator down two floors
7. Taking the elevator up two floors
8. Taking the elevator down two floors and then up two floors
9. Taking the elevator down to the basement
10. Taking the elevator up to the highest floor and down again

Clients begin at step one and do not progress to step two until they are able to remain calm on the first. If they become bothered by anxiety, they remove themselves from the situation and regain calmness by practising muscle relaxation or focusing on soothing mental imagery. The encounter is then repeated as often as necessary to reach and sustain feelings of calmness. They then proceed to the next step, repeating the process.

Kevin was also trained to practise self-relaxation and talk calmly and rationally to himself to help him remain calm during his exposure trials. Whenever he began to feel even slightly anxious, he would tell himself to calm down and relax. He was able to counter the disruptive belief that he was going to fall apart if he was trapped in an elevator with rational self-statements such as, "Just relax. I may experience some anxiety, but it's nothing that I haven't been through before. In a few moments I'll feel relieved."

Kevin gradually overcame his phobia but still occasionally experienced some anxiety, which he interpreted as a reminder of his former phobia. He did not exaggerate the importance of these feelings. Now and then it dawned on him that an elevator he was servicing had once occasioned fear. One day following his treatment, Kevin was repairing an elevator that serviced a bank vault 30 metres underground. The experience of moving deeper and deeper underground aroused fear, but Kevin did not panic. He repeated to himself, "It's only a couple of seconds and I'll be out." By the time he took his second trip down, he was much calmer.

THE AUTHORS' FILES

Cognitive Techniques The most widely used cognitive technique is Beck's cognitive therapy, which seeks to identify dysfunctional or distorted beliefs and replace them with rational or adaptive alternatives. For example, people with social phobia might think no one at a party will want to talk with them and that they will wind up lonely and isolated for the rest of their lives. Cognitive therapists help clients recognize the logical flaws in their thinking and assist them in viewing situations rationally. Clients may be asked to gather evidence to test out their beliefs, which may lead them to alter beliefs they find are not grounded in reality. Therapists may encourage clients with social phobia to test their beliefs that they are bound to be ignored, rejected, or ridiculed by others in social gatherings by attending a party, initiating conversations, and monitoring other people's reactions. Therapists may also help clients develop social skills to improve their interpersonal effectiveness and teach them how to handle social rejection, if it should occur, without catastrophizing.

One example of cognitive techniques is **cognitive restructuring**. This involves a process in which therapists help clients pinpoint their self-defeating thoughts and generate rational alternatives so they learn to cope with anxiety-provoking situations. Kevin learned to replace self-defeating thoughts with rational alternatives and to practise speaking rationally and calmly to himself during his exposure trials. Consider the case of Phyllis, who also suffered from an elevator phobia:

cognitive restructuring Cognitive therapy method that involves replacing irrational or self-defeating thoughts and attitudes with rational alternatives.

Phyllis, a 32-year-old writer and mother of two sons, had not been on an elevator in 16 years. Her life revolved around finding ways to avoid appointments and social events on high floors. She had suffered from a fear of elevators since the age of eight, when she had been stuck between floors with her grandmother.

To help overcome her fear of elevators, Phyllis imagined herself getting stuck in an elevator and countering the self-defeating thoughts she might experience with rational self-statements. She closed her eyes and reported the thoughts that would come to mind. The psychologist encouraged her to create a rational counterpoint to each of them. She then repeated the exercise in her imagination and practised replacing the self-defeating thoughts with rational alternatives, as in the following examples:

Self-Defeating Thought	Rational Alternative
Oh, oh, I'm stuck. I'm going to lose control.	Relax. Just think coolly, what do I have to do next?
I can't take it. I'm going to pass out.	Okay, practise your deep breathing. Help will be coming shortly.
I'm having a panic attack. I can't stand it.	You've experienced all these feelings before. Just let them pass through.
If it takes an hour, that would be horrible.	That would be annoying, but it wouldn't necessarily be horrible. I've gotten stuck in traffic longer than that.
I've got to get out of here.	Stay calm. There's no real danger. I can just sit down and imagine I'm somewhere else until someone comes to help.

THE AUTHORS' FILES

Behavioural Treatment of Social Phobia Exposure therapy is also an effective form of treatment for social phobia (Cottraux, 2005; Fedoroff & Taylor, 2001). In exposure therapy, clients are instructed to enter increasingly stressful social situations and to remain in those situations until the urge to escape has lessened. The therapist may help guide them during exposure trials, gradually withdrawing direct support so clients become capable of handling the situations on their own. Exposure treatment is often combined with cognitive techniques that assist clients in replacing maladaptive anxiety-inducing thoughts with more rational alternatives and with behavioural techniques, such as training in conversational skills. The cognitive and behavioural treatments for social phobia have been shown to be effective and their benefits appear to be durable (Fedoroff & Taylor, 2001; Rowa & Antony, 2005).

Flooding is a type of exposure therapy in which subjects are exposed to intensely anxiety-provoking situations. Why? It is believed anxiety that has been conditioned to a phobic stimulus should extinguish if the individual remains in the phobic situation for a long enough period of time and nothing traumatic occurs. Typically, the phobic individual either avoids the phobic stimulus or beats a hasty retreat at the first opportunity for escape. Thus, no opportunity for unlearning (extinguishing) the fear response occurs. Flooding is just as effective as other forms of cognitive-behavioural treatments but may work faster.

Behavioural Treatment of Agoraphobia Evidence shows gradual exposure to fear-inducing stimuli to be more effective than control conditions in reducing avoidance behaviour in people with agoraphobia (Taylor, 2000). Treatment is stepwise and gradually exposes the phobic individual to increasingly fearful stimulus situations, such as walking through congested streets or shopping in department stores. A trusted companion or perhaps the therapist may accompany the person during the exposure trials. The eventual goal is for the person to be able to handle each situation alone and without discomfort or an urge to escape. The benefits of gradual exposure are typically enduring.

Behavioural Treatment of Posttraumatic Stress Disorder Exposure therapy has achieved good results in reducing symptoms of PTSD (National Institute for Clinical Excellence, 2005; Taylor, 2005). Exposure to cues associated with a trauma may involve talking about the trauma, re-experiencing the trauma in one's imagination, viewing related slides or films, or visiting the scene of the event. For combat-related PTSD, homework assignments may involve visiting war memorials or viewing war movies. The person comes to gradually re-experience the traumatic event and accompanying anxiety in a safe setting that is free of negative consequences, which allows extinction to take its course. Exposure therapy is often supplemented with cognitive restructuring that focuses on replacing dysfunctional thoughts with rational alternatives. Training in stress-management skills, such as self-relaxation, may help enhance the client's ability to cope with the troubling features of PTSD, such as heightened arousal and the desire to run away from

Virtual Therapy

Virtual reality, a computer-generated simulated environment, has become a therapeutic tool. By donning a specialized helmet and gloves that are connected to a computer, a person with a fear of heights, for example, can encounter frightening stimuli in this virtual world, such as riding a glass-enclosed elevator to the 49th floor, peering over a railing on a balcony on the 20th floor, or flying in a helicopter over a war zone (Pull, 2005). Recent findings from Canadian investigators suggest that virtual therapy is also useful for treating driving phobia (Wald & Taylor, 2003). Here, a client practises driving in a simulator under increasingly more challenging situations (e.g., on a quiet street, then in heavy traffic, then driving in the rain). By a process of exposure to a series of increasingly more frightening virtual stimuli, while progressing only when fears at each preceding step diminish, people learn to overcome fears in much the same way they would had they followed a program of graduated exposure to phobic stimuli in real-life situations. The advantage of virtual reality is that it provides an opportunity to experience situations that might be difficult or impossible to arrange in reality. Virtual therapy is a promising treatment that has been used successfully in helping people overcome many different kinds of phobias, including fears of heights, driving, flying, and spiders (Pull, 2005).

We have only begun to explore the potential therapeutic uses of this new technology. Therapists are experimenting with virtual therapy to help people overcome other types of fears, such as fear of public speaking and agoraphobia. In other applications, virtual therapy may help clients work through unresolved conflicts with significant figures in their lives by allowing them to confront these "people" in a virtual environment. Self-help therapy modules, consisting of compact discs and virtual reality helmets and gloves, may even begin to appear on the shelves of your neighbourhood computer software store in the not-too-distant future. With these self-help modules, people may be able in their own living rooms to confront objects or situations they fear, or to learn to stop smoking or lose weight, all with the help and guidance of a "virtual therapist."

Scene from driving simulator. Virtual reality therapy using a driving simulator can be useful in treating driving phobia.

trauma-related stimuli. Training in anger-management skills may also be helpful, especially with combat veterans who have PTSD (Taylor, 2005).

Additional interventions may also be required. Specialist programs may be needed for people with two or more disorders, such as PTSD combined with substance-use disorders (e.g., Najavits, 2002). Some of these programs cater to specific groups, such as the Tsow-Tun Le Lum residential program for Aboriginal adults located in Nanaimo, British Columbia. Other programs need to be very broad in focus in order to address the needs of their clients. Survivors of torture, for example—many of whom have arrived in Canada as refugees—often have PTSD combined with a host of other practical problems, such as the need for housing, education in written and spoken English, and legal aid to help with refugee claims. Organizations such as the Canadian Centre for Victims of Torture, located in Toronto, provide important assistance in these areas.

One controversial but widely used PTSD treatment is "eye movement desensitization and reprocessing" (EMDR; Shapiro, 2001). The main part of an EMDR intervention requires a patient to recall trauma-related memories while also attending to some form of external oscillatory stimulation. Stimulation is typically induced by the therapist moving a finger from side to side across the patient's field of vision, which induces eye movement. Sets of eye movements are induced until distress is reduced. There are several reasons why EMDR is controversial, including claims by its founder, Francine Shapiro, that EMDR works more rapidly and is more effective than other psychological treatments, and that it works in a fundamentally different way than behavioural treatments. These claims have not been supported by research; the most rigorous studies to date indicate that EMDR works no faster and is no more effective than other cognitive-behavioural treatments (Rothbaum, Astin, & Marsteller, 2005; Taylor et al., 2003). In fact, Taylor et al. (2003) found that behaviour therapy was more effective than EMDR, and other researchers have concluded that EMDR is simply a form of behavioural (exposure) therapy (Davidson & Parker, 2001; Rothbaum et al., 2005). Moreover, there is no compelling reason why eye movements would reduce distress. Indeed, research shows that eye movements do not contribute to treatment efficacy (Davidson & Parker, 2001).

Behavioural Treatment of Obsessive-Compulsive Disorder Behaviour therapy has achieved impressive results in treating obsessive-compulsive disorder with a combination of *exposure and response prevention* within intensive, carefully monitored programs (Clark, 2004). Exposure involves purposefully placing oneself in situations that evoke obsessive thoughts. For many people, such situations are hard to avoid. Leaving the house, for example, can trigger obsessional thoughts about whether or not the gas jets are turned off or the windows and doors are locked. Response prevention involves the effort to physically prevent a compulsive behaviour from occurring. Through exposure with response prevention, people with OCD learn to tolerate the anxiety triggered by their obsessive thoughts while they are prevented from performing their compulsive rituals. With repeated exposure, the anxiety eventually subsides and the person feels less compelled to perform the ritual. Extinction, or the weakening of the anxiety response following repeated presentation of the obsessional cues in the absence of any aversive consequences, is believed to underlie the treatment effect. Overall, many people benefit from this treatment (Clark, 2004). Cognitive therapy is often combined with exposure therapy. The therapist focuses on helping the person correct cognitive distortions such as tendencies to overestimate the likelihood and severity of feared consequences.

It appears that behavioural therapy is at least as effective as drug therapy (use of SSRI-type antidepressants) and may produce more lasting results (Antony & Swinson, 2000; Taylor, 2000). Yet it remains to be seen whether a combination of drugs and behaviour therapy is more effective than either approach alone.

Behavioural therapy may also change brain function as well as behaviour. People with obsessive-compulsive disorder who received cognitive-behavioural therapy show changes in their brain functioning, as measured by PET scans (Baxter et al., 2000). A part of the brain that is unusually active in persons with OCD showed a lessening of activity—the same kind of change seen when OCD is treated with the antidepressant Prozac.

Cognitive-Behavioural Treatment of Generalized Anxiety Cognitive-behaviour therapists use a combination of techniques to treat generalized anxiety disorder, including relaxation training; substitution of adaptive thoughts for intrusive, anxiety-inducing thoughts; and decatastrophizing (avoiding tendencies to think the worst). Studies from Concordia University, Laval University, and elsewhere indicate that cognitive-behavioural approaches are superior to control conditions and yield equivalent or better effects than alternative drug or psychological therapies (Dugas & Koerner, 2005; Ladouceur et al., 2000; Mitte, 2005).

Cognitive-Behavioural Treatment of Panic Disorder The treatment components in cognitive-behavioural therapy (CBT) for panic disorder include training in skills relating to handling panic attacks without catastrophizing, breathing retraining, exposure to situations linked to panic attacks and to bodily cues associated with panic, and training in relaxation (Taylor, 2000).

Therapists helps clients think differently about their bodily cues, such as passing sensations of dizziness or heart palpitations. Receiving corrective information that these sensations will subside naturally and are not signs of an impending catastrophe helps clients learn to cope with them without panicking (Taylor, 2000). (Persons who complain of cardiovascular symptoms should also be evaluated medically to ensure they are physically healthy.) On a cognitive level, clients are taught to replace catastrophizing thoughts and self-statements ("I'm having a heart attack") with calming, rational alternatives ("Calm down. These are panicky feelings that will soon pass").

Breathing retraining aims at restoring a normal level of carbon dioxide in the blood by having clients breathe slowly and deeply from the abdomen to avoid the shallow, rapid breathing (hyperventilation) that leads to breathing off too much carbon dioxide. In some treatment programs, people with panic disorder purposefully hyperventilate in the controlled setting of the treatment clinic in order to discover for themselves the relationship between breathing off too much carbon dioxide and cardiovascular sensations. Through these first-hand experiences, they learn to calm themselves down and cope with these sensations rather than overreacting. Some of the common elements of CBT for panic are shown in Table 5.9.

The efficacy of CBT in treating panic disorder is well established (Antony & Swinson, 2000; Taylor, 2000). Investigators find that from roughly two-thirds to about four-fifths of panic patients treated with CBT become panic-free by the end of treatment, and the gains from CBT appear to be long-lasting (Barlow, 2002). Despite the common belief that panic disorder is best treated with psychiatric drugs, CBT appears to produce even better results than drug treatment with imipramine or benzodiazepines (Taylor, 2000).

TABLE 5.9

Elements of Cognitive-Behavioural Programs for Treatment of Panic Disorder

Self-Monitoring	Keeping a log of panic attacks to help determine situational stimuli that might trigger them.
Exposure	A program of gradual exposure to situations in which panic attacks have occurred. During exposure trials, the person engages in self-relaxation and rational self-talk to prevent anxiety from spiralling out of control. In some programs, participants learn to tolerate changes in bodily sensations associated with panic attacks by experiencing these sensations within a controlled setting of the treatment clinic. The person may be spun around in a chair to induce feelings of dizziness, learning in the process that such sensations are not dangerous or signs of imminent harm.
Development of Coping Responses	Developing coping skills to interrupt the vicious cycle in which overreactions to anxiety cues or cardiovascular sensations culminate in panic attacks. Behavioural methods focus on deep, regular breathing and relaxation training. Cognitive methods focus on modifying catastrophic misinterpretations of bodily sensations. Breathing retraining may be used to help the individual avoid hyperventilation during panic attacks.

A CLOSER LOOK

Coping with a Panic Attack

People who have panic attacks usually feel their hearts pounding such that they are overwhelmed and unable to cope. They typically feel an urge to flee the situation as quickly as possible. If escape is impossible, they may become immobilized and "freeze" until the attack dissipates. What can you do if you suffer a panic attack or an intense anxiety reaction? Let us suggest a few coping responses:

- Don't let your breathing get out of hand. Breathe slowly and deeply.
- "Talk yourself down." Tell yourself to relax. Tell yourself you're not going to die. Tell yourself no matter how painful the attack is, it is likely to pass soon.

- Find someone to help you through the attack. Telephone someone you know and trust. Talk about anything at all until you regain control.
- Don't fall into the trap of making yourself housebound to avert future attacks.
- If you are uncertain as to whether or not sensations such as pain or tightness in the chest have physical causes, seek immediate medical assistance. Even if you suspect your attack may "only" be one of anxiety, it is safer to have a medical evaluation than to diagnose yourself.

You need not suffer recurrent panic attacks and fears about loss of control. When in doubt, or if attacks are persistent or frightening, consult a professional.

In this chapter, we have explored the diagnostic class of anxiety disorders. In Chapter 6, we examine dissociative and somatoform disorders, which have been historically linked to the anxiety disorders as neuroses.

Treatment of Anxiety Disorders

Review It

- **How is the treatment of anxiety disorders approached from the major contemporary theoretical perspectives?** Traditional psychoanalysis helps people work through unconscious conflicts that are thought to underlie anxiety disorders. Modern psychodynamic approaches also focus on current disturbed relationships and encourage clients to assume more adaptive behaviour patterns. The biological perspectives have led to the development of various drug therapies to treat anxiety disorders.

  Learning perspectives encompass a broad range of behavioural and cognitive-behavioural techniques to help people overcome anxiety-related problems. Exposure methods help people with phobias overcome their fears through gradual exposure to the phobic stimuli.

  Obsessive-compulsive disorder is often treated with a combination of exposure and response prevention. Relaxation training is often used to help people overcome generalized anxiety. Behavioural treatment of PTSD incorporates progressive exposure to trauma-related cues and training in stress management skills, such as self-relaxation.

  Cognitive approaches such as rational-emotive therapy and cognitive therapy help people identify and correct cognitive errors that give rise to or maintain anxiety disorders. Cognitive-behavioural approaches to panic disorder focus on helping panic-prone people learn to use deep-breathing skills to tone down their bodily alarm in anxiety-inducing situations and to avoid catastrophizing changes in bodily sensations.

Define It

fear-stimulus hierarchy
cognitive restructuring

Recall It*

1. The various psychological approaches to treating anxiety discussed in the text all share a common approach of encouraging clients to _____.
   a. use drugs to manage anxiety symptoms
   b. confront the sources of their anxieties
   c. distract themselves from their anxieties
   d. understand the childhood roots of their anxieties

2. John is seeking help for overcoming an anxiety disorder. His therapist helps him become aware of how his symptoms may be symbolizing inner conflicts of which he is unaware. The therapist is using a(n) _____ approach to conceptualize John's disorder.
   a. psychodynamic
   b. humanistic-existential
   c. behavioural
   d. cognitive

3. The most widely used drugs for treating states of tension associated with anxiety disorders are _____.
   a. antidepressants
   b. minor tranquillizers
   c. major tranquillizers
   d. analgesics

4. The type of exposure therapy involving exposure to intensely anxiety-provoking situations is _____.
   a. progressive exposure
   b. systematic desensitization
   c. overexposure
   d. flooding

5. The commonly used behavioural treatment for agoraphobia is _____.
   a. flooding
   b. response prevention
   c. gradual exposure
   d. cognitive restructuring

* Recall It answers can be found on the Companion Website for this text.

Think About It

- What are the advantages and disadvantages of using anti-anxiety drugs?
- Select a particular type of anxiety disorder and describe how its treatment would be approached by therapists representing the psychodynamic, learning-based, cognitive, and biological perspectives.

WEBLINKS

Anxiety Treatment and Research Centre
www.anxietytreatment.ca/info.htm
Information on anxiety disorders, including Canadian treatment resources.

Anxiety Disorders Association of Canada
www.anxietycanada.ca
Information and links to provincial anxiety disorder associations.

Anxiety Disorders Association of America
www.adaa.org
The ADAA's website contains information on the nature and treatment of anxiety disorders, as well as links to self-help books and other resources.

Obsessive-Compulsive Foundation
www.ocfoundation.org
This nonprofit organization provides information on obsessive-compulsive disorder and its treatment.

National Center for PTSD
www.ncptsd.org
This organization's site contains a good deal of useful information on posttraumatic stress reactions and their treatment.

Anxiety Disorders

Types of Anxiety Disorders

Panic Disorder

- Recurrent, unexpected panic attacks
- With or without agoraphobia

Agoraphobia

- Involves fear of places and situations from which it might be difficult or embarrassing to escape

Generalized Anxiety Disorder

- Excessive anxiety and worry

Phobic Disorders

Specific Phobia
- Severe fear of specific objects or situations

Social Phobia
- Severe fear of social or performance situations

Obsessive-Compulsive Disorder

- Recurrent obsessions and/or compulsions

Posttraumatic Stress Disorder

- Persistent symptoms after exposure to trauma
- Re-experiencing, avoidance, emotional numbing, hyperarousal

Acute Stress Disorder

- Similar to posttraumatic stress disorder
- Symptoms last only days or weeks after exposure to trauma

Theoretical Perspectives

Psychodynamic

- Anxiety is a signal that threatening sexual or aggressive impulses are nearing the level of awareness.
- Ego mobilizes defence mechanisms to ward off the threatening impulses.

Learning (Behavioural)

- Two-factor model: Fears are acquired by classical conditioning and maintained by operant conditioning.
- Prepared conditioning: People might be genetically predisposed to fear certain types of stimuli.

Cognitive

- Dysfunctional thinking patterns (self-defeating or irrational beliefs).

Biological

- Genetic predisposition (diathesis).
- Dysfunctional neurotransmitter systems (e.g., GABA, serotonin, or norepinephrine systems).

Treatment of Anxiety Disorders

Psychodynamic

- Traditional psychoanalysis: Aims to increase awareness of how anxiety disorders symbolize inner conflicts.
- Modern approaches: Focus more on current relationships and encourage coping skills.

Learning-based

- Behavioural treatments: Systematic desensitization; gradual exposure.
- Cognitive treatments: Rational emotive behaviour therapy; cognitive theory.

Humanistic

- Assumption: Anxiety stems from social repression of the genuine self.
- Goal: To help people get in touch with and express their genuine talents and feelings.

Biological

- Various types of medications. Example: reuptake inhibitors (e.g., sertraline).

CHAPTER 6

Dissociative and Somatoform Disorders

CHAPTER OUTLINE

Dissociative Disorders
Somatoform Disorders

Did You Know That...

See the underlined text on the pages indicated below for more information on these interesting and often misunderstood facts.

- The term *split personality* is a lay term that refers to multiple personality, not schizophrenia? (p. 220)

- At some time or another, the majority of adults have episodes of feeling detached from their own bodies or thought processes? (p. 222)

- The great majority of people with multiple personalities were physically or sexually abused as children? (p. 226)

- Some people undergo operations even though they know nothing is medically wrong with them? (p. 229)

- Some people who have lost their ability to see or move their legs have displayed a strangely indifferent attitude toward their physical condition? (p. 231)

- There was an epidemic in China in the 1980s affecting more than 3000 people who fell prey to the belief that their genitals were shrinking and retracting into their bodies? (p. 236)

IN THE MIDDLE AGES, the clergy used rites of exorcism to bring forth demons from people believed to be possessed. Curious incantations were heard during the contests for victims' souls between the exorcist and the demons believed to lurk within.

Curious phrasings were also heard more recently in 20th-century Los Angeles. They were intended to elicit another sort of demon from Kenneth Bianchi, a suspect in an investigation.

At one point, a question was put to Bianchi: "Part, are you the same thing as Ken or are you different?" The interviewer was not a member of the clergy, but a police psychiatrist. The interviewee had been dubbed the "Hillside strangler" by the press. He had terrorized the city, leaving prostitutes dead in the mountains that bank the metropolis.

Under hypnosis—not religious incantations—Bianchi claimed a hidden personality or "part" named "Steve" had committed the murders. "Ken" knew nothing of them. Bianchi claimed to be suffering from multiple personality disorder (now called *dissociative identity disorder*), one of the intriguing but perplexing psychological disorders we explore in this chapter. Dissociative identity disorder is classified as a dissociative disorder, a type of psychological disorder involving a change or disturbance in the functions of self-identity, memory, or consciousness that make the personality whole. Normally speaking, we know who we are. We may not be certain of ourselves in an existential, philosophical sense, but we know our names, where we live, and what we do for a living. We also tend to remember the salient events of our lives. We may not recall every detail, and we may confuse what we ate for dinner on Tuesday with what we had on Monday, but we generally know what we have been doing for the past days, weeks, and years. Normally speaking, there is a unity to consciousness that gives rise to a sense of self. We perceive ourselves as progressing through space and time. In the dissociative disorders, one or more of these aspects of daily living is disturbed—sometimes bizarrely so.

This chapter also focuses on *somatoform disorders*, a class of psychological disorders involving complaints of physical symptoms that are believed to reflect underlying psychological issues. In some cases there is no apparent medical basis to the physical symptoms, such as in the form of hysterical blindness or numbness (now called *conversion disorder*). In other cases, people may hold an exaggerated view of the meaning of their physical symptoms, believing them to be signs of underlying serious illnesses despite reassurances of their physicians to the contrary.

The dissociative and conversion disorders were grouped with the anxiety disorders in earlier versions of the diagnostic manual under the more general category of "neurosis." The common grouping was based on the psychodynamic model that held these various disorders involve maladaptive ways of managing anxiety. In the anxiety disorders, the appearance of disturbing levels of anxiety was expressed directly in behaviour, such as in a phobia where a person would avoid a feared object or situation. But the role of anxiety in the dissociative and somatoform disorders was inferred rather than expressed in behaviour. Persons with *dissociative disorders* may show no signs of overt anxiety. However, they manifest other psychological problems, such as loss of memory or changes in identity, that are theorized within the psychodynamic model to serve the purpose of keeping the underlying sources of anxiety out of awareness. Likewise, people with conversion disorder often show a strange indifference to physical problems (e.g., loss of vision). Here, too, it was theorized the "symptoms" mask unconscious sources of anxiety. Some theorists interpret indifference to symptoms to mean there is an underlying benefit to them; that is, they help prevent anxiety from intruding into consciousness. But, as we will see later, this interpretation has been recently challenged.

The DSM now separates the anxiety disorders from the other categories of neuroses—the dissociative and somatoform disorders—with which they were historically linked. Yet many practitioners continue to use the broad conceptualization of neuroses as a framework for classifying the anxiety, dissociative, and somatoform disorders.

DISSOCIATIVE DISORDERS

The major dissociative disorders include *dissociative identity disorder*, *dissociative amnesia*, *dissociative fugue*, and *depersonalization disorder*. In each case, there is a disruption or dissociation ("splitting off") of the functions of identity, memory, or consciousness, which normally combine to make us whole.

Dissociative Identity Disorder

In response to a newspaper inquiry, Nancy came forth to tell her story about her struggles with a dissociative identity disorder. Nancy, who resides in Ontario, gave the following account of her problems, how they arose, and how she has worked to overcome them:

The piano has a place of honour in Nancy's living room. It's a red mahogany Lesage made in Quebec. But Nancy fears that piano. She will play it only if the doors are locked or if her husband Hugh is around. When she was a girl, she loved to play the classics every day. Sonatinas, rondos, and allegros by Mozart. She concentrated so hard. She shut herself off from her surroundings. "I felt I was inside the music." And while Nancy played, her father and sometimes other men molested her. Her father touched her; he masturbated. From the time she was a toddler, he had abused her. It could happen anywhere in the house. At the piano, she had the music to take her away. But wherever she was, Nancy had grown skilled at using her mind to float away from her father's grasp. She could peel off a piece of herself, so she hardly felt the pain. That ability saved her then. But now it's a problem.

She got therapy and soon even started a self-help group. "I found out it's okay to talk about what happened, to say it out loud. I realized it really wasn't my fault." After a few years, she left the group. "I thought I was doing quite well. I'd learned to handle the flashbacks and the memories." But she started getting sick a lot again. There was something that had bothered Nancy for years—the voices inside her. And by this point, they seemed awfully persistent. "There's a saying that it's okay to talk to yourself and as long as you don't answer, you're not crazy." But Nancy noticed she was waking up at night, hearing herself talking and answering. She had said something to her husband years before, "Hughie, I think I'm going crazy. I hear all these voices. They're talking, fighting, arguing." The arguments that rattled through her head could be about something as simple as whether to serve a chicken dinner with baked potatoes or rice. Or whether to go to the mall. "It was like Siamese twins who constantly talk back and forth because they can't do anything without each other." And there was amnesia, confusion, lost time. Nancy was sure she had invited that couple to dinner. They were puzzled why she got angry when they didn't show up. We all dissociate.

We all daydream; we cruise along a straight stretch of highway and later we don't really remember the details at all. But for someone like Nancy, those moments of lost time were deeper, more frequent. Her earliest memory of abuse is from when she was about three years old. The abuse continued until she was 18, when she got married. Hugh showed up in Nancy's life and helped her. She told him about some of the past. "You need to talk about this," he told her.

Nancy said she was fine. She was married, to the right man. And she was a nurse, which she'd always wanted to be. But that fell apart one night at work. Nancy went to walk into the medication room and walked into the wall instead. She collapsed. She was sick for months. She couldn't drive, couldn't climb stairs. She vomited and had severe headaches. Nancy underwent many tests. Maybe it was a brain tumour. Or an inner-ear problem. Finally, a neurologist said, "Nancy, is it possible you've been under stress?" "It was like a light being turned on," she says. "And I said, 'Yes, I'm 36 and I've been under stress for 33 years.'"

She was then sent to two psychiatrists. Both made the diagnosis of dissociative identity disorder. There appear to be eight different parts to Nancy's personality. In her mind, each has its own physical appearance. She pictures them with different hair, different glasses. There is Malveen. She's shy, introverted, overwhelmed with guilt. This part of Nancy stopped growing when she was a teenager and met Hugh. There's Dorothy, well organized, able to do ten things at once. There's another part that's all anger. And there is Just Me, that persistent part she always argued with. Good therapy and the right medication sent that personality away. Nancy continues to work on her recovery.

Six years earlier, one of the men who abused her was convicted of assault, gross indecency, and sexual intercourse with a female under 14. The judge called the crimes abhorrent. But because of the way that the judge addressed the jury, the man was granted a new trial. He died before it took place. Nancy's mother and father, both abused as children, are gone now. Mother, a nurse, died 13 years ago in Nancy's home. Father, a postal worker then city employee, died seven years ago. Nancy had been looking after him, cleaning his apartment, getting his groceries. She had confronted him and wrung out an apology. He was about to be charged when he died.

Therapy has been hard and slow, but Nancy is not discouraged. "Each of these parts of me was beneficial. They helped me to survive. But it would be good for me now to merge these parts. It would be good to become one healthy person."

ADAPTED FROM P. WILSON (2000), KEEPING PAIN AT A DISTANCE, *THE HAMILTON SPECTATOR*, MAY 16. QUOTATIONS REPRINTED BY PERMISSION OF *THE HAMILTON SPECTATOR*.

Nancy was diagnosed with multiple personality disorder, which is now called **dissociative identity disorder**. In this disorder, sometimes referred to as *split personality*, two or more personalities—each with well-defined traits and memories—"occupy" one person. They may or may not be aware of one another. There are many variations. Sometimes two personalities vie for control. Sometimes there is one dominant or core personality and several subordinate ones. Themes of sexual ambivalence (sexual openness vs. inhibition) and shifting sexual orientations are particularly common. It is as if conflicting internal impulses cannot coexist or achieve dominance. As a result, each is expressed as the cardinal or steering trait of an alternate personality. The clinician can sometimes bring forth alternate personalities by inviting them to make themselves known, as in asking, "Is there another part of you that wants to say something to me?"

The case of Margaret illustrates the purported emergence of an alternate personality:

dissociative identity disorder
Dissociative disorder in which a person has two or more distinct or alternate personalities.

[Margaret explained that] she often "heard a voice telling her to say things and do things." It was, she said, "a terrible voice" that sometimes threatened to "take over completely." When it was finally suggested to [Margaret] that she let the voice "take over," she closed her eyes, clenched her fists, and grimaced for a few moments during which she was out of contact with those around her. Suddenly she opened her eyes and one was in the presence of another person. Her name, she said, was "Harriet." Whereas Margaret had been paralyzed, and complained of fatigue, headache and backache, Harriet felt well, and she at once proceeded to walk unaided around the interviewing room. She spoke scornfully of Margaret's religiousness, her invalidism, and her puritanical life, professing that she herself liked to drink and "go partying" but that Margaret was always going to church and reading the Bible. "But," she said impishly and proudly, "I make her miserable—I make her say and do things she doesn't want to." At length, at the interviewer's suggestion, Harriet reluctantly agreed to "bring Margaret back," and after more grimacing and fist clenching, Margaret reappeared, paralyzed, complaining of her headache and backache, and completely amnesiac for the brief period of Harriet's release from prison.

NEMIAH, 1978, PP. 179–180

As with Margaret, the dominant personality is often unaware of the existence of the alternate personalities. This seems to suggest that the mechanism of dissociation is controlled by unconscious processes. Although the dominant personality lacks insight into the existence of the other personalities, she or he may vaguely sense that something is amiss. There may even be "interpersonality rivalry," in which one personality aspires to do away with another, usually in blissful ignorance of the fact that this would result in the death of all.

Celebrated cases of multiple personality have been depicted in the popular media. One became the subject of the film *The Three Faces of Eve*. In the film, Eve White is a timid housewife who harbours two other personalities: Eve Black, a sexually provocative, antisocial personality, and Jane, a balanced, developing personality who could reconcile her sexual needs with the demands of social acceptability (see Figure 6.1). The three faces eventually merged into one—Jane, providing a "happy ending." The real-life Eve, whose name was Chris Sizemore, failed to maintain this integrated personality. Her personality split into 22 subsequent personalities, purportedly after she learned that another famous case—Sybil—had 16 personalities (Kihlstrom, 2005). As for the celebrated case of Sybil, which was also made into a movie, recent evidence, including tape recordings of sessions with a psychiatrist who claimed to have elicited Sybil's multiple personalities, indicates that Sybil was highly suggestible to the psychiatrist's suggestions that there were multiple personalities, but is unlikely to have had genuine multiple personality disorder (Borch-Jacobsen, 1997; Rieber, Takoosian, & Iglesias, 2002).

FIGURE 6.1 The three faces of Eve.
In the film *The Three Faces of Eve*, a timid housewife, Eve White (A), harbours two alternative personalities. Eve Black (B), a libidinous antisocial personality; and Jane (C), an integrated personality who can accept her sexual and aggressive urges but still engage in socially appropriate behaviour.

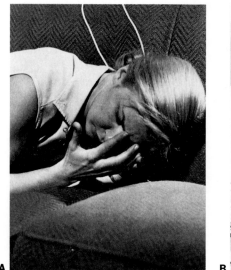

A   B   C

The diagnostic features of dissociative identity disorder are listed in Table 6.1 below.

The 1970s witnessed an "epidemic" of dissociative identity disorder cases. The number of alter egos reported by patients has also risen over time. It was almost as if there was some kind of contest to determine who could have (or be) the patient with the greatest number of alternative personalties (Kihlstrom, 2005). In the 1980s and '90s, it also became common for multiple-personality patients to talk with their therapists about previously unheard-of phenomena: alters of races or sexes different from the hosts; alters of different species, including cats, dogs, panthers, gorillas, and lobsters; alters of demons, angels, and even God (Piper & Merskey, 2004).

Although dissociative identity disorder is generally considered rare, the very existence of the disorder continues to arouse debate. The DSM cautions that the disorder has lately become overdiagnosed in people who are highly suggestible, leading them to be overly compliant with suggestions that they might have it (APA, 2000a). Increased public attention paid to the disorder in recent years may also account for the perception that its prevalence is greater than was commonly believed.

The disorder does appear to be culture-bound and largely restricted to North America (Spanos, 2001). Very few cases have been reported elsewhere (Piper & Merskey, 2004)—even in North America, few psychologists and psychiatrists have ever encountered a case of multiple personality. Most cases of multiple personality are reported by a relatively small number of investigators and clinicians who strongly believe in the existence of the disorder. Surveys in Canada and the United States reveal that many mental health professionals are skeptical of the validity of the concept of dissociative identity disorder (e.g., Lalonde, Hudson, Gigante, & Pope, 2001). Critics such as the University of Western Ontario's Harold Merskey and colleagues wonder whether some overzealous clinicians might be helping to manufacture that which they are seeking (Merskey, 1992; Piper & Merskey, 2004).

Some other leading authorities agree, most notably the late psychologist Nicholas Spanos, who worked at Carleton University. To Spanos and other psychologists (e.g., Lilienfeld & Lynn, 2003), multiple personality is not a distinct disorder, but a form of role-playing in which individuals first come to construe themselves as having multiple selves and then begin to act in ways that are consistent with their conception of the disorder. Eventually, their role-playing becomes so ingrained that it becomes a reality to them. Perhaps their therapists or counsellors, maybe unintentionally, first planted the idea in their minds that their confusing welter of emotions and behaviours may represent different personalities at work. Impressionable people may have learned how to enact the role of persons with the disorder by watching others perform the role on television and in the movies. Films like *The Three Faces of Eve* and *Sybil* have given detailed examples of the behaviours that characterize multiple personalities (Spanos, 2001). Or perhaps therapists provided cues about the features of multiple personality, enough for clients to enact the role convincingly.

TABLE 6.1

Features of Dissociative Identity Disorder (Formerly Multiple Personality Disorder)

1. At least two distinct personalities exist within the person, with each having a relatively enduring and distinct pattern of perceiving, thinking about, and relating to the environment and the self.

2. Two or more of these personalities repeatedly take complete control of the individual's behaviour.

3. There is a failure to recall important personal information too substantial to be accounted for by ordinary forgetfulness.

4. The disorder cannot be accounted for by the effects of a psychoactive substance or a general medical condition.

Source: Adapted from the DSM-IV (APA, 2000a).

Kenneth Bianchi, the so-called Hillside strangler.
Did the police psychiatrist who interviewed Bianchi suggest to him that he could role-play a person with multiple personalities?

Many reinforcers may become contingent on enacting the role of a multiple personality type. Receiving attention from others and evading accountability for unacceptable behaviour are two possible sources of reinforcement (Spanos, 2001). This is not to suggest that people with multiple personalities are "faking" any more than it would be to suggest you are faking your behaviour when you perform daily roles as a student, spouse, or worker. You may enact the role of a student (e.g., sitting attentively in class, raising your hand when you wish to talk, etc.) because you have learned to organize your behaviour according to the nature of the role and because you have been rewarded for doing so. People with multiple personalities may have come to identify so closely with the role that it becomes real for them.

In support of his belief that multiple personality represents a form of role-playing, Spanos and his colleagues showed that with proper cues, college students in a laboratory simulation of the Bianchi-type interrogation could easily enact a multiple-personality role, even attributing the blame to an alternate personality for a murder they were accused of committing (Spanos, 2001). Perhaps the manner in which the Bianchi interrogation was conducted had cued Bianchi to enact the multiple-personality role in order to evade criminal responsibility. (It didn't work, as he was eventually convicted.)

Relatively few cases of multiple personality involve criminal behaviour, in which enactment of a multiple-personality role might relieve individuals of criminal responsibility for their behaviour. But even in more typical cases, there may be more subtle incentives for enacting the role of a multiple personality, such as a therapist's expression of interest and excitement at discovering a multiple personality. People with multiple personalities were often highly imaginative during childhood. Accustomed to playing games of "make-believe," they may readily adopt alternate identities—especially if they learn how to enact the multiple-personality role and there are external sources of validation such as a clinician's interest and concern.

The social-reinforcement model may help to explain why some clinicians seem to "discover" many more cases of multiple personality than others. These clinicians may be "multiple personality magnets." They may unknowingly cue clients to enact the multiple-personality role and reinforce the performance with extra attention and concern. With the right set of cues, certain clients may adopt the role of a multiple personality to please their clinicians.

The role-playing model has been challenged by some researchers (e.g., Gleaves, Hernandez, & Warner, 2003) and it remains to be seen how many cases of the disorder in clinical practice the model can explain. Whether multiple personality is a real phenomenon or a form of role-playing, there is no question that people who display this behaviour have serious emotional and behavioural difficulties.

Multiple personality, which often is called *split personality* by laypeople, should not be confused with schizophrenia. The term split personality refers to multiple personality, not schizophrenia. Schizophrenia (which comes from roots that mean "split brain") occurs much more commonly than multiple personality, and involves the "splitting" of cognition, affect, and behaviour. There may, thus, be little agreement between thoughts and emotions, or between the individual's perception of reality and what is truly happening. The person with schizophrenia may become giddy when told of disturbing events or may experience hallucinations or delusions. In people with multiple personalities, the personality apparently divides into two or more personalities, but each of them usually shows more integrated functioning on cognitive, emotional, and behavioural levels than is true of people with schizophrenia.

Dissociative Amnesia

Dissociative amnesia is another controversial diagnostic category (Kihlstrom, 2005). *Amnesia* derives from the Greek roots *a-*, meaning "not," and *mnasthai,* meaning "to remember." In **dissociative amnesia** (formerly called *psychogenic amnesia*), a person becomes unable to recall important personal information usually involving material relating to traumatic or stressful experiences that cannot be accounted for by simple forgetfulness. Nor can the memory loss be attributed to a particular organic cause, such as a blow to the head or a particular medical condition, or to the direct effects of drugs or alcohol. Unlike some progressive forms of memory impairment (such as dementia associated with Alzheimer's disease), the memory loss in dissociative amnesia is reversible, although it may last for days, weeks, or even years. Recall of dissociated memories may happen gradually but often occurs suddenly and spontaneously, as when a soldier who has no recall of a battle for several days afterward suddenly recalls the experience after being transported to a hospital away from the battlefield.

Most types of dissociative amnesia involve localized amnesia, which means that events occurring during a specific time period are lost to memory. For example, a person cannot recall events for a number of hours or days after a stressful or traumatic incident, as in warfare or a case where there's an uninjured survivor of an accident. Other forms of dissociative amnesia include *selective amnesia* and *generalized amnesia*. In selective amnesia, people forget only the disturbing particulars that take place during a certain time period. Some people may recall the period of life during which they conducted an extramarital affair, but not the guilt-arousing affair itself. A soldier may recall most of a battle, but not the death of his or her compatriot. In generalized amnesia, people forget their entire lives—who they are, what they do, where they live, with whom they live. This form of amnesia is very rare, although you wouldn't think so if you watch daytime soap operas. Persons with generalized amnesia cannot recall personal information, but tend to retain their habits, tastes, and skills. If you had generalized amnesia, you would still know how to read, although you would not recall your elementary school teachers. You would still prefer french fries to broccoli, or vice versa. People with dissociative amnesia usually forget events or periods of life that were traumatic—ones that generated strong negative emotions such as horror or guilt.

Some researchers argue that true dissociative amnesia is exceedingly rare, and that many cases of so-called dissociative amnesia are actually caused by brain injury or disease (Kihlstrom, 2005). In some cases, this explanation is quite plausible. For example, forgetting what happened during a severe motor vehicle accident may not be dissociative amnesia; it may simply reflect the fact they you had a mild brain injury (concussion), which temporarily disrupted the brain's ability to form and retain memories. However, other cases, particularly dissociative amnesia purportedly involving the loss of one's identity (as the person's only problem), are typically very different from the memory problems caused by brain damage or disease. People with this type of amnesia have seemingly lost the most deeply ingrained of all their memories—those of who they are—while they are able to readily recall other more recent things, such as what they had for breakfast in the hospital that morning. Other cognitive functions such as reasoning skills are also unaffected. In comparison, people with brain damage or disease often have difficulty recalling recent events—even for patients with dementia associated with Alzheimer's disease, one of the last things they forget is who they are (Lezak, 2004). A simple concussive blow to the head might wipe out your memory of events in the hours or days before the concussion, but you'll likely still remember who you are and recognize friends and family.

People sometimes claim they cannot recall certain events of their lives, such as criminal acts, promises made to others, and so forth. Falsely claiming amnesia as a way of escaping responsibility is called **malingering**, which involves the attempt to fake symptoms or make false claims for personal gain. It can be sometimes be very difficult to determine whether a person's reported memory loss is dissociative amnesia, malingering, or some other problem.

Dissociative Fugue

Fugue derives from the Latin *fugere*, meaning "flight." The word *fugitive* has the same origin. Fugue is like amnesia "on the run." In **dissociative fugue** (formerly called *psychogenic fugue*), a person travels suddenly and unexpectedly from his or her home or

dissociative amnesia Type of dissociative disorder in which a person experiences memory losses in the absence of any identifiable organic cause. General knowledge and skills are usually retained.

malingering Faking illness so as to avoid or escape work or other duties, or to obtain benefits.

dissociative fugue Type of dissociative disorder in which one suddenly flies from one's life situation, travels to a new location, assumes a new identity, and has amnesia for past personal material. The person usually retains skills and other abilities and may appear to others in the new environment to be leading a normal life.

place of work, is unable to recall past personal information, and either becomes confused about his or her identity or assumes a new identity (either partially or completely) (APA, 2000a). Despite these odd behaviours, the person may appear "normal" and show no other signs of mental disturbance. The person may not think about the past, or may report a past filled with false memories but not recognize them as false.

Whereas people with amnesia appear to wander aimlessly, people in a fugue state act more purposefully. Some stick close to home. They spend the afternoon in the park or in a theatre, or they spend the night at a hotel under another name, usually having little if any contact with others during the fugue state. But the new identity is incomplete and fleeting and the individual's former sense of self soon returns in a matter of hours or a few days. Less common is a pattern in which the fugue state lasts for months or years and involves travel to distant cities or foreign lands and assumption of a new identity. These individuals may assume an identity that is more spontaneous and sociable than their former selves, which were typically "quiet" and "ordinary." They may establish new families and successful businesses. Although these cases may sound rather bizarre, the fugue state is not considered psychotic because people with the disorder can think and behave quite normally—in their new lives, that is. Then one day, quite suddenly, their awareness of their past identity returns to them, and they are flooded with old memories. Now, they typically do not recall the events that occurred during the fugue state. The new identity, the new life—including all its involvements and responsibilities—vanish from recollection.

Fugue, like amnesia, is rare, and believed to affect only about 2 people in 1000 among the general population (APA, 2000a). It is most likely to occur in the wake of an extremely stressful event such as a disaster. The underlying notion is that dissociation in the fugue state protects one from traumatic memories or other sources of emotionally painful experiences or conflict (Isaac & Chand, 2006), but the evidence favouring this hypothesis is plagued by poor methodology (Kihlstrom, 2005). Fugue can also be difficult to distinguish from malingering. That is, a number of persons who were dissatisfied with their former lives could claim to be amnesic when they are uncovered in their new locations and new identities.

Depersonalization Disorder

depersonalization Feelings of unreality or detachment from one's self or one's body, as if one were a robot or functioning on automatic pilot or observing oneself from outside.

derealization Loss of the sense of reality of one's surroundings, experienced in terms of strange changes in one's environment (e.g., people or objects changing size or shape) or in the sense of the passage of time.

Depersonalization involves a temporary loss or change in the usual sense of our own reality. In a state of depersonalization, people may feel detached from their minds or bodies. They may have the sense of living in a dream or a movie or acting like a robot (Holmes et al., 2005).

Derealization—a sense of unreality about the external world involving strange changes in perception of surroundings or in the sense of the passage of time—may also be present. People and objects may seem to change in size or shape; they may sound different. All these feelings can be associated with feelings of anxiety, including dizziness and fears of going insane, or with depression.

Although these sensations are strange, people with depersonalization maintain contact with reality. They can distinguish reality from unreality, even during the depersonalization episode. In contrast to generalized amnesia and fugue, they know who they are. Their memories are intact and they know where they are—even if they do not like their present state. Feelings of depersonalization usually come on suddenly and fade gradually.

What is even more unusual about all this is that we have thus far described only normal feelings of depersonalization. According to the DSM, single brief episodes of depersonalization are experienced by about half of all adults, usually during times of extreme stress. Estimates are that 80% to 90% of people go through dissociative experiences at one time or another (Gershuny & Thayer, 1999).

Consider Richie's experience:

"We went to Orlando with the children after school let out. I had also been driving myself hard, and it was time to let go. We spent three days 'doing' Disney World, and it got to the point where we were all wearing shirts with mice and ducks on them and singing Disney songs like 'Yo ho, yo ho, a pirate's life for me.' On the third day, I began to feel unreal and ill at ease while we were watching these teenagers singing and dancing in front of Cinderella's Castle. The day was finally cooling down, but I broke into a sweat. I became shaky and dizzy and sat down on the cement next to the four-year-old's stroller without giving [my wife] an explanation. There were strollers and kids and [adults'] legs all around me, and for some strange reason I became fixated on the pieces of popcorn strewn on the ground. All of a sudden it was like the people around me were all silly mechanical creatures, like the dolls in the It's a Small World [exhibit] or the animals on the Jungle Cruise. Things sort of seemed to slow down, the way they do when you've smoked marijuana, and there was this invisible wall of cotton between me and everyone else.

"Then the concert was over and my wife was like, 'What's the matter?' and did I want to stay for the Electrical Parade and the fireworks or was I sick? Now I was beginning to wonder if I was going crazy and I said I was sick, that my wife would have to take me by the hand and drive us back to the Sonesta Village [Motel]. Somehow, we got back to the monorail and turned in the strollers. I waited in the herd [of people] at the station like a dead person, my eyes glazed over, looking out over kids with Mickey Mouse ears and Mickey Mouse balloons. The mechanical voice on the monorail almost did me in and I got really shaky.

"I refused to go back to the Magic Kingdom. I went with the family to Sea World, and on another day I dropped [my wife] and the kids off at the Magic Kingdom and picked them up that night. My wife thought I was goldbricking or something, and we had a helluva fight about it, but we had a life to get back to and my sanity had to come first."

THE AUTHORS' FILES

Depersonalization. Episodes of depersonalization are characterized by feelings of detachment from oneself. During an episode, it may feel as if one were walking through a dream or observing the environment or oneself from outside one's body.

TABLE 6.2

Diagnostic Features of Depersonalization Disorder

1. Recurrent or persistent experiences of depersonalization, which are characterized by feelings of detachment from one's mental processes or body, as if one were an outside observer of oneself. The experience may have a dreamlike quality.

2. The individual is able to maintain reality testing (i.e., distinguish reality from unreality) during the depersonalization state.

3. The depersonalization experiences cause significant personal distress or impairment in one or more important areas of functioning, such as social or occupational functioning.

4. Depersonalization experiences cannot be attributed to other disorders or to the direct effects of drugs, alcohol, or medical conditions.

Source: Adapted from the DSM-IV (APA, 2000a).

depersonalization disorder Disorder characterized by persistent or recurrent episodes of depersonalization.

Richie's depersonalization experience was limited to the one episode and would not qualify for a diagnosis of **depersonalization disorder**. Depersonalization disorder is diagnosed only when such experiences are persistent or recurrent and cause marked distress (APA, 2000a). The DSM diagnoses depersonalization disorder according to the criteria shown in Table 6.2.

QUESTIONNAIRE

The Dissociative Experience Scale

Brief dissociative experiences, such as momentary feelings of depersonalization, are quite common. The great majority of us experience them at least some of the time (Simeon & Abugel, 2006). Dissociative disorders, by contrast, involve more persistent and severe dissociative experiences. Researchers have developed a measure, the Dissociative Experiences Scale (DES), to offer clinicians a way of measuring dissociative experiences that occur in both the general population and among people with dissociative disorders (Bernstein & Putnam, 1986). Fleeting dissociative experiences are quite common, but those reported by people with dissociative disorders are more frequent and problematic than those in the general population.

The following is a listing of some of the types of dissociative experiences drawn from the Dissociative Experiences Scale that many people encounter from time to time. Bear in mind that transient experiences like these are reported by both normal and abnormal groups in varying frequencies. Let us also suggest that if these experiences become persistent or commonplace, or cause you concern or distress, it might be worthwhile to discuss them with a professional.

Have you ever experienced the following?

1. Suddenly realizing, when you are driving the car, that you don't remember what has happened during all or part of the trip.

2. Suddenly realizing, when you are listening to someone talk, that you did not hear part or all of what the person said.

3. Finding yourself in a place and having no idea how you got there.

4. Finding yourself dressed in clothes that you don't remember putting on.

5. Experiencing a feeling that seemed as if you were standing next to yourself or watching yourself do something and actually seeing yourself as if you were looking at another person.

6. Looking in a mirror and not recognizing yourself.

7. Feeling sometimes that other people, objects, and the world around you are not real.

8. Remembering a past event so vividly that it seems like you are reliving it in the present.

9. Having the experience of being in a familiar place but finding it strange and unfamiliar.

10. Becoming so absorbed in watching television or a movie that you are unaware of other events happening around you.

11. Becoming so absorbed in a fantasy or daydream that it feels as though it were really happening to you.

12. Talking out loud to yourself when you are alone.

13. Finding that you act so differently in a particular situation compared with another that it feels almost as if you were two different people.

14. Finding that you cannot remember whether or not you have just done something or perhaps had just thought about doing it (e.g., not knowing whether you have just mailed a letter or have just thought about mailing it).

15. Feeling sometimes as if you were looking at the world through a fog such that people and objects appear far away or unclear.

Source: Bernstein, E. M., & Putnam, F. W. (1986). Development, reliability, and validity of a dissociation scale. *Journal of Nervous and Mental Disease, 174*, 727–735. Copyright © Williams & Wilkins, 1986.

In terms of observable behaviour and associated features, depersonalization may be more closely related to disorders such as phobias and panic than to dissociative disorders (Holmes et al., 2005). Unlike other forms of dissociative disorders that seem to protect the self from anxiety, depersonalization can lead to anxiety and in turn to avoidance behaviour, as we saw in the case of Richie.

Theoretical Perspectives

The dissociative disorders are fascinating and perplexing phenomena. How can one's sense of personal identity become so distorted that one develops multiple personalities, blots out large chunks of personal memory, or develops a new self-identity? Although these disorders remain in many ways mysterious, clues have emerged that provide insights into their origins.

Psychodynamic theorists believe that dissociative disorders involve the massive use of repression, which leads to the "splitting off" from consciousness of unacceptable impulses and painful memories. In dissociative amnesia and fugue, the ego protects itself from becoming flooded with anxiety by blotting out disturbing memories or by dissociating threatening impulses of a sexual or aggressive nature. In multiple personality, people may express these unacceptable impulses through the development of alternate personalities. In depersonalization, people stand outside themselves—safely distanced from the emotional turmoil within.

Learning and cognitive theorists view dissociation as a learned response that involves *not thinking* about disturbing acts or thoughts in order to avoid feelings of guilt and shame evoked by such experiences. The habit of *not thinking about these matters* is negatively reinforced by relief from anxiety or by removal of feelings of guilt or shame. Some social cognitive theorists, such as the late Nicholas Spanos (2001) and others (e.g., Lilienfeld & Lynn, 2003), propose that dissociative identity disorder is a form of role-playing acquired by means of observational learning and reinforcement. This is not quite the same as pretending or malingering; people can honestly come to organize their behaviour patterns according to particular roles they have observed. They might also become so absorbed in role-playing that they "forget" they are enacting a role.

TYING IT TOGETHER

A widely held view of dissociative identity disorder is that it represents a means of coping with and surviving severe childhood abuse (Ross, 2001). It is possible that in some cases, severely abused children may retreat into alter personalities as a psychological defence against unbearable abuse. The construction of alter personalities may allow severely abused children to escape psychologically or distance themselves from their suffering. Dissociation may offer a means of escape when no other means is available. In the face of repeated abuse, these alter personalities may become stabilized, making it difficult for the person to maintain a unified personality. In adulthood, people with multiple personalities may use their alter personalities to block out traumatic childhood memories and their emotional reactions to them—wiping the slate clean and beginning life anew in the guise of alter personalities (Ross, 2001). The alter identities or personalities may also serve as a way of coping with stressful situations or of expressing deep-seated resentments that the individual is unable to integrate within his or her primary personality. Although this theory is popular with many clinicians, the evidence comes largely from methodologically weak studies (Kihlstrom, 2005).

The great majority of people with multiple personalities report being physically or sexually abused as children, although most people abused as children do not develop multiple personalities (Piper & Merskey, 2004). Similarly, the vast majority of people exposed to trauma do not develop dissociative disorders (Kihlstrom, 2005).

Consistent with the *diathesis-stress model*, only certain individuals may be predisposed to develop dissociative disorders when exposed to severe stress. Certain personality traits, such as a proneness to fantasize, a high ability to be hypnotized, and an openness to altered states of consciousness, may predispose individuals to develop dissociative experiences in the face of extreme stress caused by events like traumatic abuse (Isaac & Chand, 2006). These personality traits themselves do not lead to dissociative disorders, but they might increase the risk that people who experience severe trauma will develop dissociative phenomena as a survival mechanism.

Perhaps most of us can divide our consciousness so we become unaware of—at least temporarily—those events we normally focus on. Perhaps most of us can thrust the unpleasant from our minds and enact various roles—parent, child, lover, business person, soldier—that help us meet the requirements of our situations. Perhaps the marvel is *not* that attention can be splintered, but that human consciousness is normally integrated into a meaningful whole.

Treatment of Dissociative Disorders

Dissociative amnesia and fugue are usually fleeting experiences that end abruptly. Episodes of depersonalization can be recurrent and persistent, and they are most likely to occur when people are undergoing periods of mild anxiety or depression. In such cases, clinicians usually focus on managing the anxiety or the depression. Much of the attention in the research literature has focused on dissociative identity disorder and specifically on bringing together an integration of the alter personalities into a cohesive personality structure.

Traditional psychoanalysis aims at helping people with dissociative identity disorder to uncover and learn to cope with early childhood traumas. The analyst can work with whatever personality dominates the therapy session. Any and all personalities can be asked to talk about their memories and dreams as best they can. Any and all personalities can be assured the therapist will help them make sense of their anxieties and to safely "relive" traumatic experiences and make them conscious. If therapy is successful, the self will be able to work through the traumatic memories and will no longer need to escape into alternate "selves" to avoid the anxiety associated with the trauma. Thus, reintegration of the personality becomes possible.

Does this sort of therapy work? Coons (1986) followed 20 "multiples" aged from 14 to 47 at time of intake for an average of 39 months. Only five of the subjects showed a complete reintegration of their personalities. Other therapists report significant improvement in measures of dissociative and depressive symptoms in treated patients (Ellason & Ross, 1997), but these studies have been criticized for methodological problems (Kihlstrom, 2005). Reports of the effectiveness of other forms of therapy, such as cognitive-behaviour therapy, rely largely on uncontrolled case studies. Nor do we have evidence showing psychiatric drugs or other biological approaches to be effective in bringing about an integration of various alternative personalities. Accordingly, it is not possible to draw firm conclusions about the safety and efficacy of psychoanalytic or other treatments for dissociative identity disorder.

Little is known about the treatment of other forms of dissociative disorder. The relative infrequency of these disorders has hampered efforts to conduct controlled experiments that compare different forms of treatment with each other and with control groups. However, preliminary evidence suggests that cognitive-behaviour therapy and some types of medication may be helpful in treating depersonalization disorder (Hunter, Baker, Phillips, Sierra, & David, 2005; Simeon & Abugel, 2006).

A CLOSER LOOK

A Recovered-Memory Controversy

A high-level business executive's comfortable life fell apart one day when his 19-year-old daughter accused him of having repeatedly molested her throughout her childhood. He lost his marriage as well as his $400 000-a-year job. But he fought back against the allegations that he insisted were untrue. He sued his daughter's therapists who had assisted her in recovering these memories. A jury sided with the father, awarding him $500 000 in damages from the two therapists.

In the Canadian case of *R. v. Francois* (1994), Francois was convicted of repeatedly raping a 13-year-old girl in 1985. The only evidence was the girl's testimony. She said that she had repressed memories of the sexual assaults, but then the recollections returned in 1990. At the time of the recollections, the police suggested that if she thought long enough about her past, she might recall something in a "flashback." The girl reported that the flashbacks occurred while doing this. The conviction was later overturned by the Supreme Court of Canada.

These are just two of many cases involving allegations made by adults who claim to have only recently become aware of memories of being sexually abused during childhood. Hundreds of people throughout North America have been brought to trial on the basis of recovered memories of childhood abuse, with many of these cases resulting in convictions and long jail sentences, even in the absence of any corroborating evidence. Recovered memories of sexual abuse in childhood may occur following suggestive probing by a therapist or hypnotist (Loftus & Davis, 2006). The issue of recovered memories continues to be hotly debated in psychology and the broader community (Prout & Dobson, 1998). At the heart of the debate is the question, "Are recovered memories believable?" No one doubts that child sexual abuse is a major problem confronting our society. But should recovered memories be taken at face value?

Several lines of evidence lead us to question the validity of recovered memories. Research evidence shows, for example, that under some circumstances people who are given plausible but false information about their childhoods may come to believe the information is true. To illustrate, consider the research by Dalhousie University psychologist Stephen Porter, who with his colleagues at the University of British Columbia demonstrated that some people can create false memories for emotional childhood events (Porter, Yuille, & Lehman, 1999; Porter, Birt, Yuille, & Lehman, 2000). Participants in this research were university students. The parents of the students were asked to provide information about six emotional events (e.g., serious accidents, medical procedures, animal attacks) that the student may or may not have experienced as a child. This information enabled the researchers to construct, for a given student, a fabricated childhood event that could form the basis of a false memory. The experiment consisted of three interviews over two weeks. In the first interview, students were interviewed about a real and a false event, with each introduced to the student as true. In the second and third interviews, students were re-interviewed about the false event. Interviewers attempted to elicit a false memory in each student, using methods such as guided imagery (e.g., asking the student to repeatedly imagine the fictitious event), mild social pressure that the event actually occurred, and by encouraging repeated attempts to recover the memory. Porter and his colleagues (1999) found that 26% of students created a false memory, 30% created a partial false memory (e.g., the student was unsure about whether the false event had occurred), and 44% created no false memory. Further results suggested that false memories are most likely to occur for people with dissociative tendencies (i.e., high scores on the Dissociative Experiences Scale) and when the interviewer is engaging, persuasive, and confident (Porter et al., 2000).

Underscoring the importance of findings such as these, a leading memory expert, psychologist Elizabeth Loftus, (1996, p. 356) wrote of the dangers of taking recovered memories at face value:

(continued)

After developing false memories, innumerable "patients" have torn their families apart, and more than a few innocent people have been sent to prison. This is not to say that people cannot forget horrible things that have happened to them; most certainly they can. But there is virtually no support for the idea that clients presenting for therapy routinely have extensive histories of abuse of which they are completely unaware, and that they can be helped only if the alleged abuse is resurrected from their unconscious.

Should we conclude, then, that all recovered memories are bogus? Not necessarily. It is possible for people in adulthood to recover memories of childhood, including memories of abuse (Chu, Frey, & Ganzel,1999). There is little doubt that abuse can be forgotten and later

remembered, although ordinary forgetting and remembering—rather than a special mechanism such as repression—seem more than adequate to account for this (Loftus & Davis, 2006). Some recovered memories may be true; others may not. Unfortunately, we don't have the tools to distinguish the true memory from the false one. Just because a "memory" report is detailed, or that a person expresses it with confidence and emotion, does not mean the event actually happened (Loftus & Davis, 2006).

We shouldn't think of the brain as a kind of mental camera that stores snapshots of events as they actually happened in the form of memories. Memory is more of a reconstructive process in which bits of information are pieced together in ways that can sometimes lead to a distorted recollection of events, even though the person may be convinced the memory is accurate.

STUDY BREAK

Dissociative Disorders

Review It

- **What are dissociative disorders?** Dissociative disorders involve changes or disturbances in identity, memory, or consciousness that affect the ability to maintain an integrated sense of self. They include dissociative identity disorder, dissociative amnesia, dissociative fugue, and depersonalization disorder.

- **What is the major feature of dissociative identity disorder?** In dissociative identity disorder, two or more distinct personalities, each possessing well-defined traits and memories, exist within a person and repeatedly take control of the person's behaviour.

- **What are the clinical features associated with dissociative amnesia, dissociative fugue, and depersonalization disorder?** Dissociative amnesia involves loss of memory for personal information that cannot be accounted for by organic causes. In dissociative fugue, a person travels suddenly away from home or place of work, shows a loss of memory for his or her personal past, and experiences identity confusion or takes on a new identity. Depersonalization disorder involves persistent or recurrent episodes of depersonalization that are of sufficient severity to cause significant distress or impairment in functioning.

- **How do psychodynamic theorists conceptualize dissociative disorders?** Psychodynamic theorists view dissociative disorders as involving a form of psychological defence by which the ego defends itself against troubling memories and unacceptable impulses by blotting them out of consciousness.

- **How do learning and cognitive theorists account for these disorders?** To learning and cognitive theorists, dissociative experiences involve ways of learning not to think about certain troubling behaviours or thoughts that might lead to feelings of guilt or shame. Relief from anxiety negatively reinforces this pattern of dissociation. Some social-cognitive theorists suggest that multiple personality may represent a form of role-playing behaviour.

- **How has dissociative identity disorder been treated?** Most therapeutic approaches help the person with dissociative identity disorder uncover and cope with dissociated painful experiences from childhood. Biological approaches focus on the use of drugs to treat the anxiety and depression often associated with the disorder, but drugs have not been able to bring about reintegration of the personality.

dissociative identity disorder   dissociative fugue
dissociative amnesia   depersonalization
malingering   derealization
   depersonalization disorder

Recall It*

1. _____ disorders are characterized by a change or disturbance in self-identity, memory, or consciousness.

   a. Somatoform
   b. Anxiety
   c. Dissociative
   d. Adjustment

2. The term *split personality* is commonly used to refer to _____.

   a. depersonalization disorder
   b. dissociative identity disorder
   c. schizophrenia
   d. bipolar disorder

3. The most frequent type of dissociative disorder is _____.

   a. dissociative fugue
   b. dissociative identity disorder

   c. depersonalization disorder
   d. dissociative amnesia

4. Harry has experiences in which he feels like he is walking through a fog and is strangely detached from his own body. This type of experience is most likely to occur in the context of _____.

   a. dissociative identity disorder
   b. dissociative fugue
   c. depersonalization disorder
   d. dissociative amnesia

5. As opposed to dissociative amnesia, dissociative fugue often involves _____.

   a. loss of memory of personal events
   b. a psychotic breakdown
   c. travel to a new place
   d. derealization

* Recall It answers can be found on the Companion Website for this text.

Think About It

- How might you apply the diathesis-stress model in accounting for the development of dissociative identity disorder?

- Do you believe that people with dissociative identity disorder are playing a role? Why or why not?

SOMATOFORM DISORDERS

The word *somatoform* derives from the Greek *soma*, meaning "body." In the **somatoform disorders**, people have physical symptoms suggestive of physical disorders, but no organic abnormalities can be found to account for them. Moreover, there is evidence or some reason to believe that the symptoms reflect psychological factors. Some people complain of problems in breathing or swallowing or of a "lump in the throat." Problems such as these can reflect overactivity of the sympathetic branch of the autonomic nervous system, which can be related to anxiety. Sometimes the symptoms take more unusual forms, as in a "paralysis" of a hand or leg that is inconsistent with the workings of the nervous system. In yet other cases, people are preoccupied with the belief that they have a serious disease, yet no evidence of a physical abnormality can be found. We consider several forms of somatoform disorders, including *conversion disorder*, *hypochondriasis*, and *somatization disorder*.

\Somatoform disorders are distinguished from malingering or purposeful fabrication of symptoms for obvious gain (like avoiding work). They are also distinguished from a **factitious disorder**, the most common form of which is **Münchausen syndrome**. Münchausen syndrome is a form of feigned illness in which people either fake being ill or make themselves ill (by ingesting toxic substances such as rat poison or injecting themselves with bacteria, for example). Münchausen syndrome is named after the fictional accounts published by Rudolf Raspe (e.g., 1860) about Baron Münchausen, an 18th-century German army officer.

Some Münchausen patients go through unnecessary surgeries, even though they know there is nothing wrong with them. Yet unlike malingering, there is no apparent purpose to

somatoform disorders Disorders in which people complain of physical (somatic) problems, although no physical abnormality can be found. See *conversion disorder*, *hypochondriasis*, and *somatization disorder*.

factitious disorder Type of psychological disorder characterized by the intentional fabrication of psychological or physical symptoms for no apparent gain.

Münchausen syndrome Type of factitious disorder characterized by the feigning of medical symptoms for no apparent purpose other than getting admitted or remaining in hospitals.

the fakery, save for the attention the person receives from medical professionals. A rare and potentially very harmful variant of this disorder is Münchausen-by-Proxy syndrome (MBPS), where the parent feigns or induces illness in a child (Ayoub, 2006). For example, the parent may attempt to poison the child in order that the child (and, by proxy, the parent) will receive medical attention. Thus, MBPS can be associated with severe and sometimes deadly child abuse.

Malingering is motivated by external incentives, and so it is not considered a psychological disorder within the DSM framework. In factitious disorders, however, the symptoms are not connected with obvious gains. The absence of external incentives in these disorders suggests that they serve a psychological need; hence, they are considered psychological disorders.

Why do patients with Münchausen syndrome feign illness or sometimes put themselves at grave risk by causing themselves to be sick or injured? This syndrome represents an extreme need for nurturance or attention (Slovenko, 2006), although the underlying reasons for this need are unclear. Perhaps enacting the sick role in the protected hospital environment provides a sense of security that was lacking in childhood. Perhaps the hospital becomes a stage on which they can act out resentments against doctors and parents that have been brewing since childhood. Perhaps they are trying to identify with a parent who was often sick. Or perhaps they learned to enact a sick role in childhood to escape repeated sexual abuse or other traumatic experiences and continue to enact the role to escape stressors in their adult lives (Trask & Sigmon, 1997). No one is really sure, and the disorder remains one of the more puzzling forms of abnormal behaviour.

Now let's consider several of the major types of somatoform disorder.

Conversion Disorder

conversion disorder Type of somatoform disorder characterized by loss or impairment of physical function in the absence of any organic causes that might account for the changes. Formerly called *hysteria* or *hysterical neurosis*.

Conversion disorder is characterized by a major change in or loss of physical functioning, although there are no medical findings to support the physical symptoms or deficits (see Table 6.3 on page 231). The symptoms are not intentionally produced. The person is not malingering. The physical symptoms usually come on suddenly in stressful situations. A soldier's hand may become "paralyzed" during intense combat, for example. The fact that conversion symptoms first appear in the context of or are aggravated by conflicts or stressors the individual encounters gives credence to the view that they relate to psychological factors (APA, 2000a).

Conversion disorder is so named because of the psychodynamic belief that it represents the channelling or *conversion* of repressed sexual or aggressive energies into physical symptoms. Conversion disorder was formerly called *hysteria* or *hysterical neurosis* and played an important role in Freud's development of psychoanalysis (see Chapter 1). Hysterical or

Tall Tales. Baron Münchausen, who, according to the fictional accounts published by Rudolf Raspe, regaled his friends with tales of his incredible feats. In one of his tall tales, depicted here, he claimed that he had fallen asleep inside a cannon and was inadvertently shot across the Thames River.

TABLE 6.3

Diagnostic Features of Conversion Disorder

1. At least one symptom or deficit involving voluntary motor or sensory functions that suggests the presence of a physical disorder.

2. Psychological factors are judged to be associated with the disorder because the onset or exacerbation of the physical symptom is linked to the occurrence of psychosocial stressors or conflict situations.

3. The person does not purposefully produce or fake the physical symptom.

4. The symptom cannot be explained as a cultural ritual or response pattern, nor can it be explained by any known physical disorder on the basis of appropriate testing.

5. The symptom causes significant emotional distress; impairment in one or more important areas of functioning, such as social or occupational functioning; or is sufficient to warrant medical attention.

6. The symptom is not restricted to complaints of pain or problems in sexual functioning, nor can it be accounted for by another psychological disorder.

Source: Adapted from the DSM-IV (APA, 2000a).

conversion disorders seem to have been more common in Freud's day but are relatively rare today.

According to the DSM, conversion symptoms mimic neurological or general medical conditions involving problems with voluntary motor (movement) or sensory functions. Some of the "classic" symptom patterns involve paralysis, epilepsy, problems in coordination, blindness and tunnel vision, loss of the sense of hearing or of smell, or loss of feeling in a limb (anaesthesia). The bodily symptoms found in conversion disorders often do not match the medical conditions they suggest. For example, conversion epileptics, unlike true epileptic patients, may maintain control over their bladders during an attack. People whose vision is supposedly impaired may wend their ways through the physician's office without bumping into the furniture. People who become "incapable" of standing or walking may nevertheless perform other leg movements normally. Nonetheless, there are some cases in which hysteria or conversion disorder was incorrectly diagnosed in people who turned out to have underlying medical conditions that went unrecognized and untreated.

If you suddenly lost your vision, or if you could no longer move your legs, you would probably be very upset. But some people with conversion disorders, like those with dissociative amnesia, show a remarkable indifference to their symptoms, a phenomenon termed **la belle indifférence** ("beautiful indifference"). This was once thought to be an important feature that distinguished conversion disorders from real physical disorders. However, accumulating evidence shows that many people cope with real physical disorders by denying their pain or concern, which provides the semblance of indifference and relieves anxieties—at least temporarily. In fact, people with conversion disorder are no more likely than people with real physical disorders to display *la belle indifférence*, suggesting that this feature is of little diagnostic value (Stone, Smyth, Carson, Warlow, & Sharpe, 2006).

la belle indifférence French term describing the lack of concern over one's symptoms displayed by some people with conversion disorder but also by people with real physical disorders.

Hypochondriasis

The core feature of hypochondriasis is a preoccupation or fear that one's physical symptoms are due to an underlying serious illness, such as cancer or a heart problem. The fear persists despite medical reassurances that it is groundless (see Table 6.4).

People with hypochondriasis do not consciously fake their physical symptoms. They generally experience physical discomfort, often involving the digestive system or an assortment of aches and pains. Unlike conversion disorder, hypochondriasis does not involve the loss or distortion of physical function. Unlike the attitude of indifference toward one's symptoms that is sometimes found in conversion disorders, people who

TABLE 6.4

Diagnostic Features of Hypochondriasis

1. The person is preoccupied with a fear of having a serious illness or with the belief that one has a serious illness. The person interprets bodily sensations or physical signs as evidence of physical illness.

2. Fears of physical illness or beliefs of having a physical illness persist despite medical reassurances.

3. The preoccupations are not of a delusional intensity (the person recognizes the possibility that these fears and beliefs may be exaggerated or unfounded) and are not restricted to concerns about appearance.

4. The preoccupations cause significant emotional distress or interfere with one or more important areas of functioning, such as social or occupational functioning.

5. The disturbance has persisted for six months or longer.

6. The preoccupations do not occur exclusively within the context of another psychological disorder.

Source: Adapted from the DSM-IV (APA, 2000a).

develop hypochondriasis are very concerned, indeed unduly concerned, about their symptoms and what they fear they may represent. About 1% to 5% of the population develop hypochondriasis at some point in their lives (APA, 2000a). The disorder appears to be about equally common in men and women. It most often begins between the ages of 20 and 30, although it can begin at any age.

People with hypochondriasis may be overly sensitive to slight changes in heartbeat and minor aches and pains. Anxiety about physical symptoms can produce its own physical sensations, however—for example, heavy sweating and dizziness, even fainting. Thus, a vicious cycle may ensue. People with hypochondriasis may become resentful when their doctors tell them how their own fears may be causing their physical symptoms. They frequently go "doctor shopping" in the hope that a competent and sympathetic physician will heed them before it is too late. Physicians, too, can develop hypochondriasis, as we see in the following case example:

A 38-year-old radiologist has just returned from a ten-day stay at a famous diagnostic centre where he has undergone extensive testing of his entire gastrointestinal tract. The evaluation proved negative for any significant physical illness, but rather than feel relieved, the radiologist appeared resentful and disappointed with the findings. The radiologist has been bothered for several months with various physical symptoms, which he describes as symptoms of mild abdominal pain, feelings of "fullness," "bowel rumblings," and a feeling of a "firm abdominal mass." He has become convinced that his symptoms are due to colon cancer and has become accustomed to testing his stool for blood on a weekly basis and carefully palpating his abdomen for "masses" while lying in bed every several days. He has also secretly performed X-ray studies on himself after regular hours. There is a history of a heart murmur that was detected when he was 13 and his younger brother died of congenital heart disease in early childhood. When the evaluation of his murmur proved to be benign, he nonetheless began to worry that something might have been overlooked. He developed a fear that something was actually wrong with his heart, and while the fear eventually subsided, it has never entirely left him. In medical school he worried about the diseases that he learned about in pathology. Since graduating, he has repeatedly experienced concerns about his health that follow a typical pattern: noticing certain symptoms, becoming preoccupied with what the symptoms might mean, and undergoing physical evaluations that prove negative. His decision to seek a psychiatric consultation was prompted by an incident with his nine-year-old son. His son accidentally walked in on him while he was palpating his abdomen and asked, "What do you think it is this time, Dad?" He becomes tearful as he relates this incident, describing his feelings of shame and anger—mostly at himself.

ADAPTED FROM SPITZER, FIRST, & WILLIAMS, 1994, PP. 88–90

People who develop hypochondriasis have more health worries, more psychiatric symptoms, and perceive their health to be worse than do other people. They are also more likely than other psychiatric patients to report being sick as children, having missed school because of health reasons, and having experienced childhood trauma, such as sexual abuse or physical violence. Hypochondriasis may fluctuate in severity over time or it may persist in a severe form for many years (Strassnig, Stowell, First, & Pincus, 2006; Taylor & Asmundson, 2004). Many people with this disorder also have other psychological disorders, especially major depression and anxiety disorders (Taylor & Asmundson, 2004).

Somatization Disorder

Somatization disorder, formerly known as Briquet's syndrome, is characterized by multiple and recurrent somatic complaints that begin prior to the age of 30 (most commonly during the teen years), persist for at least several years, and result in the seeking of medical attention and significant impairment in fulfilling social or occupational roles. Complaints usually involve various organ systems (Hiller, Rief, & Brähler, 2006). Seldom does a year pass without some physical complaint that prompts a trip to the doctor. People with somatization disorder are heavy users of medical services; people with somatization symptoms, compared to non-somatizing patients, use twice as many inpatient and outpatient medical services, resulting in twice the annual medical costs (Strassnig et al., 2006). The complaints cannot be explained by physical causes or exceed what would be expected from a known physical problem. Complaints seem vague or exaggerated, and the person frequently receives medical care from a number of physicians, sometimes at the same time.

Somatization disorder usually begins in adolescence or young adulthood and appears to be a lifelong disorder involving major disability (Kirmayer & Looper, 2006). It usually occurs in the context of other psychological disorders, especially anxiety disorders and depressive disorders (APA, 2000a). Estimates are that 1 person in 1000 is affected by somatization disorder, with ten times as many cases found among women than men (APA, 2000a). Not much is known of the childhood backgrounds of people with somatization disorder. Although a number of studies found high rates of childhood sexual abuse among patients with somatoform disorders, several recent studies found that other aspects of negative parenting style have a stronger association with somatization; for example, childhood physical and emotional abuse and an unsupportive (e.g., hostile and rejecting/neglectful) family environment (Kirmayer & Looper, 2006).

The essential feature of hypochondriasis is fear of disease, of what bodily symptoms may portend. Persons with somatization disorder, by contrast, are pestered by the symptoms themselves. Both diagnoses may be given to the same individual if the diagnostic criteria for both disorders are met.

Other Somatoform Disorders

Two other somatoform disorders, which we will briefly mention, are *body dysmorphic disorder* and *pain disorder*. Body dysmorphic disorder is diagnosed when a person is preoccupied with some imagined defect in his or her appearance. The person is typically preoccupied with a facial feature, and may become highly upset about some minor feature ("My lips are too thin" or "My ears aren't symmetrical"). In some cases, this preoccupation can lead the person to repeatedly seek plastic surgery. The preoccupation with the body part far exceeds normal worries about physical imperfections. People with body dysmorphic disorder

somatization disorder Type of somatoform disorder involving recurrent multiple complaints that cannot be explained by any clear physical causes. Formerly called *Briquet's syndrome*.

may endlessly worry about their bodies and be considerably distressed as a result. Preoccupation can also interfere with work, school, or social functioning (e.g., by avoiding social gatherings because of imagined ugliness, or failing to get work assignments done because the person is spending too much time checking his or her appearance in the mirror).

Pain disorder is characterized by a preoccupation with pain in cases in which a physical cause cannot adequately explain the persistence of the person's pain. Psychological factors are judged to play an important role in creating or intensifying the person's chronic pain. For example, receiving sympathy and attention from others can motivate the person to focus on and complain excessively of pain. In other cases, complaints of pain may be reinforced because they enable the person to get out of arduous or boring tasks (e.g., household chores). Such incentives often perpetuate pain complaints. Stressful life events may also contribute to the pain experienced in people diagnosed with pain disorder. This can arise because stressors can lead the person to experience prolonged muscle tension, resulting in muscle cramps or headaches.

Theoretical Perspectives

Conversion disorder, or "hysteria," was known to Hippocrates, who attributed the strange bodily symptoms to a wandering uterus, which created internal chaos. The term *hysterical* derives from the Greek *hystera*, meaning "uterus." Hippocrates noticed that these complaints were less common among married women. He prescribed marriage as a "cure" on the basis of these observations, and also on the theoretical assumption that pregnancy would satisfy uterine needs and fix the organ in place. Pregnancy fosters hormonal and structural changes that are of benefit to some women with menstrual complaints, but Hippocrates's belief in the "wandering uterus" has contributed throughout the centuries to degrading interpretations of complaints by women of physical problems. Despite Hippocrates's belief that hysteria is exclusively a female concern, it also occurs in men.

Modern theoretical accounts of the somatoform disorders, like those of the dissociative disorders, have most often sprung from psychodynamic and learning theories. Although not much is known about biological underpinnings of somatoform disorders, evidence indicates that somatization disorder tends to run in families, and a recent twin

What to take? Hypochondriasis involves persistent concerns or fears that one is seriously ill, although no organic basis can be found to account for the person's physical complaints. People with this disorder frequently medicate themselves with over-the-counter preparations and find little, if any, reassurance in doctors' assertions that their health is not in jeopardy.

study conducted at the University of British Columbia indicates that hypochondriacal features—such as excessive health-related worry and the unfounded belief that one has a serious, undiagnosed disease—are caused by a combination of environmental and genetic factors (Taylor, Thordarson, Jang, & Asmundson, 2006). Environmental factors include learning experiences such as episodes of childhood illness that teach the child that he or she is sickly and frail (Taylor & Asmundson, 2004). Such experiences can give rise to unrealistic beliefs (e.g., "My health is in constant jeopardy"), which can cause people to focus their attention on their bodies and thereby notice and misinterpret the significance of minor bodily aches and pains or other bodily changes (Marcus, Gurley, Marchi, & Bauer, 2007). Such factors also appear to play a role in somatization (Brown, 2004). Thus, an accumulating body of research supports learning theories of hypochondriasis and other somatoform disorders, although the results indicate that biological factors such as genes also play a role (Kirmayer & Looper, 2006; Rief & Barsky, 2005; Taylor, Thordarson, Jang, & Asmundson, 2006).

Hysterical disorders provided an arena for some of the debate between the psychological and biological theories of the 19th century. The alleviation—albeit often temporarily—of hysterical symptoms through hypnosis by Charcot, Breuer, and Freud contributed to the belief that hysteria was rooted in psychological rather than physical causes and led Freud to the development of a theory of the unconscious mind. Freud held that the ego manages to control unacceptable or threatening sexual and aggressive impulses arising from the id through defence mechanisms such as repression. Such control prevents the outbreak of anxiety that would occur if the person were to become aware of them. In some cases, the leftover emotion or energy that is "strangulated" or cut off from the threatening impulses becomes *converted* into a physical symptom, such as hysterical paralysis or blindness. Although the early psychodynamic formulation of hysteria is still widely held, empirical evidence has been lacking. One problem with the Freudian view is that it does not explain how energies left over from unconscious conflicts become transformed into physical symptoms (Miller, 1987). A further problem is that psychodynamic theory does not consider the role of learning factors (e.g., sympathy or other forms of positive reinforcement for expressing symptoms) or biological factors in the disorder (Stonnington, Barry, & Fisher, 2006; Wald, Taylor, & Scamvougeras, 2004).

According to psychodynamic theory, hysterical symptoms are functional: they allow the person to achieve **primary gains** and **secondary gains**. The primary gains consist of allowing the individual to keep internal conflicts repressed. The person is aware of the physical symptom, but not of the conflict it represents. In such cases, the "symptom" is symbolic of, and provides the person with a "partial solution" of, the underlying conflict. For example, the hysterical paralysis of an arm might symbolize and also prevent the individual from acting out on repressed unacceptable sexual (e.g., masturbatory) or aggressive (e.g., murderous) impulses. Repression occurs automatically, so the individual remains unaware of the underlying conflicts. *La belle indifférence*, first noted by Charcot, is believed to occur because the physical symptoms help relieve rather than cause anxiety. From the psychodynamic perspective, conversion disorders, like dissociative disorders, serve a purpose.

Secondary gains may allow the individual to avoid burdensome responsibilities and to gain the support—rather than condemnation—of those around them. For example, soldiers sometimes experience sudden "paralysis" of their hands, which prevents them from firing their guns in battle. They may then be sent to recuperate at a hospital rather than face enemy fire. The symptoms in such cases are not considered contrived, as would be the case in malingering. A number of World War II bomber pilots suffered hysterical "night blindness" that prevented them from carrying out dangerous nighttime missions. In the psychodynamic view, their "blindness" may have achieved a primary gain of shielding them from guilt associated with dropping bombs on civilian areas. It may also have achieved a secondary purpose of helping them avoid dangerous missions.

Psychodynamic theory and learning theory concur that the symptoms in conversion disorders relieve anxiety. Psychodynamic theorists, however, seek the causes of anxiety in unconscious conflicts. However, there is little evidence to support psychodynamic theories that propose that medically unexplained symptoms such as those found in somatoform disorders are the expression of unconscious psychological conflicts (Brown, 2004).

Learning theorists focus on the more direct reinforcing properties of the symptom and its secondary role in helping the individual avoid or escape uncomfortable or anxiety-evoking situations. From the learning perspective, the symptoms in conversion and other somatoform disorders may also carry the benefits or reinforcing properties of the "sick role" (Speed & Mooney, 1997). Persons with conversion disorders may be relieved of chores and responsibilities like going to work or performing household tasks. Being sick also usually earns sympathy and support. People who received such reinforcers during past illnesses are likely to learn to adopt a sick role even when they are not ill. We are not suggesting that people with conversion disorders are fakers. We are merely pointing out that people may learn to adopt roles that lead to reinforcing consequences, regardless of whether or not they deliberately seek to enact these roles.

A leading cognitive explanation of hypochondriasis focuses on the role of distorted thinking (Marcus et al., 2007; Taylor & Asmundson, 2004). People who develop hypochondriasis have a tendency to "make mountains out of molehills" by exaggerating the importance of their physical complaints. They misinterpret relatively minor physical complaints as signs of a serious illness, creating anxiety and leading them to chase down one doctor after another in an attempt to uncover the dreaded disease they fear they have. The anxiety itself may lead to unpleasant physical symptoms, which are likewise exaggerated in importance, leading to more worrisome thoughts.

primary gains In psychodynamic theory, the relief from anxiety obtained through the development of a neurotic symptom.

secondary gains Side benefits associated with neuroses or other disorders, such as expressions of sympathy and increased attention from others, and release from ordinary responsibilities.

Koro and Dhat Syndromes: Far Eastern Somatoform Disorders?

In Canada, it is common for people who develop hypochondriasis to be troubled by the idea that they have serious illnesses, such as cancer. The Koro and Dhat syndromes of the Far East share some clinical features with hypochondriasis. Although these syndromes may seem strange to most North American readers, they are each connected through folklore within their Far Eastern cultures.

Koro Syndrome

Koro syndrome is a culture-bound syndrome found primarily in China and some other Far Eastern countries, although Koro-like cases also have been described in Africa, India, and Western countries, including Canada (Dzokoto & Adams, 2005). People with Koro fear their genitals are shrinking and retracting into the body, which they believe will result in death (Cheng, 1996). The syndrome, which tends to be short-lived, has been identified mainly in young men, although some cases have also been reported in women, who fear that their genitals or breasts are shrinking or retracting into the body (Chowdhury, 1996; Dzokoto & Adams, 2005). Physiological signs of anxiety that approach panic proportions are common, including profuse sweating, breathlessness, and heart palpitations. Men who suffer from Koro have been known to use mechanical devices such as chopsticks to try to prevent the penis from retracting into the body (Cheng, 1996).

[4]The word Dhat can be loosely translated as "the elixir of life."

Epidemics involving hundreds or thousands of people have been reported in parts of Asia such as China, Singapore, Thailand, and India (Dzokoto & Adams, 2005). For example, in southern China an epidemic of Koro involving more than 3000 people occurred during 1984–1985, with incidence in the most severely afflicted villages ranging from 6 to 19% (Cheng, 1996). People who fall victim to Koro tend to be poorly educated, lacking in proper sex information, and accepting of Koro-related folk beliefs (such as the belief that shrinkage of the penis will be lethal) (Cheng, 1996; Chowdhury, 1996; Dzokoto & Adams, 2005). Medical reassurance that such fears are unfounded often quell Koro episodes. Similar reassurance generally fails to dent the concerns of Westerners who develop hypochondriasis, however (Taylor & Asmundson, 2004). Koro episodes among those who do not receive corrective information tend to pass with time but may recur.

Koro has been classified in various ways—as a form of anxiety disorder, depersonalization, body-image disturbance, or an atypical somatoform disorder (Chowdhury, 1996; Dzokoto & Adams, 2005).

Dhat Syndrome

Dhat syndrome[4] is found among young males in India and involves excessive fears over the loss of seminal fluid during nocturnal emissions (Ranjith & Mohan, 2006). Some men with this syndrome also believe (incorrectly) that semen mixes with urine and is excreted through urination. Men with Dhat syndrome may roam from physician to physician seeking help to prevent nocturnal emissions or the (imagined) loss of

Koro syndrome Culture-related somatoform disorder, found primarily in China, in which people fear their genitals are shrinking and retracting into the body.

Dhat syndrome Usually diagnosed among young Indian men who describe an intense fear or anxiety over the loss of semen.

Cognitive theorists have recently speculated that hypochondriasis and panic disorder, with which it often occurs concurrently, may share a common cause, namely a cognitive bias to misinterpret changes in bodily cues or sensations as signs of catastrophic harm (Salkovskis & Clark, 1993). Differences between the two disorders may hinge on whether the misinterpretation of bodily cues carries a perception of imminent threat leading to a rapid spiralling of anxiety (panic disorder) or of a longer-range threat in the form of an underlying disease process (hypochondriasis). Research into cognitive processes involved in hypochondriasis deserves further study. Given the linkages that may exist between hypochondriasis and anxiety disorders such as panic disorder and OCD, it remains unclear whether hypochondriasis should be classified as a somatoform disorder or an anxiety disorder.

semen mixed with excreted urine. There is a widespread belief within Indian culture (and other Near- and Far Eastern cultures) that the loss of semen is harmful because it depletes the body of physical and mental energy (Ranjith & Mohan, 2006). Like other culture-bound syndromes, Dhat must be understood within its cultural context. Based on the cultural belief in the life-preserving nature of semen, it is not surprising that some Indian males experience extreme anxiety over the involuntary loss of the fluid through nocturnal emissions.

According to Ranjith and Mohan (2006), Dhat is a form of health anxiety similar to hypochondriasis: under stress, people who are predisposed to worry about their health may focus their attention on bodily products or changes, such as turbidity of urine and tiredness. And, in light of widely held beliefs in their community, they may misattribute these bodily products or changes to loss of semen.

Culture-bound disorders such as Koro and Dhat are unlikely to remain static. The prevalence and features of such disorders probably shift along with changes in the pertinent cultures. In recent years, there have been several reports of cases of Dhat in various countries, including Western countries, which raise doubt about whether we should still consider Koro and Dhat to be culture-bound syndromes (Chandrashekar & Math, 2006).

Culture-Bound Dissociative Conditions

Commonalities also exist between the Western concept of dissociative disorders and certain culture-bound syndromes found in other parts of the world. For

Dhat syndrome. Found principally in India, Dhat syndrome afflicts young men with an intense fear or anxiety over the loss of semen.

example, *amok* is a culture-bound syndrome occurring primarily in Southeast Asian and Pacific island cultures that describes a trancelike state in which a person suddenly becomes highly excited and violently attacks other people or destroys objects (see Chapter 3). People who "run amok" may later claim to have no memory of the episode or recall feeling as if they were acting like a robot. Another example is *zar*, a term used in North African and Middle Eastern countries to describe spirit possession in people who experience dissociative states during which they engage in unusual behaviour, ranging from shouting to banging their heads against a wall. The behaviour itself is not deemed abnormal, because it is believed to be controlled by spirits.

Treatment of Somatoform Disorders

The treatment approach that Freud pioneered—psychoanalysis—began with the treatment of hysteria, which is now termed *conversion disorder*. Psychoanalysis seeks to uncover and bring unconscious conflicts that originated in childhood into conscious awareness. Once the conflict is aired and worked through, the symptom is no longer needed as a "partial solution" to the conflict and should disappear. The psychoanalytic method is supported by case studies, some reported by Freud and others by his followers. However, the infrequency of conversion disorders in contemporary times has made it difficult to mount controlled studies of the psychoanalytic technique.

The behavioural approach to treating conversion disorders and other somatoform disorders may focus on removing sources of secondary reinforcement (or secondary gain) that may become connected with physical complaints. Family members and others, for example, often perceive individuals with somatization disorder as sickly and infirm and as incapable of carrying normal responsibilities. Other people may be unaware of how they reinforce dependent and complaining behaviours when they relieve the sick person of responsibilities. The behaviour therapist may teach family members to reward attempts to assume responsibility and ignore nagging and complaining. The behaviour therapist may also work more directly with the person who has a somatoform disorder, for example, helping the person to learn more adaptive ways of handling stress or anxiety through relaxation and cognitive restructuring (e.g., Wald et al., 2004). A lack of controlled studies in this area limits any general conclusions about the effectiveness of behavioural methods. A growing number of studies, however, indicates that cognitive-behavioural therapy (CBT) is effective in treating hypochondriasis and somatization disorder (Greeven et al., 2007; Janca, 2005; Taylor, Asmundson, & Coons, 2005). CBT is used to help modify the exaggerated illness-related beliefs of patients with the disorder.

Attention has recently turned to the use of antidepressants, especially SSRI medications such as fluoxetine (Prozac) and paroxetine (Paxil), in treating some types of somatoform disorder. Although we lack specific drug therapies for conversion disorder, several studies suggest that hypochondriasis can be successfully treated with SSRI medications (Greeven et al., 2007; Taylor, Asmundson, & Coons, 2005). We lack any systematic studies of approaches to treating factitious disorder (Münchausen's syndrome) and are a limited to a few isolated case examples; for the most part, Münchausen's syndrome is extremely difficult to treat and the prognosis is poor (Huffman & Stern, 2003; Slovenko, 2006).

The dissociative and somatoform disorders remain among the most intriguing and least-understood patterns of abnormal behaviour.

STUDY BREAK

Somatoform Disorders

Review It

- **What are somatoform disorders?** In somatoform disorders, there are physical complaints that cannot be accounted for by organic causes. Thus, the symptoms are theorized to reflect psychological rather than organic factors. Three types of somatoform disorders are considered: conversion disorder, hypochondriasis, and somatization disorder.

- **What are the major features of conversion disorder, hypochondriasis, and somatization disorder?** In conversion disorder, symptoms or deficits in voluntary motor or sensory functions occur that suggest an underlying physical disorder, but no apparent medical basis for the condition can be found. Hypochondriasis is a preoccupation with the fear of having or the belief that one has a serious medical illness, but no medical basis for the complaints can be found and fears of illness persist despite medical reassurances. Formerly known as Briquet's syndrome, somatization disorder involves multiple and recurrent complaints of physical symptoms that persist for many years and usually begian prior to the age of 30—most typically during adolescence.

- **How are somatoform disorders conceptualized by the various theoretical perspectives?** The psychodynamic view holds that conversion disorders represent the conversion into physical symptoms of the left-over emotion or energy cut off from unacceptable or threatening impulses that the ego has prevented from reaching awareness. The symptom is functional, allowing the person to achieve both primary gains and secondary gains. Learning theorists focus on reinforcements that are associated with conversion disorders, such as the reinforcing effects of adopting a "sick role." Cognitive factors in hypochondriasis include unrealistic beliefs about health and disease.

- **How is the treatment of conversion disorder approached by the various theoretical perspectives?** Psychodynamic therapists attempt to uncover and bring to the level of awareness the unconscious conflicts, originating in childhood, that are believed to be at the root of the problem. Once the conflict is uncovered and worked through, the symptoms should disappear because they are no longer needed as a partial solution to the underlying conflict. Behavioural approaches focus on removing underlying sources of reinforcement that may be maintaining the abnormal behaviour pattern. More generally, behaviour therapists assist people with somatoform disorders to learn to handle stressful or anxiety-arousing situations more effectively.

Define It

somatoform disorders   somatization disorder
factitious disorder   primary gains
Münchausen syndrome   secondary gains
conversion disorder   Koro syndrome
la belle indifférence   Dhat syndrome

Recall It*

1. The word *somatoform* derives from the Greek word meaning _____.

    a. "body"
    b. "illness"
    c. "split"
    d. "deviation"

2. Which of the following is NOT a classic symptom of conversion disorder?

    a. epilepsy
    b. blindness
    c. paranoia
    d. paralysis

3. Richard is preoccupied with the idea that his physical symptoms are signs of cancer, even though he has been reassured by his doctors that his fears are unfounded. He is most likely to be diagnosed with _____.

    a. conversion disorder
    b. somatization disorder
    c. hypochondriasis
    d. Münchausen's syndrome

4. Cognitive theorists propose that the physical complaints of people with hypochondriasis may represent a type of _____ strategy.

    a. passive-aggressive
    b. repressive
    c. withdrawal
    d. self-handicapping

5. In treating people with somatoform disorders, behaviour therapists often focus on _____.

    a. rewarding sources of primary gain
    b. punishing hysterical complaints
    c. removing sources of secondary gain
    d. restricting the stimulus field

* Recall It answers can be found on the Companion Website for this text.

Think About It

- Why is conversion disorder considered a treasure trove in the annals of abnormal psychology? What role did the disorder play in the development of psychological models of abnormal behaviour?
- People often become labelled as hypochondriacs when others don't believe that their symptoms are real. Based on your reading of the text, why is this belief unfounded?

WEBLINKS

Sidran Institute
www.sidran.org
The Sidran Institute's website contains information on dissociative disorders, including links to books and educational materials.

Imaginary Crimes
http://members.shaw.ca/imaginarycrimes/repressedmemory.htm
Information and links on repressed memory.

Recovered Memories
http://psych.athabascau.ca/html/aupr/psyclaw.shtml#Recovered%20Memories
Contains useful links on recovered memories.

False-Memory Syndrome Foundation
www.fmsonline.org
Further useful information on repressed and recovered memories and dissociative disorders.

Psychology Works for Intense Illness Concern (Hypochondriasis)
www.cpa.ca/cpasite/userfiles/Documents/factsheets/hypo.pdf
Fact sheet and links on hypochondriasis from the Canadian Psychological Association.

Dissociative and Somatoform Disorders

Dissociative Disorders

Dissociative Identity Disorder (formerly called Multiple Personality Disorder)

Features
- At least two distinct personalities
- Different personalities repeatedly take control
- Failure to recall important personal info
- Not due to drugs, alcohol, or medical condition

Theories
- Psychodynamic: Massive repression
- Diathesis-stress model
- Spanos: Disorder is a form of well-engrained role-playing, reinforced by others

Treatments
- Psychodynamic: Goal of uncovering trauma and reintegrating personalities
- Effectiveness of any treatment remains to be established
- Other

Other important points
- Existence of disorder is controversial
- Suggestible individuals may be led to "reveal" multiple personalities by hypnosis or leading questions by overzealous therapists

Dissociative Amnesia

Features
- Unable to recall important personal info
- Usually triggered by traumatic or stressful experiences
- Not due to simple forgetfulness
- Not due to drugs, alcohol, or medical condition

Theories
- Psychodynamic: Massive repression
- Learning theory: Learned avoidance
- Diathesis-stress model

Treatments
- Amnesia is usually short-lived and so treatment is usually unnecessary

Other important points
- Amnesia can be selective or generalized
- Can be difficult to distinguish dissociative amnesia from malingering

Dissociative Fugue

Features
- Dissociative amnesia "on the run"
- Person travels suddenly and unexpectedly away from home and assumes new identity
- Amnesia for past identity

Theories
- Psychodynamic: Massive repression
- Learning theory: Learned avoidance
- Diathesis-stress model

Treatments
- Amnesia is usually short-lived so treatment is usually unnecessary

Other important points
- Flight is purposeful, not aimless wandering
- Person is not psychotic
- Disorder often spontaneously ends
- Need to rule out malingering

Depersonalization Disorder

Features
- Recurrent/persistent depersonalization
- Reality testing is intact
- Depersonalization causes distress or impairment
- Not due to drugs, alcohol, or medical condition

Theories
- Psychodynamic: Massive repression
- Learning theory: Learned avoidance
- Diathesis-stress model

Treatments
- Cognitive-behavioural treatments and some medications show promise

Other important points
- Depersonalization may be associated with derealization
- Isolated episodes of depersonalization and derealization are common experiences in normal people

Somatoform Disorders

Conversion Disorder (formerly called Hysteria)

Features
- Symptoms/deficits suggesting a physical disorder
- Psychological factors are judged to contribute to the disorder
- Not due to purposefully producing the symptoms
- Not due to other factors (e.g., not a physical disorder)
- Symptoms cause significant distress/impairment

Theories
- Psychodynamic: Expression of unconscious conflict
- Learning theory: Reinforcement for sick role

Treatments
- Psychodynamic, cognitive-behavioural, and other treatments, although little is known about the efficacy of these interventions

Other important points
- Not due to malingering or factitious disorder, or an undiagnosed physical disorder such as a neurological disease

Hypochondriasis

Features
- Persistent fear/preoccupation that one has a serious illness
- Fear/preoccupation persists despite medical reassurance
- Causes significant distress/impairment
- Not due to some other disorder

Theories
- Psychodynamic: Expression of unconscious conflict
- Learning theory: Reinforcement for sick role
- Cognitive theory: Role of dysfunctional beliefs and misinterpretations of harmless bodily sensations

Treatments
- Cognitive-behaviour therapy
- Particular medications such as SSRIs

Other important points
- Not due to malingering or factitious disorder

Somatization Disorder (formerly Briquet's Syndrome)

Features
- Multiple, recurrent medically unexplained physical symptoms involving multiple organ systems
- Persists for many years
- Causes significant distress/impairment and frequent medical consultations

Theories
- Psychodynamic: Expression of unconscious conflict
- Learning theory: Reinforcement for sick role
- Cognitive theory: Role of dysfunctional beliefs and misinterpretations of harmless bodily sensations

Treatments
- Cognitive-behaviour therapy
- Particular medications such as SSRIs

Other important points
- Not due to malingering or factitious disorder

CHAPTER 7

Mood Disorders and Suicide

CHAPTER OUTLINE

Types of Mood Disorders
Theoretical Perspectives
Treatment
Suicide

Did You Know That...

See the underlined text on the pages indicated below for more information on these interesting and often misunderstood facts.

- Feeling depressed is perfectly normal in some circumstances? (p. 243)

- Most people who become severely depressed will suffer additional episodes later in life? (p. 246)

- The bleak light of winter casts some people into a diagnosable state of depression? (p. 248)

- Some people ride an emotional roller coaster, swinging from the heights of elation to the depths of depression without any external cause? (p. 251)

- The ancient Greeks and Romans used a chemical that is still used today to curb turbulent mood swings? (p. 273)

- The most widely used remedy for depression in Germany is not a drug but an herb? (p. 274)

- It is untrue that people who threaten to commit suicide are only seeking attention? (p. 279)

LIFE HAS ITS UPS and downs. Most of us feel elated when we have earned high grades, a promotion, or the affections of Ms. or Mr. Right. Most of us feel down or depressed when we are rejected by a date, flunk a test, or suffer financial losses. It is normal and appropriate to be happy about uplifting events. It is just as normal, just as appropriate, to feel depressed by dismal events. It might very well be "abnormal" if we were not depressed by life's miseries.

Our **moods** are enduring states of feeling that colour our psychological lives. Feeling down or depressed is not abnormal in the context of depressing events or circumstances. But people with **mood disorders** experience disturbances in mood that are unusually severe or prolonged and impair their ability to function in meeting their normal responsibilities. Some people become severely depressed even when things appear to be going well or when they encounter mildly upsetting events that others take in stride. Still others experience extreme mood swings. They ride an emotional roller coaster with dizzying heights and abysmal depths when the world around them remains largely on an even keel.

mood Pervasive quality of an individual's emotional experience, as in depressed mood, anxious mood, or elated mood.

mood disorder Type of disorder characterized by disturbances of mood, as in depressive disorders (*major depressive disorder* or *dysthymic disorder*) or bipolar disorders (*bipolar disorder* and *cyclothymic disorder*).

TYPES OF MOOD DISORDERS

In this chapter, we focus on several kinds of mood disorders, including two kinds of depressive disorders—major depressive disorder and dysthymic disorder—and two kinds of mood swing disorders—bipolar disorder and cyclothymic disorder (see Table 7.1). Table 7.2 on page 244 lists some of the common features of depression. The depressive disorders are considered **unipolar** because the disturbance lies in only one emotional direction or pole—down. Disorders that involve mood swings are **bipolar**. They involve excesses of both depression and elation, usually in an alternating pattern.

Many of us, probably most of us, have periods of sadness from time to time. We may feel down in the dumps, cry, lose interest in things, find it hard to concentrate, expect the worst to happen, or even consider suicide. To illustrate the prevalence of sadness and

unipolar Pertaining to a single pole or direction, as in unipolar (depressive) disorders. Contrast with *bipolar disorder*.

bipolar Characterized by opposites, as in *bipolar disorder*.

TABLE 7.1	
Types of Mood Disorders	
Depressive Disorders (Unipolar Disorders)	
Major Depressive Disorder	Occurrence of one or more periods or episodes of depression (called major depressive episodes) without a history of naturally occurring manic or hypomanic episodes. People may have one major depressive episode, followed by a return to their usual state of functioning. The majority of people with a major depressive episode have recurrences that are separated by periods of normal or perhaps somewhat impaired functioning.
Dysthymic Disorder	A pattern of mild depression (but perhaps an irritable mood in children or adolescents) that occurs for an extended period of time—in adults, typically for many years.
Bipolar Disorders	
Bipolar Disorders	Disorders with one or more manic or hypomanic episodes (episodes of inflated mood and hyperactivity in which judgment and behaviour are often impaired). Manic or hypomanic episodes often alternate with major depressive episodes with intervening periods of normal mood.
Cyclothymic Disorder	A chronic mood disturbance involving numerous hypomanic episodes (episodes with manic features of a lesser degree of severity than manic episodes) and numerous periods of depressed mood or loss of interest or pleasure in activities, but not of the severity to meet the criteria for a major depressive episode.

Source: Adapted from the DSM-IV (APA, 2000a).

TABLE 7.2

Common Features of Depression

Changes in Emotional States	Changes in mood (persistent periods of feeling down, depressed, sad, or blue) Tearfulness or crying Increased irritability or loss of temper
Changes in Motivation	Feeling unmotivated, or having difficulty getting going in the morning or even getting out of bed Reduced level of social participation or interest in social activities Loss of enjoyment or interest in pleasurable activities Reduced interest in sex Failure to respond to praise or rewards
Changes in Functioning and Motor Behaviour	Moving about or talking more slowly than usual Changes in sleep habits (sleeping too much or too little, awakening earlier than usual and having trouble getting back to sleep in early morning hours—so-called early morning awakening) Changes in appetite (eating too much or too little) Changes in weight (gaining or losing weight) Functioning less effectively than usual at work or school
Cognitive Changes	Difficulty concentrating or thinking clearly Thinking negatively about oneself and one's future Feeling guilty or remorseful about past misdeeds Lack of self-esteem or feelings of inadequacy Thinking of death or suicide

major depressive disorder Severe mood disorder characterized by the occurrence of major depressive episodes in the absence of a history of manic episodes. Major depressive disorder is characterized by a range of features such as depressed mood, lack of interest or pleasure in usual activities, lack of energy or motivation, and changes in appetite or sleep patterns.

depression, a survey of nearly 5000 high school students in Ontario found that 16% had often felt sad in the preceding seven days and 12% had felt depressed during this period (Adlaf & Paglia, 2001). For most of us, mood changes pass quickly or are not severe enough to interfere with our lifestyle or ability to function.

Among people with mood disorders, including depressive disorders and bipolar disorders, mood changes are more severe or prolonged and affect daily functioning.

Major Depressive Disorder

The diagnosis of **major depressive disorder** (also called *major depression*) is based on the occurrence of one or more *major depressive episodes* in the absence of a history of

Major depression versus bereavement. Major depression is distinguished from a normal grief reaction to the death of a loved one, which is termed bereavement. But major depression may occur in people whose bereavement becomes prolonged or seriously interferes with normal functioning.

When are changes in mood considered abnormal? Although changes in mood in response to the ups and downs of everyday life may be quite normal, persistent or severe changes in mood or cycles of extreme elation and depression may suggest the presence of a mood disorder.

manic or **hypomanic episodes.** In a major depressive episode, the person experiences either a depressed mood (feeling sad, hopeless, or "down in the dumps") or loss of interest or pleasure in all or virtually all activities for a period of at least two weeks (APA, 2000a). The diagnostic features of a major depressive episode are listed in Table 7.3 below.

manic Relating to mania, as in the manic phase of a bipolar disorder.

hypomanic episodes Mild manic episodes.

People with major depressive disorder may also have poor appetite, lose or gain substantial amounts of weight, and become physically agitated or—at the other extreme—show a marked slowing down in their motor activity. They may lose interest in most of their usual activities and pursuits, have difficulty concentrating and making decisions, have pressing thoughts of death, and may attempt suicide. Although depression is a diagnosable psychological disorder, many people polled in surveys perceive it to be a sign of personal weakness (Jorm et al., 2006). Many people don't seem to understand that people who are clinically depressed can't simply "shake it off" or "snap out of it." This attitude may explain why, despite the availability of safe and effective treatments, many people who are clinically depressed remain untreated (Beck et al., 2005). Many people with untreated depression believe that they should be able to handle the problem themselves (Jorm et al., 2006). In fact, it can be very difficult to handle major depression without receiving professional help. Major depressive disorder is the most common type of mood disorder, affecting—at some point in their lives—about 12% of Canadian adults living in the community (Patten et al., 2006). Depression may be even more prevalent in other countries such as the United States (Patten et al., 2006). At least 1 in 20 people can be diagnosed with major depression at any given time—it is so common that it's been dubbed the "common cold" of psychological problems. Effective treatment for depression is available and leads not only to psychological improvement but also to increased income, as people are able to return to a more productive level of functioning. In our clinical practices, we have seen college students who were on the verge of dropping out of school because of major depression receive effective treatment and become able to complete their degrees.

Major depression, particularly in more severe episodes, may be accompanied by psychotic features, such as delusions that one's body is rotting from illness (Meyers, 2006).

bereavement Normal experience of suffering following the loss of a loved one.

TABLE 7.3

Diagnostic Features of a Major Depressive Episode

A major depressive episode is denoted by the occurrence of five or more of the following features or symptoms during a two-week period, which represents a change from previous functioning. At least one of the features must involve either (1) depressed mood, or (2) loss of interest or pleasure in activities. Moreover, the symptoms must cause either clinically significant levels of distress or impairment in at least one important area of functioning, such as social or occupational functioning, and must not be due directly to the use of drugs or medications, or to a medical condition, or accounted for by another psychological disorder.* Nor can it represent a normal grief reaction to the death of a loved one—that is, **bereavement**.

1. Depressed mood during most of the day, nearly every day; can be irritable mood in children or adolescents

2. Greatly reduced sense of pleasure or interest in all or almost all activities, nearly every day for most of the day

3. A significant loss or gain of weight (more than 5% of body weight in a month) without any attempt to diet, or an increase or decrease in appetite

4. Daily (or nearly daily) insomnia or hypersomnia

5. Excessive agitation or slowing down of movement responses nearly every day

6. Feelings of fatigue or loss of energy nearly every day

7. Feelings of worthlessness or misplaced or excessive or inappropriate guilt nearly every day

8. Reduced ability to concentrate or think clearly or make decisions nearly every day

9. Recurrent thoughts of death or suicide without a specific plan, or occurrence of a suicidal attempt or specific plan for committing suicide

* The DSM includes separate diagnostic categories for mood disorders due to medical conditions or due to the use of substances such as drugs of abuse.

Source: Adapted from the DSM-IV (APA, 2000a).

People with severe depression may also experience hallucinations, such as "hearing" the voices of others, or of demons, condemning them for perceived misdeeds or telling them to kill themselves.

Sarah Hamid, an undergraduate at Simon Fraser University in Vancouver, provided the following illustration of some of the features of her unipolar depression:

> The symptoms of mental illness crept over Sarah like a cold, damp fog. Cloaked in her dark world, Sarah was sleeping 12 to 16 hours a day. She would weep in class, so much that she'd sneak off to the bathroom so no one could see. "Almost like someone with an addiction," says Sarah, "I was finding places to hide my habit." She ate little and was losing weight. "It got to the point where I was driving home one day and I really wanted to drive the car over the yellow line into oncoming traffic," says Sarah. "I was like, Okay, I really have to tell someone." Her doctor diagnosed severe depression. Now 24, Sarah takes an effective anti-depressant, and the crying fits that would overwhelm her for hours once or twice a day now happen only every few months or so and last only maybe ten minutes.
>
> ADAPTED FROM HAWALESHKA, 2002

A major depressive disorder, if left untreated, usually lasts for six months or longer and possibly even two or more years (APA, 2000a). Some people experience a single episode with a full return to previous levels of functioning. However, the majority of people with major depression, at least 50%, have repeated occurrences (Health Canada, 2002a). Given a pattern of repeated occurrences of major depressive episodes and prolonged symptoms, many professionals have come to view major depression as a chronic, indeed lifelong, disorder.

Risk Factors for Major Depression Factors that place people at greater risk of developing major depression include the following: age (initial onset is more common among younger adults than older ones), socioeconomic status (people on the lower rungs of the socioeconomic ladder are at greater risk than those who are better off), and marital status (people who are not in an intimate relationship tend to be at greater risk than those who are in such a relationship) (Afifi, Cox, & Enns, 2006; Patten et al., 2006).

Women are nearly twice as likely as men to develop major depression, although the difference becomes smaller with advancing age (Health Canada, 2002a; Patten et al., 2006) (see Figure 7.1). Although hormonal or other biologically linked gender differences may be involved, the gender difference may be due to the greater amount of stress that women encounter in contemporary life (Hammen, 2005). Women are more likely than men to encounter such stressful life factors as physical and sexual abuse, poverty, single parenthood, and sexism.

Differences in coping styles may also help explain women's greater proneness toward depression. Regardless of whether or not the initial precipitants of depression are biological, psychological, or social, one's coping responses may either worsen or reduce the severity and duration of depressive episodes. Nolen-Hoeksema and

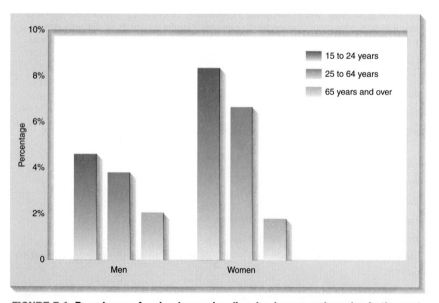

FIGURE 7.1 Prevalence of major depressive disorder, by age and gender, in the past 12 months in Canada.

Source: Adapted from Statistics Canada, "Canadian Community Health Survey-Mental Health and Well-Being," 2002. Catalogue 82-617, September 9, 2004.

Corte have found that men are more likely to distract themselves when they are depressed, whereas women are more likely to amplify depression by ruminating about their feelings and possible causes (Nolen-Hoeksema & Corte, 2004). Women may be more likely to sit at home when they are depressed and think about how they feel or try to understand the reasons they feel the way they do, whereas men may try to distract themselves by doing something they enjoy, such as by going to a favourite hangout to get their mind off their feelings. Men often distract themselves by turning to alcohol as a form of self-medication, which can lead to another set of psychological and social problems (Nolen-Hoeksema & Corte, 2004).

Rumination is not limited to women, although they tend to do so more than men. Both men and women who repeatedly ruminate about the loss of loved ones or when feeling down or sad are more likely to become depressed and to suffer longer and more severe depression than those who ruminate less (Nolen-Hoeksema & Corte, 2004).

Although the gender gap in depression continues, more men are seeking help for depression. The male ego also seems to be battered by assaults from corporate downsizing to growing financial insecurity. Although long viewed by men as a sign of personal weakness, the stigma associated with depression shows signs of lessening although not disappearing.

Risks of major depression also vary with ethnicity. Aboriginal Canadians (i.e., First Nations, Inuit, and Métis), compared to non-Aboriginal groups, have higher rates of depression and suicide, although there is some fluctuation from one Aboriginal community to another (Health Canada, 2002a; Kirmayer, Brass, & Tait, 2000). According to a 2002 Health Canada report, there are several contributing factors: Because of conflicting messages about the value of their own culture, many Aboriginal people do not have a strong sense of self. Also, cultural instability has led to sexual abuse, family violence, and substance abuse, which are associated with a high risk of depression and suicide. Childhood separation, poverty, and access to firearms are also contributing factors.

Women and depression. Women are more likely to suffer from major depression than men. The higher rates of depression among women may be due to factors such as unhappy marriages, physical and sexual abuse, impoverishment, single parenthood, sexism, hormonal changes, childbirth, and the burden of being a primary caregiver to children.

Major depression generally develops in young adulthood (people in their 20s and 30s) (APA, 2000a). It can affect children, but depression is more common in adults (Costello, Erkanli, & Angold, 2006). A multinational study of nine countries,[5] which is the largest study of its kind so far, showed that rates of major depression have been rising in Canada and elsewhere (Cross-National Collaborative Group, 1992). The greatest increases were found in Florence, Italy; the least in Christchurch, New Zealand. In all countries, rates for depression were higher among woman than men.

No one knows why depression has been on the rise in many cultures, but speculation focuses on social and environmental changes, such as increasing fragmentation of families due to relocations, exposure to wars and civil conflicts, and increased rates of violent crimes, as well as possible exposure to toxins or infectious agents in the environment that might affect mental as well as physical health (Cross-National Collaborative Group, 1992). One example is the dramatic increase in depression that occurred during 1950–1960 in Beirut, Lebanon. This was a period of chaotic political and demographic change in that country. Depression dropped sharply in the following decade, 1960 to 1970, a time of relative prosperity and stability, but increased again between 1970 and 1980 during a time of social upheaval and internal warfare.

Seasonal Affective Disorder Are you glum on gloomy days? Is your temper short during the brief days of winter? Are you dismal during the dark of long winter nights? Do you feel up when the long sunny days of spring and summer return?

[5]Canada, the United States, Puerto Rico, Italy, France, Germany, Lebanon, Taiwan, and New Zealand.

Many people report that their moods vary with the weather. For some people, the changing of the seasons from summer into fall and winter leads to a type of depression called seasonal affective (mood) disorder—SAD.[6]

The features of SAD include fatigue, excessive sleep, craving for carbohydrates, and weight gain. SAD tends to lift with the early buds of spring. It affects women more often than men and is most common among young adults. SAD possibly occurs in children but not as commonly as in young adults (Magnusson & Partonen, 2005).

Seasonal affective disorder is more prevalent the further one goes from the equator, because there are greater seasonal variations in daylight hours (Lam & Levitt, 1999). In a survey of a community sample in Toronto, for example, it was found that 11% of people with major depression had the seasonal subtype (Levitt, Boyle, Joffe, & Baumal, 2000). This suggests that seasonal affective disorder is not uncommon.

Although the causes of SAD remain unknown, one possibility is that seasonal changes in light may alter the body's biological rhythms that regulate such processes as body temperature and sleep–wake cycles (Sohn & Lam, 2005). Another possibility is that some parts of the central nervous system may have deficiencies in transmission of the mood-regulating neurotransmitter serotonin during the winter months (Sohn & Lam, 2005). Whatever the underlying cause, a trial of intense light therapy, called *phototherapy*, often helps relieve depression (Lam et al., 2006). Phototherapy typically consists of exposure to a range of 30 minutes to 3 hours of bright artificial light a day. The artificial light supplements the meagre sunlight the SAD-afflicted person otherwise receives. People can generally carry out some of their daily activities (e.g., eating, reading, writing) during their phototherapy sessions. Improvement typically occurs within several days of phototherapy, but treatment is likely required throughout the course of the winter season. Light directed at the eyes tends to be more successful than light directed at the skin.

We still don't know how phototherapy works. Mobilizing expectations of improvement (a placebo effect) may be involved in explaining at least a part of the effect, although research has shown that phototherapy is more effective than placebo (Golden et al., 2005; Lam et al., 2006). Phototherapy does not help all people with SAD. Fortunately, however, other treatments are effective. For example, a group of Canadian researchers led by Raymond Lam at the University of British Columbia has shown that SAD can be effectively treated with the antidepressant medication fluoxetine (trade name Prozac) (Lam et al., 2006).

Postpartum Depression Many, perhaps even most, new mothers experience mood changes, periods of tearfulness, and irritability following the birth of a child. These mood changes are commonly called the "maternity blues," "postpartum blues," or "baby blues." They usually last for a couple of days and are believed to be a normal response to hormonal changes that accompany childbirth. Given these turbulent hormonal shifts, it would be "abnormal" for most women *not* to experience some changes in feeling states shortly following childbirth.

Some mothers, however, undergo severe mood changes that may persist for months or even a year or more. These problems in mood are referred to as **postpartum depression** (PPD). *Postpartum* derives from the Latin roots *post*, meaning "after," and *papere*, meaning "to bring forth." The DSM-IV does not treat postpartum depression as a unique form of depression. Rather, it is recognized as a subtype of major depression affecting women shortly after childbirth. PPD is often accompanied by disturbances in appetite and sleep, low self-esteem, and difficulties in maintaining concentration or attention. The prevalence of PPD is widely believed to be in the range of 10% to 15%, although there are considerable variations across different cultures (Halbreich & Karkun, 2006). This variation could be due to any of a variety of reasons, including cultural differences in the stigma associated with depression (which would influence the person's willingness to report

postpartum depression Persistent and severe mood changes that occur following childbirth. Abbreviated *PPD*.

---

[6] Seasonal affective disorder is not classified as a diagnostic category in its own right in the DSM-IV but is designated as a specifier of mood disorders in which major depressive episodes occur. For example, major depressive disorder that occurs seasonally would be given a diagnosis of major depressive disorder *with seasonal pattern*.

depressive symptoms), along with further cultural differences in risk factors for depression such as the prevalence of stressful life events and the availability of social support (Halbreich & Karkun, 2006). PPD typically remits during the first three months after childbirth—although, as we saw earlier, some cases persist for years (Verkerk, Pop, Van Son, & Van Heck, 2003). Tragically, some women with this disorder commit suicide (Lindahl, Pearson, & Colpe, 2005).

In what is considered to be an especially severe case of postpartum depression, Dr. Suzanne Killinger-Johnson killed herself and her six-month-old baby Cuyler by jumping in front of an oncoming subway train. The night before—Thursday, August 10, 2000—Suzanne was clutching her baby in a Toronto subway station. She had been standing by the platform for quite some time. Transit officials became concerned, so they called the police. Officers spoke with Suzanne and she left. About 90 minutes later, a similar thing happened at another subway station. This time the police drove her home, leaving her in the care of her husband and relatives. During rush hour the next morning, Suzanne slipped out of the house with her baby and went to yet another subway station. Commuters watched in horror as Suzanne dived in front of an oncoming train, clutching her baby. The infant was killed instantly. Suzanne died several days later.

Although PPD may involve chemical or hormonal imbalances brought on by childbirth (Bloch, Rotenberg, Koren, & Ehud, 2006), psychosocial factors such as financial problems, a troubled marriage, lack of social or emotional support from partners and family members, a history of depression, or an unwanted or sick baby all increase a woman's vulnerability to PPD (Boyce & Hickey, 2005; Halbreich, 2005). Having PPD also appears to increase a woman's risk of future depressive episodes (Bloch et al., 2006).

? QUESTIONNAIRE

Are You Depressed?

Screening tests for depression, such as the following, are offered annually by the organizers of the National Depression Screening Day (www.mentalhealthscreening.org). Tests like the one below can help you assess whether you are suffering from a serious depression. Such screening tests are not intended for you to diagnose yourself, but rather to raise your awareness of concerns you may want to discuss with a professional.

	Yes	No
1. I feel downhearted, blue, and sad.	___	___
2. I don't enjoy the things that I used to.	___	___
3. I feel that others would be better off if I were dead.	___	___
4. I feel that I am not useful or needed.	___	___
5. I notice that I am losing weight.	___	___
6. I have trouble sleeping through the night.	___	___
7. I am restless and can't keep still.	___	___
8. My mind isn't as clear as it used to be.	___	___
9. I get tired for no reason.	___	___
10. I feel hopeless about the future.	___	___

Rating your responses: if you agree with at least five of the statements, including either item 1 or 2, and if you have had these complaints for at least two weeks, professional help is strongly recommended. If you answered "yes" to statement 3, seek consultation with a professional immediately. If you don't know whom to turn to, contact your college or university counselling centre, neighbourhood mental health centre, or health provider.

Source: Adapted from Brody (1992©), "Myriad masks hide an epidemic of depression," *New York Times*, September 30, 1992, p. C12.

Dysthymic Disorder

dysthymic disorder Mild but chronic type of depressive disorder.

Major depressive disorder is severe and marked by a relatively abrupt change from one's pre-existing state. In comparison, **dysthymic disorder** (also called *dysthymia*), a milder form of depression, seems to follow a chronic course of development that often begins in childhood or adolescence (APA, 2000a). The term *dysthymia* derives from Greek roots *dys-*, meaning "bad" or "hard," and *thymos*, meaning "spirit."

Persons with dysthymic disorder feel "bad spirited" or "down in the dumps" most of the time but they are not so severely depressed as those with major depressive disorder. Whereas major depressive disorder tends to be severe and time limited, dysthymic disorder is relatively mild and nagging, typically lasting for years (Klein & Santiago, 2003).

About 3% to 6% of Canadian adults have dysthymia at some point in their lives (Health Canada, 2002a). Like major depressive disorder, dysthymic disorder is more common in women than men. Similar findings have been reported in other Western countries (Klein & Santiago, 2003).

In dysthymic disorder, complaints of depression may become such a fixture of people's lives that they seem to be part of their personality. The persistence of complaints may lead others to perceive them as whining and complaining. Although dysthymic disorder is less severe than major depressive disorder, persistent depressed mood and low self-esteem can affect a person's occupational and social functioning, as we see in the following case:

> The woman, a 28-year-old junior executive, complained of chronic feelings of depression since the age of 16 or 17. Despite doing well in college, she brooded about how other people were "genuinely intelligent." She felt she could never pursue a man she might be interested in dating because she felt inferior and intimidated. While she had extensive therapy through college and graduate school, she could never recall a time during those years when she did not feel somewhat depressed. She got married shortly after college graduation to the man she was dating at the time, although she didn't think that he was anything "special." She just felt she needed to have a husband for companionship and he was available. But they soon began to quarrel and she's lately begun to feel that marrying him was a mistake. She has had difficulties at work, turning in "slipshod" work and never seeking anything more than what was basically required of her and showing little initiative. While she dreams of acquiring status and money, she doesn't expect that she or her husband will rise in their professions because they lack "connections." Her social life is dominated by her husband's friends and their spouses and she doesn't think that other women would find her interesting or impressive. She lacks interest in life in general and expresses dissatisfaction with all facets of her life—her marriage, her job, her social life.
>
> ADAPTED FROM SPITZER, FIRST, & WILLIAMS, 1994, PP. 110–112

double depression Term applied to persons diagnosed with both *major depressive disorder* and *dysthymic disorder*.

Some people are affected by both dysthymic disorder and major depression at the same time. The term **double depression** applies to those who have a major depressive episode superimposed on a longer-standing dysthymic disorder. Major depressive episodes tend to occur more frequently and to be longer in duration in people with double depression than those with major depression alone (Dunner, 2005).

We noted that major depressive disorder and dysthymic disorder are depressive disorders in the sense that the disturbance of mood is only in one direction—down. Yet some people with mood disorders may have fluctuations in mood in both directions that exceed the usual ups and downs of everyday life. These types of disorders are called bipolar disorders. Here, we focus on the two types of bipolar disorder: (1) bipolar disorder and (2) cyclothymic disorder.

Bipolar Disorder

People with **bipolar disorder** ride an emotional roller coaster, swinging from the heights of elation to the depths of depression without external cause. The first episode may be either manic or depressive. Manic episodes, typically lasting from a few weeks to several months, are generally shorter in duration and end more abruptly than major depressive episodes. More than 90% of people who experience manic episodes eventually experience a recurrence (APA, 2000a). Some people with recurring bipolar disorder attempt suicide "on the way down" from the manic phase. They report that they would do nearly anything to escape the depths of depression they know lie ahead.

The DSM distinguishes between two general types of bipolar disorder, *bipolar I disorder* and *bipolar II disorder* (APA, 2000a). The essential feature of bipolar I disorder is the occurrence of one or more manic episodes. A disorder can thus be labelled "bipolar" even if it consists of manic episodes without any past or present major depressive episodes. In such cases, it is possible that a major depressive disorder will eventually appear or has been overlooked. In a few cases of bipolar I disorder, called the mixed type, both a manic episode and a major depressive episode occur simultaneously (i.e., rapidly alternating between mania and depression). More frequently, though, cycles of elated and depressed mood states alternate with intervening periods of normal mood.

Bipolar II disorder is associated with a milder form of mania. In bipolar II, the person has experienced one or more major depressive episodes and at least one hypomanic episode, but never a full-blown manic episode. Whether bipolar I and bipolar II represent qualitatively different disorders or different points along a continuum of severity of bipolar disorder remains to be determined.

Bipolar disorder is relatively uncommon, with reported lifetime prevalence rates from community surveys of 0.4% to 2.2% for bipolar I disorder and 0.5% for bipolar II disorder (APA, 2000a; Health Canada, 2002a; Schaffer, Cairney, Cheung, Veldhuizen, & Levitt, 2006). Unfortunately, it appears that many people with bipolar disorder are not adequately treated (Beck et al., 2005).

Unlike major depression, rates of bipolar I disorder appear about equal in men and women, although women tend to have more depressive episodes (Miklowitz & Johnson, 2006). Gender differences in rates of bipolar II disorder are not well established. The typical age of onset of bipolar disorder is in the 20s (Schaffer et al., 2006), but sometimes the disorder does not appear until a person's 40s or 50s.

Sometimes, cases involve periods of "rapid cycling" in which the individual experiences two or more full cycles of mania and depression within a year without any intervening normal periods. Rapid cycling is associated with an earlier age of onset and is relatively uncommon (Miklowitz & Johnson, 2006).

Manic Episode

Manic episodes, or periods of mania, typically begin abruptly, gathering force within days. During a manic episode, the person experiences a sudden elevation or expansion of mood and feels unusually cheerful, euphoric, or optimistic. The person seems to have boundless energy and is extremely sociable, although perhaps to the point of becoming overly demanding and overbearing toward acquaintances. Other people recognize the sudden shift in mood to be excessive in light of the person's circumstances. It's one thing to feel elated if you've just won the lottery; it is another to feel euphoric "because" it's Wednesday.

People in a manic episode or phase are excited and may strike others as silly, by carrying jokes too far, for example. They tend to show poor judgment and to become argumentative, sometimes going so far as destroying property. Roommates may find manic people abrasive and avoid them. They tend to speak very rapidly (with **pressured speech**). Their thoughts and speech may jump from topic to topic (in a **rapid flight of ideas**). Others find it difficult to get a word in edgewise. Manic people may also become extremely generous and make large charitable contributions they can ill afford or give away costly possessions. They may not be able to sit still or sleep restfully. They almost always show less need for sleep. They tend to awaken early yet feel well rested and full of energy. They sometimes go for days without sleep and without feeling tired. Although they may have

bipolar disorder Disorder characterized by mood swings between states of extreme elation and severe depression. Formerly called *manic-depression*.

manic episode Period of unrealistically heightened euphoria, extreme restlessness, and excessive activity characterized by disorganized behaviour and impaired judgment. Alternates with major depressive episodes in bipolar disorder.

pressured speech Outpouring of speech in which words seem to surge urgently for expression, as in a manic state.

rapid flight of ideas Characteristic of manic behaviour involving rapid speech and changes of topics.

abundant stores of energy, they seem unable to organize their efforts constructively. Their elation impairs their ability to work and maintain normal relationships.

People in a manic episode generally experience an inflated sense of self-esteem that may range from extreme self-confidence to wholesale delusions of grandeur. They may feel capable of solving the world's problems or of composing symphonies despite a lack of any special knowledge or talent. They may spout off about matters on which they know little, such as how to solve world hunger or how to prevent global warming. It soon becomes clear that they are disorganized and incapable of completing their projects. They become highly distractible. Their attention is easily diverted by irrelevant stimuli like the sounds of a ticking clock or of people talking in the next room. They tend to take on multiple tasks, more than they can handle. They may suddenly quit their jobs to enroll in art school, wait tables at night, organize charity drives on weekends, and work on a best-selling novel in their "spare time." They tend to exercise poor judgment and fail to weigh the consequences of their actions. As a result, they may get into trouble as a consequence of lavish spending, reckless driving, or sexual escapades. In severe cases, they may experience disorders of thinking similar to those of people with schizophrenia. They may experience hallucinations or become grossly delusional, believing, for example, that they have a special relationship with God.

The following case provides an account of a manic episode, documented by Toronto psychiatrist Dr. Virginia Edwards:

Brian began acting quite strangely shortly after his brother's wife had a son. He told his wife, Wanda, he had invented a motor that could run on propane only, and he thought General Motors would buy his invention. He became more and more talkative, with monologues running far into the night, which Wanda found exhausting. Wanda called her father-in-law, who talked quietly to Brian. Brian then broke into tears, rocking back and forth and lamenting what a failure he was. They took Brian to the local hospital and he agreed to be admitted. After he calmed down, he said he felt great, as if his ideas were brilliant. He needed little sleep and his thoughts raced. Brian said that he had never felt so wonderful in his life, but that he also felt he was on a roller coaster that he couldn't get off.

ADAPTED FROM EDWARDS, 2002, P. 37

Cyclothymic Disorder

Cyclothymia is derived from the Greek *kyklos*, which means "circle," and *thymos* ("spirit"). The notion of a circular-moving spirit is an apt description because this disorder involves a chronic cyclical pattern of mood disturbance characterized by mild mood swings of at least two years (one year for children and adolescents). **Cyclothymic disorder** usually begins in late adolescence or early adulthood and persists for years. Few, if any, periods of normal mood last for more than a month or two. Neither the periods of elevated or depressed mood are severe enough to warrant a diagnosis of bipolar disorder, however. Estimates from community studies indicate lifetime prevalence rates for cyclothymic disorder of between 0.4% and 1% (4 to 10 people in 1000), with men and women about equally likely to be affected (APA, 2000a).

The periods of elevated mood are called hypomanic episodes, from the Greek prefix *hypo-*, meaning "under" or "less than." *Hypo* manic episodes are less severe than manic episodes and are not accompanied by the severe social or occupational problems associated with full-blown manic episodes. During hypomanic episodes, people may have an inflated sense of self-esteem, feel unusually charged with energy and alert, and may be more restless and irritable than usual. They may be able to work long hours with little fatigue or need for sleep. Their projects may be left unfinished when their moods reverse, however. Then they enter a mildly depressed mood state and find it difficult to summon the energy or interest to persevere. They feel lethargic and depressed, but not to the extent typical of a major depressive episode.

cyclothymic disorder Mood disorder characterized by a chronic pattern of mild mood swings between depression and mania that are not of sufficient severity to be classified as bipolar disorder.

Social relationships may become strained by shifting moods, and work may suffer. Social invitations, eagerly sought during hypomanic periods, may be declined during depressed periods. Phone calls may not be returned as the mood slumps. Sexual interest waxes and wanes with the person's moods.

The boundaries between bipolar disorder and cyclothymic disorder are not yet clearly established. Some forms of cyclothymic disorder may represent a mild, early type of bipolar disorder. About one-third of people with cyclothymia go on to develop full-fledged bipolar disorder. People with cyclothymia, compared to other people in the general population, are more likely to have family members that suffer from bipolar disorder. Cyclothymia also responds to similar medications to those used to treat bipolar disorder. Findings such as these suggest that cyclothymia and bipolar disorder may have etiological factors in common (Akiskal, 2001).

The following case presents an example of the mild mood swings that typify cyclothymic disorder:

> The man, a 29-year-old car salesman, reports that since the age of 14 he has experienced alternating periods of "good times and bad times." During his "bad" periods, which generally last between four and seven days, he sleeps excessively and feels a lack of confidence, energy, and motivation, as if he were "just vegetating." Then his moods abruptly shift for a period of three or four days, usually upon awakening in the morning, and he feels flushed with confidence and sharpened mental ability. During these "good periods," he engages in promiscuous sex and uses alcohol, in part to enhance his good feelings and in part to help him sleep at night. The good periods may last upwards of seven to ten days at times, before shifting back into the bad periods, generally following a hostile or irritable outburst.
>
> ADAPTED FROM SPITZER ET AL., 1994, PP. 155–157

STUDY BREAK

Types of Mood Disorders

Review It

- **What are mood disorders?** Mood disorders are disturbances in mood that are unusually prolonged or severe and serious enough to impair daily functioning.

- **What are the major types of mood disorders?** There are various kinds of mood disorders, including depressive (unipolar) disorders such as major depressive disorder and dysthymic disorder, and disorders involving mood swings, such as bipolar disorder and cyclothymic disorder.

- **What are the features associated with major depression?** People with major depressive disorder experience a profound change in mood that impairs their ability to function. There are many associated features of major depressive disorder, including downcast mood; changes in appetite; difficulty sleeping; reduced sense of pleasure in formerly enjoyable activities; feelings of fatigue or loss of energy; sense of worthlessness; excessive or misplaced guilt; difficulties concentrating, thinking clearly, or making decisions; repeated thoughts of death or suicide; attempts at suicide; and even psychotic behaviours (hallucinations and delusions).

- **What is dysthymic disorder?** Dysthymic disorder is a form of chronic depression that is milder than major depressive disorder but may nevertheless be associated with impaired functioning in social and occupational roles.

- **What are the types of bipolar disorder?** Bipolar I disorder is defined by the occurrence of one or more manic episodes, which generally but not necessarily occur in persons who have experienced major depressive episodes. In bipolar II disorder, depressive episodes occur along with hypomanic episodes, but without the occurrence of a full-blown manic episode.

Manic episodes are characterized by sudden elevation or expansion of mood and sense of self-importance, feelings of almost boundless energy, hyperactivity, and extreme sociability, which often take a demanding and overbearing form. People in manic episodes tend to exhibit pressured or rapid speech, rapid "flight of ideas," and decreased need for sleep.

- **What is cyclothymic disorder?** Cyclothymic disorder is a type of bipolar disorder characterized by a chronic pattern of mild mood swings that sometimes progresses to bipolar disorder.

Define It

mood	postpartum depression
mood disorder	dysthymic disorder
unipolar	double depression
bipolar	bipolar disorder
major depressive disorder	manic episode
	pressured speech
manic	rapid flight of ideas
hypomanic episodes	cyclothymic disorder
bereavement	

Recall It*

1. _____ are enduring feeling states that colour our psychological lives.

   a. Needs
   b. Drives
   c. Moods
   d. Traits

2. The most common type of mood disorder is _____.

   a. minor depression
   b. major depression
   c. dysthymia
   d. bipolar disorder

3. Every winter, Cathy begins to feel "down in the dumps," becomes easily fatigued, overly sleepy, and develops a craving for carbohydrates. Her symptoms lift in early spring. She is most likely suffering from _____.

   a. cyclical dysthymic disorder
   b. cyclothymic disorder
   c. seasonal bipolar disorder
   d. seasonal affective disorder

4. The term *postpartum blues* refers to _____.

   a. normally occurring mood fluctuations in women following childbirth
   b. prolonged mood changes in new mothers
   c. a bipolar disorder affecting women following childbirth
   d. a postpartum depression that represents a form of major depression

5. Keith has mood swings from periods of extreme elation and hyperactivity to deep depression. He probably is suffering from _____.

   a. double depression
   b. dysthymic disorder
   c. cyclothymic disorder
   d. bipolar disorder

* Recall It answers can be found on the Companion Website for this text.

Think About It

- Agree or disagree with this statement and support your answer: "Women are just naturally more inclined to depression than men."

- Where would you draw the line between a person with a naturally exuberant personality and someone with a bipolar disorder?

THEORETICAL PERSPECTIVES

Multiple factors—biological, psychological, social, and environmental—appear to be involved in the development of mood disorders. In this section, we first consider the relationship between stress and mood disorders. Then we consider psychological and biological perspectives on depression.

Stress and Mood Disorders

Research indicates that there is a robust and causal association between stressful life events and major depressive episodes (Hammen, 2005); major depression is often preceded by stressful events, although not everyone who experiences such events will become depressed. Stressors such as the loss of a loved one, prolonged unemployment, physical illness, marital or relationship problems, economic hardship, pressure at work, racism, and discrimination may all contribute to the development and recurrence of mood disorders, especially major depression (Hammen, 2005; Kendler & Prescott, 2006). To illustrate physical illness as a stressor, results from an Ontario study of 297 people with HIV/AIDS revealed that 54% were currently suffering from clinically significant depression (Williams et al., 2005). As we saw earlier, this is much higher than the rate of depression in the general population.

Although stress appears to contribute to the risk of becoming depressed, research indicates that not all cases of major depression are preceded by stressful life events (Kendler & Prescott, 2006). People are also more likely to become depressed when they hold themselves responsible for undesirable events, such as school problems, financial difficulties, unwanted pregnancy, interpersonal problems, and problems with the law (Hammen, 2005). Research by Kate Harkness at Queen's University in Ontario, as well as the work of other investigators, suggests that stressors may interact with one another to influence a person's risk of depression. For example, the experience of childhood abuse and neglect appears to increase the odds that future stressful events (e.g., in adolescence) will lead to depression (Harkness, Bruce, & Lumley, 2006).

People are also more likely to become depressed if they have a particular genetic makeup that leaves them vulnerable to stress. In such a case, a person might possess the short allele (variant) of a gene involved in the regulation of the neurotransmitter serotonin (Caspi & Moffitt, 2006; Kendler & Prescott, 2006).

To complicate matters, the relationship between stress and depression may cut both ways: stressful life events may contribute to depression, and depressive symptoms in themselves may be stressful or lead to additional sources of stress, such as divorce or loss of employment. When you're depressed, for example, you may find it more difficult to keep up with your work at school or on the job, which can lead to more stress as your work piles up. The closer the stressful event taps the person's core concerns (failing at work or school, for instance), the more likely it is to precipitate a relapse in people who have a history of depression (Hammen, 2005). Stressful events may also play a role in trigger episodes of bipolar disorder (Miklowitz & Johnson, 2006).

Coping Styles and Social Support: Resources for Handling Stress Some people seem better able to withstand stress or recover from losses than others. Investigators find that psychosocial factors such as social support and coping styles may serve as buffers against depression in times of stress (Hammen, 2005). To illustrate, research conducted at the University of Manitoba and University of Calgary indicates that depression is more prevalent among people who live alone, such as women who are separated or divorced, or elderly men who never married (Afifi et al., 2006; Patten et al., 2006). Close relationships, such as with marital partners, may provide a source of support during times of stress. The availability of social support is also associated with quicker recoveries and better outcomes in cases of major depression (Nasser & Overholser, 2005).

Evidence also shows that people with major depression are less likely to use active problem-solving strategies to alleviate stress than nondepressed people (Matheson & Anisman, 2003). People with major depression also show deficits in skills needed to solve interpersonal problems with friends, co-workers, or supervisors (Haugh, 2006). People who are better able solve their problems in daily life are morel likely to overcome their depression (Nezu, Wilkins, & Nezu, 2004).

Psychodynamic Perspectives The classic psychodynamic theory of depression of Freud (1917/1957) and his followers (e.g., Abraham, 1916/1948) holds that depression represents anger directed inward rather than against significant others. Anger may become directed against the self following either the actual or threatened loss of these important others.

Freud believed that **mourning** or normal bereavement is a healthy process by which one eventually comes to psychologically separate oneself from a person who is lost

mourning Normal feelings or expressions of grief following a loss. See *bereavement.*

through death, separation, divorce, or other reason. Pathological mourning, however, does not promote healthy separation. Rather, it fosters lingering depression. Pathological mourning is likely to occur in people who hold powerful *ambivalent* feelings—a combination of positive (love) and negative (anger, hostility) feelings—toward the person who has departed or whose departure is feared. Freud theorized that when people lose, or even fear losing, an important figure about whom they feel ambivalent, their feelings of anger toward the other person turn to rage. Yet rage triggers guilt, which in turn prevents the person from venting anger directly at the lost person (called an "object").

To preserve a psychological connection to the lost object, people *introject* or bring inward a mental representation of the object. They thus incorporate the other person into the self. Now anger is turned inward, against the part of the self that represents the inward representation of the lost person. This produces self-hatred, which in turn leads to depression.

While also emphasizing the importance of loss, more recent psychodynamic models focus more on issues relating to the individual's sense of self-worth or self-esteem. One model, called the *self-focusing model*, considers how people allocate their attentional processes after a loss (death of a loved one, a personal failure, and so on) (Pyszczynski & Greenberg, 1992). According to this model, depression-prone people experience a period of intense self-examination (self-focusing) following a major loss or disappointment. They become preoccupied with thoughts about the lost object (loved one) or personal failure and remain unable to surrender hope of somehow regaining it.

Consider a person who must cope with the termination of a failed romantic relationship. It may be clear to all concerned that the relationship is beyond hope of revival. The self-focusing model proposes, however, that the depression-prone individual persists in focusing attention on restoring the relationship, rather than recognizing the futility of the effort and getting on with life. Moreover, the lost partner was someone who was a source of emotional support and upon whom the depression-prone individual had relied to maintain feelings of self-esteem. Following the loss, the depression-prone individual feels

What happens when we lose our sense of direction?
According to the humanistic-existential perspective, depression may result from the inability to find meaning and purpose in one's life.

stripped of hope and optimism because these positive feelings that had depended on the other person are now lost. The loss of self-esteem and feelings of security, not of the relationship itself, precipitates depression. If depression-prone people peg their self-worth to a specific occupational goal, such as success in a modelling career, failure triggers self-focusing and consequent depression. Only by surrendering the object or lost goal and fostering alternate sources of identity and self-worth can the cycle be broken.

Research Evidence Psychodynamic theorists focus on the role of loss in depression. Research does show that the losses of significant others (through death or divorce, for example) are often (but not invariably) associated with the onset of depression (Kendler & Prescott, 2006). Such losses may also lead to other psychological disorders, however. There is yet a lack of research to support Freud's view that repressed anger toward a departed loved one is turned inward in depression.

Research on the utility of the self-focusing model has been mixed. On one hand, people suffering from depression have been shown to engage in higher levels of self-focusing following failure experiences than others, and in relatively lower levels of self-focusing following successes (Pyszczynski & Greenberg, 1992). On the other hand, self-focused attention has been linked to disorders other than depression, including anxiety disorders, alcoholism, mania, and schizophrenia (Ingram, 1990, 1991). The general linkage between self-focused attention and psychopathology may limit the model's value as an explanation of depression (Ingram, 1991).

Humanistic Perspectives

From a humanistic perspective, people become depressed when they cannot imbue their existence with meaning and make authentic choices that lead to self-fulfillment. The world for them is a drab place. People's search for meaning gives colour and substance to their lives. Guilt may arise when people believe they have not lived up to their potentials. Humanistic psychologists challenge us to take a long hard look at our lives. Are they worthwhile and enriching? Or are they drab and routine? If the latter, it may be we have frustrated our needs for self-actualization. We may be settling, coasting through life. Settling can give rise to a sense of dreariness that becomes expressed in depressive behaviour—lethargy, sullen mood, and withdrawal.

Like psychodynamic theorists, humanistic theorists also focus on the loss of self-esteem that can arise when people lose friends or family members or suffer occupational setbacks or losses. We tend to connect our personal identity and sense of self-worth with our social roles as parents, spouses, students, or workers. When these role identities are lost, through the death of a spouse, the departure of children to college, or loss of a job, our sense of purpose and self-worth can be shattered. Depression is a frequent consequence of such losses. It is especially likely when we base our self-esteem on our occupational role or success. The loss of a job, a demotion, or a failure to achieve a promotion are all common precipitants of depression, especially when we are reared to value ourselves on the basis of occupational success.

Learning Perspectives

Whereas psychodynamic perspectives focus on inner, often unconscious, determinants of mood disorders, learning perspectives dwell more on situational factors, such as the loss of positive reinforcement. We perform best when levels of reinforcement are commensurate with our efforts. Changes in the frequency or effectiveness of reinforcement can shift the balance so that life becomes unrewarding.

Reinforcement and Depression Peter Lewinsohn (e.g., Lewinsohn, Sullivan, & Grosscup, 1980) suggested that depression may result when a person's behaviour receives too little reinforcement from the environment. Lack of reinforcement can sap motivation and induce feelings of depression. A vicious cycle may ensue: inactivity and social withdrawal deplete opportunities for reinforcement; lesser reinforcement exacerbates withdrawal. The low rate of activity typical of depression may also be a source of secondary reinforcement. Family members and other people may rally around people suffering from depression and release them from their responsibilities. Rather than help people who are struggling with depression regain normal levels of productive behaviour, sympathy may thus backfire and maintain depressed behaviour.

Reduction in reinforcement levels can occur for many reasons. A person who is recuperating at home from a serious illness or injury may find little that is reinforcing to do. Social reinforcement may plummet when people close to us, who were suppliers of reinforcement, die or leave us. People who suffer social losses are more likely to become depressed when they lack the social skills to form new relationships. Some first-year university students are homesick and depressed because they lack the skills to form rewarding new relationships. Widows and widowers may be at a loss as to how to ask someone for a date or start a new relationship.

Changes in life circumstances may also alter the balance of effort and reinforcement. A prolonged layoff may reduce financial reinforcements, which may in turn force painful cutbacks in lifestyle. A disability or an extended illness may also impair one's ability to ensure a steady flow of reinforcements.

Lewinsohn's model is supported by research findings that connect depression to a low level of positive reinforcement. For example, Lewinsohn and Libet (1972) noted a correspondence between depressed moods and lower rates of participation in potentially reinforcing activities. People with depressive disorders were also found to report fewer pleasant activities than nondepressed people (MacPhillamy & Lewinsohn, 1974). It remains unclear, however, whether depression precedes or follows a decline in the level of reinforcement (J. M. Williams, 1984). It may be that people who become depressed lose interest in pleasant activities or withdraw from potentially reinforcing social interactions, and not that inactivity leads to depression. Regardless of the causes of depression, behavioural treatment approaches that encourage people who become depressed to increase their levels of pleasant activities and provide them with the skills to do so are often helpful in alleviating depression (DeRubeis & Crits-Christoph, 1998; Dimidjian et al., 2006; Jacobson et al., 1996).

Interactional Theory The interactions between depressed persons and other people may help explain the former group's shortfall in positive reinforcement. Interactional theory (Coyne, 1999) proposes that the adjustment to living with a depressed person can become so stressful that the partner or family member becomes progressively less reinforcing toward the depressed person.

Interactional theory is based on the concept of reciprocal interaction. People's behaviour influences and is influenced by the behaviour of others. The theory holds that depression-prone people react to stress by demanding greater social support and reassurance. At first, people who become depressed may succeed in garnering support. Over time, however, their demands and behaviour begin to elicit anger or annoyance. Although loved ones may keep their negative feelings to themselves so as not to further upset the depressed person, these feelings may surface in subtle ways that spell rejection. Depressed people may react to rejection with deeper depression and greater demands, triggering a vicious cycle of further rejection and more profound depression. They may also feel guilty about distressing their family members, which can exacerbate negative feelings about themselves.

Evidence shows that people who become depressed tend to encounter rejection in long-term relationships (Marcus & Nardone, 1992). Family members may find it stressful to adjust to the behaviour of the person who is depressed, especially to such behaviours as withdrawal, lethargy, fretfulness, and despair. Similarly, evidence suggests people with depressed spouses tend to have negative attitudes toward the spouse if the depressed person is constantly seeking reassurance about his or her self-worth (Van Orden & Joiner, 2006).

All in all, research evidence generally supports Coyne's belief (1999) that people who suffer from depression elicit rejection from others, but there remains a lack of evidence to show this rejection is mediated by negative emotions (anger and annoyance) that the depressed person induces in others. Rather, a growing body of literature suggests that depressed people may lack effective social skills, which may account for the fact that others often reject them. In some cases, these deficits in social skills may be long-standing (i.e., present even when the person is not depressed), while in other cases the deficits may be present only when the person is depressed (and perhaps a consequence of depression) (Petty, Sachs-Ericsson, & Joiner, 2004). People with major depression tend to be unresponsive, uninvolved, and even impolite when they interact with others. In conversation, for example, they tend to gaze very little at the other person, take an excessive amount of time to respond, show very little approval or validation of the other person, and dwell on their problems and negative feelings. They even dwell on negative feelings when interacting with strangers. In effect, they turn other people off, setting the stage for rejection.

Whether social skills deficits are a cause or a symptom of depression remains to be determined. Whatever the case, impaired social behaviour likely may play an important role in determining the persistence or recurrence of depression. As we shall see, some psychological approaches to treating depression (e.g., interpersonal psychotherapy and Lewinsohn's social-skills-training approach—discussed later) focus on helping people with depression better understand and overcome their interpersonal problems. This may help, in turn, alleviate depression or perhaps prevent future recurrences.

Cognitive Perspectives

Cognitive theorists relate the origin and maintenance of depression to the ways in which people see themselves and the world around them.

Aaron Beck's Cognitive Theory One of the most influential cognitive theorists, psychiatrist Aaron Beck (Beck, 1976; Beck, Rush, Shaw, & Emery, 1979), relates the development of depression to the adoption early in life of a negatively biased or distorted way of thinking—the **cognitive triad of depression** (see Table 7.4). The cognitive triad includes negative beliefs about oneself (e.g., "I'm no good"), the environment or the world at large (e.g., "This school is awful"), and the future (e.g., "Nothing will ever turn out right for me"). Cognitive theory holds that people who adopt this negative way of thinking are at greater risk of becoming depressed in the face of stressful or disappointing life experiences, such as getting a poor grade or losing a job.

Beck views these negative concepts of the self and the world as mental templates or *cognitive schemas* that are adopted in childhood on the basis of early learning experiences. Children may find that nothing they do is good enough to please their parents or teachers. As a result, they may come to regard themselves as basically incompetent and to perceive their future prospects as dim. These beliefs may sensitize them later in life to interpret any failure or disappointment as a reflection of something basically wrong or inadequate about themselves. Minor disappointments and personal shortcomings become "blown out of proportion."

The tendency to magnify the importance of minor failures is an example of an error in thinking that Beck labels a *cognitive distortion*. He believes cognitive distortions set the stage for depression in the face of personal losses or negative life events. Psychiatrist David Burns (1980) enumerated a number of the cognitive distortions associated with depression:

1. *All-or-nothing thinking.* Seeing events in black and white, as either all good or all bad. For example, one may perceive a relationship that ended in disappointment as a totally negative experience, despite any positive feelings or experiences that may have occurred along the way. Perfectionism is an example of all-or-nothing thinking. Perfectionists judge any outcome other than perfect success to be complete failure. They may consider a grade of B+ or even A– to be tantamount to an F. They may feel like abject failures if they fall a few dollars short of their sales quotas or receive a very fine (but less than perfect) performance evaluation. Perfectionism is connected with an increased vulnerability to depression (Flett & Hewitt, 2002).

2. *Overgeneralization.* Believing that if a negative event occurs, it is likely to occur again in similar situations in the future. One may come to interpret a single negative event as foreshadowing an endless series of negative events. For example, receiving a letter of rejection from a potential employer leads one to assume that all other job applications will similarly be rejected.

cognitive triad of depression In Aaron Beck's theory, the view that depression derives from the adoption of negative views of oneself, the world, and the future.

TABLE 7.4		
The Cognitive Triad of Depression		
Negative view of oneself	Perceiving oneself as worthless, deficient, inadequate, unlovable, and as lacking the skills necessary to achieve happiness.	
Negative view of the environment	Perceiving the environment as imposing excessive demands and/or presenting obstacles that are impossible to overcome, leading continually to failure and loss.	
Negative view of the future	Perceiving the future as hopeless and believing that one is powerless to change things for the better. All that one expects of the future is continuing failure and unrelenting misery and hardship.	
According to Aaron Beck, depression-prone people adopt a habitual style of negative thinking—the so-called cognitive triad of depression.		

Source: Adapted from Beck & Young, 1985; Beck et al., 1979.

3. *Mental filter.* Focusing only on negative details of events, thereby rejecting the positive features of one's experiences. Like a droplet of ink that spreads to discolour an entire beaker of water, focusing only on a single negative detail can darken one's vision of reality. Beck called this cognitive distortion **selective abstraction**, meaning the individual selectively abstracts the negative details from events and ignores their positive features. One's self-esteem is thus based on perceived weaknesses and failures rather than on positive features or on a balance of accomplishments and shortcomings. For example, a person receives a job evaluation that contains positive and negative comments but he or she focuses only on the negative.

4. *Disqualifying the positive.* This refers to the tendency to snatch defeat from the jaws of victory by neutralizing or denying your accomplishments. An example is dismissal of congratulations for a job well done by thinking and saying, "Oh, it's no big deal. Anyone could have done it." By contrast, taking credit where credit is due may help people overcome depression by increasing their belief they can make changes that will lead to a positive future (Needles & Abramson, 1990).

5. *Jumping to conclusions.* Forming a negative interpretation of events, despite a lack of evidence. Two examples of this style of thinking are *mind reading* and the *fortune teller error*. In mind reading, you arbitrarily jump to the conclusion that others don't like or respect you, as in interpreting a friend's not calling for a while as a rejection. The fortune teller error involves the prediction that something bad is always about to happen to oneself. The person believes the prediction of calamity is factually based even though there is an absence of evidence to support it. For example, the person concludes that a passing tightness in the chest *must* be a sign of heart disease, discounting the possibility of more benign causes.

6. *Magnification and minimization.* Magnification or *catastrophizing* refers to the tendency to make mountains out of molehills—to exaggerate the importance of negative events, personal flaws, fears, or mistakes. Minimization is the mirror image, a type of cognitive distortion in which one minimizes or underestimates one's good points.

7. *Emotional reasoning.* Basing reasoning on emotions—thinking, for example, "If I feel guilty, it must be because I've done something really wrong." One interprets feelings and events on the basis of emotions rather than a fair consideration of evidence.

8. *Should statements.* Creating personal imperatives or self-commandments— *should*s or *must*s. For example, "I *should* always get my first serve in!" or, "I *must* make Chris like me!" By creating unrealistic expectations, the person may become depressed when he/she falls short.

9. *Labelling and mislabelling.* Explaining behaviour by attaching negative labels to oneself and others. You may explain a poor grade on a test by thinking you were "lazy" or "stupid" rather than simply unprepared for the specific exam or, perhaps, ill. Labelling other people as "stupid" or "insensitive" can engender hostility toward them. Mislabelling involves the use of labels that are emotionally charged and inaccurate, such as calling yourself a "pig" because of a minor deviation from your usual diet.

10. *Personalization.* This refers to the tendency to assume you are responsible for other people's problems and behaviour. You may assume your partner or spouse is crying because of something you have done (or not done), rather than recognizing that other causes may be involved.

Consider the errors in thinking illustrated in the following case:

Christie was a 33-year-old real estate sales agent who suffered from frequent episodes of depression. Whenever a deal fell through, she would blame herself: "If only I had worked harder . . . negotiated better . . . talked more persuasively . . . the deal would have been done." After several successive disappointments, each one followed by self-recriminations, she felt like quitting altogether. Her thinking became increasingly dominated by negative thoughts, which further depressed her mood and lowered her self-esteem: "I'm a loser . . . I'll never succeed . . . It's all my fault . . . I'm no good and I'm never going to succeed at anything."

Christie's thinking included cognitive errors such as the following: (1) *personalization* (believing herself to be the sole cause of negative events); (2) *labelling and mislabelling* (labelling herself to be a loser); (3) *overgeneralization* (predicting a dismal future on the basis of a present disappointment); and (4) *mental filter* (judging her personality entirely on the basis of her disappointments). In therapy, Christie was helped to think more realistically about events and not to jump to conclusions that she was automatically at fault whenever a deal fell through, or to judge her whole personality on the basis of disappointments or perceived flaws within herself. In place of this self-defeating style of thinking, she began to think more realistically when disappointments occurred, like telling herself, "Okay, I'm disappointed. I'm frustrated. I feel lousy. So what? It doesn't mean I'll never succeed. Let me discover what went wrong and try to correct it the next time. I have to look ahead, not dwell on disappointments in the past."

THE AUTHORS' FILES

Distorted thinking tends to be experienced as automatic, as if the thoughts had just popped into one's head. These **automatic thoughts** are likely to be accepted as statements of fact rather than opinions or habitual ways of interpreting events.

Supporting Beck's model is evidence linking cognitive distortions (including the magnification of one's shortcomings) and negative thinking to depressive symptoms and clinical depression (Beck & Perkins, 2001; Clark, Beck, & Alford, 1999). People who are depressed also tend to hold more pessimistic views of the future and are more critical of themselves and others (Beck & Perkins, 2001). Such pessimistic thinking predicts future development or worsening of depression (Alloy et al., 1999).

All in all, there is broad research support for many aspects of the theory, including Beck's concept of the cognitive triad of depression and his view that people with depression think more negatively than nondepressed people about themselves, the future, and the world in general. Although dysfunctional cognitions (negative, distorted, or pessimistic thoughts) are more common among people who are depressed, the causal pathways remain unclear. We can't yet say whether dysfunctional or negative thinking causes depression or is merely a feature of depression. Perhaps the causal linkages go both ways. Our thoughts may affect our moods and our moods may affect our thoughts (Kwon & Oei, 1994). Think in terms of a vicious cycle. People who feel depressed may begin thinking in more negative, distorted ways. The more negative and distorted their thinking becomes, the more depressed they feel; the more depressed they feel, the more dysfunctional their thinking becomes. Alternatively, dysfunctional thinking may come first in the cycle, perhaps in response to a disappointing life experience, which then leads to a downcast mood. This in turn may accentuate negative thinking, and so on. We are still faced with the old "chicken or the egg" dilemma of determining which comes first in the causal sequence—distorted thinking or depression. Future research may help tease out these causal pathways. Even if it should become clear that distorted cognitions play no direct causal role in the initial onset of depression, the reciprocal interaction between thoughts and moods may play a role in maintaining depression and in determining the likelihood of recurrence (Kwon & Oei, 1994). Fortunately, evidence shows that dysfunctional attitudes tend to decrease with effective treatment for depression (Clark et al., 1999).

Learned Helplessness (Attributional) Theory

The **learned helplessness** model proposes that people may become depressed because they learn to view themselves as helpless to control the reinforcements in their environments—or to change their lives for the better.

automatic thoughts Thoughts that seem to pop into one's mind. In Aaron Beck's theory, automatic thoughts that reflect cognitive distortions induce negative feelings like anxiety or depression.

learned helplessness In Martin Seligman's model, a behaviour pattern characterized by passivity and perceptions of lack of control that develops because of a history of failure to be able to exercise control over one's environment.

The originator of the learned helplessness concept, Martin Seligman (1975), suggests that people learn to perceive themselves as helpless because of their experiences. The learned helplessness model thus straddles the behavioural and the cognitive: situational factors foster attitudes that lead to depression.

Seligman and his colleagues based the learned helplessness model on early laboratory studies of animals. In these studies, dogs exposed to an inescapable electric shock showed the "learned helplessness effect" by failing to learn to escape when the shock was later made escapable (Overmier & Seligman, 1967; Seligman & Maier, 1967). Exposure to uncontrollable forces apparently taught the animals they were helpless to change their situation. Animals that developed learned helplessness showed behaviours that were similar to those of people with depression, including lethargy, lack of motivation, and difficulty acquiring new skills (Maier & Seligman, 1976).

Seligman (1975, 1991) proposed that some forms of depression in humans might result from exposure to apparently uncontrollable situations. Such experiences can instill the expectation that future reinforcements will also be beyond the individual's control. A vicious cycle may come into play in many cases of depression. A few failures may produce feelings of helplessness and expectations of further failure. Perhaps you know people who have failed certain subjects, such as mathematics. They may come to believe themselves incapable of succeeding in math. They may thus decide that studying for the quantitative section of the Graduate Record Exam is a waste of time. They then do poorly, completing the self-fulfilling prophecy by confirming their expectations, which further intensifies feelings of helplessness, leading to lowered expectations and so on in a vicious cycle.

Although it stimulated much interest, Seligman's model failed to account for the low self-esteem typical of people who are depressed. Nor did it explain variations in the persistence of depression. Seligman and his colleagues (Abramson, Seligman, & Teasdale, 1978) offered a reformulation of the theory to meet such shortcomings. The revised theory held that perception of lack of control over reinforcement alone did not explain the persistence and severity of depression. It was also necessary to consider cognitive factors, especially the ways in which people explain their failures and disappointments to themselves.

Seligman and his colleagues recast the helplessness theory in terms of the social psychology concept of **attributional style**. An attributional style is a personal style of explanation. When disappointments or failures occur, we may explain them in various characteristic ways. We may blame ourselves (an **internal attribution**) or our circumstances (an **external attribution**). We may see bad experiences as typical events (a **stable attribution**) or as isolated events (an **unstable attribution**). We may see them as evidence of broader problems (a **global attribution**) or as evidence of precise and limited shortcomings (a **specific attribution**). The revised helplessness theory—called the reformulated helplessness theory—holds that people who explain the causes of negative events (like failure in work, school, or romantic relationships) according to these three types of attributions are most vulnerable to depression:

1. *Internal factors* or beliefs that failures reflect their personal inadequacies, rather than external factors or beliefs that failures are caused by environmental factors;
2. *Global factors* or beliefs that failures reflect sweeping flaws in personality, rather than specific factors or beliefs that failures reflect limited areas of functioning; and
3. *Stable factors* or beliefs that failures reflect fixed personality factors, rather than unstable factors or beliefs that the factors leading to failures are changeable.

Let us illustrate these attributional styles with the example of a university student who goes on a disastrous date. Afterward, he shakes his head in wonder and tries to make sense of his experience. An internal attribution for the calamity would involve self-blame, as in, "I really messed it up." An external attribution would place the blame elsewhere, as in, "Some couples just don't hit it off" or, "She must have been in a bad mood." A stable attribution would suggest a problem that cannot be changed, as in, "It's my personality." An unstable attribution, on the other hand, would suggest a transient condition, as in, "It was probably the head cold." A global attribution for failure magnifies the extent of the

attributional style Personal style for explaining cause-and-effect relationships between events.

internal attribution In the reformulated helplessness theory, a type of attribution involving the belief that the cause of an event involved factors within oneself. Contrast with *external attribution*.

external attribution In the reformulated helplessness theory, a type of attribution involving the belief that the cause of an event involves factors outside the self. Contrast with *internal attribution*.

stable attribution In the reformulated helplessness theory, a type of attribution involving the belief that the cause of an event involved stable rather than changeable factors. Contrast with *unstable attribution*.

unstable attribution In the reformulated helplessness theory, a type of attribution involving the belief that the cause of an event involved changeable rather than stable factors. Contrast with *stable attribution*.

global attribution In the reformulated helplessness theory, a type of attribution involving the belief that the cause of an event involved generalized rather than specific factors. Contrast with *specific attribution*.

specific attribution In the reformulated helplessness theory, a type of attribution involving the belief that the cause of an event involved specific rather than generalized factors. Contrast with *global attribution*.

problem, as in, "I really have no idea what I'm doing when I'm with people." A specific attribution, in contrast, chops the problem down to size, as in, "My problem is how to make small talk to get a relationship going."

The revised theory holds that each attributional dimension makes a specific contribution to feelings of helplessness. Internal attributions for negative events are linked to lower self-esteem. Stable attributions help explain the persistence—or, in medical terms, the chronicity—of helplessness cognitions. Global attributions are associated with the generality or pervasiveness of feelings of helplessness following negative events. Attributional style should be distinguished from negative thinking (Gotlib, Lewinsohn, Seeley, Rohde, & Redner, 1993). You may think negatively (pessimistically) or positively (optimistically), but still hold yourself to blame for your perceived failures. An example of pessimistic self-blame for perceived failures would be, "I messed up, and this is further evidence that I'm a loser." An example of more optimistic self-blame would be, "I messed up but I can learn from this experience so it doesn't happen again."

Research is generally but not completely supportive of the reformulated helplessness (attributional) model. There is much evidence that people who are depressed are more likely than nondepressed people to attribute the causes of failures to internal, stable, and global factors (Alloy, Abramson, Walshaw, & Neeren, 2006a; Sturman, Mongrain, & Kohn, 2006). Longitudinal studies show that this attributional style, even in people who are currently not depressed, also predicts the person's future risk for the first onset or recurrence of future depressive episodes (Alloy et al., 2006b). Further research, however, is needed to determine whether this attributional style truly causes depression. It could be that some other variable, correlated with depressive attributional style, is the actual causal agent.

Biological Perspectives

Evidence has accumulated pointing to the important role of biological factors, especially genetics and neurotransmitter functioning, in the development of mood disorders. Recent investigations are examining the biological roots of depression at the neurotransmitter level as well as the genetic, molecular, and cellular levels.

Genetic Factors A growing body of research implicates genetic factors in mood disorders (Jang, 2005; Kendler & Prescott, 2006). For one thing, we know that mood disorders tend to run in families. Families, however, share environmental similarities as well as genes. Family members may share blue eyes (an inherited attribute) but also a common religion (a cultural attribute). Yet strengthening the genetic link are findings showing the closer the genetic relationship one shares with a person with a major mood disorder such as major depression or bipolar disorder, the greater the likelihood that one will also suffer from a major mood disorder (Jang, 2005; Kendler & Prescott, 2006).

Twin studies and adoptee studies provide additional evidence of a genetic contribution. A higher concordance (agreement) rate among monozygotic (MZ) twins than dizygotic (DZ) twins for a given disorder is taken as supportive evidence of genetic factors. Both types of twins share common environments, but

Is it me? According to reformulated helplessness theory, the kinds of attributions we make concerning negative events can make us more or less vulnerable to depression. Attributing the break-up of a relationship to internalizing ("It's me"), globalizing ("I'm totally worthless"), and stabilizing ("Things are always going to turn out badly for me") causes can lead to depression.

MZ twins share 100% of their genes as compared to approximately 50% for DZ twins. Twin studies suggest that major depression is moderately heritable (Jang, 2005; Kendler & Prescott, 2006). However, individual depressive symptoms vary widely in their heritabilities. Symptoms such as depressed mood or tearfulness do not appear to be heritable, whereas other symptoms (e.g., loss of libido and appetite) have a heritable basis (Jang, Livesley, Taylor, Stein, & Moon, 2004). Data from twin studies suggest that dysthymic disorder may be relatively less influenced by genetic factors than either major depression or bipolar disorder. Genetic factors are particularly important in bipolar disorder, accounting for roughly 80% of the risk for developing this disorder, although the specific genes remain to be identified (Farmer, Elkin, & McGuffin, 2007).

All in all, researchers believe that heredity plays a contributing role in major depression in both men and women (Jang, 2005; Kendler & Prescott, 2006). However, genetics isn't the only, nor is it even the major, determinant of risk of major depression. Environmental factors, such as exposure to stressful life events, appear to play an important role in determining the risk of the disorder (Kendler & Prescott, 2006).

Biochemical Factors and Brain Abnormalities in Depression If there is a genetic component to depression, just what is inherited? Perhaps the genetic vulnerability expresses itself in abnormalities in neurotransmitter activity. These malfunctions may involve either an overabundance or oversensitivity of receptor sites on receiving (postsynaptic) neurons where neurotransmitters dock. Antidepressant drugs may work by gradually reducing the number and sensitivity of these receptors. Although early speculation focused mainly on the role of norepinephrine in depression, investigators today believe that we also need to take into account irregularities in other neurotransmitters as well, especially serotonin, in explaining depression (Southwick, Vythilingam, & Charney, 2005).

One line of research uses brain imaging techniques such as the PET scan (to measure metabolic activity) and the MRI (to examine structural differences) that peer into the brains of the people with depression. It turns out that the metabolic activity of the *prefrontal cortex* (the area of the frontal lobes lying in front of the motor areas) is typically lower in clinically depressed groups than in healthy controls (Damasio, 1997; Drevets et al., 1997). The prefrontal cortex is involved in regulating neurotransmitters believed to be involved in mood disorders, including serotonin and norepinephrine, so it is not surprising that evidence points to irregularities in this region of the brain. Abnormalities in the emotional centres of the brain (the limbic system) have also been observed. Other investigators find that MRI scans of the brains of people with bipolar disorder show evidence of structural abnormalities in parts of the brain involved in regulating mood states, such as the limbic system (Miklowitz & Johnson, 2006).

Research, including work done at the University of Toronto, indicates that the brain abnormalities in depression can be corrected with either drugs and/or cognitive therapy. Both treatments can correct the abnormalities in activity in the prefrontal cortex and limbic system (Goldapple et al., 2004).

TYING IT TOGETHER

Depression and other mood disorders involve interplay of multiple factors. Consistent with the *diathesis-stress model* (see Figure 7.2 on page 265), depression may reflect an interaction of biological factors (such as genetic factors, neurotransmitter irregularities, or brain abnormalities), psychological factors (such as cognitive distortions or learned helplessness), and social and environmental stressors (such as divorce or loss of a job).

Consistent with this formulation, evidence suggests that genes interact with the environment; people with a particular genetic makeup (e.g., a particular version of a gene involved in serotonin regulation) are most likely to become depressed and suicidal in response to stressful life events (Caspi & Moffitt, 2006; Kendler & Prescott, 2006). In fact, there is a growing body of evidence that many forms of psychological disorder,

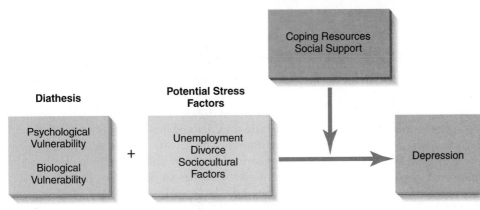

Potential Protective Factors

Coping Resources
Social Support

Diathesis

Psychological
Vulnerability

Biological
Vulnerability

+

**Potential Stress
Factors**

Unemployment
Divorce
Sociocultural
Factors

Depression

**FIGURE 7.2 Diathesis-stress
model of depression.**

including major depression, are the result of interactions between genes and the environment (Caspi & Moffitt, 2006; Rutter, 2006). In other words, both genes and environmental events are important in shaping a person's risk for developing major depression and other psychological disorders.

Stressful life events, such as prolonged unemployment or a divorce, may have a depressing effect by reducing neurotransmitter activity in the brain. These biochemical effects may be more likely to occur or be more pronounced in people with a certain genetic predisposition or *diathesis* for depression. However, a depressive disorder may not develop, or may develop in a milder form, in people with more effective coping resources for handling stressful situations. For example, people who receive emotional support from others may be better able to withstand the effects of stress than those who have to go it alone. So too for people who make active coping efforts to meet the challenges they face in life.

Sociocultural factors may be major sources of stress that impact the development of mood disorders. These factors include poverty; overcrowding; exposure to racism, sexism, and prejudice; violence in the home or community; unequal stressful burdens placed on women; and family disintegration. These factors may figure prominently in either precipitating mood disorders or accounting for their recurrence. Other sources of stress include negative life events such as the loss of a job, the development of a serious illness, the break-up of a romantic relationship, and the loss of a loved one.

The diathesis for depression may take the form of a psychological vulnerability involving a depressive thinking style, one characterized by tendencies to exaggerate the consequences of negative events, to heap blame on oneself, and to perceive oneself as helpless to effect positive change. This cognitive diathesis may increase the risk of depression in the face of negative life events. These cognitive influences may also interact with a genetically based diathesis to further increase the risk of depression following stressful life events. Then too, the availability of social support from others may help bolster a person's resistance to stress during difficult times. People with more effective social skills may be better able to garner and maintain social reinforcement from others and thus be better able to resist depression than people lacking social skills. But biochemical changes in the brain might make it more difficult for the person to cope effectively and bounce back from stressful life events. Lingering biochemical changes and feelings of depression may exacerbate feelings of helplessness, compound the effects of the initial stressor, and so on.

Gender-related differences in coping styles may also come into play. Men and women may respond differently to feelings of depression. According to Nolen-Hoeksema, women are more likely to ruminate over emotional problems, and men are more likely to distract themselves, such as seeking refuge in a bottle. Differences in coping styles may propel women into longer and more severe bouts of depression while setting the stage for the development of alcohol-related problems in men. As you can see, a complex web of factors may be involved in the development of mood disorders.

Theoretical Perspectives

Review It

- **How are mood disorders conceptualized within the psychodynamic model?** In classic psychodynamic theory, depression is viewed in terms of inward-directed anger. People who hold strongly ambivalent feelings toward people they have lost, or whose loss is threatened, may direct unresolved anger toward the inward representations of these people that they have incorporated or introjected within themselves, producing self-loathing and depression. Bipolar disorder is understood in psychodynamic theory in terms of the shifting balances between the ego and superego. More recent psychodynamic models, such as the self-focusing model, incorporate both psychodynamic and cognitive aspects in explaining depression in terms of the continued pursuit of lost love objects or goals that it would be more adaptive to surrender.

- **How do humanistic and learning theorists view depression?** In the existential-humanistic framework, feelings of depression reflect the lack of meaning and authenticity in a person's life. Learning perspectives focus on situational factors in explaining depression, such as changes in the level of reinforcement. When reinforcement is reduced, the person may feel unmotivated and depressed, which can occasion inactivity and further reduces opportunities for reinforcement. Coyne's interactional theory focuses on the negative family interactions that can lead family members of people with depression to become less reinforcing toward them.

- **What are two major cognitive models of depression?** Beck's cognitive model focuses on the role of negative or distorted thinking in depression. Depression-prone people hold negative beliefs toward themselves, the environment, and the future. This cognitive triad of depression leads to specific errors in thinking, or cognitive distortions, in response to negative events, which in turn lead to depression.

  The learned helplessness model is based on the belief that people may become depressed when they come to view themselves as helpless to control the reinforcements in their environment or to change their lives for the better. A reformulated version of the theory held that the ways in which people explain events—their attributions—determine their proneness toward depression in the face of negative events. The combination of internal, global, and stable attributions for negative events renders one most vulnerable to depression.

- **What role do biological factors play in mood disorders?** Genetic factors appear to play a role in mood disorders, especially in explaining major depressive disorder and bipolar disorder. Imbalances in neurotransmitter activity in the brain appear to be involved in depression and mania. The diathesis-stress model is used as an explanatory framework to illustrate how biological or psychological diatheses may interact with stress in the development of depression.

Define It

mourning	internal attribution
cognitive triad of depression	external attribution
selective abstraction	stable attribution
automatic thoughts	unstable attribution
learned helplessness	global attribution
attributional style	specific attribution

Recall It*

1. In the classic psychodynamic formulation, depression represents _____.

    a. loss of self-worth or self-esteem
    b. perceptions of existence lacking in meaning
    c. failure of the ego to dominate the id
    d. anger turned inward

2. Behavioural theorists emphasize the role of _____ in explaining depression.

    a. person variables
    b. unconscious conflicts
    c. self-esteem factors
    d. reinforcement

3. _____ is based on the belief that depressed people impose unrealistic demands on others, leading others to reject them.

    a. Self-focusing theory
    b. Situational theory
    c. Interactional theory
    d. Behavioural deficit theory

4. The "cognitive triad of depression" refers to a set of negative beliefs about each of the following except _____.

    a. oneself
    b. the past

c. the future

d. the environment

5. Genetic factors are believed to play a greater role in _____.

    a. dysthymic disorder than major depression

    b. major depression than bipolar disorder

    c. bipolar disorder than major depression

    d. cyclothymic disorder than bipolar disorder

* Recall It answers can be found on the Companion Website for this text.

TREATMENT

Just as theoretical perspectives suggest that many factors may be involved in the development of mood disorders, there are various approaches to treatment that derive from psychological and biological models. Here we focus on several of the leading contemporary approaches.

Psychodynamic Approaches

Traditional psychoanalysis aims to help people who become depressed understand their ambivalent feelings toward important people (objects) in their lives they have lost or whose loss was threatened. By working through feelings of anger toward these lost objects, they can turn anger outward—through verbal expression of feelings, for example—rather than leave it to fester and turn inward.

Traditional psychoanalysis can take years to uncover and deal with unconscious conflicts. Modern psychoanalytic approaches also focus on unconscious conflicts, but they are more direct, relatively brief, and focus on present as well as past conflicted relationships. According to a recent review, patients treated with psychodynamic therapy tended to improve, although most of the research studies had important methodological problems, which makes it difficult to determine whether psychodynamic psychotherapy is any more effective than placebo (Bond, 2006). Eclectic psychodynamic therapists may also use behavioural methods to help clients acquire the social skills they need to develop a broader social network.

Newer models of psychotherapy for depression have emerged from the interpersonal school of psychodynamic therapy derived initially from the work of Harry Stack Sullivan (see Chapter 2) and other neo-Freudians, such as Karen Horney. One contemporary example is **interpersonal psychotherapy** (IPT) (Weissman & Markowitz, 2000). IPT is a brief form of therapy (usually no more than 9 to 12 months) that focuses on the client's current interpersonal relationships. The developers of ITP believe that depression occurs within an interpersonal context and that relationship issues need to be emphasized in treatment. IPT has been shown to be an effective treatment for major depression and shows promise in treating other psychological disorders, including dysthymic disorder and bulimia (Harkness et al., 2002; Markowitz, 2006a,b). Although IPT shares some features with traditional psychodynamic approaches (principally the belief that early life experiences and persistent personality features are important issues in psychological adjustment), it differs from traditional psychodynamic therapy by focusing primarily on clients' current relationships, rather than helping them acquire insight into unconscious internal conflicts of childhood origins. Although unconscious factors and early childhood experiences are recognized, therapy focuses on the present—the here and now.

interpersonal psychotherapy A brief, psychodynamic form of therapy that focuses on helping people resolve interpersonal problems.

Interpersonal psychotherapy (IPT). IPT is a brief, psychodynamic form of therapy that focuses on issues in a person's current interpersonal relationships. Like traditional psychodynamic approaches, IPT assumes that early life experiences are key issues in adjustment, but IPT focuses on the present—the here and now.

Interpersonal psychotherapy helps clients deal with unresolved or delayed grief reactions following the death of a loved one as well as role conflicts in present relationships (Weissman & Markowitz, 2000). The therapist helps clients express grief and come to terms with their loss while assisting them in developing new activities and relationships to help renew their lives. The therapist also helps clients identify areas of conflict in their present relationships, understand the issues that underlie them, and consider ways of resolving them. If the problems in a relationship are beyond repair, the therapist helps the client consider ways of ending it and establishing new relationships. In the case of Sal, a 31-year-old television repairman's assistant, depression was associated with marital conflict:

Sal began to explore his marital problems in the fifth therapy session, becoming tearful as he recounted his difficulty expressing his feelings to his wife because of feelings of being "numb." He felt that he had been "holding on" to his feelings, which was causing him to become estranged from his wife. The next session zeroed in on the similarities between himself and his father, in particular how he was distancing himself from his wife in a similar way to how his father had kept a distance from him. By session seven, a turning point had been reached. Sal expressed how he and his wife had become "emotional" and closer to one another during the previous week and how he was able to talk more openly about his feelings, and how he and his wife had been able to make a joint decision concerning a financial matter that had been worrying them for some time. When later he was laid off from his job, he sought his wife's opinion, rather than picking a fight with her as a way of thrusting his job problems on her. To his surprise he found that his wife responded positively—not "violently" as he had expected—to times when he expressed his feelings. In his last therapy session (session 12), Sal expressed how therapy had led to a "reawakening" within himself with respect to the feelings he had been keeping to himself—an openness that he hoped to create in his relationship with his wife.

ADAPTED FROM KLERMAN, WEISSMAN, ROUNSAVILLE, & CHEVRON, 1984, PP. 111–113

Behavioural Approaches

Behavioural treatment approaches presume that depressive behaviours are learned and can be unlearned. Behaviour therapists aim to directly modify behaviours rather than seeking to foster awareness of possible unconscious causes of these behaviours. Behaviour therapy has been shown to produce substantial benefits in treating depression both in adults and adolescents (Dimidjian et al., 2006; Hopko et al., 2003).

One illustrative behavioural program was developed by Lewinsohn and colleagues (Hops & Lewinsohn, 1995; Lewinsohn al., 1984). It consists of a 12-session, 8-week group therapy program organized as a course—the *Coping with Depression (CWD) Course*. The course helps clients acquire relaxation skills, increase pleasant activities, and build social skills that enable them to obtain social reinforcement. For example, students learn how to accept rather than deny compliments and how to ask friends to join them in activities to raise the frequency and quality of their social interactions. Participants are taught to generate a self-change plan, to think more constructively, and to develop a lifetime plan for maintaining treatment gains and preventing recurrent depression. The therapist is considered a teacher; the client, a student; the session, a class. Each participant is treated as a responsible adult who is capable of learning. The structure involves lectures, activities, and homework, and each session follows a structured lesson plan. Here is one example:

Liz Foster, a 27-year-old woman diagnosed as suffering from major depressive disorder, participated in an eight-member *Coping with Depression Course*. Prior to therapy, Liz had been feeling depressed for two months, eating poorly, sleeping excessively, and experiencing suicidal thoughts. She had had similar bouts of depression during the previous eight years. When she was depressed, she would spend most of her time alone at home—watching television, reading, or just sitting. She engaged in a low rate of pleasant activities.

Liz had been laid off from work 11 months earlier and had few social contacts other than her boyfriend. She rarely saw her family, and two of her closest friends had moved away. Her remaining friends rarely visited, and she made no effort to see them.

With the eight other women in her class, Liz learned to focus on behaviours that she could change to increase her level of pleasant activities. At first she complained, "I don't feel like doing anything." The group instructors acknowledged that it would be hard, at first, to select desired reinforcers. Group members were encouraged to try out activities they had formerly enjoyed to see if they still found pleasure in them. Group members were instructed to identify stressful situations or hassles that increased their level of daily stress and were trained in relaxation techniques that they could use to cope with these stresses. They were given Pleasant Events Schedules to complete and encouraged to increase their frequency of pleasant activities.

Liz and the other group members plotted on a graph their level of pleasant activities from week to week and rated their mood levels on a daily basis. Most group members, including Liz, noticed a relationship between their moods and pleasant activities. Liz, whose initial rate of pleasant activities was about eight per day, decided to increase her rate to 15–20 activities a day, and devised a plan to reinforce herself with rewards of 25 cents for each activity she completed over 13, pooling her rewards until she had earned $8, which she then used to buy a record album. Liz was able to increase her rate to 20 and noticed that her mood had improved.

The course also exposed participants to various techniques for controlling their thoughts. Liz selected the technique of self-reward/self-punishment: She rewarded herself with money for positive thoughts and charged herself (a nickel a thought) for negative thoughts. In tracking her thoughts, Liz found that she was able to increase her daily average of positive thoughts from six to eleven and decrease her negative thoughts from seven to two. By the eighth session, Liz was reporting that she was no longer depressed and felt more in control of her thoughts and feelings. In later class sessions, group members learned assertive techniques for handling conflicts, such as dealing with aggressive salespeople, and for starting conversations with strangers.

In later sessions, group members prepared life plans that they could use to deal with major life events and maintain the progress they had made. Liz recognized that she needed to maintain her frequency of pleasant activities at a high level, and she continued to monitor these activities to ensure that the frequency remained above a critical level. At a class reunion six months following the course, she reported that she continued to use the techniques she had learned. Follow-up evaluations through a period of one and a half years showed that Liz had maintained her gains.

ADAPTED FROM LEWINSOHN, TERI, & WASSERMAN, 1983, PP. 94–101

Cognitive Approaches

cognitive therapy (1) Name of Aaron Beck's kind of psychotherapy, which challenges the distorted thought patterns that give rise to or exacerbate clients' problems. (2) More generally, a form of psychotherapy that addresses clients' cognitive processes, usually their self-defeating attitudes.

Cognitive theorists believe that distorted thinking plays a key role in the development of depression. Aaron Beck and his colleagues have developed a multicomponent treatment approach called **cognitive therapy**, which focuses on helping people with depression learn to recognize and change their dysfunctional thinking patterns. Depressed people tend to focus on how they are feeling rather than on the thoughts that may underlie their feeling states. That is, they usually pay more attention to how bad they feel than to the thoughts that may trigger or maintain their depressed moods.

Cognitive therapy, like behaviour therapy, involves a relatively brief therapy format, frequently 14 to 16 weekly sessions. Therapists use a combination of behavioural and cognitive techniques to help clients identify and change dysfunctional thoughts and develop more adaptive behaviours (Dobson & Khatri 2002). For example, they assist clients in connecting thought patterns to negative moods by having them monitor the automatic negative thoughts they experience throughout the day by means of a thought diary or daily record. They note when and where negative thoughts occur and how they feel at the time. Once these disruptive thoughts are identified, the therapist helps the client challenge their validity and replace them with more adaptive thoughts. The following case example shows how a cognitive therapist works with a client to dispute the validity of thoughts reflecting the cognitive distortion called selective abstraction (the tendency to judge oneself entirely on the basis of specific weaknesses or flaws in character). The client judged herself to be completely lacking in self-control because she ate a single piece of candy while she was on a diet.

Client: I don't have any self-control at all.

Therapist: On what basis do you say that?

C: Somebody offered me candy and I couldn't refuse it.

T: Were you eating candy every day?

C: No, I just ate it this once.

T: Did you do anything constructive during the past week to adhere to your diet?

C: Well, I didn't give in to the temptation to buy candy every time I saw it at the store . . . Also, I did not eat any candy except that one time when it was offered to me and I felt I couldn't refuse it.

T: If you counted up the number of times you controlled yourself versus the number of times you gave in, what ratio would you get?

C: About 100 to 1.

T: So if you controlled yourself 100 times and did not control yourself just once, would that be a sign that you are weak through and through?

C: I guess not—not *through* and *through* (smiles).

ADAPTED FROM BECK ET AL., 1979, P. 68

There is ample evidence supporting the effectiveness of cognitive therapy in treating major depression (Hollon, 2006). Depressive symptoms often lift within 8 to 12 sessions. The benefits achieved appear to be at least equal to those achieved from antidepressant medication in treating mild to moderate depression. Questions remain about how effective cognitive or cognitive-behavioural approaches may be in treating severe depression, however (Jacobson & Hollon, 1996). Another open question is whether a combination approach involving antidepressant medication and psychotherapy is preferable to either approach alone (Craighead, Craighead, & Ilardi, 1998). Cognitive therapy or cognitive-behavioural therapy appears to produce about the same level of benefit as interpersonal psychotherapy or antidepressant medications (Hollon, 2006; Shapiro et al., 1995).

There is less research on the psychological treatment of dysthymia, although techniques used in treating major depression, such as cognitive therapy and interpersonal psychotherapy, have shown some promising results (Dunner, 2005). Cognitive theorists suggest that cognitive errors can lead to depression if they are left to rummage around unchallenged in the individual's mind. They help assist clients to recognize cognitive distortions and replace them with more rational alternative thoughts.

Table 7.5 shows some common examples of automatic thoughts, the types of cognitive distortions they represent, and some rational alternative responses.

TABLE 7.5

Cognitive Distortions and Rational Responses

Automatic Thought	Kind of Cognitive Distortion	Rational Response
I'm all alone in the world.	All-or-Nothing Thinking	It may feel like I'm all alone, but there are some people who care about me.
Nothing will ever work out for me.	Overgeneralization	No one can look into the future. Concentrate on the present.
My looks are hopeless.	Magnification	I may not be perfect looking, but I'm far from hopeless.
I'm falling apart. I can't handle this.	Magnification	Sometimes I just feel overwhelmed. But I've handled things like this before. Just take it a step at a time and I'll be okay.
I guess I'm just a born loser.	Labelling and Mislabelling	Nobody is destined to be a loser. Stop talking yourself down.
I've only lost four kilograms on this diet. I should just forget it. I can't succeed.	Negative Focusing/Minimization/Disqualifying the Positive/Jumping to Conclusions/All-or-Nothing Thinking	Four kilograms is a good start. I didn't gain all this weight overnight, and I have to expect that it will take time to lose it.
I know things must really be bad for me to feel this awful.	Emotional Reasoning	Feeling something doesn't make it so. If I'm not seeing things clearly, my emotions will be distorted too.
I know I'm going to flunk this course.	Fortune Teller Error	Give me a break! Just focus on getting through this course, not jumping to negative conclusions.
I know John's problems are really my fault.	Personalization	Stop blaming yourself for everyone else's problems. There are many reasons why John has these problems that have nothing to do with me.
Someone my age should be doing better than I am.	Should Statements	Stop comparing yourself to others. All anyone can be expected to do is their best. What good does it do to compare myself to others? It only leads me to get down on myself, rather than get motivated.
I just don't have the brains for college.	Labelling and Mislabelling	Stop calling yourself names like stupid. I can accomplish a lot more than I give myself credit for.
Everything is my fault.	Personalization	There you go again. Stop playing this game of pointing blame at yourself. There's enough blame to go around. Better yet, forget placing blame and try to think through how to solve this problem.
It would be awful if Sue turns me down.	Magnification	It might be upsetting. But it needn't be awful unless I make it so.
If people really knew me, they would hate me.	Mind Reader	What evidence is there for that? More people who get to know me like me than don't like me.
If something doesn't get better soon, I'll go crazy.	Jumping to Conclusions/Magnification	I've dealt with these problems this long without falling apart. I just have to hang in there. Things are not as bad as they seem.
I can't believe I got another pimple on my face. This is going to ruin my whole weekend.	Mental Filter	Take it easy. A pimple is not the end of the world. It doesn't have to spoil my whole weekend. Other people get pimples and seem to have a good time.

Biological Approaches

The most common biological approaches to treating mood disorders involve the use of antidepressant drugs and electroconvulsive therapy for depression and lithium carbonate for bipolar disorder.

Antidepressant Drugs Drugs used to treat depression include several classes of antidepressants: tricyclic antidepressants (TCAs), monoamine oxidase (MAO) inhibitors, and selective serotonin-reuptake inhibitors (SSRIs). All of these drugs increase brain levels and, perhaps, the actions of neurotransmitters. The increased availability of key neurotransmitters in the synaptic cleft may alter the sensitivity of postsynaptic neurons to these chemical messengers. It is not precisely known how antidepressant medications work in relieving depression. Given that there are many different types of these drugs working on various types (and subtypes) of neurotransmitters, it seems likely that there are several different ways in which the various antidepressant medications exert their therapeutic effects. Antidepressants tend to have a delayed effect, typically requiring several weeks of treatment before a therapeutic benefit is achieved. SSRIs not only lift mood, but in many cases also eliminate delusions that may accompany severe depression (Zanardi et al., 1996). Antidepressant medication is clearly effective in helping relieve major depression in many cases (Kupfer, 1999). Evidence also shows that antidepressant medication is helpful in treating dysthymia as well (Dunner, 2005).

The different classes of antidepressants increase the availability of neurotransmitters, but in different ways (see Figure 7.3). The tricylics, which include imipramine (trade name Tofranil), amitriptyline (Elavil), desipramine (Norpramin), and doxepin (Sinequan), are so named because of their three-ringed molecular structure. They increase levels in the brain of the neurotransmitters norepinephrine and serotonin by interfering with the reuptake (reabsorption by the transmitting cell) of these chemical messengers. As a result, more of these neurotransmitters remain available in the synapse, which induces the receiving cell to continue to fire, prolonging the volley of nerve impulses travelling through the neural highway in the brain.

The selective serotonin-reuptake inhibitors (SSRIs) (fluoxetine, trade name Prozac, is one) work in a similar fashion but have more specific effects on raising the levels of serotonin in the brain. The MAO inhibitors increase the availability of neurotransmitters by inhibiting the action of monoamine oxidase (MAO), an enzyme that normally breaks down or degrades neurotransmitters in the synaptic cleft. MAO inhibitors are used less widely than other antidepressants because of potentially serious interactions with certain foods and alcoholic beverages.

The potential side effects of tricyclics and MAO inhibitors include dry mouth, constipation, blurred vision, and, less frequently, urinary retention, paralytic ileus (a paralysis of the intestines, which impairs the passage of intestinal contents), confusion, delirium, and

FIGURE 7.3 The actions of various types of antidepressants at the synapse.
Tricyclic antidepressants and serotonin-reuptake inhibitors both increase the availability of neurotransmitters by preventing their reuptake by the presynaptic neuron. Tricyclic antidepressants impede the reuptake of both norepinephrine and serotonin. MAO inhibitors work by inhibiting the action of monoamine oxidase, an enzyme that normally breaks down neurotransmitters in the synaptic cleft.

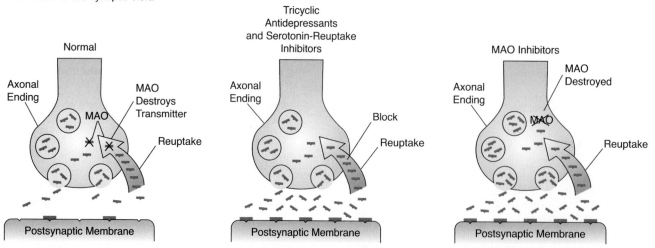

cardiovascular complications such as reduced blood pressure. Tricyclics are also highly toxic in very high doses, which raises the prospect of suicidal overdoses if the drugs are used without close supervision.

Compared to the older generation of tricylics, SSRIs such as Prozac and Zoloft have two major advantages: first, they are less toxic and so are less dangerous when taken in very high doses (as in overdose); second, they have fewer of the common side effects (such as dry mouth, constipation, and weight gain) associated with the tricylics and MAO inhibitors. Still, Prozac and other SSRIs may produce side effects such as upset stomach, headaches, agitation, insomnia, lack of sexual drive, and delayed orgasm. Moreover, SSRIs are only moderately effective in treating depression (Taylor & Stein, 2006), and may be less effective than tricylics (Montgomery, 2006).

Another promising class of medications are the serotonin noradrenaline reuptake inhibitors (SNRIs), such as Effexor (venlafaxine). SNRIs are similar to tricylics in that they increase the availability of both serotonin and norepinephrine. Although SNRIs have not been studied as extensively as SSRIs, the evidence so far suggests that in high doses, SNRIs appear to be more effective than SSRIs, but not at low doses (Montgomery, 2006). SNRIs appear to be as effective as tricylics but with milder side effects (Montgomery, 2006). Patients who fail to respond to a particular SNRI may benefit from another SNRI, or they may benefit from some other medication, such as an SSRI (Blier, 2006).

One issue we need to address in discussing drug therapy is the high rate of relapse following discontinuation of medication. A review of drug withdrawal studies showed relapse rates of 25% to 75% when antidepressants were withdrawn (Petersen, 2006). Continued (maintenance) medication can help reduce the rate of relapse. Psychologically based therapies appear to provide greater protection against a recurrence of depression following termination of treatment, presumably because the learning that occurs during therapy carries past the end of active treatment (Petersen, 2006).

Research, such as studies conducted by Zindel Segal and colleagues at the University of Toronto, suggests that mindfulness-based cognitive therapy (MBCT) is a particularly useful way of preventing relapse, regardless of whether the patient's depression was first treated with either medication or psychotherapy (Carney & Segal, 2005). MBCT involves training the person in meditation exercises, including exercises that increase their awareness of the things in the present (e.g., "What I am doing right now") instead of ruminating about bad things that happened in the past or might happen in the future. MBCT also teaches people to simply observe their unwanted thoughts as they float through the stream of consciousness, without attaching evaluative judgments (e.g., "I've just had the thought, 'I'll always fail'—I don't need to get upset about the thought or believe it; all I need to do is to notice that the thought comes and goes.") (Segal, Williams, & Teasdale, 2002).

Overall, evidence shows that most people with major depressive disorder will respond favourably to cognitive therapy, cognitive-behavioural therapy, or interpersonal psychotherapy, or to antidepressant medications (APA, 2000b; Hollon & Shelton, 2001). It is currently a matter of debate as to whether drugs or psychotherapy are most appropriate for severe depression (APA, 2000b; Hollon, 2006), although drugs would be indicated if the depressed person was experiencing delusions and hallucinations. Some people who fail to respond to drug therapy may respond favourably to psychotherapy, and vice versa.

Other interventions also can be useful as adjuncts or alternatives to medication or psychotherapy. For example, research indicates that physical exercise is useful for alleviating depressive symptoms in people with mild to moderate depression (Martinsen, 2005).

Lithium The drug lithium carbonate, a powdered form of the metallic element lithium, is the most widely used and one of the most recommended treatments for bipolar disorder (Yatham et al., 2006). It could be said that the ancient Greeks and Romans were among the first to use lithium as a form of chemotherapy. They prescribed mineral water that contained lithium for people with turbulent mood swings.

Lithium is effective in stabilizing moods in people with bipolar disorder and reducing recurrent episodes of mania and depression. People with bipolar disorder may need to use lithium indefinitely to control their mood swings, just as diabetics use insulin continuously to control their illness. Lithium is given orally in the form of a natural mineral salt, lithium carbonate. Despite more than 40 years of use, we still can't say how lithium works, although there is emerging evidence that it influences the communication between neurons (Miklowitz & Johnson, 2006).

Lithium treatment must be closely monitored because of potential toxic effects and other side effects. Lithium is not a panacea; many patients fail to respond or cannot tolerate the side effects (e.g., stomach irritation, weight gain, increased thirst). Fortunately, there are other effective medications for bipolar disorder, including some antipsychotic and anticonvulsant medications that happen to have mood stabilizing properties (e.g., Zyprexa, Tegretol; Yatham et al., 2006). These alternative medications usually cause fewer or less severe side effects than lithium. However, some patients have only a partial response to lithium or other drugs and some fail to respond at all. Thus, there remains a need for alternative treatments or drug strategies to be developed, perhaps involving a combination of these or other drugs.

Electroconvulsive Therapy More commonly called shock therapy, *electroconvulsive therapy (ECT)* continues to evoke controversy. The idea of passing an electric current through someone's brain may seem barbaric. Yet ECT is a generally safe and effective treatment for severe depression, and can help relieve depression in many cases in which alternative treatments have failed.

Electroconvulsive therapy involves the administration of an electrical current to the head. A current of between 70 to 130 volts is used to induce a convulsion that is similar to a grand mal epileptic seizure. ECT is usually administered in a series of 6 to 12 treatments over a period of several weeks. The patient is put to sleep with a brief-acting general anaesthetic and given a muscle relaxant to avoid wild convulsions that might result in injury. As a result, spasms may be barely perceptible to onlookers. The patient awakens soon after the procedure and generally remembers nothing. Although ECT had earlier been used in the treatment of a wide variety of psychological disorders, including schizophrenia and bipolar disorder, ECT is typically used only to treat major depressive disorder in people who do not respond to antidepressant medication.

A CLOSER LOOK

St. John's Wort—A Natural "Prozac"?

Might a humble herb be a remedy for depression? The herb, called St. John's wort or *Hypericum perforatum*, has been used for centuries to help heal wounds. Now people are using it to relieve depression. Nowhere is it more popular than Germany, where high-strength versions of the herb are among the most widely used antidepressants on the market. The benefits of St. John's wort are currently unclear and have been the subject of much debate. Some studies provide support for the benefits of St. John's wort in treating major depressive disorder with fewer reported side effects than medications. For example, Alpert et al. (2005) found that the herb was more effective than fluoxetine (Prozac). Another study found that the herb was at least as effective as the SSRI drug proxetine (Paxil) in moderate to severe major depression (Szegedi et al., 2005). However, other studies have raised doubts about the herb's efficacy. According to a review of several recent placebo-controlled studies, St. John's wort has minimal beneficial effects on major depression,

although it might be useful in treating milder forms of depression (Linde, Berner, Egger, & Mulrow, 2005). More promising treatments for major depression include cognitive-behaviour therapy or selective serotonin reuptake inhibitors. Regardless of the effects of St. John's wort on depressive symptoms, the herb appears to increase the levels of serotonin in the brain by interfering with its reabsorption, the same mechanism believed to account for Prozac's benefits. Yet we don't know about the herb's long-term safety. Evidence suggests that it should not be combined with conventional antidepressant medications such as Prozac because St. John's wort interacts with these drugs to produce an excess of serotonin in the brain. This is called the serotonin syndrome, which can progress from dizziness, headaches, and vomiting to coma and death (Vermani, Milosevic, Smith, & Katzman, 2005). St John's wort also should be used with caution in patients receiving anticoagulants (blood thinners), oral contraceptives, or antiviral drugs because St. John's wort can alter the blood levels of these medications by means of its effects on the liver (Vermani et al., 2005).

A highly effective treatment for depression, ECT is used particularly for people who have failed to respond to other treatments (Pagnin, de Queiroz, Pini, & Cassano, 2004). ECT results in shorter and less costly hospitalizations for major depression (Olfson, Marcus, Sackheim, Thompson, & Pincus, 1998). Although it often produces a dramatic relief of symptoms, no one knows exactly how ECT works. ECT produces such mammoth chemical and electrical changes in the body that it is difficult to pinpoint the mechanism of therapeutic action. It is possible that ECT may work by normalizing brain levels of certain neurotransmitters (Grover, Mattoo, & Gupta, 2005). Although ECT can be an effective short-term treatment of severe depression, it too is no panacea. Depression often returns at some later point, even among people who continue to be treated with antidepressant medication (Bourgon & Kellner, 2000).

Electroconvulsive therapy may be administered to either both sides of the head (*bilateral ECT*) or to only one (*unilateral ECT*). Unilateral ECT is applied to the nondominant hemisphere of the brain, which, for most people, is the right side. Bilateral ECT tends to produce a somewhat greater clinical benefit than unilateral ECT, but also greater short-term memory impairment (Reisner, 2003).

There is an understandable concern among patients, relatives, and professionals themselves concerning the possible risk of brain damage from ECT. Much of this concern has focused on potential memory loss. The evidence so far suggests that ECT does not result in structural damage to the human brain, and any memory losses suffered as the result of treatment are temporary except for events occurring shortly before or after ECT administration (Reisner, 2003). Earlier memories or those formed weeks after ECT do not appear to be affected. Still, many professionals view ECT as a treatment of last resort, to be used only after other treatment approaches have been tried and failed. Moreover, it is not possible to definitively rule out the possibility that ECT may cause brain damage in a small proportion of people (Reisner, 2003).

In summing up, let us note that experts have described clinical practice guidelines for depression. The guidelines were based on evidence from controlled studies showing the following treatments to be effective in treating depression (American Psychiatric Association, 2000; Hollon, 2006; Hollon & Skelton, 2001):

- Antidepressant medication (tricyclics, SSRIs, SNRIs)
- Three specific forms of psychotherapy: cognitive therapy, behaviour therapy, and interpersonal psychotherapy
- A combination of one of the recommended forms of psychotherapy and antidepressant medication
- Other specified forms of treatment, including ECT for very severe depression and phototherapy for seasonal depression

Treatments for depression are continually evolving, and researchers have been seeking to identify and investigate new treatments. Combinations of particular medications have been examined. As noted by depression researchers Sidney Kenney (University of Toronto) and Raymond Lam (University of British Columbia), for patients who have failed to respond to conventional depression treatments, it may be useful to add drugs that are used in the treatment of schizophrenia, such as respiridone (Kennedy & Lam, 2003).

Another promising treatment approach is called *repetitive transcranial magnetic stimulation (rTMS)*. This is a non-invasive way of stimulating particular regions of the brain. It involves the use of a device containing a powerful electromagnet, which is placed next to the person's head in order to induce weak electric currents in particular regions of the brain at particular frequencies for a few minutes per day for several days or weeks. It is thought that this can induce enduring changes (i.e., stimulating or calming down) the activity of particular brain regions (Fitzgerald, Fountain, & Daskalakis, 2006). When used in the treatment of depression, brain regions that are thought to play a role in depression are repeatedly stimulated, typically the left prefrontal cortex. Although there is some preliminary evidence for the benefits of rTMS, more research is needed to evaluate the magnitude of its effects (Fitzgerald, Benitez, et al., 2006; Mitchell & Loo, 2006).

Recent research suggests that rTMS is not as effective as ECT for severe depression (Eranti et al., 2007).

Other innovative methods have also been developed for the treatment of depression, such as deep brain stimulation (involving the placement of electrodes deep within the brain) and vagus nerve stimulation (i.e., stimulating the vagus nerve with electrical signals). These methods show promise in the treatment of severely depressed people who have not benefited from other treatments. However, more research is required to determine whether these methods are safe and effective (Nemeroff, 2007).

One of the big challenges—and controversies—in recent years concerns the treatment of depressed children and adolescents. It is widely believed that SSRIs and SNRIs are associated with a worsening of suicidal thoughts and behaviours in children and adolescents. Drug-related suicidal ideation may emerge suddenly, without warning, even in people who have not had previous episode of suicidal ideation. Agitation and restlessness may be early signs of danger (Simon, 2006). Health Canada and health agencies in other countries such as the United States and United Kingdom have issued warnings about the use of these drugs (Whittington, Kendall, & Pilling, 2005). Health Canada advises that patients (or their caregivers) should consult the treating physician to confirm that the benefits of the drug still outweigh its potential risks. According to a recent review by University of British Columbia psychiatrist Jane Garland (2004), there is also evidence suggesting that these medications may not be effective in children and adolescents.

Not all clinicians are convinced that these medications are ineffective and harmful, and so the issue remains controversial (Simon, 2006). Adverse effects, when they do occur, appear to be rare. Alternatives to drugs are available, such as psychotherapies like cognitive-behaviour therapy. These treatments do not have the side effects associated with drugs. However, psychotherapies are only moderately effective in treating depression in children and adolescents (Weisz, McCarty, & Valeri, 2006). Clearly, much more research needs to be done in order to find ways of effectively helping depressed youth. Preliminary evidence suggests that the combination of psychotherapy and SSRIs may be both effective and protective against the increased risk of suicide-related thoughts and behaviours (Whittington et al., 2005).

STUDY BREAK

Treatment

Review It

- **What are the approaches taken by the major theoretical perspectives in treating depression?** Psychodynamic treatment of depression has traditionally focused on helping the depressed person uncover and work through ambivalent feelings toward the lost object, thereby lessening the anger directed inward. Modern psychodynamic approaches tend to be more direct and briefer and focus more on developing adaptive means of achieving self-worth and resolving interpersonal conflicts. Learning theory approaches have focused on helping people with depression increase the frequency of reinforcement in their lives through such means as increasing the rates of pleasant activities in which they participate and assisting them in developing more effective social skills to increase their ability to obtain social reinforcements from others. Cognitive therapists focus on helping the person identify and correct distorted or dysfunctional thoughts and learn more adaptive behaviours. Biological approaches have focused on the use of antidepressant drugs and other biological treatments, such as electroconvulsive therapy (ECT). Antidepressant drugs may help normalize neurotransmitter functioning in the brain. Bipolar disorder is commonly treated with lithium.

Define It

interpersonal psychotherapy
cognitive therapy

Recall It*

1. Modern approaches to psychoanalytic treatment focus on helping depressed patients _____.

   a. channel their anger outwardly through verbal confrontations
   b. resolve problems in present conflicted relationships

c. expand awareness of their authentic feelings

d. change their behaviours to increase sources of reinforcement

2. A depressed patient who blows negative events out of proportion shows a type of cognitive distortion called _____.

a. labelling

b. magnification

c. overgeneralization

d. dismissing the positives

3. Which of the following drugs (or drug groups) is used in the treatment of bipolar disorder?

a. selective serotonin-reuptake inhibitors

b. MAO inhibitors

c. lithium

d. tricyclics

4. Prozac is a type of _____.

a. selective serotonin-reuptake inhibitor (SSRI)

b. MAO inhibitor

c. endorphin

d. tricyclic

5. Which of the following statements is NOT true?

a. Both psychotherapy and antidepressant drugs have been shown to be effective in treating depression.

b. Antidepressant drugs appear to have more lasting benefits than psychotherapy in the treatment of depression.

c. Psychotherapy appears to have more lasting benefits than antidepressant drugs in the treatment of depression.

d. Phototherapy has been found to be effective in treating seasonal depression.

* Recall It answers can be found on the Companion Website for this text.

Think About It

- What are the advantages and disadvantages of drug therapy for depression? If you were to become clinically depressed, which course of treatment would you prefer—medication, psychotherapy, or a combination? Explain.

SUICIDE

Suicidal thoughts are common enough. According to University of Waterloo, Ontario, psychologist Donald Meichenbaum (2005), a practicing clinical psychologist will see an average of five patients per month who have suicidal thoughts. Under great stress, many, if not most, people have considered suicide. One Canadian survey found that 10% of men and 13% of women had contemplated suicide at some point in their lives, and 2% of men and 6% of women had attempted suicide (Weissman et al., 1999). Thus, most people who have suicidal thoughts do not act on them. Even so, far too many people kill themselves. In 1998, for example, nearly 4000 Canadians took their lives (Health Canada, 2002a). The rates of completed suicide, according to the most recent data, are shown in Figure 7.4, where it can be seen that men are more likely than women to actually kill themselves in suicide attempts.

Who Commits Suicide

Suicide is one of the leading causes of death in both men and women from adolescence to middle age (Spirito & Esposito-Smythers, 2006; Health Canada, 2002a). Disturbingly, suicide rates among Canadian adolescents have doubled over the past 30 years (Stewart, Manion, & Davidson, 2002). Suicide accounts for 24% of all deaths among 15- to 24-year-olds, and 16% among 25- to 44-year-olds (Health Canada, 2002a). Although the problem of teenage suicide often grabs the headlines, suicide rates are as high or higher in middle-aged and elderly men (see Figure 7.4).

Despite life-extending advances in medical care, some older adults may find the quality of their lives is less than satisfactory. With longer life, older people are more susceptible to diseases such as cancer and Alzheimer's disease, which can leave them with feelings of helplessness and hopelessness that can give rise to suicidal thinking. Many older adults

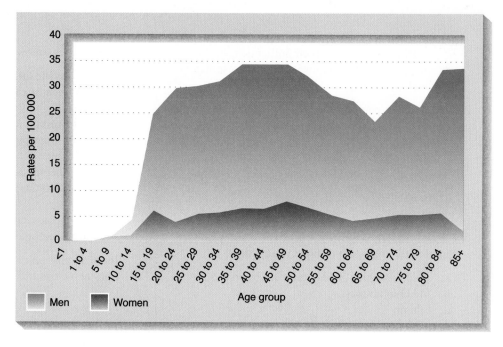

FIGURE 7.4 Suicide rates according to age and gender.
Although adolescent suicides may be more widely publicized, adults, especially middle-aged and elderly men, tend to have high suicide rates.

Source: Health Canada (2002a). *A Report on Mental Illness in Canada*. Public Health Agency of Canada ©. Reproduced with the permission of the Minister of Public Works and Government Services Canada, 2007.

also suffer a mounting accumulation of losses of friends and loved ones as time progresses, leading to social isolation. These losses, as well as the loss of good health and of a responsible role in the community, may wear down the will to live. Not surprisingly, the highest suicide rates in older men are among those who are widowed or lead socially isolated lives. Whatever the causes, suicide has become an increased risk for elderly people (Szanto et al., 1996). Perhaps society should focus its attention as much on the quality of life that is afforded our elderly and not simply on providing them the medical care that helps make longer life possible.

Although more women than men, by a ratio of 1.5 to 1, attempt suicide, men are four times more likely to "succeed" (Health Canada, 2002a). More males succeed, in large part, because they tend to choose quicker acting and more lethal means, such as firearms or hanging, whereas women are more likely to overdose on pills (Health Canada, 2002a).

Gender differences in suicide risk may mask underlying factors. The common finding that men are more likely to take their own lives may be due to the fact that men are also more likely to have a history of alcohol and drug abuse and less likely to have children in the home. When these two factors were taken into account in one study, gender differences in suicide risk disappeared (Young et al., 1994).

Why Do People Commit Suicide?

To many lay observers, suicide seems so extreme an act that they believe only "insane" people (meaning people who are out of touch with reality) would commit suicide. However, suicidal thinking does not necessarily imply loss of touch with reality, deep-seated unconscious conflict, or a personality disorder. Having thoughts about suicide generally reflects a narrowing of the range of options people think are available to them to deal with their problems (Brent & Mann, 2006). That is, they are discouraged by their problems and see no other way out. This is illustrated by the following example:

> Sue Goodwin left work one day with a simple, spontaneous plan: She intended to die. Midway through a regular shift at a regular office, she walked calmly into a Toronto subway station. "I remember standing on the platform, thinking, 'This will show all the people who've hurt me. This will show them what they've done to me.'" The rush of air was coming. The train hurtled toward the station. "And

Many suicides are associated with major depression or bipolar disorder (Joiner, Brown, & Wingate, 2005; Miklowitz & Johnson, 2006), which is why we include the topic in this chapter. Attempted or completed suicide is also connected with other psychological disorders such as alcoholism and drug dependence, schizophrenia, and personality disorders including antisocial personality disorder and borderline personality disorder (Joiner et al., 2005; Renaud, Chagnon, Turecki, & Marquette, 2005).

Stress is also implicated in many suicides (Renaud et al., 2005). Suicide attempts often occur following highly stressful life events, especially "exit events" such as the death of a spouse, close friend, or relative; divorce or separation; a family member's leaving home; or the loss of a close friend. People who consider taking their lives in response to stressful events appear to have poorer problem-solving skills than those who do not consider suicide (Brent & Mann, 2006). People who consider suicide in times of stress may be less able to find alternative ways of coping with the stressors they face.

Theoretical Perspectives on Suicide

The classic psychodynamic model views depression as the turning inward of anger against the internal representation of a lost love object. Suicide then represents inward-directed anger that turns murderous. Suicidal people, then, do not seek to destroy themselves. Instead, they seek to vent their rage against the internalized representation of the love object. In so doing, they destroy themselves as well, of course. In his later writings, Freud speculated that suicide may be motivated by the "death instinct," a tendency to return to the tension-free state that preceded birth. Existential and humanistic theorists relate suicide to the perception that life is meaningless and hopeless.

In the last century, sociologist Emile Durkheim (1958) noted that people who experience **anomie**—who feel lost, without identity, rootless—are more likely to commit suicide. Sociocultural theorists likewise believe that alienation in today's society may play a role in suicide. In our modern, mobile society, people frequently move hundreds or thousands of kilometres for school and jobs. Executives and their families may be relocated every two years or so. Military personnel and their families may be shifted about yet more rapidly. Many people are thus socially isolated or cut off from their support groups. Moreover, city dwellers tend to limit or discourage informal social contacts because of crowding, overstimulation, and fear of crime. It is thus understandable that many people find few sources of support in times of crisis. In some cases, the availability of family support may not be helpful. Family members may be perceived as part of the problem, not part of the solution.

anomie Lack of purpose or identity; aimlessness.

Learning theorists point to the reinforcing effects of prior suicide threats and attempts and to the effects of stress, especially when combined with inability to solve personal problems. People who threaten or attempt suicide may also receive sympathy and support from loved ones and others, perhaps making future—and more lethal—attempts more likely. This is not to suggest that suicide attempts or gestures should be ignored. It is not the case that people who threaten suicide are merely seeking attention. Although people who threaten suicide might not carry out the act, their threats should be taken seriously. People who commit suicide often tell others of their intentions or leave clues beforehand (Joiner, 2006).

Social-cognitive theorists suggest that suicide may be motivated by positive expectancies and by approving attitudes toward the legitimacy of suicide (Joiner, 2006). People who kill themselves may expect they will be missed or eulogized after death, or that survivors will feel guilty for mistreating them. Suicidal psychiatric patients hold more positive expectancies concerning suicide than do nonsuicidal psychiatric samples. They more often expressed the belief that suicide would solve their problems, for example (Linehan, Camper, Chiles, Strosahl, & Shearin, 1987). Suicide may represent a desperate attempt to deal with one's problems in one fell swoop rather than piecemeal.

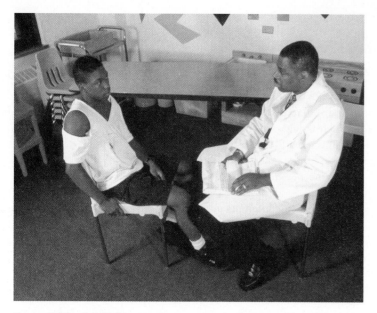

Teen suicide. Suicidal teenagers may see no other way of handling their life problems. The availability of counselling and support services may help prevent suicide by assisting troubled teens in learning alternate ways of reducing stress and resolving conflicts with others.

Social-cognitive theorists also focus on the potential modelling effects of observing suicidal behaviour in others, especially among teenagers who feel overwhelmed by academic and social stressors. A *social contagion*, or spreading of suicide in a community, may occur in the wake of suicides that receive widespread publicity. Teenagers, who seem to be especially vulnerable to these modelling effects, may even romanticize the suicidal act as one of heroic courage, and may expect their demise to have a profound impact on their community. A suicide of a close friend or sibling does not usually increase the risk of a suicide attempt; such imitation is more likely to be triggered by a suicidal model who is not personally known to the imitator, such as a famous musician, actor, or other celebrity (Brent & Mann, 2006).

Biological factors also appear to be involved in suicide. Evidence shows reduced serotonin activity in people who attempt or commit suicide (Brent & Mann, 2006). Serotonin deficits have been implicated in depression, so the relationship with suicide is not surprising. Yet serotonin acts to curb or inhibit nervous system activity, so perhaps decreased serotonin function leads to a *disinhibition* or release of impulsive behaviour that takes the form of a suicidal act in vulnerable individuals. Consistent with this, serotonin deficits have also been linked to impulsive aggression (Brent & Mann, 2006).

Evidence from twin studies suggest that genetic factors influence, to some extent, the risk of suicidal behaviour (Joiner, 2006). Suicidal behaviour that occurs before 25 years of age is highly familial; the greater the number of family members with a history of suicidal behaviour, the earlier the age of the appearance of suicidal acts in offspring (Brent & Mann, 2006).

Suicide is connected with a complex web of factors, and its prediction is not simple. Yet it is clear that many suicides could be prevented if people with suicidal feelings would receive treatment for the disorders that underlie suicidal behaviour, including depression, schizophrenia, and alcohol and substance abuse (Brent & Mann, 2006; Joiner, 2006).

Predicting Suicide

"I don't believe it. I saw him just last week and he looked fine."

"She sat here just the other day, laughing with the rest of us. How were we to know what was going on inside her?"

"I knew he was depressed, but I never thought he'd do something like this. I didn't have a clue."

"Why didn't she just call me?"

Friends and family members often respond to news of a suicide with disbelief or guilt that they failed to pick up signs of the impending act. Yet even trained professionals find it difficult to predict who is likely to commit suicide.

Evidence points to the role of hopelessness as an important predictor or perhaps contributor to suicidal thinking and behaviour (Brent & Mann, 2006; Joiner, 2006). In one study, psychiatric outpatients with hopelessness scores above a certain cut-off were 11 times more likely to commit suicide than those with scores below the cut-off (Beck et al., 1990). But *when* does hopelessness lead to suicide?

People who commit suicide tend to signal their intentions, often quite explicitly, such as by telling others about their suicidal thoughts. Some attempt to cloak their intentions. Behavioural clues may still reveal suicidal intent, however. Edwin Shneidman (1994), a leading researcher on suicide, found that 90% of the people who committed suicide had left clear clues, such as disposing of their possessions. People contemplating suicide may also suddenly try to sort out their affairs, as in drafting a will or buying a cemetery plot. They may purchase guns despite lack of prior interest in firearms. When troubled people decide to commit suicide, they may seem to be suddenly at peace; they feel relieved of having to contend with life problems. This sudden calm may be misinterpreted as a sign of hope.

The prediction of suicide is not an exact science, even for experienced professionals. Many observable factors, such as hopelessness, do seem to be connected with suicide, but we cannot predict *when* a hopeless person will attempt suicide, if at all.

A CLOSER LOOK

Suicide Prevention

Imagine yourself having an intimate conversation with a close campus friend, Chris. You know that things have not been good. Chris's grandfather died six weeks ago, and the two were very close. Chris's grades have been going downhill, and his romantic relationship also seems to be coming apart at the seams. Still, you are unprepared when he says very deliberately, "I just can't take it any more. Life is just too painful. I don't feel like I want to live anymore. I've decided that the only thing I can do is to kill myself."

When somebody discloses that he or she is contemplating suicide, you may feel bewildered and frightened, as if a great burden has been placed on your shoulders. It has. If someone confides suicidal thoughts to you, your goal should be to persuade him or her to see a professional or to get the advice of a professional yourself as soon as you can. But if the suicidal person declines to talk to another person and you sense you can't break away for such a conference, there are some things you can do then and there (Shneidman, 1985; Shneidman et al., 1994):

1. *Draw the person out.* Frame questions like, "What's going on?" "Where do you hurt?" "What would you like to see happen?" Such questions may prompt people to verbalize thwarted psychological needs and offer some relief. They also grant you the time to appraise the risk and contemplate your next move.

2. *Be sympathetic.* Show that you fathom how troubled the person is. Don't say something like, "You're just being silly. You don't really mean it."

3. *Suggest that means other than suicide can be discovered to work out the person's problems*, even if they are not apparent at the time. Suicidal people can usually see only two solutions to their predicaments—either suicide or some kind of magical resolution. Professionals try to broaden the available alternatives of people who are suicidal.

4. *Inquire as to how the person expects to commit suicide.* People with explicit methods who also possess the means (e.g., a gun or drugs) are at greater risk. Ask if you may hold on to the gun, drugs, or whatever for a while. Sometimes the person agrees.

5. *Propose that the person accompany you to consult a professional right now.* Many campuses have hotlines that you or the suicidal individual can call. Many towns and cities have such hotlines and they can be called anonymously. Other possibilities include the emergency room of a general hospital, a campus health centre or counselling centre, or the campus or local police. If you are unable to maintain contact with the suicidal person, get professional assistance as soon as you separate.

6. *Don't say something like "You're talking crazy."* Such comments are degrading and injurious to the individual's self-esteem. Don't press the suicidal person to contact specific people, such as parents or a spouse. Conflict with them may have given rise to the suicidal thoughts.

Above all, keep in mind that your primary goal is to confer with a helping professional. Don't go it alone any longer than you have to.

STUDY BREAK

Suicide

Review It

- **What are some of the factors linked to suicide?** Mood disorders are often linked to suicide. Although women are more likely to attempt suicide, more men actually succeed, probably because they select more lethal means. The elderly—not the young—are more likely to commit suicide, and the rate of suicide among the elderly appears to be increasing. People who attempt suicide are often depressed, but they are generally in touch with reality. They may, however, lack effective problem-solving skills and see no way to deal with their life stress other than suicide. A sense of hopelessness figures prominently in suicides.

- **Why should you never ignore a person's threat to commit suicide?** Although certainly not all people who threaten suicide go on to commit the act, many do. People who commit suicide often signal their intentions by telling others about their suicidal thoughts, for example.

Define It

anomie

Recall It*

1. Suicide is most likely to occur among _____.

   a. teenagers
   b. adults in their 20s
   c. middle-aged adults
   d. older adults

2. Which of the following is NOT true of people who attempt or commit suicide?

   a. People who commit suicide usually have deep-seated personality disorders.
   b. People who commit suicide often leave clues beforehand.
   c. Suicide often follows exit events in people's lives.
   d. Many people who take their own lives have problems with alcohol or substance abuse.

3. The term *anomie*, as used by the theorist Emile Durkheim, refers to _____.

   a. rootlessness or loss of identity
   b. anger turned inward
   c. feelings of despair
   d. a deep sense of hopelessness

4. The neurotransmitter _____ has been implicated as playing a role in suicidal behaviour.

   a. acetylcholine
   b. norepinephrine
   c. serotonin
   d. dopamine

* Recall It answers can be found on the Companion Website for this text.

Think About It

- Did your reading of the text change your ideas about how you might deal with a suicidal threat by a friend or loved one? If so, how?

WEBLINKS

Mood Disorders Society of Canada
www.mooddisorderscanada.ca
The Mood Disorders Society of Canada is a national, not-for-profit organization that is committed to improving the quality of life for people affected by depression, bipolar disorder, and other related disorders. The site provides information and treatment resources for mood disorders, including major depression and bipolar disorder.

PsychDirect
www.psychdirect.com
PsychDirect's website provides evidence-based mental health education and information, including links to self-assessment measures of depression.

Internet Mental Health
www.mentalhealth.com/dis/p20-md02.html
Good source of information and numerous links on major depression and bipolar disorder.

First Nations Health Links
http://hsl.mcmaster.ca/tomflem/firstnations.html
Contains numerous links to articles on mood disorders and suicide among Canada's First Nations people.

Mood Disorders and Suicide

Types of Mood Disorders

Unipolar

Major Depressive Disorder (MDD)
- Features
  - One or more major depressive episodes
  - No history of manic or hypomanic episodes
- Lifetime prevalence: 12%
  - More common in women than men
  - Types of MDD include postpartum depression and seasonal affective disorder (SAD)
- Important theoretical perspectives
  - Diathesis-stress model
  - Genetic and other biological factors
  - Learning and cognitive factors
- Treatments
  - Psychotherapies (cognitive-behaviour therapy, interpersonal psychotherapy)
  - Medications (tricylics, SSRIs, SNRIs)
  - ECT

Dysthymic Disorder
- Features
  - A chronic pattern of mild depression
  - Typically lasts for many years
- Lifetime prevalence: 3% to 6%
- More common in women than men
- Important theoretical perspectives
  - Similar to MDD
- Treatments
  - Psychotherapies and medications used for MDD

Bipolar

Bipolar Disorders
- Features
  - One or more manic or hypomanic episodes, that often alternate with depressive episodes
- Lifetime prevalence: 0.4% to 2.2%
- Equally common in women and men
- Important theoretical perspectives
  - Importance of genetic and other biological factors
  - Role of stress
- Treatments
  - Lithium, anticonvulsants, antipsychotics

Cyclothymia
- Features
  - Recurrent hypomanic and depressive episodes
  - Depressive episodes are not sufficiently severe to meet criteria for major depressive episodes
- Lifetime prevalence: 0.4% to 1%
- Equally common in women and men
- Important theoretical perspectives
  - Similar to bipolar disorders
- Treatments
  - Little is known about optimal treatment
  - Medications used for bipolar disorder may be effective

CHAPTER 8

Personality Disorders

CHAPTER OUTLINE

Types of Personality Disorders
Theoretical Perspectives
Treatment

Did You Know That...

See the underlined text on the pages indicated below for more information on these interesting and often misunderstood facts.

- Warning signs of personality disorders may begin appearing in childhood, even during the preschool years? (p. 285)

- People with schizoid personalities may develop stronger attachments to animals than to people? (p. 287)

- Not all people with psychopathic personalities are lawbreakers; some are very successful in their chosen, lawful occupations? (p. 291)

- Many notable figures in history, from Lawrence of Arabia to Adolf Hitler and even Marilyn Monroe, have been depicted as borderline personalities? (p. 295)

- Adults with dependent personalities may have such difficulty making independent decisions that they allow their parents to decide whom they will or will not marry? (p. 301)

- It is often difficult to draw the line between normal variations in behaviour and personality disorders? (p. 304)

- The conceptualization of certain types of personality disorders may be sexist? (p. 305)

- Despite a veneer of self-importance, people with narcissistic personalities may harbour deep feelings of insecurity? (p. 308)

- Identical twins reared apart show remarkable similarity in psychopathic traits? (p. 312)

ALL OF US HAVE particular styles of behaviour and ways of relating to others. Some of us are orderly; others sloppy. Some of us prefer solitary pursuits; others are more social. Some of us are followers; others leaders. Some of us seem immune to rejection by others, whereas others avoid social initiatives for fear of getting shot down. When behaviour patterns become so inflexible or maladaptive that they cause significant personal distress or impair people's social or occupational functioning, they may be diagnosed as personality disorders.

TYPES OF PERSONALITY DISORDERS

In most of us by the age of thirty, the character has set like plaster, and will never soften again.

WILLIAM JAMES

Personality disorders are excessively rigid patterns of behaviour or ways of relating to others. Their rigidity prevents people from adjusting to external demands; thus, they ultimately become self-defeating. Disordered personality traits become evident by adolescence or early adulthood and continue through much of adult life, becoming so deeply ingrained that they are highly resistant to change. The warning signs of personality disorders may be detected during childhood, even in the troubled behaviour of preschoolers. Children with childhood behaviour problems such as conduct disorder, depression, anxiety, and immaturity are at greater than average risk of developing personality disorders during adolescence (Bernstein, Cohen, Skodol, Bezirganian, & Brook, 1996).

Despite the self-defeating consequences of their behaviour, people with personality disorders do not generally perceive a need to change. Using psychodynamic terms, the DSM notes that people with personality disorders tend to perceive their traits as **ego syntonic**—as natural parts of themselves. As a result, persons with personality disorders are more likely to be brought to the attention of mental health professionals by others than to seek services themselves. In contrast, persons with anxiety disorders or mood disorders tend to view their disturbed behaviour as **ego dystonic**. They do not see their behaviour as parts of their self-identities and are thus more likely to seek help to relieve the distress caused by them.

The DSM groups clinical syndromes on Axis I and personality disorders on Axis II. Both clinical syndromes and personality disorders may thus be diagnosed in clients whose behaviours meet the criteria for both classes of disorders. A person may have an Axis I mood disorder, for example, like major depression, and also show the more enduring characteristics associated with an Axis II personality disorder.

The DSM groups personality disorders into three clusters:

Cluster A: People who are perceived as odd or eccentric. This cluster includes paranoid, schizoid, and schizotypal personality disorders.

Cluster B: People whose behaviour is overly dramatic, emotional, or erratic. This grouping consists of antisocial, borderline, histrionic, and narcissistic personality disorders.

Cluster C: People who often appear anxious or fearful. This cluster includes avoidant, dependent, and obsessive-compulsive personality disorders.

Personality Disorders Characterized by Odd or Eccentric Behaviour

This group of personality disorders includes paranoid, schizoid, and schizotypal disorders. People with these disorders often have difficulty relating to others, or may show little or no interest in developing social relationships.

personality disorders Types of abnormal behaviour patterns involving excessively rigid patterns of behaviour or ways of relating to others that ultimately become self-defeating because their rigidity prevents adjustment to external demands.

ego syntonic Behaviour or feelings that are perceived as natural or compatible parts of the self.

ego dystonic Behaviour or feelings that are perceived to be foreign or alien to one's self-identity.

paranoid personality disorder Type of personality disorder characterized by persistent suspiciousness of the motives of others, but not to the point of holding clear-cut delusions.

Paranoid Personality Disorder The defining trait of **paranoid personality disorder** is pervasive suspiciousness—the tendency to interpret other people's behaviour as deliberately threatening or demeaning. People with the disorder are excessively mistrustful of others, and their relationships suffer for it. They may be suspicious of co-workers and supervisors but can generally maintain employment.

The following case illustrates the unwarranted suspicion and reluctance to confide in others that typifies people with paranoid personalities:

> An 85-year-old retired businessman was interviewed by a social worker to determine the health-care needs for himself and his infirm wife. The man had no history of treatment for a mental disorder. He appeared to be in good health and mentally alert. He and his wife had been married for 60 years, and it appeared that his wife was the only person he'd ever really trusted. He had always been suspicious of others. He would not reveal personal information to anyone but his wife, believing that others were out to take advantage of him. He had refused offers of help from other acquaintances because he suspected their motives. When called on the telephone, he would refuse to give out his name until he determined the nature of the caller's business. He'd always involved himself in "useful work" to occupy his time, even during the 20 years of his retirement. He spent a good deal of time monitoring his investments and had altercations with his stockbroker when errors on his monthly statement prompted suspicion that his broker was attempting to cover up fraudulent transactions.
>
> ADAPTED FROM SPITZER, GIBBON, SKODOL, WILLIAMS, & FIRST, 1994, PP. 211–213

People who have paranoid personalities tend to be overly sensitive to criticism, whether real or imagined. They take offence at the smallest slight. They are readily angered and hold grudges when they think they have been mistreated. They are unlikely to confide in others because they believe that personal information may be used against them. They question the sincerity and trustworthiness of friends and associates. A smile or a glance may be viewed with suspicion. As a result, they have few friends and intimate relationships. When they do form an intimate relationship, they may suspect infidelity, although there is no evidence to back up their suspicions. They tend to remain hypervigilant, as if they must be on the lookout against harm. They deny blame for misdeeds, even when warranted, and are perceived by others as cold, aloof, scheming, devious, and humourless. They tend to be argumentative and may launch repeated lawsuits against those who they believe have mistreated them.

Clinicians need to weigh cultural and sociopolitical factors when arriving at a diagnosis of paranoid personality disorder. They may find members of immigrant or ethnic minority groups, political refugees, or people from other cultures to be guarded or defensive in their behaviour. This behaviour may reflect unfamiliarity with the language, customs, or rules and regulations of the majority culture or a cultural mistrust arising from a history of neglect or oppression. Such behaviour should not be confused with paranoid personality disorder (APA, 2000a).

Although the suspicions of people with paranoid personality disorder are exaggerated and unwarranted, there is an absence of the outright paranoid delusions that characterize the thought patterns of people with paranoid schizophrenia (e.g., believing the RCMP are out to get them). People who have paranoid personalities are unlikely to seek treatment for themselves; they see others as causing their problems. The reported prevalence of paranoid personality disorder in the general population ranges from 0.5% to 2.5% (APA, 2000a). The disorder is diagnosed in clinical samples more often in men than women.

Schizoid Personality Disorder Social isolation is the cardinal feature of **schizoid personality disorder**. Often described as a loner or an eccentric, the person with a schizoid personality lacks interest in social relationships. The emotions of persons with schizoid personalities appear shallow or blunted, but not to the degree found in schizophrenia (see

schizoid personality disorder Type of personality disorder characterized by a persistent lack of interest in social relationships, flattened affect, and social withdrawal.

Chapter 12, "Schizophrenia"). People with this disorder seem to rarely, if ever, experience strong anger, joy, or sadness. They look distant and aloof. Their faces tend to show no emotional expression, and they rarely exchange social smiles or nods. They seem indifferent to criticism or praise and appear to be wrapped up in abstract ideas rather than in thoughts about people. Although they prefer to remain distant from others, they maintain better contact with reality than people with schizophrenia. The prevalence of the disorder in the general population remains unknown. Men with schizoid personality disorder rarely date or marry. Women who have it are more likely to accept romantic advances passively and marry, but they seldom initiate relationships or develop strong attachments to their partners.

Akhtar (1987, 2003) claims there may be discrepancies between outer appearances and the inner lives of people with schizoid personalities. Although they may appear to have little appetite for sex, for example, they may harbour voyeuristic wishes and become attracted to pornography. Akhtar also suggests that the distance and social aloofness of people with schizoid personalities could be somewhat superficial. They may also harbour exquisite sensitivity, deep curiosities about people, and wishes for love that they cannot express. In some cases, sensitivity is expressed in deep feelings for animals rather than people:

Schizoid personality. It is normal to be reserved about displaying one's feelings, especially when one is among strangers, but people with schizoid personalities rarely express emotions and are distant and aloof. Yet the emotions of people with schizoid personalities are not as shallow or blunted as they are in people with schizophrenia.

> John, a 50-year-old retired police officer, sought treatment a few weeks after his dog was hit by a car and died. Since the dog's death, John felt sad and tired. He had difficulty concentrating and sleeping. John lives alone and prefers to be by himself, limiting his contacts with others to a passing "Hello" or "How are you?" He thinks social conversation is a waste of time and feels awkward when others try to initiate friendship. Although he avidly reads newspapers and keeps abreast of current events, he has no real interest in people. He works as a security guard and is described by his co-workers as a "loner" and a "cold fish." The only relationship he had was with his dog, with which he felt he could exchange more sensitive and loving feelings than he could share with people. At Christmas, he would "exchange gifts" with his dog, buying presents for the dog and wrapping a bottle of Scotch for himself as a gift from the animal. The only event that ever saddened him was the loss of his dog. In contrast, the loss of his parents failed to evoke an emotional response. He considers himself to be different from other people and is bewildered by the displays of emotionality that he sees in others.
>
> ADAPTED FROM SPITZER, GIBBON, SKODOL, WILLIAMS, & FIRST, 1989, PP. 249–250

Schizotypal Personality Disorder Schizotypal personality disorder usually becomes evident by early adulthood. The diagnosis applies to people who have difficulties forming close relationships and whose behaviour, mannerisms, and thought patterns are peculiar or odd, but not disturbed enough to merit a diagnosis of schizophrenia. They may be especially anxious in social situations, even when interacting with familiar people. Their social anxieties seem to be associated with paranoid thinking (e.g., fears that others mean them harm) rather than concerns about being rejected or evaluated negatively by others (APA, 2000a).

Schizotypal personality disorder is believed to be slightly more common in males and is thought to affect about 3% of the general population (APA, 2000a). Clinicians need to

schizotypal personality disorder Type of personality disorder characterized by eccentricities or oddities of thought and behaviour but without clearly psychotic features.

be careful not to label certain behaviour patterns that reflect culturally determined beliefs or religious rituals as schizotypal, such as beliefs in voodoo and other magical beliefs.

The eccentricity associated with the schizoid personality is limited to a lack of interest in social relationships. Schizotypal personality disorder refers to a wider range of odd behaviour, beliefs, and perceptions. Persons with the disorder may experience unusual perceptions or illusions, such as feeling the presence of a deceased family member in the room. They realize, however, that the person is not actually there. They may become unduly suspicious of others or paranoid in their thinking. They may develop **ideas of reference**, such as the belief that other people are talking about them. They may engage in "magical thinking," such as believing they possess a "sixth sense" (i.e., can foretell the future) or that others can sense their feelings. They may attach unusual meanings to words. Their own speech may be vague or unusually abstract but not so it becomes incoherent or filled with the loose associations that characterize schizophrenia. They may appear unkempt, display unusual mannerisms, and engage in unusual behaviour such as talking to themselves in the presence of others. Their faces may register little emotion. Like people with schizoid personalities, they may fail to exchange smiles with or nod at others. They may appear silly and smile and laugh at the wrong times. They tend to be socially withdrawn and aloof, with few if any close friends or confidants. They seem to be especially anxious around unfamiliar people.

Some of these features are found in the case of Jonathan:

> Jonathan, a 27-year-old auto mechanic, had few friends and preferred science fiction novels to socializing with other people. He seldom joined in conversations. At times, he seemed to be lost in his thoughts, and his co-workers would have to whistle to get his attention when he was working on a car. He often showed a "queer" expression on his face. Perhaps the most unusual feature of his behaviour was his reported intermittent experience of "feeling" his deceased mother standing nearby. These illusions were reassuring to him, and he looked forward to their occurrence. Jonathan realized they were not real. He never tried to reach out to touch the apparition, knowing it would disappear as soon as he drew closer. It was enough, he said, to feel her presence.
>
> THE AUTHORS' FILES

Despite the DSM's grouping of schizotypal behaviour with personality disorders, the schizotypal behaviour pattern may fall within a spectrum of schizophrenia-related disorders that also includes paranoid and schizoid personality disorders, schizoaffective disorder (discussed in Chapter 12), and schizophrenia itself. Schizotypal personality disorder may actually share a common genetic basis with schizophrenia (Kendler & Walsh, 1995; Siever & Davis, 2004). Let us note, however, that schizotypal personality disorder tends to follow a chronic course, and relatively few people diagnosed with the disorder go on to develop schizophrenia or other psychotic disorders (APA, 2000a). Perhaps the emergence of schizophrenia in persons with this shared genetic predisposition is determined by such factors as stressful early family relationships.

Personality Disorders Characterized by Dramatic, Emotional, or Erratic Behaviour

This cluster of personality disorders includes the antisocial, borderline, histrionic, and narcissistic types. The behaviour patterns of these types are excessive, unpredictable, or self-centred. People with these disorders have difficulty forming and maintaining relationships.

Much of our attention in this section focuses on antisocial personality disorder. Historically, it is the personality disorder that has been most extensively studied by scholars and researchers.

ideas of reference Form of delusional thinking in which a person reads personal meaning into the behaviour of others or external events that are completely independent of the person.

Antisocial Personality Disorder (and Psychopathy) People with **antisocial personality disorder** (APD) persistently violate the rights of others and often break the law. They disregard social norms and conventions, are impulsive, and fail to live up to interpersonal and vocational commitments. Yet they often show a superficial charm and are at least average in intelligence (Cleckley, 1976). Perhaps the features that are most striking about them are their low levels of anxiety in threatening situations and lack of guilt or remorse following wrongdoing. Punishment seems to have little if any effect on their behaviour. Although parents and others have usually punished them for their misdeeds, they persist in leading irresponsible and impulsive lives.

Men are more likely than women to receive diagnoses of APD (Cale & Lilienfeld, 2002). The prevalence rate for the disorder in Canada is estimated to be about 1.7% to 3.7% (Bland, Newman, & Orn, 1988a, 1988b; Offord et al., 1996) (see Table 8.1 on page 290). In a study of psychiatric disorders in Ontario, Offord and colleagues (1996) found a one-year prevalence rate of 2.9% in males and 0.5% in females. Although the prevalence of the disorder has been rising in both genders in recent years, it has been climbing even more sharply among women (APA, 2000a). For a diagnosis of APD to be applied, the person must be at least 18 years of age. The alternate diagnosis of conduct disorder is used for younger people (see Chapter 13, "Abnormal Behaviour in Childhood and Adolescence"). Many children with conduct disorders do not continue to show antisocial behaviour as adults.

We once used terms like *psychopath* and *sociopath* to refer to the type of people who are commonly classified as having antisocial personalities—people whose behaviour is amoral and asocial, impulsive, and lacking in remorse and shame. The roots of the word *psychopath* focus on the idea that something is amiss (pathological) in the individual's psychological functioning. The roots of *sociopathy* centre on the person's social deviance. The DSM criteria for APD focus more on elements of criminal actions (e.g., that involve antisocial behaviour and social deviance) than on the traditional elements of **psychopathy** that emphasize emotional (e.g., callousness and a lack of the normal pangs of guilt, anxiety, and remorse) and interpersonal traits (e.g., superficial charm and manipulative behaviour) (Hare, 1996; Harpur & Hare, 1994). The pattern of behaviour that characterizes both APD and *psychopathic* personality begins in childhood or adolescence and extends into adulthood.

With the widespread clinical use of the DSM-III, the traditional conception of the personality construct *psychopathy* was overshadowed (Hare, Hart, & Harper, 1991). University of British Columbia psychologist Robert Hare devised the *Psychopathy Checklist-Revised* (PCL-R), which is used to identify and diagnose psychopaths and determine their degree of psychopathy. The PCL-R measures interpersonal and affective traits such as callousness, selfishness, and the remorseless use of others (known as Factor 1 subfactors, which are closely related to the traditional concept of psychopathy). It also measures impulsive lifestyle and antisocial behaviour traits (known as Factor 2 subfactors, which are associated with the concept of the antisocial personality). Although the two factors are related, they have important distinctions that have significant implications for mental health treatment and recidivism rates of dangerous criminal offenders (Hare, 1996; Serin, 1998).

PROFILE OF THE ANTISOCIAL PERSONALITY Common features of people with APD include failure to conform to social norms, irresponsibility, aimlessness and lack of long-term goals or plans, impulsive behaviour, outright lawlessness, violence, chronic unemployment, marital problems, lack of remorse or empathy, substance abuse, a history of alcoholism, and a disregard for the truth and for the feelings and needs of others (Patrick, Cuthbert, & Lang, 1994; Robins, Tipp, & Przybeck, 1991; Smith & Newman, 1990). Irresponsibility may be seen in a personal history dotted by repeated,

antisocial personality disorder Type of personality disorder characterized by a chronic pattern of antisocial and irresponsible behaviour and lack of remorse.

psychopathy Type of personality pattern characterized by affective and interpersonal traits, such as shallow emotions, selfishness, arrogance, superficial charm, deceitfulness, manipulativeness, irresponsibility, sensation-seeking, and a lack of empathy, anxiety, and remorse, combined with persistent violations of social norms, a socially deviant and nomadic lifestyle, and impulsiveness.

Antisocial personality. Serial killer Paul Bernardo killed without feeling or remorse and also displayed some of the superficial charm seen in some people with antisocial personality disorder.

TABLE 8.1

Estimates of Lifetime Prevalence of Antisocial Personality Disorder in the Canadian General and Forensic Populations (percentage with disorder)

General Population	Males		Females	
	General Population	Incarcerated	General Population	Incarcerated
1.7% to 3.7%	3%	37.8% to 56.9% (meets stringent criteria)	1% to 1.2%	29% to 36.8% (meets stringent criteria)

Sources: Blanchette (1996); Bland, Newman, & Orn (1988); Bland, Orn, & Newman (1988); Correctional Services Canada (2002b); Gove (1979); Motiuk & Poporino (1991); Offord et al. (1996).

unexplained absences from work, abandonment of jobs without having other job opportunities to fall back on, or long stretches of unemployment despite available job opportunities. Irresponsibility extends to financial matters, where there may be repeated failure to repay debts, pay child support, or meet other financial responsibilities to one's family and dependents. The diagnostic features of APD, as defined in the DSM, are shown in Table 8.2 on page 291.

The following case represents a number of antisocial characteristics:

> A 19-year-old male is brought by ambulance to a hospital emergency room in a state of cocaine intoxication. He's wearing a hard-rock T-shirt . . . and sports a punk-style haircut. His mother is called and sounds groggy and confused on the phone; the doctors must coax her to come to the hospital. She later tells the doctors that her son has arrests for shoplifting and driving while intoxicated. She suspects that he takes drugs, although she has no direct evidence. She believes that he is performing fairly well at school and has been a star member of the basketball team.
>
> It turns out that her son has been lying to her. In actuality, he never completed high school and never played on the basketball team. A day later, his head cleared, the patient tells his doctors, almost boastfully, that his drug and alcohol use started at the age of 13, and that by the time he was 17, he was regularly using a variety of psychoactive substances, including alcohol, speed, marijuana, and cocaine. Lately, however, he has preferred cocaine. He and his friends frequently participate in drug and alcohol binges. At times they each drink a case of beer in a day along with downing other drugs. He steals car radios from parked cars and money from his mother to support his drug habit, which he justifies by adopting a (partial) "Robin Hood" attitude—that is, taking money only from people who have lots of it.
>
> ADAPTED FROM SPITZER ET AL., 1994, PP. 81–83

Although this case is suggestive of APD, the diagnosis was maintained as provisional because the interviewer could not determine that the deviant behaviour (lying, stealing, skipping school) began before the age of 15.

PROFILE OF THE PSYCHOPATHIC PERSONALITY Hervey Cleckley (1941) showed that the characteristics defining the psychopathic personality—self-centredness, irresponsibility, impulsivity, and insensitivity to the needs of others—exist not only among criminals but also among many respected members of the community, including doctors, lawyers, politicians, and business executives. Robert Hare's *Psychopathy Checklist-Revised* (PCL-R) has been shown to be a valid and reliable predictor of psychopathy in both criminal and non-criminal populations (Hart & Hare, 1997; Hare, 1996; Hare, Hart, & Harpur, 1991). The PCL-R measures the main aspects of psychopathy and it was found that the *Factor 1* personality traits associated with psychopathy seem to remain stable across a lifespan. In

TABLE 8.2

Diagnostic Features of Antisocial Personality Disorder

(a) The person is at least 18 years old.

(b) There is evidence of a conduct disorder prior to the age of 15 as shown by such behaviour patterns as truancy, running away, initiating physical fights, use of weapons, forcing someone into sexual activities, physical cruelty to people or animals, deliberate destruction of property or fire setting, lying, stealing, or mugging.

(c) Since the age of 15, there has been general indifference to and violation of the rights of other people, as shown by several of the following:

(1) Lack of conformity to social norms and legal codes, as shown by law-breaking behaviour that may or may not result in arrest, such as destruction of property, engaging in unlawful occupations, stealing, or harassing others.

(2) Aggressive and highly irritable style of relating to others, as shown by repeated physical fights and assaults with others, possibly involving abuse of one's spouse or children.

(3) Consistent irresponsibility, as shown by failure to maintain employment due to chronic absences, lateness, abandonment of job opportunities, or extended periods of unemployment despite available work; and/or by failure to honour financial obligations, such as failing to maintain child support or defaulting on debts; and/or by lack of a sustained monogamous relationship.

(4) Failure to plan ahead or impulsivity, as shown by travelling around without prearranged employment or clear goals.

(5) Disregard for the truth, evidenced by repeated lying, conning others, or use of aliases for personal gain or pleasure.

(6) Recklessness with regard to personal safety or the safety of other people, as shown by driving while intoxicated or repeated speeding.

(7) Lack of remorse for misdeeds, as shown by indifference to the harm done to others, and/or by rationalizing that harm.

Source: Adapted from the DSM-IV-TR (APA, 2000a).

contrast, the *Factor 2* antisocial behaviours that more closely associated with APD as diagnosed by the DSM criteria tend to decline with age and may actually disappear by the time a person reaches the age of 40 (Harpur & Hare 1994).

ANTISOCIAL BEHAVIOUR, PSYCHOPATHY, AND CRIMINALITY We may tend to think of psychopathic behaviour as synonymous with criminal behaviour. Although there is a strong relationship between the two, not all criminals show signs of psychopathy and only a minority of people with psychopathic personalities become criminals (Hare, 1996; Lilienfeld & Andrews, 1996). Many psychopaths are law-abiding and quite successful in their chosen occupations, yet they possess a personality style characterized by a callous disregard of the interests and feelings of others.

Investigators have begun to view psychopathic personality as composed of two somewhat independent factors. The first is a personality factor. It consists of such traits as superficial charm, selfishness, lack of empathy, and callous and remorseless use of others and disregard of their feelings and welfare. This psychopathic personality factor applies to people who have these kinds of psychopathic traits but generally manage to avoid coming into contact with the law. In one study, Hart and Hare (1989) estimated that only 12.5% of a Canadian correctional population sample was rated as psychopathic, in comparison to 50% who were diagnosed with APD. In fact, psychopathic individuals possess those very qualities that allow them to charm and take advantage of co-workers on their way to the top chief executive positions in business, politics, and other social institutions (Babiak, 1995; Hare 1996). In recent years, media accounts have abounded trying to explain how a number of top corporate executives could have arrived at the point where they fraudulently reaped millions, and in some cases billions, of dollars from their own companies, which not only devastated employees, shareholders, and other stakeholders, but undermined the world economy. A common question is whether or not, or to what extent, these corrupt albeit exceedingly wealthy leaders were psychopathic (English 2002; Gettler, 2003; Hercz, 2001).

The second factor is considered a behavioural dimension. It is characterized by the adoption of an unstable and antisocial lifestyle, including frequent problems with the law, poor employment history, and unstable relationships, and is more closely aligned with APD (Brown & Forth, 1997; Cooke & Michie, 1997; Hare, Hart, & Harpur, 1991). These two factors are not entirely separate—many psychopathic individuals show evidence of both sets of traits.

We should also note that people may become criminals or delinquents not because of a disordered personality but because they were reared in environments or subcultures that encouraged and rewarded criminal behaviour (Hare, 1986). The criminal behaviour of a professional thief or drug pusher, although antisocial, does not in itself justify a diagnosis of APD. Canadian studies indicate that criminal and aggressive behaviour have multiple causes and represent many personality styles in both male and female offenders (Laishes, 2002; Motiuk & Porporino, 1991). Although the behaviour of criminals is deviant to society at large, it may be normal by the standards of their subcultures. We should also recognize that lack of remorse, a cardinal feature of APD, does not characterize all criminals. Some criminals regret their crimes, and evidence of remorse is considered when a sentence is passed.

Nearly twice as many males as females are diagnosed with APD in Canadian prisons (see Table 8.1 on page 290). Proportionally, far fewer psychopaths than APD individuals are imprisoned. Psychopaths who do enter the correctional system, such as Clifford Olson, Paul Bernardo, and Karla Homolka, are much more likely to have committed serious, violent, cold-blooded serial offences (Hare, 1996; Hare, Hart, & Harpur, 1991). It should not come as a surprise that psychopaths are overrepresented in maximum-security penitentiaries in Canada (Motiuk & Porporino, 1991). In addition, psychopaths who scored high on the PCL-R had the highest rates of both recidivism (80%) and violent recidivism (25%). They re-offended within an average span of 30 months (Correctional Services Canada, 2002a).

SOCIOCULTURAL FACTORS AND ANTISOCIAL PERSONALITY DISORDER Antisocial personality disorder cuts across all racial and ethnic groups. Researchers find no evidence of ethnic or racial differences in the rates of the disorder (Robins, Tipp, & Przybeck, 1991). The disorder is more common, however, among people with lower socioeconomic status (SES). One explanation is that people with APD may drift downward occupationally, perhaps because their antisocial behaviour makes it difficult for them to hold steady jobs or progress upward. It is possible, too, that people from lower SES levels are more likely to have been reared by parents who themselves modelled antisocial behaviour. However, it is also possible that the diagnosis is misapplied to people living in hard-pressed communities who may engage in seemingly antisocial behaviour as a type of defence strategy in order to survive (APA, 2000a).

PSYCHOPHYSIOLOGICAL AND BIOLOGICAL FACTORS ASSOCIATED WITH ANTISOCIAL PERSONALITY AND PSYCHOPATHY There are several psychophysiological and biological factors that are related to antisocial personality and psychopathy:

1. *Lack of emotional responsiveness.* People with antisocial personalities can maintain their composure in stressful situations that would induce anxiety in most people (Cleckley, 1976). Lack of anxiety in response to threatening situations may help explain the failure of punishment to induce antisocial people to relinquish their behaviour. For most of us, the fear of getting caught and being punished is sufficient to inhibit antisocial impulses. People with antisocial personalities, however, often fail to inhibit behaviour that has led to punishment in the past (Arnett, Smith, & Newman, 1997). They may not learn to inhibit antisocial or aggressive behaviour because they experience little if any fear or anticipatory anxiety about being caught and punished.

    In an early classic study, Lykken (1957) showed that prison inmates with antisocial personalities performed more poorly than normal controls on a shock-avoidance task, although their general learning ability did not differ from that of normals. The shock-avoidance task involved learning responses to avoid getting a mild electric shock. Lykken reasoned that the inmates who had antisocial personalities were less able to learn avoidance responses because they experienced unusually low levels of anxiety in anticipation of the shock.

When people get anxious, their palms tend to sweat. This skin response, called the *galvanic skin response* (GSR), is a sign of activation of the sympathetic branch of the autonomic nervous system (ANS). In an early study, Hare (1965) showed that people with antisocial personalities had lower GSR levels when they were expecting painful stimuli than did normal controls. Apparently, people with antisocial personalities experienced little anxiety in anticipation of impending pain.

Hare's findings of a weaker GSR response in anticipation of an aversive stimulus in people with antisocial personalities has been replicated a number of times (e.g., Arnett, 1997; Patrick, Cuthbert, & Lang, 1994). Other research generally supports the view that people with antisocial personalities are generally less aroused than others both at times of rest and in situations in which they are faced with stress (Fowles, 1993). This lack of emotional responsivity may help explain why the threat of punishment seems to have little effect on deterring their antisocial behaviour. It is conceivable that the autonomic nervous systems of people with antisocial personalities are underresponsive to threatening stimuli.

2. *The craving-for-stimulation model.* Other investigators have attempted to explain the antisocial personality's lack of emotional response in terms of the levels of stimulation necessary to maintain an **optimum level of arousal**. Our optimum levels of arousal are the degrees of arousal at which we feel best and function most efficiently.

optimum level of arousal Level of arousal associated with peak performance and maximum feelings of well-being.

Psychopathic individuals appear to have exaggerated cravings for stimulation (Arnett et al., 1997). Perhaps they require a higher-than-normal threshold of stimulation to maintain an optimum state of arousal (Quay, 1965). That is, they may need more stimulation than other people to function normally.

A need for higher levels of stimulation may explain why people with psychopathic traits tend to become bored more easily than other people and more often gravitate to more stimulating but potentially dangerous activities, such as the use of intoxicants like drugs or alcohol, motorcycling, skydiving, high-stakes gambling, or sexual adventures. A higher-than-normal threshold for stimulation would not directly cause antisocial or criminal behaviour; after all, part of the "right stuff" of respected astronauts includes sensation seeking. However, threat of boredom and inability to tolerate monotony may influence some sensation seekers to drift into crime or reckless behaviour (R. J. Smith, 1978).

3. *Lack of restraint on impulsivity.* Other research on brain wave functions shows lower levels of activity in the frontal lobes of the cerebral cortex in men with APD (Deckel, Hesselbrock, & Bauer, 1996). The frontal cortex plays a key role in inhibiting impulsive behaviour, which may help explain why people with antisocial personalities have difficulty controlling impulsive or aggressive behaviour. Some theorists have speculated that the cerebral cortex may mature more slowly in people with antisocial personalities (Reid, 1986).

4. *Limbic abnormalities.* As described above, one of the distinguishing features of psychopathic personalities is a dysfunctional processing of emotional information. A recent study of the brain's limbic system using magnetic resonance imaging (MRI) compared both criminal nonpsychopaths and noncriminal control participants with criminal psychopaths while they performed an affective memory task (Kiehl et al., 2001). Results revealed that criminal psychopaths showed significantly less brain activity in the emotional parts of the brain found within the limbic system, but showed overstimulation in areas of the frontal-temporal lobes that are associated with processing and regulating emotional information. This suggests that the emotional irregularities found in psychopathic offenders may be tied to diminished input from brain structures within the limbic system.

Borderline Personality Disorder Borderline personality disorder (BPD) is primarily characterized by a pervasive pattern of instability in relationships, self-image, mood, and a lack of control over impulses. People with BPD tend to be uncertain about their values, goals, loyalties, careers, choices of friends, and perhaps even their sexual orientations. This instability in self-image or identity leaves them with persistent feelings of emptiness and boredom. They cannot tolerate being alone and will make desperate attempts to avoid feelings of abandonment (Gunderson, 1996). Fear of abandonment renders them clinging and demanding in their social relationships, but their clinging often pushes away the people on whom they depend. Signs of rejection may enrage them, straining their relationships further. Their feelings toward others are consequently intense and shifting. They alternate between extremes of adulation (when their needs are met) and loathing (when

? QUESTIONNAIRE

The Sensation-Seeking Scale

Do you crave stimulation or seek sensation? Are you satisfied by reading or watching television, or must you ride the big wave or bounce your motorbike over desert dunes? Zuckerman (1980) finds four factors related to sensation seeking: (1) pursuit of thrill and adventure, (2) disinhibition (that is, proclivity to express impulses), (3) pursuit of experience, and (4) susceptibility to boredom. Although some sensation seekers get involved with drugs or encounter trouble with the law, many are law-abiding and limit their sensation seeking to sanctioned activities. Thus, sensation seeking should not be interpreted as criminal or antisocial in itself.

Zuckerman developed several sensation-seeking scales that assess the levels of stimulation people seek in order to feel their best and function efficiently. A brief form of one of them follows. To assess your own sensation-seeking tendencies, pick the choice, A or B, that best depicts you. Then compare your responses to those in the next Study Break box on pages 305 to 307.

1. A. I would like a job that requires a lot of travel.
   B. I would prefer a job in one location.

2. A. I am invigorated by a brisk, cold day.
   B. I can't wait to get indoors on a cold day.

3. A. I get bored seeing the same old faces.
   B. I like the comfortable familiarity of everyday friends.

4. A. I would prefer to live in an ideal society in which everyone is safe, secure, and happy.
   B. I would have preferred living in the unsettled days of our history.

5. A. I sometimes like to do things that are a little frightening.
   B. A sensible person avoids activities that are dangerous.

6. A. I would not like to be hypnotized.
   B. I would like to have the experience of being hypnotized.

7. A. The most important goal in life is to live it to the fullest and experience as much as possible.
   B. The most important goal in life is to find peace and happiness.

8. A. I would like to try parachute jumping.
   B. I would never want to try jumping out of a plane, with or without a parachute.

9. A. I enter cold water gradually, giving myself time to get used to it.
   B. I like to dive or jump right into the ocean or a cold pool.

10. A. When I go on a vacation, I prefer the change of camping out.
    B. When I go on a vacation, I prefer the comfort of a good room and bed.

11. A. I prefer people who are emotionally expressive, even if they are a bit unstable.
    B. I prefer people who are calm and even-tempered.

12. A. A good painting should shock or jolt the senses.
    B. A good painting should give one a feeling of peace and security.

13. A. People who ride motorcycles must have some kind of unconscious need to hurt themselves.
    B. I would like to drive or ride a motorcycle.

Source: Scale from M. Zuckerman (1980). Sensation seeking. In H. London & J. Exner (Eds.), *Dimensions of Personality*. New York: John Wiley & Sons. Copyright © John Wiley & Sons. Reprinted by permission of John Wiley & Sons, Inc.

Borderline personality disorder. World War II dictator Adolf Hitler lived—and died—by the Nazi principle of "death before dishonour"—arguably a form of the "all-or-nothing" thinking characteristic of BPD.

they feel neglected). They tend to view other people as all good or all bad, shifting abruptly from one extreme to the other. As a result, they may flit from partner to partner in a series of brief and stormy relationships. People they had idealized are treated with contempt when relationships end or when they feel the other person fails to meet their needs (Gunderson, 2001).

Many notable figures have been described as having personality features associated with borderline personality disorder, including Marilyn Monroe, Lawrence of Arabia, Adolf Hitler, and the philosopher Sören Kierkegaard (Sass, 1982). Some theorists believe we live in highly fragmented and alienating times that tend to create the problems in forming cohesive identities and stable relationships that characterize people with borderline personalities (Sass, 1982). "Living on the edge" or border can be seen as a metaphor for an unstable society. Borderline personality disorder is believed to occur in about 2% of the general population (APA, 2000a). Although it is diagnosed more often (about 75% of the time) in women, gender differences in prevalence rates for BPD in the general population remain undetermined.

The term *borderline personality* was originally used to refer to individuals whose behaviour appeared to be on the border between neuroses and psychoses. People with BPD generally maintain better contact with reality than people with psychoses, although they may show transient psychotic behaviour during times of stress. Generally speaking, they seem to be more severely impaired than most people with neuroses but not as dysfunctional as those with psychotic disorders.

Borderline personality disorder may actually lie closer to mood disorders than psychotic disorders. Many individuals diagnosed with BPD also meet diagnostic criteria for mood disorders, such as major depression and bipolar disorder. Some researchers, however, find weaker links between borderline personality and depression, so connections remain somewhat muddled (Gunderson & Phillips, 1991). Many people with BPD also meet criteria for other personality disorders. University of Toronto researcher Paul Links and his colleagues conducted a seven-year follow-up study of a Canadian sample of BPD patients. They found that those patients with persistent symptoms of the disorder were more likely to have coexisting personality disorders than those patients who were in remittance for BPD, including avoidant (59.2%), self-defeating (40.7%), passive-aggressive (37%), dependent (33.3%), and histrionic (25.9%) symptoms (Links, Heslegrave, & van Reekum, 1998). Other investigators have found that in addition to meeting the DSM criteria for a variety of personality disorders, patients with BPD share the personality dimensions of neuroticism, impulsivity, anxiousness, affective liability, and insecure attachment (Skodol et al., 2002a, 2002b).

Instability of moods is a central characteristic of borderline personality disorder. Moods run the gamut from anger and irritability to depression and anxiety, and may shift frequently and abruptly (Koenigsberg et al, 2002). Another feature of BPD is ongoing anger, loneliness, boredom, a deep sense of emptiness, and impulsivity (Hochhausen, Lorenz, & Newman, 2002; Zanarini, Frankenburg, Hennen, & Silk, 2003). People with BPD have difficulty controlling anger and are prone to fights or smashing things. They often act on impulse, like eloping with someone they have just met. This impulsive and unpredictable behaviour can often be self-destructive and is linked to a risk of suicidal attempts and gestures (e.g., Sanislow, Grilo, & McGlashan, 2000). It may also involve spending sprees, gambling, drug abuse, engaging in unsafe sexual activity, reckless driving, binge eating, or shoplifting. People with BPD sometimes partake in impulsive acts of self-mutilation, such as scratching their wrists or burning cigarettes on their arms, as in this young woman's case:

Client: I've got such repressed anger in me; what happens is . . . I can't *feel* it; I get anxiety attacks. I get very nervous, smoke too many cigarettes. So what happens to me is I tend to *explode*. Into tears or hurting myself or whatever . . . because I don't know how to contend with all those mixed up feelings.

Interviewer: What was the more recent example of such an explosion?

Client: I was alone at home a few months ago; I was frightened! I was trying to get in touch with my boyfriend and I couldn't. . . . He was nowhere to be found. All my friends seemed to be busy that night and I had no one to talk to. . . . I just got more and more nervous and more and more agitated. Finally, *bang*!—I took out a cigarette and lit it and stuck it into my forearm. I don't know why I did it because I didn't really care for him all that much. I guess I felt I had to do something dramatic . . . .

ADAPTED FROM STONE, 1980, P. 400

Self-mutilation is sometimes carried out as an expression of anger or a means of manipulating others. Such acts may be intended to counteract self-reported feelings of "numbness," particularly in times of stress. Not surprisingly, frequent self-mutilation among people with BPD is associated with an increased risk of suicidal thinking (Dulit, Fyer, Leon, Brodsky, & Frances, 1994).

Individuals with BPD tend to have very troubled relationships with their families of origin and others. Commonly, BPD patients remember traumatic childhood experiences, ranging from their parents being neglectful or abusive to parental losses or separations (Liotti & Pasquini 2000; Paris & Frank, 1989). Additionally, there is an association between documented childhood sexual abuse and the later development of BPD (Johnson, Cohen, Brown, Smailes, & Bernstein, 1999). Patients with BPD tend to view their relationships as rife with hostility and to perceive others as rejecting and abandoning (Benjamin & Wonderlich, 1994). They also tend to be difficult to work with in psychotherapy, demanding a great deal of support from therapists and calling them at all hours or acting suicidal to elicit support. They tend to drop out early from psychotherapy (Aronson, 1989), but those who have a coexisting mood disorder are more amenable to treatment (Pope, Jones, Hudson, Cohen, & Gunderson, 1983). Their behaviour toward therapists, as toward other people, undergoes rapid alterations between adulation and outrage. These abrupt shifts in feelings are interpreted by psychoanalysts as signs of "splitting," or an inability to reconcile the positive and negative aspects of one's experiences of oneself and others.

From the modern psychodynamic perspective, borderline individuals cannot synthesize positive and negative elements of personality into complete wholes. They therefore fail to achieve fixed self-identities or images of others. Rather than viewing important figures in their lives as sometimes loving, sometimes rejecting, they shift back and forth between viewing them as all good or all bad, between idealization and abhorrence. The psychoanalyst Otto Kernberg, a leading authority on borderline personality, tells of a woman in her 30s whose attitude toward him vacillated in such a way. According to Kernberg, the woman would respond to him in one session as if he was the most wonderful therapist, feeling that all her problems were solved. But several sessions later, she would turn against him and accuse him of being unfeeling and manipulative, become very dissatisfied with the treatment she was receiving, and threaten to drop out and never come back (Sass, 1982). A recent review by a leading BPD researcher, psychiatrist Joel Paris of McGill University (2005), found that structured psychodynamic therapies as well as a range of other interpersonal and cognitive therapies are more effective in the long-term treatment of BPD than are pharmacological interventions.

Paris conducted an extensive review of 170 recent articles on BPD and determined that about one in ten BPD patients commits suicide (Paris, 2002a). Another study found that early death from all causes approaches a rate of one in five (Paris, 2002b). As for the persistence of the disorder, Paris followed up the long-term outcomes of 64 patients with BPD at 15- and 27-year time periods. He found that in the long term, a slight majority of BPD patients no longer met the full criteria for the disorder. Moreover, most BPD patients showed improvement leading up to and beyond the ages of 40 and 50 (Paris 2002b, 2003; Paris, Brown, & Nowlis, 1987; Paris & Zweig-Frank, 2001).

Histrionic Personality Disorder

Histrionic personality disorder involves excessive emotionality and the necessity to be the centre of attention. The term is derived from the Latin *histrio*, which means "actor." People with histrionic personality disorder tend to be dramatic and emotional, but their emotions seem shallow, exaggerated, and volatile. The disorder was formerly called *hysterical* personality. The supplanting of *hysterical* with *histrionic* and the associated exchange of the roots *hystera* (meaning "uterus") and *histrio* allow professionals to distance themselves from the notion that the disorder is intricately bound up with being female. The disorder is diagnosed more frequently in women than men, however (Hartung & Widiger, 1998). Some studies, using structured interview methods, find similar rates of occurrence among men and women (APA, 2000a). Whether the gender discrepancy in clinical practice reflects true differences in the underlying rates of the disorder, diagnostic biases, or other unseen factors remains something of an open question (Corbitt & Widiger, 1995).

Despite a long-standing belief among clinicians that histrionic personality is closely related to conversion disorder, research has not borne out this connection (Kellner, 1992). People with conversion disorder are actually more likely to show features of dependent personality disorder than histrionic personality disorder.

People with histrionic personalities may become unusually upset by news of a sad event and cancel plans for the evening, inconveniencing their friends. They may exude exaggerated delight when they meet someone or become enraged when someone fails to notice their new hairstyle. They may faint at the sight of blood or blush at a slight faux pas. They tend to demand that others meet their needs for attention and play the victim when others fall short. If they feel a touch of fever, they may insist that others drop everything to rush them to a doctor. They tend to be self-centred and intolerant of delays of gratification; they want what they want when they want it. They grow quickly restless with routine and crave novelty and stimulation. They are drawn to fads. Others may see them as putting on airs or play-acting, although they may evince a certain charm. They may enter a room with a flourish and embellish their experiences with flair. When pressed for details, however, they fail to colour in the specifics of their tales. They tend to be flirtatious and seductive but are too wrapped up in themselves to develop intimate relationships or have deep feelings toward others. As a result, their associations tend to be stormy and ultimately ungratifying. They tend to use their physical appearance as a means of drawing attention to themselves. Men with the disorder may act and dress in an overly "macho" manner to draw attention to themselves; women may choose very frilly, feminine clothing. Glitter supersedes substance.

histrionic personality disorder Type of personality disorder characterized by excessive needs to be the centre of attention and to receive reassurance, praise, and approval from others. Such persons often appear overly dramatic and emotional in their behaviour.

People with histrionic personalities may be attracted to professions like modelling or acting, where they can hog the spotlight. Despite outward successes, they may lack self-esteem and strive to impress others to boost their self-worth. If they suffer setbacks or lose their place in the limelight, depressing inner doubts may emerge. The case of Marcella shows some of these features:

> Marcella was a 36-year-old attractive but overly made-up woman who was dressed in tight pants and high heels. Her hair was in a bird's nest of the type that had been popular when she was a teenager. Her social life seemed to bounce from relationship to relationship, from crisis to crisis. Marcella sought help from a psychologist at this time because her 17-year-old daughter Nancy had just been hospitalized for cutting her wrists. Nancy lived with Marcella and her mother's current boyfriend, Morris, and there were constant arguments in the apartment. Marcella recounted the disputes that took place with high drama, waving her hands, clanging the bangles that hung from her wrists, and clutching her breast. It was difficult having Nancy live at home, because Nancy had expensive tastes, was "always looking for attention," and flirted with Morris as a way of "flaunting her youth." Marcella saw herself as a doting mother and denied any possibility that she was in competition with her daughter.
>
> Marcella came for a handful of sessions, during which she basically vented her feelings and was encouraged to make decisions that might lead to a reduction of some of the pressures on her and her daughter. At the end of each session, she said, "I feel *so* much better," and thanked the psychologist profusely. At termination of "therapy," she took the psychologist's hand and squeezed it endearingly. "Thank you *so* much, doctor," she said, and made her exit.
>
> THE AUTHORS' FILES

Marcella also showed a number of features of narcissism, which we discuss next.

Narcissistic Personality Disorder *Narkissos* was a handsome youth who, according to Greek myth, fell in love with his reflection in a spring. Because of his excessive self-love, in one version of the myth he was transformed by the gods into the flower we know as the narcissus.

narcissistic personality disorder Type of personality disorder characterized by the adoption of an inflated self-image and demands for constant attention and admiration, among other features.

Persons with **narcissistic personality disorder** have an inflated or grandiose sense of themselves and an extreme need for admiration. They brag about their accomplishments and expect others to shower them with praise and notice their special qualities, even when their accomplishments are ordinary. Narcissists enjoy basking in the light of adulation; they are self-absorbed and tend to lack empathy for others. Although they share certain features with histrionic personalities, such as demanding to be the centre of attention, they have a much more inflated view of themselves and are less melodramatic than people with histrionic personality disorder. The label of borderline personality disorder is sometimes applied to them, but people with narcissistic personality disorder are generally better able to organize their thoughts and actions. They tend to be more successful in their careers and better able to rise to positions of status and power. Their relationships tend to be more stable than those of people with BPD.

Narcissistic personality disorder is believed to occur in less than 1% of the general population (APA, 2000a). Although more than half of the people diagnosed with the disorder are men, we cannot say whether there is an underlying gender difference in the prevalence rates of the general population. A certain degree of narcissism or self-aggrandizement may represent a healthful adjustment to insecurity, a shield from criticism and failure, or a motive for achievement (Goleman, 1988). Excessive narcissistic qualities can become unhealthy, especially when cravings for adulation are insatiable. Table 8.3 on page 299 compares "normal" self-interest with self-defeating extremes of narcissism. Up to a point, self-interest fosters success and happiness. In more extreme cases, as with narcissism, it can compromise relationships and careers.

Narkissos. According to one version of the Greek myth, Narkissos fell in love with his reflection in a spring. Because of his excessive self-love, the gods transformed him into a flower—the narcissus.

A person with a narcissistic personality? People with narcissistic personalities are often preoccupied with fantasies of success and power, ideal love, or recognition for their brilliance or beauty. They may pursue careers that provide opportunities for public recognition and adulation, such as acting, modelling, or politics. They may become deeply wounded by the slightest hint that they are not as special as they believe themselves to be.

TABLE 8.3

Features of Normal Self-Interest as Compared to Self-Defeating Narcissism

Normal Self-Interest	Self-Defeating Narcissism
Appreciating acclaim, but not requiring it in order to maintain self-esteem.	Craving adoration insatiably; requiring acclaim in order to feel momentarily good about oneself.
Being temporarily wounded by criticism.	Being inflamed or crushed by criticism and brooding about it extensively.
Feeling unhappy but not worthless following failure.	Having enduring feelings of mortification and worthlessness triggered by failure.
Feeling "special" or uncommonly talented in some way.	Feeling incomparably better than other people, and insisting upon acknowledgment of that pre-eminence.
Feeling good about oneself, even when other people are being critical.	Needing constant support from other people in order to maintain one's feelings of well-being.
Being reasonably accepting of life's setbacks, even though they can be painful and temporarily destabilizing.	Responding to life's wounds with depression or fury.
Maintaining self-esteem in the face of disapproval or denigration.	Responding to disapproval or denigration with loss of self-esteem.
Maintaining emotional equilibrium despite lack of special treatment.	Feeling entitled to special treatment and becoming terribly upset when one is treated in an ordinary manner.
Being empathic and caring about the feelings of others.	Being insensitive to other people's needs and feelings; exploiting others until they become fed up.

Source: Based on Goleman, 1988, p. C1.

People with narcissistic personalities tend to be preoccupied with fantasies of success and power, ideal love, or recognition for brilliance or beauty. They, like people with histrionic personalities, may gravitate toward careers in which they can receive adulation, such as modelling, acting, or politics. Although they tend to exaggerate their accomplishments and abilities, many people with narcissistic personalities are quite successful in their occupations, but envy those who achieve even greater success. Insatiable ambition may prompt them to devote themselves tirelessly to work. They are driven to succeed, not so much for money as for the adulation that attends success.

Interpersonal relationships are invariably strained by the demands they impose on others and by their lack of empathy with and concern for other people. They seek the company of flatterers and are often superficially charming and friendly and able to draw people to them. But their interest in people is one-sided: they seek people who will serve their interests and nourish their sense of self-importance (Goleman, 1988). They have a sense of entitlement that leads them to exploit others. They treat sex partners as devices for their own pleasure or to brace their self-esteem.

The case of Bill illustrates several features of the narcissistic personality:

Most people agreed that Bill, a 35-year-old investment banker, had a certain charm. He was bright, articulate, and attractive. He possessed a keen sense of humour that drew people to him at social gatherings. He would always position himself in the middle of the room, where he could be the centre of attention. The topics of conversation invariably focused on his "deals," the "rich and famous" people he had met, and his outmanoeuvring of opponents. His next project was always bigger and more daring than the last. Bill loved an audience. His face would light up when others responded to him with praise or admiration for his business successes, which were always inflated beyond their true measure. But when the conversation shifted to other people, he would lose interest and excuse himself to make a drink or to call his answering machine. When hosting a party, he would urge guests to stay late and feel hurt if they had to leave early; he showed no sensitivity to or awareness of the needs of his friends.

The few friends he had maintained over the years had come to accept Bill on his own terms. They recognized that he needed to have his ego fed or that he would become cool and detached.

Bill had also had a series of romantic relationships with women who were willing to play the adoring admirer and make the sacrifices that he demanded—for a time. But they inevitably tired of the one-sided relationship or grew frustrated by Bill's inability to make a commitment or feel deeply toward them. Lacking empathy, Bill was unable to recognize other people's feelings and needs. His demands for constant attention from willing admirers did not derive from selfishness, but from a need to ward off underlying feelings of inadequacy and diminished self-esteem. It was sad, his friends thought, that Bill needed so much attention and adulation from others and that his many achievements were never enough to calm his inner doubts.

THE AUTHORS' FILES

Personality Disorders Characterized by Anxious or Fearful Behaviour

This cluster of personality disorders includes the avoidant, dependent, and obsessive-compulsive types. Although the features of these disorders differ, they share a component of fear or anxiety.

avoidant personality disorder Type of personality disorder characterized by avoidance of social relationships due to fears of rejection.

Avoidant Personality Disorder Persons with **avoidant personality disorder** are so terrified of rejection and criticism that they are generally unwilling to enter relationships without ardent reassurances of acceptance. As a result, they may have few close relationships outside their immediate families. They also tend to avoid group occupational or recreational activities for fear of rejection. They prefer to eat lunch alone at their desks. They shun company picnics and parties, unless they are perfectly sure of acceptance. Avoidant personality disorder, which appears to be equally common in men and women, is believed to affect between 0.5% and 1.0% of the general population (APA, 2000a).

Unlike people with schizoid qualities, with whom they share the feature of social withdrawal, individuals with avoidant personalities have interest in and feelings of warmth toward other people. However, fear of rejection prevents them from striving to meet their needs for affection and acceptance. In social situations, they tend to hug the walls and avoid conversing with others. They fear public embarrassment—the thought that others might see them blush, cry, or act nervously. They tend to stick to their routines and exaggerate the risks or effort involved in trying new things. They may refuse to attend a party that is an hour away on the pretext the late drive home would be too taxing.

The case of Harold illustrates several of the features of the avoidant personality:

> Harold, a 24-year-old accounting clerk, had dated only a few women, and he had met them through family introductions. He never felt confident enough to approach a woman on his own. Perhaps it was his shyness that first attracted Stacy. A 22-year-old secretary, she worked alongside Harold and asked him if he would like to get together some time after work. At first Harold declined, claiming some excuse, but when Stacy asked again a week later, Harold agreed, thinking she must really like him if she were willing to pursue him. The relationship developed quickly, and soon they were dating virtually every night. The relationship was strained, however. Harold interpreted any slight hesitation in her voice as a lack of interest. He repeatedly requested reassurance that she cared about him and evaluated every word and gesture for evidence of her feelings. If Stacy said she could not see him because of fatigue or illness, Harold assumed she was rejecting him and sought reassurance. After several months, Stacy decided she could no longer accept Harold's nagging, and the relationship ended. Harold assumed that Stacy had never truly cared for him.
>
> THE AUTHORS' FILES

There is a good deal of overlap between avoidant personality disorder and social phobia, particularly with a severe subtype of social phobia that involves a generalized pattern of social phobia (excessive, irrational fear of most social situations) (Herbert, Hope, & Bellack, 1992; Turner, Beidel, & Townsley, 1992; Widiger, 1992). Although research evidence shows that many cases of generalized social phobia occur in the absence of avoidant personality disorder (Holt, Heimberg, & Hope, 1992), relatively fewer cases of avoidant personality occur in the absence of generalized social phobia (Widiger, 1992). Thus, avoidant personality disorder may represent a more severe form of social phobia (Hoffman, Newman, Ehlers, & Roth, 1995). Still, the scientific jury is out on the question of whether avoidant personality disorder should be considered a severe form of generalized social phobia or a distinct diagnostic category as it is presently classified.

Dependent Personality Disorder

Dependent personality disorder describes people who have an excessive need to be taken care of by others. This leads them to be overly submissive and clinging in their relationships and extremely fearful of separation. People with this disorder find it very difficult to do things on their own. They seek advice in making even the smallest decision. Children or adolescents with the problem may look to their parents to select their clothes, diets, schools or colleges, even their friends. Adults with the disorder allow others to make important decisions for them. Sometimes, they are so dependent on others for making decisions that they allow their parents to determine whom they will or will not marry, as in the case of Matthew:

dependent personality disorder Type of personality disorder characterized by difficulties making independent decisions and by overly dependent behaviour.

Matthew, a 34-year-old single accountant who lives with his mother, sought treatment when his relationship with his girlfriend came to an end. His mother had objected to marriage because his girlfriend was of a different religion, and—because "blood is thicker than water"—Matthew acceded to his mother's wishes and ended the relationship. Yet he was angry with himself and at his mother because he felt that she was too possessive to ever grant him permission to get married. He describes his mother as a domineering woman who "wears the pants" in the family and is accustomed to having things her way. Matthew alternates between resenting his mother and thinking that perhaps she knows what's best for him.

Matthew's position at work is several levels below what would be expected of someone of his talent and educational level. Several times, he has declined promotions in order to avoid increased responsibilities that would require him to supervise others and make independent decisions. He has maintained close relationships with two friends since early childhood and has lunch with one of them every working day. On days his friend calls in sick, Matthew feels lost. Matthew has lived his whole life at home, except for one year away at college. He returned home because of homesickness.

ADAPTED FROM SPITZER ET AL., 1994, PP. 179–180

After marriage, people with dependent personality disorder may rely on their spouses to make decisions such as where they should live, which neighbours they should befriend, how they should discipline their children, what jobs they should take, how they should budget money, and where they should vacation. Like Matthew, individuals with dependent personality disorder avoid positions of responsibility. They turn down challenges and promotions and work beneath their potentials. They tend to be overly sensitive to criticism and are preoccupied with fears of rejection and abandonment. They may be devastated by the end of a close relationship or by the prospect of living on their own. Because of a fear of rejection, they often subordinate their wants and needs to those of others. They may agree with outlandish statements about themselves and do degrading things in order to please others.

Although dependent personality disorder is diagnosed more frequently in women (Bornstein, 1997; APA, 2000a), it is not clear that there is an underlying difference in the prevalence of the disorder between men and women (Corbitt & Widiger, 1995). The diagnosis is often applied to women who, for fear of abandonment, tolerate husbands who openly cheat on them, abuse them, or gamble away family resources. Underlying feelings of inadequacy and helplessness discourage them from taking effective action. In a vicious circle, their passivity encourages further abuse, leading them to feel yet more inadequate and helpless. The diagnosis of women with this disorder is controversial and may be seen as unfairly "blaming the victim" because women in our society are often socialized into more dependent roles. A panel convened by the American Psychological Association noted that women also encounter greater stress than men in contemporary life (Goleman, 1990). Women are more likely than men to be subjected to second-class citizenship, which may set the stage for dependency.

Dependent personality disorder has been linked to other psychological disorders, including major depression, bipolar disorder, and social phobia, and to physical problems such as hypertension, cancer, and gastrointestinal disorders like ulcers and colitis (Bornstein, 1999b; Loranger, 1996; Reich, 1996). There also appears to be a link between dependent personality and what psychodynamic theorists refer to as "oral" behaviour problems, such as smoking, eating disorders, and alcoholism (Bornstein, 1993, 1999b). Psychodynamic writers trace dependent behaviour to the utter dependence of a newborn baby and the baby's seeking of nourishment through oral means (suckling). From infancy, they suggest, people associate provision of food with love. Food may come to symbolize love, and persons with dependent personalities may overeat to symbolically ingest love (Greenberg & Bornstein, 1988a, 1988b).

Research shows that people with dependent personalities are more reliant on other people for support and guidance than the average person (Greenberg & Bornstein,

1988a). People with dependent personalities often attribute their problems to physical rather than emotional causes and seek support and advice from medical experts rather than psychologists or counsellors (Greenberg & Bornstein, 1988b).

Obsessive-Compulsive Personality Disorder The defining features of **obsessive-compulsive personality disorder** involve an excessive degree of orderliness, perfectionism, rigidity, difficulty coping with ambiguity, difficulties expressing feelings, and meticulousness in work habits. About 1% of people in community samples are diagnosed with the disorder (APA, 2000a). The disorder is about twice as common in men than women. Unlike obsessive-compulsive anxiety disorder, people with obsessive-compulsive personality disorder do not necessarily experience outright obsessions or compulsions. If they do, both diagnoses may be deemed appropriate.

Persons with obsessive-compulsive personality disorder are so preoccupied with perfection that they cannot complete things in a timely fashion. Their efforts inevitably fall short of their expectations and they force themselves to redo their work. Or they may ruminate about how to prioritize their assignments and never seem to get started working. They focus on details that others perceive as trivial. As the saying goes, they often fail to see the forest for the trees. Their rigidity impairs their social relationships; they insist on doing things their way rather than compromising. Their zeal for work keeps them from participating in or enjoying social and leisure activities. They tend to be stingy with money. They find it difficult to make decisions and postpone or avoid them for fear of making the wrong choice. They tend to be overly rigid in issues of morality and ethics because of inflexibility in personality rather than deeply held convictions. They tend to be overly formal in relationships and find it difficult to express feelings. It is hard for them to relax and enjoy pleasant activities; they worry about the costs of such diversions.

Consider the case of Jerry:

"A place for everything, and everything in its place?" People with obsessive-compulsive personalities may have invented this maxim. Many such people have excessive needs for orderliness in their environment.

obsessive-compulsive personality disorder Type of personality disorder characterized by rigid ways of relating to others, perfectionistic tendencies, lack of spontaneity, and excessive attention to details.

> Jerry, a 34-year-old systems analyst, was perfectionistic, overly concerned with details, and rigid in his behaviour. Jerry was married to Marcia, a graphic artist. He insisted on scheduling their free time hour by hour and became unnerved when they deviated from his agenda. He would circle a parking lot repeatedly in search of just the right parking spot to ensure that another car would not scrape his car. He refused to have the apartment painted for over a year because he couldn't decide on the colour. He had arranged all the books on their bookshelf alphabetically and insisted that every book be placed in its proper position.
>
> Jerry never seemed to be able to relax. Even on vacation, he was bothered by thoughts of work that he had left behind and by fears that he might lose his job. He couldn't understand how people could lie on a beach and let all their worries evaporate in the summer air. Something can always go wrong, he figured, so how can people let themselves go?
>
> THE AUTHORS' FILES

Problems with the Classification of Personality Disorders

Questions remain about the reliability and validity of the diagnostic categories for personality disorders. There may be too much overlap among the diagnoses to justify so many different categories. Agreement between raters on personality disorder diagnoses remains modest at best (Coolidge & Segal, 1998). The classification system also seems to blur the distinctions between normal and abnormal variations in personality. Moreover, some categories of personality disorder may be based on sexist presumptions.

Undetermined Reliability and Validity The present DSM system sought to remove ambiguities in the diagnostic criteria of personality disorders in earlier editions by providing descriptive criteria that more tightly define particular disorders. The reliability and validity of the definitions used in the DSM-IV remains to be fully tested, however (Livesley, 2001).

Problems Distinguishing Axis I from Axis II Disorders Some commentators on the DSM system question whether there is sufficient justification for placing personality disorders and clinical syndromes on separate axes—Axis I and Axis II, respectively (Farmer, 2000; Livesley, Schroeder, Jackson, & Jang, 1994). University of British Columbia psychiatrist John Livesley, a leading expert on personality disorders, and his colleagues question the assumption that personality disorders are discriminable from clinical syndromes like anxiety or depressive disorders. First, for example, it may be difficult to distinguish in actual practice between obsessive-compulsive disorder and obsessive-compulsive personality disorder. Second, clinical syndromes are believed to be variable over time, whereas personality disorders are held to be generally more enduring patterns of disturbance. Yet evidence indicates that features of personality disorders may vary over time with changes in circumstances. On the other hand, some Axis I clinical syndromes (dysthymia, for example) follow a more or less chronic course.

Overlap Among Disorders Psychologists Brian O'Connor of Lakehead University and Jamie Dyce at Concordia University College of Alberta contend that not only are the diagnostic criteria for any given category of personality disorder broader than they are for other psychological disorders, there is also a high degree of overlap among the personality disorders. Moreover, a person does not have to satisfy all of the diagnostic criteria in order to be diagnosed with a personality disorder (O'Connor & Dyce, 2001). Overlap undermines the DSM's conceptual clarity or purity by increasing the number of cases that seem to fit two or more diagnostic categories (Livesley, 1998, 2001; Livesley, West, & Tanney, 1986). Although some personality disorders have distinct features, many appear to share common traits. For example, the same person may have traits suggestive of dependent personality disorder (inability to make decisions or initiate activities independently) and of avoidant personality disorder (extreme social anxiety and heightened sensitivity to criticism). One study found that as many as 25% of people with schizoid personality disorders could also be diagnosed as having avoidant personality disorder (Reich & Noyes, 1986). Another reported that in a sample of people with borderline personality disorder, nearly one in four (23%) also met criteria for APD (Hudziak et al., 1996). Overall, roughly two out of three people with personality disorders meet diagnostic criteria for more than one type of personality disorder (Widiger, 1991). The high degree of overlap suggests that the personality disorders included in the DSM system may not be sufficiently distinct from one another (Westen & Shedler, 1999). Some so-called disorders may thus represent different aspects of the same disorder, not separate diagnostic categories.

Difficulty in Distinguishing Between Variations in Normal Behaviour and Abnormal Behaviour Another problem with the diagnosis of personality disorders is that they involve traits that, in lesser degrees, describe the behaviour of most normal individuals. Feeling suspicious now and then does not mean you have a paranoid personality disorder. The tendency to exaggerate your own importance does not mean you are narcissistic. You may avoid social interactions for fear of embarrassment or rejection without having an avoidant personality disorder, and you may be especially conscientious in your work without having an obsessive-compulsive personality disorder. Because the defining attributes of these disorders are commonly occurring personality traits, clinicians should apply these diagnostic labels only when the patterns are so pervasive that they interfere with the individual's functioning or cause significant personal distress. Yet it can be difficult to know where to draw the line between normal variations in behaviour and personality disorders. We continue to the lack data to more precisely determine the point at which a trait becomes sufficiently inflexible or maladaptive to justify a personality disorder diagnosis (Livesley, 2001; Widiger & Costa, 1994).

Livesley and his colleagues (Livesley, Jang, & Vernon, 1998; Livesley et al., 1994) provide evidence that personality traits sit on a continuum and the extremes of some personality dimensions may signal dysfunction or maladjustment. From this dimensional perspective, disordered patterns of personality are considered variations of normal personality patterns. But it's not just extremeness that distinguishes normal from disordered personality patterns. For instance, being extremely sociable may not be such a bad thing. Livesley (1998) suggests that the definition of personality disorder should also include measurable dysfunctions in one or more of the following three domains: the self system (the stable and integrated sense of oneself and others), interpersonal relationships (intimate relationships and affiliation with others), and societal relationships (prosocial behaviours and co-operative relationships).

Sexist Biases The construction of certain personality disorders may have sexist underpinnings. For example, diagnostic criteria for personality disorders label stereotypical feminine behaviour as pathological with greater frequency than is the case with stereotypical masculine behaviour. The concept of the histrionic personality, for example, seems a caricature of the traditional stereotype of the feminine personality: flighty, emotional, shallow, seductive, attention seeking. But if the feminine stereotype corresponds to a mental disorder, shouldn't we also have a diagnostic category that reflects the masculine stereotype of the "macho male"? It may be possible to show that overly masculinized traits are associated with significant distress or impairment in social or occupational functioning in certain males. Highly masculinized males often get into fights and experience difficulties working for female bosses. There is no personality disorder that corresponds to the macho male stereotype, however.

The diagnosis of dependent personality disorder may also unfairly stigmatize women who are socialized into dependent roles as having a "mental disorder." Women may be at a greater risk of receiving diagnoses of histrionic or dependent personality disorders because clinicians perceive these patterns as existing more commonly among women or because women are more likely than men to be socialized into these behaviour patterns. Clinicians may also be biased in favour of perceiving women as having histrionic personality disorder and men as having antisocial personality disorder even when the men and women in question do not differ in symptomatology (Garb, 1997).

Clinicians may also have a gender bias when it comes to diagnosing borderline personality disorder. In one study, researchers presented a hypothetical case example to a sample of 311 psychologists, social workers, and psychiatrists (Becker & Lamb, 1994). Half of the sample was presented with a case identified as a female; the other half read the identical case except it was identified as male. The gender of the case for half of the respondents was male. Clinicians more often diagnosed the case identified as female as having borderline personality disorder.

All in all, personality disorders are convenient labels for identifying common patterns of ineffective and ultimately self-defeating behaviour, but labels do not explain their causes. Still, the development of an accurate descriptive system is an important step toward scientific explanation. The establishment of reliable diagnostic categories sets the stage for valid research into causation and treatment.

Types of Personality Disorders

Review It

- **What are personality disorders?** Personality disorders are maladaptive or rigid behaviour patterns or personality traits associated with states of personal distress that impair a person's ability to function in social or occupational roles. People with personality disorders do not generally recognize a need to change themselves.

- **What are the classes of personality disorders within the DSM system?** The DSM categorizes personality disorders according to the following clusters of characteristics: odd or eccentric behaviour; dramatic, emotional, or erratic behaviour; anxious or fearful behaviour.

- **What are the features associated with personality disorders characterized by odd or eccentric behaviour?** People with paranoid personality disorder are unduly suspicious and mistrustful of others, to the point that their relationships suffer. But they do not hold the more flagrant paranoid delusions typical of schizophrenia. Schizoid personality disorder describes people who have little if any interest in social relationships, show a restricted range of emotional expression, and appear distant and aloof. People with schizotypal personalities appear odd or eccentric in their thoughts, mannerisms, and behaviour, but not to the degree found in schizophrenia.

- **What are the features associated with personality disorders characterized by dramatic, emotional, or erratic behaviour?** Antisocial personality disorder describes people who persistently engage in behaviour that violates social norms and the rights of others and who tend to show no remorse for their misdeeds. The psychopathic personality includes affective and interpersonal traits that when combined with criminality are often associated with persistent, senseless, and violent behaviour. Borderline personality disorder is defined in terms of instability in self-image, relationships, and mood. People with borderline personality disorder often engage in impulsive acts, which are frequently self-destructive. People with histrionic personality disorder tend to be highly dramatic and emotional in their behaviour, whereas people diagnosed with narcissistic personality disorder have an inflated or grandiose sense of self, and like those with histrionic personalities, they demand to be the centre of attention.

- **What are the features associated with personality disorders characterized by anxious or fearful behaviour?** Avoidant personality disorder describes people who are so terrified of rejection and criticism that they are generally unwilling to enter relationships without unusually strong reassurances of acceptance. People with dependent personality disorder are overly dependent on others and have extreme difficulty acting independently or making even the smallest decisions on their own. People with obsessive-compulsive personality disorder have vari-

ous traits such as orderliness, perfectionism, rigidity, and excessive attention to detail, but are without the true obsessions and compulsions associated with obsessive-compulsive (anxiety) disorder.

- **What are some problems associated with the classification of personality disorders?** Various controversies and problems attend the classification of personality disorders, including a lack of demonstrated reliability and validity, too much overlap among the categories, difficulty in distinguishing between variations in normal behaviour and abnormal behaviour, and underlying sexist biases in certain categories.

Define It

personality disorders	optimum level of arousal
ego syntonic	borderline personality
ego dystonic	disorder
paranoid personality	histrionic personality
disorder	disorder
schizoid personality	narcissistic
disorder	personality disorder
schizotypal personality	avoidant personality
disorder	disorder
ideas of reference	dependent personality
antisocial personality	disorder
disorder	obsessive-compulsive
psychopathy	personality disorder

Recall It*

1. Personality disorders involve patterns of behaviour that ultimately prove self-defeating because of their _____.

   a. immorality
   b. instability
   c. rigidity
   d. deviance

2. Harriet is very sensitive to criticism, even to the point of taking offence at the most trivial slight, whether real or imagined. She angers easily and doesn't trust anyone. She has few friends and holds grudges for years. Her pattern of behaviour most closely resembles _____ personality disorder.

   a. paranoid
   b. antisocial
   c. histrionic
   d. avoidant

3. The major characteristic of schizoid personality disorder is _____.

    a. bizarre thinking
    b. social isolation
    c. the flagrant disregard for others' rights
    d. obsessive thinking

4. The term _____ is often associated with an antisocial personality.

    a. *psychotic*
    b. *psychopath*
    c. *schizotypal*
    d. *borderline*

5. From the DSM perspective, each personality disorder is a distinct category. Other theorists contend that personality consists of dimensions that are on _____ between normal and abnormal traits.

    a. an axis
    b. the boundary
    c. a pendulum
    d. a continuum

* Recall It answers can be found on the Companion Website for this text.

Think About It

- Have you known people whose personality traits or styles caused continuing difficulties in their relationships with others? Did their personalities relate to any one of the types of personality disorders discussed in this chapter? Did the person ever seek help from a mental health professional? If so, what was the outcome? If not, why not?

Key for Sensation-Seeking Scale (page 294)

- Because this is an abbreviated version of a questionnaire, no norms are applicable. However, answers that agree with the following key are suggestive of sensation seeking:

1. A	8. A
2. A	9. B
3. A	10. A
4. B	11. A
5. A	12. A
6. B	13. B
7. A	

THEORETICAL PERSPECTIVES

In this section, we consider the theoretical perspectives on personality disorders. Many of the theoretical accounts of disturbed personality derive from the psychodynamic model. We thus begin with a review of traditional and modern psychodynamic models.

Psychodynamic Perspectives

Traditional Freudian theory focused on problems arising from the Oedipus complex as the foundation for many abnormal behaviours, including personality disorders. Freud believed that children normally resolve the Oedipus complex by forsaking incestuous wishes for the parent of the opposite gender and identifying with the parent of the same gender. As a result, they incorporate the parent's moral principles in the form of a personality structure called the superego. Many factors may interfere with appropriate identification, however, such as having a weak or absent father or an antisocial parent. These factors may sidetrack the normal developmental process, preventing children from developing the moral constraints that prevent antisocial behaviour and the feelings of guilt or remorse that normally follow behaviour that is hurtful to others.

More recent psychodynamic theories have generally focused on the earlier, pre-Oedipal period of about 18 months to 3 years, during which infants are theorized to begin to develop their identities as separate from those of their parents. These recent advances in psychodynamic theory focus on the development of the sense of self in explaining such disorders as narcissistic and borderline personality disorders.

Heinz Kohut One of the principal shapers of modern psychodynamic concepts was Heinz Kohut (1913–1981), whose views are labelled **self psychology.** Kohut focused much of his attention on the development of the narcissistic personality.

self psychology Heinz Kohut's theory, which describes processes that normally lead to the achievement of a cohesive sense of self, or in narcissistic personality disorder, to a grandiose but fragile sense of self.

Kohut (1966) believed that people with narcissistic personalities may mount a façade of self-importance to cover up deep feelings of inadequacy. Kohut maintained that early childhood is characterized by a normal stage of "healthful narcissism." Infants feel powerful, as though the world revolves around them. Infants also normally perceive older people, especially parents, as idealized towers of strength and wish to be one with them to share their power. Empathic parents reflect their children's inflated perceptions by making them feel that anything is possible and by nourishing their self-esteem (e.g., telling them how terrific and precious they are). Even empathic parents are critical from time to time, however, and puncture their children's grandiose sense of self. Or they fail to measure up to their children's idealized views of them. Gradually, unrealistic expectations dissolve and are replaced by more realistic appraisals. This process of childhood narcissism that eventually gives way to more realistic appraisals of self and others is perfectly normal. Earlier grandiose self-images form the basis for assertiveness later in childhood and set the stage for ambitious striving in adulthood. In adolescence, childhood idealization is transformed into realistic admiration for parents, teachers, and friends. In adulthood, these ideas develop into a set of internal ideals, values, and goals.

Lack of parental empathy and support, however, sets the stage for pathological narcissism in adulthood. Children who are not prized by their parents may fail to develop a sturdy sense of self-esteem. They may be unable to tolerate even slight blows to their self-worth. They develop damaged self-concepts and feel incapable of being loved and admired because of perceived inadequacies or flaws. Pathological narcissism involves the construction of a grandiose facade of self-perfection that is merely a shell to cloak perceived inadequacies. The facade always remains on the brink of crumbling, however, and must be continually shored up by a constant flow of reassurance that one is special and unique. This leaves the person vulnerable to painful blows to self-esteem following failure to achieve social or occupational goals. So needy of constant approval, a person with a narcissistic personality may fly into a rage when he or she feels slighted in any way.

Otto Kernberg Modern psychodynamic views of the borderline personality also trace the disorder to difficulties in the development of the self in early childhood. Kernberg (1975), a leading psychodynamic theorist (born 1928), views borderline personality in terms of a pre-Oedipal failure to develop a sense of constancy and unity in one's image of the self and others. Kernberg proposes that childhood failure to synthesize these contradictory images of good and bad results in a failure to develop a consistent self-image and in tendencies toward **splitting**—shifting back and forth between viewing oneself and other people as "all good" or "all bad."

In Kernberg's view, parents, even excellent parents, invariably fail to meet all their children's needs. Infants therefore face the early developmental challenge of reconciling images of the nurturing, comforting "good mother" with those of the withholding, frustrating "bad mother." Failure to reconcile these opposing images into a realistic, unified, and stable parental image may fixate children in the pre-Oedipal period. As adults, then, they may retain these rapidly shifting attitudes toward their therapists and others.

Margaret Mahler Mahler (1897–1985), another influential modern psychodynamic theorist, explained borderline personality disorder in terms of childhood separation from the mother figure. Mahler and her colleagues (Mahler & Kaplan, 1977; Mahler, Pine, & Bergman, 1975) believed that during the first year, an infant develops a **symbiotic** attachment to its mother. *Symbiosis* is a biological term derived from the Greek root meaning "to live together"; it describes life patterns in which two species lead interdependent lives. In psychology, symbiosis is likened to a state of oneness in which a child's identity is fused with its mother's. Normally, children gradually differentiate their own identities or senses of self from their mothers. The process is called **separation-individuation**. Separation is developing a separate psychological and biological identity from the mother. Individuation involves recognizing the personal characteristics that define one's self-identity. Separation-individuation may be a stormy process. Children may vacillate between seeking greater independence and moving closer to, or "shadowing," their mother, which is seen as a wish for reunion. The mother may disrupt normal separation-individuation by refus-

splitting Term describing the inability of some persons (especially people with borderline personalities) to reconcile the positive and negative aspects of themselves and others into a cohesive integration, resulting in sudden and radical shifts between strongly positive and strongly negative feelings.

symbiotic (1) In biology, the living together of two different but interdependent organisms. (2) In Mahler's object-relations theory, the term used to describe the state of oneness that normally exists between a mother and infant in which the infant's identity is fused with the mother's.

separation-individuation In Margaret Mahler's theory, the process by which young children come to separate psychologically from their mothers and to perceive themselves as separate and distinct persons.

ing to let go of the child or by too quickly pushing the child toward independence. The tendencies of people with borderline personalities to react to others with ambivalence and to alternate between love and hate are suggestive to Mahler of earlier ambivalences during the separation-individuation process. Borderline personality disorder may arise from a failure to master this developmental challenge.

Further on in this chapter, we underscore the links between abuse in childhood and the later development of personality disorders. These linkages suggest that failure to form close-bonding relationships with parental caregivers in childhood plays a critical role in developing many of the maladaptive personality patterns classified as personality disorders.

Learning Perspectives

Learning theorists tend to focus more on the acquisition of behaviour than on the notion of enduring personality traits. Similarly, they think more in terms of maladaptive behaviour than of disorders of "personality" or "personality traits." Trait theorists believe that personality traits steer behaviour, providing a framework for consistent behaviour in diverse situations. Many critics (e.g., Mischel, 1979), however, argue that behaviour is actually less consistent across situations than trait theorists would suggest. Behaviour may depend more on situational demands than on inherent traits. For example, we may describe a person as lazy and unmotivated. But is this person always lazy and unmotivated? Aren't there some situations in which the person may be energetic and ambitious? What differences in these situations may explain differences in behaviour? Learning theorists are generally interested in defining the learning histories and situational factors that give rise to maladaptive behaviour and the reinforcers that maintain them.

Learning theorists suggest that in childhood, many important experiences occur that shape the development of the maladaptive habits of relating to others that constitute personality disorders. For example, children who are regularly discouraged from speaking their minds or exploring their environments may develop a dependent personality behaviour pattern. Obsessive-compulsive personality disorder may be connected with excessive parental discipline or overcontrol in childhood. Theodore Millon (1981) suggests that children whose behaviour is rigidly controlled and punished by parents, even slight transgressions, may develop inflexible, perfectionistic standards. As these children mature, they may strive to develop in an area in which they excel, such as schoolwork or athletics, as a way of avoiding parental criticism or punishment. But excessive attention to a single area of development may prevent them from becoming well-rounded. They may thus squelch spontaneity and avoid new challenges or risks. They may also place perfectionistic demands on themselves so as to avoid any risk of punishment or rebuke, and develop other behaviour associated with the obsessive-compulsive personality pattern.

Millon suggests that histrionic personality disorder may be rooted in childhood experiences in which social reinforcers, such as parental attention, are connected to a child's appearance and willingness to perform for others, especially in cases where reinforcers are dispensed inconsistently. Inconsistent attention teaches children not to take approval for granted and to strive for it continually. People with histrionic personalities may also have

What are the origins of antisocial personality disorder? Here, we see two young men who are members of a gang. Are youth who develop antisocial personalities largely unsocialized because early learning experiences lack the consistency and predictability that help other children connect their behaviour with rewards and punishments? Or are they very "socialized"—but socialized to imitate the behaviour of other antisocial youth? Are we confusing antisocial behaviour with antisocial personality disorder? To what extent does criminal behaviour or membership in gangs overlap with antisocial personality disorder? Can environmental factors explain how people with antisocial personality disorder maintain their composure (their relatively low levels of arousal) under circumstances that would induce anxiety in most of us?

identified with parents who are dramatic, emotional, and attention-seeking. Extreme sibling rivalry would further heighten motivation to perform for attention from others.

Behaviour theories emphasize the role of reinforcement in explaining the origins of antisocial behaviour. Ullmann and Krasner (1975) proposed, for example, that people with antisocial personalities may have failed to learn to respond to other people as potential reinforcers. Most children learn to treat others as reinforcing agents because others reinforce them with praise when they behave appropriately and punish them for misbehaviour. Reinforcement and punishment provide feedback (information about social expectations) that helps children modify their behaviour to maximize the chances of future rewards and minimize the risks of future punishment. As a consequence, children become socialized. They become sensitive to the demands of powerful others, usually parents and teachers, and learn to regulate their behaviour accordingly. They thus adapt to social expectations. They learn what to do and what to say, how to dress and how to act to obtain social reinforcement or approval from others.

People with antisocial personalities, by contrast, may not have become socialized because their early learning experiences lacked the consistency and predictability that helped other children connect their behaviour with rewards and punishments. Perhaps they were sometimes rewarded for doing the "right thing," but just as often not. They may have borne the brunt of harsh physical punishments that depended more on parental whims than on their own conduct. As adults they may not place much value on what other people expect because there was no clear connection between their own behaviour and reinforcement in childhood. They may have learned as children that there was little they could do to prevent punishment and so perhaps lost the motivation to try. Although Ullmann and Krasner's views may account for some features of antisocial personality disorder, they may not adequately address the development of the "charming" type of antisocial personality, which describes people who are skilful at reading social cues produced by other people and using them for personal advantage.

Family Perspectives

Many theorists have argued that disturbances in family relationships underlie the development of personality disorders. Consistent with psychodynamic formulations, researchers find that people with borderline personality disorder *remember* their parents as having been more controlling and less caring than do reference subjects with other psychological disorders (Zweig-Frank & Paris, 1991). When people with borderline personality disorder recall their earliest memories, they are more likely than other people to paint significant others as malevolent or evil. They portray their parents and others close to them as having been more likely to injure them deliberately or to fail to help them escape injuries by others (Nigg, Lohr, Western, Gold, & Silk, 1992).

A number of researchers have linked a history of physical or sexual abuse or neglect in childhood to the development of personality disorders, including borderline personality disorder, in adulthood (e.g., Johnson et al., 1999; Weaver & Clum, 1995; Zanarini et al., 1997). Perhaps the "splitting" observed in people with the disorder is a function of having learned to cope with unpredictable and harsh behaviour from parental figures or other caregivers.

Again consistent with psychodynamic theory, family factors such as parental overprotection and authoritarianism have been implicated in the development of dependent personality traits that may hamper the development of independent behaviour (Bornstein, 1992). Extreme fears of abandonment may also be involved, perhaps resulting from a failure to develop secure bonds with parental attachment figures in childhood due to parental neglect, rejection, or death. Subsequently, a chronic fear of being abandoned by other people with whom one has close relationships may develop, leading to the clinginess that typifies dependent personality disorder. Theorists also suggest that obsessive-compulsive personality disorder may emerge within a strongly moralistic and rigid family environment, which does not permit even minor deviations from expected roles or behaviour (e.g., Oldham, 1994).

As in the case of borderline personality disorder, researchers find that childhood abuse or neglect is a risk factor in the development of antisocial personality disorder in adulthood (Luntz & Widom, 1994). In a view that straddles the psychodynamic and learning theories, the McCords (McCord & McCord, 1964) focus on the role of parental rejection or neglect in the development of antisocial personality disorder. They suggest that children normally learn to associate parental approval with conformity to parental practices and values, and disapproval with disobedience. When tempted to transgress, children feel anxious for fear of losing parental love.

Anxiety serves as a signal that encourages a child to inhibit antisocial behaviour. Eventually, the child identifies with parents and internalizes these social controls in the form of a conscience. When parents do not show love for their children, this identification does not occur. Children do not fear loss of love because they have never had it. The anxiety that might have served to restrain antisocial and criminal behaviour is absent.

Children who are rejected or neglected by their parents may not develop warm feelings of attachment to others. They may lack the ability to empathize with the feelings and needs of others, developing instead an attitude of indifference. Or perhaps they still retain a wish to develop loving relationships but lack the ability to experience genuine feelings.

Although family factors may be implicated in some cases of antisocial personality disorder, many neglected children do not later show antisocial or other abnormal behaviour. We are left to develop other explanations to predict which deprived children will develop antisocial personalities or other abnormal behaviour, and which will not.

Cognitive-Behavioural Perspectives

Social-cognitive theorist Albert Bandura (1973, 1986) has studied the role of observational learning in aggressive behaviour, which is one of the common components of antisocial behaviour. He and his colleagues (e.g., Bandura, Ross, & Ross, 1963) have shown that children acquire skills, including aggressive skills, by observing the behaviour of others. Exposure to aggression may come from watching violent television programs or observing parents who act violently toward one another. Bandura does not believe children and adults display aggressive behaviour in a mechanical way, however. Rather, people usually do not imitate aggressive behaviour unless they are provoked and believe they are more likely to be rewarded than punished for it. When models get their way with others by acting aggressively, children may be more likely to imitate them. Children may also acquire antisocial behaviour such as cheating, bullying, or lying by direct reinforcement if they find such behaviour helps them avoid blame or manipulate others.

Cognitive-behaviour oriented psychologists have shown that the ways in which people with personality disorders interpret their social experiences influence their behaviour. Antisocial adolescents, for example, tend to incorrectly interpret other people's behaviour as threatening (Dodge, Laird, Lochman, & Zelli, 2002). Perhaps because of family and community experiences, they tend to presume that others intend them ill when they do not. In a promising cognitive therapy method based on such findings—**problem-solving therapy**—antisocial adolescent boys have been encouraged to reconceptualize their social interactions as problems to be solved rather than as threats to be responded to with aggression (Kazdin & Whitely, 2003). They then generate nonviolent solutions to social confrontations and, like scientists, test out the most promising ones. In the section on biological perspectives, we also see that the antisocial personality's failure to profit from punishment is connected with a cognitive factor: the *meaning* of the aversive stimulus.

problem-solving therapy Form of therapy that focuses on helping people develop more effective problem-solving skills.

Biological Perspectives

Our knowledge about biological factors in most personality disorders has progressed rapidly in recent years with advances in genetics and neuroimaging technologies. We have suggestive evidence of genetic factors based in part on findings that the first-degree biological relatives (parents and siblings) of people with certain personality disorders, especially antisocial, schizotypal, and borderline types, are more likely to be diagnosed with these disorders than are members of the general population (APA, 2000a; Battaglia, Bernardeschi, Franchini, Bellodi, & Smeraldi, 1995; Nigg & Goldsmith, 1994). Recent studies using fMRI technology have also provided evidence for neurological differences in personality traits (Gray and Braver, 2002; Reuter et al., 2004).

Genetic Factors The establishment of well-defined criteria or dimensions is considered the essential first step in the search for the genetic underpinnings of personality disorders (Jang, Livesley, & Vernon, 2002). To that end, Kerry Jang and John Livesley initiated the UBC Twin Project in 1991 to help build valid diagnostic systems and measurements for major forms of personality disorders. With over 1000 adult twin pairs, it is Canada's largest twin study and the only one dedicated to the study of psychiatric disorders.

Studies of familial transmission are limited because family members share common environments as well as genes. Hence, researchers have turned to twin and adoptee studies to tease out genetic and environmental effects. Evidence from twin studies suggests that dimensions of personality associated with particular personality disorders may have an inherited component (Livesley, Jang, Jackson, & Vernon, 1993). Researchers examined the genetic contribution to 18 dimensions that underlie various personality disorders, including callousness, identity problems, anxiousness, insecure attachment, narcissism, social avoidance, self-harm, and oppositionality (negativity) (Livesley et al., 1993). Genetic influences were suggested by findings of greater correlations of a given trait among identical (monozygotic or MZ) twins than among fraternal (dizygotic or DZ) twins. A statistical measure of heritability, reflecting the percentage of variability on a given trait that is accounted for by genetics, was computed for each personality dimension. The results showed that 12 of the 18 dimensions had heritabilities in the 40%-to-60% range, indicating a substantial genetic contribution to these characteristics. The highest heritabilities were for narcissism (64%) and identity problems (59%), and the lowest were for conduct problems (0%) and submissiveness (25%).

The findings suggest that genetics play a role in varying degrees in the development of the traits that underlie personality disorders. Certainly, not all people possessing these traits develop personality disorders. It is possible, however, that people with a genetic predisposition for these traits may be more vulnerable to developing personality disorders if they encounter certain environmental influences, such as being reared in a dysfunctional family.

In fact, it may be the case that genetically based behaviour dictates what environments and situations a person will seek out (Jang, Vernon, & Livesley, 2001). Jang and his colleagues at UBC argue that people do not just passively respond to nor are merely shaped by their environment, but that personality plays a role in the kinds of environments that will be actively sought out. For instance, a person with a genetic predisposition for sensation seeking may gravitate toward exhilarating situations such as bungee jumping, heli-skiing/boarding, or street racing. In this regard, genetic personality traits and the environment act cyclically (e.g., thrill seekers gravitate to thrilling environments and thrilling environments serve to reinforce the thrill seeking) and thus the person's personality becomes self-reinforcing and well-ingrained. The question remains: to what extent is the influence of the environment dependant upon pre-existing genetic factors?

Evidence from adoption studies shows that biological and adopted children of people with antisocial personality disorder are more likely to develop the disorder themselves, which is consistent with the view that both genetics and environment play a role in its development (APA, 2000a). Consistent with a genetic contribution, evidence shows striking similarities between identical twins reared apart on some personality dimensions, including a psychopathic personality dimension (DiLalla, Carey, Gottesman, & Bouchard, 1996). A Danish study found four to five times greater incidence of psychopathy among the biological relatives of antisocial adoptees than among the adoptive relatives (Schulsinger, 1972). However, the size of the genetic contribution was relatively small. Environmental influences also contribute to antisocial behaviour. Evidence from adoption studies links criminal behaviour to genetics, although environmental factors also play a role (Carey, 1992; Carey & DiLalla, 1994; DiLalla & Gottesman, 1991; Mednick, Moffitt, & Stack, 1987).

Neuropsychological Factors The neuroscience theory of personality can be traced back to physiologist Ivan Pavlov, who introduced the concept of nervous system excitation (e.g., a conditioned pleasure response) and inhibition (e.g., a conditioned fear response) (recall Chapter 2) (Corr, 2004; Corr & Perkins, 2005). Later, personality theorist Hans Eysenck incorporated Pavlov's ideas of excitatory and inhibitory processes into his theory of personality and suggested that *extroverts*—active, socially outgoing people—differ from *introverts*—socially withdrawn, introspective people—with respect to differences in cortical arousal sensitivity. Eysenck believed that extroverts have a lower level of arousal and seek out stimulating activity to increase their arousal. Contrariwise, introverts have higher levels of arousal and are more easily aroused, and thus seek to avoid sensory stimulation. Because social behaviour is arousing, in social situations, you may expect an extrovert to be the "life of the party," whereas an introvert may prefer to avoid parties altogether.

Over a 40-year period, theorist Jeffrey Gray has woven the theories of Pavlov and Eysenck into what is now known as *reinforcement sensitivity theory* (RST) (Corr, 2004). Gray's RST has evolved into a biological personality theory that focuses on three distinct neuropsychological systems: (1) the behavioural approach system (BAS), (2) the fight-flight-freeze system (FFFS), and (3) the behavioural inhibition system (BIS) (Gray, 1970; Gray & McNaughton, 2000). New evidence supporting the neurological basis of personality comes from a growing body of molecular genetics (e.g., Gray & Braver, 2002; Gray et al., 2005; Canli et al., 2006; Caspi et al., 2003; Ebstein, Benjamin, & Belmaker, 2003), as well as neuroimaging research studies (e.g., McCloskey, Phan, & Coccaro, 2005; McNaughton & Corr, 2004; Reuter, Schmitz, Corr, & Hennig, 2006; Reuter et al., 2004; Schaefer et al., 2006).

Gray suggests that each neuropsychological system functions in a unique way. The BAS, for instance, is sensitive to and anticipates rewards; it acts to seek out pleasure. It has been linked with personality traits characterized by positive affect, extroversion, and impulsivity, but it may also underlie addictive behaviours, hypomania, and mania (Franken & Muris, 2006; Gomez & Gomez, 2002, 2005; Kambouropoulos & Staiger, 2007; Segarra et al., 2007; Smits & Boeck, 2006). The fight-flight-freeze system (FFFS) is a fear response to punishing stimuli; it acts to avoid pain. The FFFS is tied to defensive escape (panic) and avoidance (fear) behaviours and is linked to panic disorders and phobias (Corr, 2004). The BIS is sensitive to potential conflicts caused by the expected rewards and punishments in a situation. When there is a goal conflict, the BIS is activated to resolve any potential or anticipated threat and to bring the person back to a nonconflict state. Let's say, for example, you and your friends are vacationing in a foreign country and you are excited (BAS activation) about going into a raucous nightclub that is quite a distance from your hotel. Although you are out to have a fun time, you may initially tend to be alert to your surroundings, looking for potential danger in this novel situation (BIS activation). If all goes well, the BIS relaxes and you and your extroverted friends are free to enjoy the evening's events (BAS activity). If someone were actually to threaten you, however, the FFFS would immediately kick in and you would be ready to respond to the danger. As for any introverted friends among your group, chances are they'd be on high alert before, during, and even after your night out on the town. Thus, as you can see from this illustration, the BIS acts as an alarm signal and is characterized by risk assessment, worry, rumination, and vigilance. Traits associated with the BIS include negative affect, neuroticism, low self-esteem, and anxiety (Gomez & Gomez, 2002; Segarra et al., 2007; Smits & Boeck, 2006), and conditions such as generalized anxiety and obsessive-compulsive disorder (Corr & Perkins, 2006).

Sociocultural Views

The sociocultural perspective leads us to examine the social conditions that may contribute to the development of the behaviour patterns identified as personality disorders. For instance, a Canadian study found that socioeconomic status (SES) risk factors, such as low family income, teenage-parent family, lone-parent family, low parental education, and family dysfunction are associated with an increased vulnerability to one or more behavioural problems in young children, especially when the children are exposed to hostile/ineffective parenting (Landy & Tam, 1998). Because antisocial personality disorder is reported more frequently among people from lower socioeconomic classes, we might examine the role that the kinds of stressors encountered by disadvantaged families play in developing problem behaviour patterns. Some Canadian neighbourhoods and communities are beset by social problems such as alcohol and drug abuse, teenage pregnancy, and disorganized and disintegrating families. These stressors are associated with an increased likelihood of child abuse and neglect, which may in turn contribute to lower self-esteem and breed feelings of anger and resentment in children. Neglect and abuse may be translated into the lack of empathy and callous disregard for the welfare of others that are associated with antisocial personalities.

Little information is available about the rates of personality disorders outside North America. One initiative in this direction involved a joint program sponsored by the World Health Organization (WHO) and the Alcohol, Drug Abuse, and Mental Health Administration (ADAMHA) of the U.S. government. The goal of the program was to develop and standardize diagnostic instruments that could be used to arrive at psychiatric diagnoses worldwide. The result of this effort was the development of the International Personality Disorder Examination (IPDE), a semistructured interview protocol for diagnosing personality disorders (Loranger et al., 1994). The IPDE was pilot-tested by psychiatrists and clinical psychologists in 11 different countries (India, Switzerland, the Netherlands, the United Kingdom, Luxembourg, Germany, Kenya, Norway, Japan, Austria, and the United States). The interview protocol had reasonably good reliability for diagnosing personality disorders among the different languages and cultures that were sampled. Although more research is needed to determine the rates of particular personality disorders in other parts of the world, investigators found borderline and avoidant types to be the most frequently diagnosed. Perhaps the characteristics associated with these personality disorders reflect some dimensions of personality disturbance that are commonly encountered throughout the world.

STUDY BREAK

Theoretical Perspectives

Review It

- **How do traditional Freudian concepts of disturbed personality development compare with more recent psychodynamic approaches?** Traditional Freudian theory focused on unresolved Oedipal conflicts in explaining normal and abnormal personality development. More recent psychodynamic theorists have focused on the pre-Oedipal period in explaining the development of such personality disorders as narcissistic and borderline personality.

- **How do learning theorists view personality disorders?** Learning theorists view personality disorders in terms of maladaptive patterns of behaviour rather than personality traits. Learning theorists seek to identify the early learning experiences and present reinforcement patterns that may explain the development and maintenance of personality disorders.

- **What is the role of family relationships in personality disorders?** Many theorists have argued that disturbed family relationships play a formative role in the development of many personality disorders. For example, theorists have connected antisocial personality to parental rejection or neglect and parental modelling of antisocial behaviour.

- **How do cognitive encoding strategies of antisocial adolescents differ from those of their peers?** Antisocial adolescents are more likely to interpret social cues as provocations or intentions of ill will. This cognitive bias may lead them to be confrontative in their relationships with peers.

- **What roles might biological factors play in personality disorders?** Genetics plays a role in varying degrees to the development of traits that underlie personality disorders. Some people with a genetic predisposition for these traits may be more vulnerable to developing personality disorders if they encounter certain environmental influences. In others, genetically based behaviour can dictate what environments a person will seek out. Reinforcement sensitivity theory (RST), backed up by genetic and neuropsychological evidence, helps explain and describe the psychophysiological basis of personality differences.

- **What role do sociocultural factors play in the development of personality disorders?** The effects of poverty, urban blight, and drug abuse can lead to family disorganization and disintegration, making it less likely that children will receive the nurturance and support they need to develop more socially adaptive behaviour patterns. Sociocultural theorists believe that such factors may underlie the development of personality disorders, especially antisocial personality disorder.

Define It

self psychology
splitting
symbiotic text

separation-individuation
problem-solving therapy

Recall It*

1. The theorist Heinz Kohut believed that narcissism in early childhood is _____.

    a. normal and sets the stage for healthy development, but only if combined with strict discipline from parents
    b. normal and sets the stage for healthy development, but only when combined with parental empathy
    c. abnormal and should be corrected early before patterns of behaviour become ingrained
    d. abnormal if it involves the child's belief that the world revolves around him or her

2. According to Otto Kernberg, the term *splitting* refers to _____.

    a. failure to individuate one's own identity from that of the maternal figure
    b. failure to develop a clear or cohesive sense of self as a separate person
    c. failure to synthesize contradictory images of good and bad in themselves and others
    d. a tendency to separate parts of the self that meet with social disapproval

3. Clarence has been diagnosed with antisocial personality disorder. According to social-cognitive theorists, his problems are likely to have arisen from _____ when he was a child.

    a. an absence of parental discipline
    b. overcontrol on the part of the parents
    c. a lack of consistency and predictability in his learning experiences
    d. a lack of encouragement for early exploratory behaviour

4. Researchers report links between borderline personality disorder and _____.

    a. birth trauma
    b. death of a parent during early adolescence
    c. childhood trauma
    d. rejection by peers in early adolescence

5. According to Gray's reinforcement sensitivity theory, which neuropsychological system is sensitive to situations that offer both potential rewards and punishments?

    a. the flight or fright system (FFS)
    b. the behavioural approach system (BAS)
    c. the reticular activating system (RAS)
    d. the behavioural inhibition system (BIS)

* Recall It answers can be found on the Companion Website for this text.

Think About It

- Have you known anyone who you believe might fit the profile of an antisocial personality? What factors do you believe may have shaped this individual's personality development? How did the individual's personality affect his or her relationships with others?

TREATMENT

We began the chapter with a quote from the eminent psychologist William James, who suggested that people's personalities seem to be "set in plaster" by a certain age. His view may be especially applicable to many people with personality disorders, who are typically highly resistant to change.

People with personality disorders usually see their behaviour, even maladaptive, self-defeating behaviour, as natural parts of themselves. Although they may be unhappy and distressed, they are unlikely to perceive their own behaviour as causative. Like Marcella on page 298, whom we described as showing features of a histrionic personality disorder, they may condemn others for their problems and believe others, not themselves, need to change. Thus, they usually do not seek help on their own. Or they begrudgingly acquiesce to treatment at the urging of others but drop out or fail to co-operate with a therapist. Or they may go for help when they feel overwhelmed by anxiety or depression and terminate treatment as soon as they find some relief rather than probing more deeply for the underlying causes of their problems. People with personality disorders also tend to respond more poorly to treatment of problems like depression than others, perhaps because of the negative influence of their maladaptive behaviour patterns (Shea, Widiger, & Klein, 1992). For many reasons, observers have widely believed that personality disorders have been difficult to treat, yet recent evidence suggests that both psychodynamic and cognitive-behavioural therapies are equally effective in producing long-term improvement in personality disorders (Leichsenring, Hiller, Weissberg, & Leibing, 2006; Leichsenring & Leibing, 2003; Livesley, 2005).

Psychodynamic Approaches

Psychodynamic approaches are often used to help people with personality disorders become more aware of the roots of their self-defeating behaviour patterns and learn more adaptive ways of relating to others. Progress in therapy may be hampered by difficulties in working therapeutically with people who have personality disorders, especially clients with borderline and narcissistic personality disorders. Psychodynamic therapists often report that people with borderline personality disorder tend to have turbulent relationships with them, sometimes idealizing them, sometimes denouncing them as uncaring. Case studies suggest that therapists feel manipulated and exploited by borderline clients' needs to test their approval, such as by calling them at all hours or threatening suicide. Such clients can be exhausting and frustrating, although some successes have been reported among therapists who can handle clients' demands.

Promising results have been reported based on a brief, structured form of psychodynamic therapy pioneered at New York's Beth Israel Medical Center (Bateman & Fonagy, 2001; Svartberg, Stiles, & Seltzer, 2004; Winston et al., 1991). There, researchers reported that a relatively brief form of psychodynamically oriented psychotherapy that averaged 40 weeks of treatment resulted in significant improvement in symptom complaints and social adjustment of people with personality disorders (Winston et al., 1994). The treatment emphasized interpersonal behaviour and used a more active, confrontational style in addressing clients' defences than is the case in traditional psychoanalysis.

Behaviour Approaches

Behaviour therapists see their task as changing clients' behaviour rather than personality structures. Many behaviour theorists do not think in terms of clients' "personalities" at all, but rather in terms of acquired maladaptive behaviour that is maintained by reinforcement contingencies. Behaviour therapists therefore focus on attempting to replace maladaptive behaviour with adaptive behaviour through techniques such as extinction, modelling, and reinforcement. If clients are taught behaviour likely to be reinforced by other people, the new behaviour may well be maintained.

Behavioural marital therapists, for example, may encourage clients not to reinforce their spouses' histrionic behaviour. Techniques for treating social phobia, such as those described in Chapter 5, have also been of benefit in treating people with avoidant personality disorder (Renneberg, Goldstein, Phillips, & Chambless, 1990). This may include social-skills training to help clients function more effectively in social situations, such as dating and meeting new people. Cognitive methods may be incorporated to help socially avoidant individuals offset catastrophizing beliefs, such as the exaggerated fear of being shot down or rejected by dates.

Despite the difficulties in treating borderline personality disorder, two groups of therapists headed by Aaron Beck (e.g., Beck, Freeman, Davis, & Associates, 2003) and Marsha Linehan (Koerner & Linehan 2002; Linehan, 1993) report promising results using cognitive-behaviour techniques specifically adapted to the problems encountered in working with clients with borderline personality disorder. Beck's approach focuses on helping the individual correct cognitive distortions that underlie tendencies to see oneself and others as either all good or all bad. Linehan's technique, called *dialectical* behaviour therapy (DBT), combines behaviour therapy and supportive psychotherapy. Behaviour techniques are used to help clients develop more effective social skills and problem-solving skills, which can help improve their relationships with others and their ability to cope with negative events. Because people with borderline personality disorder tend to be overly sensitive to even the slightest cues of rejection, therapists provide continuing acceptance and support, even when clients push the limits by becoming manipulative or overly demanding.

Biological Approaches

Drug therapy does not directly treat personality disorders. Antidepressants or anti-anxiety drugs are sometimes used to treat the emotional distress that individuals with personality disorders may encounter, however. Drugs do not alter the long-standing patterns of maladaptive behaviour that may give rise to distress. However, a study indicates that the antidepressant Prozac can reduce aggressive behaviour and irritability in impulsive and aggressive individuals with personality disorders (Coccaro & Kavoussi, 1997; Rivas-Vazquez & Blais, 2002). Researchers suspect that impulsive aggressive behaviour may be related to serotonin deficiencies. Prozac and similar drugs act to increase the availability of serotonin in the synaptic connections in the brain.

Canadian Treatment Services

Paris (1998) takes the approach that personality disorders are clusters of traits that can be viewed as amplifications of normal personality traits. The therapy implications of this premise are as such: First, psychotherapy should focus on reducing the extremeness of the traits in part by identifying maladaptive behavioural patterns and bringing them to the attention of the patient. Second, the maladaptive behaviours should be given some historical perspective so that the patient can see how his or her behaviour is shaped by past experiences more than current realities and how this leads to inappropriate consequences. Third, treatment involves change. Patients are given the skills to practise alternative and more adaptive behaviour patterns. Still, the treatment goals for patients with personality disorders remain modest, and therapy sessions should be spaced out because their chronic nature precludes quick change.

Because of the diversity of problems associated with personality disorders, no single therapy modality works with all patients. Add this to the cost-containment constraints on mental health services across Canada and the need for service-delivery mechanisms that must be comprehensive and flexible yet efficient and effective (Links, 1998). Livesley (2005) suggests that just such a system of care for personality-disordered patients needs to be grounded in evidence-based therapies and it requires an integrated and systematic approach. Treatment phases would focus on safety and crisis support (e.g., telephone and mobile crisis support and hospital emergency support), containment of psychological distress through continuing care (e.g., outpatient treatment, daycare, and community-based care), control and regulation (e.g., improving self-management skills, coping skills, and problem-solving skills), exploration and change (e.g., changing maladaptive beliefs and interpersonal behaviours), and long-term treatment that focuses on the integration of clear boundaries between self and others (e.g., through goal-setting and experimenting with new behaviours).

Much remains to be learned about working with people who have personality disorders. The major challenges involve recruiting people who do not see themselves as being disordered into treatment and prompting them to develop insight into their self-defeating or injurious behaviour. Current efforts to help such people are too often reminiscent of an old couplet:

> He that complies against his will,
> Is of his own opinion still.
>
> SAMUEL BUTLER, HUDIBRAS

In this chapter, we have considered a number of problems in which people act out on maladaptive impulses yet fail to see how their behaviour is disrupting their lives. In the next chapter, we explore other maladaptive behaviours that are frequently connected with lack of self-insight: behaviours involving substance abuse.

Treatment

Review It

- **How do therapists approach the treatment of personality disorders?** Experts from different schools of therapy try to assist people with personality disorders to gain better awareness of their self-defeating behaviour patterns and learn more adaptive ways of relating to others. Despite the difficulties in working therapeutically with these clients, promising results are emerging from the use of relatively short-term psychodynamic therapy and cognitive-behaviour treatment approaches. The delivery of mental health services across Canada needs to be comprehensive and flexible yet efficient and effective.

Recall It*

1. A therapist helps a client with a personality disorder explore the childhood roots of the problem and develop more adaptive methods of relating to others. This therapist is probably a _____ therapist.

   a. psychodynamic
   b. behaviour
   c. cognitive
   d. humanistic

2. _____ is a technique that combines behaviour therapy and supportive psychotherapy in the treatment of borderline personality disorder.

   a. Object-relations therapy
   b. Cognitive restructuring
   c. Attachment therapy
   d. Dialectical behaviour therapy

3. Research points to links between the type of impulsive aggressive behaviour seen in some types of personality disorders and deficiencies in _____.

   a. epinephrine
   b. acetylcholine
   c. serotonin
   d. dopamine

4. Evidence suggests that the drug _____ may help reduce aggressive and irritable behaviour in individuals with personality disorders who have difficulties with aggressive and impulsive behaviour.

   a. Valium
   b. Lithium
   c. Haldol
   d. Prozac

5. Paris suggests that a comprehensive and flexible system of care for personality-disordered patients requires the following: crisis support, continuing care, psychoeducational programs for family members, and other integrated types of care such as _____.

   a. substance-abuse therapy
   b. antipsychotic drug therapy
   c. intensive brief therapy
   d. expanded hospital care

* Recall It answers can be found on the Companion Website for this text.

Think About It

- What factors make it difficult to treat people with personality disorders? If you were a therapist, how might you attempt to overcome these difficulties?

WEBLINKS

Psych Links
www.psychlinks.ca/pages/personalitydisorder.htm
An Ottawa psychologist developed this website, which provides links to mental health and self-help resources, including personality disorders.

Personality Disorders
www.phac-aspc.gc.ca/publicat/miic-mmac/pdf/chap_5_e.pdf
This site links to a chapter on personality disorders from Health Canada's *A Report on Mental Illness in Canada*.

Personality Profile Comparisons Between Homeless and Housed Adults
www.camh.net/hsrcu/pdfs/APHA99pp97.pdf
This site from the Centre for Addiction and Mental Health (CAMH) looks at psychological disorders in homeless people.

Internet Mental Health
http://mentalhealth.com/p20-grp.html
This site includes a list of personality disorders linked to relevant information about description, diagnosis, treatment, and research.

Mental Help Net
mentalhelp.net/poc/center_index.php?id=8
This site includes a list of personality disorders linked to information about symptoms and treatment.

Personality Disorders

Types of Personality Disorders

Types of abnormal behaviour patterns involving excessively rigid patterns of behaviour, or ways of relating to others, that ultimately become self-defeating because their rigidity prevents adjustment to external demands.

Personality Disorders Characterized by Odd or Eccentric Behaviour

Paranoid Personality Disorder
- Persistent suspiciousness of the motives of others, but not to the point of holding clear-cut delusions

Schizoid Personality Disorder
- Persistent lack of interest in social relationships, flattened affect, and social withdrawal

Schizotypal Personality Disorder
- Eccentricities or oddities of thought and behaviour but without clearly psychotic features

Personality Disorders Characterized by Dramatic, Emotional, or Erratic Behaviour

Antisocial Personality Disorder
- Chronic pattern of antisocial and irresponsible behaviour and lack of remorse

Borderline Personality Disorder
- Abrupt shifts in mood, lack of a coherent sense of self, and unpredictable, impulsive behaviour

Histrionic Personality Disorder
- Excessive need to be the centre of attention and to receive reassurance, praise, and approval from others. Such persons often appear overly dramatic and emotional in their behaviour

Narcissistic Personality Disorder
- Adoption of an inflated self-image and demands for constant attention and admiration, among other features

Personality Disorders Characterized by Anxious or Fearful Behaviour

Avoidant Personality Disorder
- Avoidance of social relationships due to fears of rejection

Dependent Personality Disorder
- Difficulties making independent decisions and overly dependent behaviour

Obsessive-Compulsive Personality Disorder
- Rigid ways of relating to others, perfectionistic tendencies, lack of spontaneity, and excessive attention to details

Problems with the Classification of Personality Disorders

Undetermined Reliability and Validity
- The reliability and validity of the definitions used in the DSM-IV remains to be fully tested

Problems Distinguishing Axis I from Axis II Disorders
- The assumption that personality disorders are discriminable from clinical syndromes like anxiety or depressive disorders is questionable

Overlap Among Disorders
- Although some personality disorders have distinct features, many appear to share common traits

Difficulty in Distinguishing Between Variations in Normal Behaviour and Abnormal Behaviour
- Personality disorders involve traits that, in lesser degrees, describe the behaviour of most normal individuals

Sexist Bias
- Diagnostic criteria for personality disorders label stereotypical feminine behaviour as pathological with greater frequency than is the case with stereotypical masculine behaviour

Theoretical Perspectives

Psychodynamic Perspectives

- *Self psychology:* Heinz Kohut's theory that describes processes that normally lead to the achievement of a cohesive sense of self.
- *Object-relations theory:* Margaret Mahler used the term *symbiotic* to describe the state of oneness that normally exists between mother and infant in which the infant's identity is fused with the mother's. Mahler's *separation-individuation* is the process by which young children come to separate psychologically from their mothers and come to perceive themselves as separate and distinct persons.

Learning Perspectives

- Focus more on the acquisition of behaviour than on the notion of enduring personality traits. Many important experiences occur in childhood that shape the development of the maladaptive habits of relating to others that constitute personality disorders.

Family Perspectives

- Disturbances in family relationships underlie the development of personality disorders.

Cognitive-Behavioural Perspectives

- Albert Bandura noted that children acquire skills, including aggressive skills, by observing the behaviour of others. The ways in which people with personality disorders interpret their social experiences influence their behaviour.

Biological Perspectives

- Genetics plays a role in varying degrees in the development of traits that underlie personality disorders.
- Jeffrey Gray's *Reinforcement Sensitivity Theory* is based on the Behavioural Approach System (BAS), the Fight-Flight-Freeze System (FFFS), and the Behavioural Inhibition System (BIS).

Sociocultural Views

- Social conditions contribute to the development of the behaviour patterns identified as personality disorders.

Treatment

Psychodynamic Approaches

- Help people with personality disorders become more aware of the roots of their self-defeating behaviour patterns and learn more adaptive ways of relating to others.

Behaviour Approaches

- Focus on replacing maladaptive behaviour with adaptive behaviour through techniques such as extinction, modelling, and reinforcement. If clients are taught behaviours that are likely to be reinforced by other people, the new behaviour may well be maintained.

Biological Approaches

- Drug therapy does not directly treat personality disorders. Antidepressants or anti-anxiety drugs are sometimes used to treat the emotional distress that individuals with personality disorders may encounter.

Canadian Treatment Services

- John Livesley proposes a systematic, integrated, multi-perspective, evidence-based treatment approach.

Substance Abuse and Dependence

Did You Know That...

See the underlined text on the pages indicated below for more information on these interesting and often misunderstood facts.

- You can become psychologically dependent on a drug without becoming physically addicted? (p. 328)

- Alcohol "goes to women's heads" more rapidly than men's? (p. 331)

- Light to moderate alcohol intake is associated with a reduced risk of heart disease and lower death rates? (p. 336)

- Coca-Cola originally contained cocaine? (p. 338)

- Habitual smoking is a form of physical addiction, not just a bad habit? (p. 340)

- Being able to "hold your liquor" better than most people may put you at risk of developing a drinking problem? (p. 348)

- A widely used treatment for heroin addiction involves the substitution of another addictive drug? (p. 356)

THE PLANET IS A supermarket of psychoactive chemicals or drugs. The Western world is flooded with substances that alter the mood and twist perceptions—substances that lift you up, cool you down, and turn you upside down. Many people use these substances because their friends do. Some adolescents use them because their parents and authority figures tell them not to. Some users are seeking pleasure or temporary relief from emotional pain. Others are searching for inner truth.

Throughout North America, psychoactive drugs are widely used. A recent Ontario survey revealed that 45% of people aged 15 and older had used marijuana at some point in their lives, and 79% had used alcohol (Adlaf, Begin, & Sawka, 2005). According to the survey, compared to marijuana and alcohol, the lifetime use of other substances is less common: hallucinogens, 11%; cocaine, 11%; amphetamines (speed), 6%; MDMA (ecstasy), 4%; and heroin, 1%. Some people consume multiple substances, which is called *polydrug use*. To illustrate, consider the following study conducted by members of Robert Pihl's research group at McGill University (Barrett, Gross, Garand, & Pihl, 2005). Pihl is an internationally acclaimed substance-abuse researcher. He and his colleagues conducted a survey of drug use of 186 people who attended "raves" in Montreal. Most participants were in their early 20s. About 80% reported using multiple psychoactive substances (excluding tobacco) at the most recent rave they attended. Cannabis, alcohol, ecstasy, amphetamines, cocaine, ketamine (Special K), and GHB (gamma-hydroxybutyrate) were the most frequently used. Frequent rave attendees tended to use more of these substances than infrequent attendees. Later in this chapter, we will discuss the brain damage and other harmful effects of these drugs, especially when used repeatedly and in large quantities.

The old standby, alcohol, is the most popular drug on campus—whether the campus is a high school or university. In fact, 90% Canadian university students report using alcohol within the past year, as compared to an estimated 25% to 33% who report using any illicit drug (CCSA/CAMH, 1999; Gliksman, Adlaf, Demers, Newton-Taylor, & Schmidt, 2000). Under certain conditions, the use of substances that affect mood and behaviour is normal enough, at least as gauged by statistical frequency and social standards. It is normal to start the day with caffeine in the form of coffee or tea, to take wine or coffee with meals, to meet friends for a drink after work, and to end the day with a nightcap. Many of us take prescription drugs that calm us down or ease our pain. Flooding the bloodstream with nicotine by means of smoking is normal in the sense that about one in five Canadians smoke (Health Canada, 2001). Some psychoactive substances are illegal and are used illicitly, like cocaine, marijuana, and heroin. Others are available by prescription, like minor tranquillizers, amphetamines, and opiate analgesics. Still others are available without prescription or over the counter, like tobacco (which contains nicotine, a mild stimulant) and alcohol (which is a depressant). The most widely and easily accessible substances—tobacco and alcohol—cause more deaths through sickness and accidents than all illicit drugs combined.

Table 9.1 on page 324 shows some results of surveys of people of various age groups across Canada. Such surveys suggest prevalence of illicit drug use has remained roughly stable over the past two decades (e.g., CCSA/CAMH, 1999), although the prevalence of marijuana use may increase if legalized.

The prevalence of tobacco use has declined to some extent over the past few decades (CCSA/CAMH, 1999; Health Canada, 2001). To illustrate, in 1965 a total of 61% of men and 38% of women were smokers. In 2001, these figures dropped to 25% and 20% respectively

(Health Canada, 2001). The decline is likely due to a range of factors, including government legislation banning smoking in various public places, restrictions on the sale of tobacco to minors, warnings on tobacco packages, and public health campaigns emphasizing the harmful effects of smoking.

Although there has been some decline in overall alcohol consumption over the years (CCSA/CAMH, 1999), problem drinking, especially binge drinking, remains widespread on university campuses and elsewhere in society. A binge drinker is someone who reports consuming five or more drinks (for men) or four or more drinks (for women) on one occasion during the preceding two-week period. A 1998 survey of sixteen Canadian universities found that 63% of students reported having five or more drinks on a single occasion, and 35% had eight or more drinks. On average, students consumed five or more drinks about twice a month (Gliksman et al., 2000). In other words, the average student was binge drinking every two weeks. The prevalence of binge drinking is higher in male than female students (Adler, 1994; Wechsler et al., 1994). The prevalence of alcohol dependence appears to be rising, due largely to increases in adolescent alcohol abuse leading eventually to outright dependence (Nelson, Heath, & Kessler, 1998).

TABLE 9.1

Drug Use in the Past Year for Selected Canadian Age Groups (in percentages)

Drug	Survey Year	Age Group							
		15–19	20–24	25–34	35–44	45–54	55–64	65–74	75+
Alcohol	1996–97	71.3	85.7	83.2	82.0	79.1	73.1	63.9	51.9
Tobacco[*]	1996–97	29.2	35.1	33.7	33.4	28.3	23.7	17.2	11.2
Marijuana	1994	24.2	19.3	9.6	5.8	1.4	0.7	0.2	—
LSD, Amphetamines, or Heroin	1994	7.0	2.8	0.6	0.2	—	—	—	—
Cocaine (including Crack)	1994	1.6	1.4	1.0	0.8	0.1	0.1	—	—

[*]Current smokers.
— Indicates that percentages were too small to be reliably estimated.

Source: Adapted from Canadian Centre on Substance Abuse and Centre for Addiction and Mental Health (1999). Canadian profile: Alcohol, tobacco and other drugs. Ottawa, ON: Author.

substance-use disorders Pattern of maladaptive behaviour involving the use of a psychoactive substance. Substance-use disorders include substance-abuse disorders and substance-dependence disorders.

substance-induced disorders Disorders induced by the use of psychoactive substances, including intoxication, withdrawal syndromes, mood disorders, delirium, and amnesia.

psychoactive Describing chemical substances or drugs that have psychological effects.

intoxication State of drunkenness.

CLASSIFICATION OF SUBSTANCE-RELATED DISORDERS

The DSM-IV classifies substance-related disorders into two major categories: **substance-use disorders** and **substance-induced disorders**. Substance-use disorders involve maladaptive use of **psychoactive** substances. These types of disorders include substance abuse and substance dependence. Substance-induced disorders involve disorders that can be induced by using psychoactive substances such as intoxication, withdrawal syndromes, mood disorders, delirium, dementia, amnesia, psychotic disorders, anxiety disorders, sexual dysfunctions, and sleep disorders. Different substances have different effects, so some of these disorders may apply to one, a few, or nearly all substances.

Substance **intoxication** is a state of drunkenness or "being high." These effects largely reflect the chemical actions of the psychoactive substances. The particular features of intoxication depend on which drug is ingested, the dose, the user's biological reactivity, and—to some degree—the user's expectations. Signs of intoxication often include confusion, belligerence, impaired judgment, inattention, and impaired motor and spatial skills. Extreme intoxication from the use of alcohol, cocaine, opiates, and PCP (phencyclidine) can even result in death (yes, you can die from an alcohol overdose), either because of the substance's biochemical effects or because of behaviour patterns—such as suicide—that are connected with psychological pain or impaired judgment brought on by use of the drug.

Substance Abuse and Dependence

Where does substance use end and abuse begin? According to the DSM, substance abuse involves a pattern of recurrent use that leads to damaging consequences. Damaging consequences may involve failing to meet one's major role responsibilities (e.g., as a student, worker, or parent), putting oneself in situations where substance use is physically dangerous (e.g., combining driving with substance use), encountering repeated problems with the law arising from substance use (e.g., multiple arrests for substance-related behaviour), or having recurring social or interpersonal problems because of substance use (e.g., repeatedly getting into fights when drinking).

When people repeatedly miss school or work because they are drunk or "sleeping it off," their behaviour may fit the definition of **substance abuse**. A single incident of excessive drinking at a friend's wedding would not qualify. Nor would regular consumption of low-to-moderate amounts of alcohol be considered abusive, so long as it is not connected with any impairment in functioning. Neither the amount nor the type of drug ingested, nor whether or not the drug is illicit, is key to defining substance abuse according to the DSM. Rather, the determining feature of substance abuse is whether a pattern of drug-using behaviour becomes repeatedly linked to damaging consequences.

Substance abuse may continue for a long period of time or progress to **substance dependence**, a more severe type of substance-use disorder in which abuse is associated with physiological signs of dependence (tolerance or withdrawal) *and/or* compulsive use of a substance. People who are compulsive users lack control over their drug use. They may be aware of how their drug use is disrupting their lives or damaging their health, but feel helpless or powerless to stop using drugs, even though they may want to. By the time they become dependent on a given drug, they've given over much of their lives to obtaining and using it. The diagnostic features associated with substance dependence are listed in Table 9.2.

Repeated use of a substance may alter the body's physiological reactions, leading to the development of *tolerance* or a physical **withdrawal syndrome** (see Table 9.2). Tolerance is a state of physical habituation to a drug such that with frequent use, higher doses are needed to achieve the same effect. A withdrawal syndrome (also called an *abstinence syndrome*) involves a characteristic cluster of withdrawal symptoms that occur when a dependent person abruptly stops using a particular substance following a period of heavy, prolonged use. People who experience a withdrawal syndrome often return to using the substance in order to relieve the discomfort associated with withdrawal, which serves to maintain the addictive pattern. Withdrawal symptoms vary with the particular type of drug. With alcohol dependence, typical withdrawal symptoms include dryness in the mouth, nausea or vomiting, weakness, **tachycardia**, anxiety and depression, headaches, insomnia, elevated blood pressure, and fleeting hallucinations.

In some cases of chronic alcoholism, withdrawal produces a state of **delirium tremens** or DTs. The DTs are usually limited to chronic, heavy users of alcohol who dramatically lower their intake of alcohol after many years of steady drinking. The DTs involve intense autonomic hyperactivity (profuse sweating and tachycardia) and **delirium**—a state of mental confusion characterized by incoherent speech, **disorientation**, and extreme restlessness. Terrifying hallucinations—frequently of creepy-crawly animals (worms, snakes, etc.)—may also be present. Substances that tend to lead to withdrawal syndromes include alcohol, opiates, cocaine, amphetamines, sedatives and barbiturates, nicotine, and antianxiety agents (minor tranquillizers). Marijuana and hallucinogens like LSD are not recognized as producing a withdrawal syndrome because of a lack of evidence that abrupt

substance abuse Continued use of a psychoactive drug despite the knowledge that it is causing or contributing to a persistent or recurrent social, occupational, psychological, or physical problem.

substance dependence Impaired control over the use of a psychoactive drug and continued or even increased use despite awareness that the substance is disrupting one's life. Substance dependence is often characterized by physiological dependence.

withdrawal syndrome Characteristic cluster of withdrawal symptoms following the sudden reduction or abrupt cessation of use of a psychoactive substance after physiological dependence has developed.

tachycardia Abnormally rapid heartbeat.

delirium tremens Withdrawal syndrome that often occurs following a sudden decrease or cessation of drinking in chronic alcoholics that is characterized by extreme restlessness, sweating, disorientation, and hallucinations. Abbreviated *DTs*.

delirium State of mental confusion, disorientation, and extreme difficulty in focusing attention.

disorientation State of mental confusion or lack of awareness with respect to time, place, or the identity of oneself or others.

TABLE 9.2

Diagnostic Features of Substance Dependence

Substance dependence is defined as a maladaptive pattern of use that results in "significant impairment or distress," as typified by the following features occurring within the same year:

(1) Tolerance for the substance, as shown by either
   (a) the need for increased amounts of the substance to achieve the desired effect or intoxication, or
   (b) marked reduction in the effects of continuing to ingest the same amounts.

(2) Withdrawal symptoms, as shown by either
   (a) the withdrawal syndrome that is considered characteristic for the substance, or
   (b) the taking of the same substance (or a closely related substance, as when methadone is substituted for heroin) to relieve or to prevent withdrawal symptoms.

(3) Taking larger amounts of the substance, or for longer periods of time than the individual intended (e.g., person had desired to take only one drink, but after taking the first, continues drinking until severely intoxicated).

(4) Persistent desire to cut down or control intake of substance, or lack of success in trying to exercise self-control.

(5) Spending a good deal of time in activities directed toward obtaining the substance (e.g., visiting several physicians to obtain prescriptions or engaging in theft), in actually ingesting the substance, or in recovering from its use. In severe cases, the individual's daily life revolves around substance use.

(6) The individual has reduced or given up important social, occupational, or recreational activities due to substance use (e.g., person withdraws from family events in order to indulge in drug use).

(7) Substance use is continued despite evidence of persistent or recurrent psychological or physical problems either caused or exacerbated by its use (e.g., repeated arrests for driving while intoxicated).

Source: Adapted from the DSM-IV (APA, 2000a).

withdrawal from these substances reliably produces clinically significant withdrawal effects (APA, 2000a).

Tolerance and withdrawal syndromes are often, but not necessarily, associated with substance dependence. Substance dependence sometimes involves a pattern of compulsive use without the development of the physiological features of dependence (tolerance and/or a withdrawal syndrome). For example, people may become compulsive users of marijuana, especially when they come to rely on the drug to help them cope with the stresses of

Two of the many faces of alcohol use—and abuse. Alcohol is our most widely used—and abused—drug. Many people use alcohol to celebrate achievements and happy occasions, as in the photograph on the left. Unfortunately, like the man in the photograph on the right, some people use alcohol to drown their sorrows, which may only worsen their problems. Where does substance use end and abuse begin? According to the DSM, use becomes abuse when it leads to damaging consequences.

daily life. Yet they may not require larger amounts of the substance to get "high" or experience distressing withdrawal symptoms when they cease using it. In most cases, however, substance dependence and physiological features of dependence occur together. Despite the fact that the DSM considers substance abuse and dependence to be distinct diagnostic categories, the boundary between the two is not always clear.

One of the most reliable estimates of the prevalence of substance dependence comes from the DSM-IV (APA, 2000a), which synthesizes data from the United States, Canada, and other countries. Estimates from the DSM-IV and elsewhere suggest that about 15% of adults in Canada and the States have a history of alcohol dependence (APA, 2000a; Ross, 1995). Up to 25% have developed nicotine dependence through the repeated use of tobacco products, most usually cigarettes (APA, 2000a). About 7.5% have developed a dependence on an illicit drug, inhalant, or nonprescription use of tranquillizers or other psychiatric (psychotropic) drugs. Table 9.3 gives the lifetime prevalence of drug dependence for other types of drugs. The table shows the estimates from the DSM-IV (APA, 2000a) and, for comparison purposes, the results from one of the most extensive epidemiologic surveys done in Canada: Roger Bland's Edmonton survey. The results of this survey are quite similar to the estimates in the DSM-IV, although the prevalence of cocaine dependence is lower in the Edmonton survey, corresponding to the lower prevalence of cocaine problems in Canada compared to the United States (APA, 2000a; CCSA/CAMH, 1999).

People can abuse or become dependent on more than one psychoactive substance at the same time. People who abuse or become dependent on heroin, for instance, may also abuse or become dependent on other drugs, such as alcohol, cocaine, or stimulants—simultaneously or successively. In fact, surveys from Canada and elsewhere indicate that most illicit users of opioids such as heroin are polydrug users involved in the intensive co-use of crack or cocaine (or both) (Fischer & Rehm, 2006). People who engage in these patterns of polydrug abuse face increased potential of harmful overdoses when drugs are used in combination. Moreover, "successful" treatment of one form of abuse may not affect, and in some cases could even exacerbate, abuse of other drugs.

Addiction, Physiological Dependence, and Psychological Dependence

The DSM uses the terms *substance abuse* and *substance dependence* to classify people whose use of these substances impairs their functioning. It does not use the term *addiction* to describe these problems, yet the concept of addiction is widespread among professionals and laypeople alike. But what is meant by addiction?

TABLE 9.3

Lifetime Prevalence of Drug Dependence by Type of Drug (in percentages)

Drug	Edmonton Survey (Russell et al., 1994)	Estimates from Canada and U.S. (APA, 2000)
Tobacco	—	up to 25.0
Alcohol	16.5	15.0
Marijuana	5.9	5.0
Amphetamines	1.5	1.5
Opiates	0.7	0.7
Barbiturates or sedatives	0.7	< 1.0
Hallucinogens	0.5	0.6
Cocaine	0.5	2.0

— Not assessed.

Source: Based on J.M. Russell, S. C. Newman, & R. C. Bland (1994). Drug abuse and dependence. *Acta Psychiatrica Scandinavica, Suppl. 376*, 54–62; American Psychiatric Association (2000a). *Diagnostic and Statistical Manual of Mental Disorders* (4th ed., text revision). Washington, DC: Author.

addiction Impaired control over the use of a chemical substance accompanied by physiological dependence.

physiological dependence State of physical dependence on a drug in which the user's body comes to depend on a steady supply.

psychological dependence Reliance, as on a substance, although one may not be physiologically dependent.

People define addiction in different ways. For our purposes, we define **addiction** as the habitual or compulsive use of a drug accompanied by evidence of physiological dependence. **Physiological dependence** means that one's body has changed as a result of the regular use of a psychoactive drug such that it comes to depend on a steady supply of the substance. The major signs of physiological dependence involve the development of tolerance and/or an abstinence syndrome. A **psychological dependence** involves a pattern of compulsive use associated with impaired control over the use of a drug.

Although physical addiction is generally associated with substance dependence, some cases of dependence involve compulsive patterns of using drugs without physical signs of addiction (Schuckit et al., 1999). As we noted earlier, you can become psychologically dependent on a drug without developing a physiological dependence or addiction.

On the other hand, people may become physiologically dependent on a drug but not become a compulsive user or psychologically dependent. For example, people recuperating from surgery are often given narcotics derived from opium as painkillers. Some may develop signs of physiological dependence—such as tolerance and a withdrawal syndrome—but they likely would not become habitual users or show a lack of control over the use of these drugs.

In recent years, the concept of addiction has also extended beyond the abuse of chemical substances to apply to many habitual forms of maladaptive behaviour, such as pathological gambling (Ladouceur, 2002). In the vernacular, we hear of people being addicted to love or shopping or to almost anything. There have even been suggestions that people can become addicted to the Internet (Beard, 2005), whereby people (usually males) lose sleep, miss meals, experience social isolation, and fail to attend classes or neglect work responsibilities because of excessive use of the Internet, such as for the purpose of using chat rooms, playing online games, or visiting gambling or sexual websites (Chou, Condron, & Belland, 2005). These people are excessively preoccupied with using the Internet, to the exclusion of everything else in their lives, and they seem to experience symptoms of withdrawal (anxiety, depression) when they are separated from it (Niemz, Griffiths, & Banyard, 2005). Preoccupation with the Internet and other so-called addictions do not involve physiological dependence on a chemical substance. In this chapter, we limit the term *addiction* to the habitual use of substances that produce physiological dependence.

Pathways to Drug Dependence

Although the progression to substance dependence varies from person to person, some common pathways can be described according to the following stages (Weiss & Mirin, 1994):

1. *Experimentation.* During the stage of experimentation, or occasional use, the drug temporarily makes users feel good, even euphoric. Users feel in control and believe they can stop at any time.

2. *Routine use.* During the next stage, a period of routine use, people begin to structure their lives around the pursuit and use of drugs. Denial plays a major role at this stage, as users mask the negative consequences of their behaviour to themselves and others. Values change. What had formerly been important, such as family and work, comes to matter less than the drugs.

   As routine drug use continues, problems mount. Users devote more of their resources to drugs. Family bank accounts are emptied, "temporary" loans are sought from friends and relatives for trumped-up reasons, and family heirlooms and jewellery are sold to pawnbrokers for a fraction of their value. Lying and manipulation become a way of life to cover up the drug use. The husband sells the television set to a pawnbroker and forces the front door open to make it look like a burglary. The wife claims to have been robbed at knifepoint to explain the disappearance of a gold chain or engagement ring. Family relationships become strained as the mask of denial shatters and the consequences of drug abuse become apparent: days lost from work, unexplained absences from home, rapid mood shifts, depletion of family finances, failure to pay bills, stealing from family members, and absence from family gatherings or children's birthday parties.

3. *Addiction or dependence.* Routine use becomes addiction or dependence when users feel powerless to resist drugs, either because they want to experience their effects or to avoid the consequences of withdrawal. Little or nothing else matters at this stage, as seen in the case of Eugene, a 41-year-old architect, who related the following conversation with his wife:

> She had just caught me with cocaine again after I had managed to convince her that I hadn't used in over a month. Of course I had been tooting (snorting) almost every day, but I had managed to cover my tracks a little better than usual. So she said to me that I was going to have to make a choice—either cocaine or her. Before she finished the sentence, I knew what was coming, so I told her to think carefully about what she was going to say. It was clear to me that there wasn't a choice. I love my wife, but I'm not going to choose *anything* over cocaine. It's sick, but that's what things have come to. Nothing and nobody comes before my coke (Weiss & Mirin, 1994, p. 55).

STUDY BREAK

Classification of Substance-Related Disorders

Review It

- **How does the DSM distinguish between substance-abuse disorders and substance-dependence disorders?** According to the DSM, substance-abuse disorders involve a pattern of recurrent use of a substance that repeatedly leads to damaging consequences. Substance-dependence disorders involve impaired control over the use of a substance and often include features of physiological dependence on the substance, as manifested by the development of tolerance or an abstinence syndrome.

- **What are meant by the terms addiction and psychological dependence?** Although various people use the term *addiction* differently, it is employed here to refer to the habitual or compulsive use of a substance together with the development of physiological dependence. Psychological dependence involves compulsive use of a substance, with or without the development of physiological dependence.

Define It

psychoactive
substance-use disorders
substance-induced disorders
intoxication
substance abuse
substance dependence
withdrawal syndrome

tachycardia
delirium tremens
delirium
disorientation
addiction
physiological dependence
psychological dependence

Recall It*

1. In the DSM system, disorders involving maladaptive patterns of use of psychoactive substances are called _____ disorders.

   a. substance-use
   b. substance-induced
   c. substance-reaction
   d. psychoactive-drug

2. _____ is not known to produce a withdrawal syndrome.

   a. Alcohol
   b. LSD
   c. Heroin
   d. Cocaine

3. The criteria for determining whether a person's use of a drug crosses the line from substance use to abuse involves _____.

   a. whether the person begins using illegal drugs
   b. the amount of the drugs the person uses
   c. the number of times the person uses drugs
   d. a repeated pattern in which drug use becomes connected to damaging consequences

4. _____ involves a process of physical habituation to the repeated use of a drug such that higher and higher dosages of the drug are needed to achieve a similar effect.

   a. Tolerance
   b. Dependence
   c. Potentiation
   d. Reverse tolerance

5. Carol has been using cocaine to the point that she experiences withdrawal symptoms when she tries to quit using it. She has become _____ on cocaine.

   a. psychologically dependent
   b. physiologically dependent
   c. both psychologically and physiologically dependent
   d. neither psychologically nor physiologically dependent

* Recall It answers can be found on the Companion Website for this text.

Think About It

• What is the basis for determining where drug use becomes abuse or dependence? Have you or someone you know crossed the line between use and abuse?

• Do you or someone you know show evidence of non-chemical forms of addiction, such as compulsive shopping, gambling, or Internet addiction? How is this behaviour affecting your (or his or her) life? What can you (or he or she) do about overcoming it?

DRUGS OF ABUSE

Drugs of abuse are generally classified into three major groupings: (1) depressants, such as alcohol and opiates; (2) stimulants, such as amphetamine and cocaine; and (3) hallucinogens.

Depressants

depressant Drug that lowers the level of activity of the central nervous system.

A **depressant** is a drug that slows down or curbs the activity of the central nervous system. It reduces feelings of tension and anxiety, causes our movements to become sluggish, and impairs our cognitive processes. In high doses, depressants can arrest vital functions and cause death. The most widely used depressant, alcohol, can lead to death when taken in large amounts because of its depressant effects on respiration (breathing). Other effects are specific to the particular kind of depressant. For example, some depressants, like heroin, produce a "rush" of pleasure. Here we will consider several of the major types of depressants.

Alcohol You may not have thought of alcohol as a drug, perhaps because it is so popular, or maybe because it is ingested by drinking rather than by smoking or injection. But alcoholic beverages like wine, beer, and hard liquor contain a depressant called *ethyl alcohol* (or *ethanol*). The concentration of the drug varies with the type of beverage (wine and beer have less pure alcohol per ounce than distilled spirits such as whiskey, gin, or vodka). Alcohol is classified as a depressant drug because it has biochemical effects similar to those of a class of minor tranquillizers, the benzodiazepines, which include the well-known drugs diazepam (Valium) and chlordiazepoxide (Librium). We can think of alcohol as a type of over-the-counter tranquillizer.

Alcohol is used in many ways. It is our mealtime relaxant, our party social facilitator, our bedtime sedative. We observe holy days, laud our achievements, and express joyful wishes with alcohol. Adolescents assert their maturity with alcohol. Pediatricians used to swab the painful gums of teething babies with alcohol. Alcohol even deals the death blow to germs on surface wounds and is the active ingredient in some antiseptic mouthwashes. In Western countries like Canada, most adults drink alcohol at least occasionally. Most people who drink do so in moderation, but many develop significant problems with alcohol use (Adlaf et al., 2005). Alcohol is the most widely abused substance in the world. Many lay and professional people use the term *alcoholism* to refer to problems of alcohol dependence. Although definitions of alcoholism vary, we use the term to refer to a state of physical dependence on or addiction to alcohol that is characterized by impaired control over the use of the drug.

The personal and social costs of alcoholism are considerable. In Canada, the economic costs of alcoholism—based on days lost from work, health problems associated with alcoholism, and costs resulting from motor vehicle accidents involving alcohol use—are staggering, amounting to more than $7.5 billion annually according to a 1992 estimate (Dingle, Samtani, Kraatz, & Solomon, 2002). Alcohol abuse is connected with lower productivity, loss of jobs, and downward movement in socioeconomic status. Estimates are that over 20% of homeless people suffer from alcohol dependence (Farrell et al., 2003). Alcohol also plays a part in about 27% of all male suicides and 17% of all female suicides in Canada (Dingle et al., 2002). It is a leading cause of death of young people. Approximately 40% of Canadian teens killed in motor-vehicle accidents have alcohol in their systems (Centre for Addictions Research, BC, 2006).

Alcohol, not cocaine or other drugs, is the drug of choice among young people today and the leading drug of abuse (CCSA/CAMH, 1999; Gliksman et al., 2000). Drinking is so integrated into university life that it has become essentially normative, as much a part of the college experience as attending a weekend hockey or basketball game.

Despite the popular image of alcoholics as skid row drunks, the truth is that only a small minority of people with alcoholism fit that stereotype. The great majority of alcoholics are the type of people you're likely to see every day—your neighbours, co-workers, friends, and members of your own family. They are found in all walks of life and from every social and economic class. Many have families, hold good jobs, and live fairly comfortably. Yet alcoholism can have just as devastating an effect on the well-to-do as the indigent, leading to wrecked careers and ruined marriages, motor-vehicle and other accidents, and severe, life-threatening physical disorders, as well as exacting an enormous emotional toll.

No single drinking pattern is exclusively associated with alcoholism. Some people with alcoholism drink heavily every day; others binge only on weekends. Still others can abstain for lengthy periods of time but periodically "go off the wagon" and engage in episodes of binge drinking that may last for days, weeks, or months.

RISK FACTORS FOR ALCOHOLISM Investigators have identified a number of factors that place people at increased risk for developing alcoholism and alcohol-related problems. These include:

1. *Gender.* The lifetime prevalence of alcohol dependence among women and men is similar according to some studies. For example, a Canadian survey reported that the lifetime prevalence among women and men was 11% and 12% respectively (Lukassen & Beaudet, 2005). However, other studies have found that alcohol abuse and dependence is more common in men (APA, 2000a). The conflicting results may have to do with when the studies were conducted; the gender gap in the prevalence of alcoholism is narrowing, with women catching up to men (Zilberman, Tavares, & el-Guebaly, 2003). This seems to be partly because social drinking has become more acceptable for women. In general, women start drinking several years later than men, but once alcohol abuse or dependence develops in women, the disorder progresses somewhat more rapidly. But in general, the clinical course of alcohol dependence is more similar than different (APA, 2000a).

    Alcohol seems to "go to women's heads" more rapidly than men's. This is apparently because women metabolize less alcohol in the stomach than men do. Why? It appears that women have less of an enzyme that metabolizes alcohol in the stomach (Lieber, 1990). Alcohol then reaches women's circulatory systems and brains relatively intact. <u>This means that gram for gram, women drinkers absorb more alcohol into their bloodstreams than their male counterparts.</u> It is almost as if women were injecting alcohol intravenously. It is not a substance to be trifled with.

2. *Age.* The great majority of cases of alcohol dependence develop in young adulthood, typically before age 40. The typical age of onset is late adolescence (Sher, Grekin, & Williams, 2005). Although alcohol-use disorders tend to develop somewhat later in women than men, women who develop these problems experience health, social, and occupational problems by middle age just like their male counterparts. Although many people who develop alcohol problems tend to "grow out" of them, a significant number of people have lifelong problems (Sher et al., 2005).

3. *Antisocial personality disorder.* Antisocial behaviour in adolescence or adulthood increases the risk of later alcoholism (Sher et al., 2005).
4. *Family history.* The best predictor of problem drinking in adulthood appears to be a family history of alcohol abuse. Family members who drink may act as models and "set a poor example." Moreover, the biological relatives of people with alcohol dependence may also inherit a predisposition that makes them more likely to develop problems with alcohol.
5. *Sociodemographic factors.* Alcohol problems are more common among people of lower income and educational levels and among people living alone (CCSA/CAMH, 1999; Khan, Murray, & Barnes, 2002). In Canada, alcohol and drug dependence are more common among Aboriginal than non-Aboriginal people (Tjepkema, 2002). We further examine ethnic group differences in alcohol use and abuse in the accompanying "Focus on Diversity: Ethnicity and Alcohol Abuse" feature.

CONCEPTIONS OF ALCOHOLISM: DISEASE, MORAL DEFECT, OR BEHAVIOUR PATTERN?
According to the medical perspective, alcoholism is a disease. E. M. Jellinek (1960), a leading proponent of the disease model, believed that alcoholism is a permanent, irreversible condition. Jellinek believed that once a person with alcoholism takes a drink, the biochemical effects of the drug on the brain create an irresistible physical craving for more. Jellinek's ideas have contributed to the view, "once an alcoholic, always an alcoholic." Alcoholics Anonymous (AA), which adopted Jellinek's concepts, views people who suffer from alcoholism as either drinking or "recovering." In other words, alcoholism is never cured. Jellinek's concepts have also supported the idea that "just one drink" will cause the person with alcoholism to "fall off the wagon." In this view, the sole path to recovery is abstinence.

QUESTIONNAIRE

How Do You Know If You Are Hooked?

Are you dependent on alcohol? If you shake and shiver and feel tormented when you go without a drink for a while, the answer is clear enough. Sometimes the clues are more subtle, however.

The following self-test can shed some light on the question. Simply place a check mark in the yes or no column for each item. Then refer to the key at the end of the next Study Break box on pages 345 to 346.

	Yes	No
1. Do you sometimes go on drinking binges?	___	___
2. Do you tend to keep away from your family or friends when you are drinking?	___	___
3. Do you become irritated when your family or friends talk about your drinking?	___	___
4. Do you feel guilty now and then about your drinking?	___	___
5. Do you often regret the things you have said or done when you have been drinking?	___	___

6. Do you find that you fail to keep the promises you make about controlling or cutting down on your drinking?	___	___
7. Do you eat irregularly or not at all when you are drinking?	___	___
8. Do you feel low after drinking?	___	___
9. Do you sometimes miss work or appointments because of drinking?	___	___
10. Do you use more and more to get drunk or high?	___	___

Source: Adapted from *Newsweek*, February 20, 1989, p. 52.

Ethnicity and Alcohol Abuse

Striking cultural differences in alcohol use and abuse have long been evident. Chinese and Jewish populations, for example, are considerably less susceptible to alcohol problems than Irish and some Aboriginal groups (Prince, 2000). In Canada, the Aboriginal population consists of three broad groups: North American Indian, Métis, and Inuit people. They encompass a diverse range of smaller groups, differing from one another in history, culture, and traditions (Tjepkema, 2002). Surveys of people living in First Nations communities reveal that more than 70% of respondents believe alcohol abuse is an important problem in their community (Rogers & Abas, 1988; Statistics Canada, 1993). Alcohol abuse in Aboriginal communities is often associated with other forms of drug abuse, such as inhalant abuse (Gfellner & Hundelby, 1995). Alcohol-related health problems, such as liver disease, are also significantly higher in Aboriginal populations (Scott, 1994).

Taken as a group, Aboriginal Canadians, compared to their non-Aboriginal counterparts, do not have more of a tendency to drink alcohol. But those who do consume alcohol are likely to drink more heavily, even when socioeconomic status is taken into consideration (Haggarty, Cernovsky, Kermeen, & Merskey, 2000; Lavallee & Bourgault, 2000; Tjepkema, 2002). Tjepkema, for example, assessed "heavy drinking" (defined as five or more drinks in a single sitting) in off-reserve Aboriginal and non-Aboriginal Canadians. Fewer Aboriginals than non-Aboriginals were weekly drinkers (27% vs. 38%). The groups did not differ in the proportion of people who were light or abstinent drinkers (both 50%), but Aboriginals had more heavy drinkers (23% vs. 16%). The same pattern was found regardless of whether the respondents lived in urban or rural areas. Similar findings were obtained in a study of women in northern Quebec: alcohol consumption was less frequent among Aboriginal women, but those who did drink consumed higher quantities of alcohol (Lavallee & Bourgault, 2000).

Group differences in alcohol use and abuse have been attributed to psychosocial factors such as cultural or religious attitudes toward drinking. The cultural traditions concerning the use of alcohol in family, religious, and social settings, particularly during childhood, can influence the risk for later alcohol problems (APA, 2000a). Jewish people, for example, tend to expose children to the ritual use of wine within a religious context and to impose strong cultural restraints on excessive and underage drinking.

Psychosocial factors within cultures also may influence drinking patterns. To illustrate, Gfellner and Hundelby (1990) investigated the predictors of drug and alcohol use in a small urban community in Manitoba. The number of a person's friends who used alcohol or drugs was the strongest predictor of alcohol or drug use for both Aboriginal and non-Aboriginal students. Peer attitudes about drug or alcohol use was also a predictor for Aboriginal students (Gfellner & Hundelby, 1990).

Many writers see the prevalence of alcoholism among Aboriginals as a consequence of the forced attempt by European colonists to eradicate tribal language and culture, leading to a loss of cultural identity that sets the stage for alcoholism, drug abuse, and depression. Kahn (1982) explains the greater incidence of psychopathology among Aboriginals in terms of the disruption in traditional culture caused by the appropriation of their lands by European powers and the attempts to sever them from their cultural traditions while denying them full access to the dominant Western culture. Aboriginals have since lived in severe cultural and social disorganization that has resulted in high rates of psychopathology and substance abuse. Beset by such problems, Aboriginal adults are prone to child abuse and neglect. Abuse and neglect contribute to feelings of hopelessness and depression among adolescents, who then seek to escape their feelings through alcohol and other drugs (Berlin, 1987).

Research into the acculturation hypothesis suggests that alcohol and drug abuse is greatest among Aboriginal youths who identify least closely with traditional values. Bicultural youth, consisting of those who felt comfortable within both their traditional culture and the larger society, showed the lowest abuse of alcohol and other drugs. These findings would suggest that the best adjustment (meaning the lowest levels of culture-related stress) is found among youth who have adapted to both cultures. Other factors, such as the poverty faced by many Aboriginals, may also contribute to stress and alcohol and drug abuse.

Biological factors also appear to contribute to ethnic differences in alcohol use and abuse. The low rates of alcohol problems in Asian countries appear to be related to a lack in some Asians of the enzyme aldehyde dehydrogenase, which is involved in the metabolizing of alcohol in the body. Roughly 50% of Asians are at least partially missing the enzyme, compared to only 5% to 15% of Caucasians (APA, 2000a; Prince, 2000). The enzyme may be partially or totally absent—an estimated 10% of Asian people completely lack the enzyme. When they drink alcohol, they experience a flushed face and palpitations, and sometimes nausea, dizziness, and headaches. This reaction can be so intense that it sometimes leads the person to abstain altogether from drinking. The other 40% of Asian people with a relative deficiency of the enzyme have less intense reactions, but still are less likely to develop an alcohol problem (APA, 2000a). The flushing response is evident even in infants (Prince, 2000) and can be a deterrent to alcohol use and abuse. However, the flushing response provides only a modest defence against excessive drinking. Among the Japanese, for example, alcohol abuse has increased considerably in recent years, despite their susceptibility to the flushing response (Prince, 2000).

Alcohol and ethnic diversity. The damaging effects of alcohol abuse appear to be taking the heaviest toll on Canada's First Nations people. Jewish people have relatively low incidences of alcohol-related problems, perhaps because they tend to expose children to the ritual use of wine in childhood and impose strong cultural restraints on excessive drinking. Asian people tend to drink less heavily than most other Canadians, in part because of cultural constraints and possibly because they have less biological tolerance of alcohol, as shown by a greater flushing response.

Although the disease model has achieved prominence and gained wide public acceptance, the nature of alcoholism continues to be debated. For most of history, immoderate drinking was seen as a moral defect. Alcoholism was first considered a disease in the 1960s. Since that time, the campaign to instill this view has been so pervasive that most people now endorse it.

Yet not all professionals regard alcoholism as a medical disease. To some, the term is used as a label to describe a harmful pattern of alcohol ingestion and related behaviours. In this view, the "just-one-drink" hypothesis is not a biochemical inevitability. For these observers, it is instead a common self-fulfilling prophecy, as we see later in the chapter.

PSYCHOLOGICAL EFFECTS OF ALCOHOL The effects of alcohol or other drugs vary from person to person. By and large, they reflect the interaction of (1) the physiological effects of the substances, and (2) our interpretations of those effects. What do most people expect from alcohol? People frequently hold stereotypical expectations that alcohol will reduce states of tension, enhance pleasurable experiences, wash away their worries, and enhance their social skills. But what *does* alcohol actually do?

At a physiological level, alcohol, like the benzodiazepines, appears to heighten the sensitivity of the gamma-aminobutyric acid (GABA) receptor sites (Suzdak, Glowa, Crawley, & Schwartz, 1986). Because GABA is an inhibitory neurotransmitter, increasing the action of GABA reduces overall nervous system activity, producing feelings of relaxation. As people drink, their senses become clouded, and balance and coordination suffer. Still higher doses act on the parts of the brain that regulate involuntary vital functions such as heart rate, respiration rate, and body temperature.

People may do many things when drinking that they would not do when sober, in part because of expectations concerning the drug, and in part because of the drug's effects on the brain. For example, they may become more flirtatious or sexually aggressive or say or do things they later regret. Their behaviour may reflect their expectation that alcohol has liberating effects and provides an external excuse for questionable behaviour. Later, they can claim, "It was the alcohol, not me." The drug may impair the brain's ability to curb impulsive behaviour, perhaps by interfering with information-processing functions (Steele & Southwick, 1985). Although alcohol may make them feel more relaxed and self-confident, it may prevent them from exercising good judgment, which can lead them to make choices they would ordinarily reject, such as engaging in risky sex (Gordon & Carey, 1996). One of the lures of alcohol is that it induces short-term feelings of euphoria and elation that can drown self-doubts and self-criticism. Alcohol may also make them less capable of perceiving the unfortunate consequences of their behaviour. Chronic use, however, may deepen feelings of depression. Alcohol dependence and other substance-use disorders are strongly correlated with depression (Currie et al., 2005; Lukassen & Beaudet, 2005). This correlation exists for various reasons, as described later in this chapter.

Alcohol in increasing amounts can dampen sexual arousal or excitement and impair our ability to perform sexually. As an intoxicant, alcohol also hampers coordination and motor ability and slurs speech. These effects help explain why alcohol use is implicated in so many road fatalities, other accidents, and violent crimes (see Figure 9.1).

PHYSICAL HEALTH AND ALCOHOL Chronic, heavy alcohol use affects virtually every organ and body system either directly or indirectly. Heavy alcohol use is linked to a higher risk of various forms of cancer, such as cancer of the throat, esophagus, larynx, stomach, colon, liver, and possibly cancer of the bowels and breasts (e.g., Fuchs et al., 1995; Kruger & Jerrells, 1992; Reichman, 1994). Heavy drinking is also linked to coronary heart disease, ulcers, hypertension, gout, and pancreatitis (painful inflammation of the pancreas) (CCSA/CAMH, 1999; USDHHS, 2001). The linkages noted here are based on a statistical association or correlation between heavy drinking, on one hand, and health problems on the other. These linkages are strongly suggestive of the damaging effects of heavy drinking. However, because they are based on correlational evidence, we cannot conclude they are necessarily causal.

Heavy drinking clearly does damage the liver, the organ that serves as the primary site of alcohol metabolism. Chronic, heavy consumption of alcohol is a leading cause of illness and death from liver disease (USDHHS, 1991). Two of the major forms of alcohol-related liver disease are *alcoholic hepatitis*, a serious and potentially life-threatening inflammation of the liver, and *cirrhosis of the liver*, a potentially fatal liver disease in which healthy liver cells are replaced with scar tissue. To a great extent, the health risks of alcohol consumption depend on the amount and duration of use. Some people may also be genetically more susceptible to the harmful effects of heavy alcohol use than others.

Habitual drinkers tend to be malnourished, which can put them at risk of complications arising from nutritional deficiencies. Chronic drinking is thus associated with nutritionally linked disorders such as cirrhosis of the liver (linked to protein deficiency) and **alcohol-induced persisting amnestic disorder** (connected with vitamin B deficiency). Alcohol-induced persisting amnestic disorder (also known as **Korsakoff's syndrome**) is characterized by glaring confusion, disorientation, and memory loss regarding recent events.

alcohol-induced persisting amnestic disorder See *Korsakoff's syndrome.*

Korsakoff's syndrome Form of brain damage associated with chronic thiamine deficiency. The syndrome is associated with chronic alcoholism and characterized by memory loss, disorientation, and the tendency to invent memories to replace lost ones (confabulation). Also called *alcohol-induced persisting amnestic disorder.*

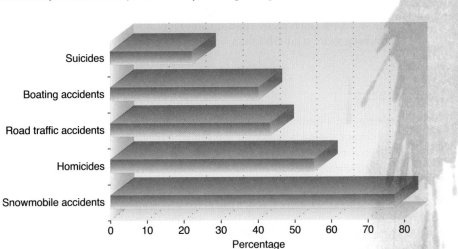

FIGURE 9.1 Estimated percentages of deaths in Canada from various causes connected with the use of alcohol.
Alcohol is a factor in over half of the homicides in Canada.

Source: Adapted from Dingle et al. (2002).

All told, it is estimated that in 1995 over 6500 Canadians lost their lives as a result of alcohol consumption, with motor vehicle accidents, liver cirrhosis, and suicide as the primary causes (CCSA/CAMH, 1999). Each year, it is estimated that thousands of Canadians die because of alcohol. After tobacco, alcohol is the second leading cause of premature death in our society. Men who drink heavily stand nearly twice the risk of dying before the age of 65 as men who abstain; women who drink heavily are more than three times as likely to die before age 65 as are women who abstain ("NIAAA Report Links Drinking and Early Death," 1990).

Mothers who drink during pregnancy put their fetuses at risk for infant mortality, birth defects, central nervous system dysfunctions, and later academic problems (Jones, 2006). Many children whose mothers drank during pregnancy develop fetal alcohol syndrome (FAS), a syndrome characterized by facial features such as a flattened nose, widely spaced eyes, an underdeveloped upper jaw, and mental retardation. Research from all over the world suggests FAS is disturbingly common, affecting 1 in 100 babies (Mukherjee, Hollins, & Turk, 2006).

We don't know whether a minimum amount of alcohol is needed to produce FAS. Some children of mothers who drank as little as two ounces of alcohol a day during their first trimesters have been found to have FAS (Astley, Clarren, Little, Sampson, & Daling, 1992). Although the question of whether there is any safe dose of alcohol during pregnancy continues to be debated, the fact remains that FAS is an entirely preventable birth defect. The safest course for women who know or suspect they are pregnant is not to drink. Period. The same applies, of course, to other substances, such as cocaine and heroin. Even tobacco smoking during pregnancy can have harmful effects, including low birth weight and sudden infant death syndrome (SIDS) (Jones, 2006).

MODERATE DRINKING: IS THERE A HEALTH BENEFIT? According to the Canadian guidelines for low-risk drinking, weekly intake should not exceed 14 drinks for men and 9 for women, and daily consumption should not exceed 2 drinks for both women and men (Adlaf et al., 2005). Despite the above list of adverse effects associated with heavy drinking, growing evidence links light-to-moderate use of alcohol with reduced risk of heart attacks and lower death rates ("Alcohol and the Heart," 1996; Thun et al., 1997). Researchers suspect that alcohol may help prevent blood clots from forming that can clog arteries and lead to heart attacks. Alcohol also appears to increase the levels of HDL cholesterol—the so-called good cholesterol—that sweeps away fatty deposits along artery walls (Ochs, 1998). Although light-to-moderate use of alcohol (about one drink per day) may have a protective effect on the heart, public health officials caution that promoting the possible health benefits of alcohol may backfire by increasing the risks of alcohol abuse and dependence (Brody, 1994b). Alcohol use is also linked to an increased risk of some forms of cancer, including breast cancer (Smith-Warner et al., 1998). Heavy drinking is clearly damaging to the heart and other organs, and any level of alcohol intake by a pregnant woman may be harmful to a developing fetus. Health-promotion efforts might be better directed toward finding safer ways of achieving the health benefits associated with moderate drinking (such as by quitting smoking, lowering dietary fat and cholesterol, and exercising more regularly) than by encouraging alcohol consumption (Gaziano et al., 1993).

Barbiturates

Estimates indicate that almost 1% of the adult population meet the criteria for a substance-abuse or dependence disorder involving the use of barbiturates, sleep medication (hypnotics), or anti-anxiety agents at some point in their lives (APA, 2000a; Russell, Newman, & Bland, 1994). **Barbiturates** such as amobarbital, pentobarbital, phenobarbital, and secobarbital are depressants or **sedatives** with several medical uses, including alleviation of anxiety and tension, anaesthetizing of pain, treatment of epilepsy and high blood pressure, and short-term treatment of insomnia. Barbiturate use quickly leads to psychological dependence and physiological dependence in the form of both tolerance and the development of a withdrawal syndrome.

barbiturates Types of depressant drugs that are sometimes used to relieve anxiety or induce sleep, but which are highly addictive.

sedatives Types of depressant drugs that reduce states of tension and restlessness and induce sleep.

In contrast to the profiles of young cocaine or narcotic abusers, most barbiturate addicts are middle-aged people who initially used sedatives to combat anxiety or insomnia and then got hooked. Because of concerns about abuse, physicians today prescribe other drugs for the temporary relief of anxiety and tension, such as minor tranquillizers like Valium and Librium. However, it is now recognized that minor tranquillizers can also create physiological dependence. Moreover, regular use of these drugs fails to help people alter the sources of stress in their lives.

Barbiturates are also popular street drugs because they are relaxing and produce a mild state of euphoria or "high." High doses of barbiturates, like alcohol, produce drowsiness, slurred speech, motor impairment, irritability, and poor judgment—a particularly deadly combination of effects when their use is combined with the operation of a motor vehicle. The effects of barbiturates last from three to six hours.

Because of synergistic effects, a mixture of barbiturates and alcohol is about four times as powerful as either drug used by itself (Combs, Hale, & Williams, 1980). A combination of barbiturates and alcohol was implicated in the deaths of the entertainers Marilyn Monroe and Judy Garland. Even such widely used anti-anxiety drugs as Valium and Librium, which have a wide margin of safety when used alone, can be dangerous and lead to overdose when their use is combined with alcohol (APA, 2000a).

Physiologically dependent people need to be withdrawn carefully and only under medical supervision from sedatives, barbiturates, and anti-anxiety agents. Abrupt withdrawal can produce states of delirium that can be life-threatening (APA, 2000a). Delirium may involve visual, tactile, or auditory hallucinations and disturbances in thinking processes and consciousness. The longer the period of use and the higher the doses used, the greater the risk of severe withdrawal effects. Grand mal epileptic seizures and even death may occur if the individual undergoes untreated, abrupt withdrawal.

Opiates

Opiates are narcotics, a term applied to addictive drugs that have pain-relieving and sleep-inducing properties. They are derived from the poppy plant and include such derivatives as morphine, heroin, and codeine. Synthetic opiates such as Demerol and Percodan are manufactured in a laboratory to have effects similar to natural opiates. The major medical application of opiates—natural or synthetic—is the relief of pain; that is, analgesia. Opiates produce a rush or intense feelings of pleasure, which is the primary reason for their popularity as street drugs. They also dull awareness of one's personal problems, which is attractive to people seeking a mental escape from stress.

The medical use of opiates is carefully regulated because overdoses can lead to comas and even death, although prescription opiates are, unfortunately, readily available on the street—and through the Internet. Street use of these drugs is associated with many fatal overdoses and accidents. Estimates are that about 0.7% of the adult population (7 people in 1000) currently have or have had an opiate abuse or dependence disorder (APA, 2000a; Russell et al., 1994). Once dependence sets in, it usually follows a chronic course, although periods of temporary abstinence are frequent (APA, 2000a).

Opiates become drugs of abuse because they are capable of producing a euphoric state of pleasure or rush. They produce pleasurable effects apparently because they stimulate brain centres that regulate sensations of pleasure and pain (USDHSS, 1986). It appears that the brain has its own natural opiate system. Two revealing discoveries were made in the 1970s. One was that neurons in the brain have receptor sites into which opiates fit—like a key in a lock. The second was that the human body produces substances similar to opiates in chemical structures that dock at those same receptor sites (Goldstein, 1976). Some of these natural substances are labelled endorphins, which is short for "endogenous morphine"—that is, morphine coming from within. Endorphins appear to play a role in regulating states of pleasure and pain. Opiates mimic the actions of endorphins by docking at receptor sites intended for them, which in turn stimulates the brain centres that produce pleasurable sensations.

The opiate heroin is usually injected either directly beneath the skin (skin popping) or into a vein (mainlining). You may be surprised to learn that heroin is not the most widely

opiates Types of depressant drugs with strong addictive properties that are derived from the opium poppy; provide feelings of euphoria and relief from pain.

narcotics Drugs, such as opiates, that are used for pain relief and treatment of insomnia, but which have strong addictive potential.

analgesia State of relief from pain without loss of consciousness.

endorphins Natural substances that function as neurotransmitters in the brain and are similar in their effects to morphine.

abused opiate. Studies from Canada and the United States indicate that prescription opiates, often illicitly obtained, such as oxycodone (OxyContin) and hydrocodone (Vicodin) are more widely abused than heroin (Fischer & Rehm, 2006; Kuehn, 2007)

The positive effects of opiates are immediate. In the case of heroin, there is a powerful rush that lasts for 5 to 15 minutes and a state of satisfaction, euphoria, and well-being that lasts for three to five hours. In this state, all positive drives seem satisfied. All negative feelings of guilt, tension, and anxiety disappear. With prolonged usage, addiction can develop. Many physiologically dependent people support their habits through dealing (selling heroin), prostitution, or selling stolen goods. Heroin is a depressant, however, and its chemical effects do not directly stimulate criminal or aggressive behaviour.

The withdrawal syndrome associated with dependence on opiates can be severe. It begins within four to six hours after the last dose. Flu-like symptoms are accompanied by anxiety, feelings of restlessness, irritability, and cravings for the drug. Within a few days, symptoms progress to rapid pulse, high blood pressure, cramps, tremors, hot and cold flashes, fever, vomiting, insomnia, and diarrhea, among other symptoms. Although these symptoms can be uncomfortable, they are usually not devastating, especially when other drugs are prescribed to relieve them. Moreover, unlike withdrawal from barbiturates, the withdrawal syndrome rarely results in death.

Stimulants

Stimulants such as amphetamines and cocaine are psychoactive substances that increase the activity of the nervous system. Effects vary somewhat from drug to drug, but some stimulants contribute to feelings of euphoria and self-confidence. Stimulants such as amphetamines, cocaine, and even caffeine (the stimulant found in coffee) increase the availability in the brain of the neurotransmitters norepinephrine and dopamine. High levels of these neurotransmitters, therefore, remain available in the synaptic gaps between neurons, which maintain high levels of nervous system activity and states of high arousal.

amphetamines Types of stimulants, such as Dexedrine and Benzedrine. Abuse can trigger an amphetamine psychosis that mimics acute episodes of schizophrenia.

Amphetamines The **amphetamines** are a class of synthetic stimulants. Street names for stimulants include speed, uppers, "bennies" (for *amphetamine sulfate*; trade name Benzedrine), "dexies" (*dextroamphetamine*; trade name Dexedrine), and "meth" (for *methamphetamine*; a street drug).

Amphetamines are used in high doses for their euphoric rush. They are often taken in pill form or smoked in a relatively pure form called "ice" or "crystal meth." The most potent form of amphetamine, liquid methamphetamine, is injected directly into the veins and produces an intense and immediate rush. Some users inject methamphetamine for days on end to maintain an extended high. Eventually, such highs come to an end. People who have been on extended highs sometimes "crash" and fall into a deep sleep or depression, and may suffer from brain damage (Maxwell, 2005). Some people commit suicide on the way down. High doses can cause restlessness, irritability, hallucinations, paranoid delusions, loss of appetite, and insomnia.

Physiological dependence can develop, leading to an abstinence syndrome characterized most often by depression and fatigue as well as unpleasant, vivid dreams, insomnia or hypersomnia (excessive sleeping), increased appetite, and either a slowing down of motor behaviour or agitation (APA, 2000a). Psychological dependence is seen most often in people who use amphetamines as a way of coping with stress or depression.

amphetamine psychosis Psychotic state induced by ingestion of amphetamines.

Violent behaviour may occur in the context of amphetamine dependence, especially when the drug is smoked or injected intravenously (APA, 2000a). The hallucinations and delusions of the **amphetamine psychosis** mimic the features of paranoid schizophrenia, which has encouraged researchers to study the chemical changes induced by amphetamines as possible causes of schizophrenia.

cocaine Stimulant derived from coca leaves.

Cocaine It might surprise you to learn that the original formula for Coca-Cola contained an extract of cocaine. In 1906, however, the company withdrew cocaine from its secret formula. The beverage was originally described as a "brain tonic and intellectual beverage," in part because of its cocaine content. Cocaine is a natural stimulant extracted from the leaves of the coca plant—the plant from which the soft drink obtained its name. Coca-Cola is still flavoured with an extract from the coca plant, but one that is not known to be psychoactive.

It was long believed that cocaine was not physically addicting. However, evidence supports the addictive properties of the drug in producing a tolerance effect and an identifiable withdrawal syndrome, consisting of depression, inability to experience pleasure, and intense cravings for the drug (APA, 2000a). Withdrawal symptoms are usually brief in duration and may involve a "crash" or period of intense depression and exhaustion following a cocaine binge.

Cocaine is brewed from coca leaves as a "tea," breathed in ("snorted") in powder form, and injected ("shot up") in liquid form. The rise in the use of **crack**, a hardened form of cocaine suitable for smoking that may contain more than 75% pure cocaine, has made cocaine—once the toy of the well-to-do—available to adolescents. Crack "rocks"—so called because they look like small white pebbles—are available in small ready-to-smoke amounts and considered the most habit-forming street drug available. Crack produces a prompt and potent rush that wears off in a few minutes.

Crack. Crack "rocks" resemble small white pebbles. Crack produces a powerful, prompt rush when smoked. Small, ready-to-smoke doses are available at prices that make them affordable to adolescents.

The rush from snorting cocaine is milder and takes a while to develop, but it tends to linger longer than the rush of crack.

Freebasing also intensifies the effects of cocaine. Cocaine in powder form is heated with ether, freeing the psychoactive chemical base of the drug, and then smoked. Ether, however, is highly flammable.

Cocaine is most commonly used by young adults, although even in Canada it is not widely used—a 1994 survey found that 1% to 2% of young adults had tried cocaine in the previous 12 months (CCSA/CAMH, 1999). The lifetime prevalence of cocaine dependence in Canada is about 0.5%, which is lower than in the United States (2%) (APA, 2000a; Russell et al., 1994). It is unclear whether Canada will eventually catch up to the States.

Cocaine abuse is characterized by periodic binges lasting perhaps 12 to 36 hours, which are then followed by two to five days of abstinence, during which time the abuser may experience cravings that prompt another binge (Gawin & Ellinwood, 1989). According to one estimate, between 10% and 15% of people who try snorting cocaine eventually develop cocaine abuse or dependence (Gawin, 1991).

EFFECTS OF COCAINE Cocaine increases the availability in the brain of the neurotransmitter dopamine, producing a pleasurable "high" (Volkow et al., 1997). The drug produces a sudden rise in blood pressure, constricts blood vessels (with associated reduction of the oxygen supply to the heart), and accelerates the heart rate. Overdoses can produce restlessness, insomnia, headaches, nausea, convulsions, tremors, hallucinations, delusions, and even sudden death. Death may result from respiratory or cardiovascular collapse. Although intravenous use of cocaine carries the greatest risk of a lethal overdose, other forms of use can also be fatal. Table 9.4 summarizes a number of the health risks of cocaine use.

Repeated and high-dose use of cocaine can lead to depression and anxiety (Weiss & Mirin, 1994). Depression may be severe enough to prompt suicidal behaviour. Both initial and routine users report episodes of "crashing" (feelings of depression after a binge), although crashing is more common among long-term high-dose users. Psychotic behaviours, which can be induced by cocaine use as well as by use of amphetamines, tend to become more severe with continued use. Cocaine psychosis is usually preceded by a period of heightened suspiciousness, depressed mood, compulsive behaviour, fault finding, irritability, and increasing paranoia (Weiss & Mirin, 1994). Psychosis may also include visual and auditory hallucinations and delusions of persecution.

crack Hardened, smokable form of cocaine.

freebasing Method of ingesting cocaine by means of heating the drug with ether to separate its most potent component (its "free base") and then smoking the extract.

TABLE 9.4

Health Risks of Cocaine Use

Physical Effects and Risks

Effects	Risks
Increased heart rate	Accelerated heart rate may give rise to heart irregularities that can be fatal, such as ventricular tachycardia (extremely rapid contractions) or ventricular fibrillation (irregular, weakened contractions).
Increased blood pressure	Rapid or large changes in blood pressure may place too much stress on a weak-walled blood vessel in the brain, which can cause it to burst, producing cerebral hemorrhage or stroke.
Increased body temperature	Can be dangerous to some individuals.
Possible grand mal seizures (epileptic convulsions)	Some grand mal seizures are fatal, particularly when they occur in rapid succession or while driving a car.
Respiratory effects	Overdoses can produce gasping or shallow irregular breathing that can lead to respiratory arrest.
Dangerous effects in special populations	Various special populations are at greater risk from cocaine use or overdose. People with coronary heart disease have died because their heart muscles were taxed beyond the capacity of their arteries to supply oxygen.

Medical Complications of Cocaine Use

Nasal problems	When cocaine is administered intranasally (snorted), it constricts the blood vessels serving the nose, decreasing the supply of oxygen to these tissues, leading to irritation and inflammation of the mucous membranes, ulcers in the nostrils, frequent nosebleeds, and chronic sneezing and nasal congestion. Chronic use may lead to tissue death of the nasal septum, the part of the nose that separates the nostrils, requiring plastic surgery.
Lung problems	Freebase smoking may lead to serious lung problems within three months of initial use.
Malnutrition	Cocaine suppresses the appetite so that weight loss, malnutrition, and vitamin deficiencies may accompany regular use.
Seizures	Grand mal seizures, typical of epileptics, may occur due to irregularities in the electrical activity of the brain. Repeated use may lower the seizure threshold, described as a type of "kindling" effect.
Sexual problems	Despite the popular belief that cocaine is an aphrodisiac, frequent use can lead to sexual dysfunctions, such as impotence and failure to ejaculate among males, and decreased sexual interest in both sexes. Although some people report initial increased sexual pleasure with cocaine use, they may become dependent on cocaine for sexual arousal or lose the ability to enjoy sex for extended periods following long-term use.
Other effects	Cocaine use may increase the risk of miscarriage among pregnant women. Sharing of infected needles is associated with transmission of hepatitis, endocarditis (infection of the heart valve), and HIV. Repeated injections often lead to skin infections as bacteria are introduced into the deeper levels of the skin.

Source: Adapted with permission from R. D. Weiss & S. M. Mirin (1987). *Cocaine*. Washington, DC. American Psychiatric Press, Inc.

Nicotine Habitual smoking is not just a bad habit. It is also a form of physical addiction to a stimulant drug, nicotine, found in tobacco products including cigarettes, cigars, and smokeless tobacco (D.A. Kessler et al., 1997). Smoking (or other tobacco use) is the means of administering the drug to the body.

More than 30 000 lives in Canada are lost each year from smoking-related causes, mostly from lung cancer, cardiovascular disease, and chronic obstructive lung disease (CCSA/CAMH, 1999). Smoking is implicated in one in three cancer deaths (Boyle, 1993). Smokers overall stand twice the risk of dying from cancer as nonsmokers; among heavy smokers, the risk is four times as great (Bartecchi, MacKenzie, & Schrier, 1994).

The World Health Organization estimates that a billion people worldwide smoke, and more than three million die each year from smoking-related causes. Smoking is expected to become the world's leading cause of death by the year 2020 ("Smoking Will Be World's Biggest Killer," 1996).

Largely because of health concerns, the percentage of Canadians who smoke declined from 61% of men and 38% of women in 1965 to 24% of men and 20% of women in

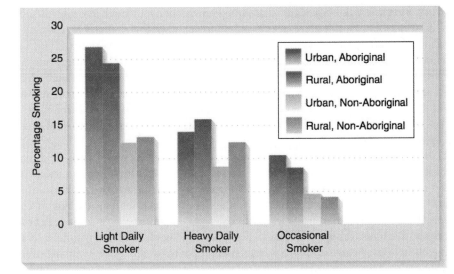

FIGURE 9.2 Smoking prevalence among people 15 years of age and older, according to off-reserve Aboriginal status and geographic region, Canada.

Source: Based on Tjepkema (2002).

2001 (Health Canada, 2001a). Teenage smoking has not decreased as dramatically. Young adults aged 20 to 24 still have the highest smoking rate of any age group, at 32%. The younger that people start to smoke, the more difficulty they have in quitting (Health Canada, 2001a).

Cigarette smoking causes cancer of the larynx, oral cavity, esophagus, and lungs, and may contribute to cancer of the bladder, pancreas, and kidneys. Pregnant women who smoke risk miscarriage, premature birth, and birth defects in their offspring. Smokers stand twice the risk of developing Alzheimer's disease and other forms of dementia as nonsmokers ("Extinguishing Alzheimer's," 1998). Lung cancer, which in 90% of cases is caused by smoking, has now surpassed breast cancer as the leading killer of women. Although quitting smoking clearly has health benefits, it unfortunately does not reduce the risks to normal (nonsmoking) levels. The lesson is clear: if you don't smoke, don't start. But if you do smoke, quit.

The prevalence of smoking among adults is higher among Aboriginal than non-Aboriginal people, regardless of whether they live rural or urban environments (see Figure 9.2). Smoking is becoming increasingly concentrated among the poorer and less well-educated segments of the population (CCSA/CAMH, 1999; Health Canada, 2001a; see Figure 9.3).

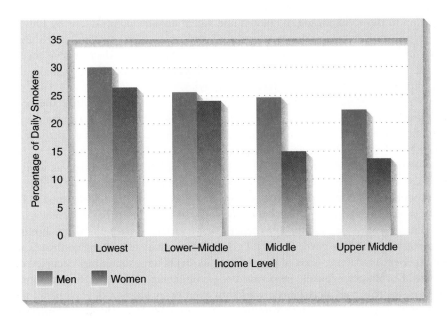

FIGURE 9.3 Cigarette smoking in Canada, according to income status.
Smoking is most prevalent among poorer (and less educated) members of society.

Source: Based on CCSA/CAMH (1999).

NICOTINE DEPENDENCE Nicotine is delivered to the body through the use of tobacco products. As a stimulant, it increases alertness but can also give rise to cold, clammy skin, nausea and vomiting, dizziness and faintness, and diarrhea—all of which account for the discomforts of novice smokers. Nicotine also stimulates the release of epinephrine, a hormone that generates a rush of autonomic activity including rapid heartbeat and release of stores of sugar into the blood. Nicotine quells the appetite and provides a sort of psychological "kick" (Grunberg, 1991). Nicotine also leads to the release of endorphins, opiate-like hormones produced in the brain. This may account for the pleasurable feelings associated with tobacco use.

Habitual use of nicotine leads to a physiological dependence on the drug (Lichtenstein & Glasgow, 1992). Nicotine dependence is associated with both tolerance (intake rises to a level of a pack or two a day before levelling off) and a characteristic withdrawal syndrome. The withdrawal syndrome for nicotine includes such features as lack of energy, depressed mood, irritability, frustration, nervousness, impaired concentration, light-headedness and dizziness, drowsiness, headaches, fatigue, irregular bowels, insomnia, cramps, lowered heart rate, heart palpitations, increased appetite, weight gain, sweating, tremors, and craving for cigarettes (APA, 2000a; Klesges et al., 1997). It is nicotine dependence, not cigarette smoking per se, that is classifiable as a psychological disorder in the DSM system. Between 80% and 90% of regular smokers have nicotine dependence (APA, 2000a).

Hallucinogens

hallucinogens Substances that give rise to hallucinations.

psychedelics Class of drugs that induce sensory distortions or hallucinations. Also called *hallucinogens*.

Hallucinogens, also known as **psychedelics**, are a class of drugs that produce sensory distortions or hallucinations. There are major alterations in colour perception and hearing. Hallucinogens may also have additional effects, such as relaxation and euphoria, or, in some cases, panic. The hallucinogens include such drugs as lysergic acid diethylamide (LSD), psilocybin, and mescaline. Psychoactive substances that are similar in effect to psychedelic drugs are marijuana (cannabis) and phencyclidine (PCP). Mescaline is derived from the peyote cactus and has been used for centuries by Native Americans in the southwest United States, Mexico, and Central America in religious ceremonies, as has psilocybin, which is derived from certain mushrooms. LSD, PCP, and marijuana are more commonly used in North America.

Although tolerance to hallucinogens may develop, we lack evidence of a consistent or characteristic withdrawal syndrome associated with their use (APA, 2000a). Cravings following withdrawal may occur, however.

LSD A powerful hallucinogenic drug. LSD is the acronym for *lysergic acid diethylamide*.

LSD LSD is the acronym for lysergic acid diethylamide, a synthetic hallucinogenic drug. In addition to the vivid parade of colours and visual distortions produced by LSD, users have claimed that it "expands consciousness" and opens new worlds—as if they were looking into some reality beyond the usual reality. Sometimes they believe they have achieved great insights during an LSD "trip," but when it wears off they usually cannot follow through or even summon up these discoveries.

LSD apparently decreases the action of serotonin, a neurotransmitter that inhibits neural firing. It may also increase utilization of dopamine. Because LSD curbs the action of an inhibiting neurotransmitter and increases dopamine activity, brain activity escalates, in this case giving rise to a flurry of colourful sensations or hallucinations.

The effects of LSD are unpredictable and depend on the amount taken as well as the user's expectations, personality, mood, and surroundings (USDHHS, 1992). The user's prior experiences with the drug may also play a role, as users who have learned to handle the effects of the drug through past experience may be better prepared than new users.

flashback (1) Vivid re-experiencing of a past event, which may be difficult to distinguish from current reality. (2) Experience of sensory distortions or hallucinations occurring days or weeks after use of LSD or another hallucinogenic drug that mimics the drug's effects.

Some users have unpleasant experiences or "bad trips" with the drug. Feelings of intense fear or panic may occur (USDHHS, 1992). Users may fear losing control or sanity. Some experience terrifying fears of death. Fatal accidents have sometimes occurred during LSD trips. **Flashbacks**, typically involving a re-experiencing of some of the perceptual distortions of the trip, may occur days, weeks, or even years afterward. Flashbacks tend to occur suddenly and often without warning. They may stem from chemical changes in the brain caused by the prior use of the drug. Triggers for flashbacks include entry into darkened environments, use of various drugs, anxiety or fatigue states, or stress (APA, 2000a). Psychological factors, such as underlying personality problems, may also be involved in explaining why some users experience flashbacks. In some cases, a flashback may involve an imagined re-enactment of the LSD experience (Matefy, 1980).

Phencyclidine (PCP) Phencyclidine or PCP—referred to as "angel dust" on the street—was developed as an anaesthetic in the 1950s but was discontinued as such when its hallucinatory side effects were discovered. A smokable form of PCP became popular as a street drug in the 1970s because it was readily manufactured and relatively inexpensive. By the mid-1980s, more than one in five young people in the 18-to-25 age range had used PCP (USDHHS, 1986). However, its popularity has since waned, largely because of its unpredictable effects.

The effects of PCP, like most drugs, are dose-related. In addition to causing hallucinations, PCP accelerates the heart rate and blood pressure and causes sweating, flushing, and numbness. PCP is classified as a *deliriant*—a drug capable of producing states of delirium. It also has dissociating effects, causing users to feel as if there is some sort of invisible barrier or wall between themselves and their environments. Dissociation can be experienced as pleasant, engrossing, or frightening, depending on the user's expectations, mood, setting, and so on. Overdoses can give rise to drowsiness and a blank stare, convulsions, and, now and then, coma; paranoia and aggressive behaviour; and tragic accidents resulting from perceptual distortion or impaired judgment during states of intoxication.

Marijuana **Marijuana** is produced from the *Cannabis sativa* plant. Marijuana sometimes produces mild hallucinations, so is regarded as a minor hallucinogen. The psychoactive substance in marijuana is **delta-9-tetrahydrocannabinol** or THC, which is found in the plant's branches and leaves but is highly concentrated in the resin of the female plant. **Hashish** or "hash" is also derived from the resin. Although it is more potent than marijuana, hashish has similar effects.

Marijuana dependence is the most common form of dependence on illicit drugs in North America, affecting an estimated 5% to 6% of the adult population at some point in their lives (APA, 2000a; Russell et al., 1994). Males are more likely than females to develop a marijuana use disorder (either abuse or dependence), and the rates of these disorders are greatest among young people aged 18 to 30 (APA, 2000a).

marijuana A mild or minor hallucinogen derived from the *Cannabis sativa* plant.

delta-9-tetrahydrocannabinol Major active ingredient in marijuana. Abbreviated *THC*.

hashish Drug derived from the resin of the marijuana plant— *Cannabis sativa*.

Marijuana. The proportion of marijuana users in Canada is much higher among young adults than the population as a whole.

Low doses of the drug can produce relaxing feelings similar to drinking a highball of liquor. Some users report that at low doses the drug makes them feel more comfortable in social gatherings. Higher doses, however, often lead users to withdraw into themselves. Some users believe the drug increases their capacity for self-insight or creative thinking, although the insights or thoughts achieved under its influence may not seem so insightful/creative once the drug's effects have passed. People may turn to marijuana, as to other drugs, to help them cope with life problems or to help them function when they are under stress. Strongly intoxicated people perceive time as passing more slowly. A song of a few minutes may seem to last an hour. There is increased awareness of bodily sensations, such as heartbeat. Smokers also report that strong intoxication heightens sexual sensations. Visual hallucinations may occur.

Strong intoxication can cause smokers to become disoriented. If their moods are euphoric, disorientation may be construed as harmony with the universe. Yet some smokers find strong intoxication disturbing. An accelerated heart rate and sharpened awareness of bodily sensations cause some smokers to fear their hearts will "run away" from them. Some smokers are frightened by disorientation and fear they will not "come back." High levels of intoxication now and then induce nausea and vomiting.

Marijuana dependence is associated more with patterns of compulsive use or psychological dependence than with physiological dependence. Although tolerance to many of the drug's effects may occur with chronic use, some users report reverse tolerance or *sensitization*. A withdrawal syndrome has not been reliably demonstrated (APA, 2000a). However, research with animals points to some disturbing similarities between marijuana and addictive drugs like heroin and cocaine (Wickelgren, 1997). In one study, researchers found that withdrawal from marijuana activated the same brain circuits involved in withdrawal from opiates, alcohol, and cocaine (Rodríguez de Fonseca, Carrera, Navarro, Koob, & Weiss, 1997). These brain circuits are also involved in producing feelings of anxiety when an animal or person is under stress (Blakeslee, 1997). In another study, researchers determined that marijuana activated the same reward circuits in the brain as heroin (Tanda et al., 1997). Although these studies were conducted with animals, researchers believe the underlying biological mechanisms may apply to humans as well (Blakeslee, 1997).

University students who are heavy users of marijuana show evidence of cognitive impairment, including diminished ability in tasks requiring attention, abstraction, and mental flexibility (Pope & Yurgelun-Todd, 1996). However, it is unclear whether these deficits are due to the drug or to characteristics of people who become heavy users (Lee, 1997).

We do know that marijuana impairs perception and motor co-ordination and thus makes driving and the operation of other machines dangerous. It also impairs short-term memory and retards learning ability. Although it induces positive mood changes in many users, some people report anxiety and confusion; there are also occasional reports of psychotic reactions. Marijuana elevates the heart rate to about 140 to 150 beats per minute and, in some people, raises blood pressure. These changes may be especially dangerous to people with heart conditions or hypertension. Finally, marijuana smoke contains carcinogenic hydrocarbons, so chronic users risk lung cancer and other respiratory diseases.

Inhalants

Many different kinds of substances fall into the category of inhalants. Substances commonly used in inhalant abuse include adhesives, aerosols, anaesthetics, benzene, carbon dioxide, cleaning fluids, correction fluid, deodorants and deodorizers, disinfectants, ether, fingernail polish, refrigeration and air conditioner coolant, lighter fluid, fuels, whiteboard markers, paint and paint removers, styrene, toluene, and transmission fluid. In cases of inhalant abuse, these substances are typically used by soaking a cloth with the substance and then either holding the cloth near the face to inhale fumes or putting the cloth in a bag and inhaling from the bag. An alternative is to pour the substance into a bag or balloon and then inhale the fumes. Inhalants can induce feelings of intoxication and euphoria. The reinforcing effects of inhalants occur mainly through their effects on GABA and dopamine neurotransmitter systems. Inhalant abuse is a serious and dangerous problem—it is associated with impairments in learning and memory. The use of inhalants, even on a single occasion, increases the risk of serious medical illness and even death (Ridenour, 2005).

Drugs of Abuse

Review It

- **What are depressants?** Depressants are drugs that depress or slow nervous system activity. They include alcohol, sedatives and minor tranquillizers, and opiates. Their effects include intoxication, impaired coordination, slurred speech, and impaired intellectual functioning. Chronic alcohol abuse is linked to alcohol-induced persisting amnestic disorder (Korsakoff's syndrome), cirrhosis of the liver, fetal alcohol syndrome, and other physical health problems. Barbiturates are depressants or sedatives that have been used medically for relief of anxiety and short-term insomnia, among other uses. Opiates such as morphine and heroin are derived from the opium poppy. Others are synthesized. Used medically for relief of pain, they are strongly addictive.

- **What are stimulants?** Stimulants increase the activity of the nervous system. Amphetamines and cocaine are stimulants that increase the availability of neurotransmitters in the brain, leading to heightened states of arousal and pleasurable feelings. High doses can produce psychotic reactions that mimic features of paranoid schizophrenia. Habitual cocaine use can lead to a variety of health problems, and an overdose can cause sudden death. Repeated use of nicotine, a mild stimulant found in cigarettes, leads to physiological dependence.

- **What are hallucinogens?** They are drugs that distort sensory perceptions and can induce hallucinations. They include lysergic acid diethylamide (LSD), psilocybin, and mescaline. Other drugs with similar effects are cannabis (marijuana) and phencyclidine (PCP). There is little evidence that these drugs induce physiological dependence, although psychological dependence may occur.

Define It

depressant	cocaine
alcohol-induced persisting amnestic disorder	crack
	freebasing
Korsakoff's syndrome	hallucinogens
barbiturates	psychedelics
sedatives	LSD

opiates	flashback
narcotics	marijuana
analgesia	delta-9-tetrahydro-
endorphins	cannabinol
amphetamines	hashish
amphetamine psychosis	

Recall It*

1. Drugs that curb the activity of the central nervous system are called _____.

   a. stimulants
   b. narcotics
   c. hallucinogens
   d. depressants

2. The factor linked most closely to alcoholism or problem drinking in adulthood is _____.

   a. ethnic background
   b. family history of alcohol abuse
   c. antisocial personality
   d. social class

3. Drugs that increase the activity of the central nervous system are called _____.

   a. stimulants
   b. narcotics
   c. hallucinogens
   d. depressants

4. Philip has recently begun smoking. He notices his skin becomes cold and clammy when he smokes and he feels nauseated, dizzy, and faint. His symptoms most likely result from the presence of _____ in the cigarette smoke he inhales.

   a. carbon monoxide
   b. caffeine
   c. nicotine
   d. hydrocarbons

5. The most widely used illegal drug in Canada is _____.

   a. marijuana
   b. cocaine
   c. amphetamine
   d. LSD

* Recall It answers can be found on the Companion Website for this text.

THEORETICAL PERSPECTIVES

People begin using psychoactive substances for various reasons. Some adolescents start using drugs because of peer pressure or because they believe drugs make them seem more sophisticated or grown up. Some use drugs as a way of rebelling against their parents or society at large. Regardless of why people get started with drugs, they continue to use them because of their pleasurable effects or because they find it difficult to stop. Most adolescents drink alcohol to "get high," not to establish that they are adults. Many people smoke cigarettes for the pleasure they provide. Others smoke to help them relax when they are tense and, paradoxically, to give them a kick or a lift when they are tired. Many would like to quit but find it difficult to break their addiction.

People who are anxious about their jobs or social lives may be drawn to the calming effects of alcohol, marijuana (in certain doses), tranquillizers, and sedatives. People with low self-confidence and self-esteem may be drawn to the ego-boosting effects of amphetamines and cocaine. Many poor young people attempt to escape the poverty, anguish, and tedium of inner-city life through using heroin and similar drugs. More well-to-do adolescents may rely on drugs to manage the transition from dependence on their parents to independence and major life changes concerning jobs, university, and lifestyles. In the next sections, we consider several major theoretical perspectives on substance abuse and dependence.

Biological Perspectives

We are beginning to learn more about the biological underpinnings of addiction. Much of the recent research has focused on neurotransmitters, especially dopamine, and on the role of genetic factors.

Neurotransmitters A common pathway in the brain involving the neurotransmitter dopamine may explain the pleasure-inducing effects of many drugs. Researchers suspect that drugs such as nicotine, alcohol, heroin, cocaine, and even marijuana produce pleasurable effects by increasing the levels of the neurotransmitter dopamine—the brain's "reward and reinforcing" agent (Chang & Haning, 2006).

We know that laboratory rats will work for injections of cocaine by repetitively pressing a lever. They will continue to work for cocaine injections even if the neural pathways that use norepinephrine are destroyed. Their work effort plummets when the neural pathways for dopamine are destroyed (Weiss & Mirin, 1994). With repeated drug use over time, the brain's ability to make dopamine on its own can diminish, leading to cravings for drugs that will provide a steady supply of dopamine (Blakeslee, 1997). This may explain the intense cravings and anxiety that accompany drug withdrawal and the difficulty people with chemical dependencies have maintaining abstinence.

Other neurotransmitters are also believed to be involved in drug use and abuse. Evidence points to the neurotransmitter serotonin playing a role in activating the brain's pleasure or reward circuits in response to use of cocaine and other drugs (Blakeslee, 1998; Rocha et al., 1998). We also know that a group of neurotransmitters called endorphins have pain-blocking properties similar to opiates such as heroin. Endorphins and opiates dock at the same receptor sites in the brain. Normally, the brain produces a certain level of endorphins that maintains a sort of psychological steady state of comfort and potential to experience pleasure. However, when the body becomes habituated to a supply of opiates, it may stop producing endorphins. This makes the user dependent on opiates for feelings of comfort, relief from pain, and feelings of pleasure. When the habitual user stops using heroin or other opiates, feelings of discomfort and little aches and pains may be magnified until the body resumes adequate production of endorphins. This discomfort might account, at least in part, for the unpleasant withdrawal symptoms experienced by opiate addicts when they attempt to quit using. However, this model remains speculative, and more research is needed to document direct relationships between endorphin production and withdrawal symptoms.

Genetic Factors Increasing evidence points to genetic factors in substance abuse and dependence. We know that alcoholism runs in families. People with a family history of alcoholism are about three or four times more likely to develop problems of alcohol abuse or dependence than others (APA, 2000a; Schuckit & Smith, 1996). The closer the genetic relationship, the greater the risk. Familial patterns provide only suggestive evidence of genetic factors because families share common environments as well as common genes. More definitive evidence comes from twin and adoptee studies.

Monozygotic (MZ) twins have identical genes, whereas fraternal or dizygotic (DZ) twins share only half of their genes. If genetic factors are involved, we would expect MZ twins to have higher concordance (agreement) rates for alcoholism than DZ twins. The evidence for higher concordance rates for alcoholism among MZ twins than DZ twins is stronger for male twin pairs than female twin pairs, which indicates the genetic factors may be more strongly involved in alcoholism in males than females (Kendler & Prescott, 2006; Jang, Livesley, & Vernon, 1997). To illustrate, research conducted at the University of British Columbia found that alcohol and drug problems were due to a combination of environmental and genetic factors in men, but were entirely due to environmental factors in women (Jang et al., 1997). Future research may help clarify these apparent gender differences.

Other evidence points to a genetic contribution in other forms of substance abuse, including opiate, marijuana, cocaine, and nicotine dependence (Kendler & Prescott, 2006; Jang et al., 1997). An emerging body of research suggests the importance of gene-environment interactions in the development of substance-use disorders, where people with a particular genetic makeup are most likely to develop drug abuse or dependence when exposed to substances such as alcohol, cocaine, or nicotine under particular environmental conditions (e.g., highly stressful conditions) (Caspi & Moffitt, 2006; van der Kam, Ellenbroek, & Cools, 2005).

If alcoholism or other forms of substance abuse and dependence are influenced by genetic factors, what is it that is inherited? Some clues have begun to emerge. Researchers have linked alcoholism, nicotine dependence, and opiate addiction to genes involved in determining the structure of dopamine receptors in the brain (Kotler, 1997). We've mentioned that dopamine is involved in regulating states of pleasure, which leads researchers to suspect that genetic factors enhance feelings of pleasure derived from alcohol, which in turn may increase cravings for the drug (Altman, 1990). In all likelihood there is not one "alcoholism gene" but a set of genes that interact with each other and with environmental factors to increase the risk of alcoholism (Kendler & Prescott, 2006).

Evidence also suggests that a genetic vulnerability to alcoholism may involve a combination of at least two factors (Sher et al., 2005). First, genetic factors influencing the ability to rapidly metabolize alcohol (some people, such as many people from Asian backgrounds, are genetically predisposed to have difficulty metabolizing alcohol, thereby leading to flushing and nausea when they drink). People who metabolize alcohol relatively quickly can tolerate larger doses and are less likely to develop upset stomachs, dizziness, and headaches when they drink. Unfortunately, a lower sensitivity to the unpleasant effects of alcohol may make it difficult to know when to say "when." Thus, people who are better able to "hold their liquor" may be at greater risk of developing drinking problems. They may need to rely on other cues, such as counting their drinks, to learn to limit their drinking. People whose bodies more readily "put the brakes" on excess drinking may be less likely to develop problems in moderating their drinking than those with better tolerance. Second, genetic factors influence the degree of reinforcement (enjoyment) obtained from consuming alcohol (Sher et al., 2005).

Despite the role of genetic factors in alcoholism, environmental factors are also important. For example, there is evidence that some types of family experiences, such as drinking at home and particular types of parenting, promote the development of alcohol problems, especially in genetically vulnerable individuals (Sher et al., 2005).

Learning Perspectives

Learning theorists propose that substance-related behaviours are largely learned and can, in principle, be unlearned. They focus on the roles of operant and classical conditioning and observational learning. Substance abuse problems are not regarded as symptoms of diseases, but rather as problem habits. Although learning theorists do not deny that genetic or biological factors may be involved in the genesis of substance abuse problems, they place a greater emphasis on the role of learning in the development and maintenance of these problem behaviours (McCrady, 1993, 1994).

Drug use may become habitual because of the pleasure or positive reinforcement that drugs produce. In the case of drugs like cocaine, which appear capable of directly stimulating pleasure mechanisms in the brain, the reinforcement is direct and powerful.

Operant Conditioning
In animal studies, injection of psychoactive drugs like cocaine has been made contingent on the performance of various tasks, such as pressing a lever (Weiss & Mirin, 1994). Laboratory animals will learn to press a lever repeatedly for cocaine. Researchers can estimate the reinforcing power of drugs by comparing the rates at which animals perform operant responses such as pressing a lever to receive them. Animals will perform to receive a wide range of drugs, including amphetamines, nicotine, barbiturates, opiates, alcohol, and PCP. Performance rates are most dramatic for cocaine, however. Rhesus monkeys will work continuously for cocaine until they die (Weiss & Mirin, 1994).

People may initially use a drug because of social influence, trial and error, or social observation. In the case of alcohol, they learn the drug can produce reinforcing effects, such as feelings of euphoria and reductions in states of anxiety and tension. Alcohol may also release behavioural inhibitions. Alcohol can thus be reinforcing when it is used to combat depression (by producing euphoric feelings, even if short-lived), to combat tension (by functioning as a tranquillizer), or to help people sidestep moral conflicts (e.g., by dulling awareness of moral prohibitions against sexual behaviour or aggression). Social reinforcers are also made available by substance abuse, such as the approval of drug-abusing companions and, in the cases of depressants and stimulants, the (temporary) overcoming of social shyness.

Alcohol and Tension Reduction
Learning theorists have long maintained that one of the primary reinforcers for using alcohol is relief from states of tension. The *tension-reduction theory* proposes that the more often one drinks to reduce tension or anxiety, the stronger or more habitual the habit becomes. Viewed in this way, alcohol use can be likened to a form of self-medication—a way of easing psychological pain—at least temporarily.

Laboratory studies have provided inconsistent support for the tension-reduction theory (Pihl & Smith, 1983), although the stressors induced in those studies tended to be mild (for ethical reasons). The occurrence of more severe stressful events, such as physical or sexual assault, is associated with an increase risk of alcohol abuse (Stewart, 1996). Thus, there is some support for the tension-reduction theory, although many other factors aside from tension reduction appear to play a role in alcohol use and abuse.

Drugs, including nicotine from cigarette smoking, may also be used as a form of self-medication for depression (Breslau, Peterson, Schultz, Chilcoat, & Andreski, 1998). Stimulants like nicotine temporarily elevate the mood, whereas depressants like alcohol quell anxiety. Although nicotine, alcohol, and other drugs may temporarily alleviate emotional distress, they cannot resolve underlying personal or emotional problems. Rather than learning to resolve these problems, people who use drugs as forms of self-medication often find themselves facing additional substance-related problems.

Negative Reinforcement and Withdrawal   Once people become physiologically dependent, *negative reinforcement* comes into play in maintaining a drug habit. In other words, people may resume using drugs to gain relief from unpleasant withdrawal symptoms. In operant conditioning terms, the resumption of drug use is negatively reinforced by relief from unpleasant withdrawal symptoms that occur following cessation of drug use. For example, the addicted smoker who quits cold turkey may shortly return to smoking to fend off the discomfort of withdrawal. Smokers who are able to quit and maintain abstinence are occasionally bothered by urges to smoke but have learned to manage them.

The Conditioning Model of Cravings   Principles of classical conditioning may help explain the cravings for drugs experienced by people with drug dependencies. Repeated exposure to cues associated with drug use (such as the sight or aroma of an alcoholic beverage or the sight of a needle and syringe) may elicit conditioned responses in the form of alcohol or drug cravings (Drummond & Glautier, 1994). Although drug cravings may have a biological basis involving a bodily need to restore levels of the addictive substance, they may also become conditioned responses triggered by a wide range of cues (conditioned stimuli) that were previously associated with use of the substance. For example, socializing with certain companions (drinking buddies) or even passing a liquor store may elicit conditioned cravings for alcohol. Sensations of anxiety or depression that were paired with use of alcohol or drugs may also elicit cravings. The following case illustrates conditioned cravings to environmental cues:

> A 29-year-old man was hospitalized for the treatment of heroin addiction. After four weeks of treatment, he returned to his former job, which required him to ride the subway past the stop at which he had previously bought his drugs. Each day, when the subway doors opened at this location, [he] experienced an enormous craving for heroin, accompanied by tearing, a runny nose, abdominal cramps, and gooseflesh. After the doors closed, his symptoms disappeared, and he went on to work.
>
> WEISS & MIRIN, 1987, P. 71. REPRINTED WITH PERMISSION.

Similarly, some people are primarily "stimulus smokers." They reach for a cigarette in the presence of smoking-related stimuli such as seeing someone smoke or smelling smoke. Smoking becomes a strongly conditioned habit because it is paired repeatedly with many situational cues—watching television, finishing dinner, driving in the car, studying, drinking or socializing with friends, sex, and, for some, using the bathroom. Environmental stimuli associated with substance use (e.g., being in a bar or seeing someone smoke) can influence tolerance, elicit withdrawal symptoms, and trigger relapse of substance use (Siegel, 2005). The conditioning model of craving is strengthened by research showing that people with alcoholism tend to salivate more than others to the sight and smell of alcohol (Monti et al., 1987). In Pavlov's classic experiment, a salivation response was conditioned in dogs by repeatedly pairing the sound of a bell (a neutral or conditioned stimulus) with the presentation of food powder (an unconditioned stimulus). Salivation among people who develop alcoholism can also be viewed as a conditioned response to alcohol-related cues. Whereas salivating to a bell may be harmless, salivating at a bottle of scotch or at a picture of a bottle in a magazine ad can throw the person who suffers from alcoholism and is trying to remain abstinent into a tailspin. People with drinking problems who show the greatest salivary response to alcohol cues may be at the highest risk of relapse. They may also profit from treatments designed to extinguish their responses to alcohol-related cues.

One such treatment, called **cue-exposure training**, holds promise in the treatment of alcohol dependence and other forms of addictive behaviour (Drummond & Glautier, 1994; Monti et al., 1994). In cue-exposure treatment, a person is repeatedly seated in front of drug- or alcohol-related cues, such as open alcoholic beverages, while prevented from using the drug. This pairing of the cue (alcohol bottle) with nonreinforcement (by dint of preventing drinking) may lead to extinction of the conditioned craving. Cue-exposure treatment may be combined with coping-skills training to help people with substance-abuse problems learn to cope with drug-use urges without resorting to drug use (Monti et al., 1994). It has also been applied to helping nondependent problem drinkers learn to stop drinking after two or three drinks (Sitharthan, Sitharthan, Hough, & Kavanagh, 1997).

cue-exposure training Treatment used for people with substance dependence, it involves exposure to cues associated with ingestion of drugs or alcoholic beverages in a controlled situation in which the person is prevented from using the drug.

Observational Learning   The role of modelling or observational learning may in part explain the increased risk of alcoholism among people with a family history of alcoholism. Teens who say their fathers imbibe more than two drinks a day have about a 75% greater risk of developing substance-abuse problems than do teens with fathers who are light drinkers or abstainers ("Teens Who Have Problems," 1999). Researchers also find that young men from families with a history of alcoholism were more strongly affected by exposure to others who modelled excessive drinking than were men without familial alcoholism (Chipperfield & Vogel-Sprott, 1988). Perhaps their parents had modelled excessive drinking and they learned to regulate their own intake by observing the drinking behaviour of others. When their drinking companions drink to excess, they may be more likely to follow their lead.

Cognitive Perspectives

Evidence supports the role of various cognitive factors in substance abuse and dependence, including expectancies, attitudes, beliefs, decision-making processes, and self-awareness.

Outcome Expectancies, Decision Making, and Substance   The beliefs and expectancies you hold concerning the effects of alcohol and other drugs clearly influence your decision to use them or not. People who hold positive expectancies about the effects of a drug are not only more likely to use the drug (Schafer & Brown, 1991) but also are more likely to use larger quantities of it (Baldwin, Oei, & Young, 1994). One of the key factors in predicting problem alcohol use in adolescents is the degree to which their friends hold positive attitudes toward alcohol use (Scheier, Botvin, & Baker, 1997). Similarly, fifth and seventh graders who hold more positive impressions of smokers (e.g., seeing them as cool, independent, or good looking) were more likely than their peers to become smokers by the time they reached the ninth grade (Dinh, Sarason, Peterson, & Onstad, 1995). Smoking prevention programs may need to focus on changing the image that young people hold of smokers long before they ever light up a cigarette themselves. Positive alcohol expectancies also appear in children even before drinking begins.

Among the most widely held positive expectancies concerning alcohol is that it reduces tension, helps divert attention from one's problems, heightens pleasure, and lessens anxiety in social situations and makes one more socially adept (MacLatchy-Gaudet & Stewart, 2001). In one study, alcohol expectancies were stronger predictors of the likelihood of drinking among adolescents than family drinking history (Christiansen & Goldman, 1983). The belief that alcohol helps make a person more socially adept (more relaxed, outgoing, assertive, and carefree in social interactions) appears to be an especially important factor in prompting drinking in adolescents and university students (Burke & Stephens, 1999; G. T. Smith, Goldman, Greenbaum, & Christiansen, 1995).

From a decision-making perspective, people choose whether or not to use drugs according to their weighing of the expected positive and negative consequences. Consider people with drinking problems who face the choice to drink or not to drink every day. They may be aware of the eventual negative consequences of drinking (e.g., getting fired or divorced or incurring serious health troubles), but expectations of immediate relief from anxiety and feelings of pleasure may be more prominent at a given moment (Cox & Klinger, 1988). They may well decide, then, to drink. The person with a drinking problem may or may not be aware of such decisions, or of decisions to engage in the chain of behaviours that lead to problem drinking—such as whether or not to take a route from work that runs past a favourite watering hole.

Self-Efficacy Expectancies Part of the appeal of substances such as alcohol lies in their ability to enhance self-efficacy expectancies (beliefs in our ability to accomplish tasks) either directly (by enhancing feelings of energy, power, and well-being) or indirectly (by reducing stressful states of arousal, such as anxiety). Cocaine also enhances self-efficacy expectancies, an outcome sought in particular by performance-conscious athletes. People may therefore come to rely on substances in challenging situations where they doubt their abilities. Alcohol can also help protect one's sense of self-efficacy by shunting criticism for socially unacceptable behaviour from the self to the alcohol. People who "screw up" while drinking can maintain their self-esteem by attributing their misdeeds to alcohol.

Does One Slip Cause People with Substance Abuse or Dependence to Go on Binges? Perhaps What You Believe Is What You Get According to the disease model of alcoholism, abstainers who binge after just one drink do so largely for biochemical reasons. Experimental research, however, suggests that cognitive factors may be more important. In fact, the one-drink hypothesis may be explained by the drinker's expectancies rather than the biochemical properties of alcohol.

Studies of the one-drink hypothesis, like many other studies on alcohol, are made possible by the fact that the taste of vodka can be cloaked by tonic water. In a classic study by Marlatt and his colleagues (Marlatt, Demming, & Reid, 1973), subjects were led to believe they were participating in a taste test. Alcohol-dependent subjects and social drinkers who were informed they were sampling an alcoholic beverage (vodka) drank significantly more than counterparts who were informed they were sampling a nonalcoholic beverage. The expectations of the alcohol-dependent subjects and the social drinkers alike turned out to be the crucial factors that predicted the amount consumed (see Figure 9.4 on page 352). *The actual content of the beverages was immaterial.*

Marlatt (1978) explains the one-drink effect as a self-fulfilling prophecy. If people with alcohol-related problems believe just one drink will cause a loss of control, they perceive the outcome as predetermined when they drink. Their drinking—even taking one drink—may thus escalate into a binge. When individuals who were formerly physiologically dependent on alcohol share this belief—which is propounded by many groups, including AA—they may interpret "just one drink" as "falling off the wagon." Marlatt's point is that the "mechanism" of falling off the wagon due to one drink is cognitive, reflecting one's expectations about the effects of the drink, and not physiological. This expectation is an example of what Aaron Beck refers to as *absolutist thinking*. When we insist on seeing the world in black and white rather than shades of grey, we may interpret one bite of dessert as proof we are off our diets, or one cigarette as proof we are hooked again. Rather than telling ourselves, "Okay, I goofed, but that's it. I don't have to have more," we encode our lapses as catastrophes and transform them into full-blown relapses. Still, alcohol-dependent people who believe they may go on a drinking binge if they have just one drink are well advised to abstain rather than place themselves in situations they feel they may not be able to manage.

Psychodynamic Perspectives

According to traditional psychodynamic theory, alcoholism reflects certain features of what is termed an *oral-dependent personality*. Alcoholism is, by definition, an oral behaviour

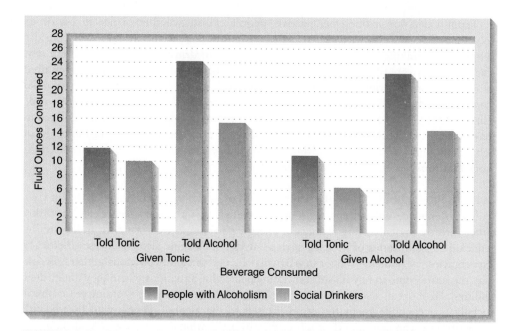

FIGURE 9.4 Must people who develop alcoholism fall off the wagon if they have one drink?
It is widely believed that people who develop alcoholism will "lose control" if they have just one drink. Will they? If so, why? Laboratory research by Marlatt and his colleagues suggests that the tendency of people who suffer from alcoholism to drink to excess following a first drink may be the result of a self-fulfilling prophecy rather than a craving. Like the dieter who eats a piece of chocolate, people who develop alcoholism may assume that they have lost control because they have fallen off the wagon, and then go on a binge. This figure shows that people with alcoholism who participated in the Marlatt study drank more when they were led to believe that the beverage contained alcohol, regardless of its actual content. It remains unclear, however, whether binge drinking by people with alcohol-related problems in real-life settings can be explained as a self-fulfilling prophecy.

Source: Adapted from Marlatt et al. (1973).

pattern. Psychodynamic theory also associates excessive alcohol use with other oral traits, such as dependence and depression, and traces the origins of these traits to fixation in the oral stage of psychosexual development. Excessive drinking in adulthood symbolizes efforts to attain oral gratification.

Psychodynamic theorists also view smoking as an oral fixation, although they have not been able to predict who will or will not smoke. Sigmund Freud smoked upward of 20 cigars a day despite several vain attempts to desist. Although he contracted oral cancer and had to have painful jaw surgery, he would still not surrender his "oral fixation." He eventually succumbed to cancer of the mouth in 1939 at the age of 83, after years of agony.

Research support for these psychodynamic concepts is mixed. Although people who develop alcoholism often show dependent traits, it is unclear whether dependence contributes to or stems from problem drinking. Chronic drinking, for example, is connected with loss of employment and downward movement in social status, both of which would render drinkers more reliant on others for support. Moreover, an empirical connection between dependence and alcoholism does not establish that alcoholism represents an oral fixation that can be traced to early development.

Then too, many—but certainly not all—people who suffer from alcoholism have antisocial personalities characterized by independence-seeking as expressed through rebelliousness and rejection of social and legal codes (Graham & Strenger, 1988). All in all, there doesn't appear to be a single alcoholic personality (Sher & Trull, 1994).

Sociocultural Perspectives

Cultural and religious factors are also related to consumption of alcohol and drugs. Rates of alcohol abuse vary across ethnic and religious groups (see the earlier "Focus on Diversity" box on pages 333 to 334). Let us note some other sociocultural factors. Church attendance, for example, is generally connected with abstinence from alcohol. Perhaps people who are more willing to engage in culturally sanctioned activities, such as churchgoing, are also more likely to adopt culturally sanctioned prohibitions against excessive drinking. Rates of alcohol use also vary across cultures. For example, alcohol use is greater in Germany than in Canada, apparently because of a cultural tradition that makes the consumption of alcohol, especially beer, normative in German society (Cockerham, Kunz, & Lueschen, 1989).

Use of alcohol and drugs often occurs within a group or social setting. We go drinking with friends or entertain over drinks at home. A good wine list is a sign of class in a restaurant. Drinking is determined, in part, by where we live, with whom we worship, and by the social or cultural norms that regulate our behaviour. Cultural attitudes can encourage or discourage problem drinking.

Peer pressure and peer drug use play important roles in the use of alcohol and drugs among adolescents (Curran, Stice, & Chassin, 1997; Farrell & White, 1998). Conversely, support from family members can reduce the negative influence of drug-using peers on an adolescent's use of tobacco and other drugs (e.g., Farrell & White, 1998; Frauenglass, Routh, Pantin, & Mason, 1997).

TYING IT TOGETHER

Substance abuse and dependence are complex patterns of behaviour that involve an interplay of biological, psychological, and environmental factors. Genetic factors and the early home environment may give rise to predispositions (diatheses) to abuse and dependence. In adolescence and adulthood, positive expectations concerning drug use, together with social pressures and a lack of cultural constraints, affect drug-use decisions and tendencies toward abuse. When physiological dependence occurs, people may use a substance to avoid withdrawal symptoms.

Genetic factors may create an inborn tolerance for certain drugs, such as alcohol, which can make it difficult to regulate usage, or to know "when to say when." Some individuals may have genetic tendencies that lead them to become unusually tense or anxious. Perhaps they turn to alcohol or other drugs to quell their nervousness. Genetic predispositions may interact with environmental factors that increase the potential for drug abuse and dependence—factors such as pressure from peers to use drugs, parental modelling of excessive drinking or drug use, and family disruption that results in a lack of effective guidance or support. Cognitive factors, especially positive drug expectancies (e.g., beliefs that using drugs will enhance one's social skills or sexual prowess), may also raise the potential for alcohol or drug problems.

Sociocultural factors need to be taken into account in this matrix of factors, such as the availability of alcohol and other drugs, presence or absence of cultural constraints that might curb excessive or underage drinking, the glamorizing of drug use in popular media, and inborn tendencies (such as among Asians) to flush more readily following alcohol intake.

Learning factors also play important roles. Drug use may be *positively* reinforced by the pleasurable effects associated with its use (mediated perhaps by release of dopamine in the brain or by activation of endorphin receptors). It may also be *negatively* reinforced by the reduction of states of tension and anxiety that depressant drugs such as alcohol, heroin, and tranquillizers can produce. Sadly, people who become dependent on drugs often continue to use them solely because of the relief from withdrawal symptoms and cravings they encounter when they go without the drug.

Problems of substance abuse and dependence are best approached by investigating the distinctive constellation of factors that apply to each individual case. No single model or set of factors will explain each case, which is why we need to understand each individual's unique characteristics and personal history.

Theoretical Perspectives

Review It

- **How are problems of substance abuse and dependence conceptualized within the major theoretical perspectives?** Biological perspectives focus on uncovering the biological pathways that may explain the mechanisms of physiological dependence. The disease model is a prominent biological perspective that treats problems of substance abuse and dependence as disease processes. Learning perspectives view substance abuse disorders as learned patterns of behaviour, with roles for classical and operant conditioning and observational learning. Cognitive perspectives focus on the roles of attitudes, beliefs, and expectancies in accounting for substance use and abuse. Sociocultural perspectives emphasize the cultural, group, and social factors that underlie drug use patterns, including the role of peer pressure in determining adolescent drug use. Psychodynamic theorists view problems of substance abuse, such as excessive drinking and habitual smoking, as signs of an oral fixation.

Define It

cue-exposure training

Recall It*

1. With increasing habituation to the use of opiates, the body reduces production of _____.

   a. endorphins
   b. testosterone
   c. prostaglandins
   d. epinephrine

2. Research on the genetic underpinnings of alcoholism and other forms of substance dependence has led to speculation that genes involved in determining the structure of _____ receptors in the brain may be involved.

   a. serotonin
   b. endorphin
   c. dopamine
   d. thyroxin

3. From a learning-theory perspective, drug use may become habitual because of the effects of _____ reinforcement.

   a. social
   b. cued
   c. negative
   d. delayed

4. Whenever Cynthia walks by a local bar where she often had drinks with her friends, she experiences cravings for alcohol. In classical conditioning terms, her cravings represent _____.

   a. unconditioned stimuli
   b. unconditioned responses
   c. conditioned stimuli
   d. conditioned responses

5. From a psychodynamic perspective, alcoholism reflects an _____ personality.

   a. oral-dependent
   b. oral-aggressive
   c. anal-retentive
   d. anal-expulsive

* Recall It answers can be found on the Companion Website for this text.

Think About It

- Do you know some people who can "hold their liquor" better than most? Why do the authors consider this talent a dubious blessing?
- How has your cultural background affected your attitudes and use of drugs such as alcohol and tobacco?
- Have you ever used an illicit drug? What factors contributed to your use?

TREATMENT

There have been and remain a vast array of nonprofessional, biological, and psychological approaches to substance abuse and dependence. However, treatment has often been a frustrating endeavour. In many, perhaps most cases, people with drug dependencies really do not want to discontinue the substances they are abusing. Most people who abuse cocaine, for example, like most abusers of alcohol and other drugs, do not seek treatment on their own. Those who do not seek treatment tend to be heavy abusers who deny the negative impact of cocaine on their lives and dwell within a social milieu that fails to encourage them to get help. When people do come for treatment, helping them through a withdrawal syndrome is usually straightforward enough, as we shall see. However, helping them pursue a life devoid of their preferred substances is more problematic. Moreover, treatment takes place in a setting—such as a therapist's office, support group, residential centre, or hospital—in which abstinence is valued and encouraged. Then the individual returns to the work, family, or street settings in which abuse and dependence were instigated and maintained. The problem of returning to abuse and dependence following treatment—that is, of *relapse*—can thus be more troublesome than the problems involved in initial treatment. For this reason, recent treatment efforts have focused on relapse prevention (Brandon, Vidrine, & Litvin, 2007). Given the difficulties encountered in treating people with substance abuse problems, it is no wonder there is much variability in the outcomes achieved in substance abuse treatment, regardless of the types of clients, treatments, or measures of outcome used (McLellan et al., 1994). One consistent finding that does emerge is that people with more severe alcohol and drug-use problems preceding treatment tend to have poorer outcomes in controlling their substance use following treatment.

Another complication is that many people with substance abuse problems also have psychological disorders and vice versa (APA, 2000a; Currie et al., 2005). Most clinics and treatment programs focus on the drug or alcohol problem, or the other psychological disorders, rather than treating all these problems simultaneously, however. This narrow focus results in poorer treatment outcomes, including more frequent rehospitalizations among those with these *dual diagnoses*.

Biological Approaches

An increasing range of biological approaches is used in treating problems of substance abuse and dependence. For people with chemical dependencies, biological treatment typically begins with **detoxification**—that is, helping them through withdrawal from addictive substances.

detoxification Process of ridding the system of alcohol or drugs under supervised conditions in which withdrawal symptoms can be monitored and controlled.

Detoxification Detoxification is often carried out in a hospital setting to provide the support needed to help the person withdraw safely from the addictive substance. In the case of addiction to alcohol or barbiturates, hospitalization allows medical personnel to monitor the development of potentially dangerous withdrawal symptoms, such as convulsions. The tranquillizing agents called benzodiazepines, such as Valium, may help block more severe withdrawal symptoms such as seizures and delirium tremens (Mayo-Smith, 1997). Behavioural treatment using monetary rewards for abstinent behaviour (judged by clean urine samples) may help improve outcomes during detoxification from opiates (Bickel, Amass, Higgins, Badger, & Esch, 1997). Detoxification from alcohol takes about a week. When tranquillizers are used to cope with subsequent urges to drink, however, people can be caught up in a game of "musical drugs."

Next, we consider other drugs used to treat people with chemical dependencies.

Disulfiram The drug *disulfiram* (brand name Antabuse) discourages alcohol consumption because the combination of the two produces a strong aversive reaction consisting of nausea, sweating, flushing, rapid heart rate, reduced blood pressure, and vomiting. In some extreme cases, drinking alcohol while taking disulfiram can lead to such a dramatic drop in blood pressure that the individual goes into shock and may even die. Although disulfiram has been used widely in alcoholism treatment, its effectiveness is limited because many patients who want to continue drinking simply stop using the drug. Others stop taking the drug in the belief they can maintain abstinence without it. Unfortunately, many return to uncontrolled drinking. Another drawback is that the drug has toxic effects in people with liver disease, a frequent ailment of people who suffer from alcoholism. Little evidence supports the efficacy of the drug in the long run (Garbutt, West, Carey, Lohr, & Crews, 1999; Schuckit, 1996).

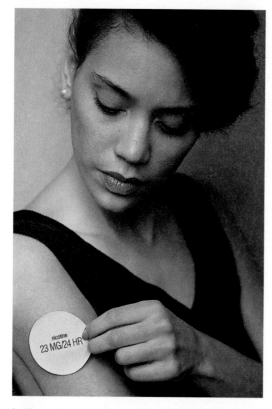

Antidepressants Antidepressants have shown some promise in reducing cravings for cocaine following withdrawal from the drug. These drugs may stimulate neural processes that regulate feelings of pleasure derived in everyday experiences. If pleasure can be more readily derived from nondrug-related activities, cocaine-addicted patients may be less likely to return to using the drug to induce pleasurable feelings. However, antidepressants have thus far failed to produce consistent results in reducing relapse rates for cocaine dependence, so it is best to withhold judgment concerning their efficacy (O'Brien, 1996). Of all the medications tested to date, disulfiram (Antabuse) has demonstrated the most consistent effect in reducing cocaine use (Vocci & Elkashef, 2005). Other medications that look promising according to controlled studies include baclofen, modafinil, tiagabine, and topiramate. All pharmacotherapy trials in cocaine-dependent patients include behaviour therapy. Therefore, these trials essentially evaluate whether the medications add to the effect of behavioural interventions (Vocci & Elkashef, 2005).

Researchers suspect that deficiencies of the neurotransmitter serotonin may underlie alcohol desires or cravings (Anton, 1994). Research is underway focusing on whether the appetite for alcohol can be curbed by using serotonin-reuptake inhibitors (e.g., Prozac) that increase the availability of serotonin in the brain. The use of these drugs in the early stages of abstinence may help people who are alcohol dependent to maintain sobriety and continue in treatment. In a recent clinical trial, Prozac improved the moods and reduced the drinking of people with coexisting (comorbid) alcohol dependence and depression (Cornelius et al., 1997). The actions of another neurotransmitter, dopamine, may account for the pleasurable or euphoric effects of alcohol. Drugs that mimic dopamine may be helpful in blocking the pleasurable reinforcing effects of alcohol.

Is the path to abstinence from smoking skin deep? Forms of nicotine-replacement therapy—such as nicotine transdermal (skin) patches and chewing gum that contains nicotine—allow people to continue to receive nicotine when they quit smoking. Though nicotine-replacement therapy is more effective than a placebo in helping people quit smoking, it does not address the behavioural components of addiction to nicotine, such as the habit of smoking while drinking alcohol. For this reason, nicotine-replacement therapy may be more effective if it is combined with behaviour therapy that focuses on changing smoking habits.

Nicotine Replacement Therapy One promising development in the pharmacological treatment of cigarette smoking is nicotine-replacement therapy in the form of prescription gum (brand name Nicorette), transdermal (skin) patches, and a recently approved nasal spray (Hurt et al., 1998). Many regular smokers, perhaps the great majority, are nicotine dependent. The use of nicotine replacements helps avert withdrawal symptoms following smoking cessation. After quitting smoking, ex-smokers can gradually wean themselves from the nicotine replacement.

Nicotine-chewing-gum treatment and the nicotine patch have been shown to be effective aids in quitting smoking (e.g., O'Brien & McKay, 1998; Skaar et al., 1997). The jury is still out on nicotine nasal sprays. However, although nicotine patches and gum may help quell the physiological components of withdrawal, they have no effect on the behavioural components of the addiction, such as the habit of smoking while drinking alcohol. As a result, nicotine replacement may be ineffective in promoting long-term changes unless it is combined with behavioural therapy that focuses on changing smoking habits ("The Last Draw for Smokers," 1996).

A non–nicotine-based antismoking drug, an antidepressant called *bupropion* (trade name Zyban), has been shown to be more effective than placebo in helping smokers quit (Hurt et al., 1997). This is the first drug that works on reducing cravings for nicotine, in much the same way that other antidepressants are being used to treat cocaine cravings.

methadone Artificial narcotic that lacks the rush associated with heroin that is used to help people addicted to heroin abstain without incurring an abstinence syndrome.

Methadone Maintenance Programs Methadone, a synthetic opiate, is widely used in treating heroin addiction. Although methadone treatment for opioid dependence gained its popularity through studies in the United States, it was first experimentally practised in the late 1950s by Dr. Robert Halliday and his addiction-treatment team in Vancouver (Fischer & Rehm, 2006). Methadone satisfies cravings for heroin and prevents the intense withdrawal symptoms that people addicted to heroin suffer upon withdrawal (O'Brien,

1996). Methadone does not produce the intense high or the stuporous state associated with heroin use, so people using it can hold jobs (O'Brien & McKay, 1998). However, like other opiates, methadone is highly addictive. For this reason, people treated with methadone can be conceptualized as swapping dependence on one drug for dependence on another. Yet methadone programs are usually publicly financed and so relieve people who are addicted to heroin of the need to engage in criminal activity to support their dependence on methadone. Although methadone can be taken indefinitely, individuals may be weaned from it without returning to using heroin.

For maximum effectiveness, methadone treatment must be combined with psychological counselling (O'Brien, 1996). Although methadone treatment produces clear benefits in improved daily functioning, not everyone succeeds with methadone, even with counselling (O'Brien & McKay, 1998). Some addicts turn to other drugs such as cocaine to get high or they return to using heroin.

Naloxone and Naltrexone Naloxone and **naltrexone** are sister drugs that block the high produced by heroin and other opiates. By blocking the opiate's effects, they may be useful in helping addicts avoid relapsing following opiate withdrawal.

Naltrexone (brand name ReVia) blocks the high from alcohol as well as from opiates, and has been approved in Canada for the treatment of alcoholism (Gianoulakis, 2001). In a double-blind placebo-control study, naltrexone in combination with behavioural treatment cut the relapse rates in people treated for alcoholism by more than half (Volpicelli et al., 1992, 1994). Naltrexone doesn't prevent the person from taking a drink, but seems to blunt cravings for the drug (O'Brien & McKay, 1998). By blocking the pleasure produced by alcohol, the drug can help break the vicious cycle in which one drink creates a desire for another, leading to episodes of binge drinking.

A nagging problem with drugs such as naltrexone, naloxone, disulfiram, and methadone is that people with substance-abuse problems may simply stop using them and return to their substance-abusing behaviour. Nor do such drugs provide alternative sources of positive reinforcement that can replace the pleasurable states produced by drugs of abuse. Drugs such as these are only effective in the context of a broader treatment program, consisting of psychological counselling and other treatment components such as job training, and stress-management training—treatments designed to help people with substance-abuse problems attain the skills they need to embark on a life in the mainstream culture (Miller & Brown, 1997).

naloxone Drug that prevents users from becoming high if they subsequently take heroin. Some people are placed on naloxone after being withdrawn from heroin to prevent return to heroin.

naltrexone Chemical cousin of naloxone that blocks the high from alcohol as well as opiates and is now approved for use in treating alcoholism.

Nonprofessional Support Groups

Despite the complexity of the factors contributing to substance abuse and dependence, these problems are frequently handled by laypeople or nonprofessionals. Such people often have or had the problems themselves. For example, self-help group meetings are sponsored by organizations like Alcoholics Anonymous (AA), Narcotics Anonymous, and Cocaine Anonymous. These groups promote abstinence and provide members with an opportunity to discuss their feelings and experiences in a supportive group setting. More experienced group members (sponsors) support newer members during periods of crisis or potential relapse. The meetings are sustained by nominal voluntary contributions.

The most widely used nonprofessional program, Alcoholics Anonymous, is based on the belief that alcoholism is a disease, not a sin. AA assumes that people who suffer from alcoholism are never "cured," regardless of how long they abstain from alcohol or how well they control their drinking. Instead of being cured, people who suffer from alcoholism are seen as "recovering." It is also assumed that people who suffer from alcoholism cannot control their drinking and need help in order to stop. There are more than 50 000 chapters of AA in North America ("Treatment of Drug Abuse and Addiction—Part 1," 1995). AA is so deeply embedded in the consciousness of health-care professionals that many of them automatically refer newly detoxified people to AA as a follow-up agency. About half of AA members have problems with illicit drugs as well as alcohol.

The AA experience is part spiritual, part group supportive, part cognitive. AA follows a 12-step approach in which the beginning steps deal with acceptance of one's powerlessness over alcohol and turning one's will and life over to a higher power. This spiritual component may be helpful to some participants but not to others who prefer not to appeal for divine support. (Other lay organizations, such as Rational Recovery, do not adopt a spiritual approach.) The later steps focus on examining one's character flaws, admitting one's wrongdoings, being open to God's help in overcoming character defects, making amends to others, and, at the 12th step, bringing the AA message to other people suffering from alcoholism (McCrady, 1994). Prayer and meditation are urged on members to help them get in touch with their higher power. The meetings themselves provide group support. So does the buddy or sponsoring system, which encourages members to call each other for support when they feel tempted to drink.

Alcoholics Anonymous claims to have a high success rate—in the neighbourhood of 75% (Wallace, 1985). Critics note that percentages this high are based on personal testimonies rather than on careful surveys or experiments. Moreover, such estimates include only persons who attend meetings for extended periods. The dropout rate is high, with as many as 70% of members dropping out within ten meetings, according to one survey. Even AA estimates that 50% of its members drop out after three months ("Treatment of Alcoholism—Part II," 1996). It has been difficult to conduct controlled studies because AA does not keep records of its members in order to protect their anonymity and also because of an inability to conduct randomized clinical trials in AA settings (McCaul & Furst, 1994). On the other hand, the greater the involvement with AA, researchers find, the better the outcome in terms of days not drinking or using drugs (Morgenstern, Langenbucher, Labouvie, & Miller, 1997). Yet we can't say for certain whether regular participation in AA or personal motivation that may contribute to both use of AA and change in substance use behaviour is responsible for better outcomes. In all likelihood, success is due to both factors. Nor can we say who is likely to succeed in AA and who is not.

Al-Anon, begun in 1951, is a spin-off of AA that supports the families and friends of people suffering from alcoholism. Another spin-off of AA, Alateen, provides support to children whose parents have alcoholism, helping them see they are not to blame for their parents' drinking and are thus undeserving of the guilt they may feel.

Residential Approaches

A residential approach to treatment involves a stay in a hospital or therapeutic residence. Hospitalization may be recommended when substance abusers cannot exercise self-control in their usual environments or cannot tolerate withdrawal symptoms, and when their behaviour is self-destructive or dangerous to others. Outpatient treatment is less costly and often indicated when withdrawal symptoms are less severe, clients are committed to changing their behaviour, and environmental support systems, such as families, strive to help clients make the transition to a drug-free lifestyle. The great majority (nearly 90%) of people treated for alcoholism are helped on an outpatient basis (McCaul & Furst, 1994).

When alcoholism was first considered a disease in the 1960s, only a few medically based treatment programs existed. Many other residential programs have since come into being, with some facilities, such as the Betty Ford Clinic, receiving a great deal of media attention. Most inpatient programs use an extended 28-day detoxification or drying-out period. Clients are helped through withdrawal symptoms in a few days. Then the emphasis shifts to counselling about the destructive effects of alcohol and combating distorted ideas or rationalizations. Consistent with the disease model, the goal of abstinence is urged (Desmond, 1987).

Researchers find that most people with alcohol use disorders do not require hospitalization, although some certainly do. Studies comparing outpatient and inpatient programs reveal no overall difference in relapse rates (Miller & Hester, 1986). However, medical insurance may not cover outpatient treatment, which may encourage many people who may benefit from outpatient treatment to admit themselves for inpatient treatment.

A number of residential therapeutic communities are also in use. Some of them have part- or full-time professional staffs. Others are run entirely by laypeople. Residents are expected to remain free of drugs and take responsibility for their actions. They are often confronted about their excuses for failing to take responsibility for themselves and about

Al-Anon Organization sponsoring support groups for family members of people with alcoholism.

their denial of the damage being done by their drug abuse. They share their life experiences to help one another develop productive ways of handling stress. As with AA, we lack evidence from controlled studies demonstrating the efficacy of residential treatment programs. Also like AA, therapeutic communities have high numbers of early dropouts. Moreover, many former members of residential treatment programs who remain substance free during their time in residence relapse upon returning to the world outside. Evidence suggests that a day treatment therapeutic community may be as effective as a residential treatment facility (Guydish, Werdegar, Sorensen, Clark, & Acampora, 1998).

Psychodynamic Approaches

Psychoanalysts view substance abuse and dependence as symptomatic of conflicts that are rooted in childhood experiences. Focusing on substance abuse or dependence per se is seen to offer, at most, a superficial type of therapy. It is assumed that if the underlying conflicts are resolved, abusive behaviour will also subside as more mature forms of gratification are sought. Traditional psychoanalysts also assume that programs directed solely at abusive behaviour will be of limited benefit because they fail to address the underlying psychological causes of abuse. Although there are many reports of successful psychodynamic case studies of people with substance abuse problems, there is a dearth of controlled and replicable research studies. The effectiveness of psychodynamic methods for treating substance abuse and dependence thus remains unsubstantiated.

Behavioural Approaches

The use of behaviour therapy or behaviour modification in treating substance abuse and dependence focuses on modifying abusive and dependent behaviour patterns. The issue to many behaviourally oriented therapists is not whether substance abuse and dependence are diseases but whether or not abusers can learn to change their behaviour when they are faced with temptation.

Self-Control Strategies Self-control training focuses on helping abusers develop skills they can use to change their abusive behaviour. Behaviour therapists focus on three components of substance abuse:

1. The *antecedent* cues or stimuli (As) that prompt or trigger abuse,
2. The abusive *behaviours* (Bs) themselves, and
3. The reinforcing or punishing *consequences* (Cs) that maintain or discourage abuse.

Table 9.5 shows the kinds of strategies used to modify the "ABCs" of substance abuse.

Aversive Conditioning In **aversive conditioning**, painful or aversive stimuli are paired with substance-abuse or abuse-related stimuli to make abuse less appealing. In the case of problem drinking, tastes of different alcoholic beverages are usually paired with chemically induced nausea and vomiting or with electric shock. As a consequence, alcohol may come to elicit an aversive conditioned response, such as fear or nausea that inhibits drinking. Relief from aversive responses then negatively reinforces avoidance of alcohol.

aversive conditioning Behaviour therapy technique in which a maladaptive response is paired with exposure to an aversive stimulus, such as electric shock or nausea, so a conditioned aversion develops toward the stimuli associated with the maladaptive response. Also termed *aversion therapy*.

Social-Skills Training Social-skills training helps people develop effective interpersonal responses in social situations that prompt substance abuse. Assertiveness training, for example, may be used to teach people with alcohol-related problems how to fend off social pressures to drink. Behavioural marital therapy seeks to improve marital communication and a couple's problem-solving skills to relieve marital stresses that can trigger abuse. Couples may learn how to use written behavioural contracts. One such contract might stipulate that the person with a substance-abuse problem agrees to abstain from drinking or to start taking Antabuse, and his or her spouse agrees to refrain from making comments about past drinking and the probability of future lapses. The available evidence supports the utility of social-skills training and behavioural marital therapy approaches in treating alcoholism (Finney & Monahan, 1996; O'Farrell et al., 1996).

TABLE 9.5

Self-Control Strategies for Modifying the "ABCs" of Substance Abuse

1. Controlling the As (Antecedents) of Substance Abuse:

People who abuse or become dependent on psychoactive substances become conditioned to a wide range of external (environmental) and internal stimuli (body states). They may begin to break these stimulus-response connections by:

- Removing drinking and smoking paraphernalia from the home—all alcoholic beverages, beer mugs, carafes, ashtrays, matches, cigarette packs, lighters, etc.

- Restricting the stimulus environment in which drinking or smoking is permitted. Using the substance only in a stimulus-deprived area of their homes, such as the garage, bathroom, or basement. All other stimuli that might be connected to using the substance are removed—there is no television, reading materials, radio, or telephone. In this way, substance abuse becomes detached from many controlling stimuli.

- Not socializing with others with substance-abuse problems, by avoiding situations linked to abuse—bars, the street, bowling alleys, etc.

- Frequenting substance-free environments—lectures or concerts, a gym, museums, evening classes—by socializing with nonabusers, sitting in nonsmoking cars of trains, eating in restaurants without liquor licences.

- Managing the internal triggers for abuse by practising self-relaxation or meditation and not taking the substance when tense; by expressing angry feelings by writing them down or self-assertion, not by taking the substance; and by seeking counselling for prolonged feelings of depression, not alcohol, pills, or cigarettes.

2. Controlling the Bs (Behaviours) of Substance Abuse

People can prevent and interrupt substance abuse by:

- Using response prevention—breaking abusive habits by physically preventing them from occurring or making them more difficult—by not bringing alcohol home or cigarettes to the office.

- Using competing responses when tempted by being prepared to handle substance-related situations with appropriate ammunition—mints, sugarless chewing gum, etc.; and by taking a bath or shower, walking the dog, walking around the block, taking a drive, calling a friend, spending time in a substance-free environment, practising meditation or relaxation, or exercising when tempted rather than using the substance.

- Making abuse more laborious—buying one can of beer at a time; storing matches, ashtrays, and cigarettes far apart; wrapping cigarettes in foil to make smoking more cumbersome; pausing for ten minutes when struck by the urge to drink, smoke, or use another substance and asking oneself, "Do I really need this one?"

3. Controlling the Cs (Consequences) of Substance Abuse

Substance abuse has immediate positive consequences such as pleasure, relief from anxiety and withdrawal symptoms, and stimulation. People can counter these intrinsic rewards and alter the balance of power in favour of nonabuse by:

- Rewarding themselves for nonabuse and punishing themselves for abuse.

- Switching to brands of beer and cigarettes they don't like.

- Setting gradual substance-reduction schedules and rewarding themselves for sticking to them.

- Punishing themselves for failing to meet substance-reduction goals. People with substance-abuse problems can assess themselves at say, 10 cents for each slip, and donate the cash to an unpalatable cause, such as a brother-in-law's birthday present.

- Rehearsing motivating thoughts or self-statements—like writing reasons for quitting smoking on index cards. For example:

    Each day I don't smoke adds another day to my life.

    Quitting smoking will help me breathe deeply again.

    Foods will smell and taste better when I quit smoking.

    Think how much money I'll save by not smoking.

    Think how much cleaner my teeth and fingers will be by not smoking.

    I'll be proud to tell others that I kicked the habit.

    My lungs will become clearer each and every day I don't smoke.

Smokers can carry a list of 20 to 25 such statements and read several of them at various times throughout the day. The statements can become parts of one's daily routine, a constant reminder of one's goals.

Relapse-Prevention Training

The word **relapse** derives from Latin roots meaning "to slide back." From 50% to 90% of people who are successfully treated for substance abuse problems eventually relapse (Leary, 1996). Relapses often occur in response to negative mood states such as depression or anxiety, to interpersonal conflict, or to social pressures to resume drinking (Cooney et al., 1997). People with drinking problems who relapse are more likely than those who do not to have encountered stress, such as the loss of a loved one or economic problems. They are also more likely than those who maintain sobriety to rely on avoidance methods of coping, such as denial. Successful abstainers from alcohol tend to have more social and family resources and support to draw on in handling stress (Havassy, Hall, & Wasserman, 1991).

relapse Recurrence of a problem behaviour or disorder.

controlled social drinking Controversial approach to treating problem drinkers in which the goal of treatment is the maintenance of controlled social drinking in moderate amounts, rather than total abstinence.

A CLOSER LOOK

The Controlled Social Drinking Controversy

The disease model of alcoholism contends that people who suffer from the disease who have just one drink will lose control and go on a binge. Some professionals, however, like Linda and Mark Sobell, have argued that behaviour modification self-control techniques can teach many people who abuse alcohol or have a dependence to engage in **controlled social drinking**—to have a drink or two without necessarily falling off the wagon.

The contention that people who develop alcoholism can learn to drink moderately remains controversial. The proponents of the disease model of alcoholism, who have wielded considerable political strength, stand strongly opposed to attempts to teach controlled social drinking.

To support their contention, the Sobells, who did a good deal of their research at Toronto's Addiction Research Foundation, published the results of an experiment in which people who suffered from alcoholism were either taught to control their drinking or were encouraged to abstain from alcohol. The Sobells (1973, 1976, 1984) reported that 85% of their 20 controlled-drinking subjects remained in control of their drinking at a two-year follow-up. However, a research group critical of the Sobells (Pendery, Maltzman, & West, 1982) published its own ten-year follow-up of the Sobells' subjects. The group claimed that only 1 in 20 people remained successful at controlled social drinking. Most had returned to uncontrolled drinking on many occasions, and four of the group had died from alcohol-related causes.

Despite the controversy it caused, Pendery et al.'s study was flawed. The researchers reported results for only the controlled drinking group without reporting data for the Sobells' control group (the abstinence-based treatment condition). Without some kind of control

group, it is impossible to assess the effects of controlled drinking. A ten-year follow-up of the Sobells' study reported by Dickens et al. (1982) found that there were more deaths in the abstinence group (30%) than in the controlled drinking group (20%).

Other investigators have found that controlled social drinking is a reasonable treatment goal for younger people with problem drinking who are less alcohol dependent but are headed on the road toward chronic alcoholism (e.g., Miller & Muñoz, 1983; Sanchez-Craig, Annis, Bornet, & MacDonald, 1984; Sanchez-Craig & Wilkinson, 1986/1987). Evidence supporting controlled social drinking programs for people with chronic alcoholism, however, remains lacking. Interest in controlled social drinking programs has also waned, largely because of strong opposition from professionals and lay organizations committed to the abstinence model. Nevertheless, as noted by University of Calgary psychologist David Hodgins (2006), controlled drinking is feasible for some people and so we should consider how best to integrate it into our treatment systems. Controlled-drinking programs may be best suited for younger people with early-stage alcoholism or problem drinking, as well as those who reject goals of total abstinence or have failed in programs requiring abstinence, and those who do not show severe withdrawal symptoms (Marlatt, Larimer, Baer, & Quigley, 1993; Rosenberg, 1993; Sobell et al., 1990). Researchers also find that women tend to do better than men in controlled drinking programs (Marlatt et al., 1993). By offering moderation as a treatment goal, controlled drinking programs may also reach many people with alcohol use disorders who might otherwise go untreated because they refuse to participate in abstinence-only treatment programs (Marlatt et al., 1993).

Controlled drinking programs may actually represent a pathway to abstinence for people who would not otherwise enter abstinence-only treatment programs

(continued)

(Marlatt et al., 1993). That is, treatment in a controlled drinking program may be the first step in the direction of giving up drinking completely. A large percentage (about one out of four in one study; Miller et al., 1993) enters with the goal of achieving controlled drinking but becomes abstinent by the end of treatment. On the other hand, controlled social drinking may not be appropriate for people with established alcohol dependence and those who are taking medications that interact with alcohol or have other medical risks that might be aggravated by alcohol (Lawson, 1983; "Treatment of Alcoholism— Part II," 1996).

relapse-prevention training Cognitive-behavioural technique used in the treatment of addictive behaviours that involves the use of behavioural and cognitive strategies to resist temptations and prevent lapses from becoming relapses.

Because of the prevalence of relapse, behaviourally oriented therapists have devised a number of methods referred to as **relapse-prevention training**. Such training helps people with substance abuse problems cope with temptations and high-risk situations to prevent *lapses*—that is, slips—from becoming full-blown relapses (Marlatt & Gordon, 1985). High-risk situations include negative mood states, such as depression, anger, or anxiety; interpersonal conflict (e.g., marital problems or conflicts with employers); and socially conducive situations such as "the guys getting together." Participants learn to cope with these situations, for example, by learning self-relaxation skills to counter anxiety and learning to resist social pressures to resume use of the substance. Trainees are also taught to avoid practices that might prompt a relapse, such as keeping alcohol on hand for friends.

Although it contains many behavioural strategies, relapse-prevention training is a cognitive-behavioural technique in that it also focuses on the person's *interpretations* of any lapses or slips that may occur, such as smoking a first cigarette or taking a first drink following quitting. Clients are taught how to avoid the so-called **abstinence-violation effect** (AVE)—the tendency to overreact to a lapse—by learning to reorient their thinking about lapses and slips. People who have a slip may be more likely to relapse if they attribute their slip to personal weakness and experience shame and guilt rather than attributing the slip to an external or transient event (Curry, Marlatt, & Gordon, 1987). For example, consider a skater who slips on the ice (Marlatt & Gordon, 1985). Whether or not the skater gets back up and continues to perform depends largely on whether he or she sees the slip as an isolated and correctable event or as a sign of complete failure. Evidence shows that the best predictor of progression from a first to a second lapse among ex-smokers was the feeling of giving up after the first lapse (Shiffman et al., 1996). But those who responded to a first lapse by using coping strategies were more likely to succeed in averting a subsequent lapse on the same day.

abstinence-violation effect Tendency in people trying to maintain abstinence from a substance, such as alcohol or cigarettes, to overreact to a lapse with feelings of guilt and a sense of resignation that may then trigger a full-blown relapse. Abbreviated *AVE*.

In contrast to the disease model, which contends that people who suffer from alcoholism automatically lose control if they take a single drink, the relapse-prevention model assumes that whether or not a lapse becomes a relapse depends on the person's interpretation of the lapse (Marlatt & Gordon, 1985). Self-defeating attributions such as, "What's the use? I'm just doomed to fail" trigger depression, resignation, and resumption of problem drinking. Participants in relapse-prevention training programs are encouraged to view lapses as temporary setbacks that provide opportunities to learn what kinds of situations lead to temptation and how they can avoid or cope with such situations. If they can learn to think, "Okay, I had a slip, but that doesn't mean all is lost unless I believe it is," they are less likely to catastrophize lapses and subsequently relapse. Other relapse-prevention techniques focus on training smokers' spouses or partners to be more helpful in maintaining abstinence. Social support appears to play a key role in determining relapse in abstinence-based programs for alcoholism, drug abuse, and cigarette smoking (e.g., Nides et al., 1995).

All in all, efforts to treat people with substance abuse and dependence problems have been mixed at best. Many abusers really do not want to discontinue use of these substances, although they would prefer, if possible, to avoid their negative consequences. The more effective substance abuse treatment programs involve intensive, multiple treatment approaches that address the wide range of problems that people with substance abuse disorders frequently present, including co-occurring (comorbid) psychiatric problems like depression (Brown et al., 1997; Crits-Christoph & Siqueland, 1996; D. A. Kessler et al., 1997). Comorbidity (co-occurrence) of substance use disorders and other psychiatric disorders has become the rule in treatment facilities rather than the exception (Brems & Johnson, 1997). Substance abusers who have comorbid disorders or more severe psychological problems typically fare more poorly in treatment for their drug or alcohol problems (Kranzler et al., 1996; Simpson et al., 1999). For people with alcoholism and other substance abuse problems, a number of different therapies, including 12-step and cognitive-behavioural approaches, often work well (Breslin, Li, Sdao-Jarvie, Tupker, & Ittig-Deland, 2002; Conrod et al., 2000; Project MATCH Research Group, 1997).

The major problem is that many people with alcohol use disorders have no contact whatsoever with alcohol treatment programs or self-help organizations (Institute of Medicine, 1990). Clearly, more needs to be done to help people whose use of alcohol and other drugs puts them at risk. In the case of inner-city youth who have become trapped within a milieu of street drugs and hopelessness, the availability of culturally sensitive counselling and job-training opportunities would be of considerable benefit in helping them assume more productive social roles. The challenge is clear: to develop cost-effective ways of helping people recognize the negative effects of substances and forgo the powerful and immediate reinforcements they provide.

STUDY BREAK

Treatment

Review It

- **What treatment approaches are used to help people overcome problems of substance abuse and dependence?** Biological approaches to substance-abuse disorders include detoxification; the use of drugs such as disulfiram, methadone, naloxone, naltrexone, and antidepressants; and nicotine replacement therapy. Residential-treatment approaches include hospitals and therapeutic residences. Nonprofessional support groups, like Alcoholics Anonymous, promote abstinence within a supportive group setting. Psychodynamic therapists focus on uncovering the inner conflicts, originating in childhood, that are believed to be at the root of substance-abuse problems. Behavioural therapists focus on helping people with substance-related problems change problem behaviours through such techniques as self-control training, aversive conditioning, and skills training. Regardless of the initial success of a treatment technique, relapse remains a pressing problem in treating people with substance-abuse problems. Relapse-prevention training employs cognitive-behavioural techniques to help ex-abusers cope with high-risk situations and to prevent lapses from becoming relapses by helping participants interpret lapses in less damaging ways.

Define It

detoxification
methadone
naloxone
naltrexone
Al-Anon

aversive conditioning
controlled social drinking
relapse
relapse-prevention training
abstinence-violation effect

Recall It*

1. The initial step in treating problems of chemical dependence generally involves _____.

   a. insight-oriented therapy
   b. detoxification
   c. behavioural counselling
   d. relapse-prevention training

2. Howard has been fighting his addiction to heroin. He has been given an alternative drug to help him withdraw from heroin without experiencing unpleasant withdrawal symptoms. The alternative drug is also an opiate, but it doesn't produce the rush provided by heroin. The drug he is taking is _____.

   a. naloxone
   b. methadone
   c. disulfiram
   d. diazepam

3. _____ is a drug that blocks the high produced by heroin and other opiates.

    a. Naloxone
    b. Methadone
    c. Disulfiram
    d. Diazepam

4. The behavioural technique in which painful or aversive stimuli are paired with substance abuse or abuse-related stimuli is called _____.

    a. behavioural reconditioning
    b. aversive conditioning
    c. contingent punishment
    d. relapse-prevention training

5. Sally is involved in a therapy program for problem drinkers. Her therapist helps her learn how to deal more assertively with her "drinking buddies," who are always pressuring her to drink. The technique the therapist is using is called _____.

    a. self-control training
    b. behavioural reconditioning
    c. cognitive retraining
    d. social-skills training

* Recall It answers can be found on the Companion Website for this text.

Think About It

- Do you know anyone who has received treatment for a drug-abuse problem? What was the outcome?
- Many teenagers today have parents who themselves smoked marijuana or used other drugs when they were younger. If you were one of those parents, what would you tell your kids about drugs?
- What do you think of the concept of using methadone, a narcotic drug, to treat problems of addiction to another narcotic drug, heroin? What are the advantages and disadvantages of this approach? Do you believe the government should support methadone maintenance programs? Why or why not?

WEBLINKS

Centre for Addiction and Mental Health (CAMH)
www.camh.net
This is a public hospital providing direct patient care for people with mental health and addiction problems. CAMH is also a research facility, an education and training institute, and a community-based organization providing health promotion and prevention services across Ontario.

Canadian Centre on Substance Abuse
www.ccsa.ca
This website provides statistics and other information on substance use disorders.

Alcoholics Anonymous
www.alcoholics-anonymous.org
AA's website provides information on the nature and treatment of alcohol problems.

Mothers Against Drunk Driving (MADD)
www.madd.ca
MADD's Canadian site provides information on the prevalence and cost of alcohol abuse.

National Council on Alcohol and Drug Dependence
www.ncadd.org
This site contains numerous links providing information on the nature and treatment of substance use disorders.

FASworld
www.fasworld.com
A Canadian-based website providing information about fetal alcohol spectrum disorder.

Substance Abuse and Dependence

Classification of Substance-Related Disorders

Substance-Use Disorders

Substance Abuse
- Features
  - Pattern of repeated drug-using behaviour that has damaging consequences
  - May develop into substance dependence

Substance Dependence
- Features
  - Physiological signs of dependence (tolerance or withdrawal), and/or
  - Compulsive use of substance (e.g., lack of control over substance use)

Substance-Induced Disorders

- Induced by psychoactive substances:
  - Intoxication
  - Withdrawal syndromes
  - Mood disorders, anxiety disorders, psychotic disorders
  - Delirium, dementia, amnesia
  - Sexual dysfunction, sleep disorders

Pathways to Drug Dependence

- Experimentation
- Routine use
- Addiction or dependence

Drugs of Abuse

Depressants

- Alcohol
- Barbiturates (sedatives; e.g., amobarbital)
- Opiates (narcotics; e.g., heroin)

Hallucinogens

- LSD ("acid" or lysergic acid diethylamide)
- PCP ("angel dust" or phencyclidine)
- Marijuana (e.g., "hash")

Stimulants

- Amphetamines (e.g., "meth" or methamphetamine)
- Cocaine (e.g., "crack")
- Nicotine

Inhalants

- Diverse group of substances (e.g., aerosols)

Theoretical Perspectives

Treatment

Eating Disorders and Sleep Disorders

Did You Know That...

See the underlined text on the pages indicated below for more information on these interesting and often misunderstood facts.

- Although others see them as "skin and bones," young women with anorexia nervosa still see themselves as too fat? (p. 369)

- Some bulimic women force themselves to vomit after every meal? (p. 373)

- Drugs used to treat depression may also help curb bulimic binges? (p. 375)

- Nutrition management and psychoeducational programs are important in the treatment of eating disorders? (p. 377)

- Some people have sleep attacks in which they suddenly fall asleep without any warning? (p. 382)

- Some people literally gasp for breath hundreds of times during sleep without realizing it? (p. 383)

- Sleeping pills are only a short-term solution for the treatment of sleeping disorders and can actually worsen insomnia? (p. 387)

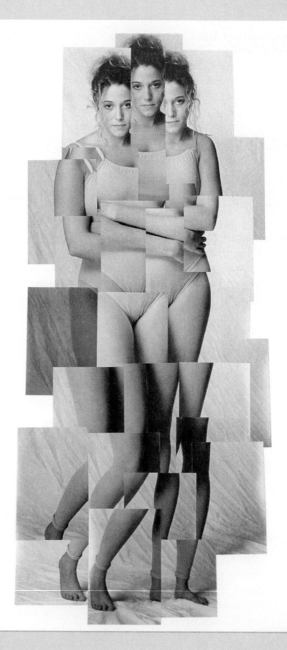

JESSICA WAS A 20-year-old communications major when she consulted a psychologist for the first time. For years she had kept a secret from everyone, including her fiancé Ken. She and Ken were planning to get married in three months. She had decided that it was time to finally confront her problem. She told the psychologist she didn't want to bring the problem into the marriage with her, that it wouldn't be fair to Ken. She said, "I don't want him to have to deal with this. I want to stop this before the marriage. I have to stop bingeing and throwing up." Jessica went on to describe her problem: "I go on binges and then throw it all up. It makes me feel like I am in control, but really I'm not." To conceal her secret, she would lock herself in the bathroom, run the water in the sink to mask the sounds, and induce vomiting. She would then clean up after herself and spray an air deodorant to mask any telltale odours. "The only one who suspects," she said with embarrassment, "is my dentist. He said my teeth are beginning to decay from stomach acid."

Jessica had *bulimia nervosa*, an eating disorder characterized by recurrent cycles of binge-ing and purging. Eating disorders like bulimia nervosa and *anorexia nervosa* often affect young people of high school or college age, especially young women. Although rates of diag-nosable eating disorders in college and university students are not as high as you might think, chances are you have known people with anorexia or bulimia or with disturbed eating patterns that fall within a spectrum of eating-related disorders, such as repeated binge eating or excessive dieting. Another class of psychological disorders that commonly affect young adults is sleep disorders. The most common form of sleep disorder, chronic insomnia, affects many young people who are making their way in the world and tend to bring their worries and concerns to bed with them.

EATING DISORDERS

In a nation of plenty, some people literally starve themselves—sometimes to death. They are obsessed with their weight and desire to achieve an exaggerated image of thinness. Others engage in repeated cycles in which they binge on food and then attempt to purge their excess eating, such as by inducing vomiting. These dysfunctional patterns are the two major types of **eating disorders: anorexia nervosa**, and **bulimia nervosa**, respectively. Eating disorders are characterized by disturbed patterns of eating and maladaptive ways of controlling body weight. Like many other psychological disorders, anorexia and bulimia are often accompanied by other forms of psychopathology, including mood, anx-iety, impulse-control, and substance-use disorders (Hudson, Hiripi, Pope, & Kessler, 2007; Milos, Spindler, & Schnyder, 2004).

Anorexia nervosa and bulimia nervosa were once considered very rare, but they are becoming increasingly common in Canada and other developed countries. Hospitalization rates for Canadian women with eating disorders increased 20% between 1987 and 1999 (Health Canada, 2002a). The great majority of cases (about 90%) occur among women, especially young women (HealthyOntario.com, 2003). Canadian sources indicate that although these disorders may develop in middle or even late adulthood, they typically begin during adolescence or early adulthood when the pressures to be thin are the strongest (Jilek, 2001; National Institute of Nutrition, 2001). As these social pressures have increased, so too have the rates of eating disorders. Estimates are that between 1% and 2% of female adolescents and young adults in Canada develop anorexia and 3% to 10% develop bulimia (Canadian Mental Health Association, 2003; Leichner, Arnett, Rallo, Srilcamesuaran, & Vulcano, 1986; Polivy & Herman, 2002; Woodside et al., 2001). Rates of anorexia and bulimia among young Canadian males are much lower, esti-mated at roughly 0.3% (3 in 1000) (Woodside et al., 2001).

eating disorders Psychological disor-ders involving disturbed eating pat-terns and maladaptive ways of controlling body weight.

anorexia nervosa Eating disorder, pri-marily affecting young women, char-acterized by maintenance of an abnormally low body weight, distor-tions of body image, intense fears of gaining weight, and, in females, amenorrhea.

bulimia nervosa Eating disorder char-acterized by a recurrent pattern of binge eating followed by self-induced purging and accompanied by persist-ent overconcern with body weight and shape.

A much larger percentage of young women show bulimic behaviours (occasional bingeing and purging) or excessive dieting, but not to the point that they would warrant a diagnosis of an eating disorder. In one large study, researchers found that almost one-quarter of Ontario high school females were dieting to lose weight and 27% showed symptoms of an eating disorder along with reported bingeing and purging. It was also found that disordered eating attitudes and behaviours increased significantly with age. Of note, it was revealed that even in younger females (aged 12 to 15), 18.8% had binged or purged, while the reported incidence increased to 26.3% in females aged 15 and older (Jones, Bennett, Olmsted, Lawson, & Rodin, 2001). These figures are disturbing because it puts females with these eating attitudes and behaviours at risk for developing full-blown eating disorders (Fairburn, Cooper, Doll, & Davies, 2005; Patton, Selzer, Coffey, Carlin, & Wolfe, 1999).

Anorexia Nervosa

Karen was the 22-year-old daughter of a renowned English professor. She had begun her college career full of promise at the age of 17, but two years ago, after "social problems" occurred, she returned to live at home and took progressively lighter course loads at a local college. Karen had never been overweight, but about a year ago her mother noticed that she seemed to be gradually "turning into a skeleton."

Karen spent literally hours every day shopping at the supermarket, butcher, and bakeries conjuring up gourmet treats for her parents and younger siblings. Arguments over her lifestyle and eating habits had divided the family into two camps. The camp led by her father called for patience; that headed by her mother demanded confrontation. Her mother feared that Karen's father would "protect her right into her grave" and wanted Karen placed in residential treatment "for her own good." The parents finally compromised on an outpatient evaluation.

At an even five feet, Karen looked like a prepubescent 11-year-old. Her nose and cheekbones protruded crisply. Her lips were full, but the redness of her lipstick was unnatural, as if too much paint had been dabbed on a corpse for a funeral. Karen weighed only 78 pounds, but she had dressed in a stylish silk blouse, scarf, and baggy pants so that not one inch of her body was revealed.

Karen vehemently denied that she had a problem. Her figure was "just about where I want it to be" and she engaged in aerobic exercise daily. A deal was struck in which outpatient treatment would be tried as long as Karen lost no more weight and showed steady gains back to at least 90 pounds. Treatment included a day hospital with group therapy and two meals a day. But word came back that Karen was artfully toying with her food—cutting it up, sort of licking it, and moving it about her plate—rather than eating it. After three weeks Karen had lost another pound. At that point, her parents were able to persuade her to enter a residential treatment program, where her eating behaviour could be more carefully monitored.

THE AUTHORS' FILES

Anorexia derives from the Greek roots *an-*, meaning "without," and *orexis*, meaning "a desire for." *Anorexia*, thus, means "without desire for [food]," which is something of a misnomer because loss of appetite among people with anorexia nervosa is rare. However, they may be repelled by food and refuse to eat more than is absolutely necessary to maintain a minimal weight for their ages and heights. Often, they starve themselves to the point where they become dangerously emaciated. By and large, anorexia nervosa develops in early to late adolescence, between the ages of 12 and 18, although earlier and later onsets are sometimes found.

The clinical features listed in Table 10.1 on page 369 are used to diagnose anorexia nervosa. Although reduced body weight is the most obvious sign, the most prominent

TABLE 10.1

Diagnostic Features of Anorexia Nervosa

A. Refusal to maintain weight beyond the minimal normal weight for one's age and height; for example, a weight at least 15% below normal.

B. Strong fear of putting on weight or becoming fat, despite being thin.

C. A distorted body image in which one's body—or part of one's body—is perceived as fat, although others perceive the person as thin.

D. In case of females who have had menarche, absence of three or more consecutive menstrual periods.

Source: Adapted from the DSM-IV-TR (APA, 2000a).

clinical feature is an intense fear of obesity. One common pattern of anorexia begins after menarche when a girl notices added weight and insists it must come off. Extreme dieting and, often, excessive exercise continue unabated after the initial weight-loss goal is achieved, however—even after their families and others express concern. Another common pattern occurs among young women when they leave home to attend university or college and encounter difficulties adjusting to the demands of college life and independent living. Anorexia is also more common among young women involved in ballet or modelling, in which there is often a strong emphasis on maintaining an unrealistically thin body shape.

Adolescent girls and women with anorexia almost always deny that they are losing too much weight or wasting away. They may argue that their ability to engage in stressful exercise demonstrates their fitness. Women with eating disorders are more likely than normal women to view themselves as heavier than they are (Horne, Van Vactor, & Emerson, 1991; Penner, Thompson, & Coovert, 1991). Others may see them as nothing but "skin and bones," but anorexic women have a distorted body image and may still see themselves as too fat. Although they literally starve themselves, they may spend much of the day thinking and talking about food, and even preparing elaborate meals for others (Rock & Curran-Celentano, 1996).

Although anorexia in women is far more common than in men, an increasing number of young men are presenting with anorexia. Many are involved in sporting activities, like wrestling and gymnastics, in which they have experienced pressure to maintain a lower weight classification. In this regard, it seems both young men and women experience similar pressures to achieve weight loss and leanness (Ricciardelli & McCabe, 2004).

Subtypes of Anorexia Due to the earlier work of Canadian eating disorder authorities Garfinkel, Moldofsky, and Garner (1980), the DSM diagnosis of anorexia now includes two general subtypes of anorexia, a *binge-eating/purging type* and a *restrictive type*. The first type is characterized by frequent episodes of binge eating and purging; the second type is not. Although repeated cycles of binge eating and purging occur in bulimia, bulimic individuals do not reduce their weight to anorexic levels. The distinction between the subtypes of anorexia is supported by differences in personality patterns. Individuals with the eating/purging type tend to have problems relating to impulse control, which, in addition to binge-eating episodes, may involve substance abuse or stealing (Garner, 1993). They tend to alternate between periods of rigid control and impulsive behaviour.

Who's at risk? Competitive activities that emphasize endurance, aesthetics, and weight levels put athletes at risk for developing an eating disorder. Runners, wrestlers, swimmers, and dancers are among the athletes who have a high occurrence of eating disorders.

How do I see myself? A distorted body image is a key component of eating disorders.

amenorrhea Absence of menstruation—a symptom of anorexia nervosa.

osteoporosis Physical disorder caused by calcium deficiency that is characterized by extreme brittleness of the bones (from the Greek *osteon*, meaning "bone," and the Latin *porus*, meaning "pore").

Those with the restrictive type tend to be rigidly, even obsessively, controlled about their diet and appearance.

Medical Complications of Anorexia University of Toronto psychiatrists Allan Kaplan and Blake Woodside (1987) concluded that anorexia can lead to serious medical complications that in extreme cases can be fatal. Weight losses of as much as 35% of body weight may occur and anemia may develop. Females suffering from anorexia are also likely to encounter dermatological problems like dry, cracking skin; fine, downy hair; even a yellowish discoloration that may persist for years after weight is regained. Cardiovascular complications include heart irregularities, hypotension (low blood pressure), and associated dizziness upon standing, sometimes causing blackouts. Decreased food ingestion can cause gastrointestinal problems like constipation, abdominal pain, and obstruction or paralysis of the bowels or intestines. Menstrual irregularities are common, and **amenorrhea** (absence or suppression of menstruation) is part and parcel of the clinical definition of anorexia in females. Muscular weakness and abnormal growth of bones may occur, causing loss of height and **osteoporosis**.

The death rate from anorexia is estimated at 5% to 8% over a ten-year period, with most deaths due to suicide or medical complications associated with severe weight loss (Goleman, 1995b). Some studies show that people with eating disorders may have a sixfold increase in death compared to the normal population (Patton, 1988; Crisp, Callender, Halek, & Hsu, 1992).

Bulimia Nervosa

I think of how many people would like to have more than one cookie out of the bag they bring home from the supermarket. Some of them do have several cookies, savour them, then place the rest of the bag in the cupboard. Others have a harder time doing that; they eat too many cookies, half the package perhaps, then feel repentant and disgusted with themselves. But imagine ratcheting that urge up further. Imagine that you are unable to sleep because of the cookies in your cupboard, that you can't work or read or leave the house knowing the uneaten cookies are there. That feeling of anxiety begins to build in you, a desperation and a kind of anger, until you break down and cram the cookies into your mouth several at a time, devouring them until you throw up. If, after you throw up, there are still some cookies left in the bag, you have to keep eating them, even though by then you are sick of their taste and texture. If there are ten bags of cookies and no way that you can eat them all, you will have to bury the rest of them immediately at the bottom of the garbage pail—first crushing them and soaking them in water, say, to prevent your retrieving them later—in order to be rid of them.

ADAPTED FROM LAU, 2001, PP. 81–82.

LAU, E. (2001). MORE AND MORE. IN L. CROZIER & P. LANE (EDS.), *ADDICTED: NOTES FROM THE BELLY OF THE BEAST* (PP. 73–84). VANCOUVER: GREYSTONE BOOKS, A DIVISION OF DOUGLAS & MCINTYRE LTD. REPRINTED BY PERMISSION OF THE PUBLISHER.

Canadian writer Evelyn Lau describes her bulimic urges at a time in her life when she suffered from bulimia nervosa. *Bulimia* derives from the Greek roots *bous*, meaning "ox" or "cow," and *limos*, meaning "hunger." The unflattering picture inspired by the origin of the term is one of continuous eating, like a cow chewing its cud. Bulimia nervosa is an eating disorder characterized by recurrent episodes of gorging on large quantities of food followed by use of inappropriate ways to prevent weight gain, such as purging by means of self-induced vomiting or use of laxatives, diuretics, or enemas, or by fasting or engaging in excessive exercise (see Table 10.2). Two or more strategies may be used for purging, such as vomiting and use of laxatives (Tobin, Johnson, & Dennis, 1992). Although people with anorexia are extremely thin, bulimic individuals are usually of normal weight. However, they have an excessive concern about their shape and weight.

Bulimic individuals typically gag themselves to induce vomiting. Most attempt to conceal their behaviour. Fear of gaining weight is a constant factor. Although an overconcern with body shape and weight is a cardinal feature of bulimia and anorexia, bulimic individuals do not pursue the extreme thinness characteristic of anorexia. Their ideal weights are similar to those of women who do not suffer from eating disorders (Fairburn, Cooper, & Cooper, 1986).

The binge itself usually occurs in secret and most commonly at home during unstructured afternoon or evening hours (Drewnowski, 1997; Guertin, 1999). A binge typically lasts from 30 to 60 minutes and involves consumption of forbidden foods that are generally sweet and rich in fat. Binge eaters typically feel they lack control over their bingeing and may consume 5000 to 10 000 calories at a sitting. One young woman described eating everything available in the refrigerator, even to the point of scooping out margarine from its container with her finger. The episode continues until the binger is spent or exhausted, suffers painful stomach distension, induces vomiting, or runs out of food. Drowsiness, guilt, and depression usually ensue, but bingeing is initially pleasant because of release from dietary constraints.

The age range for onset of bulimia is the late teens, when concerns about dieting and dissatisfaction with bodily shape or weight are at their height. (APA, 2000a).

Medical Complications of Bulimia Bulimia is also associated with many medical complications (Kaplan & Woodside, 1987). Many of these stem from repeated vomiting. There may be irritations of the skin around the mouth due to frequent contact with stomach acid, blockage of salivary ducts, decay of tooth enamel, and dental cavities. The acid from the vomit may damage taste receptors on the palate, which might make the person less sensitive to the taste of vomit with repeated purgings (Rodin, Bartoshuk, Peterson, & Schank, 1990). Decreased sensitivity to the aversive taste of vomit may play a role in maintaining the purging behaviour (Rodin et al., 1990). Cycles of bingeing and vomiting may cause abdominal pain, hiatal hernia, and other abdominal complaints. Stress on the pancreas may produce pancreatitis (inflammation), which is a medical emergency. Disturbed menstrual function is found in as many as 50% of normal-weight women with bulimia (Weltzin, Cameron, Berga, & Kaye, 1994). Excessive use of laxatives may cause bloody diarrhea and laxative dependency, so the person cannot have normal bowel movements without laxatives. In the extreme, the bowel can lose its reflexive eliminatory response to pressure from waste material. Bingeing on large quantities of salty food may cause convulsions and swelling. Repeated vomiting or abuse of laxatives can lead to potassium deficiency, producing muscular weakness, cardiac irregularities, even sudden death—especially when diuretics are used. As with anorexia, menstruation may come to a halt.

TABLE 10.2

Diagnostic Features of Bulimia Nervosa

A. Recurrent episodes of binge eating (gorging) as shown by both:
   (1) Eating an unusually high quantity of food during a two-hour period, and
   (2) Sense of loss of control over food intake during the episode.

B. Regular inappropriate behaviour to prevent weight gain such as self-induced vomiting, abuse of laxatives, diuretics, or enemas, or by fasting or excessive exercise.

C. A minimum average of two episodes a week of binge eating and inappropriate compensatory behaviour to prevent weight gain over a period of at least three months.

D. Persistent overconcern with the shape and weight of one's body.

Source: Adapted from the DSM-IV-TR (APA, 2000a).

Causes of Anorexia and Bulimia

Like other psychological disorders, anorexia and bulimia involve a complex interplay of a host of biopsychosocial factors. Increasingly, researchers are finding that eating disorders arise when underlying genetic and neurobiological vulnerabilities interact with the social pressures felt by young people that lead them to put a high value on their physical appearance, especially their weight (Steiger, 2007; Steiger & Bruce, 2007; Treasure, 2007).

Sociocultural Factors Evidence shows that eating disorders are less common, even rare, in non-Western countries (Jilek, 2001; Ricciardelli, McCabe, Williams, & Thompson, 2007). Sociocultural theorists point to societal pressures and expectations placed on young men and, to an even greater extent, women in our society as contributing to the development of eating disorders (Ricciardelli et al., 2007; Stice, 2001). The pressure to achieve an unrealistic standard of thinness, combined with the importance attached to appearance in defining the female role in our society, can lead young women to strive toward an unrealistically thin ideal and to develop an overriding fear of gaining weight that can put them at risk of developing eating disorders. Additionally, University of Toronto psychologists Janet Polivy and Peter Herman (2002) suggest that in our culture, thinness acts as a point of focus for women's dissatisfaction and distress and its pursuit serves as an ineffective problem-solving strategy.

The media plays an important role in promoting cultural values and has been shown to exert its influence on both women's and men's reactions to thinness. For example, Canadian female university students participated in a study that examined how they responded to pictures of fashion models who represented the thin ideal. The researchers discovered that the women who viewed the pictures of models were significantly more depressed and angry than women who merely viewed pictures that did not contain human figures. This study demonstrates that viewing idealized female models has an immediate negative emotional impact and arguably gives credence to the role that media images play in the development of disordered eating attitudes and behaviours (Pinhas, Toner, Ali, Garfinkel, & Stuckless, 1999). Men, too, are experiencing greater dissatisfaction with their body image. They are under increasing media influence to look leaner and more muscular (Cohane & Pope, 2001; Leit, Gray, & Pope, 2002). The authors of one Canadian study, for example, have suggested that more males are participating in weight training and bodybuilding in an attempt to achieve the media-endorsed image of the ideal body shape (Goldfield, Blouin, & Woodside, 2006). One side effect of this trend is that male bodybuilders exhibit many eating-related characteristics of men with bulimia nervosa. Competitive bodybuilders show even higher rates of unhealthy eating and weight-control practices than do recreational bodybuilders and may be at risk of developing bulimia nervosa.

Despite the widespread belief that eating disorders, especially anorexia nervosa, are more common among affluent people, Canadian research (Jones et al., 2001) supports evidence that shows no strong linkage between socioeconomic status and eating disorders (Gard & Freeman, 1996; Wakeling, 1996). Beliefs that eating disorders are associated with high socioeconomic status may reflect the likelihood that affluent patients find treatment more accessible. Alternatively, it may be

Wanting to be Barbie. The Barbie doll has long represented a symbol of the busty but thin feminine form that has become idealized in our culture. If women were proportioned like the classic Barbie doll, they would resemble the woman in the photograph on the right. To achieve this idealized form, the average women would need to grow nearly 30 centimetres in height, reduce her waist by about 13 centimetres, and add 10 centimetres to her bustline. What message do you think the Barbie doll figure conveys to young girls?

that the social pressures on young women to strive to achieve an ultra-thin ideal have now generalized across all socioeconomic levels.

Psychosocial Factors Although cultural pressures to conform to an ultra-thin female ideal play a major role in eating disorders, the great majority of young women exposed to these pressures do not develop the disorders. Other factors must be involved. One likely factor involved in bulimic cases is a history of rigid dieting (Patton et al., 1999; Rock & Curran-Celentano, 1996). Women with bulimia typically engage in extreme dieting characterized by very strict rules about what they can eat, how much they can eat, and how often they can eat (Drewnowski, Yee, Kurth, & Krahn, 1994). Not surprisingly, they tend to spend more time thinking about their weight than non-bulimic women (Zotter & Crowther, 1991).

Bulimic women tend to have been slightly overweight preceding the development of bulimia, and the initiation of the binge–purge cycle usually follows a period of strict dieting to lose weight. In a typical scenario, the rigid dietary controls fail, which prompts initial bingeing. This sets in motion a chain reaction in which bingeing leads to fear of weight gain, which prompts self-induced vomiting or excessive exercise to reduce any added weight. <u>Some bulimic women become so concerned about possible weight gain that they resort to vomiting after every meal</u> (Lowe, Gleaves, & Murphy-Eberenz, 1998). Purging is negatively reinforced by producing relief, or at least partial relief, from anxiety over gaining weight.

Body dissatisfaction is another important factor in eating disorders (Heatherton, Mahamedi, Striepe, Field, & Keel, 1997). Body dissatisfaction may lead to maladaptive attempts—through self-starvation and purging—to attain a desired body weight or shape. Bulimic and anorexic women tend to be extremely concerned about their body weight and shape (Jacobi, Hayward, de Zwaan, Kraemer, & Agras, 2004).

Cognitive factors are also involved. University of Toronto researchers have found that women with anorexia often have significantly high perfectionistic attitudes in comparison to healthy controls, and the higher the perfectionism score, the poorer the outcome (Sutandar-Pinnock, Woodside, Carter, Olmsted, & Kaplan, 2003). Perfectionists tend to get down on themselves when they fail to meet the high standards they set, including their rigid dieting standards. Their extreme dieting may give them a sense of control and independence that they may feel they lack in other aspects of their lives. Bulimic women tend to be both perfectionistic and dichotomous ("black or white") in their thinking patterns (Fairburn, Welch, Doll, Davies, O'Connor, 1997). Thus, they expect themselves to adhere perfectly to their rigid dietary rules and judge themselves as complete failures when they deviate even slightly. They also judge themselves harshly for episodes of binge eating and purging. These cognitive factors influence each other, as illustrated in Figure 10.1. In addition, women with bulimic tendencies tend to have a dysfunctional cognitive style that may lead to exaggerated beliefs about the negative consequences of gaining weight (Poulakis & Wertheim, 1993).

Researchers have also noted linkages between bulimia and problems in interpersonal relationships. Bulimic women tend to be shy and to have few, if any, close friends (Fairburn et al., 1997). One study of 21 college women with bulimia and a matched control

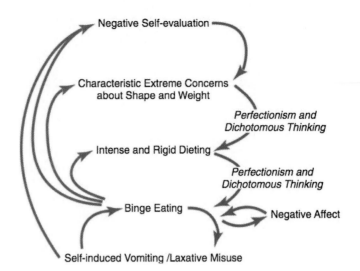

FIGURE 10.1 A cognitive model of bulimia nervosa.

Source: Fairburn, C. B. (1997). Eating disorders. In Clark, D. M. & Fairburn, C. G. (Eds.), *Science and Practice of Cognitive Behaviour Therapy* (209–241). New York: Oxford University Press. Reprinted by permission of Oxford University Press.

Bingeing. People with bulimia nervosa may cram thousands of calories during a single binge and then attempt to purge what they have consumed by forcing themselves to vomit.

group of 21 nonbulimic women found that those with bulimia had more social problems. They believed that less social support was available to them and reported more social conflict, especially with family members (Grissett & Norvell, 1992). They also rated themselves, and were judged by others, as less socially skilful than the control group. Although causal links between a lack of social skills and eating disorders remain to be elaborated, it is possible that enhancing the social skills of women with bulimia may increase the quality of their relationships and perhaps reduce their tendencies to use food in maladaptive ways.

Young women with bulimia also tend to have more psychological problems and lower self-esteem than other dieters (Fairburn et al., 1997; Jacobi et al., 2004). Canadian researchers have found that anorexia and bulimia often occur together with many kinds of psychological disorders, including affective disorders such as major depression and dysthymic disorder; anxiety disorders such as obsessive-compulsive disorder, panic disorder, phobia, generalized anxiety disorder, and posttraumatic stress disorder; and disorders found in children and adolescents such as oppositional defiant disorder and conduct disorder (Geist, Davis, & Heinmaa, 1998). Perhaps some forms of binge eating involve attempts at self-medication for emotional problems. Consistent with this view is evidence that bulimic women are more likely than other women to have experienced childhood sexual and physical abuse (Kent & Waller, 2000; Wonderlich, Brewerton, Jocic, Dansky, & Abbott, 1997). Bulimia may develop in some cases as an ineffective means of coping with abuse.

What we have gained from this research is the understanding that bulimia often develops within a context of extreme, rigid dieting overlaying psychological, interpersonal, and cognitive factors.

Family Factors and Eating Disorders Eating disorders frequently develop against a backdrop of family conflicts (Fairburn et al., 1997; Wonderlich et al., 1997). Some theorists focus on the brutal effect of self-starvation on parents. They suggest that some adolescents use their refusal to eat to punish parents for feelings of loneliness and alienation they experience in the home. One related study compared the mothers of adolescent girls with eating disorders to the mothers of other girls. Mothers of the adolescents with eating disorders were more likely to be unhappy about their families' functioning, to have their own problems with eating and dieting, to believe their daughters ought to lose weight, and to regard their daughters as unattractive (Pike & Rodin, 1991). Moreover, mothers of daughters with eating disorders showed high levels of perfectionism and an overconcern about shape and weight (Woodside et al., 2002). Is binge eating, as suggested by Humphrey (1986), a metaphoric effort to gain the nurturance and comfort that the mother is denying her daughter? Does purging represent the symbolic upheaval of negative feelings toward the family?

Families of young women with eating disorders tend to be more often conflicted, while at the same time less cohesive and nurturing and more overprotective and critical than reference groups (Fairburn et al., 1997; Rattit, Humphrey, & Lyons, 1996). The parents seem less capable of promoting independence in their daughters (Strober & Humphrey, 1987). Conflicts with parents over issues of autonomy are often implicated in the development of both anorexia nervosa and bulimia (Rattit et al., 1996). Yet it remains uncertain whether these family patterns contribute to the initiation of eating disorders or whether eating disorders go on to disrupt family life. The truth probably lies in an interaction between the two.

From the **systems perspective**, families are systems that regulate themselves in ways that minimize the open expression of conflict and reduce the immediate need for overt change. Within this perspective, girls who develop anorexia may be seen as helping maintain the shaky balances and harmonies found in dysfunctional families by displacing attention from family conflicts and marital tensions onto themselves (Minuchin, Rosman, & Baker, 1978). The girl may become the *identified patient*, although the family unit is actually dysfunctional.

Regardless of the factors that initiate eating disorders, social reinforcers may maintain them. Children with eating disorders may quickly become the focus of attention of their families, and receive attention from their parents that might otherwise be lacking.

systems perspective View that problems reflect the systems (family, social, school, ecological, etc.) in which they are embedded.

Biological Factors   Interest in the biological underpinnings of eating disorders, especially bulimia, has largely focused on the role of the neurotransmitter serotonin. Serotonin is involved in regulating mood and appetite, especially appetite for carbohydrates.

Decreased serotonin activity or responsivity may be involved in prompting binge eating in bulimic individuals, especially carbohydrate bingeing (Levitan, Kaplan, Joffe, Levitt, & Brown, 1997). This line of thinking is buttressed by evidence that antidepressants, such as Prozac, which increase serotonin activity, can decrease binge-eating episodes in bulimic women (Walsh, Fairburn, Mickley, Sysko, & Parides, 2004). We also know that many women with eating disorders are depressed or have a history of depression, and imbalances of serotonin are implicated in depressive disorders. It may be that bulimia is related to depression, perhaps at a genetic level.

Evidence also supports a genetic link with eating disorders (Lamberg, 2003). A large-scale study of more than 2000 female twins showed a much higher concordance rate for the disorder—23% versus 9%—among monozygotic (MZ) twins than among dizygotic (DZ) twins (Kendler et al., 1991). Greater concordance for anorexia is also found among MZ than DZ twins—50% versus 5%—suggesting that genetics plays a role in anorexia as well (Holland, Sicotte, & Treasure, 1988). Eating disorders also tend to run in families, which is further suggestive of a genetic component. However, genetic factors cannot fully account for the development of eating disorders. Eating disorder researchers Howard Steiger and Kenneth Bruce (2007) of the McGill University–affiliated Douglas Hospital Research Centre propose that, as in the diathesis-stress model, a genetic predisposition involving a dysfunction of neurotransmitter activity interacts with family, social, cultural, and environmental pressures, thereby leading to the development of eating disorders.

? QUESTIONNAIRE

The Fear of Fat Scale

The fear of becoming fat is a prime factor underlying eating disorders like anorexia and bulimia. The Goldfarb Fear of Fat Scale (Goldfarb, Dykens, & Gerrard, 1985) measures the degree to which people fear becoming fat. The scale may help identify individuals at risk of developing eating disorders. It differentiates between anorexic and normal women, and between bulimic and nonbulimic women. Dieters, however, also score higher on the scale than nondieters.

_____ 1. My biggest fear is becoming fat.

_____ 2. I am afraid to gain even a little weight.

_____ 3. I believe there is a real risk that I will become overweight someday.

_____ 4. I don't understand how overweight people can live with themselves.

_____ 5. Becoming fat would be the worst thing that could happen to me.

_____ 6. If I stopped concentrating on controlling my weight, chances are I would become very fat.

To complete the Fear of Fat Scale, read each of the following statements and write in the number that best represents your own feelings and beliefs. Then check the key on pages 379 to 380 in the next Study Break section.

1 = very untrue
2 = somewhat untrue
3 = somewhat true
4 = very true

_____ 7. There is nothing that I can do to make the thought of gaining weight less painful and frightening.

_____ 8. I feel like all my energy goes into controlling my weight.

_____ 9. If I eat even a little, I may lose control and not stop eating.

_____ 10. Staying hungry is the only way I can guard against losing control and becoming fat.

Source: Goldfarb, L. A., Dykens, E. M. & Gerrard, M. (1985). The Goldfarb fear of fat scale. _Journal of Personality Assessment_, 49, 329–332. Reprinted with permission.

Canadian studies have also shown that adolescent girls with type-1 diabetes were twice as likely to develop eating disorders as their nondiabetic peers (Frankenfield, 2000). A long-term follow-up of young diabetic women with eating disorders found that they had a threefold higher risk of developing diabetic retinopathy (a potentially blinding complication of diabetes that damages the eye's retina) (Rodin et al., 2002). It was recommended that young women with diabetes who have poor metabolic control and who are concerned about their shape and weight should be monitored for a potential eating disorder.

Treatment of Anorexia Nervosa and Bulimia Nervosa

Eating disorders are difficult to treat and treatment efforts are often met with ongoing denial and resistance by patients with such disorders, especially anorexia (Kaplan & Garfinkel, 1999). People with anorexia may be hospitalized, especially when weight loss is severe or body weight is falling rapidly. In a hospital, they are usually placed on a closely monitored refeeding regimen. Dalhousie University philosopher Chris MacDonald (2002) alerts us to the ethical dilemma that results when caregivers are confronted with patients who resist treatment. It forces caregivers to decide which interventions, such as tube-feeding or chemical restraints, justify a violation of the patient's autonomy and right to refuse treatment, especially when the patient's well-being is at stake.

Kaplan (2002) contends that psychotherapy is still a common treatment for anorexia, but by itself, its efficacy remains in question. The best outcomes result from treatment that involves psychotherapy combined with nutritional management and family interventions (Geist, Heinmaa, Stephens, Davis, & Katzman, 2000; Kaplan, 2002). Cognitive analytic therapy has been shown to benefit anorexic patients (Treasure & Ward, 1997). Behaviour therapy has also been shown to be effective in promoting weight gain in anorexic patients (Johnson, Tsoh, & Varnado, 1996). Behaviour therapy is commonly used with rewards made contingent on adherence to the refeeding protocol (Rock & Curran-Celentano, 1996). Individual or family therapy following hospitalization has also shown favourable long-term benefits (Eisler et al., 1997). Family therapy may also be employed to help resolve underlying family conflicts. Family group psychoeducation (FGP) has been shown to be a cost-effective alternative to family therapy during the first months of treatment for severely anorexic teens (Geist et al., 2000). FGP provides patients and parents with information about the nature of eating disorders, developmental issues, and weight-regulation issues, and also provides them with opportunities to discuss the information.

Hospitalization may also be used to help break the binge–purge cycle in bulimia, but appears to be necessary only in cases in which eating behaviours are clearly out of control and outpatient treatment has failed, or where there is evidence of severe medical complications, suicidal thoughts or attempts, or substance abuse (APA, 2000a).

Cognitive-behavioural therapy (CBT) is useful in helping bulimic individuals challenge self-defeating thoughts and beliefs, such as unrealistic, perfectionistic expectations regarding dieting and body weight. Another common dysfunctional thinking pattern is dichotomous (all-or-nothing) thinking that predisposes them to purge when they slip even a little from their rigid diets. CBT also challenges tendencies to overemphasize appearance in determining self-worth. To eliminate self-induced vomiting, therapists may use the behavioural technique of *exposure with response prevention* that was developed for treatment of people with obsessive-compulsive disorder. In this technique, the bulimic patient is exposed to eating forbidden foods while the therapist stands by to prevent vomiting until the urge to purge passes. Bulimic individuals thus learn to tolerate violations of their dietary rules without resorting to purging.

Cognitive-behavioural therapy has been shown to have therapeutic benefits in treating bulimia (Fairburn, 1997; Lewandowski, Gebing, Anthony, & O'Brien, 1997; Walsh et al., 1997; Wilson & Fairburn, 1998). Another psychologically based treatment, interpersonal psychotherapy, has also shown good success and may be used as an alternative treatment in cases where CBT proves unsuccessful (Cooper & Steere, 1995; Wilson & Fairburn, 1998). Interpersonal therapy focuses on resolving interpersonal problems in the belief that more effective interpersonal functioning will lead to healthier food habits and attitudes.

Canadian studies have also found that brief therapy interventions are effective for reducing symptoms in bulimic patients. For instance, as a first step in their treatment, Carter et al. (2003) found that bulimic patients who were not well informed about bulimia, had more problems with intimacy, and higher compulsivity scores benefited from self-help manuals that provided information about the disorder or focused on self-assertion skills. In another study, it was shown that group psychoeducation by itself provided therapeutic benefits in five sessions (Davis, Olmsted, Rockert, Marques, & Dolhanty, 1997).

The pharmacological treatment of eating disorders has generally been disappointing (Zhu & Walsh, 2002). Antidepressant drugs have been shown to provide short-term therapeutic benefits in treating bulimia, but have not been very successful in treating anorexia (Johnson, Tsoh, & Varnado, 1996; Wilson & Fairburn, 1998; Zhu & Walsh, 2002). They are believed to work by decreasing the urge to binge through normalizing serotonin—the brain chemical involved in regulating appetite.

A review of the available evidence suggests that cognitive-behavioural therapy is more effective than antidepressant medication in treating bulimia nervosa and carries a lower rate of relapse (Johnson, Tsoh, & Varnado, 1996; Wilson & Fairburn, 1998; Zhu & Walsh, 2002). It appears that CBT should be the first treatment choice for bulimia, followed by use of antidepressant medication if psychological treatment is not successful (Compas, Haaga, Keefe, Leitenberg, & Williams, 1998; Wilson & Fairburn, 1998). Studies examining whether a combined CBT–medication treatment approach is more effective than either treatment component alone have thus far produced inconsistent results (Johnson, Tsoh, & Varnado, 1996; Walsh et al., 1997).

Treatment of eating disorders in Canada has moved away from relying on long-term hospitalization, psychotherapy, and drugs that have risky side effects. Treatment has progressed toward a team approach that focuses on nutritional stabilization along with brief forms of psychotherapy, group and family psychoeducation, and outpatient care that is tailored to different stages of recovery (Geist et al., 2000; Health Canada, 2002a; Kaplan, 2002; Wilkins, 1998). Although progress has been made in treating eating disorders (Health Canada, 2002a), there is considerable room for improvement. Even in CBT, about half of treated patients show continued evidence of bulimic behaviour (Compas et al., 1998; Wilson & Fairburn, 1998). Eating disorders can be a tenacious and enduring problem, especially when excessive fears of body weight and distortions of body image are maintained. A recent study reported that ten years after an initial presentation with bulimia, approximately 30% of women still showed either recurrent binge-eating or purging behaviours (Keel, Mitchell, Miller, Davis, & Crow, 1999). Recovery from anorexia also tends to be a long process. A recent study of 88 German patients with anorexia showed that 50% of the patients did not recover sooner than six years after their first hospitalization (Herzog, Schellberg, & Deter, 1997).

Binge-Eating Disorder

People with **binge-eating disorder** (BED) have recurrent eating binges but do not purge themselves of the excess food afterward. Binge-eating disorder is classified in the DSM as a potential disorder requiring further study. We currently know too little about the characteristics of people with BED to warrant its inclusion as an official diagnostic category. The criteria used for diagnosing the disorder also need further evaluation.

binge-eating disorder Proposed psychological disorder characterized by repeated episodes in which binge eating occurs but is not followed by purging.

The available evidence indicates that unlike bulimia, BED is more commonly found among obese individuals (Spitzer et al., 1992). It is frequently associated with people suffering from depression who have a history of unsuccessful attempts at losing excess weight and keeping it off. People with BED tend to be older than those with anorexia or bulimia (Arnow, Kenardy, & Agras, 1992). Like other eating disorders, it is found more frequently among women, although of all the eating disorders, men are most likely to experience BED (Health Canada, 2002a). Overall, about 2% of the population report frequent eating binges.

People with BED are often described as "compulsive overeaters." During a binge, they feel a loss of control over their eating. BED may fall within a broader domain of compulsive behaviours characterized by impaired control over maladaptive behaviours, such as pathological gambling and substance-abuse disorders. A history of dieting may play a role in some cases of BED, although it appears to be a less important factor in BED than in bulimia (Howard & Porzelius, 1999).

Cognitive-behavioural techniques have shown some positive effects in treating binge-eating disorder (Carter & Fairburn, 1998; Peterson et al., 1998; Wilson & Fairburn,

---

A CLOSER LOOK

Other Eating Problems and Related Conditions

Many other disordered conditions that involve food, eating, and body image have been identified. Some have a formal diagnosis while others are somewhat controversial.

Some feeding and eating problems associated with infancy and childhood include the following:

- *Pica.* The persistent craving or eating of items that are not food, such as clay, dirt, stones, feces, paint chips, plastic, and so forth.

- *Rumination disorder.* Characterized by repeated eating, regurgitation, and then rechewing and re-eating of food.

Bigorexia. People with muscle dysmorphia, also known as reverse anorexia nervosa, are preoccupied with the belief that they are not muscular enough, and will go to extreme lengths to build muscle.

- *Feeding disorder of infancy or early childhood.* Persistent failure to consume foods that provide adequate nutrition, which results in weight loss or a failure to gain weight appropriately for development.

- *Prader-Willi syndrome.* A disorder of chromosome 15, which is characterized by a severe loss of muscle tone and feeding difficulties in early infancy, followed in later childhood by an insatiable appetite, excessive eating, and gradual development of life-threatening obesity.

- *Cyclic vomiting syndrome* (also known as *abdominal migraine*). Characterized by recurrent bouts of severe nausea and vomiting that last for hours or even days and alternate with longer periods without symptoms.

Eating and body-image disorders associated with adolescents and adults include the following:

- *Anorexia athletica.* Exercising for an amount of time or intensity that is well beyond normal (in association with an obsessive preoccupation with diet and weight).

- *Muscle dysmorphia* (also known as *bigorexia* or *reverse anorexia nervosa*). Common in bodybuilders, a chronic preoccupation with the belief and insecurity that one is not muscular enough accompanied by a variety of muscle-bulking strategies.

- *Orthexia nervosa.* Obsession with eating "pure" or "superior" foods and "proper" food preparation to the point that it interferes with a person's life.

- *Night-eating syndrome.* A form of compulsive eating whereby more than half the person's daily food intake is consumed after dinner and before breakfast; accompanied by feelings of anxiety and guilt.

- *Nocturnal sleep-related eating disorder.* A rare type of sleepwalking disorder characterized by recurrent episodes of eating during sleep that can lead to significant weight gain.

- *Gourmand syndrome.* An eating disorder that is linked to damage of the right hemisphere of the brain that results in the person becoming obsessed with shopping for specialty foods and engaging in elaborate food preparation and dining rituals associated with gourmet food.

1998). Antidepressants, especially antidepressants of the SSRI family, may also reduce the frequency of binge-eating episodes by helping regulate serotonin levels in the brain (Hudson et al., 1998).

Behaviour modification leads to modest weight losses that are generally well maintained for at least a year after treatment (Brownell & Wadden, 1992). However, a look at longer-term outcomes reveals a dimmer picture. As many as 90% to 95% of people who lose weight by dieting or behaviour modification return to their baseline weight levels within five years (Wilson, 1994). The problem appears to be that the changes in diet, exercise patterns, and eating habits that led to the initial weight loss do not generally carry over into changes in lifestyles that would promote long-term maintenance of weight loss. Clearly, to maintain weight loss, people need to make healthy changes in dietary and exercise patterns a part of their lifestyle.

STUDY BREAK

Eating Disorders

Review It

- **What are the major types of eating disorders?** There are two major types of eating disorders included in the DSM: anorexia nervosa and bulimia nervosa. Anorexia nervosa involves maintenance of weight at least 15% below normal levels, intense fears of becoming overweight, distorted body image, and, in females, amenorrhea. In comparison, people with bulimia nervosa are usually of normal weight, but because of a preoccupation with weight control and body shape, they engage in repeated binges and regular purging to keep weight down. Another type of eating disorder called binge-eating disorder is listed as a potential disorder requiring further study.

- **What are some of the factors involved in these types of eating disorders?** They tend to begin in adolescence and affect many more females than males. They both involve preoccupations with weight control and maladaptive ways of trying to keep weight down. Many factors have been implicated in their development, including social pressures on young women to adhere to unrealistic standards of thinness, issues of control, underlying psychological problems, and conflict within the family—especially over issues of autonomy. People with binge-eating disorder tend to be older than those with anorexia or bulimia and to suffer from obesity.

Define It

eating disorders	osteoporosis
anorexia nervosa	systems perspective
bulimia nervosa	binge-eating disorder
amenorrhea	

Recall It*

1. Deaths associated with anorexia most commonly result from _____.

   a. cancer
   b. suicide or direct complications from severe weight loss
   c. pancreatic disorders caused by calcium deficiencies
   d. thrombosis

2. Samantha has an intense fear of gaining weight. She diets constantly, but frequently loses control and binges on whatever food is available at the time. Afterward, she forces herself to vomit. These behaviours are most consistent with a diagnosis of _____.

   a. amenorrhea
   b. bulimia nervosa
   c. anorexia nervosa
   d. binge-eating disorder

3. The behaviour technique of _____ is used to help people with bulimia nervosa tolerate eating forbidden foods without resorting to purging.

   a. relapse-prevention training
   b. cognitive restructuring
   c. exposure with response prevention
   d. response-contingent reinforcement

4. The diagnosis of binge-eating disorder is applied most often to _____.

   a. young women with a history of anorexia
   b. young women without a history of anorexia
   c. women who are typically older than those with anorexia or bulimia
   d. men and women in about equal proportions

5. Treatment of eating disorders in Canada has moved away from reliance on _____.

    a. nutritional stabilization
    b. long-term hospitalization
    c. brief forms of psychotherapy
    d. family psychoeducation

* Recall It answers can be found on the Companion Website for this text.

Think About It

- How are sociocultural factors related to the development of eating disorders? How might we as a society change the social influences that lead many young women to develop disordered eating habits?
- Do you believe that high-risk anorexic patients who resist or refuse treatment should be forced to accept medical intervention? Why or why not?

Norms for the Fear of Fat Scale

Comparative scores are available for women only. You may compare your own score on the Fear of Fat Scale to those obtained by the following groups:

Group	Number	Mean
Non-dieting college women (women satisfied with their weight)	49	17.30
General female college population	73	18.33
College women who are dissatisfied with their weight and have been on three or more diets during the past year	40	23.90
Bulimic college women (actively bingeing and purging)	32	30.00
Anorexic women in treatment	7	35.00

Source of data: Goldfarb, L. A., Dykens, E. M., & Gerrard, M. (1985). The Goldfarb fear of fat scale. *Journal of Personality Assessment*, 49, 329–332. Reprinted with permission.

Keep the following in mind as you interpret your score:

1. The Goldfarb samples are quite small.
2. A score at a certain level does not place you in that group; it merely means that you report an equivalent fear of fat. In other words, a score of 33.00 does not indicate you have bulimia or anorexia. It means that your self-reported fear of fat approximates those reported by bulimic and anorexic women in the Goldfarb study.

SLEEP DISORDERS

Sleep is a biological function that remains in many ways a mystery. We know sleep is restorative and that most of us need at least seven or more hours of sleep a night to function at our best. Yet we cannot identify the specific biochemical changes occurring during sleep that account for its restorative function. We also know that many of us are troubled by sleep problems, although the causes of some of these problems remain obscure. Sleep problems of sufficient severity and frequency that lead to significant personal distress or impaired functioning in social, occupational, or other roles are classified in the DSM system as **sleep disorders**.

Highly specialized diagnostic facilities, called sleep disorders centres, have been established throughout Canada to provide a more comprehensive assessment of sleep problems. The Canadian Sleep Society (2003) provides a list of about 90 sleep centres across Canada (see www.css.to/sleep/centers.htm). People with sleep disorders typically spend a few nights at a sleep centre, where they are wired to devices that track their physiological responses during sleep or attempted sleep—brainwaves, heart and respiration rates, and so on. This form of assessment is termed **polysomnographic (PSG) recording**, because it involves simultaneous measurement of diverse physiological response patterns, including brainwaves, eye movements, muscle movements, and respiration. Information obtained from physiological monitoring of sleep patterns is combined with that obtained from medical and psychological evaluations, subjective reports of sleep disturbance, and sleep diaries (i.e., daily logs compiled by the problem sleeper that track the length of time between retiring to bed and falling asleep, number of hours slept, nightly awakenings, daytime naps, and so on). Multidisciplinary teams of physicians and psychologists in sleep centres sift through this information to arrive at a diagnosis and suggest treatment approaches to address the presenting problem.

sleep disorders Diagnostic category representing persistent or recurrent sleep-related problems that cause significant personal distress or impaired functioning.

polysomnographic (PSG) recording Relating to the simultaneous measurement of multiple physiological responses during sleep or attempted sleep.

The DSM groups sleep disorders into two major categories: **dyssomnias** and **parasomnias**.

Dyssomnias

Dyssomnias are characterized by disturbances in the amount, quality, or timing of sleep. There are five specific types of dyssomnias: primary insomnia, primary hypersomnia, narcolepsy, breathing-related sleep disorder, and circadian rhythm sleep disorder.

Insomnia **Insomnia** derives from the Latin *in-*, meaning "not" or "without," and, of course, *somnus*, meaning "sleep." Occasional bouts of insomnia, especially during times of stress, are not abnormal. All the same, more than an estimated 3.3 million Canadians aged 15 and older suffer from insomnia, averaging just 6.5 hours of sleep a night—a full hour less than those who don't have insomnia (Tjepkema, 2005). Although chronic insomnia affects older people in greater numbers, young people usually complain it takes too long to get to sleep, whereas older people are more likely to complain of waking frequently during the night or of waking too early in the morning. Many seniors also have more chronic health problems that interfere with their sleep patterns (Tjepkema, 2005; Williams, 2001). Overall, there are a host of factors that can have a negative impact on the odds of Canadians getting a good night's sleep, including, for example, high levels of life stress; shift work; heavy drinking or cannabis use; obesity; being divorced/separated or widowed; being female; and lower levels of education and income (Morin, LeBlanc, Daley, Gregoire, & Merette, 2006; Tjepkema, 2005).

Chronic insomnia lasting a month or longer is often a sign of an underlying physical problem or a psychological disorder such as depression. If the underlying problem is treated successfully, chances are that normal sleep patterns will be restored. Chronic insomnia that cannot be accounted for by another psychological or physical disorder or by the effects of drugs or medications is classified as a sleep disorder called *primary insomnia*. People with primary insomnia have persistent difficulty falling asleep, remaining asleep, or achieving restorative sleep (sleep that leaves the person feeling refreshed and alert) for a period of a month or longer. The sleep disturbance or associated daytime fatigue causes significant levels of personal distress or difficulties performing usual social, occupational, student, or other roles. Not surprisingly, there is a high rate of comorbidity (co-occurrence) between insomnia and other psychological problems, especially anxiety and depression (Morin et al., 2006; Toward Optimized Practice (TOP), 2007). Although the prevalence of primary insomnia is unknown, it is considered the most common form of sleep disturbance.

Psychological factors play a prominent role in primary insomnia. For example, University of Ottawa psychologists found that high levels of anxiety were associated with moderate to severe sleep-onset chronic insomnia (Viens, De Koninck, Mercier, St-Onge, & Lorrain, 2003). People troubled by primary insomnia tend to bring their anxieties and worries to bed with them, which raises their bodily arousal to a level that prevents natural sleep. Then they worry about not getting enough sleep, which only compounds their sleep difficulties. They may try to force themselves to sleep, which tends to backfire by creating more anxiety and tension, making sleep even less likely to occur. Sleep cannot be forced. Trying to make yourself fall asleep is likely to backfire. We can set the scene for sleep only by retiring when we are tired and relaxed and allowing sleep to occur naturally.

Hypersomnia The word *hypersomnia* is derived from the Greek *hyper*, meaning "over" or "more than normal," and the Latin *somnus*, meaning "sleep." Primary **hypersomnia** involves a pattern of excessive sleepiness during the day that continues for a period of a month or longer. The excessive sleepiness (sometimes referred to as "sleep drunkenness") may take the form of difficulty awakening following a prolonged sleep period (typically 8 to 12 hours). Or there may be a pattern of daytime sleep episodes occurring virtually every day in the form of intended or unintended napping (such as inadvertently falling asleep while watching television). Despite the fact that daytime naps often last an hour or more, the person does not feel refreshed upon awakening. The disorder is considered primary

dyssomnias Category of sleep disorders involving disturbances in the amount, quality, or timing of sleep.

parasomnias Category of sleep disorders involving the occurrence of abnormal behaviours or physiological events during sleep or at the transition between wakefulness and sleep.

insomnia Term applying to difficulties falling asleep, remaining asleep, or achieving restorative sleep.

hypersomnia Condition relating to a pattern of excessive sleepiness during the day.

because it cannot be accounted for by inadequate amounts of sleep during the night due to insomnia or other factors (like loud neighbours keeping the person up), by another psychological or physical disorder, or by drug or medication use.

Although many of us feel sleepy during the day from time to time, and may even drift off occasionally while reading or watching television, the person with primary hypersomnia has more persistent and severe periods of sleepiness that typically lead to difficulties in daily functioning, such as missing important meetings because of difficulty awakening. Although the prevalence of the disorder is unknown, surveys of the general population show complaints related to daytime sleepiness affecting between 0.5% and 5% of the adult population (APA, 2000a).

Narcolepsy

narcolepsy Sleep disorder characterized by sudden, irresistible episodes of sleep (sleep attacks).

cataplexy Brief, sudden loss of muscular control, typically lasting from a few seconds to as long as two minutes.

REM sleep REM (rapid eye movement) sleep is the stage of sleep associated with dreaming that is characterized by the appearance of rapid eye movements under closed eyelids.

Narcolepsy The word **narcolepsy** derives from the Greek *narke*, meaning "stupor," and *lepsis*, meaning "an attack." People with narcolepsy experience sleep attacks in which they suddenly fall asleep without any warning at various times during the day. They remain asleep for an average period of about 15 minutes. The person can be in the midst of a conversation at one moment and slump to the floor fast asleep a moment later. The diagnosis is made when sleep attacks occur daily for a period of three months or longer and are combined with the presence of one or both of the following conditions: (1) **cataplexy** (a sudden loss of muscular control), and (2) intrusions of **REM sleep** in the transitional state between wakefulness and sleep (APA, 2000a). REM or rapid eye movement sleep is the stage of sleep associated with dreaming. It is so named because the sleeper's eyes tend to dart about rapidly under their closed lids. Narcoleptic attacks are associated with an almost immediate transition into REM sleep from a state of wakefulness. In normal sleep, REM typically follows several stages of non-REM sleep.

Cataplexy typically follows a strong emotional reaction such as joy or anger. It can range from a mild weakness in the legs to a complete loss of muscle control that results in the person suddenly collapsing (Dahl, 1992; Siegel, 2004). People with narcolepsy may also experience *sleep paralysis*, a temporary state following awakening in which the person feels incapable of moving or talking. The person may also report frightening hallucinations, called *hypnagogic hallucinations*, which occur just before the onset of sleep and tend to involve visual, auditory, tactile, and kinesthetic (body movement) sensations.

Narcolepsy affects men and women equally and is a relatively uncommon disorder, affecting an estimated 0.02% (2 in 10 000) to 0.16% (16 in 10 000) people within the general adult population (APA, 2000a). Unlike hypersomnia, in which daytime sleep episodes follow a period of increasing sleepiness, narcoleptic attacks occur abruptly and are experienced as refreshing upon awakening. The attacks can be dangerous and frightening, especially if they occur when the person is driving or using heavy equipment or sharp implements. About two out of three people with narcolepsy have fallen asleep while driving and four out of five have fallen asleep on the job (Aldrich, 1992). Household accidents resulting from falls are also common (Cohen, Ferrans, & Eshler, 1992). Not surprisingly, the disorder is associated with a lower quality of life in terms of general health and daily functioning (Ferrans, Cohen, & Smith, 1992). Scientists have recently discovered that narcolepsy with cataplexy is related to low levels of a **neuropeptide**, *hypocretin*, in the cerebrospinal fluid in the brain (Baumann, Khatami, Werth, & Bassetti, 2006; Fronczek, van der Zande, van Dijk, Overeem, & Lammers, 2007; Overeem, Mignot, van Dijk, & Lammers, 2001). The hypocretin deficiency is due to a loss of hypocretin-producing neurons, but the exact cause of the loss remains unknown.

neuropeptide An amino acid found in cerebrospinal fluid that plays a role in neuronal transmission and the modulation of brain circuits or regions.

Breathing-Related Sleep Disorder

breathing-related sleep disorder Sleep disorder in which sleeping is repeatedly disrupted due to difficulties breathing normally.

apnea Temporary cessation of breathing.

Breathing-Related Sleep Disorder People with a **breathing-related sleep disorder** experience repeated disruptions of sleep due to respiratory problems (APA, 2000a). These frequent disruptions of sleep result in insomnia or excessive daytime sleepiness.

The subtypes of the disorder are distinguished in terms of the underlying causes of the breathing problem. The most common type is *obstructive sleep apnea*, which involves repeated episodes of either complete or partial obstruction of breathing during sleep (Canadian Lung Association, 2006). The word **apnea** derives from the Greek prefix *a-*, meaning "not, without," and *pneuma*, meaning "breath." The breathing difficulty results from the blockage of air flow in the upper airways, which is often due to a structural defect, such as an overly thick palate or enlarged tonsils or adenoids. In cases of complete obstruction, the sleeper may literally stop breathing for periods of 15 to 90 seconds as many as 30 times an hour, or more in severe cases (APA, 2000a; Fleetham et al., 2006). When these lapses of breathing occur, the sleeper may suddenly sit up, gasp for air, take a few deep breaths, and fall back asleep without awakening or realizing that breathing was interrupted. The narrowing of the air passages also produces loud snoring, which alternates with these momentary silences when breathing is suspended (Phillipson, 1993).

Although a biological reflex kicks in to force a gasping breath after these brief interruptions of breathing, the frequent disruptions of normal sleep resulting from apneas can leave people feeling sleepy the following day, making it more difficult for them to function effectively. Obstructive sleep apnea is a relatively common problem, affecting an estimated 2% to 4% of the adult population (Banno, Walld, & Kryger, 2005). The disorder is more common in younger men than women, but the rates increase and become more

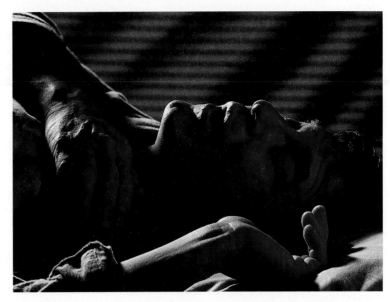

Sleep apnea. Loud snoring may be a sign of obstructive sleep apnea, a breathing-related sleep disorder in which a person may temporarily stop breathing as many as 500 times during a night's sleep. Loud snoring, described by bed partners as reaching levels of industrial noise pollution, may alternate with momentary silences when breathing is suspended.

similar in both men and women as they approach age 50 (Bardwell, Moore, Ancoli-Israel, & Dimsdale, 2003; Tishler, Larkin, Schluchter, & Redline, 2003). It is also much more common among people who are obese (e.g., because of a narrowing of the upper airways due to an enlargement of soft tissue) and, along with rising obesity rates in people across North America, we are now seeing an associated rise in the incidence of sleep apnea (Banno et al., 2005). Alcohol use before bedtime can also cause snoring due to a narrowing of the breathing passageways into outright blockages, resulting in sleep apneas (Phillipson, 1993).

People with sleep apnea may gasp for breath hundreds of times during the night without realizing it. They may only become aware of the problem when it is diagnosed or when their bed partners point it out to them. The person's bed partner is usually very aware of the problem because the loudness of the person's snoring can reach levels associated with industrial noise pollution (Alain, 1986). Bed partners commonly look for other sleeping places to obtain a good night's sleep. Not surprisingly, people who have sleep apnea report a poorer quality of life than unaffected people; they are vulnerable to excessive daytime sleepiness, impaired intellectual and memory functioning, and depression—factors that can contribute to the loss of employment, marriage break-ups, and accidents at work and on the road (Banno & Kryger, 2007; Canadian Lung Association, 2006). Sleep apnea is also associated with an increased risk of high blood pressure, heart attacks, strokes, and even sudden death.

Not only does obstructive sleep apnea result in personal suffering, there is a high cost to the health-care system when it goes undiagnosed. Meir Kryger and others at the St. Boniface General Hospital Research Centre in Winnipeg, North America's first sleep disorder breathing lab, tracked medical system usage of sleep apnea patients before and after treatment (Kryger, 2001). In studies that looked at the two-year and ten-year time spans preceding diagnosis, it was shown that sleep apnea patients used about two times the medical resources as the general population (Kryger, Roos, Delaive, Walld, & Horrocks, 1996; Ronald et al., 1999). Prior to diagnosis for apnea, patients were being treated for cardiovascular diseases, chronic obstructive airways disease, and depression, which accounted for most of the increased medical resource utilization (Smith et al., 2002). The good news is that once apnea patients are diagnosed and they follow a treatment regime, there is a significant reduction in medical care costs (Bahammam et al., 1999). Toronto Western Hospital psychiatrists conducted a review of the sleep apnea literature and concluded that the disorder has serious medical, socioeconomic, and psychological consequences, although it remains largely undiagnosed (Chung, Jairam, Hussain, & Shapiro, 2002). They contend that by detecting and treating obstructive sleep apnea, morbidity and mortality rates and health-care costs associated with the disorder will be reduced. Consequently, they strongly recommend that primary care physicians need to be prepared to screen patients who have symptoms of obstructive sleep apnea and refer them for an overnight (polysomnographic) assessment at a sleep clinic.

Circadian Rhythm Sleep Disorder Most bodily functions follow a cycle or an internal rhythm—called a circadian rhythm—that lasts about 24 hours. Even when people are relieved of scheduled activities and work duties and placed in environments that screen the time of day, they usually follow relatively normal sleep–wake schedules. Our circadian rhythm appears to be partially genetically based—we tend to be either morning people (early risers who are more alert early in the day) or evening people (late risers who are more alert at night) (Hur, 2007).

In **circadian rhythm sleep disorder**, this rhythm becomes grossly disturbed because of a mismatch between the sleep schedule demands imposed on the person and the person's internal sleep–wake cycle. The disruption in normal sleep patterns caused by the mismatch can lead to insomnia or hypersomnia. Like other sleep disorders, the mismatch must be persistent and severe enough to cause significant levels of distress or impair one's ability to function in social, occupational, or other roles. The jet lag that can accompany travel between time zones does not qualify because it is usually transient. However, frequent changes of time zones and frequent changes of work shifts (as encountered, for example, by nursing personnel) can induce more persistent or recurrent problems adjusting sleep patterns to scheduling demands, resulting in a circadian rhythm sleep disorder. Treatment may involve a program of making gradual adjustments in the sleep schedule to allow the person's circadian system to become aligned with changes in the sleep–wake schedule (Dahl, 1992).

Parasomnias

The parasomnias involve abnormal behaviours or physiological events taking place during sleep or at the threshold between wakefulness and sleep. Among the more common parasomnias are nightmare disorder, sleep terror disorder, and sleepwalking disorder.

Nightmare Disorder **Nightmare disorder** involves recurrent awakenings from sleep because of frightening dreams (nightmares). The nightmares are typically lengthy story-like dreams that involve threats of imminent physical danger to the individual, such as being chased, attacked, or injured. The nightmare is usually recalled vividly upon awakening.

Although alertness is regained quickly after awakening, anxiety and fear may linger and prevent a return to sleep. In a major poll, nearly one in five Canadians reported that they often (3.6%) or sometimes (14.7%) have nightmares that disturb their sleep (Leger Marketing, 2002). The actual percentages of people having the intense, recurrent nightmares that produce the kind of emotional distress or difficulties in functioning that would lead to a diagnosis of nightmare disorder remains unknown (APA, 2000a).

Nightmares are often associated with traumatic experiences and are generally more frequent when the individual is under stress. Supporting the general link between trauma and nightmares, researchers report that the incidence of nightmares was greater among survivors of the 1989 San Francisco earthquake in the weeks following the quake than among comparison groups (Wood et al., 1992). An increased frequency of nightmares was also observed among children who were exposed to the 1994 Los Angeles earthquake (Kolbert, 1994).

Nightmares generally occur during REM sleep. REM tends to become longer and the dreams occurring during REM more intense in the latter half of sleep, so nightmares usually occur late at night or toward morning. Although nightmares may contain great motor activity, as in fleeing from an assailant, drzzeamers show little muscle activity. The same biological processes that activate dreams—including nightmares—inhibit body movement,

circadian rhythm sleep disorder Sleep disorder characterized by disruption of sleep due to a mismatch in sleep schedules between the body's internal sleep–wake cycle and the demands of the environment. Formerly called *sleep–wake schedule disorder*.

nightmare disorder Sleep disorder characterized by recurrent awakenings from sleep due to the occurrence of frightening nightmares. Formerly called *dream anxiety disorder*.

Nightmares. Although frightening dreams are common in people of all ages, they occur more frequently during times of stress.

causing a type of paralysis. This is indeed fortunate, as it prevents the dreamer from jumping out of bed and running into a dresser or a wall in an attempt to elude the pursuing assailants from a dream.

Sleep Terror Disorder It typically begins with a loud, piercing cry or scream in the night. Even the most soundly asleep parent will be summoned to their child's bedroom as if shot from a cannon. The child (most cases involve children) may be sitting up, appear frightened and show signs of extreme arousal—profuse sweating with rapid heartbeat and respiration. The child may start talking incoherently or thrash about wildly, but remain asleep. If the child awakens fully, he or she may not recognize the parent or may attempt to push the parent away. After a few minutes, the child falls back into a deep sleep and upon awakening in the morning remembers nothing of the experience. These terrifying attacks, called *sleep terrors*, are more intense than ordinary nightmares. Unlike nightmares, sleep terrors tend to occur during the first third of nightly sleep and during deep non-REM sleep (Dahl, 1992).

A **sleep terror disorder** involves repeated episodes of sleep terrors resulting in abrupt awakenings that begin with a panicky scream (APA, 2000a). If awakening occurs during a sleep terror episode, the person will usually appear confused and disoriented for a few minutes. The person may feel a vague sense of terror and be able to report some fragmentary dream images, but not the sort of detailed dreams typical of nightmares. Most of the time the person falls back to sleep and remembers nothing of the experience the following morning.

Sleep terror disorder in children is typically outgrown during adolescence. More boys than girls are affected by the disorder, but among adults the gender ratio is about even. In adults, the disorder tends to follow a chronic course during which the frequency and intensity of the episodes waxes and wanes over time. Prevalence data on the disorder is lacking, but episodes of sleep terror are estimated to occur in 1% to 6% of children but in less than 1% of adults (APA, 2000a). The cause of sleep terror disorder remains a mystery.

Sleepwalking Disorder **Sleepwalking disorder** involves repeated episodes in which the sleeper arises from bed and walks about the house while remaining fully asleep. Because these episodes tend to occur during the deeper stages of sleep, when there is an absence of dreaming, it does not appear that a sleepwalking episode involves the enactment of a

sleep terror disorder Sleep disorder characterized by repeated episodes of sleep terror resulting in abrupt awakenings.

sleepwalking disorder Type of sleep disorder involving repeated episodes of sleepwalking.

dream. In sleepwalking disorder, the occurrence of repeated episodes of sleepwalking are of sufficient severity to cause significant levels of personal distress or impaired functioning. Sleepwalking disorder is more common in children, affecting between 1% and 5%, according to some estimates (APA, 2000a). Between 10% and 30% of children are believed to have had at least one episode of sleepwalking. The prevalence of the disorder among adults is unknown, as are its causes. However, perhaps as many as 7% of adults have experienced occasional sleepwalking episodes (APA, 2000a). The causes of sleepwalking remain obscure, although both genetic and environmental factors are believed to be involved (Hublin, Kaprio, Partinen, Heikkila, & Koskenvuo, 1997).

Although sleepwalkers typically avoid walking into things, accidents occasionally happen. Sleepwalkers tend to have a blank stare on their faces during these episodes. They are generally unresponsive to others and difficult to awaken. When they do awaken the following morning, they typically have little if any recall of the experience. If they are awakened during the episode, they may be disoriented or confused for a few minutes (as is the case with sleep terrors), but full alertness is soon restored. There is no basis to the belief that it is harmful to sleepwalkers to awaken them during episodes.

Isolated incidents of violent behaviour have been associated with sleepwalking, but these are rare occurrences and may well involve other forms of psychopathology. For instance, Canadian psychiatrists describe a distinct parasomnia that they have coined *sexsomnia* (Shapiro, Trajanovic, & Fedoroff, 2003). The researchers suggest that sexsomnia is distinct from pure sleepwalking and involves complex sexual behaviour, which can include sexual activity with other people, while asleep. Look at the case of D. W.:

> D. W. is a 43-year-old divorced police officer. He has an extensive sleep history of parasomnias. A few years earlier, he had stood trial for impaired driving and driving under the influence of alcohol. His defence was parasomnia, based on a previous history of sleepwalking and sleep talking that had intensified in the two years prior to his offence. Many features surrounding the case supported the parasomnia (sleepwalking) claim.
>
> Subsequently, it was discovered that Mr. W had another manifestation of his parasomnia, namely sexsomnia. This emerged at a "routine" follow-up in which the [interviewer] commented to Mr. W that his "sleep-driving" was being rivalled as the most unusual of parasomnias. A description of sexsomnia was given, and Mr. W responded by saying, "Oh, but I do that." The disingenuous response by the interviewer—"But you never told me"—was followed by Mr. W saying, "But you never asked." Mr. W's two current girlfriends independently confirmed that he frequently engages in sexual behaviour while asleep. One describes him as a "different person" during these activities—apparently, he is a more amorous and gentle lover and more oriented toward satisfying his partner when he is asleep.
>
> ADAPTED FROM SHAPIRO, TRAJANOVIC, & FEDOROFF, 2003

Treatment of Sleep Disorders

The most common pharmacologic method for treating sleep disorders in Canada is the use of sleep medications called **anxiolytics**. However, because of problems associated with these drugs, nonpharmacological treatment approaches, principally cognitive behaviour therapy, have come to the fore.

anxiolytics Drugs, such as sedatives and anaesthetics, that induce partial or complete unconsciousness and are commonly used in the treatment of sleep disorders.

Biological Approaches Various anxiolytic (anti-anxiety) drugs are frequently used to treat insomnia, including a class of minor tranquillizers called benzodiazepines (e.g., Dalmane, Halcion, and Restoril) and to a lesser extent, barbiturates (e.g., Seconal, Nembutal, and Amytal) (Health Canada, 2000b; Holbrook, Crowther, Lotter, Cheng, & King, 2000). (These drugs are also widely used in the treatment of anxiety disorders, as we saw in Chapter 5.) When Canadians were polled in 2002, the results indicated that nearly one in ten takes a sleeping pill to help with sleep (Leger Marketing, 2002). The use of sleeping pills by Canadians increases with age and two-thirds more women than men use them (Health Canada, 1995). However, McMaster University researchers caution that the overall benefit of anxiolytic drugs in comparison to a placebo is relatively minor (Holbrook et al., 2000). <u>Prudent use of these drugs is recommended, as they can produce adverse side effects as well as dependence if used regularly over time.</u>

When used for the short-term treatment of insomnia, anxiolytics are generally effective in reducing the time it takes to get to sleep, increasing total length of sleep and reducing nightly awakenings (Nowell, Buysse, Morin, Reynolds, & Kupfer, 1998). They work by reducing arousal and inducing feelings of calmness, thereby making the person more receptive to sleep. However, as many as 10% of sleep disorder patients take sleeping pills for months or years, despite a lack of evidence from controlled studies supporting their long-term efficacy.

A number of problems are associated with using drugs to combat insomnia (Kryger, Roth, & Dement, 2005). Sleep-inducing drugs tend to suppress REM sleep, which may interfere with some of the restorative functions of sleep. They can also lead to a carryover or "hangover" the following day, which is associated with daytime sleepiness and reduced performance. Rebound insomnia can also follow discontinuation of the drug, causing worse insomnia than was originally the case. Rebound insomnia may be lessened, however, by tapering off the drug rather than abruptly discontinuing it. These drugs quickly lose their effectiveness at a given dosage level, so progressively larger doses must be used to achieve the same effect. High doses can be dangerous, especially if they are mixed with alcoholic beverages at bedtime. Regular use can also lead to physical dependence (addiction). Once dependence is established, withdrawal symptoms following cessation of use may occur, including agitation, tremors, nausea, headaches, and, in severe cases, delusions or hallucinations.

Users can also become *psychologically* dependent on sleeping pills. That is, they can develop a psychological need for the medication and assume they will not be able to get to sleep without them. Because worry about going without drugs heightens bodily arousal, such self-doubts are likely to become self-fulfilling prophecies. Moreover, users may attribute their success in falling asleep to the pill and not to themselves, which strengthens reliance on the drugs and makes it harder to forgo using them.

Not surprisingly, there is little evidence of long-term benefits of drug therapy after withdrawal (Morin & Wooten, 1996). Relying on sleeping pills does nothing to resolve the underlying cause of the problem or help the person learn more effective ways of coping with it. If anxiolytic drugs like benzodiazepines are to be prescribed at all for sleep problems, they should be used only for a brief period of time (a few weeks at most) and at the lowest possible dose (Holbrook et al., 2000). The aim should be to provide a temporary respite so the clinician can help the client find effective ways of handling the sources of stress and anxiety that contribute to insomnia.

Minor tranquillizers of the benzodiazepine family and tricyclic antidepressants are also used to treat the deep-sleep disorders—sleep terrors and sleepwalking. They seem to have a beneficial effect by decreasing the length of deep sleep and reducing partial arousals between sleep stages (Dahl, 1992). Use of sleep medications for these disorders, as for primary insomnia, also incurs the risk of physiological and psychological dependence and thus should be used only in severe cases and only as a temporary means of "breaking the cycle."

Narcolepsy is predominantly a neurological disorder and sleep apnea involves physiological factors. Thus, both disorders are commonly treated using medical interventions. The excessive daytime sleepiness that accompanies narcolepsy is commonly treated with psychostimulants, such as *Modafinil*, but prospective new therapies are emerging (e.g., hypocretin gene therapy and stem cell transplantation) (Thorpy, 2007). Treatments for sleep apnea range from the use of medical assistive devices (e.g., continuous positive airway pressure—a technique of delivering pressurized air via a face mask to prevent the airway from collapsing, or oral appliances that expand the size of the upper airway) to lifestyle changes (e.g., weight loss, avoiding alcohol and sleeping pills, and a regular sleep routine) to surgery in some cases (e.g., to expand the upper airway by removing excess tissue from inside the roof of the mouth) (Banno & Kryger, 2007; Canadian Lung Association, 2006; Fleetham et al., 2006).

Psychological Approaches Psychological approaches have by and large been limited to treatment of primary insomnia. Overall, cognitive-behavioural treatment approaches have produced substantial benefits in treating chronic insomnia, as measured by both reductions in sleep latency and improvement of perceived sleep quality (Nowell et al., 1998; Viens et al., 2003). As many as 60% to 80% of patients respond favourably. Still, only about a third become good sleepers.

Cognitive-behavioural techniques are short term in emphasis and focus on directly lowering states of physiological arousal, modifying maladaptive sleeping habits, and changing dysfunctional thoughts. Cognitive-behavioural therapists typically use a combination of techniques, including stimulus control, relaxation training, and anxiety-management training. Stimulus control involves changing the stimulus environment associated with sleeping. Under normal conditions, we learn to associate stimuli relating to lying down in bed with sleeping, so that exposure to these stimuli comes to induce feelings of sleepiness. But when people use their beds for many other activities—such as eating, reading, and watching television—the bed may lose its association with sleepiness. Moreover, the longer the person with insomnia lies in bed tossing and turning, the more the bed becomes associated with cues related to anxiety and frustration. Stimulus control techniques attempt to strengthen the connection between the bed and sleep by restricting as much as possible the activities spent in bed to sleeping and by limiting the time spent in bed trying to fall asleep to 10 or 20 minutes at a time. If sleep does not occur within the designated time period, the person is instructed to leave the bed and go to another room to restore a relaxed frame of mind before returning to bed, such as by sitting quietly, reading, watching television, or practising relaxation exercises. Relaxation techniques, such as the Jacobson progressive relaxation approach, may be practised before bedtime to help reduce the level of physiological arousal. Biofeedback training may also be used as a way of teaching self-relaxation skills. Based on a meta-analysis of outcome studies, it does not appear that the combination of stimulus control and relaxation training produces any larger benefit than either approach alone (Murtagh & Greenwood, 1995).

Cognitive restructuring involves substituting rational alternatives for self-defeating, maladaptive thoughts or beliefs (see the accompanying "A Closer Look" box for examples). The belief that failing to get a good night's sleep will lead to unfortunate, even disastrous, consequences the next day reduces the chances of falling asleep because it raises the level of anxiety and can lead the person to try unsuccessfully to force sleep to happen. Most of us do reasonably well if we lose sleep or even miss a night of sleep, even though we might like more.

A CLOSER LOOK

To Sleep, Perchance to Dream

Many of us have difficulty falling asleep or remaining asleep from time to time. Although sleep is a natural function and cannot be forced, we can develop more adaptive sleep habits that help us become more receptive to sleep. However, if insomnia or other sleep-related problems persist or become associated with difficulties functioning during the day, it would be worthwhile to have the problem checked out with a professional. Here are some techniques to help you acquire more adaptive sleep habits:

1. Retire to bed only when you feel sleepy.
2. Limit as much as possible your activities in bed to sleeping. Avoid watching television or reading in bed.
3. If after 10 to 20 minutes of lying in bed you are unable to fall asleep, get out of bed, leave the bedroom, and put yourself in a relaxed mood by reading, listening to calming music, or practising self-relaxation.

(continued)

4. Establish a regular routine. Sleeping late to make up for lost sleep can throw off your body clock. Set your alarm for the same time each morning and get up, regardless of how many hours you have slept.

5. Avoid naps during the daytime. You'll feel less sleepy at bedtime if you catch Zs during the afternoon.

6. Avoid ruminating in bed. Don't focus on solving your problems or organizing the rest of your life as you're attempting to sleep. Tell yourself that you'll think about tomorrow tomorrow. Help yourself enter a more sleepful frame of mind by engaging in a mental fantasy or mind trip, or just let all thoughts slip away from consciousness. If an important idea comes to you, don't rehearse it in your mind. Jot it down on a handy pad so you won't lose it. But if thoughts persist, get up and follow them elsewhere.

7. Put yourself in a relaxed frame of mind before sleep. Some people unwind before bed by reading; others prefer watching television or just resting quietly. Do whatever you find most relaxing. You may find it helpful to incorporate in your regular bedtime routine techniques for lowering your level of arousal (discussed in Chapter 5) such as meditation or progressive relaxation.

8. Establish a regular daytime exercise schedule. Regular exercise during the day (not directly before bedtime) can help induce sleepiness upon retiring.

9. Avoid use of caffeinated beverages, such as coffee and tea, in the evening or late afternoon. Also, avoid drinking alcoholic beverages. Alcohol can interfere with normal sleep patterns (reduced total sleep, REM sleep, and sleep efficiency) even when consumed six hours before bedtime.

10. Practise rational restructuring. Substitute rational alternatives for self-defeating thoughts. Here are some examples:

Is your bed a cue for sleeping? People who use their beds for many activities, including eating, reading, and watching television, may find that lying in bed loses its association with sleeping. Behaviour therapists use stimulus control techniques to help people with insomnia create a stimulus environment associated with sleeping.

Self-Defeating Thoughts	Rational Alternatives
"I must fall asleep right now or I'll be a wreck tomorrow."	"I may feel tired, but I've been able to get by with little sleep before. I can make up for it tomorrow by getting to bed early."
"What's the matter with me that I can't seem to fall sleep?"	"Stop blaming yourself. You can't control sleep. Just let whatever happens, happen."
"If I don't get to sleep right now, I won't be able to concentrate tomorrow on the exam (conference, meeting, etc.)."	"My concentration may be off a bit, but I'm not going to fall apart. There's no point blowing things out of proportion. I might as well get up for a while and watch a little television rather than lie here ruminating."

Sleep Disorders

Review It

- **What are the major types of sleep disorders?** Sleep disorders are classified into two major categories: dyssomnias and parasomnias. Dyssomnias involve disturbances in the amount, quality, or timing of sleep. They include five specific types: primary insomnia, primary hypersomnia, narcolepsy, breathing-related sleep disorder, and circadian rhythm sleep disorder. Parasomnias involve disturbed behaviours or abnormal physiological responses occurring either during sleep or at the threshold between wakefulness and sleep. They include three major types: nightmare disorder, sleep terror disorder, and sleepwalking disorder.

- **What are the major forms of treatment for sleep disorders?** The most common form of treatment for sleep disorders involves the use of anxiolytic drugs. However, use of these drugs should be time limited because of the potential for psychological and/or physical dependence, among other problems associated with their use. Cognitive-behavioural interventions have produced substantial benefits in helping people with chronic insomnia.

Define It

sleep disorders	breathing-related sleep
polysomnographic	disorder
(PSG) recording	apnea
dyssomnias	neuropeptide
parasomnias	circadian rhythm sleep
insomnia	disorder
hypersomnia	nightmare disorder
cataplexy	sleepwalking disorder
REM sleep	anxiolytics
	sleep terror disorder

Recall It*

1. The most common type of sleep disorder is _____.

   a. hypersomnia
   b. primary insomnia
   c. narcolepsy
   d. sleep apnea

2. People who suddenly fall asleep without any warning at various times during the day suffer from _____.

   a. apnea
   b. hypersomnia
   c. circadian rhythm sleep disorder
   d. narcolepsy

3. Parasomnias involve _____.

   a. abnormal behaviours or physiological events that occur during sleep or during the threshold between wakefulness and sleep
   b. difficulties falling asleep or remaining asleep
   c. disturbances in the body's regulation of the sleep–wake cycle
   d. excessive sleepiness during the day

4. Seven-year-old Timothy calls out occasionally in the middle of the night and appears extremely frightened and highly aroused. He thrashes about wildly but remains asleep and remembers nothing of the episode the following morning. He is most likely to be suffering from a sleep disorder called _____.

   a. nightmare disorder
   b. sleep terror disorder
   c. circadian rhythm sleep disorder
   d. sleepwalking disorder

5. Which of the following statements concerning the use of drugs in treating insomnia is true?

   a. The most commonly used drugs for treating insomnia are antidepressants.
   b. There is little evidence of long-term benefits of drug therapy after withdrawal.
   c. There is little evidence of rebound insomnia following drug withdrawal.
   d. The overall benefit of anxiolytic drugs in comparison to a placebo is relatively large.

* Recall It answers can be found on the Companion Website for this text.

Think About It

- Do your sleep habits help or hinder your sleeping patterns? Explain.
- What are the drawbacks of relying on sleep medications to combat chronic insomnia? Do you get enough sleep? If not, what can you do about it?

WEBLINKS

Eating Disorders
www.phac-aspc.gc.ca/publicat/miic-mmac/pdf/chap_6_e.pdf
This site links to the chapter on eating disorders from Health Canada's *A Report on Mental Illness in Canada*.

Internet Mental Health
http://mentalhealth.com/dis/p20-et01.html
The Internet Mental Health site has links to information about anorexia nervosa and bulimia.

Anorexia Nervosa and Bulimia Association
www.phe.queensu.ca/anab
This site offers Canadian-focused information and support for eating disorders.

National Eating Disorder Information Centre (NEDIC)
www.nedic.ca
This site provides Canadian information and resources on eating disorders and weight preoccupation.

Canadian Sleep Society (CSS)
www.css.to
The CSS's website has information on research and links to treatment centres.

Sleepnet.com
www.sleepnet.com
A comprehensive sleep disorder site that includes a sleep test.

Eating Disorders and Sleep Disorders

Eating Disorders

Disorders involving disturbed eating patterns and maladaptive ways of controlling body weight.

Anorexia Nervosa

- Maintenance of an abnormally low body weight
- Distortions of body image
- Intense fears of gaining weight
- Amenorrhea in females

Medical Complications of Anorexia
- Menstrual irregularities
- Muscular weakness
- Abnormal growth of bones
- Estimated 5% to 8% mortality rate

Bulimia Nervosa

- Recurrent pattern of binge eating followed by self-induced purging
- Persistent overconcern with body weight and shape

Medical Complications of Bulimia
- Irritations of the skin around the mouth due to frequent contact with stomach acid
- Blockage of salivary ducts
- Decay of tooth enamel and dental cavities
- Pancreatitis and muscular weakness
- Cardiac irregularities
- Sudden death

Causes of Anorexia and Bulimia

Sociocultural
- Pressure to achieve an unrealistic standard of thinness or an ideal body shape

Psychosocial
- High perfectionistic attitudes and comorbidity with psychological disorders

Family
- Family conflicts and issues of autonomy

Biological
- Genetic predisposition

Treatment of Anorexia Nervosa and Bulimia Nervosa

- Nutritional management
- Family interventions
- Cognitive-behavioural therapy
- Interpersonal psychotherapy

Binge-Eating Disorder

- Repeated episodes in which binge eating occurs but is not followed by purging

Sleep Disorders

Persistent or recurrent sleep-related problems that cause significant personal distress or impaired functioning.

Dyssomnias
Disturbances in the amount, quality, or timing of sleep

Insomnia
- Difficulties falling asleep, remaining asleep, or achieving restorative sleep

Hypersomnia
- Pattern of excessive sleepiness during the day

Narcolepsy
- Sudden, irresistible episodes of sleep (sleep attacks)

Breathing-Related Sleep Disorder
- Breathing difficulties that disrupt sleep

Circadian Rhythm Sleep Disorder
- Mismatch in sleep schedules between the body's internal sleep-wake cycle and the demands of the environment

Parasomnias
Occurrence of abnormal behaviours or physiological events occurring during sleep or at the transition between wakefulness and sleep

Nightmare Disorder
- Recurrent awakenings from sleep due to the occurrence of frightening nightmares

Sleep Terror Disorder
- Repeated episodes of sleep terror resulting in abrupt awakenings

Sleepwalking Disorder
- Repeated episodes of sleepwalking

Treatment of Sleep Disorders

Biological Approaches
- Anxiolytic drugs for insomnia
- Stimulant drugs for narcolepsy
- Surgery and assistive devices for sleep apnea

Psychological Approaches
- Focus on directly lowering states of physiological arousal
- Modifying maladaptive sleeping habits
- Changing dysfunctional thoughts

CHAPTER 11

Gender Identity Disorder, Paraphilias, and Sexual Dysfunctions

Did You Know That...

See the underlined text on the pages indicated below for more information on these interesting and often misunderstood facts.

- Unlike people with gender identity disorder, gay and lesbian people do not perceive themselves as members of the opposite sex? (p. 398)

- Homosexuality is no longer considered a psychological disorder? (p. 398)

- Professional strippers are not classified as exhibitionists? (p. 401)

- Becoming sexually aroused by watching your partner disrobe or viewing an X-rated movie are not forms of voyeurism? (p. 403)

- Some people cannot become sexually aroused unless others subject them to pain or humiliation? (p. 406)

- In most cases of sexual assault, the woman was acquainted with the assailant? (p. 409)

- Orgasm is a reflex? (p. 416)

- Premature ejaculation affects about one out of three men? (p. 416)

- Both men and women have the male sex hormone testosterone circulating in their bodies? (p. 417)

- The drug *Viagra*, used in the treatment of erectile dysfunction, became the fastest-selling drug in history when it was introduced? (p. 424)

OFF THE FOG-BOUND shore of Ireland lies the isle of Inis Beag.[7] From the air it is an emerald jewel, warm and enticing. From the ground, the perspective is different.

The inhabitants of Inis Beag believe that normal women do not have orgasms and that those who do must be deviant (Messenger, 1971). Premarital sex is virtually unknown. Women participate in sexual relations in order to conceive children and pacify their husbands' lustful urges. They need not be concerned about being called on for frequent performances because the men of Inis Beag believe, groundlessly, that sex saps their strength. Relations on Inis Beag take place in the dark—literally and figuratively, and with nightclothes on. Consistent with local standards of masculinity, the man ejaculates as quickly as he can. Then he rolls over and goes to sleep, without concern for his partner's satisfaction. Women do not complain, however, as they are reared to believe it is abnormal for them to experience sexual pleasure.

If Inis Beag is not your cup of tea, perhaps the ambience of the island of Mangaia will strike you as more congenial. Mangaia is a Polynesian pearl. Languidly, Mangaia lifts out of the azure waters of the Pacific. Inis Beag and Mangaia are on opposite sides of the world— literally and figuratively.

From childhood, Mangaian children are expected to explore their sexuality through masturbation (Marshall, 1971). Mangaian teenagers are encouraged by their elders to engage in sexual relations. They are often found on hidden beaches or beneath the sheltering fronds of palms, industriously practising skills acquired from their elders. Mangaian women usually reach orgasm numerous times before their partners do. Young men vie to see who is more skilful in helping their partner attain multiple orgasms.

The inhabitants of Mangaia and Inis Beag have identical anatomic features and the same hormones pulsing through their bodies. Their attitudes and cultural values about what is normal and abnormal differ vastly, however. Their attitudes affect their sexual behaviour and the enjoyment they attain—or do not attain—from sex. In sex, as in other areas of behaviour, the lines between normal and abnormal are not always drawn precisely. Sex, like eating, is a natural function. Yet this natural function has been profoundly affected by cultural, religious, and moral beliefs, custom, folklore, and superstition.

Even in Canada today, we find attitudes as diverse as those on Inis Beag and Mangaia. Some people feel guilty about any form of sexual activity and thus reap little if any pleasure from sex. Others, who see themselves as sexually liberated, may worry about whether they have become free enough or skilful enough in their sexual activity.

In the realm of sexual behaviour, our conceptions of what is normal and what is not are clearly influenced by sociocultural factors. Various patterns of sexual behaviour that might be considered abnormal in Inis Beag, such as masturbation, premarital intercourse, and oral-genital sex, are normal in Western society from the standpoint of statistical frequency. For example, a survey of a representative sample of 3432 males and females between the ages of 18 and 59 found that 63% of adult men and 42% of adult women questioned reported that they had masturbated during the previous year (Laumann, Gagnon, Michael, & Michaels, 1994). It is likely that many more practised masturbation but were hesitant to admit so to interviewers.

Behaviour may be labelled abnormal because it deviates from the norms of one's society. For example, kissing is a highly popular form of mild petting in Western cultures but is considered

[7] Inis Beag is actually a pseudonym for an Irish folk community.

deviant behaviour in some societies, such as the Siriono of Bolivia and the Thonga of Africa. The Thonga tribesmen were shocked when they first observed European visitors kissing, and one man exclaimed, "Look at them—they eat each other's saliva and dirt."

Sexual behaviour may also be considered abnormal if it is self-defeating, harms others, causes personal distress, or interferes with one's ability to function. The disorders we feature in this chapter—gender identity disorder, paraphilias, and sexual dysfunctions—meet one or more of the criteria of abnormality. In exploring these disorders, we touch on questions that probe the boundaries between abnormality and normality. For example, is gay or lesbian sexual orientation a psychological disorder? Are some instances of voyeurism or exhibitionism normal and others abnormal? When is it considered abnormal to have difficulty becoming sexually aroused or reaching orgasm?

GENDER IDENTITY DISORDER

gender identity One's psychological sense of being female or being male.

gender identity disorder Disorder in which an individual believes that her or his anatomic gender is inconsistent with her or his psychological sense of being female or male.

Our **gender identity** is our sense of being male or female. Gender identity is normally based on anatomic gender, and in the normal run of things, our gender identity is consistent with our anatomic gender. In **gender identity disorder**, however, there is a conflict between one's anatomic gender and one's gender identity.

Gender identity disorder may begin in childhood. Children with the disorder find their anatomic gender to be a source of persistent and intense distress. The diagnosis is not used simply to label "tomboyish" girls and "sissyish" boys. It is applied to children who persistently repudiate their anatomic traits (girls might insist on urinating standing up or assert that they do not want to grow breasts; boys may find their penis and testes revolting) or who are preoccupied with clothing or activities that are stereotypic of the other gender (see Table 11.1).

TABLE 11.1

Clinical Features of Gender Identity Disorder

(a) A strong, persistent identification with the other gender. At least four of the following features are required to make the diagnosis in children:

   (1) Repeated expression of the desire to be a member of the other gender (or expression of the belief that the child does belong to the other gender)
   (2) Preference for wearing clothing stereotypical of members of the other gender
   (3) Presence of persistent fantasies about being a member of the other gender, or assumption of parts played by members of the other gender in make-believe play
   (4) Desire to participate in leisure activities and games considered stereotypical of the other gender
   (5) Strong preference for playmates who belong to the other gender (at ages when children typically prefer playmates of their own gender)

   Adolescents and adults typically express the wish to be of the other gender, frequently "pass" as a member of the other gender, and wish to live as a member of the other gender, or believe that their emotions and behaviour typify the other gender.

(b) A strong, persistent sense of discomfort with one's anatomic gender or with the behaviours that typify the gender role of that gender.

   In children, these features are commonly present: Boys state that their external genitals are repugnant or that it would be better not to have them, and show aversion to "masculine" toys, games, and rough-and-tumble play. Girls prefer not to urinate while sitting, express wishes not to grow breasts or to menstruate, or show an aversion to "feminine" clothing.

   Adolescents and adults typically state that they were born the wrong gender and express the wish for medical intervention (e.g., hormone treatments or surgery) to rid them of their own sex characteristics and simulate the characteristics of the other gender.

(c) There is no "intersex condition," such as ambiguous sexual anatomy, that might give rise to such feelings.

(d) The features cause serious distress or impair key areas of occupational, social, or other functioning.

Source: Adapted from the DSM-IV (APA, 2000a).

About five times as many boys as girls have gender identity disorder (Zucker & Green, 1992). The disorder takes many paths. It can come to an end or abate markedly by adolescence, with the child becoming more accepting of her or his gender identity. It may persist into adolescence or adulthood. The child may also develop a gay or lesbian sexual orientation at about the time of adolescence (Zucker & Green, 1992).

The diagnosis of *gender identity disorder* (formerly called *transsexualism*) applies to both children and adults who perceive themselves psychologically as members of the opposite gender and who show persistent discomfort with their anatomic gender. These people may seek out sex-reassignment surgery. In these procedures, surgeons attempt to construct external genitalia that are as close as possible to those of the opposite gender. People who undergo these operations can engage in sexual activity, even achieve orgasm, yet they are incapable of conceiving or bearing children because they lack the internal reproductive organs of their reconstructed gender.

Gender reassignment surgery. In 1953, George Jorgensen (left), later Christine Jorgensen (right), became one of the first people to undergo gender reassignment surgery.

Men seeking gender reassignment outnumber female applicants. Recent clinical studies show generally favourable psychological outcomes following gender reassignment surgery (e.g., De Cuypere et al., 2005; Smith, Van Goozen, Kuiper, & Cohen-Kettenis, 2005), especially when safeguards are taken to restrict surgical treatment to the most appropriate candidates. In one recent study of 162 transsexuals, the majority were found to be functioning well socially and psychologically postoperatively with only two expressing regrets about the procedure (Smith et al., 2005). Unfavourable outcome was predicted by being a nonhomosexual male-to-female transsexual who also had other significant psychological problems.

Holly Devor was, by Aaron Devor's account, a strange, conspicuous woman. Even though she did a pretty good "woman" act, it became increasingly like a contortionist's work and, ultimately, not very persuasive to others. "I never fit well as a girl or woman," said Dr. Devor, whose announcement that he was going to live as a man swept the University of Victoria campus in 2003 (Smith, 2003). Currently a professor of sociology, from 2002 to 2007 he was the university's dean of graduate studies, and appeared happy to conform to a conservative image more typical of men who run $3 million enterprises: Striding into his spare, elegant office, Dr. Devor projected confidence and control, wearing a dark grey suit and black tie with a blue shirt just over-large enough to hide any shape that might suggest he was once a woman. When interviewed in 2003 by *Globe and Mail* reporter Vivian Smith, Aaron Devor looked much younger than 51, with smooth skin, thick hair and light blue eyes behind large-lensed glasses. In the manner of men used to commanding space, even at 5'6", his hand gestures were expansive, the right leg crossed the left widely as he sat, and he shrugged his shoulders loosely. Aaron Devor had become a man in full, if not in anatomy. Like many people hitting 50, Holly Devor wanted sweeping changes in her life. So the sociologist was thrilled to win her big, new job as graduate studies dean at the University of Victoria. Then she announced her name would be Aaron H. Devor and she would be living as a man. Holly Devor always dressed in pants and presented herself as a masculine woman. The only change people on campus seemed to notice in the dean was a shorter haircut. His voice is clearly male. There is only one thing that Dr. Devor misses in his life as a man: he told the *Globe*'s

Gender identity should not be confused with sexual orientation. <u>Gay and lesbian individuals have erotic interest in members of their own gender, but their gender identity (sense of being male or female) is consistent with their anatomic sex.</u> They do not desire to become members of the opposite gender or despise their own genitalia, as we may find in people with gender identity disorder. <u>Nor is homosexuality any longer considered a psychological disorder.</u> In 1973, it was dropped from the DSM listing of psychological disorders. Yet people who are persistently distressed or confused about their sexual orientation, whether they are gay, bisexual, or heterosexual, may continue to be diagnosed with a definable type of sexual disorder called *Sexual Disorder Not Otherwise Specified*.[8] In practice, however, this diagnosis has been applied almost exclusively to people with a gay, lesbian, or bisexual sexual orientation.

Unlike a gay or lesbian sexual orientation, gender identity disorder is very rare. People with gender identity disorder who are sexually attracted to members of their own anatomic gender are unlikely to consider themselves gay or lesbian, however. Nature's gender assignment is a mistake in their eyes. From their perspective, they are trapped in the body of the wrong gender.

Theoretical Perspectives

No one knows what causes gender identity disorder (Zucker, 2005). Psychodynamic theorists point to extremely close mother–son relationships, parents with empty relationships, and fathers who were absent or detached (Stoller, 1969). These family circumstances may foster strong identification with the mother in young males, leading to a reversal of expected gender roles and identity. Girls with weak, ineffectual mothers and strong, masculine fathers may overly identify with their fathers and develop a psychological sense of themselves as "little men."

Learning theorists similarly point to father absence in the case of boys—to the unavailability of a strong male role model. Socialization patterns might have affected children who were reared by parents who had wanted children of the other gender and who strongly encouraged cross-gender dressing and patterns of play.

Learning history or childhood rearing experiences by themselves are probably insufficient to shape gender identity or to produce gender identity disorder. This point is underscored by the case of a Winnipeg boy, originally known as Bruce, who was raised as a girl (Colapinto, 2000). When he was eight months old, his doctor badly botched a circumcision, resulting in the loss of Bruce's penis. The family was persuaded by the leading sexologist John Money to raise Bruce as a girl. Even though Bruce received hormones to promote female appearance, the results were disastrous. Renamed Brenda and wearing a dress, he was clearly masculine in his appearance, interests, and behaviour, and he always felt that he was really a boy. "She" was teased at school because of his masculine appear-

Is homosexuality a psychological disorder? Gay, lesbian, and bisexual people as a group are about as well adjusted as heterosexuals. Homosexuality is no longer considered a psychological disorder in the DSM system.

[8] We refer to *gay* and *lesbian* people rather than *homosexuals*. There are several problems with the label *homosexual*: (1) because it has been historically associated with concepts of deviance and mental illness, it may perpetuate negative stereotypes of gay men and lesbians; (2) the term is often used to refer to men only, thus rendering lesbians invisible; and (3) it is often ambiguous in meaning—that is, does it refer to sexual behaviour or sexual orientation?

ance and behaviour, and life was miserable. At age 14, he was told of the botched operation, and shortly thereafter he changed his name to David and began living in the male role. He later married and adopted three children. Thus, years of socialization into the female gender role were unsuccessful in altering his gender identity. But even life as a male was not easy for him. David suffered from marital difficulties and bouts of depression. Tragically, he committed suicide in 2004, at age 38.

The great majority of people with these types of family histories described by psychodynamic and learning theorists do not develop gender identity disorder. Perhaps family factors play a role in combination with a biological predisposition. We know that people with gender identity disorder often showed cross-gender preferences in toys, games, and clothing very early in childhood. If there are critical early learning experiences in gender identity disorder, they may occur very early in life. Prenatal hormonal imbalances may also be involved. Perhaps the brain is "masculinized" or "feminized" by sex hormones during certain stages of prenatal development. The brain could become differentiated as to gender identity in one direction while the genitals develop in the other direction (Money, 1987). Researchers suspect that gender identity disorders may develop as the result of an interaction in utero between the developing brain and the release of sex hormones (Zhou, Hofman, Gooren, & Swaab, 1995). Yet speculations about the origins of gender identity disorder remain unsubstantiated by hard evidence.

STUDY BREAK

Gender Identity Disorder

Review It

- **What is gender identity disorder?** People with gender identity disorder find their anatomic gender to be a source of persistent and intense distress. People with the disorder may seek to change their sex organs to resemble those of the opposite gender, and many undergo gender reassignment surgery to accomplish this purpose.

- **How is gender identity disorder different from sexual orientation?** Gender identity disorder involves a mismatch between one's psychological sense of being male or female and one's anatomic sex. Sexual orientation relates to the direction of one's sexual attraction—toward members of one's own or the opposite gender. Unlike people with gender identity disorder, people with a gay or lesbian sexual orientation have a gender identity consistent with their anatomic gender.

Define It

gender identity   gender identity disorder

Recall It*

1. People with _____ have a basic conflict between their anatomical gender and their gender identity.

   a. a bisexual sexual orientation
   b. gender identity disorder
   c. a gay or lesbian sexual orientation
   d. transvestic fetishism

2. Which of the following is true of gender identity disorder?

   a. It is the most common type of sexual disorder.
   b. It occurs more commonly in boys than girls.
   c. It almost always continues into adulthood in the form of transsexualism.
   d. It is caused by a lack of communication in the family of origin.

3. People with a gay or lesbian sexual orientation _____.

   a. almost always experienced gender identity disorder in childhood
   b. secretly harbour a wish to become members of the opposite gender
   c. have a gender identity that is consistent with their anatomic sex
   d. have a basic mismatch between their anatomic sex and their sense of maleness or femaleness

4. Which of the following is true?

   a. The causes of gender identity disorder remain unknown.
   b. The closeness of the relationship between a boy and his mother is the major causal factor in gender identity disorder in boys.
   c. Genetic factors play a larger role in determining gender identity in females than males.
   d. Few adults with gender identity disorder showed

cross-gender preferences and behaviours in childhood.

5. Researchers suspect that prenatal _____ may lead the brain to become differentiated with respect to gender identity in one direction while the genitals develop in the other direction.

   a. trauma
   b. release of specific antibodies
   c. hormonal imbalances
   d. release of the neurotransmitter serotonin

* Recall It answers can be found on the Companion Website for this text.

Think About It

• Do you believe that how children are reared by their parents plays a causative role in the development of gender identity disorder? Why or why not?

• Do you think that anyone requesting a sex-change operation should be entitled to receive one? If not, what criteria should apply?

PARAPHILIAS

paraphilias Sexual deviations or types of sexual disorders in which a person experiences recurrent sexual urges and sexually arousing fantasies involving nonhuman objects (such as articles of clothing), inappropriate or nonconsenting partners (e.g., children), or situations producing humiliation or pain to oneself or one's partner. The person has either acted upon such urges or is strongly distressed by them.

exhibitionism Type of paraphilia almost exclusively occurring in males in which the man experiences persistent and recurrent sexual urges and sexually arousing fantasies involving the exposure of his genitals to a stranger and either has acted on these urges or feels strongly distressed by them.

The word *paraphilia* was coined from the Greek roots *para*, meaning "to the side of," and *philos*, meaning "loving." In the **paraphilias**, people show sexual arousal ("loving") in response to atypical stimuli ("to the side of" normally arousing stimuli). According to the DSM-IV, paraphilias involve recurrent, powerful sexual urges and fantasies lasting six months or longer that centre on either (1) nonhuman objects such as underwear, shoes, leather, or silk; (2) humiliation or experience of pain in oneself or one's partner; or (3) children and other persons who do not or cannot grant consent. Although acting out on paraphilic urges is not required for a diagnosis (the person might be distressed by the urges but not act on them), people with paraphilias often engage in overt paraphilic behaviours like exhibitionism and voyeurism.

Some people who receive the diagnosis can function sexually in the absence of paraphilic stimuli or fantasies. Others resort to paraphilic stimuli under stress. Still others cannot become sexually aroused unless these stimuli are used, in actuality or in fantasy. For some individuals, the paraphilia is their exclusive means of attaining sexual gratification.

The majority of people with paraphilias are men (APA, 2000a). However, studies in Canada, England, and the United States have identified women who have paraphilias (Denov, 2001; Fedoroff, Fishell, & Fedoroff, 1999; Litman, 2003) and raise the possibility that paraphilias in women may have been previously overlooked by researchers and clinicians. Little is known about the prevalence of paraphilias in women, although they are probably rare. According to the Canadian Centre for Justice Statistics, in 1999 only 2% of convicted sex offenders were women.

Some paraphilias are relatively harmless and victimless. Among these are fetishism and transvestic fetishism. Others, such as exhibitionism and pedophilia, have unwilling victims. A most harmful paraphilia is sexual sadism when acted out with a nonconsenting partner. Voyeurism falls somewhere in between because the "victim" does not typically know he or she is being watched.

Exhibitionism. Exhibitionism is a type of paraphilia that characterizes people who seek sexual arousal or gratification through exposing themselves to unsuspecting victims. People with this disorder are usually not interested in actual sexual contact with their victims.

Exhibitionism

Exhibitionism involves recurrent, powerful urges to expose one's genitals to an unsuspecting stranger in order to surprise, shock, or sexually arouse the victim. The person may masturbate while fantasizing about, or actually, exposing oneself. Almost all cases involve men (Freund & Blanchard, 1986). The victims are almost always women.

According to Toronto investigators Ron Langevin and Rubin Lang (1987), most exhibitionists are married and have generally satisfactory relationships with women. The person diagnosed with exhibitionism is typically not interested in actual sexual contact with the victim and therefore is not usually dangerous. Nevertheless, victims may believe themselves in great danger and may be traumatized by the act. Victims are probably best advised to show no reaction to people who expose themselves but to just continue on their way, if possible. It would be unwise to insult the person who exposed himself, lest it provoke a violent reaction. Nor do we recommend an exaggerated show of shock or fear—it tends to reinforce the person for the act of exposing himself.

Some researchers view exhibitionism as a means for perpetrators to indirectly express hostility toward women, perhaps because of perceptions of having been wronged by women in the past or of not being noticed or taken seriously by them (Geer, Heiman, & Leitenberg, 1984; Lee, Jackson, Pattison, & Ward, 2002). Men with this disorder tend to be shy, dependent, and lacking in social and sexual skills—even socially inhibited (Allen et al., 2004; Dwyer, 1988). Some doubt their masculinity and harbour feelings of inferiority (Blair & Lanyon, 1981). Their victims' revulsion or fear boosts their sense of mastery of the situation and heightens their sexual arousal. Consider the case of Michael:

Michael was a 26-year-old, handsome, boyish-looking married male with a three-year-old daughter. He had spent about a quarter of his life in reform schools and prison. As an adolescent, he had been a fire-setter. As a young adult, he had begun to expose himself. He came to the clinic without his wife's knowledge because he was exposing himself more and more often—up to three times a day—and was afraid he would eventually be arrested and thrown into prison again.

Michael said he liked sex with his wife, but it wasn't as exciting as exposing himself. He couldn't prevent his exhibitionism, especially now, when he was between jobs and worried about where the family's next month's rent was coming from. He loved his daughter more than anything and couldn't stand the thought of being separated from her.

Michael's method of operation was as follows: he would look for slender adolescent females, usually near the junior and senior high schools. He would take his penis out of his pants and play with it while he drove up to a girl or a small group of girls. He would lower the car window, continuing to play with himself, and ask them for directions. Sometimes the girls didn't see his penis. That was okay. Sometimes they saw it and didn't react. That was okay, too. When they saw it and became flustered and afraid, that was best of all. He would start to masturbate harder, and now and then he managed to ejaculate before the girls had departed.

Michael's history was unsettled. His father had left home before he was born, and his mother had drunk heavily. He was in and out of foster homes throughout his childhood. Before he was ten years old he was involved in sexual activities with neighbourhood boys. Now and then, the boys forced neighbourhood girls into petting, and Michael had mixed feelings when the girls got upset. He felt bad for them, but he also enjoyed it. A couple of times girls seemed horrified at the sight of his penis, and it made him "really feel like a man. To see that look, you know, with a girl, not a woman, but a girl—a slender girl, that's what I'm after."

THE AUTHORS' FILES

Wearing revealing bathing suits is not a form of exhibitionism in the clinical sense of the term. Nearly all people diagnosed with exhibitionism disorder are men, and they are motivated by the wish to shock and dismay unsuspecting observers, not to show off the attractiveness of their bodies. Nor do professional strippers typically meet the clinical criteria for exhibitionism. Although they may seek to show off the attractiveness of their bodies, they are generally not motivated by the desire to expose themselves to unsuspecting strangers in order to arouse them or shock them. The chief motive of the stripper, of course, may simply be to earn a living.

Fetishism

fetishism Type of paraphilia in which a person uses an inanimate object or a body part (*partialism*) as a focus of sexual interest and as a source of arousal.

The French *fetiche* is thought to derive from the Portuguese *feitico*, referring to a "magic charm." In this case, the "magic" lies in the object's ability to sexually arouse. The chief feature of **fetishism** is recurrent, powerful sexual urges and arousing fantasies involving inanimate objects, such as an article of clothing (bras, panties, hosiery, boots, shoes, leather, silk, and the like) or a body part (e.g., feet). It is normal for men to like the sight, feel, and smell of their lovers' undergarments. Men with fetishism, however, may prefer the object to the person and may not be able to become sexually aroused without it. They often experience sexual gratification by masturbating while fondling the object, rubbing or smelling it, or by having their partners wear it during sexual activity.

The origins of fetishism can sometimes be traced to early childhood experiences. But although research suggests that early learning experiences may be important, the origin of fetishes is likely to be more complex, involving an interplay of learning experiences and various biological (e.g., hormonal) factors (Pfaus, Kippin, & Centeno, 2001; Quinsey, 2003).

Transvestic Fetishism

transvestic fetishism Type of paraphilia in heterosexual males characterized by recurrent sexual urges and sexually arousing fantasies involving dressing in female clothing, in which the person has either acted on these urges or is strongly distressed by them. Also termed *transvestism*.

The chief feature of **transvestic fetishism** is recurrent, powerful urges and related fantasies involving cross-dressing for purposes of sexual arousal. Other people with fetishes can be satisfied by handling objects such as women's clothing while they masturbate; people with transvestic fetishism want to wear them. They may wear full feminine attire and makeup or favour one particular article of clothing, such as women's stockings. Men with transvestic are typically heterosexual. Typically, the man cross-dresses in private and imagines himself to be a woman who he is stroking as he masturbates. Some men frequent transvestite clubs or become involved in transvestic subcultures.

Gay men may cross-dress to attract other men or because it is fashionable to masquerade as women in some social circles, not because they are sexually aroused by cross-dressing. Males with gender identity disorder cross-dress because of gender discomfort associated with wearing men's clothing. Because cross-dressing among gay men and men with gender identity disorder is performed for other reasons than sexual arousal or gratification, it is not considered a form of transvestic fetishism. Nor are female impersonators who cross-dress for theatrical purposes considered to have a form of transvestism. For reasons such as these, the diagnosis is usually limited to heterosexuals.

Most men with transvestism are married and engage in sexual activity with their wives, but they seek additional sexual gratification through dressing as women, as in the case of Archie:

Archie was a 55-year-old plumber who had been cross-dressing for many years. There was a time when he would go out in public as a woman, but as his prominence in the community grew, he became more afraid of being discovered in public. His wife Myrna knew of his "peccadillo," especially since he borrowed many of her clothes, and she also encouraged him to stay at home, offering to help him with his "weirdness." For many years, his paraphilia had been restricted to the home.

The couple came to the clinic at the urging of the wife. Myrna described how Archie had imposed his will on her for 20 years. Archie would wear her undergarments and masturbate while she told him how disgusting he was. (The couple also regularly engaged in "normal" sexual intercourse, which Myrna enjoyed.) The cross-dressing situation had come to a head because a teenaged daughter had almost walked into the couple's bedroom while they were acting out Archie's fantasies.

With Myrna out of the consulting room, Archie explained that he had grown up in a family with several older sisters. He described how underwear had been perpetually hanging all around the one bathroom to dry. As an adolescent, Archie experimented with rubbing against articles of underwear, then with trying them on. On one occasion a sister walked in while he was modelling panties before the mirror. She told him he was one of the "dregs of society" and he straightaway experienced unparalleled sexual excitement. He masturbated when she left the room, and his orgasm was the strongest of his young life.

Archie did not think that there was anything wrong with wearing women's undergarments and masturbating. He was not about to give it up, regardless of whether his marriage was destroyed as a result. Myrna's main concern was finally separating herself from Archie's "sickness." She didn't care what he did any more, so long as he did it by himself. "Enough is enough," she said.

That was the compromise the couple worked out in marital therapy. Archie would engage in his fantasies by himself. He would choose times when Myrna was not at home, and she would not be informed of his activities. He would also be very, very careful to choose times when the children would not be around.

Six months later the couple was together and content. Archie had replaced Myrna's input into his fantasies with transvestic-sadomasochistic magazines. Myrna said, "I see no evil, hear no evil, smell no evil." They continued to have sexual intercourse. After a while, Myrna even forgot to check to see which underwear had been used.

THE AUTHORS' FILES

Transvestic fetishism should be distinguished from gender identity disorder. Transvestic fetishists do not consider themselves to be women, and transsexuals are not sexually aroused by cross-dressing. Even so, the two disorders appear to be connected; transvestic fetishism sometimes develops into gender identity disorder. In fact, transsexualism is often preceded by transvestic fetishism (Freund, Watson, & Dickey, 1991; Zucker & Blanchard, 1997). According to Ray Blanchard, the head of the Clinical Sexology Program at the University of Toronto and a leading researcher in the subject, gender identity disorders may be uncommon in women because the precursor—transvestic fetishism—is rare in women (Blanchard, 1989). Although gender identity disorders seem to be more common in children than adults, they occur in only 3% of boys and 1% of girls (Green & Blanchard, 1995).

Voyeurism

The chief feature of **voyeurism** is either acting on or being strongly distressed by recurrent, powerful sexual urges and related fantasies involving watching unsuspecting people, generally strangers, who are undressed, disrobing, or engaging in sexual activity. The purpose of watching or "peeping" is to attain sexual excitement. The person who engages in voyeurism does not typically seek sexual activity with the person or persons being observed.

Are the acts of watching one's partner disrobe or viewing sexually explicit films forms of voyeurism? The answer is no. The people who are observed know they are being observed by their partners or will be observed by film audiences. Voyeuristic acts involve watching unsuspecting persons disrobing or engaging in sexual activities. Note that feelings of sexual arousal while watching our partners undress or observing sex scenes in R- and X-rated films fall within the normal spectrum of human sexuality.

During voyeuristic acts, the person usually masturbates while watching or fantasizing about watching. Peeping may be the person's exclusive sexual outlet. Some people engage in voyeuristic acts in which they place themselves in risky situations—the prospect of being found out or injured apparently heightens the excitement.

voyeurism Type of paraphilia characterized by recurrent sexual urges and sexually arousing fantasies involving the act of watching unsuspecting others who are naked, in the act of undressing, or engaging in sexual activity, in which the person has either acted on these urges or is strongly distressed by them.

Frotteurism

The French *frottage* refers to the artistic technique of making a drawing by rubbing against a raised object. The chief feature of the paraphilia of **frotteurism** is recurrent, powerful sexual urges and related fantasies involving rubbing against or touching a non-consenting person. Frotteurism or "mashing" generally occurs in crowded places, such as subway cars, buses, or elevators. It is the rubbing or touching, not the coercive aspect of the act, that is sexually arousing. Almost all people diagnosed with frotteurism are male. He may imagine himself enjoying an exclusive, affectionate sexual relationship with the victim. Because the physical contact is brief and furtive, people who commit frotteuristic acts stand only a small chance of being caught by authorities. Even the victims may not realize at the time what has happened or register much protest (Spitzer, Gibbon, Skodol, Williams, & First, 1994). In the following case example, a man victimized about 1000 women over a period of years but was arrested only twice:

> Charles, 45, was seen by a psychiatrist following his second arrest for rubbing against a woman in the subway. He would select as his target a woman in her 20s as she entered the subway station. He would then position himself behind her on the platform and wait for the train to arrive. He would then follow her into the subway car and when the doors closed would begin bumping against her buttocks, while fantasizing that they were enjoying having intercourse in a loving and consensual manner. About half of the time he would reach orgasm. He would then continue on his way to work. Sometimes, when he hadn't reached orgasm, he would change trains and seek another victim. While he felt guilty for a time after each episode, he would soon become preoccupied with thoughts about his next encounter. He never gave any thought to the feelings his victims might have about what he had done to them. While he has been married to the same woman for 25 years, he appears to be rather socially inept and unassertive, especially with women.
>
> ADAPTED FROM SPITZER ET AL., 1994, PP. 164–165.
> REPRINTED FROM NEVID, FICHNER-RATHUS, & RATHUS, 1995, P. 570.

Pedophilia

Pedophilia derives from the Greek *paidos*, meaning "child." The chief feature of pedophilia is recurrent, powerful sexual urges and related fantasies involving sexual activity with prepubescent children (typically 13 years old or younger). Some pedophiles may not have actually molested children, because the diagnosis can be made on the basis of recurrent fantasies without the person necessarily acting on those fantasies (Barbaree & Seto, 1997). To be diagnosed with pedophilia, the person must be at least 16 years of age and at least five years older than the child or children toward whom he or she is sexually attracted or has victimized. In some cases of pedophilia, the person is attracted only to children. In other cases, the person is attracted to adults as well.

Although some persons with pedophilia restrict their pedophilic activity to looking at or undressing children, others engage in exhibitionism, kissing, fondling, oral sex, anal intercourse, and, in the case of girls, vaginal intercourse (Knudsen, 1991). Not being worldly wise, children are often exploited by molesters who inform them they are "educating" them, "showing them something," or doing something they will "like." Some men with pedophilia limit their sexual activity with children to incestuous relations with family members; others molest children only outside the family. Not all child molesters have pedophilia, however. The clinical definition of pedophilia is brought to bear only when sexual attraction to children is recurrent and persistent. Some molesters engage in these acts or experience pedophilic urges only occasionally or during times of opportunity.

Despite the stereotype, most cases of pedophilia do not involve "dirty old men" who hang around schoolyards in raincoats. Men with this disorder are usually (otherwise) law-

frotteurism Type of paraphilia characterized by recurrent sexual urges or sexually arousing fantasies involving bumping and rubbing against nonconsenting victims for sexual gratification. The person has either acted on these urges or is strongly distressed by them.

pedophilia Type of paraphilia involving sexual attraction to children.

abiding, respected citizens in their 30s or 40s. Most are married or divorced and have children of their own. They are usually well acquainted with their victims, who are typically either relatives or friends of the family. Many cases of pedophilia are not isolated incidents. They may be a series of acts that begin when children are very young and continue for many years until they are discovered or the relationship is broken off (Finkelhor, Hotaling, Lewis, & Smith, 1990).

Nearly all pedophiles are men, although the disorder is occasionally seen in women (Denov, 2001; Fedoroff et al., 1999; Seto, 2004). In recent years, there have been a number of widely publicized newspaper and television reports of female high school teachers in their late 20s, 30s, or older having affairs with adolescent students (e.g., Denov, 2001). Such reports have come from schools in British Columbia, Ontario, and elsewhere. Some of these may be cases of pedophilia, especially where the female teacher persistently seeks sexual encounters with young students.

The origins of pedophilia are complex and varied. Some cases fit the stereotype of a weak, shy, socially inept, and isolated person who is threatened by mature relationships and turns to children for sexual gratification because children are less critical and demanding (Ames & Houston, 1990). In other cases, it may be that childhood sexual experiences with other children were so enjoyable that the person, as an adult, is attempting to recapture the excitement of earlier years. Or perhaps in some cases of pedophilia, people who were sexually abused in childhood by adults may now be reversing the situation in an effort to establish feelings of mastery. Consistent with the latter possibility, research indicates that pedophilic men, compared to other kinds of sex offenders, are more likely to have been sexually abused as children (Marshall, Serran, & Cortoni, 2000; Seto, 2004). This suggests that early sex-related experiences may be somehow linked to pedophilia. Men whose pedophilic acts involve incestuous relationships with their own children tend to fall at one extreme or the other on the dominance spectrum, either being very dominant or passive (Ames & Houston, 1990).

Effects of Child Sexual Abuse Child survivors of sexual abuse are more likely than nonabused children to develop psychological problems, including anxiety, depression, anger and aggressive behaviour, eating disorders, premature sexual behaviour or promiscuity, drug abuse, self-destructive behaviour such as suicide attempts, lack of trust, low self-esteem, social withdrawal, psychosomatic problems such as stomach aches and headaches, and symptoms of posttraumatic stress disorder (PTSD) (e.g., Boney-McCoy & Finkelhor, 1996; Mian, Marton, & LeBaron, 1996; Swanston, Tebbutt, O'Toole, & Oates, 1997). Regressive behaviour in the form of thumb-sucking or recurrences of childhood fears, such as fear of the dark or of strangers, are not uncommon. Although the effects of child sexual abuse are more similar than not between boys and girls (e.g., both genders tend to experience fears and sleep disturbances), there are some important differences. The clearest gender difference is that boys tend to develop "externalized" behaviour problems, such as excessive aggressive behaviour, whereas girls tend to experience "internalized" problems, such as depression (Finkelhor et al., 1990; Gomez-Schwartz, Horowitz, & Cardarelli, 1990).

Late adolescence and early adulthood is a particularly difficult time for survivors of child sexual abuse, because unresolved feelings of anger and guilt and a deep sense of mistrust can prevent survivors from developing intimate relationships (Jackson, Calhoun, Amick, Maddever, & Habif, 1990). Research and scientific reviews conducted throughout the world, including at universities in Ontario and Manitoba, indicate that there are many serious long-term consequences of childhood sexual abuse (Abdulrehman & De Luca, 2001; Lipman, MacMillan, & Boyle, 2001; MacMillan et al., 2001; Rumstein-McKean & Hunsley, 2001). Adult survivors of childhood sexual abuse, compared to people who were never abused, are more likely to have psychological disorders (e.g., anxiety disorders, mood disorders, suicidal behaviour, substance abuse, and antisocial behaviour), relationship problems, tend to have fewer friends, have more social adjustment problems, and tend to have greater problems in sexual functioning. Martin Kruze is a tragic case in point. He, along with many other young hockey players, was sexually abused by men working in Toronto's Maple Leaf Gardens from the 1970s to the 1990s (Vine & Challen,

2002). Many boys were traumatized. Martin, who as an adult blew the whistle on the abuse, later committed suicide.

Sexual Masochism

sexual masochism Type of paraphilia characterized by sexual urges and sexually arousing fantasies involving receiving humiliation or pain, in which the person has either acted on these urges or is strongly distressed by them.

hypoxyphilia Paraphilia in which a person seeks sexual gratification by being deprived of oxygen by means of using a noose, plastic bag, chemical, or pressure on the chest.

sexual sadism Type of paraphilia or sexual deviation characterized by recurrent sexual urges and sexually arousing fantasies involving inflicting humiliation or physical pain on sex partners, in which the person has either acted on these urges or is strongly distressed by them.

sadomasochism Sexual activities between partners involving the attainment of gratification by means of inflicting and receiving pain and humiliation.

Sexual masochism derives its name from the Austrian novelist Ritter Leopold von Sacher Masoch (1835–1895), who wrote stories and novels about men who sought sexual gratification from women inflicting pain on them, often in the form of flagellation (being beaten or whipped). Sexual masochism involves strong, recurrent urges and fantasies relating to sexual acts that involve being humiliated, bound, flogged, or made to suffer in other ways. The urges are either acted on or cause significant personal distress. In some cases of sexual masochism, the person cannot attain sexual gratification in the absence of pain or humiliation.

In some cases, sexual masochism involves binding or mutilating oneself during masturbation or sexual fantasies. In others, a partner is engaged to restrain (bondage), blindfold (sensory bondage), paddle, or whip the person. Some partners are prostitutes; others are consensual partners who are asked to perform the sadistic role. In some cases, the person may desire, for purposes of sexual gratification, to be urinated or defecated on or subjected to verbal abuse.

A most dangerous expression of masochism is **hypoxyphilia** (also known as autoerotic asphyxiation), in which participants are sexually aroused by being deprived of oxygen—for example, by using a noose, plastic bag, chemical, or pressure on the chest during a sexual act, such as masturbation. The oxygen deprivation is usually accompanied by fantasies of asphyxiating or being asphyxiated by a lover. People who engage in this activity generally discontinue it before they lose consciousness, but occasional deaths due to suffocation have resulted from miscalculations (Blanchard & Hucker, 1991; Cosgray, Hanna, Fawley, & Money, 1991).

To illustrate the nature of this paraphilia, an Alberta study of 19 cases of death due to hypoxyphilia revealed that the person is often a single male aged 15 to 29 years, who performed the act repetitively and when alone. Accidental death typically occurred when there was a failure of the "safety" mechanism designed to restore oxygen (Tough, Butt, & Sanders, 1994). According to Stephen Hucker, a Toronto psychiatrist and expert on paraphilias, people who engage in hypoxyphilia also tend to practise other forms of sexual masochism, such as self-administered electrical shocks (Hucker, 1985).

Sexual Sadism

Sexual sadism is named after the infamous Marquis de Sade, the 18th-century Frenchman who wrote stories about the pleasures of achieving sexual gratification by inflicting pain or humiliation on others. Sexual sadism is the flip side of sexual masochism. It involves recurrent, powerful urges and related fantasies of engaging in acts in which the person is sexually aroused by inflicting physical suffering or humiliation on another person. People with this paraphilia either act out their fantasies or are disturbed by them. They may recruit consenting partners, who may be lovers or wives with a masochistic streak, or prostitutes. Still others—known as sadistic rapists—stalk and assault nonconsenting victims and become aroused by inflicting pain or suffering on their victims. The experience of power and control may be as important as inflicting pain (Hucker, 1997). Most rapists, however, do not seek to become sexually aroused by inflicting pain on their victims; they may even lose sexual interest when they see their victims in pain.

Many people have occasional sadistic or masochistic fantasies or engage in sex play involving simulated or mild forms of **sadomasochism** with their partners. Sadomasochism describes a mutually gratifying sexual interaction involving both sadistic and masochistic acts. Simulation may take the form of using a feather brush to strike one's partner, so

S&M paraphernalia. Some of the devices used by people who engage in sadomasochism.

that no actual pain is administered. People who engage in sadomasochism frequently switch roles during their encounters or from one encounter to another. The clinical diagnosis of sexual masochism or sadism is not usually brought to bear unless such people become distressed by their behaviour or fantasies or act them out in ways that are harmful to themselves or others.

Other Paraphilias

There are many other paraphilias. These include making obscene phone calls ("telephone scatologia"), necrophilia (sexual urges or fantasies involving sexual contact with corpses), partialism (sole focus on part of the body), zoophilia (sexual urges or fantasies involving sexual contact with animals), and sexual arousal associated with feces (coprophilia), enemas (klismaphilia), and urine (urophilia).

Theoretical Perspectives

Psychodynamic theorists see many paraphilias as defences against leftover castration anxiety from the Oedipal period. The thought of the penis disappearing into the vagina is unconsciously equated with castration.

The man who develops a paraphilia may avoid this threat of castration anxiety by displacing sexual arousal into other activities—for example, undergarments, children, or watching others. By sequestering his penis under women's clothes, the man with transvestic fetishism engages in a symbolic act of denial that women do not have penises, which eases castration anxiety by unconsciously providing evidence of women's (and his own) safety. The shock and dismay shown by the victim of a man who exposes himself provides unconscious reassurance that he does, after all, have a penis. Sadism involves an unconscious identification with the man's father—the "aggressor" of his Oedipal fantasies—and relieves anxiety by giving him the opportunity to enact the role of the castrator. Some psychoanalytic theorists see masochism as a way of coping with conflicting feelings about sex. Basically, the man feels guilty about sex but is able to enjoy it so long as he is being punished for it. Others view masochism as the redirection inward of aggressive impulses originally aimed at the powerful, threatening father. Like the child who is relieved when his inevitable punishment is over, the man gladly accepts bondage and flagellation in place of castration. These views remain speculative and controversial. We lack any direct evidence that men with paraphilias are handicapped by unresolved castration anxiety.

Learning theorists explain paraphilias in terms of conditioning and observational learning (Pfaus, Kippin, & Centeno, 2001; Seto, 2004). Some object or activity becomes inadvertently associated with sexual arousal. The object or activity then gains the capacity to elicit sexual arousal. For example, a boy who glimpses his mother's stockings on the towel rack while he is masturbating may go on to develop a fetish for stockings (Breslow, 1989). Orgasm in the presence of the object reinforces the erotic connection, especially when it occurs repeatedly. Yet if fetishes were acquired by mechanical association, we would expect people to develop fetishes to stimuli that are inadvertently and repeatedly connected with sexual activity, such as bedsheets, pillows, even ceilings (Breslow, 1989; Marshall & Eccles, 1993). Such is not the case. The *meaning* of the stimulus also apparently plays a role. Perhaps the development of fetishes depends on people's ability to eroticize certain types of stimuli (like women's undergarments) and incorporate them into their erotic and masturbatory fantasies. Fetishes can often be traced to experiences in early childhood. Like other patterns of abnormal behaviour, paraphilias may involve multiple biological, psychological, and sociocultural factors. Money and Lamacz (1990) hypothesize a multifactorial model that traces the development of paraphilias to childhood. They suggest that childhood experiences etch a pattern or "lovemap" that can be likened to a software program in the brain that determines the kinds of stimuli and behaviours that come to arouse people sexually. In the case of paraphilias, lovemaps become "vandalized" by early traumatic experiences, such as incest, physical abuse, or neglect, and excessively harsh antisexual child-rearing. Yet not all children who undergo such experiences develop paraphilias. Nor do all people with paraphilias have such traumatic experiences. Perhaps

Origins of fetishism? The conditioning model of the origins of fetishism suggests that men who develop fetishisms involving women's undergarments may have had experiences in childhood in which sexual arousal was repeatedly paired with exposure to their mother's undergarments. The developing fetish may have been strengthened by the boy incorporating the object into his erotic fantasies or masturbatory activity.

some children are more vulnerable to developing distorted lovemaps than others. The precise nature of such vulnerability remains to be defined.

Treatment of Paraphilias

Therapists of various theoretical persuasions have attempted to treat clients with paraphilias. Psychoanalysts, for example, attempt to bring childhood sexual conflicts (typically of an Oedipal nature) into awareness so they can be resolved in the light of the individual's adult personality. Favourable results from individual case studies appear in the literature from time to time, but there is a dearth of controlled investigations to support the efficacy of psychodynamic treatment of paraphilias.

Behaviour therapists have used aversive conditioning to induce a negative emotional reaction to paraphilic stimuli or fantasies. In aversive conditioning, the stimulus that elicits sexual arousal (e.g., panties) is paired repeatedly with an aversive stimulus (e.g., electric shock) in the belief the stimulus will acquire aversive properties. A basic limitation of aversive conditioning is that it does not help the individual acquire more adaptive behaviours in place of maladaptive response patterns. This may explain why researchers find that a broad-based, cognitive-behavioural program for treating exhibitionism that emphasizes the development of adaptive thoughts, the building of social skills, and the development of stress-management skills is more effective than an alternative program based on aversion therapy (Marshall, Eccles, & Barbaree, 1991).

Maletzky (1991, 1998; Maletzky & Steinhauser, 2002) reported on the success rates of the largest treatment program study to date, based on more than 7000 cases of rapists and sex offenders with paraphilias. Treatment procedures incorporated a variety of behavioural techniques, including aversive and nonaversive methods, which were tailored to the particular type of paraphilia.

Success rates for treatment of various paraphilias are reported in Table 11.2. Several cautions are advised in interpreting these data, however. Criteria for success were at least partly dependent on self-reports of an absence of deviant sexual interests or behaviour, and self-reports may be biased, especially in offender groups. Second, with the lack of a control group, we cannot discount the possibility that other factors, such as fears of legal consequences or nonspecific factors unrelated to the specific behavioural techniques used, influenced the outcome. Nonetheless, these data are among the strongest sources of evidence supporting the effectiveness of behavioural techniques in treating paraphilias.

Some promising results are also reported in using selective serotonin reuptake inhibitors (SSRIs) such as Prozac in treating voyeurism and fetishism (Greenberg & Bradford, 1997). Why SSRIs? These medications have been used effectively in treating obsessive-compulsive disorder (see Chapter 5). Researchers speculate that paraphilias may fall within an obsessive-compulsive spectrum (Kruesi, Fine, Valladares, Phillips, & Rapoport, 1992). Many people with paraphilias report feeling compelled to carry out paraphilic acts in much the same way that people with obsessive-compulsive disorder feel driven to perform compulsive acts. Paraphilias also tend to have an obsessional quality. The person experiences intrusive, repetitive urges to engage in paraphilic acts or thoughts that relate to the paraphilic object or situation. However, Maletzky (1998) cautions that these drugs may act to reduce sexual drives rather than specifically target deviant sexual fantasies.

Sexual Assault

Although sexual assaults are not diagnosable psychological disorders, they certainly meet several of the criteria used to define abnormal behaviour. Rape, pedophilia, and other forms of sexual assault are socially unacceptable, violate social norms, and are grievously harmful to their victims. Sexual assault may also be associated with some clinical syndromes, especially some forms of sexual sadism.

TABLE 11.2

Percentages of Sex Offenders Successfully Treated

Paraphilia	No. of Cases Treated	% of Cases Treated Successfully
Situational pedophilia (heterosexual)	3012	95.6
Predatory pedophilia (heterosexual)	864	88.3
Situational pedophilia (homosexual)	717	91.8
Predatory pedophilia (homosexual)	596	80.1
Exhibitionism	1130	95.4
Rape	543	75.5
Voyeurism	83	93.9
Public masturbation	77	94.8
Frotteurism	65	89.3
Fetishism	33	94.0
Transvestic fetishism	14	78.6
Obscene telephoning	29	93.1
Zoophilia	23	95.6

A treatment success was defined as an offender who completed all treatment sessions, reported no covert or overt deviant sexual behaviour at the end of treatment or at any follow-up session, demonstrated no deviant sexual arousal at the end of treatment or at any follow-up session, and had no repeat legal charges for any sexual crime at the end of treatment or at any follow-up session.

Source: Maletzky, B. M. The paraphilias: Research and treatment. In P. E. Nathan & J. M. Gorman (Eds.), *A Guide to Treatments That Work* (Table 24–8). Copyright © 1998 by Peter E. Nathan and Jack M. Gorman. Used by permission of Oxford University Press, Inc.

Forcible rape refers to the use of force, violence, or threats of violence to coerce someone into sexual intercourse. **Statutory rape** is defined as sexual intercourse with a person who is unable to give consent, either because of being under the age of consent or because of mental disability, even though the person may co-operate with the rapist.

forcible rape Legal term for rape or forced sexual intercourse with a non-consenting person.

statutory rape Legal term referring to sexual intercourse with a minor, even with the minor's consent.

Incidence of Rape and Other Forms of Sexual Assault Sexual assault, including rape, is disturbingly common. To illustrate, a Winnipeg survey of 551 women revealed that 6% reported that they had been raped, and 21% reported being sexually assaulted (e.g., unwanted touching) at some point in their lives (Brickman & Briere, 1984). In a later and larger survey of students from colleges and universities across Canada, 28% of women reported being sexually abused in the previous year, and 11% of men reported having victimized a female dating partner in this way during the same period (DeKeseredy, 1997). Similar results have been reported from campuses in the United States (e.g., Gross, Winslett, Roberts, & Gohm, 2006). In the Canadian population in general, it has been estimated that more than 30% of men and over 50% of women have been sexually assaulted (Canadian Committee on Sexual Offences Against Children and Youth, 1984).

In over 80% of rape cases overall, the woman is acquainted with the assailant (Cole, 2006; Gibbs, 1991). Rape is the most common violent crime on campus. Most *rapes* occur in social situations, such as at a party or when students study together in a dormitory room, and roughly half of perpetrators and *rape* survivors are drinking alcohol at the time of the assault (Cole, 2006). Some men may use alcohol intoxication as an excuse for sexual assault, and some men perceive women who drink alcohol to be more sexually available and therefore appropriate targets for sexual aggression. Regardless of the motives or perceptions of a man or a woman, rape is never justified. Although male rapes do occur, especially in prisons, the great majority of cases involve women as the victim.

Theoretical Perspectives There is no single kind of perpetrator of sexual assault. Sexual assailants are no more likely than other offenders to have the kinds of psychological disorders coded on Axis I of the DSM-IV (Polaschek, Ward, & Hudson, 1997). Rape has more to do with violent impulses and issues of power and control than sexual gratification. According to DeKeseredy's (1997) survey of Canadian undergraduates, men who had sexually abused tended to hold beliefs that women should be obedient, respectful, dependent, and sexually submissive toward men. Such beliefs may increase the odds that a man will become sexually abusive. Many sex offenders were sexually abused themselves as children (Seto, 2004). Some rapists who were abused as children may humiliate women as a way of expressing anger and power over them and of taking revenge. For still other rapists, violent cues appear to enhance sexual arousal, so they are motivated to combine sex with aggression (Marshall & Moulden, 2001). Sadistic rapes frequently employ torture and **bondage**, merging sex and aggression. Sadistic rapists are most likely to mutilate their victims.

William L. Marshall, a psychologist at Queen's University and an expert on paraphilias, argues that the risk of committing sexual offences is increased by early learning experiences that cause the person to have low self-confidence and poor social skills. Possessing poor social skills mean that the person will have difficulty attracting dating partners. Sexual offences involve the domination or humiliation of victims, and thereby may give a sense of power to men who are otherwise lacking in power and self-confidence. Offensive sexual behaviours are maladaptive attempts to achieve intimacy through sex. These efforts are invariably unsuccessful and self-defeating; they merely serve to isolate the person further from society. Paradoxically, the pattern may become deeply ingrained because it results in the momentary pleasure associated with orgasm and because it offers the illusory hope of eventually achieving intimacy with another person. These and other factors are implicated in Marshall's theory (see, for example, Marshall, 2001; Marshall, Anderson, & Champagne, 1997; Marshall, Hudson, & Hodkinson, 1993).

Marshall and others emphasize the role of attachment problems in sexual offenders (Beech & Mitchell, 2005; Marshall, 2001). Many sexual offenders report having had sexually or physically abusive childhood experiences; they also in many cases did not have safe, loving relationships (bondings) with one or both parents, because the parents were abusive, rejecting, or emotionally cold. These experiences are thought to increase the chances that a child will as an adult either seek out intimate, sexual attachments with children, perhaps confusing sex with intimacy, or become sexually aggressive with women (Beech & Mitchell, 2005).

Does pornography lead to sexual aggression? Given the seriousness of sexual assault and the growing size of the pornography industry, it is important to understand the role of pornography and sex offending. Psychologist Michael Seto and colleagues from the Centre for Addiction and Mental Health in Toronto recently reviewed the evidence regarding this important question (Seto, Maric, & Barbaree, 2001). They concluded that the existing evidence suggests people who are already predisposed to sexually offend are most likely to show an effect of pornography exposure (e.g., to be stimulated or encouraged by violent pornography or more likely to engage in sexual violence). Subsequent research lends support for this conclusion (e.g., Carr & VanDeusen, 2004).

Sociocultural factors also need to be considered. Although many rapists show evidence of psychopathology on psychological tests, especially psychopathic traits (Beech & Mitchell, 2005), many do not (Brown & Forth, 1997; Herkov, Gynther, Thomas, & Myers, 1996). The very normality of many rapists on psychological instruments suggests that socialization factors play an important role. Some sociocultural theorists argue that our culture actually breeds rapists by socializing men into sexually dominant and aggressive roles associated with stereotypical concepts of masculinity (e.g., Hall & Barongan, 1997; Lisak, 1991). Sexually coercive college men tend to have an excessively masculinized personality orientation, adhere more strictly to traditional gender roles, view women as adversaries in the "mating game," and hold more accepting attitudes toward the use of violence against women than do noncoercive men (e.g., O'Donohue, McKay, & Schewe, 1996; Polaschek et al., 1997). They are also more prone to blame rape survivors over rapists and become more sexually aroused by portrayals of rape than are men who hold

bondage Form of sadomasochism involving the binding of the arms or legs of oneself or one's partner during sexual activity.

less rigid stereotypes. Sociocultural influences also reinforce themes that may underlie rape, such as the cultural belief that a masculine man is expected to be sexually assertive and overcome a woman's resistance until she "melts" in his arms (Stock, 1991).

Date rape is a form of acquaintance rape. College men on dates frequently perceive their dates' protests as part of an adversarial sex game. One male undergraduate said, "Hell, no," when asked whether a date had consented to sex. He added, "But she didn't say no, so she must have wanted it, too. It's the way it works" (Celis, 1991). Consider the comments of Jim, a man who raped a woman he had just met at a party (Trenton State College, 1991):

> She looked really hot, wearing a sexy dress that showed off her great body. We started talking right away. I knew that she liked me by the way she kept smiling and touching my arm while she was speaking. She seemed pretty relaxed so I asked her back to my place for a drink. . . . When she said yes, I knew that I was going to be lucky!
>
> When we got to my place, we sat on the bed kissing. At first, everything was great. Then, when I started to lay her down on the bed, she started twisting and saying she didn't want to. Most women don't like to appear too easy, so I knew that she was just going through the motions. When she stopped struggling, I knew that she would have to throw in some tears before we did it.
>
> She was still very upset afterwards, and I just don't understand it! If she didn't want to have sex, why did she come back to the room with me? You could tell by the way she dressed and acted that she was no virgin, so why she had to put up such a big struggle I don't know.

Let us rebut these beliefs. Accepting a date is not the equivalent of consenting to intercourse. Accompanying a man to his room or apartment is not the equivalent of consenting to intercourse. Kissing and petting are not the equivalent of consenting to intercourse. When a woman fails to consent or says no, the man must take no for an answer.

Effects of Sexual Assault Women who are sexually assaulted suffer more than the assault itself. They report loss of appetite, headaches, irritability, anxiety and depression, and menstrual irregularity in the wake of a sexual assault. Some become sullen, withdrawn, and mistrustful. In some cases, women show an unrealistic composure, which often gives way to venting of feelings later on. Because of society's tendency to blame the victim for the assault, some survivors also have misplaced feelings of guilt, shame, and self-blame. Survivors often develop sexual dysfunctions such as lack of sexual desire and difficulty becoming sexually aroused (Letourneau, Resnick, Kilpatrick, Saunders, & Best, 1996). Many survivors show signs of PTSD, including intrusive memories of the rape, nightmares, emotional numbing, and heightened autonomic arousal (Taylor, 2006).

Psychological problems experienced by rape survivors often continue through at least the first year following the sexual assault (Kimerling & Calhoun, 1994). About one in four rape survivors continues to encounter psychological problems such as depression and anxiety for a number of years after the attack (Calhoun & Atkeson, 1991; Koss et al., 1994).

Treatment of Rape Survivors Treatment of rape survivors is often a two-phase process that first assists women in coping with the immediate aftermath of rape and then helps them with their long-term adjustment. Crisis intervention provides women with emotional support and information to help them see to their immediate needs as well to help them develop strategies for coping with the trauma (Taylor, 2005). Longer-term treatment may be designed to help rape survivors cope with undeserved feelings of guilt and shame, lingering feelings of anxiety and depression, and the interpersonal and sexual problems they may develop with the men in their lives. Unfortunately, most rape survivors do not seek help from mental health professionals, rape crisis centres, or rape survivor assistance programs (Kimerling & Calhoun, 1994). The cultural stigma associated with seeking help for mental health problems may discourage a fuller utilization of psychological services.

Rape Prevention

Given the incidence of rape, it is important to be aware of strategies that may prevent it. By listing strategies for rape prevention, we do not mean to imply that rape survivors are somehow responsible for falling prey to an attack. The responsibility for any act of sexual violence lies with the perpetrator, not with the person who is assaulted, and perhaps with society for fostering attitudes that underlie sexual violence. On a societal level, we need to do a better job of socializing young men to acquire prosocial and respectful attitudes toward women. Exposure to feminist, egalitarian, and multicultural education, as well as educating men about the often devastating impact of rape on the person who is assaulted, may help promote more respectful attitudes in young men (Foubert & Perry, 2007; Hall & Barongan, 1997; Kershner, 1996).

Preventing Stranger Rape

- Establish signals and plans with other women in the building or neighbourhood.
- List first initials only in the phone directory and on the mailbox.
- Use dead-bolt locks.
- Lock windows and install iron grids on first-floor windows.
- Keep doorways and entries well lit.
- Have keys handy for the car or the front door.
- Do not walk by yourself after dark.
- Avoid deserted areas.
- Do not allow strange men into the apartment or the house without checking their credentials.
- Keep the car door locked and the windows up.
- Check out the backseat of the car before getting in.
- Don't live in a risky building.

- Don't give rides to hitchhikers (that includes female hitchhikers).
- Don't converse with strange men on the street.
- Shout "Fire!" not "Rape!" People flock to fires but circumvent scenes of violence.

Preventing Date Rape

- Avoid getting into secluded situations until you know your date very well.
- Be wary when a date attempts to control you in any way, such as frightening you by driving rapidly or taking you some place you would rather not go.
- Stay sober. We often do things we would not otherwise do—including sexual activity with people we might otherwise reject—when we have had too many drinks. Be aware of your limits. And if you do drink, don't leave your drink unattended. Many women have been sexually assaulted as a result of their drinks being spiked with drugs.
- Be very assertive and clear concerning your sexual intentions. Some rapists, particularly date rapists, tend to misinterpret women's wishes. If their dates begin to implore them to stop during kissing or petting, they construe pleading as "female game playing." So if kissing or petting is leading where you don't want it to go, speak up.
- When dating a person for the first time, try to date in a group.
- Encourage your college or university to offer educational programs about date rape.
- Talk to your date about his attitudes toward women. If you get the feeling that he believes men are in a war with women, or that women try to "play games" with men, you may be better off dating someone else.

Sources: Adapted from Nevid, Fichner-Rathus, & Rathus 1995.

Paraphilias

Review It

- **What are paraphilias?** Paraphilias are sexual deviations involving patterns of arousal to stimuli such as nonhuman objects (e.g., shoes or clothes), humiliation, the experience of pain in oneself or one's partner, or children.

- **What are the major types of paraphilia?** Paraphilias include exhibitionism, fetishism, transvestic fetishism, voyeurism, frotteurism, pedophilia, sexual masochism, and sexual sadism. Although some paraphilias are essentially harmless (such as fetishism), others, such as pedophilia and sexual sadism, often harm nonconsenting victims.

- **What causes paraphilias and what makes them so difficult to treat?** Paraphilias may be caused by the interaction of biological, psychological, and social factors. Efforts to treat paraphilias are compromised by the fact that most people with these disorders do not wish to change.

- **What factors underlie tendencies to rape?** The desires to dominate women or express hatred toward them may be more prominent motives for rape than sexual desire. Although some men who rape show clear evidence of underlying psychopathology, many do not.

  Rape has more to do with violent impulses and issues of power than with pursuit of sexual gratification. From a sociocultural perspective, we should examine cultural attitudes, such as stereotypes of male aggressiveness and social dominance, which underlie propensities to rape.

Define It

paraphilias	sexual masochism
exhibitionism	hypoxyphilia
fetishism	sexual sadism
transvestic fetishism	sadomasochism
voyeurism	forcible rape
frotteurism	statutory rape
pedophilia	bondage

Recall It*

1. All of the following are examples of objects or situations that relate to the focus of paraphilic urges or fantasies EXCEPT _____.

   a. humiliation experienced during sexual encounters
   b. persons who dress in revealing or sexually oriented clothing
   c. persons engaged in sexual acts who are unaware of being observed
   d. shoes or other nonhuman objects

2. Jamie has strong, recurrent sexual urges and fantasies involving desires to caress women's undergarments. This pattern of behaviour most closely resembles _____.

   a. frotteurism
   b. voyeurism
   c. fetishism
   d. pedophilia

3. Which of the following is considered a form of voyeurism?

   a. Using binoculars to watch a person undress through a bedroom window.
   b. Becoming aroused while watching a sexually explicit movie.
   c. Becoming aroused while observing your partner undress in front of you.
   d. All three of the above acts are considered forms of voyeurism.

4. According to classic psychodynamic theory, paraphilias in men represent a defence against _____.

   a. conflicts arising from the oral stage of psychosexual development
   b. castration anxiety
   c. repressed memories of incest
   d. hateful feelings toward the self

5. Each of the following is true concerning the psychological effects of rape EXCEPT _____.

   a. survivors often show lasting effects that continue beyond a year
   b. many survivors show evidence of posttraumatic stress disorder
   c. survivors rarely show evidence of sexual dysfunctions
   d. about one in four survivors continue to have psychological problems for years afterward

Think About It

- Do you think our culture is to blame for socializing boys and young men into sexually aggressive roles? Why or why not?

- Do you believe exhibitionists, voyeurs, and pedophiles should be punished, treated, or both? Explain.

- Where does the boundary lie between normal and abnormal forms of sexual arousal?

SEXUAL DYSFUNCTIONS

sexual dysfunctions Psychological disorders involving persistent difficulties with sexual interest, arousal, or response.

Sexual dysfunctions involve problems with sexual interest, arousal, or response. Sexual dysfunctions are widespread in our society, affecting over 40% of women and roughly 33% of men (Hayes, Bennett, Fairley, & Dennerstein, 2006; Laumann, Paik, & Rosen, 1999). They are often significant sources of distress to the affected person and his or her partner. There are various types of sexual dysfunctions, but they tend to share some common features, as outlined in Table 11.3. Table 11.4 on page 415 shows the estimated rates of several major types of sexual dysfunction based on community samples.

Some cases of sexual dysfunction have existed throughout the individual's lifetime, and are thus labelled *lifelong dysfunctions*. In the case of *acquired dysfunctions*, the problem begins following a period (or at least one occurrence) of normal functioning. In the case of a *situational dysfunction*, the problem occurs in some situations (e.g., with one's spouse), but not in others (e.g., with a lover or when masturbating), or at some times but not others. In the case of a *generalized dysfunction*, the problem occurs in all situations and at all times the individual engages in sexual activity.

Types of Sexual Dysfunctions

The DSM-IV groups most sexual dysfunctions into the following categories:

1. Sexual desire disorders
2. Sexual arousal disorders
3. Orgasm disorders
4. Sexual pain disorders

The first three categories correspond to the first three phases of the sexual response cycle.

TABLE 11.3	
Common Features of Sexual Dysfunction	
Fear of failure	Fears relating to failure to achieve or maintain erection or failure to reach orgasm.
Assumption of a spectator role rather than a performer role	Monitoring and evaluating your body's reactions during sex.
Diminished self-esteem	Thinking less of yourself for failure to meet your standard of normality.
Emotional effects	Guilt, shame, frustration, depression, anxiety. Avoiding sexual contacts for fear of failure to perform adequately; making excuses to your partner.
Avoidance behaviour	Fears relating to failure to achieve or maintain erection or failure to reach orgasm.

Source: Reprinted with permission from Nevid, J. S., Fichner-Rathus, L., & Rathus, S. A. (1995). *Human Sexuality in a World of Diversity.* (2nd ed.). Boston: Allyn & Bacon, p. 454.

TABLE 11.4

Estimated Prevalence of Various Current Sexual Dysfunctions (percentage of respondents reporting any problem)

Premature ejaculation	36–38
Erectile dysfunction	4–9
Male orgasmic disorder	4–10
Female orgasmic disorder	5–10

Source: Adapted from Spector, I. M., & Carey, M. P. (1990). Incidence and prevalence of the sexual dysfunctions: A critical review of the empirical evidence. *Archives of Sexual Behavior, 1,* 389–408.

Sexual Desire Disorders Sexual desire disorders involve disturbances in sexual appetite or an aversion to genital sexual activity. People with **hypoactive sexual desire disorder** have an absence or lack of sexual interest or desire. Typically, there is either a complete or virtual absence of sexual fantasies. However, clinicians have not reached any universally agreed upon criteria for determining the level of sexual desire that is considered normal. Individual clinicians must weigh various factors in reaching a diagnosis in cases of low sexual desire, such as the client's lifestyle (e.g., the lack of sexual energy or interest in parents contending with the demands of infants or young children is to be expected), sociocultural factors (e.g., culturally restrictive attitudes may restrain sexual desire or interest), the quality of the relationship between the client and her or his partner (declining sexual interest or activity may reflect relationship problems rather than diminished drive), and the client's age (desire normally declines but does not disappear with increasing age). Couples usually seek help when one or both partners recognize that the level of sexual activity in the relationship is deficient or has waned to the point that little desire or interest remains. Sometimes the lack of desire is limited to one partner. In other cases, both partners may feel sexual urges, but anger and conflict concerning other issues inhibit sexual interaction. Although problems in sexual desire were first included in the DSM in 1980, the diagnosis of hypoactive sexual desire disorder has become one of the most commonly diagnosed sexual dysfunctions in women today (Hayes et al., 2006; Letourneau & O'Donohue, 1993). Giving lie to the myth that men are always ready for sex, the number of men presenting with hypoactive sexual desire disorder appears to be on the rise (Letourneau & O'Donohue, 1993; Spector & Carey, 1990). However, premature ejaculation is still the most common sexual dysfunction in men (Hellstrom, Nehra, Shabsigh, & Sharlip, 2006).

People with **sexual aversion disorder** have a strong aversion to genital sexual contact and avoid all or nearly all genital contact with a partner. They may, however, desire and enjoy affectionate contact or nongenital sexual contact. Their disgust with any form of genital contact may stem from childhood sexual abuse, rape, or other traumatic experiences. In other cases, deep-seated feelings of sexual guilt or shame may impair sexual response. In men, the diagnosis is often connected with a history of erectile failures. Such men may associate sexual opportunities with failure and shame. Their partners may also develop aversions to sexual contact because their sexual contacts have been so frustrating or emotionally painful.

Sexual Arousal Disorders Disorders of sexual arousal comprise an inability to achieve or maintain the physiological responses involved in sexual arousal or excitement—vaginal lubrication in the woman or penile erection in the man—that are needed to allow completion of sexual activity.

In women, sexual arousal is characterized by lubrication of the vaginal walls that makes entry by the penis possible. In men, sexual arousal is characterized by erection. Almost all women now and then have difficulty becoming or remaining lubricated. Almost all men have occasional difficulty attaining or maintaining an erection through intercourse. The diagnoses of **female sexual arousal disorder** and **male erectile disorder**

hypoactive sexual desire disorder Persistent or recurrent lack of sexual interest or sexual fantasies.

sexual aversion disorder Type of sexual dysfunction characterized by aversion to, and avoidance of, genital sexual contact.

female sexual arousal disorder Type of sexual dysfunction in women involving difficulties becoming sexually aroused, as defined by a lack of vaginal lubrication or failure to maintain sufficient lubrication to complete the sexual act or lack of sexual excitement or pleasure during sexual activity.

male erectile disorder Sexual dysfunction in males characterized by difficulty in achieving or maintaining erection during sexual activity.

(also called *sexual impotence* or erectile dysfunction) are reserved for persistent or recurrent problems in becoming genitally aroused.

Orgasm Disorders Orgasm or sexual climax is an involuntary reflex that results in rhythmic contractions of the pelvic muscles and is usually accompanied by feelings of intense pleasure. In men, these contractions are accompanied by expulsion of semen. There are three specific types of orgasm disorders: **female orgasmic disorder**, **male orgasmic disorder**, and **premature ejaculation**.

Orgasmic disorder refers to persistent or recurrent delay in reaching orgasm or the absence of orgasm following a normal level of sexual interest and arousal. The clinician needs to make a judgment about whether there is an "adequate" amount and type of stimulation to achieve an orgasmic response. There is a broad range of normal variation in sexual response that needs to be considered. Many women, for example, require direct clitoral stimulation (by means of stimulation by her own hand or her partner's) in order to achieve orgasm during vaginal intercourse. This should not be considered abnormal, because the clitoris, not the vagina, is the woman's most erotically sensitive organ.

In men, recurrent or persistent difficulty achieving orgasm following a normal pattern of sexual interest and excitement is termed male orgasmic disorder. This disorder is relatively rare and has received very little attention in the clinical literature (Dekker, 1993; Rosen & Leiblum, 1995). Men with this problem can usually reach orgasm through masturbation but not through intercourse.

Premature ejaculation is defined as a recurrent or persistent pattern of ejaculation with minimal sexual stimulation. It can occur prior to, upon, or shortly after penetration, but before the man desires it. Note the subjective elements. In making the diagnosis, the clinician weighs the man's age, the novelty of the partner, and the frequency of sexual activity. Occasional experiences of rapid ejaculation, such as when the man is with a new partner, has had infrequent sexual contacts, or is very highly aroused, fall within the normal spectrum. More persistent patterns of premature ejaculation would occasion a diagnosis of the disorder. About one in three men experience premature ejaculation (Hellstrom et al., 2006).

Sexual Pain Disorders In **dyspareunia**, sexual intercourse is associated with recurrent pain in the genital region. The pain cannot be explained fully by an underlying medical condition and so is believed to have a psychological component. However, many, perhaps even most, cases of pain during intercourse are traceable to an underlying medical condition, such as insufficient lubrication or a urinary tract infection. The DSM classifies these cases under a different diagnostic label, "Sexual Dysfunction Due to Medical Condition."

Dyspareunia can occur in both men and women, but is more common in women (Meana & Binik, 1994). Women who seek treatment for this disorder are often afraid of intercourse and vaginal penetration (Reissing, Binik, & Khalife, 1999). McGill University psychologist Yitzchak Binik and colleagues argue that dyspareunia is primarily a pain syndrome rather than a sexual dysfunction (Binik, 2005; Meana, Binik, Khalife, & Cohen, 1997).

Vaginismus involves an involuntary spasm of the muscles surrounding the vagina when vaginal penetration is attempted, making sexual intercourse painful or impossible.

Theoretical Perspectives

As emphasized by internationally renowned University of British Columbia sexologist Rosemary Basson (2001, 2005), sexual dysfunctions, like most psychological disorders, reflect a complex interplay of biological, psychological, and other factors.

Biological Perspectives Deficient testosterone production and thyroid overactivity or underactivity are among the many biological conditions that can lead to impaired sexual desire (Kresin, 1993). Medical conditions can also impair sexual arousal in both men and women (Graber, 1993). Diabetes, for instance, is the most common organic cause of erectile dysfunction, with estimates indicating that half of diabetic men eventually suffer some

---

female orgasmic disorder Type of sexual dysfunction in women involving difficulties achieving orgasm.

male orgasmic disorder Type of sexual dysfunction in men involving persistent difficulties achieving orgasm.

premature ejaculation Type of sexual dysfunction involving a persistent or recurrent pattern of ejaculation occurring during sexual activity at a point before the man desires it.

dyspareunia Persistent or recurrent pain experienced during or following sexual intercourse.

vaginismus Type of sexual dysfunction characterized by the recurrent or persistent contraction of the muscles surrounding the vaginal entrance, making penile entry while attempting intercourse difficult or impossible.

degree of erectile dysfunction (Thomas & LoPiccolo, 1994). Diabetes may also impair sexual response in women, with decreased vaginal lubrication being the most common consequence.

Biological factors may play a prominent role in as many as 70% to 80% of cases of erectile dysfunction (Brody, 1995). Other biological factors that can impair sexual desire, arousal, and orgasm include nerve-damaging conditions such as multiple sclerosis, lung disorders, kidney disease, circulatory problems, damage caused by sexually transmitted diseases, and side effects of various drugs (Brody, 1995; Segraves, 1988). Yet even in cases of sexual dysfunction that are traced to physical causes, emotional problems such as anxiety, depression, and marital conflict can compound the problem.

The male sex hormone testosterone plays a pivotal role in sexual interest and functioning in women as well as men (both genders produce testosterone in varying amounts) (Meston & Bradford, 2006). Men with deficient production of testosterone may lose sexual interest and the capacity for erections (Kresin, 1993). The adrenal glands and ovaries are the sites of testosterone production in women. Women who have these organs surgically removed because of invasive disease no longer produce testosterone and may gradually lose sexual interest and the capacity for sexual response. Although hormonal deficiencies may play a role in sexual dysfunction in such cases, researchers find that most men and women with sexual dysfunctions have normal hormone levels (Schreiner-Engel, Schiavi, White, & Ghizzani, 1989; Stuart, Hammond, & Pett, 1987).

Many temporary physical conditions can lead to problems in desire, arousal, and orgasm—even to sexual pain. Fatigue impairs sexual response and can lead to genital pain if the couple persists in attempting intercourse. Depressants such as tranquillizers, alcohol, and narcotics can lessen sexual response (Segraves, 1988). These effects are normally isolated unless people do not recognize their causes and attach too much meaning to them. That is, if you are intoxicated and do not know that alcohol can suppress your sexual response, you may wonder whether there is something wrong with you. Biological factors may thus interact with psychological factors in leading to the development of a persistent problem. Because of your concern, you may try to bear down during your next sexual opportunity, causing anxiety that may further interfere with normal sexual response. A second failure may strengthen self-doubts, creating more anxiety, which in turn stems performance, which may lead to a vicious cycle resulting in repeated failure experiences.

Psychodynamic Perspectives Psychodynamic hypotheses generally revolve around presumed conflicts of the phallic stage (Fenichel, 1945). Mature genital sexuality is believed to require successful resolution of the Oedipus and Electra complexes. Men with sexual dysfunctions are presumed to suffer from unconscious castration anxiety. Sexual intercourse elicits an unconscious fear of retaliation by the father, rendering the vagina unsafe. Erectile dysfunction "saves" the man from having to enter the vagina. Premature ejaculation allows him to "escape" rapidly and may also represent unconscious hatred of women (Kaplan, 1974). Orgasmic disorder prevents him from completing the act and unconsciously minimizes his guilt and fear. Rapid ejaculation serves the unconscious purpose of expressing hatred through soiling the woman and denying her sexual pleasure.

In women, unresolved penis envy engenders hostility toward men. The woman who remains fixated in the phallic stage punishes her partner for having a penis by not permitting the organ to bring her pleasure, as in female sexual arousal disorder. The clamping down of the vaginal muscles in vaginismus may express an unconscious wish to castrate her partner (Kaplan, 1974). In orgasmic disorder, she has failed to overcome penis envy and to develop mature sexuality, which involves transferring erotic feelings from the clitoris to the

When a source of pleasure becomes a source of anxiety. Sexual dysfunctions can be a source of intense personal distress and lead to friction between partners. Problems in communication can give rise to or exacerbate sexual dysfunctions.

vagina. She thus prevents orgasm from occurring through intercourse. It is difficult to test the validity of the psychoanalytic concepts because they involve unconscious conflicts, like castration anxiety and penis envy, that cannot be scientifically observed. Evidence for these views relies on case studies that involve interpretation of patients' histories. Case-study accounts are open to rival interpretations. We can say with certainty, however, that despite the traditional psychoanalytic conception, clitoral stimulation remains a key part of the woman's erotic response as she matures and is not a sign of an immature fixation.

Learning Perspectives

Learning theorists focus on the role of conditioned anxiety in the development of sexual dysfunctions. The occurrence of physically or psychologically painful experiences associated with sexual activity may cause a person to respond to sexual encounters with anxiety that is strong enough to counteract sexual pleasure and performance. A history of sexual abuse or rape plays a role in many cases in women with sexual arousal disorder, sexual aversion disorder, orgasmic disorder, or vaginismus. People who were sexually traumatized earlier in life may find it difficult to respond sexually when they develop intimate relationships. They may be flooded with feelings of helplessness, unresolved anger, or misplaced guilt, or experience flashbacks of the abusive experiences when they engage in sexual relations with their partners, preventing them from becoming sexually aroused or achieving orgasm.

Sexual fulfillment is also based on learning sexual skills. Sexual skills or competencies, like other types of skills, are acquired through opportunities for new learning. We learn about how our bodies and our partners' bodies respond sexually in various ways, including trial and error with our partners, learning about our own sexual response through self-exploration (as in masturbation), reading about sexual techniques, and perhaps by talking to others or viewing sex films or videos. Yet children who are raised to feel guilty or anxious about sex may have lacked such opportunities to develop sexual knowledge and skills. Consequently, they may respond to sexual opportunities with feelings of anxiety and shame rather than arousal and pleasure.

Cognitive Perspectives Irrational beliefs and attitudes may contribute to sexual dysfunctions (Barlow, 1986; Cyranowski et al., 1999; Meston & Bradford, 2006). Consider the irrational beliefs that we must have the approval at all times of everyone who is important to us and we must be thoroughly competent at everything we do. If we cannot accept the occasional disappointment of others, we may catastrophize the significance of a single frustrating sexual episode. If we insist that every sexual experience must be perfect, we set the stage for inevitable failure.

Helen Singer Kaplan (1974) noted problems that can occur with our ability to regulate our levels of sexual arousal. Men who ejaculate prematurely, for example, may have difficulty gauging their level of sexual arousal. As a consequence, they may not be able to temporarily suspend stimulation in time to delay ejaculation. Most men respond to sexual arousal with positive emotions, such as joy and warmth. But for men with sexual dysfunctions, sexual arousal becomes disconnected from positive emotions (Rowland, Cooper, & Slob, 1996). Psychologist David Barlow (1986) proposed that anxiety may have inhibiting or arousing effects on sexual response depending on the man's thought processes (see Figure 11.1). For men with sexual dysfunctions, anxiety has inhibiting effects. Perhaps because they expect to fail in sexual encounters, their thoughts are focused on anticipated feelings of shame and embarrassment rather than on erotic stimuli. Concerns about failing increase autonomic arousal or anxiety, which leads men to focus even more attention on the consequences of failure, which in turn leads to dysfunctional performance. Failure experiences in turn lead to avoidance of sexual encounters because these situations have become encoded as opportunities for repeated failure, frustration, and self-defeat. Functional men, by contrast, expect to succeed and focus their attention on erotic stimuli, not on fears of failure. Their erotic attentional focus increases autonomic arousal or anxiety, but not to the point that it interferes with their sexual response. Mild anxiety may actually enhance their sexual arousal. By focusing on erotic cues, functional men become more aroused, successfully engage in sexual activity, and heighten their expectations of a future successful performance—all leading to increased approach tendencies.

The cognitive model formulated by Barlow highlights the role of interfering cognitions in sexual dysfunctions. Interfering cognitions include expectancies of failure that are evoked by performance demands. They heighten anxiety to the point of impairing sexual performance. In a vicious cycle, the more people focus on these interfering cognitions, the more difficult it will be for them to perform sexually— and the more likely they will focus on interfering cognitions in the future. Although the model was derived from research on men, Barlow believes it may also help explain sexual dysfunctions in women.

Problems in Relationships
"It takes two to tango," as they say. Sexual relations are usually no better than other facets of relationships or marriages (Perlman & Abramson, 1982). Couples who harbour resentments toward one another may choose the sexual arena for combat. Communication problems, moreover, are linked to general marital dissatisfaction. Couples who find it difficult to communicate their sexual desires may lack the means to help their partners become more effective lovers.

Sociocultural Perspectives
At around the turn of the last century, an Englishwoman was quoted as saying she would "close her eyes and think of England" when her husband engaged her in sexual relations. This old-fashioned stereotype suggests how sexual pleasure was once considered exclusively a male preserve—that sex, for women, was primarily a duty. Mothers usually informed their daughters of the conjugal duties before the wedding, and girls encoded sex as just one of the ways in which women serviced the needs of others. Women who harbour such stereotypical attitudes toward female sexuality may be unlikely to become aware of their sexual potentials. In addition, sexual anxieties may transform negative expectations into self-fulfilling prophecies. Sexual dysfunctions in men, too, may be linked to severely restricted sociocultural beliefs and sexual taboos.

Modern psychodynamic theorists recognize that anger and other negative feelings women may hold toward men can lead to sexual dysfunctions. Yet they believe these negative emotions stem from sociocultural factors rather than penis envy. Women in our society are often socialized to sacrifice for and submit to their husbands, which may engender rebellion through becoming sexually unresponsive.

Sociocultural factors also play an important role in erectile dysfunction. Investigators find a greater incidence of erectile dysfunction in cultures with more restrictive sexual attitudes toward premarital sex among females, sex in marriage, and extramarital sex (Welch & Kartub, 1978). Men in these cultures may be prone to develop sexual anxiety or guilt that may interfere with sexual performance.

Psychological Factors
Various psychological factors such as depression, anxiety, guilt, and low self-esteem can impair

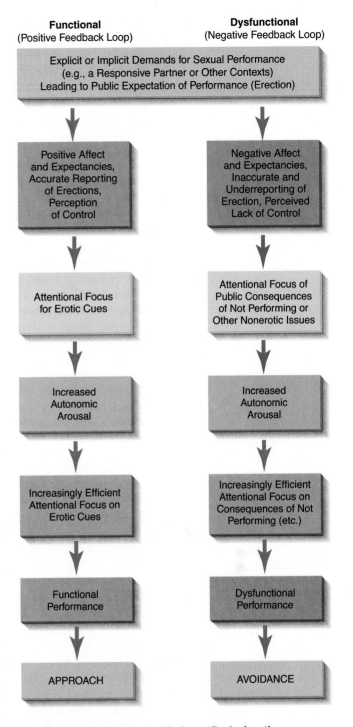

FIGURE 11.1 Barlow's model of erectile dysfunction.
In this model, past experience with erectile dysfunction leads men to expect that they will fail again. They consequently focus on anticipated feelings of shame and embarrassment when they engage in sexual relations rather than on erotic stimuli. These concerns heighten their anxiety, impairing their performance and distracting them from erotic cues. Functional men, by contrast, expect to succeed and focus more of their attention on erotic stimuli, which heightens their sexual response. Although they too may experience anxiety, it is not severe enough to distract them from erotic cues or impair their performance.

Source: Barlow, D. H. (1986). Causes of sexual dysfunction. The role of anxiety and cognitive interference. *Journal of Consulting and Clinical Psychology, 54,* 140–148. Copyright © 1986 by the American Psychological Association. Reprinted with permission.

sexual interest or performance. One principal culprit is **performance anxiety**, a type of anxiety that involves an excessive concern about whether we will be able to perform successfully. People troubled by performance anxiety become spectators during sex rather than performers. Their attention is focused on how their bodies are responding (or not responding) to sexual stimulation and on concerns they have about the negative consequences of failing to perform adequately, rather than absorbing themselves in their erotic experiences. Men with performance anxiety may have difficulty achieving or maintaining an erection or may ejaculate prematurely; women may fail to become adequately aroused or have difficulty achieving orgasm. A vicious cycle may ensue in which each failure experience instills deeper doubts, which lead to more anxiety during sexual encounters, which occasions repeated failure, and so on.

In Western cultures, the connection between a man's sexual performance and his sense of manhood is deeply ingrained. The man who repeatedly fails to perform sexually may suffer a loss of self-esteem, become depressed, or feel he is no longer a man (Carey, Wincze, & Meisler, 1998). He may see himself as a total failure, despite other accomplishments in life. Sexual opportunities are construed as tests of his manhood and he may respond to them by bearing down and trying to will (force) an erection. Willing an erection may backfire because erection is a reflex that cannot be forced. With so much of his self-esteem riding on the line whenever he makes love, it is little wonder that anxiety about the quality of his performance—performance anxiety—may mount to a point that it inhibits erection. The erectile reflex is controlled by the parasympathetic branch of the autonomic nervous system. Activation of the sympathetic nervous system, which occurs when we are anxious, can block parasympathetic control, preventing the erectile reflex from occurring. Ejaculation, in contrast, is under sympathetic nervous system control, so heightened levels of arousal, as in the case of performance anxiety, can trigger premature ejaculation.

One client who suffered erectile dysfunction described his feelings of sexual inadequacy this way:

> I always felt inferior, like I was on probation, having to prove myself. I felt like I was up against the wall. You can't imagine how embarrassing this was. It's like you walk out in front of an audience that you think is a nudist convention and it turns out to be a tuxedo convention.
>
> THE AUTHORS' FILES

Another man described how performance anxiety led him to prepare for sexual relations as though he were psyching himself up for a big game:

> At work I have control over what I do. With sex, you don't have control over your sex organ. I know that my mind can control what my hands do. But the same is not true of my penis. I had begun to view sex as a basketball game. I used to play in college. When I would prepare for a game, I'd always be thinking, "Who was I guarding that night?" I'd try to psych myself up, sketching out in my mind how to play this guy, thinking through all possible moves and plays. I began to do the same thing with sex. If I were dating someone, I'd be thinking the whole evening about what might happen in bed. I'd always be preparing for the outcome. I'd sketch out in my mind how I was going to touch her, what I'd ask her to do. But all the time, right through dinner or the movies, I'd be worrying that I wouldn't get it up. I kept picturing her face and how disappointed she'd be. By the time we did go to bed, I was paralyzed with anxiety.
>
> THE AUTHORS' FILES

Women, too, may equate their self-esteem with their ability to reach frequent and intense orgasms. Yet when men and women try to bear down to will arousal or lubrication or to force an orgasm, they may find that the harder they try, the more these responses elude them. Forty years ago the pressures concerning sex often revolved around the issue "Should I or shouldn't I?" Today, however, the pressures for both men and women are often based more on achieving performance goals relating to proficiency at reaching orgasm and satisfying one's partner's sexual needs.

Sex Therapy

Until the groundbreaking work of sex researchers William Masters and Virginia Johnson in the 1960s, there was no effective treatment for most sexual dysfunctions. Psychoanalytic forms of therapy approached sexual dysfunctions indirectly, for example. It was assumed that sexual dysfunctions represented underlying conflicts, and the dysfunctions might abate if the underlying conflicts—the presumed causes of the dysfunctions—were resolved through psychoanalysis. A lack of evidence that psychoanalytic approaches reversed sexual dysfunctions led clinicians and researchers to develop other approaches that would focus more directly on the sexual problems themselves.

Most contemporary sex therapists assume sexual dysfunctions can be treated by directly modifying a couple's sexual interactions. Pioneered by Masters and Johnson, sex therapy employs a variety of relatively brief, cognitive-behavioural techniques that centre on enhancing self-efficacy expectancies, improving a couple's ability to communicate, fostering sexual competencies (sexual knowledge and skills), and reducing performance anxiety. Therapists may also work with couples to help them iron out problems in their relationship that may impede sexual functioning. When feasible, both sex partners are involved in therapy. In some cases, however, individual therapy may be preferable, as we shall see.

Significant changes have occurred in the treatment of sexual dysfunctions in the past 20 years. There is greater emphasis now on the role of biological or organic factors in the development of sexual problems and greater use of medical treatments, such as the use of the drugs Viagra, Cialis, and Levitra, in treating male erectile dysfunction. But even men whose erectile problems can be traced to physical causes can benefit from sex therapy along with medical intervention (Bach, Barlow, & Wincze, 2004).

Let us briefly survey some of the more common sex-therapy techniques for particular types of disorders.

Sexual Desire Disorders Sex therapists may try to help people with low sexual desire kindle their sexual appetite through the use of self-stimulation (masturbation) exercises together with erotic fantasies (Leiblum, 2006). Or in working with couples, the therapist might prescribe mutual pleasuring exercises the couple could perform at home or encourage them to expand their sexual repertoire in order to add novelty and excitement to their sex life. When a lack of sexual desire is connected with depression, the treatment would probably focus on relieving the underlying depression in the hope that sexual interest would rebound when the depression lifts. When problems of low sexual desire or sexual aversion appear to be rooted in deep-seated causes, sex therapist Helen Singer Kaplan (1987) has recommended the use of insight-oriented approaches to help uncover and resolve underlying issues. Some cases of hypoactive sexual desire involve hormonal deficiencies, especially lack of testosterone. Testosterone replacement is effective only in the relatively few cases in which production of the hormone is truly deficient (Simpkins & Van Meter, 2005). A lack of sexual desire may also reflect relationship problems that may need to be addressed through couples therapy. Couples therapy might also be used when sexual dysfunction develops from problems in the relationship (McCarthy & Bodnar, 2005). In other cases of sexual aversion, a program of mutual pleasuring, beginning with partner stimulation in nongenital areas and gradually progressing to genital stimulation, may help desensitize fears about sexual contact.

Masters and Johnson. Sex therapists William Masters and Virginia Johnson.

Disorders of Arousal Women who have difficulty becoming sexually aroused and men with erectile problems are first educated to the fact that they need not "do" anything to become aroused. As long as their problems are psychological, not organic, they need only experience sexual stimulation under relaxed, nonpressured conditions, so that disruptive cognitions and anxiety do not inhibit reflexive responses.

Masters and Johnson have the couple counter performance anxiety by engaging in **sensate focus exercises**. These are nondemand sexual contacts—sensuous exercises that do not demand sexual arousal in the form of vaginal lubrication or erection. Partners begin by massaging one another without touching the genitals. The partners learn to "pleasure" each other and to "be pleasured" by means of following and giving verbal instructions and by guiding each other's hands. The method fosters both communication and sexual skills and countermands anxiety because there is no demand for sexual arousal. After several sessions, direct massage of the genitals is included in the pleasuring exercise. Even when obvious signs of sexual excitement are produced (lubrication or erection), the couple does not straightaway engage in intercourse, because intercourse might create performance demands. After excitement is achieved consistently, the couple engages in a relaxed sequence of other sexual activities, culminating eventually in intercourse.

A number of similar sex-therapy methods were employed in the case of Victor P.:

> Victor P., a 44-year-old concert violinist, was eager to show the therapist reviews of his concert tour. A solo violinist with a distinguished orchestra, Victor's life revolved around practice, performances, and reviews. He dazzled audiences with his technique and the energy of his performance. As a concert musician, Victor had exquisite control over his body, especially his hands. Yet he could not control his erectile response in the same way. Since his divorce seven years earlier, Victor had been troubled by recurrent episodes of erectile failure. Time and time again he had become involved in a new relationship, only to find himself unable to perform sexually. Fearing repetition, he would sever the relationship. He was unable to face an audience of only one. For a while, he dated casually, but then he met Michelle.
>
> Michelle was a writer who loved music. They were a perfect match because Victor, the musician, loved literature. Michelle, a 35-year-old divorcee, was exciting, earthy, sensual, and accepting. The couple soon grew inseparable. He would practise while she would write—poetry mostly, but also short magazine pieces. Unlike some women Victor met who did not know Bach from Bartok, Michelle held her own in conversations with Victor's friends and fellow musicians over a late night dinner. They kept their own apartments; Victor needed his own space and solitude for practice.
>
> In the nine months of their relationship, Victor was unable to perform on the stage that mattered most to him—his canopied bed. It was just so frustrating. He said, "I would become erect and then just as I approach her to penetrate, pow! It collapses on me." Victor's history of nocturnal erections and erections during light petting suggested that he was basically suffering from performance anxiety. He was bearing down to force an erection, much as he might try to learn the fingering of a difficult violin piece. Each night became a command performance in which Victor served as his own harshest critic. Victor became a spectator to his own performance, a role that Masters and Johnson refer to as **self-spectatoring**. Rather than focusing on his partner, his attention was riveted on the size of his penis. As noted by the late great pianist Vladimir Horowitz, the worst thing a pianist can do is watch his fingers. Perhaps the worst thing a man with erectile problems can do is watch his penis.
>
> To break the vicious cycle of anxiety, erectile failure, and more anxiety, Victor and Michelle followed a sex-therapy program (Rathus & Nevid, 1977) modelled after the Masters and Johnson–type treatment. The aim was to restore the pleasure of sexual activity, unfettered by anxiety. The couple was initially instructed to abstain from attempts at intercourse to free Victor from any pressure to perform. The couple progressed through a series of steps:

sensate focus exercises In sex therapy, mutual pleasuring activities between partners that is focused on the partners taking turns giving and receiving physical pleasure.

self-spectatoring Tendency to observe one's behaviour as if one were a spectator of oneself. People with sexual dysfunctions often become self-spectators in the sense of focusing their attention during sexual activity on the response of their sex organs rather than on their partners or the sexual stimulation itself.

1. Relaxing together in the nude without any touching, such as when reading or watching television together.
2. Sensate focus exercises.
3. Genital stimulation of each other manually or orally to orgasm.
4. Nondemand intercourse (intercourse performed without any pressure on the man to satisfy his partner). The man may afterward help his partner achieve orgasm by using manual or oral stimulation.
5. Resumption of vigorous intercourse (intercourse involving more vigorous thrusting and use of alternative positions and techniques that focus on mutual satisfaction). The couple is instructed not to catastrophize occasional problems that may arise.

The therapy program helped Victor overcome his erectile disorder. Victor was freed of the need to prove himself by achieving erection on command. He surrendered his post as critic. Once the spotlight was off the bed, he became a participant and not a spectator.

THE AUTHORS' FILES

Disorders of Orgasm Women with orgasmic disorder often harbour underlying beliefs that sex is dirty or sinful. They may have been taught not to touch themselves. They are often anxious about sex and have not learned, through trial and error, what kinds of sexual stimulation will arouse them and help them reach orgasm. Treatment in these cases includes modification of negative attitudes toward sex. When orgasmic disorder reflects the woman's feelings about, or relationship with, her partner, treatment requires working through these feelings or enhancing the relationship.

In either case, Masters and Johnson work with the couple and first use sensate focus exercises to lessen performance anxiety, open channels of communication, and help the couple acquire pleasuring skills. Then during genital massage and, later, during intercourse, the woman directs her partner to use caresses and techniques that stimulate her. By taking charge, the woman becomes psychologically freed from the stereotype of the passive, submissive female role.

Many researchers find that a program of directed masturbation is most effective in helping *preorgasmic* women—women who have never achieved orgasm through any means (Baucom, Shoham, Mueser, Daiuto, & Stickle, 1998; Heiman & LoPiccolo, 1987; LoPiccolo & Stock, 1986). Masturbation provides a chance to learn about one's own body and give oneself pleasure without reliance on a partner or need to attend to a partner's needs. Directed masturbation programs educate women about their sexual anatomy and encourage them to experiment with self-caresses in the privacy of their own homes. Women proceed at their own pace and are encouraged to incorporate sexual fantasies and imagery during self-stimulation exercises designed to heighten their level of sexual arousal. They gradually learn to bring themselves to orgasm, sometimes with the help of a vibrator. Once women can masturbate to orgasm, additional couples-oriented treatment can facilitate but does not guarantee transference to orgasm with a partner (Heiman & LoPiccolo, 1987; LoPiccolo & Stock, 1986).

Although scant attention in the scientific literature has been focused on male orgasmic disorder, the standard treatment, barring any underlying organic problem, focuses on increasing sexual stimulation and reducing performance anxiety (LoPiccolo, 1990; LoPiccolo & Stock, 1986).

The most widely used approach to treating premature ejaculation, called the *stop–start* or *stop-and-go* technique, was introduced in 1956 by the urologist James Semans. The man and his partner just suspend sexual activity when he is about to ejaculate and then resume stimulation when his sensations subside. Repeated practice enables the man to regulate ejaculation by sensitizing him to the cues that precede the ejaculatory reflex (making him more aware of his "point of no return," the point at which the ejaculatory reflex is triggered).

Vaginismus and Dyspareunia Vaginismus is a conditioned reflex involving the involuntary constriction of the vaginal opening. It involves a psychologically based fear of penetration, rather than a physical defect or disorder (LoPiccolo & Stock, 1986). Treatment for vaginismus involves a combination of cognitive-behavioural exercises such as relaxation techniques and the use of vaginal dilators to gradually desensitize the vaginal musculature. The woman herself regulates the insertion of dilators (plastic rods) of increasing diameter, always proceeding at her own pace to avoid any discomfort (LoPiccolo & Stock, 1986). The method is generally successful as long as it is unhurried. Because women with vaginismus often have histories of sexual molestation or rape, psychotherapy may be part of the treatment program in order to deal with the psychological consequences of traumatic experiences (LoPiccolo & Stock, 1986). In cases of painful intercourse or dyspareunia, treatment focuses on attempting to resolve the underlying psychological or medical conditions that give rise to the pain.

Research from McGill University supports the value of cognitive-behavioural therapy for dyspareunia, but also suggests that a surgical intervention called vestibulectomy may be very effective (Bergeron et al., 2001). Vestibulectomy involves the surgical removal of the vulvar tissue that appears to be the source of pain in dyspareunia.

Evaluation of Sex Therapy Success rates for sex therapy have been more impressive for some disorders than others. High levels of success are reported in treating vaginismus in women and premature ejaculation in men (J. G. Beck, 1993; O'Donohue, Letourneau, & Geer, 1993). Reported success rates in treating vaginismus have ranged as high as 80% (Hawton & Catalan, 1990) to 100% (Masters & Johnson, 1970). Success rates in treating premature ejaculation with the stop–start or squeeze procedures have been reported as high as 95%, but relapse rates tend to be high (Segraves & Althof, 1998). Success rates in treating erectile dysfunction with sex therapy techniques are more variable (Rosen, 1996), and we still lack the methodologically sound studies needed to support the effectiveness of these techniques (O'Donohue, Swingen, Dopke, & Regev, 1999). Outcomes of treatment for male orgasmic disorder also vary and are often disappointing (Dekker, 1993).

Although some progress has been made in treating sexual desire disorders, we would benefit from new treatment methods because current techniques often fail to resolve the problem (J. G. Beck, 1995; Hawton, 1991). Better results are generally reported from directed masturbation programs for preorgasmic women, with success rates (percentage of women achieving orgasm) reported in a range of 70% to 90% (Rosen & Leiblum, 1995). However, much lower rates are reported when measured in terms of percentages of women reporting orgasm during sexual intercourse with their partners (Segraves & Althof, 1998). Some researchers believe that the final determination of the effectiveness of directed masturbation as a treatment alternative remains to be made (O'Donohue, Dopke, & Swingen, 1997).

Biological Treatments of Male Sexual Dysfunctions

Biological treatments of erectile disorder have included silicone implants, hormonal treatments, injections of muscle relaxants, vascular surgery, and medications that promise to help men with erectile dysfunction achieve erections. The popularity of penile implants (semirigid or inflatable silicone rods) has fallen off over the years because of its invasiveness and potential complications, and because less intrusive treatments are now available (Rosen, 1996; Thomas & LoPiccolo, 1994). In 1998, the first drug was approved for the treatment of erectile dysfunction (Morrow, 1998). Called Viagra, the drug expands blood vessels in the penis, which increases the flow of blood to the penis and in turn causes erection (Goldstein et al., 1998; Kolata, 1998). Taken about an hour before sexual relations, the drug has helped 70% to 80% of patients achieve erections. Similar findings have been reported with related drugs such as Cialis and Levitra. In the first few weeks following its release to the public, Viagra became the fastest-selling new drug in history. Viagra and some related drugs have also been tried to help women with sexual dysfunctions, but so far the results suggest that they is no better than placebos (Basson, McInnes, Smith, Hodgson, & Koppiker, 2002; Meston & Bradford, 2006).

Hormone treatments may be helpful to men with abnormally low levels of male sex hormones but not those whose hormone levels are within normal limits (Simpkins & Van Meter, 2005). Because hormone treatments can have side effects, such as liver damage, they should not be undertaken lightly.

Vascular surgery may be effective in rare cases in which blockage in the blood vessels prevents blood from swelling the penis or in which the penis is structurally defective (LoPiccolo & Stock, 1986; Mohr & Beutler, 1990).

Evidence indicates that SSRI-type antidepressant drugs may also help delay ejaculation in men with premature ejaculation (Kim & Seo, 1998; Segraves & Althof, 1998). These drugs affect the availability of neurotransmitters that may play a role in the brain's regulation of the ejaculatory reflex.

All in all, the success rates reported for treating sexual dysfunctions through psychological or biological approaches are quite encouraging, especially when we remember that only a generation or two ago there were no effective treatments available.

STUDY BREAK

Sexual Dysfunctions

Review It

- **What are the major types of sexual dysfunctions?** Sexual dysfunctions include sexual desire disorders (hypoactive sexual desire disorder and sexual aversion disorder), sexual arousal disorders (female sexual arousal disorder and male erectile disorder), orgasm disorders (female and male orgasmic disorders and premature ejaculation), and sexual pain disorders (dyspareunia and vaginismus).

- **What causes sexual dysfunctions?** Sexual dysfunctions can stem from biological factors (such as disease or the effects of alcohol and other drugs), psychological factors (such as performance anxiety, unresolved conflicts, or lack of sexual competencies), and sociocultural factors (such as sexually restrictive cultural learning).

- **What are the major goals of sex therapy?** Sex therapists help people overcome sexual dysfunctions by enhancing self-efficacy expectancies, teaching sexual competencies, improving sexual communication, and reducing performance anxiety.

Define It

sexual dysfunctions
hypoactive sexual desire disorder
sexual aversion disorder
female sexual arousal disorder
male erectile disorder
female orgasmic disorder
male orgasmic disorder
premature ejaculation
dyspareunia
vaginismus
performance anxiety
sensate focus exercises
self-spectatoring

Recall It*

1. Sexual dysfunctions involve problems with _____.

   a. sexual interest or arousal
   b. sexual interest, arousal, or response
   c. sexual arousal or response
   d. none of the above

2. A sexual dysfunction that begins following a period (or at least one occurrence) of normal functioning is labelled _____.

   a. acquired
   b. situational
   c. lifelong
   d. generalized

3. Jim rarely has any interest in sexual activity or experiences sexual fantasies or desires. He doesn't find sexual relations revolting. Nor does he have trouble performing sexually. Yet he doesn't understand why people seem so interested in sex. When he consults a psychologist at the urging of his wife, the most likely diagnosis would be _____.

   a. dyspareunia
   b. sexual aversion disorder
   c. hypoactive sexual desire disorder
   d. male erectile disorder

4. Monica frequently fantasizes about sex and has had frequent sexual relations. However, she has been unable to achieve orgasm with her partners or through masturbation no matter how long she is sexually stimulated, despite the fact that she becomes vaginally lubricated. Her problem would most likely be diagnosed as _____.

   a. dyspareunia
   b. vaginismus

c. female orgasmic disorder

d. female sexual arousal disorder

5. Sally has vaginismus. If she were to consult a sex therapist for help, the treatment most likely to be used would consist of _____.

   a. long-term insight-oriented therapy to get at the roots of the problem

   b. antidepressant medication to relieve the depression that often underlies the problem

   c. the use of vaginal dilators to desensitize the vaginal musculature gradually to allow penetration

   d. directed masturbation exercises

* Recall It answers can be found on the Companion Website for this text.

Think About It

- Can you think of examples in your own life in which you have been hampered by performance anxiety of one kind or another? What did you do about it?

- When does a sexual problem become a sexual dysfunction?

WEBLINKS

Notes on Gender Role Transition
www.avitale.com
This website contains information on gender identity disorder and some paraphilias.

The Lesbian, Gay, Bisexual, and Transgender Community Center
www.gaycenter.org
This site provides information on gender identity disorder.

Gender Identity Clinic
www.camh.net/Care_Treatment/Program_Descriptions/Mental_Health_Programs/
Gender_Identity_Clinic
This site describes treatment options for gender dysphoria from Toronto's Centre for Addiction and Mental Health.

Sexuality and Sexual Relationships
www.psychnet-uk.com/counselling_psychology/counselling_psychology_sexuality.htm
Visit this site for detailed coverage of human sexuality, including sexual dysfunctions.

Sexual Counselling
www.sexualcounselling.com
This site offers answers to a range of questions about sex, and specific questions can be submitted online.

Gender Identity Disorder, Paraphilias, and Sexual Dysfunctions

Gender Identity Disorder

Theoretical Perspectives

Paraphilias

Exhibitionism

- Recurrent, powerful urges to expose genitals to unsuspecting strangers
- Intended to shock, surprise, or arouse victim

Fetishism

- Recurrent, powerful urges and arousing fantasies involving either inanimate objects or a particular body part

Transvestic Fetishism

- Recurrent, powerful sexual urges and fantasies involving cross-dressing
- Not to be confused with gender identity disorder (transsexualism)

Voyeurism

- Acting on or being strongly distressed by recurrent, powerful sexual urges and fantasies about watching unsuspecting people undressing or engaging in sex

Frotteurism

- Recurrent, powerful sexual urges and fantasies involving rubbing against or touching a nonconsenting person

Pedophilia

- Recurrent, powerful sexual urges and fantasies involving sexual activity with prepubescent children

Sexual Masochism

- Recurrent, powerful sexual urges and fantasies about sexual acts involving humiliation or suffering

Sexual Sadism

- Recurrent, powerful sexual urges and fantasies involving the humiliation or suffering of others

Sexual Dysfunctions

Sexual Desire Disorders

- Hypoactive sexual desire disorder
- Sexual aversion disorder

Sexual Arousal Disorders

- Female sexual arousal disorder
- Male erectile disorder

Orgasm Disorders

- Female orgasmic disorder
- Male orgasmic disorder
- Premature ejaculation

Sexual Pain Disorders

- Dyspareunia
- Vaginismus

Schizophrenia

CHAPTER OUTLINE

Did You Know That...

See the underlined text on the pages indicated below for more information on these interesting and often misunderstood facts.

- You cannot be diagnosed with schizophrenia for months even though you show all the signs of the disorder? (p. 431)

- Despite wide differences in cultures, the rate of schizophrenia is similar in both developed and developing nations throughout the world? (p. 432)

- Auditory hallucinations may be a form of inner speech? (p. 437)

- Some people with schizophrenia maintain unusual, seemingly uncomfortable positions for hours during which they will not respond to questions or communicate with others? (p. 439)

- A 54-year-old hospitalized woman diagnosed with schizophrenia was conditioned to cling to a broom by being given cigarettes as reinforcers? (p. 444)

- Even if you have two parents with schizophrenia, your chances of developing the disorder are less than one in two? (p. 450)

- Living in a family environment that is hostile, critical, and unsupportive increases the risk of relapse among people with schizophrenia? (p. 453)

- Drugs can help control but cannot cure schizophrenia? (p. 456)

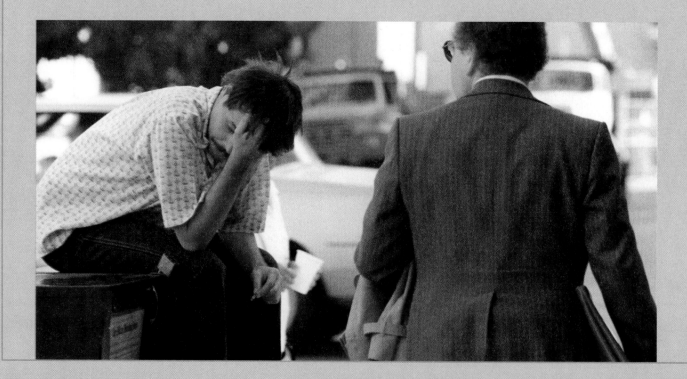

SCHIZOPHRENIA IS PERHAPS the most puzzling and disabling clinical syndrome. It is the psychological disorder that best corresponds to popular conceptions of madness or lunacy. It often elicits fear, misunderstanding, and condemnation rather than sympathy and concern. Accordingly, social stigma is an important problem associated with schizophrenia. The disorder strikes at the heart of a person, stripping the mind of the intimate connections between thoughts and emotions and filling it with distorted perceptions, false ideas, and illogical conceptions, as in the case of Marilyn:

> For someone who lives in total isolation, Marilyn R. has a lot of company. She's got the Cabir brothers. All five of them, all abusive, callous and unrelenting in their insults. Marilyn recalls a beating she suffered at the hands of a Cabir: "He just went crazy and said, 'I hate you.' And he grabbed an ashtray and just—pow!—hit me over the head with it. Put his teeth in my face and was going for the knife. . . . "
>
> Marilyn starts to weep. It's a memory so vivid, so real, that the Cabirs' place of residence comes as a shock. "They're all in the wall. They just stand there and keep giving me slurs all the time. They say am I ever ugly, say 'I can't stand the sight of her,'" she explains. "Strange, isn't it?"
>
> Marilyn finds a bi-weekly injection she gets at a downtown Toronto drop-in centre helps quiet the Cabirs. But it doesn't make them go away. They're in the walls every day and every night. They even follow her on the bus. The Cabirs—very real to Marilyn but invisible to a visitor—are only part of the story. The room she lives in is just as surreal—and far more frightening. It is crawling with cockroaches.
>
> A swarm of hatchlings has taken over the table—probing every square millimetre of the surface. Marilyn sits, flyswatter in hand, trying to get as many as she can. Her conversation is interrupted frequently by the slap of her weapon. "I wish they'd go away," she says of the Cabirs. (Swat!) "He just stands there in the wall. He just stands there with his hands on his hips. He's there now. The whole family's there." (Swat!) In addition to the cockroaches, Marilyn has caught nine mice in her room. Scattered rodent droppings dot the thick shag carpet, a rug so heavily infested with insects, a visitor is grateful the room is partially dark.
>
> The date is December 17. Marilyn has no plans for Christmas. And despite her appalling living conditions, she has no hope of finding anything better. She's been there five years. "I guess I'll be here the rest of my life," she says. In the spring of the following year, however, the City of Toronto got a look at 136 Jones Ave.—a look that convinced inspectors it was unfit for human habitation.
>
> Marilyn was hooked up with a mental health worker, a woman who was astonished at the conditions in which she lived. The worker helped find her a new place; a considerable feat in a city where people like Marilyn languish on waiting lists for up to five years. Marilyn moved to a self-contained subsidized apartment in the Sherbourne–Dundas Streets area. Not exactly prime real estate, but conditions are a world apart from her old place. "It was awful. Unbearable. I left a lot behind because those cockroaches used to get in my clothes." For her new apartment, Marilyn pays $300 a month—$30 less than her old place. And, she says, the surroundings have made a tremendous improvement in her mental health. "Oh, 100 per cent better!" she smiles. And she's still got company. "The Cabirs are here," she says. "There's five of them in the wall."
>
> SIMMIE, S. (1998). EXCERPT FROM "I'D SIT IN THE KITCHEN AND JUST SHAKE." *TORONTO STAR*, OCTOBER 4.

Schizophrenia touches every facet of an affected person's life. Acute episodes of schizophrenia are characterized by delusions, hallucinations, illogical thinking, incoherent speech, and bizarre behaviour. Between acute episodes, people with schizophrenia may still be unable to think clearly and may lack appropriate emotional responses to people and events in their lives. They may speak in a flat tone and show little if any facial expressiveness. Although researchers are immersed in probing the psychological and biological foundations of schizophrenia, the disorder remains in many ways a mystery. In this chapter, we examine how research has illuminated our understanding of schizophrenia.

CLINICAL FEATURES OF SCHIZOPHRENIA

Although various forms of "madness" have afflicted people throughout the course of history, no one knows how long the behaviour pattern we now label **schizophrenia** existed before it was first described as a medical syndrome by Emil Kraepelin in 1893. Modern conceptualizations of schizophrenia have been largely shaped by the contributions of Kraepelin, Eugen Bleuler, and Kurt Schneider.

Historical Contributions to Concepts of Schizophrenia

Emil Kraepelin (1856–1926), one of the fathers of modern psychiatry, called the disorder we recognize today as schizophrenia *dementia praecox*. The term was derived from the Latin *dementis*, meaning "out" (*de-*) of one's "mind" (*mens*), and the roots that form the word *precocious*, meaning "before" one's level of "maturity." Dementia praecox thus refers to premature impairment of mental abilities. Kraepelin believed that dementia praecox was a disease process caused by specific, although unknown, pathology in the body.

Kraepelin wrote that dementia praecox involves the "loss of the inner unity of thought, feeling, and acting." The syndrome begins early in life, and the course of deterioration eventually results in complete "disintegration of the personality" (Kraepelin, 1909–1913, p. 943). Kraepelin's description of dementia praecox includes delusions, hallucinations, and odd motor behaviours—things that typically characterize the disorder today.

In 1911, the Swiss psychiatrist Eugen Bleuler (1857–1939) renamed dementia praecox *schizophrenia*, from the Greek *schistos*, meaning "cut" or "split," and *phren*, meaning "brain." In doing so, Bleuler focused on the major characteristic of the syndrome: the splitting of the brain functions that give rise to cognition, feelings or affective responses, and behaviour. A person with schizophrenia, for example, might giggle inappropriately when discussing an upsetting event, or might show no emotional expressiveness in the face of tragedy.

Although Bleuler accepted Kraepelin's description of the symptoms of schizophrenia, he did not accept Kraepelin's views that schizophrenia necessarily begins early in life and inevitably follows a deteriorating course. Bleuler proposed that schizophrenia follows a more variable course. In some cases, acute episodes occur intermittently. In others, there might be limited improvement rather than inevitable deterioration. Bleuler believed that schizophrenia could be recognized on the basis of four primary features or symptoms. Today, we refer to them as the **four As**:

1. **Associations.** Associations or relationships among thoughts become disturbed. We now call this type of disturbance *thought disorder* or *looseness of associations*. Looseness of associations means ideas are strung together with little or no relationship among them; nor does the speaker appear to be aware of the lack of connectedness. The person's speech appears to others to become rambling and confused.
2. **Affect.** Affect or emotional response becomes flattened or inappropriate. The individual may show a lack of response to upsetting events or burst into laughter upon hearing that a family member or friend has died.
3. **Ambivalence.** People with schizophrenia hold ambivalent or conflicting feelings toward others, such as by loving and hating them at the same time.
4. **Autism.** Autism is withdrawal into a private fantasy world that is not bound by principles of logic. (Note that autism, as a feature of schizophrenia, is different from the disorder of childhood known as autism, which is discussed in Chapter 13.)

schizophrenia Enduring psychosis that involves failure to maintain integrated personality functioning, impaired reality testing, and disturbances in thinking. Common features of schizophrenia include delusions, hallucinations, flattened or inappropriate affect, and bizarre behaviour. Also see *schizophreniform disorder*, *schizotypal personality disorder*, and *brief reactive psychosis*.

four As In Bleuler's view, the primary characteristics of schizophrenia: *(loose) associations, (blunted or inappropriate) affect, ambivalence,* and *autism.*

associations Linkages or relationships among thoughts or utterances.

affect Emotion or feeling state that is attached to objects, ideas, or life experiences. Pronounced *AF-fect.*

ambivalence A state in which a person holds conflicting feelings toward others, such as loving and hating a person at the same time.

autism (1) An absorption into daydreaming and fantasy. (2) A disorder in childhood characterized by failure to relate to others, lack of speech, disturbed motor behaviours, intellectual impairment, and demands for sameness in the environment. Also one of Bleuler's *Four As*, describing one of the primary symptoms of schizophrenia.

In Bleuler's view, hallucinations and delusions represent "secondary symptoms," symptoms that accompany the primary symptoms but do not define the disorder.

Another influential developer of modern concepts of schizophrenia was German psychiatrist Kurt Schneider (1887–1967). Schneider believed Bleuler's criteria (his four As) were too vague for diagnostic purposes and that they failed to distinguish schizophrenia adequately from other disorders. Schneider (1957) distinguished between two sets of symptoms: **first-rank symptoms**, which he believed are central to diagnosis, and **second-rank symptoms**, which he believed are found not only in schizophrenia, but also in other psychoses and in some nonpsychotic disorders such as personality disorders. In contrast to Bleuler, Schneider proposed that hallucinations and delusions are key or first-rank features of schizophrenia (1957). He considered disturbances in mood and confused thinking to be second-rank symptoms because they are also found in other disorders. Although Schneider's ranking of disturbed behaviours helped distinguish schizophrenia from other disorders, we now know that first-rank symptoms are sometimes found among people with other disorders, especially bipolar disorder. Although first-rank symptoms are clearly associated with schizophrenia, they are not unique to it.

Hallucinations. According to Kurt Schneider, hallucinations and delusions are numbered among the first-rank symptoms of schizophrenia—that is, the symptoms of schizophrenia that are central to the diagnosis. So-called second-rank symptoms are found in other disorders as well. Schneider considered confusion and disturbances in mood to be second-rank symptoms.

Today, the contributions of Kraepelin, Bleuler, and Schneider are expressed in modified form in the present DSM diagnostic system. However, the diagnostic code for schizophrenia is not limited, as Kraepelin had proposed, to cases where there is a course of progressive deterioration. The present code is also tighter than earlier conceptualizations and separates into other diagnostic categories cases in which there are disturbances of mood combined with psychotic behaviour and those involving schizophrenic-like thinking but without overt psychotic behaviour (schizotypal personality disorder). <u>The DSM-IV criteria for schizophrenia also require that psychotic behaviours be present at some point during the course of the disorder and that signs of the disorder be present for at least six months.</u> People with briefer forms of psychosis are placed in diagnostic categories that may be connected with more favourable outcomes. Table 12.1 describes the major clinical criteria for schizophrenia.

first-rank symptoms In Kurt Schneider's view, the primary features of schizophrenia, such as hallucinations and delusions, that distinctly characterize the disorder.

second-rank symptoms In Schneider's view, symptoms associated with schizophrenia that also occur in other psychological disorders.

TABLE 12.1

Major Clinical Features of Schizophrenia

A. Two or more of the following must be present for a significant portion of time over the course of a one-month period:

   (1) delusions
   (2) hallucinations
   (3) speech that is either incoherent or characterized by marked loosening of associations
   (4) disorganized or catatonic behaviour
   (5) negative features (e.g., flattened affect)

B. Functioning in such areas as social relations, work, or self-care during the course of the disorder is markedly below the level achieved prior to the onset of the disorder. If the onset develops during childhood or adolescence, there is a failure to achieve the expected level of social development.

C. Signs of the disorder have occurred continuously for a period of at least six months. This six-month period must include an active phase lasting at least a month in which psychotic symptoms (listed in A) characteristic of schizophrenia occur.

D. The disorder cannot be attributed to the effects of a substance (e.g., substance abuse or prescribed medication) or to a general medical condition.

Source: Adapted from the DSM-IV (APA, 2000a).

Prevalence and Costs of Schizophrenia

According to the best estimates, about 1% of the adult Canadian population suffers from schizophrenia at some point in their lives (Health Canada, 2006). The rates of schizophrenia appear to be similar in both developed and developing countries (APA, 2000a; Jablensky et al., 1992). Schizophrenia is the fifth leading cause of disability worldwide and the most common diagnosis of people who are involuntarily hospitalized (Bland, 1998; Health Canada, 2006). Although some people with schizophrenia have healthy relationships, most (60% to 70%) do not marry, and most have limited social contacts (Health Canada, 2006). The chronic course of the disorder contributes to ongoing social problems, and so people with schizophrenia are greatly overrepresented in prison and homeless populations. About 40% to 60% of people with schizophrenia attempt suicide, and about 10% die from suicide. They are between 15 and 25 times more likely than the general population to die from a suicide attempt (Health Canada, 2006).

Phases of Schizophrenia

Schizophrenia usually afflicts young people, and often does so at the very time that they are making their way from the family into the outside world (APA, 2000a). People who develop schizophrenia become increasingly disengaged from society. They fail to function in the expected roles of student, worker, or spouse, and their families and communities grow intolerant of their deviant behaviour. The disorder typically develops in the late teens or early 20s, a time at which the brain is reaching full maturation (Andreasen, 1999). In about three-quarters of cases, the first signs of schizophrenia appear by the age of 25 (Keith, Regier, & Rae, 1991). Men and women are affected equally by schizophrenia but men usually develop the disorder earlier (Health Canada, 2006).

In some cases, the onset of the disorder is acute. It occurs suddenly, within a few weeks or months. The individual may have been well adjusted and shown few if any signs of behavioural disturbance. Then a rapid transformation in personality and behaviour leads to an acute psychotic episode.

In most cases, however, there is a slower, more gradual decline in functioning. It may take years before psychotic behaviours emerge, although early signs of deterioration may be observed. This period of deterioration is called the **prodromal phase**. It is characterized by waning interest in social activities and increasing difficulty in meeting the responsibilities of daily living. At first, such people seem to take less care of their appearance. They fail to bathe regularly or they wear the same clothes repeatedly. Over time, their behaviour may become increasingly odd or eccentric. There are lapses in job performance or schoolwork. Their speech may become increasingly vague and rambling. These changes in personality may start out so gradually that they raise little concern among friends and families. They may be attributed to "a phase" that the person is passing through. But as behaviour becomes more bizarre—like hoarding food, collecting garbage, or talking to oneself on the street—the acute phase of the disorder begins. Finally, psychotic symptoms develop, such as wild hallucinations, delusions, and increasingly bizarre behaviour.

Following acute episodes, people who develop schizophrenia may enter the **residual phase**, in which their behaviour returns to the level that was characteristic of the prodromal phase. Although flagrant psychotic behaviours may be absent during the residual phase, the person may continue to be impaired by a deep sense of apathy, difficulties in thinking or speaking clearly, and the harbouring of unusual ideas, such as beliefs in telepathy or clairvoyance. Such patterns of behaviour make it difficult for the person to meet expected social roles as wage earners, marital partners, or students. Full return to normal behaviour is uncommon but may occur. More commonly, a chronic pattern characterized by occasional relapses and continued impairment between acute episodes develops (Wiersma, Nienhuis, Slooff, & Giel, 1998).

The chronic course of the disorder contributes to ongoing social problems. As a result, people with schizophrenia are greatly overrepresented in prison and homeless populations. Up to 80% of people with schizophrenia abuse substances at some point in their lives. Substance abuse in people with schizophrenia is associated with poorer functional

prodromal phase (1) Stage in which the early features or signs of a disorder become apparent. (2) In schizophrenia, the period of decline in functioning that precedes the development of the first acute psychotic episode.

residual phase In schizophrenia, the phase of the disorder that follows an acute phase, characterized by a return to a level of functioning typical of the prodromal phase.

adjustment, suicidal behaviour, and violence (Health Canada, 2006). However, because of their behavioural problems (such as odd or socially inappropriate behaviour), people with schizophrenia are more often the victims than the perpetrators of violence (Health Canada, 2006).

Public misunderstanding and fear contribute to the serious stigma associated with schizophrenia. Contrary to popular opinion, most people with the disorder are withdrawn and not violent. In fact, when adequately treated, people with the disorder are no more violent than the general population. Even so, the stigma of violence interferes with schizophrenics' ability to acquire housing, employment, and treatment, and also makes it difficult for them to make friends or enter intimate relationships. The stigma associated with schizophrenia also adds to the burden of the people caring for the person with the disorder, such as families and caregivers (Health Canada, 2006; Sartorius & Schulze, 2005). Public education about the nature of schizophrenia is an important step toward reducing the stigma associated with the disorder.

Major Features of Schizophrenia

Schizophrenia is a pervasive disorder that affects a wide range of psychological processes involving cognition, affect, and behaviour. People with schizophrenia show a marked decline in occupational and social functioning. They may have difficulty holding a conversation, forming friendships, holding a job, or taking care of their personal hygiene. Yet no single behaviour pattern is unique to schizophrenia, nor is any one behaviour pattern invariably present among people with schizophrenia. People with schizophrenia may exhibit delusions, problems with associative thinking, and hallucinations at one time or another, but not necessarily all at once. There are also different kinds or types of schizophrenia, characterized by different behaviour patterns.

Let us consider how schizophrenia affects thinking, speech, attentional and perceptual processes, emotional processes, and voluntary behaviour.

Disturbances of Thought and Speech

Schizophrenia is characterized by disturbances in thinking and in the expression of thoughts through coherent, meaningful speech. Disturbances in thinking may be found in both the content and form of thought.

Disturbances in the Content of Thought The most prominent disturbance in the content of thought involves *delusions*, or false beliefs that remain fixed in the person's mind despite their illogical bases and lack of supporting evidence. They tend to remain unshakable even in the face of disconfirming evidence. Delusions may take many forms, including *delusions of persecution* (e.g., "The police are out to get me"), *delusions of reference* ("People on the bus are talking about me," or "People on television are making fun of me"), *delusions of being controlled* (believing one's thoughts, feelings, impulses, or actions are controlled by external forces, such as agents of the devil), and *delusions of grandeur* (believing oneself to be Jesus or believing one is on a special mission, or having grand but illogical plans for saving the world). People with delusions of persecution may think they are being pursued by the Mafia, terrorists, the RCMP, or some other group. A woman we treated who had delusions of reference believed television news correspondents were broadcasting coded information about her. A man with delusions of this type expressed the belief that his neighbours had bugged the walls of his house. Other delusions include beliefs that one has committed unpardonable sins or is rotting from some horrible disease. Common delusions include *thought broadcasting* (believing one's thoughts are somehow transmitted to the external world so that others can overhear them), *thought insertion* (believing one's thoughts have been planted in one's mind by an external source), and *thought withdrawal* (believing that thoughts have been removed from one's mind).

Mellor (1970) offers the following examples of thought broadcasting, thought insertion, and thought withdrawal:

Thought Broadcasting: A 21-year-old student reported, "As I think, my thoughts leave my head on a type of mental ticker-tape. Everyone around has only to pass the tape through their mind and they know my thoughts" (p. 17).

Thought Insertion: A 29-year-old housewife reported that when she looks out of the window, she thinks, "The garden looks nice and the grass looks cool, but the thoughts of [a man's name] come into my mind. There are no other thoughts there, only his . . . . He treats my mind like a screen and flashes his thoughts on it like you flash a picture" (p. 17).

Thought Withdrawal: A 22-year-old woman experienced the following: "I am thinking about my mother, and suddenly my thoughts are sucked out of my mind by a phrenological vacuum extractor, and there is nothing in my mind, it is empty" (pp. 16–17).

Disturbances in the Form of Thought Unless we are engaged in daydreaming or purposefully letting our thoughts wander, our thoughts tend to be tightly knit together. The connections (or associations) between our thoughts tend to be logical and coherent. People with schizophrenia tend to think in a disorganized, illogical fashion, however. In schizophrenia, the form or structure of thought processes as well as their content is often disturbed. Clinicians label this type of disturbance a **thought disorder**.

Thought disorder is recognized by a breakdown in the organization, processing, and control of thoughts. Looseness of associations, which we now regard as a chief sign of thought disorder, was one of Bleuler's four As. The speech pattern of people with schizophrenia is often disorganized or jumbled, with parts of words combined incoherently or words strung together to make meaningless rhymes. Their speech may jump from one topic to another, but show little interconnectivity between the ideas or thoughts that are expressed. People with thought disorder are usually unaware that their thoughts and behaviour appear abnormal. In severe cases, their speech may become completely incoherent or incomprehensible.

Another common sign of thought disorder is poverty of speech; that is, speech that is coherent but is so limited in production or vague that little informational value is conveyed. Less commonly occurring signs include **neologisms** (a word made up by the speaker that has little or no meaning to others), **perseveration** (inappropriate but persistent repetition of the same words or train of thought), **clanging** (stringing together of words or sounds on the basis of rhyming, such as, "I know who I am but I don't know Sam"), and **blocking** (involuntary abrupt interruption of speech or thought). Disconnected speech is more common and more severe among younger patients; poverty of speech is found more often and is more severe among older patients (Harvey et al., 1997).

Many but not all people with schizophrenia show evidence of thought disorder. Some appear to think and speak coherently, but have disordered content of thought as seen by the presence of delusions. Nor is disordered thought unique to schizophrenia; it has even been found in milder form among people without psychological disorders (Bachman & Cannon, 2005), especially when they are tired or under stress. Disordered thought is also found among other diagnostic groups, such as persons with mania. Thought disorders in people experiencing a manic episode tend to be short-lived and reversible, however. In those with schizophrenia, thought disorder tends to be more persistent or recurrent—it occurs most often during acute episodes, but may linger into residual phases. Thought disorders that persist beyond acute episodes are connected with poorer prognoses, perhaps because lingering thought disorders reflect more severe disorders (Marengo & Harrow, 1997).

Attentional Deficiencies

To read this book, you must screen out background noises and other environmental stimuli. The ability to focus on relevant stimuli is basic to learning and thinking. Kraepelin and Bleuler suggested that schizophrenia involves a breakdown in the processes of attention. People with schizophrenia appear to have difficulty filtering out irrelevant distracting stimuli, a deficit that makes it nearly impossible to focus their attention and organize their thoughts (Bergida & Lenzenweger, 2006; Wang et al., 2007).

thought disorder Disturbances in thinking characterized by various features, especially a breakdown in logical associations between thoughts.

neologisms Type of disturbed thinking associated with schizophrenia involving the coining of new words.

perseveration Persistent repetition of the same thought or response.

clanging In people with schizophrenia, the tendency to string words together because they rhyme or sound alike.

blocking (1) Disruption of self-expression of threatening or emotionally laden material. (2) In people with schizophrenia, a condition of suddenly becoming silent with loss of memory for what they had just discussed.

The mother of a son who had schizophrenia provided the following illustration of her son's difficulties in filtering out extraneous sounds:

> [H]is hearing is different when he's ill. One of the first things we notice when he's deteriorating is his heightened sense of hearing. He cannot filter out anything. He hears each and every sound around him with equal intensity. He hears the sounds from the street, in the yard, and in the house, and they are all much louder than normal. (Anonymous, 1985, p. 1; cited in Freedman et al., 1987, p. 670)

People with schizophrenia also appear to be *hypervigilant* or acutely sensitive to extraneous sounds, especially during the early stages of the disorder. During acute episodes, they may become flooded by these stimuli, overwhelming their ability to make sense of their environments. Through measuring the brain's involuntary brainwave responses to auditory stimuli, researchers find the brains of people with schizophrenia are less able than those of other people to inhibit or screen out responses to distracting sounds (Bergida & Lenzenweger, 2006).

Investigators suspect that attentional deficits associated with schizophrenia are, to a certain extent, inherited (Ettinger, Joober, De Guzman, & O'Driscoll, 2006; Goldberg et al., 2006). Although the underlying mechanism is not entirely clear, attentional deficits may be related to dysfunction in the subcortical parts of the brain that regulate attention to external stimuli, such as the basal ganglia (Cornblatt & Kelip, 1994). Scientists suspect there may be a "gating" mechanism in the brain responsible for filtering extraneous stimuli, much like the closing of a gate in a road can stem the flow of traffic (de Bruin, van Luijtelaar, Cools, & Ellenbroek, 2003). Evidence suggests that training in attention skills may help reduce attentional deficits in schizophrenia patients (Medalia et al., 1998).

Perceptual Disturbances

> Every so often during the interview, Sally would look over her right shoulder in the direction of the office door and smile gently. When asked why she kept looking at the door, she said that the voices were talking about the two of us just outside the door and she wanted to hear what they were saying. "Why the smile?" Sally was asked. "They were saying funny things," she replied, "like maybe you thought I was cute or something."
>
> Eugene was flailing his arms wildly in the hall of the psychiatric unit. Sweat seemed to pour from his brow, and his eyes darted about with agitation. He was subdued and injected with haloperidol (brand name Haldol) to reduce his agitation. When he was about to be injected he started shouting, "Father, forgive them for they know not . . . forgive them . . . father . . . " His words became jumbled. Later, after he had calmed down, he reported that the ward attendants had looked to him like devils or evil angels. They were red and burning, and steam issued from their mouths.
>
> THE AUTHORS' FILES

Hallucinations, the most common form of perceptual disturbance in schizophrenia, are images perceived in the absence of external stimulation. They are difficult to distinguish from reality. For Sally, the voices coming from outside the consulting room were real enough, even though no one was there. Hallucinations may involve any of the senses. Auditory hallucinations ("hearing voices") are most common. Tactile hallucinations (such as tingling, electrical, or burning sensations) and somatic hallucinations (feeling like snakes are crawling inside one's belly) are also common. Visual hallucinations (seeing things that are not there), gustatory hallucinations (tasting things that are not present), and olfactory hallucinations (sensing odours that are not present) are rarer.

A painting by a man with schizophrenia.

Auditory hallucinations occur in over 60% of cases of schizophrenia (Cleghorn et al., 1992; Rector & Seeman, 1992). In auditory hallucinations, the voices may be experienced as female or male and as originating inside or outside one's head (APA, 2000a). When hallucinating, schizophrenic people may hear voices conversing about them in the third person, debating their virtues or faults.

Some people with schizophrenia experience *command hallucinations*, voices that instruct them to perform certain acts, such as harming themselves or others. Joanne, for example, was instructed by "devils" to commit suicide, and so she attempted to jump from a bridge. People with schizophrenia who experience command hallucinations are often hospitalized for fear they may harm themselves or others. There is a good reason for this. One study found that four out of five people with command hallucinations reported obeying them, with nearly half reporting they had obeyed commands to harm themselves during the past month (Kasper, Rogers, & Adams, 1996). Yet command hallucinations often go undetected by professionals because command hallucinators deny them or are unwilling to discuss them.

Hallucinations are not unique to schizophrenia. People with major depression and mania sometimes experience hallucinations. Nor are hallucinations invariably a sign of psychopathology. Cross-cultural evidence shows they are common and socially valued in some developing countries (Bentall, 1990). Even in developed countries, about 5% of respondents in nonpatient samples report experiencing hallucinations during the preceding year, mostly auditory hallucinations (Honig et al., 1998). Hallucinations in people without psychiatric conditions are often triggered by unusually low levels of sensory stimulation (lying in the dark in a soundproof room for extended time) or low levels of arousal (Teunisse, Craysberg, Hoefugels, Verboek, & Zitman, 1996). Unlike psychotic individuals, these people realize their hallucinations are not real and feel in control of them.

People who are free of psychological disorders sometimes experience hallucinations during the course of a religious experience or ritual (Asaad & Shapiro, 1986). Participants in such experiences may report fleeting trancelike states with visions or other perceptual aberrations. All of us hallucinate nightly, if we consider dreams to be a form of hallucination (perceptual experience in the absence of external stimuli).

Hallucinations may also occur in response to hallucinogenic drugs, such as LSD. They may also occur during grief reactions, when images of the deceased may appear, and in other stressful conditions. In most cases, grief-induced hallucinations can be differentiated from psychotic ones in that the individual can distinguish the former type from reality. Bentall (1990) views the hallucinations of psychiatric patients as involving the lack of ability to distinguish between real and imaginary events. They tend to confuse real and imaginary (hallucinatory) events, that is.

Drug-induced hallucinations tend to be visual and often involve abstract shapes such as circles or stars or flashes of light. Schizophrenic hallucinations, in contrast, tend to be more fully formed and complex. Hallucinations (e.g., of bugs crawling on one's skin) are common during delirium tremens, which often occur as part of the withdrawal syndrome for chronic alcoholism. Hallucinations may also occur as side effects of medications or in neurological disorders, such as Parkinson's disease.

Causes of Hallucinations The causes of psychotic hallucinations remain unknown, but speculations abound. Disturbances in brain chemistry are suspected as playing a role. The neurotransmitter dopamine has been implicated because antipsychotic drugs that block dopamine activity also tend to reduce hallucinations. Conversely, drugs that lead to increased production of dopamine tend to induce hallucinations. Because hallucinations resemble dreamlike states, it is also possible that hallucinations are types of daytime dreams connected with a failure of brain mechanisms that normally prevent dream images from intruding on waking experiences.

Hallucinations may also represent a type of subvocal inner speech (Stephane, Barton, & Boutros, 2001). Many of us talk to ourselves from time to time, although we usually keep our mutterings beneath our breath (subvocal) and recognize the voice as our own. Might auditory hallucinations that occur among people with schizophrenia be projections of their own internal voices or self-speech onto external sources? In one experiment, 14 of 18 hallucinators who suffered from schizophrenia reported the voices disappeared when they engaged in a procedure that prevented them from talking to themselves under their breath (Bick & Kinsbourne, 1987). Similar results were obtained for 18 of 21 normal subjects who reportedly experienced hallucinations in response to hypnotic suggestions.

Researchers find that activity in Broca's area, a part of the brain involved in controlling speech, was greater in people with schizophrenia when they were hearing voices than at a later time when they were no longer hallucinating (McGuire, Shah, & Murray, 1993). This same area is known to become active when people engage in inner speech (Paulesu, Frith, & Frackowisk, 1993). Researchers also find evidence of similar electrical activity in the auditory cortex of the brain during auditory hallucinations and in response to hearing real sounds (Stephane et al., 2001). This evidence supports the view that auditory hallucinations may be a form of inner speech (silent self-talk) that for some unknown reason is attributed to external sources rather than to one's own thoughts (Johns, Gregg, Allen, & McGuire, 2006).

Even if theories linking subvocal speech to auditory hallucinations stand up to further scientific inquiry, however, they cannot account for hallucinations in other sensory modalities, such as visual, tactile, or olfactory hallucinations (Laroi, 2006).

The brain mechanisms responsible for hallucinations are likely to involve a number of interconnected brain systems. One intriguing possibility is that defects in deeper brain structures may lead the brain to create its own reality, which goes unchecked because of a failure of the higher thinking centres in the brain, located in the frontal lobes of the cerebral cortex, to perform a reality check on these images to determine whether they are real, imagined, or hallucinated (Begley, 1995; Collerton, Perry, & McKeith, 2005). Consequently, people may misattribute their own internally generated voices to outside sources. As we'll see later, evidence from other brain-imaging studies points to abnormalities in the frontal and temporal lobes in at least some people with schizophrenia.

Emotional Disturbances

Disturbances of affect or emotional response in schizophrenia are typified by blunted affect—also called *flat affect*—and by inappropriate affect. Flat affect is inferred from the absence of emotional expression in the face and voice. People with schizophrenia may speak in a monotone and maintain an expressionless face or "mask." They may not experience a normal range of emotional response to people and events. Or their emotional responses may be inappropriate, like giggling at bad news.

It is not fully clear, however, whether emotional blunting in people with schizophrenia is a disturbance in their ability to express emotions, to report the presence of emotions, or to actually experience emotions (Berenbaum & Oltmanns, 2005). They may, in other words, experience emotions even if their experiences are not communicated to the world outside through such means as facial expression. Support along these lines is found in research showing that people with schizophrenia displayed less facial expression of positive and negative emotions when viewing emotion-eliciting films than did control subjects, but they reported experiencing as much positive or negative emotion (Kring, Kerr, Smith, & Neale, 1993). It may be that people with schizophrenia experience emotions internally but lack the capacity to express them outwardly (Kring & Neale, 1996).

Other Types of Impairment

People who suffer from schizophrenia may become confused about their personal identities—the cluster of attributes and characteristics that define themselves as individuals and give meaning and direction to their lives. They may fail to recognize themselves as unique individuals and be unclear as to how much of what they experience is part of themselves. In psychodynamic terms, this phenomenon is sometimes referred to as loss of *ego boundaries*. They may also have difficulty adopting a third-party perspective and fail to perceive their own behaviour and verbalizations as socially inappropriate in a given situation because they are unable to see things from another person's point of view (Carini & Nevid, 1992; Penn, Combs, & Mohamed, 2001).

Disturbances of volition are most often seen in the residual or chronic state and are characterized by loss of initiative to pursue goal-directed activities. People with schizophrenia may be unable to carry out plans and may lack interest or drive. Apparent ambivalence toward choosing courses of action may block goal-directed activities.

People with schizophrenia may show highly excited or wild behaviour or slow to a state of **stupor**. They may exhibit odd gestures and bizarre facial expressions, or become unresponsive and curtail spontaneous movement. In extreme cases, as in catatonic schizophrenia, the person may seem unaware of the environment or maintain a rigid posture. Or the person may move about in an excited but seemingly purposeless manner.

People with schizophrenia also tend to show significant impairment in their interpersonal relationships. They tend to withdraw from social interactions and become absorbed in private thoughts and fantasies. Or they cling so desperately to others that they make them uncomfortable. They may become so dominated by their own fantasies that they essentially lose touch with the outside world. They also tend to have been introverted and peculiar even before the appearance of psychotic behaviour (Berenbaum & Fujita, 1994; Metsanen et al., 2004). These early signs may be associated with a vulnerability to schizophrenia, at least in people with a genetic risk of developing the disorder.

Subtypes of Schizophrenia

The belief that there are different forms or types of schizophrenia traces back to Kraepelin, who listed three types of schizophrenia: paranoid, catatonic, and hebephrenic (now called disorganized type). The DSM-IV lists three specific types of schizophrenia: *disorganized*, *catatonic*, and *paranoid*. People with schizophrenia who display active psychotic features, such as hallucinations, delusions, incoherent speech, or confused or disorganized behaviour, but who do not meet the specifications of the other types are considered to be of an *undifferentiated type*. Others who have no prominent psychotic features at the time of evaluation but have some residual features (e.g., social withdrawal, peculiar behaviour, blunted or inappropriate affect, strange beliefs or thoughts) would be classified as having a *residual type* of schizophrenia.

Let us consider the specific types of schizophrenia recognized by the DSM system.

Disorganized Type The **disorganized type** is associated with such features as confused behaviour, incoherent speech, vivid, frequent hallucinations, flattened or inappropriate affect, and disorganized delusions that often involve sexual or religious themes. Social impairment is frequent among people with disorganized schizophrenia. They also display silliness and giddiness of mood, giggling and talking nonsensically. They often neglect their appearance and hygiene and lose control of their bladders and bowels.

Consider the case of Emilio:

A 40-year-old man who looks more like 30 is brought to the hospital by his mother, who reports that she is afraid of him. It is his twelfth hospitalization. He is dressed in a tattered overcoat, baseball cap, and bedroom slippers, and sports several medals around his neck. His affect ranges from anger (hurling obscenities at his mother) to giggling. He speaks with a childlike quality and walks with exaggerated hip movements and seems to measure each step very carefully. Since stopping his medication about a month ago, his mother reports, he had been hearing voices and looking and acting more bizarrely. He tells the interviewer he

stupor State of relative or complete unconsciousness in which a person is not generally aware of or responsive to the environment, as in a *catatonic stupor*.

disorganized type Subtype of schizophrenia characterized by disorganized behaviour, bizarre delusions, and vivid hallucinations. Formerly *hebephrenic schizophrenia*.

A person diagnosed with disorganized schizophrenia. One of the features of disorganized schizophrenia is grossly inappropriate affect, as shown by this young man who continuously giggles and laughs for no apparent reason.

A person diagnosed with catatonic schizophrenia. People with catatonic schizophrenia may remain in unusual, difficult positions for hours, even though their limbs become stiff or swollen. They may seem oblivious to their environment, even to people who are talking about them. Yet they may later say that they heard what was being said. Periods of stupor may alternate with periods of agitation.

has been "eating wires and lighting fires." His speech is generally incoherent and frequently falls into rhyme and clanging associations. His history reveals a series of hospitalizations since the age of 16. Between hospitalizations, he lives with his mother, who is now elderly, and [he] often disappears for months at a time, but is eventually picked up by the police for wandering in the streets.

ADAPTED FROM SPITZER, GIBBON, SKODOL, WILLIAMS, & FIRST, 1994, PP. 189–190

Catatonic Type   The **catatonic type** is a subtype of schizophrenia characterized by markedly impaired motor behaviour and a slowing down of activity that progresses to a stupor but may switch abruptly into an agitated phase. People with catatonic schizophrenia may show unusual mannerisms or grimacing, or maintain bizarre, apparently strenuous postures for hours, even though their limbs become stiff or swollen. <u>A striking but less common feature is **waxy flexibility**, which involves the adoption of a fixed posture into which they have been positioned by others.</u> They will not respond to questions or comments during these periods, which can last for hours. Later, they may report they heard what others were saying at the time.

A 24-year-old man had been brooding about his life. He professed that he did not feel well, but could not explain his bad feelings. While hospitalized, he initially sought contact with people, but a few days later was found in a statuesque position, his legs contorted in an awkward-looking position. He refused to talk to anyone and acted as if he couldn't see or hear anything. His face was an expressionless mask. A few days later, he began to talk, but in an echolalic or mimicking way. For example,

catatonic type Subtype of schizophrenia characterized by gross disturbances in motor activity, such as catatonic stupor.

waxy flexibility Feature of catatonic schizophrenia in which a person's limbs are moved into a certain posture or position that the person then rigidly maintains for a lengthy period of time.

> he would respond to the question, "What is your name?" by saying, "What is your name?" He could not care for his needs and required to be fed by spoon.
>
> ADAPTED FROM ARIETI, 1974, P. 40

Although catatonia is associated with schizophrenia, it may also occur in other physical and psychological disorders, including brain disorders, states of drug intoxication, metabolic disorders, and mood disorders (Moskowitz, 2004).

Paranoid Type The paranoid type is characterized by preoccupations with one or more delusions or with the presence of frequent auditory hallucinations (APA, 2000a). The behaviour and speech of someone with paranoid schizophrenia does not show the marked disorganization typical of the disorganized type, nor is there a prominent display of flattened or inappropriate affect or catatonic behaviour. Their delusions often involve themes of grandeur, persecution, or jealousy. They may believe, for example, that their spouse or lover is unfaithful despite a lack of evidence. They may also become highly agitated, confused, and fearful.

> Myra, a 25-year-old woman, was visibly frightened. She was shaking badly and had the look of someone who feared that she might be attacked at any moment. The night before, she had been found cowering in a corner of the local bus station, mumbling to herself incoherently, having arrived in town minutes earlier on a bus. The station manager had called the police, who took her to the hospital. She told the interviewer that she had to escape because the Mafia was closing in on her. She was a schoolteacher, she explained, at least until the voices started bothering her. The voices would tell her she was bad and had to be punished. Sometimes the voices were in her head; sometimes they spoke to her through the electrical wires in her apartment. The voices told her that someone from the Mafia would come to kill her. She felt that one of her neighbours, a shy man who lived down the hall, was in league with the Mafia. She felt the only hope she had was to escape. To go somewhere, anywhere. So she hopped on the first bus leaving town, heading nowhere in particular, except away from home.
>
> THE AUTHORS' FILES

Type I vs. Type II Schizophrenia

Some investigators have gone beyond the DSM typology in proposing other ways of categorizing schizophrenia. One alternative typology distinguishes between two basic types of schizophrenia: Type I and Type II (Crow, 1980a, 1980b, 1980c). Type I schizophrenia is characterized by more flagrant symptoms called **positive symptoms**, such as hallucinations, delusions, and looseness of associations, as well as by an abrupt onset, preserved intellectual ability, and a more favourable response to antipsychotic medication (Penn, 1998). Type II schizophrenia corresponds to a pattern consisting largely of deficit or **negative symptoms** of schizophrenia, such as flat affect, low motivation, loss of pleasure in activities, social withdrawal, and poverty of speech. Type II is also characterized by a more gradual onset, intellectual impairment, and poorer response to antipsychotic drugs (Selten, Gernaat, Nolen, Wiersma, & van den Bosch, 1998).

One intriguing possibility is that Type I and Type II schizophrenia represent different pathological processes. The Type I pattern may involve a defect in the inhibitory (blocking) mechanisms in the brain that would normally control excessive or distorted behaviours. Underlying this malfunction may be a disturbance in the supply or regulation of dopamine in the brain, because antipsychotic drugs that regulate dopamine function gen-

positive symptoms The more flagrant features of schizophrenia characterized by the *presence* of abnormal behaviour, such as hallucinations, delusions, thought disorder, disorganized speech, and inappropriate affect.

negative symptoms Features of schizophrenia characterized by the *absence* of normal behaviour. Negative symptoms are deficits or behavioural deficiencies, such as social-skills deficits, social withdrawal, flattened affect, poverty of speech and thought, psychomotor retardation, and failure to experience pleasure in pleasant activities.

erally have a favourable impact on positive symptoms. The negative symptoms associated with Type II schizophrenia represent the more enduring or persistent characteristics of schizophrenia. The Type II pattern is associated with poorer **premorbid functioning** and with a more progressive decline in functioning leading to enduring disability (Earnst & Kring, 1997; McGlashan & Fenton, 1992): One possibility is that Type II schizophrenia is caused by structural damage or atrophy in the brain.

The Type I–Type II distinction remains controversial, because evidence does not clearly support the existence of two distinct behaviour patterns in schizophrenia. Some investigators (e.g., Kay, 1990; Mortimer et al., 1990) find that only a minority of people with schizophrenia can be classified as exhibiting either predominantly positive or negative symptoms. Positive and negative symptoms may not define distinct subtypes of schizophrenia but rather separate dimensions that can coexist in the same individual.

Perhaps, as other research suggests, a three-dimensional model is most appropriate for grouping schizophrenic symptoms (Andreasen et al., 1995; Liddle, 1999). One dimension, a *psychotic dimension*, consists of delusional thinking and hallucinations. A *negative dimension* comprises negative symptoms such as flat affect and poverty of speech and thought. The third dimension, labelled a *disorganized dimension*, includes inappropriate affect and thought disorder (disordered thought and speech). Although schizophrenic symptoms seem to cluster into these three dimensions, there is considerable overlap. Thus, it does not appear these dimensions represent distinct subtypes of schizophrenia. Still, it remains an open question whether or not different underlying neurobiological processes give rise to different constellations of symptoms.

premorbid functioning Level of functioning before the onset of a disorder.

On the run? People with paranoid schizophrenia hold systematized delusions that commonly involve themes of persecution and grandeur. They usually do not show the degree of confusion, disorganization, or disturbed motor behaviour seen in people with disorganized or catatonic schizophrenia. Unless they are discussing the areas in which they are delusional, their thought processes may appear to be relatively intact.

Clinical Features of Schizophrenia

Review It

• **What is schizophrenia and how prevalent is it?** Schizophrenia is a chronic psychotic disorder characterized by acute episodes involving a break with reality, as manifested by such features as delusions, hallucinations, illogical thinking, incoherent speech, and bizarre behaviour. Residual deficits in cognitive, emotional, and social areas of functioning persist between acute episodes. Schizophrenia is believed to affect about 1% of the population.

• **What key historical figures in psychiatry influenced our conceptions of schizophrenia?** Emil Kraepelin was the first to describe the syndrome we identify as schizophrenia. He labelled the disorder *dementia praecox* and believed it was a disease that develops early in life and follows a progressively deteriorating course. Eugen Bleuler renamed the disorder *schizophrenia* and believed its course is more variable. He also distinguished between primary symptoms (the four As) and secondary symptoms. Kurt Schneider distinguished between first-rank symptoms that define the disorder and second-rank symptoms that occur in schizophrenia and other disorders.

- **What are the major phases of schizophrenia?** Schizophrenia usually develops in late adolescence or early adulthood. Its onset may be abrupt or gradual. The period of deterioration preceding the onset of acute symptoms is called the prodromal phase. An acute episode involves the emergence of clear psychotic features. A level of functioning that was typical of the prodromal phase characterizes the residual phase.

- **What are the most prominent features of schizophrenia?** Among the more prominent features of schizophrenia are disorders in the content of thought (delusions) and form of thought (thought disorder), as well as the presence of perceptual distortions (hallucinations) and emotional disturbances (flattened or inappropriate affect). There are also dysfunctions in the brain processes that regulate attention to the external world.

- **What are the various subtypes of schizophrenia?** The disorganized type describes a version of schizophrenia associated with grossly disorganized behaviour and thought processes. The catatonic type describes a version of the disorder associated with grossly impaired motor behaviours, such as maintenance of fixed postures and muteness for long periods of time. The paranoid type involves the presence of paranoid delusions or frequent auditory hallucinations. The undifferentiated type is a catch-all category that applies to cases involving schizophrenic episodes that don't clearly fit the other types. The residual type applies to individuals with schizophrenia who do not have prominent psychotic behaviours at the time of evaluation. Researchers have also distinguished between two general types of schizophrenia: Type I, characterized by positive symptomatology, more abrupt onset, better response to antipsychotic medication, and better preserved intellectual ability; and Type II, characterized by negative symptomatology, more gradual onset, poorer response to antipsychotic medication, and greater cognitive impairment.

Define It

schizophrenia	neologisms
four As	perseveration
associations	clanging
affect	blocking
ambivalence	stupor
autism	disorganized type
first-rank symptoms	catatonic type

second-rank symptoms	waxy flexibility
prodromal phase	positive symptoms
residual phase	negative symptoms
thought disorder	premorbid functioning

Recall It*

1. The term *schizophrenia* was introduced by _____.
   a. Kraepelin
   b. Kaplan
   c. Bleuler
   d. Schneider

2. To receive a diagnosis of schizophrenia, signs of the disorder must be present for a period of at least _____.
   a. two weeks
   b. one month
   c. six months
   d. one year

3. The major feature of a thought disorder is _____.
   a. obsessional thinking
   b. hallucinations
   c. paranoid delusions
   d. looseness of associations

4. People with schizophrenia who adopt a fixed posture, into which they have been positioned by others, are said to demonstrate _____.
   a. perseveration
   b. waxy flexibility
   c. *la belle indifférence*
   d. autistic paralysis

5. Research suggests that auditory hallucinations in people with schizophrenia may represent a form of _____.
   a. obsessive-compulsive behaviour
   b. drug-induced hysteria
   c. subvocal inner speech
   d. perceptual blocking

* Recall It answers can be found on the Companion Website for this text.

Think About It

- The authors state that schizophrenia is perhaps the most disabling type of mental or psychological disorder. What makes it so?

THEORETICAL PERSPECTIVES

The understanding of schizophrenia has been approached from each of the major theoretical perspectives. Although the underlying causes of schizophrenia have not been identified, they are presumed to involve biological abnormalities in combination with psychosocial and environmental influences.

Psychodynamic Perspectives

According to the psychodynamic perspective, schizophrenia represents the overwhelming of the ego by primitive sexual or aggressive drives or impulses arising from the id. These impulses threaten the ego and give rise to intense intrapsychic conflict. Under such a threat, the person regresses to an early period in the oral stage, referred to as *primary narcissism*. In this period, the infant has not yet learned that it and the world are distinct entities. Because the ego mediates the relationship between the self and the outer world, this breakdown in ego functioning accounts for the detachment from reality that is typical of schizophrenia. Input from the id causes fantasies to become mistaken for reality, giving rise to hallucinations and delusions. Primitive impulses may also carry more weight than social norms and be expressed in bizarre, socially inappropriate behaviour.

Freud's followers, such as Erik Erikson and Harry Stack Sullivan, placed more emphasis on interpersonal than intrapsychic factors. Sullivan (1962), for example, who devoted much of his life's work to schizophrenia, emphasized the importance of impaired mother–child relationships, arguing they can set the stage for gradual withdrawal from other people. In early childhood, anxious and hostile interactions between the child and parent lead the child to take refuge in a private fantasy world. A vicious cycle ensues: The more the child withdraws, the less opportunity there is to develop a sense of trust in others and the social skills necessary to establish intimacy. Then the weak bonds between the child and others prompt social anxiety and further withdrawal. This cycle continues until young adulthood. Then, faced with increasing demands at school or work and in intimate relationships, the person becomes overwhelmed with anxiety and withdraws completely into a world of fantasy.

Critics of Freud's views point out that schizophrenic behaviour and infantile behaviour are not much alike, so that schizophrenia cannot be explained by regression. Freud's detractors and modern psychodynamic theorists note that psychodynamic explanations are *post hoc* or retrospective. Early child–adult relationships are recalled from the vantage point of adulthood rather than observed longitudinally. Psychoanalysts have not been able to demonstrate that hypothesized early childhood experiences or family patterns lead to schizophrenia.

Learning Perspectives

Although learning theory may not account for schizophrenia, the principles of conditioning and observational learning may play a role in the development of some forms of schizophrenic behaviour. From this perspective, people may learn to "emit" schizophrenic behaviours when they are more likely to be reinforced than normal behaviour.

Ullmann and Krasner (1975) focused on the reinforcement value of social stimulation. Children who later develop schizophrenia may grow up in nonreinforcing environments because of disturbed family patterns or other environmental influences. Thus, they never learn to respond appropriately to social stimuli. Instead, as Sullivan, too, argued, they increasingly attend to private or idiosyncratic stimuli. Other people perceive them as strange, and they suffer social rejection. In a vicious cycle, rejection spurs feelings of alienation; alienation, in turn, engenders more bizarre behaviour. Patterns of bizarre behaviour may be maintained by the unintentional reinforcement they receive from some people in the form of attention and expressions of sympathy.

Support for this view is found in operant conditioning studies in which bizarre behaviour is shaped by reinforcement. Experiments involving people with schizophrenia show, for example, that reinforcement affects the frequency of bizarre versus normal verbalizations and that hospital patients can be shaped into performing odd behaviours. In a classic case example, Haughton and Ayllon (1965) conditioned a 54-year-old woman with chronic schizophrenia to cling to a broom. A staff member gave her the broom to hold, and when she did, another staff member gave her a cigarette. This pattern was repeated several times. Soon, the woman could not be parted from the broom. But the fact that reinforcement can influence people to engage in peculiar behaviour does not demonstrate that bizarre behaviours characterizing schizophrenia are learned behaviours determined by reinforcement.

There are other shortcomings to these behavioural explanations. For example, many of us grow up in harsh or punishing circumstances, but do not retreat into private worlds of fantasy or display bizarre behaviour. Many people with schizophrenia also grow up in homes that are supportive and socially reinforcing. Moreover, schizophrenic behaviours fall into patterns that are unlikely to occur by chance and then be reinforced to the point that they become learned habits.

Social-cognitive theorists suggest that modelling of schizophrenic behaviour can occur within mental hospitals. In that setting, patients may begin to model themselves after fellow patients who act strangely. Hospital staff may inadvertently reinforce schizophrenic behaviour by paying more attention to those patients who exhibit more bizarre behaviour. This understanding is consistent with the observation that schoolchildren who disrupt class garner more attention from their teachers than do well-behaved children.

Perhaps some forms of schizophrenic behaviour can be explained by the principles of modelling and reinforcement. However, many people come to display schizophrenic behaviour patterns without prior exposure to other people with schizophrenia. In fact, the onset of schizophrenic behaviour patterns is more likely to lead to hospitalization than to result from it.

Biological Perspectives

Although we still have much to learn about the biological underpinnings of schizophrenia, most investigators today recognize that biological factors play a determining role.

Genetic Factors
We now have compelling evidence that schizophrenia is strongly influenced by genetic factors (DeLisi & Fleischhaker, 2007; Kendler & Prescott, 2006). One source of evidence of genetic factors is based on familial studies. Schizophrenia, like many other disorders, tends to run in families. Overall, people with biological relatives with schizophrenia have about a tenfold greater risk of developing the disorder than do members of the general population (APA, 2000a).

Further supporting a genetic linkage, evidence shows that the closer the genetic relationship between people diagnosed with schizophrenia and their family members, the greater the likelihood (or concordance rate) of schizophrenia in their relatives. Figure 12.1 shows the pooled results of European studies on family incidence of schizophrenia conducted from 1920 to 1987. However, the fact that families share common environments as well as common genes requires that we dig deeper to examine the genetic underpinnings of schizophrenia.

More support for a genetic contribution to schizophrenia is found in twin studies, which show concordance rates for the disorder among identical or monozygotic (MZ) twins is more than twice the rate found among fraternal or dizygotic (DZ) twins (Kendler & Prescott, 2006).

We should be cautious, however, not to overinterpret the results of twin studies. MZ twins not only share 100% genetic similarity, but they may also be treated more alike than DZ twins. Thus, environmental factors may play a role in explaining the higher concordance rates found among MZ twins. To help sort out environmental from genetic factors, investigators have turned to adoption studies in which high-risk (HR) children (children of one or more biological parents with schizophrenia) were adopted away shortly after birth and reared apart from their biological parents.

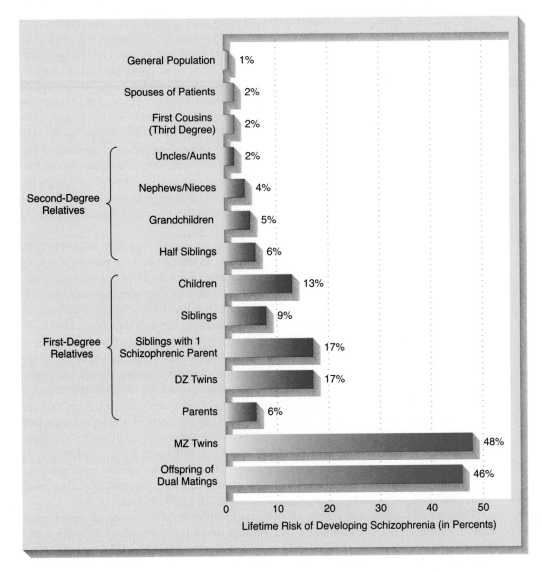

FIGURE 12.1 The familial risk of schizophrenia.
Generally speaking, the more closely one is related to people who have developed schizophrenia, the greater the risk of developing the disorder oneself. Monozygotic (MZ) twins, whose genetic heritages overlap fully, are much more likely than dizygotic (DZ) twins, whose genes overlap by 50%, to be concordant for schizophrenia.

Source: Adapted from Gottesman, McGuffin, & Farmer. (1987).

Adoption studies provide stronger evidence for a genetic contribution to schizophrenia (Gottesman, McGuffin, & Farmer, 1987). In perhaps the best-known example, researchers in Denmark examined official registers and found 39 high-risk (HR) adoptees who had been reared apart from their biological mothers who had schizophrenia (Rosenthal et al., 1968, 1975). Three of the 39 HR adoptees (8%) were diagnosed with schizophrenia, as compared to none of a reference group of 47 adoptees whose biological parents had no psychiatric history.

Other investigators have approached the question of heredity in schizophrenia from the opposite direction. Kety and colleagues (1968, 1975, 1978) used official records to find 33 index cases of children in Copenhagen, Denmark, who had been adopted early in life and were later diagnosed with schizophrenia. They compared the rates of diagnosed schizophrenia in the biological and adoptive relatives of the index cases with those of the relatives of a matched reference group that consisted of adoptees with no psychiatric history. The results strongly supported the genetic explanation. The incidence of diagnosed schizophrenia was greater among the biological relatives of the adoptees who had schizophrenia than among the biological relatives of the control adoptees. Adoptive relatives of both the index and control cases showed similar *low* rates of schizophrenia. Similar results were found in later research that extended the scope of the investigation to the rest of Denmark (Kety et al., 1994). It thus appears that family linkages in schizophrenia follow shared genes, not shared environments.

cross-fostering study Method of determining heritability of a trait or disorder by examining differences in prevalence among adoptees reared by either adoptive parents or biological parents who possessed the trait or disorder in question. Evidence that the disorder followed biological rather than adoptive parentage favours the heritability of the trait or disorder.

Still another approach, the **cross-fostering study**, has yielded additional evidence of genetic factors in schizophrenia. In this approach, investigators compare the incidence of schizophrenia among children whose biological parents either had or didn't have schizophrenia and who were reared by adoptive parents who either had or didn't have schizophrenia. Another Danish study by Wender and colleagues (Wender, Rosenthal, Kety, Schulsinger, & Welner, 1974) found the incidence of schizophrenia related to the presence of the disorder in the children's biological parents, but not in their adoptive parents. High-risk children (children whose biological parents had schizophrenia) were almost twice as likely to develop schizophrenia as those of nonschizophrenic biological parents, regardless of whether or not they were reared by a parent with schizophrenia. It is also notable that adoptees whose biological parents did not suffer from schizophrenia were placed at no greater risk of developing the disorder by being reared by an adoptive parent with schizophrenia than by a nonschizophrenic parent. In sum, a genetic relationship with a person with schizophrenia seems to be the most prominent risk factor for developing the disorder.

Although it is recognized that genetic factors play an important role in schizophrenia, the mode of genetic transmission remains unknown. Evidence points to an interaction of multiple genes involved in determining risk for schizophrenia (Kendler & Prescott, 2006). Researchers have identified several chromosomes, including chromosomes 6, 8, 13, 15, and 22, that appear to contain genes linked to the disorder (Detera-Wadleigh & McMahon, 2006; Harrison & Law, 2006; Severinsen et al., 2006; Vazza et al., 2007).

York University psychologist R. Walter Heinrichs (2001, 2005) argued that schizophrenia may be an umbrella term for several different disorders, each arising from different mechanisms manifesting themselves primarily in cognitive disturbances. It is possible that there are several different sets of genetic aberrations, with each independently causing schizophrenia. Preliminary findings support this idea. For example, Anne Bassett and her colleagues at the University of Toronto have found that one form of schizophrenia seems to be associated with abnormalities specifically on chromosome 22 (Bassett & Chow, 1999; Bassett et al., 1998, 2003; Chow, Watson, Young, & Bassett, 2006). About 25% of people with this genetic abnormality develop a psychotic disorder such as schizophrenia. These people also tend to have unusual facial features (e.g., long, narrow face, prominent nose, small ears and mouth) and congenital defects (e.g., heart defects).

Genetics alone does not determine risk of schizophrenia. For one thing, people may carry a high genetic risk of schizophrenia and not develop the disorder. For another, the rate of concordance among MZ twins, as noted earlier, is well below 100%, even though identical twins carry identical genes. The prevailing view today, which we discuss later, is the *diathesis-stress model*, which holds that schizophrenia involves a complex interplay of genetic and environmental factors.

Biochemical Factors Contemporary biological investigations of schizophrenia have focused on the role of the neurotransmitter dopamine. The **dopamine theory** posits that schizophrenia involves an overreactivity of dopamine receptors in the brain—the receptor sites on postsynaptic neurons into which molecules of dopamine lock (Abi-Dargham, 2004; Haber & Fudge, 1997).

dopamine theory Biochemical theory of schizophrenia that proposes that schizophrenia involves the action of dopamine.

People with schizophrenia do not appear to produce more dopamine. Instead, they appear to *utilize* more of it. But why? Research suggests that people with schizophrenia may have a greater than normal number of dopamine receptors in their brains or have receptors that are overly sensitive to dopamine (Davis, Kahn, Ko, & Davidson, 1991; Gur & Pearlson, 1993; Seeman & Kapur, 2001).

The major source of evidence for the dopamine model is found in the effects of antipsychotic drugs called major tranquillizers or *neuroleptics*. The most widely used neuroleptics belong to a class of drugs called *phenothiazines*—this class includes such drugs as Largactil and Mellaril. Neuroleptic drugs block dopamine receptors, thereby reducing the level of dopamine activity (Kane, 1996). As a consequence, neuroleptics inhibit excessive transmission of neural impulses that may give rise to schizophrenic behaviour.

Another source of evidence supporting the role of dopamine in schizophrenia is based on the actions of amphetamines, a class of stimulant drugs. These drugs increase the concentration of dopamine in the synaptic cleft by blocking its reuptake by presynaptic neurons. When given in large doses to normal people, these drugs can lead to abnormal behaviour states that mimic paranoid schizophrenia.

Overall, evidence points to irregularities in schizophrenia patients in the neural pathways in the brain that utilize dopamine (Meador-Woodruff et al., 1997; Seeman & Kapur, 2001). The specific nature of this abnormality remains unclear. We can't yet say whether the abnormality involves overreactivity of particular dopamine pathways or more complex interactions among dopamine systems. One possibility is that overreactivity of dopamine receptors may be involved in producing more flagrant behaviour patterns (positive symptoms) but not the negative symptoms or deficits associated with schizophrenia. Decreased rather than increased dopamine reactivity may be connected with some of the negative symptoms of schizophrenia (Bodkin et al., 1996; Earnst & Kring, 1997; Okubo et al., 1997). We should also note that other neurotransmitters, such as norepinephrine, serotonin, and GABA, also appear to be involved in the disorder (Busatto et al., 1997; Kapur & Remington, 1996).

Viral Infections Might schizophrenia be caused by a slow-acting virus that attacks the developing brain of a fetus or newborn child? Prenatal rubella (German measles), a viral infection, is a cause of later mental retardation. Could another virus give rise to schizophrenia?

Viral infections are more prevalent in the winter months. Viral infection during pregnancy or infancy could account for findings of an excess number of people with schizophrenia being born in the winter (Muller, 2004). However, we have yet to find an identified viral agent we can link to schizophrenia. Moreover, there is some evidence to suggest that many different sorts of infectious agents—not just viruses—are linked to schizophrenia, raising the possibility that some cases of schizophrenia are the result of a reaction by the immune system of a developing child (Muller, 2004). But such infections probably account for only a fraction of the number of cases of schizophrenia (Muller, 2004).

Brain Abnormalities Despite the widely held belief that schizophrenia is a brain disease, researchers are still asking the question, "Where is the pathology?" Researchers are trying to find an answer by using modern brain-imaging techniques, including PET scans, EEGs, CT scans, and MRIs, to probe the inner workings of the brains of people with schizophrenia. Evidence from these types of studies shows various abnormalities in the brains of people with schizophrenia.

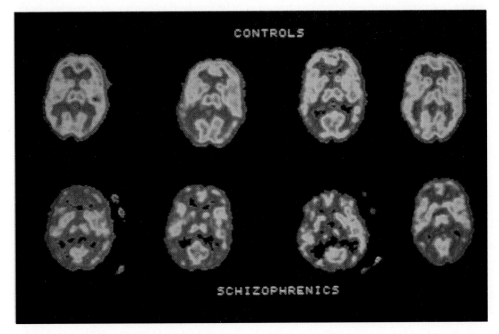

FIGURE 12.2 PET scans of people with schizophrenia versus normals. Positron emission tomography (PET scan) evidence of the metabolic processes of the brain shows relatively less metabolic activity (indicated by less yellow and red) in the frontal lobes of the brains of people with schizophrenia. PET scans of the brains of four normal people are shown in the top row, and PET scans of the brains of four people with schizophrenia are shown below.

The most prominent finding involves enlargements of brain ventricles (the hollow spaces in the brain) (Dwork, 1997; Lauriello et al., 1997; Nopoulos, Flaum, & Andreasen, 1997). Ventricular enlargement is a sign of structural damage involving loss of brain cells. It is found in about three out of four schizophrenia patients (Coursey, Alford, & Safarjan, 1997). Still, not all people with schizophrenia show evidence of enlarged ventricles or other signs of brain damage. Research conducted at the University of Toronto and York University, for example, shows that only some people with schizophrenia seem to have abnormalities in the frontal or temporal lobes (Zakzanis, Poulin, Hansen, & Jolic, 2000; Zakzanis & Heinrichs, 1999). This leads researchers to suspect that there may be several forms of schizophrenia that have different causal processes. Perhaps one form involves a degenerative loss of brain tissue (Knoll, Ramberg, Kingsbury, Croissant, & McDermott, 1998).

Structural damage to the brains of some schizophrenia patients may have occurred long before the initial onset of the disorder, most probably either prenatally or very early in life (Akbarian et al., 1996; Gur et al., 1998). One theory points to prenatal complications occurring during the period of 13 to 15 weeks of fetal development when certain brain structures are forming (Davis & Bracha, 1996). Consistent with this possibility, a cross-national group of Canadian investigators have found that schizophrenia tends to be associated with poor fetal growth, premature birth, and low birth weight (Smith et al., 2001).

The source of brain damage in schizophrenia remains an open question. Among the suspected causes are prenatal infections, birth complications such as anoxia (oxygen deprivation), brain traumas suffered early in life or during prenatal development, environmental influences in childhood, or genetic defects leading to abnormal brain development (van Os, Krabbendam, Myin-Germeys, & Delespaul, 2005).

Another line of research points to possible neurotransmitter disturbances. By tracking blood flow in the brain and using brain-imaging techniques such as PET scans, EEGs, and MRIs, researchers find evidence that some people with schizophrenia have reduced brain activity in the frontal lobes, specifically in the prefrontal cortex, the area of the frontal lobes in the cerebral cortex that lies in front of the motor cortex (Zakzanis & Heinrichs, 1999) (see Figure 12.2 on page 447). The prefrontal cortex is involved in performing various cognitive and emotional functions, the kinds of functions that are often impaired in people with schizophrenia. Among its functions, the prefrontal cortex serves as a kind of mental clipboard for holding information needed to guide organized behaviour (Casanova, 1997). Abnormalities in the complex circuitry of the frontal lobes may explain why people with schizophrenia have difficulty organizing their thoughts and behaviour and performing higher-level cognitive tasks, such as formulating concepts, prioritizing information, and formulating goals and plans (Barch, 2005). Imbalances in neurotransmitter functioning in these neural pathways may be involved in explaining disturbed brain circuitry (Goldman-Rakic & Selemon, 1997). The prefrontal cortex is also involved in regulating attention, so findings of reduced activity coincide with research evidence of deficits in attention among people with schizophrenia. These are intriguing findings that may provide clues as to the biological bases of schizophrenia.

Other evidence points to defects in brain circuitry involving brain regions lying below the cortex, especially the **hippocampus** and **amygdala**, two structures in the *limbic system* (Barch, 2005; Boos, Aleman, Cahn, Pol, & Kahn, 2007). The limbic system plays a key role in regulating emotions and higher mental functions, including memory. These structures send projections to the prefrontal cortex, which interprets information received from lower brain centres. Imbalances in neurotransmitter function may also be involved in disrupting these brain circuits.

hippocampus One of a pair of structures in the limbic system that are involved in processes of memory.

amygdala One of a pair of almond-shaped structures in the limbic system that are involved in emotion and memory.

TYING IT TOGETHER

The Diathesis-Stress Model

In 1962, psychologist Paul Meehl proposed an integrative model that led to the development of the diathesis-stress model. Meehl suggested that certain people possess a genetic predisposition to schizophrenia that is expressed behaviourally only if they are reared in stressful environments (Meehl, 1962, 1972).

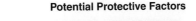

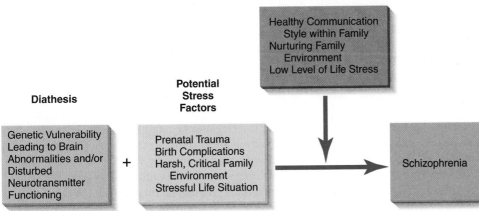

FIGURE 12.3 Diathesis-stress model of schizophrenia.

Later, Zubin and Spring (1977) formulated the diathesis-stress model, which views schizophrenia in terms of the interaction or combination of a *diathesis* in the form of a genetic predisposition to develop the disorder, with environmental stress that exceeds the individual's stress threshold or coping resources. Environmental stressors may include psychological factors such as family conflict, child abuse, emotional deprivation, or loss of supportive figures, as well as physical environmental influences, such as early brain trauma or injury. On the other hand, if environmental stress remains below the person's stress threshold, schizophrenia may never develop—even in persons at genetic risk (see Figure 12.3).

More recently, University of Western Ontario psychologist Richard W. J. Neufeld developed a comprehensive dynamic vulnerability model, which posits that genetic factors and environmental stressors interact in complex, mutually reinforcing ways (Neufeld, 1999; Nicholson & Neufeld, 1992; Neufeld, Vollick, Carter, Boksman, & Jette, 2002). According to this model, genetic vulnerability to schizophrenia influences the person's ability to cope and affects the way she or he appraises (interprets) stressful events. In turn, coping is said to influence the genetically mediated vulnerability to develop schizophrenia symptoms. To illustrate, a genetic predisposition leads to odd behaviour and thinking problems, which leads to environmental stress (e.g., school failure, rejection by peers). In turn, this creates distress for the person, which impairs coping and worsens schizophrenic symptoms.

What is the biological basis for the diathesis? No one has yet been able to find any specific brain abnormality present in all individuals who receive a schizophrenia diagnosis (Jablensky, 2006). Perhaps it shouldn't surprise us that a "one-size-fits-all" model doesn't apply. Schizophrenia is a complex disorder characterized by different subtypes and symptom complexes. There may be different causal processes in the brain explaining different forms of schizophrenia or even different *schizophrenias* (Jablensky, 2006).

We noted two possible causal processes, one involving structural damage to brain tissue, the other involving disturbed neurotransmitter functioning that disrupts complex brain circuits involved in thought, perception, emotions, and attention. The welter of confusing thoughts and perceptions, social withdrawal, and bizarre behaviour that characterize schizophrenia may be the result of disturbed neurotransmitter functioning in brain circuits involving the prefrontal cortex and its connections to lower brain regions (Barch, 2005; Goldman-Rakic & Selemon, 1997; Weinberger, 1997). These neural networks are involved in processing information efficiently and turning it into meaningful thoughts and behaviour. A defect in this circuitry may be involved in explaining the more flagrant, positive features of schizophrenia such as hallucinations, delusions, and thought disorder.

Another potential causal process involves structural damage to the brain, as evidenced by the presence of enlarged ventricles. Ventricular enlargement may play a greater role in explaining negative symptoms and chronic cognitive impairment than the more flagrant features of the disorder (Antonova, Sharma, Morris, & Kumari, 2004).

Research Evidence Supporting the Diathesis-Stress Model

Several lines of evidence support the diathesis-stress model. Evidence suggests that stress predicts the initial onset of schizophrenia occurring in genetically vulnerable individuals (van Os et al., 2005). Such sources of stress may involve sociocultural factors associated with poverty, such as overcrowding, poor diet and sanitation, impoverished housing, and inadequate health care (Selton, Cantor-Graae, & Kahn, 2007; van Os et al., 2005). Research from several countries, including Canada, has shown that the incidence of schizophrenia is higher among immigrants than among those who are native-born. The high rate of schizophrenia among immigrants is thought to be a result of the stress that is often associated with immigration, such as discrimination, difficulty coping because of language problems, and feeling isolated within one's new community (Smith et al., 2006). Such stressors appear to trigger schizophrenia in genetically vulnerable individuals.

Research on gene–environment interactions provides further support for the diathesis-stress model. To illustrate, consider the research on cannabis use and schizophrenia (Caspi & Moffitt, 2006). Here, cannabis use can be considered to be an environmental stimulus. People who possess particular forms of the COMT gene are liable to develop psychotic symptoms (delusions and hallucinations) when they consume cannabis, and sometimes these symptoms persist to the point that the person develops schizophrenia. In comparison, people with other forms of the COMT gene do not experience these reactions to cannabis. COMT genes are involved in the regulation of dopamine. Thus, an environmental stimulus (cannabis use) may trigger schizophrenia only in genetically vulnerable individuals. In other words, there is a gene–environment interaction.

Perhaps the strongest support for the diathesis-stress model comes from longitudinal studies of "high-risk" (HR) children who are at increased genetic risk of developing the disorder by virtue of having one or more parents with schizophrenia. *Longitudinal studies* of high-risk children (offspring of parents with schizophrenia) support the central tenet of the diathesis-stress model that heredity interacts with environmental influences in determining vulnerability to schizophrenia. Longitudinal studies track individuals over extended periods of time. Ideally, they begin before the emergence of the disorder or behaviour pattern in question and follow its course. In this way, investigators may identify early characteristics that predict the later development of a particular disorder, such as schizophrenia. These studies require a commitment of many years and substantial cost. Because schizophrenia occurs in only about 1% of the general population, researchers have focused on high-risk children because they are more likely to develop the disorder. Children with one schizophrenic parent have about a 10% to 25% chance of developing schizophrenia, and those with two parents have about a 45% risk (Erlenmeyer-Kimling, Adamo et al., 1997; Gottesman, 1991). <u>Still, even children who have two biological parents with schizophrenia stand a better than even chance of not developing the disorder themselves.</u>

Finnish researchers followed 112 high-risk (HR) children (index cases who were adopted away at birth) (Tienari et al., 1987, 1990, 2006). These index cases, which were compared with a reference group of 135 cases, matched adopted children of nonschizophrenic biological parents. Evidence showed a much higher rate of schizophrenia in the index cases than the control cases, 5% versus 1% respectively (Tienari, 1991, 1992).

Consistent with the diathesis-stress model, environmental factors appear to have played a role in the Finnish study. Disturbed rearing in adoptive families predicted the development of schizophrenia (Tienari, Wahlberg, & Wynne, 2006). Moreover, index children reared by disturbed adoptive families were more likely to have developed other serious psychological problems, such as borderline personality, than those reared by more functional families. Some of the disturbed families were rigid and tended to cope with family conflict by denying it. Others were chaotic; they showed low levels of trust and high levels of anxiety. The evidence from the Finnish study indicates that a combination of genetic factors and a disruptive family environment increases the risk of schizophrenia. A drawback of the Finnish study, however, was that it was not possible to determine whether disturbed family relationships represented the reaction of the families to the emergence of behavioural problems in their troubled offspring, or, instead, were a contributing factor in their own right (Kendler & Prescott, 2006; Miklowitz, 2004).

Researchers have also compared HR children and other children to search for factors or *markers* that may predispose HR children to schizophrenia (e.g., Szymanski, Kane, & Lieberman, 1991). If we understand these early indicators, we may be able to understand the processes that lead to schizophrenia. We may also be able to identify children at greatest risk and devise intervention programs that may possibly prevent the development of the disorder.

The best-known longitudinal study of HR children was undertaken by Sarnoff Mednick and his colleagues in Denmark. In 1962, the Mednick group identified 207 HR children (those whose mothers had schizophrenia) and 104 reference subjects who were matched for factors such as gender, social class, age, and education but whose mothers did not have schizophrenia (Mednick, Parnas, & Schulsinger, 1987). The children from both groups ranged in age from 10 to 20 years, with a mean of 15 years. None showed signs of disturbance when first interviewed.

Later, at an average age of 20, the children were re-examined. By then, 20 of the HR children were found to have demonstrated abnormal behaviour, although not necessarily a schizophrenic episode (Mednick & Schulsinger, 1968). The children who showed abnormal behaviour, referred to as the HR "sick" group, were then compared with a matched group of 20 HR children from the original sample who remained well functioning (an HR "well" group)

Protective factors in high-risk children. A supportive and nurturing environment may reduce the likelihood of developing schizophrenia among high-risk children.

and a matched group of 20 low-risk (LR) subjects. It turned out that the mothers of the HR "well" offspring had experienced easier pregnancies and deliveries than those of the HR "sick" group or the LR group. Seventy percent of the mothers of the HR "sick" children had serious complications during pregnancy or delivery. Perhaps, consistent with the diathesis-stress model, complications during pregnancy, childbirth, or shortly after birth cause brain damage (a stress factor) that in combination with a genetic vulnerability leads to severe psychological disorders in later life. A study in Finland provided a supportive link in showing an association between fetal and postnatal abnormalities and the development of schizophrenia in adulthood (Jones et al., 1998). The low rate of complications during pregnancy and birth in the HR "well" group in the Danish study suggests that normal pregnancies and births may actually help protect HR children from developing abnormal behaviour patterns (Mednick, Parnas, & Schulsinger, 1987).

Evaluation of these same HR subjects in the late 1980s, when they averaged 42 years of age and had passed through the period of greatest risk for development of schizophrenia, showed a significantly higher percentage of schizophrenia in the HR group than the LR comparison group, 16% versus 2% respectively (Parnas et al., 1993). These results, like those of the Finnish study, show a strong familial association for schizophrenia between mothers and their children. An Israeli study paralleled the Danish and Finnish studies in finding a significantly greater risk of schizophrenia in a sample of HR children (8% with diagnosed schizophrenia) as compared to LR controls (0%) by the age of 30 (Ingraham et al., 1995).

Evidence from longitudinal studies of HR children indicates that environmental factors, including quality of parenting and possible complications occurring prenatally or shortly after birth, may interact with genetic factors in the causal pathway leading to schizophrenia. Certain environmental factors, such as good parenting, may actually have a protective role in preventing the development of the disorder in people at increased genetic risk. In support of the role of early environmental influences, Mednick and his colleagues found that HR children who developed schizophrenia had poorer relationships with their parents than did HR children who did not go on to develop the disorder (Mednick et al., 1987). The presence of childhood behaviour problems may also be a marker for the later development of schizophrenia-related disorders in HR children (Amminger et al., 1999).

In the next section, we go on to consider the role of family factors in schizophrenia.

Family Theories

Disturbed family relationships have long been regarded as playing a role in the development and course of schizophrenia (Miklowitz, 2004). Early family theories of schizophrenia focused on the role of a "pathogenic" family member, such as the **schizophrenogenic mother** (Fromm-Reichmann, 1948, 1950). In what some feminists view as historic psychiatric sexism, the schizophrenogenic mother was described as cold, aloof, overprotective, and domineering. She was characterized as stripping her children of self-esteem, stifling their independence, and forcing them into dependency on her. Children reared by such mothers were believed to be at special risk for developing schizophrenia if their fathers were passive and failed to counteract the pathogenic influences of the mother. Despite extensive research, however, mothers of people who develop schizophrenia do not fit the stereotypical picture of the schizophrenogenic mother (Neill, 1990).

In the 1950s, family theorists began to focus on the role of disturbed communications in the family. One of the more prominent theories, put forth by Gregory Bateson and his colleagues (Bateson, Jackson, Haley, & Weakland, 1956), was that **double-bind communications** contributed to the development of schizophrenia. A double-bind communication transmits two mutually incompatible messages. In a double-bind communication with a child, a mother might freeze up when the child approaches her and then scold the child for keeping a distance. Whatever the child does, she or he is wrong. With repeated exposure to such double binds, the child's thinking may become disorganized and chaotic. The double-binding mother prevents discussion of her inconsistencies because she cannot admit to herself that she is unable to tolerate closeness. Note this vignette:

> A young man who had fairly well recovered from an acute schizophrenic episode was visited in the hospital by his mother. He was glad to see her and impulsively put his arm around her shoulders whereupon she stiffened. He withdrew his arm and she asked, "Don't you love me anymore?" He then blushed and she said, "Dear, you must not be so easily embarrassed and afraid of your feelings." The patient was able to stay with her only a few minutes more and following her departure he assaulted an aide.
>
> BATESON ET AL., 1956, P. 251

Perhaps double-bind communications serve as a source of family stress that increases the risk of schizophrenia in genetically vulnerable individuals. In more recent years, investigators have broadened the investigation of family factors in schizophrenia by viewing the family in terms of a system of relationships among the members, rather than singling out mother–child or father–child interactions. Research has begun to identify stressful factors in the family that may interact with a genetic vulnerability in leading to the development of schizophrenia. Two principal sources of family stress that have been studied are patterns of deviant communications and negative emotional expression in the family.

Communication Deviance Communication deviance describes a pattern characterized by unclear, vague, disruptive, or fragmented parental communication and by parental inability to focus in on what the child is saying (Kymalainen, Weisman, Resales, & Armesto, 2006). Parents high in communication deviance tend to attack their children personally rather than offer constructive criticism and may subject them to double-bind communications. They also tend to interrupt the child with intrusive, negative comments. They are prone to telling the child what she or he "really" thinks rather than allowing the child to formulate her or his own thoughts and feelings. Parents of people with schizophrenia show higher levels of communication deviance than parents of people without schizophrenia (Kymalainen et al., 2006).

Communication deviance may be one of the stress-related factors that increase the risk of development of schizophrenia in genetically vulnerable individuals (Kymalainen et al., 2006). Then, too, the causal pathway may work in the opposite direction. Perhaps communication deviance is a parental reaction to the behaviour of disturbed children. Parents

schizophrenogenic mother Type of mother, described as cold but also overprotective, who was believed to be capable of causing schizophrenia in her children. Research has failed to support the validity of this concept.

double-bind communications Pattern of communication involving the transmission of contradictory or mixed messages without acknowledgment of the inherent conflict; posited by some theorists to play a role in the development of schizophrenia.

may learn to use odd language as a way of coping with children who continually interrupt and confront them (Miklowitz, 2004). Or perhaps parents and children share genetic traits that become expressed as disturbed communications and increased vulnerability toward schizophrenia, without there being a causal link between the two.

Expressed Emotion Another measure of disturbed family communications is called expressed emotion (EE). EE involves the tendency of family members to be hostile, critical, and unsupportive of their schizophrenic family members. <u>People with schizophrenia whose families are high in EE tend to show poorer adjustment and have higher rates of relapse following release from the hospital than those with more supportive families</u> (Miklowitz, 2004). Expressed emotion in relatives is also associated with a greater risk of relapse from other disorders, such as major depression and eating disorders (Butzlaff & Hooley, 1998).

Low-EE families may actually serve to protect or buffer the family member with schizophrenia from the adverse impact of outside stressors and help prevent recurrent episodes (Strachan, 1986) (see Figure 12.4 below). Yet family interactions are a two-way street. Family members and patients influence each other and are influenced in turn. Disruptive behaviours by the schizophrenic family member frustrate other members of the family, prompting them to respond to the person in a less supportive and more critical and hostile way. This in turn can exacerbate the schizophrenia patient's disruptive behaviour (Miklowitz, 2004).

Families of people with schizophrenia tend to have little if any preparation or training for coping with the stressful demands of caring for them. Rather than focusing so much on the negative influence of high-EE family members, we should learn to better understand the negative day-to-day interactions between people with schizophrenia and their family members that lead to high levels of expressed emotion. Recent evidence shows that families can be helped to reduce the level of expressed emotion (Miklowitz, 2004).

Research on expressed emotion and family stress factors helps focus attention on the need for family-intervention programs (reviewed on page 459 in this chapter) that help prepare families for the burdens of caregiving and assist them in learning more adaptive ways of relating to one another. This, in turn, may reduce the stress imposed on the family member with schizophrenia and improve family harmony.

Family Factors in Schizophrenia: Causes or Sources of Stress? No evidence supports the belief that family factors, such as negative family interactions, lead to schizophrenia in children who do not have a genetic vulnerability. What then is the role of family factors in schizophrenia? In the diathesis-stress model, disturbed patterns of emotional interaction and communication in the family represent a source of potential stress that may increase the risks of developing schizophrenia among people with a genetic predisposition for the disorder. Perhaps these increased risks could be minimized or eliminated if families are taught to handle stress and to be less critical and more supportive of the members of their families with schizophrenia. Counselling programs that help family members of people with chronic schizophrenia learn to express their feelings without attacking or criticizing the person with the disorder may prevent family conflicts that damage the person's adjustment (Miklowitz, 2004). The family member with schizophrenia may also benefit from efforts to reduce the level of contact with relatives who fail to respond to family interventions.

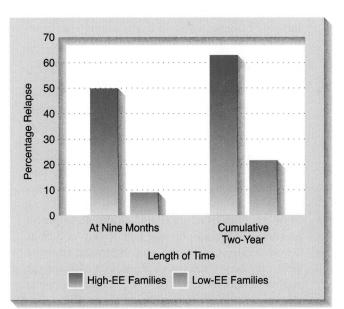

FIGURE 12.4 Relapse rates of people with schizophrenia in high- and low-EE families.
People with schizophrenia whose families are high in expressed emotion (EE) are at greater risk of relapse than those whose families are low in EE. Whereas low-EE families may help protect the family member with schizophrenia from environmental stressors, high-EE families may impose additional stress.

Source: Adapted from Leff & Vaughn (1981).

Theoretical Perspectives

Review It

- **How is schizophrenia conceptualized in traditional psychodynamic theory and learning perspectives?** In the traditional psychodynamic model, schizophrenia represents a regression to a psychological state corresponding to early infancy in which the proddings of the id produce bizarre, socially deviant behaviour and give rise to hallucinations and delusions. Learning theorists propose that some form of schizophrenic behaviour may result from a lack of social reinforcement, which leads to gradual detachment from the social environment and increased attention to an inner world of fantasy. Modelling and selective reinforcement of bizarre behaviour may explain some schizophrenic behaviours in a hospital setting.

- **What do we know about the biological bases of schizophrenia?** Compelling evidence for a strong genetic component in schizophrenia comes from studies of family patterns of schizophrenia, twin studies, and adoption studies. The mode of genetic transmission remains unknown. Most researchers believe the neurotransmitter dopamine plays a role in schizophrenia, especially in the more flagrant features of the disorder. Viral factors may also be involved, but definite proof of viral involvement is lacking. Evidence of brain dysfunctions and structural damage in schizophrenia is accumulating, but researchers are uncertain about causal pathways.

- **How is schizophrenia conceptualized in the diathesis-stress model?** The diathesis-stress model posits that schizophrenia results from an interaction of a genetic predisposition (the diathesis) and environmental stressors (e.g., family conflict, child abuse, emotional deprivation, loss of supportive figures, early brain trauma).

- **How are family factors related to the development and course of schizophrenia?** Family factors such as communication deviance and expressed emotion (EE) may act as sources of stress that increase the risk of development or recurrence of schizophrenia among people with a genetic predisposition.

Define It

cross-fostering study   schizophrenogenic mother
dopamine theory   double-bind communications
hippocampus   amygdala

Recall It*

1. Derek is receiving treatment for schizophrenia in a psychiatric hospital. His therapist notices that much of his peculiar behaviour on the ward is modelled after the behaviour of other patients who receive reinforcement from staff members in the form of extra attention. His therapist most likely identifies with a _____ orientation.

   a. psychodynamic
   b. humanistic
   c. social-cognitive
   d. biological

2. European studies on family incidence of schizophrenia are limited because _____.

   a. twins are not representative of people in general
   b. families share common environments as well as common genes
   c. there was no attempt to examine the degree of genetic relationships among family members
   d. schizophrenia occurred so rarely that it was impossible to examine genetic factors

3. The methodological approach, in which investigators compare the incidence of schizophrenia in adopted children whose biological parents either had or didn't have schizophrenia and who were reared by adoptive parents who either had or didn't have schizophrenia, is called a _____.

   a. twin-concordance study
   b. familial association study
   c. cross-fostering study
   d. cross-generational study

4. The _____ model posits that schizophrenia involves an interaction of a genetic predisposition with exposure to levels of stress that exceed the individual's stress tolerance.

   a. bivariate causal
   b. diathesis-stress
   c. distinct heterogeneity
   d. multifactorial-polygenic

5. A family factor linked to an increased risk of relapse in people with schizophrenia is _____.

   a. communication deviance
   b. family size
   c. sibling rivalry
   d. expressed emotion

* Recall It answers can be found on the Companion Website for this text.

TREATMENT APPROACHES

There is no cure for schizophrenia. Treatment of schizophrenia is generally multifaceted, incorporating pharmacological, psychological, and rehabilitative approaches. Most people treated for schizophrenia in organized mental health settings receive some form of antipsychotic medication, which is intended to control more flagrant behaviour patterns such as hallucinations and delusions and decrease the risk of recurrent episodes.

Biological Approaches

The advent in the 1950s of antipsychotic drugs—also referred to as major tranquillizers or *neuroleptics*—revolutionized the treatment of schizophrenia and provided the impetus for large-scale releases of mental patients into the community (deinstitutionalization). The first of these drugs, chlorpromazine (Largactil) was introduced to North America by McGill University psychiatrist Heinz Lehmann (Lehmann & Hanrahan, 1954). Antipsychotic medication helped control the more flagrant behaviour patterns of schizophrenia and reduced the need for long-term hospitalization when taken on a maintenance basis (Sheitman, Kinon, Ridgway, & Lieberman, 1998). Yet for many chronic schizophrenia patients today, entering a hospital is like going through a revolving door. That is, they are repeatedly admitted and discharged within a relatively brief time frame. Many are simply discharged to the streets once they are stabilized on medication and receive little if any follow-up care or available housing. This often leads to a pattern of chronic homelessness punctuated by brief stays in the hospital. Only a small proportion of people with schizophrenia who are discharged from long-term care facilities are successfully reintegrated into the community (Bellack & Mueser, 1990).

Commonly used antipsychotic drugs include the following phenothiazines: *chlorpromazine* (Largactil), *thioridazine* (Mellaril), *trifluoperazine* (Stelazine), and *fluphenazine* (Moditen), as well as *haloperidol* (Haldol), which is chemically distinct from the phenothiazines but produces similar effects.

Although we can't say with certainty how these drugs work, it appears they derive their therapeutic effect from blocking dopamine receptors in the brain. This reduces dopamine activity, which seems to quell the more flagrant signs of schizophrenia such as hallucinations and delusions. The effectiveness of antipsychotic drugs has been repeatedly demonstrated in double-blind, placebo-controlled studies (Kane, 1996). Yet a substantial minority of people with schizophrenia receive little benefit from traditional neuroleptics, and no clear-cut factors determine who will best respond (Kane & Marder, 1993).

The major risk of long-term treatment with neuroleptic drugs (possibly excluding clozapine and other new-generation drugs) is a potentially disabling side effect called **tardive dyskinesia** (TD). TD is an involuntary movement disorder that can affect any body part (Hansen, Casey, & Hoffman, 1997). It is irreversible in many cases, even when the neuroleptic medication is withdrawn. It occurs most often in patients who are treated with neuroleptics for six months or longer. TD can take different forms, the most common of which is frequent eye blinking. Common signs of the disorder include involuntary chewing and eye movements, lip smacking and puckering, facial grimacing, and involuntary movements of the limbs and trunk. In some cases, the movement disorder is so severe

tardive dyskinesia Movement disorder characterized by involuntary movements of the face, mouth, neck, trunk, or extremities caused by long-term use of antipsychotic medications.

that patients have difficulties breathing, talking, or eating. Overall, about one in four people receiving long-term treatment with neuroleptics eventually develop TD (Jeste & Caligiuri, 1993).

Tardive dyskinesia is more common among older people and women (Hansen et al., 1997). Unfortunately, we lack a safe and effective treatment for TD (Egan, Apud, & Wyatt, 1997; Sheitman et al., 1998). Although TD tends to improve gradually or stabilize over a period of years, many people with TD remain persistently and severely disabled.

The risk of these potentially disabling side effects requires physicians to carefully weigh the risks and benefits of long-term treatment with these drugs. Investigators have altered drug regimens in an attempt to reduce the risk of TD, such as by stopping medication in stable outpatients and starting it again when early symptoms reappear. However, intermittent medication schedules are associated with a twofold increase in the risk of relapse and have not been shown to lower the risk of TD (Kane, 1996).

A new generation of drugs, called atypical antipsychotic drugs (clozapine, risperidone, and olanzapine are examples), have been introduced and offer the promise of controlling schizophrenic symptoms with fewer neurological side effects than conventional antipsychotics (Kapur & Remington, 2001). They may also be more effective in treating negative symptoms of schizophrenia than conventional antipsychotics. One of these atypical antipsychotics, clozapine, is the only known drug that carries a minimal risk of TD (Conley & Buchanan, 1997; Kane, 1996). Clozapine appears to be more effective than conventional antipsychotics in reducing the symptoms of schizophrenia patients, including patients who have failed to respond to other antipsychotics (Breier et al., 1999; Wahlbeck, Cheine, Essali, & Adams, 1999). However, other side effects limit its use, especially the risk of agranulocytosis, a potentially lethal disorder in which the body produces inadequate supplies of white blood cells. The disorder affects 1% to 2% of patients who use the drug (Kane & Marder, 1993). There are also promising findings that olanzapine may reduce the risk of TD relative to conventional antipsychotics (Tollefson, Beasley, Tamura, Tran, & Potvin, 1997), but more research is needed to reach a more definitive conclusion (Egan et al., 1997).

A panel of Canadian experts on schizophrenia (psychologists and psychiatrists) published a set of clinical practice guidelines on the treatment of the disorder (Working Group for the Canadian Psychiatric Association and Canadian Alliance for Research on Schizophrenia, 1998). The guidelines, based on the current state of knowledge, are similar to those of other countries. According to the guidelines, antipsychotic medications are the most effective treatment available, especially when combined with psychoeducational interventions. Antipsychotic drugs help control the more flagrant or bizarre features of schizophrenia, but are not a cure. People with chronic schizophrenia typically receive maintenance doses of antipsychotic drugs once their flagrant symptoms abate. The working group notes that the relapse rate may be as high as 90% in the first year after hospital discharge if the patient discontinues medication. Staying on medication can reduce the relapse rate to about 40% (Hogarty, 1993). Still, not all people with schizophrenia require antipsychotic medication to maintain themselves in the community. Unfortunately, no one can yet predict which patients can manage effectively without continued medication.

Drug therapy needs to be supplemented with psychoeducational programs that help schizophrenia patients develop better social skills and adjust to demands of community living. A wide array of treatment components are needed within a comprehensive model of care, including such elements as antipsychotic medication, medical care, family therapy, social skills training, crisis intervention, rehabilitation services, and housing and other social services (Marder et al., 1996; Penn & Mueser, 1996). Programs also need to ensure a continuity of care between the hospital and the community.

Psychoanalytic Approaches

Freud did not believe traditional psychoanalysis was well suited to the treatment of schizophrenia. The withdrawal into a fantasy world that typifies schizophrenia prevents the individual with schizophrenia from forming a meaningful relationship with the psychoanalyst. The techniques of classical psychoanalysis, Freud wrote, must "be replaced by others; and we do not know yet whether we shall succeed in finding a substitute" (Arieti, 1974, p. 532).

Other psychoanalysts such as Harry Stack Sullivan and Frieda Fromm-Reichmann adapted psychoanalytic techniques specifically for the treatment of schizophrenia. However, research has failed to demonstrate the effectiveness of psychoanalytic or psychodynamic therapy for schizophrenia. In light of negative findings, some critics have argued that further research on the use of psychodynamic therapies for treating schizophrenia is not warranted (e.g., Klerman, 1984).

Learning-Based Approaches

Although few behaviour therapists believe faulty learning causes schizophrenia, learning-based interventions have been shown to be effective in modifying schizophrenic behaviour and assisting people with the disorder in developing more adaptive behaviours that can help them adjust more effectively to living in the community. Therapy methods include techniques such as (1) selective reinforcement of behaviour (like providing attention for appropriate behaviour and extinguishing bizarre verbalizations through withdrawal of attention); (2) the token economy, in which individuals on inpatient units are rewarded for appropriate behaviour with tokens, such as plastic chips, that can be exchanged for tangible reinforcers such as desirable goods or privileges; and (3) social-skills training, in which clients are taught conversational skills and other appropriate social behaviours through coaching, modelling, behaviour rehearsal, and feedback.

Promising results have emerged from studies applying intensive learning-based approaches in hospital settings. A classic study by Paul and Lentz (1977) showed that a psychosocial treatment program based on a token-economy system improved adaptive behaviour in the hospital, decreased need for medication, and lengthened community tenure following release in relation to a traditional, custodial-type treatment condition and a *milieu* approach that emphasized patient participation in decision making (see Figure 12.5).

Overall, token economies have proven to be more effective than intensive milieu treatment and traditional custodial treatment in improving social functioning and reducing psychotic behaviour (Glynn & Mueser, 1992; Mueser & Liberman, 1995). However, the many prerequisites may limit the applicability of this approach. Such programs require strong administrative support, skilled treatment leaders, extensive staff training, and continuous quality control (Glynn & Mueser, 1986).

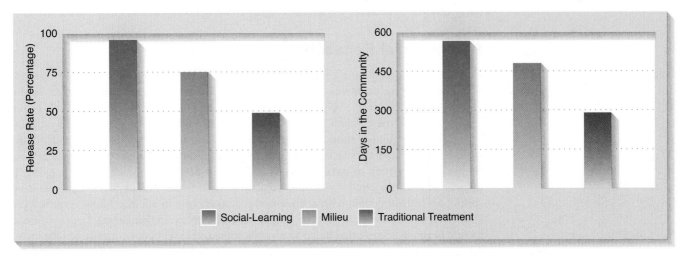

FIGURE 12.5 Some measures of outcome from the Paul and Lentz study.
This figure shows the release rates and community tenure (days in the community) of people with schizophrenia in the three conditions studied by Paul and Lentz: (1) social-learning-based treatment, (2) milieu treatment, and (3) traditional hospital treatment. Nearly all of the subjects in the social-learning program (97.5%) were able to be discharged and to remain in the community for a minimum of 90 days, as compared to 71% of the milieu-therapy participants and 45% of the control (standard treatment) participants. Subjects in the social-learning program also remained in the community longer than subjects who received the other conditions.

Source: Glynn & Mueser (1986).

Social-Skills Training Social-skills training (SST) involves programs that help individuals acquire a range of social and vocational skills. People with schizophrenia are often deficient in basic social skills involving assertiveness, interview skills, and general conversational skills—skills that may be needed to adjust successfully to community living. Controlled studies have shown that SST can improve a wide range of social skills, increase social adjustment, and reduce psychiatric symptoms in persons with schizophrenia and improve community functioning (Hunter, Bedell, & Corrigan, 1997; Marder et al., 1996; Penn, 1998). Social-skills training has also been shown to reduce relapse rates during the first year following treatment (Bellack & Mueser, 1993). Researchers in Calgary found that the benefits of a short (nine-week) social-skills training program tended to be lost over time (Dobson, McDougall, Busheikin, & Aldous, 1995), suggesting that long-term programs may be required, at least for some people with schizophrenia. It remains to be seen whether social-skills training can produce a substantial payoff in helping patients adapt to community living (Dilk & Bond, 1996; Penn, 1998).

Although different approaches to skills training have been developed, the basic model uses role-playing exercises in a group format. Participants practise skills such as starting or maintaining conversations with new acquaintances and receive feedback and reinforcement from the therapist and other group members. The first step might be a dry run in which the participant role-plays the targeted behaviour, such as asking strangers for bus directions. The therapist and other group members then praise the effort and provide constructive feedback. Role-playing is augmented by techniques such as modelling (observation of the therapist or other group members enacting the desired behaviour), direct instruction (specific directions for enacting the desired behaviour), shaping (reinforcement for successive approximations to the target behaviour), and coaching (therapist use of verbal or nonverbal prompts to elicit a particular desired behaviour in the role play). Participants are given homework assignments to practise the behaviours in the settings in which they live, such as on the hospital ward or in the community. The aim is to enhance generalization or transfer of training to other settings. Training sessions may also be run in stores, restaurants, schools, and other real-life settings.

Multifaceted cognitive-behavioural interventions, which can include social-skills training and other techniques, appear to be helpful (Norman & Townsend, 1999; Rector & Beck, 2001). Cognitive-behavioural interventions can include teaching patients skills for managing the stress in their lives and showing them ways of managing their symptoms. For example, they can include helping patients identify triggers that make their symptoms worse (e.g., anxiety, family conflicts) and teaching them skills for dealing with the triggers (e.g., relaxation training, cognitive restructuring, conflict-negotiating skills).

Psychosocial Rehabilitation

People with schizophrenia typically have difficulties functioning in social and occupational roles. These problems limit their ability to adjust to community life even in the absence of overt psychotic behaviour. Many older, long-hospitalized individuals who have been resettled in the community are particularly ill-prepared to handle the tasks of daily living, such as cooking, shopping, or travelling around town. Many younger individuals with schizophrenia have markedly deficient social skills, even though they have spent only short periods of time in mental hospitals (Anthony & Liberman, 1986). As a result, a number of self-help groups and more structured psychosocial rehabilitation centres have sprung up to help people with schizophrenia find a place in society. Many centres were launched by nonprofessionals or by people with schizophrenia themselves, largely because mental health agencies often failed to provide comparable services (Anthony & Liberman, 1986).

Social-skills training can be incorporated into cognitive-behaviour therapy for schizophrenia. Research from investigators around the world, including studies done at the University of Western Ontario and the University of Toronto, have shown that cognitive-behavioural treatment programs (involving stress management, social-skills training, and other techniques) can be useful, especially for people with schizophrenia who have failed to benefit fully from antipsychotic medication (Rathod & Turkington, 2005). This, combined with family intervention programs and community programs, can reduce the risk of relapse (Rathod & Turkington, 2005).

Community programs typically offer services such as housing, as well as job and educational opportunities. These programs often make use of skills-training approaches to help clients learn how to handle money, resolve disputes with family members, develop friendships, take buses, cook their own meals, shop, and so on.

The rehabilitation model teaches that people with emotional or physical disabilities can achieve their potentials if they are given the support and structure they need and if the expectations and demands placed on them are consistent with their capabilities. Both the client and the family should be helped to adjust their expectations to attainable levels (Anthony & Liberman, 1986).

Family-Intervention Programs

Family conflicts and negative family interactions can heap stress on family members with schizophrenia, increasing the risk of recurrent episodes (Addington, Collins, McCleery, & Addington, 2005). Researchers and clinicians have worked with families of people with schizophrenia to help them cope with the burdens of care and assist them in developing more co-operative, less confrontational ways of relating to others. The specific components involved in family interventions vary among programs, but they tend to share certain common features, such as a focus on the practical aspects of everyday living, educating family members about schizophrenia, teaching them how to relate in a less hostile way to family members with schizophrenia, improving communication in the family, and fostering effective problem-solving and coping skills for handling family problems and disputes.

Structured family-intervention programs have been shown to reduce rates of relapse among schizophrenia patients (Addington et al., 2005). However, the benefits appear to be modest and questions remain about whether recurrences are prevented or merely delayed. We should also note that not all people with schizophrenia live with their families. Perhaps similar psychoeducational programs can be applied to nonfamily environments where people live with schizophrenia, such as foster-care homes or board-and-care homes.

In sum, no single treatment approach meets all the needs of people with schizophrenia. The conceptualization of schizophrenia as a lifelong disability underscores the need for long-term treatment interventions involving antipsychotic medication, family interventions, psychological interventions, vocational training, and social-system support such as provision of decent housing. These interventions should be co-ordinated and integrated within a comprehensive model of treatment to be most effective in helping the individual achieve maximal social adjustment (Coursey et al., 1997). Treatment services are also more likely to improve client functioning in certain areas, such as improving work or independent living, when they are specifically targeted toward those areas (Brekke, Long, Nesbitt, & Sobel, 1997). This model may consist of drug therapy, hospitalization as needed, inpatient learning-based programs, family-intervention programs, skills-training programs, social self-help clubs, and rehabilitation programs.

Early-Intervention Programs

The treatment approaches described so far in this chapter were all intended for people with full-blown schizophrenia. More recently, there have been important developments in treating symptoms before they become very severe. Such programs are important because the earlier a person receives treatment, the better the outcome in terms of reducing symptoms and improving daily functioning (Killackey & Yung, 2007). There are two main forms of early intervention. The first is to initiate treatment as early as possible once the person has developed schizophrenia, using the treatments described above. The second is to intervene *before* the onset of schizophrenia (i.e., prevention programs). This involves accurately identifying people at high risk for schizophrenia, as suggested by (a) a high-risk age (late teens or early 20s), (b) recent deterioration in social functioning, and (c) a family history of psychosis. Such high-risk people are then offered treatment—typically cognitive-behaviour therapy or antipsychotic medication (Killackey & Yung, 2007).

Research suggests that treating the symptoms as early as possible is important in improving outcomes (Malla, Norman, & Joober, 2005). However, further studies are needed to fully evaluate the benefits of treatments aimed at preventing schizophrenia (Killackey & Yung, 2007; Malla et al., 2005).

STUDY BREAK

Treatment Approaches

Review It

- **How does the treatment of schizophrenia involve a multifaceted approach?** Contemporary treatment approaches tend to be multifaceted, incorporating pharmacological and psychosocial approaches. Antipsychotic medication is not a cure but tends to stem the more flagrant aspects of the disorder and to reduce the need for hospitalization and the risk of recurrent episodes.

- **What types of psychosocial interventions have shown promising results?** These are principally learning-based approaches, such as token economy systems and social-skills training. They help increase the adaptive behaviour of schizophrenia patients. Psychosocial-rehabilitation approaches help people with schizophrenia adapt more successfully to occupational and social roles in the community. Family-intervention programs help families cope with the burdens of care, communicate more clearly, and learn more helpful ways of relating to the patient.

Define It

tardive dyskinesia

Recall It*

1. The most common treatment for people with schizophrenia involves _____.
   a. electroconvulsive therapy
   b. antipsychotic medication
   c. psychosurgery
   d. insight-oriented therapy

2. The neurological disorder caused by exposure to antipsychotic drugs and characterized by involuntary movements such as eye blinking, lip smacking, and facial grimacing is called _____.
   a. tardive dyskinesia
   b. Wernicke's syndrome
   c. institutionalization syndrome
   d. Huntington's chorea

3. Each of the following is an example of a learning-based therapeutic technique used in the treatment of schizophrenia EXCEPT _____.
   a. reinforcement of desirable behaviours
   b. token economy programs
   c. social-skills training
   d. aversive conditioning to eliminate undesirable behaviours

4. Structured family intervention programs have been shown to _____.
   a. prevent the development of schizophrenia in people at risk
   b. reduce the costs of hospitalization
   c. reduce the rates of relapse in schizophrenia patients
   d. increase the effectiveness of antipsychotic medication

* Recall It answers can be found on the Companion Website for this text.

Think About It

- What are the relative risks and benefits of antipsychotic medication? Do you believe that people with schizophrenia should be treated indefinitely with these drugs? Why or why not?
- Why is medication alone not sufficient to treat schizophrenia?

WEBLINKS

Schizophrenia Society of Canada
www.schizophrenia.ca
This site offers information in both English and French about the causes and treatments of schizophrenia. Contains a number of useful links.

NIMH's Schizophrenia Page
www.nimh.nih.gov/healthinformation/schizophreniamenu.cfm
The National Institutes of Mental Health's schizophrenia page provides useful information on the disorder.

Schizophrenia Resources
www.chovil.com/six.html
This site contains numerous links to sites offering information about various aspects of schizophrenia, including descriptions of the experience of having schizophrenia from people who suffer from the disorder.

Schizophrenia.com
www.schizophrenia.com
Another informationally rich website, containing many links concerning schizophrenia.

Schizoaffective Disorder
www.noah-health.org/en/mental/disorders/schizo.html
This website provides information on schizoaffective disorder.

Schizophrenia

Main Types of Schizophrenia Symptoms
(Organized according to the 3-dimensional model)

Psychotic Dimension

Examples
- Hallucinations
- Delusions

Negative Dimension

Examples
- Flat affect
- Poverty of speech and thought

Disorganized Dimension

Examples
- Inappropriate affect
- Disordered thought and speech

Subtypes of Schizophrenia

Paranoid Type

- Preoccupation with one or more delusions, or preoccupation with frequent auditory hallucinations
- Does not have disorganized behaviour or flat or inappropriate affect

Disorganized Type

- Confused behaviour, incoherent speech, hallucinations, disorganized delusions, inappropriate (e.g., silly) affect

Catatonic Type

- Markedly impaired motor behaviour, stupor, mannerisms, bizarre postures, waxy flexibility

Undifferentiated Type

- Fails to meet specifications for any of single one of the above three types, or has features of more than one of the above types

Residual Type

- No prominent psychotic features but still has features of a previous episode of schizophrenia (e.g., blunted affect)

CHAPTER 13

Abnormal Behaviour in Childhood and Adolescence

CHAPTER OUTLINE

Pervasive Development Disorders
Mental Retardation
Learning Disorders
Attention-Deficit and Disruptive Behaviour Disorder
Anxiety and Depression

Did You Know That...

See the underlined text on the pages indicated below for more information on these interesting and often misunderstood facts.

- Many behaviour patterns considered normal for children would be considered abnormal in adults? (p. 465)

- Maternal smoking during pregnancy may contribute to the development of attention-deficit/hyperactivity disorder (ADHD) in children? (p. 475)

- Some people can recall verbatim every story they read in a newspaper? (p. 476)

- Most children with ADHD are given stimulants to help calm them down? (p. 486)

- Major depression can occur in young children? (p. 492)

- Some children refuse to go to school because they believe terrible things may happen to their parents while they are away? (p. 493)

PSYCHOLOGICAL PROBLEMS IN childhood and adolescence often have a special poignancy. They affect children at ages when they have little capacity to cope. Some of these problems, such as autism and mental retardation, prevent children from fulfilling their developmental potentials. Some psychological problems in childhood and adolescence mirror the types of problems found in adults—problems such as mood and anxiety disorders. In some cases, the problems are unique to childhood, such as separation anxiety; in others, like attention-deficit/hyperactivity disorder (ADHD), the problems manifest differently in childhood than in adulthood.

To determine what is normal and abnormal among children and adolescents, not only do we consider the criteria outlined in Chapter 1, we also weigh what is to be expected given a child's age, gender, family and cultural background, and the sundry developmental transformations that are taking place. Many problems are first identified when a child enters school. They may have existed earlier but were tolerated or unrecognized as problematic in the home. Sometimes, the stress of starting school contributes to their onset. Keep in mind, however, that what is socially acceptable at one age, such as intense fear of strangers at about nine months, may be socially unacceptable at more advanced ages. Many behaviour patterns that would be considered abnormal among adults—such as intense fear of strangers and lack of bladder control—are perfectly normal for children at certain ages.

Psychotherapy with children has been approached from various perspectives and differs in important respects from therapy for adults. Children may not have the verbal skills to express their feelings through speech or the ability to sit in a chair through a therapy session. Therapy methods must be tailored to the level of the child's cognitive, physical, social, and emotional development. For example, psychodynamic therapists have developed techniques of **play therapy** in which children enact family conflicts symbolically through their play activities, such as by playacting with dolls or puppets. Or they might be given drawing materials and asked to draw pictures, in the belief that their drawings will reflect their underlying feelings.

Just how common are mental health problems among Canada's children and adolescents? Although we lack nationwide statistics, University of British Columbia researchers reviewed studies from Ontario, Quebec, the United States, and the United Kingdom that indicated that about 14% of children and adolescents have a mental disorder (Waddell, McEwan, Shepard, Offord, & Hua, 2005; Waddell & Shepherd, 2002). The four most common categories—anxiety disorders, conduct disorders, ADHD, and depressive disorders—account for nearly 90% of those mental disorders.

Despite the prevalence of psychological disorders among the young, fewer than a quarter of children and youth with mental disorders received specialized clinical services (Waddell et al., 2005; Waddell, Offord, Shepherd, Hua, & McEwan, 2002). Children who have internalized problems, such as anxiety and depression, are at higher risk of going untreated than are children with externalized problems (problems involving acting out or aggressive behaviour) that tend to be disruptive or annoying to others.

In this chapter, we examine a number of psychological disorders affecting children and adolescents. We examine the features of these disorders, their causes, and the treatments used to help children who suffer from them.

play therapy Form of psychodynamic therapy with children in which play activities and objects are used as a means of helping children symbolically enact family conflicts or express underlying feelings or personal problems.

PERVASIVE DEVELOPMENTAL DISORDERS

Pervasive developmental disorders (PPDs), which are also referred to as autistic spectrum disorders (Alberta Learning, 2003), involve markedly impaired behaviour or functioning in multiple areas of development. These disorders generally become evident in the first few years of life and are often associated with mental retardation (APA, 2000a). They were generally classified as forms of *psychoses* in early editions of the DSM, and were thought to reflect childhood forms of adult psychoses like schizophrenia because they share features such as social and emotional impairment, oddities of communication, and stereotyped motor behaviours. Research has shown that they are distinct from schizophrenia and other psychoses, however, and PPDs are now classified separately from psychotic disorders. The label of schizophrenia with childhood onset is reserved for the relatively rare instances in which schizophrenia develops in childhood (Jacobsen et al., 1997).

McGill University child research psychiatrist Eric Fombonne (2005; Fombonne, Zakarian, Bennett, Meng, & McLean-Heywood, 2006) estimates that the prevalence of all forms of PDDs is 0.6% to 0.7%. The DSM (APA, 2000a) includes the following PDDs: autistic disorder, Rett's disorder, childhood disintegrative disorder, Asperger's disorder, and pervasive developmental disorder not otherwise specified. The major type of pervasive developmental disorder, which is our focus here, is autism or autistic disorder.

Autism

Peter nursed eagerly, sat, and walked at the expected ages. Yet some of his behaviour made us vaguely uneasy. He never put anything in his mouth. Not his fingers nor his toys—nothing. . . . More troubling was the fact that Peter didn't look at us, or smile, and wouldn't play the games that seemed as much a part of babyhood as diapers. He rarely laughed, and when he did, it was at things that didn't seem funny to us. He didn't cuddle, but sat upright in my lap, even when I rocked him. But children differ and we were content to let Peter be himself. We thought it hilarious when my brother, visiting us when Peter was eight months old, observed, "That kid has no social instincts, whatsoever." Although Peter was a first child, he was not isolated. I frequently put him in his playpen in front of the house, where the schoolchildren stopped to play with him as they passed. He ignored them, too.

It was Kitty, a personality kid, born two years later, whose responsiveness emphasized the degree of Peter's difference. When I went into her room for the late feeding, her little head bobbed up and she greeted me with a smile that reached from her head to her toes. And the realization of that difference chilled me more than the wintry bedroom. Peter's babbling had not turned into speech by the time he was three. His play was solitary and repetitive. He tore paper into long thin strips, bushel baskets of it every day. He spun the lids from my canning jars and became upset if we tried to divert him. Only rarely could I catch his eye, and then saw his focus change from me to the reflection in my glasses. . . .

[Peter's] adventures in our suburban neighbourhood had been unhappy. He had disregarded the universal rule that sand is to be kept in sandboxes, and the children themselves had punished him. He walked around a sad and solitary figure, always carrying a toy airplane, a toy he never played with. At that time, I had not heard the word that was to dominate our lives, to hover over every conversation, to sit through every meal beside us. That word was *autism*.

ADAPTED FROM EBERHARDY, 1967

Autism or *autistic disorder* is one of the severest disorders of childhood. It is a chronic, lifelong condition. Children with autism, like Peter, seem utterly alone in the world, despite parental efforts to bridge the gulf that divides them.

Autism derives from the Greek *autos*, meaning "self." The term *autism* was first used in 1906 by Swiss psychiatrist Eugen Bleuler to refer to a peculiar style of thinking among people with schizophrenia. (Autism is one of Bleuler's *four As*.) Autistic thinking is the tendency to view oneself as the centre of the universe, to believe that external events somehow refer to oneself. In 1943, another psychiatrist, Leo Kanner, applied the diagnosis "early infantile autism" to a group of disturbed children who seemed unable to relate to others, as if they lived in their own private worlds. Unlike children suffering from mental retardation, children with autism seemed to shut out any input from the outside world, creating a kind of "autistic aloneness" (Kanner, 1943).

Autism is a lifelong condition that spans all socioeconomic levels (Fombonne, 2005). It typically becomes evident in toddlers between 18 and 30 months of age (Rapin, 1997), and is four times more common in boys (Fombonne, 2005).

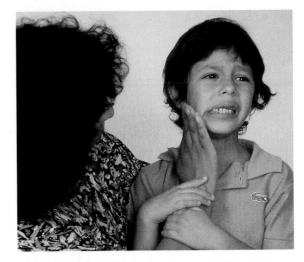

Autism. Autism, one of the most severe childhood disorders, is characterized by pervasive deficits in the ability to relate to and communicate with others, and by a restricted range of activities and interests. Children with autistic disorder lack the ability to relate to others and seem to live in their own private worlds.

Features of Autism Perhaps the most poignant feature of autism is the child's utter aloneness (see Table 13.1). Other features include language and communication problems and ritualistic or stereotyped behaviour. The child may also be mute, or if some language skills are present, they may be characterized by peculiar usage, as in echolalia (parroting back what the child has heard in a high-pitched monotone); pronoun reversals (using "you" or "he" instead of "I"); use of words that have meaning only to those who have intimate knowledge of the child; and tendencies to raise the voice at the end of sentences, as if asking a question. Nonverbal communication may also be impaired or absent. For example, children with autistic disorder may not engage in eye contact or display facial expressions. Although they may be unresponsive to others, researchers find

---

TABLE 13.1

Diagnostic Features of Autistic Disorder

A. Diagnosis requires a combination of features from the following groups. Not all of the features from each group need be present for a diagnosis to be made.

Impaired social interactions	1. Impairment in the nonverbal behaviours that normally regulate social interaction, such as facial expressiveness, posture, gestures, and eye contact 2. Does not develop age-appropriate peer relationships 3. Failure to express pleasure in the happiness of other people 4. Does not show social or emotional reciprocity (give and take)
Impaired social communication	1. Delay in development of spoken language (and no effort to compensate for this lack through gestures) 2. When speech development is adequate, there is nevertheless lack of ability to initiate or sustain conversation 3. Shows abnormalities in form or content of speech (e.g., stereotyped or repetitive speech, as in echolalia; idiosyncratic use of words; speaking about the self in the second or third person—using "you" or "he" to mean "I") 4. Does not show spontaneous social or imaginative (make-believe) play
Restricted, repetitive, and stereotyped behaviour patterns	1. Shows restricted range of interests 2. Insists on routines (e.g., always uses same route to go from one place to another) 3. Shows stereotyped movements (e.g., hand flicking, head banging, rocking, spinning) 4. Shows preoccupation with parts of objects (e.g., repetitive spinning of wheels of toy car) or unusual attachments to objects (e.g., carrying a piece of string)

B. Onset occurs prior to the age of three through a display of abnormal functioning in at least one of the following: social behaviour, communication, or imaginative play.

Source: Adapted from the DSM-IV-TR (APA, 2000a).

they are capable of displaying strong emotions, especially strong negative emotions like anger, sadness, and fear (Capps et al., 1993; Kasari, Sigman, Yirmiya, & Mundy, 1993).

A primary feature of autism is interminable, repeated, purposeless, stereotyped movements—twirling, flapping the hands, or rocking back and forth with the arms around the knees. Some children with autism mutilate themselves, even as they cry out in pain. They may bang their heads, slap their faces, bite their hands and shoulders, or pull out their hair. They may also throw sudden tantrums or panics. Another feature of autism is an aversion to environmental changes—a feature termed *preservation of sameness*. When familiar objects are moved even slightly from their usual places, children with autism may throw tantrums or cry continually until their placement is restored. Children with autistic disorder may also insist on eating the same food every day.

Children with autism are bound by ritual. The teacher of a five-year-old girl with autistic disorder learned to greet her every morning by saying, "Good morning, Lily, I am very, very glad to see you" (Diamond, Baldwin, & Diamond, 1963). Although Lily would not respond to the greeting, she would shriek if the teacher omitted even one of the *very*s.

Children who develop autism appear to have failed to develop a differentiated self-concept—a sense of themselves as distinct individuals (Toichi et al., 2002). Despite their unusual behaviour, autistic children are often quite attractive and can have an "intelligent look" about them. However, as measured by scores on standardized tests, their intellectual development tends to lag below the norm. International studies indicate that 30% of autistic subjects had mild to moderate levels of mental retardation and 40% had severe to profound levels (Fombonne, 2005). Even those who function at an average level of intelligence show deficits in activities requiring the ability to symbolize, such as recognizing emotions, engaging in symbolic play, and conceptual problem solving (Yirmiya & Sigman, 1991). They also display difficulty in attending to tasks that involve interacting with other people.

Theoretical Perspectives

Early views of autism focused on pathological family relationships. Kanner and his colleagues (e.g., Kanner & Eisenberg, 1955) suggested that children with autism were reared by cold, detached parents who were dubbed "emotional refrigerators." Psychoanalyst Bruno Bettelheim (1967) also focused on the family by suggesting that extreme self-absorption is the child's defence against parental rejection. The parents rear the child in an emotionally and socially desolate atmosphere in which the child's efforts to develop language and social skills wither. The child surrenders efforts to develop mastery over the external world and withdraws into a world of fantasy. The pathological insistence on preservation of sameness represents the child's rigid, defensive efforts to impose order and predictability.

Research, however, has not supported the assumption—devastating to many parents—that they are frosty and remote (Hoffmann & Prior, 1982). Of course, there is truth to the notion that children with autism and their parents do not relate to one another very well, but causal connections are clouded. Rather than rejecting their children and thus fostering autism, parents may grow somewhat aloof because their efforts to relate to their children repeatedly meet with failure. Aloofness then becomes a result of autism, not a cause.

Psychologist O. Ivar Lovaas and his colleagues (Lovaas, Koegel, & Schreibman, 1979) offer a cognitive-behavioural perspective on autism. They suggest that children with autism have perceptual deficits that limit them to processing only one stimulus at a time. As a result, they are slow to learn by means of classical conditioning (association of stimuli). From the learning theory perspective, children become attached to their primary caregivers because they are associated with primary reinforcers like food and hugging. Children with autism, however, attend either to the food or the cuddling and do not connect it with the parent.

Cognitive theorists have focused on the kinds of cognitive deficits shown by children with autism and the possible relationships among these deficits. Children with autism appear to have difficulty integrating information from various senses (Rutter, 1983). At times, they seem hypersensitive to stimulation. At other times they are so insensitive that an observer might wonder whether or not they are deaf. Perceptual and cognitive deficits seem to diminish their capacity to make use of information—to comprehend and apply social rules. This may impede the development of what psychologists call a **theory of mind**. Theory of mind is the ability to appreciate that other people have a mental state that is different from one's own. Autistic children show deficits in their ability to infer beliefs, intentions, and emotions in others (Baron-Cohen, 1995, 1998). Not being able to readily see the world from another person's perspective interferes with the normal give and take of social relationships.

theory of mind The ability to appreciate that other people have a mental state that is different from one's own.

But what is the basis of these perceptual and cognitive deficits? Canadian experts who have reviewed the research into the causes of autism have concluded that the many impairments associated with autism, including mental retardation, communications deficits, repetitive bizarre motor behaviour, and even seizures, suggest an underlying neurobiological basis (Nicolson & Szatmari, 2003; Szatmari, 2003). MRI scans show that as compared to normal children, autistic children have a period of overgrowth of brain size early in postnatal development, especially in the frontal regions. This period is followed by significantly slowed growth resulting in a brain volume smaller than average for children aged 5 to 16. The brain tissue that connects the two halves of the brain, the corpus callosum, is smaller than normal in autistic patients, which may affect **lateralization** of brain function. The area of the brain that regulates motor function, the cerebellum, also shows abnormal development in autistic individuals.

lateralization The developmental process by which the left hemisphere specializes in verbal and analytic functions and the right hemisphere specializes in nonverbal, spatial functions.

Nicolson and Szatmari's (2003) review of the research indicates that there is substantial support for the suggestion that genetics plays a significant role in the neurodevelopment of autistic children, with susceptible genes on chromosomes 2 and 7 in particular. It may be that multiple genes are involved and that they interact with other factors, possibly environmental or biological in origin, leading to autism (McBride, Anderson, & Shapiro, 1996; McIntosh, 1999). Still, the cause of autism remains unknown and some theorists argue that emerging behavioural, cognitive, and neurological evidence shows there is no single cause to explain the diverse symptoms that define autism (Happé & Plomin, 2006).

Treatment Although there is no cure for autism, structured treatment programs have yielded the best results. The most effective treatment programs focus on behavioural, educational, and communication deficits and are highly intensive and structured, offering a great deal of individual instruction (Rapin, 1997). In a classic study conducted by O. Ivar Lovaas (1987) at UCLA, children suffering from autism received more than 40 hours of one-to-one behaviour modification each week for at least two years. Significant intellectual and educational gains were reported for 9 of the 19 children (47%) in the program. The children who improved achieved normal IQ scores and were able to succeed in the first grade. Only 2% of a control group that did not receive the intensive treatment achieved similar gains. Treatment gains were well maintained at the time of a follow-up when the children were 11 years old (McEachin, Smith, & Lovaas, 1993).

The results of these psychological intervention programs are effective for many children with autism. We should also note that some children make great progress and others do not (Smith, 1999). Children who are better functioning at the start of treatment typically gain the most.

Biological approaches have had only limited impact in the treatment of autism. One line of research has focused on drugs normally used to treat schizophrenia, such as Haldol, which blocks dopamine activity. Several controlled studies show Haldol to be helpful in many cases in reducing social withdrawal and repetitive motor behaviour (such as rocking), aggression, hyperactivity, and self-injurious behaviour (McCracken et al., 2002). We have not seen drugs lead to consistent improvement in cognitive and language development in children with autism, however.

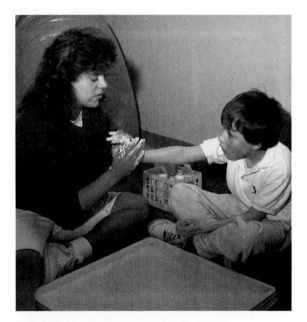

Establishing contact. One of the principal therapeutic tasks in working with autistic children is the establishment of interpersonal contact. Behaviour therapists use reinforcers to increase adaptive social behaviours, such as paying attention to the therapist and playing with other children. Behaviour therapists may also use punishments to suppress self-mutilative behaviour.

The Cost of Autism Treatment in Canada

Dalhousie University psychologist Susan Bryson and her colleagues have emphasized the importance of early intervention, saying, "Early intervention in autism needs to be seen as similar to teaching language to deaf children or to teaching mobility and Braille to blind children—a necessary, publicly funded, rehabilitative service, without which outcomes cannot be meaningfully discussed" (Bryson, Rogers, & Fombonne, 2003, p. 511). Moreover, the Autism Society of Canada as well as provincial cost-benefit estimates have shown that the clinical benefit achieved through early **intensive behavioural intervention** (IBI) would cut by half the lifetime cost of providing service to patients with autism. The Lovaas model of early IBI helps autistic children under the age of six catch up with their school-aged peers. The program can cost upwards of $60 000 per year for 40 hours a week of one-to-one therapy. Except for Nunavut, all jurisdictions in Canada provide at least some funding to cover the costs of treatment. Recent Supreme Court of Canada rulings, however, have left it up to our elected officials to legislate a national autism strategy, such as recommended in the

Senate Committee Final Report *Pay Now or Pay Later: Autism Families in Crisis* (Eggleton & Keon, 2007).

Although we know that early intervention with intensive behavioural treatment can enhance the development of children with autism, especially in the areas of intelligence and language, several challenges remain (Bryson et al., 2003). First, early identification is possible for children as young as age two to three, but, in practice, most children are not formally diagnosed before the age of four, which means they miss a critical window of opportunity for improvement in that human development occurs most rapidly before the age of six. Second, if full recovery is not possible, there is the question of which outcomes are the most important to address. Should treatment target "social skills, language, tested IQ scores, decreases in autism symptoms, or low levels of adaptive behaviour?" (Bryson et al., 2003, p. 511). Finally, in Canada, where we prefer to integrate all children into the regular public education system, there is the concern that the potential gains of early intervention may be compromised by the lack of an intensive, coordinated, evidence-based method of treatment by parents, teachers, and other professional supports.

intensive behavioural intervention A systematic behavioural teaching method that is unique to the needs of the child. It is typically a long-term, one-to-one approach ranging from 25 to 40 hours per week.

Autistic traits generally continue into adulthood to one degree or another. Yet some autistic children do go on to achieve college degrees and are able to function independently (Rapin, 1997). Others need continuing treatment throughout their lives, even institutionalized care. Even the highest-functioning adults with the disorder manifest deficient social and communication skills and a highly limited range of interests and activities (APA, 2000a).

STUDY BREAK

Pervasive Developmental Disorders

Review It

- **What are pervasive developmental disorders?** Pervasive developmental disorders involve marked deficiencies in multiple areas of development. They develop within the first years of life and are often associated with mental retardation. Autistic disorder is the most prominent type of pervasive developmental disorder.

- **What are the clinical features of autism?** Children with autism shun affectionate behaviour, engage in stereotyped behaviour, attempt to preserve sameness, and tend to have peculiar speech habits such as echolalia, pronoun reversals, and idiosyncratic speech. The causes of autism remain unknown, but gains in academic and social functioning have been obtained through the use of early intensive behaviour therapy.

MENTAL RETARDATION

Mental retardation involves a broad delay in the development of cognitive and social functioning. The course of development of children with mental retardation is variable. Many improve over time, especially if they receive support, guidance, and enriched educational opportunities. Children with mental retardation who are reared in impoverished environments may fail to improve or may deteriorate further in relation to other children.

Mental retardation is generally assessed by a combination of formal intelligence tests and observation of adaptive functioning. The DSM-IV-TR uses three criteria in diagnosing mental retardation: (1) an IQ score of approximately 70 or below on a test like the Wechsler Intelligence Scale for Children (WISC) or the Stanford-Binet; (2) evidence of impaired functioning in adaptive behaviour; and (3) onset of the disorder before age 18. People whose behaviour is impaired fail to meet the standards of behaviour that are expected of someone of the same age within a given cultural setting. They do not develop comparable social and communication skills or become adequately independent and self-sufficient. For infants, task-related judgments of subaverage intellectual functioning may be used in place of IQ scores because tests of infant intelligence either do not yield reliable IQ scores or any IQ scores at all.

The DSM-IV-TR classifies mental retardation according to level of severity. Table 13.2 provides a description of the deficits and abilities associated with various degrees of mental retardation. Children with mild mental retardation are generally capable of meeting basic academic demands such as learning to read simple passages. As adults, they are generally capable of independent functioning, although they may require some guidance and support.

TABLE 13.2

Levels of Retardation, Typical Ranges of IQ Scores, and Types of Adaptive Behaviours Shown

Approximate IQ Range	Preschool Age 0–5 Maturation and Development	School Age 6–21 Training and Education	Adult 21 and Over Social and Vocational Adequacy
Mild 50–70	Often not noticed as retarded by casual observer, but is slower to walk, feed self, and talk than most children.	Can acquire practical skills and useful reading and arithmetic to a 3rd-to-6th grade level with special education. Can be guided toward social conformity.	Can usually achieve social and vocational skills adequate for self-maintenance; may need occasional guidance and support when under unusual social or economic stress.
Moderate 35–49	Noticeable delays in motor development, especially in speech; responds to training in various self-help activities.	Can learn simple communication, elementary health and safety habits, and simple manual skills; does not progress in functional reading or arithmetic.	Can perform simple tasks under sheltered conditions; participates in simple recreation; travels alone in familiar places; usually incapable of self-maintenance.
Severe 20–34	Marked delay in motor development; little or no communication skills; may respond to training in elementary self-help—e.g., self-feeding.	Usually walks, barring specific disability; has some understanding of speech and some response; can profit from systematic habit training.	Can conform to daily routines and repetitive activities; needs continuing direction and supervision in a protective environment.
Profound Below 20	Gross retardation; minimal capacity for functioning in sensorimotor areas; needs nursing care.	Obvious delays in all areas of development; shows basic emotional responses; may respond to skilful training in use of legs, hands, and jaws; needs close supervision.	May walk, may need nursing care, may have primitive speech; will usually benefit from regular physical activity; incapable of self-maintenance.

Source: Rathus, S. A. (1996). *Psychology in the New Millennium* (6th ed.). Copyright © 1996 by Holt, Rinehart, & Winston. Reproduced by permission of the publisher.

A 2002 study of adolescents conducted in the Niagara Region found results comparable to earlier Canadian and international studies (Bradley, Thompson, & Bryson, 2002). The researchers identified the overall prevalence of mental retardation as 7.18 in 1000. Using broad criteria, they found that the prevalence for mild mental retardation (MMR; IQ = 50 to 75) was 3.54 in 1000, and for severe mental retardation (SMR; IQ under 50) it was 3.64 in 1000. Although the overall rates of mild and severe mental retardation in adolescents were nearly equivalent, the number of individuals with MMR declined slightly with age whereas the rates of SMR remained constant. The authors caution that the lower than expected rate of MMR may be related to Ontario's integration policy for education, which has made individuals with MMR less visible as they adapt to the mainstream classroom, albeit with a modified program of study. Moreover, once formal schooling is completed, people with MMR blend into the community much more readily than people with SMR. Males in the study outnumbered females 1.3:1.0, but more females fell in the range of SMR.

Not all systems of classification of mental retardation are based on level of severity. The American Association on Mental Retardation (AAMR), an organization composed of leading professionals in the field, classifies mental retardation according to the intensity of support needed by the individual in various areas of functioning (AAMR, 1992). Some individuals need only intermittent support that varies in intensity from time to time on an *as needed basis*, whereas others require more constant or pervasive support involving extensive commitment of staff and resources. This system of classification attempts to match the level of support needed to the individual's ability to function in work, school, and home environments.

Causes of Mental Retardation

In many cases, mental retardation can be traced to biological causes, including chromosomal and genetic disorders, infectious diseases, and brain damage. However, more than half of the cases of mental retardation remain unexplained, with most of these falling in the mild range of severity (Flint et al., 1995). These unexplained cases might involve cultural or familial causes, such as being raised in an impoverished home environment, or perhaps they involve an interaction of environmental and genetic factors, the nature of which remains poorly understood (Thapar et al., 1994).

Down Syndrome and Other Chromosomal Abnormalities The most common chromosomal abnormality resulting in mental retardation is **Down syndrome** (formerly called Down's syndrome in Canada), which is characterized by an extra or third chromosome on the 21st pair of chromosomes, resulting in 47 chromosomes rather than the normal complement of 46. Down syndrome occurs in about 1 in 800 births. It usually occurs when the 21st pair of chromosomes in either the egg or the sperm fails to divide normally, resulting in an extra chromosome. Chromosomal abnormalities become more likely as parents age, so expectant couples in their mid-30s or older often undergo prenatal genetic tests to detect Down syndrome and genetic abnormalities. Down syndrome can be traced to a defect in the mother's chromosomes in about 95% of cases (Antonarakis et al., 1991), with the remainder attributable to defects in the father's sperm.

People with Down syndrome are recognizable by certain physical features, such as a round face; broad, flat nose; and small, downward-sloping folds of skin at the inside corners of the eyes that give the impression of slanted eyes. A protruding tongue; small, squarish hands and short fingers; a curved fifth finger; and disproportionately small arms and legs in relation to their bodies also characterize children with Down syndrome. Nearly all of these children have mental retardation and many suffer from physical problems, such as malformations of the heart and respiratory difficulties. Sadly, most die by middle age. In their later years, they tend to suffer memory losses and experience childish emotions that represent a form of senility.

Children with Down syndrome suffer various deficits in learning and development. They tend to be unco-ordinated and to lack proper muscle tone, which makes it difficult for them to carry out physical tasks and engage in play activities like other children. Down syndrome children suffer memory deficits, especially for information presented verbally, which makes it difficult for them to learn in school. They also have difficulty following instructions from teachers and expressing their thoughts or needs clearly in speech. Despite their disabilities, most can learn to read, write, and perform simple arithmetic if they receive appropriate schooling and the right encouragement.

Although less common than Down syndrome, chromosomal abnormalities on the sex chromosome may also result in mental retardation, such as in Klinefelter's syndrome and Turner's syndrome. Klinefelter's syndrome, which occurs only in males, is characterized by the presence of an extra X sex chromosome, resulting in an XXY sex chromosomal pattern rather than the XY pattern that men normally have. Estimates of the prevalence of Klinefelter's syndrome range from 1 in 500 to 1 in 1000 male births (Brody, 1993). Men with this XXY pattern fail to develop appropriate secondary sex characteristics, resulting in small, underdeveloped testes, low sperm production, enlarged breasts, poor muscular development, and infertility. Mild retardation or learning disabilities frequently occur among these men. Men with Klinefelter's syndrome often don't discover they have the condition until they undergo tests for infertility.

Turner's syndrome is found exclusively in females, and is characterized by the presence of a single X sex chromosome instead of the normal two. Although such girls develop normal external genitals, their ovaries remain poorly developed, producing reduced amounts of estrogen. As women, they tend to be shorter than average and infertile. They also tend to show evidence of mild retardation, especially in skills relating to math and science.

Fragile X Syndrome and Other Genetic Abnormalities Fragile X syndrome is the most common type of inherited (genetic) mental retardation. It is the second most common form

Down syndrome Condition caused by a chromosomal abnormality involving an extra chromosome on the 21st pair ("trisomy 21"); it is characterized by mental retardation and various physical abnormalities. Formerly called *mongolism* and *Down's syndrome* in Canada.

of retardation overall after Down syndrome ("Blood Test Can Detect Retardation," 1993; Plomin, Owen, & McGuffin, 1994). The disorder is believed to be caused by a mutated gene on the X sex chromosome (Huber, Gallagher, Warren, & Bear, 2002). The defective gene is located in an area of the chromosome that appears fragile, hence the name *fragile X syndrome*. Fragile X syndrome causes mental retardation in about 1 in every 1000 to 1500 males and (generally less severe) mental handicaps in about 1 in every 2000 to 2500 females (Angier, 1991b; Rousseau et al., 1991). The effects of fragile X syndrome range from mild learning disabilities to retardation so profound that those affected can hardly speak or function.

Females normally have two X sex chromosomes, whereas males have only one. For females, having two X sex chromosomes seems to provide some protection against the disorder if the defective gene turns up on one of the two chromosomes (Angier, 1991b). This may explain why the disorder usually has more profound effects on males than on females. Yet the mutation does not always manifest itself. Many males and females carry the fragile X mutation but show no clinical evidence of it. Nevertheless, they can pass along the syndrome to their offspring.

A genetic test can detect the presence of the mutation by direct DNA analysis and may help prospective parents who seek out genetic counselling. Prenatal testing of the fetus is also available. Although there is no treatment for fragile X syndrome, identifying the defective gene is the first step toward understanding how the protein produced by the gene functions to create the disability—which may lead to the development of treatments (Huber et al., 2002).

phenylketonuria Genetic disorder that prevents the metabolization of phenylpyruvic acid, leading to mental retardation. Abbreviated *PKU*.

Phenylketonuria (PKU) is a genetic disorder that occurs in 1 in 10 000 births (Plomin et al., 1994). It is caused by a recessive gene that prevents the child from metabolizing the amino acid *phenylalanine (phe)*, which is found in many foods. Consequently, phenylalanine and its derivative, phenylpyruvic acid, accumulate in the body, causing damage to the central nervous system that results in mental retardation and emotional disturbance. PKU can be detected among newborns by analyzing blood or urine samples. Although there is no cure for PKU, children with the disorder may suffer less damage or develop normally if they are placed on a diet low in phenylalanine soon after birth (Brody, 1990). Such children receive protein supplements that compensate for their nutritional loss.

University of Toronto researchers Mary Lou Smith and her colleagues tested children with PKU who had either high or low levels of *phe* (Smith, Klim, & Hanley, 2000). They found that PKU children with low *phe* levels were indistinguishable from non-PKU controls on several cognitive tasks. In contrast, however, the higher the levels of *phe* in school-aged children with PKU, the greater the impairment in cognitive performance on specific problem-solving and verbal memory tasks.

Smith-Lemli-Opitz syndrome An autosomal recessive disease resulting in low levels of cholesterol. It is characterized by varying degrees of multiple facial and bodily malformations, mental retardation, and autism-spectrum disorder behaviours. Abbreviated *SLOS*.

Smith-Lemli-Opitz syndrome (SLOS) is an inherited disease caused by an inability to make cholesterol, which affects development before and after birth. It results in varying degrees of multiple facial and bodily malformations, mental retardation, and autism-spectrum disorder behaviours. McMaster University researchers suggest that after PKU, SLOS is the second most common treatable recessive gene metabolic disease (Nowaczyk, Whelan, Heshka, & Hill, 1999). The incidence of the disorder is highest in Caucasians with northern or central European heritage, affecting about 1 in every 29 000 Canadians. In addition, 1 in 70 Canadians may be carriers of the chromosome 11 gene that interferes with normal cholesterol production in the body (Nowaczyk, 2001a, 2001b). Genetic counselling to provide reproductive choices for parents who are high-risk carriers and prenatal genetic diagnostic testing as early as 11 to 12 weeks of gestation are important preventive measures but can be overlooked because the disease is relatively unknown to primary-care physicians (Nowaczyk et al., 1999). Pre- and postnatal treatment of SLOS, including cholesterol supplements, reportedly reduces many of the physical and behavioural symptoms but has less of an effect on the level of mental retardation (Nowaczyk et al., 1999; Nowaczyk, 2001a, 2001b).

Tay-Sachs disease Disease of lipid metabolism that is genetically transmitted and usually results in death in early childhood.

Tay-Sachs disease is caused by recessive genes on chromosome 15. A fatal degenerative disease of the central nervous system, it mostly afflicts Jews of Eastern European ancestry and also French Canadians of the Gaspé region of Quebec (Triggs-Raine, Richard, Wasel, Prence, & Natowicz, 1995). About 1 in 14 French Canadians in Eastern Quebec is a carrier of the recessive gene responsible for the disorder (Chodirker et al., 2001; Kaback et al.,

1993). Children afflicted by Tay-Sachs suffer gradual loss of muscle control, deafness and blindness, retardation and paralysis, and usually die before the age of five.

Today, various prenatal diagnostic tests can detect the presence of chromosomal abnormalities and genetic disorders. In *amniocentesis*, which is usually conducted about 14 to 15 weeks following conception, a sample of amniotic fluid is drawn with a syringe from the amniotic sac that contains the fetus. With *chorionic villus sampling* (CVS), cells are extracted from the placenta outside the sac where the fetus develops. CVS is best performed between 10 and 12 weeks into a woman's pregnancy. Depending upon the procedure, cells from the fetus or the placenta can then be examined for abnormalities, including Down syndrome, X-linked disorders, PKU, SLOS, and Tay-Sachs.

In the future, it may be possible to control the impact of defective genes during prenatal development. For now, expectant couples rely on genetic counselling. It offers a complete and accurate view of the options available and can assist couples in making informed decisions about terminating a pregnancy, or alternatively help them prepare for a baby who has congenital defects.

Prenatal Factors Some cases of mental retardation are caused by maternal infections or substance abuse during pregnancy. Rubella (German measles) in the mother, for example, can be passed along to the unborn child, causing brain damage that results in retardation, and may play a role in autism. Although the mother might experience only mild symptoms or none at all, the effects on the fetus can be tragic. Other maternal diseases that can cause retardation in the child include syphilis, **cytomegalovirus**, and genital herpes.

Widespread programs that immunize women against rubella before pregnancy and tests for syphilis during pregnancy have reduced the risk of transmission of these infections to children. Most children who contract genital herpes from their mothers do so during delivery by coming into contact with the herpes simplex virus that causes the disease in the birth canal. Caesarean sections (C-sections) reduce the risk of the baby's coming into contact with the virus during outbreaks. Drugs the mother ingests during pregnancy are able to pass through the placenta to the child. Some can cause severe birth deformities and mental retardation. Children whose mothers drink alcohol during pregnancy are often born with fetal alcohol syndrome (FAS, described in Chapter 9). FAS is among the most prominent causes of mental retardation. Maternal smoking during pregnancy has also been linked to the development of attention-deficit/hyperactivity disorder in children (Milberger, Biederman, Faraone, Chen, & Jones, 1996).

Birth complications, such as oxygen deprivation or head injuries, place children at increased risk for neurological disorders, including mental retardation. Prematurity also places children at risk of retardation and other developmental problems. Brain infections, such as encephalitis and meningitis, or traumas during infancy and early childhood can cause mental retardation and other health problems. Children who ingest toxins, such as paint chips containing lead, may also suffer brain damage that produces mental retardation.

Cultural-Familial Causes Children with mental retardation fall mainly into the mild range of severity and there is no apparent biological cause or distinguishing physical feature that sets these children apart from other children. Psychosocial factors, such as an impoverished home, a social environment that is intellectually unstimulating, or parental neglect or abuse, may play a causal or contributing role in the development of mental retardation in such children. Supporting a family linkage is evidence from a study in Atlanta in which mothers who failed to finish high school were four times more likely than better educated mothers to have children with mild retardation (Drews, Yeargin-Allsopp, Decouflé, & Murphy, 1995).

These cases are considered **cultural-familial retardation**. Children in impoverished families may lack toys, books, or opportunities to interact with adults in intellectually stimulating ways. Consequently, they may fail to develop appropriate language skills or become unmotivated to learn the skills that are valued in contemporary society. Economic burdens, such as the need to hold multiple jobs, may prevent the parents from spending time reading to them, talking to them at length, and exposing them to creative play or trips to museums and parks. They may spend most of their days glued to the television set.

cytomegalovirus Maternal disease of the herpes virus group that carries a risk of mental retardation to the unborn child.

cultural-familial retardation Milder form of mental retardation that is believed to result, or at least be influenced by, impoverishment in the child's home environment

Savant Syndrome

Got a minute? Try the following:

1. Without referring to a calendar, calculate the day of the week that March 15, 2079 will fall on.

2. List the prime numbers between 1 and 1 billion. (Hint: the list starts 1, 2, 3, 5, 7, 11, 13, 17 . . .)

3. Repeat verbatim the newspaper stories you read over coffee this morning.

4. Sing accurately every note played by the first violin in Beethoven's Ninth Symphony.

These tasks are impossible for all but a very few. Ironically, people who are most likely to be able to accomplish these feats suffer from autism, mental retardation, or both. Such a person is commonly called an *idiot savant*. The term *savant* is derived from the French *savoir*, meaning "to know." The label *savant syndrome* is preferable to the pejorative *idiot savant*, in referring to someone with severe mental deficiencies who possesses some remarkable mental abilities. The prevalence of savant syndrome among people with mental retardation is estimated at about 0.06% or about 1 case in 2000 (Hill, 1987). The emergence of the savant syndrome is also closely linked to infantile autism (Miller, 1999). Most people with savant syndrome, like most people with autism, are male (Treffert, 1988). Among a sample of 5400 people with autism, 531 cases (9.8%) were reported by parents to have the savant syndrome (Rimland, 1978). Because they want to think of their children as special, however, parents might overreport the incidence of savant syndrome.

Several hundred people with savant syndrome have been described in this century. They are reported to have shown remarkable but circumscribed mental skills, such as calendar calculating, rare musical talent, even accomplished poetry (Dowker, Hermelin, & Pring, 1996)—all of which stand in contrast to their limited general intellectual abilities. People with savant syndrome also have outstanding memories. Just as we learn about health by studying illness, we may be able to learn more about normal mechanisms of memory by studying people in whom memory stands apart from other aspects of mental functioning (e.g., Kelly, Macaruso, & Sokol, 1997).

The savant syndrome phenomenon occurs more frequently in males by a ratio of roughly 6 to 1. The special skills of people with savant syndrome tend to appear out of the blue and may disappear as suddenly. Some people with the syndrome engage in lightning calculations. Thomas Fuller, a 19th-century enslaved man in Virginia, "was able to calculate the number of seconds in 70 years, 17 days, and 12 hours in a minute and one half, taking into account the 17 leap years that would have occurred in the period" (Smith, 1983). There are also cases of persons with the syndrome who were blind but could play back any musical piece, no matter how complex, or repeat long passages of foreign languages without losing a syllable. Some people with the syndrome make exact estimates of elapsed time. One could reportedly repeat verbatim the contents of a newspaper he had just heard; another could repeat backward what he had just read (Tradgold, 1914).

The parents, most of whom were also reared in poverty, may lack the reading or communication skills to help shape the development of these skills in their children. A vicious cycle of poverty and impoverished intellectual development may be repeated from generation to generation.

Children with this form of developmental delay may respond dramatically when provided with enriched learning experiences, especially at earlier ages. For example, the Health Canada–funded Aboriginal Head Start (AHS) was instituted in 114 urban centres and northern communities across Canada to promote education and school readiness, Aboriginal culture and language, parental involvement, health, nutrition, and social support (Health Canada, 2002c). To date, the AHS program has been highly successful and has exceeded program expectations as major gains have been achieved in all areas of children's development (Health Canada, 2000c; Indian and Northern Affairs, 2003; Ottawa Aboriginal Head Start Program, 1998).

Intervention

The services that children with mental retardation require to meet the developmental challenges they face depend in part on the type of retardation and the level of severity (Dykens

Various theories have been presented to explain savant syndrome (Treffert, 1988). Some believe that children with the savant syndrome have unusually well-developed memories that allow them to record and scan vast amounts of information. It has been suggested that people with savant syndrome may inherit two sets of hereditary factors, one for retardation and the other for special abilities. Perhaps it is coincidental that their special abilities and their mental handicaps were inherited in common. Other theorists suggest that the left and right hemispheres of their cerebral cortexes are organized in an unusual way. This latter belief is supported by research suggesting that the special abilities they possess often involve skills associated with right hemisphere functioning. Still other theorists suggest they learn special skills to compensate for their lack of more general skills, perhaps as a means of coping with their environment or of earning social reinforcements. It could be that their skills in concrete functions, like calculation, compensate for their lack of abstract thinking ability. Linguists like Noam Chomsky theorize that people are neurologically "prewired" to grasp the deep structure that underlies all human languages. Perhaps, as the neurologist Oliver Sacks speculates, the brain circuits of some people with savant syndrome are wired with a "deep arithmetic"—an innate structure for perceiving mathematical relationships that is analogous to the prewiring that allows people to perceive and produce language.

Some earlier research has pointed to possible gender-linked left hemisphere damage occurring prenatally or

Savant syndrome. Dustin Hoffman (left) won the best actor Oscar for his portrayal in the 1988 film Rain Man of a man with autism who showed a remarkable capacity for numerical calculation. Tom Cruise (right) played his brother. Hoffman was able to capture a sense of emotional detachment and isolation in his character.

congenitally. Compensatory right hemisphere development might then take place, establishing specialized brain circuitry that processes concrete and narrowly defined kinds of information (Treffert, 1988). An environment that reinforces savant abilities and provides opportunities for practice and concentration would give further impetus to the development of these unusual abilities. As it stands, savant syndrome remains a mystery.

& Hodapp, 1997; Snell, 1997). With appropriate training, children with mild retardation may approach a grade six level of competence. They can acquire vocational skills that allow them to support themselves minimally through meaningful work. In Canada, most mildly mentally retarded children are integrated into the regular classroom, typically with a modified curriculum. Children with more severe forms of retardation, on the other hand, may be placed in special schools or classes if the caregiver prefers (Bradley et al., 2002).

Controversy remains over the **mainstreaming** of children with mental retardation into regular classes. Although some children with mild retardation may achieve better when they are mainstreamed, others may not do so well in regular classes. Some of these children find regular classes be overwhelming and withdraw from their schoolmates. There has also been a trend in Canada and the United States toward deinstitutionalization of people with more severe mental retardation, a policy shift motivated in large part by public outrage over the appalling conditions that existed in many institutions serving this population.

People with mental retardation who are capable of functioning in the community have the right to receive less restrictive care than is provided in large institutions. Many are capable of living outside an institution and have been placed in supervised group homes. Residents typically share household responsibilities and are encouraged to participate in

mainstreaming The practice of having all students with disabilities included in the regular classroom. Also referred to as *integration* or *inclusion*.

meaningful daily activities, such as training programs or sheltered workshops. Others live with their families and attend structured day programs. Adults with mild retardation often work in outside jobs and live in their own apartments or share apartments with other persons who have mild retardation. Although the large-scale dumping of mental patients into the community from psychiatric institutions resulted in massive social problems and swelled the ranks of the homeless population, deinstitutionalization of people with mental retardation has largely been a success story achieved, mostly, with rare dignity (Winerip, 1991).

Behavioural approaches can be used to teach persons with more severe retardation such basic hygienic behaviours as toothbrushing, self-dressing, and hair combing. In demonstrating toothbrushing, the therapist might first define the component parts of the targeted behaviour (e.g., picking up the toothbrush, wetting the toothbrush, taking the cap off the tube, putting the paste on the brush, and so on) (Kissel, Whitman, & Reid, 1983). The therapist might then shape the desired behaviour by using such techniques as *verbal instruction* (e.g., "Jim, pick up the toothbrush"); *physical guidance* (physically guiding the client's hand in performing the desired response); and *reward* (use of positive verbal reinforcement) for successful completion of the desired response ("That's really good, Jim"). Such behavioural techniques have been shown to be effective in teaching a simple but remunerative vocational skill (for example, stamping return addresses on envelopes) to a group of adult women with such severe mental retardation that they were essentially nonverbal (Schepis, Reid, & Fitzgerald, 1987). These techniques may also help people with severe mental retardation develop adaptive capacities that can enable them to perform more productive roles.

Other behavioural treatment techniques include social-skills training, which focuses on increasing the individual's ability to relate co-operatively with others, and anger-management training to help individuals develop more effective ways of handling conflicts than aggressively acting out (Huang & Cuvo, 1997; Nezu & Nezu, 1994; Rose, 1996).

Children with mental retardation stand perhaps a three to four times greater chance of developing other psychological disorders, such as attention-deficit/hyperactivity disorder (ADHD), depression, or anxiety disorders (Borthwick-Duffy, 1994). Mental health professionals have been slow to recognize the prevalence of mental health problems among people with mental retardation, perhaps because of a long-held conceptual distinction between emotional impairment on one hand and intellectual deficits on the other (Nezu, 1994; Ollendick & Ollendick, 1982). Many professionals even assumed (wrongly) that

Inclusion. Across Canada, most children with special learning needs typically remain in regular classrooms and are provided with educational programs that meet their individual needs.

people with mental retardation were worry free and somehow immune from psychological problems (Nezu, 1994). Given these commonly held beliefs, it is perhaps not surprising that many of the psychological problems of people with mental retardation have gone unrecognized and untreated (Reiss & Valenti-Hein, 1994).

Children and adults with mental retardation may need psychological counselling to help them adjust to life in the community. Many have difficulty making friends and may become socially isolated. Problems with self-esteem are also common, especially because people who have mental retardation are often demeaned and ridiculed. Supportive counselling may be supplemented with behavioural techniques to help those with developmental disabilities acquire skills in areas such as personal hygiene, work, and social relationships.

STUDY BREAK

Mental Retardation

Review It

- **What is mental retardation and how is it assessed?** Mental retardation is a general delay in the development of intellectual and adaptive abilities. It is assessed through evaluation of performance on intelligence tests and measures of functional ability. Most cases fall in the range of mildly retarded.

- **What are the causes of mental retardation?** There are many causes of mental retardation, including chromosomal abnormalities such as Down syndrome, genetic disorders such as fragile X syndrome, phenylketonuria, Smith-Lemli-Opitz syndrome, and Tay-Sachs disease, prenatal factors such as maternal diseases and alcohol (and other drug) use, and familial/cultural factors associated with intellectually impoverished home environments.

Define It

Down syndrome
phenylketonuria
Smith-Lemli-Opitz
  syndrome
Tay-Sachs disease

cytomegalovirus
cultural-familial
  retardation
mainstreaming

Recall It*

1. To be diagnosed with mental retardation, a person must meet all of the following criteria EXCEPT _____.

    a. receive an IQ score of approximately 70 or below
    b. show evidence of brain abnormalities
    c. show evidence of impaired functioning in adaptive behaviour
    d. show evidence of impaired functioning before the age of 18

2. Maura is diagnosed with mental retardation. Although she needs occasional help when she experiences stressful life situations, she can generally function on her own. She is capable of reading at a grade six level and has a tested IQ of 54. Her level of retardation is best described as _____.

    a. mild
    b. moderate
    c. severe
    d. profound

3. Most cases of mental retardation involve _____.

    a. Down syndrome
    b. chromosomal abnormalities other than Down syndrome
    c. brain damage
    d. unknown causes

4. A chromosomal abnormality in men that results in a failure to develop appropriate male secondary sexual characteristics is called _____.

    a. Klinefelter's syndrome
    b. Down syndrome
    c. Turner's syndrome
    d. phenylketonuria

5. Maternal drinking during pregnancy can result in _____, one of the most common causes of mental retardation.

    a. fetal distress syndrome
    b. fetal alcohol syndrome
    c. Klinefelter's syndrome
    d. fetal alcohol dependence

* Recall It answers can be found on the Companion Website for this text.

Think About It

- Do you think children with mental retardation should be mainstreamed into regular classes? Why or why not?

LEARNING DISORDERS

Many famous scientists, leaders, and celebrities have been thought to have what are now considered learning disorders. Among their number are Albert Einstein, Alexander Graham Bell, Winston Churchill, Agatha Christie, and Tom Cruise. These highly creative and successful people suffered from **dyslexia** and related disorders. The term *dyslexia* is derived from the Greek roots *dys-*, meaning "bad," and *lexikon*, meaning "of words." Dyslexia is the most common type of **learning disorder** (also called a *learning disability*) (Shaywitz, 1998). It accounts for roughly 80% of learning-disability cases. People with learning disorders have average or higher intelligence, and may even be gifted, but show inadequate development in reading, math, or writing skills that impairs school performance or daily activities (see the accompanying "A Closer Look" box for a Canadian definition of learning disabilities).

About 12% of children in Canadian schools are identified as having a learning disorder (Lipps & Frank, 1997). Learning disorders tend to run a chronic course and are the most common long-term conditions of children up to age 14 (Cossette & Duclos, 2002). The more severe the problem is in childhood, the more likely it is to affect adult development (Spreen, 1988). Children with learning disorders tend to perform poorly in school; about half of all children who received remedial education were identified as having a learning disability (Lipps & Frank, 1997).

dyslexia Type of learning disorder characterized by impaired reading ability that may involve difficulty with the alphabet or spelling.

learning disorder Deficiency in a specific learning ability, which is noteworthy because of the individual's general intelligence and exposure to learning opportunities.

Types of Learning Disorders

The several types of learning disorders include *mathematics disorder*, *disorder of written expression*, and *reading disorder*.

Mathematics Disorder Mathematics disorder describes children with deficiencies in arithmetic skills. They may have problems understanding basic mathematical terms or operations, such as addition or subtraction; decoding mathematical symbols (+, =, etc.); or learning sequential facts by rote memory, such as multiplication tables. The problem may become apparent as early as grade one (age six) but is not generally recognized until about grade three (age eight).

A CLOSER LOOK

A Canadian Definition of Learning Disabilities

On January 30, 2002, after years of deliberation, the Learning Disabilities Association of Canada (LDAC) adopted an official definition of *learning disabilities* that is the culmination of a thorough review of learning disabilities research and input from hundreds of individuals in all provinces and territories—the LDAC National Legal Committee and the LDAC "Think Tank" (Learning Disabilities Association of Canada, 2002):

Learning disabilities refer to a number of disorders that may affect the acquisition, organization, retention, understanding, or use of verbal or nonverbal information. These disorders affect learning in individuals who otherwise demonstrate at least average abilities essential for thinking and/or reasoning. As such, learning disabilities are distinct from global intellectual deficiency.

Learning disabilities result from impairments in one or more processes related to perceiving, thinking, remembering, or learning. These include but are not limited to: language processing; phonological processing; visual spatial processing; processing speed; memory and attention; and executive functions (e.g. planning and decision-making).

Learning disabilities range in severity and may interfere with the acquisition and use of one or more of the following:

- oral language (e.g., listening, speaking, understanding);

- reading (e.g., decoding, phonetic knowledge, word recognition, comprehension);

(continued)

- written language (e.g., spelling and written expression); and

- mathematics (e.g., computation, problem solving).

Learning disabilities may also involve difficulties with organizational skills, social perception, social interaction, and perspective taking.

Learning disabilities are lifelong [disorders]. The way in which they are expressed may vary over an individual's lifetime, depending on the interaction between the demands of the environment and the individual's strengths and needs. Learning disabilities are suggested by unexpected academic underachievement or achievement that is maintained only by unusually high levels of effort and support.

Learning disabilities [occur] due to genetic and/or neurobiological factors or injury that alters brain functioning in a manner that affects one or more processes related to learning. These disorders are not due primarily to hearing and/or vision problems, socio-economic

factors, cultural or linguistic differences, lack of motivation, or ineffective teaching, although these factors may further complicate the challenges faced by individuals with learning disabilities. Learning disabilities may co-exist with various conditions including attentional, behavioural, and emotional disorders, sensory impairments, or other medical conditions.

For success, individuals with learning disabilities require early identification and timely specialized assessments and interventions involving home, school, community, and workplace settings. The interventions need to be appropriate for each individual's learning disability subtype and, at a minimum, include the provision of:

- specific skill instruction;

- accommodations;

- compensatory strategies; and

- self-advocacy skills.

Source: Reprinted with permission from the Learning Disabilities Association of Canada (2002).

Disorder of Written Expression Disorder of written expression refers to children with grossly deficient writing skills. The deficiency may be characterized by errors in spelling, grammar, or punctuation, or by difficulty in composing sentences and paragraphs. Severe writing difficulties generally become apparent by age seven (grade two), although milder cases may not be recognized until the age of ten (grade five) or later.

Reading Disorder Reading disorder—dyslexia— characterizes children who have poorly developed skills in recognizing letters and words and comprehending written text. Children with dyslexia may read slowly with difficulty, and distort, omit, or substitute words when reading aloud. They may have trouble decoding letters. They may perceive letters upside down (*w* for *m*) or in reversed images (*b* for *d*). Dyslexia is usually apparent by the age of seven, coinciding with grade two, but is sometimes recognized in six-year-olds. Although it was earlier believed that the problem affected mostly boys, more recent studies find similar rates among boys and girls (APA, 2000a; Shaywitz, 1998). Yet boys with dyslexia are more likely than girls to exhibit disruptive behaviour and so are more likely to be referred for evaluation. Children and adolescents with dyslexia tend to be more prone than their peers to depression, to have lower self-worth and feelings of competence in their academic work, and to have signs of ADHD (Boetsch, Green, & Pennington, 1996).

Dyslexia. Children with dyslexia have difficulty decoding words. Note the reversal of the letters w and l in the word owl in this photo of a dyslexic girl completing a writing exercise.

Theoretical Perspectives Canadian neuropsychologists contend that the origins of learning disorders are primarily based on neurobiological factors (Fiedorowicz, 1999; Fiedorowicz et al., 1999, 2002). Many children with learning disorders have problems with visual or auditory sensation and perception. They may lack the capacity to copy words or to discriminate geometric shapes. Other children have short attention spans or show hyperactivity, which is also suggestive of an underlying brain abnormality.

Much of the research on learning disorders has focused on dyslexia. Mounting evidence points to underlying brain dysfunctions (Shaywitz et al., 1998). Cross-cultural language research has now shown that dyslexia is a universal neuroanatomical disorder that causes the same reading disabilities (Paulesu et al., 2001). There is evidence of impaired visual processing in people with dyslexia that would be consistent with a defect in a major visual relay station in the brain involved in sequencing the flow of visual information from the retina to the visual cortex (Livingstone, Rosen, Drislane, & Galaburda, 1991). Inspection of the autopsied brains of people who had dyslexia showed this relay station was smaller and less well organized than in other people.

As a result, the brains of people with dyslexia are not likely to be able decipher a rapid succession of visual stimuli, such as those involved in decoding letters and words. Words may thus become blurry, fuse together, or seem to jump off the page—all problems reported by people with dyslexia (Blakeslee, 1991).

Dysfunctions in other sensory pathways involving the sense of hearing and even the sense of touch may also be involved in learning disorders. For example, research suggests that some forms of dyslexia may be traceable to an abnormality in the brain circuits responsible for processing rapidly flowing auditory information (Blakeslee, 1994b). This flaw in brain circuitry may make it difficult to understand rapidly occurring speech sounds, such as the sounds corresponding to the letters *b* and *p* in syllables like *ba* and *pa*. Problems discerning the differences between many basic speech sounds can make it difficult for people with dyslexia to learn to speak correctly and later, perhaps, to learn to read. They continue to have problems distinguishing between words like *boy* and *toy* or *pet* and *bet* in rapid speech. If defects in brain circuitry responsible for relaying and processing sensory data are involved in learning disorders, as the evidence suggests, it may lead the way to the development of specialized treatment programs to help children adjust to their sensory capabilities.

Genetic factors appear to be involved in brain abnormalities associated with dyslexia (Fiedorowicz et al., 1999, 2002). People whose parents have dyslexia are at greater risk themselves (see Figure 13.1) (Vogler, DeFries, & Decker, 1985). Moreover, higher rates of concordance (agreement) for dyslexia are found between identical (MZ) than fraternal (DZ) twins—70% versus 40% respectively (Plomin et al., 1994). Suspicion has focused

FIGURE 13.1 Familial risk of developmental reading disorder (dyslexia).
Boys are at greater risk than girls of developing dyslexia, and children of both genders whose parents have dyslexia are at relatively greater risk. Although these data are consistent with a genetic explanation of the etiology of dyslexia, it is also possible that parents with dyslexia do not provide their children with the types of stimulation that foster reading skills, such as books and the reading of bedtime stories.

Source: Adapted from Vogler et al. (1985).

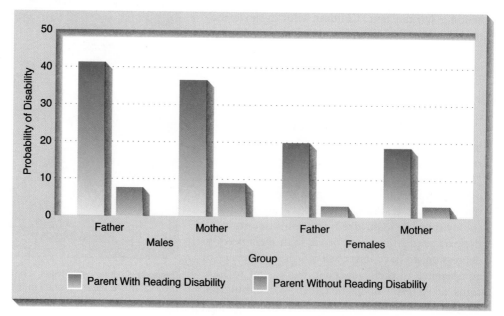

on the role that particular genes may play in causing subtle defects in the brain circuitry involved in reading.

Intervention

With the growing recognition of the neurobiological nature of learning disabilities, our approach to treatment in Canada now involves support and intervention strategies that focus on a child's information processing style and academic strengths. The support aspect focuses on bolstering the child's self-esteem and increasing motivation, developing close teacher–parent partnerships, and in older children, the development of effective self-advocacy skills. Second, once an **individual education plan (IEP)** is in place, intervention can be accomplished through language re-education, a variety of mixed-ability teaching methods, academic accommodations such as alternate learning and testing methods, development of compensatory skills, and the use of assistive technologies such as computers, spell checkers, and calculators (Bos & Van Reusen, 1991; Brazeau-Ward, 2003; Drover & Owen, 2000; Learning Disabilities Association of Canada, 2003a, 2003b).

individual education plan A contractual document that contains learning and behavioural outcomes for a student, a description of how the outcomes will be achieved, and how the outcomes will be evaluated. Acronym is *IEP*.

STUDY BREAK

Learning Disorders

Review It

- **What are learning disorders?** Learning disorders (also called learning disabilities) are specific deficits in the development of arithmetic, writing, or reading skills.

- **What are the causes of learning disorders and approaches to treatment?** The causes remain under study but most probably involve underlying neurobiological brain dysfunctions that make it difficult to process or decode visual and auditory information. Intervention focuses mainly on the remediation and accommodation of specific skill deficits.

Define It

dyslexia
individual education plan (IEP)
learning disorder

Recall It*

1. _____ is the most common form of learning disorder.

   a. Mathematics disorder
   b. Reading disorder
   c. Disorder of written expression
   d. Articulation disorder

2. The Learning Disabilities Association of Canada states that _____.

   a. *dyslexia* is another term for *learning disability*
   b. learning disabilities are largely a result of an impoverished home environment

   c. learning disabilities are likely due to heredity, neurobiological factors, or injury
   d. interventions are best delivered in special education classes

3. Evidence indicates that the rate of concordance (agreement) for dyslexia between identical twins is _____%.

   a. 30
   b. 50
   c. 70
   d. 90

4. Learning-disorder interventions in Canada focus on _____.

   a. providing support and strategies that focus on a child's information-processing style and academic strengths
   b. modifying the standard curriculum so that a child is working on material at a lower grade level
   c. placing the child in enrichment programs so he/she can outgrow his/her disability more quickly
   d. placing the child in a special education setting within the school along with the other special-needs students

* Recall It answers can be found on the Companion Website for this text.

Think About It

- Do you think people with learning disorders should be given special consideration when given standardized tests like provincial achievement tests, such as having extra time? Why or why not?

ATTENTION-DEFICIT AND DISRUPTIVE BEHAVIOUR DISORDERS

The category of *attention-deficit* and *disruptive behaviour disorders* refers to a diverse range of problem behaviours, including *attention-deficit/hyperactivity disorder* (ADHD), *conduct disorder* (CD), and *oppositional defiant disorder* (ODD). These disorders are socially disruptive and usually more upsetting to other people than to the children who receive the diagnoses. Although there are differences among these disorders, the rate of comorbidity (co-occurrence) among them is very high (Jensen, Martin, & Cantwell, 1997).

Attention-Deficit/Hyperactivity Disorder

attention-deficit/hyperactivity disorder Behaviour disorder of childhood characterized by excessive motor activity and inability to focus one's attention. Acronym is *ADHD*.

hyperactivity Abnormal behaviour pattern found most often in young boys that is characterized by extreme restlessness and difficulty maintaining attention.

Many parents believe their children are not attentive toward them—that they run around on whim and do things in their own way. Some inattention, especially in early childhood, is normal enough. In **attention-deficit/hyperactivity disorder** (ADHD), however, children display impulsivity, inattention, and **hyperactivity** that are considered inappropriate to their developmental levels.

ADHD is divided into three subtypes: a predominantly inattentive type; a predominantly hyperactive or impulsive type; and a combination type characterized by high levels of both inattention and hyperactivity-impulsivity (APA, 2000a). The disorder is usually first diagnosed during elementary school, when problems with attention or hyperactivity-impulsivity make it difficult for the child to adjust to school. Although signs of hyperactivity are often observed earlier, many overactive toddlers do not go on to develop ADHD.

ADHD is far from rare. Canadian studies have found the prevalence rates of ADHD to be between 5% and 10% in children aged 6 to 14 (Romano, Baillargeon, & Tremblay, 2002). Boys were two to three times more likely than girls to be identified as having ADHD and 6- to 8-year-olds had higher rates than 12- to 14-year-olds. Although inattention appears to be the basic problem, there are associated problems such as an inability to sit still for more than a few moments, bullying, temper tantrums, stubbornness, and failure to respond to punishment (see Table 13.3).

TABLE 13.3

Diagnostic Features of Attention-Deficit/Hyperactivity Disorder (ADHD)

Kind of Problem	Specific Behaviour Pattern
Lack of attention	Fails to attend to details or makes careless errors in schoolwork, etc.
	Has difficulty sustaining attention in schoolwork or play
	Doesn't appear to pay attention to what is being said
	Fails to follow through on instructions or to finish work
	Has trouble organizing work and other activities
	Avoids work or activities that require sustained attention
	Loses work tools (e.g., pencils, books, assignments, toys)
	Becomes readily distracted
	Forgetful in daily activities
Hyperactivity	Fidgets with hands or feet or squirms in his or her seat
	Leaves seat in situations such as the classroom in which remaining seated is required
	Is constantly running around or climbing on things
	Has difficulty playing quietly
Impulsivity	Frequently "calls out" in class
	Fails to wait his/her turn in line, games, etc.

In order to receive a diagnosis of ADHD, the disorder must begin by the age of seven; must have significantly impaired academic, social, or occupational functioning; and must be characterized by a designated number of clinical features shown in this table occurring over a six-month period in at least two settings such as at school, at home, or at work.

Source: Adapted from the DSM-IV-TR (APA, 2000a)..

Activity and restlessness impair the ability of children with ADHD to function in school. They seem incapable of sitting still. They fidget and squirm in their seats, butt into other children's games, have outbursts of temper, and may engage in dangerous behaviour, such as running into the street without looking. All in all, they can drive parents and teachers to despair.

Where does "normal" age-appropriate overactivity end and hyperactivity begin? Assessment of the degree of hyperactive behaviour is crucial because many normal children are called "hyper" from time to time. Some critics of the ADHD diagnosis argue that it merely labels children who are difficult to control as mentally disordered or sick. Most children, especially boys, are highly active during the early school years. Proponents of the diagnosis counter that there is a difference in quality between normal overactivity and ADHD. Normally, overactive children are goal directed and can exert voluntary control over their own behaviour. But children with ADHD appear hyperactive without reason and do not seem to be able to conform their behaviour to the demands of teachers and parents. Put it another way: Most children can sit still and concentrate for a while when they want to; children who are ADHD seemingly cannot.

Children with ADHD tend to do more poorly in school than their peers despite being, for the most part, of average or above average intelligence. They may fail to follow or remember instructions and complete assignments. They are more likely than their peers to have learning disabilities, to repeat grades, and to be placed in special-education classes (Faraone et al., 1993; Leibson, Katusic, Barbaresi, Ransom, & O'Brien, 2001). They also stand a greater risk of having mood disorders, anxiety disorders, and problems getting along with family members (Biederman et al., 1996). They are frequently disruptive in the classroom and tend to get into fights (especially the boys). Not surprisingly, they are frequently unpopular with their classmates. Although ADHD symptoms tend to decline with age, the disorder can persist into adolescence and adulthood (Asherson, Chen, Craddock, & Taylor, 2007; Weiss & Murray, 2003).

Theoretical Perspectives Although the causes of ADHD are not known, both biological and environmental influences are believed to be involved (Arnold, O'Leary, & Edward, 1997; Seidman, Biederman, Faraone, Weber, & Ouelette, 1997). Increasing evidence points to a complex genetic vulnerability to ADHD wherein multiple genes have a singularly small, albeit additive, impact (Faraone & Khan, 2006). Hereditary evidence comes from findings of higher concordance rates for ADHD among monozygotic (MZ) twins than DZ (dizygotic) twins, supporting a genetic linkage (Sherman, McGue, & Ianoco, 1997).

Attention-deficit/hyperactivity disorder (ADHD). ADHD is more common in boys than girls and is characterized by attentional difficulties, restlessness, impulsivity, excessive motor behaviour (continuous running around or climbing), and temper tantrums.

Neuropsychological testing, EEG studies, and MRI studies of children and adolescents with ADHD point to abnormalities in the areas of the brain involved in regulating the processes of attention, inhibition of motor (movement) behaviour, and executive control (i.e., the ability to focus, plan, and act) (Serene, Ashtari, Szeszko, & Kumra, 2007; Bush, Valera, & Seidman, 2005; Castellanos, Glaser, & Gerhardt, 2006; Seidman, Valera, & Makris, 2005). We shall also see that the effects of stimulants on children with ADHD offer some support to the hypothesis of organic causes. Despite evidence suggestive of biological factors, we lack a definitive biological explanation of ADHD. In fact, some theorists suggest that the mounting evidence from neuropsychological studies challenges the long-held belief that ADHD is a single coherent clinical entity (Stefanatos & Baron, 2007).

ADHD has also been linked with exposure to environmental toxins. Children who have ADHD were found to be 2.5 times more likely than other children to have had prenatal exposure to environmental tobacco smoke (ETS) (Braun, Khan, Froehlich, Auinger, & Lanphear, 2006). Moreover, a significant dose–response relationship was found—the greater the exposure to ETS the higher the risk of ADHD, especially for girls. These researchers also found a significant dose–response relationship between higher levels of lead in the blood and ADHD.

Treatment   It seems odd that the drugs used to help ADHD children calm down and attend better in school belong to a class of stimulants that include Ritalin (methylphenidate) and longer-acting variants, such as Ritalin SR and Concerta. These stimulants have a paradoxical effect of calming down children with ADHD and increasing their attention spans. Although the use of stimulant medication is not without criticism, it is clear that these drugs can help many children with ADHD calm down and concentrate better on tasks and schoolwork, perhaps for the first times in their lives (Goldman, Genel, Bezman, & Slanetz, 1998; Greenhill, 1998; Spencer et al., 1996). These drugs not only improve attention in ADHD children, but also reduce impulsivity, overactivity, and disruptive, annoying, or aggressive behaviour (Gillberg et al., 1997; Hinshaw, 1992). Stimulant medication appears to be safe and effective when carefully monitored, and successful in helping about three out of four children with ADHD ("Attention Deficit Disorder—Part II," 1995; Hinshaw, 1992; Spencer et al., 1996). Improvements are noted at home as well as in school. The normal (voluntary) high activity levels shown in physical education classes and on weekends are not disrupted, however.

We do not know what accounts for the seemingly paradoxical effects of stimulants in calming children with ADHD, although it is suspected that these drugs work on neurotransmitter systems in the brain ("Attention Deficit Disorder—Part II," 1995). Although the precise mechanisms are not well understood, we know these drugs heighten dopamine and norepinephrine activity in the prefrontal cortex of the brain, the area that regulates attention and control of impulsive behaviour (Faraone, 2003a, 2003b). Thus, the drugs may help ADHD children focus their attention and avoid acting out impulsively. Stimulant medication has become so popular that its use increased more than sevenfold during the 1990s (Gibbs, 1998). Currently, an estimated 82 in 1000 Canadian children are using these types of drugs as treatment for ADHD (Romano et al., 2005). The rate of usage climbs from 0.58% in four- to five-year-old boys to a peak of 6.31% in ten- to eleven-year-old boys. By comparison, girls are much less likely to use these drugs—the highest usage is at age eight to nine (1.09%).

Although stimulant medication can help reduce restlessness and increase attention, it is hardly a panacea. Canadian pediatric researchers caution that although Ritalin has a significant short-term effect on the symptoms of ADHD, there is a lack of evidence that demonstrates its usefulness beyond four weeks of treatment. Research is needed to determine the long-term effectiveness (Schachter, Pham, King, Langford, & Moher, 2001). Moreover, no solid evidence has shown that stimulant medication improves academic performance or leads to better outcomes in adulthood ("Attention Deficit Disorder—Part II," 1995; Rapport et al., 1994; Rutter, 1997). As in the case of Eddie, the range of effectiveness is limited:

Nine-year-old Eddie is a problem in class. His teacher complains that he is so restless and fidgety that the rest of the class cannot concentrate on their work. He hardly ever sits still. He is in constant motion, roaming the classroom, talking to other children while they are working. He has been suspended repeatedly for outrageous behaviour, most recently swinging from a fluorescent light fixture, from which he was unable to get himself down. His mother reports that Eddie has been a problem since he was a toddler. By the age of three he had become unbearably restless and demanding. He has never needed much sleep and always awakened before anyone else in the family, making his way downstairs and wrecking things in the living room and kitchen. Once, at the age of four, he unlocked the front door and wandered into traffic, but was rescued by a passerby.

Psychological testing shows Eddie to be average in academic ability, but to have a "virtually nonexistent" attention span. He shows no interest in television or in games or toys that require some concentration. He is unpopular with peers and prefers to ride his bike alone or to play with his dog. He has become disobedient at home and at school and has stolen small amounts of money from his parents and classmates.

Eddie has been treated with methylphenidate (Ritalin), but it was discontinued because it had no effect on his disobedience and stealing. However, it did seem to reduce his restlessness and increase his attention span at school.

ADAPTED FROM SPITZER ET AL., 1989, PP. 315–317

Then there is the question of side effects. Although short-term side effects (e.g., loss of appetite or insomnia) usually subside within a few weeks of treatment or may be eliminated by lowering the dose, concerns have been raised about whether stimulants might retard a child's growth. Although these drugs do slow growth for a few years, researchers found that the drug delays but does not stunt a youngster's growth (Gittelman-Klein & Mannuzza, 1990; Gorman, 1998). Recently, Health Canada (2006a) posted a drug advisory warning Canadians with high blood pressure, heart disease, and cardiovascular conditions or an overactive thyroid to avoid any stimulant drugs to manage symptoms of ADHD. In rare cases, these drugs can result in cardiac arrest, strokes, or sudden death. A subsequent Health Canada (2006b) information update also indicated the potential for adverse psychiatric effects, such as agitation and hallucinations in children who use ADHD drugs.

With so many children on Ritalin and similar drugs, critics claim we are too ready to seek a "quick fix" for problem behaviour in children rather than examining other factors contributing to the child's problem, such as dysfunctions in the family (Gibbs, 1998). As one pediatrician put it, "It takes time for parents and teachers to sit down and talk to kids . . . . It takes less time to get a child a pill" (Hancock, 1996, p. 52). Whatever the benefits of stimulant medication, medication alone typically fails to bring the social and academic behaviour of children with ADHD into a normal range (Hinshaw, 1992). Drugs cannot teach new skills. So, attention has focused on whether a combination of stimulant medication and behavioural or cognitive-behavioural techniques can produce greater benefits than either approach alone. Cognitive-behavioural treatment of ADHD combines behaviour modification, typically based on the use of reinforcement (e.g., a teacher praising the child with ADHD for sitting quietly) and cognitive modification (e.g., training the child to silently talk himself or herself through the steps involved in solving challenging academic problems). Thus far, the evidence favours a combination approach. A McMaster University–based review of 14 studies involving nearly 1400 participants found that a combination of medication and behavioural interventions yielded better outcomes than either type of treatment alone (Schachar et al., 2002).

Conduct Disorder

Although they both involve disruptive behaviour, **conduct disorder** differs in important ways from ADHD. Whereas children with ADHD seem literally incapable of controlling

conduct disorder Pattern of abnormal behaviour in childhood characterized by disruptive, antisocial behaviour.

their behaviour, children with conduct disorders purposefully engage in patterns of antisocial behaviour that violate social norms and the rights of others. Whereas children with ADHD throw temper tantrums, children diagnosed as conduct disordered are intentionally aggressive and cruel. Like antisocial adults, many conduct-disordered children are callous and apparently do not experience guilt or remorse for their misdeeds. They may steal or destroy property. In adolescence, they may commit rape, armed robbery, or even homicide. They may cheat in school—when they bother to attend—and lie to cover their tracks. They frequently engage in substance abuse and sexual activity.

The prevalence of conduct disorder in Canadian children and youth is estimated to be 3.3% (Waddell & Shepard, 2002). Conduct disorders are much more common among boys than girls, especially the childhood-onset type in which characteristic features of the disorder appear before age ten (APA, 2000a). Conduct disorder typically takes a somewhat different form in boys than girls. In boys, it is more likely to be manifested in stealing, fighting, vandalism, or disciplinary problems at school, whereas in girls the disorder is more likely to involve lying, truancy, running away, substance use, and prostitution (APA, 2000a). Although there are differences between ADHD and conduct disorder, some children with conduct disorder also display a pattern of short attention span and hyperactivity that may justify a double diagnosis.

Conduct disorder is typically a chronic or persistent disorder (Lahey et al., 1995). Longitudinal studies show that Canadian elementary schoolchildren with conduct disorders are more likely than other children to engage in delinquent acts as early adolescents (Tremblay et al., 1992). Antisocial behaviour in the form of delinquent acts (stealing, truancy, vandalism, fighting or threatening others, and so on) during early adolescence (ages 14 to 15) has also been found to predict alcohol and substance abuse in late adolescence, especially among boys (Boyle et al., 1992). Another form of conduct disorder may involve a cluster of personality traits that have different origins than antisocial behaviour (Wootton, Frick, Shelton, & Silverthorn, 1997). These traits include callousness (uncaring, mean, and cruel behaviour) and an unemotional way of relating to others.

Oppositional Defiant Disorder

oppositional defiant disorder
Disorder in childhood or adolescence characterized by excessive oppositionality or tendencies to refuse requests from parents and others.

Debate continues among professionals over the issue of whether conduct disorder (CD) and **oppositional defiant disorder** (ODD) are separate disorders or variations of a common disruptive behaviour disorder (Rey, 1993). Or perhaps ODD is a precursor or milder form of conduct disorder (Abikoff & Klein, 1992; Biederman et al., 1996). Currently, the two disorders are conceptualized as related but separate disorders. ODD is more closely related to nondelinquent (negativistic) conduct disturbance, and conduct disorder involves more outright delinquent behaviour in the form of truancy, stealing, lying, and aggressiveness (Rey, 1993). University of British Columbia researchers have found a strong association between oppositional defiant disorder symptoms and generalized anxiety symptoms in preadolescent children (Garland & Garland, 2001). However, they noted reluctance on the part of clinicians to give a diagnosis of ODD to children with anxiety disorders. This reluctance can have an impact on treatment and outcomes.

Children with ODD tend to be negativistic or oppositional. They are defiant of authority, which is exhibited by their tendency to argue with parents and teachers and refuse to follow requests or directives from adults. They may deliberately annoy other people, become easily angered or lose their temper, become touchy or easily annoyed, blame others for their mistakes or misbehaviour, feel resentful toward others, or act in spiteful or vindictive ways toward others (Angold & Costello, 1996; APA, 2000a). The disorder typically begins before age eight and develops gradually over a period of months or years. It typically starts in the home environment but may extend to other settings, such as school.

ODD is one of the most common diagnoses among children (Doll, 1996). Studies show that among children diagnosed with a psychological disorder, about one in three are judged to meet the criteria for ODD (Rey, 1993). An estimated 6% to 12% of school-aged children display ODD (Frick & Silverthorn, 2001). ODD is more common overall among boys than girls. However, this overall effect masks a gender shift over age. Among children 12 years of age or younger, ODD appears to be more than twice as common among boys. Yet among adolescents, a higher prevalence is reported in girls (Rey, 1993). By contrast, most studies find conduct disorder to be more common in boys than girls across all age groups.

Theoretical Perspectives   The causal factors in ODD remain obscure. Some theorists believe that oppositionality is an expression of an underlying child temperament described as the "difficult-child" type (Rey, 1993). Others believe that unresolved parent–child conflicts or overly strict parental control may lie at the root of the disorder. Psychodynamic theorists look at ODD as a sign of fixation at the anal stage of psychosexual development, when conflicts between the parent and child may emerge over toilet training. Leftover conflicts may later become expressed in the form of rebelliousness against parental wishes (Egan, 1991). Learning theorists view oppositional behaviours as arising from parental use of inappropriate reinforcement strategies. In this view, parents may inappropriately reinforce oppositional behaviour by "giving in" to the child's demands whenever the child refuses to comply with the parent's wishes, which can become a pattern.

McMaster University researchers have found that family and parenting factors are also implicated in the development of disruptive behaviour disorders such as oppositional defiant disorder and conduct disorder (Cunningham & Boyle, 2002). Some forms of disruptive behaviour disorders appear to be linked to unassertive and ineffective parenting styles, such as failure to provide positive reinforcement for appropriate behaviour and use of harsh and inconsistent discipline for misbehaviour. Families of children with CD tend to be characterized by negative, coercive interactions (Dadds, Sanders, Morrison, & Rebgetz, 1992). Children with CD are often very demanding and noncompliant in relating to their parents and other family members.

Oppositional defiant disorder (ODD). A common childhood disorder that engenders a "no-win" situation for everyone concerned.

Family members often reciprocate by using negative behaviours, such as threatening or yelling at the child or using physical means of coercion. Parental aggression against children with conduct behaviour problems is common, including pushing, grabbing, slapping, spanking, hitting, or kicking (Jouriles, Mehta, McDonald, & Francis, 1997). Parents of children with oppositional defiant disorders or severe conduct disorder display high rates of antisocial personality disorder and substance abuse (Frick, Lahey, Loeber, & Stouthamer-Loeber, 1992). It's not too much of a stretch to speculate that parental modelling of antisocial behaviours can lead to antisocial conduct in their children.

Disruptive behaviour disorders often occur in a context of parental distress, such as marital conflict. Another factor is maternal depression. Depressed mothers tend to display poor parenting behaviours—such as vague and interrupted commands—that may foster disruptive behaviour in their children (Forehand et al., 1988). Mothers of children with conduct disorders are also more likely than other mothers to be inconsistent in their use of discipline and less able to supervise their childrens' behaviour (Frick et al., 1992). Maternal smoking during pregnancy has also been linked to a greater likelihood of conduct disorder in sons (Wakschlag et al., 1997).

Some investigations focus on the ways in which children with disruptive behaviour disorders process information. For example, children who are overly aggressive in their behaviour tend to be biased in their processing of social information: They may assume that others intend them ill when they do not (Akhtar & Bradley, 1991; Lochman, 1992). They usually blame others for the scrapes they get into. They believe they are misperceived and treated unfairly. They may believe that aggression will lead to favourable results (Dodge et al., 1997). They are also less able than their peers to generate alternate (nonviolent) responses to social conflicts (Lochman & Dodge, 1994).

Genetic factors may interact with family or other environmental factors in the development of conduct disorder in children and antisocial behaviour in adolescence (O'Connor, McGuire, Reiss, Hetherington, & Plomin, 1998; Slutske et al., 1997, 1998). Genetic factors may also be involved in the development of oppositional defiant disorder.

Treatment The treatment of conduct disorders remains a challenge. Although there is not an established pharmacological treatment approach, Toronto psychiatrist Lindley Bassarath (2003) reviewed recent studies that indicate that certain antipsychotic and stimulant drugs may be effective in reducing antisocial behaviour in CD children and adolescents. Psychotherapy has not generally been shown to help disruptive children change their behaviour. Placing children with conduct disorders in programs or treatment settings with explicit rules and clear rewards for obeying them may offer greater promise (e.g., Barkley, Hastings, Tousel, & Tousel, 1976; Henggeler et al., 1986). Such programs usually rely on operant conditioning procedures that involve systematic use of rewards and punishments.

Many children with conduct disorders, especially boys, display aggressive behaviour and have problems controlling their anger. Many can benefit from programs designed to help them learn anger coping skills that they can use to handle conflict situations without resorting to violent behaviour. Cognitive-behavioural therapy has been used to teach boys who engage in antisocial and aggressive behaviour to reconceptualize social provocations as problems to be solved rather than as challenges to their manhood that must be answered with violence. They have been trained to use calming self-talk to inhibit impulsive behaviour and control anger whenever they experience social taunts or provocations and to generate and try out nonviolent solutions to social conflicts (Lochman & Lenhart, 1993). Other programs present child models on video demonstrating skills of anger control. The results of these programs appear promising (Kazdin & Weisz, 1998; Webster-Stratton & Hammond, 1997). Sometimes the disruptive child's parents are brought into the treatment process (Kazdin & Whitley, 2003).

Henggeler and his colleagues (Henggeler et al., 1986) have developed a "family-ecological" approach based on Urie Bronfenbrenner's (1979) ecological theory. Like Bronfenbrenner, Henggeler sees children as embedded within various social systems—family, school, criminal justice, community, and so on. He focuses on how youth offenders affect and are affected by the systems with which they interact. The techniques themselves are not unique. Rather, the family-ecological approach tries to change childrens' relationships with multiple systems to end disruptive interactions. This multiple systems approach or *multisystemic therapy (MST) approach* has shown promising results in the treatment of youth offenders in terms of reducing the frequency of subsequent arrests in comparison with youths who received typical youth services from a county youth services department (Henggeler, Melton, & Smith, 1992; Henggeler, Melton, Brondino, Scherer, & Hanley, 1997; Kazdin, 1998; Kazdin & Weisz, 1998).

The following example illustrates the involvement of the parents in the behavioural treatment of a case of oppositional defiant disorder:

> Billy was a seven-year-old second-grader referred by his parents. The family relocated frequently because the father was in the navy. Billy usually behaved when his father was taking care of him, but he was noncompliant with his mother and yelled at her when she gave him instructions. His mother was incurring great stress in the effort to control Billy, especially when her husband was at sea.
>
> Billy had become a problem at home and in school during the first grade. He ignored and violated rules in both settings. Billy failed to carry out his chores and frequently yelled at and hit his younger brother. When he acted up, his parents would restrict him to his room or the yard, take away privileges and toys, and spank him. But all of these measures were used inconsistently. He also played on the railroad tracks near his home and twice the police had brought him home after he had thrown rocks at cars.

A home observation showed that Billy's mother often gave him inappropriate commands. She interacted with him as little as possible and showed no verbal praise, physical closeness, smiles, or positive facial expressions or gestures. She paid attention to him only when he misbehaved. When Billy was noncompliant, she would yell back at him and then try to catch him to force him to comply. Billy would then laugh and run from her.

Billy's parents were informed that the child's behaviour was a product of inappropriate cueing techniques (poor directions), a lack of reinforcement for appropriate behaviour, and lack of consistent sanctions for misbehaviour. They were taught the appropriate use of reinforcement, punishment, and **time out**. The parents then charted Billy's problem behaviours to gain a clearer idea of what triggered and maintained them. They were shown how to reinforce acceptable behaviour and use time out as a contingent punishment for misbehaviour. Billy's mother was also taught relaxation training to help desensitize her to Billy's disruptions. Biofeedback was used to enhance the relaxation response.

During a 15-day baseline period, Billy behaved in a noncompliant manner about four times per day. When treatment was begun, Billy showed an immediate drop to about one instance of noncompliance every two days. Follow-up data showed that instances of noncompliance were maintained at a bearable level of about one per day. Fewer behavioural problems in school were also reported, even though they had not been addressed directly.

ADAPTED FROM KAPLAN, 1986, PP. 227–230

time out Behavioural technique in which an individual who emits an undesired behaviour is removed from an environment in which reinforcers are available and placed in an unreinforcing environment for a period of time as a form of punishment. Time out is frequently used in behavioural programs for modifying behaviour problems in children, in combination with positive reinforcement for desirable behaviour.

In Canada, as in most other industrialized nations, the emphasis is more on treatment than prevention. This usually means that by the time a conduct-disordered youth gets into care, his or her problem behaviour is well established and therefore it is more resistant and more expensive to treat. A failure to implement effective prevention programs may have more to do with short-sighted political agendas and rigid service-delivery systems than it does with program costs or a desire to serve long-term needs to prevent future conduct-disordered youth (Moretti et al., 1997).

STUDY BREAK

Attention-Deficit and Disruptive Behaviour Disorders

Review It

- **What are attention-deficit and disruptive behaviour disorders?** This category includes attention-deficit/hyperactivity disorder (ADHD), conduct disorder, and oppositional defiant disorder. ADHD is characterized by impulsivity, inattention, and hyperactivity. Children with conduct disorders intentionally engage in antisocial behaviour. Children with ODD show negativistic or oppositional behaviour but not outright delinquent or antisocial behaviour characteristic of conduct disorder. However, ODD may represent an early stage of development of conduct disorder.

- **How are these disorders treated?** Stimulant medication is generally effective in reducing hyperactivity, but has not led to general academic gains. Behaviour

therapy may help ADHD children adapt better to school. Behaviour therapy may also be helpful in modifying behaviours of children with conduct disorders and oppositional defiant disorder.

Define It

attention-deficit/ hyperactivity disorder	conduct disorder
	oppositional defiant disorder
hyperactivity	time out

Recall It*

1. All of the following are diagnostic features of attention-deficit/hyperactivity disorder EXCEPT _____.

   a. lack of attention
   b. impulsivity
   c. intentional cruelty
   d. hyperactivity

2. Brain-imaging studies and neuropsychological testing of children with attention-deficit/hyperactivity disorder (ADHD) _____.

   a. fail to show any signs of brain abnormalities
   b. show clear evidence of structural defects in areas of the brain involved in regulating attention
   c. show possible signs of subtle brain abnormalities
   d. show evidence of brain abnormalities, but only in boys

3. The most widely used treatment for attention-deficit/hyperactivity disorder is _____.

   a. insight therapy
   b. cognitive-behavioural therapy
   c. tranquillizing medication
   d. stimulant medication

4. Conduct disorder in boys is more likely to be shown by behaviours such as _____ and _____, whereas in girls it is more likely to involve _____ and _____.

   a. truancy and running away; stealing and fighting
   b. hyperactivity and distractibility; suicidal behaviour and panic attacks

   c. vandalism and disciplinary problems; lying and substance abuse
   d. lying and substance abuse; vandalism and disciplinary problems

5. Theoretical views of oppositional defiant disorder (ODD) have focused on all of the following EXCEPT _____.

   a. parental use of inappropriate reinforcement strategies
   b. underlying child temperament
   c. fixation at the anal stage of psychosexual development
   d. ambivalence over issues of sexual identity

* Recall It answers can be found on the Companion Website for this text.

Think About It

- What are the risks and benefits of using stimulant medication like Ritalin in treating ADHD in children?
- If you had a child with ADHD, would you consider using these drugs? Why or why not?

ANXIETY AND DEPRESSION

Anxieties and fears are a normal feature of childhood, just as they are a normal feature of adult life. Childhood fears—of the dark or of small animals—are commonplace and are usually outgrown naturally. Anxiety is considered abnormal, however, when it is excessive and interferes with normal academic or social functioning or becomes troubling or persistent. Children, like adults, may suffer from different types of diagnosable anxiety disorders, including specific phobias, social phobias, and generalized anxiety disorder (GAD). Although these disorders may develop at any age, we will consider a type of anxiety disorder that typically develops during early childhood: *separation anxiety disorder*.

Children may also show a more general pattern of avoidance of social interactions that characterizes *avoidant personality disorder*. Although children who are socially avoidant or have social phobias may have warm relationships with family members, they tend to be shy and withdrawn around others. Their avoidance of people outside the family interferes with their development of social relationships with their peers. Their distress at being around other children at school can also impede their academic progress. Such problems tend to develop after normal fear of strangers fades, at age two and a half or later.

We often think of childhood as the happiest time of life. Most children are protected by their parent(s) and are unencumbered by adult responsibilities. From the perspective of aging adults, their bodies seem made of rubber and free of aches. They have apparently boundless energy. Despite the stereotype of a happy childhood, clinical depression is found in children and adolescents. Estimates indicate that slightly more than 2% of Canadian children experience a depressive disorder (Waddell & Shepard, 2002). Although rare, major depression has even been found among preschoolers. Although there is no discernible gender difference in the risk of depression in childhood, a prominent gender difference appears after the age of 15 with adolescent girls becoming about twice as likely to become depressed as adolescent boys (Hankin et al., 1998; Lewinsohn,

Rohde, & Seeley, 1994; Nolen-Hoeksema & Girgus, 1994). Nationwide surveys have revealed that, of Canadian youth aged 15 to 19 years, 12% of the females and 3% to 6% of the males have had a major depressive episode (Shaw & Grenier, 2001).

Separation Anxiety Disorder

It is normal for children to show anxiety when they are separated from their caregivers (Ainsworth & Bowlby, 1991). Mary Ainsworth (1989), who has chronicled the development of attachment behaviours, notes that separation anxiety is a normal feature of the child–caregiver relationship and begins during the first year of life. The sense of security normally provided by bonds of attachment apparently encourages children to explore their environments and become progressively independent of their caregivers (Bowlby, 1988).

Separation anxiety disorder is diagnosed when separation anxiety is persistent and excessive or inappropriate for the child's developmental level. That is, three-year-olds ought to be able to attend preschool without nausea and vomiting brought on by anxiety. Six-year-olds ought to be able to attend grade one without persistent dread that something awful will happen to themselves or their parents. Children with this disorder tend to cling to their parents and follow them around the house. They may voice concerns about death and dying and insist that someone stay with them while they are falling asleep. Other features of the disorder include nightmares, stomach aches, nausea and vomiting when separation is anticipated (as on school days), pleading with parents not to leave, or throwing tantrums when parents are about to depart. <u>They may refuse to attend school for fear that something will happen to their parents while they are away.</u> The disorder affects about 4% of children and young adolescents and occurs more frequently, according to community-based studies, among females (APA, 2000a). The disorder may persist into adulthood, leading to an exaggerated concern about the well-being of one's children and spouse and difficulty tolerating any separation from them.

In the past, separation anxiety disorder was usually referred to as *school phobia*. Separation anxiety disorder may occur at preschool ages, however. Today, most cases in which younger children refuse to attend school are viewed as forms of separation anxiety. In adolescence, however, refusal to attend school is also frequently connected with academic and social concerns, in which case the label of separation anxiety disorder would not apply. The development of separation anxiety disorder frequently follows a stressful life event, such as illness, the death of a relative or pet, or a change of schools or homes. Alison's problems followed the death of her grandmother:

separation anxiety disorder
Childhood disorder characterized by extreme fears of separation from parents or others on whom the child is dependent.

Alison's grandmother died when Alison was seven years old. Her parents decided to permit her request to view her grandmother in the open coffin. Alison took a tentative glance from her father's arms across the room, then asked to be taken out of the room. Her five-year-old sister took a leisurely close-up look, with no apparent distress.

Alison had been concerned about death for two or three years by this time, but her grandmother's passing brought on a new flurry of questions: "Will I die?"; "Does everybody die?"; and so on. Her parents tried to reassure her by saying, "Grandma was very, very old, and she also had a heart condition. You are very young and in perfect health. You have many, many years before you have to start thinking about death."

Alison also could not be alone in any room in her house. She pulled one of her parents or her sister along with her everywhere she went. She also reported nightmares about her grandmother and, within a couple of days, insisted on sleeping in the same room with her parents. Fortunately, Alison's fears did not extend to school. Her teacher reported that Alison spent some time talking about her grandmother, but her academic performance was apparently unimpaired.

Alison's parents decided to allow Alison time to "get over" the loss. Alison gradually talked less and less about death, and by the time three months had passed, she was able to go into any room in her house by herself. She wanted to continue to sleep in her parents' bedroom, however, so her parents "made a deal" with her. They would put off the return to her own bedroom until the school year had ended (a month away), if Alison would agree to return to her own bed at that time. As a further incentive, a parent would remain with her until she fell asleep for the first month. Alison overcame the anxiety problem in this fashion with no additional delays.

THE AUTHORS' FILES

Perspectives on Anxiety Disorders in Childhood

Theoretical understandings of excessive anxiety in children to some degree parallel explanations of anxiety disorders in adults. Psychoanalytic theorists argue that childhood anxieties and fears, like their adult counterparts, symbolize unconscious conflicts. Cognitive theorists focus on the role of cognitive biases underlying anxiety reactions. In support of the cognitive model, investigators find that highly anxious children show cognitive biases in processing information, such as interpreting ambiguous situations as threatening, expecting negative outcomes, thinking poorly of themselves and of their ability to cope, and engaging in negative self-talk (e.g., Kazdin, 2003; Weems, Costa, Watts, Taylor, & Cannon, 2007). Expecting the worst, combined with low self-confidence, encourages avoidance of feared activities—with friends, in school, and elsewhere. Negative expectations may also heighten feelings of anxiety to the point where they impede performance. Learning theorists suggest that the occurrence of generalized anxiety may touch on broad themes, such as fears of rejection or failure, that carry across situations. Underlying fears of rejection or self-perceptions of inadequacy may generalize to most areas of social interaction and achievement.

Whatever the causes, overanxious children may profit from the anxiety-control techniques we discussed in Chapter 5, such as gradual exposure to phobic stimuli and relaxation training. Cognitive techniques such as replacing anxious self-talk with coping self-talk may also be helpful (Kendall, 1994). Cognitive-behavioural approaches appear to be effective in treating various childhood anxiety disorders (Kazdin, 2003; Kendall, Safford, Flannery-Schroeder, & Webb, 2004).

Depression in Childhood and Adolescence

The basic features of depression in children and adolescents are similar to those in adults (Kovacs, 1996). Depressed children and adolescents typically show a greater sense of hopelessness, display more cognitive errors and negative attributions (e.g., blaming themselves for negative events), have lower perceived competence or self-efficacy, and lower self-esteem than do their nondepressed peers (Lewinsohn et al., 1994; Tems, Stewart, Skinner, Hughes, & Emslie, 1993). They often report episodes of sadness, crying, and apathy, as well as insomnia, fatigue, and poor appetite. They may refuse to attend school, express fears of their parents' dying, and cling to their parents or retreat to their rooms. They may have suicidal thoughts or attempt suicide.

The average length of a major depressive episode in childhood or adolescence is about 11 months, but an individual episode may last for as long as 18 months in some cases (Goleman, 1994a). Moderate levels of depression, however, may persist for years, severely impacting school performance and social functioning (Nolen-Hoeksema & Girgus, 1994). Adolescent depression is associated with an increased risk of future major depressive episodes and suicide attempts in adulthood (Weissman, 1999). About three out of four children who become depressed from age 8 to 13 have a recurrence later in life (Goleman, 1994a).

Children who experience depression may also lack skills in various domains, including academic performance, social acceptance by peers, and athletic performance (Seroczynski, Cole, & Maxwell, 1997). They may find it hard to concentrate in school and may suffer from impaired memory, making it difficult for them to keep their grades up (Goleman, 1994a). They often keep their feelings to themselves, which may prevent their parents from recognizing the problem and seeking help for them. Negative feelings may also be expressed in the form of anger, sullenness, or impatience, leading to conflicts with parents that in turn can accentuate and prolong depression in the child.

Childhood depression rarely occurs by itself (Hammen & Compas, 1994). Depressed children typically experience other psychological disorders, especially anxiety disorders and conduct or oppositional defiant disorders (Hammen & Compas, 1994). Eating disorders are also common among depressed adolescents, at least among females (Rohde, Lewinsohn, & Seeley, 1991). Overall, childhood depression increases the chances that a child will develop another psychological disorder by at least twentyfold (Angold & Costello, 1993).

We should recognize that depressed children or adolescents may fail to label what they are feeling as depression. They may not report feeling sad even though they appear sad to others and may be tearful (Goleman, 1994a). Part of the problem is cognitive-developmental. Children are not usually capable of recognizing internal feeling states until about the age of seven. They may not be able to identify negative feeling states in themselves, including depression, until adolescence (Larson, Raffaelli, Richards, Ham, & Jewell, 1990). Even adolescents may not recognize what they are experiencing as depression.

Is this child too young to be depressed? Although we tend to think of childhood as the happiest and most carefree time of life, depression is actually quite common among children and adolescents. Depressed children may report feelings of sadness and lack of interest in previously enjoyable activities. Many, however, do not report, or are not aware of, feelings of depression, even though they may look depressed to observers. Depression may also be masked by other problems such as conduct/school-related problems, physical complaints, and overactivity.

Depression in childhood may also be masked by behaviours that do not appear directly related to depression. Conduct disorders, academic problems, physical complaints, and even hyperactivity may stem now and then from unrecognized depression. Among adolescents, aggressive and sexual *acting out* may also be signs of underlying depression.

Correlates and Treatment of Depression in Childhood and Adolescence

Depression and suicidal behaviour in childhood are frequently related to family problems and conflicts. Children who are exposed to stressful life events affecting the family, such as parental conflict or unemployment, stand an increased risk of depression, especially younger children (Nolen-Hoeksema, Girgus, & Seligman, 1992). Stressful life events and a lack of social support from friends and family also figure into the profile of adolescents who become depressed (Lewinsohn et al., 1994). Depression in adolescents may be triggered by such stressful life events as conflicts with parents and dissatisfaction with school grades. Interestingly, the relationship between loss of a parent in childhood and later depression during childhood or adolescence is not a consistent finding; some studies show a connection, whereas others do not (Lewinsohn et al., 1994).

As children mature and their cognitive abilities increase, however, cognitive factors, such as attributional styles, appear to play a stronger role in the development of depression. Older children (sixth- and seventh-graders) who adopt a more helpless or pessimistic explanatory style (attributing negative events to internal, stable, and global causes, and who attribute positive events to external, unstable, and specific causes) are more likely than children with a more optimistic explanatory style to develop depression (Nolen-Hoeksema, Girgus, & Seligman, 1992). Researchers also find that adolescents who are depressed tend to hold more dysfunctional attitudes and to adopt a more helpless explanatory style than their nondepressed peers (Lewinsohn et al., 1994). Like their adult counterparts, children and adolescents with depression tend to adopt a cognitive style characterized by negative attitudes toward themselves and the future (Garber, Weiss, & Shanley, 1993). All in all, the distorted cognitions of depressed children include the following:

1. Expecting the worst (pessimism)
2. Catastrophizing the consequences of negative events

3. Assuming personal responsibility for negative outcomes, even when it is unwarranted
4. Selectively attending to the negative aspects of events

Although there are links between cognitive factors and depression, it remains to be determined whether children become depressed because they think depressing thoughts, whether depression causes changes in cognitive style, or whether depression and cognitive styles interact in more complex ways. Genetic factors also appear to play a role in explaining depressive symptoms, at least among adolescents (O'Connor et al., 1998). The role of genetics in childhood depression requires further study, however (Kovacs, Devlin, Pollock, Richards, & Mukerji, 1997).

Adolescent girls may face a greater risk of depression because they tend to face more social challenges than boys during adolescence—challenges such as pressures to narrow their interests and pursue feminine-typed activities (Nolen-Hoeksema & Girgus, 1994). It may be that girls who adopt a more passive, ruminative style of coping as children may be at greatest risk of becoming depressed when they face socially restrictive attitudes that devalue their accomplishments and abilities in relation to those of boys, when they face restrictions placed on the social roles and activities deemed appropriate for their gender, and when they encounter sexual pressures or abuse.

Accumulating evidence supports the effectiveness of cognitive-behavioural therapy (CBT) in treating depression in childhood and adolescence (Braswell & Kendall, 2001; Lewinsohn & Clarke, 1999). Although individual approaches vary, CBT usually involves a coping skills model in which children or adolescents receive social skills training (e.g., learning how to start a conversation or make friends) to increase the likelihood of obtaining social reinforcement (Kazdin & Weisz, 1998). CBT typically also includes training in problem-solving skills and ways of increasing the frequency of rewarding activities and countering depressive styles of thinking. In addition, family therapy may be useful in helping families resolve underlying conflicts and reorganize their relationships in ways that members can become more supportive of each other.

The earlier generation of antidepressants failed to show superior results to placebos in treating childhood or adolescent depression (Rutter, 1997; Sommers-Flanagan & Sommers-Flanagan, 1996). We cannot assume drugs that may be effective with adults will work as well or be as safe when used with children (Bitiello & Jensen, 1997). However, the drug Prozac, one of the new generation of SSRI antidepressants, has been shown in at least one study to produce better results than a placebo control in relieving severe and persistent depression in children and adolescents (Emslie et al., 1997). Still, the complete elimination of depressive symptoms was rare.

Suicide Among Children and Adolescents Suicide is relatively uncommon among children under the age of ten in Canada. However, for youth aged 10 to 19 years, Health Canada (1999c) reports that after traffic fatalities, suicide is the second leading cause of death, accounting for almost one in five deaths. The rates of suicide climb with age; from 2 in 100 000 between the ages of 10 and 14 years rising to 11.5 between the ages of 15 and 19. Males are about three-and-a-half times as likely to complete a suicide. These official statistics only account for reported suicide; some apparent accidental deaths, such as those due to falling from a window, may be suicides as well.

Despite the commonly held view that children and adolescents who talk about suicide are only venting their feelings, young people who do intend to kill themselves may very well talk about it beforehand (Brody, 1992b). In fact, those who discuss their plans are the ones most likely to carry them out. Moreover, children and adolescents who have survived suicide attempts are most likely to try again (Brody, 1992b). Unfortunately, parents tend not to take their children's suicidal talk seriously. They often refuse treatment for their children or terminate treatment prematurely.

Several factors are associated with an increased risk of suicide among children and adolescents (Levy, Jurkovic, & Spirito, 1995; Lewinsohn et al., 1994; Neiger, 1988):

1. *Gender.* Girls, like women, are three times more likely than boys to attempt suicide. Boys, like men, are more likely to succeed, however, perhaps because boys, like

men, are more apt to use lethal means, such as guns. The presence of a loaded handgun in the house turns out to be the greatest risk factor for completed suicide among children, even those as young as five (Brody, 1992b).

2. *Age.* Young people in late adolescence or early adulthood (ages 15 to 24) are at greater risk than younger adolescents.

3. *Ethnicity.* The suicide rate for Canadian Aboriginal youth is three to four times higher than for youth in the general population (Health Canada, 1999c). The rates of suicide in some First Nations communities are among the highest in the world (Canadian Aboriginal, 1999).

4. *Depression and hopelessness.* Depression and hopelessness, especially when combined with low self-esteem, are major risk factors for suicide among adolescents, as for adults.

5. *Previous suicidal behaviour.* A quarter of adolescents who attempt suicide are repeaters. More than 80% of adolescents who take their lives have talked about it before doing so. Suicidal teenagers may carry lethal weapons, talk about death, make suicide plans, or engage in risky or dangerous behaviour. A family history of suicide also increases risk of teenage suicide (Mann, Underwood, & Arango, 1996).

6. *Family problems.* Family problems are present among about 75% of adolescent suicide attempters. Problems include family instability and conflict, physical or sexual abuse, loss of a parent due to death or separation, and poor parent–child communication (Asarnow, Carlson, & Guthrie, 1987; Wagner, 1997).

7. *Stressful life events.* Many suicides among young people are directly preceded by stressful or traumatic events, such as the break-up of a relationship with a girlfriend or boyfriend, unwanted pregnancy, getting arrested, having problems at school, moving to a new school, or having to take an important test.

8. *Substance abuse.* Addiction in the adolescent's family or by the adolescent is a factor.

9. *Social contagion.* Adolescent suicides sometimes occur in clusters, especially when a suicide or a group of suicides receives widespread publicity (Kessler, Downey, Milavsky, & Stipp, 1988; Phillips & Carstensen, 1986). Adolescents may romanticize suicide as a heroic act of defiance. There are often suicides or attempts among the siblings, friends, parents, or adult relatives of suicidal adolescents. Adolescent suicides may occur in bunches in a community, especially when adolescents are subjected to mounting academic pressures, such as competing for admission to university. Perhaps the suicide of a family member or schoolmate renders suicide a more "real" option for managing stress or punishing others. Perhaps the other person's suicide gives the adolescent the impression that he or she is "doomed" to commit suicide. Note the case of Pam:

Pam was an exceptionally attractive 17-year-old who was hospitalized after cutting her wrists.

"Before we moved to [an upper-middle-class U.S. town in Westchester County]," she told the psychologist, "I was the brightest girl in the class. Teachers loved me. If we had had a yearbook, I'd have been the most likely to succeed. Then we moved, and suddenly I was hit with it. Everybody was bright, or tried to be. Suddenly I was just another ordinary student planning to go to college.

"Teachers were good to me, but I was no longer special, and that hurt. Then we all applied to college. Do you know that 90 percent of the kids in the high school go on to college? I mean four-year colleges? And we all knew—or suspected—that the good schools had quotas on kids from here. I mean you can't have 30 kids from our senior class going to Yale or Princeton or Wellesley, can you? You're better off applying from Utah.

"Then Kim got her early-acceptance rejection from Brown. Kim was number one in the class. Nobody could believe it. Her father had gone to Brown and Kim had scored almost 1500 on her SATs. Kim was out of commission for a few days—I mean she didn't come to school or anything—and then, boom, she was gone. She offed herself, kaput, no more, the end. Then Brian was rejected from Cornell. A few days later, he was gone, too. And I'm like, 'These kids were better than me.' I mean their grades and their SATs were higher than mine, and I was going to apply to Brown and Cornell. I'm like, 'What chance do I have? Why bother?'"

THE AUTHORS' FILES

You can identify how catastrophizing cognitions can play a role in such tragic cases. Consistent with the literature on suicide among adults, suicidal children and adolescents make less use of active problem-solving strategies in handling stressful situations. They may see no other way out of their perceived failures or stresses. As with adults, one approach to working with suicidal children and adolescents involves helping them challenge distorted thinking and generate alternate strategies for handling the problems and stressors they face.

STUDY BREAK

Anxiety and Depression

Review It

- **What types of anxiety disorders affect children?** Anxiety disorders that occur commonly among children and adolescents include specific phobias, social phobia, and generalized anxiety disorder. Children may also show separation anxiety disorder, which involves excessive anxiety at times when they are separated from their parents. Cognitive biases such as expecting negative outcomes, negative self-talk, and interpreting ambiguous situations as threatening figure prominently in anxiety disorders in children and adolescents, as they often do among adults.

- **What are the distinguishing features of depression in childhood and adolescence?** Depressed children, especially younger children, may not report or be aware of feeling depressed. Depression may also be masked by seemingly unrelated behaviours, such as conduct disorders. Depressed children also tend to show cognitive biases associated with depression in adulthood, such as adoption of a pessimistic explanatory style and distorted thinking. Although rare, suicide in children does occur and threats should be taken seriously. Risk factors for adolescent suicide include gender, age, geography, race, depression, past suicidal behaviour, strained family relationships, stress, substance abuse, and social contagion.

Define It

separation anxiety disorder

Recall It*

1. Fears of the dark or of small animals in young children are _____.

   a. normal and are typically outgrown naturally
   b. abnormal and may set the stage for other phobias later in life
   c. common but are not typically outgrown unless they are treated
   d. generally a sign of underlying depression

2. The proportion of Canadian females in the 15- to 19-year age range who are likely to experience major depression is about _____.

   a. 25%
   b. 12%
   c. 3% to 6%
   d. nominal

3. Each of the following is a feature of separation anxiety disorder EXCEPT _____.

   a. clingingness to parents
   b. concerns about death and dying
   c. physical symptoms such as stomach aches, nausea, and vomiting
   d. involuntary soiling of clothes

4. Depressed children show evidence of the following types of distorted cognitions EXCEPT _____.

   a. expecting the worst
   b. catastrophizing the consequences of negative events
   c. attributing negative events to unstable causes
   d. selectively attending to the negative aspects of events

5. The factor most strongly linked to the risk of completed suicide among children is _____.

    a. physical abuse
    b. relocation to another part of the country
    c. the presence of a loaded handgun in the house
    d. the occurrence of suicide in classmates

* Recall It answers can be found on the Companion Website for this text.

WEBLINKS

Autism Society Canada
http://autismsocietycanada.ca
This website is a primary source for Canadian information about autism spectrum disorders, services, and resources.

Canadian Association for Community Living
www.cacl.ca
This site provides information about Canadian community supports and services for persons of all ages who have an intellectual disabilities.

Special Olympics Canada
www.specialolympics.ca
Homepage for Special Olympics Canada, a nonprofit organization dedicated to enriching the lives of Canadians with intellectual disabilities.

Learning Disabilities Association of Canada (LDAC)
www.ldac-taac.ca
This site is Canada's central repository for information about learning disabilities, resources, and supports.

Children and Adults with Attention Deficit Disorders (CHADD)
www.vcn.bc.ca/chaddvan/chaddcanada
This Canadian site is dedicated to the support, education, and betterment of the lives of children and adults with attention deficit disorders.

Children and Youth
www.ontario.cmha.ca/children_and_youth.asp
This page from the Canadian Mental Health Association provides information about a wide range of mental and emotional problems of children and youth.

Abnormal Behaviour in Childhood and Adolescence

Pervasive Developmental Disorders

Autism
One of the most severe disorders of childhood, autism is a chronic lifelong condition

Features
- Impaired social communications
- Impaired social interactions
- Restricted, repetitive and stereotyped behaviour patterns

Theoretical perspectives
- The cause of autism remains unknown

Treatment
- Early intervention is important
- Intensive behavioural treatment (IBT)

Mental Retardation
Broad delay in the development of cognitive and social functioning

Causes of Mental Retardation
- Chromosomal and genetic disorders
- Prenatal infectious diseases and brain injuries
- Cultural or familial causes, such as being raised in an impoverished home environment

Intervention
- Mainstreaming: having all students with disabilities included in the regular classroom
- Behavioural techniques that help them acquire skills in areas such as personal hygiene, work, and social relationships

Learning Disorders
Average or higher intelligence, but shows inadequate development in reading, math, or writing skills that impairs school performance or daily activities

Types of Learning Disorders
- Mathematics disorder
- Disorder of written expression
- Reading disorder (dyslexia is most common)

Intervention
- Remediation and accommodation of specific skill deficits
- Target information processing style and academic strengths
- Individual education plan (IEP): learning and behaviour outcomes contract

Theoretical Perspectives
- Neurobiological problems with visual or auditory sensation and perception
- Genetic factors in dyslexia

Anxiety and Depression

Separation Anxiety Disorder
- Characterized by extreme fears of separation from parents or others on whom the child is dependent
- Persistent and excessive or inappropriate for the child's developmental level

Perspectives on Anxiety Disorders in Childhood
- Psychoanalytic theorists: anxiety symbolizes unconscious conflicts
- Cognitive model: expecting negative outcomes, negative self-talk, and interpreting ambiguous situations as threatening
- Learning therapies: anxiety-control techniques
- Cognitive-behavioural therapies: coping self-talk

Depression in Childhood and Adolescence
- Sense of hopelessness, displays cognitive errors and negative attributions, lower perceived competence or self-efficacy, and lower self-esteem
- Episodes of sadness, crying, and apathy, as well as insomnia, fatigue, and poor appetite
- Suicide is the second leading cause of death in youth aged 10 to 19 years

Correlates and Treatment of Depression in Childhood and Adolescence
- Frequently related to family problems and conflicts
- Stressful life events and a lack of social support from friends and family
- Cognitive-behavioural therapy
- Family therapy

Attention-Deficit and Disruptive Behaviour Disorders

Attention-Deficit/Hyperactivity Disorder (ADHD)
Characterized by excessive motor activity and inability to focus one's attention

Theoretical Perspectives
- Biological and environmental influences
- Brain abnormalities involved in regulating the processes of attention, inhibition of motor (movement) behaviour, and executive control
- Neuropsychological studies challenge the long-held belief that ADHD is a single coherent clinical entity
- Linked with exposure to environmental toxins

Intervention
- Stimulant drugs
- Cognitive-behavioural treatment combined with medication

Conduct Disorder
Pattern of purposeful antisocial behaviour that violates social norms and the rights of others

Oppositional Defiant Disorder
Characterized by excessive oppositionality or tendencies to refuse requests from parents and others

Theoretical Perspectives
- Family and parenting factors
- Biased processing of social information

Treatment
- Cognitive-behavioural therapy
- Multisystemic therapy (MST) approach

CHAPTER 14

Abnormal Psychology and Society

CHAPTER OUTLINE

Psychiatric Commitment and
    Patients' Rights
The Insanity Defence

Did You Know That...

See the underlined text on the pages indicated below for more information on these interesting and often misunderstood facts.

- People can't be committed to a psychiatric hospital just because they're eccentric? (p. 505)

- Psychologists and other mental health professionals are not very accurate when it comes to predicting dangerousness? (p. 506)

- Therapists may be obligated by law to breach client confidentiality to warn intended victims of threats of violence made against them by their clients? (p. 509)

- The person who attempted to assassinate former prime minister Jean Chrétien was found to be not criminally responsible by a court of law? (p. 514)

- Despite beliefs to the contrary, the insanity defence is used in very few trials and is successful in fewer still? (p. 515)

- It is possible for a defendant to be held competent to stand trial but still be judged not guilty of a crime by reason of insanity? (p. 517)

As a youngster, Edmond Yu showed he had the drive to achieve great things. He was an excellent student, leaving home early for classes and studying in his room late every night. Yet he balanced his rigorous academic work with a variety of hobbies. After emigrating from Hong Kong to Canada, Edmond spent two years at York University in pre-med classes, and later earned a scholarship to study medicine at the University of Toronto.

In his first term, Edmond's marks were excellent. But during the second term, he started to become reclusive; he began studying from home, avoiding campus except for exams or group projects. The initial signs that all was not well were detected an ocean away by his sister, Katherine Yu, who was living in Hong Kong. She got a phone call saying there had been a serious fight between Edmond and his elder brother. Edmond had been asked to leave the house. There were other calls from Edmond, too, in which he would ramble about someone stealing his wallet at the university. He sounded incoherent, illogical; not himself. "I realized at that point there was something wrong with him," his sister recalls. She flew to Canada.

Things began to quickly spiral downward. Katherine remembers going to his apartment to check up on him. "He said the people in his building, as well as in nearby buildings, were spies," she says. "He believed there were satellites planted in his building—even in his own apartment—watching him." Likely unaware he was suffering from an illness, Edmond rejected Katherine's attempts to get him to seek help.

Katherine went to Edmond, demanding he accept help, see a doctor, take medication. He refused. "I knew there was something wrong with him. He asked me to leave, but I insisted and kept on talking. And then he slapped me in the face." It was painful for Katherine to use the incident against her brother, but she felt his best interests were at stake. The police apprehended Edmond and he was taken to the Clarke Institute of Psychiatry, where he was diagnosed as having paranoid schizophrenia. He was persuaded that, if he accepted treatment, he might still be able to return to medical school. He consented.

At least initially, Edmond tried to stick with the treatment, which consisted of antipsychotic drugs to quell the delusions. Unfortunately, some people experience severe side effects with psychotropic drugs. Edmond was one of them. "When he was on medication, he seemed to be a totally different person," Katherine says. "All he could do was eat and sleep. He was completely non-communicative. His hands were so shaky he couldn't even hold a bowl of soup properly. The soup would always spill."

It was clear to Edmond he would not be able to attend school while on medication. It was equally clear he would not be able to attend school without it. Edmond requested that a doctor certify him fit for medical school. But because he would not take his medication, the doctor refused.

With no classes to attend, no career as a doctor, Edmond again flew back to Hong Kong. Within a month, he was picked up by police on a charge of disturbing the peace. Edmond was sent to a psychiatric hospital. The hospital then decided to impose treatment on Edmond—to force medication. When he returned to Canada, he immediately stopped taking the drugs. His non-compliance marked the start of a long struggle with his family over treatment.

Edmond's illness deepened, and his behaviour worsened. He was overtaken by paranoia and suspicion. He would talk non-stop. He felt he had special influence over world affairs. He feared those around him were conspiring to harm him. On occasion, he would be verbally abusive. And he began burning things—clothes, books, photographs. He would take them out on to the driveway and put a match to them. Edmond also started to meditate in front of the family's Scarborough home, sometimes for hours. On two occasions, he threw a knife at a dartboard he set up outside the garage door. Neighbours called police both times. Other times, they just stared from their windows.

Edmond began to drift, from housing to hostels—where he says he was beaten and robbed—to the street. He made the occasional visit home, his deterioration more evident each time. His clothes were becoming ragged. The family later found him living in a public washroom in Grange Park, behind the Art Gallery of Ontario. His family managed to obtain a court order for him to be assessed by a psychiatrist. As a result, he was involuntarily committed to the Clarke Institute of Psychiatry for more than three months. Doctors declared him incapable of making his own treatment decisions, and his mother was appointed a substitute decision-maker. She had the power to authorize forced medication.

Over the next few years, a pattern set in: arrest, often for some form of assault, incarceration, release. The combination of winter, homelessness, and illness were beginning to wear Edmond down. Late one afternoon, he was at the bus loop at the foot of Spadina Ave. Unaccountably, he struck a woman in the face, then boarded a bus. The police were called. The driver ordered everyone off the bus and left Edmond alone with the doors locked. Three police officers boarded the bus and tried to persuade Edmond to leave with them. At one point, he did agree to leave, but then took a hammer out of his jacket.

"I watched while he waggled his right wrist with the hammer in it," said a witness, who watched from an adjacent streetcar. "Then the movement of his wrist stopped, and seconds passed, when I heard what I thought initially was a cap gun. I could see the red flash of the gun, and the body slumped."

Constable Lou Pasquino fired six shots. One hit Edmond in the throat, his head twisting as the shots continued. A second hit his ear and entered the side of his head. The third hit the back of his skull. Edmond was dead before he hit the floor.

SCOTT SIMMIE, "REALITY IS SOMETIMES PAINFUL," *TORONTO STAR*, OCTOBER 3, 1998.

THE CASE OF EDMOND YU touches on many important issues, including the issue of balancing the rights of the individual with the rights of society. Do people have the right to live on the streets under unsanitary conditions? There are those who argue that a just and humane society has the right and responsibility to care for people who are perceived incapable of protecting their own best interests, even if "care" means involuntarily committing them to a psychiatric institution. Do people who are obviously mentally disturbed have the right to refuse treatment? Do psychiatric institutions have the right to inject them with antipsychotic and other drugs against their will? Should mental patients with a history of disruptive or violent behaviour be hospitalized indefinitely or permitted to live in supervised residences in the community once their conditions are stabilized? When severely disturbed people break the law, should society respond to them with the criminal justice system or with the mental health system?

In this chapter, we consider psychiatric commitment and other issues that arise from society's response to abnormal behaviour, such as the rights of patients in institutions, the use of the insanity defence in criminal cases, and the responsibility of professionals to warn individuals who may be placed at risk by the dangerous behaviour of their clients.

Mandatory medication? Should people suffering from serious mental illnesses, like Edmond Yu, be required to receive treatment?

PSYCHIATRIC COMMITMENT AND PATIENTS' RIGHTS

Legal placement of people in psychiatric institutions against their will is called **civil** or psychiatric **commitment.** Through civil commitment, individuals deemed to be mentally disordered and a threat to themselves or others may be involuntarily confined to psychiatric institutions to provide them with treatment and help ensure their own safety and that of others. Civil commitment should be distinguished from legal or criminal commitment, in which an individual who has been acquitted of a crime by reason of insanity—that is, found to be "not criminally responsible on account of a mental disorder"—is placed in a psychiatric institution for treatment. In **legal commitment**, a criminal's unlawful act is judged by a court of law to be the result of a mental disorder or defect that should be dealt with by having the individual committed to a psychiatric hospital where treatment can be provided, rather than having the individual incarcerated in a prison.

Civil commitment should also be distinguished from voluntary hospitalization, in which a person voluntarily seeks treatment in a psychiatric institution, and can, with adequate notice, leave the institution when she or he so desires. Even in such cases, however, when hospital staffers believe that a voluntary patient presents a threat to her or his own welfare or to others, the staff may petition the court to change the patient's legal status from voluntary to involuntary.

Involuntary placement of an individual in a psychiatric hospital usually requires that a petition be filed by a relative or a physician. Psychiatric review panels may be empowered by the court to evaluate the person in a timely fashion. In the event of commitment, the law usually requires periodic legal review and recertification of the patient's involuntary status. The legal process is intended to ensure that people are not indefinitely "warehoused" in psychiatric hospitals. Hospital staff must demonstrate the need for continued inpatient treatment.

Legal safeguards are usually in place to protect people's civil rights in commitment proceedings. Defendants have the right to due process and to be assisted by a lawyer, for example. But when individuals are deemed to present a clear and imminent threat to themselves or others, the court may order immediate hospitalization until a more formal commitment hearing can be held. Such emergency powers are usually limited to a specific period, like 72 hours. During this time, a formal commitment petition must be filed with the court or the individual has a right to be discharged.

Standards for psychiatric commitment have been tightened over the past generation, and the rights of individuals who are subject to commitment proceedings are more strictly protected. In the past, psychiatric abuses were more commonplace. People were often committed without clear evidence that they posed a threat. These days, civil commitment is based on standards that give greater weight to patients' rights. The current criteria for civil commitment differ to some extent across Canadian provinces and territories. However, all require that the person be mentally ill *and* pose an *imminent* risk of harm or danger to him- or herself or others (Schuller & Ogloff, 2000). Thus, people cannot be committed or forced to take medication because of their eccentricity. People must be judged mentally ill and to present a clear and present danger to themselves or others in order for them to be psychiatrically committed.

Contemporary tightening of civil commitment laws provides greater protection of the rights of the individual. Even so, some critics of the psychiatric system have called for the complete abolition of psychiatric commitment on the grounds that commitment deprives the individual of liberty in the name of therapy, and that such a loss of liberty cannot be justified in a free society. Perhaps the most vocal and persistent critic of the civil commitment statutes is psychiatrist Thomas Szasz. In the 1960s, Szasz argued that the label of *mental* illness is a societal invention that transforms social deviance into medical illness. In Szasz's view, which he still maintains today (Szasz, 2006), people should not be deprived of their liberty because their behaviour is perceived to be socially deviant or disruptive. According to Szasz, people who violate the law should be prosecuted for criminal behaviour, not confined to a psychiatric hospital. Although psychiatric commitment may prevent

civil commitment Legal process involved in placing an individual in a mental institution, even against his or her will. Also called *psychiatric commitment.*

legal commitment Legal process involved in confining a person found "not criminally responsible on account of a mental disorder" in a mental institution; also called *criminal commitment.*

some people from acting violently, it *does* violence to many more by depriving them of liberty:

> The mental patient, we say, *may be* dangerous: he may harm himself or someone else. But we, society, *are* dangerous: we rob him of his good name and of his liberty, and subject him to tortures called "treatments" (Szasz, 1970, p. 279).

Szasz's strident opposition to institutional psychiatry and his condemnation of psychiatric commitment have focused attention on abuses in the mental health system. Szasz has also persuaded many professionals to question the legal, ethical, and moral bases of coercive psychiatric treatment in the forms of involuntary hospitalization and forced medication. Many caring and concerned professionals draw the line at abolishing psychiatric commitment, however. They argue that people may not be acting in their considered best interests when they threaten suicide or harm to others or when their behaviour becomes so disorganized that they cannot meet their basic needs. Indeed, investigations, including research by Daniel Frank and colleagues (Frank, Perry, Kean, Sigman, & Geagea, 2005) at McGill University, have shown that court orders mandating severely ill psychotic patients to undergo compulsory treatment have resulted in those patients tending to spend less time in hospital and therefore receiving increased personal freedom.

Predicting Dangerousness

In order to be psychiatrically committed, people must be judged to be at imminent risk of harming themselves or others. Professionals are thus responsible for making accurate predictions of dangerousness to determine whether people should be involuntarily hospitalized or maintained involuntarily in a hospital. But how accurate are professionals in predicting dangerousness? Do professionals have special skills or clinical wisdom that renders their predictions accurate, or are their predictions no more accurate than those of laypeople?

Unfortunately, psychologists and other mental health professionals who rely on their clinical judgments are not very accurate when it comes to predicting the dangerousness of the people they treat. Mental health professionals tend to *overpredict* dangerousness—that is, to label many individuals as dangerous when they are not (Monahan, 1981). Clinicians tend to err on the side of caution in overpredicting the potential for dangerous behaviour, perhaps because they believe that failure to predict violence may have more serious consequences than overprediction. Overprediction of dangerousness does deprive many people of liberty on the basis of fears that turn out to be groundless. According to Szasz and other critics of the practice of psychiatric commitment, the commitment of the many to prevent the violence of the few is a form of preventive detention that violates the basic principles on which democracies like Canada were founded. A leading authority in the field, John Monahan put the issue this way: "When it comes to predicting violence, our crystal balls are terribly cloudy" (Rosenthal, 1993, p. A1).

Predictions of dangerousness based on the clinical judgments of psychologists and psychiatrists may be somewhat more accurate than predictions based on chance alone (Bloom, Webster, Hucker, & De Freitas, 2005). The accuracy of predicting violence, especially violence in the long term, is improved if clinicians use the Psychopathy Checklist or similar instruments (Bloom et al., 2005). The Psychopathy Checklist was developed by psychologist Robert Hare and his colleagues at the University of British Columbia (e.g., Hart, Cox, & Hare, 1995). People with high scores on the checklist are classified as psychopaths. According to Hare (1996), psychopaths are

> predators who use charm, manipulation, intimidation, and violence to control others and to satisfy their own selfish needs. Lacking in conscience and in feelings for others, they cold-bloodedly take what they want and do as they please, violating social norms and expectations without the slightest sense of guilt or regret (p. 26).

Psychopaths, particularly the ones who are highly intelligent and not impulsive, can have ruthlessly successful careers in the corporate world, in government, or both. Hare and his colleague Paul Babiak refer to such individuals as "snakes in suits" (Babiak & Hare, 2006).

One famous example of a psychopath, according to Hare, is Paul Bernardo, the serial rapist and murderer. In Hare's view, "Bernardo was a cold-blooded predator lacking in remorse.... He is a perfect example of a psychopath" (Kaihla, 1996, pp. 50–51).

Psychopathy is similar to antisocial personality disorder (as described in Chapter 8). Psychopathy predicts future violence in part because it assesses past violence, which is one of the better predictors of future violence (Bloom et al., 2005). To measure a person's level of psychopathy, the clinician conducts an interview-based evaluation and checks the person's criminal record.

Although scores on the Psychopathy Checklist and similar instruments can improve the clinician's ability to predict violence, the accuracy is far from perfect, and predictive errors are often made. Unfortunately, although past violent behaviour may be the best predictor of future violence, hospital staff may not be permitted access to criminal records or may lack the time or resources to track them down. A further problem is that it is much more difficult to predict imminent violence (e.g., Will the person be violent within the next 48 hours?) than it is to predict long-term violence (e.g., Will the person be violent in the next 12 months?). The prediction problem has been cited by some as grounds for the abandonment of dangerousness as a criterion for civil commitment.

Although their crystal balls may be cloudy, mental health professionals who work in institutional settings continue to be called on to make these predictions—deciding whom to commit and whom to discharge based largely on how they appraise the potential for violence. Clinicians may be more successful in predicting violence, especially long-term violence, by basing predictions on the patient's level of psychopathy. Another variable that may improve predictability is substance abuse. The potential for violence is heightened in people with serious psychiatric disorders when they use alcohol, crack, or other drugs (Friedman, 2006). Various factors may lead to inaccurate predictions of dangerousness, including the following.

The Post Hoc Problem Recognizing violent tendencies after a violent incident occurs (*post hoc*) is easier than predicting it (*ad hoc*). It is often said that hindsight is 20/20; it is easier to piece together fragments of people's prior behaviours as evidence of their violent tendencies *after* they have committed acts of violence. Predicting a violent act before the fact is a more difficult task, however.

The Problem in Leaping from the General to the Specific Generalized perceptions of violent tendencies may not predict specific acts of violence. Most people who have "general tendencies" toward violence may never act on them. Nor is classification within a diagnostic category associated with aggressive or dangerous behaviour, such as psychopathy or antisocial personality disorder, a sufficient basis for predicting *specific* violent acts in individuals (Bloom & Rogers, 1987; Friedman, 2006). In other words, psychopathy predicts the general tendency to be violent, but it does not tell us when or how the person might become violent.

Problems in Defining Dangerousness One difficulty in assessing the predictability of dangerousness is the lack of agreement in defining the criteria for labelling behaviour as violent or dangerous. There is no universal agreement on the definition of violence or dangerousness. Most people would agree that crimes such as murder, rape, and assault are acts of violence. There is less agreement, even among authorities, for labelling other acts—for example, driving recklessly, harshly criticizing one's spouse or children, destroying property, selling drugs, shoving into people at a bar, or stealing cars—as violent or dangerous. Consider also the dangerous (but legal) behaviour of business owners and corporate executives who produce and market cigarettes despite widespread knowledge of the death and disease caused by these substances. Clearly, the determination of which behaviours are regarded as dangerous involves moral and political judgments within a given social context.

Base-Rate Problems The prediction of dangerousness is complicated by the fact that violent acts like murder, assault, and suicide are infrequent or rare events at the individual level within the general population, even if newspaper headlines sensationalize them regularly. Other rare events—like earthquakes—are also difficult to predict with any degree of certainty concerning when or where they will strike.

The relative difficulty of making predictions of infrequent or rare events is known as the *base-rate problem*. Consider as an example the problem of suicide prediction. If the suicide rate in a given year has a low base rate of about 1% of a clinical population, the likelihood of accurately predicting that any given person in this population will commit suicide is very difficult. You would be correct 99% of the time if you predicted that any given individual in this population would *not* commit suicide in a given year. But to predict the nonoccurrence of suicide in every case would mean you would fail to predict the relatively few cases in which suicide does occur, even though virtually all of your predictions would likely be correct. Yet predicting the one likely case of suicide among each 100 people in the population is sure to be tricky. You are bound to be wrong more often than not if you made predictions of suicide in a given year in only three cases out of 100 (even if one of the three did commit suicide).

When clinicians make predictions, they weigh the relative risks of incorrectly failing to predict the occurrence of a behaviour (a *false negative*) against the consequences of incorrectly predicting it (a *false positive*). Clinicians often err on the side of caution by overpredicting dangerousness. From the clinician's perspective, erring on the side of caution might seem like a no-lose situation. Yet many people committed to an institution under such circumstances are denied their liberty when they would not actually have acted violently against themselves or others.

The Unlikelihood of Disclosure of Direct Threats of Violence How likely is it that truly dangerous people will disclose their intentions to health professionals who are evaluating them or to their own therapists? The client in therapy is not likely to inform a therapist of a clear threat such as, "I'm going to kill _____ next Wednesday morning." Threats are more likely to be vague and nonspecific, as in, "I'm so sick of _____; I could kill her," or "I swear he's driving me to murder." In such cases, therapists must infer dangerousness from hostile gestures and veiled threats. Vague, indirect threats of violence are less reliable indicators of dangerousness than specific and direct threats.

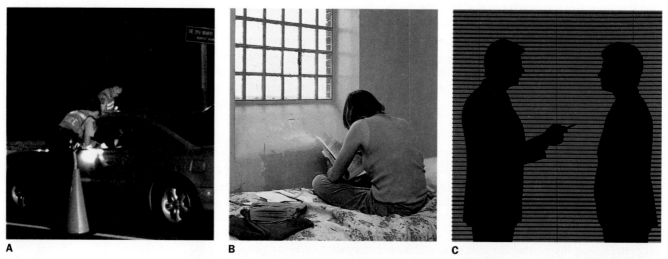

A **B** **C**

Who is the most dangerous? Is it the apparently drunk driver (A)? Is it the institutionalized psychiatric patient (B)? Or is it the scheming corporate executive (C)? Critics of the mental health system, such as psychiatrist Thomas Szasz, point out that drunk drivers account for more injuries and deaths than do people with paranoid schizophrenia, although the latter are more likely to be committed. Others have suggested that corporate executives who knowingly make decisions that jeopardize the health of employees and consumers to maximize profits are guilty of corporate violence that accounts for more deaths and injuries than other types of crime.

The Difficulty of Predicting Behaviour in the Community from Behaviour in the Hospital Much of the research on the accuracy of clinical predictions of dangerousness is based on the predictions of the long-term dangerousness of hospitalized patients when they are discharged. Clinicians often base such predictions on patients' behaviour in the hospital. Violent or dangerous behaviour may be situation specific, however. A model patient who is able to adapt to a structured environment like that of a psychiatric hospital may be unable to cope with the pressures of independent life in the community. Accuracy is improved when predictions of potential violence are based on the person's past community behaviour, such as a history of violent incidents, rather than on the person's behaviour in the hospital setting (Bloom et al., 2005).

As we explore in the accompanying "A Closer Look" box, the problem of predicting dangerousness also arises when therapists need to evaluate the seriousness of threats made by their patients against others.

Patients' Rights

We have considered society's right to hospitalize involuntarily people who are judged to be mentally ill and to pose a threat to themselves or others. What happens following commitment, however? Do involuntarily committed patients have the right to receive or demand treatment? Or can society just warehouse them in psychiatric facilities indefinitely without treating them? Consider the opposite side of the coin as well: May people who are involuntarily committed refuse treatment? Such issues fall under the umbrella of *patients' rights*. Generally speaking, the history of abuses in the mental health system, as highlighted in such popular books and movies as *One Flew Over the Cuckoo's Nest*, have led to a tightening of standards of care and adoption of legal guarantees to protect patients' rights. The legal status of some issues, such as aspects of the right to treatment, remain unsettled, however.

duty to warn Obligation imposed on therapists to warn third parties of threats made against them by the therapists' clients. In the U.S., the *Tarasoff* case established the legal basis for duty-to-warn provisions. Although U.S. law does not apply in Canada, the Canadian Psychological Association states that, ethically, therapists have a duty to warn.

A CLOSER LOOK

The Duty to Warn

One of the most difficult dilemmas a therapist may face is whether or not to disclose confidential information that could protect third parties from harm. Part of the difficulty lies in determining whether or not the client has made a bona fide threat against another person.

The other part of the dilemma is that the information a client discloses in psychotherapy is generally considered to be confidential. But this right is not absolute. The therapist is obliged to breach confidentiality under certain conditions, such as when there is clear and compelling evidence that an individual poses a serious threat to others. Under such conditions, the therapist could, for example, call the police to prevent the patient from causing harm to him- or herself or others.

In addition, an important Californian case, *Tarasoff v. the Regents of the University of California*, established a basis for the therapist's **duty to warn** the patient's potential victims. In 1969, a graduate student at the University of California at Berkeley, Prosenja Poddar, a native of India, became depressed when his romantic overtures toward a young woman, Tatiana Tarasoff,

were rebuffed. Poddar entered psychotherapy with a psychologist at a student health facility, during the course of which he informed the psychologist that he intended to kill Tatiana when she returned from her summer vacation. The psychologist, concerned about Poddar's potential for violence, first consulted with his colleagues and then notified the campus police. He informed them that Poddar was dangerous and recommended he be taken to a facility for psychiatric treatment.

Poddar was subsequently interviewed by the campus police. They believed he was rational and released him after he promised to keep his distance from Tatiana. Poddar then terminated treatment with the psychologist, and shortly afterward killed Tatiana. He shot her with a pellet gun when she refused to allow him entry to her home and then repeatedly stabbed her as she fled into the street. Poddar was found guilty of the lesser sentence of voluntary manslaughter, rather than murder, based on testimony of three psychiatrists that Poddar suffered from diminished mental capacity and paranoid schizophrenia. Under California law, his diminished capacity prevented the finding of malice that was necessary for conviction on a charge of first- or second-degree murder.

(continued)

Following a prison term, Poddar returned to India, where he reportedly made a new life for himself (Schwitzgebel & Schwitzgebel, 1980). Tatiana's parents, however, sued the university. They claimed that the university health centre had failed in its responsibility to warn Tatiana of the threat made against her by Poddar. The Supreme Court of the State of California agreed with the parents. They ruled that a therapist who has reason to believe a client poses a serious threat to another person is obligated to warn the potential victim. This obligation is not met by notifying police. This ruling imposed on therapists a duty-to-warn obligation when their clients show the potential for violence by making threats against others. The ruling recognized that the rights of the intended victim outweigh the rights of confidentiality. Under *Tarasoff*, the therapist does not merely have a *right* to breach confidentiality and warn potential victims of danger, but is *obligated* by law to divulge such confidences to the victim.

Does the *Tarasoff* decision influence Canadian mental health practitioners? Since U.S. court decisions do not apply in Canada, the *Tarasoff* ruling does not necessarily have sway in this country. Some Canadian civil lawsuits have raised arguments similar to those in the *Tarasoff* case, but there has yet to be a legal precedent like the *Tarasoff* ruling (Glancy & Chaimowitz, 2003; Schuller & Ogloff, 2000). Even so, it could be argued that it is ethical for mental health practitioners to warn third parties of impending harm. Accordingly, a duty to warn has been included in the code of ethics for the Canadian Psychological Association (2000). The code states that psychologists should

> do everything reasonably possible to stop or off-set the consequences of actions by others when these actions are likely to cause serious physical harm or death. This may include reporting to appropriate authorities (e.g., the police) or an intended victim, and would be done even when a confidential relationship is involved (p. 19).

The duty-to-warn provision poses ethical and practical dilemmas for psychologists and other psychotherapists. Psychotherapists have an ethical duty to assess the potential violence of their clients, *even though professionals are not generally able to predict dangerousness with a high degree of accuracy*. This means that therapists may actually feel obliged to protect their personal interests and those of others by breaching confidentiality on the mere suspicion that their clients harbour violent intentions toward third parties.

Because there are very few cases in which clients' threats are carried out, the *Tarasoff* ruling may serve to

deny many clients their rights to confidentiality in order to prevent such rare instances. Although some clinicians may "overreact" to *Tarasoff* and breach confidentiality without sufficient cause, it can be argued that the interests of the few potential victims outweigh the interests of the many who may suffer a loss of confidentiality.

Although therapists have difficulty accurately predicting dangerousness, the duty-to-warn provision obliges them to judge whether or not their clients' disclosures indicate a clear intent to harm others. In the *Tarasoff* case, the threat was obvious enough to prompt the therapist to breach confidentiality by requesting the help of campus police. In most cases, however, threats are not so clear-cut. There remains a lack of clear criteria for determining whether or not a therapist "should have known" that a client was dangerous before a violent act occurs (Fulero, 1988). In the absence of guidelines that specify the criteria therapists should use to fulfill their duty to warn, they must rely on their best subjective judgments. Although the intent of the *Tarasoff* decision was to protect potential victims, it may inadvertently increase the risks of violence when applied to clinical practice (Stone, 1976). For example,

1. *Clients may be less willing to confide in their therapists.* Under the obligations imposed on therapists by *Tarasoff*, clients may be less willing to confide violent urges to their therapists, making it more difficult for therapists to help them diffuse these feelings before they are acted on.

2. *Potentially violent people may be less likely to enter therapy.* People with violent tendencies may be less willing to enter therapy for fear that disclosures made to a therapist may be revealed.

3. *Therapists may be less likely to probe violent tendencies for fear of legal complications.* To protect themselves and their careers, therapists may avoid asking clients questions concerning potential violence in the belief that they are legally protected if they remain ignorant of them (Wise, 1978). Therapists might also avoid accepting patients for treatment who are believed to have violent tendencies.

It is unclear whether *Tarasoff* has protected or endangered lives. It is clear, however, that *Tarasoff* has raised concerns for clinicians who are trying to meet both ethical and clinical responsibilities to their clients. Therapists must not lose sight of the primary therapeutic responsibility to their clients when ethical or legal issues arise. They must balance the obligation to meet their responsibilities under duty-to-warn guidelines with the need to help their clients resolve the feelings of rage and anger that give rise to violent threats.

Right to Treatment We might assume that mental health institutions that accept people for treatment will provide them with treatment. However, it is only in the past two decades that Canada has adequately extended civil rights to people in psychiatric hospitals. Patient-advocacy groups and precedent-setting court cases have been required to establish important patient rights, such as the right to treatment in the least restrictive environment (Olley & Ogloff, 1995).

Treatment in the least restrictive environment involves, among other things, not hospitalizing a patient when he or she can be appropriately treated as an outpatient. This is important because it allows the person to continue living in the community. Thus, the state provides mandatory care when necessary, such as involuntary hospitalization, but care must not be unduly restrictive.

A problem in implementing this approach concerns the availability of treatment resources. A person might benefit from either inpatient treatment or a less restricting alternative, such as treatment in a group home in the community. But what happens when the less restrictive alternatives are not available? Even in wealthy countries like Canada, there are insufficient resources for treating patients in the community. Unfortunately, some patients are treated in psychiatric hospitals when they could be living in supervised accommodation in the community.

What are the rights of mental patients? Popular books and films such as *One Flew Over the Cuckoo's Nest* starring Jack Nicholson have highlighted many of the abuses of psychiatric hospitals. In recent years, a tightening of standards of care and the adoption of legal safeguards have led to better protection of the rights of patients in psychiatric hospitals.

To make matters more complicated, patients have the right to be treated in the community even when they might be more appropriately treated in a psychiatric hospital. If community resources are unavailable, then the family sometimes assumes the onus of care, even though they may be ill prepared. This can be highly stressful for the family, as illustrated in the following example:

> The sturdy oak bar snaps snugly across the door leading to Robbi-Lynn Jessop's bedroom. Her parents, Bob and Pamela, place it there each night to prevent their daughter from killing them. Once a gifted student at Riverside Secondary School in Windsor, Ontario, Robbi, 18, has for two years spiralled into the deepest abyss of schizophrenia. In 2000, she tried to set the family home on fire. Last year, she admitted to visions of stabbing her parents and two sisters, arranging their bodies like toppled dominoes in a pool of their own blood. Unable to find a residential treatment centre for their daughter, the Jessops took the extraordinary step of barricading Robbi's bedroom each night and taking turns standing watch. Where once they lovingly tucked her in, now they fearfully lock her in. "Right now there are nights when I am so mentally tired I want to say, 'Here Robbi, here's a knife, just put an end to it,'" says Pamela Jessop. "If only we could get proper help for her, things might be different. But the system sucks and if you're mentally ill, God help you."
>
> Veronique Mandal, "Families of mentally ill pay terrible toll," *The Vancouver Sun*, October 7, 2002, pp. A1–A2. Material reprinted with permission of "Pacific Newspaper Group Inc," a CanWest Partnership.

Presumably, Robbi was not deemed by her psychiatrist to be of imminent risk for harming her family, otherwise she would have been involuntarily committed to a psychiatric hospital. Although she would have received good care in hospital, a less restrictive alternative would be to treat her in a group home. That is, a home in the community where a small number of patients with similar problems would reside under the constant care of mental health professionals, such as live-in staff, who are trained to care for people like Robbi. Sadly, this resource was not available, leaving Robbi's parents to shoulder the burden of care.

Right to Refuse Treatment Consider the following scenario: a person, John Citizen, is involuntarily committed to a psychiatric hospital for treatment. The hospital staff determines that John suffers from a psychotic disorder, paranoid schizophrenia, and should be treated with antipsychotic medication. John, however, decides not to comply with treatment. He claims that the hospital has no right to treat him against his will. The hospital staff seeks a court order to mandate treatment, arguing it makes little sense to commit people involuntarily unless the hospital is empowered to treat them as the staff deems fit.

Does an involuntary patient like John have the right to refuse treatment? If so, does this right conflict with the rights of the state to commit people to mental institutions to receive treatment for their disorders? One might also wonder whether people who are judged in need of involuntary hospitalization are competent enough to make decisions about which treatments are in their best interests.

Some mental health professionals have raised the concern that involuntarily committed patients who refuse medications would be "rotting with their rights on"—incarcerated but untreated (Pinals & Appelbaum, 2004). Fortunately, this does not often happen—at least in Canada. Since the proclamation of the 1982 Canadian Charter of Rights and Freedoms, there has been increasing recognition across the provinces and territories of the right for competent, involuntary patients to refuse treatment (Gray & O'Reilly, 2005). Today, provincial mental health legislation generally does not allow for institutionalization and compulsory treatment of people who refuse treatment, unless that person poses a threat to him- or herself or to the general public (Steller, 2003). A person like Edmond Yu, from our chapter-opening case study, would not be involuntarily hospitalized and treated unless he was judged to be at imminent risk of harming himself or others. As we saw earlier, Edmond refused treatment and was generally allowed to do so, even though he was psychotic and would have benefited from treatment.

Fortunately, most people in need of psychiatric treatment do not refuse. Less than 10% persistently refuse treatment (Gratzer & Matas, 1994). But the treatment refusers pose an important dilemma for health-care professionals: How do we balance the rights of the patients with the responsibility to provide competent care for their psychiatric disorders? Should we allow patients to refuse treatment even when that means they are unfit for living in the community? Will this lead to an increase in homelessness for people with serious mental disorders, like Edmond Yu?

Psychiatric Commitment and Patients' Rights

Review It

- **What is the difference between civil commitment and legal commitment?** The legal process by which people are placed in psychiatric institutions against their will is called civil or psychiatric commitment. Civil commitment is intended to provide treatment to people who are deemed to suffer from mental disorders and to pose a threat to themselves or others. Legal or criminal commitment, by comparison, involves placement in a psychiatric institution for treatment of a person who has been found to be not criminally responsible on account of having a mental disorder. In voluntary hospitalization, people voluntarily seek treatment in a psychiatric facility, and can leave of their own accord, unless a court rules otherwise.

- **How successful are mental health professionals in predicting dangerousness of patients they evaluate?** Although people must be judged dangerous to be placed involuntarily in a psychiatric facility, mental health professionals often make errors in predicting dangerousness. Factors that may account for the failure to predict dangerousness include: (1) recognizing violent tendencies post hoc is easier than predicting it; (2) generalized perceptions of violent tendencies may not predict specific acts of violence; (3) a lack of agreement in defining violence or dangerousness; (4) base-rate problems; (5) the unlikelihood of direct threats of violence; and (6) predictions based on hospital behaviour may not generalize to community settings.

- **What is meant by the duty to warn?** Although information disclosed by a client to a therapist generally carries a right to confidentiality, California's *Tarasoff* ruling held that therapists have a duty or obligation to warn third parties of threats made against them by their clients. Although U.S. laws do not apply to Canada, the Canadian Psychological Association includes the duty to warn in its code of ethics.

- **What are the rights of psychiatric patients?** According to the 1982 Canadian Charter of Rights and Freedoms, people with mental disorders have the same rights and privileges as other Canadians. They have the right to psychiatric treatment and the right to treatment in the least restrictive environment. Patients typically also have the right to refuse treatment, although most involuntary patients do not persistently refuse.

Define It

civil commitment   duty to warn
legal commitment

Recall It*

1. Civil commitment to a psychiatric hospital is made when _____.

   a. a person has a severe mental disorder in need of emergency treatment
   b. a person is unfit to live in the community
   c. a person has a psychotic disorder such as paranoid schizophrenia
   d. a person has a mental disorder and poses a threat to him- or herself or others

2. Legal commitment involves the involuntary placement in psychiatric hospitals of people who _____.

   a. have been judged to be not criminally responsible on account of a mental disorder, and pose a threat to the public

   b. have been determined by the courts to be in need of hospitalization
   c. have been judged to be mentally ill but not dangerous to themselves or others
   d. have been acquitted of all criminal charges against them, but nonetheless deemed to be in need of treatment

3. The psychiatrist Thomas Szasz argues that _____.

   a. involuntary hospitalization is needed, but only when there is a clear and present risk of harm to self or others
   b. statutes governing involuntary hospitalization should be broadened to include people who fail to attend to their basic needs, even if they are not currently threatening themselves or others
   c. involuntarily hospitalization should be abolished
   d. involuntary hospitalization should be used only as a last resort

4. Predictions of dangerousness by mental health professionals tend to _____.

   a. be biased in favour of underpredicting dangerousness
   b. be biased in favour of overpredicting dangerousness
   c. be accurate when predicting behaviour in the community on the basis of behaviour observed in the hospital
   d. be generally accurate except in cases of severe personality disorders

5. The *Tarasoff* case led to the establishment of _____.

   a. the duty of psychiatric hospitals to provide treatment to people in need
   b. minimum standards of care in psychiatric hospitals
   c. the duty of hospitals to release involuntarily held patients who are no longer considered dangerous
   d. the duty to warn

* Recall It answers can be found on the Companion Website for this text.

Think About It

- Do you believe we should abolish psychiatric commitment? Why or why not?
- If you were called on to evaluate whether an individual posed an imminent danger to him- or herself or others, on what criteria would you base your judgment?
- Have you ever known anyone who was confined to a psychiatric hospital? What was the experience like for him or her?

THE INSANITY DEFENCE

Society has long held to the doctrine of free will as a basis for determining responsibility for wrongdoing. The doctrine of free will, as applied to criminal responsibility, requires that people can be held guilty of a crime only if they are judged to have been in control of their actions at the time of committing the crime. Not only must it be determined by a court of law that a defendant has committed a crime beyond a reasonable doubt, but the issue of the individual's state of mind must be considered as well in determining whether the person can be held accountable for his or her crime. Thus, the court must rule not only on whether a crime was committed, but also on whether or not an individual is held *morally* responsible and *deserving* of punishment. The insanity defence is based on the belief that when a criminal act derives from a distorted state of mind, and not from the exercise of free will, the individual should not be punished but rather treated for the underlying mental disorder.

Armed with a knife, 34-year-old André Dallaire, a thin, bespectacled, former convenience-store worker, broke into the home of Prime Minister Jean Chrétien. It was the early hours of November 5, 1995. André climbed the fence surrounding Chrétien's residence, smashed a window, and entered the house. He intended to cut the prime minister's throat. An inner voice commanded him to kill Chrétien, while another voice told him to stop. André believed he was a secret agent whose mission was to avenge the "No" side's victory in the Quebec referendum on independence (Fisher, 1996). André believed he would be glorified for liberating Canada from a "traitorous" prime minister.

Outside the bedroom where the prime minister was sleeping, André encountered Chrétien's wife, Aline. She fled to the bedroom, locked the door, and called the police. The RCMP arrived shortly afterward and took André into custody. A psychiatric assessment revealed that he was delusional and hallucinating. He had been suffering from paranoid schizophrenia since the age of 16. The judge ruled that André's intent to kill was the product of a severe mental disorder. <u>Although Andre was found guilty of attempted murder, he was not held criminally responsible for his actions because he was suffering from a mental disorder at the time, which prevented him from appreciating the nature and wrongfulness of his actions.</u> Thus, André was judged to be "not criminally responsible on account of a mental disorder" (NCRMD). This is Canada's version of the insanity defence, which is similar to the "not guilty by reason of insanity" defence used in other countries.

Sixty-year-old Dorothy Joudrie, a wealthy Calgary socialite, was estranged from her husband, Earl. The two had had a rocky, often violent marriage. Earl hit her on several occasions, once breaking her nose. Dorothy had begun using alcohol excessively, even drinking as early as 9:00 a.m., and suffered from depression, anxiety, and panic attacks. Earl had an affair, and eventually they separated.

On January 21, 1995, Earl went to Dorothy's condominium to exchange papers about their pending divorce. The two had coffee and Dorothy showed Earl an album of their wedding pictures and some family Christmas letters that she had written. As he began to leave, she asked Earl whether he still wanted a divorce. He said yes. Dorothy began to cry, saying "It's easier for you. I'm alone and you have someone." As Earl went to leave, Dorothy redirected him to the garage. She pulled out a .25 calibre Beretta and fired six shots into him, narrowly missing his heart. As Earl lay there bleeding, Dorothy said, "I told you I wouldn't let you get away with this.... How long will it take you to die?... I'll just load you into the car and dump you in a ditch somewhere." Uncharacteristically, Dorothy showed no emotion at the time, and Earl later testified that she was

Was she insane when she committed her crime? Dorothy Joudrie, a Calgary socialite, attempted to kill her estranged husband in 1995. She pumped six shots into him with a Berretta handgun. She was later found to be not criminally responsible by reason of a mental disorder. At the time she was in a dissociative state.

acting and speaking like a completely different person. Eventually, she said, "Oh, my God, what have I done?" and then called for an ambulance. According to her testimony, Dorothy had no recollection of the shooting, but "sort of came to" when Earl was lying on the garage floor.

In her trial, the court found that Dorothy was in a dissociative state at the time of the shooting, triggered by her realization that the marriage was over and combined with the effects of alcoholism and her emotional problems. Dorothy was found guilty, but NCRMD (Andrews, 1999; McSherry, 1998).

Dorothy Joudrie and André Dallaire were suffering from quite different psychological problems; Dorothy was in a severe dissociative state, whereas André was suffering from hallucinations and delusions. Both were found guilty but not criminally responsible because they were suffering from a mental disorder at the time of their crimes.

How often is the **insanity defence** used? Do people using this defence really "get away with murder" or attempted murder? <u>The defence is not often used, and even when it is used few people are judged to be NCRMD.</u> From 1992 to 1998 in British Columbia, for example, an average of only 46 people per year were found NCRMD (Livingston, Wilson, Tien, & Bond, 2003). People found NCRMD are typically hospitalized until they are safe to be released into the community, although some may not be hospitalized if they no longer are suffering from a serious mental disorder.

insanity defence Form of legal defence in which a defendant in a criminal case pleads guilty but not criminally responsible on the basis of having a mental disorder.

Legal Bases of the Insanity Defence

The insanity defence has a long legal history. The ancient Greeks believed that insanity limits a person's responsibility for crimes committed. In early English law, which formed a basis for Canadian law, the insanity defence was also used. An important legal precedent for modern laws was set in the 1843 legal defence that led to the *M'Naughten rule*. This was based on a case in England of a Scotsman, Daniel M'Naughten, who had intended to assassinate the prime minister of England, Sir Robert Peel. Instead, he killed Peel's secretary, whom he had mistaken for the prime minister. M'Naughten claimed that the voice of God had commanded him to kill Lord Peel. The English court acquitted M'Naughten on the basis of insanity, finding that the defendant had been "labouring under such a defect of reason, from disease of the mind, as not to know the nature and quality of the act he was doing; or, if he did know it, that he did not know what he was doing was wrong." The M'Naughten rule, as it has come to be called, holds that people do not bear criminal responsibility if, by reason of a mental disease or defect, they either have no knowledge of their actions or are unable to tell right from wrong.

Another important legal precedent was the *irresistible impulse test*, which was introduced in the 19th century to broaden the insanity defence. According to this test, the defendant could be found insane if a mental disease prevented that person from controlling his or her actions. In other words, if a person cannot control his or her actions, then that person cannot be held accountable for any crimes committed, and the commission of crimes would not be deterred by the prospects of punishment. This test was used in the U.S., although it did not gain popularity in Canada.

In terms of more recent developments in the insanity defence, the 1985 Criminal Code of Canada allowed a person to be found *not guilty by reason of insanity* (NGRI). People found NGRI were automatically placed in a secure psychiatric facility, indefinitely, "until the pleasure of the Lieutenant Governor is known"—meaning that a person was detained until the mental disorder had improved to an extent that would justify release. A person could be detained for a longer period than he or she would have served in prison if convicted for the crime (Gray & O'Reilly, 2005). Some people judged to be NGRI were held in psychiatric hospitals without receiving adequate treatment. Later changes to the Criminal Code rectified this problem.

Changes came with the case of *R. v. Swain* (1991), which challenged the insanity defence in a number of ways. Owen Swain was charged with aggravated assault after attacking his wife and two children. At the time, he was psychotic; he believed his family was being attacked by devils and that he had to perform certain rituals to protect them, including physically assaulting them. Owen was hospitalized, successfully treated with antipsychotic medication, and then released on bail. At his trial, the Crown raised the issue of insanity, despite Owen's objections and those of his lawyer. Owen was judged NGRI, which meant that he would be involuntarily placed in a psychiatric hospital. He appealed the decision, arguing that it violated his rights for the Crown to raise the issue of insanity and to automatically incarcerate people judged to be NGRI. Owen's appeal was successful, which led to important reforms in the Canadian version of the insanity defence.

As a result, the Canadian Criminal Code was amended to give the accused person greater procedural and civil rights. The amendment was an attempt to balance the goals of fair and humane treatment of the offender against the safety of the public (Schneider et al., 2000). Major changes included reductions in how long an accused person could be detained in a psychiatric facility and changes in the procedures for making appeals. The mental disorder defence was also changed, with NGRI being replaced with *not criminally responsible on account of a mental disorder* (NCRMD). Thus, the Canadian Criminal Code now states that,

> no person is criminally responsible for an act committed or an omission made while suffering from a mental disorder that rendered the person incapable of appreciating the nature and quality of the act or omission or of knowing that it was wrong.

Moreover,

> Although personality disorders or psychopathic [antisocial] personalities are capable of constituting a disease of the mind, the defence of insanity is not made out where the accused has the necessary understanding of the nature, character and consequences of the act, but merely lacks appropriate feelings for the victim or lacks feelings of remorse or guilt for what he [or she] has done, even though such lack of feeling stems from a disease of the mind (Greenspan, 1998, p. 50).

NGRI and NCRMD share many similarities, although there are some important differences. Under NCRMD, for example, the defendant is now considered to be "not criminally responsible" instead of "not guilty." This change more explicitly recognizes that the defendant committed the offence as opposed to being not guilty (Davis, 1993). Dorothy Joudrie, for example, actually did try to murder her estranged husband, so she was guilty of the crime. But she was found to be not criminally responsible because she was in a dissociative state at the time.

Under NCRMD, the defendant or his or her legal counsel may raise the insanity defence at any time. The prosecution (i.e., the Crown) can raise this defence only after the accused has been found guilty. The side raising the possibility of NCRMD bears the burden of proving it.

Unlike NGRI, under NCRMD an indeterminate confinement in a psychiatric facility is not allowed. There are three possible outcomes under NCRMD:

- *Absolute discharge.* This is required by law if the person is not a significant threat to the public.

- *Conditional discharge.* For example, discharge in the community on the proviso that the person receive appropriate treatment for his or her mental disorder.

- *Detention in hospital, with periodic assessment to determine whether continued confinement is warranted.* The decision for continued detention is based on several considerations, including the need to protect the public and the mental condition of the person.

What happened to André Dallaire and Dorothy Joudrie? After Dorothy was found NCRMD, she was committed to a psychiatric hospital in Edmonton, Alberta, on the grounds that she continued to pose a threat to public safety (McSherry, 1998). She was released after an unusually brief stay of only five months. Some years later, she developed health problems and died. After his arrest, André was sent to the Royal Ottawa Hospital and placed on antipsychotic medication. After a period of treatment, he was no longer delusional or hearing voices, and expressed remorse for his actions. After finding him NCRMD, the court ordered a conditional discharge under which André was released to an Ottawa-area group home and allowed to come and go so long as he was escorted by a group home staff member (Fisher, 1996). He remained there until a review board decided that he was no longer a threat and so then he was free to move about unsupervised. However, he was not permitted to go within 500 metres of the prime minister or his residence, and he was required to continue seeing a psychiatrist and to remain on antipsychotic medication.

Perspectives on the Insanity Defence

The insanity defence places special burdens on juries. In assessing criminal responsibility, the jury is expected to determine not only that a crime was committed by the accused, but also the defendant's state of mind at the time of commission of the crime. The task imposed on the jury is made even more difficult by the mandate to decide whether or not the defendant was mentally *incapacitated* at the time of the crime. To add to the complexity, expert witnesses such as psychologists and psychiatrists often disagree with one another as to whether the accused had a mental disorder at the time of the crime that prevented him or her from appreciating the nature or wrongfulness of the crime. The defendant's courtroom behaviour may bear little resemblance to his or her behaviour during the crime.

Thomas Szasz and others who deny the existence of mental illness itself have raised another challenge to the insanity defence. If mental illness does not exist, then the insanity defence becomes groundless. Szasz argues that the insanity defence is ultimately degrading because it strips people of personal responsibility for their behaviour. People who break laws are criminals, Szasz argues, and should be prosecuted and sentenced accordingly. Acquittal of defendants by reason of insanity treats them as nonpersons, as unfortunates who are not deemed to possess the basic human qualities of free choice, self-determination, and personal responsibility. We are each responsible for our behaviour, Szasz contends, and we should each be held accountable for our misdeeds.

Szasz argues that the insanity defence has historically been invoked in crimes that were particularly heinous or perpetrated against persons of high social rank. When persons of low social rank commit crimes against persons of higher status, Szasz argues, the effect of the insanity defence is to direct attention away from the social ills that may have motivated the crime. Despite Szasz's contention, the insanity defence is invoked in many cases of less shocking crimes or in cases involving persons from similar social classes.

How, then, are we to evaluate the insanity defence? To abolish the insanity defence in all forms would be to reverse hundreds of years of a legal tradition that has recognized that people are not to be held responsible for their criminal behaviour when their ability to control themselves is impaired by a mental disorder or defect.

Consider a hypothetical example. John Citizen commits a crime, say a heinous crime like murder, while acting on a delusional belief that the victim was intent on assassinating him. The accused claims that voices from his television set informed him of the identity of the assailant and commanded him to kill the assailant to save himself and other potential victims. Cases like this are thankfully rare. Few mentally disturbed persons, even few people with psychotic features, commit violent crimes, and even fewer commit murder.

In reaching a judgment on the insanity plea, we need to consider whether we believe the law should allow special standards to apply in cases such as our hypothetical case, or whether one standard of criminal responsibility should apply to all. If we assert the legitimacy of the insanity defence in some cases, we still need a standard of insanity that can be interpreted and applied by juries of ordinary citizens.

Competency to Stand Trial

There is a basic rule of law that those who stand accused of crimes must be able to understand the charges and proceedings brought against them and be able to participate in their own defence. The concept of competency to stand trial should not be confused with the legal defence of insanity. A defendant can be held competent to stand trial but still be judged not criminally responsible on account of a mental disorder. A clearly delusional person, for example, may understand the court proceedings and be able to confer with defence counsel, but still be acquitted by reason of insanity. On the other hand, a person may be incapable of standing trial at a particular time, but be tried and acquitted or convicted at a later time when competency is restored.

In Canada, a judge can order compulsory treatment if the defendant in a criminal trial is found unfit to stand trial due to a mental disorder. It is presumed that every defendant is fit to stand trial unless the court is convinced otherwise. In order to verify the accused's fitness, a psychiatric assessment is needed. The issue of fitness is adjudicated in a separate trial. A defendant is held unfit to stand trial when he or she meets one or more of the following (Bal & Koenraadt, 2000) criteria:

- Is not capable of conducting his or her defence
- Can't distinguish between available pleas
- Doesn't understand the nature and purpose of the proceedings, including the respective roles of the judge, jury, and counsel
- Is unable to communicate with counsel rationally or make critical decisions on counsel's advice
- Is unable to take the stand to testify if necessary

An accused found unfit to stand trial can be committed to compulsory treatment in a psychiatric hospital. The case is adjourned until the accused has recovered to such an extent that he or she can be found fit. Mentally ill offenders can be committed to a psychiatric hospital on the verdict of unfitness to stand trial for an unlimited time without their criminal case being tried. Consequently, these accused offenders form a relatively large part of the population in psychiatric hospitals (Bal & Koenraadt, 2000).

Abuses may occur if defendants are kept incarcerated for indefinite periods awaiting trial. In earlier years, it was not uncommon for people who were declared incompetent to have their trials delayed for months or years until they were judged ready to stand trial, if indeed they were ever judged to be competent. These days, if it does not seem the person would ever become competent, even with treatment, the individual would have to be either released or committed under the procedures for civil commitment.

At the outset of this book, we remarked on the public impression that abnormal behaviour affects only the few; it actually affects nearly every one of us in some way or another. Let us close by suggesting that if we all work together to foster research into the causes, treatment, and prevention of abnormal behaviour, perhaps we can meet the multifaceted challenges that abnormal behaviour poses to so many of us and to our society at large.

STUDY BREAK

The Insanity Defence

Review It

- **What are the legal bases of Canada's insanity defence?** The M'Naughten rule, based on a case in England in 1843, treated the failure to appreciate the wrongfulness of one's action as the basis of legal insanity. This rule was adapted and modified over the years to become "not guilty by reason of insanity" (NGRI) and, more recently, "not criminally responsible on account of a mental disorder" (NCRMD). A person found guilty of a crime is judged to be NCRMD if he or she was suffering from a mental disorder that rendered the person incapable of appreciating the nature and quality of the act or omission or of knowing that it was wrong.

- **What is meant by the legal concept of competency to stand trial?** People who are accused of crimes but are incapable of understanding the charges against them or assisting in their own defence can be found incompetent to stand trial and remanded to a psychiatric facility.

Define It

insanity defence

Recall It*

1. The general public tends to _____ the number of defendants who are actually acquitted by reason of insanity.

a. underestimate
b. overestimate
c. estimate fairly accurately
d. estimate more accurately than mental health professionals

2. One of the possible outcomes for a person who is judged to be not criminally responsible on account of a mental disorder is _____.

a. jail
b. absolute discharge
c. involuntary commitment at "the Lieutenant Governor's pleasure"
d. always some form of mandatory treatment

3. Which of the following disorders is most likely to be associated with a judgment of not criminally responsible on account of a mental disorder?

a. psychopathic (antisocial) personality disorder
b. panic disorder
c. paranoid schizophrenia
d. phobia

4. If a defendant is judged to be unable to understand the charges and proceedings brought against him or her in a criminal action, he or she _____.

a. is tried by a judge rather than a jury
b. is judged not guilty of a crime but is then committed to a psychiatric hospital for treatment
c. is deemed incompetent to stand trial
d. is deemed not guilty by reason of insanity and then may be hospitalized under civil commitment proceedings

5. A person who is competent to stand trial _____.

a. cannot be legally sane at the time of the crime
b. may be legally insane when the crime is committed
c. must be released on bail
d. need not receive psychiatric treatment

* Recall It answers can be found on the Companion Website for this text.

Think About It

- Do you think we should abolish the verdict of "not criminally responsible on account of mental disorder"? Should it be replaced with another type of verdict, like "not guilty by reason of insanity"? Why or why not?

WEBLINKS

Abnormal Psychology and Society

Psychiatric Commitment and Patients' Rights

Legal Commitment

- Legal process of confining in a mental institution a person found to be "not criminally responsible on account of a mental disorder"

Predicting Dangerousness

- Difficult to predict, although methods such as the psychopathy checklist are useful
- Duty to warn potential victim

Civil Commitment

- Legal process involved in placing a person in a mental institution, even against his or her will

Patients' Rights

- Right to treatment
- Right to refuse treatment

The Insanity Defence

Legal defence in which the defendant pleads guilty but not criminally responsible on account of having a mental disorder

Historical Precedents

- M'Naughten rule
- Irresistible impulse test
- Not guilty by reason of insanity

Current Canadian Version of the Insanity Defence

- Not criminally responsible on account of a mental disorder (NCRMD)
- NCRMD means that the person is guilty of the crime but that his or her actions were due to a mental disorder

Competency to Stand Trial

- A defendant can be competent to stand trial but still be judged NCRMD
- Competency involves a person being able to understand the charges against them and a person being able to participate in their defence

GLOSSARY

A

abnormal psychology Branch of psychology that deals with the description, causes, and treatment of abnormal behaviour patterns.

abstinence violation effect Tendency in people trying to maintain abstinence from a substance, such as alcohol or cigarettes, to overreact to a lapse with feelings of guilt and a sense of resignation that may then trigger a full-blown relapse.

acetylcholine Type of neurotransmitter involved in the control of muscle contractions. Abbreviated *ACh*.

acquired immunodeficiency syndrome A condition caused by the human immunodeficiency virus (HIV) that is characterized by debilitation of the immune system, leaving the body vulnerable to opportunistic diseases. Acronym is *AIDS*.

acrophobia Excessive fear of heights.

acute stress disorder Traumatic stress reaction occurring in the days and weeks following exposure to a traumatic event.

addiction Impaired control over the use of a chemical substance accompanied by physiological dependence on the substance.

adjustment disorder Maladaptive reaction to an identified stressor or stressors that occurs shortly following exposure to the stressor(s) and results in impaired functioning or signs of emotional distress that exceed what would normally be expected in the situation. The reaction may be resolved if the stressor is removed or the individual learns to adapt to it successfully.

adoptee studies Studies of adopted-away children that examine whether their behaviour patterns and psychological functioning more closely resemble those of their biological parents or adoptive parents.

affect Emotion or feeling state that is attached to objects, ideas, or life experiences. Pronounced *AF-fect*.

agoraphobia The fear of places and situations from which it might be difficult or embarrassing to escape in the event of panicky symptoms or a full-fledged panic attack; or of situations in which help may be unavailable if such problems should occur.

Al-Anon Organization sponsoring support groups for family members of people with alcoholism.

alarm reaction First stage of the general adaptation syndrome following response to a stressor; characterized by heightened sympathetic activity.

alcohol-induced persisting amnestic disorder See *Korsakoff's syndrome*

Alzheimer's disease Progressive brain disease characterized by gradual loss of memory and intellectual functioning, personality changes, and eventual loss of ability to care for oneself.

ambivalence Holding conflicting feelings toward another person or goal, such as both loving and hating the same person.

ambulatory Able to walk about on one's own.

amenorrhea Absence of menstruation—a symptom of anorexia nervosa.

amphetamine psychosis Psychotic state induced by ingestion of amphetamines.

amphetamines Types of stimulants, such as Dexedrine and Benzedrine. Abuse can trigger an amphetamine psychosis that mimics acute episodes of schizophrenia.

amygdala Named for its almond shape, it is involved in the regulation of defensive emotions like fear and anger.

anal expulsive In psychodynamic theory, a personality type characterized by excessive self-expression, such as extreme sloppiness or messiness.

anal fixation In psychodynamic theory, attachment to objects and behaviours that characterize the anal stage.

anal retentive In psychodynamic theory, a personality type characterized by excessive needs for self-control, such as extreme neatness and punctuality.

anal stage The second stage of psychosexual development in Freud's theory, in which gratification is achieved through anal activities, such as by the elimination of bodily wastes.

analgesia State of relief from pain without loss of consciousness.

analogue Something that resembles something else in many respects.

analytical psychology Jung's psychodynamic theory, which emphasizes such concepts as the collective unconscious, the existence of archetypes, and the notion of the self as a unifying force of personality.

anomie Lack of purpose or identity; aimlessness.

anorexia nervosa Eating disorder, primarily affecting young women, characterized by maintenance of an abnormally low body weight, distortions of body image, intense fears of gaining weight, and, in females, amenorrhea.

antibodies Substances produced by white blood cells that identify and target antigens for destruction.

antidepressants Types of drugs that act to relieve depression. Tricyclics, MAO inhibitors, and selective serotonin-reuptake inhibitors are the major classes of antidepressants.

antigen Substance that triggers an immune system response to it (the contraction for *anti*body *gen*erator).

antisocial personality disorder Type of personality disorder characterized by a chronic pattern of antisocial and irresponsible behaviour and lack of remorse.

anxiety Emotional state characterized by physiological arousal, unpleasant feelings of tension, and a sense of apprehension, foreboding, and dread about the future.

anxiety disorder Type of mental disorder in which anxiety is the prominent feature.

anxiety sensitivity A "fear of fear," or fear that one's emotions or states of bodily arousal will get out of control and lead to harmful consequences.

anxiolytics Drugs, such as sedatives and anaesthetics, that induce partial or complete unconsciousness and are commonly used in the treatment of sleep disorders.

apnea Temporary cessation of breathing.

archetypes Jung's concept of primitive images or concepts that reside in the collective unconscious.

arteriosclerosis Disease involving thickening and hardening of the arteries.

associations Linkages or relationships among thoughts or utterances.

atherosclerosis Disease process consisting of arteriosclerosis with the deposition of fatty substances along the walls of the arteries.

attention-deficit/hyperactivity disorder Behaviour disorder of childhood characterized by excessive motor activity and inability to focus attention.

attributional style Personal style for explaining cause-and-effect relationships between events.

autism (1) Absorption into daydreaming and fantasy. (2) A disorder in childhood characterized by failure to relate to others, lack of speech, disturbed motor behaviours, intellectual impairment, and demands for sameness in the environment. Also one of Bleuler's **four As** describing one of the primary symptoms of schizophrenia.

automatic thoughts Thoughts that seem to pop into one's mind. In Aaron Beck's theory, automatic thoughts that reflect cognitive distortions induce negative feelings like anxiety or depression.

autonomic nervous system Division of the peripheral nervous system that regulates the activities of glands and involuntary functions, such as respiration, heartbeat, and digestion. Abbreviated *ANS*. See also *sympathetic* and *parasympathetic* branches of the ANS.

aversive conditioning Behaviour therapy technique in which a maladaptive response is paired with exposure to an aversive stimulus, such as electric shock or nausea, so a conditioned aversion develops toward the stimuli associated with the maladaptive response. Also termed *aversion therapy*.

avoidant personality disorder Type of personality disorder characterized by avoidance of social relationships due to fears of rejection.

axon Long, thin part of the neuron along which nervous impulses travel.

B

barbiturates Types of depressants that are sometimes used to relieve anxiety or induce sleep, but which are highly addictive.

basal ganglia Ganglia located between the thalamus and the cerebrum in the brain that are involved in the coordination of motor activity.

baseline Period of time preceding the implementation of a treatment. Used to gather data regarding the rate of occurrence of the target behaviour before treatment is introduced.

behaviour therapy A learning-based model of therapy.

behavioural assessment Approach to clinical assessment that focuses on the objective recording or description of the problem behaviour rather than inferences about personality traits.

behavioural genetics The study of how hereditary and environmental factors interact to produce behaviour.

behavioural interview Approach to clinical interviewing that focuses on relating the problem behaviour to antecedent stimuli and reinforcement consequences.

behavioural rating scale Method of behavioural assessment that involves the use of a scale to record the frequency of occurrence of target behaviours.

behaviourism School of psychology that defines psychology as the study of observable or overt behaviour and focuses on investigating the relationships between stimuli and responses.

benzodiazepines Class of minor tranquillizers that includes Valium and Librium.

bereavement Normal experience of suffering following the loss of a loved one.

binge-eating disorder Proposed psychological disorder characterized by repeated episodes in which binge eating occurs but is not followed by purging.

biofeedback training Method of feeding back to the individual information about bodily functions so the person is able to gain better control over these functions. Abbreviated *BFT*.

biopsychosocial model A conceptual model that emphasizes that human behaviour is linked to complex interactions between biological, psychological, and sociocultural factors.

bipolar Characterized by opposites, as in **bipolar disorder.**

bipolar disorder Disorder characterized by mood swings between states of extreme elation and severe depression. Formerly called *manic-depression.*

blind In the context of research design, a state of being unaware of whether or not one has received a treatment.

blocking (1) Disruption of self-expression of threatening or emotionally laden material. (2) In people with schizophrenia, a condition of suddenly becoming silent with loss of memory for what they had just discussed.

bondage Form of sadomasochism involving the binding of the arms or legs of oneself or one's partner during sexual activity.

borderline personality disorder Type of personality disorder characterized by abrupt shifts in mood, lack of a coherent sense of self, and unpredictable, impulsive behaviour.

brain electrical activity mapping Method of brain imaging that involves the computer analysis of data from multiple electrodes that are placed on the scalp in order to reveal areas of the brain with relatively higher or lower levels of electrical activity. Acronym is *BEAM.*

breathing-related sleep disorder Sleep disorder in which sleeping is repeatedly disrupted due to difficulties breathing normally.

bulimia nervosa Eating disorder characterized by a recurrent pattern of binge eating followed by self-induced purging and accompanied by persistent overconcern with body weight and shape.

C

cardiovascular disease Disease or disorder of the cardiovascular system, such as coronary heart disease and hypertension.

case study Carefully drawn biography that is typically constructed on the basis of clinical interviews, observations, psychological tests, and, in some cases, historical records.

castration anxiety In psychodynamic theory, the boy's unconscious fear that he will be castrated as a form of punishment for having incestuous wishes for his mother.

cataplexy Brief, sudden loss of muscular control, typically lasting from a few seconds to as long as two minutes.

catastrophize To exaggerate or magnify the negative consequences of events; to "blow things out of proportion."

catatonic type Subtype of schizophrenia characterized by gross disturbances in motor activity, such as catatonic stupor.

catecholamines A group of chemically related substances that function as neurotransmitters in the brain (dopamine and norepinephrine) and as hormones (epinephrine and norepinephrine).

catharsis (1) Discharge of states of tension associated with repression of threatening impulses or material; (2) the free expression or purging of feelings. Also called *abreaction.*

causal relationship Relationship between two factors or events in which one is necessary and sufficient to bring about the other. Also called a *cause-and-effect relationship.*

central nervous system The brain and spinal cord.

cerebellum Part of the hindbrain involved in coordination and balance.

cerebral cortex Wrinkled surface area of the cerebrum, often referred to as grey matter because of the appearance produced by the high density of cell bodies. Higher mental functions, such as thinking and planning, are assumed to occur in the cerebral cortex.

cerebrum Large mass of the forebrain consisting of two hemispheres.

choleric Having or showing bad temper.

chromosomes Structures found in the nuclei of cells that carry the units of heredity or *genes*

circadian rhythm sleep disorder Sleep disorder characterized by disruption of sleep due to a mismatch in sleep schedules between the body's internal sleep-wake cycle and the demands of the environment. Formerly called *sleep–wake schedule disorder.*

civil commitment Legal process involved in placing an individual in a mental institution, even against his or her will. Also called *psychiatric commitment.*

clanging In people with schizophrenia, the tendency to string words together because they rhyme or sound alike.

claustrophobia Excessive fear of tight, small places.

client-centred therapy Another name for Carl Rogers's *person-centred therapy.*

clinical drug trials The controlled investigation of a new drug to determine how well it works, dosage limits, side effects, and safety.

clinical psychologist Person with graduate training in psychology who specializes in abnormal behaviour. They must be registered and licensed with a provincial psychological regulatory body in order to provide psychological services in that province.

closed-ended questions Questionnaire or test items that have a limited range of response options.

cocaine Stimulant derived from coca leaves.

coefficient alpha Measure of internal consistency or reliability; the average intercorrelation among the items composing a particular scale or test.

cognitive restructuring Cognitive therapy method that involves replacing irrational or self-defeating thoughts and attitudes with rational alternatives.

cognitive therapy (1) Name of Aaron Beck's kind of psychotherapy, which challenges the distorted thought patterns that give rise to or exacerbate clients' problems. (2) More generally, a form of psychotherapy that addresses clients' cognitive processes, usually their self-defeating attitudes.

cognitive triad of depression In Aaron Beck's theory, the view that depression derives from the adoption of negative views of oneself, the environment, and the future.

collective unconscious In Carl Jung's theory, the hypothesized storehouse of archetypes and racial memories.

comatose In a coma, a state of deep, prolonged unconsciousness.

compulsion Repetitive or ritualistic behaviour that the person feels compelled to perform, such as compulsive hand-washing.

compulsion to utter In psychodynamic theory, the urge to express repressed material verbally.

computerized tomography Generation of a computer-enhanced image of the internal structures of the brain by means of passing a narrow X-ray beam through the head at different angles. Abbreviated *CT scan*.

concordance Agreement.

concurrent validity Type of test validity determined on the basis of the statistical relationship or correlation between the test and a criterion measure taken at the same point in time.

conditional positive regard In Carl Rogers's theory, valuing other people on the basis of whether their behaviour meets with one's approval.

conditioned response (1) In classical conditioning, a learned or acquired response to a previously neutral stimulus. (2) A response to a conditioned stimulus. Abbreviated *CR*.

conditioned stimulus Previously neutral stimulus that comes to evoke a conditioned response following repeated pairings with a stimulus (unconditioned stimulus) that had already evoked that response. Abbreviated *CS*.

conditions of worth Standards by which one judges the worth or value of oneself or others.

conduct disorder Pattern of abnormal behaviour in childhood characterized by disruptive, antisocial behaviour.

confidentiality The principle of safeguarding information so that it remains secret and is not disclosed to other parties.

congruence In Carl Rogers's theory, the fit between one's self-concept and one's thoughts, behaviours, and feelings. One of the principal characteristics of effective person-centred therapists.

conscious Aware.

construct validity Degree to which a test or instrument measures the hypothetical construct that it purports to measure.

content validity (1) Degree to which the content of a test or measure represents the content domain of the construct it purports to measure. (2) Degree to which the content of a test or measure covers a representative sample of the behaviours associated with the construct dimension or trait in question.

contrasted groups approach Method of concurrent validity in which group membership is used as the criterion by which the validity of a test is measured. The ability of the test to differentiate between two or more comparison groups (e.g., people with schizophrenia vs. normals) is taken as evidence of concurrent validity.

control subject Subject who does not receive the experimental treatment or manipulation but for whom all other conditions are held constant.

controlled social drinking Controversial approach to treating problem drinkers in which the goal of treatment is the maintenance of controlled social drinking in moderate amounts rather than total abstinence.

conversion disorder Type of somatoform disorder characterized by loss or impairment of physical function in the absence of any organic causes that might account for the changes. Formerly called *hysteria* or *hysterical neurosis*.

corpus callosum Thick bundle of fibres that connects the two hemispheres of the brain.

correlation Relationship or association between two or more variables. A correlation between variables may suggest, but does not prove, that a causal relationship exists between them.

countertransference In psychoanalysis, the transfer of feelings that the analyst holds toward other persons in her or his life onto the client.

crack Hardened, smokable form of cocaine.

creative self In Alfred Adler's theory, the self-aware part of the personality that strives to achieve its potential.

criterion validity The degree to which a test or instrument correlates with an independent, external criterion (standard) representing the construct or trait that the test or instrument is intended to measure. There are two general types of criterion validity: concurrent validity and predictive validity.

critical thinking A style of thinking characterized by adoption of a questioning attitude and careful weighing of the available evidence to determine if claims made by others stand up to scrutiny.

cross-fostering study Method of determining heritability of a trait or disorder by examining differences in prevalence among adoptees reared by either adoptive parents or biological parents who possessed the trait or disorder in question. Evidence that the disorder followed biological, rather than adoptive parentage favours the heritability of the trait or disorder.

cue-exposure training Treatment used for people with substance dependence, it involves exposure to cues associated with ingestion of drugs or alcoholic beverages in a controlled situation in which the person is prevented from using the drug.

cultural-familial retardation Milder form of mental retardation that is believed to result, or at least be influenced by, impoverishment in the child's home environment.

culture-bound disorders Referring to patterns of behaviour that are found only within one or a few cultural contexts.

cyclothymic disorder Mood disorder characterized by a chronic pattern of mild mood swings between depression and mania that are not of sufficient severity to be classified as bipolar disorder.

cytomegalovirus Maternal disease of the herpes virus group that carries a risk of mental retardation to the unborn child.

D

debriefed Providing research participants with a full accounting of a study's aims and purposes after their participation, including information about any deception that may have been used or other information that may have been withheld from them.

defence mechanisms In psychodynamic theory, the reality-distorting strategies used by the ego to shield itself from conscious awareness of anxiety-evoking or troubling material.

deinstitutionalization Practice of discharging large numbers of hospitalized mental patients to the community and of reducing the need for new admissions through the development of alternative treatment approaches such as halfway houses and crisis intervention services.

delirium State of mental confusion, disorientation, and extreme difficulties focusing attention.

delirium tremens Withdrawal syndrome that often occurs following a sudden decrease or cessation of drinking in chronic alcoholics that is characterized by extreme restlessness, sweating, disorientation, and hallucinations. Abbreviated *DTs*.

delta-9-tetrahydrocannabinol Major active ingredient in marijuana. Abbreviated *THC*.

delusions Firmly held but inaccurate beliefs that persist despite evidence that they have no basis in reality.

dementia praecox Term given by Kraepelin to the disorder we now call schizophrenia.

demonological model The model that explains abnormal behaviour in terms of supernatural forces.

dendrites Root-like structures at the end of a neuron that receive nerve impulses from other neurons.

dependent personality disorder Type of personality disorder characterized by overly dependent behaviour and difficulties making independent decisions.

dependent variable Measure of outcome in a scientific study that is assumed to be dependent on the effects of the independent variable.

depersonalization Feelings of unreality or detachment from one's self or one's body, as if one were a robot or functioning on automatic pilot or observing oneself from outside.

depersonalization disorder Disorder characterized by persistent or recurrent episodes of depersonalization.

depressant Drug that lowers the level of activity of the central nervous system.

derealization Loss of the sense of reality of one's surroundings, experienced in terms of strange changes in one's environment (e.g., people or objects changing size or shape), or in the sense of the passage of time.

description In science, the representation of observations without interpretation or inferences as to their nature or meaning. Contrast with *inference*, which is the process of drawing conclusions based on observations.

detoxification Process of ridding the system of alcohol or drugs under supervised conditions in which withdrawal symptoms can be monitored and controlled.

deviation IQ Intelligence quotient derived by determining the deviation between the individual's score and the norm (mean).

diathesis A predisposition or vulnerability.

diathesis-stress model Model of abnormal behaviour that posits that abnormal behaviour patterns, such as schizophrenia, involve the interaction of genetic and environmental influences. In this model, a genetic or acquired predisposition or diathesis increases the individual's vulnerability to develop the disorder in response to stressful life circumstances. If, however, the level of stress is kept under the person's particular threshold, the disorder may never develop, even among people with the predisposition.

differentiate When unspecialized cells divide into any of the many cells that make up the body, such as the heart, liver, or brain.

dimensional model An approach to diagnosis that quantifies indicators on a continuous scale (e.g., from low to average to high).

disorganized type Subtype of schizophrenia characterized by disorganized behaviour, bizarre delusions, and vivid hallucinations. Formerly *hebephrenic schizophrenia*.

disorientation State of mental confusion or lack of awareness with respect to time, place, or the identity of oneself or others.

displacement In psychodynamic theory, a type of defence mechanism that involves the transferring of impulses toward threatening or unacceptable objects onto more acceptable or safer objects.

dissociative amnesia Type of dissociative disorder in which a person experiences memory losses in the absence of any identifiable organic cause; general knowledge and skills are usually retained.

dissociative fugue Type of dissociative disorder in which one suddenly flies from one's life situation, travels to a new location, assumes a new identity, and has amnesia for past personal material. The person usually retains skills and other abilities and may appear to others in the new environment to be leading a normal life.

dissociative identity disorder Dissociative disorder in which a person has two or more distinct or alter personalities.

distress The psychologically harmful and disease-producing experience that accompanies pressures or demands.

dizygotic (DZ) twins Twins who develop from separate fertilized eggs. Also called fraternal twins. Abbreviated *DZ twins*. Often contrasted with **monozygotic (MZ) twins** in studies of heritability of particular traits or disorders.

DNA Deoxyribonucleic acid (DNA) is a double-strand complex molecule of helical structure that contains the genetic instructions for building and maintaining living organisms.

dopamine Neurotransmitter of the catecholamine class that is believed to play a role in schizophrenia.

dopamine theory Biochemical theory of schizophrenia that proposes that schizophrenia involves the action of dopamine.

double-bind communications Pattern of communication involving the transmission of contradictory or mixed messages without acknowledgment of the inherent conflict; posited by some theorists to play a role in the development of schizophrenia.

double depression Term applied to persons diagnosed with both *major depressive disorder* and *dysthymic disorder*

Down syndrome Condition caused by a chromosomal abnormality involving an extra chromosome on the 21st pair ("trisomy 21"); characterized by mental retardation and various physical abnormalities. Formerly called *mongolism* and *Down's syndrome* in Canada.

downward drift hypothesis The belief that people with psychological problems may drift downward in socioeconomic status.

drive to superiority In Adler's theory, a term describing the desire to compensate for feelings of inferiority.

duty to warn Obligation imposed on therapists to warn third parties of threats made against them by the therapists' clients. In the United States, the *Tarasoff* case established the legal basis for duty-to-warn provisions. Although U.S. law does not apply in Canada, the Canadian Psychological Association states that ethically, therapists have a duty to warn.

dyslexia Type of learning disorder characterized by impaired reading ability; may involve difficulty with the alphabet or spelling.

dyspareunia Persistent or recurrent pain experienced during or following sexual intercourse.

dyssomnias Category of sleep disorders involving disturbances in the amount, quality, or timing of sleep.

dysthymic disorder Mild but chronic type of depressive disorder.

E

eating disorders Psychological disorders involving disturbed eating patterns and maladaptive ways of controlling body weight.

eclectic orientation Adoption of principles or techniques from various systems or theories.

ego In psychodynamic theory, the psychic structure corresponding to the concept of the self. The ego is governed by the reality principle and is responsible for finding socially acceptable outlets for the urgings of the id. The ego is characterized by the capacity to tolerate frustration and delay gratification.

ego analysts Psychodynamically oriented therapists who are influenced by ego psychology.

ego dystonic Behaviour or feelings that are perceived to be foreign or alien to one's self-identity.

ego ideal In Freud's view, the configuration of higher social values and moral ideals embodied in the superego.

ego psychology Approach of modern psychodynamic theorists that posits that the ego has energy and strivings of its own apart from the id. Ego psychologists focus more on the conscious strivings of the ego than on the hypothesized unconscious functioning of the id.

ego syntonic Behaviour or feelings that are perceived as natural or compatible parts of the self.

Electra complex In psychodynamic theory, the term used to describe the conflict in a young girl during the phallic stage of development involving her longing for her father and her resentment of her mother.

electroconvulsive therapy Induction of a convulsive seizure by means of passing an electric current through the head; used primarily in the treatment of severe depression. Abbreviated *ECT*.

electrodermal response Changes in the electrical conductivity of the skin following exposure to a stimulus.

electroencephalograph Instrument for measuring the electrical activity of the brain (brain waves). Abbreviated *EEG*.

electromyograph Instrument for measuring muscle tension often used in biofeedback training. Abbreviated *EMG*.

emotion-focused coping Style of coping with stress that attempts to minimize emotional responsiveness rather than deal with the source of stress directly (e.g., the use of denial to avoid thinking about the stress or the use of tranquillizers to quell feelings of anxiety).

emotional intelligence "The ability to perceive emotions, to access and generate emotions so as to assist thought, to understand emotions and emotional knowledge, and to reflectively regulate emotions so as to promote emotional and intellectual growth" (Mayer & Salovey, 1997).

empathy In Carl Rogers's theory, the ability to understand a client's experiences and feelings from the client's frame of reference. It is considered one of the principal characteristics of effective person-centred therapists.

endocrine system System of ductless glands in the body that directly secrete hormones into the bloodstream.

endorphins Natural substances that function as neurotransmitters in the brain and are similar in their effects to morphine.

epidemiological method Method of research involved in tracking the rates of occurrence of particular disorders among different groups.

epigenetics The study of the heritable and acquired changes in gene regulation (phenotype) that occur without affecting DNA sequence (genotype).

epigenome The sum total of inherited and acquired molecular variations to the genome that lead to changes in gene regulation without changing the DNA sequence of the genome itself.

erogenous zone Part of the body that is sensitive to sexual stimulation.

etiology Cause or origin; the study of causality. Plural *etiologies*.

eustress The enjoyable and curative experience that accompanies pressures or demands.

exhaustion stage Third stage of the general adaptation syndrome (GAS); characterized by a lowering of resistance, increased parasympathetic activity, and possible physical deterioration.

exhibitionism Type of paraphilia almost exclusively occurring in males in which the man experiences persistent and recurrent sexual urges and sexually arousing fantasies involving the exposure of his genitals to a stranger and either has acted on these urges or feels strongly distressed by them.

exorcism Ritual intended to expel demons or evil spirits from a person believed to be possessed.

expectancies In social-cognitive theory, a person variable describing people's predictions of future outcomes.

experimental method Scientific method that aims to discover cause-and-effect relationships by means of manipulating the independent variable(s) and observing their effects on the dependent variable(s).

experimental subject (1) In an experiment, a subject receiving a treatment or intervention, in contrast to a *control subject*. (2) More generally, one who participates in an experiment.

external attribution In the reformulated helplessness theory, a type of attribution involving the belief that the cause of an event involves factors outside the self. Contrast with *internal attribution*

extinction The gradual reduction of a behaviour through repeated non-reinforcement.

eye movement desensitization and reprocessing A controversial form of psychotherapy in which the main intervention requires the patient to recall trauma-related memories while also attending to some form of external oscillatory stimulation. Stimulation is typically induced by the therapist moving a finger from side to side across the patient's field of vision, which induces eye movements. Sets of eye movements are induced until distress is reduced. Acronym is *EMDR*.

F

face validity Aspect of content validity: the degree to which the content of a test or measure bears an apparent or obvious relationship to the constructs or traits it is purported to measure.

factitious disorder Type of mental disorder characterized by the intentional fabrication of psychological or physical symptoms for no apparent gain.

fear Unpleasant, negative emotion characterized by the perception of a specific threat, sympathetic nervous system activity, and tendencies to avoid a feared object.

fear-stimulus hierarchy Ordered series of increasingly more fearful stimuli. Used in the behavioural techniques of *systematic desensitization* and *gradual exposure*

feedback Information about one's behaviour.

female orgasmic disorder Type of sexual dysfunction in women involving difficulties achieving orgasm.

female sexual arousal disorder Type of sexual dysfunction in women involving difficulties becoming sexually aroused, as defined by a lack of vaginal lubrication or failure to maintain sufficient lubrication to complete the sexual act or lack of sexual excitement or pleasure during sexual activity.

fetishism Type of paraphilia in which a person uses an inanimate object or a body part (*partialism*) as a focus of sexual interest and as a source of arousal.

fight-or-flight reaction Hypothesized inborn tendency to respond to a threat by means of fighting the threat or fleeing.

first-rank symptoms In Kurt Schneider's view, the primary features of schizophrenia, such as hallucinations and delusions, that distinctly characterize the disorder.

fixation In psychodynamic theory, arrested development in the form of attachment to objects of an earlier stage that occurs as a result of excessive or inadequate gratification at that stage.

flashback (1) Vivid re-experiencing of a past event that may be difficult to distinguish from current reality. (2) Experience of sensory distortions or hallucinations occurring days or weeks after usage of LSD or other hallucinogenic drugs that mimics the drug's effects.

forced-choice formats Method of structuring test questions that requires respondents to select among a set number of possible answers.

forcible rape Legal term for rape or forced sexual intercourse with a nonconsenting person.

four As In Bleuler's view, the primary characteristics of schizophrenia: *(loose) associations, (blunted or inappropriate) affect, ambivalence*, and *autism*.

free association In psychoanalysis, the method of verbalizing thoughts as they occur without any conscious attempt to edit or censure them.

freebasing Method of ingesting cocaine by means of heating the drug with ether to separate its most potent component (its "free base") and then smoking the extract.

frotteurism Type of paraphilia characterized by recurrent sexual urges or sexually arousing fantasies involving bumping and rubbing against nonconsenting persons for sexual gratification. The person has either acted on these urges or is strongly distressed by them.

functional analysis Analysis of behaviour in terms of antecedent stimuli and consequent stimuli (potential reinforcers).

functional magnetic resonance imaging A form of magnetic resonance imaging of the brain that records what regions of the brain are active during specific mental activities. Acronym is *fMRI*.

G

galvanic skin response Measure of the change in electrical activity in skin caused by increased activity of the sweat glands that accompanies states of sympathetic nervous system arousal, such as when the person is anxious. Acronym is *GSR*.

gamma-aminobutyric acid An inhibitory neurotransmitter believed to play a role in regulating anxiety. Acronym is *GABA*.

gender identity One's psychological sense of being female or being male.

gender-identity disorder Disorder in which an individual believes that her or his anatomic gender is inconsistent with her or his psychological sense of being female or male.

gender roles Characteristic ways in which males and females are expected to behave within a given culture.

gene-environment interaction Occurs when the effects of genetic factors vary across different environmental conditions. For example, a person with a particular form of a serotonin-related gene might only develop symptoms of depression or anxiety under highly stressful conditions.

gene expression The process by which a gene sequence becomes activated ("turned on") and is translated into the proteins that determine the structure and functions of body cells.

gene silencing The process of preventing or suppressing ("switching off") a gene sequence from being translated into proteins.

general adaptation syndrome In Selye's view, the body's three-stage response to states of prolonged or intense stress. Acronym is *GAS*.

general paresis Degenerative brain disorder that occurs during the final stage of syphilis.

generalized anxiety disorder Type of anxiety disorder characterized by general feelings of dread and foreboding and heightened states of sympathetic arousal. Formerly referred to as *free-floating anxiety*.

genes Units found on chromosomes that carry heredity.

genetics Science of heredity.

genital stage In psychodynamic theory, the fifth stage of psychosexual development that corresponds to mature sexuality and is characterized by the expression of libido through sexual intercourse with an adult member of the opposite gender.

genotype (1) Genetic constitution of an individual or a group. (2) Sum total of traits that one inherits from one's parents.

genuineness In Carl Rogers's view, the ability to recognize and express one's true feelings. Genuineness is considered to be a characteristic of the effective person-centred therapist.

global attribution In the reformulated helplessness theory, a type of attribution involving the belief that the cause of an event involved generalized rather than specific factors. Contrast with *specific attribution*.

gradual exposure In behaviour therapy, a method of overcoming fears through a stepwise process of direct exposure to increasingly fearful stimuli.

H

hallucinations Perceptions that occur in the absence of an external stimulus that are confused with reality.

hallucinogens Substances that give rise to hallucinations.

hashish Drug derived from the resin of the marijuana plant— *Cannabis sativa*. Often called *hash*.

health psychologists Psychologists involved in the study of the interrelationships between psychological factors and physical illness.

high strain Referring to jobs that impose great stress on workers.

hippocampus Named for its sea horse shape, it plays a key role in the formation of memories. One of a pair of structures in the limbic system that are involved in processes of memory.

histrionic personality disorder Type of personality disorder characterized by excessive needs to be the centre of attention and to receive reassurance, praise, and approval from others. Such persons often appear overly dramatic and emotional in their behaviour.

hormones Substances secreted by endocrine glands that regulate bodily functions and promote the development or growth of body structures.

human immunodeficiency virus The virus that causes AIDS. Abbreviated *HIV*.

humours Historic: the vital bodily fluids considered responsible for one's disposition and health, as in Hippocrates's belief that the health of the body and mind depended on the balance of four humours in the body: phlegm, black bile, blood, and yellow bile.

hyperactivity Abnormal behaviour pattern found most often in young boys that is characterized by difficulties maintaining attention and extreme restlessness.

hypersomnia Condition relating to a pattern of excessive sleepiness during the day.

hyperventilation Pattern of overly rapid breathing, sometimes associated with anxiety, in which the amount of oxygen inhaled is in excess of metabolic requirements, leading to harmless but sometimes unpleasant sensations such as feeling faint or light-headed.

hypnosis Trancelike state induced by suggestion in which one is generally passive and responsive to the commands of the hypnotist.

hypoactive sexual desire disorder Persistent or recurrent lack of sexual interest or sexual fantasies.

hypomanic episodes Mild manic episodes.

hypothalamus Structure in the lower middle part of the brain involved in regulating body temperature, emotion, and motivation.

hypothesis Assumption that is tested through experimentation.

hypothyroidism Physical condition caused by deficiencies of the hormone thyroxin that is characterized by sluggishness and lowered metabolism.

hypoxyphilia Paraphilia in which a person seeks sexual gratification by being deprived of oxygen by means of using a noose, plastic bag, chemical, or pressure on the chest.

hysteria Former term for *conversion disorder*.

I

id In psychodynamic theory, the unconscious psychic structure that is present at birth. The id contains instinctive drives and is governed by the pleasure principle.

ideas of persecution Form of delusional thinking characterized by false beliefs that one is being persecuted or victimized by others.

ideas of reference Form of delusional thinking in which a person reads personal meaning into the behaviour of others or external events that are completely independent of the person.

identification (1) In psychodynamic theory, the process of incorporating the personality or behaviour of others. (2) In social learning theory, a process of imitation by which children acquire behaviours similar to those of role models.

immune system The body's system for recognizing and destroying antigens (foreign bodies) that invade the body, mutated cells, and worn-out cells.

incidence Number of new cases of a disorder occurring within a specific period of time.

independent variable Factor in an experiment that is manipulated so its effects can be measured or observed.

individual education plan A contractual document that contains learning and behavioural outcomes for a student, a description of how the outcomes will be achieved, and how the outcomes will be evaluated. Acronym is *IEP*.

individual psychology Psychodynamic theory developed by Alfred Adler.

inference Conclusion drawn from data.

inferiority complex In Adler's view, feelings of inferiority believed to be a central source of motivation.

informed consent Agreement by individuals to participate in research based on a prior disclosure of information about the study's purpose, methods, risks, and benefits suffi-cient to allow subjects to make informed decisions about their participation.

insanity defence Form of legal defence in which a defendant in a criminal case pleads guilty but not criminally responsible on the basis of having a mental disorder.

insight In psychotherapy, the attainment of awareness and understanding of one's true motives and feelings.

insomnia Term applying to difficulties falling asleep, remaining asleep, or achieving restorative sleep.

intelligence (1) Global capacity to understand the world and cope with its challenges. (2) Trait or traits associated with successful performance on intelligence tests.

intelligence quotient Measure of intelligence derived on the basis of scores on an intelligence test. Called a quotient because it was originally derived by dividing a respondent's *mental age* by her or his actual age. Acronym is *IQ*.

intensive behavioural intervention A systematic behavioural teaching method that is unique to the needs of a child. It is typically a long-term, one-to-one approach ranging from 25 to 40 hours per week.

internal attribution In the reformulated helplessness theory, a type of attribution involving the belief that the cause of an event involved factors within oneself. Contrast with *external attribution*

internal consistency Reliability as measured by the cohesiveness or interrelationships of the items on a test or scale.

interpersonal psychotherapy A brief, psychodynamically oriented form of therapy that focuses on helping people resolve interpersonal problems.

interrater reliability Measure of reliability of a test based on agreement between raters.

intoxication State of drunkenness.

introjection In psychodynamic theory, the process of unconsciously incorporating features of the personality of another person within one's own ego structure.

involuntary Automatic or without conscious direction, as in the cases of bodily processes like heartbeat and respiration.

K

knob Swollen ending of an axon terminal.

Koro syndrome Culture-related somatoform disorder, found primarily in China, in which people fear their genitals are shrinking and retracting into the body.

Korsakoff's syndrome Form of brain damage associated with chronic thiamine deficiency. The syndrome is associated with chronic alcoholism and characterized by memory loss, disorientation, and the tendency to invent memories to replace lost memories (confabulation). Also called *alcohol-induced persisting amnestic disorder*.

L

la belle indifférence French term describing the lack of concern over one's symptoms displayed by some people with conversion disorder.

latency stage According to psychoanalytic theory, the fourth stage of psychosexual development, which is characterized by repression of sexual impulses.

latent content In psychodynamic theory, the underlying or symbolic content of dreams.

lateralization The developmental process by which the left hemisphere specializes in verbal and analytic functions and the right hemisphere specializes in nonverbal, spatial functions.

learned helplessness In Seligman's model, a behaviour pattern characterized by passivity and perceptions of lack of control that develops because of a history of failure to be able to exercise control over one's environment.

learning disorder Noted deficiency in a specific learning ability, which is remarkable because of the individual's general intelligence and exposure to learning opportunities.

legal commitment Legal process involved in confining a person found "not criminally responsible on account of a mental disorder" in a mental institution; also called *criminal commitment*.

leukocytes White blood cells. Leukocytes comprise part of the body's immune system.

libido In psychodynamic theory, sexual drive or energy.

limbic system Group of forebrain structures, consisting of the amygdala, hippocampus, thalamus, and hypothalamus, that are involved in processes of learning and memory and basic drives involving hunger, thirst, sex, and aggression.

locus of control One's perception of the site (internal or external) of the capacity to generate reinforcement. People who believe they have the capacity to generate or attain reinforcements are said to have an internal locus of control. People who rely on others or luck for reinforcement are said to have an external locus of control.

longitudinal studies Research studies in which subjects are followed over time. Longitudinal studies have helped researchers identify factors in early life that may predict the later development of disorders such as schizophrenia.

LSD A powerful hallucinogenic drug. LSD is the acronym for *lysergic acid diethylamide*.

M

magnetic resonance imaging Formation of a computer-generated image of the anatomical details of the brain by measuring the signals that these structures emit when the head is placed in a strong magnetic field. Acronym is *MRI*.

mainstreaming The practice of having all students with disabilities included in the regular classroom. Also referred to as *integration* or *inclusion*.

major depressive disorder Severe mood disorder characterized by the occurrence of major depressive episodes in the absence of a history of manic episodes. Major depressive disorder is characterized by a range of features such as depressed mood, lack of interest or pleasure in usual activities, lack of energy or motivation, and changes in appetite or sleep patterns.

male erectile disorder Sexual dysfunction in males characterized by difficulty in achieving or maintaining erection during sexual activity.

male orgasmic disorder Type of sexual dysfunction in men involving persistent difficulties achieving orgasm.

malingering Faking illness so as to avoid or escape work or other duties or to obtain benefits.

manic Relating to mania, as in the manic phase of a bipolar disorder.

manic episode Period of unrealistically heightened euphoria, extreme restlessness, and excessive activity characterized by disorganized behaviour and impaired judgment. Alternates with major depressive episodes in *bipolar disorder*.

manifest content In psychodynamic theory, the reported content or apparent meaning of dreams.

mantra In meditation, a resonant-sounding word or sound that is repeated to induce a state of relaxation and a narrowing of consciousness.

marijuana A mild or minor hallucinogen derived from the *Cannabis sativa* plant.

medical model Biological perspective in which abnormal behaviour is viewed as symptomatic of underlying illness.

medulla Area of the hindbrain involved in the regulation of heartbeat and respiration.

melancholia State of severe depression.

mental age Age equivalent that corresponds to a person's level of intelligence, as measured by performance on the Stanford-Binet Intelligence Scale.

mental status examination Structured clinical evaluation to determine various aspects of a client's mental functioning.

meta-analysis Statistical technique for combining the results of different studies into an overall average. In psychotherapy research, meta-analysis is used to compute the average benefit or size of effect associated with psychotherapy overall or with different forms of therapy in relation to control groups.

methadone Artificial narcotic that lacks the rush associated with heroin and is used to help people addicted to heroin abstain from it without incurring an abstinence syndrome.

modelling In behaviour therapy, a technique for helping a client acquire new behaviour by means of having the therapist or members of a therapy group demonstrate a target behaviour that is then imitated by a client.

monoamine oxidase (MAO) inhibitors Antidepressants that act to increase the availability of neurotransmitters in the brain by inhibiting the actions of an enzyme, monoamine oxidase, that normally breaks down or degrades neurotransmitters (norepinephrine and serotonin) in the synaptic cleft.

monozygotic (MZ) twins Twins who develop from the same fertilized egg and therefore share identical genes. Also called identical twins. Abbreviated *MZ twins*. Contrast with fraternal or *dizygotic (DZ) twins*.

mood Pervasive quality of an individual's emotional experience, as in depressed mood, anxious mood, or elated mood.

mood disorder Type of disorder characterized by disturbances of mood, as in depressive disorders *(major depressive disorder* or *dysthymic disorder)* or bipolar disorders *(bipolar disorder* and *cyclothymic disorder)*.

moral principle In psychodynamic theory, the principle that governs the superego to set moral standards and enforce adherence to them.

moral therapy A 19th-century treatment philosophy that emphasized that hospitalized mental patients should be treated with care and understanding in a pleasant environment, not shackled in chains.

mourning Normal feelings or expressions of grief following a loss. See also *bereavement*.

Münchausen syndrome Type of factitious disorder characterized by the feigning of medical symptoms for no apparent purpose other than getting admitted or remaining in hospitals.

mutagens Any substances or conditions, such as pesticides, heavy metals, or ionizing radiation, that produce heritable changes in cellular DNA.

myocardial infarction Breakdown of the tissue of the heart due to an obstruction of the blood vessels that supply blood to the affected area—a heart attack.

N

naloxone Drug that prevents users from becoming high if they subsequently take heroin. Some people are placed on naloxone after being withdrawn from heroin to prevent return to heroin.

naltrexone Chemical cousin of naloxone that blocks the high from alcohol as well as opiates and is now approved for use in treating alcoholism.

narcissistic personality disorder Type of personality disorder characterized by the adoption of an inflated self-image and demands for constant attention and admiration, among other features.

narcolepsy Sleep disorder characterized by sudden, irresistible episodes of sleep (sleep attacks).

narcotics Drugs, such as opiates, that are used for pain relief and treatment of insomnia, but which have strong addictive potential.

naturalistic-observation method Method of scientific research in which the behaviour of subjects is carefully and unobtrusively observed and measured in their natural environments.

negative correlation Statistical relationship between two variables such that increases in one variable are associated with decreases in the other.

negative punishers Types of punishers that decrease the frequency of behaviour when they are taken away. Removal of negative punishers, such as treats, opportunity to play, and social approval, tends to decrease the rate of the immediately preceding behaviour. Contrast with *positive punishers*.

negative reinforcers Reinforcers whose removal increases the frequency of an operant behaviour. Anxiety, pain, and social disapproval often function as negative reinforcers; that is, their removal tends to increase the rate of the immediately preceding behaviour. Contrast with *positive reinforcer*.

negative symptoms Features of schizophrenia characterized by the *absence* of normal behaviour. Negative symptoms are deficits or behavioural deficiencies, such as social skills deficits, social withdrawal, flattened affect, poverty of speech and thought, psychomotor retardation, and failure to experience pleasure in pleasant activities.

neo-Freudians Term used to describe the "second generation" of theorists who followed in the Freudian tradition. On the whole, neo-Freudians (such as Jung, Adler, Horney, Sullivan) placed greater emphasis on the importance of cultural and social influences on behaviour and lesser importance on sexual impulses and the functioning of the id.

neologisms Type of disturbed thinking associated with schizophrenia involving the coining of new words.

neuroleptics Group of antipsychotic drugs used in the treatment of schizophrenia, such as the phenothiazines (e.g., Thorazine).

neurons Nerve cells.

neuropeptide An amino acid found in cerebrospinal fluid that plays a role in neuronal transmission and the modulation of brain circuits or regions.

neuropsychological assessment Methods of psychological assessment used to detect signs of underlying neurological damage or brain defects.

neurosis Type of nonpsychotic behavioural disturbance characterized chiefly by the use of defensive behaviours to control anxiety in which a person is generally able to function but is impaired in some aspect(s) of functioning. Plural: *neuroses*.

neuroticism A personality trait consisting of an enduring tendency to experience negative emotional states. People with high levels of neuroticism tend to cope poorly with stress and frequently experience feelings of anxiety, anger, guilt, and depression.

neurotransmitter Chemical substance that serves as a type of messenger by transmitting neural impulses from one neuron to another.

neustress Neither a taxing nor an enhancing experience that accompanies pressures and demands.

nightmare disorder Sleep disorder characterized by recurrent awakenings from sleep due to the occurrence of frightening nightmares. Formerly called *dream anxiety disorder*.

nonspecific treatment factors Characteristics that are not specific to any one form of psychotherapy but tend to be shared by psychotherapies, such as the attention a client receives from a therapist and the therapist's encouragement of the client's sense of hope and positive expectancies.

norepinephrine Type of neurotransmitter of the catecholamine class.

O

object-relations Person's relationships to the internalized representations or "objects" of other's personalities that have been introjected within the person's ego structure. See also *object-relations theory*.

object-relations theory In psychodynamic theory, the viewpoint that focuses on the influences of internalized representations (called "objects") within the person's ego structure of the personalities of parents and other figures of strong attachment.

objective tests Tests that allow a limited, specified range of response options or answers so they can be scored objectively.

obsession Intrusive, unwanted, and recurrent thought, image, or urge that seems beyond the individual's ability to control.

obsessive-compulsive personality disorder Type of personality disorder characterized by rigid ways of relating to others, perfectionistic tendencies, lack of spontaneity, and excessive attention to details. Acronym is *OCPD*.

Oedipus complex In psychodynamic theory, the conflict that occurs during the phallic stage of development in which the boy incestuously desires his mother and perceives his father as a rival for his mother's love and attention.

open-ended questions Type of questions that provide an unlimited range of response options.

opiates Type of depressant drug with strong addictive properties that is derived from the opium poppy and provides relief from pain and feelings of euphoria.

oppositional defiant disorder Disorder in childhood or adolescence characterized by excessive oppositionality or tendencies to refuse requests from parents and others.

optimum level of arousal Level of arousal associated with peak performance and maximum feelings of well-being.

oral stage In psychodynamic theory, the first of Freud's stages of psychosexual development, during which pleasure is primarily sought through such oral activities as sucking and biting.

osteoporosis Physical disorder caused by calcium deficiency that is characterized by extreme brittleness of the bones (from the Greek *osteon*, meaning "bone," and the Latin *porus*, meaning "pore").

P

panic disorder Type of anxiety disorder characterized by recurrent episodes of panic.

paranoid Referring to irrational suspicions.

paranoid personality disorder Type of personality disorder characterized by persistent suspiciousness of the motives of others, but not to the point of holding clear-cut delusions.

paraphilias Sexual deviations or types of sexual disorders in which a person experiences recurrent sexual urges and sexually arousing fantasies involving nonhuman objects (such as articles of clothing), inappropriate or nonconsenting partners (e.g., children), or situations producing humiliation or pain to oneself or one's partner. The person has either acted upon such urges or is strongly distressed by them.

parasomnias Category of sleep disorders involving the occurrence of abnormal behaviours or physiological events occurring during sleep or at the transition between wakefulness and sleep.

parasympathetic Relating to the activity of the parasympathetic branch of the autonomic nervous system. See also *sympathetic*.

pathogen Organism such as a bacterium or virus that can cause disease.

pedophilia Type of paraphilia involving sexual attraction to children.

performance anxiety Fear relating to the threat of failing to perform adequately.

peripheral nervous system Part of the nervous system that consists of the somatic nervous system and the autonomic nervous system.

perseveration Persistent repetition of the same thought or response.

person-centred therapy Carl Rogers's method of psychotherapy, emphasizing the establishment of a warm, accepting therapeutic relationship that frees clients to engage in a process of self-exploration and self-acceptance.

personality disorders Types of abnormal behaviour patterns involving excessively rigid patterns of behaviour or ways of relating to others that ultimately become self-defeating because their rigidity prevents adjustment to external demands.

phallic stage In psychodynamic theory, Freud's third stage of psychosexual development, characterized by sexual interest focused on the phallic region and the development of incestuous desires for the parent of the opposite gender and rivalry with the parent of the same gender (the *Oedipus complex*).

phenothiazines Group of antipsychotic drugs or "major tranquillizers" used in the treatment of schizophrenia.

phenotype Representation of the total array of traits of an organism as influenced by the interaction of nature (genetic factors) and nurture (environmental factors).

phenylketonuria Genetic disorder that prevents the metabolization of phenylpyruvic acid, leading to mental retardation. Abbreviated *PKU*.

phlegmatic Slow and stolid.

phrenologist Practitioner of the study of bumps on a person's head as indications of the individual's underlying traits or characteristics.

physiological dependence State of physical dependence on a drug in which the user's body comes to depend on a steady supply of the drug.

placebo Inert medication or form of bogus treatment intended to control for the effects of expectancies. Sometimes referred to as a "sugar pill." Pronounced *pluh-SEE-bo*.

play therapy Form of psychodynamic therapy with children in which play activities and objects are used as a means of helping children symbolically enact family conflicts or express underlying feelings or personal problems.

pleasure principle In psychodynamic theory, the governing principle of the id, involving the demands for immediate gratification of instinctive needs.

polygenic Traits or characteristics that are determined by more than one gene.

polysomnographic (PSG) recording Relating to the simultaneous measurement of multiple physiological responses during sleep or attempted sleep.

pons Brain structure located in the hindbrain that is involved in respiration.

population Total group of people, other organisms, or events.

positive correlation Statistical relationship between two variables such that increases in one variable are associated with increases in the other.

positive punishers Types of punishers that decrease the frequency of behaviour when they are presented. Physical aggression and social disapproval are generally but not always positive punishers. Contrast with *negative punishers*.

positive reinforcers Types of reinforcers that increase the frequency of behaviour when they are presented. Food and social approval are generally but not always positive reinforcers. Contrast with *negative reinforcer*.

positive symptoms The more flagrant features of schizophrenia characterized by the *presence* of abnormal behaviour, such as hallucinations, delusions, thought disorder, disorganized speech, and inappropriate affect.

positron emission tomography Brain-imaging technique in which a computer-generated image of the neural activity of regions of the brain is formed by tracing the amounts of glucose used in the various regions. Abbreviated *PET scan*.

possession In demonology, a type of superstitious belief in which abnormal behaviour is taken as a sign that the individual has become possessed by demons or the devil, usually as a form of retribution or the result of making a pact with the devil.

postpartum depression Persistent and severe mood changes that occur following childbirth.

posttraumatic stress disorder Type of anxiety disorder involving impaired functioning following exposure to a traumatic experience, such as combat, physical assault or rape, or natural or technological disasters, in which a person experiences, for at least a month, such problems as reliving or re-experiencing the trauma, intense fear, avoidance of event-related stimuli, generalized numbing of emotional responsiveness, and heightened autonomic arousal. Abbreviated *PTSD*.

preconscious In psychodynamic theory, descriptive of material that lies outside of present awareness but which can be brought into awareness by focusing attention. See also *unconscious*.

predictive validity Degree to which a test response or score is predictive of some criterion behaviour (such as school performance) in the future.

prefrontal lobotomy Form of psychosurgery in which certain neural pathways in the brain are severed in the attempt to control disturbed behaviour.

pregenital In psychodynamic theory, referring to characteristics that are typical of stages of psychosexual development that precede the genital stage.

premature ejaculation Type of sexual dysfunction involving a persistent or recurrent pattern of ejaculation occurring during sexual activity at a point before the man desires it.

premorbid functioning Level of functioning before the onset of a disorder.

prepared conditioning Belief that people are genetically prepared to acquire fear responses to certain classes of stimuli, such as fears of large animals, snakes, heights, or even strangers. Although the development of such phobias may have had survival value for prehistoric ancestors, such behaviour patterns may be less functional today.

pressured speech Outpouring of speech in which words seem to surge urgently for expression, as in a manic state.

prevalence Overall number of cases of a disorder existing in the population during a given period of time.

primary gains In psychodynamic theory, the relief from anxiety obtained through the development of a neurotic symptom.

primary process thinking In psychodynamic theory, the mental process in infancy by which the id seeks gratification of primitive impulses by means of imagining it possesses what it desires. Thinking that is illogical, magical, and fails to discriminate between reality and fantasy.

primary reinforcers Natural reinforcers or stimuli that have reinforcement value without learning. Water, food, warmth, and relief from pain are examples of primary reinforcers. Contrast with *secondary reinforcer*.

proband Initial diagnosed case of a given disorder.

problem-focused coping Form of coping with stress characterized by directly confronting the source of the stress.

problem-solving therapy Form of therapy that focuses on helping people develop more effective problem-solving skills.

prodromal phase (1) Stage in which the early features or signs of a disorder become apparent. (2) In schizophrenia, the period of decline in functioning that precedes the development of the first acute psychotic episode.

projection In psychodynamic theory, a defence mechanism in which one's own impulses are attributed to another person.

proteins Organic compounds consisting of amino acids that perform most life functions and make up the majority of cellular structures.

psychedelics Class of drugs that induce sensory distortions or hallucinations. Also called *hallucinogens*.

psychiatrist Physician who specializes in the diagnosis and treatment of mental disorders.

psychic (1) Relating to mental phenomena. (2) A person who claims to be sensitive to supernatural forces.

psychoactive Describing chemical substances or drugs that have psychological effects.

psychoanalysis (1) Theoretical model of personality developed by Sigmund Freud. (2) Method of psychotherapy developed by Sigmund Freud.

psychoanalytic theory Theoretical model of personality developed by Freud. Also called *psychoanalysis*.

psychodynamic model Theoretical model of Freud and his followers in which behaviour is viewed as the product of clashing forces within the personality.

psychological dependence Reliance, as on a substance, although one may not be physiologically dependent on the substance.

psychological disorders Disturbances of psychological functioning or behaviour associated with states of personal distress or impaired social, occupational, or interpersonal functioning. Also called *mental disorders*.

psychological hardiness Cluster of stress-buffering traits characterized by commitment, challenge, and control.

psychometric approach Method of psychological assessment that seeks to use psychological tests to identify and measure the reasonably stable traits in an individual's personality that are believed to largely determine the person's behaviour.

psychopathy Type of personality pattern characterized by affective and interpersonal traits, such as shallow emotions, selfishness, arrogance, superficial charm, deceitfulness, manipulativeness, irresponsibility, sensation-seeking, and a lack of empathy, anxiety, and remorse, combined with persistent violations of social norms, a socially deviant and nomadic lifestyle, and impulsiveness.

psychopharmacology Field of study that examines the effects of drugs on behaviour and psychological functioning and explores the use of psychoactive drugs in the treatment of emotional disorders.

psychophysiological Referring to physiological correlates or underpinnings of psychological events.

psychosexual Descriptive of the stages of human development in Freud's theory in which sexual energy (libido) becomes expressed through different erogenous zones of the body during different developmental stages.

psychosis Type of major psychological disorder in which people show impaired ability to interpret reality and difficulties in meeting the demands of daily life. Schizophrenia is a prominent example of a psychotic disorder. Plural: *psychoses*.

psychosomatic Relating to physical disorders in which psychological factors are believed to play a causal or contributing role.

psychotherapy Method of helping involving a systematic interaction between a therapist and a client that brings psychological principles to bear on influencing the client's thoughts, feelings, or behaviours in order to help that client overcome abnormal behaviour or adjust to problems in living.

punishments Unpleasant stimuli that suppress the frequency of the behaviours they follow.

R

random sample Sample drawn in such a way that every member of a population has an equal probability of being selected.

rapid flight of ideas Characteristic of manic behaviour involving rapid speech and changes of topics.

rapport In psychotherapy, the interpersonal relationship between a therapist and client that is characterized by harmony, trust, and co-operation.

reactivity Tendency for behaviour to be influenced by the process by which it is measured.

reality principle In psychodynamic theory, the governing principle of the ego that involves consideration of what is socially acceptable and practical in gratifying needs.

reality testing Ability to perceive the world accurately and to distinguish reality from fantasy.

rebound anxiety Occurrence of strong anxiety following withdrawal from a tranquillizer.

receptor site Part of a dendrite on the receiving neuron that is structured to receive a neurotransmitter.

reciprocal determinism The ongoing process of two-way interactions among personal factors (cognitive—expectancies, values, attitudes, and beliefs, affective, and biological), behaviours (skills, talents, habits, and interpersonal relations) and environmental factors (physical surroundings and other people).

rehearsal In behaviour therapy, a practice opportunity in which a person enacts a desired response and receives feedback from others.

reinforcement Stimulus that increases the frequency of the response it follows. See *positive* and *negative*, and *primary* and *secondary reinforcers*.

relapse Recurrence of a problem behaviour or disorder.

relapse-prevention training Cognitive-behavioural technique used in the treatment of addictive behaviours that involves the use of behavioural and cognitive strategies to resist temptations and prevent lapses from becoming relapses.

reliable In psychological assessment, the consistency of a measuring instrument such as a psychological test or rating scale. There are various ways of measuring reliability, such as test-retest reliability, internal consistency, and interrater reliability. See also *validity*.

REM sleep REM (rapid eye movement) sleep is the stage of sleep associated with dreaming that is characterized by the appearance of rapid eye movements under the closed eyelids.

repetitive transcranial magnetic stimulation A procedure that uses strong magnetic pulses to stimulates the brain. Acronym is *rTMS*.

repression In psychodynamic theory, a type of defence mechanism involving the ejection from awareness of anxiety-provoking ideas, images, or impulses without the conscious awareness that one has done so.

residual phase In schizophrenia, the phase of the disorder that follows an acute phase, characterized by a return to a level of functioning which was typical of the prodromal phase.

resistance During psychoanalysis, the blocking of thoughts or feelings that would evoke anxiety if they were consciously experienced. Resistance may also take the form of missed sessions by the client or the client's verbal confrontation with the analyst as threatening material is about to be uncovered.

resistance stage In Selye's view, the second stage of the general adaptation syndrome, involving the attempt to withstand prolonged stress and preserve bodily resources. Also called the *adaptation stage*.

reticular activating system Part of the brain involved in processes of attention, sleep, and arousal. Acronym is *RAS*.

reversal design An A-B-A-B type of experimental single-subject design in which treatment is instituted following a baseline phase and then withdrawn (reversal phase) so as to examine effects on behaviour.

S

sadomasochism Sexual activities between partners involving the attainment of gratification by means of inflicting and receiving pain and humiliation.

sample Part of a population.

sanguine Having a cheerful disposition.

schizoid personality disorder Type of personality disorder characterized by a persistent lack of interest in social relationships, flattened affect, and social withdrawal.

schizophrenia Enduring psychosis that involves failure to maintain integrated personality functioning, impaired reality testing, and disturbances in thinking. Common features of schizophrenia include delusions, hallucinations, flattened or inappropriate affect, and bizarre behaviour. See also *schizophreniform disorder, schizotypalpersonality disorder*, and *brief reactive psychosis*.

schizophrenogenic mother Type of mother, described as cold but also overprotective, who was believed to be capable of causing schizophrenia in her children. Research has failed to support the validity of this concept.

schizotypal personality disorder Type of personality disorder characterized by eccentricities or oddities of thought and behaviour but without clearly psychotic features.

second-rank symptoms In Schneider's view, symptoms associated with schizophrenia that also occur in other mental disorders.

secondary gains Side benefits associated with neuroses or other disorders, such as expressions of sympathy and increased attention from others, and release from ordinary responsibilities.

secondary process thinking In psychodynamic theory, the reality-based thinking processes and problem-solving activities of the ego.

secondary reinforcers Stimuli that gain reinforcement value through their association with established reinforcers. Money and social approval are typically secondary reinforcers. Contrast with *primary reinforcer*.

sedatives Types of depressant drugs that reduce states of tension and restlessness and induce sleep.

selective abstraction In Beck's theory, a type of cognitive distortion involving the tendency to focus selectively only on the parts of one's experiences that reflect on one's flaws and to ignore those aspects that reveal one's strengths or competencies.

selective serotonin-reuptake inhibitors Type of antidepressant medication that prevents serotonin from being taken back up by the transmitting neuron, thus increasing its action. Acronym is *SSRIs*.

self Centre of one's consciousness that organizes one's sensory impressions and governs one's perceptions of the world. The sum total of one's thoughts, sensory impressions, and feelings.

self-monitoring In behavioural assessment, the process of recording or observing one's own behaviour, thoughts, or emotions.

self-spectatoring Tendency to observe one's behaviour as if one were a spectator of oneself. People with sexual dysfunctions often become self-spectators in the sense of focusing their attention during sexual activity on the response of their sex organs rather than on their partners or the sexual stimulation itself.

self psychology Hans Kohut's theory that describes processes that normally lead to the achievement of a cohesive sense of self, or in narcissistic personality disorder, to a grandiose but fragile sense of self.

semi-structured interviews Type of clinical interview in which interviewers are guided by a general outline but are free to modify the order in which questions are asked and to branch off in other directions.

sensate focus exercises In sex therapy, the mutual pleasuring activities between the partners that is focused on the partners taking turns giving and receiving physical pleasure.

sensitivity Ability of a test or diagnostic instrument to identify people as having a given characteristic or disorder who truly have the characteristic or disorder.

separation anxiety disorder Childhood disorder characterized by extreme fears of separation from parents or others on whom a child is dependent.

separation-individuation In Margaret Mahler's theory, the process by which young children come to separate psychologically from their mothers and come to perceive themselves as separate and distinct persons.

serotonin Type of neurotransmitter, imbalances of which have been linked to mood disorders and anxiety.

sexual aversion disorder Type of sexual dysfunction characterized by aversion to and avoidance of genital sexual contact.

sexual dysfunctions Psychological disorders involving persistent difficulties with sexual interest, arousal, or response.

sexual masochism Type of paraphilia characterized by sexual urges and sexually arousing fantasies involving receiving humiliation or pain in which the person has either acted on these urges or is strongly distressed by them.

sexual sadism Type of paraphilia or sexual deviation characterized by recurrent sexual urges and sexually arousing fantasies involving inflicting humiliation or physical pain on sex partners in which the person has either acted on these urges or is strongly distressed by them.

significant In statistics, a magnitude of difference that is taken as indicating meaningful differences between groups because of the low probability that it occurred by chance.

single-case experimental designs Type of case study in which the subject (case) is used as his or her own control by varying the conditions to which the subject is exposed (by use of a *reversal* phase) or by means of a *multiple-baseline* design.

sleep disorders Diagnostic category representing persistent or recurrent sleep-related problems that cause significant personal distress or impaired functioning.

sleep terror disorder Sleep disorder characterized by repeated episodes of sleep terror resulting in abrupt awakenings.

sleepwalking disorder Type of sleep disorder involving repeated episodes of sleepwalking.

Smith-Lemli-Opitz syndrome An autosomal recessive disease resulting in low levels of cholesterol. It is characterized by varying degrees of multiple facial and bodily malformations, mental retardation, and autism-spectrum disorder behaviours. Acronym is *SLOS*.

social-cognitive theory A broader view of learning theory that emphasizes both situational determinants of behaviour (reinforcements and punishments) and cognitive factors (expectancies, values, attitudes, beliefs, etc.).

social phobia Excessive fear of engaging in behaviours that involve public scrutiny.

soma Cell body.

somatic nervous system Division of the peripheral nervous system that relays information from the sense organs to the brain and transmits messages from the brain to the skeletal muscles, resulting in body movements.

somatization disorder Type of somatoform disorder involving recurrent multiple complaints that cannot be explained by any clear physical causes. Formerly called *Briquet's syndrome*.

somatoform disorders Disorders in which people complain of physical (somatic) problems, although no physical abnormality can be found. See also *conversion disorder*, *hypochondriasis*, and *somatization disorder*.

specific attribution In the reformulated helplessness theory, a type of attribution involving the belief that the cause of an event involved specific, rather than generalized, factors. Contrast with *global attribution*.

specific phobia Persistent but excessive fear of a specific object or situation, such as a fear of heights or of small animals.

specificity Ability of a test or diagnostic instrument to avoid classifying people as having a characteristic or disorder who truly do not have the characteristic or disorder.

splitting Term describing the inability of some persons (especially people with borderline personalities) to reconcile the positive and negative aspects of themselves and others into a cohesive integration, resulting in sudden and radical shifts between strongly positive and strongly negative feelings.

stable attribution In the reformulated helplessness theory, a type of attribution involving the belief that the cause of an event involved stable rather than changeable factors. Contrast with *unstable attribution*.

standard scores Scores that indicate the relative standing of raw scores in relation to the distribution of normative scores. For example, raw scores on the MMPI scales are converted into standard scores that indicate the degree to which each of the individual raw scores deviates from the mean.

statutory rape Legal term referring to sexual intercourse with a minor, even with the minor's consent.

stem cells Undifferentiated cells that are capable of indefinite self-replication and differentiation into specialized cells.

steroids Group of hormones including testosterone, estrogen, progesterone, and corticosteroids.

stress The mental, emotional, or physical adaptation or adjustment an organism makes in the face of any tangible or perceived pressure or demand.

stressor Source of stress.

stroke Destruction of brain tissues resulting from the blockage of a blood vessel that serves the brain or from bleeding in the brain. Also called a cerebrovascular accident (CVA).

structural hypothesis In Freud's theory, the belief that the clashing forces within a personality could be divided into three psychic structures: the id, the ego, and the superego.

structured interviews Means by which an interviewer obtains clinical information from a client by asking a fairly standard series of questions concerning such issues as the client's presenting complaints or problems, mental state, life circumstances, and psychosocial or developmental history.

stupor State of relative or complete unconsciousness in which a person is not generally aware of or responsive to the environment, as in a *catatonic stupor*.

substance abuse Continued use of a psychoactive drug despite the knowledge that it is causing or contributing to a persistent or recurrent social, occupational, psychological, or physical problem.

substance dependence Impaired control over the use of a psychoactive drug and continued or even increased use despite awareness that the substance is disrupting one's life. Substance dependence is often characterized by physiological dependence.

substance-induced disorders Disorders induced by the use of psychoactive substances, including intoxication, withdrawal syndromes, mood disorders, delirium, and amnesia.

substance-use disorders Pattern of maladaptive behaviour involving the use of a psychoactive substance. Substance use disorders include substance abuse disorders and substance dependence disorders.

superego In psychodynamic theory, the psychic structure that represents the incorporation of the moral values of parents and important others and floods the ego with guilt and shame when it falls short of meeting those standards. The superego is governed by the moral principle and consists of two parts, the conscience and the ego ideal.

survey method Method of scientific research in which large samples of people are questioned by use of a survey instrument.

Sychoneuroimmunology Field of scientific investigation that studies relationships between psychological factors, such as coping styles, attitudes, and behaviour patterns, and immunological functioning.

symbiotic (1) In biology, the living together of two different but interdependent organisms. (2) In Mahler's object-relations theory, the term used to describe the state of oneness that normally exists between mother and infant in which the infant's identity is fused with the mother's.

sympathetic Pertaining to the division of the autonomic nervous system that becomes active to meet the demands of stress, as in adjusting to cold temperatures or in expending bodily reserves of energy through physical exertion or through emotional reactions such as anxiety or fear. See also *parasympathetic*.

synapse Junction between the terminal knob of one neuron and the dendrite or soma of another through which nerve impulses pass.

syndrome Cluster of symptoms that is characteristic of a particular disorder.

systematic desensitization Behaviour therapy technique for overcoming phobias by means of exposure (in imagination or by means of slides) to progressively more fearful stimuli while one remains deeply relaxed.

T

tachycardia Abnormally rapid heartbeat.

taijin-kyofu-sho Psychiatric syndrome found in Japan that involves excessive fear of offending or causing embarrassment to others. Abbreviated *TKS*.

tardive dyskinesia Movement disorder characterized by involuntary movements of the face, mouth, neck, trunk, or extremities caused by long-term use of antipsychotic medications.

Tay-Sachs disease Disease of lipid metabolism that is genetically transmitted and generally results in death in early childhood.

temporal stability Consistency of test responses across time, as measured by test-retest reliability.

teratogens Any substances or conditions, such as drugs, X-rays, and infectious diseases, that interfere with normal prenatal development.

terminals In neuropsychology, the small branching structures found at the tips of axons.

test-retest reliability Method for measuring the reliability of a test by means of comparing (correlating) the scores of the same test subjects on separate occasions.

thalamus Structure in the brain involved in relaying sensory information to the cortex and in processes relating to sleep and attention.

theory (1) Plausible or scientifically defensible explanation of events. (2) Formulation of the relationships underlying observed events. Theories are helpful to scientists because they provide a means of organizing observations and lead to predictions about future events.

theory of mind The ability to appreciate that other people have a mental state that is different from one's own.

thermistor Small device that is strapped to the skin for registering body temperature, as used in biofeedback training.

thought disorder Disturbances in thinking characterized by various features, especially the breakdown in logical associations between thoughts.

time-out Procedures that deny the opportunity to receive reinforcement for a specific period of time.

time out Behavioural technique in which an individual who emits an undesired behaviour is removed from an environment where reinforcers are available and placed in an unreinforcing environment for a period of time as a form of punishment. Time out is frequently used in behavioural programs for modifying behaviour problems in children in combination with positive reinforcement for desirable behaviour.

token economies Behavioural treatment programs in institutional settings in which a controlled environment is constructed such that people are reinforced for desired behaviours by receiving tokens (such as poker chips) that may be exchanged for desired rewards or privileges.

tolerance Physical habituation to a drug so that with frequent usage, higher doses are needed to attain similar effects.

transcendental meditation Popular form of meditation introduced to North America by the Maharishi Mahesh Yogi that focuses on the repeating of a mantra to induce a meditative state. Acronym is *TM*.

transference relationship In psychoanalysis, the client's transfer or generalization to the analyst of feelings and attitudes the client holds toward important figures in his or her life.

transvestic fetishism Type of paraphilia in heterosexual males characterized by recurrent sexual urges and sexually arousing fantasies involving dressing in female clothing in which the person has either acted on these urges or is strongly distressed by them. Also termed *transvestism*.

trephining Harsh, prehistoric practice of cutting a hole in a person's skull, possibly as an ancient form of surgery for brain trauma, or possibly as a means of releasing the demons that prehistoric people may have believed caused abnormal behaviour in afflicted persons.

tricyclics Group of antidepressant drugs that increase the activity of norepinephrine and serotonin in the brain by interfering with the reuptake of these neurotransmitters by transmitting neurons. Also called *TCAs* (tricyclic antidepressants).

two-factor model O. Hobart Mowrer's belief that both operant and classical conditioning are involved in the acquisition of phobic responses. Basically, the fear component of phobia is acquired by means of classical conditioning (pairing of a previously neutral stimulus with an aversive stimulus), and the avoidance component is acquired by means of operant conditioning (relief from anxiety negatively reinforces avoidance behaviour).

Type A behaviour pattern Pattern of behaviour characterized by a sense of time urgency, competitiveness, and hostility. Acronym is *TABP*.

U

unconditional positive regard In Carl Rogers's view, the expression of unconditional acceptance of another person's basic worth as a person, regardless of whether one approves of all of the behaviour of the other person. The ability to express unconditional positive regard is considered a quality of an effective person-centred therapist.

unconditioned response Unlearned response or a response to an unconditioned stimulus. Abbreviated *UR* or *UCR*.

unconditioned stimulus Stimulus that elicits an instinctive or unlearned response from an organism. Abbreviated *US* or *UCS*.

unconscious (1) In psychodynamic theory, pertaining to impulses or ideas that are not readily available to awareness, in many instances because they are kept from awareness by means of *repression*. (2) Also in psychodynamic theory, the part of the mind that contains repressed material and primitive urges of the id. (3) More generally, a state of unawareness or loss of consciousness.

unipolar Pertaining to a single pole or direction, as in unipolar (depressive) disorders. Contrast with *bipolar disorder*.

unobtrusive Not interfering.

unstable attribution In the reformulated helplessness theory, a type of attribution involving the belief that the cause of an event involved changeable rather than stable factors. Contrast with *stable attribution*.

unstructured interviews Type of clinical interview in which interviewers determine which questions to ask rather than following a standard interview format.

V

vaginismus Type of sexual dysfunction characterized by the recurrent or persistent contraction of the muscles surrounding the vaginal entrance, making penile entry while attempting intercourse difficult or impossible.

validity (1) With respect to tests, the degree to which a test measures the traits or constructs that it purports to measure. (2) With respect to experiments, the degree to which an experiment yields scientifically accurate and defensible results.

validity scales Groups of test items that serve to detect whether the results of a particular test are valid or whether a person responded in a random manner or in a way intended to create a favourable or unfavourable impression.

variables Conditions that are measured (dependent variables) or manipulated (independent variables) in scientific studies.

voyeurism Type of paraphilia characterized by recurrent sexual urges and sexually arousing fantasies involving the act of watching unsuspecting others who are naked, in the act of undressing, or engaging in sexual activity, in which the person has either acted on these urges or is strongly distressed by them.

W

waxy flexibility Feature of catatonic schizophrenia in which a person's limbs are moved into a certain posture or position which the person then rigidly maintains for a lengthy period of time.

weaning Process of accustoming a child to eat solid food rather than seeking nourishment through breast feeding or sucking a baby bottle.

withdrawal syndrome Characteristic cluster of withdrawal symptoms following the sudden reduction or abrupt cessation of use of a psychoactive substance after physiological dependence has developed.

world view Prevailing view of the times. (English translation of the German *Weltanschauung*.)

REFERENCES

A

Abdulrehman, R. Y., & De Luca, R. V. (2001). The implications of childhood sexual abuse on adult social behavior. *Journal of Family Violence, 16,* 193–203.

Abi-Dargham, A. (2004). Do we still believe in the dopamine hypothesis? New data bring new evidence. *International Journal of Neuropsychopharmacology, 7* (Suppl. 1), S1–S5.

Abikoff, H., & Klein, R. G. (1992). Attention-deficit hyperactivity and conduct disorder: Comorbidity and implications for treatment. *Journal of Consulting and Clinical Psychology, 60,* 881–892.

Aboriginal Planet (2002). *Aboriginal Planet—who are we?* Ottawa: Department of Foreign Affairs and International Trade. Retrieved February 9, 2003, from http://www.dfait-maeci.gc.ca/foreign_policy/aboriginal/talk/talk-en.asp.

Abraham, K. (1948). The first pregenital stage of the libido. In D. Bryan & A. Strachey (Eds.), *Selected papers of Karl Abraham, M. D.* London: The Hogarth Press. (Original work published in 1916.)

Abramson, L. T., Seligman, M. E. P., & Teasdale, J. D. (1978). Learned helplessness in humans: Critique and reformulation. *Journal of Abnormal Psychology, 87,* 49–74.

Achenbach, T. M. (1978). The Child Behavior Profile: I. Boys aged 6 through 11. *Journal of Consulting and Clinical Psychology, 46,* 478–488.

Achenbach, T. M., & Edelbrock, C. S. (1979). The Child Behavior Profile: I. Boys aged 12–16 and girls aged 6–11 and 12–16. *Journal of Consulting and Clinical Psychology, 47,* 223–233.

Addington, J., Collins, A., McCleery, A., & Addington, D. (2005). The role of family work in early psychosis. *Schizophrenia Research, 79,* 77–83.

Adlaf, E. M., & Paglia, A. (2001). *The mental health and well-being of Ontario students: 1991–1999.* Toronto, ON: CAMH.

Adlaf, E. M., Begin, P., & Sawka, E. (Eds.) (2005). *Canadian addiction survey (CAS): A national survey of Canadians' use of alcohol and other drugs.* Ottawa: Canadian Centre on Substance Abuse.

Adler, J. (1994, December 19). The endless binge. *Newsweek,* pp. 72–73.

Afifi, T. O., Cox, B. J., & Enns, M. W. (2006). Mental health profiles among married, never-married, and separated/divorced mothers in a nationally representative sample. *Social Psychiatry and Psychiatric Epidemiology, 41,* 122–129.

Agbayewa, M. O. (2000). Caring and the culture of mental health professionals. *Visions, 9* (Winter), 17.

Ahern, J., Galea, S., Resnick, H., Kilpatrick, D., Bucuvalas, M., Gold, J., et al. (2002). Television images and psychological symptoms after the September 11 terrorist attacks. *Psychiatry: Interpersonal and Biological Processes, 65,* 289–300.

Ainsworth, M. D. (1989). Attachments beyond infancy. *American Psychologist, 44,* 709–716.

Ainsworth, M. D. S., & Bowlby, J. (1991). An ethological approach to personality development. *American Psychologist, 46,* 333–341.

Akbarian, S., Kim, J. J., Potkin, S. G., Hetrick, W. P., Bunney, W. E., Jr., & Jones, E. G. (1996). Maldistribution of interstitial neurons in prefrontal white matter of the brains of schizophrenic patients. *Archives of General Psychiatry, 53,* 425–436.

Akhtar, A. (1987). Schizoid personality disorder: A synthesis of developmental, dynamic, and descriptive features. *American Journal of Psychotherapy, 41,* 499–517.

Akhtar, N., & Bradley, E. J. (1991). Social information processing deficits of aggressive children: Present findings and implications for social skills training. *Clinical Psychology Review, 11,* 621–644.

Akhtar, S. (2003). Things: Developmental, psychopathological, and technical aspects of inanimate objects. *Canadian Journal of Psychoanalysis, 11*(1), 1–44.

Akiskal, H. S. (2001). Dysthymia and cyclothymia in psychiatric practice a century after Kraepelin. *Journal of Affective Disorders, 62,* 17–31.

Alarcón, R. D., Bell, C. C., Kirmayer, L. J., Lin, K-M., Üstün, B., & Wisner, K. L. (2002). Beyond the funhouse mirrors. In D.J. Kupfer, M.B. First, & D.A. Regier (Eds.), *A research Agenda for DSM-V.* (pp. 219–281). Washington, DC: American Psychiatric Association.

Alberta Learning (2003). *Teaching students with autism spectrum disorders.* Edmonton: the Crown in Right of Alberta.

Alberta Mental Health Board. (2001). *A policy framework: Mental health for Alberta's children and youth.* Retrieved April 23, 2003, from http://www.amhb.ab.ca/chmh/partners/pdf/ACY.pdf.

Alberta Mental Health Board (2002). *Crosswalk development: DSM-IV-TR to ICD-10-CA.* Calgary: Author. Retrieved May 05, 2003, from http://www.amhb.ab.ca/crosswalk_development.pdf.

Alcohol and the heart: Consensus emerges. (1996, January). *Harvard Heart Letter, 6*(5).

Aldrich, M. S. (1992). Narcolepsy. *Neurology, 42 (7, Suppl. 6),* 34–43.

Allderidge, P. (1979). Hospitals, madhouses and asylums: Cycles in the care of the insane. *British Journal of Psychiatry, 134,* 1476–1478.

Allen, M., Bourhis, J., Sahlstein, E., Laskowski, K., Falato, W. L., Ackerman, J., et al. (2004). A meta-analysis of the relationship between social skills and sexual offenders. *Communication Reports, 17,* 1–10.

Alloy, L. B., Abramson, L. Y., Walshaw, P. D., & Neeren, A. M. (2006a). Cognitive vulnerability to unipolar and bipolar mood disorders. *Journal of Social & Clinical Psychology, 25,* 726–754.

Alloy, L. B., Abramson, L. Y., Whitehouse, W. G., Hogan, M. E., Panzarella, C., & Rose, D. T. (2006b). Prospective incidence of first onsets and recurrences of depression in individuals at high and low cognitive risk for depression. *Journal of Abnormal Psychology, 115,* 145–156.

Alloy, L. B., Abramson, L. Y., Whitehouse, W. G., Hogan, M. E., Tashman, N. A., Steinberg, D. L, et al. (1999). Depressogenic cognitive styles: Predictive validity, information processing and personality characteristics, and developmental origins. *Behaviour Research and Therapy, 37,* 503–531.

Alpert, J., Nierenberg, A. A., Mischoulon, D., Otto, M. W., Zajecka, J., Murck, H. et al. (2005). A double-blind, randomized trial of St John's wort, fluoxetine, and placebo in major depressive disorder. *Journal of Clinical Psychopharmacology, 25,* 441–447.

Altman, L. K. (1990, April 18). Scientists see a link between alcoholism and a specific gene. *The New York Times,* pp. A1, A18.

Altman, L. K. (1994, February 22). Stomach microbe offers clues to cancer as well as ulcers. *The New York Times,* p. C3.

American Association on Mental Retardation (AAMR). (1992). *Mental retardation: Definition, classification, and systems of supports* (9th ed.). Washington, DC: Author.

American Psychiatric Association (2000a). *Diagnostic and statistical manual of mental disorders* (4th ed., text revision). Washington, DC: Author.

American Psychiatric Association. (2000b). Practice guideline for major depressive disorder in adults. *American Journal of Psychiatry, 150 (Suppl 4),* 1–45.

Ames, M. A., & Houston, D. A. (1990). Legal, social, and biological definitions of pedophilia. *Archives of Sexual Behavior, 19,* 333–342.

Amminger, G. P., Pape, S., Rock, D., Roberts, S. A., Looser, S.,

Squires-Wheeler, E., Kestenbaum, C., & Erlenmeyer-Kimling, L. (1999). Relationship between childhood behavioral disturbance and later schizophrenia in the New York High-Risk Project. *American Journal of Psychiatry, 156,* 525–530.

Amor, D. J., Bentley, K., Ryan, J., Perry, J., Wong, L., Slater, H. et al. (2004). Human centromere repositioning 'in progress.' *Proceedings of the National Academy of Sciences of the United States of America, 101*(17), 6542–6547.

Andersen, B. L. (1992). Psychological interventions for cancer patients to enhance the quality of life. *Journal of Consulting and Clinical Psychology, 60,* 552–568.

Andersen, B. L. (1997, July). Psychological interventions for individuals with cancer. *Clinician's Research Digest, Supplemental Bulletin, 16,* pp. 1–2.

Anderson, B. L. (2002). Biobehavioral outcomes following psychological interventions for cancer patients. *Journal of Consulting and Clinical Psychology, 70*(3), 590–610.

Andersen, B. & Miranda, S. M. (2000). Transference: How past relationships emerge in the present. *The Psychologist, 13*(12), 608–609.

Anderson, E. M. & Lambert, M. J. (1995). Short-term dynamically oriented psychotherapy: A review and meta-analysis. *Clinical Psychology Review, 15,* 503–514.

Andreasen, N. C. (1999). Understanding the causes of schizophrenia. *New England Journal of Medicine, 340,* 645–647.

Andreasen, N. C., Arndt, S., Alliger, R. et al. (1995). Symptoms of schizophrenia: Methods, meanings, and mechanisms. *Archives of General Psychiatry, 52,* 341–351.

Andreasen, N. C. et al. (1997). Hypofrontality in schizophrenia: Distributed dysfunctional circuits in neuroleptic-naive patients. *Lancet, 349,* 1730–1734.

Andrews, A. (1999). *Be good, sweet maid: The trials of Dorothy Joudrie.* Ontario: Wilfrid Laurier University Press.

Angier, N. (1991a, May 30). Gene causing common type of retardation is discovered. *The New York Times,* pp. A1, B11.

Angier, N. (1991b, August 4). Kids who can't sit still. *The New York Times,* Section 4A, pp. 30–33.

Angold, A. & Costello, E. J. (1993). Depressive comorbidity in children and adolescents: Empirical, theoretical, and methodological issues. *American Journal of Psychiatry, 150,* 1779–1791.

Angold, A., & Costello, E. J. (1996). Toward establishing an empirical basis for the diagnosis of oppositional defiant disorder. *Journal of the American Academy of Child and Adolescent Psychiatry, 35,* 1205–1212.

Anthony, W. A. & Liberman, R. P. (1986). The practice of psychiatric rehabilitation: Historical, conceptual, and research base. *Schizophrenia Bulletin, 12,* 542–559.

Anton, R. F. (1994). Medications for treating alcoholism. *Alcohol Health and Research World, 18,* 265–271.

Antonarakis, S. E. (1991). Parental origin of the extra chromosome in trisomy 21 as indicated by analysis of DNA polymorphisms. Down Syndrome Collaborative Group. *The New England Journal of Medicine, 324*(13), 872–876.

Antonova, E., Sharma, T., Morris, R., & Kumari, V. (2004). The relationship between brain structure and neurocognition in schizophrenia: A selective review. *Schizophrenia Research, 70,* 117–145.

Antony, M. M. & Barlow, D. H. (2002). Specific phobias. In D. H. Barlow, *Anxiety and its disorders: The nature and treatment of anxiety and panic,* 2nd ed. (pp. 380–417). New York: Guilford.

Antony, M. M. & McCabe, R. (2005). *Overcoming animal and insect phobias.* Oakland, CA: New Harbinger.

Antony, M. M. & Swinson, R. P. (1998). *When perfect isn't good enough: Strategies for coping with perfectionism.* Oakland, CA: New Harbinger.

Antony, M. M. & Swinson, R. P. (2000). *Phobic disorders and panic attacks in adults: A guide to assessment and treatment.* Washington, DC: American Psychological Association.

Antony, M. M., Ledley, D. R., Liss, A., & Swinson, R. P. (2006). Responses to symptom induction exercises in panic disorder. *Behaviour Research and Therapy, 44,* 85–98.

Antony, M. M., Rowa, K., Liss, A., Swallow, S. R., & Swinson, R. P. (2005). Social comparison processes in social phobia. *Behavior Therapy, 36,* 65–75.

Anway, M. D., Cupp, A. S., Uzumcu, M., & Skinner, M. K. (2005). Epigenetic transgenerational actions of endocrine disruptors and male fertility. *Science, 308*(5727), 1466–1469.

Arieti, S. (1974). *Interpretation of schizophrenia* (2nd ed.). New York: Basic Books.

Arnett, J. L. (2006). Psychology and health. *Canadian Psychology, 47*(1), 19–32.

Arnett, P. A. (1997). Autonomic responsivity in psychopaths: A critical review and theoretical proposal. *Clinical Psychology Review, 17,* 903–936.

Arnett, P. A., Smith, S. S., & Newman, J. P. (1997). Approach and avoidance motivation in psychopathic criminal offenders during passive avoidance. *Journal of Personality and Social Psychology, 72,* 1413–1428.

Arnold, E. H., O'Leary, S. G., & Edward, G. H. (1997). Father involvement and self-reported parenting of children with attention deficit-hyperactivity disorder. *Journal of Consulting and Clinical Psychology, 65,* 337–342.

Arnow, B., Kenardy, J., & Agras, W. S. (1992). Binge eating among the obese: A descriptive study. *Journal of Behavioral Medicine, 15,* 155–170.

Aronson, T. A. (1989). A critical review of psychotherapeutic treatments of the borderline personality: Historical trends and future directions. *Journal of Nervous and Mental Disease, 177,* 511–528.

Arthur, N. & Stewart, J. (2001). Multicultural counselling in the new millennium: Introduction to the special theme issue. *Canadian Journal of Counselling, 35*(1), 3–14.

Arthur, N. & Januszkowski, T. (2001). The multicultural counselling competencies of Canadian counsellors. *Canadian Journal of Counselling, 35*(1), 36–48.

Asaad, G. & Shapiro, B. (1986). Hallucinations: Theoretical and clinical overview. *American Journal of Psychiatry, 143,* 1088–1097.

Asarnow, J. R., Carlson, G. A., & Guthrie, D. (1987). Coping strategies, self-perceptions, hopelessness, and perceived family environments in depressed and suicidal children. *Journal of Consulting and Clinical Psychology, 55*(3), 361–366.

Asherson, P., Chen, W., Craddock. B., & Taylor, E. (2007). Adult attention-deficit hyperactivity disorder: Recognition and treatment in general adult psychiatry. *British Journal of Psychiatry, 190*(1), 4–5.

Association for Cognitive Analytic Therapy. (2003). *ACAT Online.* Retrieved April 13, 2003, from http://www.acat.org.uk/10000.htm.

Astley, S. J., Clarren, S. K., Little, R. E., Sampson, P. D., & Daling, J. R. (1992). Analysis of facial shape in children gestationally exposed to marijuana, alcohol, and/or cocaine. *Pediatrics, 89,* 67–77.

Attention deficit disorder—Part II. (1995, May). *The Harvard Mental Health Letter, 11*(11), 1–3.

Autism Society of Canada (2001). *ABA Treatment: Evidence-based supporting literature.* Orangeville, ON: Author. Retrieved October 11, 2003, from http://www.autismsocietycanada.ca/en/ABA_document.html.

Ayoub, C. C. (2006). Munchausen by proxy. In P. G. Plante (Ed.), *Mental disorders of the new millennium: Biology and function* (vol. 3, pp. 173–193). Westport, CT: Praeger.

Azrin, N. H. & Peterson, A. L. (1989). Reduction of an eye tick by controlled blinking. *Behavior Therapy, 20,* 467–473.

B

Babiak, P. (1995). When psychopaths go to work: A case study of an industrial psychopath. *International Journal of Applied Psychology, 44*(2), 171–188.

Babiak, P. & Hare, R. D. (2006). *Snakes in suits: When psychopaths go to work.* New York: Regan.

Bach, A. K., Barlow, D. H., & Wincze, J. P. (2004). The enhancing effects of manualized treatment for erectile dysfunction among men using sildenafil: A preliminary investigation. *Behavior Therapy, 35,* 55–73.

Bachman, P. & Cannon, T. D. (2005). Cognitive and

neuroscience aspects of thought disorder. In K. J. Holyoak & R. G. Morrison (Eds.), *Cambridge handbook of thinking and reasoning* (pp. 493–526). New York: Cambridge University Press.

Baer, L. et al. (1995). Cingulotomy for intractable obsessive-compulsive disorder: Prospective long-term follow-up of 18 patients. *Archives of General Psychiatry, 52,* 384–392.

Bagby, R. M., Nicholson, R., & Buis, T. (1998). Utility of the Deceptive-Subtle items in the detection of malingering. *Journal of Personality Assessment, 70,* 405–415.

Bahammam, A., Delaive, K., Ronald, J., Manfreda, J., Roos, L., & Kryger, M. H. (1999). Health care utilization in males with obstructive sleep apnea syndrome two years after diagnosis and treatment. *Sleep, 22*(6), 740–747.

Baker, R. C. & Kirschenbaum, D. S. (1993). Self-monitoring may be necessary for successful weight control. *Behavior Therapy, 24,* 377–394.

Bal, P. & Koenraadt, F. (2000). Criminal law and mentally ill offenders in comparative perspective. *Psychology, Crime and Law, 6,* 219–250.

Balch, C., Montgomery, J. S., Paik, H. I., Kim, S., Huang, T. H., & Nephew, K. P. (2005). New anti-cancer strategies: Epigenetic therapies and biomarkers. *Frontiers in Bioscience,10*(2),1897–1931.

Baldwin, A. R., Oei, T. P., & Young, R. (1994). To drink or not to drink: The differential role of alcohol expectancies and drinking refusal self-efficacy in quantity and frequency of alcohol consumption. *Cognitive Therapy & Research, 17,* 511–530.

Balwin, D. S. (2006). Serotonin noradrenaline reuptake inhibitors. *International Journal of Psychiatry in Clinical Practice,* 12–15.

Bandura, A. (1973). *Aggression: A social learning analysis.* Englewood Cliffs, NJ: Prentice Hall.

Bandura, A. (1982). Self-efficacy mechanism in human agency. *American Psychologist, 37,* 122–147.

Bandura, A. (1986). *Social foundations of thought and action: A social-cognitive theory.* Englewood Cliffs, NJ: Prentice Hall.

Bandura A. (1989). Social Cognitive Theory. *Annals of Child Development, 6,* p1–60.

Bandura, A. (2001). Social cognitive theory: An agentic perspective. *Annual Review of Psychology, 52*(2), 1–26.

Bandura, A., Blanchard, E. B., & Ritter, B. (1969). The relative efficacy of desensitization and modeling approaches for inducing behavioral, affective, and cognitive changes. *Journal of Personality and Social Psychology, 13,* 173–199.

Bandura, A., Jeffery, R. W., & Wright, C. L. (1974). Efficacy of participant modeling as a function of response induction aids. *Journal of Abnormal Psychology, 83,* 56–64.

Bandura, A., Ross, S. A., & Ross, D. (1963). Imitation of film-mediated aggressive models. *Journal of Abnormal and Social Psychology, 66,* 3–11.

Bandura, A., Taylor, C., Williams, S. L., Mefford, I. N., & Barchas, J. D. (1985). Catecholamine secretion as a function of perceived coping self-efficacy. *Journal of Consulting and Clinical Psychology, 53*(3), 406–414.

Banno, K., Walld, R., & Kryger, M. H. (2005). Increasing obesity trends in patients with sleep-disordered breathing referred to a sleep disorders center. *Journal of Clinical Sleep Medicine, 1*(4), 364–366.

Banno, K. & Kryger, M. H. (2007). Sleep apnea: Clinical investigations in humans. *Sleep Medicine, 8*(4), 402–428.

Barbaree, H. E. & Seto, M. C. (1997). Pedophilia: Assessment and treatment. In D. R. Laws & W. T. O'Donohue (Eds.), *Handbook of sexual deviance: Theory and application.* New York: Guilford.

Barch, D. M. (2005). The cognitive neuroscience of schizophrenia. *Annual Review of Clinical Psychology, 1,* 321–353.

Bardwell, W. A., Moore, P., Ancoli-Israel, S., & Dimsdale, J. E. (2003). Fatigue in obstructive sleep apnea: Driven by depressive symptoms instead of apnea severity? *The American Journal of Psychiatry, 160*(2), 350–355.

Barkham, M. et al. (1996). Dose-effect relations in time-limited psychotherapy for depression. *Journal of Consulting and Clinical Psychology, 64,* 927–935.

Barkley, R. A., Hastings, J. E., Tousel, R. E., & Tousel, S. E. (1976). Evaluation of a token system for juvenile delinquents in a residential setting. *Journal of Behavior Therapy & Experimental Psychiatry, 7*(3), 227–230.

Barlow, D. H. (1986). Causes of sexual dysfunction: The role of anxiety and cognitive interference. *Journal of Consulting and Clinical Psychology, 54,* 140–148.

Barlow, D. H. (2002). *Anxiety and its disorders* (2nd ed.). New York: Guilford.

Baron-Cohen, S. (1995). *Mindblindness: An essay on autism and theory of mind.* Cambridge, MA: The MIT Press.

Baron-Cohen, S. (1998). *Autism and "Theory of Mind": An introduction and review.* International Symposium on Autism 1998. Toronto: Geneva Centre for Autism. Retrieved October 11, 2003, from http://www.autism.net/html/baron-cohen.html.

Barrett, S. P., Gross, S. R., Garand, I., & Pihl, R. O. (2005). Patterns of simultaneous polysubstance use in Canadian rave attendees. *Substance Use & Misuse, 40,* 1525–1537.

Barsky, A. J., Wyshak, G., & Klerman, G. L. (1992). Psychiatric comorbidity in DSM-III-R hypochondriasis. *Archives of General Psychiatry, 49,* 101–108.

Bartecchi, C. E., MacKenzie, T. D., & Schrier, R. W. (1994). The human costs of tobacco use [First of two parts]. *New England Journal of Medicine, 330,* 907–912.

Basch, M. F. (1980). *Doing psychotherapy.* New York: Basic Books.

Basoglu, M. et al. (1997). Double-blindness procedures, rater blindness, and ratings of outcome. *Archives of General Psychiatry, 54,* 744–748.

Bassarath, L. (2003). Medication strategies in childhood aggression: A review. *Canadian Journal of Psychiatry, 48*(6), 367–373.

Bassett, A. S. & Chow, E. W. C. (1999). 22q11 deletion syndrome: A genetic subtype of schizophrenia. *Biological Psychiatry, 46,* 882–891.

Bassett, A. S., Chow, E. W. C., Abdel-Malik, P., Gheorghiu, M., Husted, J., & Weksberg, R. (2003). The schizophrenia phenotype in 22q11 deletion syndrome. *American Journal of Psychiatry, 160,* 1580–1586.

Bassett, A. S., Hodgkinson, K., Chow, E. W. C., Correia, S., Scutt, L., & Weksberg, R. (1998). 22q11 deletion syndrome in adults with schizophrenia. *American Journal of Medical Genetics, 81,* 328–337.

Basson, R. (2001). Human sex-response cycles. *Journal of Sex & Marital Therapy, 27,* 33–43.

Basson, R. (2005). Women's sexual dysfunction: Revised and expanded definitions. *Canadian Medical Association Journal, 172,* 1327–1333.

Basson, R., McInnes, R., Smith, M. D., Hodgson, G., & Koppiker, N. (2002). Efficacy and safety of sildenafil citrate in women with sexual dysfunction associated with female sexual arousal disorder. *Journal of Women's Health & Gender-Based Medicine, 11,* 367–377.

Bateman, A. B. & Fonagy, P. (2001). Treatment of borderline personality disorder with psychoanalytically oriented partial hospitalization. An 18 month follow-up. *American Journal of Psychiatry, 158*(1), 36–42.

Bateson, G. D., Jackson, D., Haley, J., & Weakland, J. (1956). Toward a theory of schizophrenia. *Behavioral Science, 1,* 251–264.

Battaglia, M., Bernardeschi, L., Franchini, L., Bellodi, L., & Smeraldi, E. (1995). A family study of schizotypal disorder. *Schizophrenia Bulletin, 21*(1), 33–45.

Baucom, D. H., Shoham, V., Mueser, K. T., Daiuto, A. D., & Stickle, T. (1998). Empirically supported couple and family interventions for marital distress and adult mental health problems. *Journal of Consulting and Clinical Psychology, 66,* 53–88.

Baumann, C. R., Khatami, R., Werth, E., & Bassetti, C. L. (2006). Hypocretin (orexin) deficiency predicts severe objective excessive daytime sleepiness in narcolepsy with cataplexy. *Journal of Neurology, Neurosurgery, and Psychiatry, 77*(3), 402–404.

Baxter, L. R., Ackerman, R. F., Swerdlow, N. R., Brody, A., Saxena, S., Schwartz, J. M. et al. (2000). Specific brain system mediation of obsessive-compulsive disorder responsive to either medication or behavior therapy. In W. K. Goodman, M. V. Rudorfer, & J. D. Maser (Eds.), *Obsessive-compulsive disorder* (pp. 573–609). Mahwah, NJ: Erlbaum.

Baylis, P. J. (2002). Promoting resilience: A review of the literature. Retrieved April 23, 2003, from http://www.amhb.ab.ca/chmh/resources/page.cfm?pg=Promoting%20Resilience%20.

Beard, K. W. (2005). Internet addiction: A review of current assessment techniques and potential assessment questions. *CyberPsychology & Behavior, 8*, 7–14.

Bebbington, P. (1993). Transcultural aspects of affective disorders. *International Review of Psychiatry, 5*, 145–156.

Beck, A. T. (1976). *Cognitive therapy and the emotional disorders.* New York: International Universities Press.

Beck, A. T. & Clark, D. A. (1997). An information processing model of anxiety: Automatic and strategic processes. *Behaviour Research and Therapy, 35*, 49–58.

Beck, A. T. & Young, J. E. (1985). Depression. In D. H. Barlow (Ed.), *Clinical handbook of psychological disorders* (pp. 206–244). New York: Guilford.

Beck, A. T., Brown, G., Steer, R. A., Eidelson, J. I., & Riskind, J. H. (1987). Differentiating anxiety and depression: A test of the cognitive content-specificity hypothesis. *Journal of Abnormal Psychology, 96*, 179–183.

Beck, A. T. et al. (1990). Relationship between hopelessness and ultimate suicide: A replication with psychiatric outpatients. *American Journal of Psychiatry, 147*, 190–195.

Beck, A. T. et al. (1991). Factor analysis of the Dysfunctional Attitude Scale in a clinical population. *Psychological Assessment, 3*, 478–483.

Beck, A. T., Freeman, A., & Associates. (1990). *Cognitive therapy of personality disorders.* New York: Guilford.

Beck, A. T., Rush, A. J., Shaw, B. F., & Emery, G. (1979). *Cognitive therapy of depression.* New York: Guilford.

Beck, A. T., Ward, C. H., Mendelson, M., Mock, J., & Erbaugh, J. (1961). An inventory for measuring depression. *Archives of General Psychiatry, 4*, 561–571.

Beck, A.T., Freeman, A., Davis, D.D., & Associates. (2003). *Cognitive therapy of personality disorders* (2nd ed.). New York: Guilford.

Beck, C. A., Patten, S. B., Williams, J. V. A., Wang, J. L., Currie, S. R., Maxwell, C. J. et al. (2005). Antidepressant utilization in Canada. *Social Psychiatry and Psychiatric Epidemiology, 40*, 799–807.

Beck, C. A., Williams, J. V. A., Wang, J. L., Kassam, A., El-Guebaly, N., Currie, S. R. et al. (2005). Psychotropic medication use in Canada. *Canadian Journal of Psychiatry, 50*, 605–613.

Beck, J. G. (1993). Vaginismus. In W. O'Donohue & J. H. Geer (Eds.), *Handbook of sexual dysfunctions: Assessment and treatment* (pp. 381–397). Boston: Allyn & Bacon.

Beck, J. G. (1995). Hypoactive sexual desire disorder: An overview. *Journal of Consulting and Clinical Psychology, 63*, 919–927.

Beck, R. & Perkins, T. S. (2001). Cognitive content-specificity for anxiety and depression: A meta-analysis. *Cognitive Therapy and Research, 25*, 651–663.

Becker, A. J., McCulloch, E. A., & Till, J. E. (1963). Cytological demonstration of the clonal nature of spleen colonies derived from transplanted mouse marrow cells. *Nature, 197*(4866), 452–454.

Becker, D. & Lamb, S. (1994). Sex bias in the diagnosis of borderline personality disorder and posttraumatic stress disorder. *Professional Psychology: Research and Practice, 25*, 55–61.

Beech, A. R. & Mitchell, I. J. (2005). A neurobiological perspective on attachment problems in sexual offenders and the role of selective serotonin re-uptake inhibitors in the treatment of such problems. *Clinical Psychology Review, 25*, 153–182.

Begley, S. (1995, November 20). Lights of madness. *Newsweek*, pp. 76–77.

Behar, E. & Borkovec, T. D. (2006). The nature and treatment of generalized anxiety disorder. In B. O. Rothbaum (Ed.), *Pathological anxiety* (pp. 181–196). New York: Guilford.

Beidel, D. C. & Turner, S. M. (1986). A critique of the theoretical bases of cognitive-behavioral theories and therapy. *Clinical Psychology Review, 6*, 177–199.

Beiser, M. (2003a). Culture and psychiatry, or "the tale of the hole and the cheese." *Canadian Journal of Psychiatry, 48*(3), 143–144.

Beiser, M. (2003b). Why should researchers care about culture? *Canadian Journal of Psychiatry, 48*(3), 154–160.

Beitman, B. D., Goldfried, M. R., & Norcross, J. C. (1989). The movement toward integrating the psychotherapies: An overview. *American Journal of Psychiatry, 146*, 138–147.

Bellack, A. S. & Mueser, K. T. (1990). Schizophrenia. In A. S. Bellack, M. Hersen, & A. E. Kazdin (Eds.), *International handbook of behavior modification and therapy* (2nd ed., pp. 353–370). New York: Plenum.

Bellack, A. S. & Mueser, K. T. (1993). Psychosocial treatment for schizophrenia. *Schizophrenia Bulletin, 19*, 317–336.

Benjamin, L. S. & Wonderlich, S. A. (1994). Social perceptions and borderline personality disorder: The relation to mood disorders. *Journal of Abnormal Psychology, 103*, 610–624.

Bennett, D. (1985). Rogers: More intuition in therapy. *APA Monitor, 16*, 3.

Bennett-Baker, P. E., Wilkowski, J., & Burke, D. T. (2003). Age-associated activation of epigenetically repressed genes in the mouse. *Genetics, 165*(4), 2055–2062.

Benson, H. (1975). *The relaxation response.* New York: Morrow.

Benson, H., Manzetta, B. R., & Rosner, B. (1973). Decreased systolic blood pressure in hypertensive subjects who practiced meditation. *Journal of Clinical Investigation, 52*, 8.

Bentall, R. P. (1990). The illusion of reality: A review and integration of psychological research on hallucinations. *Psychological Bulletin, 107*, 82–95.

Berczi, I. (2001). Neuroimmune biology—An introduction. In I. Berczi & R. M. Gorczynski (Eds.), *New foundation of biology* (pp. 3–45). New York: Elsevier Science.

Berenbaum, H. & Fujita, F. (1994). Schizophrenia and personality: Exploring the boundaries and connections between vulnerability and outcome. *Journal of Abnormal Psychology, 103*, 148–158.

Berenbaum, H. & Oltmanns, T. F. (2005). Emotional experience and expression in schizophrenia and depression. In E. L. Rosenberg (Ed.), *What the face reveals: Basic and applied studies of spontaneous expression using the facial action coding system* (2nd ed., pp. 441–458). New York: Oxford University Press.

Bergeron, S., Binik, Y. M., Kalife, S., Pagidas, K., Glazer, H. I., Meana, M., & Amsel, R. (2001). A randomized comparison of group cognitive-behavioral therapy, surface electromyographic biofeedback, and vestibulectomy in the treatment of dyspareunia resulting from vulvar vestibulitis. *Pain, 91*, 297–306.

Bergida, H. & Lenzenweger, M. F. (2006). Schizotypy and sustained attention: Confirming evidence from an adult community sample. *Journal of Abnormal Psychology, 115*, 545–551.

Bergner, R. M. (1997). What is psychopathology? And so what? *Clinical Psychology: Science and Practice, 4*, 235–248.

Berkman, L. F. & Breslow, L. (1983). *Health and ways of living: The Alameda County Study.* New York: Oxford University Press.

Berkman, L. F. & Syme, S. L. (1979). Social networks, host resistance, and mortality: A nine-year follow-up study of Alameda County residents. *American Journal of Epidemiology, 109*, 186–204.

Berlim, M. T. & Turecki, G. (2007). Definition, assessment, and staging of treatment-resistant refractory major depression: a review of current concepts and methods. *Canadian Journal of Psychiatry, 52*(1), 46–54.

Berlin, I. N. (1987). Suicide among American Indian adolescents: An overview. *Suicide & Life-Threatening Behavior, 17*(3), 218–232.

Bernreuther, C., Dihne, M., Johann, V., Schiefer, J., Cui, Y., Hargus, G. et al. (2006). Neural Cell Adhesion Molecule L1-Transfected Embryonic Stem Cells Promote

Functional Recovery after Excitotoxic Lesion of the Mouse Striatum. *The Journal of Neuroscience, 26*(45), 11532–11539.

Bernstein, D. P., Cohen, P., Skodol, A., Bezirganian, S., & Brook, J. S. (1996). Childhood antecedents of adolescent personality disorders. *American Journal of Psychiatry, 153*(7), 907–913.

Bernstein, E. M. & Putnam, F. W. (1986). Development, reliability, and validity of a dissociation scale. *Journal of Nervous and Mental Disease, 174,* 727–735.

Bettelheim, B. (1967). *The empty fortress.* New York: Free Press.

Bibby, R. W. (2006). *The boomer factor: What Canada's most famous generation is leaving behind.* Toronto: Bastian Books.

Bibeau, G., Rousseau, C., Corin, E., Kirmayer, L. J., Lock, M., Pedersen, D., Young, A., & Zarowsky, C. (1999). *Modernity, suffering and psychopathology.* Ottawa: Canadian Institute of Health research. Retrieved April 20, 2003, from http://www.chsrf.ca/docs/finalrpts/HIDG/bibeau.pdf.

Bick, P. A. & Kinsbourne, M. (1987). Auditory hallucinations and subvocal speech in schizophrenic patients. *American Journal of Psychiatry, 144,* 222–225.

Bickel, W. K., Amass, L., Badger, G. J., & Esch, R. A. (1997). Effects of adding behavioral treatment to opioid detoxification with buprenorphine. *Journal of Consulting and Clinical Psychology, 65,* 803–810.

Biederman, J., Biederman, J., Faraone, S. V., Milberger, S., Garcia Jetton, J., Chen, L., Mick, E. et al. (1996). Is childhood oppositional defiant disorder a precursor to adolescent conduct disorder? Findings from a four-year follow-up study of children with ADHD. *Journal of the American Academy of Child and Adolescent Psychiatry, 35,* 1193–1204.

Binder, J. L. & Strup, H. H. (1997). Negative process: A recurrently discovered and underestimated facet of therapeutic process and outcome in the individual psychotherapy of adults. *Clinical Psychology: Science and Practice, 4,* 121–139.

Binik, Y. M. (2005). Should dyspareunia be retained as a sexual dysfunction in DSM-V? A painful classification decision. *Archives of Sexual Behavior, 34,* 11–21.

Biran, M. (1988). Cognitive and exposure treatment for agoraphobia: Re-examination of the outcome research. *Journal of Cognitive Psychotherapy: An International Quarterly, 2,* 165–178.

Bitiello, B. & Jensen, P. S. (1997). Medication development, testing in children and adolescents. *Archives of General Psychiatry, 54,* 871–876.

Blair, C. D. & Lanyon, R. I. (1981). Exhibitionism: A critical review of the etiology and treatment. *Psychological Bulletin, 89,* 439–463.

Blakeslee, S. (1991, September 15). Study ties dyslexia to brain flaw affecting vision and other senses. *The New York Times,* pp. A1, A30.

Blakeslee, S. (1994, August 16). New clue to cause of dyslexia seen in mishearing of fast sounds. *The New York Times,* pp. C1, C10.

Blakeslee, S. (1997, June 27). Brain studies tie marijuana to other drugs. *The New York Times,* p. A16.

Blakeslee, S. (1998, May 14). Two studies shed new light on cocaine's effect on brain. *The New York Times,* p. A20.

Blanchard, E. B., & Diamond, S. (1996). Psychological treatment of benign headache disorders. *Professional Psychology, 27,* 541–547.

Blanchard, E. B., Appelbaum, K. A., Radnitz, C. L., Morrill, B., Michultka, D., Kirsch, C., Guarnieri, P., Hillhouse, J., Evans, D.D., Jaccard, J. et al. (1990). A controlled evaluation of thermal biofeedback and thermal feedback combined with cognitive therapy in the treatment of vascular headache. *Journal of Consulting and Clinical Psychology, 58*(2), 216–224.

Blanchard, R. (1989). The classification and labeling of nonhomosexual gender dysphorias. *Archives of Sexual Behavior, 18,* 315–334.

Blanchard, R. & Hucker, S. J. (1991). Age, transvestism, bondage, and concurrent paraphilic activities in 117 fatal cases of autoerotic asphyxia. *British Journal of Psychiatry, 159,* 371–377.

Blanchette, K. (1996). *The relationships between criminal history, mental disorder, and recidivism among federally sentenced female offenders.* Unpublished Masters Thesis, Carleton University, Ottawa.

Bland, R. C. (1998). Psychiatry and the burden of mental illness. *Canadian Journal of Psychiatry, 43,* 801–810.

Bland, R. C., Newman, S. C., & Orn, H. (1988a). Lifetime prevalence of psychiatric disorders in Edmonton. *Acta Psychiatrica Scandinavica, 77* (Suppl. 338), 24–32.

Bland, R. C., Newman, S. C., & Orn, H. (1988b). Period prevalence of psychiatric disorders in Edmonton. *Acta Psychiatrica Scandinavica, 77* (Suppl. 338), 33–42.

Blankstein, K. R. & Segal, Z. V. (2001). Cognitive assessment: Issues and methods. In K.S. Dobson (Ed.), *Handbook of cognitive-behavioral therapies* (2nd ed., pp. 40–85). New York: Guilford Press.

Blazer, D.G. (1997). Generalized anxiety disorder and panic disorder in the elderly: A review. *Harvard Review of Psychiatry, 5,* 18–27.

Blier, P. (2006). Dual serotonin and noradrenaline reuptake inhibitors: Focus on their differences. *International Journal of Psychiatry in Clinical Practice, 10 (Suppl 2),* 22–32.

Blier, P., Habib, R., & Flament, M. F. (2006). Pharmacotherapies in the management of obsessive-compulsive disorder. *Canadian Journal of Psychiatry, 51,* 417–430.

Bloch, M., Rotenberg, N., Koren, D., & Ehud, K. (2006). Risk factors for early postpartum depressive symptoms. *General Hospital Psychiatry, 28,* 3–8.

Block, D. R., Kelly, M. M., & Carpenter, L. L. (2006). Generalized anxiety disorder. *Directions in Psychiatry, 26,* 171–181.

Blood test can detect retardation. (1993, October 6). *The New York Daily News,* p. 10.

Bloom, B. L. (1992). Computer assisted psychological intervention: A review and commentary. *Clinical Psychology Review, 12,* 169–197.

Bloom, H., Webster, C., Hucker, S., & De Freitas, K. (2005). The Canadian contribution to violence risk assessment: History and implications for current psychiatric practice. *Canadian Journal of Psychiatry, 50,* 3–11.

Bloom, J. D. & Rogers, J. L. (1987). The legal basis of forensic psychiatry: Statutorily mandated psychiatric diagnosis. *American Journal of Psychiatry, 144,* 847–853.

Bodkin, J., *Alexander, M. D., Cohen, Bruce M., Salomon, M. S., Cannon, S. E., Zornberg, G. L., & Cole, J. O.* (1996). Treatment of negative symptoms in schizophrenia and schizoaffective disorder by selegiline augmentation of antipsychotic medication. *Journal of Nervous and Mental Disease, 184,* 295–301.

Boetsch, E. A., Green, P. A., & Pennington, B. F. (1996). Psychosocial correlates of dyslexia across the lifespan. *Development and Psychopathology, 8,* 539–562.

Bond, M. (2006). Psychodynamic psychotherapy in the treatment of mood disorders. *Current Opinion in Psychiatry, 19,* 40–43.

Boney-McCoy, S. & Finkelhor, D. (1996). Is youth victimization related to trauma symptoms and depression after controlling for prior symptoms and family relationships? A longitudinal, prospective study. *Journal of Consulting and Clinical Psychology, 64,* 1406–1416.

Bonnano, G. A. (2005). Resilience in the face of potential trauma. *Current Directions in Psychological Science, 14,* 135–138.

Boos, H. B., Aleman, A., Cahn, W., Pol, H. H., & Kahn, R. S. (2007). Brain volumes in relatives of patients with schizophrenia: A meta-analysis. *Archives of General Psychiatry, 64,* 297–304.

Booth-Kewley, S. & Friedman, H. S. (1987). Psychological predictors of heart disease: A quantitative review. *Psychological Bulletin, 101,* 343–362.

Borch-Jacobsen, M. (1997). Sybil—the making of a disease: An interview with Dr. Herbert Spiegel. *New York Review of Books, 44,* 60–64.

Boren, T., Faulk, P., Roth, K. A., Larson, G., & Normark, S. (1993). Attachment of *Helicobacter pylori* to human gastric epithelium mediated by blood group antigens. *Science, 262,* 1892–1895.

Bornstein, M. R., Bellack, A. S., & Hersen, M. (1977). Social-skills training for unassertive children: A multiple-baseline analysis. *Journal of Applied Behavior Analysis, 10,* 183–195.

Bornstein, R. F. (1992). The dependent personality: Developmental, social, and clinical perspectives. *Psychological Bulletin, 112,* 3–23.

Bornstein, R. F. (1993). *The dependent personality.* New York: Guilford Press.

Bornstein, R. F. (1997). Dependent personality disorder in the DSM-IV and beyond. *Clinical Psychology: Science and Practice, 4,* 175–187.

Bornstein, R. F. (1999a). Criterion validity of objective and projective dependency tests: A meta-analytic assessment of behavioral prediction. *Psychological Assessment, 11,* 48–57.

Bornstein, R. F. (1999b). Dependent and histrionic personality disorders. In T. Millon, et al. (Eds.), *Oxford textbook of psychopathology. Oxford textbooks in clinical psychology, Vol.4* (pp. 535–554). New York: Oxford University Press.

Bornstein, R. F. (2001). Clinical utility of the Rorschach Inkblot method: Reframing the debate. *Journal of Personality Assessment, 77*(1), 39–47.

Borthwick-Duffy, S. A. (1994). Epidemiology and prevalence of psychopathology in individuals with dual diagnoses. *Journal of Consulting and Clinical Psychology, 62,* 17–27.

Bos, C. S. & Van Reusen, A. K. (1991). Academic interventions with learning disabled students. In J. E. Obrzut & G. W. Hynd (Eds.). *Neuropsychological foundations of learning disabilities: A handbook of issues, methods and practices* (pp. 659–683). San Diego, CA: Academic Press.

Boston Women's Health Book Collective. (1984). *The new our bodies, ourselves.* New York: Simon & Schuster.

Bouchard, C., Shephard, R. J., & Stephens, T. (Eds.). (1993). *Physical activity, fitness, and health: Consensus statement,* p. 61. Proceedings of the Second International Consensus Symposium on Physical Activity, Fitness, and Health, Toronto, Ontario, May 1992. Champaign, IL: Human Kinetics.

Bouchard, S., Paquin, B., Payeur, R., Allard. M., Rivard. V., Fournier, T. et al. (2004). Delivering cognitive-behavior therapy for panic disorder

with agoraphobia in videoconference. *Telemedicine and E-Health,* 10(1), 13–25.

Bourgon, L. N. & Kellner, C. H. (2000). Relapse of depression after ECT: A review. *Journal of ECT, 16,* 19–31.

Bowers, T. G. & Clum, G. A. (1988). Relative contribution of specific and nonspecific treatment effects: Meta-analysis of placebo-controlled behavior therapy research. *Psychological Bulletin, 103,* 315–323.

Bowlby, J. (1988). *A secure base.* New York: Basic Books.

Boyce, P. & Hickey, A. (2005). Psychosocial risk factors to major depression after childbirth. *Social Psychiatry and Psychiatric Epidemiology, 40,* 605–612.

Boyle, M. H., Offord, D. R., Racine, Y. A., Szatmari, P., Fleming, J. E., & Links, P. S. (1992). Predicting substance use in late adolescence: Results from the Ontario Child Health Study Follow-up. *American Journal of Psychiatry, 149,* 761–767.

Boyle, P. (1993). The hazards of passive—and active—smoking. *New England Journal of Medicine, 328,* 1708–1709.

Bradley, E. A., Thompson, A., & Bryson, S. E. (2002). Mental retardation in teenagers: Prevalence data from the Niagara Region, Ontario. *Canadian Journal of Psychiatry, 47*(7), 652–659.

Brandon, T. H., Vidrine, J. I., & Litvin, E. B. (2007). Relapse and relapse prevention. *Annual Review of Clinical Psychology, 3,* 29–56.

Brass, G. M. (2001). Healing the Aboriginal offender: Identity construction through therapeutic practice. In L. J. Kirmayer, M. E. MacDonald, & G. M. Brass, (Eds.). *Proceedings of the advanced study institute: The mental health of indigenous peoples.* Montreal, Quebec: McGill Summer Program in Social & Cultural Psychiatry.

Braswell, L. & Kendall, P. C. (2001). Cognitive-behavioral therapy with children. In K. Dobson (Ed.) *Handbook of cognitive-behavioral therapies* (2nd ed., pp.246–294). New York: Guilford.

Braun, J. M., Kahn, R. S., Froehlich, T., Auinger, P., & Lanphear, B. P. (2006). Exposures to environmental toxicants and attention deficit hyperactivity disorder in U.S.

children. *Environmental Health Perspectives,* 114(12), 1904–1909.

Braxton, L. E., Calhoun, P. S., Williams, J. E., & Boggs, C. D. (2007). Validity rates of the Personality Assessment Inventory and the Minnesota Multiphasic Personality Inventory–2 in a VA medical center setting. *Journal of Personality Assessment,* 88(1), 5–15.

Brazeau-Ward, L. (2003). *I'm confused, is it dyslexia or is it learning disability?* Ottawa: Canadian Dyslexia Society.

Breier, A. F., Malhotra, A. K., Su, T-P, Pinals, D. A., Elman, I., Adler, C. M. et al. (1999). Clozapine and risperidone in chronic schizophrenia: Effects on symptoms, Parkinsonian side effects, and neuroendocrine response. *American Journal of Psychiatry, 156,* 294–298.

Brekke, J., Long, J. D., Nesbitt, N., & Sobel, E. (1997). The impact of service characteristics on functional outcomes from community support programs for persons with schizophrenia: A growth curve analysis. *Journal of Consulting and Clinical Psychology,* 65, 464–475.

Brems, C. & Johnson, M. E. (1997). Clinical implications of the co-occurrence of substance use and other psychiatric disorders. *Professional Psychology: Research and Practice, 28,* 437–447.

Brent, D. A. & Mann, J. J. (2006). Familial pathways to suicidal behavior—Understanding and preventing suicide among adolescents. *New England Journal of Medicine, 355,* 2719–2721.

Breslau, N., Peterson, E. L., Schultz, L. R., Chilcoat, H. D., & Andreski, P. (1998). Major depression and stages of smoking: A longitudinal investigation. *Archives of General Psychiatry, 55,* 161–166.

Breslin, C., Li, S., Sdao-Jarvie, K., Tupker, E., & Ittig-Deland, V. (2002). Brief treatment for young substance abusers: A pilot study in an addiction treatment setting. *Psychology of Addictive Behaviors, 16,* 10–16.

Breslow, N. (1989). Sources of confusion in the study and treatment of sadomasochism. *Journal of Social Behavior and Personality, 4,* 263–274.

Brewin, C. R. & Andrews, B. (2000). Psychological defence mechanisms: The example of

repression. *The Psychologist,* 13(12), 615–617.

Brickman, J. & Briere, J. (1984). Incidence of rape and sexual assault in an urban Canadian population. *International Journal of Women's Studies, 7,* 195–206.

Brody, J. E. (1990, June 7). A search to bar retardation in a new generation. *The New York Times,* p. B9.

Brody, J. E. (1992a, May 15). Study finds liquid diet works (but not for the 50% who quit). *The New York Times,* p. B17.

Brody, J. E. (1992b, June 16). Suicide myths cloud efforts to save children. *The New York Times,* pp. C1, C3.

Brody, J. E. (1992c, September 30). Myriad masks hide an epidemic of depression. *The New York Times,* p. C12.

Brody, J. E. (1993, December 15). Living with a common genetic abnormality. *The New York Times,* p. C17.

Brody, J. E. (1994a, January 5). Heart diseases are persisting in study's second generation. *The New York Times,* p. C12.

Brody, J. E. (1994b, December 28). Wine for the heart: Overall, risks may outweigh benefits. *The New York Times,* p. C10.

Brody, J. E. (1995, August 2). With more help available for impotence, few men seek it. *The New York Times,* p. C9.

Brody, J. E. (1996a, August 7). Relaxation method may aid health. *The New York Times,* p. C10.

Brody, J. E. (1996b, November 20). Controlling anger is good medicine for the heart. *The New York Times,* p. C15.

Bronfenbrenner, U. (1979). *The ecology of human development: Experiments by nature and design.* Cambridge, MA: Harvard University Press.

Brown, R. A. et al. (1997). Cognitive-behavioral treatment for depression in alcoholism. *Journal of Consulting and Clinical Psychology,* 65, 715–726.

Brown, R. J. (2004). Psychological mechanisms of medically unexplained symptoms: An integrative conceptual model. *Psychological Bulletin, 130,* 793–812.

Brown, S. L. & Forth, A. E. (1997). Psychopathy and sexual assault: Static risk factors, emotional precursors, and rapist subtypes. *Journal of*

Consulting and Clinical Psychology, 65, 848–857.

Brown, T. A., Di Nardo, P. A., Lehman, C. L., & Campbell, L. A. (2001). Reliability of DSM-IV anxiety and mood disorders: Implications for the classification of emotional disorders. *Journal of Abnormal Psychology, 110*(1), 49–58

Brownell, K. D. & Wadden, T. A. (1992). Etiology and treatment of obesity: Understanding a serious, prevalent, and refractory disorder. *Journal of Consulting and Clinical Psychology, 60*, 505–517.

Bryson, S. E., Rogers, S. J., & Fombonne, E. (2003). Autism spectrum disorders: Early detection, intervention, education, and psychopharmacological management. *Canadian Journal of Psychiatry, 48*(8), 506–516.

Buhr, K. & Dugas, M. J. (2006). Investigating the construct validity of intolerance of uncertainty and its unique relationship with worry. *Journal of Anxiety Disorders, 20*, 222–236.

Burke, R. S. & Stephens, R. S. (1999). Social anxiety and drinking in college students: A social cognitive theory analysis. *Clinical Psychology Review, 19*, 513–530.

Burns, D. D. (1980). *Feeling good: The new mood therapy.* New York: Morris.

Burns, D. D. & Beck, A. T. (1978). Modification of mood disorders. In J. P. Foreyt & D. P. Rathjen (Eds.), *Cognitive behavior therapy: Research and application* (pp. 109–134). New York: Plenum.

Busatto, G. F., Pilowsky, L. S., Costa, D. C., Ell, P. J., David, A. S., Lucey, J. V., & Kerwin, R.W. (1997). Correlation between reduced in vivo benzodiazepine receptor binding and severity of psychotic symptoms in schizophrenia. *American Journal of Psychiatry, 154*, 56–63.

Bush, G., Valera, E. M., & Seidman, L. J. (2005). Functional neuroimaging of attention deficit/hyperactvity disorder: A review and suggested future directions. *Biological Psychiatry, 57*(11), 1273–1284.

Butzlaff, R. L. & Hooley, J. M. (1998). Expressed emotion and psychiatric relapse. *Archives of General Psychiatry, 55*, 547–552.

C

Cable News Network. (1998, April 6). Alcohol remains large factor in violent crime. *CNN Interactive* [Online].

Cale, E. M. & Lilienfeld, S. O. (2002). Sex differences in psychopathology and antisocial personality disorder. A review and integration. *Clinical Psychology Review, 22*(8), 1179–1207.

Calhoon, S. K. (1996). Confirmatory factor analysis of the Dysfunctional Attitude Scale in a student sample. *Cognitive Therapy and Research, 20*, 81–91.

Calhoun, K. S. & Atkeson, B. M. (1991). *Treatment of rape victims: Facilitating social adjustment.* New York: Pergamon.

Callinan, P. A. & Feinberg, A. P. (2006). The emerging science of epigenomics. *Human Molecular Genetics, 15*(Review Issue No. 1), 95–101.

Camara, W. J., Nathan, J. S., & Puente, A. E. (2000). Psychological test usage: Implications in Professional Psychology. *Professional Psychology: Research and Practice, 31*(2), 141–154.

Canadian Aboriginal (1999). Federal paternalism angers Pikangikum. *Canadian Aboriginal News.* Retrieved October 24, 2001, from http://www.canadianaboriginal.com/news/news131a.htm.

Canadian Alliance on Mental Illness and Mental Health. (2000). *Building Consensus for a National Action Plan on Mental Illness and Mental Health.* Ottawa: Canadian Psychiatric Association.

Canadian Cancer Society (2003). *Risk reduction.* Retrieved May 17, 2003, from http://www.cancer.ca/ccs/internet/standard/0,3182,3172_10139__langId-en,00.html.

Canadian Cancer Society (2006). *Canadian Cancer Statistics 2006.* Retrieved February 8, 2007, from http://www.cancer.ca/vgn/images/portal/cit_86751114/31/21/935505792cw_2006stats_en.pdf.pdf.

Canadian Centre for Justice Statistics (1999). Crime statistics in Canada. *Juristat, 20*(5).

Canadian Committee on Sexual Offences Against Children and Youth (1984). *Report of the committee.* Ottawa: National Health and Welfare.

Canadian Health Network. (1999, January). *Is mental illness related to poverty?* Retrieved April 20, 2003, from http://www.canadian-health-network.ca/faq-faq/mental_health-sante_mentale/7e.html.

Canadian Institute for Health Information. (2001). *The Canadian enhancement of ICD-10* (ISBN No. 1-894766-01-6). Ottawa: Author. Also known as the ICD-10-CA.

Canadian Lung Association. (2006). *Sleep apnea.* Ottawa, ON: Author. Retrieved May 4, 2007, from http://www.lung.ca/diseases-maladies/apnea-apnee_e.php.

Canadian Mental Health Association (2003). *Eating disorders.* Retrieved July 31, 2003, from http://www.cmha.ca/english/info_centre/mh_pamphlets/mh_pamphlet_ed.pdf.

Canadian Mental Health Association. (1999). *Health promotion tool kit: What's the tool kit about?* Retrieved April 23, 2003, from http://www.cmha.ca/mh_toolkit/intro/intro_1.htm.

Canadian Mental Health Association. (n.d.). *Fast facts.* Retrieved April 23, 2003, from http://www.cmha.ca/english/info_centre/fast_facts.htm.

Canadian Psychological Association (2000). *Canadian code of ethics for psychologists (3rd ed.).* Ottawa, ON: Author.

Canadian Psychological Association. (2002, September). *The clinical psychologist in Canada: How can we help?* Retrieved April 20, 2003, from http://www.cpa.ca/clinical/advancing/brochureE.pdf.

Canadian Sleep Society (2003). Sleep centres in Canada. Retrieved July 31, 2003, from http://www.css.to/sleep/centers.htm.

Canli, T., Qiu, M., Omura, K., Congdon, E., Haas, B.W., Amin, Z. et al. (2006). Neural correlates of epigenesis. *Proceedings of the National Academy of Sciences of the United States of America, 103*(43), 16033–16038.

Cao, Q., Xu, X-M., DeVries, W. H., Enzmann, G. U., Ping, P., Tsoulfas, P. et al. (2005). Functional recovery in traumatic spinal cord injury after transplantation of multineurotrophin-expressing glial-restricted precursor cells.

Journal of Neuroscience, 25(30), 6947–6957.

Capps, L., Kasari C., Yirmiya N., & Sigman M. (1993). Parental perception of emotional expressiveness in children with autism. *Journal of Consulting and Clinical Psychology, 61*, 475–484.

Carey, G. (1992). Twin imitation for antisocial behavior: Implications for genetic and family environment research. *Journal of Abnormal Psychology, 101*, 18–25.

Carey, K. B., Carey, M. P., Maisto, S. A., & Henson, J. M. (2006). Brief motivational interventions for heavy college drinkers: A randomized controlled trial. *Journal of Consulting and Clinical Psychology, 74*(5), 943–954.

Carey, M.P., Carey, K.B., Maisto, S.A., Gordon, C.M., Schroder, K.E., Vanable, P.A. (2004). Reducing HIV-risk behavior among adults receiving outpatient psychiatric treatment: results from a randomized controlled trial. *Journal of Consulting and Clinical Psychology, 72*(2), 252–268.

Carey, G. & DiLalla, D. L. (1994). Personality and psychopathology: Genetic perspectives. *Journal of Abnormal Psychology, 103*, 32–43.

Carey, M. P., Wincze, J. P., & Meisler, A. W. (1998). Sexual dysfunction: Male erectile disorder. In D. H. Barlow (Ed.), *Clinical handbook for psychological disorders* (pp. 442–480). New York: Guilford.

Carini, M. A. & Nevid, J. S. (1992). Social appropriateness and impaired perspective in schizophrenia. *Journal of Clinical Psychology, 48*, 170–177.

Carney, C. E. & Segal, Z. V. (2005). Mindfulness-based cognitive therapy for depression. In L. VandeCreek (Ed.), *Innovations in clinical practice: Focus on adults* (pp. 5–17). Sarasota, FL: Professional Resource Press.

Carr, J. L. & VanDeusen, K. M. (2004). Risk factors for male sexual aggression on college campuses. *Journal of Family Violence, 19*, 279–289.

Carter, J. C. & Fairburn, C. G. (1998). Cognitive-behavioral self-help for binge eating disorder: A controlled effectiveness study. *Journal of Consulting and Clinical Psychology, 66*, 616–623.

Carter, J. C., Olmsted, M. P., Kaplan, A. S., McCabe, R. E., Mills, J. S., & Aime, A. (2003). Self-help for bulimia nervosa: A randomized control trial. *American Journal of Psychiatry, 160*(5), 973–978.

Carver, C. S. & Gaines, J. G. (1987). Optimism, pessimism, and postpartum depression. *Cognitive Therapy & Research, 11*, 449–462.

Casanova, M. R. (1997). Functional and anatomical aspects of prefrontal pathology in schizophrenia. *Schizophrenia Bulletin, 23*, 517–519.

Caspi, A., Sugden, K., Moffitt, T. E., Taylor, A., Craig, I. W., Harrington, H. et al. (2003). Influence of life stress on depression: Moderation by a polymorphism in the 5-HTT gene. *Science, 301*(5631), 386–389.

Caspi, A. & Moffitt, T. E. (2006). Gene-environment interactions in psychiatry: Joining forces with neuroscience. *Nature Reviews Neuroscience, 7*, 583–590.

Castellanos, F. X., Glaser, P. E. A., & Gerhardt, G. A. (2006). Towards a neuroscience of attention-deficit/hyperactivity disorder: Fractionating the phenotype . *Journal of Neuroscience Methods, 151*(1), 1–4.

Castelnuovo, G., Gaggioli, A., Mantovani, F., & Riva, G. (2003). New and old tools in psychotherapy: The use of technology for the integration of traditional clinical treatments. *Psychotherapy: Theory, Research, Practice, Training, 40*(1–2), 33–44.

Catz, S. L. & Kelly, J. A. (2001). Living with HIV disease. In A. Baum, T. A. Revenson, & J. E. Singer (Eds.), *Handbook of Health Psychology* (pp. 841–850). Mahwah, NJ: Erlbaum.

CCSA/CAMH (Canadian Centre on Substance Abuse and Centre for Addiction and Mental Health) (1999). *Canadian profile: Alcohol, tobacco and other drugs.* Ottawa, ON: Author.

Celis, W. (1991, January 2). Students trying to draw line between sex and an assault. *The New York Times*, pp. 1, B8.

Centre for Addictions Research, BC (2006). *Responding to your teen's alcohol use.* Victoria, BC: Author.

Centre for Addition and Mental Health. (2002, September).

Educating Students About Mental Health and Mental Illness Curriculum Support for the Ontario Curriculum. Retrieved April 23, 2003, from http://sano.camh.net/curriculum/intro.htm.

Centre for Addiction and Mental Health. (2006). *Epigenomics.* Retrieved on January 25, 2007, from http://www.camh.net/Research/Areas_of_research/Epigenomics.

Chaimowitz, G. (2000). Aboriginal mental health—Moving forward. *Canadian Journal of Psychiatry, 45*(7), 605–606.

Chan, D. W. (1991). The Beck Depression Inventory: What difference does the Chinese version make? *Psychological Assessment, 3*, 616–622.

Chandrashekar, C. R. & Math, S. B. (2006). Psychosomatic disorders in developing countries: Current issues and future challenges. *Current Opinion in Psychiatry, 19*, 201–206.

Chang, L. & Haning, W. (2006). Insights from recent positron emission tomographic studies of drug abuse and dependence. *Current Opinion in Psychiatry, 19*, 246–252.

Chang, S. C. (1984). Review of I. Yamashita's "Taijinkyofu." *Transcultural Psychiatric Research Review, 21*, 283–288.

Charney, D. S., Nemeroff, C. B., Lewis, L., Laden, S. K., Gorman, J. M., Laska, E. M. et al. (2002). National depressive and manic-depressive association consensus statement on the use of placebo in clinical trials of mood disorders. *Archives of General Psychiatry,59*(3), 262–270.

Chen, Y., Johansen, H., Thillaiampalam, S., & Sambell, C. (2005). *Asthma.* (Catalogue no. 82-003-XIE, Vol. 16, No. 2, pp. 43–46). Ottawa: Minister of Industry.

Cheng, S. T. (1996). A critical review of Chinese Koro. *Culture, Medicine and Psychiatry,20*, 67–82.

Cheung, F. M. & Ho, R. M. (1997). Standardization of the Chinese MMPI-A in Hong Kong: A preliminary study. *Psychological Assessment, 9*, 499–502.

Cheung, F., Song, W., & Butcher, J. N. (1991). An infrequency scale for the Chinese MMPI. *Psychological Assessment, 3*, 648–653.

Chipperfield, B. & Vogel-Sprott, M. (1988). Family history of problem drinking among young male social drinkers: Modeling effects on alcohol consumption. *Journal of Abnormal Psychology, 97*, 423–428.

Chodirker, B. N., Cadrin, C., Davies, G. A. L., Summers, A. M., Wilson, R. D., Winsor, E. J. T., & Young, D. (2001). Canadian guidelines for prenatal diagnosis: Genetic indications for prenatal diagnosis. *Journal Society of Obstetricians and Gynaecologists of Canada, 105*(6), 1–7.

Chomsky, N. (1959). A review of B. F. Skinner's *Verbal Behavior. Language, 35*(1), 26–58.

Chou, C., Condron, L., & Belland, J. C. (2005). A review of the research on Internet addiction. *Educational Psychology Review, 17*, 363–388.

Chow, E. W. C., Watson, M., Young, D. A., & Bassett, A. S. (2006). Neurocognitive profile in 22q11 deletion syndrome and schizophrenia. *Schizophrenia Research, 87*, 270–278.

Chowdhury, A. N. (1996). The definition and classification of Koro. *Culture, Medicine and Psychiatry, 20*, 41–65.

Christiansen, B. A. & Goldman, M. S. (1983). Alcohol related expectancies versus demographic/background variables in the prediction of adolescent drinking. *Journal of Consulting and Clinical Psychology, 52*, 249–257.

Chu, J. A., Frey, L. M., & Ganzel, B. L. (1999). Memories of childhood abuse: Dissociation, amnesia, and corroboration. *American Journal of Psychiatry, 156*, 749–755.

Chung, S. A., Jairam, S., Hussain, M. R., & Shapiro, C. M. (2002). How, what, and why of sleep apnea. Perspectives for primary care physicians. *Canadian Family Physician, 48*(6), 1073–1080.

Clark, D. A. (2004). *Cognitive-behavior therapy for OCD.* New York: Guilford.

Clark, D. A., Beck, A. T., & Alford, B. A. (1999). *Scientific foundations of cognitive theory and therapy of depression.* New York: John Wiley & Sons.

Clark, D. M. (1986). A cognitive approach to panic. *Behaviour Research and Therapy, 24*, 461–470.

Clarke, B. M., Upton, A. R., Kamath, M. V., Al-Harbi, T.,

& Castellanos, C. M. (2006). Transcranial magnetic stimulation for migraine: clinical effects. *Journal of Headache and Pain, 7*(5):341–346.

Cleckley, H. (1941). *The mask of sanity: An attempt to reinterpret the so-called psychopathic personality.* St. Louis: Mosby.

Cleckley, H. (1976). *The mask of sanity* (5th ed.). St. Louis: Mosby.

Cleghorn, J. M., Franco, S., Szechtman, B., Kaplan, R. D., Szechtman, H., Brown, G. M., Nahnias, C., & Garnett, E. S. (1992). Toward a brain map of auditory hallucinations. *American Journal of Psychiatry, 149*, 1062–1069.

Cloos, J.-M. (2005). The treatment of panic disorder. *Current Opinion in Psychiatry, 18*, 45–50.

Coccaro, E. F. & Kavoussi, R. J. (1997). Fluoxetine and impulsive aggressive behavior in personality-disordered subjects. *Archives of General Psychiatry, 54*, 1081–1088.

Cockerham, W. C., Kunz, G., & Lueschen, G. (1989). Alcohol use and psychological distress: A comparison of Americans and West Germans. *International Journal of the Addictions, 24*, 951–961.

Cohane, G. H. & Pope, H. G., Jr. (2001). Body image in boys: A review of the literature. *International Journal of Eating Disorders, 29*(4), 373–379.

Cohen, F. L., Ferrans, C. E., & Eshler, B. (1992). Reported accidents in narcolepsy. *Loss, Grief and Care, 5*, 71–80.

Cohen, S., Doyle, W. J., Skoner, D. P., Rabin, B. S., & Gwaltney, J. M., Jr. (1997). Social ties and susceptibility to the common cold. *Journal of the American Medical Association, 277*(24), 1940–1944.

Cohen, S., Frank, E., Doyle, W. J., Skoner, D. P., Rabin, B. S., & Gwaltney, J. M., Jr. (1998). Types of stressors that increase susceptibility to the common cold in healthy adults. *Health Psychology, 17*(3), 214–223.

Cohen, S., Tyrell, D. A. J., & Smith, A. P. (1991). Psychological stress and susceptibility to the common cold. *New England Journal of Medicine, 325*, 606–612.

Colapinto, J. (2000). *As nature made him: The boy who was raised as a girl.* New York: HarperCollins.

Cole, S. W., Kemeny, M. E., & Taylor, S. E. (1997). Social identity and physical health: Accelerated HIV progression in rejection-sensitive gay men. *Journal of Personality and Social Psychology, 72,* 320–335.

Cole, T. B. (2006). Rape at US colleges often fueled by alcohol. *JAMA: Journal of the American Medical Association, 296,* 504–505.

Collerton, D., Perry, E., & McKeith, I. (2005). Why people see things that are not there: A novel perception and attention deficit model for recurrent complex visual hallucinations. *Behavioral and Brain Sciences, 28,* 737–794.

Compas, B. E., Haaga, D. A., Keefe, F. J., Leitenberg, H., & Williams, D.A. (1998). Sampling of empirically supported psychological treatments from health psychology: Smoking, chronic pain, cancer, and bulimia nervosa. *Journal of Consulting and Clinical Psychology, 66*(1), 89–112.

Concepts, research, and interventions relating to the self and shyness. New York: John Wiley & Sons.

Conley, R. R. & Buchanan, R. W. (1997). Evaluation of treatment-resistant schizophrenia . *Schizophrenia Bulletin, 23,* 663–674.

Connors, G. J. et al. (1997). The therapeutic alliance and its relationship to alcoholism treatment participation and outcome. *Journal of Consulting and Clinical Psychology, 65,* 588–598.

Conrod, P. J., Stewart, S. H., Pihl, R. O., Cote, S., Fontaine, V., & Dongier, M. (2000). Efficacy of brief coping skills interventions that match different personality profiles of female substance abusers. *Psychology of Addictive Behaviors, 14,* 231–242.

Cooke, D. J. & Michie, C. (1997). An item response theory analysis of the Hare Psychopathy Checklist—Revised. *Psychological Assessment, 9,* 3–14.

Coolidge, F. L. & Segal, D. L. (1998). Evolution of personality disorder diagnosis in the Diagnostic and Statistical Manual of Mental Disorders. *Clinical Psychology Review, 18,* 585–599.

Cooney, N. L. et al. (1997). Alcohol cue reactivity, negative-mood reactivity, and relapse in treated alcoholic men. *Journal of Abnormal Psychology, 106,* 243–250.

Coons, P. M. (1986). Treatment progress in 20 patients with multiple personality disorder. *Journal of Nervous and Mental Disease, 174,* 715–721.

Cooper, P. J. & Steere, J. (1995). A comparison of two psychological treatments for bulimia nervosa: Implications for models of maintenance. *Behaviour Research and Therapy, 33,* 875–885.

Corbitt, E. M. & Widiger, T. A. (1995). Sex differences among the personality disorders: An exploration of the data. *Clinical Psychology: Science and Practice, 2,* 225–238.

Cordes, C. (1985). Common threads found in suicide. *APA Monitor, 16*(10), 11.

Cornblatt, B. A. & Kelip, J. G. (1994). Impaired attention, genetics, and the pathophysiology of schizophrenia. *Schizophrenia Bulletin, 20,* 31–46.

Cornelius, J. R. et al. (1997). Fluoxetine in depressed alcoholics: A double-blind, placebo-controlled trial. *Archives of General Psychiatry, 54,* 700–705.

Coronary disease: Taking emotions to heart. (1996, October). *Harvard Health Letter, 21*(11), 1–3.

Corr, P. J. (2004). Reinforcement sensitivity theory and personality. *Neuroscience and Biobehavioral Reviews, 28*(3), 317–332.

Corr, P. J. & Perkins, A. M. (2006). The role of theory in the psychophysiology of personality: From Ivan Pavlov to Jeffrey Gray. *International Journal of Psychophysiology, 62*(3), 367–376.

Correctional Services Canada (2002a). Recidivism. Ottawa: Author. Retrieved July 16, 2003, from http://www.cscscc.gc.ca/text/pblct/forum/e052/e052h_e.shtml.

Correctional Services Canada (2002b). A mental health profile of federally sentenced offenders. Ottawa: Author. Retrieved July 16, 2003, from http://www.csc-scc.gc.ca/text/pblct/forum/e02/e021d_e.shtml.

Cosgray, R. E., Hanna, V., Fawley, R., & Money, M. (1991). Death from auto-erotic asphyxiation in a long-term psychiatric setting. *Perspectives in Psychiatric Care, 27,* 21–24.

Cossette, L. & Duclos, E. (2002). *A profile of disability in Canada, 2001* (Catalogue No. 89-577-XIE). Ottawa: Statistics Canada. Retrieved August 13, 2007, from http://www.statcan.gc.ca/english/freepub/89-577-XIE/pdf/89-577-XIE01001.pdf.

Costello, E. J., Erkanli, A., & Angold, A. (2006). Is there an epidemic of child or adolescent depression? *Journal of Child Psychology and Psychiatry, 47,* 1263–1271.

Cottraux, J. (2005). Recent developments in research and treatment for social phobia (social anxiety disorder). *Current Opinion in Psychiatry, 18,* 51–54.

Coursey, R. D., Alford, J., & Safarjan, B. (1997). Significant advances in understanding and treating serious mental illness. *Professional Psychology: Research and Practice, 28,* 205–216.

Cox, B. J. & Taylor, S. (1999). Anxiety disorders: Panic and phobias. In T. Millon, P. Blaney, & R. Davis (Eds.), *Oxford textbook of psychopathology* (pp. 81–113). Oxford: Oxford University Press.

Cox, W. M. & Klinger, E. (1988). A motivational model of alcohol use. *Journal of Abnormal Psychology, 97,* 168–180.

Coyne, J. C. (1999). Thinking interactionally about depression: A radical restatement. In T. Joiner & J. C. Coyne (Eds.), *The interactional nature of depression: Advances in interpersonal approaches* (pp. 365–392). Washington, DC: American Psychological Association.

Craighead, W. E., Craighead, L. W., & Ilardi, S. S. (1998). Psychosocial treatments for major depressive disorder. In P. E. Nathan & J. M. Gorman (Eds.), *A guide to treatments that work* (pp. 226–239). New York: Oxford University Press.

Craske, M. G. & Waters, A. M. (2005). Panic disorder, phobias, and generalized anxiety disorder. *Annual Review of Clinical Psychology, 1,* 197–225.

Crisp, A. H., Callender, J. S., Halek, C., & Hsu, L. K. (1992). Long-term mortality in anorexia nervosa: A 20-year follow-up of the St. George's and Aberdeen cohorts. *British Journal of Psychiatry, 161*(1), 104–107.

Crits-Christoph, P. (1992). The efficacy of brief dynamic psychotherapy: A meta-analysis. *American Journal of Psychiatry, 149,* 151–158.

Crits-Christoph, P. & Siqueland, L. (1996). Psychosocial treatment for drug abuse: Selected review and recommendations for national health care. *Archives of General Psychiatry, 53,* 749–756.

Cross-National Collaborative Group. (1992). The changing rate of major depression: Cross-national comparisons. *Journal of the American Medical Association, 268,* 3098–3105.

Crow, T. J. (1980a). Molecular pathology of schizophrenia: More than one disease process? *British Medical Journal, 280,* 66–68.

Crow, T. J. (1980b). Positive and negative schizophrenic symptoms and the role of dopamine. *British Journal of Psychiatry, 137,* 383–386.

Crow, T. J. (1980c). Positive and negative schizophrenic symptoms and the role of dopamine: A debate. *British Journal of Psychiatry, 137,* 379–383.

Crozier, W. R., & Alden, L. E. (2001). *International handbook of social anxiety: Concepts, research, and interventions relating to the self and shyness.* New York: John Wiley & Sons.

Cunningham C. E. & Boyle, M. H. (2002). Preschoolers at risk for attention-deficit hyperactivity disorder and oppositional defiant disorder: Family, parenting, and behavioral correlates. *Journal of Abnormal Child Psychology, 30*(6), 555–569.

Curran, P. J., Stice, E., & Chassin, L. (1997). The relation between adolescent alcohol use and peer alcohol use: A longitudinal random coefficients model. *Journal of Consulting and Clinical Psychology, 65,* 130–140.

Currie, S. R., Patten, S. B., Williams, J. V. A., Wang, J., Beck, C. A., El-Guebaly, N. et al. (2005). Comorbidity of major depression with substance use disorders. *Canadian Journal of Psychiatry, 50,* 660–666.

Curry, S., Marlatt, G. A., & Gordon, J. R. (1987). Abstinence violation effect: Validation of an attributional construct with smoking cessation. *Journal of Consulting and Clinical Psychology, 55,* 145–149.

Cyranowski, J. M., Aarestad, S. L., & Andersen, B. L. (1999). The role of sexual self-schema in a diathesis-stress model of sexual dysfunction. *Applied and Preventive Psychology, 8,* 217–228.

D

Dadds, M. R., Sanders, M. R., Morrison, M., & Rebgetz, M. (1992). Childhood depression and conduct disorder: II. An analysis of family interaction patterns in the home. *Journal of Abnormal Psychology, 101,* 505–513.

Dahl, R. E. (1992). The pharmacologic treatment of sleep disorders. *Psychiatric Clinics of North America, 15,* 161–178.

Daley, S. E. et al. (1997). Predictors of the generation of episodic stress: A longitudinal study of late adolescent women. *Journal of Abnormal Psychology, 106,* 251–259.

Daly, L. E., Kirke, P. N., Molloy, A., Weir, D. G., & Scott, J. M. (1995). Folate levels and neural tube defects: Implications for prevention. *Journal of the American Medical Association, 274*(21), 1698–1702.

Damasio, A. R. (1997). Towards a neuropathology of emotion and mood. *Nature, 386,* 769–770.

Davidson, P. R. & Parker, K. C. H. (2001). Eye movement desensitization and reprocessing (EMDR): A meta-analysis. *Journal of Consulting and Clinical Psychology, 69,* 305–316.

Davis, J. O., & Bracha, H. S. (1996). Prenatal growth markers in schizophrenia: A monozygotic co-twin control study. *American Journal of Psychiatry, 153,* 1166–1172.

Davis, K. C., Morris, J., George, W. H., Martell, J., & Heiman, J. R. (2006). Men's likelihood of sexual aggression: The influence of alcohol, sexual arousal, and violent pornography. *Aggressive Behavior, 32,* 581–589.

Davis, K. L., Kahn, R. S., Ko, G., & Davidson M. (1991). Dopamine in schizophrenia: A review and reconceptualization. *American Journal of Psychiatry, 148,* 1474–1486.

Davis, R., Olmsted, M., Rockert, W., Marques, T., & Dolhanty, J. (1997). Group psychoeducation for bulimia nervosa with and without additional psychotherapy process sessions.

International Journal of Eating Disorders, 22(1), 25–34.

Davis, S. (1993). Changes to the *Criminal Code* provisions for mentally disordered offenders and their implications for Canadian psychiatry. *Canadian Journal of Psychiatry, 38,* 122–126.

de Bruin, N. M., van Luijtelaar, E. L., Cools, A. R., & Ellenbroek, B. A. (2003). Filtering disturbances in schizophrenic patients. *Current Neuropharmacology, 1,* 47–87.

De Cuypere, G., T'Sjoen, G., Beerten, R., Selvaggi, G., De Sutter, P., Hoebeke, P. et al. (2005). Sexual and physical health after sex reassignment surgery. *Archives of Sexual Behavior, 34,* 679–690.

De Koninck, J. (1997). Sleep, the common denominator for psychological adaptation. *Canadian Psychology, 38,* 191–195.

Deckel, A. W., Hesselbrock, V., & Bauer, L. (1996). Antisocial personality disorder, childhood delinquency, and frontal brain functioning: EEG and neuropsychological findings. *Journal of Clinical Psychology, 52,* 639–650.

Decker, T.W., Cline-Elsen, J., & Gallagher, M. (1992). Relaxation therapy as an adjunct in radiation oncology. *Journal of Clinical Psychology, 48,* 388–393.

Deffenbacher, J. L., Dahlen, E. R., Lynch, R. S., Morris, C. D., & Gowensmith, W. N. (2000). An Application of Beck's Cognitive Therapy to General Anger Reduction. *Cognitive Theory and Research, 24*(6), 689–697.

DeKeseredy, W. S. (1997). Measuring sexual abuse in Canadian university/college dating relationships. In M. D. Schwartz (Ed.), *Researching sexual violence against women* (pp. 43–53). Thousand Oaks, CA: Sage.

Dekker, J. (1993). Inhibited male orgasm. In W. O'Donohue & J. H. Geer (Eds.), *Handbook of sexual dysfunctions: Assessment and treatment* (pp. 279–301). Boston: Allyn & Bacon.

DeLisi, L. E. & Fleischhaker, W. (2007). Schizophrenia research in the era of the genome, 2007. *Current Opinion in Psychiatry, 20,* 109–110.

Dell'Osso, B., Nestadt, G., Allen, A., & Hollander, E. (2006). Serotoin-norepinephrine reuptake inhibitors in the treatment of obsessive-compulsive

disorder. *Journal of Clinical Psychiatry, 67,* 600–610.

DeLongis, A. (1985). *The relationship of everyday stress to health and well-being: Inter- and intraindividual approaches.* Unpublished doctoral dissertation. University of California, Berkeley.

DeLongis, A., Folkman, S., & Lazarus, R. S. (1988). The impact of daily stress on health and mood: Psychological and social resources as mediators. *Journal of Personality and Social Psychology, 54*(3), 486–495.

Denollet, J. et al. (1996). Personality as independent predictor of long-term mortality in patients with coronary heart disease. *Lancet, 347,* 417–421.

Denov, M. S. (2001). Culture of denial: Exploring professional perspectives on female sex offending. *Canadian Journal of Criminology, 43,* 303–329.

Denys, D., van Nieuwerburgh, F., Deforce, D., & Westenberg, H. G. M. (2006). Association between serotonergic candidate genes and specific phenotypes of obsessive compulsive disorder. *Journal of Affective Disorders, 91,* 39–44.

DeRubeis, R. J. & Crits-Cristoph, P. (1998). Empirically supported individual and group psychological treatments for adult mental disorders. *Journal of Consulting and Clinical Psychology, 66,* 37–52.

Deshpande, D. M., Kim, Y-S., Martinez, T., Carmen, J., Dike, S., Shats, I. et al. (2006). Recovery from Paralysis in Adult Rats Using Embryonic Stem Cells. *Annals of Neurology, 60*(1), 22–34.

Desmond, E. W. (1987, November). Out in the open: Changing attitudes and new research give fresh hope to alcoholics. *Time,* pp. 80–90.

Detera-Wadleigh, S. D. & McMahon, F. J. (2006). G72/G30 in schizophrenia and bipolar disorder: Review and meta-analysis. *Biological Psychiatry, 60,* 106–114.

Devanand, D. P. et al. (1994). Does ECT alter brain structure? *American Journal of Psychiatry, 151,* 957–970.

Diamond, S., Baldwin, R., & Diamond, R. (1963). *Inhibition and choice.* New York: Harper & Row.

Dickens, B. M., Doob, A. N., Warwick, O. H., & Winegard, W. C. (1982). *Report of the Committee of Enquiry into*

Allegations Concerning Drs. Linda and Mark Sobell. Toronto: Addiction Research Foundation.

DiLalla, D. L., Carey, G., Gottesman, I. I., & Bouchard, T. J., Jr. (1996). Heritability of MMPI personality indicators of psychopathology in twins reared apart. *Journal of Abnormal Psychology, 105,* 491–499.

DiLalla, L. F. & Gottesman, I. I. (1991). Biological and genetic contributors to violence: Widom's untold tale. *Psychological Bulletin, 109,* 125–129.

Dilk, M. N. & Bond, G. R. (1996). Meta-analytic evaluation of skills training research for individuals with severe mental illness. *Journal of Consulting and Clinical Psychology, 64,* 1337–1346.

Dimidjian, S., Hollon, S. D., Dobson, K. S., Schmaling, K. B., Kohlenberg, R. J., Addis, M. E., et al. (2006).Randomized trial of behavioral activation, cognitive therapy, and antidepressant medication in the acute treatment of adults with major depression. *Journal of Consulting and Clinical Psychology, 74,* 658–670.

Dingle, G., Samtani, P., Kraatz, J., & Solomon, R. (2002). *The real facts on alcohol use, injuries and deaths.* Mississauga, ON: MADD.

Dinh, K. T., Sarason, I. G., Peterson, A. V., & Onstad, L. E. (1995). Children's perceptions of smokers and nonsmokers: A longitudinal study. *Health Psychology, 14,* 32–40.

Dobson, D. J. G., McDougall, G., Busheikin, J., & Aldous, J. (1995). Effects of social skills training and social milieu treatment on symptoms of schizophrenia. *Psychiatric Services, 46,* 376–380.

Dobson, K. S. & Dozois, D. J. A. (2001). Historical and philosophic bases of the cognitive-behavioral therapies. In K. S. Dobson (Ed.), *Handbook of Cognitive-Behavioral Therapies* (2nd ed., pp. 3–39). New York: The Guilford Press.

Dobson, K. S. & Khatri, N. (2002). Major depressive disorder. In M. Hersen (Ed.), *Clinical behavior therapy: Adults and children* (pp. 37–51). New York: John Wiley & Sons.

Dodge, K. A. et al. (1997). Reactive and proactive aggression in school children and psychiatrically impaired chronically assaultive youth. *Journal of*

Abnormal Psychology, 106, 37–51.

Dodge, K. A., Laird, R., Lochman, J. E., & Zelli, A. (2002). Multidimensional latent-construct analysis of children's social information processing patterns. *Psychological Assessment, 14*(1), 60–73.

Dohrenwend, B. P., Turner, J. B., Turse, N. A., Adams, B. G., Koenen, K. C., & Marshall, R. (2006). The psychological risks of Vietnam for U.S. veterans: A revisit with new data and methods. *Science, 313,* 979–982.

Doidge, N. (2006). Sigmund Freud: The doctor is back in. *Maclean's, 119*(19), 40–43.

Doll, B. (1996). Prevalence of psychiatric disorders in children and youth: An agenda for advocacy by school psychology. *School Psychology Quarterly, 11,* 20–46.

Donker, F. J. (2000). Cardiac rehabilitation: a review of current developments. *Clinical Psychology Review, 20*(7), 923–943.

Dowker, A., Hermelin, B., & Pring, L. (1996). A savant poet. *Psychological Medicine, 26,* 913–924.

Drevets, W. C., Price, J. L., Simpson, J. R., Todd, R. D. et al. (1997). Subgenual prefrontal cortex abnormalities in mood disorders. *Nature, 386,* 824–827.

Drewnowski, A. (1997). Taste preferences and food intake. *Annual Review of Nutrition, 17,* 237–253.

Drewnowski, A., Yee, D. K., Kurth, C. L., & Krahn, D. D. (1994). Eating pathology and DSM-III-R bulimia nervosa: A continuum of behavior. *American Journal of Psychiatry, 151*(8), 1217–1219.

Drews, C. D., Yeargin-Allsopp, M., Decouflé, P., & Murphy, C. C. (1995). Variation in the influence of selected sociodemographic risk factors for mental retardation. *American Journal of Public Health, 85*(3), 329–334.

Drover, J. & Owen, L. (2000). *Fact Sheet. They can get there from here: Students with learning disabilities in Canadian colleges & universities.* Ottawa: Learning Disabilities Association of Canada. Retrieved October 18, 2003, from http://www.ldac-taac.ca/english/indepth/post-sec/getthere.pdf.

Drummond, D. C. & Glautier, S. (1994). A controlled trial of cue exposure treatment in alcohol dependence. *Journal of Consulting and Clinical Psychology, 62,* 809–817.

Dryden, J., Johnson, B. R., Howard, S., & McGuire, A. (1998). *Resiliency: A Comparison arising from conversations with 9–12-year-old children and their teachers.* Paper given at the Annual Meeting of the American Educational Research Association, San Diego, April 13–17.

Dryden, W. (1984). *Rational-emotive therapy: Fundamentals and innovations.* London: Croom Helm.

Duffy, F. H. (1994). In G. Dawson & K. W. Fischer (Eds.), *Human behavior and the developing brain* (pp. 93–132). New York: Guilford.

Dugas, M. J. & Koerner, N. (2005). Cognitive-behavioral treatment for generalized anxiety disorder: Current status and future directions. *Journal of Cognitive Psychotherapy, 19,* 61–81.

Dugas, M. J., Gagnon, F., Ladouceur, R., & Freeston, M. H. (1998). Generalized anxiety disorder: A preliminary test of a conceptual model. *Behaviour Research and Therapy, 36,* 215–226.

Dugas, M. J., Hedayati, M., Karavidas, A., Buhr, K., Francis, K., & Phillips, N. A. (2005). Intolerance of uncertainty and information processing: Evidence of biased recall and interpretations. *Cognitive Therapy and Research, 29,* 57–70.

Dugas, M. J., Marchand, A., & Ladouceur, R. (2005). Further validation of a cognitive-behavioral model of generalized anxiety disorder. *Journal of Anxiety Disorders, 19,* 329–343.

Dulit, R. A., Fyer, M. R., Leon, A. C., Brodsky, B. S., & Frances, A. J. (1994). Clinical correlates of self-mutilation in borderline personality disorder. *American Journal of Psychiatry, 151*(9), 1305–1311.

Dunner, D. L. (2005). Dysthymia and double depression. *International Review of Psychiatry, 17,* 3–8.

Durkheim, E. (1958). *Suicide: A study in sociology.* New York: Free Press.

Dwork, A. J. (1997). Postmortem studies of the hippocampal formation in schizophrenia. *Schizophrenia Bulletin, 23,* 385–402.

Dwyer, M. (1988). Exhibitionism/voyeurism. *Journal of Social Work and Human Sexuality, 7,* 101–112.

Dykens, E. M. & Hodapp, R. M. (1997). Treatment issues in genetic mental retardation syndromes. *Professional Psychology: Research and Practice, 28,* 263–270.

Dzokoto, V. A. & Adams, G. (2005). Understanding genital-shrinking epidemics in West Africa: Koro, Juju, or mass psychogenic illness? *Culture, Medicine and Psychiatry, 29,* 53–78.

E

Earnst, K. S. & Kring, A. M. (1997). Construct validity of negative symptoms: An empirical and conceptual review. *Clinical Psychology Review, 17,* 167–189.

Eaton, W. W. et al. (1997). Natural history of diagnostic interview schedule/DSM-IV major depression: The Baltimore Epidemiologic Catchment Area follow-up. *Archives of General Psychiatry, 54,* 993–999.

Eberhardy, F. (1967). The view from "the couch." *Journal of Child Psychological Psychiatry, 8,* 257–263.

Ebstein, R. H., Benjamin, J., & Belmaker, R. H. (2003). Behavioral genetics, genomics and personality. In R. Plomin, J. C. DeFries, I. W. Craig & P. McGuffin (Eds.), *Behavioral genetics in the postgenomic era.* Washington, DC: American Psychological Association.

Eckhardt, C. I. & Deffenbacher, J. L. (1995). Diagnosis of anger disorders. In H. Kassinove (Ed.), *Anger disorders: Definition, diagnosis, and treatment* (pp. 27–47). Washington, DC: Taylor & Francis.

Eckhardt, C. I., Barbour, K. A., & Stuart, G. L. (1997). Anger and hostility in maritally violent men: Conceptual distinctions, measurement issues, and literature review. *Clinical Psychology Review, 17,* 333–358.

Eckhardt, F., Beck, S., Gut, I. G., & Berlin, K. (2004). Future potential of the Human Genome Project. *Expert Review of Molecular Diagnostics, 4*(5), 609–618.

Edelson, E. (1998, March 9). Migraines come into focus. *New York Newsday,* p. C7.

Edwards, H. P. (2000, January 4). *Regulatory requirements for registration in psychology across Canada: A comparison of acts, regulations, by-laws and guidelines in view of the AIT.* Retrieved April 20, 2003, from http://www.cpa.ca/documents/PSWAIT%20Report.PDF.

Edwards, V. (2002). *Depression and bipolar disorders.* Toronto: Key Porter.

Egan, J. (1991). Oppositional defiant disorder. In J. M. Wiener (Ed.), *Textbook of child and adolescent psychiatry.* Washington, DC: American Psychiatric Press.

Egan, M. F., Apud, J., & Wyatt, R. J. (1997). Treatment of tardive dyskinesia. *Schizophrenia Bulletin, 23,* 583–609.

Egger, G., Liang, G., Aparicio, A., & Jones, P. A. (2004). Epigenetics in human disease and prospects for epigenetic therapy. *Nature, 429*(6990), 457–463.

Eggleton, A. & Keon, W. J. (2007). *Final report on: The enquiry on the funding for the treatment of autism. Pay now or pay later. Autism families in crisis.* Ottawa, ON: The Standing Senate Committee on Social Affairs, Science and Technology. Retrieved April 28, 2007, from http://www.parl.gc.ca/39/1/parlbus/commbus/senate/com-e/soci-e/rep-e/repfinmar07-e.htm.

Eisler, I., Dare, C., Russell, G. F., Szmukler, G., le Grange, D., & Dodge, E. (1997). Family and individual therapy in anorexia nervosa: A 5-year follow-up. *Archives of General Psychiatry, 54*(11), 1025–1030.

Ellason, J. W. & Ross, C. A. (1997). Two-year follow-up of inpatients with dissociative identity disorder. *American Journal of Psychiatry, 154,* 832–839.

Ellerby, J. H., McKenzie, J., McKay, S., Gariépy, G. J., & Kaufert, J. M. (2000). Bioethics for clinicians: 18. Aboriginal culture. *Canadian Medical Association Journal, 163*(7), 845–850.

Elliot, R., Watson, J. C., Goldman, R. N., & Greenberg, L. S. (2004). *Learning emotion-focused therapy: The process-experiential approach to change.* Washington, DC: American Psychological Association.

Elliott, A. J., Uldall, K. K., Bergam, K., Russo, J., Claypoole, K., & Roy-Byrne, P. P. (1998). Randomized, placebo-controlled trial of paroxetine versus imipramine in depressed HIV-positive outpatients. *American Journal of Psychiatry, 155*(3), 367–372.

Ellis, A. (1977). *Anger: How to live with and without it.* Secaucus, NJ: Citadel.

Ellis, A. (1993). Reflections on rational-emotive therapy. *Journal of Consulting and Clinical Psychology, 61,* 199–201.

Ellis, A. (2003). Early theories and practices of rational emotive behavior theory and how they have been augmented and revised during the last three decades. *Journal of Rational-Emotive & Cognitive-Behavior Therapy, 21*(3/4), 219–243.

Ellis, A. & Dryden, W. (1987). *The practice of rational emotional therapy.* New York: Springer.

Ellis, A., Young, J., & Lockwood, G. (1989). Cognitive therapy and rational-emotive therapy: A dialogue. *Journal of Cognitive Psychotherapy, 1,* 205–256.

Emslie, G. J., Weinberg, W. A., Kowatch, R. A., Hughes, C. W., Carmody, T., & Rintelmann, J. (1997). A double-blind, randomized, placebo-controlled trial of fluoxetine in children and adolescents with depression. *Archives of General Psychiatry, 54*(11), 1031–1037.

Engelsmann, F. F. (2000). Transcultural psychiatry: Goals and challenges. *Canadian Journal of Psychiatry, 45*(5), 429–430.

English, S. (2002, October 29). Psycho at the top? *The Age.* Retrieved July 21, 2003, from http://www.theage.com.au/articles/2002/10/28/1035683360087.html.

Epping-Jordan, J. E., Compas, B. E., & Howell, D. C. (1994). Predictors of cancer progression in young adult men and women: Avoidance, intrusive thoughts, and psychological symptoms. *Health Psychology, 13,* 539–547.

Epping-Jordan, J. E., Compas, B. E., Osowiecki, D. M., Oppedisano, G., Gerhardt, C., Primo, K., & Krag, D. N. (1999). Psychological adjustment in breast cancer: Processes of emotional distress. *Health Psychology, 18*(4), 315–326.

Eranti, S., Mogg, A., Pluck, G., Landau, S., Purvis, R., Brown, R. G. et al. (2007). A randomized, controlled trial with 6-month follow-up of repetitive transcranial magnetic stimulation and electroconvulsive therapy for severe depression. *American Journal of Psychiatry, 164,* 73–81.

Erikson, E. H. (1985). *Childhood and society: 35th anniversary edition.* New York: Norton (Original work published 1963 and 1950).

Erlenmeyer-Kimling, L., Adamo, U. H. et al. (1997). The New York high-risk project: Prevalence and comorbidity of Axis I disorders in offspring of schizophrenic parents at 25-year follow-up. *Archives of General Psychiatry, 54,* 1096–1102.

Esteller, M. (2006). The necessity of a human epigenome project. *Carcinogenesis, 27*(6), 1121–1125.

Etkin, A., Egner, T., Peraza, D. M., Kandel, E. R., & Hirsch, J. (2006). Resolving emotional conflict: a model for amygdalar modulation by the rostral anterior cingulate cortex, *Neuron, 51*(6), 871–872.

Ettinger, U., Joober, R., De Guzman, R., & O'Driscoll, G. A. (2006). Schizotypy, attention deficit hyperactivity disorder, and dopamine genes. *Psychiatry and Clinical Neurosciences, 60,* 764–767.

Everett, B. (2002, December 5). Mental health reform. *Canadian Mental Health Association.* Retrieved February 6, 2003, from http://www.ontario.cmha.ca/content/policy_and_action/everett_20021205.asp.

Everett, B. (2006). *Stigma: The hidden killer: Background Paper and Literature Review.* Mood Disorders Society of Canada. Retrieved November 4, 2006, from http://www.mooddisorderscanada.ca/Stigma/pdfs/STIGMA_TheHiddenKiller_MDSC_May2006.pdf.

Exner, J. E. (1991). *The Rorschach: A comprehensive system: Vol. 2. Interpretation.* New York: John Wiley & Sons.

Exner, J. E. (1993). *The Rorschach: A comprehensive system: Vol. 1. Basic foundations* (3rd ed.). New York: John Wiley & Sons.

Extinguishing Alzheimer's. (1998, June 23). *The New York Times,* p. F7.

F

Fairburn, C. G. (1997). Eating disorders. In D. M. Clark & C. G. Fairburn (Eds.), *Science and practice of cognitive behaviour therapy* (pp. 209–241). New York: Oxford University Press.

Fairburn, C. G., Cooper, Z., & Cooper, P. J. (1986). The clinical features and maintenance of bulimia nervosa. In K. D. Brownell & J. P. Foreyt (Eds.), *Handbook of eating disorders* (pp. 389–404). New York: Basic Books.

Fairburn, C. G., Welch, S. L., Doll, H. A., Davies, B. A., & O'Connor, M. E. (1997). Risk factors for bulimia nervosa: A community-based case-control study. *Archives of General Psychiatry, 54*(6), 509–517.

Fairburn, C. G., Cooper, Z., Doll, H. A., & Davies, B. A. (2005). Identifying dieters who will develop an eating disorder: A prospective, population-based study. *The American Journal of Psychiatry, 162*(12), 2249–2255.

Faraone, S. V., Biederman, J., Lehman, B. K., Spencer, T., Norman, D., Sediman, L. J. et al. (1993). Intellectual performance and school failure in children with attention deficit hyperactivity disorders and their siblings. *Journal of Abnormal Psychology, 102,* 616–623.

Faraone, S. V. (2003a, August). *ADHD: Facts and fiction.* Paper presented at the meeting of the American Psychological Association, Toronto, ON.

Faraone, S. V. (2003b, August). *The persistence of attention-deficit/hyperactivity disorder through adolescence and adulthood.* Paper presented at the meeting of the American Psychological Association, Toronto, ON.

Faraone, S. V. & Khan. S. A. (2006). Candidate gene studies of attention-deficit/hyperactivity disorder. *Journal of Clinical Psychiatry, 67*(Supplement 8), 13–20.

Farber, B. A., Brink, D. C., & Raskin, P. M. (1996). *The psychotherapy of Carl Rogers: Cases and commentary* (pp. 74–75). New York: Guilford.

Farberman, R. K. (1997). Public attitudes about psychologists and mental health care: Research to guide the American Psychological Association Public Education Campaign. *Professional Psychology: Research and Practice, 28,* 128–136.

Farley, M., Lynne, J., & Cotton, A. J. (2005). Prostitution in Vancouver: Violence and colonization of First Nations women. *Transcultural Psychiatry, 42,* 242–271.

Farmer, A., Elkin, A., & McGuffin, P. (2007). The genetics of bipolar affective disorder. *Current Opinion in Psychiatry, 20,* 8–12.

Farmer, R.F. (2000). Issues in the assessment and conceptualization of personality disorders. *Clinical Psychology Review, 20*(7), 823–851.

Farrell, A. D., Camplair, P. S., & McCullough, L. (1987). Identification of target complaints by computer interview: Evaluation of the Computerized Assessment System for Psychotherapy Evaluation and Research. *Journal of Consulting and Clinical Psychology, 55,* 691–700.

Farrell, A. D. & White, K. S. (1998). Peer influences and drug use among urban adolescents: Family structure and parent/adolescent relationship as protective factors. *Journal of Consulting and Clinical Psychology, 66,* 248–258.

Farrell, M., Howes, S., Taylor, C., Lewis, G., Jenkins, R., Bebbington, P. et al. (2003). Substance misuse and psychiatric comorbidity: An overview of the OPCS National Psychiatric Morbidity Survey. *International Review of Psychiatry, 15,* 43–49.

Fawzy, F. I. & Fawzy, N. W. (1994). A structured psychoeducational intervention for cancer patients. *General Hospital Psychiatry, 16,* 149–192.

Fedoroff, J. P., Fishell, A., & Fedoroff, B. (1999). A case series of women evaluated for paraphilic sexual disorders. *Canadian Journal of Human Sexuality, 8,* 127–140.

Fedoroff, I. C., & Taylor, S. (2001). Psychological and pharmacological treatments for social phobia: A meta-analysis. *Journal of Clinical Psychopharmacology, 21,* 311–324.

Fenichel, O. (1945). *The psychoanalytic theory of neurosis.* New York: Norton.

Fernald, D. (1997). *Psychology.* Upper Saddle River, NJ: Prentice Hall.

Ferrans, C. E., Cohen, F. L., & Smith, K. M. (1992). The quality of life of persons with narcolepsy. *Loss, Grief and Care, 5,* 23–32.

Fiedorowicz, C. (1999). Neurobiological basis of learning

disabilities: An overview. Linking Research to Practice: Second Canadian Forum Proceedings Report, Canadian Child Care Federation Symposium (pp. 64–67). Ottawa: Canadian Child Care Federation.

Fiedorowicz, C., Benezra, E., MacDonald, W., McElgunn, B., & Wilson, A. (1999). Neurobiological Basis of Learning Disabilities. Ottawa: Learning Disabilities Association of Canada.

Fiedorowicz, C., Benezra, E., MacDonald, W., McElgunn, B., Wilson, A., & Kaplan, B. (2002). The neurobiological basis of learning disabilities: An update. *Learning Disabilities: A Multidisciplinary Focus, 11*(2), 61–73.

Fiez, J. A. (2001). Bridging the gap between neuroimaging and neuropsychology: Using working memory as a case-study . *Journal of Clinical & Experimental Neuropsychology, 23*(1), 19–31.

Finkelhor, D., Hotaling, G., Lewis, I. A., & Smith, C. (1990). Sexual abuse in a national survey of adult men and women: Prevalence, characteristics, and risk factors. *Child Abuse and Neglect, 14*, 19–28.

Finney, J. W. & Monahan, S. C. (1996). The cost-effectiveness of treatment for alcoholism: A second approximation. *Journal of Studies on Alcohol, 57*, 229–243.

Fischer, B. & Rehm, J. (2006). Illicit opioid use and treatment for opioid dependence: Challenges for Canada and beyond. *Canadian Journal of Psychiatry, 51*, 621–623.

Fisher, J. D., Fisher, W. A., Williams, S. S. & Malloy, T. E. (1994). Empirical tests of an information-motivation-behavioral skills model of AIDS-preventive behavior with gay men and heterosexual university students. *Health Psychology, 13*(3), 238–250.

Fisher, L. (1996). Bizarre right from Day 1. *Maclean's, 109*(28), 14.

Fitzgerald, P. B., Benitez, J., de Castella, A., Daskalakis, Z. J., Brown, T. L., & Kulkarni, J. (2006a). A randomized, controlled trial of sequential bilateral repetitive transcranial magnetic stimulation for treatment-resistant depression. *American Journal of Psychiatry, 163*(1), 88–94.

Fitzgerald, P. B., Huntsman, S., Gunewardene, R., Kulkarni, J., & Daskalakis, Z. J. (2006b). A randomized trial of low-frequency right-prefrontal-cortex Transcranial magnetic stimulation as augmentation in treatment-resistant major depression. *International Journal of Neuropsychopharmacology, 9*(6), 655–666.

Fitzgerald, P. B., Fountain, S., & Daskalakis, Z. J. (2006c).A comprehensive review of the effects of rTMS on motor cortical excitability and inhibition. Clinical Neurophysiology, 117 , 2584–2596.

Flanagan, J. M., Popendikyte, V., Pozdniakovaite, N., Sobolev, M., Assadzadeh, A., Schumacher, A. et al. (2006). Intra- and interindividual epigenetic variation in human germ cells. *American Journal of Human Genetics, 79*(1), 67–84.

Fleetham, J., Ayas, N., Bradley, D., Ferguson, K., Fitzpatrick, M., George, C. et al. (2006). Canadian Thoracic Society guidelines: Diagnosis and treatment of sleep disordered breathing in adults. *Canadian Respiratory Journal: Journal of the Canadian Thoracic Society, 13*(7), 387–392.

Flett, G. L. & Hewitt, P. L. (2002). *Perfectionism: Theory, research, and treatment.* Washington, DC: American Psychological Association.

Flint, J., Wilkie, A. O. M., Buckle, V. J., Winter, R. M., Holland, A. J., & McDermid, H. E. (1995). The detection of subtelomeric chromosomal rearrangements in idiopathic mental retardation. *Nature Genetics, 9*, 132–140.

Fogarty, F., Russell, J. M., Newman, S. C., & Bland, R. C. (1994). Mania. *Acta Psychiatrica Scandinavica, Suppl. 376*, 16–23.

Fombonne, E. (2005). Epidemiology of autistic disorder and other pervasive developmental disorders. *The Journal of Clinical Psychiatry, 66*(Supplement 10), 3–8.

Fombonne, E., Zakarian, R., Bennett, A., Meng, L., & McLean-Heywood, D. (2006). Pervasive developmental disorders in Montreal, Quebec, Canada: Prevalence and links with immunizations. *Pediatrics, 118*(1), 139–150.

Forehand, R., Brody, G., Slotkin, J., Fauber, R., McCombs, A., & Long, N. (1988). Young adolescent and maternal depression: Assessment, interrelations, and family predictors. *Journal of Consulting and Clinical Psychology, 56*, 422–426.

Foster, S. L. & Cone, J. D. (1986). Design and use of direct observation procedures. In A. R. Ciminiero, K. S. Calhoun, & H. E. Adams (Eds.), *Handbook of behavioral assessment* (2nd ed., pp. 253–324). New York: John Wiley & Sons.

Foubert, J. D. & Perry, B. C. (2007). Creating lasting attitude and behavior change in fraternity members and male student athletes: The qualitative impact of an emphathy-based rape prevention program. *Violence Against Women, 13*, 70–86.

Fowles, D. C. (1993). Electrodermal activity and antisocial behavior: Empirical findings and theoretical issues. In J. C. Roy et al. (Eds.), *Psychological theories of drinking and alcoholism* (pp. 181–226). New York: Guilford.

Fox, N. A., Nichols, K. E., Henderson, H. A., Rubin, K. Schmidt, L., Hamer, D. et al. (2005). Evidence for a gene-environment interaction in predicting behavioral inhibition in middle childhood. *Psychological Science, 16*, 921–926.

Fraga, M. F., Ballestar, E., Paz, M. F., Ropero, S., Setien, F., Ballestar, M. L. et al. (2005). Epigenetic differences arise during the lifetime of the monozygotic twins. *Proceedings of the National Academy of Sciences of the United States of America,102*(30), 10604–10609.

Frank, D., Perry, J. C., Kean, D., Sigman, M., & Geagea, K. (2005). Effects of compulsory treatment orders on time to hospital readmission. *Psychiatric Services, 56*, 867–869.

Franken, I. H. A., & Muris, P. (2006). BIS/BAS personality characteristics and college students' substance use. *Personality and Individual Differences, 40*(7), 1497–1503.

Frankenfield, G. (2000). Eating disorders more likely in diabetic girls. *WebMD*. Retrieved July 31, 2003, from http://my.webmd.com/content/Article/26/1728_58622.htm.

Fraser, F. (1994). The partnership of aboriginal and other cultural minorities in cultural development. *Canadian Journal of Communications, 19*(3/4).

Frauenglass, S., Routh, D. K., Pantin, H. M., & Mason, C. A. (1997). Family support decreases influence of deviant peers on Hispanic adolescents' substance use. *Journal of Clinical Child Psychology, 26*, 15–23.

Freedman, R., Adler, L. E., Gerhardt, G. A., Waldo, M., Baker, N., Rose, G. M. et al. (1987). Neurobiological studies of sensory gating in schizophrenia. *Schizophrenia Bulletin, 13*, 669–678.

Fregni, F., Marcolin, M. A., Myczkowski, M., Amiaz, R., Hasey, G., Rumi, D. O. et al. (2006). Predictors of antidepressant response in clinical trials of transcranial magnetic stimulation. *International Journal of Neuropsychopharmacology, 9*(6), 641–654.

Freud, S. (1957). Mourning and melancholia. In J. Rickman (Ed.), *A general selection from the works of Sigmund Freud.* Garden City, NY: Doubleday. (Original work published in 1917.)

Freud, S. (1959). Analysis of a phobia in a 5-year-old boy. In A. & J. Strachey (Ed. & Trans.), *Collected papers* (Vol. 3). New York: Basic Books. (Original work published in 1909.)

Freud, S. (1964). New introductory lectures. In *Standard edition of the complete psychological works of Sigmund Freud* (Vol. 22). London: Hogarth Press. (Original work published in 1933).

Freund, K. & Blanchard, R. (1986). The concept of courtship disorder. *Journal of Sex and Marital Therapy, 12*, 79–92.

Freund, K., Watson, R. J., & Dickey, R. (1991). The types of gender identity disorder. *Annals of Sex Research, 14*, 93–105.

Frick, P. J., Lahey, B. B., Loeber, R., & Stouthamer-Loeber, M. (1992). Familial risk factors to oppositional defiant disorder and conduct disorder: Parental psychopathology and maternal parenting. *Journal of Consulting and Clinical Psychology, 60*, 49–55.

Frick, P. J. & Silverthorn, P. (2001). Psychopathology in children and adolescents. In H. E. Adams (Ed.), *Comprehensive handbook of psychopathology* (3rd ed., pp. 879–919). New York: Plenum Press.

Friedlander. L. & Desrocher, M. (2006). Neuroimaging studies of obsessive-compulsive disorder in adults and children. *Clinical Psychology Review, 26*, 32–49.

Friedman, M. & Rosenman, R. H. (1974). *Type A behavior and your heart.* New York: Harper & Row.

Friedman, M. & Ulmer, D. (1984). *Treating type A behavior and your heart.* New York: Fawcett Crest.

Friedman, M., Thoresen, C. E., Gill, J. J., Ulmer, D., Powell, L. H., Price, V. A. et al. (1986). Alteration of type A behavior and its effect on cardiac recurrences in postmyocardial infarction patients: Summary results of the recurrent coronary prevention project. *American Heart Journal, 112*(4), 653–665.

Friedman, R. A. (2006). Violence and mental illness—How strong is the link? *New England Journal of Medicine, 355,* 2064–2066.

Fromm-Reichmann, F. (1948). Notes on the development of treatment of schizophrenics by psychoanalytic psychotherapy. *Psychiatry, 11,* 263–273.

Fromm-Reichmann, F. (1950). *Principles of intensive psychotherapy.* Chicago: University of Chicago Press.

Fronczek, R., van der Zande, W. L., van Dijk, J. G., Overeem, S., & Lammers, G. J. (2007). [Narcolepsy: A new perspective on diagnosis and treatment]. *[Dutch Journal of Medicine], 151*(15), 856–861.

Fuchs, C. S., Stampfer, M. J., Colditz, G. A., Giovannucci, E. L., Manson, J. E., Kawachi, I. et al. (1995). Alcohol consumption and mortality among women. *New England Journal of Medicine, 332,* 1245–1250.

Fulero, S. M. (1988). Tarasoff: 10 years later. *Professional Psychology: Research and Practice, 19,* 184–190.

Fumal, A., Coppola, G., Bohotin, V., Gerardy, P. Y., Seidel, L., Donneau, A. F. et al. (2006). Induction of long-lasting changes of visual cortex excitability by five daily sessions of repetitive transcranial magnetic stimulation (rTMS) in healthy volunteers and migraine patients. *Cephalalgia, 26*(2), 143–149.

G

Galea, S., Ahern, J., Resnick, H., Kilpatrick, D., Bucuvalas, M., Gold, J. et al. (2002). Psychological sequelae of the September 11 terrorist attacks in New York City. *New England Journal of Medicine, 346,* 982–987.

Galea, S., Nandi, A., & Vlahov, D. (2005). The epidemiology of post-traumatic stress disorder after disasters. *Epidemiologic Reviews, 27,* 78–91.

Garb, H. N. (1997). Race bias, social class bias, and gender bias in clinical judgment. *Clinical Psychology: Science and Practice, 4,* 99–120.

Garb, H.N. (2003). Incremental validity and the assessment of psychopathology in adults. *Psychological Assessments, 15*(4), 508–520.

Garber, J., Weiss, B., & Shanley, N. (1993). Cognitions, depressive symptoms, and development in adolescents. *Journal of Abnormal Psychology, 102,* 47–57.

Garbutt, J. C., West, S. L., Carey, T. S., Lohr, K. N., & Crews, F. T. (1999). Pharmacological treatment of alcohol dependence. *Journal of the American Medical Association, 281,* 1318–1325.

Gard, M. C. E. & Freeman, C. P. (1996). The dismantling of a myth: A review of eating disorders and socio-economic status. *International Journal of Eating Disorders, 20,* 1–12.

Garfield, S. L. (1994). Eclecticism and integration in psychotherapy: Development and issues. *Clinical Psychology: Science and Practice, 1,* 123–137.

Garfinkel, P. E. (2002). Eating Disorders. *Canadian Journal of Psychiatry, 47*(3), 225–226.

Garfinkel, P. E. & Dorian, B. J. (2000). Psychiatry in the new millennium. *Canadian Journal of Psychiatry, 45*(), 40–47.

Garfinkel, P. E., Moldofsky, H., & Garner, D. M. (1980). The heterogeneity of anorexia nervosa. *Archives of General Psychiatry, 37*(9), 1036–1040.

Garland, E. J. (2004). Facing the evidence: Antidepressant treatment in children and adolescents. *Canadian Medical Association Journal, 170,* 490–491.

Garland, E. J. & Garland, O. M. (2001). Correlation between anxiety and oppositionality in a children's mood and anxiety disorder clinic. *Canadian Journal of Psychiatry, 46*(10), 953–958.

Garner, D. M. (1993). Binge eating in anorexia nervosa. In C. G. Fairburn & G. T. Wilson (Eds.), *Binge eating: Nature, assessment, and treatment* (pp. 50–76). New York: Guilford.

Gatchel, R. J. (2001). Biofeedback and self-regulation of physio-logical activity: A major adjunctive treatment modality in health psychology. In A. Baum, T. A. Revenson, & J. E. Singer (Eds.), *Handbook of Health Psychology* (pp. 95–104). Mahwah, NJ: Erlbaum.

Gatehouse, J. (2002). The echoes of terror. *Maclean's, 115*(37), 18.

Gauthier, J. G. (1999). Bridging the gap between biological and psychological perspectives in the treatment of anxiety disorders. *Canadian Psychology, 40*(1), 1–11.

Gauthier, J. G., Ivers, H., & Carrier, S. (1996). Nonpharmacological approaches in the management of recurrent headache disorders and their comparison and combination with pharmacotherapy. *Clinical Psychology Review, 16,* 543–571.

Gawin, F. H. (1991). Cocaine addiction: Psychology and neurophysiology. *Science, 251,* 1581.

Gawin, F. H. & Ellinwood, E. H. (1989). Cocaine dependence. *Annual Review of Medicine, 40,* 149–161.

Gawin, F. H. et al. (1989). Desipramine facilitation of initial cocaine abstinence. *Archives of General Psychiatry, 46,* 117–121.

Gaziano, J. M., Buring, J. E., Breslow, J. L., Goldhaber, S. Z., Rosner, B., VanDenburgh, M. et al (1993). Moderate alcohol intake, increased levels of high-density lipoprotein and its subfractions, and decreased risk of myocardial infarction. *New England Journal of Medicine, 329,*1829–1834.

Geer, J., Heiman, J., & Leitenberg, H. (1984). *Human sexuality.* Englewood Cliffs, NJ: Prentice Hall.

Geist, R., Davis, R., & Heinmaa, M. (1998). Binge/purge symptoms and Comorbidity in adolescents with eating disorders. *Canadian Journal of Psychiatry, 43*(5), 507–512.

Geist, R., Heinmaa, M., Stephens, D., Davis, R., & Katzman, D. K. (2000). Comparison of family therapy and family group psychoeducation in adolescents with anorexia nervosa. *Canadian Journal of Psychiatry, 45*(2), 173–178.

Geringer, W. M., Marks, S., Allen, W. J., & Armstrong, K. A. (1993). Knowledge, attitudes, and behavior related to condom use and STDs in a high-risk population. *Journal of Sex Research, 30*(1), 75–83.

Gershuny, B. S. & Thayer, J. F. (1999). Relations among psychological trauma, dissociative phenomena, and trauma-related distress: A review and integration. *Clinical Psychology Review, 19,* 631–657.

Gettler, L. (2003, February 21). Psychopath in a suit. *The Age,* Retrieved July 21, 2003, from http://www.theage.com.au/articles/2003/02/20/1045638423969.html.

Gfellner, B. M. & Hundelby, J. D. (1990). Family and peer predictors of substance use among Aboriginal and non-Aboriginal adolescents. *Canadian Journal of Native Studies, 10,* 267–294.

Gfellner, B. M. & Hundelby, J. D. (1995). Patterns of drug use among native and white adolescents: 1990–1993. *Canadian Journal of Public Health, 86,* 95–97.

Gianoulakis, C. (2001). Influence of the endogenous opioid system on high alcohol consumption and genetic predisposition to alcoholism. *Journal of Psychiatry and Neuroscience, 26,* 304–318.

Gibbs, N. (1991, June 3). When is it rape? *Time,* pp. 48–54.

Gibbs, N. (1998, November 30). The age of Ritalin. *Time,* pp. 84–94.

Gidron, Y. & Davidson, K. (1996). Development and preliminary testing of a brief intervention for modifying CHD-predictive hostility components. *Journal of Behavioral Medicine, 19,* 203–220.

Gidron, Y., Davidson, K., & Bata, I. (1999). The short-term effects of a hostility-reduction intervention on male coronary heart disease patients. *Health Psychology, 18,* 416–420.

Gil, K. M., Williams, D. A., Keefe, F. J., & Beckham, J. C. (1990). The relationship of negative thoughts to pain and psychological distress. *Behavior Therapy, 21*(3), 349–362.

Gilbert, S. (1997, June 25). Social ties reduce risk of a cold. *The New York Times,* p. C11.

Gillberg, C., Melander, H., von Knorring, A. L. et al. (1997). Long-term stimulant treatment of children with attention-deficit hyperactivity disorder symptoms: A randomized, double-blind, placebo-controlled trial. *Archives of General Psychiatry, 54,* 857–864.

Gittelman-Klein, R., & Mannuzza, S. (1990). Hyperactive boys almost grown up. *Archives of General Psychiatry, 45*, 1131–1134.

Glancy, G. D. & Chaimowitz, G. (2003). Letter. *Journal of the American Academy of Psychiatry and the Law, 31*, 524–525.

Glaser, R., Kiecolt-Glaser, J. K., Speicher, C. E., & Holiday, J. E. (1985). Stress, loneliness, and changes in herpes virus latency. *Journal of Behavioral Medicine, 8*(3), 249–260.

Glaser, R., Rice, J., Sheridan, J., Fertel, R., Stout, J., Speicher, C. E., Pinsky, D., Kotur, M., Post, A., Beck, M., & Kiecolt-Glaser, J. K. (1987). Stress-related immune suppression: Health implications. *Brain, Behavior, and Immunity, 1*(1), 7–20.

Gleaves, D. H., Hernandez, E., & Warner, M. S. (2003). The etiology of dissociative identity disorder. *Professional Psychology: Research and Practice, 34*, 116–118.

Gliksman, L., Adlaf, E., Demers, A., Newton-Taylor, B., & Schmidt, K. (2000). *Canadian Campus Survey.* Toronto: CAMH.

Glynn, S. & Mueser, K. T. (1986). Social learning for chronic mental inpatients. *Schizophrenia Bulletin, 12*, 648–668.

Glynn, S. & Mueser, K. T. (1992). Social learning. In R. P. Liberman (Ed.), *Handbook of psychiatric rehabilitation* (pp. 127–152). New York: Macmillan.

Goeree, R., O'Brien, B. J., Goering, P., Blackhouse, G., Agro, K., Rhodes, A., & Watson, J. (1999). The economic burden of schizophrenia in Canada. *Canadian Journal of Psychiatry, 44*, 464–472.

Goering, P. N. & Morrell-Bellai, T. L. (1998). Pathways project: Integrating qualitative and quantitative findings in describing pathways to homelessness. In *Mental Illness and Pathways into Homelessness: Findings and Implications. Proceedings and Recommendations, from A Workshop of the Mental Health Policy Research Group.* Toronto: CMHA Ontario Division Clarke Institute of Psychiatry, Ontario Mental Health Foundation. Retrieved February 15, 2003, from http://www.camh.net/hsrcu/resources/proceedings/html_documents/pathways_proceedings.html.

Gold, J. H., Lalinec-Michaud, M., & Bernazzani, O. (1995). *Pioneers all: Women psychiatrists in Canada: A history.* Ottawa: Canadian Psychiatric Association.

Goldapple, K., Segal, Z., Garson, C., Lau, Mark, Bieling, P., Kennedy, S., & Mayberg, H. (2004). Modulation of cortical-limbic pathways in major depression. *Archives of General Psychiatry, 61*, 34–41.

Goldberg, T. E., Straub, R. E., Callicott, J. H., Hariri, A., Mattay, V. S., Bigelow, L. et al. (2006). The G72/G30 gene complex and cognitive abnormalities in schizophrenia. *Neuropsychopharmacology, 31*, 2022–2032.

Golden, A., Currie, W. H., Greaves, E., & Latimer, L. (1999). *Report of the Mayor's Homelessness Action Task Force: Taking Responsibility for Homelessness: An Action Plan for Toronto.* Toronto: City of Toronto.

Golden, C. J., Hammeke, T. A., & Purisch, A. D. (1980). *The Luria-Nebraska Neuropsychological Battery: Manual.* Los Angeles: Western Psychological Services.

Golden, R. N., Gaynes, B. N., Ekstrom, R. D., Hamer, R. M., Jacobsen, F. M., Suppes, T., et al. (2005). The efficacy of light therapy in the treatment of mood disorders: A review and meta-analysis of the evidence. *American Journal of Psychiatry, 162*, 656–662.

Goldfarb, L. A., Dykens, E. M., & Gerrard, M. (1985). The Goldfarb fear of fat scale. *Journal of Personality Assessment, 49*, 329–332.

Goldfield, G. S., Blouin, A. G., & Woodside, D. B. (2006). Body image, binge eating, and bulimia nervosa in male bodybuilders. *Canadian Journal of Psychiatry, 51*(3), 160–168.

Goldman, L. S., Genel, M., Bezman, R. J., & Slanetz, P. J. (1998). Diagnosis and treatment of attention-deficit/hyperactivity disorder in children and adolescents. *Journal of the American Medical Association, 279*, 1100–1107.

Goldman, S. & Windrem, M. (2006). Cell replacement therapy in neurological disease. *Philosophical Transactions of the Royal Society of London. Series B, Biological Sciences, 361*(1473), 1463–1475.

Goldman-Rakic, P. S. & Selemon, L. D. (1997). Functional and anatomical aspects of prefrontal pathology in schizophrenia. *Schizophrenia Bulletin, 23*, 437–458.

Goldstein, A. (1976). Opioid peptides (endorphins) in pituitary and brain. *Science, 193*, 1081–1086.

Goldstein, I., Lue, T. F., Padma-Nathan, H., Rosen, R. C., Steers, W. D., & Wicker, P. A. (1998). Oral sildenafil in the treatment of erectile dysfunction. *New England Journal of Medicine, 338*, 1397–1404.

Goleman, D. (1985, January 15). Pressure mounts for analysts to prove theory is scientific. *The New York Times*, p. C1.

Goleman, D. (1988, November 1). Narcissism looming larger as root of personality woes. *The New York Times*, pp. C1, C16.

Goleman, D. (1990, December 6). Women's depression is higher. *The New York Times.*

Goleman, D. (1993, December 7). Stress and isolation tied to a reduced life span. *The New York Times*, p. C5.

Goleman, D. (1994a, January 11). Childhood depression may herald adult ills. *The New York Times*, pp. C1, C10.

Goleman, D. (1995a, June 21). "Virtual reality" conquers fear of heights. *The New York Times*, p. C11.

Goleman, D. (1995b, October 4). Eating disorder rates surprise the experts. *The New York Times*, p. C11.

Gomez, A. & Gomez, R. (2002). Personality traits of the behavioural approach and inhibition systems: Associations with processing of emotional stimuli. *Personality and Individual Differences, 32*(8), 1299–1316.

Gomez, R. & Gomez, A. (2005). Convergent, discriminant and concurrent validities of measures of the behavioural approach and behavioural inhibition systems: Confirmatory factor analytic approach. *Personality and Individual Differences, 38*(1), 87–102.

Gomez-Schwartz, B., Horowitz, J., & Cardarelli, A. (1990). *Child sexual abuse: The initial effects.* Newbury Park, CA: Sage.

Goode, E. (1998, November 24). How much therapy is enough? It depends. *The New York Times*, p. F1.

Gordon, C. M. & Carey, M. P. (1996). Alcohol's effects on requisites for sexual risk reduction in men: An initial experimental investigation. *Health Psychology, 15*, 56–60.

Gorman, C. (1998, November 30). How does it work? *Time*, p. 92.

Gorman, J., Kent, J. M., Sullivan, G. M., & Coplan, J. D. (2000). Neuroanatomical hypothesis of panic disorder, revised. *American Journal of Psychiatry, 157*, 493–505.

Gotlib, I. H., Lewinsohn, P. M., Seeley, J. R., Rohde, P., & Redner, J. E. (1993). Negative cognitions and attributional style in depressed adolescents: An examination of stability and specificity. *Journal of Abnormal Psychology, 102*, 607–615.

Gottesman, I. I. (1991). *Schizophrenia genetics: The origins of madness.* New York: Freeman.

Gottesman, I. I., McGuffin, P., & Farmer, A. E. (1987). Clinical genetics as clues to the "real" genetics of schizophrenia. *Schizophrenia Bulletin, 13*, 23–47.

Gove, W. (1979). Sex differences in the epidemiology of mental disorder: Evidence and explanations. In E. Gomberg & V. Franks (Eds.), *Gender and disordered behavior.* New York: Brunner/Mazel.

Graber, B. (1993). Medical aspects of sexual arousal disorders. In W. O'Donohue & J. H. Geer (Eds.), *Handbook of sexual dysfunctions: Assessment and treatment* (pp. 103–156). Boston: Allyn & Bacon.

Graham, J. R. (1993). *MMPI-2: Assessing personality and psychopathology* (2nd ed.). New York: Oxford University Press.

Graham, J. R. (2000). *MMPI-2: Assessing personality and psychopathology.* New York: Oxford University Press.

Graham, J. R. & Strenger, V. E. (1988). MMPI characteristics of alcoholics: A review. *Journal of Consulting and Clinical Psychology, 56*, 197–205.

Grant, B. F., Hasin, D. S., Stinson, F. S., Dawson, D. A., Goldstein, R. B., Huang, B. et al. (2006). The epidemiology of DSM-IV panic disorder and agoraphobia in the United States: Results from the national epidemiologic survey on alcohol and related conditions. *Journal of Clinical Psychiatry, 67*, 363–374.

Gratzer, T. G. & Matas, M. (1994). The right to refuse treatment: Recent Canadian developments. *Bulletin of the*

American Academy of Psychiatry and Law, 22, 249–256.

Gravel, R., Connolly, D., & Bédard, M. (2004). *Canadian Community Health Survey: Mental Health and Wellbeing.* (Catalogue no. 82-617-XIE). Ottawa, ON: Statistics Canada. Retrieved November 12, 2006, from http://www.statcan.ca/bsolc/english/bsolc?catno=82-617-X.

Gray, J. A. (1970). The psychophysiological basis of introversion-extraversion. *Behaviour Research & Therapy, 8*(3), 249–266.

Gray, J. A. & McNaughton, N. (2000). *The neuropsychology of anxiety: An enquiry into the functions of the septo-hippocampal system.* (2nd ed.). Oxford: Oxford University Press.

Gray, J. E. & O'Reilly, R. L. (2005). Canadian compulsory community treatment laws: Recent reforms. *International Journal of Law and Psychiatry, 28,* 13–22.

Gray, J. R. & Braver, T.S. (2002). Personality predicts working-memory-related activation in the caudal anterior cingulate cortex. *Cognitive and Affective Behavioral Neuroscience, 2*(1), 64–75.

Gray, J. R., Burgess, G.C., Schaefer, A., Yarkoni, T., Larsen, R. J., & Braver, T. S. (2005). Affective personality differences in neural processing efficiency confirmed using fMRI. *Cognitive, Affective & Behavioral Neuroscience, 5*(2), 182–190.

Green, R. & Blanchard, R. (1995). Gender identity disorders. In H. I. Kaplan & B. J. Sadock (Eds.), *Comprehensive textbook of psychiatry* (pp. 1345–1360). Baltimore, MD: Williams & Wilkins.

Greenberg, D. M. & Bradford, J. M. W. (1997). Treatment of the paraphilic disorders: A review of the role of selective serotonin reuptake inhibitors. *Sexual Abuse: Journal of Research and Treatment, 9,* 349–360.

Greenberg, L. S. (2002a). *Emotion-focused therapy: Coaching clients to work through their feelings.* Washington, DC: American Psychological Association.

Greenberg, L. S. (2002b). Integrating an emotion-focused approach to treatment into psychotherapy integration. *Journal of Psychotherapy Integration, 12*(2), 154–189.

Greenberg, L. (2006). Emotion-Focused Therapy: A synopsis. *Journal of Contemporary Psychotherapy, 36*(2), 87–93.

Greenberg, L. S. & Safran, J. D. (1987). *Emotion in psychotherapy: Affect, cognition, and the process of change.* New York: Guilford Press.

Greenberg, R. P. & Bornstein, R. F. (1988a). The dependent personality: I. Risk for physical disorders. *Journal of Personality Disorders, 2,* 126–135.

Greenberg, R. P. & Bornstein, R. F. (1988b). The dependent personality: II. Risk for psychological disorders. *Journal of Personality Disorders, 2,* 136–143.

Greenberg, R. P., Bornstein, R. F., Greenberg, M. D., & Fisher, S. (1992). A meta-analysis of antidepressant outcome under "blinder" conditions. *Journal of Consulting and Clinical Psychology, 60,* 664–669.

Greenberg, R. P. et al. (1994). A meta-analysis of fluoxetine outcome in the treatment of depression. *Journal of Nervous and Mental Disease, 182,* 547–551.

Greenhill, L. L. (1998). Childhood attention deficit hyperactivity disorder: Pharmacological treatments. In P. E. Nathan & J. M. Gorman (Eds.), *A guide to treatments that work* (pp. 42–64). New York: Oxford University Press.

Greenland, C., Griffin, J. D., & Hoffman, B. F. (2001). Psychiatry in Canada from 1951 to 2001. In Q. Rae-Grant (Ed.), *Psychiatry in Canada: 50 years* (pp. 1–16). Ottawa: Canadian Psychiatric Association.

Greenspan, E. L. (Ed.) (1998). *Annotations at Section 16 of Martin's Criminal Code.* Ontario: Canada Law Book Inc.

Greeven, A., van Balkom, A. J. L. M., Visser, S. Merkelbach, J. W., van Rood, Y. R., van Dyck, R. et al. (2007). Cognitive behavior therapy and paroxetine in the treatment of hypochondriasis: A randomized controlled trial. *American Journal of Psychiatry, 164,* 91–99.

Griffin, J. D. (1993, December). A historical oversight. *Newsletter of the Ontario Psychiatric Association,* pp. 9–10.

Griffiths, M. (2005). Online therapy for addictive behaviors. *Cyberpsychology and Behavior, 8*(6), 555–561.

Grissett, N. I. & Norvell, N. K. (1992). Perceived social support, social skills and quality of relationships in bulimic women. *Journal of Consulting and Clinical Psychology, 60,* 293–299.

Gross, A. M., Winslett, A., Roberts, M., & Gohm, C. L. (2006). An examination of sexual violence against college women. *Violence Against Women, 12,* 288–300.

Grover, S., Mattoo, S. K., & Gupta, N. (2005). Theories on mechanism of action of electroconvulsive therapy. *German Journal of Psychiatry, 8,* 70–84.

Grunberg, N. E. (1991). Smoking cessation and weight gain. *New England Journal of Medicine, 324,* 768–769.

Guertin, T. L. (1999). Eating behavior of bulimics, self-identified binge eaters, and non-eating disordered individuals: What differentiates these populations? *Clinical Psychology Review, 19,* 1–24.

Gullette, E. C. D. et al. (1997). Effects of mental stress on myocardial ischemia during daily life. *Journal of the American Medical Association, 277,* 1521–1526.

Gunderson, J. G. (1996). The borderline patient's intolerance of aloneness: Insecure attachments and therapist availability. *American Journal of Psychiatry, 153,* 752–758.

Gunderson, J. G. (2001). *Borderline personality disorder: A clinical guide.* Washington, DC: American Psychiatric Press.

Gunderson, J. G. & Phillips, K. A. (1991). A current view of the interface between borderline personality disorder and depression. *American Journal of Psychiatry, 148,* 967–975.

Gur, R. E. & Pearlson, G. D. (1993). Neuoimaging in schizophrenia research. *Schizophrenia Bulletin, 19,* 337–353.

Gur, R. E., Cowell, P., Turetsky, B. I., Gallacher, F., Cannon, T., Bilker, W., & Gur, R. C. (1998). A follow-up magnetic resonance imaging study of schizophrenia: Relationship of neuroanatomical changes to clinical and neurobehavioral measures. *Archives of General Psychiatry, 55,* 145–152.

Guthrie, P. C., & Mobley, B. D. (1994). A comparison of the differential diagnosis efficiency of three personality disorder inventories. *Journal of Clinical Psychology, 50*(4), 656–665.

Guydish, J., Werdegar, D., Sorensen, J. L., Clark, W., & Acampora, A. (1998). Drug abuse day treatment: A randomized clinical trial comparing day and residential treatment programs. *Journal of Consulting and Clinical Psychology, 66,* 280–289.

H

Haber, S. N. & Fudge, J. L. (1997). The interface between dopamine neurons and the amygdala: Implications for schizophrenia. *Schizophrenia Bulletin, 23,* 471–482.

Haggarty, J., Cernovsky, Z., Kermeen, P., & Merskey, H. (2000). Psychiatric disorders in an Arctic community. *Canadian Journal of Psychiatry, 45,* 357–362.

Halbreich, U. (2005). Postpartum disorders: Multiple interacting underlying mechanisms and risk factors. *Journal of Affective Disorders, 88,* 1–7.

Halbreich, U. & Karkun, S. (2006). Cross-cultural and social diversity of prevalence of postpartum depression and depressive symptoms. *Journal of Affective Disorders, 91,* 97–111.

Hall, G. C. & Barongan, C. (1997). Prevention of sexual aggression: Sociocultural risk and protective factors. *American Psychologist, 52,* 5–14.

Hall, T. M. (2001). *Index of culture-bound syndromes: By culture.* Retrieved May 05, 2003, from http://weber.ucsd.edu/~thall/cbs_cul.html#US.

Hamid, S. (2000). Culture-specific syndromes: It's all relative. *Visions, 9* (Winter), 5–6.

Hammen, C. (2005). Stress and depression. *Annual Review of Clinical Psychology, 1,* 293–319.

Hammen, C. & Compas, B. E. (1994). Unmasking unmasked depression in children and adolescents: The problem of comorbidity. *Clinical Psychology Review, 14,* 585–603.

Hancock, L. (1996, March 18). Mother's little helper. *Newsweek,* pp. 51–56.

Hankin, B. L., Abramson, L. Y., Moffitt, T. E., Silva, P. A., McGee, R. et al. (1998). Development of depression from preadolescence to young adulthood: Emerging gender differences in a 10-year longitudinal study. *Journal of Abnormal Psychology, 107,* 128–140.

Hansen, T. E., Casey, D. E., & Hoffman, W. F. (1997). Neuroleptic intolerance. *Schizophrenia Bulletin, 23,* 567–582.

Happé, F., Ronald, A., & Plomin, R. (2006). Time to give up on a single explanation for autism. *Nature Neuroscience*, 9(10), 1218–1220.

Hare, R. D. (1965). Temporal gradient of fear arousal in psychopaths. *Journal of Abnormal Psychology*, 70, 442–445.

Hare, R. D. (1986). Criminal psychopaths. In J. C. Yuille (Ed.), *Polica selection and training: The role of psychology* (pp. 187–206). Dordrecht, Netherlands: Martinos Nijhoff.

Hare, R. D. (1996). Psychopathology and antisocial personality disorder: A case of diagnostic confusion. *Psychiatric Times*, 13(2), Retrieved July 16, 2003, from http://www.psychiatrictimes.com/p960239.html.

Hare, R. D. (1996). Psychopathy: A clinical construct whose time has come. *Criminal Justice and Behavior*, 23, 25–54.

Hare, R. D. (2003). *Hare Psychopathology Checklist—Revised (PCL—R™*, 2nd ed. Toronto: MHS.

Hare, R. D., Hart, S. D., & Harpur, T. J. (1991). Psychopathy and the DSM-IV criteria for antisocial personality disorder. *Journal of Abnormal Psychology*, 100, 391–398.

Hariri, A. R., Brown, S. M., & Tamminga, C. A. (2006). Images in neuroscience: Serotonin. *American Journal of Psychiatry*, 163, 12.

Harkness, K. L., Bruce, A. E., & Lumley, M. N. (2006). The role of childhood abuse and neglect in the sensitization to stressful life events in adolescent depression. *Journal of Abnormal Psychology*, 115, 730–741.

Harkness, K. L., Frank, E., Anderson, B., Houck, P. R., Luther, J., & Kupfer, D. J. (2002). Does interpersonal psychotherapy protect women from depression in the face of stressful life events? *Journal of Consulting and Clinical Psychology*, 70, 908–915.

Harpur, T. J. & Hare, R. D. (1994). Assessment of psychopathy as a function of age. *Journal of Abnormal Psychology*, 103, 604–609.

Harris, S., Davies, M. F., & Dryden, W. (2006). An experimental test of a core REBT hypothesis: evidence that irrational beliefs lead to physiological as well as psychological arousal. *Journal of Rational-Emotive & Cognitive-Behavior Therapy*, 24(2), 101–111.

Harrison, P. J. & Law, A. J. (2006). Neuregulin 1 and schizophrenia: Genetics, gene expression, and neurobiology. *Biological Psychiatry*, 60, 132–140.

Hart, S. D. & Hare, R. D. (1989). Discriminant validity of the Psychopathy Checklist in a forensic psychiatric population. *Psychological Assessment: A Journal of Consulting and Clinical Psychology*, 1, 211–218.

Hart, S. D. & Hare, R. D. (1997). Psychopathy: Assessment and association with criminal conduct. In D.M. Stoff, J. Breiling, & J. Maser (Eds.), *Handbook of antisocial behavior* (pp. 22–35). New York: John Wiley & Sons.

Hart, S. D., Cox, D. N., & Hare, R. D. (1995). *Manual for the Hare Psychopathy Checklist: Screening Version*. Toronto: Multi-Health Systems.

Hartung, C. M. & Widiger, T. A. (1998). Gender differences in the diagnosis of mental disorders: Conclusions and controversies of the DSM-IV. *Psychological Bulletin*, 123, 260–278.

Harvey, A. G. & Bryant, R. A. (2002). Acute stress disorder: A synthesis and critique. *Psychological Bulletin*, 128, 886–902.

Harvey, P. D., Lombardi, J., Leibman, M., Parrella, M., White, L., Powchik, P. et al. (1997). Age-related differences in formal thought disorder in chronically hospitalized schizophrenic patients: A cross-sectional study. *American Journal of Psychiatry*, 154, 205–210.

Haugh, J. A. (2006). Specificity and social problem-solving: Relation to depressive and anxious symptomatology. *Journal of Social and Clinical Psychology*, 25, 392–403.

Haughton, E. & Ayllon, T. (1965). Production and elimination of symptomatic behavior. In L. P. Ullmann & L. Krasner (Eds.), *Case studies in behavior modification*. New York: Holt, Rinehart and Winston.

Havassy, B. E., Hall, S. M., & Wasserman, D. A. (1991). Social support and relapse: Commonalities among alcoholics, opiate users, and cigarette smokers. *Addictive Behaviors*, 16, 235–246.

Hawaleshka, D. (2002, October 21). New national survey data shows that many health problems are getting worse. *Maclean's*.

Hawkrigg, J. J. (1975). Agoraphobia. *Nursing Times*, 71, 1280–1282.

Hawton, K. (1991). Sex therapy. Special issue: The changing face in behavioral psychotherapy. *Behavioral Psychotherapy*, 19, 131–136.

Hawton, K. & Catalan, J. (1990). Sex therapy for vaginismus: Characteristics of couples and treatment outcomes. *Sexual and Marital Therapy*, 5, 39–48.

Hayes, R. D., Bennett, C. M., Fairley, C. K., & Dennerstein, L. (2006). What can prevalence studies tell us about female sexual difficulty and dysfunction? *Journal of Sexual Medicine*, 3, 589–595.

Health & Welfare Canada. (1988). *Mental health for Canadians: Striking a balance* (Cat. H39-128/1988E). Ottawa, Ontario: Minister of Supply and Service Canada.

Health Canada (1995). *Canada's alcohol and other drugs survey* (Catalogue No. H39-338/1995E). Ottawa: Author. Retrieved August 3, 2003, from http://www.hc-sc.gc.ca/hecs-sesc/cds/pdf/aods_e.pdf.

Health Canada (1999a). *Toward a healthy future: Second report on the health of Canadians* (Cat H39-468/1999E). Ottawa: Minister of Public Works and Government Services Canada. Retrieved April 12, 2003 from http://www.hc-sc.gc.ca/hppb/phdd/report/toward/pdf/english/toward_a_healthy_english.PDF.

Health Canada (1999b). *Measuring up. A health surveillance update on Canadian children and youth. Suicide*. Ottawa: Author, Retrieved October 18, 2003, from http://www.hc-sc.gc.ca/pphb-dgspsp/publicat/meas-haut/mu_y_e.html.

Health Canada (2000a). *Canada's physical activity guide to healthy active living*. Retrieved May 21, 2003, from http://www.hc-sc.gc.ca/hppb/paguide/pdf/guideEng.pdf.

Health Canada (2000b). *Straight facts about drugs & drug abuse* (Catalogue No. H39-65/2000E). Ottawa: Author. Retrieved August 3, 2003, from http://www.hc-sc.gc.ca/hecs-sesc/cds/pdf/straight_facts.pdf.

Health Canada (2001a). *Canadian Tobacco Use Monitoring Survey*. Retrieved March 18, 2003, from http://www.hc-sc.gc.ca/hecs-sesc/tobacco/research/ctums/2001/2001overview.html.

Health Canada (2001b, June 26). *Centres of Excellence for Children's Well Being*. Retrieved April 26, 2003, from http://www.hc-sc.gc.ca/hppb/childhood-youth/centres/index2.html.

Health Canada (2002a). *A Report on Mental Illnesses in Canada* (Catalogue No. 0-662-32817-5). Ottawa: Health Canada Editorial Board Mental Illnesses in Canada. Retrieved January 31, 2003, from http://www.hc-sc.gc.ca/pphb-dgspsp/publicat/miic-mmac/pdf/men_ill_e.pdf.

Health Canada (2002b). *Canada's food guide to healthy eating*. Retrieved May 21, 2003, from http://www.hc-sc.gc.ca/hpfb-dgpsa/onpp-bppn/food_guide_rainbow_e.html.

Health Canada (2002c). *Aboriginal Head Start in Urban and Northern Communities*. Ottawa: Author. Retrieved October 18, 2003, from http://www.hc-sc.gc.ca/dca-dea/programs-mes/ahs_overview_e.html#top.

Health Canada (2003a). *Heart/cardiovascular disease*. Retrieved May 17, 2003, from http://www.hc-sc.gc.ca/english/diseases/heart.html.

Health Canada (2003b). *Deaths in Canada due to smoking*. Retrieved May 20, 2003, from http://www.hc-sc.gc.ca/english/media/releases/1996/deathe.htm.

Health Canada (2003c). *Canada's report on HIV/AIDS 2002. Lessons learned: Reframing the response*. Retrieved May 17, 2003, from http://www.hc-sc.gc.ca/hppb/hiv_aids/report02/sec1.html#epidemic.

Health Canada. (2006a). Advisory. *New cautions regarding rare heart-related risks for all ADHD drugs*. Ottawa, ON: Author. Retrieved on April 29, 2007, from: http://www.hc-sc.gc.ca/ahc-asc/media/-advisories-avis/2006/2006_35_e.html.

Health Canada. (2006b). *New information regarding uncommon psychiatric adverse events for all ADHD Drugs*. Ottawa, ON: Author. Retrieved on April 29, 2007, from http://www.hc-sc.gc.ca/ahc-asc/media/advisories-avis/2006/2006_91_e.html.

Health Canada. (2006c). *The human face of mental health and mental illness in Canada*.

Ottawa: Minister of Public Works and Government Services.

Health Reports (1999). How healthy are Canadians? A special issue (Catalogue No. 82-003-XPB). *Statistics Canada, 11*(3), 25–34.

Health Reports (2002). How healthy are Canadians? 2002 Annual Report (Catalogue No. 82-003-SPE). *Health Reports, 13*(Supplement), 73–88.

HealthyOntario.com (2003). *Eating disorders: The facts.* Retrieved July 31, 2003, from http://www.healthyontario.com/english/printVersion.asp?which=features&text_id=91&channel_id=0.

Healy, D. (2002). *The creation of psychopharmacology.* Cambridge, MA: Harvard University Press.

Heart and Stroke Foundation of Canada (2003a). *General Info—Incidence of Cardiovascular Disease.* Retrieved May 17, 2003, from http://ww1.heartandstroke.bc.ca.

Heart and Stroke Foundation of Canada (2003b). *Risk factors: Coronary heart disease risk factors.* Retrieved May 20, 2003, from http://ww1.heartandstroke.bc.ca/Page.asp?.

Heatherton, T. F., Mahamedi, F., Striepe, M., Field, A. E., & Keel, P. (1997). A 10-year longitudinal study of body weight, dieting, and eating disorder symptoms. *Journal of Abnormal Psychology, 106*(1), 117–125.

Hebb, D. O. (1949, 2002). *The organization of behavior: A neuropsychological theory.* Mahwah, New Jersey: Lawrence Erlbaum Associates. (Original work published 1949.)

Heckman, T. G., Anderson, E. S., Sikkema, K. J., Kochman, A., Kalichman, S. C., & Anderson, T. (2004). Emotional distress in nonmetropolitan persons living with HIV disease enrolled in a telephone-delivered, coping improvement group intervention. *Health Psychology, 23*(1), 94–100.

Hector, I. (2001). Changing funding patterns and the effect on mental health care in Canada. In Q. Rae-Grant (Ed.), *Psychiatry in Canada: 50 years* (pp. 59–75). Ottawa: Canadian Psychiatric Association.

Heidrich, S. M., Forsthoff, C. A., & Ward, S. E. (1994). Psychological adjustment in

adults with cancer: The self as mediator. *Health Psychology, 13,* 346–353.

Heiman, J. R. & LoPiccolo, J. (1987). *Becoming orgasmic* (2nd ed.). Englewood Cliffs, NJ: Prentice Hall.

Heinrichs, R. W. (2001). *In search of madness: Schizophrenia and neuroscience.* London: Oxford University Press.

Heinrichs, R. W. (2005). The primacy of cognition in schizophrenia. *American Psychologist, 60,* 229–242.

Hellstrom, W. J. G., Nehra, A., Shabsigh, R., & Sharlip, I. D. (2006). Premature ejaculation: The most common male sexual dysfunction. *Journal of Sexual Medicine, 3* (Suppl. 11), 1–3.

Henggeler, S. W., Rodick, D., Borduin, C. M., Hanson, C., Watson, S., & Urey, J. (1986). Multisystemic treatment of juvenile offenders: Effects on adolescent behavior and family interaction. *Developmental Psychology, 22,* 132–141.

Henggeler, S. W., Melton, G. B., Brondino, M. J., Scherer, D. G., & Hanley, J. H. (1997). Multisystemic therapy with violent and chronic juvenile offenders and their families: The role of treatment fidelity in successful dissemination. *Journal of Consulting and Clinical Psychology, 65*(5), 821–833.

Henggeler, S. W., Melton, G. B., & Smith, L. A. (1992). Family preservation using multisystemic therapy: An effective alternative to incarcerating serious juvenile offenders. *Journal of Consulting and Clinical Psychology, 60,* 953–961.

Herbert, J. D., Hope, D. A., & Bellack, A. S. (1992). Validity of the distinction between generalized social phobia and avoidant personality disorder. *Journal of Abnormal Psychology, 101,* 332–339.

Hercz, R. (2001, September 8). Psychopaths among us. *Saturday Night, 116*(4).

Herkov, M. J., Gynther, M. D., Thomas, S., & Myers, W. C. (1996). MMPI differences among adolescent inpatients, rapists, sodomists, and sexual abusers. *Journal of Personality Assessment, 66,* 81–90.

Hertz, M. R. (1986). Rorschach bound: A 50-year memoir. *Journal of Personality Assessment, 50,* 396–416.

Herzog, W., Schellberg, D., & Deter, H. C. (1997). First

recovery in anorexia nervosa patients in the long-term course: A discrete-time survival analysis. *Journal of Consulting and Clinical Psychology, 65,* 169–177.

Hilchey, T. (1994, November 11). High anxiety raises risk of heart failure in men, study finds. *The New York Times,* p. A17.

Hill, A. L. (1987). Idiot savants: The rate of incidence. *Perceptual and Motor Skills, 44,* 161–162.

Hiller, W., Rief, W., & Brähler, E. (2006). Somatization in the population: From mild bodily misperceptions to disabling symptoms. *Social Psychiatry and Psychiatric Epidemiology, 41,* 704–712.

Hiltunen, M. O., Turunen, M. P., Hakkinen, T. P., Rutanen, J. H., Makinen, M., Turunen, A. et al. (2002). DNA hypomethylation and methyltransferase expression in atherosclerotic lesions. Vascular Medicine, 7(1), 5–11.

Hinshaw, S. P. (1992). Academic underachievement, attention deficits, and aggression: Comorbidity and implications for intervention. *Journal of Consulting and Clinical Psychology, 60,* 893–903.

Hochhausen, N. M., Lorenz, A. R., & Newman, J. P. (2002). Specifying the impulsivity of female inmates with borderline personality disorder. *Journal of Abnormal Psychology, 111*(3), 495–501.

Hodgins, D. (2006). Can patients with alcohol use disorders return to social drinking? Yes, so what should we do about it? *Canadian Journal of Psychiatry, 50,* 264–265.

Hofmann, S. G., Newman, M. G., Ehlers, A., & Roth, W. T. (1995). Psychophysiological differences between subgroups of social phobia. *Journal of Abnormal Psychology, 104*(1), 224–231.

Hoffman, W. & Prior, M. (1982). Neuropsychological dimensions of autism in children: A test of the hemispheric dysfunction hypothesis. *Journal of Clinical Neuropsychology, 4,* 27–42.

Hogan, E. P. & Barlow, C. A. (2000). Delivering counsellor training to First Nations: Emerging issues. *Canadian Journal of Counselling, 34*(1), 55–67.

Hogarty, G. E. (1993). Prevention of relapse in chronic schizo-

phrenic patients. *Journal of Clinical Psychiatry, 54 (Suppl.),* 18–23.

Hogg, R. S. et al. (1998). Improved survival among HIV-infected individuals following initiation of antiretroviral therapy. *Journal of the American Medical Association, 279,* 450–454.

Holahan, C. J., Moos, R. H., Holahan, C. K., & Brennan, P. L. (1995). Social support, coping, and depressive symptoms in a late-middle-aged sample of patients reporting cardiac illness. *Health Psychology, 14*(2), 152–163.

Holbrook, A. M., Crowther, R., Lotter, A., Cheng, C., & King, D. (2000). The diagnosis and management of insomnia in clinical practice: A practical evidence-based approach. *Canadian Medical Association Journal, 162*(2), 216–220.

Holland, A. J., Sicotte, N., & Treasure, J. (1988). Anorexia nervosa: Evidence of a genetic basis. *Journal of Psychosomatic Research, 32,* 561–571.

Hollon, S. D. (2006). Cognitive therapy in the treatment and prevention of depression. In T. E. Joiner, J. S. Brown, & J. Kistner (Eds.), *The interpersonal, cognitive, and social nature of depression* (pp. 133–151). Mahwah, NJ: Erlbaum.

Hollon, S. D. & Kendall, P. C. (1980). Cognitive self-statements in depression: Development of an automatic thoughts questionnaire. *Cognitive Therapy and Research, 4,* 383–395.

Hollon, S. D. & Shelton, R. C. (2001). Treatment guidelines for major depressive disorder. *Behavior Therapy, 32,* 235–258.

Holmes, E. A., Brown, R. J., Mansell, W., Fearon, R. P., Hunter, E. C. M., Frasquilho, F. et al. (2005). Are there two qualitatively distinct forms of dissociation? A review and some clinical implications. *Clinical Psychology Review, 25,* 1–23.

Holt, C. S., Heimberg, R. G., & Hope, D. A. (1992). Avoidant personality disorder and the generalized subtype of social phobia. *Journal of Abnormal Psychology, 101,* 318–325.

Holroyd, K. A. (2002). Assessment and Psychological Management of Recurrent Headache Disorders. *Journal of Consulting and Clinical Psychology, 70*(3), 656–677.

Honig, A., Romme, M., Ensink, B., Escher, S., Pennings, M., & Devries, M. W. (1998). Auditory hallucinations: A comparison between patients and non- patients. *Journal of Nervous and Mental Disease, 186*(10), 646–651.

Hopko, D. R., Lejuez, C. W., Ruggiero, K. J., & Eifert, G. H. (2003). Contemporary behavioral activation treatments for depression: Procedures, principles and progress. *Clinical Psychology Review, 23,* 699–717.

Hops, H. & Lewinsohn, P. M. (1995). A course for the treatment of depression among adolescents. In K. D. Craig & K. S. Dobson (Eds.), *Anxiety and depression in adults and children* (pp. 230–245). Thousand Oaks, CA: Sage.

Horne, L. R., Van Vactor, J. C., & Emerson, S. (1991). Disturbed body image in patients with eating disorders. *American Journal of Psychiatry, 148,* 211–215.

Hospital for Sick Children (2003, February 6). *Infant mental health promotion project (IMP).* Retrieved April 27, 2003, from http://www.sickkids.on.ca/imp.

House, J. S., Robbins, C., & Metzner, H. L. (1982). The association of social relationships and activities with mortality: Prospective evidence from the Tecumseh Community Health Study. *American Journal of Epidemiology, 116,* 123–140.

Howard, C. E. & Porzelius, L. K. (1999). The role of dieting in binge eating disorder: Etiology and treatment implications. *Clinical Psychology Review, 19,* 25–44.

Howard, K. I., Kopta, S. M., Krause, M. S., & Orlinksy, D. E. (1986). The dose-effect relationship in psychotherapy. *American Psychologist, 41,* 159–164.

Huang, W., & Cuvo, A. J. (1997). Social skills training for adults with mental retardatoin in job-related settings. *Behavior Modification, 21,* 3–44.

Huber, K. M., Gallagher, S. M., Warren, S. T., & Bear, M. F. (2002). Altered synaptic plasticity in a mouse model of fragile X mental retardation. *Proceedings of the National Academy of Sciences of the United States of America, 99*(11), 7746–7750.

Hublin, C., Kaprio, J., Partinen, M., Heikkila, K., & Koskenvuo, M. (1997). Prevalence and genetics of sleepwalking: A population-based twin study. *Neurology, 48*(1), 177–181.

Hucker, S. J. (1985). Self-harmful sexual behavior. *Psychiatric Clinics of North America, 8,* 323–328.

Hucker, S. J. (1997). Sexual sadism: Theory and psychopathology. In D. R. Laws & W. T. O'Donohue (Eds.), *Handbook of sexual deviance: Theory and application.* New York: Guilford.

Hudson, J. I., McElroy, S. L., Raymond, N. C., Crow, S., Keck, P. E., Jr, Carter, W. P. et al. (1998). Fluvoxamine in the treatment of binge-eating disorder: A multicenter placebo-controlled, double-blind trial. *American Journal of Psychiatry, 155*(12), 1756–1762.

Hudson, J. I., Hiripi, E., Pope, H. G., Jr., & Kessler, R. C. (2007). The prevalence and correlates of eating disorders in the national comorbidity survey replication. *Biological Psychiatry, 61*(3), 348–358.

Hudziak, J. J., Boffeli, T. J., Kreisman, J. J., Battaglia, M. M., Stanger, C., & Guze, S. B. (1996). Clinical study of the relation of borderline personality disorder to Briquet's syndrome (hysteria), somatization disorder, antisocial personality disorder, and substance abuse disorders. *American Journal of Psychiatry, 153*(12), 1598–1606.

Huffman, J. C. & Stern, T. A. (2003). The diagnosis and treatment of Munchausen's syndrome. *General Hospital Psychiatry, 25,* 358–363.

Humphrey, L. L. (1986). Family dynamics in bulimia. In S. C. Feinstein et al. (Eds.), *Adolescent psychiatry.* Chicago: University of Chicago Press.

Hunsley, J. & Bailey, J. M. (1999). The clinical utility of the Rorschach: Unfulfilled promises and an uncertain future. *Psychological Assessment, 11,* 266–277.

Hunter, E. C. M., Baker, D., Phillips, M. L., Sierra, M., & David, A. S. (2005). Cognitive-behaviour therapy for depersonalization disorder: An open study. *Behaviour Research and Therapy, 43,* 1121–1130.

Hunter, R. H., Bedell, J. R., & Corrigan, P. W. (1997). Current approaches to assessment and treatment of persons with serious mental illness. *Professional Psychology: Research & Practice, 28,* 217–228.

Hur, Y.-M., (2007). Stability of genetic influence on morningness-eveningness: A cross-sectional examination of South Korean twins from preadolescence to young adulthood. *Journal of Sleep Research, 16*(1), 17–23.

Hurd, H M., Drewry, W. F., Dewey, R., Pilgrim, C. W., Blumer, G. A., & Burgess, T. J. W. (1916). *The institutional care of the insane in the United States and Canada.* Baltimore, MD: Johns Hopkins Hospital Press.

Hurt, R. D., Sachs, D. P., Glover, E. D., Offord, K. P., Johnston, J. A., Dale, L. C. et al. (1997). A comparison of sustained-release bupropion and placebo for smoking cessation. *New England Journal of Medicine, 337,* 1195–1202.

Hurt, R. D., Dale, L. C., Croghan, G. A., Croghan, I. T., Gomez-Dahl, L. C., & Offord, K. P. (1998). Nicotine nasal spray for smoking cessation. *Mayo Clinic Proceedings, 73,* 118–125.

Hwang, S. W. (2001). Homelessness and health. *Canadian Medical Association Journal, 164*(2), 229–233.

I

Indian and Northern Affairs Canada (2003). Statement by Mr. Keith Conn delegation of Canada to the second session of the UN permanent forum on indigenous issues on agenda item: Health. Ottawa: Author. Retrieved October 18, 2003, from http://www.ainc-inac.gc.ca/nr/spch/unp/hea_e.html.

Ingraham, L. J., Kugelmass, S., Frenkel, E. et al. (1995). Twenty-five year follow-up of the Israeli high-risk study: Current and lifetime psychopathology. *Schizophrenia Bulletin, 21,* 183–192.

Ingram, R. E. (1990). Self-focused attention in clinical disorders: Review and a conceptual model. *Psychological Bulletin, 107,* 156–176.

Ingram, R. E. (1991). Tilting at windmills: A response to Pyszczynski, Greenberg, Hamilton, and Nix. *Psychological Bulletin, 110,* 544–550.

Institute of Medicine. (1990). *Broadening the base of treatment for alcohol problems.* Washington, DC: National Academy Press.

Integration of cognitive, behavioral, and systemic therapy. In S. Leiblum & R. Rosen (Eds.), *Sexual desire disorders.* New York: Guilford.

International Society for Existential Psychology and Psychotherapy (ISEPP). (2006). Retrieved January 2, 2007, from http://www.existentialpsychology.org.

Irle, E. et al. (1998). Obsessive-compulsive disorder and ventromedial frontal sessions: Clinical and neuropsychological findings. *American Journal of Psychiatry, 155,* 255–263.

Ironson, G., Wynings, C., Schneiderman, N., Baum, A., Rodriguez, M., Greenwood, D., Benight, C., Antoni, M., LaPerriere, A., Huang, H. S., Klimas, N., & Fletcher, M. A. (1997). Posttraumatic stress symptoms, intrusive thoughts, loss, and immune function after Hurricane Andrew. *Psychosomatic Medicine, 59*(2), 128–141.

Isaac, M. & Chand, P. K. (2006). Dissociative and conversion disorders: Defining boundaries. *Current Opinion in Psychiatry, 19,* 61–66.

J

Jablensky, A. (2006). Subtyping schizophrenia: Implications for genetic research. *Molecular Psychiatry, 11,* 815–836.

Jablensky, A., Sartorius, N., Ernberg, G., Anker, M. et al. (1992). Schizophrenia: Manifestations, incidence and course in different cultures: A World Health Organization ten-country study. *Psychological Medicine, 20* (Monograph Suppl.), 1–97.

Jackson, J., Calhoun, K. S., Amick, A. E., Maddever, H. M., & Habif, V. L. (1990). Young adult women who report childhood intrafamilial sexual abuse: Subsequent adjustment. *Archives of Sexual Behavior, 19,* 211–221.

Jacobi, C., Hayward, C., de Zwaan, M., Kraemer, H. C., & Agras, W.S. (2004). Coming to terms with risk factors for eating disorders: Application of risk terminology and suggestions for a general taxonomy. *Psychological Bulletin, 130*(1), 19–65.

Jacobsen, L. K., Frazier, J. A., Malhotra, A. K., Karoum, F., McKenna, K., Gordon, C. T., Hamburger et al. (1997). Cerebrospinal fluid monoamine metabolites in childhood-onset schizophrenia. *American Journal of Psychiatry, 154,* 69–74.

Jacobson, N. S. & Hollon, S. D. (1996). Cognitive-behavior therapy versus pharmacotherapy: Now that the jury's returned its verdict, it's time to present the rest of the evidence. *Journal of Consulting and Clinical Psychology, 64,* 74–80.

Jacobson, N. S., Dobson, K. S., Truax, P. A., Addis, M. E., Koerner, K., Gollan, J. K. et al. (1996). A component analysis of cognitive-behavioral treatment for depression. *Journal of Consulting and Clinical Psychology, 64,* 295–304.

Jaenisch, R., & Bird, A. (2003). Epigenetic regulation of gene expression: how the genome integrates intrinsic and environmental signals. *Nature Genetics 33*(3), 245–254.

Janca, A. (2005). Rethinking somatoform disorders. *Current Opinion in Psychiatry, 18,* 65–71.

Janeck, A. S., Calamari, J. E., Riemann, B. C., & Heffelfinger, S. K. (2003). Too much thinking about thinking? Metacognitive differences in obsessive-compulsive disorder. *Journal of Anxiety Disorders, 17,* 181–195.

Jang, K. L. (2005). *The behavioral genetics of psychopathology.* Mahwah, NJ: Erlbaum.

Jang, K. L., Livesley, W. J., Taylor, S., Stein, M. B., & Moon, E. C. (2004). Heritability of individual depressive symptoms. *Journal of Affective Disorders, 80,* 125–133.

Jang, K. L., Stein, M. B., Taylor, S., Asmundson, G. J. G., & Livesley, W. J. (2003). Exposure to traumatic events and experiences: Aetiological relationships with personality function. *Psychiatry Research, 120,* 61–69.

Jang, K. L., Stein, M. B., Taylor, S., & Livesley, W. J. (1999). Gender differences in the etiology of anxiety sensitivity: A twin study. *Journal of Gender Specific Medicine, 2,* 39–44.

Jang, K. L., Livesley, W. J., & Vernon, P. A. (1997). Gender-specific etiological differences in alcohol and drug problems: A behavioural genetic analysis. *Addiction, 92,* 1265–1276.

Jang, K. L., Livesley, W. J., & Vernon, P. A. (2002). The etiology of personality function: the University of British Colombia Twin Project. *Twin Research, 5*(5), 342–346.

Jang, K. L., Vernon, P. A., & Livesley, W. J. (2001). Behav-

ioural-genetic perspectives on personality function. *Canadian Journal of Psychiatry, 46*(3), 234–244.

Januzzi, J. L. & DeSantis, R. W. (1999). Looking into the brain to save the heart. Cerebrum, 1(1), 31–43.

Jellinek, E. M. (1960). *The disease concept of alcoholism.* New Haven, CT: College and University Press.

Jemmott, J. B., Borysenko, J. Z., Borysenko, M., McClealland, D. C., Chapman, R., Meyer, D., & Benson, H. (1983, June 25). Academic stress, power motivation, and decrease in secretion rate of salivary secretory immunoglobin A. *Lancet,* 1400–1402.

Jenkins, C. D. (1988). Epidemiology of cardiovascular diseases. *Journal of Consulting and Clinical Psychology, 56,* 324–332.

Jensen, P. S., Martin, D., & Cantwell, D. P. (1997). Comorbidity in ADHD: Implications for research practice, and DSM-V. *Journal of the American Academy of Child and Adolescent Psychiatry, 36,* 1065–1079.

Jeste, D. V. & Caligiuri, M. P. (1993). Tardive dyskinesia. *Schizophrenia Bulletin, 19,* 303–315.

Jian, W. et al. (1996). Mental stress-induced myocardial ischemia and cardiac events. *Journal of the American Medical Association, 275,* 1651–1656.

Jilek, W. G. (2001). *Anorexia nervosa: Cultural factors in psychiatric disorders.* Paper presented at the 26th Congress of the World Federation for Mental Health, July, 2001. Retrieved July 31, 2003, from http://www.mentalhealth.com/mag1/wolfgangex.html.

Jirtle, R. L. & Skinner, M. K. (2007). Environmental epigenomics and disease susceptibility. *Nature reviews. Genetics, 8*(4):253–262.

Joffe, R. T. & Gardner, D. M. (2000). *The Canadian psychotropic handbook.* Mississauga, ON: Sudler & Hennessey.

Johns, L. C., Gregg, L., Allen, P., & McGuire, P. K. (2006). Impaired verbal self-monitoring in psychosis: Effects of state, trait and diagnosis. *Psychological Medicine, 36,* 465–474.

Johnson, J. G. & Bornstein, R. F. (1991). Does daily stress inde-

pendently predict psychopathology? *Journal of Social and Clinical Psychology, 10*(1), 58–74.

Johnson, J. G. & Sherman, M. F. (1997). Daily hassles mediate the relationship between major life events and psychiatric symptomatology. *Journal of Social & Clinical Psychology, 16*(4), 389–404.

Johnson, J. G., Cohen, P., Brown, J., Smailes, E. M., & Bernstein, D. P. (1999). Childhood maltreatment increases risk for personality disorders during early adulthood. *Archives of General Psychiatry, 56*(7), 600–606.

Johnson, J. G., Cohen, P., Dohrenwend, B. P., Link, B. G., & Brook, J. S. (1999). A longitudinal investigation of social causation and social selection processes involved in the association between socioeconomic status and psychiatric disorders. *Journal of Abnormal Psychology, 108*(3), 490–499.

Johnson, P. A. (1989). *Wellness Behaviour Specialist Program Proposal for the Ontario Ministry of Colleges and Universities.* Unpublished manuscript, Confederation College, Thunder Bay, ON.

Johnson, W. G., Tsoh, J. Y., & Varnado, P. J. (1996). Eating disorders: Efficacy of pharmacological and psychological interventions. *Clinical Psychology Review, 16,* 457–478.

Joiner, T. E. (2006). *Why people die by suicide.* Cambridge, MA: Harvard University Press.

Joiner, T. E., Brown, J. S., & Wingate, L. R. (2005). The psychology and neurobiology of suicidal behavior. *Annual Review of Psychology, 56,* 287–314.

Joiner, T. E. et al. (1997). The modified scale for suicidal ideation: Factors of suicidality and their relation to clinical and diagnostic variables. *Journal of Abnormal Psychology, 106,* 260–265.

Jones, E. (1953). *The life and work of Sigmund Freud.* New York: Basic Books.

Jones, H. E. (2006). Drug addiction during pregnancy. *Current Directions in Psychological Science, 15,* 126–130.

Jones, J. M., Bennett, S., Olmsted, M. P., Lawson, M. L., & Rodin, G. (2001). Disordered eating attitudes and behaviours

in teenaged girls: A school-based study. *Canadian Medical Association Journal, 165*(5), 547–552.

Jones, P. B., Rantakallio, P., Hartikainen, A-L, Isohanni, M. & Sipila, P. (1998). Schizophrenia as a long-term outcome of pregnancy, delivery, and perinatal complications: A 28-year follow-up of the 1966 North Finland general population birth cohort. *American Journal of Psychiatry, 155,* 355–364.

Jorm, A. F., Kelly, C. M., Wright, A., Parslow, R. A., Harris, M. G., & McGorry, P. D. (2006). Belief in dealing with depression alone: Results from community surveys of adolescents and adults. *Journal of Affective Disorders, 96,* 59–65.

Jouriles, E. N., Mehta, P., McDonald, R., Francis, D. J. (1997). Psychometric properties of family members' reports of parental physical aggression toward clinic-referred children. *Journal of Consulting and Clinical Psychology, 65,* 309–318.

K

Kaback, M., Lim-Steele, J., Dabholkar, D., Brown, D., Levy, N., & Zeiger, K., (1993). Tay-Sachs disease: Carrier screening, prenatal diagnosis, and the molecular era. *Journal of the American Medical Association, 270*(19), 2307–2315.

Kahan, B. & Goodstadt, M. (2002, April). *The IDM manual for using the Interactive Domain Model approach to health promotion.* Centre for Health Promotion, University of Toronto. Retrieved April 20, 2003, from http://www.utoronto.ca/chp/download.

Kahn, M. W. (1982). Cultural clash and psychopathology in three aboriginal cultures. *Academic Psychology Bulletin, 4,* 553–561.

Kaihla, P. (1996). No conscience, no remorse: A British Columbian psychologist probes the inner workings of psychopaths' brains. *Maclean's, 109*(4), 50–51

Kajander, R. (2004, February 3). Personal communication.

Kambouropoulos, N. & Staiger, P. K. (2007). Personality, behavioural and affective characteristics of hazardous drinkers. *Personality and Individual Differences, 42*(2), 213–224.

Kandel, E.R. (1999). Biology and the Future of Psychoanalysis: A New Intellectual Framework for Psychiatry Revisited. *American Journal of Psychiatry* 156(4), 505–524.

Kane, J. M. (1996). Drug therapy: Schizophrenia. *New England Journal of Medicine, 334,* 34–41.

Kane, J. M. & Marder, S. R. (1993). Psychopharmalogic treatment of schizophrenia. *Schizophrenia Bulletin, 19,* 287–302.

Kanner, L. (1943). Autistic disturbances of affective content. *Nervous Child, 2,* 217–240.

Kanner, L. & Eisenberg, L. (1955). Notes on the follow-up studies of autistic children. In P. Hoch & J. Zubin (Eds), *Psychopathology of childhood.* New York: Grune & Stratton.

Kaplan, A. S. (2002). Psychological treatments for anorexia nervosa: A review of published studies and promising new directions. *Canadian Journal of Psychiatry, 47*(3), 235–242.

Kaplan, A. S. & Garfinkel, P. E. (1999). Difficulties in treating patients with eating disorders: A review of patient and clinical variables. *Canadian Journal of Psychiatry, 44*(7), 665–670.

Kaplan, A. S. & Woodside, D. B. (1987). Biological aspects of anorexia nervosa and bulimia nervosa. *Journal of Consulting and Clinical Psychology, 55,* 645–653.

Kaplan, H. S. (1974). *The new sex therapy: Active treatment of sexual dysfunctions.* New York: Brunner/Mazel.

Kaplan, H. S. (1987). *Sexual aversion, sexual phobias, and panic disorder.* New York: Brunner/Mazel.

Kaplan, S. J. (1986). *The private practice of behavior therapy: A guide for behavioral practitioners.* New York: Plenum.

Kapur, S. & Remington, G. (1996). Serotonin-dopamine interaction and its relevance to schizophrenia. *American Journal of Psychiatry, 153,* 466–476.

Kapur, S. & Remington, G. (2001). Atypical antipsychotics: New directions and new challenges in the treatment of schizophrenia. *Annual Review of Medicine, 52,* 503–517.

Kasari, C., Sigman, M., Yirmiya, N., & Mundy, P. (1993). Affective development and communication in children with autism. In A. P. Kaiser & D. B. Gray (Eds.), *Enhancing children's communication: Research foundation for intervention* (pp. 201–222). New York: Paul H. Brookes.

Kasper, M. E., Rogers, R., & Adams, P. A. (1996). Dangerousness and command hallucinations: An investigation of psychotic inpatients. *Bulletin of the American Academy of Psychiatry and the Law, 24,* 219–224.

Kawachi, I., Colditz, G. A., Ascherio, A., Rimm, E. B., Giovannucci, E., Stampfer, M. J., & Willett, W. C. (1994). Prospective study of phobic anxiety and risk of coronary heart disease in men. *Circulation, 89*(5), 1992–1997.

Kay, S. R. (1990). Significance of the positive-negative distinction in schizophrenia. *Schizophrenia Bulletin, 16,* 635–652.

Kazdin, A. E. (1992). *Research design in clinical psychology* (2nd ed.). Boston: Allyn & Bacon.

Kazdin, A. E. (1998). Psychosocial treatments for conduct disorder in children. In P. E. Nathan & J. M. Gorman (Eds.), *A guide to treatments that work* (pp. 65–89). New York: Oxford University Press.

Kazdin, A.E. (2003). Psychotherapy for children and adolescents. *Annual Review of Psychology, 54,* 253–276.

Kazdin, A. E. & Weisz, J. R. (1998). Identifying and developing empirically supported child and adolescent treatments. *Journal of Consulting and Clinical Psychology, 66,* 19–36.

Kazdin, A. E. & Whitely, M. K. (2003). Treatment of parental stress to enhance therapeutic change among children referred for aggressive and antisocial behavior. *Journal of Consulting and Clinical Psychology, 71*(3), 504–515.

Keane, T. M., Marshall, A. D., & Taft, C. T. (2006). Posttraumatic stress disorder: Etiology, epidemiology, and treatment outcome. *Annual Review of Clinical Psychology, 2,* 161–197.

Kearins, J. M. (1981). Visual spatial memory in Australian Aboriginal children in desert regions. *Cognitive Psychology, 13,* 434–460.

Keel, P. K., Mitchell, J. E., Miller, K. B., Davis, T. L., & Crow, S. J. (1999). Long-term outcome of bulimia nervosa. *Archives of General Psychiatry, 56*(1), 63–69.

Keiller, S. W. & Graham, J. R. (1993). The meaning of low scores on MMP-2 Clinical Scales of normal subjects. *Journal of Personality Assessment, 62,* 211–223.

Keith, S. J., Regier, D. A., & Rae, D. S. (1991). Schizophrenic disorders. In L. N. Robins & D. A. Regier (Eds.), *Psychiatric disorders in America: The Epidemiologic Catchment Area Study* (pp. 33–52). New York: Free Press.

Kellner, R. (1992). Diagnosis and treatment of hypochondriacal syndromes. *Psychosomatics, 33,* 278–289.

Kelly, J. A., Brasfield, T. L., & St. Lawrence, J. S. (1991). Predictors of vulnerability to AIDS risk behavior relapse. *Journal of Consulting and Clinical Psychology, 59,* 163–166.

Kelly, J. A. & Kalichman, S. C. (1995). Increased attention in human sexuality can improve HIV-AIDS prevention efforts: Key research issues and directions. *Journal of Consulting and Clinical Psychology, 63,* 907–918.

Kelly, J. A., Sikkema, K. J., Winett, R. A., Solomon, L. J., Roffman, R. A., Heckman, T. G., et al. (1995). Factors predicting continued high-risk behavior among gay men in small cities: Psychological, behavioral, and demographic characteristics related to unsafe sex. *Journal of Consulting and Clinical Psychology, 63*(1), 101–107.

Kelly, J. A. et al. (1998). Implications of HIV treatment advances for behavioral research on AIDS: Protease inhibitors and new challenges in HIV secondary prevention. *Health Psychology, 17,* 310–319.

Kelly, J. A. & Kalichman, S. C. (2002). Behavioral research in HIV/AIDS primary and secondary prevention: recent advances and future directions. *Journal of Consulting and Clinical Psychology,70*(3), 626–639.

Kelly, S. J., Macaruso, P., & Sokol, S. M. (1997). Mental calculation in an autistic savant: A case study. *Journal of Clinical and Experimental Neuropsychology, 19,* 172–184.

Kemeny, M. E. (2003). The psychobiology of stress. *Current Directions in Psychological Science, 12*(4), 124–129.

Kendall, P. C., Safford, S., Flannery-Schroeder, E., & Webb, A. (2004). Child anxiety treatment: Outcomes in adolescence and impact on substance use and depression at 7.4-year follow-up. *Journal of Consulting and Clinical Psychology, 72*(2), 276–287.

Kendell, R. & Jablensky, A. (2003). Distinguishing between the validity and utility of psychiatric diagnoses. *American Journal of Psychiatry, 160*(1), 4–12.

Kendler, K. S. & Gardner, C. O. (1998). Boundaries of major depression: An evaluation of DSM-IV criteria. *American Journal of Psychiatry, 155,* 172–177.

Kendler, K. S. & Prescott, C. A. (2006). *Genes, environment, and psychopathology: Understanding the causes of psychiatric and substance use disorders.* New York: Guilford.

Kendler, K. S., & Walsh, D. (1995). Schizotypal personality disorder in parents and the risk for schizophrenia in siblings. *Schizophrenia Bulletin, 21,* 47–52.

Kendler, K. S., MacLean, C., Neale, M., Kessler, R., Heath, A., & Eaves, L. (1991). The genetic epidemiology of bulimia nervosa. *American Journal of Psychiatry, 148*(12), 1627–1637.

Kendler, K. S. et al. (1994). A twin-family study of alcoholism in women. *American Journal of Psychiatry, 151,* 707–715.

Kendler, K. S. et al. (1996). The identification and validation of distinct depressive syndromes in a population-based sample of female twins. *Archives of General Psychiatry, 53,* 391–399.

Kennedy, S. H., & Lam, R. W. (2003). Enhancing outcomes in the management of treatment resistant depression: A focus on atypical antipsychotics. *Bipolar Disorders, 5 (Suppl 2),* 36–47.

Kent, A. & Waller, G. (2000). Childhood emotional abuse and eating psychopathology. *Clinical Psychology Review, 20*(7), 887–903.

Kernberg, O. F. (1975). *Borderline conditions and pathological narcissism.* New York: Jason Aronson.

Kerr, D. A., Llado, J., Shamblott, M., Maragakis, N., Irani, D.

N., Dike, S. et al. (2001). Human embryonic germ cell derivatives facilitate motor recovery of rats with diffuse motor neuron injury. *The Journal of Neuroscience*, 23(12):5131–5140.

Kershner, R. (1996). Adolescent attitudes about rape. *Adolescence*, 31, 29–33.

Kessler, D. A. et al. (1997). The legal and scientific basis for FDA's assertion of jurisdiction over cigarettes and smokeless tobacco. *Journal of the American Medical Association*, 277, 405–409.

Kessler, R. C., Downey, G., Milavsky, J. R., Stipp, H. (1988). Clustering of teenage suicides after television news stories about suicides: A reconsideration. *American Journal of Psychiatry*, 145(11), 1379–1383.

Kessler, R. C., Crum, R. M., Warner, L. A., Nelson, C. B., Schulenberg, J., & Anthony, J. C. (1997). Lifetime co-occurrence of DSM-III-R alcohol abuse and dependence with other psychiatric disorders in the National Comorbidity Survey. *Archives of General Psychiatry*, 54, 313–321.

Kessler, R. C., Chiu, W. T., Jin, R., Ruscio, A. M., Shear, K., & Walters, E. E. (2006). The epidemiology of panic attacks, panic disorder, and agoraphobia in the national comorbidity survey replication. *Archives of General Psychiatry*, 63, 415–424.

Kety, S. S., Rosenthal, D., Wender, P. H., & Schulsinger, F. (1968). The types of prevalence of mental illness in the biological and adoptive families of adopted schizophrenics. In D. Rosenthal & S. S. Kety (Eds.), *The transmission of schizophrenia*. Oxford: Pergamon.

Kety, S. S., Rosenthal, D., Wender, P. H., Schulsinger, F., & Jacobsen, B. (1975). Mental illness in the biological and adoptive families of adoptive individuals who have become schizophrenic: A preliminary report based on psychiatric interviews. In R. R. Fieve, D. Rosenthal, & H. Brill (Eds.), *Genetic research in psychiatry*. Baltimore: Johns Hopkins University Press.

Kety, S. S., Rosenthal, D., Wender, P. H., Schulsinger, F., & Jacobsen, B. (1978). The biological and adoptive families of adopted individuals who become schizophrenic. In C.

Wynne, R. L. Cromwell, & S. Mathysse (Eds.), *The nature of schizophrenia* (pp. 25–37). New York: John Wiley & Sons.

Kety, S., Wender, P. H., Jacobsen, B. et al. (1994). Mental illness in the biological and adoptive relatives of schizophrenic adoptees: Replication of the Copenhagen study in the rest of Denmark. *Archives of General Psychiatry*, 51, 442–455.

Khan, S., Murray, R. P., & Barnes, G. E. (2002). A structural equation model of the effect of poverty and unemployment on alcohol abuse. *Addictive Behaviors*, 27, 405–423.

Kiecolt-Glaser, J. K. & Glaser, R. (1992). Psychoneuroimmunology: Can psychological interventions modulate immunity? *Journal of Consulting and Clinical Psychology*, 60, 569–575.

Kiecolt-Glaser, J. K., Speicher, C. E., Holliday, J. E., & Glaser, R. (1984). Stress and the transformation of lymphocytes in Epstein-Barr virus. *Journal of Behavioral Medicine*, 7(1), 1–12.

Kiecolt-Glaser, J. K., Fisher, L. D., Ogrocki, P., Stout, J. C., Speicher, C. E., & Glaser, R. (1987). Marital quality, marital disruption, and immune function. *Psychosomatic Medicine*, 49(1), 13–34.

Kiecolt-Glaser, J. K., Kennedy, S., Malkoff, S., Fisher, L., Speicher, C. E., & Glaser, R. (1988). Marital discord and immunity in males. *Psychosomatic Medicine*, 50(3), 213–229.

Kiecolt-Glaser, J. K., Marucha, P. T., Malarkey, W. B., Mercado, A. M., & Glaser, R. (1995). Slowing of wound healing by psychological stress. *Lancet*, 346(8984), 1194–1196.

Kiecolt-Glaser, J. K., McGuire, L., Robles, & T. F, Glaser, R. (2002). Emotions, morbidity, and mortality: New perspectives from psychoneuroimmunology. *Annual Review of Psychology*, 53, 83–107.

Kiehl, K. A., Smith, A. M., Hare, R. D., Mendrek, A., Forste, B. B., Brink, J., & Liddle, P. F. (2001). Limbic abnormalities in affective processing by criminal psychopaths as revealed by functional magnetic resonance imaging. *Biological Psychiatry*, 50(9), 678–684.

Kihlstrom, J. K. (2005). Dissociative disorders. *Annual Review*

of Clinical Psychology, 1, 227–253.

Killackey, E. & Yung, A. R. (2007). Effectiveness of early intervention in psychosis. *Current Opinion in Psychiatry*, 20, 121–125.

Kim, S. C. & Seo, K. K. (1998). Efficacy and safety of fluoxetine, sertraline, and clomipramine in patients with prompter ejaculation: A double-blind, placebo-controlled study. *Journal of Urology*, 159, 425–427.

Kimerling, R. & Calhoun, K. S. (1994). Somatic symptoms, social support, and treatment seeking among sexual assault victims. *Journal of Consulting and Clinical Psychology*, 62, 333–340.

Kimmins, S. & Sassone-Corsi, P. (2005). Chromatin remodelling and epigenetic features of germ cells. *Nature*, 434(7033), 583–589.

King, L. A., King, D. W., Fairbank, J. A., Keane, T. M., & Adams, G. (1998). Resilience-recovery factors in posttraumatic stress disorder among female and male Vietnam veterans: Hardiness, postwar social support, and additional stressful life events. *Journal of Personality and Social Psychology*, 74(2), 420–434.

Kirby, M. J. L. & Keon, W. J. (2004). *Report 1. Mental health, mental illness and addiction: Overview of policies and programs in Canada.* Interim Report of The Standing Senate Committee On Social Affairs, Science And Technology. Ottawa, ON: Senate of Canada. Retrieved November 1, 2006, from http://www.parl.gc.ca/38/1/parlbus/commbus/senate/com-e/soci-e/rep-e/report1/repintnov04vol1-e.pdf.

Kirby, M. J. L. & Keon, W. J. (2006). *Out of the shadows at last: Transforming mental health, mental illness and addiction services in Canada. The Standing Senate Committee on Social Affairs, Science and Technology.* Ottawa, ON: Senate of Canada. Retrieved November 1, 2006, from http://www.parl.gc.ca/39/1/parlbus/commbus/senate/com-e/soci-e/rep-e/pdf/rep02may06part2-e.pdf.

Kirmayer, L. J. (2001). Cultural variations in the clinical presentation of depression and anxiety: Implications for diagnosis and treatment. *The Journal of Clinical Psychiatry*, 62(Supplement 13), 22–28.

Kirmayer, L. J., Brass, G. M., & Tait, C. L. (2000). The mental health of Aboriginal peoples: Transformations of identity and community. *Canadian Journal of Psychiatry*, 45, 607–616.

Kirmayer, L. J., Groleau, D., Guzder, J., Blake, C., & Jarvis, E. (2003). Cultural consultation: A model of mental health service for multicultural societies. *Canadian Journal of Psychiatry*, 48(3), 145–153.

Kirmayer, L. J. & Looper, K. J. (2006). Abnormal illness behaviour: Physiological, psychological and social dimensions of coping with distress. *Current Opinion in Psychiatry*, 19, 54–60.

Kirmayer, L. J, MacDonald, M. E., & Brass, G. M. (2001). In Kirmayer, L. J., MacDonald, M. E., & Brass, G. M. (Eds.). *Proceedings of the Advanced Study Institute: The Mental Health of Indigenous Peoples.* Montreal: McGill Summer Program in Social & Cultural Psychiatry.

Kirmayer, L. J. & Minas, H. (2000). The future of cultural psychiatry: An international perspective. *Canadian Journal of Psychiatry*, 45(5), 438–446.

Kissel, R. C., Whitman, T. L., & Reid, D. H. (1983). An institutional staff training and self-management program for developing multiple self-care skills in severely-profoundly retarded individuals. *Journal of Applied Behavior Analysis*, 16, 395–415.

Klein, D. N. & Santiago, N. J. (2003). Dysthymia and chronic depression: Introduction, classification, risk factors, and course. *Journal of Clinical Psychology*, 59, 807–816.

Klein, D. N., Taylor, E. B., Dickstein, S., & Harding, K. (1988). Primary early-onset dysthymia: Comparison with primary nonbipolar nonchronic major depression on demographic, clinical, familial, personality, and socioenvironmental characteristics and short-term outcome. *Journal of Abnormal Psychology*, 97, 387–398.

Kleinman, A. (1987). Anthropology and psychiatry: The role of culture in cross-cultural research on illness. *British Journal of Psychiatry*, 151, 447–454.

Klepinger, D. H., Billy, J. O., Tanfer, K., & Grady, W. R. (1993). Perceptions of AIDS risk and severity and their association with risk-related behavior among U.S. men. *Family Planning Perspectives, 25*(2), 74–82.

Klerman, G. L. (1984). Ideology & science in the individual psychotherapy of schizophrenia. *Schizophrenia Bulletin, 10,* 608–612.

Klerman, G. L., Weissman, M. M., Rounsaville, B. J., & Chevron, E. S. (1984). *Interpersonal psychotherapy of depression.* New York: Basic Books.

Klesges, R. C., Winders, S. E., Meyers, A. W., Eck, L. H., Ward, K. D., Hultquist, C. M. et al. (1997). How much weight gain occurs following smoking cessation? A comparison of weight gain using both continuous and point prevalence abstinence. *Journal of Consulting and Clinical Psychology, 65,* 286–291.

Knoll, J. L., IV, Ramberg, J. E., Kingsbury, S. J., Croissant, D., & McDermott, B. (1998). Heterogeneity of the psychoses: Is there a neurodegenerative psychosis? *Schizophrenia Bulletin, 24,* 365–379.

Knudsen, D. D. (1991). Child sexual coercion. In E. Grauerholz & M. A. Koralewski (Eds.), *Sexual coercion: A sourcebook on its nature, causes, and prevention* (pp. 17–28). Lexington, MA: Lexington.

Kobak, K. A. et al. (1996). Computer-administered clinical rating scales: A review. *Psychopharmacology, 127,* 291–301.

Kobak, K. A. et al. (1997). A computer-administered telephone interview to identify mental disorders. *Journal of the American Medical Association, 278,* 905–910.

Kobasa, S. C. (1979). Stressful life events, personality, and health: An inquiry into hardiness. *Journal of Personality and Social Psychology, 37,* 1–11.

Kobasa, S. C., Maddi, S. R., & Kahn, S. (1982). Hardiness and health: A prospective study. *Journal of Personality and Social Psychology, 42,* 168–177.

Kobasa, S. C., Maddi, S. R., & Zola, M. A. (1983). Type A and hardiness. *Journal of Behavioral Medicine, 6,* 41–51.

Koenigsberg, H.W., Harvey, P.D., Mitropoulou, V., Schmeidler, J., New, A.S., Goodman, M. et al. (2002). Characterizing

affective instability in borderline personality disorder. *American Journal of Psychiatry, 159*(5), 784–788.

Koerner, K. & Linehan, M. M. (2002). Research on dialectical behavior therapy for patients with borderline personality disorder. *The Psychiatric clinics of North America, 23*(1), 151–167.

Kogon, M. M., Biswas, A., Pearl, D., Carlson, R. W., & Spiegel, D. (1997). Effects of medical and psychotherapeutic treatment on the survival of women with metastatic breast carcinoma. *Cancer, 80*(2), 225–230.

Kohut, H. (1966). Forms and transformations of narcissism. *Journal of the American Psychoanalytic Association, 14,* 243–272.

Kolata, G. (1998, March 28). U.S. approves sale of impotence pill; huge market seen. *The New York Times,* pp. A1, A8.

Kolbert, E. (1994, January 21). Demons replace dolls and bicycles in world of children of the quake. *The New York Times,* p. A19.

Kolko, D. J. & Rickard-Figueroa, J. L. (1985). Effects of video games on the adverse corollaries of chemotherapy in pediatric oncology patients: A single-case analysis. *Journal of Consulting and Clinical Psychology, 53,* 223–228.

Kopta, S. M. et al. (1994). Patterns of symptomatic recovery in psychotherapy. *Journal of Consulting and Clinical Psychology, 62,* 1009–1016.

Koss, M. P. et al. (1994). *No safe haven: Male violence against women at home, at work, and in the community.* Washington, DC: American Psychological Association.

Koss, M. P., Gidycz, C. A., & Wisniewski, N. (1987). The scope of rape: Incidence and prevalence of sexual aggression and victimization in a national sample of higher education students. *Journal of Consulting and Clinical Psychology, 55,* 162–170.

Kotler, M. (1997). Excess dopamine D4 receptor (D4DR) exon III seven repeat allele in opioid-dependent subjects. *Molecular Psychiatry, 2,* 251–254.

Kovacs, M. (1996). Presentation and course of major depressive disorder during childhood and later years of the lifespan. *Journal of American Academy*

of Children and Adolescent Psychiatry, 35, 705–715.

Kovacs, M., Devlin, B., Pollock, M., Richards, C., & Mukerji, P. (1997). A controlled family history study of childhood-onset depressive disorder. *Archives of General Psychiatry, 54*(7), 613–623.

Kraepelin, E. (1909–1913). *Psychiatrie* (8th ed.). Leipzig: Barth.

Krantz, D. S., Contrada, R. J., Hills, D. R., & Friedler, E. (1988). Environmental stress and biobehavioral antecedents of coronary heart disease. *Journal of Consulting and Clinical Psychology, 56,* 333–341.

Kranzler, H. R. et al. (1996). Comorbid psychiatric diagnosis predicts three-year outcomes in alcoholics: A posttreatment natural history study. *Journal of Studies in Alcohol, 57,* 619–626.

Kresin, D. (1993). Medical aspects of inhibited sexual desire disorder. In W. O'Donohue & J. H. Geer (Eds.), *Handbook of sexual dysfunctions: Assessment and treatment* (pp. 15–52). Boston: Allyn & Bacon.

Kring, A. M. & Neale, J. M. (1996). Do schizophrenic patients show a disjunctive relationship among expressive, experiential, and psychophysiological components of emotion? *Journal of Abnormal Psychology, 105,* 249–257.

Kring, A. M., Kerr, S. L., Smith, D. A., & Neale, J. M. (1993). Flat affect in schizophrenia does not reflect diminished subjective experience of emotion. *Journal of Abnormal Psychology, 102,* 507–517.

Krueger, R. F. & Markon, K. E. (2006). Reinterpreting comorbidity: A model-based approach to understanding and classifying psychopathology. *Annual Review of Clinical Psychology, 2,* 111–133.

Kruesi, M. J., Fine, S., Valladares, L., Phillips, R. A., Jr., & Rapoport, J. L. (1992). Paraphilias: A double-blind crossover comparison of clomipramine versus desipramine. *Archives of Sexual Behavior, 21,* 587–593.

Kruger, T. E. & Jerrells, T. R. (1992). Potential role of alcohol in human immunodeficiency virus infection. *Alcohol Health & Research World, 16,* 57–63.

Kryger, M. H. (2001). Waking up to the consequences of sleep disorders. *St. Boniface General Hospital Research Centre.* Retrieved August 3, 2003, from http://www.sbrc.umanitoba.ca/framekryger.htm.

Kryger, M. H., Roos, L., Delaive, K., Walld, R., & Horrocks, J. (1996). Utilization of health care services in patients with severe obstructive sleep apnea. *Sleep, 19*(9), 111–116.

Kryger, M. H., Roth, T., & Dement, W. C. (Eds.). (2005). *Principles and practice of sleep medicine* (4th ed.). Toronto, ON: W.B. Saunders Canada.

Kuehn, B. M. (2007). Opiod prescriptions soar. *New England Journal of Medicine, 297,* 249–251.

Kuiper, N. A. & Martin, R. A. (1993). Humor and self-concept. *Humor: International Journal of Humor Research, 6*(3), 251–270.

Kuiper, N. A. & Martin, R. A. (1998). Is sense of humor a positive personality characteristic? In Ruch, Willibald (ed.), *The sense of humor: Explorations of a personality characteristic.* Berlin/New York: Mouton de Gruyter, 159–178.

Kuiper, N. A., Grimshaw, M., Leite, C., & Kirsh, G. (2004). Humor is not always the best medicine: Specific components of sense of humor and psychological well-being. *Humor: International Journal of Humor Research, 17*(1/2), 135–168.

Kupfer, D. J. (1999). Research in affective disorders comes of age [Editorial]. *American Journal of Psychiatry, 156,* 165–167.

Kupfersmid, J. (1995). Does the Oedipus complex exist? *Psychotherapy, 32,* 535–547.

Kurtz, J. E. & Blais, M. A. (2007). Introduction to the special issue on the Personality Assessment Inventory. *Journal of Personality Assessment, 88*(1), 1–4.

Kwon, S. & Oei, T. P. S. (1994). The roles of two levels of cognitions in the development, maintenance, and treatment of depression. *Clinical Psychology Review, 14,* 331–358.

Kymalainen, J. A., Weisman, A. G., Resales, G. A., & Armesto, J. C. (2006). Ethnicity, expressed emotion, and communication deviance in family members of patients with schizophrenia. *Journal of Nervous and Mental Disease, 194,* 391–396.

L

LaCroix, A. Z. & Haynes, S. G. (1987). Gender differences in the stressfulness of workplace roles: A focus on work and health. In R. Barnett, G. Baruch, & L. Biener (Eds.), *Gender and stress* (pp. 96–121). New York: Free Press.

Ladouceur, R. (2002). *Understanding and treating the pathological gambler.* NewYork: John Wiley & Sons.

Ladouceur, R., Dugas, M. J., Freeston, M. H., Léger, E., Gagnon, F., & Thibodeau, N. (2000). Efficacy of a cognitive-behavioral treatment for generalized anxiety disorder: Evaluation in a controlled clinical trial. *Journal of Consulting and Clinical Psychology, 68,* 957–964.

Lahey, B. B., Loeber, R., Hart, E. L., Frick, P. J., Applegate, B., Zhang, Q. et al. (1995). Four-year longitudinal study of conduct disorder in boys: Patterns and predictors of persistence. *Journal of Abnormal Psychology, 104,* 83–93.

Laird, P. W. (2005). Cancer epigenetics. *Human Molecular Genetics, 14*(Review Issue 1), R65–R76.

Laishes, J. (2002). The 2002 mental health strategy for women offenders. Ottawa: Correctional Services Canada. Retrieved July 21, 2003, from http://www.csc-scc.gc.ca/text/prgrm/fsw/mhealth/mhealth_e.rtf.

Lalonde, J. K., Hudson, J. I., Gigante, R. A., & Pope, H. G. (2001). Canadian and American psychiatrists' attitudes toward dissociative disorders diagnoses. *Canadian Journal of Psychiatry, 46,* 407–412.

Lam, R. W. & Levitt, A. J. (1999). *Canadian consensus guidelines for the treatment of seasonal affective disorder.* Vancouver, BC: Clinical and Academic Publishing.

Lam, R. W., Levitt, A. J., Levitan, R. D., Enns, M. W., Morehouse, R., Michalak, E. E. et al. (2006). The CAN-SAD study: Randomized controlled trial of the effectiveness of light therapy and fluoxetine in patients with winter seasonal affective disorder. *American Journal of Psychiatry, 163,* 805–812.

Lamberg, L. (2003). Advances in eating disorders offer food for thought. *Journal of the American Medical Association, 290*(11), 1437–1442.

Lambert, M. J. & Bergin, A. E. (1994). The effectiveness of psychotherapy. In A. E. Bergin & S. L. Garfield (Eds.), *Handbook of psychotherapy and behavior change* (4th ed., pp. 72–113). New York: John Wiley & Sons.

Lambert, M. J. & Okiishi, J. C. (1997). The effects of the individual psychotherapist and implications for future research. *Clinical Psychology: Science and Practice, 4,* 66–75.

Landy, S. & Tam, K. K. (1998). Understanding the contribution of multiple risk factors on child development at various ages (Catalogue No. W-98_22E). Ottawa: Human Resources Development Canada. Retrieved July 21, 2003, from http://www.hrdc-drhc.gc.ca/arb/publications/research/w-98-22e.pdf.

Lang, P. J. (1968). Fear reduction and fear behavior: Problems in treating a construct. In J. M. Schlein (Ed.), *Research in psychotherapy* (Vol. 3, pp. 90–102). Washington, DC: American Psychological Association.

Lang, P. J. & Lazovik, A. D. (1963). Experimental desensitization of phobia. *Journal of Abnormal and Social Psychology, 66,* 519–525.

Langenbucher, J., Martin, C. S., Labouvie, E., Sanjuan, P. M., Bavly, L., & Pollock, N. K. (2000). Toward the DSM-V: The Withdrawal-Gate Model Versus the DSM-IV in the Diagnosis of Alcohol Abuse and Dependence. *Journal of Consulting & Clinical Psychology. 68*(5), 799–809.

Langevin, R. & Lang, R. (1987). The courtship disorders. In G. D. Wilson (Ed.), *Variant sexuality: Research and theory* (pp. 202–228). London: Croom Helm.

Lanius, R. A., Williamson, P. C., & Menon, R. S. (2002). Post-traumatic stress disorder: Neuroimaging of hyperaroused and dissociative states in post-traumatic stress disorder. *Canadian Psychiatric Association Bulletin 34*(4), 22–25.

Lanius, R. A., Williamson, P. C., Boksman, K., Densmore, M., Gupta, M., Neufeld, R.W., Gati, J.S., & Menon, R. S. (2002). Brain activation during script-driven imagery induced dissociative responses in PTSD: A functional magnetic resonance imaging investigation. *Biological Psychiatry, 52*(4), 305–11.

Lanius, R. A., Williamson, P. C., Densmore, M., Boksman, K., Neufeld, R. W., Gati, J.S., & Menon, R. S. (2004). The nature of traumatic memories: A 4-T FMRI functional connectivity analysis. *American Journal of Psychiatry, 161*(1), 36–44.

Lanius, R. A., Williamson, P. C., Hopper, J., Densmore, M., Boksman, K., Gupta, M. A., Neufeld, R. W. J., Gati, J. S., & Menon, R. S. (2003). *Recall of emotional states in post-traumatic stress disorder: An fMRI investigation. Biological Psychiatry, 53*(3), 204–210.

Laroi, F. (2006). The phenomenological diversity of hallucinations: Some theoretical and clinical implications. *Psychologica Belgica, 46,* 163–183.

Larson, R. W., Raffaelli, M., Richards, M. H., Ham, M., & Jewell, L. (1990). Ecology of depression in late childhood and early adolescence: A profile of daily states and activities. *Journal of Abnormal Psychology, 99,* 92–102.

Lau, E. (2001). More and more. In L. Crozier & P. Lane (Eds.), *Addicted: Notes from the belly of the beast* (pp. 73–84). Vancouver: Greystone.

Laumann, E. O., Gagnon, J. H., Michael, R. T., & Michaels, S. (1994). *The social organization of sexuality: Sexual practices in the United States.* Chicago: University of Chicago Press.

Laumann, E. O., Paik, A., & Rosen, R. C. (1999). Sexual dysfunction in the United States: Prevalence and predictors. *Journal of the American Medical Association, 281,* 537–544.

Lauriello, J., Hoff, A., Wieneke, M. H., Blankfeld, H., Faustman, W. O., Rosenbloom, M. et al. (1997). Similar extent of brain dysmorphology in severely ill women and men with schizophrenia. *American Journal of Psychiatry, 154,* 819–825.

Lavallee, C., & Bourgault, C. (2000). The health of Cree, Inuit and southern Quebec women: Similarities and differences. *Canadian Journal of Public Health, 91,* 212–216.

Lawson, D. M. (1983). Alcoholism. In M. Hersen (Ed.), *Outpatient behavior therapy: A clinical guide* (pp. 143–172). New York: Grune & Stratton.

Lazarus, R. S. & Folkman, S. (1984). *Stress, appraisal, and coping.* New York: Springer.

Learning Disabilities Association of Canada (2002).Official definition of learning disabilities. Ottawa: Author. Retrieved January 25, 2003, from http://www.ldac-taac.ca/english/defined/jan02eng.pdf.

Learning Disabilities Association of Canada (2003a). *Advocating for Your Child with Learning Disabilities.* IV. *Programming plans, placement options.* Ottawa: Learning Disabilities Association of Canada. Retrieved October 18, 2003, from http://www.ldac-taac.ca/english/indepth/advocacy/yorchild/6.htm.

Learning Disabilities Association of Canada, (2003b). *Fact Sheet. Assistive technology and learning disabilities.* Ottawa: Learning Disabilities Association of Canada. Retrieved October 18, 2003, from http://www.ldac-taac.ca/english/indepth/assistiv/ATandLD.pdf.

Leary, W. E. (1996, December 18). Responses of alcoholics to therapies seem similar. *The New York Times,* p. A17.

Leavitt, F. & Labott, S. M. (1997). Criterion-related validity of Rorschach analogues of dissociation. *Psychological Assessment, 9,* 244–249.

Lee, J. K. P., Jackson, H. J., Pattison, P., & Ward, T. (2002). Developmental risk factors for sexual offending. *Child Abuse & Neglect, 26,* 73–92.

Lee, T. H. (1997, May). Marijuana's cognitive effects persist. *Journal Watch for Psychiatry, 2*(5), 41.

Lefcourt, H. M. & Martin, R. A. (1986). *Humor and life stress: Antidote to adversity.* New York: Springer-Verlag.

Leff, J. & Vaughn, C. (1981). The role of maintenance therapy and relatives' expressed emotion in relapse of schizophrenia: A two-year follow-up. *British Journal of Psychiatry, 139,* 102–104.

Lefley, H. P. (1990). Culture and chronic mental illness. *Hospital and Community Psychiatry, 41,* 277–286.

Leger Marketing, 2002). Canadians and Sleep: Report. *Canadian Press/Leger Marketing* (2002, January 21). Retrieved August 3, 2003, from http://www.legermarketing.com/documents/spclm/020121eng.pdf.

Lehmann, H. E. & Hanrahan, G. E. (1954). Chlorpromazine: New inhibiting agent for psychomotor excitement and manic states. *Archives of Neurology and Psychiatry, 71,* 227–237.

Lehrer, P. M., Hochron, S. M., Mayne, T., Isenberg, S., Carlson, V., Lasoski, A. M. et al. (1994). Relaxation and music therapies for asthma among patients prestabilized on asthma medication. *Journal of Behavioral Medicine, 17*(1), 1–24.

Lehrer, P. M., Sargunaraj, D., & Hochron, S. (1992). Psychological approaches to the treatment of asthma. *Journal of Consulting and Clinical Psychology, 60,* 639–643.

Lehtinen, V., Ozamiz, A., Underwood, L., & Weiss, M. (2005). The intrinsic value of mental health. In H. Herrman, S. Saxena, & R. Moodie (Eds.), *Promoting mental health: Concepts, emerging evidence, practice* (pp. 46–58). Geneva, Switzerland: World Health Organization.

Leiblum, S. R. (2006). *Principles and practice of sex therapy* (4th ed.). New York: Guilford.

Leibson, C. L., Katusic, S. K., Barbaresi, W. J., Ransom, J., & O'Brien, P. C. (2001). Use and costs of medical care for children and adolescents with and without attention-deficit/hyperactivity disorder. *Journal of the American Medical Association, 285*(1), 60–66.

Leichner, P., Arnett, J., Rallo, J. S., Srilcamesuaran, S., & Vulcano, B. (1986). An epidemiological study of maladaptive eating attitudes in a Canadian school-aged population. *International Journal of Eating Disorders, 5,* 969–982.

Leichsenring, F. & Leibing, E. (2003). The effectiveness or psychodynamic therapy and cognitive therapy in the treatment of personality disorders: A meta-analysis. *American Journal of Psychiatry, 160*(7), 1223–1232.

Leichsenring, F., Hiller, W., Weissberg, M., & Leibing, E. (2006). Cognitive-behavioral therapy and psychodynamic psychotherapy: Techniques, efficacy, and indications. *American Journal of Psychotherapy, 60*(3), 233–259.

Leit, R. A., Gray, J. J., Pope, H. G., Jr. (2002). The media's representation of the ideal male body: A cause for muscle dysmorphia? *International Journal of Eating Disorders, 31*(3), 334–338.

Leonardo, E. D. & Hen, R. (2006). Genetics of affective and anxiety disorders. *Annual Review of Psychology, 57,* 117–137.

Leszcz, M., MacKenzie, R., el-Guebaly, N., Atkinson, M. J., & Wiesenthal, S. (2002). Part V: Canadian psychiatrists' use of psychotherapy. *Canadian Psychiatric Association: The Bulletin, 34*(5), 28–31.

Letendre, A.D. (2002). Aboriginal traditional medicine: Where does it fit? *Crossing Boundaries—An Interdisciplinary Journal, 1*(2), 78–87.

Letourneau, E. J., Resnick, H. S., Kilpatrick, D. G., Saunders, B. E., & Best, C. L. (1996). Comorbidity of sexual problems and posttraumatic stress disorder in female crime victims. *Behavior Therapy, 27,* 321–336.

Letourneau, E. & O'Donohue, W. (1993). Sexual desire disorders. In W. O'Donohue & J. H. Geer (Eds.), *Handbook of sexual dysfunctions: Assessment and treatment* (pp. 53–81). Boston: Allyn & Bacon.

Levenson, J. L. & Bemis, C. (1991). The role of psychological factors in cancer onset and progression. *Psychosmatics, 32,* 124–132.

Levenstein, S., Ackerman, S., Kiecolt-Glaser, J. K., & Dubois, A. (1999). Stress and peptic ulcer disease. *Journal of the American Medical Association, 281*(1), 10–11.

Levine, J., Warrenburg, S., Kerns, R., Schwartz, G., Delaney, R., Fontana, A., Gradman, A., Smith, S., Allen, S., & Cascione, R. (1987). The role of denial in recovery from coronary heart disease. *Psychosomatic Medicine, 49*(2), 109–117.

Levitan, R. D., Kaplan, A. S., Joffe, R. T., Levitt, A. J., & Brown, G. M. (1997). Hormonal and subjective responses to intravenous metachlorophenylpiperazine in bulimia nervosa. *Archives of General Psychiatry, 54*(6), 521–527.

Levitt, A. J., Boyle, M. H., Joffe, R. T., & Baumal, Z. (2000). Estimated prevalence of the seasonal subtype of major depression in a Canadian community sample. *Canadian Journal of Psychiatry, 45,* 650–654.

Levy, S. R., Jurkovic, G. L., & Spirito, A. (1995). A multisystems analysis of adolescent suicide attempters. *Journal of Abnormal Child Psychology, 23,* 221–234.

Lewandowski, L. M., Gebing, T. A., Anthony, J. L., & O'Brien, W. H. (1997). Meta-analysis of cognitive-behavioral treatment studies for bulimia. *Clinical Psychology Review, 17*(7), 703–718.

Lewinsohn, P. M. & Clarke, G. N. (1999). Psychosocial treatments for adolescent depression. *Clinical Psychology Review, 19,* 329–342.

Lewinsohn, P. M. & Libet, J. M. (1972). Pleasant events, activity schedules and depression. *Journal of Abnormal Psychology, 79,* 291–295.

Lewinsohn, P. M., Antonuccio, D., Steinmetz, J., & Terry, L. (1984). *The coping with depression course: A psychoeducational intervention for unipolar depression.* Eugene, OR: Castalia.

Lewinsohn, P. M., Rohde, P., & Seeley, J. R. (1994). Psychosocial risk factors for future adolescent suicide attempts. *Journal of Consulting and Clinical Psychology, 62,* 297–305.

Lewinsohn, P. M., Sullivan, J. M., & Grosscup, S. J. (1980). Changing reinforcing events: An approach to the treatment of depression. *Psychotherapy: Theory, Research, & Practice, 17,* 322–334.

Lewinsohn, P. M., Teri, L., & Wasserman, D. (1983). Depression. In M. Hersen (Ed.), *Outpatient behavior therapy: A practical guide* (pp. 81–108). New York: Grune & Stratton.

Lezak, M. D. (2004). *Neuropsychological assessment* (4th ed.). New York: Oxford University Press.

Liberman, R. P. (1994). Treatment and rehabilitation of the seriously mentally ill in China: Impressions of a society in transition. *American Journal of Orthopsychiatry, 64,* 68–77.

Lichtenstein, E. & Glasgow, R. E. (1992). Smoking cessation: What have we learned over the past decade? *Journal of Consulting and Clinical Psychology, 60,* 518–527.

Liddle, P. F. (1999). The multidimensional phenotype of schizophrenia. In C. A. Tamminga (Ed.), *Schizophrenia in a molecular age* (pp. 1–28). Washington, DC: American Psychiatric Association.

Lieber, C. S. (1990, January 14). Cited in "Barroom biology: How alcohol goes to a woman's head." *The New York Times,* p. E24.

Lightner, D. L. (1999). *Asylum, prison, and poorhouse.* Illinois: Southern Illinois University Press.

Lilienfeld, S. O. & Andrews, B. P. (1996). Identifying noncriminal psychopaths. *Journal of Personality Assessment, 66,* 488–524.

Lilienfeld, S. O. & Lynn, S. J. (2003). Dissociative identity disorder: Multiple personalities, multiple controversies. In S. O. Lilienfeld & S. J. Lynn (Eds.), *Science and pseudoscience in clinical psychology* (pp. 109–142). New York: Guilford.

Lilienfeld, S. O. & Marino, L. (1995). Mental disorder as a Roschian concept: A critique of Wakefield's "harmful dysfunction" analysis. *Journal of Abnormal Psychology, 104,* 411–420.

Lindahl, V., Pearson, J. L., & Colpe, L. (2005). Prevalence of suicidality during pregnancy and the postpartum. *Archives of Women's Mental Health, 8,* 77–87.

Linde, K., Berner, M., Egger, M., & Mulrow, C. (2005). St John's wort for depression: Meta-analysis of randomised controlled trials. *British Journal of Psychiatry, 186,* 99–107.

Lindvall, O. (2003). Stem cells for cell therapy in Parkinson's disease. *Pharmacological Research, 47*(4), 279–287.

Linehan, M. M. (1993). *Cognitive-behavioral treatment of borderline personality disorder.* New York: Guilford.

Linehan, M. M., Camper, P., Chiles, J. A., Strosahl, K., & Shearin, E. (1987). Interpersonal problem solving and parasuicide. *Cognitive Therapy and Research, 11,* 1–12.

Links, P. S. (1998). Developing effective services for patients with personality disorders. *Canadian Journal of Psychiatry, 43*(3), 251–259.

Links, P. S., Heslegrave, R., & van Reekum, R. (1998). Prospective follow-up study of borderline personality disorder: Prognosis, prediction of outcome, and Axis II Comorbidity. *Canadian Journal of Psychiatry, 43*(3), 265–270.

Liotti, G. & Pasquini, P. (2000). Predictive factors for borderline personality disorder: Patients' early traumatic experiences and losses suffered by the attachment figure. *Acta Psychiatrica Scandinavica, 102*(4), 282–289.

Lipman, E. L., MacMillan, H. L., & Boyle, M. H. (2001). Childhood abuse and psychiatric disorders among single and married mothers. *American Journal of Psychiatry, 158*, 73–77.

Lipps, G. & Frank, J. (1997). The National Longitudinal Survey of Children and Youth, 1994–1995: Initial results from the school component (Catalogue no. 81-003-XPB). *Education Quarterly Review, Statistics Canada, 4*(2), 43–57.

Lipsey, M. W. & Wilson, D. B. (1993). The efficacy of psychology, educational, and behavioral treatment: Confirmation from meta-analysis. *American Psychologist, 48*, 1181–1209.

Lipsey, M. W. & Wilson, D. B. (1995). Reply to comments on Lispey and Wilson (1993). *American Psychologist, 50*, 113–115.

Lipton, R. B., Stewart, W. F., Ryan, R. E., Jr, Saper, J., Silberstein, S., & Sheftell, F. (1998). Efficacy and safety of acetaminophen, aspirin, and caffeine in alleviating migraine headache pain. *Archives of Neurology, 55*(2), 210–217.

Lipton, R. B., Stewart, W. F., Stone, A. M., Lainez, M. J., & Sawyer, J. P. (2000). Stratified care vs step care strategies for migraine: the Disability in Strategies of Care (DISC) Study: A randomized trial. *Journal of the American Medical Association, 284*(20), 2599–2605.

Lisak, D. (1991). Sexual aggression, masculinity, and fathers. *Signs, 16*, 238–262.

Litman, L. C. (2003). Sexual sadism with lust-murder proclivities. *Canadian Journal of Psychiatry, 48*, 127.

Livesley, W. J. (1998). Suggestions for a framework for an empirically based classification of personality disorder. *Canadian Journal of Psychiatry, 43*(2), 137–147.

Livesley, W. J. (2001). Conceptual and taxonomic issues. In W. J. Livesley (Ed.), *Handbook of personality disorders: Theory, research, and treatment* (pp. 3–38). New York: Guilford Press.

Livesley, W. J. (2005). Principles and strategies for treating personality disorder. *Canadian*

Journal of Psychiatry, 50(8), 442–450.

Livesley, W. J., Jang, K. L., Jackson, D. N., & Vernon, P. A. (1993). Genetic and environmental contributions to dimensions of personality disorder. *American Journal of Psychiatry, 150*(12), 1826–1831.

Livesley, W. J., Schroeder, M. L., Jackson, D. N., & Jang, K. L. (1994). Categorical distinctions in the study of personality disorder: Implications for classification. *Journal of Abnormal Psychology, 103*(1), 6–17.

Livesley, W. J., Jang, K. L., & Vernon, P. A. (1998). Phenotypic and genetic structure of traits delineating personality disorders. *Archives of General Psychiatry, 55*(1), 941–948.

Livesley, W. J., Schroeder, M. L., Jackson, D. N., & Jang, K. L. (1994). Categorical distinctions in the study of personality disorder: Implications for classification. *Journal of Abnormal Psychology, 103*(1), 6–17.

Livesley, W. J., West, M., & Tanney, A. (1986). Doctor Livesley and associates reply. *American Journal of Psychiatry, 143*, 1062–1063.

Livingston, J. D., Wilson, D., Tien, G., & Bond, L. (2003). A follow-up study of persons found not criminally responsible on account of mental disorder in British Columbia. *Canadian Journal of Psychiatry, 48*, 408–415.

Livingstone, M. S., Rosen, G. D., Drislane, F. W., & Galaburda, A. M. (1991). Physiological and anatomical evidence for a magnocellular defect in developmental dyslexia. *Proceedings of the National Academy of Sciences, 88*, 7943–7947.

Lo, H. & Fung, K. P. (2003). Culturally competent psychotherapy. *Canadian Journal of Psychiatry, 48*(3), 161–170.

Lochman, J. E. & Dodge, K. A. (1994). Social-cognitive processes of severely violent, moderately aggressive, and nonaggressive boys. *Journal of Consulting and Clinical Psychology, 62*, 366–374.

Lochman, J. E. & Lenhart, L. (1993). Anger coping intervention for aggressive children: Conceptual models and outcome effects. *Clinical Psychology Review, 13*, 785–805.

Loftus, E. F. (1996). The myth of repressed memory and the realities of science. *Clinical*

Psychology: Science and Practice, 3, 356–365.

Loftus, E. F. & Davis, D. (2006). Recovered memories. *Annual Review of Clinical Psychology, 2*, 469–498.

Lohman, J. J. (2001). Treatment strategies for migraine headache. *Journal of the American Medical Association,* 285(8):1014–1015.

Loo, C., McFarquhar, T., & Walter, G. (2006). Transcranial magnetic stimulation in adolescent depression. *Australian Psychiatry, 14*(1), 81–85.

LoPiccolo, J. (1990). Sexual dysfunction. In A. S. Bellack, M. Hersen, & A. E. Kazdin (Eds.), *International handbook of behavior modification and therapy* (2nd ed., pp. 575–564). New York: Plenum.

LoPiccolo, J. & Stock, W. E. (1986). Treatment of sexual dysfunction. *Journal of Consulting and Clinical Psychology, 54*, 158–167.

Loranger, A. W. (1996). Dependent personality disorder: Age, sex, and Axis I comorbidity. *Journal of Nervous and Mental Disease, 184*, 17–21.

Loranger, A. W., Sartorius, N., Andreoli, A., Berger, P., Buchheim, P., Channabasavanna, S. M., et al. (1994). The international personalty disorder examination: The World Health Organization/Alcohol, Drug, Abuse and Mental Health Administration International Pilot Study of Personality Disorders. *Archives of General Psychiatry, 51*(3), 215–224.

Lovaas, O. I. (1987). Behavioral treatment and normal educational and intellectual functioning in young autistic children. *Journal of Consulting and Clinical Psychology, 55*, 3–9.

Lovaas, O. I., Koegel, R. L., & Schreibman, L. (1979). Stimulus overselectivity in autism: A review of the research. *Psychological Bulletin, 86*, 1236–1254.

Lowe, M. R., Gleaves, D. H., & Murphy-Eberenz, K. P. (1998). On the relation of dieting and bingeing in bulimia nervosa. *Journal of Abnormal Psychology, 107*, 263–271.

Luch, A. (2005). Nature and nurture—Lessons from chemical carcinogenesis. *Nature Reviews Cancer, 5*(2), 113–125.

Lukassen, J. & Beaudet, M. P. (2005). Alcohol dependence

and depression among heavy drinkers in Canada. *Social Science & Medicine, 61*, 1658–1667.

Luntz, B. K. & Widom, C. S. (1994). Antisocial personality disorder in abused and neglected children grown up. *American Journal of Psychiatry, 151*, 670–674.

Lutgendorf, S. K., Antoni, M. H., Ironson, G., Klimas, N., Kumar, M., Starr, K. et al. (1997). Cognitive-behavioral stress management decreases dysphoric mood and herpes simplex virus-type 2 antibody titer in symptomatic HIV-seropositive gay men. *Journal of Consulting and Clinical Psychology, 65*(1), 31–43.

Luthar, S. & Cicchetti, D. (2000). The construct of resilience: Implications for interventions and social policies. *Development and Psychopathology, 12*, 857–885.

Lydiard, R. B. (2003). The role of GABA in anxiety disorders. *Journal of Clinical Psychiatry, 64* (Suppl. 3), 21–27.

Lykken, D. T. (1957). A study of anxiety in the sociopathic personality. *Journal of Abnormal and Social Psychology, 55*, 6–10.

Lyons, M. J., Goldberg, J., Eisen, S. A., True, W., Tsuang, M. T., Meyer, J. M., & Henderson, W. G. (1993). Do genes influence exposure to trauma? A two study of combat. *American Journal of Medical Genetics, 48*, 22–27.

M

MacDonald, C. (2002). Treatment resistance in anorexia nervosa and the pervasiveness of ethics in clinical decision making. *Canadian Journal of Psychiatry, 47*(3), 267–270.

MacLatchy-Gaudet, H. A. & Stewart, S. H. (2001). The context-specific positive alcohol outcome expectancies of university women. *Addictive Behaviors, 26*, 31–49.

MacMillan, H. L., Fleming, J. E., Streiner, D. L., Lin, E., Boyle, M. H., Jamieson, E., Duku, E. K., Walsh, C. A., & Wong, M. Y. Y. (2001). Childhood abuse and lifetime psychopathology in a community sample. *American Journal of Psychiatry, 158*, 1878–1883.

MacMillan, H. L., MacMillan, A. B., Offord, D. R., & Dingle, J. L. (1996). Aboriginal health. *Canadian Medical Association Journal, 155*(11), 1569–1578.

Macnaughton, E. (2000). Cultural competence and "the knowledge resource base." *Visions, 9*(Winter), 14–15.

MacPhillamy, D. J. & Lewinsohn, P. M. (1974). Depression as a function of levels of desired and obtained pleasure. *Journal of Abnormal Psychology, 83,* 651–657.

Maddi, S. R. & Khoshaba, D. M. (1994). Hardiness and mental health. *Journal of Personality Assessment, 63,* 265–274.

Maddi, S. R. & Kobasa, S. C. (1984). *The hardy executive: Health under stress.* Homewood, IL: Dow Jones-Irwin.

Magnusson, A. & Partonen, T. (2005). The diagnosis, symptomatology, and epidemiology of seasonal affective disorder. *CNS Spectrums, 10,* 625–634.

Maher, W. B. & Maher, B. A. (1985). Psychopathology: I. From ancient times to the eighteenth century. In G. A. Kimble & K. Schlesinger (Eds.), *Topics in the history of psychology* (Vol. 2). Hillsdale, NJ: Erlbaum.

Mahler, M. S., Pine, F., & Bergman, A. (1975). The borderline syndrome: The role of the mother in the genesis and psychic structure of the borderline personality. *International Journal of Psychoanalysis, 56,* 163–177.

Mahler, M. & Kaplan, L. (1977). Developmental aspects in the assessment of narcissistic and so-called borderline personalities. In P. Hartocollis (Ed.), *Borderline personality disorders: The concept, the syndrome, the patient* (pp. 71–85). New York: International Universities Press.

Maier, S. F. & Seligman, M. E. P. (1976). Learned helplessness: Theory and evidence. *Journal of Experimental Psychology (General), 105,* 3–46.

Maier, S. F., Watkins, L. R., & Fleshner, M. (1994). Psychoneuroimmunology: The interface between behavior, brain, and immunity. *American Psychologist, 49,* 1004–1017.

Maitra, A., Arking, D. E., Shivapurkar, N., Ikeda, M., Stastny, V., Kassauei, K. et al. (2005). Genomic alterations in cultured human embryonic stem cells. *Nature Genetics 37*(10), 1099–1103.

Maletzky, B. M. (1991). *Treating the sexual offender.* Newbury Park, CA: Sage.

Maletzky, B. M. (1998). The paraphilias: Research and treatment. In P. E. Nathan & J. M. Gorman (Eds.), *A guide to treatments that work* (pp. 472–500). New York: Oxford University Press.

Maletzky, B. M. & Steinhauser, C. (2002). A 25-year follow-up of cognitive/behavioral therapy with 7,275 sexual offenders. *Behavior Modification, 26,* 123–147.

Malla, A. K., Norman, R. M. G., & Joober, R. (2005). First-episode psychosis, early intervention, and outcome: What have we learned? *Canadian Journal of Psychiatry, 50,* 881–891.

Mandal, V. (2002, October 7). Families of mentally ill pay terrible toll. *The Vancouver Sun,* pp. A1–A2.

Mann, J. J., Underwood, M. D., & Arango, V. (1996). Postmortem studies of suicide victims. In S. J. Watson (Ed.), *Biology of schizophrenia and affective disease* (pp. 179–221). Washington, DC: American Psychiatric Press.

Marcus, D. K. & Nardone, M. E. (1992). Depression and interpersonal rejection. *Clinical Psychology Review, 12,* 433–449.

Marcus, D. K., Gurley, J. R., Marchi, M. M., & Bauer, C. (2007). Cognitive and perceptual variables in hypochondriasis and health anxiety: A systematic review. *Clinical Psychology Review, 27,* 127–139.

Marder, S. R., Wirshing, W. C., Mintz, J., McKenzie, J., Johnston, K., Eckman, T. A., et al. (1996). Two-year outcome of social skills training and group psychotherapy for outpatients with schizophrenia. *American Journal of Psychiatry, 153,* 1585–1592.

Marengo, J. T. & Harrow, M. (1987). Schizophrenic thought disorder at follow-up: A persistent or episodic course? *Archives of General Psychiatry, 44,* 651–659.

Marengo, J. T. & Harrow, M. (1997). Longitudinal courses of thought disorder in schizophrenia and schizoaffective disorder. *Schizophrenia Bulletin, 23,* 273–285.

Marin, A. (2001). *Report to the Minister of National Defence: Systematic treatment of CF members with PTSD.* Ottawa: Canadian Department of National Defence.

Mark, D. H. (1998). Editor's note. *Journal of the American Medical Association, 279,* 151.

Markovitz, J. H. et al. (1993). Psychological predictors of hypertension in the Framington study: Is there tension in hypertension? *Journal of the American Medical Association, 270,* 2439–2443.

Markowitz, J. C. (2006a). Adaptations of interpersonal psychotherapy. *Psychiatric Annals, 36,* 559–563.

Markowitz, J. C. (2006b). Interpersonal psychotherapy for depression and dysthymic disorder. In D. J. Stein, D. J. Kupfer, & A. F. Schatzberg (Eds.), *American Psychiatric Publishing textbook of mood disorders* (pp. 373–388). Washington, DC: American Psychiatric Publishing.

Markowitz, J. C. et al. (1998). Treatment of depressive symptoms in human immunodeficiency virus-positive patients. *Archives of General Psychiatry, 55,* 452–457.

Marks, I., Shaw, S., & Parkin, R. (1998). Computer-aided treatments of mental health problems. *Clinical Psychology: Science and Practice, 5,* 151–170.

Marlatt, G. A. (1978). Craving for alcohol, loss of control, and relapse: A cognitive-behavioral analysis. In P. E. Nathan, G. A. Marlatt, & T. Loberg (Eds.), *Alcoholism: New directions in behavioral research and treatment* (pp. 271–314). New York: Plenum.

Marlatt, G. A. & Gordon, J. R. (1985). *Relapse prevention: Maintenance strategies in the treatment of addictive behaviors.* New York: The Guilford.

Marlatt, G. A., Demming, B., & Reid, J. B. (1973). Loss of control drinking in alcoholics: An experimental analogue. *Journal of Abnormal Psychology, 81,* 233–241.

Marlatt, G. A., Marlatt, G. A., Larimer, M. E., Baer, J. S., Quigley, L. A. (1993). Harm reduction for alcohol problems: Moving beyond the controlled drinking controversy. *Behavior Therapy, 24,* 461–504.

Marshall, D. (1971). Sexual behavior on Mangaia. In D. Marshall & R. Suggs (Eds.), *Human sexual behavior: Variations in the ethnographic spectrum.* Englewood Cliffs, NJ: Prentice Hall.

Marshall, W. L. (2001). Attachment problems in the etiology and treatment of sexual offenders. In W. Everaerd, E. Laan, & S. Both (Eds.), *Sexual appetite, desire and motivation* (pp. 135–143). Amsterdam, The Netherlands: Koninklijke Nederlandse Akademie van Wetenschappen.

Marshall, W. L. & Eccles, A. (1993). Pavlovian conditioning processes in adolescent sex offenders. In H. E. Barbaree, W. L. Marshall, & S. M. Hudson (Eds.), *The juvenile sex offender* (pp. 118–142). New York: Guilford.

Marshall, W. L. & Moulden, H. (2001). Hostility toward women and victim empathy of rapists. *Sexual Abuse: A Journal of Research and Treatment, 13,* 249–255.

Marshall, W. L., Anderson, D., & Champagne, F. (1997). Self-esteem and its relationship to sexual offending. *Psychology, Crime, and Law, 3,* 161–186.

Marshall, W. L., Eccles, A., & Barbaree, H. E. (1991). The treatment of exhibitionists: A focus on sexual deviance versus cognitive and relationship features. *Behaviour Research and Therapy, 29,* 129–135.

Marshall, W. L., Hudson, S. M., & Hodkinson, S. (1993). The importance of attachment bonds in the development of juvenile sex offending. In H. E. Barbaree, W. L. Marshall, & S. M. Hudson (Eds.), *The juvenile sex offender* (pp. 164–181). New York: Guilford.

Marshall, W. L., Serran, G. A., & Cortoni, F. A. (2000). Childhood attachments, sexual abuse, and their relationship to adult coping in child molesters. *Sexual Abuse: Journal of Research and Treatment, 12,* 17–26.

Martin, G. M. (2005). Epigenetic drift in aging identical twins. *Proceedings of the National Academy of Sciences of the United States of America, 102*(30), 10413–10414.

Martin, P. R. & Seneviratne, H. M. (1997). Effects of food deprivation and a stressor on head pain. *Health Psychology, 16,* 310–318.

Martin, R. A. (1996). The situational humor response questionnaire (SHRQ) and coping humour scale (CHS): A decade of research findings. *Humour, 9,* 251–272.

Martin, R. A. (2001). Humor, laughter, and physical health methodological issues and research findings. *Psychological Bulletin, 127*(4), 504–519.

Martin, R. A. (2007). *The psychology of humor: An integrative approach.* Burlington, MA: Elsevier Academic Press.

Martin, R. A. & Lefcourt, H. M. (1983). Sense of humor as a moderator of the relation between stressors and moods. *Journal of Personality and Social Psychology, 45,* 1313–1324.

Martin, R. A. et al. (1993). Humor, coping with stress, self-concept, and psychological well–being. *Humor: International Journal of Humor Research, 6,* 89–104.

Martin, R. L. et al. (1985). Mortality in a follow-up of 500 psychiatric outpatients: I. Total mortality. *Archives of General Psychiatry, 42,* 47–54.

Martin, S. (2001). Prevalence of migraine headache in Canada. *Canadian Medical Association Journal, 164*(10), 1481.

Martinsen, E. W. (2005). Exercise and depression. *International Journal of Sport and Exercise Psychology, 3,* 469–483.

Marzuk, P. M. & Barchas, J. D. (1997). Psychiatry. *Journal of American Medical Association, 277,* 1892–1894.

Mason, M. (1994, September). Why ulcers run in families. *Health,* pp. 44, 48.

Masten, A. S. (2001). Ordinary magic: Resilience processes in development . *American Psychologist, 56*(3), 227–238.

Masters, W. H. & Johnson, V. E. (1970). *Human sexual inadequacy.* Boston: Little, Brown.

Maté, G. (2003). *When the body says no: The cost of hidden stress.* Toronto: Knopf Canada.

Matefy, R. (1980). Role-playing theory of psychedelic drug flashbacks. *Journal of Consulting and Clinical Psychology, 48,* 551–553.

Mathers, J. C. & Hesketh, J. E. (2007). The biological revolution: Understanding the impact of SNPs on diet-cancer interrelationships. *The Journal of Nutrition, 137*(1), 253S–258S.

Matheson, K. & Anisman, H. (2003). Systems of coping associated with dysphoria, anxiety and depressive illness: A multivariate profile perspective. *Stress: The International Journal on the Biology of Stress, 6,* 223–234.

Mathews, A. & MacLeod, C. (2005). Cognitive vulnerability to emotional disorders.

Annual Review of Clinical Psychology, 1, 167–195.

Mattson, S. & Riley, E. (2000). Parent ratings of behavior in children with heavy prenatal alcohol exposure and IQ-matched controls. *Alcoholism: Clinical and Experimental Research, 24*(2), 226–231.

Maxwell, J. C. (2005). Emerging research on methamphetamine. *Current Opinion in Psychiatry, 18,* 235–242.

Mayer, J. D. & Salovey, P. (1997). What is emotional intelligence? In P. Salovey & D. Sluyter (Eds.), *Emotional development and emotional intelligence: Implications for educators* (pp. 3–31). New York: Basic Books.

Mayo-Smith, M. F. (1997). Pharmacological management of alcohol withdrawal. A meta-analysis and evidence-based practice guideline. American Society of Addiction Medicine Working Group on Pharmacological Management of Alcohol Withdrawal. *Journal of the American Medical Association, 278,* 144–151.

McBride, P. A., Anderson, G. M., & Shapiro, T. (1996). Autism research: Bringing together approaches to pull apart the disorder. *Archives of General Psychiatry, 53,* 980–983.

McCarthy, B. W. & Bodnar, L. E. (2005). Couple sex therapy: Assessment, treatment, and relapse prevention. In J. L. Lebow (Ed.), *Handbook of clinical family therapy* (pp. 464–493). New York: John Wiley & Sons.

McCaul, M. E., & Furst, J. (1994). Alcoholism treatment in the United States. *Alcohol Health & Research World, 18,* 253–260.

McClellan, J. M., Susser, E., & King, M. (2006). Maternal famine, de novo mutations, and schizophrenia. *The Journal of the American Medical Association, 296*(5), 582–584.

McClelland, D. C., Alexander, C., & Marks, E. (1982). The need for power, stress, immune functions, and illness among male prisoners. *Journal of Abnormal Psychology, 91,* 61–70.

McCloskey, M. S., Phan, K. L., & Coccaro, E. F. (2005). Neuroimaging and personality disorders. *Current Psychiatry Reports, 7*(1), 65–72.

McCord, W., & McCord, J. (1964). *The psychopath: An essay on the criminal mind.* New York: Van Nostrand.

McCormick, R. M. (2000). Aboriginal traditions in the treatment of substance abuse. *Canadian Journal of Counselling, 34*(1), 25–32.

McCracken, J. T., McGough, J., Shah, B., Cronin, P., Hong, D., Aman, M. G., et al. (2002). Risperidone in children with autism and serious behavioral problems. *New England Journal of Medicine, 347*(5), 314–321.

McCrady, B. S. (1993). Alcoholism. In D. H. Barlow (Ed.), *Clinical handbook of psychological disorders* (2nd ed., pp. 362–393). New York: Guilford.

McCrady, B. S. (1994). Alcoholics Anonymous and behavior therapy: Can habits be treated as diseases? Can diseases be treated as habits? *Journal of Consulting and Clinical Psychology, 62,* 1159–1166.

McCulloch, E. A. & Till, J. E. (1960). The radiation sensitivity of normal mouse bone marrow cells, determined by quantitative marrow transplantation into irradiated mice. *Radiation Research, 13*(1), 115–125.

McDougall, C. & Arthur, N. (2001). Applying racial identity models in multicultural counselling. *Canadian Journal of Counselling, 35*(1), 122–136.

McEachin, J. J., Smith, T., & Lovaas, O. I. (1993). Long-term outcome for children with autism who received early intensive behavioral treatment. *American Journal on Mental Retardation, 97,* 359–372.

McGlashan, T. H. & Fenton, W. S. (1992). The positive-negative distinction in schizophrenia: Review of natural history validators. *Archives of General Psychiatry, 49,* 63–72.

McGovern, P. G., Pankow, J. S., Shahar, E., Doliszny, K. M., Folsom, A. R., Blackburn, H. et al. (1996). Recent trends in acute coronary heart disease. *New England Journal of Medicine, 334*(14), 884–890.

McGrath, R. E., Pogge, D. L., & Stokes, J. M. (2002). Incremental validity of selected MMPI—A content scales in an inpatient setting. *Psychological Assessment, 14*(4), 401–409.

McGuire, P. K., Shah, G. M. S., & Murray, R. M. (1993). Increased blood flow in Broca's area during auditory hallucinations in schizophrenia. *Lancet, 342,* 703–706.

McIntosh, D. E. (1999). Identifying at-risk preschoolers: The

discriminant validity of the Differential Ability Scales. *Psychology in the Schools, 36,* 1–10.

McLellan, A. T., Alterman, A. I., Metzger, D. S., Grissom, G. R., Woody, G. E., Luborsky, L., et al. (1994). Similarity of outcome predictors across opiate, cocaine, and alcohol treatments: Role of treatment services. *Journal of Consulting and Clinical Psychology, 62,* 1141–1158.

McNally, R. J., Cassiday, K. L., & Calamari, J. E. (1990). Taijin-kyofu-sho in a Black American woman: Behavioral treatment of a "culture-bound" anxiety disorder. *Journal of Anxiety Disorders, 4,* 83–87.

McNaughton, N. & Corr, P. J. (2004). A two-dimensional neuropsychology of defense: Fear/anxiety and defensive distance. *Neuroscience and Biobehavioral Reviews, 28*(3), 285–305.

McSherry, B. (1998). Getting away with murder? Dissociative states and criminal responsibility. *International Journal of Law and Psychiatry, 21,* 163–176.

Mead, M. (1935). *Sex and temperament in three primitive societies.* New York: Morrow.

Meador-Woodruff, J. H., Haroutunian, V., Powchik, P., Davidson, M., Davis, K. L., Watson, S. J. et al. (1997). Dopamine receptor transcript expression in striatum and prefrontal and occipital cortex: Focal abnormalities in orbitofrontal cortex in schizophrenia. *Archives of General Psychiatry, 54,* 1089–1095.

Meana, M. & Binik, Y.M. (1994). Painful coitus: A review of female dyspareunia. *Journal of Nervous and Mental Disease, 182,* 264–272.

Meana, M., Binik, Y. M., Khalife, S., & Cohen, D. (1997). Dyspareuia: Sexual dysfunction or pain syndrome? *Journal of Nervous and Mental Disease, 185,* 561–569.

Medalia, A., Aluma, M., Tryon, W., & Merriam, A. E. (1998). Effectiveness of attention training in schizophrenia. *Schizophrenia Bulletin, 24,* 147–152.

Medical Society of Nova Scotia (1997). *Chronic daily headache—medication-induced headache: Epidemiology.* Retrieved May 20, 2003, from http://www.digital-fx.ca/cme/neuro/neur-virtprof3.html.

Mednick, S. A. (1970). Breakdown in individuals at high risk for schizophrenia: Possible predispositional perinatal factors. *Mental Hygiene, 54,* 50–63.

Mednick, S. A. & Schulsinger, F. (1968). Some pre-morbid characteristics related to breakdown in children with schizophrenic mothers. In D. Rosenthal & S. S. Kety (Eds.), *The transmission of schizophrenia* (pp. 267–291). New York: Pergamon.

Mednick, S. A., Moffitt, T. E., & Stack, S. (1987). *The causes of crime: New biological approaches.* New York: Cambridge University Press.

Mednick, S. A., Parnas, J., & Schulsinger, F. (1987). The Copenhagen High-Risk project, 1962–86. *Schizophrenia Bulletin, 13,* 485–495.

Meehl, P. E. (1962). Schizotaxia, schizotypy, schizophrenia. *American Psychologist, 17,* 827–838.

Meehl, P. E. (1972). A critical afterword. In I. I. Gottesman & J. Shields (Eds.), *Schizophrenia and genetics: A twin study vantage point* (pp. 367–415). New York: Academic.

Meichenbaum, D. (1976). Toward a cognitive theory of self-control. Chapter included in G. Schwartz & D. Shapiro (Eds.), *Consciousness and self-regulation: Advances in research.* New York: Plenum Press.

Meichenbaum, D. (1977). *Cognitive-behavior modification: An integrative approach.* New York: Plenum Press.

Meichenbaum, D. (1993). Changing conceptions of cognitive behavior modification: Retrospect and prospect. *Journal of Consulting and Clinical Psychology, 61,* 202–204.

Meichenbaum. D. (2005). 35 years of working with suicidal patients: Lessons learned. *Canadian Psychology, 46,* 64–72.

Mellings, T. M. B. & Alden, L. E. (2000). Cognitive processes in social anxiety: The effects of self-focus, rumination and anticipatory processing. *Behaviour Research and Therapy, 38,* 243–257.

Mellor, C. S. (1970). First rank symptoms of schizophrenia. *British Journal of Psychiatry, 177,* 15–23.

Mental Health Promotion. (2003). *Frequently Asked Questions.* Retrieved April 23, 2003, from http://www.hc-sc.gc.ca/hppb/mentalhealth/mhp/faq.html.

Merikangas, K. R. (2003). Will the genomics revolution revolutionize psychiatry? *American Journal of Psychiatry,160*(4), 625–635.

Merikangas, K. R. & Risch, N. (2003). Genomic priorities and public health. *Science, 302*(24), 599–601.

Merskey, H. (1992). The manufacture of personalities: The production of multiple personality disorder. *British Journal of Psychiatry, 160,* 327–340.

Messenger, J. (1971). Sex and repression in an Irish folk community. In D. Marshall & R. Suggs (Eds.), *Human sexual behavior: Variations in the ethnographic spectrum.* Englewood Cliffs, NJ: Prentice Hall.

Meston, C. M. & Bradford, A. (2006). Sexual dysfunctions in women. *Annual Review of Clinical Psychology, 3,* 81–104.

Metsanen, M., Wahlberg, K.-E., Saarento, O., Tarvainen, T., Miettunen, J., Koistinen, P. et al. (2004). Early presence of thought disorder as a prospective sign of mental disorder. *Psychiatry Research, 125,* 193–203.

Meyer, G. J. (1997). Assessing reliability: Critical corrections for a critical examination of the Rorschach comprehensive system. *Psychological Assessment, 9,* 480–489.

Meyer, T. J. & Mark, M. M. (1995). Effects of psychosocial interventions with adult cancer patients: A meta-analysis of randomized experiments. *Health Psychology, 14,* 101–108.

Meyers, B. S. (2006). Psychotic depression. *Psychiatric Annals, 36,* 7–9.

Mian, M., Marton, P., & LeBaron, D. (1996). The effects of sexual abuse on 3- to 5-year-old girls. *Child Abuse and Neglect, 20,* 731–745.

Miklowitz, D. J. (2004). The role of family systems in severe and recurrent psychiatric disorders: A developmental psychopathology view. *Development and Psychopathology, 16,* 667–688.

Miklowitz, D. J. & Johnson, S. L. (2006). The psychopathology and treatment of bipolar disorder. *Annual Review of Clinical Psychology, 2,* 199–235.

Milberger, S., Biederman, J., Faraone, S., Chen, L., & Jones, J. (1996). Is maternal smoking during pregnancy a risk factor for attention deficit hyperactivity disorder in children? *American Journal of Psychiatry, 153,* 1138–1142.

Millar, W. J. & Hill, G. B. (1998). Childhood asthma. *Health Reports, 10*(3), 9–21.

Miller, E. (1987). Hysteria: Its nature and explanation. *British Journal of Clinical Psychology, 26,* 163–173.

Miller, L. K. (1999). The savant syndrome: Intellectual impairment and exceptional skills. *Psychological Bulletin, 125,* 31–46.

Miller, T. Q., Turner, C. W., Tindale, R. S., Posavac, E. J. & Dugoni, B. L. (1991). Reasons for the trend toward null findings in research on Type A behavior. *Psychological Bulletin, 110*(3), 469–485.

Miller, W. R., & Hester, R. K. (1986). Inpatient alcoholism treatment: Who benefits? *American Psychologist, 41,* 794–805.

Miller, W. R., & Muñoz, R. F. (1983). *How to control your drinking* (2nd ed.). Albuquerque: University of New Mexico Press.

Miller, W. R., Leckman, A. L., Delaney, H. D., & Tinkcom, M. (1993). Long-term follow-up of behavioral self-control training. *Journal of Studies on Alcohol, 53,* 249–261.

Millon, T. (1981). *Disorders of personality DSM-III: Axis II.* New York: John Wiley & Sons.

Millon, T. (1982). *Millon Clinical Multiaxial Inventory manual* (3rd ed.). Minneapolis: National Computer Systems.

Millon, T. (2003). It's time to rework the blueprints: building a science for clinical psychology. *American Psychologist, 58*(11):949–961.

Millon, T., Millon, C., Meagher, S., Grossman, S., & Ramnath, R. (2004). *Personality disorders in modern life* (2nd ed.). Hoboken, NJ: John Wiley & Sons, 2004.

Milner, P. (2006). Trains of Neural Thought. *Canadian Psychology/Psychologie canadienne, 47*(1), 36–43.

Milos, G., Spindler, A., & Schnyder, U. (2004). Psychiatric comorbidity and Eating Disorder Inventory (EDI) profiles in eating disorder patients. *Canadian Journal of Psychiatry, 49*(3), 179–184.

Milstone, C. (1995). *The mentally ill and the criminal justice system: Innovative community-based programs.* Mental health Division, Health Services Directorate, Health Programs and Services. Ottawa, ON: Health Canada.

Mineka, S., & Zinbarg, R. (2006). A contemporary learning theory perspective on the etiology of anxiety disorders. *American Psychologist, 61,* 10–26.

Minuchin, S. (1974). *Families and family therapy.* Cambridge, MA: Harvard University Press.

Minuchin, S., Rosman, B. L., & Baker, L. (1978). *Psychosomatic families: Anorexia nervosa in context.* Cambridge, MA: Harvard University Press.

Mischel, W. (1979). On the interface of cognition and personality: Beyond the person-situation debate. *American Psychologist, 34,* 740–754.

Mitchell, P. B. & Loo, C. K. (2006). Transcranial magnetic stimulation for depression. *Australian and New Zealand Journal of Psychiatry, 40,* 406–413.

Mitte, K. (2005). Meta-analysis of cognitive-behavioral treatments for generalized anxiety disorder: A comparison with pharmacotherapy. *Psychological Bulletin, 131,* 785–795.

Moffitt, T. E., Caspi, A., & Rutter, M. (2006). Measured gene-environment interactions in psychopathology. *Perspectives on Psychological Science, 1,* 5–27.

Mohr, D. C., & Beutler, L. E. (1990). Erectile dysfunction: A review of diagnostic and treatment procedures. *Clinical Psychology Review, 10,* 123–150.

Monahan, J. (1981). *A clinical prediction of violent behavior.* (DHHS Publication No. ADM. 81-921). Rockville, MD: National Institute of Mental Health.

Money, J. (1987). Sin, sickness, or status? Homosexual gender identity and psychoneuroendocrinology. *American Psychologist, 42,* 384–399.

Money, J. & Lamacz, M. (1990). *Vandalized lovemaps.* Buffalo, NY: Prometheus.

Montgomery, S. (2006). Serotonin noradrenaline reuptake inhibitors: Logical evolution of antidepressant development. *International Journal of Psychiatry in Clinical Practice, 10* (Suppl 2), 5–11.

Monti, P. M., Binkoff, J. A., Abrams, D. B., Zwick, W. R., Nirenberg, T. D., & Liepman, M. R. (1987). Reactivity of alcoholics and nonalcoholics to drinking cues. *Journal of Abnormal Psychology, 96,* 122–126.

Monti, P. M. et al. (1994). Cue exposure with coping skills treatment for male alcoholics: A preliminary investigation. *Journal of Consulting and Clinical Psychology, 61,* 1011–1019.

Moran, M. G. (1991). Psychological factors affecting pulmonary and rheumatologic diseases: A review. *Psychosomatics, 32,* 14–23.

Moretti, M. M., Emmrys, C., Grizenko, N., Holland, R., Moore, K., Shamsie, J., & Hamilton, H. (1997). The Treatment of Conduct Disorder: Perspectives from across Canada. *Canadian Journal of Psychiatry, 42*(6), 637–648.

Morgenstern, J., Langenbucher, J., Labouvie, E., Miller, K. J. (1997). The comorbidity of alcoholism and personality disorders in a clinical population: Prevalence rates and relation to alcohol typology variables. *Journal of Abnormal Psychology, 106,* 74–84.

Morin, C. M. & Wooten, V. (1996). Psychological and pharmacological approaches to treating insomnia: Critical issues in assessing their separate and combined effects. *Clinical Psychology Review, 16,* 521–542.

Morin, C. M., LeBlanc, M., Daley, M., Gregoire, J. P., & Merette, C. (2006). Epidemiology of insomnia: Prevalence, self-help treatments, consultations, and determinants of help-seeking behaviors. *Sleep Medicine, 7*(2), 123–130.

Morrow, D. J. (1998, April 21). Pfizer drug for impotence leads market. *The New York Times,* pp. D1, D4.

Mortimer, A. M. et al. (1990). The positive-negative dichotomy in schizophrenia. *British Journal of Psychiatry, 157,* 41–49.

Moskowitz, A. K. (2004). "Scared stiff": Catatonia as an evolutionary-based fear response. *Psychological Review, 111,* 984–1002.

Motiuk, L. L., & Porporino, F. J. (1991). *The Prevalence, Nature and Severity of Mental Health Problems Among Male Inmates in Canadian Penitentiaries* (Catalogue No. R-24). Ottawa: Correctional Service of Canada, Research and Statistics Branch.

Mowrer, O. H. (1948). Learning theory and the neurotic paradox. *American Journal of Orthopsychiatry, 18,* 571–610.

Muckle, W. & Turnbull, J. (2006). Sheltering the homeless. *Canadian Medical Association Journal, 175*(10), 1177.

Mueser, K. T., & Liberman, R. P. (1995). Behavior therapy in practice. In B. Bongar & L. E. Beutler (Eds.), *Comprehensive textbook of psychotherapy: Theory and practice* (pp. 84–110). New York: Oxford.

Mukherjee, R. A. S., Hollins, S., & Turk, J. (2006). Psychiatric comorbidity of foetal alcohol syndrome. *Psychiatric Bulletin, 30,* 194–195.

Muller, N. (2004). Immunological and infectious aspects of schizophrenia. *European Archives of Psychiatry and Clinical Neuroscience, 254,* 1–3.

Muris, P. (2006). Freud was Right... About the origins of abnormal behavior. *Journal of Child and Family Studies, 15*(1), 1–12.

Murray, H. A. (1943). *Thematic Apperception Test: Pictures and manual.* Cambridge, MA: Harvard University Press.

Murstein, B. I. & Mathes, S. (1996). Projection on projective techniques and pathology: The problem that is not being addressed. *Journal of Personality Assessment, 66,* 337–349.

Murtagh, D. R. R. & Greenwood, K. M. (1995). Identifying effective psychological treatments for insomnia: A meta-analysis. *Journal of Consulting and Clinical Psychology, 63,* 79–89.

N

Najavits, L. M. (2002). Seeking safety: A treatment manual for PTSD and substance abuse. New York: Guilford.

Nasser, E. H. & Overholser, J. C. (2005). Recovery from major depression: The role of support from family, friends, and spiritual beliefs. Acta Psychiatrica Scandinavica, 111, 125–132.

National Asthma Control Task Force (2000). The prevention and management of asthma in Canada: A major challenge now and in the future (Catalogue No. H49-138/2000E). Ottawa, ON: Author. Retrieved February 8, 2007, from http://www.phac-aspc.gc.ca/publicat/pma-pca00/pdf/asthma00e.pdf.

National Council on Ethics in Human Research (NCEHR) (2002). Who we are. Retrieved February 15, 2003, from http://ncehr-cnerh.org/english/mstr_frm.html.

National Institute for Clinical Excellence. (2005). Post-traumatic stress disorder. London: Royal College of Psychiatrists and British Psychological Society.

National Institute of Mental Health (NIMH) (2003, December 22). Mental Illness Genetics Among Science's Top "Breakthroughs" for 2003. NIMH Press Office. Retrieved December 16, 2006, from http://www.nimh.nih.gov/Press/runnersup.cfm.

National Institute of Nutrition (2001). Giving adolescents a fighting chance against eating disorders. Retrieved July 31, 2003, from http://www.nin.ca/public_html/Publications.

Needles, D. J. & Abramson, L. Y. (1990). Positive life events, attributional style, and hopefulness: Testing a model of recovery from depression. Journal of Abnormal Psychology, 99, 156–165.

Neiger, B. L. (1988). Adolescent suicide: Character traits of high-risk teenagers. Adolescence, 23, 469–475.

Neill, J. (1990). Whatever became of the schizophrenogenic mother? American Journal of Psychotherapy, 44, 499–505.

Nelson, C. B., Heath, A. C., & Kessler, R. C. (1998). Temporal progression of alcohol dependence symptoms in the U.S. household population: Results from the National Comorbidity Survey. Journal of Consulting and Clinical Psychology, 66, 474–483.

Nemeroff, C. B. (2007). The burden of severe depression: A review of diagnostic challenges and treatment alternatives. Journal of Psychiatric Research, 41, 189–206.

Nemiah, J. C. (1978). Psychoneurotic disorders. In A. M. Nicholi (Ed.), Harvard guide to modern psychiatry. Cambridge, MA: Harvard University Press.

Neufeld, R. W. J. (1999). Dynamic differentials of stress and coping. Psychological Review, 106, 385–397.

Neufeld, R. W. J., Vollick, D., Carter, J. R., Boksman, K., & Jette, J. (2002). Application of stochastic modeling to the assessment of group and individual differences in cognitive functioning. Psychological Assessment, 14, 279–298.

Neugebauer, R. (1979). Medieval and early modern theories of mental illness. Archives of General Psychiatry, 36, 477–484.

Nevid, J. S., Fichner-Rathus, L., & Rathus, S. A. (1995). Human sexuality in a world of diversity (2nd ed.). Boston: Allyn & Bacon.

Nezu, A. M. (1994). Introduction to special section: Mental retardation and mental illness. Journal of Consulting and Clinical Psychology, 62, 4–5.

Nezu, A. M., Wilkins, V. M., & Nezu, C. M. (2004). Social problem solving, stress, and negative affect. In E. C. Chang, T. J. D'Zurilla, & L. J. Sanna (Eds.), Social problem solving: Theory, research, and training (pp. 49–65). Washington, DC: American Psychological Association.

Nezu, C. M., & Nezu, A. M. (1994). Outpatient psychotherapy for adults with mental retardation and concomitant psychopathology: Research and clinical imperatives. Journal of Consulting and Clinical Psychology, 62, 34–42.

NIAAA report links drinking and early death. (1990, October). The Addiction Letter, 6, 5.

Niagara Region, Ontario. Canadian Journal of Psychiatry, 47(7), 652–659.

Niaura, R., Todaro, J. F., Stroud, L., Spiro, A. Ward, K. D., & Weiss, S. (2002). Hostility, the metabolic syndrome, and incident coronary heart disease. Health Psychology, 21(6), 588–593.

Nicholson, I. R. & Neufeld, R. W. J. (1992). A dynamic vulnerability perspective on stress and schizophrenia. American Journal of Orthopsychiatry, 62, 117–130.

Nicholson, R. A. et al. (1997). Utility of MMPI-2 indicators of response distortion: Receiver operating characteristic analysis. Psychological Assessment, 9, 471–479.

Nicolson, R. & Szatmari, P. (2003). Genetic and Neurodevelopmental influences in autistic disorder. Canadian Journal of Psychiatry, 48(8), 526–537.

Nides, M. A., Rakos, R. F., Gonzales, D., Murray, R. P., Tashkin, D. P., Bjornson-Benson, W. M., et al. (1995). Predictors of initial smoking cessation and relapse through the first 2 years of the Lung Health Study. *Journal of Consulting and Clinical Psychology, 63,* 60–69.

Niemz, K., Griffiths, M., & Banyard, P. (2005). Prevalence of pathological Internet use among university studies and correlations with self-esteem, the general health questionnaire (GHQ), and disinhibition. *CyberPsychology & Behavior, 8,* 562–570.

Nigg, J. T. & Goldsmith, H. H. (1994). Genetics of personality disorders: Perspectives from personality and psychopathology research. *Psychological Bulletin, 115,* 346–380.

Nigg, J. T., Lohr, N. E., Western, D., Gold, L. J., & Silk, K. R. (1992). Malevolent object representations in borderline personality disorder and major depression. Journal of Abnormal Psychology, 101(1), 61–67.

Nolen-Hoeksema, S. & Corte, C. (2004). Gender and self-regulation. In R. F. Baumeister & K. D. Vohs (Eds.), Handbook of self-regulation: Research, theory, and applications (pp. 411–421). New York: Guilford.

Nolen-Hoeksema, S. & Girgus, J. S. (1994). The emergence of gender differences in depression during adolescence. Psychological Bulletin, 115, 424–443.

Nolen-Hoeksema, S., Girgus, J. S., & Seligman, M. E. P. (1992). Predictors and consequences of childhood depressive symptoms: A 5-year longitudinal study. Journal of Abnormal Psychology, 101, 405–422.

Nopoulos, P., Flaum, M., & Andreasen, N. C. (1997). Sex differences in brain morphology in schizophrenia. American Journal of Psychiatry, 154, 1648–1654.

Norman, R. M. G. & Townsend, L. A. (1999). Cognitive-behavioural therapy for psychosis: A status report. Canadian Journal of Psychiatry, 44, 245–252.

Norton, G. R., Cox, B. J., & Malan, J. (1992). Nonclinical panickers: A critical review. Clinical Psychology Review, 12, 121–139.

Nowaczyk, M. J. M. (2001a). Smith-Lemli-Opitz syndrome.

Canadian Paediatric Surveillance Program. Results 2000 (pp. 38–40). Ottawa: Canadian Paediatric Society.

Nowaczyk, M. J. M. (2001b). DHCR7 and Smith-Lemli-Opitz syndrome. Clinical and Investigative Medicine, 26(6), 311–317.

Nowaczyk, M. J. M., Whelan, D. T., Heshka, T. W., & Hill, R. E. (1999). Smith-Lemli-Opitz syndrome: A treatable inherited error of metabolism causing mental retardation. Canadian Medical Association Journal, 161(2), 165–170.

Nowell, P. D., Buysse, D. J., Morin, C., Reynolds, C F., III, & Kupfer, D. J. (1998). Effective treatments for selected sleep disorders. In P.E. Nathan & J. M. Gorman (Eds.), A guide to treatments that work (pp. 531–543). New York: Oxford University Press.

Nunes, J. & Simmie, S. (2002). Beyond crazy: Journeys through mental illness. Toronto, ON: McClelland & Stewart.

O

O'Brien, C. P. (1996). Recent developments in the pharmacotherapy of substance abuse. *Journal of Consulting and Clinical Psychology, 64,* 677–686.

O'Brien, C. P. & McKay, J. (1998). Psychopharmacological treatments of substance use disorders. In P. E. Nathan & J. M. Gorman (Eds.), *A guide to treatments that work* (pp. 127–155). New York: Oxford University Press.

O'Connor, B. P. & Dyce, J. A. (2001). Personality Disorders. In M. Hersen & V.B. Van Hasselt (Eds.), *Advanced Abnormal Psychology* (pp. 399–417). New York: Kluwer Academic/Plenum Press.

O'Connor, T. G., McGuire, S., Reiss, D., Hetherington, E. M., & Plomin, R. (1998). Co-occurrence of depressive symptoms and antisocial behavior in adolescence: A common genetic liability. *Journal of Abnormal Psychology, 107,* 27–37.

O'Donohue, W., Dopke, C. A., & Swingen, D. N. (1997). Psychotherapy for female sexual dysfunction: A review. *Clinical Psychology Review, 17,* 537–566.

O'Donohue, W., Letourneau, E., & Geer, J. H. (1993). Prema-

ture ejaculation. In W. O'Donohue & J. H. Geer (Eds.), *Handbook of sexual dysfunctions: Assessment and treatment* (pp. 303–333). Boston: Allyn & Bacon.

O'Donohue, W., McKay, J. S., & Schewe, P. A. (1996). Rape: The roles of outcome expectancies and hypermasculinity. *Sexual Abuse Journal of Research and Treatment, 8,* 133–141.

O'Donohue, W., Swingen, D. N., Dopke, C. A., & Regev, L. G. (1999). Psychotherapy for male sexual dysfunction: A review. *Clinical Psychology Review, 19,* 591–630.

O'Farrell, T. J., Choquette, K. A., Cutter, H. S. G., Floyd, F. J., et al. (1996). Cost-benefit and cost-effectiveness analyses of behavioral marital therapy as an addition to outpatient alcoholism treatment. *Journal of Substance Abuse, 8,* 145–166.

O'Leary, A. (1990). Stress, emotion, and human immune functions. *Psychological Bulletin, 108,* 382–383.

O'Neil, P. (2004). The ethics of problem definition. *Canadian Psychology/Psychologie canadienne, 46(1),* 13–20.

Ochs, R. (1998, March 9). Alcohol: Sorting the contradictions. *New York Newsday.*

Offord, D. R., Boyle, M. H., Campbell, D., Goering, P., Lin, E., Wong, M., & Racine, Y. A. (1996). One-year prevalence of psychiatric disorders in Ontarians 15 to 64 years of age. *Canadian Journal of Psychiatry, 41(9),* 559–563.

Okubo, Y., Suhara, T., Suzuki, K., Kobayashi, K., Inoue, O., Terasaki, O., et al. (1997). Decreased prefrontal dopamine D1 receptors in schizophrenia revealed by PET. *Nature, 385,* 634–636.

Oldham, J. M. (1994). Personality disorders: Current perspectives. *Journal of the American Medical Association, 272,* 1770–1776.

Olesen, J. & Goadsby, P. J. (2000). Synthesis of migraine mechanisms. In J. Olesen, P. Tfelt-Hansen, & K. M. A. Welch (Eds.), *The headaches* (2nd ed., pp. 331–336). Philadelphia: Lippincott Williams and Wilkins.

Olfson, M., Marcus, S., Sackheim, H. A., Thompson, J., & Pincus, H. A. (1998). Use of ECT for the inpatient treatment of recurrent major depression. *American Journal of Psychiatry, 155,* 22–29.

Ollendick, T. H. & Ollendick, D. G. (1982). Anxiety disorders. In J. L. Matson & R. P. Barrettt (Eds.), *Psychopathology in the mentally retarded* (pp. 77–119). Orlando, FL: Grune & Stratton.

Olley, M. C. & Ogloff, J. R. P. (1995). Patient's rights advocacy: Implications for program design and implementation. *Journal of Mental Health Administration, 22,* 368–376.

Osborne. K. (2001, May 6). Regional disturbances. *New York Times Magazine,* 98–102.

Öst, L. (1987). Age of onset in different phobias. *Journal of Abnormal Psychology, 96,* 223–229.

Öst, L. (1992). Blood and injection phobia: Background and cognitive, physiological, and behavioral variables. *Journal of Abnormal Psychology, 101,* 68–74.

Ottawa Aboriginal Head Start Program (1998). Evaluation Report 1997–1998. Ottawa: Author. Retrieved October 18, 2003, from http://www.aboriginalcanada.com/headstart/docs/report2c.pdf.

Overeem, S., Mignot, E., van Dijk, J. G., & Lammers, G. J. (2001). Narcolepsy: Clinical features, new pathophysiologic insights, and future perspectives. *Journal of Clinical Neurophysiology, 18(2),* 78–105.

Overmier, J. B. L. & Seligman, M. E. P. (1967). Effect of inescapable shock upon subsequent escape and avoidance learning. *Journal of Comparative and Physiological Psychology, 63,* 28–33.

P

Pagnin, D., de Queiroz, V., Pini, S., & Cassano, G. B. (2004). Efficacy of ECT in depression: A meta-analytic review. *Journal of ECT, 20,* 13–20.

Paris, J. (1998). Psychotherapy for personality disorders: Working with traits. *Bulletin of the Menninger Clinic, 62(3),* 287–297.

Paris, J. (2002a). Chronic suicidality among patients with borderline personality disorder. *Psychiatric Services. 53(6),* 738–742.

Paris, J. (2002b). Implications of long-term outcomes research for the management of patients with borderline personality disorder. *Harvard Review of Psychiatry, 10(6),* 315–323.

Paris, J. (2003). *Personality disorders over time.* Washington, DC: American Psychiatric Press.

Paris, J. (2005). Recent advances in the treatment of borderline personality disorder. *Canadian Journal of Psychiatry, 50*(8), 435–441.

Paris, J. & Frank, H. (1989). Perceptions of parental bonding in borderline patients. *American Journal of Psychiatry, 146*(11), 1498–1499.

Paris, J. & Zweig-Frank, H. (2001). A 27-year follow-up of patients with borderline personality disorder. *Comprehensive Psychiatry, 42*(6), 482–487.

Paris, J., Brown, R., & Nowlis, D. (1987). Long-term follow-up of borderline patients in a general hospital. *Comparative Psychiatry, 28*(6), 530–535.

Parker, K. C. H., Hanson, R. K., & Hinsley, J. (1988). MMPI, Rorschach, and WAIS: A meta-analytic comparison of reliability, stability, and validity. *Psychological Bulletin, 103*, 367–373.

Parnas, D. J., Cannon, T. D., Jacobsen, B., Schulsinger, H., Schulsinger, F., & Mednick, S. A. (1993). Lifetime DSM-III-R diagnostic outcomes in the offspring of schizophrenic mothers: Results from the Copenhagen High-Risk Study. *Archives of General Psychiatry, 50*, 707–714.

Patrick, C. J., Cuthbert, B. N., & Lang, P. J. (1994). Emotion in the criminal psychopath: Fear image processing. *Journal of Abnormal Psychology, 103*, 523–534.

Patrick, J. (1988). Concordance of the MCMI and the MMPI in the diagnosis of three DSM-III Axis I disorders. *Journal of Clinical Psychology, 44*(2), 186–190.

Patten, S. B., Wang, J. L., Williams, J. V. A., Currie, S., Beck, C. A., Maxwell, C. J. et al. (2006). Descriptive epidemiology of major depression in Canada. *Canadian Journal of Psychiatry, 51*, 84–90.

Patton, G. C. (1988). Mortality in eating disorders. *Psychological Medicine, 18*(4), 947–951.

Patton, G. C., Selzer, R., Coffey, C., Carlin, J. B., & Wolfe, R. (1999). Onset of adolescent eating disorders: Population based cohort study over 3 years. *British Medical Journal, 318*(7186), 765–768.

Paul, G. L. & Lentz, R. J. (1977). *Psychosocial treatment of chronic mental patients: Milieu versus social-learning programs.* Cambridge, MA: Harvard University Press.

Paulesu, E., Demonet, J. F., Fazio, F., McCrory, E., Chanoine, V., Brunswick, N., Cappa, S. F., Cossu, G., Habib, M., Frith, C. D., & Frith, U. (2001). Dyslexia: Cultural diversity and biological unity. *Science, 291*(5511), 2165–2167.

Paulesu, E., Frith, C. D., & Frackowisk, R. S. J. (1993). The neural correlates of the verbal component of working memory. *Nature, 362*, 342–344.

Peaston, A. E. & Whitelaw, E. (2006). Epigenetics and phenotypic variation in mammals. *Mammalian Genome, 17*(5), 365–374.

Peedicayil, J. (2006). Epigenetic therapy: A new development in pharmacology. *The Indian Journal of Medical Research, 123*(1), 17–24.

Peltzer, K. & Machleidt, W. (1992). A traditional (African) approach towards the therapy of schizophrenia and its comparison with Western models. *Therapeutic Communities International Journal for Therapeutic and Supportive Organizations, 13*, 229–242.

Pendery, M. L., Maltzman, I. M., & West, L. J. (1982). Controlled drinking by alcoholics: New findings and a re-evaluation of a major affirmative study. *Science, 217*, 169–174.

Penn, D. L. (1998, June). Assessment and treatment of social dysfunction in schizophrenia. *Clinician's Research Digest,* Supplemental Bulletin 18.

Penn, D. L. & Mueser, K. T. (1996). Research update on the psychosocial treatment of schizophrenia. *American Journal of Psychiatry, 153*, 607–617.

Penn, D. L., Combs, D., & Mohamed, S. (2001). Social cognition and social functioning in schizophrenia. In P. W. Corrigan & D. L. Penn (Eds.), *Social cognition and schizophrenia* (pp. 97–121). Washington, DC: American Psychological Association.

Penner, L. A., Thompson, J. K., & Coovert, D. L. (1991). Size overestimation among anorexics: Much ado about very little? *Journal of Abnormal Psychology, 100*, 90–93.

Perlman, J. D. & Abramson, P. R. (1982). Sexual satisfaction among married & cohabitating individuals. *Journal of Consulting and Clinical Psychology, 50*, 458–460.

Perry, B. D. (2002). Stress, trauma and post-traumatic stress disorders in children: An introduction. Houston, TX: ChildTrauma Academy. Retrieved February 7, 2004, from http://www.childtrauma.org/CTAMATERIALS/PTSDfn_03_v2.pdf.

Perry, B. D., Pollard, R., Blakely, T., Baker, W., & Vigilante, D. (1995). Childhood trauma, the neurobiology of adaptation and "use-dependent" development of the brain: how "states" become "traits." *Infant Mental Health Journal, 16*(4), 271–291.

Perry, B. D., & Szalavitz, M. (2007). *The boy who was raised as a dog and other stories from a child psychiatrist's notebook: What traumatized children can teach us about loss, love and healing.* New York: Basic Books.

Petersen, T. J. (2006). Enhancing the efficacy of antidepressants with psychotherapy. *Journal of Psychopharmacology, 30 (Suppl 3)*, 19–28.

Peterson, C. B., Mitchell, J. E., Engbloom, S., Nugent, S., Mussell, M. P., & Miller, J. P. (1998). Group cognitive-behavioral treatment of binge eating disorder: A comparison of therapist-led versus self-help formats. *International Journal of Eating Disorders, 24*(2), 125–136.

Peterson, N. D. J., Henke, P. G., & Hayes, Z. (2002). Limbic System Function and Dream Content in University Students. *Journal of Neuropsychiatry Clinical Neurosciences, 14*(3), 283–288.

Petronis, A. (2003). Epigenetics and bipolar disorder: New opportunities and challenges. *American Journal of Medical Genetics, 123*(1), 65–75.

Petronis, A. (2004). The origin of schizophrenia: genetic thesis, epigenetic antithesis, and resolving synthesis. *Biological Psychiatry, 55*(10), 965–970.

Petronis, A., Gottesman, I. I., Crow, T. J., DeLisi, L. E., Klar, A. J., Macciardi, F., et al. (2000). Psychiatric epigenetics: A new focus for the new century. *Molecular Psychiatry, 5*(4), 342–346.

Petronis, A., Popendikyte, V., Kan, P., & Sasaki, T. (2002). Major psychosis and chromosome 22: genetics meets epigenetics. *CNS Spectrums, 7*(3), 209–214.

Pettifor, J. L. (2001). Are professional codes of ethics relevant for multicultural counselling? *Canadian Journal of Counselling, 35*(1), 26–35.

Pettingale, K. W. (1985). Towards a psychobiological model of cancer: Biological considerations. Special issue: Cancer and the mind. *Social Science and Medicine, 20*, 779–787.

Petty, S. C., Sachs-Ericsson, N., & Joiner, T. E. (2004). Interpersonal functioning deficits: Temporary or stable characteristics of depressed individuals? *Journal of Affective Disorders, 81*, 115–122.

Pezawas, L., Meyer-Lindenberg, A., Drabant, E. M., Verchinski, B. A., Munoz, K. E., Kolachana, B. S., et al. (2005). 5-HTTLPR polymorphism impacts human cingulate-amygdala interactions. *Nature Neuroscience, 8*, 828–834.

Pfaus, J. G., Kippin, T. E., & Centeno, S. (2001). Conditioning and sexual behavior: A review. *Hormones and Behavior, 40*, 291–321.

Phillips, D. P. & Carstensen, L. S. (1986). Clustering of teenage suicide after television news stories about suicide. *New England Journal of Medicine, 315*, 685–689.

Phillipson, E. A. (1993). Sleep apnea—a major public health problem [Editorial]. *New England Journal of Medicine, 328*, 1271–1273.

Pianta, R. C. & Egeland, B. (1994). Relation between depressive symptoms and stressful life events in a sample of disadvantaged mothers. *Journal of Consulting and Clinical Psychology, 62*, 1229–1234.

Piersma, H.L. (1987). The MCMI as a measure of DSM-III Axis II diagnoses: An empirical comparison. *Journal of Clinical Psychology, 43*(5), 478–483.

Pihl, R. O. & Smith, S. (1983). Of affect and alcohol. In L. A. Pohorecky & J. Brick (Eds.), *Stress and alcohol use* (pp. 203–228). New York: Elsevier.

Pike, K. M. & Rodin, J. (1991). Mothers, daughters, and disordered eating. *Journal of Abnormal Psychology, 101*, 198–204.

Pinals, D. A. & Appelbaum, P. S. (2004). Risk management regulatory concerns. *Essential Psychopharmacology, 5*, 289–295.

Pine, D. S., Alegria, M., Cook Jr. E. H., Costello, E. J., Dahl, R. E., Koretz, D. et al. (2002). Advances in Developmental Science and DSM-V. In D.J. Kupfer, M. B. First, & D. A. Regier (Eds.), *A research Agenda for DSM-V*. (pp. 85–122). Washington, DC: American Psychiatric Association.

Pinhas, L., Toner, B. B., Ali, A., Garfinkel, P. E., & Stuckless, N. (1999). The effects of the ideal of female beauty on mood and body satisfaction. *International Journal of Eating Disorders, 25*(2), 223–226.

Piotrowki, C. (2000). How popular is the Personality Assessment Inventory in practice and training? *Psychological Reports, 86*(1), 65–66.

Piper, A. & Merskey, H. (2004). The persistence of folly: A critical examination of dissociative identity disorder. Part I. The excesses of an improbable concept. *Canadian Journal of Psychiatry, 49*, 592–600.

Plomin, R. & Kovas, Y. (2005). Generalist genes and learning disabilities. *Psychological Bulletin, 131*(4), 592–617.

Plomin R, McGuffin P. (2003). Psychopathology in the postgenomic era. *Annual Review of Psychology, 54*, 205–228.

Plomin, R., Owen, M. J., & McGuffin P. (1994). The genetic basis of complex human behaviors. *Science, 264*, 1733–1739.

Podymow, T., Turnbull, J., Tadic, V., & Muckle, W. (2006). Shelter-based convalescence for homeless adults. *Canadian Journal of Public Health, 97*(5):379–383.

Polaschek, D. L. L., Ward, T., & Hudson, S. M. (1997). Rape and rapists: Theory and treatment. *Clinical Psychology Review, 17*, 117–144.

Polivy, J. & Herman, P. (2002). Causes of eating disorders. *Annual Review of Psychology, 53*, 187–213.

Poonwassie, A. & Charter, A. (2001). An Aboriginal world view of helping: Empowering approaches. *Canadian Journal of Counselling, 35*(1), 63–73.

Pope, H. G., Jr. & Yurgelun-Todd, D. (1996). The residual cognitive effects of heavy marijuana use in college students. *Journal of the American Medical Association, 275*, 521–527.

Pope, H. G., Jr., Jones, J. M., Hudson, J., Cohen, B. M., & Gunderson, J. G. (1983). The validity of DSM-III borderline personality disorder. *Archives of General Psychiatry, 40*, 23–30.

Porter, S., Birt, A. R., Yuille, J. C., & Lehman, D. R. (2000). Negotiating false memories: Interviewer and rememberer characteristics relate to memory distortion. *Psychological Science, 11*, 507–510.

Porter, S., Yuille, J. C., & Lehman, D. R. (1999). The nature of real, implanted, and fabricated childhood emotional events: Implications for the recovered memory debate. *Law and Human Behavior, 23*, 517–537.

Poulakis, Z. & Wertheim, E. H. (1993). Relationships among dysfunctional congitions, depressive symptoms, and bulimic tendencies. *Cognitive Therapy and Research, 17*, 549–559.

Power, M. (2000). Freud and the unconscious. *The Psychologist, 13*(12), 612–614.

Prevention-Dividend Project. (2003). *Encouraging the understanding, and use, of economic evaluations in Canada's non-profit and public sectors*. Retrieved April 23, 2003, from http://prevention-dividend. com/en/welcome.

Prince, R. H. (2000). Transcultural psychiatry: Personal experiences and Canadian perspectives. *Canadian Journal of Psychiatry, 45*(2), 195–196.

Project MATCH Research Group. (1997). Matching alcoholism treatments to client heterogeneity: Project MATCH post-treatment drinking outcomes. *Journal of Studies on Alcohol, 58*, 7–29.

Prout, P. I. & Dobson, K. S. (1998). Recovered memories of childhood sexual abuse: Searching for the middle ground in clinical practice. *Canadian Psychology, 39*, 257–265.

Public Health Agency of Canada. (2006). *HIV and AIDS in Canada*. Retreived on February 8, 2007, from http://www.phac-aspc.gc.ca/publicat/aids-sida/haic-vsac0606/pdf/haic-vsac0606.pdf.

Pull, C. B. (2005). Current status of virtual reality exposure therapy in anxiety disorders. *Current Opinion in Psychiatry, 18*, 7–14.

Pull, C. B. (2007). Combined pharmacotherapy and cognitive-behavioural therapy for anxiety disorders. *Current Opinion in Psychiatry, 20*, 30–35.

Purdon, C. (2004). Empirical investigations of thought suppression in OCD. *Journal of Behavior Therapy and Experimental Psychiatry, 35*, 121–136.

Purdon, C. & Clark, D. A. (1993). Obsessive intrusive thoughts in nonclinical subjects. Part I. Content and relation with depressive, anxious and obsessional symptoms. *Behaviour Research and Therapy, 31*, 713–720.

Purdon, C., Rowa, K., & Antony, M. M. (2005). Thought suppression and its effects on thought frequency, appraisal and mood state in individuals with obsessive-compulsive disorder. *Behaviour Research and Therapy, 43*, 93–108.

Pyszczynski, T. & Greenberg, J. (1992). *Hanging on and letting go: Understanding the onset, progression, and remission of depression*. New York: Springer.

Q

Quay, H. C. (1965). Psychopathic personality as pathological stimulation seeking. *American Journal of Psychiatry, 122*, 180–183.

Quinsey, V. L. (2003). The etiology of anomalous sexual preference in men. *Annals of the New York Academy of Sciences, 989*, 105–117.

R

R.*v. Swain* (1991), 63 C.C.C. (3d) 481 (S.C.C.).

Rabheru, K. (2001). The Use of Electroconvulsive Therapy in Special Patient Populations. *Canadian Journal of Psychiatry, 46*(8), 710–719.

Rabkin, J. G. et al. (1997). Stability of mood despite HIV illness progression in a group of homosexual men. *American Journal of Psychiatry, 154*, 231–238.

Radomsky, A. S., Gilchrist, P. T., & Dussault, D. (2006). Repeated checking really does cause memory distrust. *Behaviour Research and Therapy, 44*, 305–316.

Räikkönen, K., Matthews, K. A., Flory, J. D., & Owens, J. F. (1999). Effects of hostility on ambulatory blood pressure and mood during daily living in healthy adults. *Health Psychology, 18*(1), 44–53.

Ranjith, G. & Mohan, R. (2006). Dhat syndrome as a functional somatic syndrome: Developing a sociosomatic model. *Psychiatry, 69*, 142–150.

Rapin, I. (1997). Autism. *New England Journal of Medicine, 337*, 97–104.

Rapoport, M. J., Mamdani, M., & Herrmann, N. (2006). Electroconvulsive Therapy in Older Adults: 13-Year Trends, *Canadian Journal of Psychiatry, 51*(6), 616–619.

Rapport, M. D., Denny C., DuPaul G. J. et al. (1994). Attention deficit disorder and methylphenidate: Normalization rates, clinical effectiveness, and response prediction in 76 children. *Journal of the American Academy of Child & Adolescent Psychiatry, 33*, 882–893.

Raspe, R. E. (1860). *Baron Munchausen's narrative of his marvelous travels*. New York: Hurst.

Rathod, S. & Turkington, D. (2005). Cognitive-behaviour therapy for schizophrenia: A review. *Current Opinion in Psychiatry, 18*, 159–163.

Rathus, S. A. (1996). *Psychology* (6th ed.). Fort Worth: Harcourt Brace Jovanovich.

Rathus, S. A. & Nevid, J. S. (1977). *Behavior therapy*. Garden City, NY: Doubleday.

Rattit, L. A., Humphrey, L. L., & Lyons, J. S. (1996). Structural analysis of families with a polydrug-dependent, bulimic, or normal adolescent daughter. *Journal of Consulting & Clinical Psychology, 64*, 1255–1262.

Ravitz, P. (2004). The interpersonal fulcrum—Interpersonal therapy for the treatment of depression. *Canadian Psychiatric Association Bulletin, 36*(1), 15–19.

Reason, J. (2000). The Freudian slip revisited. *The Psychologist, 13*(12), 610–611.

Rector, N. A., & Beck, A. T. (2001). Cognitive behavioral therapy for schizophrenia: An empirical review. *Journal of Nervous and Mental Disease, 189*, 278–287.

Rector, N. A. & Seeman, M. V. (1992). Auditory hallucinations in women and men. *Schizophrenia Research, 7*, 233–236.

Redd, W. H. (1995). Behavioral research in cancer as a model for health psychology. *Health Psychology, 14,* 99–100.

Reich, J. (1996). The morbidity of DSM-III-R dependent personality disorder. *Journal of Nervous and Mental Disease, 184,* 22–26.

Reich, J. & Noyes, R. (1986). Differentiating schizoid and avoidant personality disorders [Letter to the editor]. *American Journal of Psychiatry, 143,* 1061–1063.

Reichman, M. E. (1994). Alcohol and breast cancer. *Alcohol Health and Research World, 18,* 182–183.

Reid, W. J. (1986). Antisocial personality. In R. Michels & J. O. Cavenar, Jr. (Eds.), *Psychiatry* (Vol. 1). New York: Basic Books.

Reisner, A. D. (2003). The electroconvulsive therapy controversy: Evidence and ethics. *Neuropsychology Review, 13,* 199–219.

Reiss, S. & Valenit-Hein, D. (1994). Development of a psychopathology rating scale for children with mental retardation. *Journal of Consulting and Clinical Psychology, 62,* 28–33.

Reissing, E. D., Binik, Y. M., & Khalife, S. (1999). Does vaginismus exist? A critical review of the literature. *Journal of Nervous and Mental Disease, 187,* 261–274.

Renaud, J., Chagnon, F., Turecki, G., & Marquette, C. (2005). Completed suicides in a Youth Centres population. *Canadian Journal of Psychiatry, 50,* 690–694.

Renneberg, B., Goldstein, A. J., Phillips, D., & Chambless, D. J. (1990). Intensive behavioral group treament of avoidant personality disorder. *Behavior Therapy, 21*(3), 363–377.

Renner, M. J. & Mackin, R. S. (1998). A life stress instrument of classroom use. *Teaching of Psychology, 25*(1), 46–48.

Reuter, M., Stark, R., Hennig, J., Walter, B., Kirsch, P., Schienle, A., et al. (2004). Personality and emotion: Test of Gray's personality theory by means of an fMRI study. *Behavioral Neuroscience, 118*(3), 462–469.

Reuter, M., Schmitz, A., Corr, P., & Hennig, J. (2006). Molecular genetics support Gray's personality theory: The interaction of COMT and DRD2 polymorphisms predicts the behavioural approach system.

International Journal of Neuropsychopharmacololgy, 9(2), 155–166.

Rey, J. M. (1993). Oppositional defiant disorder. *American Journal of Psychiatry, 150,* 1769–1778.

Ricciardelli, L. A. & McCabe, M. P. (2004). A biopsychosocial model of disordered eating and the pursuit of muscularity in adolescent boys. *Psychological Bulletin, 130*(2), 179–205.

Ricciardelli, L. A., McCabe, M. P., Williams, R. J., & Thompson, J. K. (2007). The role of ethnicity and culture in body image and disordered eating among males. *Clinical Psychology Review, 27*(5), 582–606.

Richardson, B. (2003). Impact of aging on DNA methylation. *Ageing Research Reviews 2*(3), 245–261.

Ridenour, T. A. (2005). Inhalants: Not to be taken lightly anymore. *Current Opinion in Psychiatry, 18,* 243–247.

Rieber, R. W., Takoosian, H., & Iglesias, H. (2002). The case of Sybil in the teaching of psychology. *Journal of Social Distress and the Homeless, 11,* 355–360.

Rief, W. & Barsky, A. J. (2005). Psychobiological perspectives on somatoform disorders. *Psychoneuroendocrinology, 30,* 996–1002.

Riley, V. (1981). Psychoneuroendocrine influences on immunocompetence and neoplasia. *Science, 212,* 1100–1109.

Rimland, B. (1978). The savant capabilities of autistic children and their cognitive implications. In G. Serban (Ed.), *Cognitive defects in the development of mental illness.* New York: Brunner-Mazel.

Rivas-Vazquez, R. A. & Blais, M. A. (2002). Pharmacologic treatment of personality disorder. *Professional Psychology: Research and Practice, 33*(1), 104–107.

Robins, L. N., Tipp, J., & Przybeck, T. (1991). Antisocial personality. In L. N. Robins & D. A. Regier (Eds.), *Psychiatric disorders in America: The Epidemiologic Catchment Area Study* (pp. 258–290). New York: Free Press.

Rocha, B. A., Scearce-Levie, K., Lucas, J. J., Hiroi, N., Castonon, N., Nestler, E. J., et al. (1998). Increased vulnera-

bility to cocaine in mice lacking the serotonin-1B receptor [Letter]. *Nature, 393,* 175.

Rochlen, A. B., Zack, J. S., & Speyer, C. (2004). Online therapy: Review of relevant definitions, debates, and current empirical support. *Journal of Clinical Psychology, 60*(3), 269–283.

Rock, C. L. & Curran-Celentano, J. (1996). Nutritional management of eating disorders. *The Psychiatric Clinics of North America, 19,* 701–713.

Rodin, G., Olmsted, M. P., Rydall, A. C., Maharaj, S. I., Colton, P. A., Jones, J. M., Biancucci, L. A., & Daneman, D. (2002). Eating disorders in young women with type 1 diabetes mellitus. *Journal of Psychosomatic Research, 53*(4), 943–949.

Rodin, J., Bartoshuk, L., Peterson, C., & Schank, D. (1990). Bulimia and taste: Possible interactions. *Journal of Abnormal Psychology, 99,* 32–39.

Rodenhiser, D. & Mann, M. (2006). Epigenetics and human disease: translating basic biology into clinical applications. *Canadian Medical Association Journal, 174*(3), 341–348.

Rodriguez, N. et al. (1997). Posttramautic stress disorder in adult female survivors of childhood sexual abuse: A comparison study. *Journal of Consulting and Clinical Psychology, 65,* 53–59.

Rodríguez de Fonseca, F., Carrera, M. R., Navarro, M., Koob, G. F., & Weiss, F. (1997). Activation of corticotropin-releasing factor in the limbic system during cannabinoid withdrawal. *Science, 276,* 2050–2054.

Roemer, I., Reik, W., Dean, W., & Klose, J. (1997). Epigenetic inheritance in the mouse. *Current Biology, 7*(4), 277–280.

Rogers, C. R. (1951). *Client-centered therapy.* Boston: Houghton Mifflin.

Rogers, D. D. & Abas, N. (1988). A survey of native mental health needs in Manitoba. *Arctic Medical Research, 47* (Suppl. 1), 576–580.

Rohde, P., Lewinsohn, P. M., & Seeley, J. R. (1991). Comorbidity of unipolar depression: II. Comorbidity with other mental disorders in adolescents and adults. *Journal of Abnormal Psychology, 101,* 214–222.

Romano, E., Baillargeon, R. H., & Tremblay, R. E. (2002). Prevalence of hyperactivity-impulsivity and inattention among Canadian children: Findings from the first data collection cycle (1994–1995) of the National Longitudinal Survey of Children and Youth (Catalogue No. RH63-1/561-01-03E). Ottawa: Human Resources Development Canada.

Romano, E., Baillargeon, R. H., Fortier, I., Wu, H. X., Robaey, P., Zoccolillo, M., Tremblay, R. E. (2005). Individual change in methylphenidate use in a national sample of children aged 2 to 11 years. *Canadian Journal of Psychiatry, 50*(3),144–152.

Romanow, R.J. (2002). *Building On Values: The Future of Health Care in Canada.* Ottawa: Commission on the Future of Health Care in Canada.

Ronald, J., Delaive, K., Roos, L., Manfreda, J., Bahammam, A., & Kryger, M.H. (1999). Care utilization in the 10 years prior to diagnosis in obstructive sleep apnea syndrome patients. *Sleep 22*(2), 225–229.

Rosa, M. A., Gattaz, W. F., Pascual-Leone, A., Fregni, F., Rosa, M. O., Rumi, D. O. et al. (2006). Comparison of repetitive transcranial magnetic stimulation and electroconvulsive therapy in unipolar non-psychotic refractory depression: a randomized, single-blind study. *International Journal of Neuropsychopharmacology. 9*(6), 667–676.

Rose, J. (1996). Anger management: A group treatment program for people with mental retardation. *Journal of Developmental and Physical Disabilities, 8,* 133–149.

Rosen, R. C. (1996). Erectile dysfunction: The medicalization of male sexuality. *Clinical Psychology Review, 16,* 497–519.

Rosen, R. C. & Leiblum, S. R. (1995). Treatment of sexual disorders in the 1990s: An integrated approach. *Journal of Consulting and Clinical Psychology, 63,* 877–890.

Rosenberg, H. (1993). Prediction of controlled drinking by alcoholics and problem drinkers. *Psychological Bulletin, 113,* 129–130.

Rosenthal, D., Wender, P. H., Kety, S. S., Schulsinger, F., Welner, J., & Ostergaard, L.

(1968). Schizophrenics' off-spring reared in adoptive homes. In D. Rosenthal & S. S. Kety (Eds.), *The transmission of schizophrenia*. Oxford: Pergamon.

Rosenthal, D., Wender, P. H., Kety, S. S., Schulsinger, F., Welner, J., & Ostergaard, L. (1975). Parent–child relationships and psychopathological disorder in the child. *Archives of General Psychiatry, 32,* 466–476.

Rosenthal, E. (1993, April 9). Who will turn violent? Hospitals have to guess. *The New York Times,* pp. A1, C12.

Ross, C. A. (2001). *Dissociative identity disorder: Diagnosis, clinical features, and treatment of multiple personality* (2nd ed.). New York: John Wiley & Sons.

Ross, H. E. (1995). DSM-III-R alcohol abuse and dependence and psychiatric comorbidity in Ontario: Results from the Mental Health Supplement to the Ontario Health Survey. *Drug and Alcohol Dependence, 39,* 111–128.

Ross, C. A., Norton, G. R., & Wozney, K. (1989). Multiple personality disorder: An analysis of 236 cases. *Canadian Journal of Psychiatry, 34,* 413–418.

Rossman, T. G. (2003). Mechanism of arsenic carcinogenesis: an integrated approach. *Mutation Research/Fundamental and Molecular Mechanisms of Mutagenesis, 533*(1–2), 37–65.

Rothbaum, B. O. (1996). Virtual reality exposure therapy in the treatment of fear of flying: A case report. *Behaviour Research and Therapy, 34,* 477–481.

Rothbaum, B. O., Astin, M. C., & Marsteller, F. (2005). Prolonged exposure versus eye movement desensitization and reprocessing (EMDR) for PTSD rape victims. *Journal of Traumatic Stress, 18,* 607–616.

Rotter, J. B. (1966). Generalized expectancies for internal vs. external control of reinforcement. *Psychological Monographs, 1,* 210–609.

Rotter, J. B. (1972). Beliefs, social attitudes, and behavior: A social learning analysis. In J. B. Rotter, J. E. Chance, & E. J. Phares (Eds.), *Applications of a social learning theory of personality.* New York: Holt, Rinehart and Winston.

Rounsaville, B. J., Alarcón, R. D., Andrews, G., Jackson, J. S., Kendell, R. E., & Kendler, K.

(2002). Basic Nomenclature Issues for DSM-V. In D. J. Kupfer, M. B. First, & D. A. Regier (Eds.), *A research Agenda for DSM-V.* (pp. 1–29). Washington, DC: American Psychiatric Association.

Rousseau, F., Heitz, D., Biancalana, V., Blumenfeld, S., Kretz, C., Boue, J., et al. (1991). Direct diagnosis by DNA analysis of the fragile X syndrome of mental retardation. *New England Journal of Medicine, 325,* 1673–1681.

Rowa, K. & Antony, M. M. (2005). Psychological treatments for social phobia. *Canadian Journal of Psychiatry, 50,* 308–316.

Rowland, D. L., Cooper, S. E., & Slob, A. K. (1996). Genital and psychoaffective response to erotic stimulation in sexually functional and dysfunctional men. *Journal of Abnormal Psychology, 105,* 194–203.

Rumstein-McKean, O. & Hunsley, J. (2001). Interpersonal and family functioning of female survivors of childhood sexual abuse. *Clinical Psychology Review, 21,* 471–490.

Ruskin, P. E., Silver-Aylaian, M., Kling, M. A., Reed, S. A., Bradham, D. D., Hebel, J. R., et al. (2004). Treatment outcomes in depression: Comparison of remote treatment through telepsychiatry to in-person treatment. *American Journal of Psychiatry, 161*(8), 1471–1476.

Russell, J. M., Newman, S. C., & Bland, R. C. (1994). Drug abuse and dependence. *Acta Psychiatric Scandinavica, Suppl.* 376, 54–62.

Russell, L. B., Hubley, A., & Palepu, A. (2005). *What is important to the quality of life of homeless or hard-to-house Canadian adults and street youth? A multi-site study.* Poster presented at Canadian Conference on Homelessness, May 17–20, 2005, Toronto, ON. Retrieved November 18, 2006, from http://educ.ubc.ca/faculty/hubley/pdfs/CCH_poster_text.pdf.

Rutter, M. (1983). Cognitive deficits in the pathogenesis of autism. *Journal of Child Psychology & Psychiatry, 24,* 513–531.

Rutter, M. (1997). Implications of genetic research for child psychiatry. *Canadian Journal of Psychiatry, 42,* 569–576.

Rutter, M. (1999). Resilience concepts and findings: Implications for family therapy. *Journal of Family Therapy, 21*(2), 119–144.

Rutter, M. (2006). *Genes and behavior: Nature-nurture interplay examined.* Oxford: Blackwell.

Ryle, A. (1982). *Psychotherapy. A cognitive integration of theory and practice.* London: Academic press.

Ryle, A. & Kerr, I. B. (2001). *Introduction to Cognitive-Analytic Therapy: Principles and practice.* New York: John Wiley & Sons.

S

Sachdev, P. & Hay, P. (1996). Site and size of lesion and psychosurgical outcome in obsessive-compulsive disorder: A magnetic resonance imaging study. *Biological Psychiatry, 39,* 739–742.

Salkovskis, P. M. & Clark, D. M. (1993). Panic disorder and hypochondriasis. Special Issue: Panic, cognitions and sensations. *Advances in Behaviour Research and Therapy, 15,* 23–48.

Sanchez-Craig, M., & Wilkinson, D. A. (1986/1987). Treating problem drinkers who are not severely dependent on alcohol. *Drugs and Society, 1,* 39–67.

Sanchez-Craig, M., Annis, H. M., Bornet, A. R., & MacDonald, K. R. (1984). Random assignment to abstinence or controlled drinking: Evaluation of a cognitive-behavioral program for problem drinkers. *Journal of Consulting and Clinical Psychology, 52,* 390–403.

Sanislow, C.A., Grilo, C.M., & McGlashan, T.H. (2000). Factor analysis of the DSM-III-R borderline personality disorder criteria in psychiatric inpatients. *American Journal of Psychiatry, 157*(10), 1629–1633.

Santos-Rebouças, C. B. & Pimentel, M. M. G. (2007). Implication of abnormal epigenetic patterns for human diseases. *European Journal of Human Genetics.15*(1), 10–17.

Sartorius, N. & Schulze, H. (2005). *Reducing the stigma of mental illness: A report from a global programme of the World Psychiatric Association.* New York: Cambridge University Press.

Sass, L. (1982, August 22). The borderline personality. *The*

New York Times Magazine, pp. 12–15, 66–67.

Satir, V. (1967). *Conjoint family therapy.* (rev. ed.). Palo Alto, CA: Science and Behavior Books.

Schachar, R., Jadad, A. R., Gauld, M., Boyle, M., Booker, L., Snider, A., Kim, M., & Cunningham, C. (2002). Attention-deficit hyperactivity disorder: Critical appraisal of extended treatment studies. *Canadian Journal of Psychiatry, 47*(4), 337–348.

Schachter, H. M., Pham, B., King, J. Langford, S., & Moher, D. (2001). How efficacious and safe is short- acting methylphenidate for the treatment of attention-deficit disorder in children and adolescents? A meta-analysis. *Canadian Medical Association Journal, 165*(11), 1475–1488.

Schaefer, A., Braver, T. S., Reynolds, J. R., Burgess, G. C., Yarkoni, T., & Gray, J. R. (2006). Individual differences in amygdala activity predict response speed during working memory. *Journal of Neuroscience,* 26(40), 10120–10128.

Schafer, J. & Brown, S. (1991). Marijuana and cocaine effect expectancies and drug use patterns. *Journal of Consulting and Clinical Psychology, 59,* 558–565.

Schaffer, A., Cairney, J., Cheung, A., Veldhuizen, S., & Levitt, A. (2006). Community survey of bipolar disorder in Canada: Lifetime prevalence and illness characteristics. *Canadian Journal of Psychiatry, 51,* 9–16.

Scheier, L. M., Botvin, G. J., & Baker, E. (1997). Risk and protective factors as predictors of adolescent alcohol involvement and transitions in alcohol use: A prospective analysis. *Journal of Studies on Alcohol, 58,* 652–667.

Scheier, M. F. & Carver, C. S. (1985). Optimism, coping, and health: Assessment and implications of generalized outcome expectancies. *Health Psychology, 4,* 219–247.

Scheier, M. F. & Carver, C. S. (1992). Effects of optimism on psychological and physical well-being: Theoretical overview and empirical update. Special issue: Cognitive perspectives in health psychology. *Cognitive Therapy and Research, 16,* 201–228.

Scheier, M. F., Matthews, K. A., Owens, J. F., Schulz, R.,

Bridges, M. W., Magovern, G. J., & Carver, C. S. (1999). Optimism and rehospitalization after coronary artery bypass graft surgery. *Archives of Internal Medicine, 159*(8), 829–935.

Schepis, M. R., Reid, D. H., & Fitzgerald, J. R. (1987). Group instruction with profoundly retarded persons: Acquisition, generalization, and maintenance of a remunerative work skill. *Journal of Applied Behavior Analysis, 20,* 97–105.

Schmidt, N. B., Zvolensky, M. J., & Maner, J. K. (2006). Anxiety sensitivity: Prospective prediction of panic attacks and Axis I pathology. *Journal of Psychiatric Research, 40,* 691–699.

Schneider, K. (1957). Primäre und sekundäre symptome bei der schizophrenia. *Fortschritte der Neurologie Psychiatrie, 25,* 487–490.

Schneider, R. D., Glancy, G. D., Bradford, J. McD., & Seibenmorgen, E. (2000). Canadian landmark case, *Winko v. British Columbia*: Revisiting the conundrum of the mentally disordered accused. *Journal of the American Academy of Psychiatry and Law, 28,* 206–212.

Schoenman, T. J. (1984). The mentally ill witch in textbooks of abnormal psychology: Current status and implications of a fallacy. *Professional Psychiatry, 15,* 299–314.

Schreiner-Engel, P., Schiavi, R. C., White, D., & Ghizzani, A. (1989). Low sexual desire in women: The role of reproductive hormones. *Hormones and Behavior, 23,* 221–234.

Schruers, K., Koning, K., Luermans, J., Haack, M. J., & Griez, E. (2005). Obsessive-compulsive disorder: A critical review of therapeutic perspectives. *Acta Psychiatrica Scandinavica, 111,* 261–271.

Schuckit, M. A. (1996). Recent developments in the pharmacotherapy of alcohol dependence. *Journal of Consulting and Clinical Psychology, 64,* 669–676.

Schuckit, M. A., & Smith, T. L. (1996). An 8-year follow-up of 450 sons of alcoholic and control subjects. *Archives of General Psychiatry, 53,* 202–210.

Schuckit, M. A., Daeppen, J-B, Danko, G. P., Tripp, M. L., Smith, T. L., Li, T-K et al. (1999). Clinical implications for four drugs of the DSM-IV distinction between substance dependence with and without a physiological component. *American Journal of Psychiatry, 156,* 41–49.

Schuller, R. A. & Ogloff, J. R. P. (2000). *Introduction to psychology and law: Canadian perspectives.* Toronto: University of Toronto Press.

Schulsinger, F. (1972). Psychopathy: Heredity and environment. *International Journal of Mental Health, 1,* 190–206.

Schulze, B. & Angermeyer, M. C. (2003). Subjective experiences of stigma. A focus group study of schizophrenic patients, their relatives and mental health professionals. *Social Sciences and Medicine, 56*(2), 299–312.

Schulze-Rauschenbach, S. C., Harms, U., Schlaepfer, T. E., Maier, W., Falkai, P., & Wagner M. (2005). Distinctive neurocognitive effects of repetitive transcranialmagnetic stimulation and electroconvulsive therapy in major depression. *British Journal of Psychiatry, 186*(5), 410–416.

Schumacher, A. & Petronis, A. (2006). Epigenetics of complex diseases: from general theory to laboratory experiments. *Current Topics in Microbiology and Immunology, 310,* 81–115.

Schwitzgebel, R. L. & Schwitzgebel, R. K. (1980). *Law and psychological practice.* New York: John Wiley & Sons.

Scott, K. (1994). Substance use among indigenous Canadians. In D. McKenzie (Ed.), *Research issues: Substance abuse among indigenous Canadians.* Ottawa: Canadian Centre on Substance Abuse.

Sealy, P. & Whitehead, P. C. (2004). Forty years of deinstitutionalization of psychiatric services in Canada: An empirical assessment. *Canadian Journal of Psychiatry, 49*(4), 249–257.

Seeman, P. & Kapur, S. (2001). The dopamine receptor basis of psychosis. In A. Breier, P. V. Tran, J. M. Herrera, G. D. Tollefson, & F. P. Bymaster (Eds.), *Current issues in the psychopharmacology of schizophrenia* (pp. 73–84). Philadelphia, PA: Lippincott Williams & Wilkins.

Segal, Z. V., Williams, M., & Teasdale, J. D. (2002). *Mindfulness-based cognitive therapy for depression: A new approach to preventing relapse.* New York: Guilford.

Segarra, P., Ross, S. R., Pastor, M. C., Montañés, S., Poy, R., & Moltó, J. (2007). MMPI-2 predictors of Gray's two-factor reinforcement sensitivity theory. *Personality and Individual Differences, 43*(3) 437–448.

Segerstrom, S. C., Taylor, S. E., Kemeny, M. E., & Fahey, J. L. (1998). Optimism is associated with mood, coping, and immune change in response to stress. *Journal of Personality and Social Psychology, 74*(6), 1646–1655.

Segraves, R. (1988). Drugs and desire. In S. Leiblum & R. Rosen (Eds.), *Sexual desire disorders.* New York: Guilford.

Segraves, R. T. & Althof, S. (1998). Psychotherapy and pharmacotherapy of sexual dysfunctions. In P. E. Nathan & J. M. Gorman (Eds.), *A guide to treatments that work* (pp. 447–471). New York: Oxford University Press.

Seidman, L. J., Biederman, J., Faraone, S. V., Weber, W., & Ouelette, C. (1997). Toward defining a neuropsychology of attention deficit-hyperactivity disorder: Performance of children and adolescents from a large clinically referred sample. *Journal of Consulting and Clinical Psychology, 65*(1), 150–160.

Seidman, L. J., Valera, E. M., & Makris, N. (2005). Structural brain imaging of attention deficit/hyperactivity disorder. *Biological Psychiatry, 57*(11), 1263–1272.

Seligman, M. E. P. (1975). *Helplessness*: On depression, development, and death. San Francisco: Freeman.

Seligman, M. E. P. (1990). *Learned optimism: How to change your mind and your life.* New York: Simon & Schuster.

Seligman, M. E. P. (1991). *Learned optimism.* New York: Knopf.

Seligman, M. E. P., & Maier, S. F. (1967). Failure to escape traumatic shock. *Journal of Experimental Psychology, 74,* 1–9.

Selten, J. P., Gernaat, HB, Nolen, WA, Wiersma, D, van den Bosch, RJ. (1998). Experience of negative symptoms: Comparisons of schizophrenic patients to patients with a depressive disorder and to normal subjects. *American Journal of Psychiatry, 155,* 350–354.

Selten, J.-P., Cantor-Graae, E., & Kahn, R. S. (2007). Migration and schizophrenia. *Current Opinion in Psychiatry, 20,* 111–115.

Selye, H. (1974). *Stress without distress.* New York: Harper & Row

Selye, H. (1976). *The stress of life* (rev. ed.) New York: McGraw-Hill.

Serene, J. A, Ashtari, M., Szeszko, P. R., & Kumra, S. (2007). Neuroimaging studies of children with serious emotional disturbances: A selective review. *Canadian Journal of Psychiatry, 52*(3), 135–145.

Serin, R. C. (1998). Treatment responsivity, intervention, and reintegration: A conceptual model. *Forum on Corrections Research, 10,* 29–32.

Seroczynski, A. D., Cole, D. A., & Maxwell, S. E. (1997). Cumulative and compensatory effects of competence and incompetence on depressive symptoms in children. *Journal of Abnormal Psychology, 106*(4), 586–597.

Seto, M. C. (2004). Pedophilia and sexual offenses against children. *Annual Review of Sex Research, 15,* 321–361.

Seto, M. C., Maric, A., & Barbaree, H. E. (2001). The role of pornography in the etiology of sexual aggression. *Aggression and Violent Behavior, 6,* 35–53.

Severinsen, J. E., Bjarkam, C. R., Kiaer-Larsen, S., Olsen, I. M., Nielsen, M. M., Holm, I. E., et al. (2006). Evidence implicating BRD1 with brain development and susceptibility to both *schizophrenia* and bipolar affective disorder. *Molecular Psychiatry, 11,* 1126–1138.

Shadish, W. R. et al. (1997). Evidence that therapy works in clinically representative conditions. *Journal of Consulting and Clinical Psychology, 65,* 355–365.

Shapiro, C. M., Trajanovic, N. N., & Fedoroff, J. P. (2003). Sexsomnia—A new parasomnia? *Canadian Journal of Psychiatry, 48*(5), 311–317.

Shapiro, D. A. et al. (1995). Effects of treatment duration and severity of depression on the maintenance of gains after cognitive-behavioral and psychodynamic interpersonal psychotherapy. *Journal of Consulting and Clinical Psychology, 63,* 378–387.

Shapiro, F. (2001). *Eye movement desensitization and reprocessing,* 2nd ed. New York: Guilford.

Shaw, E. & Grenier, D. (2001). Taking the pulse of Canadian children—A health report card for the millennium. *Paediatrics & Child Health, 6*(4). Ottawa: Canadian Paediatric Association. Retrieved October 20, 2003, from http://www.pulsus.com/Paeds/06_04/shaw_ed.htm.

Shaw, R., Cohen, F., Doyle, B., & Palesky, J. (1985). The impact of denial and repressive style on information gain and rehabilitation outcomes in myocardial infarction patients. *Psychosomatic Medicine, 47,* 262–273.

Shaywitz, S. E. (1998). Dyslexia. *New England Journal of Medicine, 338,* 307–312.

Shaywitz, S. E., Shaywitz, B.A., Pugh, K.R. et al. (1998). Functional disruption in the organization of the brain for reading in dyslexia. *Proceedings of the National Academy of Sciences of the United States of America, 95,* 2636–2641.

Shea, M. T., Widiger, T. A., & Klein, M. H. (1992). Comorbidity of personality disorders and depression: Implications for treatment. *Journal of Consulting and Clinical Psychology, 60,* 857–868.

Sheitman, B. B., Kinon, B. J., Ridgway, B. A., & Lieberman, J. A. (1998). Pharmacological treatments of schizophrenia. In P.E. Nathan & J. M. Gorman (Eds.), *A guide to treatments that work* (pp. 167–189). New York: Oxford University Press.

Sher, K. J., & Trull, T. J. (1994). Personality and disinhibitory psychopathology: Alcoholism and antisocial personality disorder. *Journal of Abnormal Psychology, 103,* 92–102.

Sher, K. J., Grekin, E. R., & Williams, N. A. (2005). The development of alcohol use disorders. *Annual Review of Clinical Psychology, 1,* 493–523.

Sherman, D. K., McGue, M. K., & Ianoco W. G. (1997). Twin concordance for attention deficit hyperactivity disorder: A comparison of teachers' and mothers' reports. *American Journal of Psychiatry, 154*(4), 532–535.

Shields, M. (2004). Social anxiety disorder—beyond shyness. *Health Reports, 15 (Suppl.),* 47–81.

Shields, M. (2004). *Stress, health and the benefit of social support.* (Catalogue no. 82-003-XPE, Vol. 15, No. 1, pp. 9–38). Ottawa: Minister of Industry.

Shiffman, S., et al. (1996). Progression from a smoking lapse to relapse: Prediction from abstinence violation effects, nicotine dependence, and lapse characteristics. *Journal of Consulting and Clinical Psychology, 64,* 993–1002.

Shneidman, E. S. (1985). *Definition of suicide.* New York: John Wiley & Sons.

Shneidman, E. S. (1994). Clues to suicide reconsidered. *Suicide and Life-Threatening Behavior, 24,* 395–397.

Shneidman, E. S., Farberow, N. L., & Litman, R. E. (1994). *The psychology of suicide: A clinician's guide to evaluation and treatment.* Northvale, NJ: Aronson.

Shweder, R. (1985). Cross-cultural study of emotions. In A. Kleinman & B. Good (Eds.), *Culture and depression.* Berkeley: University of California Press.

Siegel, J. M. (2004). Hypocretin (orexin): Role in normal behavior and neuropathology. *Annual Review of Psychology, 55,* 125–148.

Siegel, S. (2005). Drug tolerance, drug addiction, and drug anticipation. *Current Directions in Psychological Science, 14,* 296–300.

Siever, L. J., & Davis, K. L. (2004). The pathophysiology of schizophrenia disorders: Perspectives from the spectrum. *American Journal of Psychiatry, 161*(3), 398–413.

Silberstein, R. B., et al. (1998). Functional brain electrical activity mapping in boys with attention-deficit/hyperactivity disorder. *Archives of General Psychiatry, 55,* 1105–1112.

Simeon, D., & Abugel, J. (2006). *Feeling unreal: Depersonalization disorder and the loss of the self.* New York: Oxford University Press.

Siminovitch, L., McCulloch, E. A., & Till, J. E. (1963). The distribution of colony-forming cells among spleen colonies. *Journal of Cellular and Comparative Physiology, 62*(12), 327–336.

Simmie, S. (1998, October 4). I'd sit in the kitchen and just shake. *Toronto Star.*

Simmons, H. G. (1987). Psychosurgery and the abuse of psychiatric authority in Ontario. *Journal of Health Politics, Policy and Law, 12*(3), 537–550.

Simon, G. E. (2006). The antidepressant quandary—considering suicide risk when treating adolescent depression. *New England Journal of Medicine, 355,* 2722–2723.

Simpkins, J. W., & Van Meter, R. (2005). Potential testosterone therapy for hypogonadal sexual dysfunction in women. *Journal of Women's Health, 14,* 449–451.

Simpson, D. D., et al. (1999). A national evaluation of treatment outcomes for cocaine dependence. *Archives of General Psychiatry, 57,* 507–514.

Singh, N. N., McKay, J. D., & Singh, A. N. (1998). Culture and mental health: Nonverbal communication. *Journal of Child and Family Studies, 7*(4), 403–409.

Sitharthan, T., Sitharthan, G., Hough, M. J., & Kavanagh, D. J. (1997). Cue exposure in moderation drinking: A comparison with cognitive-behavior therapy. *Journal of Consulting and Clinical Psychology, 65,* 878–882.

Skaar, K. L., et al. (1997). Smoking cessation: 1. An overview of research. *Behavioral Medicine, 23,* 5–13.

Skinner, B. F. (1938). *The behavior of organisms: An experimental analysis.* New York: Appleton.

Skodol, A. E., Gunderson, J. G., Pfohl, B., Widiger, T. A., Livesley, W. J., & Siever, L. J. (2002a). The borderline diagnosis I: Psychopathology, Comorbidity, and personality structure. *Biological Psychiatry, 51*(12), 936–950.

Skodol, A. E., Gunderson, J. G., Pfohl, B., Widiger, T. A., Livesley, W. J., & Siever, L. J. (2002b). The borderline diagnosis II: Biology, genetics, and clinical course. *Biological Psychiatry, 51*(12), 951–963.

Slovenko, R. (2006). Patients who deceive. *International Journal of Offender Therapy and Comparative Criminology, 50,* 241–244.

Slutske, W. S., Heath, A. C., Dinwiddie, S. H., Madden, P. A. F., Bucholz, K. K., Dunne, M. P., et al. (1997). Modeling genetic and environmental influences in the etiology of conduct disorder: A study of 2,682 adult twin pairs. *Journal of Abnormal Psychology, 106,* 266–279.

Slutske, W. S., Heath, A. C., Dinwiddie, S. H., et al. (1998). Common genetic risk factors for conduct disorder and alcohol dependence. *Journal of Abnormal Psychology, 107,* 363–374.

Smith, D. (1982). Trends in counseling and psychotherapy. *American Psychologist, 37,* 802–809.

Smith, D. B. & Morrissette, P. J. (2001). The experiences of white male counsellors who work with First Nations clients. *Canadian Journal of Counselling, 35*(1), 74–88.

Smith, G. N., Boydell, J., Murray, R. M., Flynn, S. McKay, K., Sherwood, M., et al. (2006). The incidence of schizophrenia in European immigrants to Canada. *Schizophrenia Research, 87,* 205–211.

Smith, G. N., Flynn, S. W., McCarthy, N., Meistrich, B., Ehmann, T. S., MacEwan, W. G., Kopala, L. C., & Honer, W. G. (2001). Low birthweight in schizophrenia: Prematurity or poor fetal growth? *Schizophrenia Research, 47,* 177–184.

Smith, G. T., Goldman, M. S., Greenbaum, P. E., & Christiansen, B. A. (1995). Expectancy for social facilitation from drinking: The divergent paths of high-expectancy and low-expectancy adolescents. *Journal of Abnormal Psychology, 104,* 32–40.

Smith, M. L., & Glass, G. V. (1977). Meta-analysis of psychotherapy outcome studies. *American Psychologist, 32,* 752–760.

Smith, M. L., Glass, G. V., & Miller, T. I. (1980). *The benefits of psychotherapy.* Baltimore: Johns Hopkins University Press.

Smith, M. L., Klim, P., & Hanley, W. B. (2000). Executive function in school-aged children with phenylketonuria. *Journal of Developmental and Physical Disabilities. 12*(4), 317–332.

Smith, R. J. (1978). *The great mental calculators.* New York: Columbia University Press.

Smith, R., Ronald, J., Delaive, K., Walld, R., Manfreda, J., & Kryger, M. H. (2002). What are obstructive sleep apnea patients being treated for prior to this diagnosis? *Chest, 121*(1), 164–172.

Smith, S. C. (1983). *The great mental calculators.* New York: Columbia University Press.

Smith, S. S., & Newman, J. P. (1990). Alcohol and drug abuse-dependence disorders in psychopathic and nonpsychopathic criminal offenders. *Journal of Abnormal Psychology, 99,* 430–439.

Smith, T. (1999). Outcome of early intervention for children with autism. *Clinical Psychology: Science and Practice, 6,* 33–49.

Smith, V. (2003, January 4). I never fit well as a girl. *The Globe and Mail.*

Smith, Y. L. S., Van Goozen, S. H. M., Kuiper, A. J., & Cohen-Kettenis, P. T. (2005). Sex reassignment: Outcomes and predictors of treatment for adolescent and adult transsexuals. *Psychological Medicine, 35,* 89–99.

Smith-Warner, S. A., Spiegelman, D., Yuan, S-S, van den Brandt, P. A., Folsom, A. R., Goldbohm, R. A., et al. (1998). Alcohol and breast cancer in women: A pooled analysis of cohort studies. *Journal of the American Medical Association, 279,* 535–540.

Smits, D. J. M., & Boeck, P. D. (2006). From BIS/BAS to the big five. *European Journal of Personality, 20(4),* 255–270.

Smoking will be world's biggest killer. (1996, September 17). *New York Newsday,* p. A21.

Snell, M. E. (1997). Teaching children and young adults with mental retardation in school programs: Current research. *Behaviour Change, 14,* 73–105.

Snodgrass, M., Bernat, E., & Shevrin, H. (2004). Unconscious perception: A model-based approach to method and evidence. *Perception & Psychophysics, 66(5),* 846–867.

Sobell, L. C., et al. (1990). Behavior therapy. In A. S. Bellack & M. Hersen (Eds.), *Comparative treatment of adult disorders* (pp. 479–505). New York: John Wiley & Sons.

Sobell, M. B., & Sobell, L. C. (1973). Alcoholics treated by individualized behavior therapy: One year treatment outcome. *Behaviour Research and Therapy, 11,* 599–618.

Sobell, M. B., & Sobell, L. C. (1976). Second year treatment outcome of alcoholics treated by individualized behavior therapy: Results. *Behaviour Research and Therapy, 14,* 195–215.

Sobell, M. B., & Sobell, L. C. (1984). The aftermath of heresy: A response to Pendery et al.'s critique of "Individualized behavior therapy for alcoholics." *Behaviour Research and Therapy, 22,* 413–440.

Söchting, I. (2004). Painful pasts: Post-traumatic stress in women survivors of Canada's Indian residential schools. *Visions Journal, 2(4),* 13–14.

Social Services Ottawa. (1999). *Ottawa Homelessness in Ottawa-Carleton.* Ottawa: Policy, Planning and Performance Management Services Branch Strategic and Operational Support Directorate Social Services. Retrieved February 6, 2003, from http://ottawa.ca/city_services/housing/pdf/12_2_2_en.pdf.

Sohn, C.-H., & Lam, R. W. (2005). Update on the biology of seasonal affective disorder. *CNS Spectrums, 10,* 635–646.

Solano, L., Costa, M., Salvati, S., Coda, R., Aiuti, F., Mezzaroma, I., et al. (1993). Psychosocial factors and clinical evolution in HIV-1 infection: A longitudinal study. *Journal of Psychosomatic Research, 37(1),* 39–51.

Solms, M. (2000). Freudian dream theory. *The Psychologist, 13(12),* 618–619.

Solms, M. (2004). Freud returns. *Scientific American, 290(5),* 82–88.

Solms, M., & Turnbull, O. (2002). *The brain and the inner world: An introduction to the neuroscience of subjective experience.* New York: Other Press.

Solomon, D. A., Keller, M. B., Leon, A. C., Mueller, T. I., Shea, M. T., Warshaw, M., Maser, J. D., Coryell, W., & Endicott, J. (1997). Recovery from major depression: A 10-year prospective follow-up across multiple episodes. *Archives of General Psychiatry, 54(11),* 1001–1006.

Somers, J. M., Goldner, E. M., Waraich, P., & Hsu, L. (2006). Prevalence and incidence studies of anxiety disorders: A systematic review of the literature. *Canadian Journal of Psychiatry, 51,* 100–113.

Sommers-Flanagan, J., & Sommers-Flanagan, R. (1996). Efficacy of antidepressant medication with depressed youth: What psychologists should know. *Professional Psychology: Research & Practice, 27,* 145–153.

Southwick, S. M., Vythilingam, M., & Charney, D. S. (2005). The psychobiology of depression and resilience to stress: Implications for prevention and treatment. *Annual Review of Clinical Psychology, 1,* 255–291.

Spanos, N. P. (1978). Witchcraft in histories of psychiatry: A critical analysis and an alternative conceptualization. *Psychological Bulletin, 85,* 417–439.

Spanos, N. P. (2001). *Multiple identities and false memories: A sociocognitive perspective.* Washington, DC: American Psychological Association.

Spector, I. P., & Carey, M. P. (1990). Incidence and prevalence of the sexual dysfunctions: A critical review of the empirical literature. *Archives of Sexual Behavior, 19,* 389–408.

Speed, J., & Mooney, G. (1997). Rehabilitation of conversion disorders: An operant approach . *Neurorehabilitation, 8,* 175–181.

Spencer, D. J. (1983). Psychiatric dilemmas in Australian Aborigines. *International Journal of Social Psychiatry, 29(3),* 208–214.

Spencer, T., Biederman, J., Wilens, T., et al. (1996). Pharmacotherapy of attention-deficit hyperactivity disorder across the life cycle. *Journal of the American Academy of Child and Adolescent Psychiatry, 35,* 409–432.

Spiegel, D., et al. (1989, October 14). Effect of psychosocial treatment on survival of patients with metastatic breast cancer. *Lancet,* pp. 888–891.

Spirito, A., & Esposito-Smythers, C. (2006). Attempted and completed suicide in adolescence. *Annual Review of Clinical Psychology, 2,* 237–266.

Spitzer, R. L., Devlin, M. J., Walsh, B. T., Hasin, D., Wing, R. R., Marcus, M. D., et al. (1992). Binge eating disorder: A multisite field trial of the diagnostic criteria. *International Journal of Eating Disorders, 11(3),* 191–203.

Spitzer, R. L., Gibbon, M., Skodol, A. E., Williams, J. B. W., & First, M. B. (1989). *DSM-III-R casebook.* Washington, DC: American Psychiatric Press.

Spitzer, R. L., Gibbon, M., Skodol, A. E., Williams, J. B. W., & First, M. B. (1994). *DSM-IV casebook* (4th ed.). Washington, DC: American Psychiatric Press.

Spreen, O. (1988). Prognosis of learning disability. *Journal of Consulting and Clinical Psychology, 56,* 836–842.

St. Lawrence, J. S., et al. (1995a). Comparison of education versus behavioral skills training interventions in lowering sexual HIV-risk behavior of substance-dependent adolescents. *Journal of Consulting and Clinical Psychology, 63,* 154–157.

St. Lawrence, J. S., et al. (1995b). Cognitive-behavioral intervention to reduce African American adolescents' risk for HIV infection. *Journal of Consulting and Clinical Psychology, 63,* 221–237.

Stable trait components of hopelessness: Baseline and sensitivity to depression. *Journal of Abnormal Psychology, 105,* 155–165.

Statistics Canada (1993). *Language, health and lifestyle issues: 1991 Aboriginal Peoples Survey* (Catalogue no. 89-533). Ottawa: Statistics Canada.

Statistics Canada (1999). *Statistical report on the health of Canadians* (Catalogue Number: 82-570-X1E). Ottawa: Author. Retrieved November 23, 2001, from http://www.statcan.ca/english/freepub/82-570-XIE/82-570-XIE.pdf.

Statistics Canada (2002). *A Profile of disability in Canada, 2001* (Catalogue No. 89-577-XIE). Ottawa: Author. Retrieved October 18, 2003, from http://www.statcan.ca/english/freepub/89-577-XIE/pdf/89-577-XIE01001.pdf.

Statistics Canada (2003a). *2001 Census: analysis series. Aboriginal peoples of Canada: A demographic profile* (Catalogue no. 96F0030XIE2001007). Ottawa: Author. Retrieved February 09, 2003, from http://www12.statcan.ca/english/census01/products/analytic/companion/abor/pdf/96F0030XIE2001007.pdf.

Statistics Canada (2003b, January 21). *Canada's ethnocultural portrait: The changing mosaic.* Retrieved April 23, 2003, from http://www12.statcan.ca/english/census01/products/analytic/companion/etoimm/canada.cfm.

Steele, C. M., & Southwick, L. (1985). Alcohol and social behavior: I. The psychology of drunken excess. *Journal of Personality and Social Psychology, 48,* 18–34.

Steer, R. A., et al. (1994). Psychometric properties of the Cognition Checklist with psychiatric outpatients and university students. *Psychological Assessment, 6,* 67–70.

Stefanatos, G. A., & Baron, I. S. (2007). Attention-deficit/hyperactivity disorder: A neuropsychological perspective towards DSM-V. *Neuropsychology Review, 17*(1), 5–38.

Steiger, H. (2007). Eating disorder paradigms for the new millennium: Do "attachment" and "culture" appear on brain and genome scans? *Canadian Journal of Psychiatry, 52*(4), 209–211.

Steiger, H., & Bruce, K. R. (2007). Phenotypes, endophenotypes, and genotypes in bulimia spectrum eating disorders. *Canadian Journal of Psychiatry, 52*(4), 220–227.

Stein, D. J., Solms, M., & van Honk, J. (2006). The cognitive-affective neuroscience of the unconscious. *CNS Spectrums, 11*(8), 580–583.

Stein, M. B., & Walker, J. R. (2002). *Triumph over shyness*. New York: McGraw-Hill.

Stein, M. B., et al. (1998). Paroxetine treatment of generalized social phobia (social anxiety disorder). *Journal of the American Medical Association, 280*, 708–713.

Stein, M. B., Jang, K. L., & Livesley, W. J. (2002). Heritability of social anxiety-related concerns and personality characteristics: A twin study. *Journal of Nervous and Mental Disease, 190*, 219–224.

Stein, M. B., Jang, K. L., Taylor, S., Vernon, P. A., & Livesley, W. J. (2002). Genetic and environmental influences on trauma exposure and posttraumatic stress disorder symptoms: A general population twin study. *American Journal of Psychiatry, 159*, 1675–1681.

Stein, M. B., Torgrud, L. J., & Walker, J. R. (2000). Social phobia symptoms, subtypes, and severity: Findings from a community survey. *Archives of General Psychiatry, 57*, 1046–1052.

Stein, M. B., Walker, J. R., Hazen, A. L., & Forde, D. R. (1997). Full and partial posttraumatic stress disorder: Findings from a community survey. *American Journal of Psychiatry, 154*, 1114–1119.

Steller, S. (2003). *Special study on mentally disordered accused in the criminal justice system*. Ottawa, ON: Statistics Canada.

Stephane, M., Barton, S., & Boutros, N. N. (2001). Auditory verbal hallucinations and dysfunction of neural substrates of speech. *Schizophrenia Research, 50*, 61–78.

Stephens, T., & Joubert, N. (2001). The economic burden of mental health problems in Canada. *Chronic Diseases in Canada, 22*(1), 18–23.

Stephens, T., Dulberg, C., & Joubert, N. (1999). Mental health of the Canadian population: A comprehensive analysis. *Chronic Diseases in Canada, 20*(3), 118–126.

Stewart, S. E., Manion, I. G., & Davidson, S. (2002). Emergency management of the adolescent suicide attempter: A review of the literature. *Journal of Adolescent Health, 30*, 312–325.

Stewart, S. H. (1996). Alcohol abuse in individuals exposed to trauma: A critical review. *Psychological Bulletin, 120*, 83–112.

Stewart, S. H., Taylor, S., Jang, K. L., Cox, B. J., Watt, M. C., Fedoroff, I. C., & Borger, S. C. (2001). Causal modeling of relations among learning history, anxiety sensitivity, and panic attacks. *Behaviour Research and Therapy, 39*, 443–456.

Stice, E. (2001). A prospective test of the dual-pathway model of bulimic pathology: Mediating effects of dieting and negative affect. *Journal of Abnormal Psychology, 110*(1), 124–135.

Stock, W. E. (1991). Feminist explanations: Male power, hostility, and sexual coercion. In E. Grauerholz & M. A. Koralewski (Eds.), *Sexual coercion: A sourcebook on its nature, causes, and prevention* (pp. 61–73). Lexington, MA: Lexington.

Stolberg, S. G. (1998). Rise in smoking by young blacks erodes a success story. *The New York Times*, p. A24.

Stoller, R. J. (1969). Parental influences in male transexualism. In R. Green & J. Money (Eds.), *Transexualism and Sex Reassignment*. Baltimore: Johns Hopkins University Press.

Stone, A. (1976). The Tarasoff decisions: Suing psychotherapists to safeguard society. *Harvard Law Review, 90*, 358–378.

Stone, A. A., Neale, J. M., Cox, D. S., Napoli, A., Valdimarsdottir, H., & Kennedy-Moore, E. (1994). Daily events are associated with a secretory immune response to an oral antigen in men. *Health Psychology, 13*(5), 440–446.

Stone, J., Smyth, R., Carson, A., Warlow, C., & Sharpe, M. (2006). La belle indifférence in conversion symptoms and hysteria: Systematic review. *British Journal of Psychiatry, 188*, 204–209.

Stone, M. H. (1980). *The borderline syndromes: Constitution, personality, and adaptation*. New York: McGraw-Hill.

Stonnington, C. M., Barry, J. J., & Fisher, R. S. (2006). Conversion disorder. *American Journal of Psychiatry, 163*, 1510–1517.

Strachan, A. M. (1986). Family intervention for the rehabilitation of schizophrenia: Toward protection and coping. *Schizophrenia Bulletin, 12*, 678–698.

Strassnig, M., Stowell, K. R., First, M. B., & Pincus, H. A. (2006). General medical and psychiatric perspectives on somatoform disorders: Separated by an uncommon language. *Current Opinion in Psychiatry, 19*, 194–200.

Stricker, G., & Gold, J. R. (1999). The Rorschach: Toward a nomothetically based, idiographically applicable configurational model. *Psychological Assessment, 11*, 240–250.

Strober, M., & Humphrey, L. L. (1987). Familial contributions to the etiology and course of anorexia nervosa and bulimia. *Journal of Consulting and Clinical Psychology, 55*, 654–659.

Strupp, H. H. (1992). The future of psychodynamic psychotherapy. *Psychotherapy, 29*, 21–27.

Stuart, F., Hammond, C., & Pett, M. (1987). Inhibited sexual desire in women. *Archives of Sexual Behavior, 16*, 91–106.

Stuart, H. L. (2005). Fighting stigma and discrimination is fighting for mental health. *Canadian Public Policy, 31* (Supplement 1), 21–28. Retrieved November 4, 2006, from http://economics.ca/cgi/jab?journal=cpp&view=v31s1/CPPv31s1p021.pdf.

Stuart, H. L. & Arboleda-Florez, J. (2000). Homeless shelter users in the postdeinstitutionalization era. *Canadian Journal of Psychiatry, 45*(1), 55–62.

Sturman, E. D., Mongrain, M., & Kohn, P. M. (2006). Attributional style as a predictor of hopelessness depression. *Journal of Cognitive Psychotherapy, 20*, 447–458.

Suinn, R. M. (2001). The terrible twos—anger and anxiety. Hazardous to your health. *American Psychologist, 56*(1):27–36.

Sullivan, H. S. (1962). *Schizophrenia as a human process*. New York: Norton.

Sulloway, F. J. (1983). *Freud: Biologist of the mind*. New York: Basic Books.

Sussman, S. (1998). The first asylums in Canada: A response to neglectful community care and current trends. *Canadian Journal of Psychiatry, 43*, 260–264.

Sussman, S. (1999). *Dr. Ruth Kajander: A pioneer of Canadian psychiatry*. London, ON: Sussco Publishing Company.

Sutandar-Pinnock, K., Woodside, D. B., Carter, J. C., Olmsted, M. P., & Kaplan, A. S. (2003). Perfectionism in anorexia nervosa: A 6–24-month follow-up. *International Journal of Eating Disorders, 33*(2), 225–229.

Suzdak, P. D., Glowa, J. R., Crawley, J. N., & Schwartz, R. D. (1986). A selective imidazobenzodiazepine antagonist of ethanol in the rat. *Science, 225*, 1243–1247.

Svartberg, M., Stiles, T. C., & Seltzer, M. H. (2004). Randomized, controlled trial of the effectiveness of short-term dynamic psychotherapy and cognitive therapy for cluster C personality disorders. *American Journal of Psychiatry, 161*(5), 810–817.

Swanston, H. Y., Tebbutt, J. S., O'Toole, B. I., & Oates, R. K. (1997). Sexually abused children 5 years after presentation: A case-control study. *Pediatrics, 100*, 600–608.

Swinson, R. P. (2005). Social anxiety disorder. *Canadian Journal of Psychiatry, 50*, 305–307.

Szanto, K., Reynolds, C. F., Frank, E., Stack, J., et al. (1996). Suicide in elderly depressed patients. Is active vs. passive suicidal ideation a clinically valid distinction? *American Journal of Geriatric Psychiatry, 4*, 197–207.

Szasz, T. (2006). The pretense of psychology as science: The myth of mental illness in statu nascendi. *Current Psychology: Developmental, Learning, Personality, Social, 25*, 42–49.

Szasz, T. S. (1961). *The myth of mental illness*. New York: Harper & Row.

Szasz, T. S. (1970). *Ideology and insanity: Essays on the psychiatric dehumanization of man.* New York: Doubleday Anchor.

Szatmari, P. (2003). The causes of autism spectrum disorders. *British Medical Journal, 326*(7382), 173–174.

Szechtman, H., & Woody, E. (2004). Obsessive-compulsive disorder as a disturbance of security motivation. *Psychological Review, 111,* 111–127.

Szegedi, A., Kohnen, R., Dienel, A., & Kieser, M. (2005). Acute treatment of moderate to severe depression with hypericum extract WS 5570 (St John's wort): Randomised controlled double blind non-inferiority trial versus paroxetine. *British Medical Journal, 330,* 503–509.

Szyf, M. (2004). Toward a discipline of pharmacoepigenomics. *Current Pharmacogenomics, 2*(4), 357–377.

Szyf, M. (2006). Letter from the editor. *Epigenetics, 1*(1), i.

Szymanski, S., Kane, J. M., & Lieberman, J. A. (1991). A selective review of biological markers in schizophrenia. *Schizophrenia Bulletin, 17,* 99–111.

T

Tae-gyu, K. (2006, October 22). Stem cells may help treat mental illness. *Korea Times.* Retrieved on August 1, 2007, from http://www.koreatimes.co.kr/www/news/nation/news_view.asp?newsIdx=2995874.

Talan, J. (1994, May 24). Is panic attack a false alarm? *New York Newsday,* pp. B27, B33.

Talbot, J. D., & McMurray, L. (2004). Combining Cognitive-Behavioural Therapy and Pharmacotherapy in the Treatment of Anxiety Disorders. *Canadian Psychiatric Association Bulletin, 36*(1), 20–22.

Tanda, G., et al. (1997). Cannabinoid and heroin activation of mesolimbic dopamine transmission by a common opioid receptor mechanism. *Science, 276,* 2048–2050.

Taupin, P. (2006). Derivation of embryonic stem cells for cellular therapy: Challenges and new strategies. *Medical Science Monitor, 12*(4), 75–78.

Taylor, C. T., & Alden, L. E. (2005). Social interpretation bias and generalized social phobia: The influence of developmental experiences.

Behaviour Research and Therapy, 43, 759–777.

Taylor, S. (1999). *Anxiety sensitivity.* Mahwah, NJ: Erlbaum.

Taylor, S. (2000). *Understanding and treating panic disorder: Cognitive-behavioural approaches.* New York: John Wiley & Sons.

Taylor, S. (2002). Cognition in obsessive-compulsive disorder: An overview. In R. O. Frost & G. Steketee (Eds.), *Cognitive approaches to obsessions and compulsions: Theory, assessment, and treatment* (pp. 1–12). Oxford: Elsevier.

Taylor, S. (2005). *Clinician's guide to PTSD.* New York: Guilford.

Taylor, S., & Asmundson, G. J. G. (2004). *Treating Health Anxiety.* New York: Guilford.

Taylor, S., & Stein, M. B. (2006). The future of selective serotonin reuptake inhibitors (SSRIs) in psychiatric treatment. *Medical Hypotheses, 66,* 14–21.

Taylor, S., Abramowitz, J. S., & McKay, D. (2006). Cognitive-behavioral models of obsessive-compulsive disorder. In M. M. Antony, C. Purdon, & L. Summerfeldt (Eds.), *Psychological treatment of OCD* (pp. 9–29). Washington, DC: American Psychological Association Press.

Taylor, S., Asmundson, G. J. G., & Coons, M. J. (2005). Current directions in the treatment of hypochondriasis. *Journal of Cognitive Psychotherapy, 19,* 291–310.

Taylor, S., Fedoroff, I. C., Koch, W. J., Thordarson, D. S., Fecteau, G., & Nicki, R. (2001). Posttraumatic stress disorder arising after road traffic collisions: Patterns of response to cognitive-behavior therapy. *Journal of Consulting and Clinical Psychology, 69,* 541–551.

Taylor, S., McKay, D., & Abramowitz, J. S. (2005). Is obsessive-compulsive disorder a disturbance of security motivation? *Psychological Review, 112,* 650–657.

Taylor, S., Thordarson, D. S., Jang, K. L., & Asmundson, G. J. G. (2006). Genetic and environmental origins of health anxiety: A twin study. *World Psychiatry, 5,* 47–50.

Taylor, S., Thordarson, D. S., Maxfield, L., Fedoroff, I. C., Lovell, K., & Ogrodniczuk, J. (2003). Comparative efficacy, speed, and adverse effects of

three treatments for PTSD: Exposure therapy, EMDR, and relaxation training. *Journal of Consulting and Clinical Psychology, 71,* 330–338.

Teens who have problems with fathers use drugs more. (1999, August 30). *Cable News Network, Inc.,* website posting.

Teicher, M. H. (2002). Scars that won't heal: The neurobiology of child abuse. *Scientific American, 286*(3), 68–75.

Tems, C. L., et al. (1993). Cognitive distortions in depressed children and adolescents: Are they state dependent or trait-like? *Journal of Clinical Child Psychology, 22,* 316–326.

Tems, C. L., Stewart, S. M., Skinner, J. R., Jr., Hughes, C. W., & Emslie, G. (1993). Cognitive distortions in depressed children and adolescents: Are they state dependent or trait-like? *Journal of Clinical Child Psychology, 22*(3), 316–326.

Teunisse, R. J., Craysberg, J. R., Hoefnagels, W. H., Verbeek, A. I., & Zitman, F. G. (1996). Visual hallucinations in psychologically normal people: Charles Bonnnet's Syndrome. *Lancet, 347,* 794–797.

Thakker, J., & Ward, T. (1998). Culture and classification: the cross-cultural application of the DSM-IV. *Clinical Psychology Review, 18*(5), 501–529.

Thapar, A., Gottesman, I. I., Owen, M. J., O'Donovan, M.C., & McGuffin, P. (1994). The genetics of mental retardation. *British Journal of Psychiatry, 164,* 747–758.

The last draw for smokers. (1996, October). *UC Berkeley Wellness Letter, 13,* 2–3.

Theorell, T. (1992). Critical life changes: A review of research. *Psychotherapy and Psychosomatics, 57,* 108–117.

Thoits, P. A. (1983). Dimensions of life events as influences upon the genesis of psychological distress and associated conditions: An evaluation and synthesis of the literature. In H. B. Kaplan (Ed.), *Psychosocial stress: Trends in theory and research.* New York: Academic Press.

Thomas, A. M., & LoPiccolo, J. (1994). Sexual functioning in persons with diabetes: Issues in research, treatment, and education. *Clinical Psychology Review, 14,* 61–86.

Thorpy, M. (2007). Therapeutic advances in narcolepsy. *Sleep Medicine, 8*(4), 430–443.

Thun, M. J., Peto, R,. Lopez, A. D., Monaco, J. H., Henley, S. J., Heath, C. W., et al. (1997). Alcohol consumption and mortality among middle-aged and elderly U.S. adults. *New England Journal of Medicine, 337,* 1705–1714.

Tienari, P. (1991). Interaction between genetic vulnerability and family environment: The Finnish adoptive family study of schizophrenia. *Acta Psychiatrica Scandinavica, 84,* 460–465.

Tienari, P. (1992). Implications of adoption studies on schizophrenia. *British Journal of Psychiatry, 161*(18, Suppl.) 52–58.

Tienari, P., et al. (1987). Genetic and psychosocial factors in schizophrenia: The Finnish Adoptive Family Study. *Schizophrenia Bulletin, 13,* 477–484.

Tienari, P., et al. (1990). Adopted-away offspring of schizophrenics and controls: The Finnish adoptive family study of schizophrenia. In L. Robbins & M. Rutter (Eds.), *Straight and devious pathways from childhood to adulthood.* New York: Cambridge University Press.

Tienari, P., Wahlberg, K.-E., & Wynne, L. C. (2006). Finnish adoption study of schizophrenia: Implications for family interventions. *Families, Systems, and Health, 24,* 442–451.

Till, J. E., & McCulloch, E. A. (1961). A direct measurement of the radiation sensitivity of normal mouse bone marrow cells. Radiation Research, 14(2), 213–222.

Tishler, P. V., Larkin, E. K., Schluchter, M. D., & Redline, S. (2003). Incidence of sleep-disordered breathing in an urban adult population: The relative importance of risk factors in the development of sleep-disordered breathing. *Journal of the American Medical Association, 289*(17), 2230–2237.

Tjepkema, M. (2002). The health of the off-reserve Aboriginal population. *Health Reports, 13 (Suppl.),* 73–86.

Tjepkema, M. (2005). Insomnia. *Health Reports, 17*(1), 9–25.

Tobin, D. L., Johnson, C. L., & Dennis, A. B. (1992). Divergent forms of purging behavior in bulimia nervosa patients. *International Journal of Eating Disorders, 11,* 17–24.

Toichi, M., Kamio, Y., Okada, T., Sakihama, M., Youngstrom,

E. A., Findling, R. L., et al. (2002). A lack of self-consciousness in autism. *The American Journal of Psychiatry, 159*(8), 1422–1424.

Tolin, D. F., & Foa, E. B. (2006). Sex differences in trauma and posttraumatic stress disorder: A quantitative review of 25 years of research. *Psychological Bulletin, 132*, 959–992.

Tollefson, G. D., Beasley, C. M., Tamura, R. N., Tran, P. V., Potvin, J. H., et al. (1997). Blind, controlled, long-term study of the comparative incidence of treatment-emergent tardive dyskinesia with olanzapine or halperidol. *American Journal of Psychiatry, 154*, 1248–1254.

Tolomiczenko, G.S & Goering, P.N. (1998). Pathways to homelessness: Broadening the perspective. *Psychiatry Rounds 1998; 2*(8), 1–6.

Toward Optimized Practice. (2007). Clinical practice guideline adult insomnia: Assessment to diagnosis. Edmonton, AB: Author. Retrieved May 3, 2007, from http://www.topalbertadoctors.org/NR/rdonlyres/70F6F2EE-D568-4CD5-9C68-771E4A171DBE/0/insomnia_assessment_guideline.pdf.

Tough, S. C., Butt, J. C., & Sanders, G. L. (1994). Autoerotic asphyxial deaths: Analysis of nineteen fatalities in Alberta, 1978 to 1989. *Canadian Journal of Psychiatry, 39*, 157–160.

Tradgold, A. F. (1914). *Mental deficiency.* New York: Wainwood.

Transport Canada (2003). *Headaches: Tension and migraine headaches.* Retrieved May 17, 2003, from http://www.tc.gc.ca/CivilAviation.

Trask, P. C., & Sigmon, S. T. (1997). Munchausen syndrome: A review and new conceptualization. *Clinical Psychology: Science and Practice, 4*, 346–358.

Traven, N. D., Kuller, L. H., Ives, D. G., Rutan, G. H., & Perper, J. A. (1995). Coronary heart disease mortality and sudden death: Trends and patterns in 35- to 44-year-old white males, 1970–1990. *American Journal of Epidemiology, 142*(1), 45–52.

Treasure, J., & Ward, A. (1997). Cognitive analytic therapy in the treatment of anorexia nervosa. *Clinical Psychology & Psychotherapy, 4*(1), 62–71.

Treasure, J. L. (2007). Getting beneath the phenotype of anorexia nervosa: The search for viable endophenotypes and genotypes. *Canadian Journal of Psychiatry, 52*(4), 212–219.

Treatment of alcoholism—Part II. (1996, September). *The Harvard Mental Health Letter, 13,* 1–5.

Treatment of drug abuse and addiction—Part I. (1995, August). *The Harvard Mental Health Letter, 12,* 1–4.

Treffert, D. A. (1988). The idiot savant: A review of the syndrome. *American Journal of Psychiatry, 145,* 563–572.

Tremblay, R. E., Masse, B., Perron, D., Leblanc, M., Schwartzman, A. E., & Ledingham, J. E. (1992). Early disruptive behavior, poor school achievement, delinquent behavior, and delinquent personality: Longitudinal analyses. *Journal of Consulting and Clinical Psychology, 60,* 64–72.

Trenton State College. (1991, Spring). *Sexual Assault Victim Education and Support Unit (SAVES-U) Newsletter.*

Trigger, B. G. and Swagerty, W. R. (1996). Entertaining strangers: North America in the sixteenth century. In B. G. Trigger and W. E. Washburn (Eds.), *The Cambridge History of the Native Peoples of the Americas: Volume 1, North America, Part 1* (Vol. 1, pp. 325–398). New York: University of Cambridge.

Triggs-Raine, B., Richard, M., Wasel, N., Prence, E. M., & Natowicz, M. R. (1995). Mutational analyses of Tay-Sachs disease: Studies on Tay-Sachs carriers of French Canadian background living in New England. *American Journal of Human Genetics, 56*(4), 870–879.

Trimble, J. E., Manson, S. E., Dinges, N. G. & Medicine, B. (1984). American Indian concepts of mental health: Reflections and directions. In P. Pederson, N. Sartorius & A. Marsella, (Eds.), *Mental Health services: The Cross-Cultural Context* (pp. 199–220). Beverly Hills: Sage Publications.

True, W. R., Rice, J., Eisen, S. A., Heath, A. C., Goldberg, J., Lyons, M. J., & Nowak, J. (1993). A twin study of genetic and environmental contributions to liability for posttraumatic stress symptoms. *Archives of General Psychiatry, 50,* 257–265.

Trull, T. J., Tragesser, S. L., Solhan, M., & Schwartz-Mette, R. (2007). Dimensional models of personality disorder: Diagnostic and Statistical Manual of Mental Disorders Fifth Edition and beyond. *Current Opinion in Psychiatry, 20*(1), 52–56.

Turk, D. C., Meichenbaum, D., & Genest, M. (1983). *Pain and Behavioral Medicine: A cognitive-behavioral perspective.* New York: The Guilford Press.

Turnbull, J., Muckle, W., & Tadic, V. (2004). *Promoting Social Inclusion through a Harm Reduction Approach.* A Community Forum on Homelessness: Linking Ottawa Research With Action And Policy. Retrieved November 18, 2006, from http://www.endhomelessnessottawa.ca/pdf/Research_at_Alliance_Forum_Nov_22_2004.pdf.

Turner, S. M., Beidel, D. C., & Jacob, R. G. (1994). Social phobia: A comparison of behavior therapy and atenolol. *Journal of Consulting and Clinical Psychology, 62,* 350–358.

Turner, S. M., Beidel, D. C., & Townsley, R. M. (1992). Social phobia: A comparison of specific and generalized subtypes and avoidant personality disorder. *Journal of Abnormal Psychology, 101,* 326–331.

Turner, S. M., Beidel, D. C., Dancu, C. V., & Keys, D. J. (1986). Psychopathology of social phobia and comparison to avoidant personality disorder. *Journal of Abnormal Psychology, 95,* 389–394.

Turner, S. M., McCann, B. S., Beidel, D. C., & Mezzich, J. E. (1986). DSM-III classification of the anxiety disorders: A psychometric study. *Journal of Abnormal Psychology, 95,* 168–172.

Tyhurst, J. S., Chalke, F. C. R., Lawson, F. S., McNeel, B. H., Roberts, C. A., Taylor, G. C., et al. (1963). *More for the mind: A study of psychiatric services in Canada.* Toronto: Canadian Mental Health Association.

U

U.S. Department of Health and Human Services (USDHHS). (1986). *NIDA Capsules: Designer drugs.* No. 10. U.S. Department of Health and Human Services (USDHSS),

Public Health Service, Alcohol Drug Abuse and Mental Health Administration, National Institute on Drug Abuse. Rockville, MD: National Institute on Drug Abuse.

U.S. Department of Health and Human Services (USDHHS). (1992). *NIDA Capsules: LSD (Lysergic acid diethylamide)* No. 39. U.S. Department of Health and Human Services, Public Health Service, Alcohol Drug Abuse and Mental Health Administration, National Institute on Drug Abuse. Rockville, MD: National Institute on Drug Abuse.

U.S. Department of Health and Human Services (USDHHS). (1999). *Mental health: A report of the Surgeon General.* Rockville, MD: U.S. Department of Health and Human Services. (pp. 3–25).

U.S. Department of Health and Human Services (USDHHS). (2001). *Healthy people 2000: National health promotion and disease prevention objectives.* Washington, DC: U.S. Government Printing Office.

Ullmann, L. P., & Krasner, L. (1975). *A psychological approach to abnormal behavior* (2nd ed.). Englewood Cliffs, NJ: Prentice Hall.

V

van Ameringen, M., Mancini, C., Pipe, B., & Boyle, M. (October, 2004). *Canadian PTSD epidemiology study.* Paper presented at the annual convention of the Canadian Psychiatric Association, Montreal, QC.

van der Kam, E. L., Ellenbroek, B. A., & Cools, A. R. (2005). Gene-environment interactions determine the individual variability in cocaine self-administration. *Neuropharmacology, 48,* 685–695.

van Etten, M., & Taylor, S. (1998). Comparative efficacy of treatments for posttraumatic stress disorder: A meta-analysis. *Clinical Psychology and Psychotherapy, 5,* 126–145.

Van Orden, K. A., & Joiner, T. E. (2006). The inner and outer turmoil of excessive reassurance seeking: From self-doubts to social rejection. In K. D. Vohs & E. J. Finkel (Eds.), *Self and relationships: Connecting intrapersonal and interpersonal processes* (pp. 104–129). New York: Guilford.

van Os, J., Krabbendam, L., Myin-Germeys, I., &

Delespaul, P. (2005). The schizophrenia envirome. *Current Opinion in Psychiatry, 18*, 141–145.

Vazza, G., Bertolin, C., Scudellaro, E., Vettori, A., Boaretto, F., Rampinelli, S., et al. (2007). Genome-wide scan supports the existence of a susceptibility locus for *schizophrenia* and bipolar disorder on *chromosome* 15q26. *Molecular Psychiatry, 12*, 87–93.

Verkerk, G. J. M., Pop, V. J. M., Van Son, M. J. M., & Van Heck, G. L. (2003). Prediction of depression in the postpartum period: A longitudinal follow-up study in high-risk and low-risk women. *Journal of Affective Disorders, 77*, 159–166.

Vermani, M., Milosevic, I., Smith, F., & Katzman, M. A. (2005). Herbs for mental illness: Effectiveness and interaction with conventional medicines. *Journal of Family Practice, 54*, 789–800.

Viens, M., De Koninck, J., Mercier, P., St-Onge, M., & Lorrain, D. (2003). Trait anxiety and sleep-onset insomnia. Evaluation of treatment using anxiety management training. *Journal of Psychosomatic Research, 54*(1), 31–37.

Viglione, D. J. (1999). A review of recent research addressing the utility of the Rorschach. *Psychological Assessment, 11*, 251–265.

Vine, C., & Challen, P. (2002). *Gardens of shame: The tragedy of Martin Kruze and the sexual abuse at Maple Leaf Gardens.* Vancouver, BC: Greystone Books.

Vocci, F. J., & Elkashef, A. (2005). Pharmacotherapy and other treatments for cocaine abuse and dependence. *Current Opinion in Psychiatry, 18*, 265–270.

Vogler, G. P., DeFries, J. C., & Decker, S. N. (1985). Family history as an indicator of risk for reading disability. *Journal of Learning Disabilities, 18*, 419–421.

Volkow, N. D., Wang, G. J., Fischman, M. W., Foltin, R. W., Fowler, J. S., Abumrad, N. N., et al. (1997). Relationship between subjective effects of cocaine and dopamine transporter occupancy. *Nature, 386*, 827–830.

Volpicelli, J. R., Alterman, A. I., Hayashida, M., & O'Brien, C. P. (1992). Naltrexone in the treatment of alcohol dependence. *Archives of General Psychiatry, 49*, 876–880.

Volpicelli, J. R., Clay, K. L., Watson, N. T., & Volpicelli, L. A. (1994). Naltrexone and the treatment of alcohol dependence. *Alcohol Health & Research World, 18*, 272–278.

W

Waddell, C., & Shepherd, C. (2002). Prevalence of mental disorders in children and youth. A research update prepared for the British Columbia Ministry of Children and Family Development: October 2002. Vancouver: The University of British Columbia.

Waddell, C., Offord, D. R., Shepherd, C. A., Hua, J. M., & McEwan, K. (2002). Child psychiatric epidemiology and Canadian public policy-making: The state of the science and the art of the possible. *Canadian Journal of Psychiatry, 47*(9), 825–832).

Waddell, C., McEwan, K., Shepherd, C.A., Offord, D.R., & Hua, J.M. (2005). A public health strategy to improve the mental health of Canadian children. *Canadian Journal of Psychiatry, 50*(4), 226–233.

Wagner, B. M. (1997). Family risk factors for child and adolescent suicidal behavior. *Psychological Bulletin, 121*, 246–298.

Wahlbeck, K., Cheine, M., Essali, A., & Adams, C. (1999). Evidence of clozapine's effectiveness in schizophrenia: A systematic review and meta-analysis of randomized trials. *American Journal of Psychiatry, 156*, 990–999.

Wakefield, J. C. (1992a). The concept of mental disorder: On the boundary between biological facts and social values. *American Psychologist, 47*, 373–388.

Wakefield, J. C. (1992b). Disorder as harmful dysfunction: A conceptual critique of DSM-III-R's definition of mental disorder. *Psychological Review, 99*, 232–247.

Wakefield, J. C. (1997). Normal inability versus pathological disability: Why Ossorio's definition of mental disorder is not sufficient. *Clinical Psychology: Science and Practice, 4*, 249–258.

Wakefield, J. C. (2001). Evolutionary history versus current causal role in the definition of disorder: Reply to McNally.

Wakeling, A. (1996). Epidemiology of anorexia nervosa. *Psychiatry Research, 62*, 3–9.

Wakschlag, L. S., Lahey, B. B., Loeber, R., Green, S. M., Gordon, R. A., & Leventhal, B. L. (1997). Maternal smoking during pregnancy and the risk of conduct disorder in boys. *Archives of General Psychiatry, 54*, 670–676.

Wald, J., & Taylor, S. (2003). Preliminary research on the efficacy of virtual reality exposure therapy to treat driving phobia. *Cyberpsychology and Behavior, 6*, 459–465.

Wald, J., Taylor, S., & Scamvougeras, A. (2004). Cognitive-behavioural and neuropsychiatric treatment of posttraumatic conversion disorder: A case study. *Cognitive Behaviour Therapy 33*, 12–20.

Waldram, J.B. (2001). The problem of "culture" and the counselling of Aboriginal Peoples. In Kirmayer, L.J., MacDonald, M.E., & Brass, G.M. (Eds.). *Proceedings of the Advanced Study Institute: The Mental Health of Indigenous Peoples.* Montreal: McGill Summer Program in Social & Cultural Psychiatry.

Waldram, J. B. (2004). *Revenge of the Windigo: The construction of the mind and mental health of North American Aboriginal peoples.* Toronto, ON: University of Toronto Press.

Wallace, J. (1985). The alcoholism controversy. *American Psychologist, 40*, 372–373.

Walsh, B. T., et al. (1997). Medication and psychotherapy in the treatment of bulimia nervosa. *American Journal of Psychiatry, 154*, 523–531.

Walsh, B. T., Fairburn, C. G., Mickley, D., Sysko, R., & Parides, M. K. (2004). Treatment of bulimia nervosa in a primary care setting. *American Journal of Psychiatry, 161*(3), 556–561.

Wampold, B. E., et al. (1997a). A meta-analysis of outcome studies comparing bona fide psychotherapies: Empirically, "All must have prizes." *Psychological Bulletin, 122*, 203–215.

Wampold, B. E., et al. (1997b). The flat earth as a metaphor for the evidence for uniform efficacy of bona fide psychotherapies: Reply to Crits-Christoph (1997) and Howard

et al. (1997). *Psychological Bulletin, 122*, 226–230.

Wang, Q., Chan, R., Sun, J., Yao, J., Deng, W., Sun, X., et al. (2007). Reaction time of the continuous performance test is an endophenotypic marker for schizophrenia: A study of first-episode neuroleptic-naïve schizophrenia, their non-psychotic first-degree relatives and healthy population controls. *Schizophrenia Research, 89*, 293–298.

Wang, Y. T. (2006). Novel Therapeutic Strategies to Repair Abnormalities in Psychiatric Disorders. Neuroscience Canada. Retrieved on February 2, 2007, from http://www.neurosciencecanada.ca/docs/2006/Fiche%20NScience-recto-Wang-angl.pdf.

Warme, G. (2006). *Daggers of the mind: Psychiatry and the myth of mental disease.* Toronto, ON: House of Anansi Press.

Wasylenki, D. (2001). The paradigm shift from institution to community. In Q. Rae-Grant (Ed.), *Psychiatry in Canada: 50 years* (pp. 95–110). Ottawa: Canadian Psychiatric Association.

Weaver, T. L., & Clum, G. A. (1995). Psychological distress associated with interpersonal violence: A meta-analysis. *Clinical Psychology Review, 15*, 115–140.

Webster-Stratton, C., & Hammond, M. (1997). Treating children with early-onset conduct problems: A comparison of child and parent training interventions. *Journal of Consulting and Clinical Psychology, 65*, 93–109.

Wechsler, D. (1975). Intelligence defined and undefined: A relativistic appraisal. *American Psychologist, 30*, 135–139.

Wechsler, H., et al. (1994). Health and behavioral consequences of binge drinking in college: A national survey of students at 140 campuses. *Journal of the American Medical Association, 272*, 1672–1677.

Weems, C.F., Costa, N.M., Watts, S.E., Taylor, L.K., & Cannon, M.F. (2007). Cognitive errors, anxiety sensitivity, and anxiety control beliefs: Their unique and specific associations with childhood anxiety symptoms. *Behavior Modification, 31*(2), 174–201.

Weinberger, D. R. (1997). On localizing schizophrenic neuropathology. *Schizophrenia Bulletin, 23*, 537–540.

Weinberger, J. (1995). Common factors aren't so common: The common factors dilemma. *Clinical Psychology: Science and Practice, 2*, 45–69.

Weiner, I. B. (2000). Using the Rorschach properly in practice and research. *Journal of Clinical Psychology, 56*(3), 435–438.

Weiner, M. F. (1997). Current status of the Rorschach inkblot method. *Journal of Personality Assessment, 68*, 5–19.

Weinhold, B. (2006). Epigenetics: The science of change. *Environmental Health Perspectives, 114*(3), A160–A167.

Weiss, M., & Murray, C. (2003). Assessment and management of attention-deficit hyperactivity disorder in adults. *Canadian Medical Association Journal, 168*(6), 715–722.

Weiss, R. D., & Mirin, S. M. (1994). *Cocaine (2nd ed.)*. Washington, DC: American Psychiatric Press.

Weissman, A. N., & Beck, A. T. (1978, November). Development and validation of the Dysfunctional Attitudes Scale: A preliminary investigation. Paper presented at the meeting of the American Educational Research Association, Toronto.

Weissman, M. M. (1999). Depressed adolescents grown up. *Journal of the American Medical Association, 281*, 1707–1713.

Weissman, M. M., & Markowitz, J. C. (2000). *Comprehensive guide to interpersonal psychotherapy*. New York: Basic Books.

Weissman, M. M., Bland, R. C., Canino, G. J., Greewald, S., Hwu, H.-G., Joyce, P. R., Karam, E. G., Lee, C.-K., Lellouch, J., Lepine, J.-P., Newman, S. C., Rubio-Stipec, M., Wells, J. E., Wickramaratne, P. J., Witten, H.-U., & Yeh, E.-K. (1999). Prevalence of suicide ideation and suicide attempts in nine countries. *Psychological Medicine, 29*, 9–17.

Weisz, J. R., McCarty, C. A., & Valeri, S. M. (2006). Effects of psychotherapy for depression in children and adolescents: A meta-analysis. *Psychological Bulletin, 132*, 132–149.

Welch, M. R., & Kartub, P. (1978). Socio-cultural correlates of incidence of impotence: A cross-cultural study. *Journal of Sex Research, 14*, 218–230.

Weltzin, T. E., Cameron, J., Berga, S., & Kaye, W. H. (1994). Prediction of reproductive status in women with bulimia nervosa by past high weight. *American Journal of Psychiatry, 151*(1), 136–138.

Wender, P. H., Rosenthal, D., Kety, S. S., Schulsinger, F., & Welner, J. (1974). Cross-fostering: A research strategy for clarifying the role of genetic and experiential factors in the etiology of schizophrenia. *Archives of General Psychiatry, 30*, 121–128.

Wente, M. (2006). Post-traumatic stress is felling more troops than the enemy. *The Globe and Mail*, July 6, p. A15.

Westen, D., & Shedler, J. (1999). Revising and assessing Axis II: I. Developing a clinically and empirically valid assessment method. *American Journal of Psychiatry, 156*, 258–272.

Whitelaw, N. C., & Whitelaw, E. (2006). How lifetimes shape epigenotype within and across generations. *Human Molecular Genetics, 15* (Review Issue No. 2),131–137.

Whittington, C. J., Kendall, T., & Pilling, S. (2005). Are the SSRIs and atypical antidepressants safe and effective with children and adolescents? *Current Opinion in Psychiatry, 18*, 21–25.

Wickelgren, I. (1997, June 27). Marijuana: Harder than thought? *Science, 276*, 1967.

Widiger, T. A. (1991). DSM-IV reviews of the personality disorders: Introduction to special series. *Journal of Personality Disorder, 5*, 122–134.

Widiger, T. A. (1992). Generalized social phobia versus avoidant personality disorder: A commentary on three studies. *Journal of Abnormal Psychology, 101*, 340–343.

Widiger, T. A., & Costa, P. T., Jr. (1994). Personality and personality disorders. *Journal of Abnormal Psychology, 103*, 78–91.

Widiger, T. A., & Clark, L. A. (2000). Toward DSM-V and the classification of psychopathology. *Psychological Bulletin, 126*(6), 946–963.

Wieman, C. (2001). An overview of Six Nations mental health services. In Kirmayer, L. J., MacDonald, M.E., & Brass, G.M. (Eds.). *Proceedings of the Advanced Study Institute: The Mental Health of Indigenous Peoples*. Montreal: McGill Summer Program in Social & Cultural Psychiatry.

Wiersma, D., Nienhuis,F. J., Slooff,C. J., & Giel, R. (1998). Natural course of schizophrenic disorders: A 15-year follow-up of a Dutch incidence cohort. *Schizophrenia Bulletin, 24*, 75–85.

Wilbur, C. B. (1986). Psychoanalysis and multiple personality disorder. In B. G. Braun (Ed.), *Treatment of multiple personality disorder*. Washington, DC: American Psychiatric Press.

Wilkins, J. (1998). Anorexia nervosa: Self sabotage in adolescence. *Pro-Teen: Canadian Association for Adolescent Health, 7*(4), 9–12.

Williams, C. (2001). You snooze, you lose? Sleep patterns in Canada (Catalogue No. 11-008). *Canadian Social Trends, Spring*, 10–14.

Williams, J. B., et al. (1992). The Structured Clinical Interview for DSM-III-(SCID): II. Multisite test-retest reliability. *Archives of General Psychiatry, 49*, 630–636.

Williams, J. M. (1984). *The psychological treatment of depression: A guide to the theory and practice of cognitive-behavior therapy*. New York: Free Press.

Williams, P. G., Wiebe, D. J., & Smith, T. W. (1992). Coping processes as mediators of the relationship between hardiness and health. *Journal of Behavioral Medicine, 15*, 237–255.

Williams, P., Narciso, L., Browne, G., Roberts, J., Weir, R., & Gafni, A. (2005). The prevalence, correlates, and costs of depression in people living with HIV/AIDS in Ontario: Implications for service directions. *AIDS Education and Prevention, 17*, 119–130.

Williams, R. B., Barefoot, J. C., Blumenthal, J. A., Helms, M. J., Luecken, L., Pieper, C. F., et al. (1997). Psychosocial correlates of job strain in a sample of working women. *Archives of General Psychiatry, 54*(6), 543–548.

Wills, T. A., & Filer Fegan, M. (2001). Social networks and social support. In A. Baum, T. A. Revenson, & J. E. Singer (Eds.), *Handbook of Health Psychology* (pp. 3–18). Mahwah, NJ: Erlbaum.

Wilson, G. T. (1994). Behavioral treatment of childhood obesity: Theoretical and practical implications. *Health Psychology, 13*, 371–372.

Wilson, G. T., & Fairburn, C. G. (1998). Treatments for eating disorders. In P. E. Nathan & J. M. Gorman (Eds.), *A guide to treatments that work* (pp. 501–530). New York: Oxford University Press.

Wilson, P. (2000, May 16). Keeping pain at a distance. *The Hamilton Spectator*.

Winerip, M. (1991, December 18). Soldier in battle for the retarded. *The New York Times*, pp. B1, B6.

Winston, A. P. (2000). Recent developments in borderline personality disorder. *Advances in Psychiatric Treatment, 6*(3), 211–218.

Winston, A., Laikin, M., Pollack, J., Samstag, L. W., McCullough, L., & Muran, J. C. (1994). Short-term psychotherapy of personality disorders. *American Journal of Psychiatry, 151*(2), 190–194.

Winston, A., Pollack, J., McCullough, L., Flegenheimer, W., Kestenbaum, R., & Trujillo, M. (1991). Brief psychotherapy of personality disorders. *Journal of Nervous and Mental Disease, 179*(4), 188–193.

Wise, T. P. (1978). Where the public peril begins: A survey of psychotherapists to determine the effects of Tarasoff. *Stanford Law Review, 135*, 165–190.

Wolfe, B. E., & Goldfried, M. R. (1988). Research on psychotherapy integration: Recommendations and conclusions from an NIMH workshop. *Journal of Consulting and Clinical Psychology, 56*, 448–451.

Wolpe, J. (1958). *Psychotherapy by reciprocal inhibition*. Stanford, CA: Stanford University Press.

Wolpe, J., & Lazarus, A. A. (1966). *Behavior therapy techniques*. New York: Pergamon.

Wonderlich, S. A., Brewerton, T. D., Jocic, Z., Dansky, B. S., & Abbott, D. W. (1997). Relationship of childhood sexual abuse and eating disorders. *Journal of the American Academy of Child and Adolescent Psychiatry, 36*(8), 1107–1115.

Wong, T. P. T. (2002, June 2). INPM: Who we are and what

we do. International Network on Personal Meaning. Retrieved April 13, 2003, from http://www.meaning.ca/about_us/june02_letter.htm.

Wood, J. M., et al. (1992). Effects of 1989 San Francisco earthquake on frequency and content of nightmares. *Journal of Abnormal Psychology, 101,* 219–234.

Wood, J. M., Nezworski, M. T., & Stejskal, W. J. (1996). The comprehensive system for the Rorschach: A critical examination. *Psychological Science, 7,* 3–10.

Wood, J. M., Nezworski, M. T., & Stejskal, W. J. (1997). The reliability of the comprehensive system for the Rorschach: A comment on Meyer. *Psychological Assessment, 9,* 490–494.

Woodside, D. B., Bulik, C. M., Halmi, K. A., Fichter, M. M., Kaplan, A. S., Berrettini, W. H., Strober, M., Treasure, J., Lilenfeld, L., Klump, K., & Kaye, W. H. (2002). Personality, perfectionism, and attitudes toward eating in parents of individuals with eating disorders. *International Journal of Eating Disorders, 31*(3), 290–299.

Woodside, D. B., Garfinkel, P. E., Lin, E., Goering, P., Kaplan, A. S., Goldbloom, D. S., & Kennedy, S. H. (2001). Comparisons of men with full or partial eating disorders, men without eating disorders, women with eating disorders in the community. *American Journal of Psychiatry, 158*(4), 570–574.

Woody, S. R. (1996). Effects of focus of attention on anxiety levels and social performance of individuals with social phobia. *Journal of Abnormal Psychology, 105,* 61–69.

Wootton, J. M., Frick, P. J., Shelton, K. K., & Silverthorn, P. (1997). Ineffective parenting and childhood conduct problems: The moderating role of callous-unemotional traits. *Journal of Consulting and Clinical Psychology, 65*(2), 301–308.

Working Group for the Canadian Psychiatric Association and Canadian Alliance for Research on Schizophrenia (1998). Canadian clinical practice guidelines for the treatment of schizophrenia. *Canadian Journal of Psychiatry, 43* (Suppl. 2), 25S–39S.

World Health Organization (2001a, June 25). ICD-10 Description. Geneva, Switzerland: Author. Retrieved May 5, 2003, from http://www.who.int/whosis/icd10/descript.htm. Full title is the International Statistical Classification of Diseases and Related Health Problems.

World Health Organization, (2001b, November). Strengthening mental health promotion. Retrieved April 23, 2003, from http://www.who.int/inf-fs/en/fact220.html.

World Health Organization, (2003). WHO definition of health. Retrieved April 27, 2003, from http://www.who.int/about/definition/en.

Y

Yatham, L. N., Kennedy, S. H., O'Donovan, C., Parikh, S. V., MacQueen, G., McIntyre, R. S., et al. (2006). Canadian Network for Mood and Anxiety Treatments (CANMAT) guidelines for the management of patients with bipolar disorder: Update 2007. *Bipolar Disorders, 8,* 721–739.

Yeni, P. G., Hammer, S. M., Carpenter, C. C., Cooper, D. A., Fischl, M. A., Gatell, J. M., et al. (2002). Antiretroviral treatment for adult HIV infection in 2002: Updated recommendations of the International AIDS Society-USA Panel. *Journal of the American Medical Association, 288*(2), 222–235.

Yirmiya, N., & Sigman, M. (1991). High functioning individuals with autism: Diagnosis, empirical findings, and theoretical issues. *Clinical Psychology Review, 11,* 669–683.

Young, M. A., et al. (1994). Interactions of risk factors in predicting suicide. *American Journal of Psychiatry, 51,* 434–435.

Young, T., et al. (1996). The gender bias in sleep apnea diagnosis. *Archives of Internal Medicine, 156,* 2445–2451.

Z

Zakzanis, K. K., & Heinricks, R. W. (1999). Schizophrenia and the frontal brain: A quantitative review. *Journal of the International Neuropsychological Society, 5,* 556–566.

Zakzanis, K. K., Poulin, P., Hansen, K. T., & Jolic, D. (2000). Searching the schizophrenic brain for temporal lobe deficits: A systematic review and meta-analysis. *Psychological Medicine, 30,* 491–504.

Zanardi, R., et al. (1996). Double-blind controlled trial of sertraline versus paroxetine in the treatment of delusional depression. *American Journal of Psychiatry, 153,* 1631–1633.

Zanarini, M. C., Williams, A. A., Lewis, R. E., Reich, R. B., Vera, S. C., Marino, M. F., et al. (1997). Reported pathological childhood experiences associated with the development of borderline personality disorder. *American Journal of Psychiatry, 154*(8), 1101–1106.

Zanarini, M.C., Frankenburg, F.R., Hennen, J., & Silk, K.R. (2003). The longitudinal course of borderline psychopathology: Six-year prospective follow-up of the phenomenology of borderline personality disorder. *American Journal of Psychiatry, 160*(2), 274–283.

Zhong, C.-B., & Liljenquist, K. (2006). Washing away your sins: Threatened morality and physical cleansing. *Science, 313,* 1451–1452.

Zhou, J-N, Hofman, M. A., Gooren, L. J., Swaab D. F. (1995). A sex difference in the human brain and its relation to transsexuality. *Nature, 378,* 68–70.

Zhu, A. J., & Walsh, B. T. (2002). Pharmacologic treatment of eating disorders. *Canadian Journal of Psychiatry, 47*(3), 227–234.

Zilberman, M., Tavares, H., & el-Guebaly, N. (2003). Gender similarities and differences: The prevalence and course of alcohol- and other substance-related disorders. *Journal of Addictive Diseases, 22,* 61–74.

Zimmerman, B.J., & Schunk, D. H. (2002). Albert Bandura: The Man and his Contributions to Educational Psychology. In B.J. Zimmerman, & H. Schunk (Eds.), *Educational psychology : a century of contributions* (pp. 431–459). Mahwah, N.J. : L. Erlbaum Associates.

Zotter, D. L., & Crowther, J. H. (1991). The role of cognitions in bulimia nervosa. *Cognitive Therapy & Research, 15,* 413–426.

Zubin, J., & Spring, B. (1977). Vulnerability—New view of schizophrenia. *Journal of Abnormal Psychology, 86,* 103–126.

Zucker, K. J. (2005). Gender identity disorder in children and adolescents. *Annual Review of Clinical Psychology, 1,* 467–492.

Zucker, K. J., & Blanchard, R. (1997). Tranvestic fetishism: Psychopathology and theory. In D. R. Laws & W. T. O'Donohue (Eds.), *Handbook of sexual deviance: Theory and application.* New York: Guilford.

Zucker, K. J., & Green, R. (1992). Psychosexual disorders in children and adolescents. *Journal of Child Psychology and Psychiatry, 33,* 107–151.

Zuckerman, M. (1980). Sensation seeking. In H. London & J. Exner (Eds.), *Dimensions of personality.* New York: John Wiley & Sons.

Zweig-Frank, H., & Paris, J. (1991). Parents' emotional neglect and overprotection according to the recollections of patients with borderline personality disorder. *American Journal of Psychiatry, 148,* 648–651.

Kuiper, N.A., 153–154
Kulkarni, J., 275\276
Kuller, L.H., 163
Kumari, V., 449
Kumra, S., 486
Kunz, G., 353
Kupfer, D.J., 272, 387
Kupfersmid, J., 59
Kurtz, J.E., 126
Kwang-soo, 81
Kwon, S., 261
Kymalainen, J.A., 452

L
LaBlanc, M., 381
Labott, S.M., 127
Labouvie, E., 358
Ladouceur, R., 195, 207, 328
Lahey, B.B., 488, 489
Lainez, M.J., 159
Laird, P.W., 44
Laird, R., 311
Laishes, J., 292
Lalinec-Michaud, M., 14, 16
Lalonde, J.K., 219
Lam, R.W., 79, 248, 275
Lamb, S., 305
Lambert, M.J., 95
Lammers, G.J., 382
Landy, S., 313
Lang, P.J., 132, 135, 289, 293
Lang, R., 401
Langenbucher, J., 109, 358
Langevin, R., 401
Langford, S., 486
Lanius, R.A., 146
Lanphear, B.P., 486
Lanyon, R.I., 401
Larimer, M.E., 361
Larkin, E.K., 383
Laroi, F., 437
Larson, G., 158
Larson, R.W., 495
Lau, E., 370, 370
Laumann, E.O., 395, 414
Lauriello, J., 448
Lavallee, C., 333
Law, A.J., 446
Lawson, D.M., 362
Lawson, M.L., 368
Lazarus, A.A., 166
Lazarus, R.S., 151
Lazovik, A.D., 132
Leary, W.E., 361
Leavitt, F., 127
LeBaron, D., 405
Ledley, D.R., 198
Lee, J.K.P., 401
Lee, T.H., 344
Lefcourt, H.M., 153
Lefley, H.P., 8
Lefton, L.A., 149
Lehman, D.R., 227
Lehmann, H.E., 14, 16, 455
Lehrer, P.M., 167
Lehtinen, V., 143, 157
Leibing, E., 316
Leiblum, S.R., 416, 421, 424
Leibson, C.L., 485
Leichner, P., 367

Leichsenring, F., 316
Leit, R.A., 372
Leite, C., 153
Leitenberg, H., 168, 377, 401
Lenhart, L., 490
Lentz, R.J., 457
Lenzenweger, M.F., 434, 435
Leon, A.C., 296
Leonardo, E.D., 197
Leszez, M., 49
Letendre, A.D., 6
Letourneau, E.J., 411, 415, 424
Levenson, J.L., 167
Levenstein, S., 158
Levine, J., 151
Levitan, R.D., 375
Levitt, A., 251
Levitt, A.J., 248, 375
Levy, S.R., 496
Lewandowski, L.M., 376
Lewinsohn, P.M., 257, 263, 268–269, 269, 492, 494, 495, 496
Lewis, I.A., 405
Lezak, M.D., 221
Li, S., 363
Liang, G., 43, 81
Liberman, R.P., 457, 458, 459
Libert, J.M., 257\258
Lichtenstein, E., 342
Liddle, P.F., 441
Lieber, C.S., 331
Lieberman, J.A., 455
Lightner, D.L., 13
Lilienfeld, S.O., 104, 219, 225, 289, 291
Liljenquist, K., 194
Lindahl, V., 249
Linde, K., 274
Lindvall, O., 81
Linehan, M.M., 279, 316
Links, P.S., 295–317
Liotti, G., 296
Lipman, E.L., 405
Lipps, G., 480
Lipsey, M.W., 94
Lipton, R.B., 159
Lisak, D., 410
Liss, A., 183, 198
Litman, L.C., 400
Little, R.E., 336
Litvin, E.B., 355
Livesley, W.J., 195, 196, 264, 304–312, 316, 317
Livingston, J.D., 515
Livingstone, M.S., 482
Lo, H., 96
Lochman, 489
Lochman, J.E., 311, 489, 490
Lockwood, G., 91
Loeber, R., 489
Loftus, E.F., 227, 228
Lohman, J.J., 159
Lohr, K.N., 355
Lohr, N.E., 310
London, H., 294
Long, J.D., 459
Long, P., 99
Loo, C., 81
Loo, C.K., 275

Looper, K.J., 233, 234
LoPiccolo, J., 417, 423, 424, 425
Loranger, A.W., 302, 314
Lorenz, A.R., 296
Lorrain, D., 381
Lotter, A., 386
Lovaas, O.I., 468, 469
Lowe, M.R., 373
Luch, A., 75
Luermans, J., 202
Lueschen, G., 353
Lukassen, J., 331, 335
Lumley, M.N., 255
Luntz, B.K., 310
Luria, A.R., 129
Lutgendorf, S.K., 169
Luthar, S., 71
Lydiard, R.B., 197
Lykken, D.T., 292
Lynch, R.S., 162
Lynn, S.J., 219, 225
Lynne, J., 188
Lyons, M.J., 196, 197

M
Macaruso, P., 476
MacDonald, C., 376
MacDonald, K.R., 361
MacDonald, M.E., 6
MacKenzie, T.D., 340
MacLatchy-Gaudet, H.A., 350
MacLeod, C., 196
MacMillan, H.L., 6, 405
Macnaughton, E., 96, 97
MacPhillamy, D.J., 257
Maddever, H.M., 405
Maddi, S.R., 152
Magiskan, A., 7
Magnusson, A., 248
Mahamedi, F., 373
Maher, B.A., 10
Maher, M.S., 308
Maher, W.B., 10
Mahler, M., 57, 58, 85
Mahler, M.S., 308
Maier, S.F., 146, 148, 262
Maitra, A., 44
Malarkey, W.B., 148
Maletzky, B.M., 408, 409
Malla, A.K., 460
Malloy, T.E., 170
Maltzman, I.M., 361
Mamdani, M., 79
Mancini, C., 188
Mandal, V., 511
Maner, J.K., 195
Manion, I.G., 277
Mann, J.J., 278, 279, 280, 497
Mann, M., 43, 44
Mannuzza, S., 487
Manson, S.E., 110
Mantovani, F., 120
Manzetta, B.R., 165
Marchand, A., 195
Marchi, M.M., 234
Marcus, D.K., 234, 235, 258
Marcus, S., 275
Marder, S.R., 455, 456, 458
Marengo, J.T., 434
Maric, A., 410
Marin, A., 187

Marino, L., 104
Mark, D.H., 159
Mark, M.M., 168
Markon, K.E., 197
Markovitz, J.H., 162
Markowitz, J.C., 169, 267, 268
Marks, E., 128
Marks, S., 170
Marlatt, G.A., 351, 352, 361–362
Marques, T., 377
Marquette, C., 279
Marshall, A.D., 188
Marshall, D., 395
Marshall, W.L., 405, 407, 408, 410
Marsteller, F., 207
Martin, D., 484
Martin, G.M., 74, 75
Martin, P.R., 159
Martin, R.A., 153–154, 159
Martin. R.L., 79
Martinsen, E.W., 273
Marton, P., 405
Marucha, P.T., 148
Maslow, A., 63, 65
Mason, C.A., 353
Mason, M., 158
Masten, A.S., 71
Masters, W.H., 421, 422, 423, 424
Matas, M., 512
Maté, G., 145\146
Matefy, R., 343
Math, S.B., 237
Mathers, J.C., 75
Mathes, S., 128
Matheson, K., 255
Mathews, A., 196
Mathews, K.A., 162
Mattoo, S.K., 275
Mattson, S., 43
Maxwell, J.C., 338
Maxwell, S.E., 494
Mayer, J.D., 65
Mayo-Smith, M.F., 355
McBride, P.A., 469
McCabe, M.P., 369, 372
McCabe, R., 203
McCarthy, B.W., 421
McCarty, C.A., 276
McCaul, M.E., 358
McCleery, A., 459
McClellan, J.M., 43
McClelland, D.C., 128
McCloskey, M.S., 313
McCord, J., 311
McCord, W., 311
McCormick, R.M., 6, 7
McCracken, J.T., 469
McCrady, B.S., 348, 358
McCulloch, E.A., 44
McDermott, B., 448
McDonald, R., 489
McDougall, C., 7
McDougall, G., 458
McEachin, J.J., 469
McEwan, K., 465
McFarquhar, T., 80–81
McGlashan, T.H., 296, 441
McGovern, P.G., 163
McGrath, R.E., 124
McGue, M.K., 485

McGuffin, P., 49, 264, 445, 474
McGuire, L., 162
McGuire, P.K., 437
McGuire, S., 490
McInnes, R., 424
McIntosh, D.E., 469
McKay, D., 193
McKay, J., 356, 357
McKay, J.D., 96
McKay, J.S., 410
McKeith, I., 437
McLean-Heywood, D., 466
McLellan, A.T., 355
McMahon, F.J., 446
McMurray, L., 78
McNally, R.J., 110
McNaughton, N., 313
McSherry, B., 515, 516
Mead, M., 4
Meador-Woodruff, J.H., 447
Meana, M., 416
Medalia, A., 435
Medicine, B., 110
Mednick, S.A., 25, 312, 451
Meehl, P.E., 448
Mehta, P., 489
Meichenbaum, D., 68, 89, 91, 159, 277
Meisler, A.W., 420
Mellings, T.M.B., 183
Mellor, C.S., 433
Melton, G.B., 490
Meng, L., 466
Menon, R.S., 146
Mercado, A.M., 148
Mercier, P., 381
Merette, C., 381
Merikangas, K.R., 49
Merskey, H., 219, 226, 333
Messenger, J., 395
Meston, C.M., 417, 418, 424
Metsanen, M., 438
Metzner, H.L., 154
Meyer, G.J., 127
Meyer, T.J., 168
Meyers, B.S., 245
Mian, M., 405
Michael, R.T., 395
Michaels, S., 395
Michie, C., 291–292
Mickley, D., 375
Miklowitz, D.J., 251, 255, 264, 274, 279, 450, 452–453
Milavsky, J.R., 497
Milberger, S., 475
Millar, W.J., 166
Miller, 357
Miller, E., 235
Miller, K.B., 377
Miller, K.J., 358
Miller, L.K., 476
Miller, T.I., 94, 95
Miller, T.Q., 161
Miller, W.R., 358, 361–362
Millon, T., 124–125, 309
Milner, P., 66
Milos, G., 367
Milosevic, I., 274
Milstone, C., 18

584 NAME INDEX

computerized tomography (CT scan), 135, 136f
conclusions, 23
concordance, 29
concurrent validity, 114
conditional positive regard, 64
conditioned response (CR), 60
conditioned stimulus (CS), 60
conditioning model of cravings, 349–350
conditions of worth, 64
conduct disorder
    described, 487–488
    theoretical perspectives, 489–490
    treatment, 490–491
confidentiality, 24, 509
congruence, 88
conscious mind, 51
construct validity, 115
content analysis, 127
content of thought, disturbances in, 433–434
content validity, 114
contrasted groups approach, 124
contrived measures, 132
control
    controlling behaviour, 22
    in scientific method, 22–23
    subject expectancies, 26–27
control subjects, 26
controlled social drinking, 361–363
controlling behaviour, 22
conversion disorder
    described, 230–231
    diagnostic features, 231t
    history of, 234
    hypnosis and, 17
    la belle indifference, 231
    physical symptoms, 215
coping styles, 151–152, 255, 265
Coping with Depression (CWD) Course, 268–269
corpus callosum, 48
correlation, 24–25, 33
cortical steroids, 149
corticosteroids, 147
countertransference, 84
CPA Code of Ethics, 519
crack, 339
craving-for-stimulation model, 293
creative self, 56
Criminal Code of Canada, 515–516
criminal commitment, 505
criterion validity, 114–115
critical thinking
    and abnormal psychology, 32
    assumptions and premises, 32–33
    correlation vs. causation, 33
    defined, 32
    definitions of terms, 32
    evidence, consideration of, 33
    features of, 32–33
    online information, 33–34
    overgeneralization, 33
    oversimplification, 33
    and skepticism, 32
cross-fostering study, 446
cue-exposure training, 350
Cullen, William, 177
cultural-familial retardation, 475
cultural stereotypes, 6

culture
    see also sociocultural perspectives
    depression, 8
    and normal behaviour, 6–8
    and schizophrenia, 8
culture-bound disorders, 110, 110t, 219, 236–237
culture-bound dissociative conditions, 236–237
cyclic vomiting syndrome, 378
cyclothymic disorder, 252–253
cystic fibrosis, 43
cytomegalovirus, 475

D
Daily Record of Dysfunctional Thoughts, 133
dangerous behaviour, 5
dangerousness, 506–509
date rape, 411–412
debriefed, 24
defence mechanisms, 52, 53t, 191
definitions of terms, 32
deinstitutionalization, 14
deliriant, 343
delirium, 325
delirium tremens, 325
delta-9-tetrahydrocannabinol (THC), 343
delusions, 5, 186, 433
delusions of being controlled, 433
delusions of grandeur, 433
delusions of persecution, 433
delusions of reference, 433
dementia praecox, 16
demonological model, 9–10, 16
dendrites, 45
denial, 151
dependent personality disorder, 301–303
dependent variables, 26, 26t
depersonalization, 222
depersonalization disorder, 222–225, 224t
deplorable hospital conditions, 13
depressants
    alcohol, 330–336
    barbiturates, 336–337
    defined, 330
    opiates, 337–338
depression
    see also mood disorders
    adolescence, 494–496
    and attributions, 262–263
    Beck Depression Inventory (BDI), 122
    biochemical factors, 264
    brain abnormalities, 264
    in childhood, 494–496
    cognitive triad of depression, 259, 259t
    common features, 244t
    cultural differences, 8
    diagnostic features of major depressive episode, 245
    diathesis-stress model, 264–265, 265f
    double depression, 250
    electroconvulsive therapy (ECT), 79
    major depressive disorder, 244–247, 245f, 246f

prevalence of major depressive disorder, 246f
    questionnaire, 249
    reinforcement, 257–258
    risk factors for major depression, 246–247
    St. John's Wort, 274
    and stress, 255
    treatment-resistant depression (TRD), 79
derealization, 222
description, 22
detoxification, 355
deviation IQ, 121
Dhat syndrome, 111, 236–237
diagnosis, 109
    see also assessment
Diagnostic and Statistical Manual of Mental Disorders, 4th Edition, Text Revision (DSM-IV-TR). See DSM-IV-TR
dialectical behaviour therapy (DBT), 316
diathesis, 73, 265
diathesis-stress model
    depression, 264–265, 265f
    interactionist perspectives, 73–74, 74f
    schizophrenia, 448–451, 449f
    shyness, 184
    stress and dissociative disorders, 226
diazepam, 77
differentiate, 44
dimensional model, 109, 155, 156t
direct observation, 130
diseases of adaptation, 149
disinhibition, 280
disorder of written expression, 481
disorganized type, 438
disorientation, 325
displacement, 83
disqualification of the positive, 260
disruptive behaviour disorders
    conduct disorder, 487–488
    oppositional defiant disorder (ODD), 488
    theoretical perspectives, 489–490
    treatment, 490–491
dissociation, 189
dissociative amnesia, 220–221
dissociative disorders
    and anxiety, 215
    depersonalization disorder, 222–225, 224t
    described, 216
    dissociative amnesia, 220–221
    Dissociative Experiences Scale (DES), 224–225
    dissociative fugue, 221–222
    dissociative identity disorder, 216–220, 218f, 219t, 225–226
    theoretical perspectives, 225–226
    treatment, 226–228
Dissociative Experiences Scale (DES), 224–225
dissociative fugue, 221–222
dissociative identity disorder
    as culture-bound syndrome, 110

described, 216–220, 218f, 219t
    severe childhood abuse, 225–226
    treatment, 226–227
distress, 143
distressors, 155, 157t
disturbances of thought and speech, 433–434
disulfiram, 355
Dix, Dorothea, 13
dizygotic (DZ) twins, 29
DNA (deoxyribonucleic acid), 42
dopamine, 46
dopamine theory, 446–447
double-bind communications, 452
double-blind placebo design, 27
double depression, 250
Down syndrome, 43, 473
downward drift hypothesis, 70
dramatic behaviour, 288–300
dream analysis, 83
drive to superiority, 56
drug dependence. See substance dependence
drug therapy
    anti-anxiety drugs, 77–78
    antidepressants, 78–79, 272–273, 356
    antipsychotic drugs, 78
    anxiety disorders, 201–202
    anxiolytics, 386–387
    attention-deficit/hyperactivity disorder, 486–487
    disulfiram, 355
    lithium, 79, 273–274
    methadone maintenance programs, 356–357
    naloxone, 357
    naltrexone, 357
    personality disorders, 317
    Ritalin, 486–487
    schizophrenia, 455–456
    sleeping disorders, 386–388
    somatoform disorders, 238
    tolerance, 77
drug use, 323, 324t
drugs of abuse
    see also substance-related disorders
    alcohol, 330–336
    amphetamines, 338
    barbiturates, 336–337
    classification of, 330
    cocaine, 339–340t
    crack, 339
    depressants, 330–338
    hallucinogens, 342–344
    inhalants, 344–345
    LSD, 342–343
    marijuana, 343–344
    narcotics, 337–338
    nicotine, 340–342, 341f
    opiates, 337–338
    phencyclidine (PCP), 343
    sedatives, 336
    stimulants, 338–342
DSM-IV-TR
    see also classification of abnormal behaviour; specific disorders
    advantages, 109
    Axis I, 105
    Axis II, 106
    Axis III, 106

learning perspectives
  anxiety disorders, 191–193
  behaviour modification, 63
  behaviour therapy, 63
  behaviourism, 60
  classical conditioning, 60–61,
    62f
  conditioning model of cravings,
    349–350
  cue-exposure training, 350
  described, 60
  dissociative disorders, 225
  evaluation of, 63
  gender identity disorder,
    398–399
  interactional theory, 258
  mood disorders, 257–258
  negative reinforcement and
    withdrawal, 349
  observational learning, 350
  operant conditioning, 61–63,
    348
  paraphilias, 407–408
  personality disorders, 309–310
  prepared conditioning, 192
  reinforcement, 257–258
  schizophrenia, 443–444
  sexual dysfunctions, 418
  situational factors, 60
  somatoform disorders, 235
  substance-related disorders,
    348–350
  tension-reduction theory,
    348–349
  two-factor model, 191–192
legal commitment, 505
Lehmann, Heinz, 14, 16
Lesbian, Gay, Bisexual, and
  Transgender Community
  Center, 426
leukocytes, 147
libido, 53
life changes, 150–151
Life Orientation Test (LOT),
  153, 154, 158
life stressors, 148
lifelong dysfunctions, 414
limbic abnormalities, 293
limbic system, 48
lithium, 79, 273–274
Little Hans, 191
lobotomy, prefrontal, 82
locus of control, 152
longitudinal study, 25, 450
looseness of associations, 430
lowering arousal, 163–165
LSD, 342–343
Luria, A.R., 129
Luria Nebraska Test Battery, 129

M
magical thinking, 288
magnetic resonance imaging
  (MRI), 136, 137f
magnification, 67, 260
Mahler, Margaret, 57, 85, 308
mainstreaming, 477
major depression, 244–247, 245f
  see also depression
major depressive disorder,
  244–247, 245f, 246f
  see also depression
maladaptive behaviour, 5
male. *See* men
male erectile disorder, 415–416,
  424–425

male orgasmic disorder, 416
male sexual dysfunctions, 424–425
malingering, 221, 229
Mangaia, 395
mania, 10
manic-depression. *See* bipolar
  disorder
manic episode, 245, 251–252
manifest content, 83
mantras, 165
marijuana, 343–344
marital therapy, 93–94, 316
markers, 451
Maslow, Abraham, 63, 65
mathematics disorder, 480
medical model
  see also biological perspectives
  vs. biological perspectives, 41
  defined, 3
  described, 16–17
  diagnosis, 109
  origins of, 10
  support for, 16
  terminology, influence on, 17
medical terminology, 17
medieval times, 10–11
meditation, 165
medulla, 47
Meichenbaum, Donald, 68,
  91–92
melancholia, 10
memory lymphocytes, 147
men
  see also gender differences
  gender reassignment surgery,
    397
  Klinefelter's syndrome, 473
  male erectile disorder,
    415–416, 424–425
  male orgasmic disorder, 416
  male sexual dysfunctions,
    424–425
mental age (MA), 120–121
mental disorders, 104
  see also psychological disorders
mental filter, 260
Mental Health Info Source, 139
mental health legislation, 15
mental health professionals,
  76–77
mental health promotion, 71–72,
  72f
Mental Health Promotion Branch
  (MHP), 72
Mental Help Net, 139, 319
mental illness, 16
mental retardation
  adaptive behaviours, types of,
    472t
  assessment, 471
  causes, 473–476
  chromosomal abnormalities,
    473
  classification of, 472
  cultural-familial retardation,
    475
  cytomegalovirus, 475
  described, 471
  Down syndrome, 473
  fragile X syndrome, 473–475
  genetic abnormalities, 473–475
  intervention, 477–479
  levels of retardation, 472t
  mainstreaming, 477
  other psychological disorders,
    478–479

phenylketonuria (PKU), 474
prenatal factors, 475
savant syndrome, 476
Smith-Lemli-Optiz syndrome
  (SLOS), 474
Tay-Sachs disease, 475
Turner's syndrome, 473
typical ranges of IQ scores,
  472t
mental status examination, 119
mental wellness continuum, 72f,
  155–157, 156t
meprobamate, 77
meta-analysis, 94–95, 98
methadone, 356–357
methadone maintenance
  programs, 356–357
methods of treatment. *See*
  treatment methods
Middle Ages, 10–11
migraine headaches, 159
Millon Clinical Multiaxial
  Inventory (MCMI),
  124–125
mind, structure of, 51, 51f
mind-body relationships, 143,
  145–146
  see also stress
mind reading, 260
mindfulness-based cognitive
  therapy (MBCT), 273
minimization, 260
Minnesota Multiphase
  Personality Inventory
  (MMPI-2), 114, 123–124,
  125f
misattributions for panic
  sensations, 195–196
mislabelling, 260
M'Naughten rule, 515
modelling, 31, 86
models
  see also theoretical perspectives
  biopsychosocial (systems)
    model, 74–75, 155
  craving-for-stimulation model,
    293
  demonological model, 9–10,
    16
  described, 5
  diathesis-stress model, 73–74,
    74f, 226, 264
  dimensional model, 109, 155,
    156t
  medical model. *See* medical
    model
  psychodynamic model, 17
  sociocultural models, 19
moderate drinking, 336
Money, John, 398
Moniz, António Egas, 82
monoamine oxidase (MAO)
  inhibitors, 78, 272–273
monozygotic (MZ) twins, 29
mood disorders
  adolescence, 494–496
  antidepressants, 272–273
  attributional theory, 262–263
  automatic thoughts, 261
  Beck's cognitive therapy,
    259–261
  behavioural therapies,
    268–269
  biochemical factors, 264
  biological perspectives,
    263–265

biological therapies, 272–276
bipolar disorder, 243,
  251–252
brain abnormalities, 264
in childhood, 494–496
cognitive-behavioural
  perspectives, 258–263
cognitive therapies, 270–271,
  271t
cyclothymic disorder, 252–253
defined, 243
depression. *See* depression
dysthymic disorder, 250, 271
electroconvulsive therapy
  (ECT), 274–276
genetics, 263–264
humanistic-existential
  perspectives, 257
hypomanic episode, 245, 252
interactional theory, 258
learned helplessness, 261–263
learning perspectives, 257–258
lithium, 273–274
major depressive disorder,
  244–247, 245f, 246f
manic episode, 245, 251–252
mindfulness-based cognitive
  therapy (MBCT), 273
multiple factors, 264–265
postpartum depression,
  248–249
psychodynamic perspectives,
  255–256
psychodynamic therapies,
  267–268
reinforcement, 257–258
seasonal affective disorder,
  247–248
St. John's Wort, 274
and stress, 254–255
theoretical perspectives,
  254–265
treatment, 267–276
types of, 243–244, 243t
unipolar disorders, 243
Mood Disorders Society of
  Canada, 282
moods, 243
moral principle, 52
moral therapy, 12–13
Mothers Against Drunk Driving
  (MADD), 364
motor cortex, 48
mourning, 255
multiaxial classification system,
  106
multicultural issues in
  psychotherapy, 96–97, 96t
multiple-baseline design, 31
multiple personality disorder. *See*
  dissociative identity disorder
multipotent stem cells, 44, 45
Münchausen syndrome, 229–230
Mundugumor, 4
muscle dysmorphia, 378
must statements, 260
mutagens, 43
myocardial infarction, 160

N
naloxone, 357
naltrexone, 357
narcissistic personality disorder,
  298–300, 300t
narcolepsy, 382
narcotics, 337–338

schizotypal personality
  disorders, 287–288
self psychology, 307–308
Sensation-Seeking Scale,
  294–295, 307
separation-individuation, 308
sexist biases, 305
sociocultural views, 313–314
splitting, 308
theoretical perspectives,
  307–314
treatment, 315–317
types of, 285
undetermined reliability and
  validity of classification, 304
variations in normal behaviour
  vs. abnormal behaviour,
  304–305
personality tests
  contrasted groups approach,
    124
  described, 122–126
  intelligence tests, 123t
  Millon Clinical Multiaxial
    Inventory (MCMI), 124–125
  Minnesota Multiphase
    Personality Inventory
    (MMPI-2), 123–124, 125f
  objective tests, 122–123
  Personality Assessment
    Inventory (PAI), 125–126
  projective personality tests,
    122, 126–128
  Rorschach inkblot test,
    126–127, 127f
  self-report tests, 122, 126
  standard scores, 124
  Thematic Apperception Test
    (TAT), 127–128, 128f
  validity scales, 124
personalization, 260
pervasive developmental disorders
  autism, 466–469, 467t, 470
  described, 466
pessimistic thoughts, 153
phallic stage, 54
phencyclidine (PCP), 343
phenelzine, 78
phenomenological perspective,
  64
phenothiazines, 14, 15–16
phenotype, 28
phenylketonuria (PKU), 474
phlegmatic, 10
phobia. See phobic disorders
phobic disorders
  acrophobia, 182
  agoraphobia, 205–206
  behavioural treatment, 205
  classical conditioning, 60,
    198–199
  claustrophobia, 182, 203
  described, 182
  learning perspective and, 192
  social phobia, 183–184, 184f,
    205
  specific phobias, 182–183
  typical age of onset, 183t
phototherapy, 248
phrenitis, 10
phrenologists, 115
physical disorders
  acquired immunodeficiency
    syndrome (AIDS), 169–170
  asthma, 163–167
  cancer, 167–169

cardiovascular disease,
  160–163
headaches, 159–160
human immunodeficiency virus
  (HIV), 169–170
ulcers, 158
physiological dependence,
  327–328
physiological measurement
  ambulatory blood pressure,
    135
  brain electrical activity
    mapping (BEAM), 136–137,
    137f
  brain imaging techniques,
    135–137
  computerized tomography (CT
    scan), 135, 136f
  described, 134–135
  electrodermal response, 134
  electroencephalograph (EEG),
    135, 135f
  electromyograph (EMG), 135
  functional magnetic resonance
    imaging (fMRI), 136
  galvanic skin response (GSR),
    134
  magnetic resonance imaging
    (MRI), 136, 137f
  positron emission tomography
    (PET scan), 135–136, 136f
  response systems, 135
  workings of the brain,
    135–137
physiological response system,
  135
physiological variables, 26t
pibloktoq, 110
pica, 378
Pinel, Philippe, 12–13
placebo, 27
placebo effect, 248
play therapy, 465
pleasure principle, 51
pluripotent stem cells, 44, 45
polygenic traits, 28
polysomnographic (PSG)
  recording, 380
pons, 47
populations, 28
pornography, 410
positive correlation, 24
positive life events, 150
positive punishers, 62
positive reinforcers, 61
positive symptoms, 440
positron emission tomography
  (PET scan), 135–136, 136f
possession, 9, 10, 16
post hoc problem, 507
postpartum depression, 248–249
postsynaptic, 46
posttraumatic stress disorder
  behavioural treatment,
    205–207
  conditioning, 61
  defined, 61, 186
  described, 186–188
  eye movement desensitization
    and reprocessing (EMDR),
    207
  neuroimmune biology, 146
  prepared conditioning, 192
  traumatic stress reactions,
    188–189
  twin studies, 196, 197f

Prader-Willi syndrome, 378
precepts, 126
preconscious mind, 51
predicting suicide, 280–281
prediction, 22–23, 25
predictive validity, 107, 115
prefrontal cortex, 48, 264
prefrontal lobotomy, 82
pregenital fixations, 55
pregnancy
  alcohol during, 336
  birth complications, 475
  prenatal factors, and mental
    retardation, 475
premature ejaculation, 416
premises, 32–33
premorbid functioning, 441
prenatal factors, 475
preorgasmic women, 423
prepared conditioning, 192
prescription opiates, 337
pressured speech, 251
presynaptic, 46
prevalence, 27
prevention
  AIDS, 169–170
  date rape, 411–412
  efforts and strategies, 71
  rape, 411–412
  stranger rape, 412
  suicide, 281
primary gains, 235
primary insomnia, 381
primary narcissism, 443
primary process thinking, 51
primary reinforcers, 61
proband, 29
problem-focused coping, 151–152
problem-solving therapy, 311
prodromal phase, 432
product claims, 34
progressive relaxation, 163–166
projection, 191
projective personality tests, 122,
  126–128
proteins, 43
provincial psychiatric hospitals,
  14–15
Prozac, 79
PsychDirect, 282
psychedelics, 342
  see also hallucinogens
psychiatric commitment. See civil
  commitment
psychiatric homeless, 18
psychiatrist, 2
psychiatrists, 77
Psychiatry Online, 139
psychic structures, 51
PsychLinks, 318
psychoactive drugs, 323
  see also drugs of abuse
psychoanalysis, 52, 82, 267,
  456–457
psychoanalysts, 82
psychoanalytic theory, 51
  see also psychodynamic
    perspectives
psychodynamic model, 17
psychodynamic perspectives
  abnormal behaviour,
    perspective on, 55–58
  analytical psychology, 56
  anxiety disorders, 191
  defence mechanisms, 52, 53t
  described, 51

dissociative disorders, 225
ego psychology, 56
evaluation of, 58–59
individual psychology, 56
mood disorders, 255–256
neo-Freudians, 55–57, 56t
normality, perspective on,
  55–58
object-relations theory, 57
other psychodynamic theorists,
  55–57
paraphilias, 407
personality disorders, 307–308
psychoanalysis, 52
psychoanalytic theory, 51
psychosocial ego psychology, 57
schizophrenia, 443
self-focusing model, 256
self psychology, 307–308
self-system, 56
self-theory, 56
separation-individuation, 308
sexual dysfunctions, 417
somatoform disorders, 235
splitting, 308
stages of psychosexual
  development, 53–55
structural hypothesis, 51
structure of personality, 51–52
structure of the mind, 51, 51f
substance-related disorders,
  351–352
psychodynamic therapies
  anxiety disorders, 201
  described, 82–83
  dream analysis, 83
  free association, 83
  interpersonal psychotherapy,
    267
  modern approaches, 84–85
  mood disorders, 267–268
  personality disorders, 316
  psychoanalysis, 52, 82, 267
  somatoform disorders, 237
  substance-related disorders,
    359
  transference, 83–84
psychogenic amnesia, 220–221
psychological dependence,
  327–328, 387
psychological disorders
  adjustment disorders, 143,
    144–145
  anxiety disorders. See anxiety
    disorders
  childhood psychological
    disorders. See childhood
    psychological disorders
  culture-bound disorders, 110,
    110t, 219
  defined, 2
  dissociative disorders. See
    dissociative disorders
  eating disorders, 367–378
  factitious disorder, 229
  gender identity disorder,
    396–399
  genetic predisposition, 28
  vs. mental disorder, 104
  paraphilias, 400–411
  personality disorders. See
    personality disorders
  preference for term, 2–3
  prevalence, 3t
  schizophrenia. See
    schizophrenia

sexual dysfunctions, 414–425
sleeping disorders, 380–388
somatoform disorders. *See* somatoform disorders
substance-related disorders. *See* substance-related disorders
Western words used to described, 7
psychological factors
performance anxiety, 419–420
and physical disorders. *See* psychosomatic disorders
sexual dysfunctions, 419–421
stress, 151–154
ulcers, 158
psychological hardiness, 152
psychological models, 17
psychological perspectives
see also specific perspectives
cognitive-behavioural perspectives, 66–68
described, 50
humanistic-existential perspectives, 63–65
learning perspectives, 60–63
psychodynamic perspectives, 51–59
psychological tests
described, 119
intelligence tests, 119–122, 121*t*, 122*t*, 123*t*
personality tests, 122–128
psychometric approach, 129
psychoneuroimmunology, 146
psychopath, 289
psychopathic personality profile, 290–292
Psychopathology of Everyday Life (Freud), 52
psychopathy, 289, 291–292
see also antisocial personality disorder (APD)
Psychopathy Checklist-Revised (PCL-R), 289, 290, 506–507
psychopharmacology, 77, 169
see also drug therapy
psychophysiological, 158, 292–293
see also psychosomatic disorders
psychoses, 177
psychosexual, 53
psychosexual development stages, 53–55
psychosis, 57
psychosocial ego psychology, 57
psychosocial problems, 107*t*
psychosocial rehabilitation, 458–459
psychosocial stages, 58*t*
psychosomatic disorders, 158
see also physical disorders
psychosurgery, 81–82
psychotherapy
see also psychodynamic therapies
defined, 76
multicultural issues, 96–97, 96*t*
Public Health Agency of Canada, 72
punishments, 62–63
pure innocents, 58
Pussin, Jean-Baptiste, 12

R
R. v. Francois, 227
R. v. Swain, 515–516
random assignment, 26, 28
random sampling, 28
rape, 408–412
rape prevention, 411–412
rape survivors, 411
rapid flight of ideas, 251
rapport, 118
rational-emotive behaviour therapy (REBT), 66–67, 89–90
rational responses, 271*t*
reactivity, 131, 132
reactors, 63
reading disorder, 481, 482*f*
reality principle, 52
reality testing, 127
rebound anxiety, 78
receptor site, 46
reciprocal determinism, 67–68
reciprocal interaction, 258
recombinant DNA techniques, 80
recovered memories, 227–228, 239
reflection, 87
rehearsal, 31
reinforcement, 61, 257–258, 310
reinforcement sensitivity theory (RST), 313
Reitan, Ralph, 128
relapse, 361
relapse-prevention training, 361, 362
relationship problems, 419
reliability
of assessment, 113–114
coefficient alpha, 113
of DSM-IV-TR, 107
interjudge reliability, 114
internal consistency, 113–114
interrater reliability, 114
personality disorders, classification of, 304
temporal stability, 114
test-retest reliability, 114
REM sleep, 382
the Renaissance, 11
repetitive transcranial magnetic stimulation (rTMS), 275
repression, 52, 58, 59
research
see also research methods
control, 22–23
description, 22
ethics in research, 23–24
explanation, 22–23
hypothesis, 23
inference, 22
objectives of science, 22–23
prediction, 22–23, 25
research question, 23
scientific method, 23
significant differences, 23
theories, 22
research ethics boards (REBs), 24
research methods
adoptee studies, 29–30
case-study method, 30
cause-and-effect relationship, 25
correlation, 24–25
epidemiological method, 27–28
experimental method, 25–27
kinship studies, 28–30

longitudinal study, 25
naturalistic-observation method, 24
random assignment, 26
reversal design, 30, 31
single-case experimental designs, 30–32
survey method, 27
twin studies, 29
research question, 23
residential approaches, 358–359
residual phase, 432
resilience, 71–72
resistance, 83
resistance stage, 149
response biases, 130
response systems, 135
reticular activating system (RAS), 47
reuptake process, 46
reversal design, 30, 31
reverse anorexia nervosa, 378
Rhythm Test, 129
right to refuse treatment, 512
right to treatment, 511–512
risk factors
alcoholism, 331–332
described, 71
major depression, 246–247
socioeconomic status (SES), 313
Ritalin, 486–487
Rogers, Carl, 63, 64, 65, 87–88
Roman Catholic Church, 11
Rorschach, Hermann, 126
Rorschach inkblot test, 126–127, 127*f*
routine use, 328
rubella, 475
rumination disorder, 378

S
Sade, Marquis de, 406
sadism, sexual, 406–407
sadomasochism, 406–407
samples, 28
sanguine, 10
Sartre, Jean-Paul, 63
savant syndrome, 476
schizoaffective disorder, 461
schizoid personality disorders, 286–287
schizophrenia
affect, 430
ambivalence, 430
antipsychotic drugs, 455–456
associations, 430
attentional deficiencies, 434–435
autism, 430
behavioural therapies, 457–458
biochemical factors, 446–447
biological perspectives, 444–448
biological therapies, 455–456
brain abnormalities, 447–448, 447*f*
catatonic type, 439–440
clinical features, 430–441, 431*t*
cognitive-behavioural therapies, 458
communication deviance, 452
content of thought, disturbances in, 433–434

costs, 432
cross-fostering study, 446
culture and, 8
delusions, 433
described, 433
diathesis-stress model, 448–451, 449*f*
disorganized dimension, 441
disorganized type, 438
disturbances of thought and speech, 433–434
dopamine theory, 446–447
double-bind communications, 452
drug therapy, 455–456
DSM-IV criteria, 431
early-intervention programs, 459–460
emotional disturbances, 437
expressed emotion, 453
family-intervention programs, 459
family perspectives, 452–453
fear, 433
first-rank symptoms, 431
form of thought, disturbances in, 434
four As, 430
genetics, 444–446, 445*f*
hallucinations, 431, 435–437
historical perspectives, 430–431
and interpersonal relationships, 438
learning perspectives, 443–444
longitudinal study, 450
major features, 433–438
negative dimension, 441
negative symptoms, 440
other types of impairment, 437–438
paranoid type, 440
perceptual disturbances, 435–437
phases, 432–433
positive symptoms, 440
premorbid functioning, 441
prevalence, 432
prodromal phase, 432
psychoanalysis, 456–457
psychodynamic perspectives, 443
psychosocial rehabilitation, 458–459
psychotic dimension, 441
public misunderstanding, 433
residual phase, 432
schizoaffective disorder, 461
schizophrenogenic mother, 452
second-rank symptoms, 431
social-skills training, 458
stigma, 433
stupor, 438
substance abuse, 432
subtypes, 438–441
theoretical perspectives, 443–453
thought disorder, 434
three-dimensional model, 441
treatment, 455–460
Type I schizophrenia, 440–441
Type II schizophrenia, 440–441
viral infections, 447
waxy flexibility, 439

sleeping disorders, 386–388
somatoform disorders,
    237–238
substance-related disorders,
    354–363
treatment methods
    behaviour therapy, 86
    biological therapies, 77–79
    clinical psychologists, 76–77
    cognitive therapies, 89
    comparison of approaches, 95
    computer-assisted treatments,
        120
    eclectic therapy, 92
    evaluation of, 94–95
    family therapy, 93–94
    group therapy, 93–94
    humanistic-existential
        therapies, 87–89
    marital therapy, 93–94
    mental health professionals,
        types of, 76–77
    meta-analysis, 94–95, 98
    multicultural issues in
        psychotherapy, 96–97, 96t
    nonspecific treatment factors,
        95
    psychiatrists, 77
    psychodynamic therapies,
        82–85
    psychotherapy, 76
    sex therapy, 421–424
    social workers, 77
    virtual therapy, 206
treatment-resistant depression
    (TRD), 79
trephining, 9
triazolam, 77
tricyclics, 78, 272–273
trisomy 21, 43
Tuke, William, 13
Turner syndrome, 43
Turner's syndrome, 473
twin studies, 29
two-factor model, 191–192
Type A behaviour pattern (TABP),
    152–161, 164
Type I schizophrenia, 440–441
Type II schizophrenia, 440–441

U
ulcers, 158
unconditional positive regard, 87
unconditioned response (UR), 60
unconditioned stimulus (US), 60
unconscious mind, 51
unfit to stand trial, 518
unilateral ECT, 275
unipolar disorders, 243
unipotent stem cells, 44, 45
unobtrusive observations, 24
unstable attribution, 262
unstructured interviews,
    118–119

unusual behaviour, 3
unwanted intrusive thoughts,
    193t

V
vaginismus, 416, 424
validity
    of assessment, 114–115
    concurrent validity, 114
    construct validity, 115
    content validity, 114
    criterion validity, 114–115
    of DSM-IV-TR, 107
    face validity, 114
    personality disorders,
        classification of, 304
    predictive validity, 107, 115
    of Rorschach inkblot test, 127
validity scales, 124
variables
    behavioural variables, 26t
    defined, 24
    dependent variables, 26, 26t
    independent variables, 26, 26t
    physiological variables, 26t
    self-report variables, 26t
vascular surgery, 425
verbal response system, 135
violence, and sleepwalking, 386
viral infections, 447
virtual therapy, 206
volition, disturbances, 438
voluntary hospitalization, 505
voyeurism, 403
vulnerability factors, 188

W
warm-up effect, 114
Watson, John B., 60
waxy flexibility, 439
weaning, 53
websites
    Alcoholics Anonymous (AA),
        364
    Anorexia Nervosa and Bulimia
        Association, 391
    Anxiety Disorders Association
        of America, 210
    Anxiety Disorders Association
        of Canada, 210
    Anxiety Treatment and
        Research Centre, 210
    Autism Society Canada, 499
    British Psychological Society
        Centre, 99
    Canadian Association for
        Community Living, 499
    Canadian Cancer Society, 171
    Canadian Centre on Substance
        Abuse, 364
    Canadian Health Network
        (CHN), 171
    Canadian Institute of Stress,
        171

Canadian Mental Health
    Association (CMHA), 36
Canadian Psychiatric
    Association (CPA), 36
Canadian Psychological
    Association (CPA), 36, 139
Canadian Sleep Society (CSS),
    391
Centre for Addiction and
    Mental Health (CAMH), 36,
    99, 364
Children and Adults with
    Attention Deficit Disorders
    (CHADD), 499
children and youth, 499
CPA Code of Ethics, 519
eating disorders, 391
False-Memory Syndrome
    Foundation, 239
FASworld, 364
First Nations Health Links,
    282
Gender Identity Clinic, 426
gender role transition, 426
Health Canada Mental Health
    page, 36
Healthy People, Healthy
    Communities, 519
Heart and Stroke Foundation
    of Canada, 171
hypochondriasis, 229,
    231–233, 234, 235, 236,
    237, 238, 239, 241
imaginary crimes, 239
International Network on
    Personal Meaning (INPM),
    99
Internet Mental Health, 99,
    282, 319, 391
Justice for All, 519
Learning Disabilities
    Association of Canada, 499
Lesbian, Gay, Bisexual, and
    Transgender Community
    Center, 426
Mental Health Info Source,
    139
Mental Help Net, 139, 319
Mood Disorders Society of
    Canada, 282
Mothers Against Drunk
    Driving (MADD), 364
National Center for PTSD,
    210
National Council on Alcohol
    and Drug Dependence, 364
National Eating Disorder
    Information Centre (NEDIC),
    391
NIMH's schizophrenia page,
    461
Obsessive-Compulsive
    Foundation, 210
personality disorders, 318

personality profile comparisons
    between homeless and housed
    adults, 319
PsychDirect, 282
Psychiatry Online, 139
PsychLinks, 318
recovered memories, 239
schizophrenia resources, 461
Schizophrenia Society of
    Canada, 461
schizophrenia.com, 461
sexual counselling, 426
sexuality and sexual
    relationships, 426
Sidran Institute, 239
Sleepnet.com, 391
Special Olympics Canada, 488
Wechsler, David, 121
Wechsler Adult Intelligence Scale,
    122t
Wechsler Intelligence Scale for
    Children (WISC), 471
Wechsler intelligence scales, 120,
    121, 123t
wellness continuum. See mental
    wellness continuum
Weyer, Johann, 12
wish-fulfillment fantasies,
    151–152
witchcraft, 11–12
withdrawal, 349
withdrawal syndrome, 325–327
women
    coping styles, 265
    female orgasmic disorder, 416
    female sexual arousal disorder,
        415
    Freud's perspective on, 59
    hospitalization for
        psychological disorders, 2
    and hysteria, 234
    and major depression,
        246–247
    penis envy, 417–418
    postpartum depression,
        248–249
    preorgasmic women, 423
    schizophrenogenic mother,
        452
    sexist biases, and personality
        disorders, 305
    Turner's syndrome, 473
working alliance, 95
World Health Organization, 8,
    103, 314
world view, 9, 96t
written expression, disorder of,
    481

Y
Yu, Edmond, 503–504

Z
zar, 111, 237